# Sociology

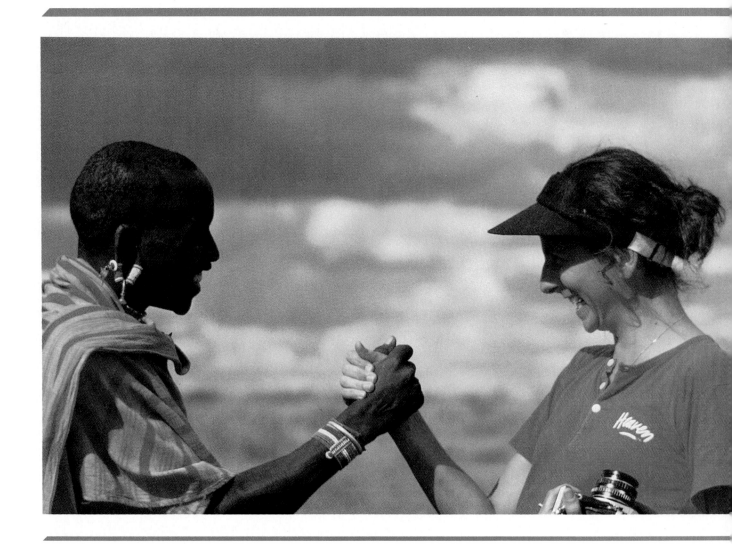

*This book is dedicated to all teachers of sociology who are
devoting their lives to helping others understand their place
in our society and in the larger world.*

John J. Macionis

# SOCIOLOGY

**FOURTH EDITION**

## John J. Macionis

*Kenyon College*

Prentice Hall, Englewood Cliffs, New Jersey 07632

*Library of Congress Cataloging-in-Publication Data*

MACIONIS, JOHN J.
    Sociology / John J. Macionis. — 4th ed.
        p.   cm.
    Includes bibliographical references and index.
    ISBN 0-13-818485-2
1. Sociology.  I. Title.
HM51.M166   1993
301—dc20                            91-29713
                                         CIP

Acquisitions Editor: Nancy Roberts
Development Editors: Susanna Lesan and Diana Drew
Production Editor: Marianne Peters
Editor-in-Chief: Charlyce Jones Owen
Marketing Manager: Tracy Augustine
Art Director: Florence Dara Silverman/Anne T. Bonanno
Interior Designer: Andrew P. Zutis
Cover Designer: Bruce Kenselaar
Prepress Buyer: Kelly Behr
Manufacturing Buyer: Mary Ann Gloriande
Photo Editor: Lorinda Morris-Nantz
Photo Researchers: Barbara Salz and Joelle Burrows
Supplements Editor: Sharon Chambliss
Page Layout: Karen Noferi
Editorial Assistant: Pat Naturale
Cover Art: *In the Luxembourg Gardens* by Adolphe Von Menzel. Pushkin, Moscow/Bridgeman
Art Library, London/Superstock, Inc., New York.

 © 1993, 1991, 1989, 1987 by Prentice-Hall, Inc.
A Simon & Schuster Company
Englewood Cliffs, New Jersey 07632

Printed in the United States of America
10  9  8  7  6  5  4  3

ISBN 0-13-818485-2

Prentice-Hall International (UK) Limited, *London*
Prentice-Hall of Australia Pty. Limited, *Sydney*
Prentice-Hall Canada Inc., *Toronto*
Prentice-Hall Hispanoamericana, S.A., *Mexico*
Prentice-Hall of India Private Limited, *New Delhi*
Prentice-Hall of Japan, Inc., *Tokyo*
Simon & Schuster Asia Pte. Ltd., *Singapore*
Editora Prentice-Hall do Brasil, Ltda., *Rio de Janeiro*

# Brief Contents

# Contents

# Boxes

## Critical Thinking

## Cross-Cultural Comparison

## A Decade of Change

## Profile

## Social Diversity

## Sociology of Everyday Life

# Global Maps: Windows on the World

# Preface

The world continues to change in surprising ways, making the revision of textbooks—especially in sociology—both necessary and challenging. The reality of the "new world order" seems to be steady transformation, as national economies become ever more linked, technology draws traditional cultures into a global conversation, and deeply rooted ethnic and religious loyalties rise from the ashes of discarded political systems.

The United States, too, is changing. Even as our economy struggles out of recession, analysts warn that many jobs may be gone for good. A postindustrial (or postmodern) era is upon us in which our society will have to adapt to new kinds of work, face up to growing inequality, contend with new forms of communication, and make new demands of our schools (and of our textbooks).

It is in this context that we are proud to offer the fourth edition of *Sociology*. This revision has taken two years of evaluation, careful planning, and intensive work. My goal has been to make this a text without equal, substantive, stimulating, and comprehensive. I invite your careful consideration of what I hope you will agree is the best edition yet—a textbook that empowers students to comprehend the many ways of life found in the United States and to understand our place in the changing world.

## The Organization of This Text

**Part I** introduces the foundations of sociology. Underlying the discipline is the *sociological perspective*—the focus of Chapter 1, which explains how this invigorating point of view illuminates the world in a new and instructive way. Chapter 2 spotlights *sociological investigation*, or the "doing of sociology," and explains how to apply the logic of science to the study of human society. We bring major research strategies to life using extended examples of well-known sociological work.

By learning how sociologists see the world and carry out research, passive readers are transformed into active, critical participants in the issues, debates, and controversies that frame subsequent chapters.

**Part II** targets the foundations of social life. Chapter 3 presents the central concept of *culture*, emphasizing the cultural diversity that makes up our society and our world. Chapter 4 links culture to the concept of *society*, and presents four enduring models for understanding the structure and dynamics of human social organization. Assigned in sequence, this unique chapter provides students with the background necessary to fully comprehend the ideas of important thinkers—including Karl Marx, Max Weber, and Emile Durkheim—that appear in subsequent chapters. Alternatively, instructors may assign each of the chapter's four parts at later points in the course. Chapter 5 focuses on *socialization*, explaining how we gain our humanity as we learn to participate in society. Chapter 6 provides a micro-level look at the patterns of *social interaction* that make up our everyday lives. Chapter 7 offers full-chapter coverage of *groups and organizations*, both of which are vital elements of social structure. Chapter 8 completes the unit by investigating how the operation of society promotes both *deviance* and *conformity*.

**Part III** provides a detailed analysis of various dimensions of social inequality. Because of its importance to human life, three chapters are devoted to *social stratification*. Chapter 9 introduces major concepts and presents fundamental theoretical analysis of social inequality. This chapter is rich with illustrations of how stratification has changed historically, and how it varies around the world today. Chapter 10 surveys *social class in the United States*, presenting common perceptions of inequality and seeing how well they square with the facts. Chapter 11 extends the analysis with *a global view of social stratification*, investigating the extent of differences in wealth and power between rich and poor societies. Both Chapters 10 and 11 explain how social stratification in the United States is linked to trends in the rest of the world, just as they explore our society's role in global stratification. *Race and ethnicity*, important dimensions of social inequality both in North America and the rest of the world, are detailed in Chapter 12. The focus of Chapter 13 is *sex and gender*. Here we explain the biological foundation of sex and sexuality, and how societies transform the distinction of sex into systems of gender stratification. *Aging and the elderly*, topics of increasing concern to members of aging societies such as the United States, are addressed in Chapter 14.

**Part IV** includes a full chapter on each social institution. Chapter 15, *the family*, underscores the diversity of family life both in the United States and in the world as a whole. Chapter 16, *education*, traces the expansion of schooling in industrial societies. Here again, educational patterns in the United States are made more meaningful through contrasts with those of many other societies. Chapter 17 discusses *religion*, revealing how the timeless human search for ultimate meaning affects social life in countless ways. Chapter 18, *politics and government*, includes discussion of the U.S. military, war, and peace. Chapter 19 focuses on *the economy and work*, highlighting industrialization, postindustrialization, the emergence of a global economy, and what these transformations mean for the U.S. labor force. Chapter 20, *health and medicine*, shows how health is a social issue just as much as it is a matter of biological processes. Paralleling the discussions of the other institutions, this chapter explains the historical emergence of medicine, analyzes current medical issues from different points of view, and compares U.S. patterns to those found in other societies.

**Part V** examines important dimensions of social change. Chapter 21 focuses on the powerful impact of *population growth and urbanization* in the United States and throughout the world. Chapter 22 explains how people seek or resist social change through various forms of *collective behavior and social movements*. Chapter 23 concludes the text with an overview of *social change and modernity*, explaining how and why world societies change, and critically analyzing the benefits and liabilities of traditional and modern ways of life.

## Continuity: Established Features of *Sociology*

Although introductory sociology texts have much in common, they are not all the same. The success of *Sociology* results from a combination of a dozen distinctive features.

*Unsurpassed writing style.* Most important, this text offers a writing style widely praised by students and faculty alike as elegant and engaging. *Sociology* is an inviting text that encourages students to read—even beyond their assignments.

*Intriguing chapter introductions.* One of the most popular features of earlier editions has been the engaging vignettes that begin each chapter. These openings—which range from the "Buy-American" campaign, to the unexpected popularity of the suicide manual *Final Exit*, to the controversy surrounding the police beating of Rodney King—spark the interest of the reader as they introduce important themes. For this edition, half of the vignettes are new.

*A celebration of social diversity.* *Sociology* invites students from all social backgrounds to discover a fresh and exciting way to see their world and themselves. Readers will hear in this text the diverse voices of our society—people of African, Asian, European, and Latino ancestry, as well as women and men of various class positions and at all points in the life course. Just as important, without flinching from the problems that marginalized people confront, this text does not treat these individuals simply as "social problems" but notes their achievements as well.

*Inclusive focus on women and men.* Beyond devoting a full chapter to the important concepts of sex and gender, *Sociology* "mainstreams" gender into *every* chapter, showing how the topic at hand affects women and men differently, and that gender affects not only our answers about how society works but also the way we frame questions in the first place.

*Rich and varied examples.* Sociologist George Herbert Mead once described the ideal teacher as a person able to transform simple information into real knowledge. Mead's insight applies as much to books as to teachers; on virtually every page of *Sociology*, therefore, rich and illuminating illustrations show students the power of applying sociology to their everyday lives.

*A global perspective.* *Sociology* has taken a leading role in expanding the horizons of our discipline beyond the United States. Each chapter contains comparative material that focuses on the social diversity of our world. Just as important, this text explains that social trends in the United States—whether they be musical tastes, the price of wheat, or growing disparity of income—are influenced by what happens elsewhere. More than ever before, then, understanding our society demands comprehending this nation's place in the larger global system.

**Theoretically clear and balanced.** *Sociology* makes theory easy. The discipline's major theoretical approaches are introduced in Chapter 1 and are systematically reapplied in later chapters. In addition to the social-conflict, structural-functional, and symbolic-interaction paradigms, various chapters incorporate social-exchange analysis, ethnomethodology, cultural ecology, and sociobiology.

Chapter 4 provides an easy-to-understand introduction to important social theorists *before* their work is discussed in later chapters. The ideas of Gerhard and Jean Lenski, Max Weber, Karl Marx, and Emile Durkheim appear in distinct sections that may be assigned together or separately at different points in the course.

**Emphasis on critical thinking.** Critical thinking skills include the ability to challenge common assumptions, formulate questions, identify and weigh appropriate evidence, and reach reasoned conclusions. This text encourages students to discover as well as to learn, to seek out contradictions as well as to formulate consistent arguments, and to make connections among the various dimensions of social life.

**Recent sociological research.** *Sociology* blends classical sociological statements with the latest research, as reported in the leading publications in the field. Hundreds of new studies are found in this revision; on average, almost three-fourths of each chapter's citations are of articles and books published since 1980. As in earlier editions of *Sociology*, the statistical data are the most recent available, including reports from the 1990 census.

**Learning aids.** This text has specific features to help students learn. In each chapter, **key concepts**, identified by boldfaced type, are followed by a *precise, italicized definition*. An alphabetical listing of key concepts and definitions appears at the end of each chapter, and a complete **Glossary** appears at the end of the book. Each chapter also contains a numbered **Summary** to assist students in reviewing material and assessing their understanding. Chapters end with lists of **Suggested Readings**, identifying books of lasting importance and spotlighting recent publications.

**Outstanding images: photography and fine art.** The author has developed a program of photography and artwork that plays a central role in this text. Not only are images of extraordinary quality, but they are the creations of artists of various social backgrounds and historical periods. In addition to widely celebrated art by George Tooker and Vincent Van Gogh, for example, this edition has paintings by African-American artists Jacob Lawrence and Henry O. Tanner, Hispanic artists Frank Romero and Diego Rivera, and the Australian painter and feminist Sally Swain.

**Thought-provoking theme boxes.** Although boxes are common to introductory texts, *Sociology* provides a wealth of uncommonly good ones. Each chapter typically contains three or four boxes, which fall into six types that strengthen central themes of the text. *Social Diversity* boxes, new to this edition, focus on multicultural issues and enhance the voices of women and people of color. A *Decade of Change* boxes, also new to this edition, use new census data to highlight important changes during the 1980s or to project trends for the 1990s. *Critical Thinking* boxes teach students to ask sociological questions about their surroundings and help them to evaluate important, controversial issues. *Cross-Cultural Comparison* boxes provoke readers to think about their own way of life by examining the fascinating cultural diversity found in our world. *Sociology of Everyday Life* boxes show that, far from being detached from daily routines, many of sociology's most important insights involve familiar, everyday experiences. Finally, *Profile* boxes introduce many of the men and women who have shaped the discipline of sociology.

# Innovation: Changes in the Fourth Edition

Each edition of *Sociology* has broken new ground, a fact that explains much of the book's remarkable success. Beginning as the most popular new text of the 1980s, *Sociology* is now the leading book in the field. A revision raises high expectations, but, with the contributions of students and faculty, I am confident that no one will be disappointed. Here is a summary of the innovations that define *Sociology, fourth edition*.

**Placing our society in global perspective.** Sociology has long revealed how individual lives are shaped by placement in their own society. As we approach the new century, sociology is extending its reach by showing how the United States is itself affected by our country's position in the world as a whole. An unfortunate fact is that, at present, our students know little about the rest of the world and the ways in which nations are linked. Consider that, of some 12 million college students in this country, only about 50,000—less than half of one percent—have first-hand experience studying abroad. At the same time, 350,000 foreign students currently study in the United States.

The fourth edition will enhance the global sophistication of students in a number of ways. First, **this edition makes careful use of language.** We have avoided using the term "American"—a word that literally refers to two continents—to refer only to people in the United States. Thus, for example, the "American economy" is now more correctly called the "U.S. economy." This may seem a small point, but it is a significant recognition that we in this country are only one part of the Americas. I have taken great care to avoid other examples of ethnocentric language.

Second, **this edition ties life in the United States to processes and trends in the larger world.** Various chapters explain, for example, how growing economic inequality in this country is linked to the globalization of the economy, and how the wealth of the United States is tied to our relations abroad. This global emphasis in no way lessens the text's focus on the United States; on the contrary, it enhances conventional scholarship and provides greater accuracy.

Third, and most significantly, **this edition includes twenty-seven global maps,** typically one or two in every chapter. **Windows on the World** are truly sociological maps that reveal global patterns such as income disparity, favored languages and religions, the power of television, the extent of prostitution, permitted marriage forms, the degree of political freedom, the incidence of HIV infection, and a host of other issues. A listing of all twenty-seven **Windows on the World** follows the table of contents.

We make a major commitment to world maps, first, because global sophistication begins by learning basic geography. Surveys tell us that our students cannot locate countries of the world. Students who do not know even in what *region* of the globe to find El Salvador, Somalia, or Bosnia obviously cannot understand the human drama that is currently unfolding in such places. Second, students need to see ways in which rich and poor nations differ. Understanding the effects of industrialization, for example, depends upon spotlighting global

wealth and poverty, birth rates, the extent of child labor, and what proportion of women are in the labor force. **Windows on the World** graphically display all these factors and more.

All maps distort reality, since they portray a three-dimensional world in two dimensions. However, some biases are better than others. Most of us are familiar with the Mercator projection (devised by the Flemish mapmaker Gerhardus Mercator, 1512–1594; see top map at right). Mercator sought to accurately present the *shape* of countries (a vital concern to early sea-faring navigators) but, in doing so, he distorted their *size*. Thus greater distance from the equator inflates a land mass, so that Europe and North America have exaggerated dimensions (and, by implication, importance). By the same token, the Mercator map renders most Third-World countries smaller than they are. **Windows on the World** are drawn in a new, non-Eurocentric projection devised by cartographer Arno Peters (*Peters', Atlas of the World*; see bottom map at right). The Peters projection distorts the shape of some countries in service to the more important goal of displaying their correct relative size.

***Highlighting the social diversity of the United States.*** College students in this country have never been as socially diverse as they are in the 1990s. This trend has brought change to disciplines, especially to sociology. The new edition of *Sociology* recognizes this diversity by incorporating variables of sex, race, ethnicity, social class, and age into each chapter. This text continuously shows how topics have different significance to various categories of people, encourages students to understand their own social identities, and helps them to intellectually reach beyond their own lives toward others who differ.

***New topics.*** The fourth edition of *Sociology* also offers dozens of new or expanded discussions. Here is a partial listing, by chapter: *Chapter 1:* The contributions of W. E. B. DuBois to sociology; *Chapter 2:* How gender affects sociological research; *Chapter 3:* Afrocentrism and the multiculturalism controversy; *Chapter 4:* The varied investment in science in global perspective; *Chapter 5:* Where and why child labor continues in the world; *Chapter 6:* How women and men use different amounts of space; *Chapter 7:* The importance of organizational environments; *Chapter 8:* Date rape and sexual violence; *Chapter 9:* Why caste remains a part of social stratification in this country; *Chapter 10:* How the 1980s redis-

The Mercator projection (top), which correctly displays the *shape* of land masses, was vital to early sea-faring navigators. But it Eurocentrically inflates the dimensions of countries (like England) that are far from the equator. The Peters projection (bottom) is used in this text because it accurately presents the *size* (and, by implication, importance) of all nations.

tributed income and wealth in the United States; *Chapter 11*: The Christopher Columbus controversy; *Chapter 12*: The coming "minority-majority"; *Chapter 13*: Why millions of Asian women are "missing"; *Chapter 14*: Why the "sandwich generation" will care for aging parents as much as for their young children; *Chapter 15*: Comparing Japan and Sweden: the most traditional and the most progressive families in the industrial world; *Chapter 16*: Schools for profit; *Chapter 17*: The global strength of major religions; *Chapter 18*: The conservative movement among African Americans; *Chapter 19*: The prospects for labor unions in the United States; *Chapter 20*: The latest look at the AIDS epidemic in global perspective; *Chapter 21*: Why birth rates are highest in the poorest countries; *Chapter 22*:

The causes behind the political transformation of Eastern Europe; *Chapter 23*: How anomie differs from alienation.

***The latest statistical data.*** Most of the 1990 Census data has been released and *Sociology, fourth edition*, has them. Each chapter has the most current statistics available—in many cases, for 1991 and even 1992—as well as hundreds of new research findings. On average, almost three-fourths of each chapter's citations refer to material published since 1980. This revision also includes recent current events, from the Rodney King incident and the L.A. riots, to the "Buy-American" movement, to the effects of the lingering recession.

# Supplements

*Sociology, fourth edition*, is the heart of an unparalleled learning package that includes a wide range of proven instructional aids as well as several new ones. As the author of the text, I maintain a keen interest in all the supplements to ensure their quality and compatibility with the text. The supplements for this revision have been thoroughly updated, improved, and expanded.

***The Annotated Instructor's Edition.*** The AIE is a complete student text annotated by the author on every page. Annotations have won praise from both new and seasoned instructors as enriching class presentations. Margin notes include summaries of research findings, statistics from the United States or other nations, insightful quotations, and high-quality survey data from the National Opinion Research Center's (NORC) General Social Survey.

***Data File.*** This is the "instructor's manual" that is of interest even to those who have shunned them in the past. The *Data File* provides far more than chapter outlines and discussion questions; it contains statistical profiles of the United States and other nations, summaries of important developments and significant research, and supplemental lecture material for every chapter of the text. The *Data File* has been prepared by Stephen W. Beach (Avila College) with the assistance of John J. Macionis.

***Social Survey Software.*** This is the supplement that is changing the way instructors teach and students learn. *Social Survey Software* is an easy yet powerful program that allows users to investigate U.S. society and other nations of the world employing the best source of survey data available, the General Social Survey. John J. Macionis and Jere Bruner (Oberlin College) have prepared more than one hundred data sets and linked them to the chapters of *Sociology, fourth edition*. Jere Bruner has written an easy-to-understand student manual and a helpful instructor's manual to accompany the software. *Social Survey Software* supports multivariate analysis, allowing investigators to analyze survey responses by sex, race, income level, education, and a host of other variables. *Social Survey Software* is executed on the CHIP-endale 1 microcomputer program developed by James A. Davis (Harvard University) and is available to operate in IBM and MacIntosh formats.

***Test Item File.*** A completely new and improved test item file for this revision, prepared by Edward Kick, University of Utah, is available in both printed and computerized forms. The file contains 2,300 items, including multiple-choice, true-false, and essay questions. Questions are divided into more simple "recall" items and more complex "inferential" items; answers to all questions are page-referenced to the text. Prentice Hall DataManager is a test generator and classroom management system designed to provide maximum flexibility in producing and grading tests and quizzes. MicroTest III, MacIntosh Version, is available to MacIntosh users.

***Seeing Ourselves: Classic, Contemporary, and Cross-Cultural Readings in Sociology, second edition.*** This best-selling collection of sixty-six readings is edited by John J. Macionis and Nijole V. Benokraitis (University of Baltimore). With a format unique among all readers, *Seeing Ourselves* provides a set of readings—classics, contemporary issues, and cross-cultural comparisons—for each chapter in *Sociology, fourth edition*. Classical statements include excerpts by Emile Durkheim, Karl Marx, George Herbert Mead, Max Weber, Georg Simmel, C. Wright Mills, W. E. B. DuBois, Mirra Komarovsky, Jessie Bernard, and others; contemporary readings highlight issues such as gender patterns in everyday speech, politics and research, how computers are changing the workplace, racial and ethnic bias in advertising, and pornography. Cross-cultural readings examine issues with an eye toward social diversity in the United States or in global perspective.

***ABC News/Prentice Hall Video Library for Sociology Series I, II, and III (Issues in Sociology).*** Video is the most dynamic supplement you can use to enhance a class. But the quality of the video material and how well it relates to your course still makes all the difference. Prentice Hall and ABC News are now working together to bring you the best and most comprehensive video ancillaries available in the college market.

Through its wide variety of award-winning programs—*Nightline, Business World, On Business, This Week with David Brinkley, World News Tonight,* and *The Health Show*—ABC offers a resource for feature and documentary-style videos related to the chapters in *Sociology*. The programs have extremely high production quality, present substantial content, and are hosted by well-versed, well-known anchors.

Prentice Hall and its authors and editors provide the benefit of having selected videos and topics that will work well with this course and text and include notes on how to use them in the classroom. An excellent video guide in the *Data File* carefully and completely integrates the videos into your lecture. The guide has a synopsis of each video showing its relation to the chapter and discussion questions to help students focus on how concepts and theories apply to real-life situations.

**A Contemporary View.** *The New York Times* and Prentice Hall are sponsoring *A Contemporary View*, a program designed to enhance student access to current information of relevance in the classroom. Through this program, the core subject matter provided in the text is supplemented by a collection of current articles from one of the world's most distinguished newspapers, *The New York Times*. These articles demonstrate the vital, ongoing connection between what is learned in the classroom and what is happening in the world around us. To enjoy the wealth of information of *The New York Times* daily, a reduced subscription rate is available. For information, call toll-free 1-800-631-1222.

Prentice Hall and *The New York Times* are proud to co-sponsor *A Contemporary View*. We hope it will make the reading of both textbooks and newspapers a more dynamic, involving process.

Other supplements available to aid in classroom teaching are:

*Prentice Hall Color Transparencies: Sociology Series I, II, and III.*
*Film/Video Guide: Prentice Hall Introductory Sociology.*
Prentice Hall's Video Library.
*Study Guide.*
*Critical Thinking* Audiocassette Tape.
*ABC News/Prentice Hall Video Library for Sociology, Series I, II, and III (Issues in Sociology).*
*A Year That Changed the World.*

## Acknowledgments

The conventional practice of designating a single author obscures the efforts of dozens of women and men that have resulted in *Sociology, fourth edition.* Nancy Rob-erts, executive editor at Prentice Hall and valued friend, has contributed enthusiasm, support, and sound advice throughout the revision process. Susanna Lesan has played a vital role in the development of this text since its first edition, with day-to-day responsibility for coordinating and supervising the editorial process. I also have a large debt to the members of the Prentice Hall sales staff, who have given this text remarkable support over the years. Thanks, especially, to Roland Hernandez and Tracy Augustine, who have headed up our marketing campaigns. I also offer heartfelt thanks to Pat Naturale, Bill Webber, Charlyce Jones Owen, Will Ethridge, and Ed Stanford for all that they have done to make this text what it is today.

The production of *Sociology* is supervised by Marianne Peters, who expends extraordinary time and energy, keeps track of countless details, and tolerates no compromises along the way. The interior design of the book is the creative work of Andrew Zutis. Karen Noferi created each of the pages with exceptional skill. Diana Drew served as the development editor; copy editing was provided by Diana Drew and Amy Macionis. Barbara Salz did an excellent job of researching photos, as did Joelle Burrows with the fine art, both under the supervision of Lorinda Morris-Nantz, head of Prentice Hall's Photo Archives. The high quality and timeliness of the supplements are due to Sharon Chambliss, Supplements Editor.

It goes without saying that every colleague knows more about many topics covered in this book than I do. For that reason, I am grateful to the hundreds of people who have written to me to offer comments and suggestions; thanks, too, to the students who have shared with me their reactions to the book. More formally, I am grateful to the following people who have reviewed some or all of this manuscript:

Peter Adler, University of Denver
Igolima Amachree, Western Illinois University
Franklyn N. Arnhoff, University of Virginia
Richard Barash, Rancho Santiago College
Stephen Beach, Avila College
Nijole Benokraitis, University of Baltimore
Paul R. Benson, Tulane University
Philip Berg, University of Wisconsin-LaCrosse
Dallas A. Blanchard, University of West Florida
Rudee Devon Boan, Gardner-Webb College
Dean A. Boldon, Maryville College
Charles Bolton, Portland State University
Brent Bruton, Iowa State University

Jean H. Cardinalli, Monroe Community College
Gregg Carter, Bryant College
Frank Clemente, Pennsylvania State University
Peter Conrad, Brandeis University
Sheila Cordray, Oregon State University
Harold Cox, Indiana State University
Harrold Curl, Mount Vernon Nazarene College
Edward Dager, University of Maryland
Dennis K. Dedrick, Georgetown College
Joseph DeMartini, Washington State University
John Farley, Southern Illinois University
Joe R. Feagin, University of Texas
Juanita M. Firestone, University of Texas at Austin
Alvin J. Fischer, Camden County College
Kevin Fitzpatrick, University of Alabama-Birmingham
Don C. Gibbons, Portland State University
Jonathan Gibralter, SUNY-Morrisville
Norval D. Glenn, University of Texas
Ann Goetting, Western Kentucky University
Phillip Gonzales, University of New Mexico
Susan Gore, University of Massachusetts-Boston
Edith E. Graber, Lindenwood College
H. James Graham, Mott Community College
Marshall J. Graney, University of Tenneseee
Linda M. Grant, Southern Illinois University
L. Sue Greer, University of Pittsburgh
Patricia A. Gwartney-Gibbs, University of Oregon
Maureen Hallinan, University of Notre Dame
Charles L. Harper, Creighton University
Jessie D. Harper, St. Cloud State University
Barbara Heisler, Cleveland State University
Cedric Herring, Texas A&M University
Gary Hodge, Collin County Community College
Paul Hsu, Austin Peay State University
Kathy Hughes, Henderson Community College
Janet C. Hunt, University of Maryland
J. Craig Jenkins, Ohio State University
Faye Johnson, Middle Tennessee State University
Norris R. Johnson, University of Cincinnati
Ronald L. Johnstone, Central Michigan University
Edward L. Kain, Southwestern University
Florence Karlstrom, Northern Arizona University
Alice A. Kemp, University of New Orleans
Harry Kitano, University of California-Los Angeles
Ross A. Klein, Skidmore College
George A. Kourvetaris, Northern Illinois University
James H. Larson, University of North Dakota
Marlene Lehtinen, University of Utah
Hugh F. Lena, Providence College
Linda Lindsey, Maryville College

Dale A. Lund, University of Utah
Larry Lyon, Baylor University
William Marsiglio, University of Florida
Wilfred G. Marston, University of Michigan
Greg Matoesian, Fontbonne College
John D. McCarthy, Catholic University
Allan McCutcheon, University of Delaware
Alan McEvoy, Wittenberg University
Meredith B. McGuire, Trinity University
Patrick McGuire, University of Toledo
Virginia McKeefrey-Reynolds, Northern Illinois University
Roger McVannan, Broome Community College
Dwayne Monette, Northern Michigan University
Wilbert E. Moore, University of Denver
Peter Morrill, Bronx Community College
Charles W. Mueller, University of Iowa
David M. Neal, University of North Texas
Sharon Nero, University of Wisconsin-Stout
Alvaro L. Nieves, Wheaton College
Anthony M. Orum, University of Texas
Brian F. Pendleton, University of Akron
Albert L. Reese, Bainbridge College
Franklyn Robbins, Community College of Rhode Island
Dorothy M. Roe, Milwaukee Area Technical College
Lawrence Rosen, Temple University
Daniel W. Rossides, Bowdoin College
Howard Sacks, Kenyon College
Beth Anne Shelton, SUNY-Buffalo
Anson Shupe, University of Texas
Richard L. Simpson, University of North Carolina at Chapel Hill
Jan Smith, Ohio Wesleyan University
Karen Cole Smith, Sante Fe Community College
Kevin B. Smith, Lamar University
Eve Spangler, Boston College
Michael Stein, University of Missouri
George F. Stine, Millersville University
Teresa A. Sullivan, University of Texas
M. L. Taylor, University of Texas-Arlington
Verta Taylor, The Ohio State University
Vickie H. Taylor, Danville Community College
Kendrick S. Thompson, Northern Michigan University
Robert Thornburrow, Paris Junior College
Susan Tiano, University of New Mexico
Andrew Treno, Clarke College
Theodore C. Wagenaar, Miami University
Pamela Barnhouse Walters, Indiana University

Philo C. Wasburn, Purdue University
David L. Westby, Pennsylvania State University
Amy S. Wharton, Washington State University
Craig C. White, Fairmont State College
John Wilson, Duke University
Richard Withers, Alderson Broaddus College
Anthony L. Wolf, Bucks County Community College
Wayne S. Wooden, California State Polytechnic University-Pomona

I also wish to thank the following colleagues for sharing their wisdom in ways that have improved this book: Doug Adams (The Ohio State University), Kip Armstrong (Bloomsburg University), Rose Arnault (Fort Hays State University), Philip Berg (University of Wisconsin, La Crosse), Bill Brindle (Monroe Community College), John R. Brouillette (Colorado State University), Karen Campbell (Vanderbilt University), Gerry Cox (Fort Hays State University), Harrold Curl (Mount Vernon Nazarene College), James A. Davis (Harvard University), Helen Rose Fuchs Ebaugh (University of Houston), Heather Fitz Gibbon (The College of Wooster), Kevin Fitzpatrick (University of Alabama-Birmingham), Dona Fletcher (Sinclair Community College), Andrew Foster (Kenyon College), Charles Frazier (University of Florida), Charlotte Gotwald (York College of Pennsylvania), Karen Lynch Frederick (Saint Anselm College), Steven Goldberg (City College, City University of New York), Jeffrey Hahn (Mount Union College), Dean Haledjian (Northern Virginia Community College), Peter Hruschka (Ohio Northern University), Glenna Huls (Camden County College), Jeanne Humble (Lexington Community College), Harry Humphries (Pittsburg State University), Cynthia Imanaka (Seattle Central Community College), Jarvis Gamble (Owen's Technical College), Patricia Johnson (Houston Community College), Ed Kain (Southwestern University), Irwin Kantor (Middlesex County College), Thomas Korllos (Kent State University), Rita Krasnow (Virginia Western Community College), Michael Levine (Kenyon College), George Lowe (Texas Tech University), Don Luidens (Hope College), Larry Lyon (Baylor University), Li-Chen Ma (Lamar University), Alan Mazur (Syracuse University), Dan McMurray (Middle Tennessee State University), Jack Melhorn (Emporia State University), Meredith McGuire (Trinity College), Joe Morolla (Virginia Commonwealth University), Craig Nauman (Madison Area Technical College), Daniel Quinn (Adrian College), Toby Parcel (The Ohio State University), Anne Peterson (Columbus State Com munity College), Nevel Razak (Fort Hays State College), Virginia Reynolds (Indiana University of Pennsylvania), Laurel Richardson (The Ohio State University), Ellen Rosengarten (Sinclair Community College), Howard Schneiderman (Lafayette College), Doug Schocke (Northern Virginia Community College), Ray Scupin (Linderwood College), Harry Sherer (Irvine Valley College), Walt Shirley (Sinclair Community College), Glen Sims (Glendale Community College), Greg Spaid (Kenyon College), Verta Taylor (The Ohio State University), Len Tompos (Lorain County Community College), Christopher Vanderpool (Michigan State University), Marilyn Wilmeth (Iowa University), Stuart Wright (Lamar University), Dan Yutze (Taylor University), Wayne Zapatek (Tarrant County Community College), and Frank Zulke (Harold Washington College).

Andrea McMahon-Peakovic, Head of Government Documents at Kenyon College, skillfully secured statistical data for this revision. Finally, beyond providing thoughtful ideas on a daily basis, Amy Marsh Macionis has made a substantial contribution to the editorial and production phases of this revision.

*Jan J. Macionis*

# The Sociological Perspective

On a spring evening in New York's Central Park in 1989, a twenty-eight-year-old woman was jogging after a day of work in the city's financial district. As she passed a grove of sycamore trees, the quiet setting suddenly exploded into a chase as a gang of more than twenty teenage boys pursued her. Flushed with terror, the woman stumbled into a gully where she fought off her attackers while being battered with a pipe and stabbed with a knife. Overpowered and seriously wounded, she was then repeatedly raped. The attackers left her for dead, and she lay helpless and broken until she was found three hours later. Having lost most of her blood, she reached a local hospital in a coma. After months of intensive medical care and rehabilitation, she has made a courageous physical recovery.

Many people reacted to this incident with disbelief. Partly, this was because of the brutality of the attack, and partly because the assailants were so young—fourteen to sixteen years of age. But most curiously, the offenders explained their crime as simply seeking excitement—what they called a night of "wilding." Thus this terrible event provoked people everywhere to confront a basic question: *What makes people do the things they do?*

There are, of course, many ways to look at human events. The *perspective*—or point of view—that people use determines which facts become important and suggests how those facts can be woven together into coherent patterns of meaning. The police officers investigating the "wilding" case used one perspective. They focused on piecing together what happened and on identifying and apprehending the individuals involved. This point of view is concerned primarily with describing an event and establishing a course of action to be undertaken in accordance with the law.

A psychiatrist offers another perspective that might be applied to the boys' behavior. From a psychiatrist's point of view, the important issue is the state of mind that leads an individual to an act of such wanton violence. In this case, the psychiatric perspective would isolate a different set of facts and prescribe a response based on appropriate medical principles.

A sociologist brings yet another perspective to understanding human behavior. A sociologist attempting to make sense of this incident might note that the offenders were males, that they were teenagers, and that they were members of an economically disadvantaged minority. Notice that the facts highlighted by the sociological perspective differ in a crucial way from those noted by law enforcement officials or psychiatrists. The police are concerned with facts that pertain to this one, specific situation. Knowing that an offender is male is useful only insofar as it leads to identifying *which* male was involved. Likewise, psychiatrists seek out the personal traumas that may have contributed to an explosive out-

We can easily grasp the power of society over the individual simply by imagining how different our life would be had we been born in place of any of these children from around the globe.

burst by a particular person. Both police and psychiatrists share the assumption that, in important respects at least, every crime and every person are unique. In contrast, a sociologist looks beyond any *particular* event or person to understand how and why one *category* of people behaves differently from another.

These brief comparisons illustrate the important idea that, to a large degree, reality depends on the perspective we use. This chapter introduces the sociological perspective, which helps us to see how social forces affect our everyday lives.

## The Sociological Perspective

A distinctive perspective is central to the discipline of **sociology,** which may be defined as *the scientific study of human society*. There are perhaps 25,000 sociologists in the United States, many of whom conduct research aimed at learning more about human behavior. In Chapter 2 ("Sociological Investigation"), we delve into how this research is carried out. As explained later in this chapter, sociologists also use various theoretical models to guide their research and teaching. But all sociologists draw on one basic point of view in their quest to understand the social world.

## Seeing the General in the Particular

Peter Berger (1963) describes the sociological perspective as *seeing the general in the particular*. This means that sociologists discern general social patterns in the behavior of particular individuals. Of course, each individual is in some ways unique, but people who fall in the same social categories—based, for instance, on sex, age, and social standing—behave in similar ways. In the "wilding" case just described, we might wonder if violent crime is more common among males, the young, and the disadvantaged, for example, than among females, older people, and the more privileged. Sociological research confirms that this is indeed the case.

To change the example slightly, what are the odds of becoming the *victim* of a violent crime resulting in death? A look at Figure 1–1 shows that some categories of people are more vulnerable to deadly violence than others. Notice, first, a general pattern involving race: *blacks* are more likely to become victims of homicide than are *whites*. The overall rate of victimization for Americans of African descent (34.1 cases for every 100,000 people in this category for the year 1988) is about six times higher than the rate for whites (5.3 per 100,000). But notice that for both races, *males* are more likely to become victims than are *females*, evidence that our sex also has important social consequences. Among whites, males (7.9) are almost three times more likely than females (2.9) to be victims of homicide. For African Americans, males (58.0) have a rate over four times higher than that for females (13.2). As Chapter 8 ("Deviance") explains, the toll of violent crime is especially heavy among disadvantaged African-American men. Clearly, our particular life experiences are shaped by the general categories of society into which we fall.

## Seeing the Strange in the Familiar

The sociological perspective can also be described as *seeing the strange in the familiar*. This does not mean that sociologists focus on the bizarre elements of society. Rather, to make sociological observations requires giving up the familiar idea that human behavior is simply a matter of what people *decide* to do, in favor of the initially strange notion that society influences our lives in key ways. Using the sociological perspective, we are likely to conclude that, in the words of Peter Berger (1963:23), "things are not what they seem."

Individualistic Americans tend to overlook how society affects our thoughts, feelings, and actions. Using the sociological perspective, therefore, takes a bit of practice. The effort is worthwhile, however, because it provides a new level of understanding far richer than simple "common sense."

Take the question of how you came to be a student at your particular college. For most people, specific reasons underlie the choice to attend one college or another:

> I wanted to stay close to home.
>
> This college has the best women's basketball team.
>
> A journalism degree from this university ensures a good job.
>
> My girlfriend goes to school here.

**Figure 1–1**  Rate of Death by Homicide, by Race and Sex, for the United States

Rates indicate the number of deaths by homicide for every 100,000 people in each category for 1988.

(*U.S. Bureau of the Census*)

African-American women and men are underrepresented on the college campuses of the United States. For this reason, these students have a heightened sociological perspective, with keen awareness of many social patterns that members of the white majority take for granted.

I wasn't accepted at the school I really wanted to attend.

Such responses are partly true, and they are certainly real to the people expressing them. But do they tell the full story? The sociological perspective provides additional insights that may not be readily apparent.

To approach the issue of college attendance sociologically, first step back from personal reasons that tell us only about *particular* choices, and think about more *general* patterns. What do students as a *category* of people have in common? A look around a college classroom suggests one answer. Although people of all ages attend college, most students are relatively young—generally between eighteen and twenty-four years of age. This is because our way of life traditionally has linked college attendance to this period of life. More than age is involved, however, because most college-age people in the United States are actually *not* enrolled in college. In fact, only about 37 percent of eighteen- to twenty-four-year-olds were enrolled in 1990.

What else do young people who go to college have in common? Consider social background, which also shapes a person's range of opportunities. Traditionally, students who attend college come from families with annual incomes that are higher than average for the United States. This helps to explain why significantly more whites in this age range (40 percent) are in college

than African Americans (31 percent) and Hispanics[1] (19 percent) (U.S. Bureau of the Census, 1991).

Of course, just as students fall into various categories, so do our nation's colleges and universities. Some colleges are much more expensive than others, and going away to school costs more than attending college while living at home.

More than three-fourths of the 13 million college students in the United States attend schools that receive government funding (U.S. Department of Education, 1991). These schools include locally supported community colleges, which generally offer two-year programs, as well as four-year state colleges and universities. In both cases, 1993 annual tuition for students living at home averaged about $2,000; for those paying room and board, the total was above $5,000. Private four-year colleges and universities, however, were even more expensive: tuition, room, and board costs averaged roughly $13,000, with the total bill at the most expensive private colleges exceeding $20,000 a year. Because most of the costs of a college education in the United States are paid by students and their families, students with modest means are likely to select local two-year colleges

---

[1] Hispanics may be of any race; about 85 percent describe their race as white. Here we are comparing Hispanics with non-Hispanic whites. The data presented here are for men and women ages twenty and twenty-one.

or four-year state schools. Older students with job and family responsibilities also favor these schools, taking advantage not only of lower costs but of part-time and evening programs. Private four-year colleges and universities are typically the choice of younger, more affluent students who are able to study full time.

Although it may initially seem strange to explain personal choices in terms of social forces, the sociological perspective empowers us as we come to understand how our own experiences—including the opportunities and barriers we face—are linked to where we are placed in the vast society around us. The box illustrates further how social forces affect a seemingly personal matter: our choice of name.

## Putting People in Social Context

Our society teaches us to view our lives in very personal terms, emphasizing personal choice. Thus everyday awareness carries a heavy load of personal responsibility, so that we pat ourselves on the back when we enjoy

success and kick ourselves when things go wrong. Proud of our individuality, even in painful times, we resist the idea that we act in socially patterned ways. Indeed, when life goes awry we are often intent on attaching personal blame to people who may not be entirely responsible for their actions.

For this reason, a tragic event such as the Central Park attack described at the beginning of this chapter often provokes controversy about how much responsibility should be attached to the offenders. The box on page 6 looks critically at the spirited debate that appeared in the press after this crime.

### Suicide: The Most Individual Act

There is perhaps no more compelling demonstration of how social forces affect human behavior than the study of suicide. What, after all, could be more personal than the act of taking one's own life? Perhaps this is why Emile Durkheim (1858–1917), a pioneer of sociology, writing a century ago, chose this as a topic of study. Durkheim was able to show that social forces are at

**SOCIAL DIVERSITY**

# What's in a Name? How Social Forces Affect Personal Choice

On the fourth of July in 1918, twins were born to Abe and Becky Friedman in Sioux City, Iowa. The first to arrive was called Esther Pauline Friedman; her sister was named Pauline Esther Friedman. Today, these women are known to almost everyone in the United States, but by new names they later adopted: Ann Landers and Abigail ("Dear Abby") Van Buren.

These two women are among the thousands of men and women who changed their names to further their careers. This practice has been especially common among celebrities. At first glance, changing one's name may seem to be little more than a matter of particular preferences. But take a closer look at the following list from a sociological point of view. Histori-

cally, women and men of various national backgrounds have tended to adopt *English-sounding* names. Why? Because the United States has long accorded high social prestige to those of Anglo-Saxon background. How many of these well-known people can you identify from their original names?

1. Michael James Vijencio Gubitosi
2. Cherilyn Sarkisian
3. Cheryl Stoppelmoor
4. Robert Allen Zimmerman
5. Patsy McClenny
6. Nathan Birnbaum
7. Frederick Austerlitz
8. George Kyriakou Panayiotou
9. Ana Mae Bullock

10. Issur Danielovitch Demsky
11. Mladen Sekulovich
12. Gerald Silberman
13. Bernadette Lazzarra
14. Karen Ziegler
15. Ramon Estevez
16. Henry John Deutschendorf, Jr.
17. Allan Stewart Konigsberg
18. Judy Cohen
19. Eugene Maurice Orowitz
20. William Claude Dukenfield

1. Robert Blake; 2. Cher; 3. Cheryl Ladd; 4. Bob Dylan; 5. Morgan Fairchild; 6. George Burns; 7. Fred Astaire; 8. George Michael; 9. Tina Turner; 10. Kirk Douglas; 11. Karl Malden; 12. Gene Wilder; 13. Bernadette Peters; 14. Karen Black; 15. Martin Sheen; 16. John Denver; 17. Woody Allen; 18. Juice Newton; 19. Michael Landon; 20. W. C. Fields

# The "Wilding" Controversy: Are Sociologists Bleeding Hearts?

In the weeks following the "wilding" incident in New York's Central Park, the press presented different views about how much personal responsibility should be assigned to the teenagers who committed the crime.

On one side of the controversy, a number of sociologists, social workers, and various other professionals pointed out that a wide range of social factors—including sex, age, race, and social background—had to be considered in assessing responsibility. But others strongly objected to this position. Indeed, several nationally known commentators took the opportunity to belittle sociology itself by arguing that the discipline's concern for social forces merely obscured the basic issue: these were *bad* kids who had committed a morally repulsive act, and they should be *punished*. Never mind, they added, what the "bleeding hearts" say.

George F. Will, a Pulitzer Prize–winning journalist, no doubt spoke for many when he denounced "psycho-socio babble" that blamed society, rather than the boys, for the attack. Sociologists, Will contended, confused the issue by "dispersing responsibility into a fog of 'socio-economic factors.'" From Will's point of view, the issue is simpler: there are good people and evil people.

Will, of course, has a point. When a particular event causes pain and anguish, people want to assign blame and exact punishment. In this case, six young boys were arrested and charged with the crimes. Thus, the perceived evil was addressed, and people's passionate sense of anger and injustice served. But is this the whole picture?

Sociologists would have to say no, and they also have a point. To begin, we must state clearly that sociological analysis is *not* a plea to turn loose people who commit violent crimes. But we must be prepared to face the truth that no human behavior is the product solely of what philosophers (and George Will) call "free will" or "simple choice." On the contrary, although human behavior involves choices, these choices are made within a constellation of influential social forces (not to mention whatever biological and psychological forces may also be at work). "Simple" is one thing human beings are not.

Consider one's sex: would anyone imagine girls to be as likely as boys to commit this kind of crime? The fact is that males in the United States engage in nine times as many violent crimes as females do, as Chapter 8 ("Deviance") explains. And what about age? Are middle-aged men as likely as teenagers to "choose" a night of wilding? Hardly, as evidenced by the fact that people between the ages of fifteen and twenty-tour represent only one-sixth of the population of the United States but account for almost half of all violent crimes. Likewise, we know that categories of people who are poor—including African Ameri-

cans and other disadvantaged minorities—are involved in more violence, both as victims and offenders, than are more affluent people. Finally, we might well consider the fact that crimes such as the Central Park attack are remarkably *American*. More assaults and murders occur in New York and other cities in the United States in a typical week than occur in most large cities in Europe in a year. And in our society, sexuality is all too often linked to rape and other brutal forms of violence.

In short, no society can exist without demanding that people take some personal responsibility for their actions. For this reason, Americans typically respond to morally outrageous behavior by seeking to attach blame to specific people. Many will agree with George Will that to blame "society" for a crime is to blame everyone and no one. But in this cultural climate of individualism, sociology injects a needed sense of balance. Embedded in society from the moment of birth, we learn to think, feel, and act as products of a larger social world. To think sociologically is not, therefore, to become a "bleeding heart." It is to understand ourselves and the world around us more fully and accurately. If our desire is to control crime effectively, we must not only punish individuals but address the situations that encourage people to make evil choices.

SOURCES: Lukas (1989), Will (1989), and Yoder (1989).

work even in the apparent isolation of a self-destructive act.

Durkheim, who lived in France, examined records of suicide in various regions of Central Europe.[2] These documents revealed that some categories of people were much more likely than others to choose to commit suicide. Specifically, Durkheim found that men, Protestants, wealthy people, and the unmarried all had significantly higher suicide rates than did women, Catholics and Jews, the poor, and married people. What factor underlies these findings? Durkheim realized that the degree of *social integration* typical of particular categories of people significantly influences the propensity to commit suicide. That is, he found that high suicide rates corresponded with categories of people who were autonomous and individualistic. By contrast, he noted, suicide was less likely among those people who commonly have stronger social bonds.

Within the male-dominated societies of nineteenth-century Europe, men certainly had more autonomy than women. Whatever advantages this freedom afforded, reasoned Durkheim, it also meant that men killed themselves with greater frequency. Likewise, Catholic and Jewish ritual fosters stronger social ties and greater conformity than do individualistic Protestant doctrines. The result, he found, was that Protestants had a higher suicide rate than Catholics or Jews. The wealthy clearly have much more freedom than do the poor, but with the predictable result in terms of suicide rates. Finally, single people are less attached to others than married people are, which, consistent with Durkheim's theory, explained their greater likelihood of suicide.

A century later, statistical evidence continues to support Durkheim's analysis (Pescosolido & Georgianna, 1989; U.S. Bureau of the Census, 1991). Figure 1–2 shows suicide rates for four categories of Americans. With 12.2 recorded instances of suicide for every 100,000 people in this category in 1988, whites have a rate twice as high as that of blacks (6.8). Also, for each racial category, suicide is more common among men than women. White men (19.8) are almost four times more likely than white women (5.1) to take their own lives. Among African Americans, men (11.8) are about five times more likely than women (2.4) to do so. Following Durkheim's argument, we conclude that the higher suicide rate among whites and men—and especially white

---

[2] This discussion is a much-abbreviated account of Durkheim's (1966; orig. 1897) considerably more complex analysis of suicide.

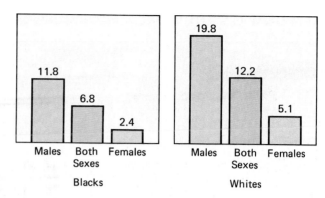

**Figure 1–2**  Rate of Death by Suicide, by Race and Sex, for the United States

Rates indicate the number of deaths by suicide for every 100,000 people in each category for 1988.

*(U.S. Bureau of the Census)*

men—is due to their greater affluence and autonomy in American society. In contrast, poorer people and those with limited social choices are more socially rooted and have correspondingly lower rates of self-destruction.

In this way, we see general social patterns in even the most personal actions of individuals. Social forces are complex, of course, as a comparison of Figures 1–1 and 1–2 shows. We can see that social forces linked to race produce very different patterns with regard to death from homicide and suicide. African Americans and other disadvantaged people suffer disproportionately from homicide; whites, as a privileged category, suffer from suicide. In contrast, gender operates consistently: men are more prone to both homicide and suicide than are women. The precise patterns may change, but in all such cases we are able to see how society is at work in our lives.

## The Importance of Global Perspective

The sociological perspective reveals that our placement in the surrounding society has profound effects on our individual experiences. In recent years, many sociologists have extended this vision a step further by investigating how the position that the United States occupies in the larger world order affects us.

In global perspective, the United States and Canada are among the world's richest societies, as Global Map

**Global Map 1–1**   Per Capita Income in Global Perspective

Comprehending the range of opportunities and obstacles that confront us depends not only on understanding our place in a single society, but also on seeing our society's position in the world as a whole. Average people in the United States and Canada, where income is far higher than in most of the world, live longer and more comfortably than people who inhabit poor societies of Latin America, Africa, and Asia.

1–1 shows. The average annual income in the United States (children as well as adults) stands at more than $10,000. This affluence creates a range of personal choices for people in the United States—in terms of housing, health care, education, and opportunities for personal recreation—that are extraordinary. By contrast, as the map suggests, billions of the world's people contend with limited choices because they live in poor, strongly traditional communities. Chapter 11 ("Global Inequality") explores the causes and consequences of wealth and poverty on a global scale. For the present, merely keep in mind that the opportunities we face and the choices we make stem from both our placement in society and our country's standing in the world of nations.

A global awareness also helps us to learn about life closer to home. Social scientists have long recognized that studying others invariably provokes insights about ourselves. We could hardly consider the life of a young woman growing up in Saudi Arabia or a man coming of age in the African nation of Botswana without thinking about what it means to live in the United States. Thus almost every chapter of this text incorporates a global perspective into the discussion at hand.

As we approach the twenty-first century, learning about our own society demands familiarity with the rest of the world. And there is a very practical reason for this: about 80 percent of new jobs created in the United States are the result of some kind of foreign trade (Council on International Educational Exchange, 1988).

## The Sociological Perspective in Everyday Life

As we have seen, members of our society often overlook the power of social forces. Yet some kinds of situations do prompt us to view the world sociologically even before we take our first course in sociology.

### Sociology and Social Diversity

A Japanese student who has just arrived on a Minnesota college campus is likely to notice social patterns that people in the United States take for granted. The strangeness of the surroundings alerts a foreigner that people's behavior reflects not only individual choice but also patterns of the larger society. In the same way, an American encountering the social diversity of the world gains a heightened awareness of social forces. Our perspective widens as well when we confront unfamiliar social environments here at home—visiting strange neighborhoods, for example, or meeting people whose beliefs and patterns of behavior are quite different from our own.

### Sociology and Social Marginality: Race, Gender, and Age

Sociologists use the term **social marginality** to refer to *the state of being excluded from social activity as an "outsider."* All people experience social marginality from time to time; for some categories of Americans, however,

being an outsider is commonplace. The more intense their social marginality, the more likely they are to make use of the sociological perspective.

No African American, for example, can live very long in the United States without being aware of how much race affects personal experiences. But because whites constitute the dominant majority in the United States, whites think about race only occasionally and tend to view race as an issue that applies only to people of African or Asian descent rather than to themselves as well.

Similarly, women of all races are more likely to see the world sociologically than are men. For several decades, women who have personally experienced the limitations that our society imposes on females have been comparing notes. The result has been a growing awareness by women that any person's particular choices, achievements, or failings reflect general social forces. Men, because of their dominant social position, generally fail to see patterns of sexual inequality as clearly and sometimes accuse women of exaggerating the problem. In the 1970s, American women described the recognition of sexual inequality as "consciousness raising." It was also one way of gaining a sociological perspective.

The elderly often perceive social patterns more acutely than do young people. While this may be partly due to wisdom gained over a lifetime, another important factor is that the elderly often experience considerable social marginality. As Chapter 14 ("Aging and the Elderly") explains, the members of our society tend to define growing old as the loss of the capacity to engage in many important human endeavors, including physical recreation, work, and even sex. Since most elderly people are indeed physically and mentally capable of all these activities, they understand more clearly than the young the degree to which society defines what individuals are and how they should think and act.

In short, people who are placed on the outside of social life—due to their race, sex, age, or a host of other factors—are usually more aware of social patterns that others take for granted. They have stepped back from society (perhaps, more accurately, society has stepped back from them) and therefore take a more sociological view of the world.

### Sociology and Social Crisis

American sociologist C. Wright Mills (1959) suggested that times of social disruption foster widespread sociological thinking. In Mills's life, the 1930s stood out as a decade of heightened sociological awareness. The Great Depression followed the stock market crash of 1929, throwing one-fourth of the labor force out of work. Under such circumstances, most unemployed people could not help but see general social forces at work in their particular lives. Rather than claiming, "Something is wrong with me; I can't find a job," they were likely to say, "There are no jobs to be found because the economy has collapsed!"

People very quickly develop a sociological perspective when the established patterns of society begin to shake and crumble. More recently, the decade of the 1960s also enhanced sociological awareness in the United States. The civil rights, women's liberation, antiwar, and hippie movements all challenged accepted social patterns in a highly visible way. This social climate called attention to the ways in which personal experiences are shaped by forces beyond the people themselves—the political, economic, military, and technological elements of "the system." Although the merits of these movements may be debated, there is no doubt that, by pointing to social forces that affect the lives of all women and men, they each incorporated an element of the sociological perspective.

Worth noting, too, is that the converse is often true: sociological thinking sometimes fosters social disruption. In other words, gaining a sociological understanding of how "the system" works may well provoke attempts to change it. For example, as more and more women and men confront the power of gender, many are actively trying to reduce the traditional separation of men's and women's lives.

As these everyday examples suggest, an introduction to sociology is an invitation to discover a new way of looking at familiar patterns of social life. At this point, we might well consider whether this invitation is worth accepting. In other words, what are the benefits of learning to use the sociological perspective?

## Benefits of the Sociological Perspective

The knowledge amassed by sociologists can be readily applied to our lives in countless ways. There are, however, four general benefits of exploring the sociological perspective.

First, we start to realize that certain ideas we have come to accept as "true" have no basis in fact. *The sociological perspective challenges familiar understandings about ourselves and others, so that we can critically assess the truth of commonly held assumptions.*

As we have already seen, a good example of a widespread but misleading "truth" is that women and men in the United States are "autonomous individuals" who are responsible for their lives. By thinking this way, we are sometimes too quick to praise particularly successful people as being personally superior to those who have not fared as well. On the other side of the coin,

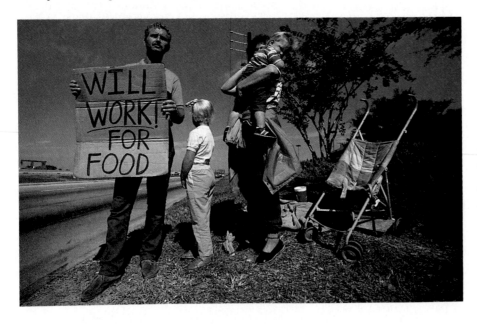

Because our way of life places such a high value on individualism and personal autonomy, we learn to think of advantaged people as especially capable and disadvantaged people as personally undeserving. The sociological perspective challenges this conclusion by showing that our life experiences also reflect larger forces, such as dramatic shifts in the economy, which may be completely beyond our control.

# C. Wright Mills (1916–1962)

Charles Wright Mills managed to cause a stir with most everything he did. Even arriving for a class at New York's Columbia University—astride his motorcycle and clad in a sweatshirt and boots—he was likely to turn some heads. During the conservative 1950s, Mills not only dressed a bit out of the mainstream; he produced a number of books that critically challenged most of the beliefs Americans took for granted. In the process, he won both followers and adversaries.

Mills's most enduring contribu-tion was his insistence that people actively use what he described as the "sociological imagination" in their daily lives. Mills rejected soci-ology as a dry enterprise detached from life in favor of a vital process by which people became engaged in their social world. His hopeful vision was for a sociologically aware society forging a more gen-tle and just way of life.

The following excerpt spells out the first step in Mills's vision.* Here he suggests that we must learn to understand our individual lives in terms of the social forces that have shaped them.

When a society becomes industrial-ized, a peasant becomes a worker; a feudal lord is liquidated or be-comes a businessman. When classes rise or fall, a man is em-ployed or unemployed; when the rate of investment goes up or down, a man takes new heart or goes

---

*In this excerpt, Mills uses male pronouns which appear as he wrote them. Of course, his point applies to all people. It is interest-ing, and even ironic, that Mills, an outspo-ken critic of society, reflected in his writing the conventional practices of his time as far as gender was concerned.

broke. When wars happen, an in-surance salesman becomes a rocket launcher; a store clerk, a radar man; a wife lives alone; a child grows up without a father. Neither the life of an individual nor the his-tory of a society can be understood without understanding both.

Yet men do not usually define the troubles they endure in terms of historical change. . . . The well-be-ing they enjoy, they do not usually impute to the big ups and downs of the society in which they live. Seldom aware of the intricate con-nection between the patterns of their own lives and the course of world history, ordinary men do not usually know what this connection means for the kind of men they are becoming and for the kinds of his-tory-making in which they might take part. They do not possess the quality of mind essential to grasp the interplay of men and society, of biography and history, of self and world. . . .

What they need . . . is a quality of mind that will help them to [see] . . . what is going on in the world and . . . what may be happening within themselves. It is this quality . . . that . . . may be called the so-ciological imagination.

SOURCE:   Mills (1959): 3–5.

---

people who do not measure up may be unfairly con-demned as personally deficient. A sociological approach encourages us to ask whether these beliefs are actually true and, to the extent that they are not, why they are so widely held.

Second, the sociological perspective helps us see that, for better or worse, our own society operates in a particular and deliberate way. This is important because no one is able to live with complete disregard for society's rules. In the game of life, we may decide how to play

our cards, but it is society that deals us the hand. The more we understand about how the game works, the more effective a player we will be. Put another way, *the sociological perspective allows us to recognize both the opportunities we have and the constraints that circum-scribe our lives.* Knowledge of this kind is power. Through it, we come to understand what we are likely and unlikely to accomplish for ourselves, and how the goals we adopt can be realized more effectively.

Third, sociological thinking encourages a more

active life. Without an awareness of how society operates, we are likely to accept passively the status quo. However, the greater our understanding of the operation of society, the more we can take an active part in shaping social life. *The sociological perspective, therefore, empowers us as active members of our world.* For some, this may mean embracing society as it is; other people, however, may attempt nothing less than changing the entire world in some way. The discipline of sociology advocates no one particular political orientation, and sociologists themselves weigh in at points all across the political spectrum. But evaluating any aspect of social life—whatever one's eventual goal—depends on the ability to identify social forces and to assess their consequences.

Some thirty years ago, C. Wright Mills (1959) pointed out the importance of what he called the "sociological imagination" in helping people to engage actively the world around them. This pioneering sociologist is highlighted in the profile box. Others will be featured in boxes throughout this book.

A fourth and final benefit of sociological thinking is learning that our world contains a remarkable variety of human social patterns. North Americans represent a scant 5 percent of the world's population and, as the remaining chapters of this book reveal, the rest of humanity lives in ways that often differ dramatically from our own. Like people elsewhere, we tend to define our own way of life as proper and "natural." But the cultural diversity of today's world presents us with countless competing versions of correct behavior. *The sociological perspective helps us to recognize human diversity and to begin to understand the challenges of living in a diverse world.*

## The Origins of Sociology

Like the "choices" made by individuals, major historical events rarely "just happen." They are typically products of powerful social forces that are always complex and only partly predictable. So it was with the emergence of sociology itself. Having described the discipline's distinctive perspective and its benefits, we now consider how and why this discipline emerged in the first place.

Although human beings have mused about society since the beginning of our history, sociology is of relatively recent origin. It is one of the youngest academic disciplines—far younger than history, physics, or economics, for example. Only in 1838 did the French social thinker Auguste Comte, introduced in the box, coin

---

## Auguste Comte (1798–1857)

What sort of person would invent *sociology?* Someone living in times of momentous change, no doubt.

Comte grew up in the shadow of the French Revolution, which brought a sweeping transformation to his country. And if that wasn't sufficient, another revolution was going on at the same time: factories were sprouting up across Europe, recasting the lives of the entire population. Just as people enduring a storm cannot help but think of the weather, so those living during Comte's turbulent era became keenly aware of the state of society.

Drawn from a small town to the bustle and energy of Paris, Comte was soon deeply involved in the exciting events of his time. More than anything else, he wanted to understand the human drama that was unfolding all around him. Once equipped with the knowledge of how society operates, Comte believed people would be able to build a better future for themselves. He divided his new discipline into two parts: how society is held together (which he called *social statics*), and how society changes (*social dynamics*). From the Greek and Latin words meaning "the study of society," Comte came to describe his work as *sociology*.

---

This medieval drawing conveys the mix of apprehension and excitement with which early scientists began to question conventional understandings of the universe. Pioneering sociologists, too, challenged many ideas that had been long taken for granted, generating new and often controversial ideas.

the term *sociology* to describe a new way of looking at the world.

## Science and Sociology

The nature of human society held the attention of the writings of virtually all the brilliant thinkers of the ancient world, including the Chinese philosopher K'ung Futzu or Confucius (551–479 B.C.E.), and the Greek philosophers Plato (427–347 B.C.E.) and Aristotle (384–322 B.C.E.).[3] Similarly, the Roman emperor Marcus Aurelius (121–180), the medieval theologian St. Thomas Aquinas (c. 1225–1274), the English playwright William Shakespeare (1564–1616), and a host of others reflected on the social world in their writings. Yet, as Emile Durkheim noted almost a century ago, none of these social thinkers approached society from a sociological point of view.

> Looking back in history . . . we find that no philosophers ever viewed matters [with a sociological perspective] until quite recently. . . . It seemed to them sufficient to ascertain

what the human will should strive for and what it should avoid in established societies. . . . Their aim was not to offer us as valid a description of nature as possible, but to present us with the idea of a perfect society, a model to be imitated. (1972:57; orig. 1918)

What made sociology different from what came before? Prior to the birth of sociology, philosophers and theologians were mostly concerned with imagining the "ideal" society, that is, life as it ought to be. None attempted an analysis of "real" society, as it actually was. Pioneers of the discipline such as Auguste Comte and Emile Durkheim reversed these priorities. Although they were certainly concerned with how human society could be improved, their major goal was to understand how society actually operates.

The key to achieving this goal, according to Comte, was the development of a scientific approach to studying society. Looking back over history, Comte sorted out efforts to understand society into three distinct stages (1975; orig. 1851–1854). The earliest era, extending through the medieval period in Europe, he termed the *theological stage*. At this point, thoughts about the world were guided by religion. More specifically, society was regarded as an expression of God's will—at least insofar as people and their religious leaders were capable of fulfilling a divine plan.

With the Renaissance, the theological approach to society gave way to what Comte called the *metaphysical*

---

[3] Throughout this text, the abbreviation B.C.E. designates "before the common era." This terminology is used in place of the traditional B.C. ("before Christ") in recognition of the religious plurality of the United States. Similarly, in place of the traditional A.D. (anno Domini, or "in the year of our Lord"), the abbreviation C.E. ("common era") is employed.

*stage*. During this period, people started to view society as a natural, rather than a supernatural, phenomenon. Human nature figured heavily in metaphysical visions of society; the English philosopher Thomas Hobbes (1588–1679), for example, suggested that society reflected not the perfection of God so much as the failings of selfish human nature.

What Comte heralded as the final, *scientific stage* in the long quest to understand society was prompted by scientists such as the Polish astronomer Copernicus (1473–1543), the Italian astronomer and physicist Galileo (1564–1642), and the English physicist and mathematician Isaac Newton (1642–1727). Comte's contribution came in applying this scientific approach—first used to study the physical world—to the study of society.

Comte was thus a proponent of **positivism**, defined as *a means to understand the world based on science*. As a positivist, Comte believed that society conforms to invariable laws, much as the physical world operates according to gravity and other laws of nature.

Sociology emerged as an academic discipline in the United States at the beginning of this century, with early sociologists such as Lester Ward (1841–1913) pursuing Comte's vision of a scientific sociology. Even today, most sociologists continue to view science as a crucial element of sociology, but we have learned that scientific techniques cannot be applied to the social world in the same way they are applied to the physical world. As we shall explain in Chapter 2 ("Sociological Investigation"), the causes of human behavior are often far more complex than the causes of events in the natural world. Put another way, human beings, unlike mere physical objects, do not always act in predictable ways. We are creatures with considerable imagination and spontaneity; thus, our behavior can never be fully explained by any rigid "laws of society."

## Social Change and Sociology

We have already suggested that the discipline of sociology sprang from revolutionary changes in society itself. European societies were buffeted by a number of great transformations during the seventeenth and eighteenth centuries. As the social ground trembled under their feet, people were understandably drawn to the study of society.

Three key factors fueled the great reshaping of society during this period. First, rapid technological innovation in eighteenth-century Europe gave rise to factories and a new industrial economy. Second, these factories drew millions of people from the countryside, causing an explosive growth of cities. Third, people in these expanding industrial cities soon began to entertain new political ideas about democracy and individual rights. We shall briefly describe each of these three interrelated changes in turn.

### A New Industrial Economy

During the Middle Ages, most people in Europe tilled fields near their homes while others engaged in small-scale *manufacturing* (a word derived from Latin words meaning "to make by hand"). Many people worked where they lived; homes were centers of commercial endeavors such as baking, furniture making, and sewing of garments.

Early in the eighteenth century, new sources of energy, especially steam power, were harnessed to large machines. Factories began to spring up. Now, instead of laboring at home, or on land that families had worked for generations, workers became part of a vast and anonymous industrial work force, toiling away from home for strangers who owned the factories. More than just a new way to produce goods, factories set loose an expanding industrial economy that soon shook medieval society to its foundations. Traditional ways of life fell victim to the sweeping changes, and countless small, closely knit communities were swallowed up by the expanding scale of life. Steadily, factories drew people from the countryside to produce gargantuan cities.

### The Growth of Cities

Factories sprouting across England and elsewhere in Western Europe became magnets attracting people in need of work. This "pull" was made all the more powerful by an additional "push" from the villages. As the English textile industry expanded, new industrialists fenced off more and more farmland to raise sheep—the source of wool. This "enclosure movement" pushed countless people from the countryside into the cities in search of jobs, which they could find in factories.

Not surprisingly, these new industrial cities soon reached unprecedented size. During the Middle Ages, towns had been small, self-contained worlds within defensive walls. As late as 1700—the dawning of the industrial era—London was the largest city in Europe with only 500,000 people. Within two centuries, that city's population had increased by *thirteen times* to 6.5 million (Chandler & Fox, 1974).

The birth of sociology came at a time of rapid social change. The discipline developed in those regions of Europe where the Industrial Revolution most disrupted traditional ways of life, drawing people from isolated villages to rapidly growing industrial cities.

Urban growth on this scale took place across the European continent, dramatically changing people's lives. Not only were cities full of strangers, but the tremendous influx of people simply overwhelmed the cities' capacity to absorb them. Widespread social problems—including pollution, crime, and inadequate housing—were the order of the day. These social crises stimulated the development of the sociological perspective.

### Political Change

During the Middle Ages, as Comte noted, most people thought of society as an expression of divine will. The feudal nobility claimed to rule by "divine right," as if the entire social order were simply God's plan for humanity. This belief is evident in lines from the old Anglican hymn "All Things Bright and Beautiful":

> The rich man in his castle,
> The poor man at his gate,
> He made them high and lowly
> And ordered their estate.

Considering, in hindsight, the new emerging economy and the rapid growth of cities, changes in political thought seem to have been inevitable. By the sixteenth century, the political conservatism that had characterized the medieval era was crumbling under a spirited attack on tradition, especially the notion that society reflected God's will. In the writings of Thomas Hobbes, John Locke (1632–1704), and Adam Smith (1723–1790), we find less concern with the moral obligations of people to society and more support for the idea that society is the product of self-interest. The key phrases in the new political climate, therefore, heralded the individual: *individual liberty* and *individual rights*. The American Declaration of Independence, which celebrated the separation of the American colonies from England, is a clear statement of these new political ideas. Here we read that each individual has "certain unalienable rights," including "life, liberty, and the pursuit of happiness." The political revolution in France that began soon afterward in 1789 was an even more dramatic effort to break with political and social traditions.

As he surveyed his society after the French Revolution, the French social analyst Alexis de Tocqueville exaggerated only slightly when he exclaimed that the changes we have described amounted to "nothing short of the regeneration of the whole human race" (1955:13; orig. 1856). In this context, it is easy to see why Auguste

Comte and other pioneers forged the new discipline of sociology. Sociology flowered in precisely those societies that had experienced the most pronounced social changes. France, Germany, and England underwent a truly revolutionary social transformation, and in all three sociology had emerged by the end of the nineteenth century. In contrast, in societies touched less by these momentous events—including Portugal, Spain, Italy, and Eastern Europe—there was little development of the sociological perspective.

Individual sociologists reacted differently to the new social order then, just as they respond differently to society today. Some found the emerging modern world deeply disturbing. Auguste Comte, for example, feared that people would be overpowered by change and uprooted from long-established local communities. Embracing social conservatism, he sought a rebirth of traditional family, community, and morality.

A different view of these massive changes characterized the thinking of German social critic Karl Marx (1818–1883), whose ideas are presented at length in Chapter 4 ("Society"). Marx worried little about the loss of traditional social patterns, which he detested. But neither could he condone the concentration of the great wealth produced by industrial technology in the hands of a small elite, while the masses faced only hunger and misery.

Clearly, Comte and Marx advanced radically different views on the problems of modernity. Yet they shared the conviction that society cannot be understood simply in terms of individual choice. The sociological perspective animates the work of each, revealing that people's individual lives are framed by the broader society in which they live. This lesson, of course, is as true today as it was in the nineteenth century.

The major issues that concern sociologists are highlighted in subsequent chapters of this book. These important social forces include culture, social class, race, ethnicity, gender, the family, and the economy. They all involve ways in which individuals are guided, united, and divided in the larger arena of society.

## Sociological Theory

Sociology involves more than adopting a distinctive point of view. Linking specific observations in a meaningful way focuses on another element of the discipline: theory. In the simplest terms, a **theory** is *the process of linking facts together in order to explain something*. To illustrate the use of theory in sociology, recall Emile Durkheim's investigation of suicide. Durkheim attempted to explain the fact that some categories of people (men, Protestants, the wealthy, and the unmarried) have higher suicide rates than others (women, Catholics, Jews, the poor, and the married). He did this by linking suicide rates to another fact—the degree of social integration typical of various categories of people. Through systematic comparisons, Durkheim refined his theory of suicide, learning that people with low social integration are more prone to take their own lives.

To illustrate further, how do we explain the fact that more men than women enroll in college science courses? Using the sociological perspective, we suspect that more than random individual choices are involved. One possible theory is that the sciences are more attractive to men than to women; perhaps men have a greater innate interest in science. A second premise is that the educational system has some formal or informal policy that limits the enrollment of women in science courses. Still another possibility is that our society encourages men to develop an interest in science while simultaneously discouraging this interest in women.

As this example shows, facts can be linked in different ways to generate a range of theoretical explanations. Merely linking facts together, therefore, hardly ensures that a theory is correct. To evaluate a theory, sociologists use methods of scientific research, described in the next chapter, to gather more information. This enables them to confirm some theories while rejecting or modifying others. Early in this century, for example, sociologists studying the rapid growth of cities theorized that urban living promoted impersonality and even mental illness. As we shall explain in Chapter 21 ("Population and Urbanization"), however, research has subsequently shown that living in a large city does not necessarily mean that people become socially isolated, nor does it diminish their mental health. Theory, then, is never static; sociologists continually refine theory through research, just as other types of scientists do.

In attempting to develop theories about human society, sociologists face a wide range of choices. What issues should they study? How should facts be linked together to form theories? Such questions are not answered haphazardly. Rather, theory building is guided by a general framework called a theoretical paradigm (Kuhn, 1970). Applied to sociology, a **theoretical paradigm** is defined as *a set of fundamental assumptions about society that guides sociological thinking and research*.

We suggested earlier that two of sociology's founders—Auguste Comte and Karl Marx—made sense of the emerging modern world in different ways. Such differences persist among sociologists today. Some are more concerned with ways societies stay the same; others focus on how societies change. Similarly, some direct attention to what joins people together, while others investigate how society divides people according to sex, race, or social class. Some sociologists seek to understand the operation of society as it is, while others see their work as encouraging what they consider to be desirable social change.

In short, sociologists often disagree about what the most interesting questions are; even when they agree about the questions, they may still differ over the answers. Nonetheless, sociological theory is far from chaotic, because sociologists share three major theoretical paradigms that allow them to analyze effectively virtually any dimension of society.

## The Structural-Functional Paradigm

The **structural-functional paradigm** is *a framework for building theory guided by the assumption that society is a complex system whose parts work together to promote stability.* As its name suggests, the structural-functional paradigm has two components. First, society is composed of numerous kinds of **social structure,** defined as *relatively stable patterns of social behavior.* Social structures range from broad patterns such as family life and economic systems to situational behaviors such as greetings and other forms of face-to-face contact. Second, this paradigm links structures together in terms of their **social functions,** which refer to *consequences for the operation of society as a whole.* Thus all the elements of society—from families to a simple handshake—have important functions that help perpetuate society, at least in its present form.

The structural-functional paradigm owes much to the ideas of Auguste Comte, who tried to imagine how his own society could remain unified while undergoing massive change. Another who advanced this theoretical approach was the English sociologist Herbert Spencer (1820–1903), introduced in the box on page 18. One of the most influential thinkers of his time, Spencer studied both the human body and society. He came to believe that the two have much in common. The structural parts of the human body include the skeleton, muscles, and various internal organs. All these elements

are interdependent, each having a function that contributes to the survival of the entire human organism. Likewise, reasoned Spencer, the elements of social life are interdependent, working to keep society operating with minimal disruption. The structural-functional approach, then, leads sociologists to identify the various parts of society, investigating the contribution of each.

Several decades after the death of Auguste Comte, Emile Durkheim expanded on the structural-functional paradigm in France. Like Spencer, his English counterpart, Durkheim investigated ways in which modern societies remain integrated. Because of the importance of his ideas to later chapters, Durkheim's analysis of social structures and their functions will be detailed in Chapter 4 ("Society").

As sociology developed in the United States, the approach of Herbert Spencer and Emile Durkheim was carried forward by Talcott Parsons (1902–1979). The chief proponent of the structural-functional paradigm in U.S. sociology, Parsons sought to identify the major functions any and all societies had to perform in order to survive, and how they accomplished them.

Another contemporary U.S. sociologist whose work falls within the structural-functional approach, Robert K. Merton (1968), has shown that social patterns can have many functions. For the same pattern, however, these functions differ depending on the point of view of specific categories of people. For example, traditional courtship behavior may benefit society by encouraging the formation of new families, but these practices may also confer advantages on men (by giving them disproportionate access to wealth and power) while limiting the opportunities of women (who may forgo professional advancement in favor of raising a family). Further, Merton points out that some of the functions of any social pattern may be more obvious than others. The **manifest functions** of any social structure are *consequences that are recognized and intended by people in the society.* By contrast, **latent functions** are *consequences that go largely unrecognized and are unintended.* To illustrate, consider the rapid increase in automobile travel during this century. One manifest consequence of this technological innovation is that people and goods are easily transported from one place to another. Cars also serve a manifest function as *status symbols,* since we sometimes judge people's social standing by the things they own. But the rise in automobile transportation also has significant latent functions. Because they allow people to travel about in relative isolation, cars reinforce our cultural emphasis on personal autonomy. This is one reason

# Herbert Spencer (1820–1903)

Herbert Spencer's most memorable idea was his assertion that the future would be characterized by "the survival of the fittest." Many people link this immortal phrase to the theory of species evolution developed by the natural scientist Charles Darwin (1809–1882). Spencer's concept of survival of the fittest, however, actually referred to society, not to living creatures. But this confusion over Spencer's remark suggests how deeply early sociological thought was influenced by comparisons between the social and natural worlds.

Spencer's view of society, which came to be known as *social Darwinism*, was built on the following principle: success would come to the most intelligent, ambitious, and productive people, who quite properly advanced their interests at the expense of the less able. Spencer endorsed the notion of the survival of the fittest, believing that this process would steadily improve society.

The key to successful social evolution, from Spencer's point of view, was simply not to meddle with society, especially its free-market economy. For this opinion, Spencer was widely applauded by early industrialists who sought to keep big business free of government regulation or social conscience. Indeed, John D. Rockefeller, who gobbled up companies to gain control of much of the American oil industry early in this century, often recited Spencer's words to young children in Sunday school, teaching them to think of the growth of giant businesses as merely the "survival of the fittest."

But others objected to the idea that society was nothing more than a jungle where people selfishly used whatever resources they could muster to their own advantage. Critics found in the new industrial United States a pressing need for social welfare programs that would assist the poor. From Spencer's point of view, however, welfare damaged society by squandering social resources on its least worthy members.

Gradually, Spencer's doctrine of social Darwinism fell out of favor among social scientists, although it remains influential in the United States. Social Darwinism was actually discredited by facts that have since come to light: we now know that an individual's ability only partially accounts for personal success, and favoring the rich and powerful is not necessarily in the interest of society as a whole. In addition, from the standpoint of values, Spencer's ideas have been widely dismissed as a remarkably heartless view of society with little room for human compassion.

---

that private automobiles have long been favored by most Americans over public transit systems.

Merton makes a further point: it is unlikely that *all* the effects of a single social structure will be useful. Merton used the term **social dysfunctions** to designate *undesirable effects of a social pattern on the operation of society.* One of the dysfunctions of our national reliance on private automobiles is that, with more than 180 million of them on the road, air quality has suffered, especially in large cities. No doubt, too, the easy travel

made possible by cars has contributed to a decline in the strength of traditional families and local neighborhoods, changes lamented by many people in the United States.

*Critical evaluation.* The positivist roots of the structural-functional paradigm are evident in this approach's tendency to see the social world as orderly and relatively fixed. The job of sociologists, from this point of view, is to employ scientific research to learn how society works.

Despite its strong influence on the discipline of sociology, however, recent decades have revealed limitations of the structural-functional paradigm.

By assuming that society operates more or less "naturally," critics point out, structural-functionalism tends to overlook ways in which social arrangements are constructed. Social patterns vary widely from place to place, and they change over time; thus, the notion that any particular arrangements are natural seems hazardous at best. Further, by emphasizing social integration, structural-functionalism tends to pay less attention to divisions based on social class, race, ethnicity, and sex, and downplays how such divisions generate tension and conflict. This focus on social stability at the expense of the important processes of conflict and social change gives the structural-functional paradigm a conservative character. As a critical response to this approach, sociologists have developed another theoretical orientation: the social-conflict paradigm.

## The Social-Conflict Paradigm

The **social-conflict paradigm** is *a framework for building theory based on the assumption that society is a complex system characterized by inequality and conflict that generate social change.* This approach complements the structural-functional paradigm by highlighting not integration but division based on social inequality. Guided by this paradigm, sociologists investigate how factors such as social class, race, ethnicity, sex, and age are linked to unequal distribution of valuable resources, including money, power, education, and social prestige. Therefore, rather than identifying how social patterns can be functional for society as a whole, this approach investigates how they are useful to some people and harmful to others. One of the pioneering U.S. sociologists, whose work was framed by a concern for racial conflict, is introduced in the box.

The social-conflict paradigm leads sociologists to view society as an arena in which conflict emerges from the incompatible interests of categories of people who occupy different positions in society. Not surprisingly, dominant categories—the rich in relation to the poor, whites in relation to people of color, and men in relation to women—typically try to protect their privileges by supporting the status quo. Those with fewer privileges commonly counter these efforts by attempting to bring about a more equitable distribution of social resources.

To illustrate, Chapter 16 ("Education") explores how secondary schools in the United States prepare some students for college and emphasize vocational training for others. Thinking in terms of the structural-functional paradigm, we might wonder if society as a whole benefits from such "tracking" to the extent that students receive education according to their academic abilities. The social-conflict paradigm provides a contrasting insight: "tracking" confers privileges on some that it denies to others, perpetuating social inequality and promoting conflict between favored and disadvantaged categories of people.

Research guided by the social-conflict paradigm has shown that schools place students in college-preparatory tracks not so much because of their superior intelligence but because of their privileged background. Virtually ensured of becoming part of the educational elite with a college degree, most of these men and women are likely to enter occupations that will provide both prestige and a high income. In the process, of course, the privileges of one generation are passed down to another. And what of the less privileged students? Schools commonly place them in vocational tracks, sometimes with little regard for their actual abilities. There they receive no preparation for college so that, like their parents before them, they will enter occupations that confer little prestige and low income. From this point of view, "tracking" amounts to using the concept of "ability" to justify a practice that merely perpetuates privilege (Bowles & Gintis, 1976; Oakes, 1982, 1985).

Other important examples of social conflict in the United States are labor strikes, the civil rights movement, and the drive for social equality for women. Overall, then, rather than viewing society as relatively stable, the social-conflict paradigm points out how social structure fosters continual conflict within a society, leading to change.

Finally, many sociologists who make use of the social-conflict paradigm attempt not only to understand society as it is but also to reduce social inequality. This was the goal of W. E. B. DuBois as well as Karl Marx, the social thinker who has had a singularly important influence on the development of the social-conflict paradigm. Marx had little patience with those who sought to use science only to understand how society works. In a well-known declaration (inscribed on his monument in London's Highgate Cemetery), Marx maintained: "The philosophers have only interpreted the world, in various ways; the point, however, is to change it."

*Critical evaluation.* The social-conflict paradigm has developed rapidly in recent decades and is now a major

# W. E. B. DuBois (1868–1963)

The discipline of sociology is built on the work of many pioneers, not all of whom have received the attention they deserve. A case in point is William Edward Burghardt DuBois, whose work both as a scientist and social critic has gained attention only in recent decades.

Born to a poor family in a small Massachusetts town, DuBois showed extraordinary aptitude as a student. After graduating from high school, he went on to college, one of only a handful of young people from his town (and the only person of African descent) to do so. After graduating from Fisk University in Nashville, Tennessee, DuBois realized a childhood ambition and enrolled at Harvard, repeating his junior and senior years and then beginning graduate study. He earned the first doctor-

ate awarded by Harvard to a person of color.

DuBois believed that social research should be linked to contemporary problems, and for him, the vexing issue of race was a paramount concern. Although he was accepted in the intellectual circles of his day, DuBois believed that blacks and whites lived in two distinct social worlds that often erupted in conflict when they came in contact with one another. DuBois maintained that research—although scientifically rigorous and fair-minded—should be directed at answering questions that would improve society. Later in his life, DuBois reflected (1940:51):

I was determined to put science into sociology through a study of the condition of my own group. I was going to study the facts, any and all facts, concerning the American Negro and his plight. . . .

After taking a position at the University of Pennsylvania in Philadelphia, he set out to conduct the research that produced a sociological classic, *The Philadelphia Negro: A Social Study* (1899). In this systematic investigation of Philadelphia's African-American community at the turn of the century, DuBois chronicled both the strengths and weaknesses of people wrestling with overwhelming social problems. Running against

the intellectual current of the times (and especially social Darwinism), DuBois rejected the widespread notion of black inferiority, explaining the problems of African Americans largely in terms of white prejudice. He was critical not only of whites, but also of successful members of the black community whom he scolded for being so eager to win white acceptance that they abandoned all ties with those still in need. "The first impulse of the best, the wisest and the richest," he lamented, "is to segregate themselves from the mass. . . ." (1899:317).

At the time *The Philadelphia Negro* was published, DuBois was optimistic about the chances of resolving the racial problems of the United States. By the end of his life, however, he had grown bitter, thinking that little had been done to advance social equality. At the age of 93, DuBois emigrated to Africa, and he died in Ghana two years later.

Although his research was not widely recognized at the time of his death, today DuBois's books are receiving the attention of a new generation of scholars. A model of sound sociology, his work also addresses many of the problems that continue to beset our society.

SOURCES: Based, in part, on Baltzell (1967) and DuBois (1967; orig. 1899).

part of sociology in the United States and elsewhere. As the paradigm itself would lead us to expect, more traditional sociological thinkers have voiced criticisms. One general concern is that this approach highlights

power struggles as the dominant trait of societies, giving little attention to social unity based on functional interdependence and shared values. In addition, the social-conflict approach is often criticized for explicitly advocating change, thereby giving up at least some claim to scientific objectivity. As Chapter 2 explains in detail, advocates of this approach respond that *all* social approaches have political consequences, albeit different ones.

An additional criticism, which applies equally to both the structural-functional and social-conflict paradigms, is that they envision society in terms of broad abstractions. A third theoretical paradigm views society more in terms of everyday, face-to-face interaction.

## The Symbolic-Interaction Paradigm

Both the structural-functional and social-conflict paradigms share a **macro-level orientation,** meaning *a focus on broad social structures that characterize society as a system.* A macro-level approach to society is rather like investigating a city from high above in a helicopter—noting, for example, that highways facilitate traffic flow from one place to another, or that there are striking contrasts between the neighborhoods of the rich and the poor. The symbolic-interaction paradigm, by contrast, uses a **micro-level orientation,** meaning *a focus on situational patterns of social interaction.* Exploring urban life in this way means being at street level, observing, for example, face-to-face interaction in public parks or how people respond to a homeless person they pass on the street. The **symbolic-interaction paradigm,** then, is *a theoretical framework based on the assumption that society is continuously recreated as human beings construct reality through interaction.*

How are millions of distinct lives intertwined into the drama of society? One answer, discussed in detail in Chapter 6 ("Social Interaction in Everyday Life"), is that we become linked to one another as we build reality in countless social situations. Humans rarely respond to things or other people in direct, physical terms, as when someone ducks to avoid a punch. Mostly, we respond based on the meanings we attach to the surrounding world. Through this process of creating meaning, we define our identities, rights, and obligations toward one another. Notice, too, that the process of reality construction is highly variable. For example, one person may define a homeless man on a city street as "just a bum looking for a handout" and ignore him. Another, however, might define him as a "fellow human being in need" and offer some assistance. In the same way, one pedestrian may respond to a police officer walking nearby with a sense of security, while another may be overcome with a feeling of nervous anxiety. Sociologists

Many women contributed to the emergence of sociology, although their achievements have long been unrecognized. Harriet Martineau (1802–1876), born to a rich English family, translated the writings of Auguste Comte from French in 1853. Soon afterward, she established her own reputation as a sociologist with studies of slavery, factory laws, and women's rights. In the United States, Jane Addams (1860–1935) was a social worker known for her writing and public activism on behalf of poor immigrants to this country. In 1889, Addams founded Hull House, a Chicago settlement house, in the heart of that city's slums. There, she presided over discussions with intellectuals and immigrants alike of the pressing problems of her day. Her contribution to the welfare of others earned Addams a Nobel Peace Prize in 1931.

guided by the symbolic-interaction approach view society as a mosaic of subjective meanings and responses.

The symbolic-interaction paradigm draws on the thinking of Max Weber (1864–1920), a German sociologist who emphasized that society is largely a matter of people's subjective perceptions. Weber's approach is considered at length in Chapter 4 ("Society").

From this general foundation, others have analyzed specific dimensions of social life. Chapter 5 ("Socialization") examines the thinking of U.S. sociologist George Herbert Mead (1863–1931), who explored how the human personality gradually emerges as a result of social experience. Chapter 6 ("Social Interaction in Everyday Life") presents the work of another U.S. sociologist, Erving Goffman (1922–1982). Goffman's contribution is described as *dramaturgical analysis* because it emphasizes the parallels between human beings and actors on a stage as we deliberately foster certain impressions in the minds of others. Other contemporary sociologists, including George Homans and Peter Blau, have created *social-exchange analysis*, which reveals how social interaction is often guided by what each person stands to gain and lose from others. Chapter 15 ("Family") applies this approach to the process of courtship, noting that individuals typically seek mates who offer at least as much—in terms of physical attractiveness, intelligence, and social background—as they provide in return.

*Critical evaluation.* Perhaps the greatest strength of the social-interaction paradigm is that it reminds us that we shape our social world just as the world, in turn, shapes us. No sociological analysis can afford to ignore the spontaneity of individuals. Put differently, the symbolic-interaction paradigm overcomes a limitation of all macro-level approaches: while broad patterns like "the family" and "social inequality" certainly exist, such abstract concepts can mask the fact that society is fundamentally *people* interacting with one another. This micro-level approach focuses more on how we as individuals actually experience society.

For just this reason, however, the symbolic-interaction paradigm sometimes leads to the error of ignoring larger social structures. Highlighting what is unique in each social scene risks overlooking the widespread effects of our culture, as well as factors like class, sex, and race.

The important characteristics of the structural-functional paradigm, the social-conflict paradigm, and the symbolic-interaction paradigm are summarized in Table 1–1. As we have explained, certain kinds of questions suggest the use of a particular theoretical paradigm. In many cases, however, the greatest benefits come from linking the sociological perspective to all three, as we shall now illustrate with an analysis of sports in the United States.

## Sports: Three Theoretical Paradigms in Action

To people in the United States, sports seem indispensable. Almost everyone has engaged in some type of sport, from gym classes throughout the school years to recreational sports by young adults to fitness programs for elderly people. In the United States, the sale of sporting goods is a multibillion-dollar industry, and most men and women observe and discuss sporting events each year. Television brings sports to millions of living rooms, not only as part of newscasts, but as regular programming averaging more than three hours a day (Coakley, 1990).

What new insights can the sociological perspective provide about this familiar element of our way of life? Each of the three major theoretical paradigms in sociology contributes part of the answer.

### The Functions of Sports

A structural-functional approach directs attention to ways in which sports help society to operate. The manifest functions of sports include providing both recreation and a relatively harmless way to "let off steam," and contributing to the physical fitness of the population. Sports have important latent functions as well, from fostering social relationships to generating tens of thousands of jobs. Perhaps the most important latent function of sports is encouraging specific attitudes and patterns of behavior that are central to our way of life.

For example, the personal effort and discipline essential to success in sports make people successful in other areas as well. Additional social skills, too, such as learning to be a team player and to play by the rules, are developed through participating or watching sporting events. And sports generate the sense of personal competition that individualistic Americans value so much in celebrating a "winner" (Spates, 1976a; Coakley, 1990). When he said, "Winning is not everything, but making

**Table 1–1   THE THREE MAJOR THEORETICAL PARADIGMS: A SUMMARY**

| Theoretical Paradigm | Orientation | Image of Society | Illustrative Questions |
|---|---|---|---|
| Structural-functional | Macro-level | A system of interrelated parts that is relatively stable based on widespread consensus as to what is morally desirable; each part has functional consequences for the operation of society as a whole | How is society integrated?<br>    What are the major parts of society?<br>    How are these parts interrelated?<br>    What are the consequences of each for the operation of society? |
| Social-conflict | Macro-level | A system characterized by social inequality; any part of society benefits some categories of people more than others; conflict-based social inequality promotes social change | How is society divided?<br>    What are major patterns of social inequality?<br>    How do some categories of people attempt to protect their privileges?<br>    How do other categories of people challenge the status quo? |
| Symbolic-interaction | Micro-level | An ongoing process of social interaction in specific settings based on symbolic communications; individual perceptions of reality are variable and changing | How is society experienced?<br>    How do human beings interact to create, sustain, and change social patterns?<br>    How do individuals attempt to shape the reality perceived by others?<br>    How does individual behavior change from one situation to another? |

the effort to win is," Vince Lombardi was speaking not only as a football coach; he was also speaking as a typical American.

Sports also have dysfunctional consequences, of course. For example, colleges and universities intent on fielding winning teams may recruit students for their athletic ability rather than for their academic aptitude. This can adversely affect the academic standards of the school and leave the athletes themselves little time to learn anything but their sport. Len Bias, a University of Maryland basketball star who died tragically from cocaine use in 1986, earned no academic credits during his last semester—a situation far from rare among athletes who must practice four to five hours a day (Bingham, 1987). The tragedy of Len Bias takes on added significance because he was part of the 1 percent of male college players who earn a professional sports contract. For too many others, the long-term benefits of attending college are minimal.

In sum, the structural-functional paradigm suggests that sports contribute in a variety of ways to the operation of American society. Perhaps the most important of these is teaching and reinforcing notions of competition and personal success, which are central to our way of life.

## Sports and Conflict

A social-conflict analysis of sports begins by pointing out that sports are closely related to patterns of social inequality. Some sports—tennis, swimming, golf, and skiing, to name a few—are expensive, so participation is largely limited to well-to-do people. By contrast, the sports with mass appeal—football, baseball, and basketball—are those accessible to people at all income levels. In short, the games people play are not simply a matter of choice; they reflect patterns of economic inequality.

In the United States, sports are also oriented toward males. Sexual discrimination has traditionally limited the opportunities of females in most sports, even when they have the talent, interest, and economic means to participate. The first modern Olympic Games held in

The painting *Pastime* by Gerald Garston suggests that baseball—the Great American Pastime—is more than mere diversion and entertainment. Baseball, like all sports, also provides valuable lessons about how members of our society expect one another to think and to behave.

1896, for example, excluded women from competition entirely (Mangan & Park, 1987). Until quite recently, Little League teams also barred girls in most parts of the country. This exclusion has been defended by ungrounded sexual stereotypes that claim that girls either lack the ability to engage in sports or risk losing their femininity if they do so. Joan Benoit, a gold medalist marathon runner in the 1984 Olympic Games, conceded that becoming a serious athlete seemed somehow "wrong" for an American woman: "When I first started running I was so embarrassed I'd walk when cars passed me. I'd pretend I was looking at the flowers" (cited in Coakley, 1986:115).

Thus, our society has encouraged males to be athletes while females are expected to be attentive observers and cheerleaders. In 1989, 57 percent of male high school seniors claimed to be active in sports, compared to 31 percent of senior females (U.S. Congress, 1989). But the fitness movement and political efforts by women are reducing this inequity. The number of high-school women in sports programs shot up from about 300,000 in 1970 to more than 2 million today. In addition, more women than ever before now play sports professionally, and women's sports enjoy growing spectator interest. Still, women continue to take a back seat to men in professional sports—particularly in those that provide the most earnings and social prestige.

Although our society traditionally excluded people of color as well from professional sports, the opportunity to earn a high income in athletics has expanded greatly in recent decades. Professional baseball was the first major American sport to admit African-American players, when Jackie Robinson broke the "color line" in 1947. By 1991, however, African Americans accounted for 18 percent of professional baseball players, 61 percent of football players, and 72 percent of basketball players (Center for the Study of Sport in Society, 1991).

The increasing proportion of people of African descent in professional sports is largely due to the fact that individual athletic performances can be measured precisely. For this reason, white prejudice cannot easily diminish the achievement of nonwhite athletes. It is no doubt also true that many people of color make a particular effort to excel in athletics, where they recognize that greater opportunity can be found (Steele, 1990). In recent years, in fact, black baseball players have earned higher salaries, on the average, than white players.

Nonetheless, racial discrimination continues to shape professional sports in the United States. For example, while people of color are now common as players, almost all managers, head coaches, and owners of sports teams are still white (Jones, 1987). In 1987, Al Campanis, a vice-president of the Los Angeles Dodgers baseball team, conceded on national television that African Americans are good athletes, but he wondered aloud if they lacked the "necessities" to become team managers and executives. The furor that followed this racist remark revealed to Americans the extent of racial prejudice in athletics forty years after Jackie Robinson's breakthrough.

Furthermore, teams tend to position people of color

in secondary positions, while whites take the starring roles. For example, about 70 percent of African-American players in the major leagues play the outfield (Staples, 1987; Center for the Study of Sport in Society, 1991). Figure 1–3 on page 26 shows the proportion of white and black players at the various positions in professional football and basketball, and includes Hispanic players in the case of baseball. The pattern is clear: in all three sports, the central positions have the highest proportion of white players.

Taking a wider view, one might also wonder who benefits most from professional sports. Although millions of fans follow their teams, the vast earnings they generate are controlled by the small number of people (again, predominantly white men) for whom teams are income-generating property. Team owners, highly competitive among themselves, together form a huge business that controls a vast national audience (Leifer, 1990). In the last decade or so, professional athletes have gained a larger share of what their teams earn. By 1990, for example, the average annual salary of major-league baseball players had risen to almost $900,000, which is thirty times the average in 1970 and far higher than the salaries of baseball's legendary greats in the past. Even so, in all professional sports, the lion's share of both power and profits remains in the hands of the few owners.

In sum, the social-conflict paradigm views professional sports in terms of patterns of social inequality. As noted earlier, sports may reflect the importance of competition and achievement to all Americans, but they are also bound up with extensive inequalities based on sex, race, and economic power.

## Sports as Interaction

At the macro-level, a sporting event can be understood as a formal system; at the micro-level, however, it is a complex drama of face-to-face interaction. In part, participants' behavior reflects their assigned positions and, of course, the rules of the game. Players also act spontaneously, however, so that the precise outcome of a game can never be predicted. According to the symbolic-interaction paradigm, sports are less a system than an ongoing process.

The symbolic-interaction paradigm also suggests that each player will look at the game at least somewhat differently. Some players, for example, thrive in a setting of stiff competition, playing the game simply for the thrill of winning. For others, however, love of the game may be greater than the need for victory; these people may actually perform worse under pressure. Still others use sports as a means to build personal friendships; they may avoid competition for fear that it will alienate people from one another (Coakley, 1986).

Beyond different attitudes toward competition, team members will also shape their particular realities according to the various prejudices, jealousies, and ambitions they bring to the field of play. Then, too, the behavior of any single player is likely to change over time. A rookie in professional baseball often feels self-conscious during the first few games in the big leagues. Eventually, however, a comfortable sense of fitting in with the team usually emerges. Coming to feel at home on the field was slow and painful for Jackie Robinson, who was initially only too aware that many white players, and millions of white baseball fans, resented his presence (Tygiel, 1983). In time, however, his outstanding performance and his confident and refined manner off the field won him the respect of the entire nation.

In spite of varied motives and perceptions, each player is expected to display team spirit and other elements of good sportsmanship. The dramaturgical approach of Erving Goffman (1959) suggests that our nation's athletes typically symbolize the ideals of honesty, hard work, and, above all, the will to win. In reality, of course, many fall far short of these ideals. For instance, frequent news accounts since the mid-1980s have documented the involvement of both amateur and professional athletes with illegal drugs, which has prompted controversial calls for mandatory drug testing. The ideal image of the athlete was also shaken in 1989 when baseball banned Cincinnati Reds manager Pete Rose. A model athlete who had earned the nickname "Charlie Hustle" for his base-running heroics, Rose was found to have engaged for years in gambling, in violation of the rules of major league baseball. He also went to prison for income-tax evasion stemming from his gambling activities.

The three theoretical paradigms certainly offer different insights, but none is more correct than the others. Applied to various social issues, each paradigm generates its own interpretations so that, to fully appreciate the sociological perspective, you should become familiar with all three. Together, they spark fascinating debates and controversies, many of which are covered in the chapters that follow.

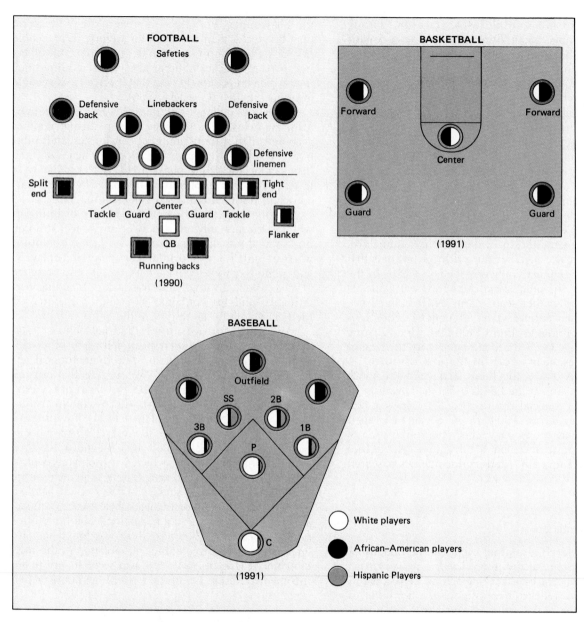

**Figure 1–3** Race and Professional Sports: Patterns of Discrimination
Professional athletics provide far greater opportunities for minorities than most other highly paid careers in the United States. Even so, a pattern of "stacking" that places white athletes in central positions (outlined in blue) is evident in professional sports. These diagrams show the proportion of black and white players at each position in professional football and basketball, and the proportion of black, Hispanic, and white players for each position in professional baseball. Professional teams apparently consider whites more suitable for the central positions—generally deemed the "thinking" roles of the games.

(*Center for the Study of Sport in Society, Northeastern University, 1991*)

# Summary

1. Using the sociological perspective we recognize that individual lives are shaped by society. This point of view may be described as "seeing the general in the particular."

2. Because people in the United States see events in terms of individual choice, the impact of society on our lives often goes unrecognized. Therefore, the sociological perspective may also be described as "seeing the strange in the familiar."

3. By discovering that suicide rates are higher among some categories of people than others, Emile Durkheim was able to show how social forces affect even the most personal of our actions.

4. The sociological perspective prompts us to recognize how our lives reflect both our position in American society and our nation's standing in the larger world.

5. The sociological perspective sometimes arises naturally, as when we enter an unfamiliar setting. Similarly, socially marginal people tend to perceive the effects of society more readily than others. During periods of social crisis, everyone is more likely to view the world sociologically.

6. There are four general benefits to using the sociological perspective. First, it challenges our familiar understandings of the world, helping us to separate fact from fiction; second, it helps us to appreciate the opportunities and constraints that frame our lives; third, it encourages more active participation in society; fourth, it makes us aware of the diversity of social behavior in the United States and in the world as a whole.

7. Auguste Comte gave sociology its name in 1838. Whereas previous social thought focused on what society ought to be, Comte's new discipline of sociology was based on the use of scientific methods to understand society as it is.

8. Sociology emerged as a reaction to the rapid transformation of European society during the eighteenth and nineteenth centuries. The rise of an industrial economy, the explosive growth of cities, and the emergence of new political ideas were three dimensions of change that directed attention to the operation of society.

9. Theory involves linking sociological insights in meaningful ways to explain social life. Theory building is guided by one or more theoretical paradigms.

10. The structural-functional paradigm is a framework for exploring how social structures promote the stability and integration of society. This approach tends to minimize the importance of social inequality, conflict, and change.

11. The social-conflict paradigm highlights social inequality, which often generates conflict resulting in change. At the same time, this approach tends to minimize the extent of social integration and social stability.

12. In contrast to these two macro-level approaches, the symbolic-interaction paradigm is a micro-level framework for studying face-to-face interaction in specific settings. At this situational level of analysis, society is viewed as people acting in variable and somewhat unpredictable ways.

13. Each of the three major theoretical paradigms provides important insights about the character of sports. The structural-functional paradigm emphasizes that sports reinforces the individualism and competition central to our way of life. The social-conflict paradigm links sports to patterns of social inequality. The symbolic-interaction paradigm portrays sports as the interplay of individuals who generate meaning as they engage one another on the field of play.

14. Because each paradigm highlights different dimensions of any social issue, the richest sociological understanding is derived from applying all three.

# Key Concepts

**latent functions** the unrecognized and unintended consequences of any social pattern

**macro-level orientation** a focus on broad social structures that characterize society as a system

**manifest functions** the recognized and intended consequences of any social pattern

**micro-level orientation** a focus on situational patterns of social interaction

**positivism** a means to understand the world based on science

**social-conflict paradigm** a framework for building theory based on the assumption that society is a complex system characterized by inequality and conflict that generate social change

**social dysfunction** the undesirable consequence of any social pattern for the operation of society

**social function** the consequence of any social pattern for the operation of society

**social marginality** the state of being excluded from social activity as an "outsider"

**social structure** a relatively stable pattern of social behavior

**sociology** the scientific study of human society

**structural-functional paradigm** a framework for building theory based on the assumption that society is a complex system whose parts work together to promote stability

**symbolic-interaction paradigm** a theoretical framework based on the assumption that society is continuously recreated as human beings construct reality through interaction

**theoretical paradigm** a set of fundamental assumptions that guides thinking and research

**theory** the process of linking facts together in order to explain something

# Suggested Readings

These two paperbacks are readable classics that describe the sociological perspective and the benefits of learning to think sociologically.

C. Wright Mills. *The Sociological Imagination*. New York: Oxford University Press, 1959.

Peter Berger. *An Invitation to Sociology*. Garden City, NY: Anchor Books, 1963.

This paperback provides sixty-six supplementary readings that follow the chapter flow of the book you're now reading. For each topic, classic essays by sociology's "greats" are accompanied by articles highlighting contemporary and cross-cultural issues.

John J. Macionis and Nijole V. Benokraitis, eds. *Seeing Ourselves: Classic, Contemporary, and Cross-Cultural Readings in Sociology*. 2nd ed. Englewood Cliffs, NJ: Prentice Hall, 1992.

This collection of essays examines the potential contribution of sociology to various areas of social life and points to factors that have limited the discipline's significance in the past.

Edgar F. Borgatta and Karen S. Cook. *The Future of Sociology*. Newbury Park, CA: Sage Publications, 1988.

This recent sociological analysis of suicide in modern Japan supports Durkheim's contention that social forces are at work in even the most personal of actions.

Mamoru Iga. *The Thorn in the Chrysanthemum: Suicide and Economic Success in Modern Japan*. Berkeley: University of California Press, 1986.

This book contains autobiographical sketches by twenty contemporary sociologists that together suggest the achievements and shortcomings of the discipline.

Bennett M. Berger. *Authors of Their Own Lives: Intellectual Autobiographies by Twenty American Sociologists*. Berkeley: University of California Press, 1990.

The following three books describe the history of sociology. The first, a general intellectual history of the discipline, delves into sociology's European roots. The second details the development of U.S. sociology at the University of Chicago in the years after World War I. The third introduces four women social scientists and explores historical barriers to the acceptance of women in sociology.

Randall Collins and Michael Makowsky. *The Discovery of Society*. New York: Random House, 1984.

Martin Bulmer. *The Chicago School of Sociology: Institutionalization, Diversity, and the Rise of Sociological Research*. Chicago: University of Chicago Press, 1984.

Ellen Fitzpatrick. *Endless Crusade: Women Social Scientists and Progressive Reform*. New York: Oxford University Press, 1990.

The first of these books is DuBois's classic study of the African-American community in Philadelphia. The second is a collection of his essays.

W. E. B. DuBois. *The Philadelphia Negro: A Social Study*. New York: Schocken Books, 1967; orig. 1899.

Dan S. Green and Edwin D. Driver, eds. *W. E. B. DuBois on Sociology and the Black Community*. Chicago: University of Chicago Press, 1978.

A comprehensive sociological analysis of sports is found in this paperback.

Jay J. Coakley. *Sport in Society: Issues and Controversies*. 4th ed. St. Louis: Times Mirror/Mosby College Publishing, 1990.

This useful paperback book for the beginning student includes a discussion of theoretical paradigms in sociology as well as information about how to gather data for writing papers.

Pauline Bart and Linda Frankel. *The Student Sociologist's Handbook*. 4th ed. New York: Random House, 1986.

Information about career possibilities in sociology is available free from the American Sociological Association, 1722 N Street NW, Washington, D.C. 20036. Ask for:

*Careers in Sociology*. Washington, D.C.: American Sociological Association.

Bettina J. Huber. *Career Possibilities for Sociology Graduates*. Washington, D.C.: American Sociological Association.

# 2

# Sociological Investigation

Linda Davis enrolled in college in 1979, full of energy and drive. She was determined to earn good grades, graduate, and begin, as she put it, "a professional career that I will use the rest of my life." She made little effort to contain her excitement when she spoke of her plans to become a physical therapist.

Davis studied hard, but soon realized that her grades were falling short of the high marks she had taken for granted in high school. As the first year came to a close, her aspirations had diminished, and she doubted her ability to gain admission to the specialized therapy program she had set her sights on for so long.

By the middle of her sophomore year, Davis no longer expressed interest in becoming a physical therapist; instead, she successfully applied to a less rigorous nursing program. She was still pleased with her accomplishments, but more than a little relieved that the pressure to achieve was now less intense than it had been. Davis began spending more and more time with her new boyfriend, Stan, and she often spoke of their future together. Those around her could see her career ambitions slowly fading.

Dorothy Holland and Margaret Eisenhart, teachers and researchers at two different universities, had followed the college career of Linda Davis, and they suspected that her experiences were not unique. Holland and Eisenhart had long wondered why so few women pursue study and occupations in the sciences. They set out to answer

this question by monitoring the changes in two dozen women by interviewing them at several points during their early college years. Using the skills of sociological investigation, the two researchers sketched the course of these women's lives in college during the 1980s, and found that their experiences were remarkably similar to those of Linda Davis. Holland and Eisenhart (1991) soon concluded that they had documented a more general pattern: the achievements and career choices of women in college—both in and out of the sciences—often fall short of their early expectations. Intrigued by this finding, Holland and Eisenhart extended their research, continuing to interview subjects in their final years of college and for five years following graduation. The general pattern of declining performance continued. Linda Davis's subsequent life exemplifies this trend.

By the time of graduation, Davis's view of herself and her future had clearly changed. The urge for career success had now taken a back seat to settling down with a husband and children. Asked how she might pursue a nursing career and care for a family, Davis responded simply, "If I had to make a decision between family and career, then there's no question—my family."

The years that followed confirmed these priorities. After graduation, Davis married Stan and found a full-time job at a local hospital. But the marriage lasted only a few years. Speaking to Holland and Eisenhart after her divorce, however, Davis explained that she was engaged to be married again. And what of her plans to work? Confident that her second marriage would be more successful, Davis looked forward to working only half time; before long she hoped to stop working entirely long enough to have at least two children.

From the life histories of Linda Davis and others, Holland and Eisenhart formulated the thesis that the college years—crucial in launching the careers of men—often are a time of compromise for women. Their research is a fascinating look at the campus scene, including insights about how women interact with faculty, the value they place on romantic attachments with men, and how college culture affects their relationships with other women.

Information of this kind stands as evidence of the power of the sociological perspective to uncover patterns (and also to identify problems) that other points of view overlook. But most important for our purposes, this research demonstrates the *doing* of sociology, the process of *sociological investigation*. We all are struck by curious social patterns, questions that all-too-often slip away unanswered. The discipline of sociology can impart a host of skills and procedures that makes us more able to find answers or, even if we never choose to conduct research ourselves, better equipped to evaluate the answers provided by others.

Many people think that scientists work only in laboratories, carefully taking measurements using complex equipment. But as Holland's and Eisenhart's study illustrates, sociologists also conduct scientific research on the campus, in neighborhoods, at workplaces, and even in prisons—in short, wherever people are living their lives.

This chapter introduces the most common methods that sociologists use to conduct research. Along the way, we shall encounter problems that test the talents of even the most seasoned women and men in this field of study. Some of these problems involve gathering information about complex and sometimes personal topics; others introduce debates about the role of personal politics and values in sociological research. The question of how facts and politics relate to one another is raised by the research by Holland and Eisenhart: should their goal be simply to *learn* about the lives of women on college campuses in the United States or, alternatively, to offer a prescription for *change* according to the researchers' own values? We shall begin the various tasks of this chapter with the basics.

# The Basics of Sociological Investigation

Sociological investigation begins with two simple requirements. The first was suggested in Chapter 1: *Look at the world using the sociological perspective.* Suddenly, from this point of view, our surroundings appear full of curious patterns of behavior that call out for further study.

Holland and Eisenhart did exactly this when they began to explore why so few women opted for careers in the sciences. But a sociological imagination prompted them to delve further into how women are influenced in their life choices by the surrounding campus culture.

This brings us to the second requirement for a sociological investigator: *Be curious and ask questions.* What patterns are evident among people living on a campus or in any other setting? Why do they live as they do? How do they understand their own lives? What factors unite and divide the community?

These two requirements—seeing the world sociologically and asking questions—are fundamental to sociological investigation. Yet they are only the beginning. They can draw us into the social world, stimulating our curiosity. But then there is the more difficult matter of finding answers to our questions. To understand the kind of answers sociology offers, consider various ways to recognize any piece of information as "true."

## Ways of Knowing: Science and "Truth"

Saying we "know" something can mean any number of things. Most Americans, for instance, claim to believe in the existence of God. Few would assert that they had had direct contact with God, but they are believers all the same. This kind of knowing is often called "faith." A second kind of truth lies in the pronouncement of some recognized expert. When we want to know how to spell a word correctly, for example, we turn to a dictionary, acknowledging the book's editors as language experts. In still other cases, ordinary people define truth through simple agreement. This way of knowing is called "consensus." We simply "know" that sexual intercourse among young children is wrong, for instance, because virtually everyone says so. Of course, people in other times and places may recognize some different "truth."

There are many kinds of truth. *The Emergence of Clowns* by U.S. artist Roxanne Swentzell presents the story of creation according to the Santa Clara Pueblo. Life began, they believe, when four clowns emerged onto the earth's surface, each facing in a different direction. All of the world's people have creation beliefs of this kind (including the Biblical accounts in *Genesis*). As members of a scientific society, we may too easily dismiss such stories as "myth." Whether or not they are entirely factual, they do convey basic truths about the way in which each society searches for human origins and struggles to find meaning in the universe. It is science, not "myth," that is powerless to address such questions.

*Heard Museum, Phoenix, AZ*

The Trobriand Islanders of New Guinea, for instance, shrug off sexual intercourse among children too young to reproduce as harmless.

As a final illustration of the variability of truth, imagine being a Peace Corps volunteer who has just arrived in a small, traditional society. With the goal of helping the local people to grow more food, you soon take to the fields, where you observe farmers carefully placing a dead fish directly on top of the ground where they have planted a seed. Curious, you ask about this practice, and they reply that the fish is a gift to the god of the harvest. A local elder adds sternly that the harvest was poor one year when no fish were offered as gifts.

From the local people's point of view, using fish as gifts to the harvest god makes sense. They believe in it, their experts endorse it, and everyone seems to agree that the system works. But, with scientific training in agriculture, you have to shake your head and wonder. The scientific "truth" in this situation is something entirely different: the decomposing fish fertilize the ground, producing a better crop.

As yet another way of knowing, **science** is defined as *a logical system that bases knowledge on direct, systematic observation*. Sometimes at odds with faith, the wis-

dom of "experts," and general agreement, scientific knowledge is based on **empirical evidence**, meaning *information we are able to verify with our senses.*

Our Peace Corps example does not mean, of course, that people in traditional societies ignore what their senses tell them, nor that members of technologically advanced societies reject all ways of knowing except science. A medical researcher seeking an effective treatment for cancer, for example, may still practice her religion as a matter of faith; she may turn to experts when making financial decisions; and she may derive political opinions from people around her. Yet none of these approaches affects her work as a scientist.

## Common Sense Versus Scientific Evidence

Here are six statements that many North Americans consider "true" based on their common sense, although each is at least partly contradicted by scientific evidence.

1. *Poor people are far more likely to break the law than rich people.* Chapter 8 ("Deviance") explains that official arrest statistics would seem to bear this out. But research also reveals that, while people

of all social backgrounds break the law, the criminal justice system is more likely to prosecute wrongdoing by poor people while treating offenses by the well-to-do more leniently.

2. *The United States is a middle-class society in which most people are more or less equal.* Studies presented in Chapter 10 ("Social Class in the United States") show that the richest 5 percent of our people control half our country's total wealth. If people are equal, then, some are much "more equal" than others.

3. *Most poor people ignore opportunities to work.* Research included in Chapter 10 indicates that this is true of some but not most poor people. In fact, about half of poor individuals in the United States are children and elderly people.

4. *Differences in the social behavior of males and females is "human nature."* Much of what we call "human nature" is created by the society in which we are raised, as Chapter 3 ("Culture") details. Further, as Chapter 13 ("Sex and Gender") argues, some societies define "masculine" and "feminine" very differently than we do.

5. *People change as they grow old, losing many former interests while becoming focused on their health.* Chapter 14 ("Aging and the Elderly") reports that researchers have learned that aging actually changes our personality very little. Problems of health do increase in old age but, on balance, elderly people retain their distinctive personalities.

6. *Most people marry because they are in love.* To members of our society, few statements are so self-evident. But as surprising as it may seem, cross-cultural research shows that, in most societies, marriage has little to do with love. Chapter 15 ("Family") explains why this is the case.

These examples confirm the old saying that "It's not the things we don't know that get us into trouble as much as the things we *do* know that just aren't so." We have all been brought up believing conventional truths, being bombarded by expert advice, and being pressured to accept the opinions of friends. As adults, we must learn to evaluate critically what we see, read, and hear to separate what is true from what is not. As a scientific discipline, sociology can help us to do that. Like any way of knowing, science has limitations, as we shall see. But scientific sociology is a useful way to assess accurately many kinds of information.

# The Elements of Science

Sociologists apply science to the study of society in much the same way that natural scientists investigate the physical world. The work of social scientists lies in identifying ways in which various dimensions of social life are interrelated. Thus a sociologist might ask questions such as:

What segments of the population are least likely to vote in national elections? Why?

Are abused children at risk of becoming child abusers themselves?

Are city dwellers less neighborly than people living in rural areas?

To answer these questions, sociologists use the elements of science to gather empirical evidence. The following sections of this chapter introduce many important components of scientific investigation.

## Concepts, Variables, and Measurement

A crucial element of science is the **concept,** *a mental construct that represents some part of the world, inevitably in a somewhat simplified form.* "Society" is itself a concept, as are the structural parts of societies, including "religion" and "the economy." Sociologists also use concepts to describe individuals, as when we speak of their "sex," "race," or "social class."

A **variable** is *a concept whose value changes from case to case.* The familiar variable "price," for example, refers to the value of items in a supermarket. Similarly, people use the sociological concept "social class" to describe (and often to evaluate) people as "upper class," "middle class," "working class," or "lower class."

The use of variables depends on **measurement,** *determining the value of a variable in a specific case.* Some variables are easy to measure; we can determine our weight simply by stepping on a scale. Measuring sociological variables, however, is often more difficult than taking physical measurements.

For example, how would you measure a person's "social class?" You might do this crudely by looking at how the person dresses, listening to patterns of speech, or by noting a home address. More precisely, you might investigate the individual's income, occupation, and edu-

# Three Useful (and Simple) Statistical Measures

Everyone talks about "averages": the average age of the U.S. population, the average price of a gallon of gasoline, or the average winning from state lotteries. In sociological research, three different statistical measures are used to describe what is average or typical.

Assume that we wish to describe the salaries paid to seven members of the local city council:

$14,250   $64,000   $21,750   $23,000
$23,000   $14,000   $18,500

The simplest statistical measure is the **mode,** defined as *the value that occurs most often in a series of numbers.* In this example, the mode is $23,000, since that value occurs twice, while each of the others occurs only once. If all the values were to occur only once, there would be no mode; if two values occurred twice, there would be two modes. Although easy to identify, the mode is rarely used in sociological research because it provides information about only some, rather than all, of the values.

A more common statistical measure, the **mean,** refers to *the arithmetic average of a series of numbers,* and is calculated by adding all the values together and dividing by the number of cases. The sum of the seven incomes is $178,500; dividing by 7 yields a mean income of $25,500. Notice that the mean income is actually higher than the income of six of the seven council members. Because the mean shows the effects of any especially high or low value (in this case, the $64,000 income), it has the drawback of giving a distorted picture of any distribution with extreme scores.

The **median** is *the value that occurs midway in a series of numbers arranged in order of magnitude or, simply, the middle case.* Here the median income for the seven people is $21,750, since three incomes are higher and three are lower. (With an even number of cases, the median is halfway between the two middle cases.) In case of one extreme score (or more), the median gives a better picture of what is "average" than the mean does.

---

cation. But in sociological investigation, researchers must recognize that a variable can be measured in more than one way. A person with very high income may seem to be "upper class." But what if the income comes from selling automobiles, an occupation most people think of as "middle class?" And if the individual has only an eighth-grade education, you might think of the person as "lower class." To resolve this dilemma, sociologists sensibly (if somewhat arbitrarily) combine these three measures—income, occupation, and education—into a single composite assessment of social class described in Chapter 9 ("Social Stratification") and Chapter 10 ("Social Class in the United States").

Another problem arises when sociologists seek to describe a number of people with respect to a variable like income. Reporting a stream of numbers does not easily convey information about the people as a whole, so sociologists use various *statistical measures* to describe people collectively. The box explains how this is done.

In conducting research, how we define a variable affects its value; therefore, researchers must specify definitions carefully. **Operationalizing a variable** means *specifying exactly what is to be measured in assigning a value to a variable.* If we were measuring the social class of particular individuals, for example, we would have to decide exactly what elements to measure. After choosing to examine several measures (such as income, occupational prestige, and education), we would then devise a way to combine them into a composite measure of "social class." When reporting the results of research, sociologists should explain how all variables are operationalized, so that readers understand the conclusions.

### Reliability and Validity of Measurement

Useful measurement involves two further considerations. **Reliability** is *the quality of consistent measurement.* A measure is reliable if repeated measurements produce the same result. An unreliable technique for measuring social class is of little use to sociologists just as a scale giving inconsistent readings of weight would be useless to a physicist.

Men who drink coffee are more likely than tea drinkers to die from a heart attack. Does this mean that coffee causes heart disease? No—the link between those two variables is spurious. Both coffee drinking and heart disease are caused by a third variable, high levels of stress.

Even consistency is no guarantee of validity, however. **Validity** means *the quality of measuring precisely what one intends to measure.* Say you want to investigate how religious people are, and you decide to do so by asking how often they attend religious services. Notice that, in trying to gauge *religiosity,* what you are actually measuring is *attendance at services,* which may or may not amount to the same thing. Generally, religious people do attend services more frequently, but people may participate in religious rituals for social reasons, out of habit, or because of a sense of duty to someone else. Moreover, many devout believers avoid organized religion altogether. Thus, even when it yields consistent results (reliability), any measurement can still miss the real, intended target (and lack validity). In sum, sociological research is no better than the quality of measurement that it employs.

### Relationships Among Variables

The real payoff in sociological investigation comes from determining the relationships among variables. Ideally,

scientists relate variables in terms of **cause and effect,** *a relationship in which change in one variable is caused by change in another.* A familiar cause-and-effect relationship occurs when a girl teases her brother until he becomes angry. *The variable that causes the change* (in this case, the teasing) is called the **independent variable.** *The variable that changes* (the behavior of the brother) is called the **dependent variable.** The value of one variable, in other words, is dependent on the value of another. Linking variables in terms of cause and effect allows researchers to *predict,* that is, to use what they do know to speculate about what they don't know.

Because science puts a premium on prediction, people may incorrectly infer cause and effect just because two variables seem to be related. But often, variables change together even though there is no causal link between them. For example, people steal more cars in the United States when the temperature goes up, but this does not mean that heat turns people into car thieves. More likely, warm weather encourages people to spend time outdoors and also prompts drivers to leave car windows open. Thus, cause and effect may be hidden within a complex web of factors, not always readily apparent.

To illustrate further, we might puzzle over the fact that juvenile delinquency is more common among young people who live in crowded housing. We could operationalize the variable "juvenile delinquency" in terms of the number of arrests of a person under the age of eighteen, and operationalize the variable "crowded housing" to mean the amount of square feet of living space per person. Because delinquency rates are high in areas that are densely populated, we would be tempted to conclude that crowding in the home (the independent variable) causes delinquency (the dependent variable). But does the fact that the two vary together indicate a causal connection?

Not necessarily. *When two (or more) variables are related in some way,* they demonstrate **correlation.** We know there is some relationship between these two variables because they change together, as shown in Part (a) of Figure 2–1 on page 37. This *may* mean that crowding causes delinquency, but there are other possibilities as well. Think for a minute about who lives in crowded housing and whose mischief is likely to attract the attention of police. The answer: people with less power and choice—the poor. Crowded housing and juvenile delinquency may be found together because *both* are caused by a third factor—poverty—as shown in Part (b) of Figure 2–1. In other words, the apparent relationship between crowding and delinquency is "explained away" by a third variable—low income—that causes them both to change. The term **spurious correlation** means *an apparent, although false, association between two (or more) variables caused by some other variable.*

Unmasking a correlation as spurious is often tricky, but it can be done using scientific **control,** meaning *the ability to neutralize the effect of one variable in order to assess the relationships among other variables.* In the example above, we can determine whether the relationship between housing density and delinquency persists if income is held the same. To do this, we measure the two variables only among persons of the same income. If the relationship between density and delinquency still exists (that is, if young people living in more crowded housing have higher rates of delinquency), we gain confidence that crowding does in fact cause delinquency. But if the relationship disappears, as shown in Part (c) of the figure, we know we have been dealing with a spurious correlation. Research has, in fact, shown that the apparent correlation between crowding and delinquency virtually disappears if the effects of income are controlled (Fischer, 1984). So we have now sorted out the relationship among the three variables, as illustrated in Part (d) of the figure. Housing density and juvenile delinquency have a spurious correlation, because our evidence suggests that both variables rise or fall according to people's income.

To sum up, correlation means only that two (or more) variables change together. Cause and effect implies not only correlation but also that change in one variable actually causes change in another. A researcher can conclude that two variables are linked by cause and effect only after demonstrating (1) the two variables are correlated; (2) the independent (or causal) variable precedes the dependent variable in time; and (3) there is no evidence that a third variable is responsible for a spurious correlation between the two.

Identifying cause-and-effect relationships enables researchers to make predictions. The natural sciences can predict with much greater accuracy than the social sciences, however, since laboratory conditions used to study the physical world allow scientists to control a number of variables. The sociologist faces a considerably more difficult task. In a world of countless social forces, to which each of us reacts at least somewhat differently, relationships of simple cause and effect are rare. Often sociologists must be satisfied with demonstrating only correlation. When relationships of cause and effect can be shown, they are usually complex, involving a large number of variables.

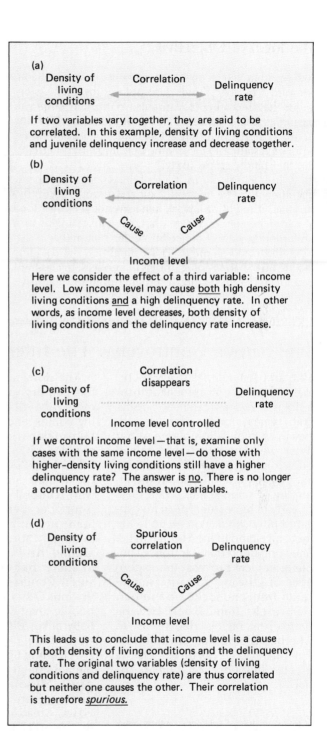

**Figure 2–1** Correlation and Cause: An Example

## The Ideal of Objectivity

Assume that ten people who work for a magazine in Broward County, Florida, are putting together a story about that area's best restaurants. With their employer paying all the expenses, they set out for a week of fine dining. Later, when they get together to compare notes, will one restaurant be everyone's clear favorite? Perhaps, but that hardly seems likely.

In scientific terms, each of the ten would probably operationalize the concept "best restaurant" differently. For one, it might be a place that serves delicious seafood at reasonable prices; for another, the choice might turn on a rooftop view of the coastline; for yet another, stunning decor and attentive service might be the deciding factor. Like so many other things in our lives, the best restaurant may well be mostly a matter of individual taste.

Personal values are fine when it comes to restaurants, but they pose a challenge to scientific research. On the one hand, sociologists and other scientists have personal opinions about whatever they study; on the other, science strives for **objectivity,** *a state of personal neutrality in conducting research.* Scientific objectivity is an ideal rather than a reality, of course, since complete impartiality is virtually impossible for any researcher to achieve. But following scientific methods promotes objectivity so that even unconscious biases will not seriously distort a researcher's work. As an additional safeguard, researchers who identify their personal leanings along with their formal findings help readers evaluate conclusions in the appropriate context.

The influential German sociologist Max Weber wrestled with the problem of personal values distorting scientific study. Weber knew the personal values of a

---

CRITICAL THINKING

# The Samoa Controversy: The Interplay of Science and Politics

Margaret Mead (1901–1978) remains the most prominent anthropologist* in American history. Several years after her death, however, replication of one of her most well-known studies raised questions about her objectivity and, more generally, about the interplay of science and politics.

Early in her career Mead investigated how children grew up in Samoa, an island in the South Pacific. She concluded that, far from a simple biological process, the experience of growing up varies significantly from one society to another. Her results immediately became part of a raging debate as to whether biology or environment ("nature" or "nurture") has a greater influence on human behavior.

---

\* Closely related to sociology, anthropology studies human culture, often with a focus on preindustrial rather than industrial societies.

The dominant position early in this century was that biology was more influential, not just in shaping adolescence but in guiding all human behavior and making some people different from others. When Mead's work was published, the United States was struggling with cultural diversity resulting from decades of immigration. Some individuals, opposed to admitting "foreigners" on the ground that they were biologically inferior, had successfully pressured Congress to restrict immigration. Other Americans thought people everywhere were essentially alike, differing only in their ways of life.

A leading figure on the environmental side of the debate was Margaret Mead's graduate school mentor, Franz Boas. Adopting his views, Mead espoused the belief that people differ only according to their environment. Not surpris-

Margaret Mead was a pioneer of social research whose work in other societies helped us to think more critically about our own. Her career also alerts us to the fact that research—especially about controversial issues—is not easy to separate from our personal values.

---

sociologist would play a part in the selection of topics to be studied. Why, after all, would one person study world hunger, another investigate the career aspirations of college women, and still another examine religious cults? While conceding that research would be *value-relevant*, Weber admonished researchers to be *value-free* in their pursuit of objective evidence. Research, he claimed, must be carried out dispassionately in order to study the world *as it is* rather than as we think *it should be*. This detachment, for Weber, set science apart from the world of politics. While politicians are committed to some particular outcome, scientists must cultivate an open-minded readiness to accept the results of their investigations, whatever they may be.

Most sociologists accept Weber's argument, even if few are confident that we can ever be entirely aware of our own biases. Social identity makes everyone—re-searchers included—think and see the world in particular ways. Moreover, sociologists are not "average" people: most are white men who are highly educated and live in cities. In addition, although the opinions of sociologists cover a broad political spectrum, they are more liberal than the population as a whole, and even more liberal than members of many other academic disciplines (Wilson, 1979). Turning the sociological perspective on the discipline itself, you should be aware that social background can and does affect sociological research, just as your own background and personal history will affect how you interpret this work.

One way to limit distortion caused by personal values is through **replication**, *repetition of research by others in order to assess its accuracy*. If other researchers repeat a study using the same procedures and obtain the same results, they can conclude that the original

---

ingly, both Boas and Mead opposed what they viewed as false biological doctrine being used to justify the exclusion and unfair treatment of some people.

Mead's first book, *Coming of Age in Samoa* (1928), was powerful ammunition for the environmental side of what Chapter 5 ("Socialization") presents as the "nature-nurture debate." If growing up in Samoa revealed little of the turbulence typical of adolescence in the United States, Mead concluded, environment must far outweigh biology in shaping humanity. Therefore, no category of people is inherently different—and certainly not better—than another.

Mead's research went a long way toward discrediting biological views of human behavior. Yet shortly after her death, Derek Freeman, who had also conducted research in Samoa, challenged Mead's conclusions about the importance of biology to human behavior. In Freeman's view, Mead had selectively represented Samoan society according to her personal politics. For his part, Freeman argued that biology plays a greater role in human behavior than Mead was willing to recognize.

Scholars still debate this issue. To those who side with Freeman, Mead was a young (twenty-four years old when she arrived in Samoa in 1925) and unseasoned researcher, prompted by her teacher to produce evidence supporting an environmental doctrine of human behavior. Her conclusions are too "neat," critics claim, suggesting that she saw only what she was looking for. In short, they assert, Mead's work is more "politically correct" than it is scientifically factual.

To others, however, Freeman stands as the villain in the controversy. Mead's defenders argue that, especially given the limited development of research skills at that time, her conclusions are basically sound. It is Freeman, they charge, who is playing politics by rigidly advocating a view of human behavior largely determined by biology. Those in Mead's camp conclude that Freeman has gained fame and fortune by unjustly attacking the work of a great scientist.

No doubt, some truth can be found on both sides of this recent controversy. One point, however, seems clear: human beings are passionate and political creatures who often fall short of the scientific goal of complete objectivity in research.

SOURCES: Based on Mead (1961; orig. 1928), Freeman (1983), Holmes (1983), and Weiner (1983).

research (as well as their own) was conducted objectively. The need for replication in scientific investigation is probably the reason that the search for knowledge is called *research* in the first place. Although only a small proportion of social science research is subjected to replication (far less than in the natural sciences), this process sometimes sparks conflict. The box on pages 38–39 describes a recent controversy arising from replication of well-known research.

## Some Limitations of Scientific Sociology

Science first revealed the operation of the natural world. People also utilize science to study the social world, but doing so requires recognizing several important limitations.

1. *Because human society is so complex, sociologists cannot predict individual behavior with precision.* Astronomers can calculate the movement of planets with remarkable precision, and they announce years in advance when a comet will next be visible from the earth. Humans, however, are more than physical beings; creative minds ensure that no two people react in exactly the same way to any event. Therefore, sociologists speak of "probabilities" that categories of people will act in some way, while rarely expressing certainty, especially about the behavior of a specific individual.

2. *Because humans respond to their surroundings, the mere presence of a researcher may affect the behavior being studied.* An astronomer gazing at the moon has no effect whatever on the celestial body, but people often react to being observed. Some may become anxious or defensive; others may try to "help" the researcher by providing the answers or actions they think are expected of them.

3. *Social patterns change constantly; what is true in one time or place may not hold in another.* Atoms and molecules do not consciously shape their environment, but human beings do, in remarkably variable ways. The study of society, therefore, must take account of diversity and change.

4. *Because sociologists are part of the social world they study, objectivity in social research is especially difficult.* Chemists are not often personally affected by what goes on in test tubes. But sociologists live in the society they study. Therefore, sociologists often have difficulty in controlling—or even recognizing—personal values that may distort their work.

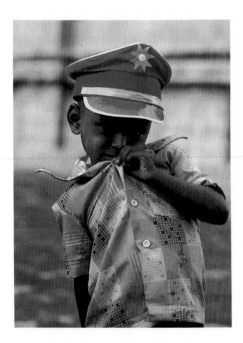

A basic lesson of social research is that being observed affects how people behave. Researchers can never be certain precisely how this will occur, however: some people become shy as the subject of attention, while others become highly animated. In neither case does the researcher witness natural behavior.

Harold E. Edgerton's celebrated photograph of a golf swing suggests a significant concern of sociological investigation: analyzing patterns of human behavior—even in minute detail—is of little value without also understanding what motivates the action and what sense people make of what they do.

## The Importance of Subjective Interpretation

The logic of science does not eliminate subjectivity from research. Nor would that be desirable, since creative thinking is vital to sociological investigation in three key ways.

First, science is basically a series of steps that guide research, rather like a recipe used in cooking. Just as more than a recipe is required to make a great chef, so scientific procedure will never, by itself, produce a great sociologist. Also needed is an inspired human imagination. Robert Nisbet (1970) points out that insight comes not from science itself but from the lively thinking of creative human beings. The genius of physicist Albert Einstein, anthropologist Margaret Mead, or sociologist Max Weber resulted not only from their use of the scientific method but also from their curiosity and imagination.

Second, science cannot embrace the vast and complex range of human motivations and feelings, including greed, love, pride, and despair. Science helps us gather facts about how people act, but it can never fully explain how people make sense of what they do (Berger & Kellner, 1981).

Third, data cannot speak for themselves. Sociologists and other scientists must always face the ultimate task of *interpretation*: creating meaning from a collection of observations. For this reason, sociology (like other disciplines) is an art as well as a science.

## Politics and Research

As Max Weber observed long ago, a narrow line separates politics from science. Most sociologists endorse Weber's goal of value-free research. But a growing number of researchers are challenging the notion that politics and science can—or should—be distinct.

Alvin Gouldner (1970a, 1970b) was among the first to claim that "value-free" research paints a "storybook picture" of sociology. All aspects of social life, he argues, have political implications since any social arrangements are likely to benefit some people more than others. In short, Gouldner concludes, what is *social* is inevitably *political*. This also holds true for research, which reflects people's political values and has political consequences.

If sociologists have no choice about their work being political, Gouldner continues, they do have a choice about *which* positions are worthy of support. Moreover, sociologists have an obligation to endorse such political objectives. Although this viewpoint is not limited to sociologists of any one political orientation, it is especially strong among those influenced by the ideas of Karl Marx. As noted in Chapter 1 ("The Sociological Perspective"), Marx asserted that while it is important to understand the world, the crucial task is to change it (1972:109; orig. 1845).

In recent years, many colleges and universities have become embroiled in what has become known as the *political correctness debate*. In simple terms, this controversy pits the Weberian defense of value-free teaching and research against the Marxist view that knowledge should be linked to needed political change.

## Gender and Research

One political dimension of research involves gender—the relative social standing of females and males. Sociologists are becoming increasingly aware that gender-related issues can play a major part in their work. Margrit Eichler (1988) identifies five dangers to sound research that relate to gender.

1. **Androcentricity.** Androcentricity (*andro* is the Greek word for "male"; *centricity* means "being centered on") refers to approaching an issue from a male perspective. Sometimes researchers approach a setting as if only the activities of men are important while ignoring what women do. For years, research in the area of occupations focused on the paid work of men while overlooking the housework traditionally performed by women (Counts, 1925; Hodge, Treiman, & Rossi, 1966). Similarly, until recently studies of status attainment were based on fathers and sons (Blau & Duncan, 1967; Sewell, Haller, & Ohlendorf, 1970). Clearly, research that seeks to understand human behavior cannot ignore half of humanity.

   Eichler notes that the parallel situation of *gynocentricity*—seeing the world from a female perspective—is equally limiting to sociological investigation. However, in male-dominated America, this problem arises much less frequently.

2. **Overgeneralizing.** This occurs when research that focuses on members of one sex is used to support conclusions about both sexes. Historically, sociologists have studied men and then made sweeping claims about "society." This approach ignores the experiences of half the population. Gathering information about a community from public officials or other prominent persons (who are likely to be

men), and then drawing conclusions about the community as a whole, would constitute overgeneralizing.

   Here, again, the problem can occur in reverse. For example, in an investigation of child-rearing practices, collecting data only from women would allow researchers to draw conclusions about "motherhood" but not about the more general issue of "parenthood."

3. **Gender insensitivity.** This refers to the failure of a researcher to consider the variable of gender at all. As is evident throughout this book, social forces often affect men and women quite differently. For example, failing to consider the importance of gender in a study of growing old in the United States would ignore important information such as the fact that most elderly men live with spouses while elderly women typically live alone.

4. **Double standards.** Researchers must be careful not to distort what they study by evaluating women and men using different standards. This might happen as a researcher investigating families describes a couple as "man and wife." This inconsistency involves more than words if the researcher defines the man as the "head of household" and treats him accordingly, while assuming that the woman simply engages in family "support work."

5. **Interference.** Beyond affecting researchers, gender often shapes the attitudes of subjects, which can also distort a study. The problem of "interference" occurs if a subject reacts to the sex of the researcher rather than to the research itself. For instance, while studying a small community in Sicily, Maureen Giovannini (1992) reported that many men responded to her as a woman to the point that she was unable to work effectively as a researcher. Gender dynamics prevented activities like private conversations with men that were deemed inappropriate for single women. In addition, local residents denied Giovannini access to places considered "off-limits" to members of her sex.

Of course researchers can choose to focus their work on one sex or the other. Indeed, pervasive attention to men at the expense of women in the past encouraged some researchers—including Dorothy Holland and Margaret Eisenhart, whose study of the college campus is presented at the beginning of this chapter—to make special efforts to investigate the lives of women. But sociologists, as well as others who read their work, should think critically about how gender affects the process of sociological investigation.

## Research Ethics

Like all investigators, sociologists must be mindful that research can be harmful as well as helpful to subjects or communities. For this reason, the American Sociological Association—the major professional association of sociologists in North America—has established formal guidelines for the conduct of research (1984).

The primary ethical guideline is that sociologists strive for technical competence and objectivity in conducting their research. Sociologists must disclose research findings in full, without omitting significant data. Further, they must include all possible interpretations of data, and they are ethically bound to make their results available to other qualified sociologists, some of whom may wish to replicate the study.

Researchers must strive to protect the rights, privacy, and safety of anyone involved in a research project. Sociologists are obligated to terminate any research, however promising it may seem, if they become aware of any potential danger to participants. Even if research is likely to cause subjects discomfort or inconvenience, sociologists must ensure in advance that all participants understand and accept any risks.

Subjects who agree to take part in research are entitled to full anonymity, even if sociologists come under legal pressure to release confidential information. Researchers should never promise such consideration, therefore, unless they are willing and able to carry through on their commitment.

Sociologists are ethically bound to present accurately the purpose of their work. They must inform subjects, in advance, of any political organization or business that they represent, and this information must also be furnished in reports of research findings. Since private or public agencies sometimes try to constrain the research process, a sociologist must never accept funding from an agency if doing so will require violating any of the ethical guidelines mentioned here. All sources of research funding must be disclosed in the publication of findings.

Finally, there is a global dimension to research ethics. Sociologists have been called on to collect data for government agencies. Professional ethics, however, demand that sociologists never use their professional role as a "cover" while gathering intelligence information for any government. In addition, when researchers do work abroad, they must understand what people in *that* setting are likely to perceive as a violation of privacy or a source of personal danger. In short, sociologists must gain familiarity with a cultural setting before they conduct research there.

# The Methods of Sociological Research

A **research method** is *a strategy for systematically conducting research*. Four commonly used methods of sociological investigation are introduced here. None is inherently better or worse than any other; but in the same way that a carpenter selects a particular tool for a particular task, distinctive strengths and weaknesses make each method suitable for certain kinds of research.

## Experiments

The logic of science is most clearly expressed in the **experiment,** *a research method for investigating cause and effect under highly controlled conditions*. Experimental research is *explanatory*, meaning that it investigates not just what happens but why. Typically, researchers devise an experiment to test a specific **hypothesis,** *an unverified statement of a relationship between variables*.

Ideally, experimental research is conducted in three steps that provide the empirical evidence needed for a researcher to accept or reject the hypothesis. First, the experimenter measures the dependent variable; second, the investigator exposes the dependent variable to the effects of the independent variable (sometimes called the "treatment"); and third, the researcher measures the dependent variable again to see if the predicted change has taken place. If the expected change has occurred, the experiment lends support to the hypothesis; if not, the hypothesis is discounted.

Successful experiments require that researchers carefully control all factors that might affect what is being measured. This is most easily accomplished in a laboratory, an artificial setting specially constructed for this purpose. Oftentimes, scientific investigators enhance experimental control by dividing subjects into an *experimental group* and a *control group*. At the outset, the dependent variable is measured for members of both groups, but only the experimental group is subjected

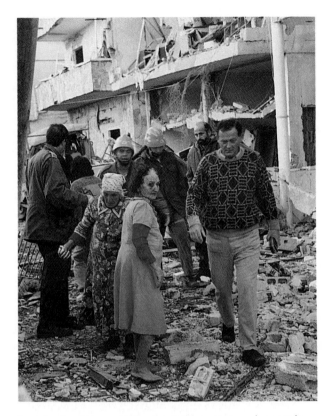

Social calamities—whether caused by nature or by people themselves—provide opportunities for field research that could never be created in a laboratory. Such studies show that disasters not only destroy property but also shred the fabric of social life, causing human suffering that may continue long after physical structures have been repaired.

to the independent variable or treatment. Then both groups are measured again. A host of factors (such as some news event) occurring during the research might cause change in the experimental group, but such factors would affect the control group as well. By comparing the before and after measurements of the two groups, the researcher is able to assess how much of the observed change is actually due to the independent variable.

Not all experimental research takes place in a laboratory. Sociologists can conduct experiments in any number of everyday locations. Such "field experiments" have the advantage of allowing researchers to observe subjects in their natural habitats. In addition, field experiments study phenomena that could never be artifically created in a laboratory. For example, sociologist Kai Erikson

(1976) investigated the aftermath of a deadly flood in Buffalo Creek, West Virginia, in 1972. Erikson found that the social damage caused by disruption of community ties was just as serious—and lasted much longer—than physical damage to property. However, the inability to control the field environment means researchers can test only hypotheses that are more general than they might be in a laboratory setting. Moreover, sociologists cannot replicate certain field experiments because precisely the same conditions (such as the Buffalo Creek flood) do not occur again.

In the field or the laboratory, subjects may change their behavior simply in response to a researcher's attention, as one classic experiment discovered. In the late 1930s, the Western Electric Company investigated productivity at its Hawthorne factory near Chicago (Roethlisberger & Dickson, 1939). One experiment tested the hypothesis that increasing the available lighting would raise worker output. First, productivity (the dependent variable) was measured; then lighting (the independent variable) was changed; finally, productivity was measured again. Productivity increased, supporting the hypothesis. But when the research team subsequently *reduced* the lighting, productivity again increased, contradicting the initial hypothesis. In time, the researchers realized that the workers were working harder simply because people were paying attention to them. Since then, social scientists have used the term **Hawthorne effect** to refer to *a change in a subject's behavior caused by the awareness of being studied.*

## A Laboratory Experiment:
## The Stanford County Prison

The social dynamics of prisons comprises an important topic of study, although social scientists are rarely able to perform this kind of research "in the field." Philip Zimbardo nonetheless sought to investigate prison violence in an artificial "laboratory" (Zimbardo, 1972; Haney, Banks, & Zimbardo, 1973).

Zimbardo was skeptical of the common-sense idea that prison violence is caused by prisoners who are in jail precisely because of antisocial or violent behavior. Also he doubted that prison guards are simply the kind of people who enjoy pushing other people around. Rather, Zimbardo suspected that, once inside a prison, even the healthiest and most emotionally stable person would be prone to violent behavior. This led to the hypothesis that *the character of prison itself, and not the personalities of prisoners and guards, causes prison violence.* Thus, the prison setting was treated as the independent variable capable of causing change in the dependent variable, people's behavior.

To test this hypothesis, Zimbardo's research team placed an ad in a local newspaper in Palo Alto, California, offering young men $15 a day to help with a two-week research project. Each of the seventy who responded was given a series of physical and psychological tests. The researchers selected the twenty-four deemed the healthiest, both physically and mentally. Then the men were randomly assigned to two groups; half were designated "prisoners" and half became "guards." The guards and prisoners were to spend the next two weeks in the "Stanford County Prison," a mock prison specially constructed in the basement of the psychology building on the Stanford University campus.

The "prisoners" were surprised when the Palo Alto police "arrested" them at their homes soon afterward. After being searched and handcuffed, they were taken to the local police station to be fingerprinted. Then they were transported to the "prison" on the Stanford campus. There each met other "prisoners," as well as the "guards," who had been instructed to keep the prison secure at all times. Zimbardo and his associates sat back with a video camera to see what would happen next.

The experiment soon became more than anyone had bargained for. The researchers observed both guards and prisoners acting in stereotypical fashion, quickly losing their sense of basic human decency. Guards insulted the prisoners, forcing them to engage in humiliating tasks such as cleaning out toilets with their bare hands. The prisoners reacted with bitterness and hostility. Within four days, five prisoners had to be removed from the study "because of extreme emotional depression, crying, rage and acute anxiety" (1973:81). Before the end of the first week, the situation had deteriorated so badly that the researchers canceled the experiment. Zimbardo explains (1972:4): "The ugliest, most base, pathological side of human nature surfaced. We were horrified because we saw some boys (guards) treat others as if they were despicable animals, taking pleasure in cruelty, while other boys (prisoners) became servile, dehumanized robots who thought only of escape, of their own individual survival and of their mounting hatred for the guards."

What unfolded in the "Stanford County Prison" supported Zimbardo's hypothesis that prison violence is rooted in the social character of prisons themselves, rather than the personalities of guards and prisoners.

His findings also raise questions about the way our society operates prisons, suggesting the need for basic prison reform. Just as important, the experiment reveals how research itself can threaten the physical and mental well-being of subjects. Such dangers are not always as immediately apparent as they were in this case. Therefore, researchers must consider carefully potential harm to subjects at all stages of their work and end any study, as Zimbardo responsibly did, if subjects appear to be threatened.

## Survey Research

A **survey** is *a research method in which subjects respond to a series of items in a questionnaire or an interview.* Perhaps the most widely used of all research methods, surveys are particularly well suited to studying what investigators cannot observe directly, such as political attitudes, religious beliefs, or the private lives of couples. Although surveys can be used to study the relationship among variables, they are most useful for *descriptive* research, in which the responses of subjects help a sociologist to understand and describe a social setting, such as an urban neighborhood or a gambling casino.

Philip Zimbardo's research helps to explain why violence has been a common element in our society's penitentiaries. Events in his simulated jail suggest that brutality is not so much a personal trait of prisoners and guards as it is a product of the dehumanization inherent in prison life.

## Population and Sample

In survey research, a **population** refers to *the people who are the focus of research*. We might wish, for example, to learn how much schooling is typical of adults living in a particular city. In this case, all the adults in the city would be the survey population. Sometimes every adult in the country is the survey population, as in the familiar polls that are taken during political campaigns. However, contacting such a vast number of people would be virtually impossible as well as extremely expensive and time-consuming. Researchers skirt this problem by using a **sample**, meaning *a part of a population selected to represent the whole*. The precise size of a sample varies. The box describes the early years of polling organizations, which learned how to study the entire population of the United States using a carefully selected sample of some fifteen hundred people.

We use the logic of sampling all the time. If you look around the classroom and notice five or six students nodding off, you might conclude that class finds the teacher to be dull. Such a conclusion involves making an inference about *all* the people (the "population") after observing *some* of the people (the "sample"). But how can we know if a sample actually represents the entire population?

The most common assurance is *random sampling*, ensuring that each element in the population has the same chance of being included in the sample. If this is the case, mathematical laws of probability make a representative sample likely within known limits. Seasoned researchers use computers to generate random samples. Novice researchers, however, sometimes assume that "randomly" walking up to people on the street produces a random sample. Unfortunately, this is unlikely for two reasons. First, any part of a city—whether a rich neighborhood or a "college town"—is likely to contain more of some kinds of people than others. Second, any researcher is apt to find some people more approachable, again introducing a bias.

Although good sampling is not simple, it offers a considerable savings in time and expense. We are spared the tedious task of contacting everyone in a population, while obtaining essentially the same results.

## SOCIOLOGY OF EVERYDAY LIFE

# National Political Surveys

About 100 million men and women voted in the presidential election of 1992. In the United States, however, political campaigns usually end with little suspense because before the first vote is cast, surveys predict the winner.

Surveys, or *polls*, form an integral part of our nation's politics. But how can information drawn from about fifteen hundred people predict what 100 million people will do? The key to accurate prediction is selecting a sample that represents the population as a whole.

The skills needed for accurate surveys came slowly. In 1936, a survey by the *Literary Digest* predicted that Republican Alfred E. Landon would handily defeat Democrat Franklin Delano Roosevelt. They could hardly have been more wrong, as Landon lost to Roosevelt in a historic landslide. The reason for such an embarrassing error was simply that the magazine's sample did not represent the voting population. The *Digest* mailed survey ballots to 20 million people (far more than would be included in a poll today), drawing names from telephone listings and automobile registrations. These sources introduced the bias, since, especially then, people who owned a telephone or car were more affluent and therefore more likely to be Republicans.

The incorrect prediction made by the *Literary Digest* did nothing for the popularity of that magazine, which soon went out of business. But a young researcher named George Gallup (1902–1984) not only correctly called the election but predicted that the *Literary Digest* would be off the mark. Gallup went on to become the best-known national survey researcher in the United States. Today, polls by the Gallup organization and others routinely provide information about elections and a host of other political issues.

SOURCE: Information on Gallup and the *Literary Digest* poll adapted from Babbie (1992).

## Questionnaires and Interviews

Selecting subjects is only the first step in carrying out a survey. Also needed is a plan for asking questions and recording answers. Surveys employ two general techniques: questionnaires and interviews.

A **questionnaire** is *a series of questions presented to subjects.* In most cases, subjects select a response from several provided by the researcher (similar to multiple-choice examination questions). Limiting responses with what is called a *closed-ended format* makes analyzing results relatively easy. In some cases, however, a researcher may want subjects to respond freely. An *open-ended format* allows subjects to express various shades of opinion. Of course, the researcher later has to make sense out of what can be a bewildering array of answers.

Deciding how to present questions to subjects forms another part of the research strategy. Most often, a questionnaire is mailed and respondents are asked to complete the form and then to mail it back. This technique is called a *self-administered survey.* Since no researcher is present when subjects read the questionnaire, it must be both inviting and clearly written. A self-administered questionnaire should always be *pretested* with a small number of people before sending it to all the subjects. This small investment of time and money may avoid the costly problem of finding out—too late—that instructions or questions were confusing.

Using the mail has the advantage of including a large number of people over a wide geographical area in the study at relatively small expense. At the same time, people may treat such questionnaires as "junk mail," so that typically fewer than half are completed and returned. Researchers often employ follow-up mailings to coax reluctant subjects.

Worth remembering, too, is that many people are not capable of completing a questionnaire on their own. Young children obviously cannot, nor can many hospital patients, and as many as one-third of adults simply have too much difficulty with reading and writing to wade through a comprehensive questionnaire (Kozol, 1985a).

An **interview** is *a series of questions administered personally by a researcher to respondents.* Generally, open-ended interviews are most useful because they allow the researcher to ask follow-up questions that probe and clarify the subject's responses. In the ensuing conversation, however, the researcher must avoid influencing the subject, which can be done by making as small a gesture as raising an eyebrow when a person begins to answer. In comparing the interview with the questionnaire, investigators have found that a subject is more

likely to complete a survey if contacted personally by the researcher. However, a disadvantage of interviews is that tracking people down and personally interrogating them is costly and time-consuming, especially if all subjects do not live in the same area.

In both questionnaires and interviews, the wording of questions has a significant effect on answers (Fowler, Jr., & Mangione, 1989). Language with an emotional charge generally sways subjects. For example, a person might endorse the statement "I approve of my child having teachers representing all political opinions" and yet reject the same statement if the words "including radicals" are added at the end. Similarly, using the term "welfare mothers" for "women who receive public assistance" injects an emotional element into a survey. In other cases, the wording of questions may suggest what other people think, thereby subtly guiding the respondent. People would be more likely to respond positively to the question "Do you *agree* that the police force is doing a good job?" than they would to the question "Do you *think* that the police force is doing a good job?" simply because the phrase "do you agree" suggests that others endorse the statement. In short, researchers must strive to use language that suggests no "correct" response.

Researchers should also avoid double-questions like "Do you think that the government should spend less money for military defense and more for domestic social programs?" The problem here is that a subject could very well agree with one part of the question but dispute the other, so that saying yes or no distorts the actual opinion the researcher is seeking.

### Surveys at Work: A Study of American Couples

Couples are a basic social unit the world over. In 1975, two seasoned sociologists, Philip Blumstein and Pepper Schwartz, began a large and complex investigation of couples in the United States: how they make decisions, the importance of sex in their lives, and how jobs and money shape their relationships. This research culminated in the publication of *American Couples* (1983), a book that provides rich insights into close human relationships.

Blumstein and Schwartz operationalized the concept "couple" to mean two individuals who (1) live together and (2) have had a sexual relationship for at least some period of time. Knowing that previous research had focused on married couples, they enlarged their study to include cohabiting heterosexual couples as well as gay and lesbian couples.

Blumstein and Schwartz faced a mammoth task in gathering data about many dimensions of intimate living, including normally private matters such as sexual relationships. Their study is an excellent example of the skillful use of questionnaires and interviews.

**Building a sample.** There is, of course, no listing of couples in the United States from which to draw a random sample. Blumstein and Schwartz were also aware that many homosexual couples are secretive about their relationships, fearing negative reaction to their sexual orientation. Thus, these researchers devised several strategies to make their sample as representative as possible.

First, Blumstein and Schwartz decided to contact a large number of subjects because, all else being equal, a larger sample better represents the entire population of couples. They were fortunate that word of their research was carried in national news reports, and they appeared on several network television shows. They were soon swamped with offers to participate from couples across the country. They sent questionnaires by return mail.

Second, Blumstein and Schwartz wanted to ensure that all types of couples were included in the study. Judging that homosexual couples were less likely to volunteer, Blumstein and Schwartz made use of contacts within the gay communities of Seattle (their own city) and San Francisco (where many homosexuals are open about their sexual orientation). They also asked participants to suggest others who might be willing to join the research. This procedure, often called *snowball sampling*, quickly increases the number of subjects.

Third, to further broaden the range of participants, Blumstein and Schwartz appeared before a variety of civic associations including the PTA and the Rotary Club, explaining their need for subjects and leaving questionnaires to be completed by those willing to do so.

Fourth and finally, the researchers alerted the general public to the study by walking through neighborhoods and by leaving flyers in supermarkets and movie theaters. In the end, they distributed almost twenty-two thousand questionnaires.

Blumstein and Schwartz's sample seemed to be diverse and it was certainly large, but they still had no guarantee that it represented the entire range of our society's couples. Mindful of this danger, they included in their report the following evaluation:

> [The sample] does not represent all of the couples in the United States, and it would be misleading if our findings were applied to all groups within the country. For instance, a large number of our couples come from the New York, San Francisco, and Seattle areas. More important, our couples are primarily white and disproportionately well educated. We have more high salaries and prestigious occupations among our couples than would be found in the general population. Thus, we need to be tentative about applying our findings to working-class or poor people, or people with only a grade-school education (1983:548).

Notice how these researchers reduced the limitations of their sample by carefully assessing their work and including this information in their formal results.

**The use of questionnaires.** Seeking a large number of participants, Blumstein and Schwartz sensibly chose a questionnaire to collect information. The questionnaire was long—some thirty-eight pages—and was painstakingly prepared and clearly worded. A closed-ended format lessened the work of compiling the responses.

Of the twenty-two thousand questionnaires Blumstein and Schwartz distributed, more than twelve thousand came back—a return rate of about 55 percent, which is excellent in light of the length of the questionnaire. Follow-up mailings might have increased the return rate, but ethical concerns led them to protect the privacy of volunteers by destroying all names and addresses after questionnaires were initially mailed.

**The use of interviews.** Blumstein and Schwartz also conducted interviews to gain a deeper understanding of the lives of couples. For example, they could not easily gather information on the history of each couple's relationship with a questionnaire. The formidable task of locating subjects and conducting interviews required the use of a research staff in this phase of the work. In all, 320 couples were interviewed for periods of time ranging from two-and-one-half to four hours.

Given the personal nature of some questions, the researchers chose to interview subjects personally rather than by telephone. This is why they limited the interviews to couples near the Seattle, San Francisco, and New York City areas. So that the couples selected for interviews would be as representative as possible, Blumstein and Schwartz categorized them according to education, duration of the relationship, and sexual orientation, and then randomly selected samples from each category.

Researchers traveled to each couple's home for the personal interviews to ensure that participants would be as comfortable as possible and also to spare them unnecessary inconvenience. Two interviewers worked together, interviewing partners separately as well as together, yielding more candid responses to many ques-

Sociologists who conduct research in other countries should be aware that what they may think are "innocent questions" may cause discomfort or even offense to others. In many societies, people rarely discuss their sexual habits with strangers or even with each other. Thus some of the questions asked by Blumstein and Schwartz would probably offend the typical Japanese couple. The growing social diversity of the United States raises the importance of this kind of sensitivity for research carried out at home as well.

tions. Couples with small homes presented a special challenge, since privacy was mandatory. Blumstein and Schwartz explain, "Some couples had only one suitable room, and so several interviews were conducted without heat, or with a flashlight, in backyards and even bathrooms. We came to call these our bathtub interviews" (1983:20).

The interviews provided the depth and detail they were hoping for. But face-to-face questions about personal topics required special skills. On the one hand, interviewers had to avoid influencing the responses of the participants, while on the other hand, they wanted to encourage openness by being nonjudgmental about what they were told. In the end, the research team concluded that they had been successful because they knew they had learned things many subjects had never revealed to anyone else, even their partners. Such candor makes the ethical issue of protecting privacy all the more important.

*Findings.* Among the more interesting conclusions of this study was that, even within a loving relationship,

money means power. The researchers found that the partner with the higher income generally steers the relationship, a blow to the common-sense notion that love encourages relational equality. In this regard, however, lesbians were an exception. Perhaps because many women in the United States do not judge their personal worth by their income, Blumstein and Schwartz reasoned, lesbian couples tended to be the most egalitarian of couples.

Another finding was striking variation regarding sex outside of the relationship, which Blumstein and Schwartz designate with the neutral term "nonmonogamy." As Table 2–1 on page 50 shows, in all types of partnerships the likelihood of nonmonogamy increases over time. But married couples tend to be more faithful than heterosexual couples simply living together. Further differences emerge among homosexual couples, none of whom can legally marry. Lesbians were found to have far less sexual involvement beyond their relationships than gay men (as noted in Chapter 20, "Health and Medicine," this pattern among gay men changed during the 1980s).

## Participant Observation

**Participant observation** is *a method in which researchers systematically observe people while joining in their routine activities.* This method allows researchers to gain an inside look at social life in settings ranging from night clubs to religious seminaries. Participant observation is commonly employed by cultural anthropologists to study other societies. Cultural anthropologists refer to participant observation as *fieldwork*; their description of an unfamiliar culture is termed an *ethnography*. Sociologists usually call the account of people in a particular setting a *case study*.

Sociologists beginning a case study may have only a vague understanding of the social patterns they wish to investigate. Thus, participant observation is *descriptive* and often *exploratory*. Researchers usually begin with few, if any, specific hypotheses to test, since they may not know initially what the important questions will turn out to be. Compared to experiments and survey research, then, participant observation has fewer hard and fast rules. A research plan must be flexible enough to adapt to unexpected circumstances. Initially, a researcher is likely to be concerned with gaining entry into what may be an unfamiliar social setting. In time, observations provoke many specific questions, and answers are organized into a detailed description of a way of life.

**Table 2–1**  SEXUAL ACTIVITY AMONG AMERICAN COUPLES, BY TYPE OF RELATIONSHIP, DURATION OF RELATIONSHIP, AND SEX OF RESPONDENT

| Married Couples | | | | | Cohabiting Heterosexual Couples | | | | | Homosexual Couples | | | | |
|---|---|---|---|---|---|---|---|---|---|---|---|---|---|---|
| | Reported Sexual Activity outside Relationship | | | | | Reported Sexual Activity outside Relationship | | | | | Reported Sexual Activity outside Relationship | | | |
| Years Together | Females Yes | No | Males Yes | No | Years Together | Females Yes | No | Males Yes | No | Years Together | Females Yes | No | Males Yes | No |
| Under 2 | 13% | 87% | 15% | 85% | Under 2 | 20% | 80% | 21% | 79% | Under 2 | 15% | 85% | 66% | 34% |
| 2–10 | 22 | 78 | 23 | 77 | 2–10 | 42 | 58 | 47 | 53 | 2–10 | 38 | 62 | 89 | 11 |
| Over 10 | 22 | 78 | 30 | 70 | Over 10* | no data | | no data | | Over 10 | 43 | 57 | 94 | 6 |

* Too few cohabiting couples had been together for more than ten years.

SOURCE: Adapted from Philip Blumstein and Pepper Schwartz, *American Couples* (New York: William Morrow, 1983), p. 276. © 1983 by Philip Blumstein and Pepper W. Schwartz. Adapted by permission of William Morrow & Co.

## CRITICAL THINKING

# Table Reading: An Important Skill

A table provides a great deal of information in a small amount of space, so learning to read tables can increase your reading efficiency. When you spot a table, look first at the title to see what information it contains. In Table 2–1, the title indicates that the table reports the sexual activity of couples in the United States. In many cases, the title also indicates the variables used in organizing the data. Here, sexual patterns are described in terms of three variables: (1) the type of relationship (married couples, cohabiting heterosexual couples, and homosexual couples); (2) the duration of the relationship (under 2 years, 2 to 10 years, over 10 years); and (3) the sex of the respondent (males and females).

These three variables form the three major parts of the table, with six categories of people found within each part. For each category, the proportion reporting sex-ual activity outside of the relationship is noted. The "yes" and "no" responses add up to 100 percent.

Looking at the first part of the table, 13 percent of females married for less than two years reported sexual activity outside of the relationship, while 87 percent reported no such activity. For women married between two and ten years, 22 percent reported nonmonogamy, while 78 percent reported none. The same percentages hold for women married for more than ten years. Comparable data are presented for other categories of people as well.

This table provides many interesting insights. First, for all types of relationships, the longer a couple has been together, the more likely nonmonogamy becomes. Second, among all couples, men are more likely than women to be nonmonogamous. Third, the likelihood of nonmonogamy varies by type of couple. Married couples are more likely to remain monogamous than cohabiting heterosexual couples. The pattern among homosexuals differs sharply by sex. Gay men are the most likely of all couples to be nonmonogamous, with lesbians falling between married women and cohabiting heterosexual women.

Finally, when reading any research results, a critical reader should be alert for clues to the overall quality of the work. Important items include the background of the researchers (are they sociologists? newspaper reporters?), as well as bibliographic information (was the research published by a respected journal? by a group with some vested interest in the topic?). The research presented here is sound on both counts. Readers need to assess the quality of the research itself with a critical eye as well as the results.

As its name suggests, participant observation has two sides. On the one hand, gaining an "insider's" look depends on becoming a participant in the setting—"hanging out" with others, attempting to act, think, and even feel the way they do. Unlike other research methods, participant observation requires a researcher to become immersed in a social setting, not for a week or two, but usually for a period of years. On the other hand, for the duration of the study, the researcher must also maintain the role of "observer," standing back from the action and applying the sociological perspective to social patterns that others take for granted. The twin roles of "insider" participant and "outsider" often come down to a series of careful compromises. Such tensions appear as a regular feature in the *field notes*, a daily record of how the research proceeds. These notes form the basis for the final research report, and should convey not only a researcher's conclusions but something of the research experience itself.

Sociologists often work alone in this kind of study, so they must remain mindful that results depend on the interpretations of a single scientist. Participant observation is typically **qualitative research**, meaning *inquiry based on subjective impressions*. Unlike surveys, participant observation usually involves little **quantitative research**, *investigation based on the analysis of numerical data*. Because personal impressions play a central role in participant observation, some scientists disparage this method as lacking in scientific rigor. Yet its personal approach can be a strength; while a highly visible team of sociologists attempting to administer formal surveys would disrupt many social settings, a sensitive participant-observer can often gain considerable insight into people's natural behavior.

## A Case Study: Street Corner Society

A classic illustration of participant observation was carried out in the late 1930s by William Foote Whyte. A graduate student at Harvard University, Whyte was fascinated by the lively street life of a nearby, rather run-down section of Boston. He embarked on a four-year study of this neighborhood, which he called "Cornerville" to protect the privacy of its inhabitants.

Cornerville was home to first- and second-generation Italian immigrants. Many were poor and lived quite unlike the more affluent Bostonians familiar to Whyte. To many, Cornerville was a place to avoid: a poor, chaotic slum that was home to racketeers. Unwilling to accept easy stereotypes, Whyte set out to discover for himself exactly what kind of life went on inside this

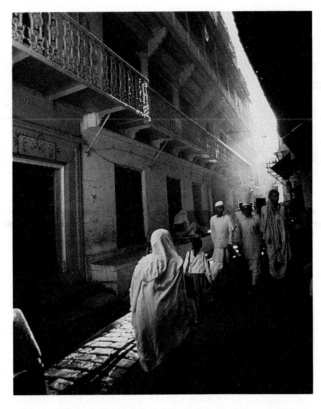

What is different often excites the sociological imagination. Participant observation is well suited for exploring an unfamiliar setting like this urban community in India. But research of this kind demands extensive preparation. To begin, investigators must acquire necessary language skills, and they need to gain at least a basic understanding of the new culture. To minimize these difficulties, researchers often study communities with which they have at least some previous experience.

community. His celebrated book, *Street Corner Society* (1981; orig. 1943), describes Cornerville as a highly organized community with its own code of values, complex social patterns, and distinctive social conflicts.

Whyte's research points up the advantages of participant-observation as well as some of its pitfalls. He could have taken his clipboard and questionnaire to one of Cornerville's community centers and asked local people to talk about their lives. Or he could have asked members of the community to come to his office at Harvard for interviews. In either case, the information he gathered would certainly have been misleading, since as we have already seen, the awareness of being observed often alters the behavior of subjects. Many Cornerville residents would probably have refused to talk to him at all under those circumstances. Whyte realized that he had to downplay the role of observer if people were to be comfortable in his presence. Therefore, he tried to become part of Cornerville's everyday social patterns.

One night early in his study, Whyte joined a group of people in Cornerville who frequented a gambling establishment. After listening to a story about how gambling was organized, Whyte asked naively, "I suppose the cops were all paid off?" The man's reaction taught Whyte something about the tension between being a participant and being an observer:

> The gambler's jaw dropped. He glared at me. Then he denied vehemently that any policeman had been paid off and immediately switched the conversation to another subject. For the rest of that evening I felt very uncomfortable.

> The next day [a local acquaintance] explained the lesson of the previous evening. "Go easy on that 'who,' 'what,' 'why,' 'when,' 'where' stuff, Bill. You ask those questions and people will clam up on you. If people accept you, you can just hang around, and you'll learn the answers in the long run without even having to ask the questions." (1981:303)

Gaining insider status—becoming a participant—was the crucial first step in Whyte's research. But how could an upper-middle-class Anglo-Saxon graduate student from Harvard become part of the life of a poor Italian immigrant community like Cornerville?

Gaining entry or "breaking in" to a strange social environment is difficult, often embarrassing, and sometimes even dangerous, as Whyte soon found out. On another evening, Whyte dropped in at a local bar, hoping to buy a woman a drink, and encourage her to talk about Cornerville. He looked around the room, but could find no woman alone. Presently, he noticed a fellow talking with two women, which he took to be an opportunity:

> I approached the group and opened with something like this:

> "Pardon me. Would you mind if I joined you?" There was a moment of silence while the man stared at me. Then he offered to throw me down the stairs. I assured him that this would not be necessary, and demonstrated as much by walking right out of there without any assistance. (1981:289)

This experience taught Whyte another important lesson: imposing on people is not only impolite, it can be hazardous to the researcher. Fortunately, however,

his luck soon took a turn for the better when he met a young man named "Doc" in the local community agency. Doc listened sympathetically to the problem and took Whyte under his wing, introducing his new friend to others in the neighborhood. This was the real start of Whyte's research because, with Doc's help, he soon became a regular among the people of Cornerville.

Whyte's friendship with Doc illustrates the importance of a *key informant* in field research. Key informants introduce a researcher to a community, and often can suggest how to find out specific information. But using a key informant has its dangers too. Because any key informant is familiar with only part of a community, such help may introduce bias into research. Moreover, once identified with a key informant, a researcher may be labeled in some way by others. In sum, while a key informant is invaluable at the outset, the participant-observer should soon seek a broader range of contacts.

Over several years of research, Whyte gradually settled in as a comfortable resident of Cornerville. He learned that it was hardly the disorganized slum some thought it to be. Many immigrants were working hard to become "established" Americans, and many were proud to have sent children to college. Whyte discovered social divisions in Cornerville, and he even found a few criminals. Yet he was able to see that this distinctive Boston neighborhood was composed mostly of people who, though poor, were working hard to build a future for themselves.

In sum, participant observation creates tensions and spotlights important contrasts. Its flexibility lets a researcher respond to an unfamiliar setting, but makes replication quite difficult. Sympathetic understanding requires involvement, while scientific observation demands detachment. Often a researcher works alone with little funding, but the time required to become familiar with a community makes this a costly type of research. Perhaps for all these reasons, participant-observation research is used less often than other methods described in this chapter. Yet the depth of understanding gained through research of this kind has greatly enriched our knowledge of many types of human communities.

## Secondary Analysis

Not all research requires investigators personally to collect their own data. In many cases, sociologists engage in **secondary analysis,** *a research method in which researchers utilize data collected by others.*

The most widely used data are statistics gathered by government agencies. The Bureau of the Census continuously gathers information about the U.S. population, much of which draws the interest of sociologists. Similar material is available from Statistics Canada, a branch of the Canadian government. Global analysis can benefit from various publications of the United Nations and the World Bank. A wide range of data is as close as the college library.

Secondary analysis may also mean using data collected by other, individual researchers. The obvious advantage of using available data—whether government statistics or the results of research studies—is a savings in time and money. This strategy enables sociologists with low budgets to undertake research that might otherwise be impossible. Just as important, the quality of government data is generally better than what even well-funded researchers could hope to obtain on their own.

Still, secondary analysis has inherent problems. For one thing, some researchers may not evaluate the accuracy of their data with a critical eye. Was information gathered in a systematic and unbiased way? Using second-hand data sometimes is a bit like buying a used car. While bargains can be found, there is potential for a poor choice.

Emile Durkheim's nineteenth-century study of suicide, described in Chapter 1 ("The Sociological Perspective"), is one of the best-known sociological investigations making use of existing records. But Durkheim's research also illustrates some of the dangers of this approach. He relied on official death records to investigate suicide rates among various types of people. But he had no way to check how many accidents were incorrectly classified as suicides, or what number of suicides were recorded as accidents or deaths due to some other cause. Sociologists who utilize others' data, then, must guard against distortions.

A second problem is that available data may have been collected for purposes different from those of a subsequent researcher. The way in which others phrased questions or selected respondents may not precisely fit the needs of a subsequent researcher. We are dealing with a trade-off here: any shortcomings in the data must be balanced against the ease by which they are obtained.

### Historical Research: A Tale of Two Cities

Since we are all trapped in the present, secondary analysis provides a key to investigating the past. The study *Puritan Boston and Quaker Philadelphia*, carried out by E. Digby

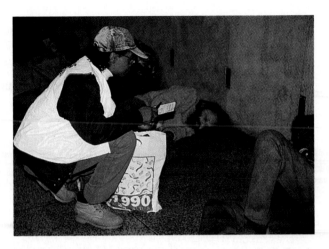

Most census data are obtained from questionnaires that officials send and receive back through the mail. This strategy, although generally quite efficient, is likely to undercount the homeless or others who lack a customary street address. To correct this problem, the Census Bureau made special efforts to count homeless people in March of 1990. They found that many individuals and families had been overlooked because they lived in converted garages, apartments added on to houses, in automobiles, or on the streets.

Baltzell (1979), exemplifies historical sociology using existing data. Visiting Bowdoin College in Maine, Baltzell was startled to learn that this small school had graduated a larger number of famous individuals than his own, much bigger University of Pennsylvania. This sparked Baltzell's sociological imagination, leading him to investigate historical patterns of achievement in New England and Pennsylvania.

Baltzell set out to test his hunch that New England had far more than its share of national leaders in diverse fields such as politics, law, and literature, while his native Pennsylvania had produced few such luminaries. Realizing that he would have to rely on historical records, Baltzell turned to the *Dictionary of American Biography*, twenty volumes of biographical data on more than thirteen thousand men and women. Baltzell knew that by using this source he could consider only those people deemed worthy by the editors of the *Dictionary*. He proceeded, accepting some inevitable bias, because he knew of no better source for the information he needed.

Baltzell's next problem was how to assess the magnitude of a person's achievement. He decided to base his ranking on the stated policy of the *Dictionary* to reflect stature in the length of each individual's biography. Such

**Table 2–2** FOUR RESEARCH METHODS: A SUMMARY

| Method | Application | Advantages | Limitations |
|---|---|---|---|
| Experiment | For explanatory research that specifies relationships among variables; generates quantitative data | Provides greatest ability to specify cause-and-effect relationships; replication of research is relatively easy | Laboratory settings have artificial quality; unless research environment is carefully controlled, result may be biased |
| Survey | For gathering information about issues that cannot be directly observed, such as attitudes and values; useful for descriptive and explanatory research; generates quantitative or qualitative data | Sampling allows surveys of large populations using questionnaires; interviews provide in-depth responses | Questionnaires must be carefully prepared and may produce low return rate; interviews are expensive and time-consuming |
| Participant observation | For exploratory and descriptive study of people in a "natural" setting; generates qualitative data | Allows study of "natural" behavior; usually inexpensive | Time-consuming; replication of research is difficult; researcher must balance roles of participant and observer |
| Secondary analysis | For exploratory, descriptive, or explanatory research whenever suitable data are available | Saves time and expense of data collection; makes historical research possible | Researcher has no control over possible bias in data; data may not be suitable for current research needs |

ratings are open to argument, of course, but Baltzell could hardly have done better entirely on his own.

By the time Baltzell had identified the seventy-five individuals with the longest biographies, a striking pattern had emerged. Massachusetts had the most top achievers, claiming twenty-one of the seventy-five. Overall, the New England states had thirty-one of the entries. By contrast, Pennsylvania had only two, and the entire Middle Atlantic region, just twelve. Closing in on the explanation, Baltzell soon discovered that almost all the great achievers from Massachusetts were actually from the city of Boston. But there turned out to be little accomplishment in the history of his own Philadelphia, a city with both more people and more money than Boston.

What could explain the disparity? Baltzell drew inspiration from the German sociologist Max Weber (1958; orig. 1904–1905), whose research linking achievement to religion is detailed in Chapter 4 ("Society"). Baltzell began contrasting the two religious environments that have historically dominated Boston and Philadelphia. Here lay the key to this historical puzzle: based on different religious convictions, the Puritan founders of Boston sought public achievement just as fervently as their Quaker counterparts in Philadelphia shunned it.

Both cities were founded by refugees fleeing religious persecution in England. But the groups viewed the world quite differently. Convinced of humanity's innate sinfulness, Baltzell explains, Boston Puritans built a rigid society in which family, church, and school controlled people's behavior. Hard work was the way to glorify God, and public prominence the most reassuring sign that one had received God's blessing. Thus, Puritanism fostered a hierarchical and disciplined life in which achievement was vigorously sought and highly respected.

Philadelphia's Quakers, however, built their way of life on the notion that human beings are inherently good. They saw little need for strong social institutions to "save" individuals from sinfulness. The Quakers vigorously pursued wealth yet, believing all people to be fundamentally equal, they celebrated personal modesty and discouraged anyone from standing apart from others by seeking fame or public office.

Baltzell's sociological imagination transformed Boston and Philadelphia into two social "test tubes": Puritanism was introduced into one, Quakerism into the other. From our vantage point centuries later, we can see what "chemical reactions" occurred in each case. Without claiming that one religion is in any sense "better" than the other, Baltzell convincingly argues that the two belief systems set in motion different orientations toward personal achievement that shaped the history of each region and the accomplishments of people who lived there.

As in all research, Baltzell's historical data do not *prove* his conclusions in any absolute sense. The best we can say is that his theory is consistent with the data, and as always, future research may support or challenge his conclusions. Especially when dealing with events far removed from the present, researchers must make considerable use of their interpretive skills. Baltzell's research reminds us that, in the end, sociological investigation encompasses a complex weave of scientific skills, personal values, and a lively and practiced imagination.

We have introduced four major methods of sociological investigation, which are summarized in Table 2–2. We now turn to our final consideration: how the specific facts obtained through sociological investigation relate to theory.

## The Interplay of Theory and Method

Methods of sociological investigation guide the discovery of facts about our social world. Facts, however, are not the final goal of research. As suggested in Chapter 1 ("The Sociological Perspective"), what sociologists really strive for is the development of theory—combining facts into cogent patterns of meaning.

In sociological investigation, researchers link facts and theory in two ways. **Deductive logical thought** is *reasoning that transforms general ideas into specific hypotheses suitable for scientific testing.* From a general understanding of some issue, in other words, the researcher *deduces* a hypothesis and selects a method by which to test it. Of course, the data collected may or may not support the hypothesis. Data supporting the hypothesis suggest that the general theory is on the right track. Faced with data refuting the hypothesis, a researcher infers that the theory should be revised or perhaps rejected entirely. The deductive logical model, then, proceeds from the general (theory) to the specific (facts used for evaluation).

Philip Zimbardo's Stanford County Prison experiment illustrates how this model operates. Zimbardo began with the general idea that prisons themselves alter human behavior. He then fashioned a specific hypothesis: placed in a prison setting, even emotionally well-balanced young men would exhibit violent behavior. Zim-

bardo confirmed this hypothesis when violence erupted soon after the experiment began. Had his experiment produced amicable behavior between "prisoners" and "guards," his original theory would clearly have required reformulation.

A second type of logical thought works in the other direction. Through **inductive logical thought**, or *reasoning that builds specific observations into general theory,* a researcher uses inductive reasoning to organize specific observations into a more general theory about human behavior.

E. Digby Baltzell's research illustrates the inductive logical model. He began noting that one New England college had produced a surprising number of high achievers. Thinking this might stem from regional differences, he collected additional facts until he discerned a distinctive pattern. Finally, he interpreted this pattern as evidence of the importance of religious values to achievement.

In most cases, researchers make use of *both* types of logical thought, as represented in Figure 2–2. Sociological investigation often begins with general ideas that lead (deductively) to hypotheses, which in turn are evaluated on the basis of specific observations. These observations then (inductively) guide the modification of the original theory.

**Figure 2–2**  Deductive and Inductive Logical Thought

## Putting It All Together: Ten Steps in Sociological Investigation

Any research project in sociology should include each of the following ten steps.

1. *Define the topic of investigation.* The ideas for social research come from all over; just remain curious and observe the world using the sociological perspective. As Max Weber suggested, the issue you choose for study is likely to have some personal significance.

2. *Find out what has already been learned about the topic.* You are probably not the first person to develop an interest in a particular issue. Spend time in the library to learn what theories and methods of sociological investigation have been applied to your topic. Theory guides the kinds of questions you ask, and research methods indicate strategies for discovering answers. In reviewing the research that has already been done, note problems that may have come up before.

3. *Assess the requirements for carrying out research on the topic.* What resources are necessary to support your research? How much time will you need? Can you do the work yourself? If not, how much help is required? What expenses will you have along the way? What sources of funding might be available to support your research? You must answer all these questions before you actually begin to design the research project.

4. *Specify the questions you are going to ask.* Are you seeking to explore an unfamiliar social setting? To describe some category of people? Or to investigate cause and effect among variables? If your study is exploratory, identify general questions that will guide the work. If it is descriptive, specify the population and the characteristics of interest. If explanatory, state the hypothesis to be tested and carefully operationalize each variable.

What we "see" in our surroundings, or in the research data we derive from them, depends on us as well as on what we study. To illustrate, examine *Target with Four Faces*, constructed of plaster, paper, cloth, and canvas by Jasper Johns. The assemblage demands that we make sense of it, especially because it places human faces and a target in menacing combination. But why are the faces the same? Why are the eyes hidden from view? The riddle of this artwork is made even more vexing by the artist's denial that it has any meaning at all. In the end, our response to all art depends on our own sensibilities. We might highlight the pleasing textures and colors that are used, the disturbing statement the work seems to make, or perhaps ponder the inconsistency between these two levels of meaning. The challenge of interpretation is as central to scientific research as it is to art.

Target with Four Faces. *1955. Encaustic on newspaper over canvas, 26 × 26" surmounted by four tinted plaster faces in wood box with hinged front. Box, closed, 3¾ × 26 × 3½". Overall dimensions with box open, 33⅝ × 26 × 3". The Museum of Modern Art, New York. Gift of Mr. and Mrs. Robert C. Scull.*

5. *Consider the ethical issues involved in the research.* Not all research raises serious ethical issues, but you should be sensitive to this matter throughout your investigation. Will you promise anonymity to the subjects? If so, how will you ensure that anonymity will be maintained? Can the research harm anyone? How might you design the study to minimize the chances for injury?

6. *Devise a research strategy.* Consider all major research strategies—as well as innovative combinations of approaches—before deciding how to proceed. Keep in mind that the appropriate method depends on the kind of questions you are asking as well as the resources available to support your research.

7. *Use the method to gather data.* The collection of data is carried out according to the research method you have chosen. Be sure to accurately record all information in a way that will make sense later (it may be some time before you actually write up the results of your work). Remain vigilant for sources of bias that may creep in and distort the research.

8. *Interpret the findings.* Scrutinize the data in terms of the initial questions and decide what answers the data suggest. If your study involved a specific hypothesis, you should be able to confirm, reject, or modify the hypothesis based on the data. Keep in mind that there may be several ways to interpret the results of your study, consistent with different theoretical paradigms, and you should consider them all. Ask other people to review your work and suggest alternative interpretations. Be on guard against the ever-present danger that personal values or expectations will affect how you make sense out of the data you have collected.

9. *Based on the findings, state your conclusions.* Prepare a final report indicating what you have learned from the research. Consider the contributions of your work both to sociological theory and to improving sociological methods of research. What is the value of your research to other people in general? Finally, evaluate your own work. What problems arose during the research process? What questions are left unanswered? Note ways in which your own biases may have affected your conclusions.

10. *Publish your research!* There are many ways to present your work including public presentations on campus and at professional meetings. The important point is to share what you have learned with others, and to let others respond to your work. Doing this, you gain a place among countless men and women who have expanded our understanding of human behavior.

## Summary

1. Sociological investigation uses the logic of science to learn about the social world.

2. Science is a fundamental part of all sociological research and, more broadly, helps us to critically evaluate information we encounter every day.

3. Two basic requirements for sociological investigation are (1) using the sociological perspective to view the surrounding world and (2) being curious and asking questions about society.

4. Science is a particular way of understanding the world based on empirical evidence. As such, science often contradicts our common sense.

5. Measurement is the process of determining the value of a variable in any specific case. Sound measurement has both reliability and validity.

6. Science seeks to specify the relationship among variables. Ideally, researchers seek relationships of cause and effect in which an independent variable can be used to predict change in a dependent variable. Often, however, research involves only correlation.

7. The scientific ideal is objectivity. Although the issues studied typically reflect personal interests, value-free research depends on suspending personal values and biases to the greatest extent possible.

8. Issues involving gender often generate bias in research. Investigators should avoid examining issues from the point of view of only one sex, or basing generalizations about humanity on data collected from only men or women.

9. The logic of science developed primarily through study of the natural world. Sociologists must recognize that the application of science to the study of human behavior has inherent limitations.

10. Curiosity and imagination, which spring from the human mind and not from science, are vital to research. Since human reality revolves around meanings, the process of interpretation stands at the core of all sociological investigation.

11. Many sociologists argue that research inevitably involves political values, and some assert that sociological research, therefore, should promote desirable social change.

12. Because sociological research has the potential to harm subjects, sociological investigators are bound by ethical guidelines.

13. Experiments attempt to specify the relationship between two (or more) variables; they are best performed under controlled conditions.

14. Surveys gather people's responses to statements or questions. Surveys utilize both questionnaires and interviews.

15. Participant observation involves directly observing a social setting for an extended period of time. In this research method, the investigator functions both as a participant in the setting and as a careful observer of it.

16. Secondary analysis, or making use of available data, is often preferable to collecting one's own data; it also allows study of historical issues.

17. Theory and research are closely linked. Deductive thought transforms general ideas into specific hypotheses suitable for testing. Inductive thought organizes specific observations into general ideas. Most sociological investigation makes use of both types of logical thought.

# Key Concepts

**cause and effect** a relationship between two variables in which change in one (the independent variable) causes change in another (the dependent variable)

**concept** a mental construct that represents some part of the world, inevitably in a somewhat simplified form

**control** the ability to neutralize the effect of one variable in order to assess the relationships among other variables

**correlation** a relationship between two (or more) variables

**deductive logical thought** reasoning that transforms general ideas into specific hypotheses suitable for scientific testing

**dependent variable** a variable that is changed by another (independent) variable

**empirical evidence** information we are able to verify with our senses

**experiment** a research method for investigating cause and effect under highly controlled conditions

**Hawthorne effect** a change in a subject's behavior caused by the awareness of being studied

**hypothesis** an unverified statement of a relationship between variables

**independent variable** a variable that causes change in another (dependent) variable

**inductive logical thought** reasoning that builds specific observations into general theory

**interview** a series of questions administered personally by a researcher to respondents

**mean** the arithmetic average of a series of numbers

**measurement** the process of determining the value of a variable in a specific case

**median** the value that occurs midway in a series of numbers arranged in order of magnitude or, simply, the middle case

**mode** the value that occurs most often in a series of numbers

**objectivity** the state of personal neutrality in conducting research

**operationalizing a variable** specifying exactly what is to be measured in assigning a value to a variable

**participant observation** a method in which researchers systematically observe people while joining in their routine activities

**population** the people who are the focus of research

**qualitative research** inquiry based on subjective impressions

**quantitative research** inquiry based on the analysis of numerical data

**questionnaire** a series of questions presented to subjects

**reliability** the quality of consistent measurement

**replication** repetition of research by others in order to assess its accuracy

**research method** a strategy for systematically conducting research

**sample** a part of a population selected to represent the whole

**science** a logical system that bases knowledge on direct, systematic observation

**secondary analysis** a research method in which a researcher utilizes data collected by others

**spurious correlation** an apparent, although false, relationship between two (or more) variables caused by some other variable

**survey** a research method in which subjects respond to a series of questions in a questionnaire or interview

**validity** the quality of measuring precisely what one intends to measure

**variable** a concept whose value changes from case to case

# Suggested Readings

The following books introduce the process of sociological investigation in terms that are easy for beginning students to understand.

Chava Frankfort–Nachmias and David Nachmias. *Research Methods in the Social Sciences*. 4th ed. New York: St. Martin's Press, 1992.

Morton M. Hunt. *Profiles of Social Research: The Scientific Study of Human Interactions*. New York: Russell Sage Foundation/Basic Books, 1986.

This book explores the development of the sociology, political science, economics, and history of the United States, highlighting how they differ from the natural sciences.

Dorothy Ross. *The Origins of American Social Science*. New York: Cambridge University Press, 1991.

The first of these books is a new edition of a classic account of interviewing. The second, described at the beginning of this chapter, applies these methods to the study of women's lives on the college campus.

Robert K. Merton, Marjorie Fiske, and Patricia Kendall. *The Focused Interview: A Manual of Problems and Procedures*. 2nd ed. The Free Press, 1990.

Dorothy Holland and Margaret Eisenhart. *Educated in Romance*. Chicago: University of Chicago Press, 1990.

The first of these books analyzes a basic research strategy; the second illustrates its use in the study of an African-American community in Philadelphia.

Danny L. Jorgensen. *Participant Observation: A Methodology for Human Studies*. Newbury Park, CA: Sage, 1989.

Elijah Anderson. *Street Wise*. Chicago: University of Chicago Press, 1990.

These books explore the neglected issue of how gender and sexism can affect the research process.

Tony Larry Whitehead and Mary Ellen Conaway, eds. *Self, Sex, and Gender in Cross-Cultural Fieldwork*. Urbana, IL: University of Illinois Press, 1986.

Margrit Eichler. *Nonsexist Research Methods: A Practical Guide*. Winchester, MA: Unwin Hyman, 1988.

"Focus groups"—small groups that interact intensively in an attempt to answer some basic questions—are widely used in industry. This book details the operation of focus groups, including how to recruit members, how to conduct group discussions, and how to analyze data.

Davis W. Stewart and Prem N. Shamdasani. *Focus Groups: Theory and Practice*. Newbury Park, CA: Sage, 1990.

All researchers need to develop skills to communicate their findings to others in a comprehensive and interesting way. These two books (the second aimed at more advanced writers) can help you to do just that.

The Sociology Writing Group. *A Guide to Writing Sociology Papers*. New York: St. Martin's Press, 1986.

Howard S. Becker, with a chapter by Pamela Richards. *Writing for Social Scientists: How to Start and Finish Your Thesis, Book, or Article*. Chicago: University of Chicago Press, 1986.

Written by a former Gallup organization official, this short book explores the role of polls in our nation's politics.

Irving Crespi. *Public Opinion, Polls, and Democracy*. Boulder, CO: Westview Press, 1989.

Sociologists continue to debate the links among research, politics, and personal values. The first book listed below is one of the best efforts to explore this controversy-filled area. The second is a recent history of the discipline suggesting that particular social values and priorities deeply influenced the work of pioneering sociologists.

Alvin W. Gouldner. *The Coming Crisis of Western Sociology*. New York: Avon Books, 1970.

Arthur J. Vidich and Stanford M. Lyman. *American Sociology: Worldly Rejections of Religion and Their Directions*. New Haven, CT: Yale University Press, 1985.

# 3

# Culture

A small aluminum motorboat chugged steadily along the muddy Orinoco River, deep within South America's vast tropical rain forest. Anthropologist Napoleon Chagnon was nearing the end of a three-day journey to the home territory of the Yąnomamö, one of the most technologically primitive societies remaining on earth.

Some twelve thousand Yąnomamö live in villages scattered along the border of Venezuela and Brazil. Their way of life could hardly be more different from our own. The Yąnomamö wear little clothing, and live without electricity, automobiles, or other conveniences people in the United States take for granted. Their traditional weapons, used for hunting and warfare, are the bow and arrow. They have had little contact with the outside world. Thus Chagnon would be as strange to them as they would be to him.

By two o'clock in the afternoon, Chagnon had almost reached his destination. The hot sun made the humid air almost unbearable. The anthropologist's clothes were soaked with perspiration; his face and hands were swollen from the bites of innumerable gnats that swarmed around him. But he hardly noticed, so preoccupied was he with the fact that in just a few moments he would be face to face with people unlike any he had ever known.

Chagnon's heart pounded as the boat slid onto the riverbank near a Yąnomamö village. Sounds of activity came from nearby. Chagnon and his guide climbed from the boat and walked toward the village, stooping as they pushed their way through the dense undergrowth. Chagnon describes what happened next:

> I looked up and gasped when I saw a dozen burly, naked, sweaty, hideous men staring at us down the shafts of their drawn arrows! Immense wads of green tobacco were stuck between their lower teeth and lips making them look even more hideous, and strands of dark green slime dripped or hung from their nostrils—strands so long that they clung to their [chests] or drizzled down their chins.

> My next discovery was that there were a dozen or so vicious, underfed dogs snapping at my legs, circling me as if I were to be their next meal. I just stood there holding my notebook, helpless and pathetic. Then the stench of the decaying vegetation and filth hit me and I almost got sick. I was horrified. What kind of welcome was this for the person who came here to live with you and learn your way of life, to become friends with you? (1983:10)

Fortunately for Chagnon, the Yąnomamö villagers recognized his guide and lowered their weapons. Reassured that he would at least survive the afternoon, Chagnon was still shaken by his inability to make any sense of the people surrounding him. And this was to be his home for a year and a half! He wondered why he had forsaken physics to study human culture in the first place.

The 5 billion people living on the earth are members of but one biological species: *Homo sapiens*. Even

61

so, any of us can be overwhelmed by how dissimilar we are from one another, differences not of biology but of culture. Entering the world of the Yanomamö, Chagnon experienced a severe case of **culture shock**: *personal disorientation that accompanies exposure to an unfamiliar way of life*. Like most of us, Chagnon had been raised to keep his clothes on, even in hot weather, and to use a handkerchief when his nose was running—especially in front of others. The Yanomamö clearly had other ideas about how to live. The nudity that embarrassed Chagnon was customary to them. The green slime hanging from their nostrils was caused by inhaling a hallucinogenic drug, a practice common among friends. The "stench" that made Chagnon recoil in disgust no doubt smelled like "Home Sweet Home" to the inhabitants of that Yanomamö village.

Human beings the world over have very different ideas about what is pleasant and repulsive, polite and rude, true and false, right and wrong. This capacity for startling difference is a wonder of our species: the expression of human culture.

## What Is Culture?

**Culture** is defined as *the beliefs, values, behavior, and material objects shared by a particular people*. But culture involves more than simply adding up all the ways people act and think, and assessing the sum of their possessions (Soyinka, 1991). Culture melds past and present, synthesizing achievement and aspiration. In short, culture comprises a complete social heritage.

To begin, however, we must divide culture into its components. Sociologists distinguish between **nonmaterial culture**, *the intangible creations of human society* (ideas ranging from altruism to zen), and **material culture**, *the tangible products of human society* (objects ranging from armaments to zippers). The terms *culture* and *society* are sometimes used interchangeably, but their precise meanings are different. Culture refers to a shared way of life. Society, the topic of the next chapter, is the organized interaction among people within a geographical or political boundary, which is guided by culture. Neither society nor culture could exist without the other.

In everyday life the way we dress, when and what we eat, where we work, and how we spend our free time are all grounded in culture. Our culture leads us

to sleep in houses of wood and brick, while people of other cultures live in huts fashioned from brush, igloos of ice, or tepees made of animal skins. In addition, culture frames the meanings we attach to our lives, indicating standards of success, beauty, and goodness, as well as reverence for a divine power, the forces of nature, or long-dead ancestors. Culture also shapes our personalities—what we commonly (yet inaccurately) describe as "human nature." The Yanomamö, who are fierce and warlike, strive to develop these "natural" qualities in their children. The Tasaday of the Philippines, by contrast, are so peace-loving that there is no word in their language for violence. The cultures of the United States and Japan stress achievement and hard work; but Americans value competition and individualism, while the Japanese emphasize cooperation and self-denying obedience to authority. In short, culture is a blueprint for virtually every dimension of our lives, from the might of enormous corporations to the meaning of a shy smile.

Sociologists, then, use the concept of culture more broadly than others do. In everyday conversation, "culture" usually refers to sophisticated art forms such as classical literature, music, dance, and painting. As used here, however, the term refers to *everything* that is part of a people's way of life—from Motown to Mozart, fish sticks to fine cuisine, ping pong to polo.

No cultural element is inherently "natural" to humanity, although most people around the world view their particular way of life that way. What sets humans apart from other species is the capacity to create culture, which we learn as members of a society. And although culture is transmitted from generation to generation, specific elements of culture are all subject to change.

Every other living species—from ants to antelopes—behaves in uniform ways. To a world traveler, the enormous diversity of human life stands out in contrast to the behavior of, say, cats, which is the same everywhere. Most living creatures respond to biological forces we call *instincts*, strategies for their survival that change only over long periods of time. A few animals—notably chimpanzees and related primates—have the capacity for basic elements of culture, as researchers have noted by observing them use tools and teach simple skills to their offspring. But the creative power of humans far exceeds that of any other form of life, so that *only people rely on culture rather than instinct to ensure the survival of their kind* (Harris, 1987).

To understand how this came to be, we must briefly review the history of our species on the earth.

A global perspective reveals that human beings create remarkably diverse ways of life. Such differences begin with outward appearance: contrast the women shown here from Iran, Kenya, New Guinea, and Egypt, and the men from Taiwan (Republic of China), Peru, India, and New Guinea. Less obvious, but of even greater importance, are internal differences, since culture also shapes our goals in life, our sense of justice, and even our inner-most personal feelings.

## Culture and Human Intelligence

In a universe perhaps 15 billion years old, our planet is a relatively young 4.5 billion years of age, and the human species is a wide-eyed infant of only 40,000. Not for a billion years after the earth was formed did the first life forms appear. Far later on—some 65 million years ago—our history took a crucial turn with the appearance of the mammals we call primates.

Primates evolved into highly intelligent life forms, with the largest brains relative to body size of all living creatures. Further change occurred as the human line diverged from that of our closest relatives, the great apes, about 12 million years ago. Our common lineage shows through, however, in traits that the human species shares with today's chimpanzees, gorillas, and orangutans: great sociability, affectionate and long-lasting bonds for child rearing and mutual protection, the ability to walk upright (normal in humans, less common among other primates), and hands that manipulate objects with great precision.

Studying fossil records, scientists conclude that the first creatures with clearly human characteristics lived about 2 million years ago. These distant ancestors, with their limited mental capacity, still grasped such cultural fundamentals as the use of fire, tools, and weapons, and the creation of simple shelters. Although these "stone age" achievements seem modest, they mark the point at which our ancestors embarked on a distinct evolution-ary course, making culture the primary strategy for human survival.

Consider for a moment what newcomers to the earth humans are. To make the time frame of human evolution clearer, Carl Sagan (1977) suggests superimposing the 15-billion-year history of our universe on a single calendar year. The life-giving atmosphere of our planet did not develop until the autumn, and the earliest human-like beings did not appear until December 31—the last day of the year—at 10:30 at night! Yet not until 250,000 years ago, which is mere minutes before the end of Sagan's "year," did our own species finally emerge. These *Homo sapiens* (derived from Latin meaning "thinking person") have continued to evolve so that, about 40,000 years ago, humans who looked very much like ourselves lived on the earth. With larger brains, these "modern" *Homo sapiens* produced culture at a rapid pace, as the wide range of tools and cave art from this period suggests. Still, what we call "civilization," based on permanent settlements and specialized occupations, began in the Middle East only about 12,000 years ago (Hamblin, 1973; Wenke, 1980). In terms of Sagan's "year," this cultural flowering occurred during the final *seconds* before midnight on New Year's Eve. And what of our modern, industrial way of life? Begun only 300 years ago, in Sagan's scheme, it amounts to a mere millisecond flash.

Human culture, then, is an evolutionary strategy for survival. Culture first evolved as our ancestors de-

A man frozen inside a glacier for some 5,300 years was recently discovered high in the European Alps. Remarkably preserved, he provides us with evidence of the development of culture among our distant ancestors. The man was about thirty years of age—old for his time—and stood just five feet, three inches tall, reflecting a lower standard of living than we have today. His reliance on animal skins is evident in his leather jacket stitched with thongs and his leather boots, which he filled with hay to insulate his feet from the cold. The man's tools included a bow and feathered arrows, a bronze-headed ax, a knife with a stone blade, and a leather pouch which held a piece of flint to spark a fire. His concern with his appearance is suggested by a stone necklace and numerous tattoos on his body.

scended from the trees into the tall grasses of central Africa, where walking upright and hunting in organized groups had clear advantages. The human capacity to create a way of life—as opposed to simply acting out biological imperatives—emerged over millions of years as the size of the human brain increased. Gradually, the biological forces we commonly call instincts were replaced by a more efficient survival scheme: humans gained the mental power *to actively fashion the natural environment for ourselves*. At this point, human nature no longer turned on instinct but on culture (Barash, 1981). Ever since, people have made and remade their worlds in countless ways, which explains today's fascinating (and, as Napoleon Chagnon's experiences show, sometimes disturbing) cultural diversity.

# The Components of Culture

Although people the world over express their humanity differently, all cultures have five common components: symbols, language, values, norms, and material culture. We begin with the one that underlies the rest: symbols.

## Symbols

The human world is grounded not in objects and action, but in *meaning*. In short, the surrounding environment is *symbolic*. A **symbol** is *anything that carries a particular meaning recognized by members of a culture*. A whistle, a wall of graffiti, a flashing red light, and a fist raised in the air all serve as symbols. We can see the human capacity to create and manipulate symbols in the simple act of winking the eye. In some settings this action conveys interest; in others, understanding; in still others, insult.

Symbols are the basis of culture, and the foundation of everyday reality. Generally, we become so fluent in the language of our culture's symbols that we take them for granted. Often, however, we sense their importance when symbols are used in an unconventional way, say, if an American flag is burned in a political demonstration. We also recognize the power of symbols when we enter a society with an unfamiliar culture. Culture shock stems from an inability to attach meaning to our surroundings. Like Napoleon Chagnon confronting the Ya̧nomamö, we feel lost, unsure of how to act, and sometimes fright-

ened—a consequence of being outside the symbolic web of culture that joins individuals in meaningful social life.

Cultural variation means that an action or object with a specific meaning in one culture may have a very different significance in another. To people in North America, a baseball bat symbolizes sport and relaxation; but the Ya̧nomamö would probably view this well-carved club with thoughts of hunting or war. A dog is a beloved household pet to millions of Americans, but a regular meal to millions of Chinese. Likewise, the cows that are sacred to millions of Hindus in India are routinely consumed as "quarter-pounders" by hungry Americans. Thus symbols not only bind people together but also separate people who live in the various societies of the world.

In practice, behavior that seems quite normal to us may spark offense among people of other societies. Women serving in the Gulf War recently discovered that simply wearing shorts in an Islamic society like Saudi Arabia was widely condemned as inappropriate. Countless gestures are imbued with different meanings in various cultures. Placing the thumb between the first and second fingers means good luck in Portugal or Brazil, yet it is an invitation to sex among the Germans. In the United States, we use the "A-OK" gesture made with thumb and forefinger to express approval and pleasure; in France and Belgium, however, the same symbol conveys the insulting meaning "You're worth zero" (Ekman et al., 1984). The lesson for travelers is obvious: understanding something about your cultural surroundings can save embarrassment—or worse.

To some degree, of course, symbolic meanings vary even within a single society. A fur coat, prized as a symbol of success by one person may represent the inhumane treatment of animals to another. Similarly, a confederate flag that represents regional pride to one individual may symbolize centuries of racial oppression to someone else.

Cultural symbols also change over time. Blue jeans were introduced as sturdy and inexpensive clothing worn by people engaged in physical labor. In the liberal political climate of the 1960s, this working-class aura made jeans popular among affluent students—many of whom wore them to identify with working people. A decade later, "designer jeans" emerged as fashionable "status symbols," signifying big clothing budgets, the opposite of their working-class roots. In recent years, jeans appear to be gaining favor once again, this time simply as comfortable apparel.

In sum, symbols allow people to make sense of their lives. In a world of cultural diversity, the use of symbols may cause embarrassment and even conflict, but without symbols human existence would be meaningless.

## Language

Helen Keller (1880–1968) was blind and deaf from birth. Cut off from the symbolic world around her, she literally lived apart from society. Only when her teacher, Anne Mansfield Sullivan, broke through her isolation with the concept of language did Helen Keller begin to realize her human potential. This remarkable woman, who later became a renowned educator herself, recalls the moment she acquired language:

> We walked down the path to the well-house, attracted by the smell of honeysuckle with which it was covered. Someone was drawing water, and my teacher placed my hand under the spout. As the cool stream gushed over one hand, she spelled into the other the word *water*, first slowly, then rapidly. I stood still, my whole attention fixed upon the motions of her fingers. Suddenly I felt a misty consciousness as of something forgotten—a thrill of returning thought; and somehow the mystery of language was revealed to me. I knew then that "w-a-t-e-r" meant the wonderful cool something that was flowing over my hand. That living word awakened my soul; gave it light, hope, joy, set it free! (1903:21–24)

**Language,** the key to entering the world of culture, is *a system of symbols that allows members of a society to communicate with one another.* All cultures have a spoken language, although some, including the Yąnomamö, have no system of writing. Written symbols themselves are culturally variable, with societies in the Western world writing left to right, those in North Africa and Western Asia writing right to left, and people in Eastern Asia writing from top to bottom.

Global Map 3–1 shows the distribution of the world's three most widely spoken languages. Chinese is spoken by 21 percent (roughly 1 billion) of the world's people. More precisely, although all Chinese people who read and write use the same characters, they speak any of several dozen Chinese dialects, each of which is marked by distinctive pronunciation. The "official" dialect, taught in schools throughout the People's Republic of China and the Republic of Taiwan, is Mandarin (the dialect of Beijing, China's historic capital city). Cantonese (the language of Canton, which differs in sound from Mandarin roughly the way French does from Span-

ish) is the second most common Chinese dialect. English is the mother tongue of about 10 percent (500 million) of the world's people, and Spanish is the official language of 6 percent (300 million) people worldwide. Notice, too, that English is steadily becoming a global language, since it is given preference as a second language in most of the world's societies.

For people throughout the world, cultural heritage is rooted in language. Thus language is the most important means of **cultural transmission,** *the process by which one generation passes culture to the next.* Just as our bodies contain the genes of our ancestors, so our everyday lives are grounded in the symbolic system of those who came before us. Through the unique power of language, we gain access to centuries of accumulated wisdom.

For most of human history, people have transmitted culture through speech, which is often termed the *oral cultural tradition.* Not until five thousand years ago did humanity devise writing, and even then only a few people learned to read and write. When the United States was founded just over two centuries ago, only a small elite was literate. Today, perhaps 25 million American adults (about one in seven) cannot read and write—an almost insurmountable barrier to opportunity in a society that increasingly demands symbolic skills. Among the poorest societies of the world, four out of five people cannot use written language.

Language skills not only put us in touch with the past, they also free the human imagination. Connecting symbols in new ways, we can conceive of life other than as it is. Language—both spoken and written—distinguishes human beings as creatures aware of our limitations and ultimate mortality, yet able to dream and hope for a future better than the present.

### Is Language Uniquely Human?

Of all the species of our world, are humans alone capable of speech and writing? Creatures great and small direct sounds and other physical cues to one another, and these are certainly forms of communication. But such signals are largely instinctual, so that humans stand alone with the mental capacity to create complex systems of symbols.

Still, research has shown that some animals have at least a rudimentary ability to use symbols in the process of communicating with one another and with humans. Allen and Beatrice Gardner taught a chimp named Washoe to use 160 different words of the American Sign Language. Washoe was able not only to attach words to objects but also to combine words to create new mean-

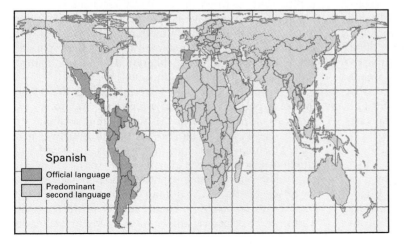

**Global Map 3–1**  Language in Global Perspective

Chinese (including Mandarin, Cantonese, and dozens of other dialects) is spoken by one-fifth of the world's people, almost all of whom live in Asia.

English is the mother tongue or official language in several world regions, and has become the preferred second language in most of the world.

The largest concentration of Spanish speakers is in Latin America, and Spanish is the preferred second language of the United States.

All animals are expressive. Only humans, however, confer symbolic meaning on facial gestures.

ings. For example, when a researcher known to Washoe as Susan accidently stepped on Washoe's doll, the chimp urgently responded: "Up Susan; mine, please up; gimme baby; shoe up; please move up." Other studies have confirmed the ability of chimps to understand complex instructions (Gardner & Gardner, 1969; Premack, 1976; Harris, 1987).

Even more remarkably, under the direction of E. Sue Savage-Rumbaugh, a four-year-old pygmy chimpanzee named Kanzi not only has spontaneously created simple sentences, but has learned to react to spoken English she has not heard before. For example, Kanzi has correctly responded to requests like "Will you get a diaper for your sister?" which is a feat until now undocumented among nonhuman primates (Eckholm, 1985).

Chimpanzees lack the physical ability to form the consonant sounds made by humans. Nor have these specially trained animals been able to teach their language skills to others of their kind. But these recent achievements suggest that we should not chauvinistically assume that humans alone can lay claim to culture. With a limited symbolic capacity, some other species share, at least partly, in a world of culture.

### Does Language Shape Reality?

If the Tasaday of the Philippines have no word for violence in their language, can they imagine deliberately hurting another person? Perhaps, but they cannot do so as readily as the Yanomamö, whose language is rich with terms for fighting. Since language provides the building-blocks of reality, linguistic differences often mean that members of one culture experience the world differently from people who inhabit another symbolic world.

Two anthropologists who specialized in linguistic studies, Edward Sapir and Benjamin Whorf, argued that language, rather than merely a series of labels, stands between us and the world; words, that is, actually shape the reality we experience (Sapir, 1929, 1949; Whorf, 1956). Sapir and Whorf challenge the common assumption that the many human languages describe a single reality. They remind us that every language has words or expressions that have no precise counterpart in other tongues. In addition, each language fuses symbols with particular emotions. Thus, as multilingual people can attest, a single idea "feels" different if spoken in Spanish rather than in English or Chinese (Falk, 1987).

Formally, then, what is now called the **Sapir-Whorf hypothesis** states that *people know the world only in terms of their language*. Using different symbolic systems, a Turk, a Brazilian, and a Filipino actually experience "distinct worlds, not merely the same world with different labels attached" (Sapir, 1949:162).

The Sapir-Whorf hypothesis does not claim that language rigidly limits human understanding. Various senses and enormous mental capacity provide us with vast perceptive power, and human creativity further enables us to generate new symbols and to use familiar ones in new ways. Thus human inventions bring with them new symbols: the development of computers, for example, has added words and phrases like *bytes, interface,* and *E-mail* to our language. In addition, people sometimes intentionally change language. The desire for social equality in a predominantly white society led African Americans to replace the word *Negro* with the term *black* or *person of color.* A generation later, such symbolic changes have helped improve white people's perceptions of African Americans. Similarly, although adult males in English-speaking societies have long been called *men,* adult females often have been condescendingly referred to as *girls.* The recent emphasis on calling women *women* is both cause and effect of growing sexual equality. In short, a system of language generates strong *tendencies* to understand the world in a particular way, but does not *determine* how we do so.

## Values

What accounts for the popularity in the United States of film characters like James Bond, Dirty Harry, Rambo, and Thelma and Louise? Each is ruggedly individualistic, suspicious of "the system," and relies primarily on personal skill and effort. Together, they suggest that Americans celebrate an ideal of sturdy individualism, especially for men. Sociologists call such patterns **values,** *standards by which members of a culture distinguish the desirable from the undesirable, what is good from what is bad, the beautiful from the ugly* (Williams, 1970:27). Values are judgments, from the standpoint of the culture, of what ought to be. People express these broad principles in most aspects of their way of life.

Cultural values shape our personalities. We learn from families, schools, and religious organizations how to think and act according to approved principles, what personal goals are worthy, and how to properly relate to our fellow human beings.

In a society as large and diverse as the United States, of course, few cultural values are shared by everyone. Over the centuries, people from throughout the world have entered the United States, producing a mosaic of cultural values. This contrasts with the greater cultural homogeneity of historically isolated societies such as Japan. Even so, the American way of life is guided by a number of values that most people recognize and that tend to persist over time.

### American Values

Sociologist Robin Williams (1970) suggests the following ten values are among the most central to our culture.

1. **Equal opportunity.** The American perception of fairness demands that everyone have the opportunity to get ahead, although, due to varying talents and efforts, people will not end up in the same situation. In other words, while not endorsing equality of *condition,* people in the United States do embrace equality of *opportunity,* by which everyone has a chance to obtain the good things in life.

2. **Achievement and success.** Our way of life encourages competition. In this way, we like to think, each person receives what is deserved on the basis of personal merit. In the United States, to be successful makes one a more worthy person—a "winner."

3. **Activity and work.** American heroes from Olympic figure skating star Kristi Yamaguchi to film's famed archeologist Indiana Jones are "doers," people who get the job done. Members of our society prefer *action* to *reflection;* through hard work we try to control events rather than passively accepting our fate. For this reason, many of us take a dim view of cultures that appear more easygoing or philosophical.

4. **Material comfort.** To be successful generally means making money and enjoying what it will buy. People in the United States may quip that "money won't buy happiness," but most diligently pursue wealth all the same.

5. **Practicality and efficiency.** Just as people in the United States value activity that earns money, so we praise solving problems with the least effort. "Building a better mousetrap" is a cultural goal, especially when it's done in the most cost-effective way.

6. **Progress.** Americans have traditionally believed that the present is better than the past, and that the future will be better still. In the United States, advertising sparks sales with claims that the "very latest" is the "very best."

7. **Science.** We often turn to scientists to solve problems, convinced that the work of scientific experts will improve our lives. We like to think of ourselves as rational people, which explains our cultural ten-

Australian artist Sally Swain alters a famous artist's painting to make fun of our culture's tendency to ignore the everyday lives of women. This spoof is entitled *Mrs. Renoir Cleans the Oven.*

dency (especially among men) to devalue emotions and intuition as sources of knowledge.

8. **Democracy and free enterprise.** Members of our society recognize various individual rights that cannot be overridden by government. Our political system is based on the ideal of free elections in which all adults express their opinions in selecting responsive leaders. Similarly, we believe that the U.S. economy meets the widely varied needs of selective, individual consumers.

9. **Freedom.** Closely related to democracy, freedom as a cultural value favors individual initiative over collective conformity. Although Americans acknowledge that everyone has responsibilities to oth-

ers, we believe that individuals should be free to pursue personal goals without unreasonable interference from anyone else.

10. **Racism and group superiority.** Despite embracing the values of equality and freedom, people in the United States also link personal worth to social categories based on social class, race, ethnicity, and sex. Our society values males above females, whites above members of other races, and more privileged people above those who are disadvantaged. Although we often describe ourselves as a nation of equals, there is little doubt that some of us are "more equal than others."

**Values: Inconsistency and Conflict**

As the listing above suggests, cultural values are sometimes inconsistent or even outright contradictory (Lynd, 1967; Bellah et al., 1986). At times, we find ourselves torn between the "me first" attitude of an individualistic, success-at-all-costs orientation and the opposing need to belong within some larger community. Similarly, the value that we place on equality of opportunity has long conflicted with our tendency to promote or degrade others because of their race, sex, or social background.

Then, too, values also change with time, sometimes as temporary trends, sometimes as new cultural orientations. For example, the traditional value placed on individual responsibility is apparently being eroded by what some observers have tagged "a new culture of victimization." The box takes a closer look.

Another dimension of value inconsistency occurs because cultural patterns vary according to people's age, sex, ethnicity, religion, race, and social class. People who are favored in one sense while disadvantaged in another (a situation that sociologists term "status inconsistency") are especially prone to contradictory values. Clarence Thomas, an African American appointed to the Supreme Court in 1991, began his climb to prominence in a poor Georgia family. His changing fortunes have left him with both an appreciation for the plight of poor minorities and a strong opposition to much of the civil rights establishment.

Further value conflict arises because dominant cultural patterns often define people—especially the poor and members of minorities—in ways that conflict with how they wish to think of themselves. Many homosexual men and women, for example, embrace mainstream cultural values in most respects while actively opposing traditional cultural stereotypes associated with their lifestyle.

# A New "Culture of Victimization?"

A New York man recently jumped in front of a subway train and survived; soon after he collected $650,000 from the city, claiming the train failed to stop in time to prevent his serious injuries. In Washington, DC, after realizing that he had been videotaped smoking crack cocaine in a hotel room, the city's mayor blamed his woman companion for "setting him up" and suggested that he was being harassed by police because he is an African American. Rose Cipollone smoked more than one pack of cigarettes each day for forty years before developing lung cancer; she sued the cigarette manufacturer, claiming the company was responsible for her illness. In the most celebrated case of its kind, Dan White gunned down the mayor of San Francisco and another man on the city council and subsequently argued that eating "junk food" (the so-called "twinkie defense") had driven him temporarily insane.

Underlying all these cases is a claim of victimization—the argument that rather than having a hand in their own mishaps, when something bad happens, the responsibility for people's misfortunes lies elsewhere. Sociologist Irving Horowitz sums up what has been called a "new culture of victimization": "Everyone is a victim these days; no one accepts responsibility for anything."

Consider the proliferation of "addictions." No longer limited to the compulsive use of drugs, we now hear about gambling addicts, compulsive overeaters, sex addicts, and even people who excuse mounting credit-card debts as a symptom of shopping addiction. Bookstores now overflow with manuals to help people come to terms with alleged medical or psychological conditions ranging from "The Cinderella Complex" and "The Casanova Complex" to "Soap Opera Syndrome." And our society's courts are becoming ever more clogged by lawsuits driven by the need to blame someone— and often to collect big money— for the kind of misfortune that we used to accept as part of life.

What's going on here? Is American culture changing? Historically, our way of life has been based on a cultural ideal of "rugged individualism," the notion that—for better or worse—people are responsible for whatever triumph or tragedy befalls them. But this value has been eroded by a number of factors. First, Americans have become more aware (partly through the work of sociologists and other social scientists) of how society itself shapes the lives of each one of us. Interestingly, the categories of people claiming the status of victim have extended well beyond those who *have* suffered historical disadvantages (like African Americans and women) to include even privileged people. In 1991, for example, *Newsweek* touted the emerging movement among white men seeking help in overcoming the alleged pressures of privilege.

Second, there has also been a small revolution in the legal system by which many lawyers—especially since gaining the right to advertise their services in 1977—now encourage a sense of injustice among clients they hope to shepherd into court. The number of million-dollar awards in such cases has risen more than twenty-five fold in the last twenty-five years.

Third, there has been a proliferation of "rights groups" that promote what Amitai Etzioni calls "rights inflation." Beyond the traditional constitutional liberties are many newly claimed rights, including those of hunters (as well as those of animals), the rights of smokers (and nonsmokers), the right of women to control their bodies (and the right of the unborn), the right to own a gun (and the right to be safe from violence). Expanding and competing claims for unmet rights, then, create victims on all sides.

Does this shift signal a fundamental realignment in our culture? In addressing this issue, we must realize that cultural trends of this kind spring from forces already at work. The current "culture of victimization" has its roots in the long-standing American belief that everyone has the right to prosperity, success, and happiness. While a heightened concern with individual rights has helped American society confront some clear cases of injustice, we also need to recognize that individualism has the potential to undermine society. As we have in the past, Americans will continue to struggle with the delicate balance between our rights as individuals and our responsibilities as members of a society.

SOURCES: Based on Taylor (1991) and Etzioni (1991).

In short, value inconsistencies and conflicts lead to strained and awkward balancing acts in how we view the world. Sometimes we decide to pursue one value at the expense of another, perhaps giving up an enjoyable area of college study for one that simply promises financial gains. At other times, we try to ignore such contradictions. National surveys, for example, show that most U.S. adults hold the clearly contradictory views that some people are born into families that confer enormous advantages over those less privileged and that the United States offers equal opportunity for all (N.O.R.C., 1991). While both views cannot be true, members of complex societies seem capable of living with significant cultural contradictions.

**Values in Action: The Games People Play**

Although we rarely think about cultural values, they affect every aspect of our lives. For example, children's games may seem like spontaneous fun, but they often provide important insights into what a culture defines as important.

Using the sociological perspective, James Spates (1976a) sees the familiar game King of the Mountain as an expression of our cultural values of achievement and success:[1]

> In this game, the King (winner) is the one who scrambles to the top of some designated area and holds it against all challengers (losers). This is a very gratifying game from the winner's point of view, for one learns what it is like (however brief is the tenure at the top before being thrown off) to be an unequivocal success, to be unquestionably better than the entire competition. (1976a:286)

Each player endeavors to become number one at the expense of all other players. But success has its price, and King of the Mountain teaches that as well.

> The King can never relax in such a pressurized position and constant vigilance is very difficult to endure, psychologically, for long. Additionally, the sole victor is likely to feel a certain alienation from others: whom can he trust? Truly, "it is lonely at the top."

Just as King of the Mountain exemplifies our cultural emphasis on winning, Tag, Keep Away, and Monkey in the Middle teach the lessons of being a loser. Spates observes that the loser in Tag, designated as "It," is singled out as unworthy of joining the group. This

---

[1] The excerpt presented here has been slightly modified on the basis of unpublished versions of the study, with the permission of the author.

experience of being excluded is so difficult to bear that other players often allow themselves to be tagged just to end "It's" ordeal. All players thus learn the importance of competing successfully, as well as the dangers of not fitting in. Drawing on these sociological observations, we can better appreciate the prominence of competitive team sports in American culture and why star athletes are often celebrated as cultural heroes.

## Norms

For most of our history, women and men in the United States viewed sex as appropriate within marriage and largely for the purpose of having children. By the 1960s, however, the rules of sexual behavior changed so that sexual activity became widely redefined as a form of recreation, sometimes involving people who hardly knew each other. By the mid-1980s, the rules changed again. Amid growing fears of sexually transmitted diseases, especially the deadly acquired immune deficiency syndrome (AIDS), the "sexual revolution" came to an end, with more men and women limiting their sexual activity to one partner (McKusick et al., 1985; Smilgas, 1987).

Such patterns illustrate what sociologists call **norms**, *rules that guide behavior*. Many norms are *proscriptive*, mandating what we should *not* do. For example, health officials now warn us to avoid casual sex. *Prescriptive* norms, on the other hand, state what we *should* do. Following practices of "safe sex," for example, has become such a norm in recent years.

Norms also apply to various settings. Some rules have broad application; for example, parents expect children to obey them regardless of the setting. Other norms, however, are situation-specific. Applauding at the completion of a musical performance is expected; applauding at the end of a classroom lecture is acceptable, but rare; applauding at the completion of a sermon by a priest or rabbi would be considered rude.

### Mores and Folkways

Norms vary in importance. William Graham Sumner (1959; orig. 1906), an early American sociologist, used the term **mores** (pronounced MORE-ays; the rarely used singular form is *mos*) to refer to *norms that have great moral significance*. Proscriptive mores, often called *taboos*, include our society's prohibition against adults having sexual relations with children. Examples of prescriptive mores are the requirements that people in public places—from beaches to workplaces—wear sufficient clothing to conform to "standards of decency."

Because they are deemed vital to social life, mores usually apply to everyone, everywhere, all the time. For the same reason, violation of mores typically brings a swift and strong reaction from others. From early childhood, for example, Americans learn that stealing, considered a serious wrong, will provoke a powerful response from the legal system.

Sumner used the term **folkways** to designate *norms of little moral significance.* Examples of folkways include norms guiding dress and polite behavior. Since they are viewed as less important than mores, folkways involve matters about which we allow people considerable personal discretion. Similarly, violations of folkways typically result in only mild penalties. For example, a man who does not wear a tie to a formal dinner party is violating one of the folkways we call "etiquette"; although the subject of some derisive comment, he is likely to be tolerated. However, if the man were to arrive at the dinner party wearing *only* a tie, he would be violating cultural mores and inviting far more serious sanctions.

Cultural norms, then, steer behavior by defining what is right and wrong, proper and improper. Although we sometimes bristle when others pressure us to conform, people generally embrace norms as part of the symbolic road map of culture that makes possible predictable and trustworthy interaction.

## Social Control

Generally, students expect to remain quiet in class, listening attentively to the teacher and taking notes as necessary. The enthusiastic student who looks for every chance to speak is therefore courting criticism as a "nerd."

Punishment and reward from others—termed *sanctions*—promote conformity to cultural norms. Sanctions are sometimes informal, illustrated by groans in the classroom when a student talks too much, and at times formal, ranging from grades in school to prosecution by the criminal justice system. Sanctions lie at the heart of a culture's system of **social control**: *various means by which members of society encourage conformity to cultural norms.*

After learning a wide range of cultural norms, we develop the capacity to respond critically to our own behavior. For most people, simply being aware of an act of theft gives rise to *guilt,* the discomfort that follows from a negative judgment we make of ourselves. Both guilt and *shame*—the painful acknowledgment of the disapproval of others—stem from internalizing cultural norms, that is, building them into our own personalities. Internalizing norms was what the writer Mark Twain had in mind when he quipped that human beings "are the only animals that blush . . . or need to."

Cultural patterns vary to some degree according to class position. Elites delight in the sounds of the violin, while ordinary people enjoy playing the fiddle. The two instruments are one and the same, of course, but one performance is defined as "high culture," while the other is termed "low culture," according to the social standing of the performers and the audience.

## "Ideal and "Real" Culture

Values and norms do not describe actual behavior as much as they state how we *should* behave. Sociologists therefore distinguish between **ideal culture**, *social patterns mandated by cultural values and norms*, and **real culture**, *social patterns that actually occur*. This distinction comes to mind when we consider, for example, that most women and men acknowledge the importance of sexual fidelity in marriage although at least one-third of married people are sexually unfaithful to their spouses at some point in the marriage. Such discrepancies, common to all cultural systems, call to mind the old saying "Do as I say, not as I do."

Like all other elements of culture, norms vary over time and among different segments of the population. The cultural values and norms brought to North America by English settlers centuries ago continue to shape our way of life, but many current interpretations of those original norms and values would strike Sir Walter Raleigh or Abigail Adams as strange indeed. In addition, immigrants from societies throughout the world have introduced myriad cultural variations into our society, modifying our culture in ways that could never have been foreseen centuries ago.

## Material Culture and Technology

In addition to intangible elements such as values and norms, every culture encompasses a wide range of tangible (from Latin meaning "touchable") human creations that sociologists term *artifacts*. The Yąnomamö gather forest materials to build huts and make hammocks. They craft bows and arrows to hunt and defend themselves, fashion tools for raising crops, and decorate their bodies with colored paints. Such examples of material culture among the Yąnomamö seem as strange to us as their language, values, and norms.

Material and nonmaterial elements of culture are closely related. The objects fashioned and used by a particular society, that is, typically express their cultural values. Because warfare is a central element of the Yąnomamö culture, they value militaristic skills and devote great care to making weapons. Poison-tipped arrows, for example, are among the Yąnomamö's most prized possessions.

In the same way, material elements of our own culture reflect the values we consider important. The cherished cultural values of individuality and independence come through in our society's high regard for privately owned automobiles and the popular disdain

Standards of beauty—including how color should be used in everyday surroundings—vary significantly from one culture to another. Members of the Ndebele in South Africa lavishly paint their homes. Members of the societies of Europe and North America, by contrast, make far less use of color so that their surroundings seem subdued by comparison.

for mass transportation. Some 140 million cars are registered in the United States today, almost one car for every licensed driver and more than one car for every two people.

Material culture reflects not only a society's values but also **technology**, *the application of cultural knowledge to the task of living in a physical environment.* Technology links the world of nature and the world of culture. The Yąnomamö, with their relatively simple level of technology, intrude little on the natural environment. Keenly aware of the cycles of rainfall and the movement of animals they hunt for food, the Yąnomamö are guided by their environment. By contrast, technologically complex societies (such as those of North America) bring to bear far greater power in contending with the forces of nature, even reshaping the environment, at times, according to their own cultural values.

Because we place a high value on science and the sophisticated technology it has produced, people in the United States tend to judge cultures with simpler technology as less advanced. Some facts would support such an assessment. Life expectancy is one good measure of a society's level of well-being. U.S. females born in 1990 can expect to live almost to the age of eighty, males to about seventy-two. Napoleon Chagnon estimated the life expectancy of the Yąnomamö at only about forty years.

We must take care, however, to avoid self-serving judgments about the quality of life of people whose cultures differ from our own. Although the Yąnomamö are eager to gain modern technology (such as steel tools and shotguns), it may surprise you to learn that they are generally well fed by world standards, and are quite satisfied with their lives (Chagnon, 1983). Like other technologically simple societies, they adapt to the natural world rather than remaking it. By contrast, our culture drives a sophisticated technology with enormous impact on the environment—for better or worse. Thus, while our advanced technology has produced work-reducing devices and seemingly miraculous forms of medical treatment, it has also contributed to unhealthy levels of stress, opened threatening holes in the planet's ozone layer, and created weapons capable of destroying in a flash everything that humankind has managed to achieve throughout history.

Finally, technology is another cultural element that varies substantially within the United States. Although many of us cannot imagine life without stereos, televisions, and microwave ovens, some members of our society cannot afford such items, and others reject them

on principle. The Amish, for example, who live in small farming communities across Pennsylvania, Ohio, and Indiana, shun most modern conveniences based on their religious beliefs. The Amish may seem like a curious relic of the past, yet their communities thrive, grounded in strong families and individuals who enjoy a sense of identity and purpose. Surely to some of the thousands of outsiders who come to observe them each year, the Amish communities must seem like "islands of sanity in a culture gripped by commercialism and technology run wild" (Hostetler, 1980:4).

# Cultural Diversity: Many Ways of Life in One World

Between 1820 (when the government began keeping track of immigration) and 1990, more than 55 million people came to the United States from other countries. Early in this century, most hailed from Europe; in the 1990s, the majority will come from Asia and Latin America. This massive immigration has made the United States—far more than most nations of the world—a land of cultural diversity.

Cultural variety appears in the distinctive ways of life of New England, the midwest, and other geographical regions of the United States; in the rich diversity of religious life among Americans; in a host of ethnic traditions; and among countless people who fashion their own individual lifestyles. Although sociologists sometimes speak of the "cloth of culture," we might more accurately characterize our society as a "patchwork quilt." To understand our nation's social patterns, then, we must move beyond dominant cultural patterns to consider cultural diversity.

## Subcultures

Sociologists use the term **subculture** to refer to *cultural patterns that distinguish some segment of a society's population.* Teenagers, Polish Americans, homeless people, and southerners all display subcultural patterns. Occupations also foster distinctive subcultures, involving specialized ways of acting, speaking, and dressing, as anyone who has ever spent time with race-car drivers, jazz musicians, or even sociologists can attest. Rural people sometimes mock the ways of "city slickers," who in turn deride their "country cousins." Sexual orientation generates yet another subculture in our society, especially in cities like San Francisco, Los Angeles, and New York, where large numbers of gay men and women live.

Most societies encompass many ethnically based subcultures. Consider Yugoslavia, a small nation in southeastern Europe. The recent conflict in this nation has been fueled by astounding cultural diversity. This *one* small country (roughly the size of the state of Wyoming, with a population of 25 million) historically has made use of *two* alphabets, *three* major religions, and *four* major languages; contains *five* major nationalities, has been divided into *six* separate republics, and absorbs cultural influences from *seven* other nations with which it shares borders. The cultural conflict that threw this nation into civil war reveals that subcultures are not only a source of pleasing variety but also of tensions and outright violence.

In the United States, children have historically been taught to view their country as a "melting pot" in which many nationalities blend into a single "American" culture. More recently, educational curricula have highlighted ethnicity and race as the basis of not only cultural diversity but also social conflict. As Chapter 12 ("Race and Ethnicity") explains, people of different cultures and colors have mixed and melded to some extent in the United States, but social divisions in our society remain powerful and persistent.

The problem here is that cultural differences involve not only *variety* but *hierarchy*. Too often, what we refer to as "dominant" cultural patterns characterize powerful segments of the U.S. population, while those we term "subcultures" are traits of disadvantaged people. This dilemma has sparked a new approach to the study of American culture—multiculturalism.

## Multiculturalism

In recent years, the United States has been facing up to the challenge of **multiculturalism,** *the recognition of past and present cultural diversity in American society coupled to efforts to promote the equality of all cultural traditions.* Historically, our society has downplayed cultural diversity, defining our way of life primarily in terms familiar to the European (and especially English) immigrants who have socially dominated the United States. The legacy of this practice is a spirited debate over whether we should continue to stress the common elements in our national experience, as some people suggest, or highlight the cultural diversity that has historically characterized the United States, as others maintain.

*E Pluribus Unum,* the familiar Latin words that appear on each piece of currency in the United States, roughly mean "out of many, one." This motto symbolizes not only our national political confederation, it also describes a widely acknowledged cultural goal—creating a single way of life for immigrants from around the world. The notion of the United States as a cultural "melting pot" is as old as the nation itself. George Washington, the first American president, confidently predicted that immigrants would learn the new nation's ways, forging a society of "one people" (Gray, 1991).

But, from the outset, reality differed sharply from this ideal: instead of melting together into a single heritage, cultures in the United States hardened into a hierarchy. Our way of life was founded on English social patterns and institutions. People of other backgrounds were advised to model themselves after "their betters," so that the "melting" was more accurately a process of Anglicization. For more than two centuries, historians in the United States have highlighted the role of descendants of the English and other Europeans, described events from their point of view, and pushed to the side the perspectives and accomplishments of Native Americans, people of African descent, and immigrants from Asia. This pattern leads multiculturalists to argue that, early in our history, the European way of life was set up as an ideal to which all should aspire and by which all should be judged. Multiculturalists describe this singular pattern in the United States as **Eurocentrism,** *the dominance of European (particularly English) cultural patterns.* Molefi Kete Asante, a leading advocate of multiculturalism, suggests that like "the fifteenth-century Europeans who could not cease believing that the earth was the center of the universe, many today find it difficult to cease viewing European culture as the center of the social universe" (1988:7).

Although few deny that our culture has wide-ranging roots, multiculturalism has generated controversy because it requires us to rethink the norms and values at the core of our society. Not surprisingly, battles over how to describe our nation's culture are now raging on many fronts.

One area of debate involves language. For a decade, Congress has debated a proposal to designate English as the official language of the United States. It has yet to decide the issue, although, by 1991, legislatures in

Conventional history has portrayed European expeditions to the so-called "New World" as sober efforts to bring religion and civilization to the child-like inhabitants of these societies. This message has long been a theme in European art, suggested here by a painting of the landfall of Columbus. More recently, historians have presented a more accurate view of events, explaining that the "explorers" were actually conquerors often intent on destroying existing civilizations in pursuit of wealth. The painting on the right suggests that the "discovery" of the Americas was more a pitched battle, illustrated by the assault on Tenochtitlán (today's Mexico City) by Hernando Cortes and his conquistadores.

sixteen states had enacted such a directive. To some, "official English" may seem unnecessary, since for centuries this language has been central to American culture. Yet, by 1990, some 30 million men and women—at least one in ten—spoke a language other than English in their homes. And their ranks will swell to an estimated 40 million by the beginning of the next century. Spanish is our second national language, and other American tongues include Italian, German, French, Filipino, Japanese, Korean, and Vietnamese.

An additional issue is how our nation's schools—from the early grades through college—should teach about culture. It is among educators that the clash over multiculturalism has been most intense. Two basic positions have emerged from this discussion.

Proponents defend multiculturalism, first, as a way to capture a more accurate picture of our nation's *past*. Proposed educational reforms seek, for example, to temper the simplistic praise directed at Christopher Columbus and other European explorers by realistically assessing the tragic impact of the European conquest on the native peoples of this hemisphere. As detailed in Chapter 12 ("Race and Ethnicity"), from the point of view of Native Americans, contact with Europeans unleashed five cen-

turies of domination and death from war and disease. In addition, a multicultural approach would recognize the achievements of many women and men whose cultural backgrounds up to now have kept them on the sidelines of history. Second, proponents claim, multiculturalism is a means to come to terms with our country's even more diverse *present*. During the 1980s, the Hispanic population of the United States increased by more than 50 percent, and the number of Asian-Americans more than doubled. Children born in the 1990s can expect that, during their lifetimes, people of African, Asian, and Hispanic ancestry will become a *majority* of this country's population. Third, proponents assert that multiculturalism is a way to strengthen the academic achievement of African-American children and others who, from this point of view, find little personal relevance in traditional educational programs. To counter pervasive Eurocentrism, some multiculturalists are calling for **Afrocentrism,** *the dominance of African cultural patterns*, which they see as a corrective for centuries of minimizing or altogether ignoring the cultural achievements of African societies. Fourth and finally, proponents see multiculturalism as worthwhile preparation for all people in the United States to live in a world that is increasingly interdependent. As various chapters of this book explain, social patterns in this country are becoming more closely linked to issues and events elsewhere in the world. Multiculturalism undermines nationalistic prejudices by pointing out global connectedness.

Although multiculturalism has found widespread favor in the last several years, it has provoked its share of criticism as well. The argument most commonly voiced by opponents of multiculturalism is that any society remains cohesive only to the extent that its cultural patterns are widely shared. Multiculturalism, say critics, fuels the "politics of difference," encouraging divisiveness as individuals identify with only their own category rather than with the nation as a whole. Opponents also charge that multiculturalism erodes the claim to common truth by maintaining that ideas should be evaluated according to the race (and sex) of those who present them. Are we to conclude that there is no common humanity, in other words, but only an "African experience," a "European experience," and so on? Second, critics are skeptical that multiculturalism actually benefits minorities as proponents say it does. On the one hand, the critics argue, multiculturalism seems to demand precisely the kind of racial segregation that our nation has struggled for decades to end. On the other hand, they add, an Afrocentric curriculum may well deny children a wide range of important knowledge and skills by forcing them to study from a single point of view. Historian Arthur Schlesinger Jr. (1991) puts the matter bluntly: "If a Kleagle of the Ku Klux Klan wanted to use the schools to handicap black Americans, he could hardly come up with anything more effective than the 'Afrocentric' curriculum." Third, critics warn, multiculturalism has a political agenda rooted in the left-wing politics of the 1960s that threatens the political and economic freedoms that have attracted diverse people to the United States in the first place.

Is there any common ground in this debate? Although sharp disagreements exist, the answer is yes. Virtually everyone agrees that all people in the United States need to gain greater appreciation of the extent of our cultural diversity. Further, because people of color will be a majority of the population during the next century, efforts in this direction are needed now. But precisely where the balance is to be struck—between the *pluribus* and the *unum*—is likely to remain a divisive issue for some time to come.

## Countercultures

Cultural diversity in a society sometimes takes the form of active opposition to at least some widely shared cultural elements. **Counterculture** refers to *social patterns that strongly oppose popular culture*. People who embrace a counterculture typically challenge the morality of the majority; when the defiance gains public attention, the majority may respond swiftly and strongly to repress what is perceived as a threat.

In many societies, youths form countercultures (Spates, 1976b, 1982, 1983). Most of us are familiar with the youth-oriented countercultures of the 1960s that attracted considerable media coverage. The hippies criticized the cultural mainstream as overly competitive, self-centered, and materialistic. Instead, they favored a cooperative lifestyle in which "being" took precedence over "doing," and the capacity for personal growth—or "expanded consciousness"—was prized over material possessions like homes and cars. Such differences led many hippies to "drop out" of the larger society, establishing new cultural centers like the Haight-Ashbury district

In a nation legally committed to racial equality and tolerance of diversity, various white supremacist groups like the Ku Klux Klan are a counterculture. Members of these groups transmit their fears and hatreds to the young, forcing yet another generation to struggle with racial problems.

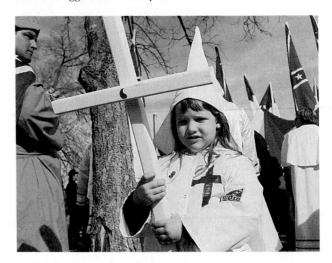

of San Francisco, perhaps the best-known hippie community in the world.

During the same period, an array of political countercultures took root in opposition to the so-called "military-industrial complex" and particularly the war in Vietnam. Political organizations such as Students for a Democratic Society (SDS) organized protest marches, while more radical groups carried out sporadic acts of violence against targets that to them exemplified the unjust and militaristic way of life in the United States. Similarly, the Black Panthers armed themselves in revolt against what they saw as pervasive racism in this country.

Countercultures develop not only their own values and political principles, but distinctive folkways, including dress, forms of greeting, and music. To many members of 1960s countercultures, for instance, blue jeans and "ethnic" clothing symbolized their identification with the "common people" of our society. Rock and roll music flourished as a countercultural anthem with far less of the middle-class respectability it enjoys today.

Countercultures still exist, but they have diminished in prominence since the 1960s. In the United States, the Ku Klux Klan and other white supremacist groups promote violence and racial hatred in order to protect what they believe are "real American values." In Europe, young "punks" express contempt for established culture through their personal appearance—shaved heads or multicolored hairstyles, black leather and chains—intended to offend more conventional members of their societies.

## Cultural Change

The Greek philosopher Aristotle asserted that "There is nothing permanent except change." Caught up in day-to-day concerns, we may not notice changes because we are busy living our lives, not observing them. But cultural change happens continuously, even though it may only be evident over a period of years. Consider, for example, some recent changes in family life. As more and more women have joined the labor force, many are delaying marriage and children, or remaining single and having children all the same. The current divorce rate is more than twice as high as it was fifty years ago. And over the last generation, the number of single-parent households more than doubled, so that a

majority of our nation's children now live with only one parent before they reach the age of eighteen.

Table 3–1 presents another dimension of change, comparing the attitudes of first-year college students in 1968 with those of men and women matriculating in

**Table 3–1 ATTITUDES AMONG STUDENTS ENTERING U.S. COLLEGES, 1968 and 1990**

|  |  | 1968 | 1990 | Change |
|---|---|---|---|---|
| REASONS TO GO TO COLLEGE (Very Important) |  |  |  |  |
| Gain a general education | male | 60 | 56 | −4 |
|  | female | 67 | 69 | +2 |
| Learn more about things | male | 69 | 68 | −1 |
|  | female | 74 | 77 | +3 |
| Get a better job | male | 74 | 78 | +4 |
|  | female | 70 | 79 | +9 |
| Prepare for graduate or professional school | male | 39 | 49 | +10 |
|  | female | 29 | 57 | +28 |
| Improve reading and writing skills | male | 22 | 38 | +16 |
|  | female | 23 | 47 | +24 |
| Make more money | male | 57 | 77 | +20 |
|  | female | 42 | 70 | +28 |
| LIFE OBJECTIVES (Essential or Very Important) |  |  |  |  |
| Develop a philosophy of life | male | 79 | 42 | −37 |
|  | female | 87 | 44 | −43 |
| Keep up with political affairs | male | 52 | 47 | −5 |
|  | female | 52 | 39 | −13 |
| Help others in difficulty | male | 50 | 51 | +1 |
|  | female | 71 | 71 | 0 |
| Raise a family | male | 64 | 68 | +4 |
|  | female | 72 | 71 | −1 |
| Be successful in my own business | male | 55 | 50 | −5 |
|  | female | 32 | 38 | +6 |
| Be well off financially | male | 51 | 78 | +27 |
|  | female | 27 | 70 | +43 |

Note: To allow comparisons, data from early 1970s rather than 1968 are used for some items.

SOURCE: Richard G. Braungart and Margaret M. Braungart, "From Yippies to Yuppies: Twenty Years of Freshmen Attitudes," Public Opinion, Vol. 11, No. 3 (September-October 1988):53–56; Alexander W. Astin, William S. Korn, and Ellyne R. Berz, The American Freshman: National Norms for Fall 1990, Los Angeles: U.C.L.A. Higher Education Research Institute, 1990.

1990. Some things have changed only slightly: about the same proportion of students come to college in order to "gain a general education" and to "learn more about things." But the students of the 1990s seem relatively more interested than the earlier generation in gaining skills, especially those that will lead to high-paying jobs. Moreover, the *political* activism of the 1960s has declined significantly in favor of pursuing *personal* success. Note that changes in attitude have generally been greater among women than among men. This, no doubt, reflects the fact that the women's movement, concerned with social equality for the two sexes, intensified after 1968.

Change in one part of a society's culture usually sparks other transformations as well. As noted earlier, for instance, women's rising participation in the labor force is linked to changing patterns of marriage. Such connections illustrate the principle of **cultural integration,** *the assertion that various parts of a cultural system are linked together.* Some parts of a cultural system, however, typically change more quickly than others. William Ogburn (1964) observed that technology moves quickly, generating new elements of material culture (like "test-tube babies") and outpacing nonmaterial culture (such as ideas about parenthood). Ogburn called this inconsistency **cultural lag,** *disruption in a cultural system resulting from the unequal rates at which different cultural elements change.* In a culture with the technical ability to allow one woman to give birth to a child by using another woman's egg, which has been fertilized in a laboratory with the sperm of a total stranger, how are we to apply the traditional terms motherhood and fatherhood?

There are three ways that such cultural changes are set in motion. The first is *invention,* the process of creating new cultural elements like video games, political parties, or polio vaccines. Consider the telephone (1876), the airplane (1903), and the aerosol spray can (1941)—all inventions that have had a tremendous impact on our culture. The process of invention goes on constantly, as indicated by the thousands of applications received by the United States Patent Office each year.

*Discovery,* a second cause of cultural change, involves recognizing and understanding something already in existence—from a distant star, to the foods of another culture, to the muscle power of American women. Discovery often results from scientific research; many medical breakthroughs occur this way. Yet discovery can also happen quite by accident, as when Marie Curie unintentionally left a rock on a piece of photographic paper in 1898 and thus discovered radium.

The third cause of cultural change is *diffusion,* the spread of cultural traits from one society to another. Missionaries and anthropologists like Napoleon Chagnon have introduced many cultural elements to the Yąnomamö. Cultural elements have likewise spread from the United States throughout the world: jazz music, with its roots deep in the culture of African Americans; computers, first built in the mid-1940s in a Philadelphia laboratory; and even the United States Constitution, used by several other countries to construct their own political systems.

Diffusion works the other way as well, so that much of what we assume is inherently "American" actually comes from other cultures. Ralph Linton (1937) explained that many commonplace elements of our way of life—most clothing and furniture, clocks, newspapers, money, and even the English language—are all derived from other cultures. As the technology of travel and communication makes the world smaller, the rate of cultural diffusion increases as well.

## Ethnocentrism and Cultural Relativity

A question in the popular game Trivial Pursuit asks which beverage is most popular in the United States. Milk? Soft drinks? Coffee? The answer is soft drinks, but all of the beverages mentioned are favored by members of our culture. If the Masai of eastern Africa were to join the game, however, their answer might well be "Blood!" To us, of course, the idea of drinking blood is revolting, if not downright unnatural. But we should keep in mind that milk (which we all know is more healthful than soft drinks or coffee) is actually detested by billions of people in the world, including the Chinese (Harris, 1985).

As Global Map 3–2 suggests, people everywhere place their society at the center of the world. Since we all favor our own way of life, how do we respond to other people's social patterns when they offend our own ideas of what is proper? Even Napoleon Chagnon, trained as an anthropologist to have an open mind, recoiled with disgust at the "naked, sweaty, and hideous" Yąnomamö. Later, Chagnon encountered several cultural practices that, from his point of view, seemed outrageous. For example, Yąnomamö men share their wives sexually with younger brothers or friends. From the point of view of Yąnomamö men, this practice symbolizes friendship and generosity. By our cultural standards, however, this behavior smacks of moral perversity and gross unfairness to women.

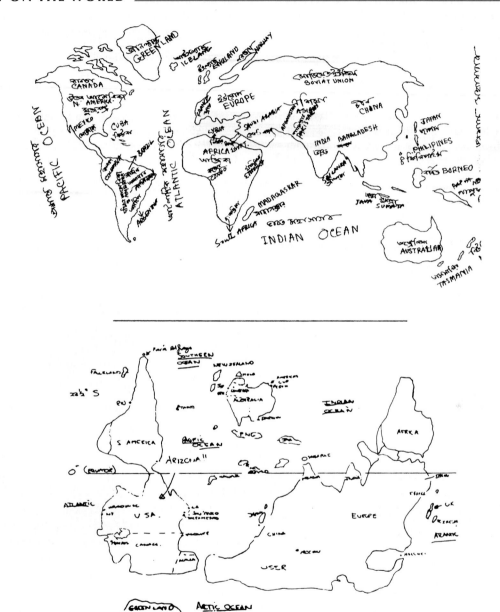

**Global Map 3–2**   Ethnocentric Images of the World

One element of culture is how a person conceives of the world. The Eurocentric map, which places Europe in the center, is common in many parts of the world, reflecting Great Britain's historical dominance of the seas. Traditionally, European sea-farers measured their east-west location using as a standard the zero meridian of longitude, which runs north and south through Greenwich (near London). The first of the maps above, drawn by a young student in India, is Eurocentric. The second map, typical of students in Australia, presents a contrasting case. Here what we in North America might call "the Far East" is placed in the center of the map; moreover, the world is drawn from the point of view of being "down under."

Common to people throughout the world is **ethnocentrism,** *the practice of judging another culture using the standards of one's own culture.* Inevitably, ethnocentrism creeps into our perceptions of other cultures because our understanding of the world is so closely tied to our own particular way of life. Why, for example, have Americans traditionally referred to the area of the world dominated by China as the "Far East?" Such a term would have little meaning to the Chinese; "Far East" is an ethnocentric expression for an area that is far east *of Europe.* For their part, the Chinese use a character to designate their nation that is translated as "the middle kingdom," suggesting that they, too, see their society as the center of the world.

Societies promote some measure of ethnocentrism

to enhance morale and solidarity among their members. But judging the cultural practices of others without understanding their cultural context yields not only a self-serving but a distorted view of other ways of life. The casual observer who puzzles at an Amish farmer tilling hundreds of acres with a team of horses rather than a tractor needs to understand the central role of hard work in the Amish way of life. From the Amish point of view, in short, tractors would be their undoing.

An alternative to ethnocentrism is **cultural relativism,** *the practice of judging a culture by its own standards.* Cultural relativism is difficult because it requires not only understanding the values and norms of another society, but also suspending cultural standards we have known all our lives. Still, the effort is worth making

## CRITICAL THINKING

# "The Traveler's Dilemma": In the Night Market of Taipei

Avoiding ethnocentrism requires resisting the temptation to judge another way of life by our own standards. But this is usually easier said than done, as American travelers often discover in disparate parts of the world.

Imagine, for instance, strolling through downtown Taipei, the capital city of Taiwan, the Republic of China. This island nation, about the size of the states of Maryland and Delaware combined, lies 150 miles off the shore of the Chinese mainland. Although it is a rapidly developing nation, its way of life is shaped by distinctive cultural traditions and a history of widespread poverty.

Taipei is a city frantic with activity. Streets are choked with people and motor scooters. From an American point of view, drivers show little concern for pedestrians, making what seem to be inten-

tional efforts to run people down. The city reaches a frenzied pace after dark, when tens of thousands of people flood into the vast "night market." In thousands of outdoor stalls, just about everything is for sale. Vendors hawk familiar items such as clothing, fruits, and jewelry to the passing crowd, but also sell "snacks" like chicken feet, and, worse still, cook dogs that people in the United States think of as pets. Children with withered limbs lie on the ground, begging from the people who swarm around them.

Wandering into the night market's infamous "Snake Alley," visitors have their sensibilities pushed to the limit. For here—from the outsider's point of view, at least—cruelty and violence are elevated to the level of a sport. People are drawn to a stall by a man beckoning over a loudspeaker. At the back of the stall, several televisions "warm up" the crowd, displaying dog fights in which one animal

tears another to pieces. The real show, however, begins as the master of ceremonies displays dozens of huge, live snakes. "Who will drink the venom?" he taunts in Chinese, again in Japanese, and then in English. One or two young men—eager to display courage to their comrades—push forward. One of the snakes, raised over-for reasons of goodwill or self-interest. As the people of the world come into increasing contact with one another, the need to fully understand other cultures grows as well.

In the ever-expanding global economy, for example, U.S. business is learning that success depends on cultural sophistication. When Coors first translated its slogan "get loose with Coors" into Spanish, would-be customers were startled to read "get the runs with Coors." Similarly, Kentucky Fried Chicken discovered that the Chinese thought that "licking one's fingers" made food seem anything but appealing. And Coca-Cola's early attempts to entice the Japanese to buy their soft drink involved a translation of "Coke adds life" that was read as "Coke brings your ancestors back from the dead," with results that are easy to imagine (Westerman, 1989:32).

Cultural sophistication underlies successful business ventures as well as a peaceful world order. But cultural relativity can also raise problems. Virtually every kind of behavior is found somewhere in a culturally diverse world, yet does that mean that anything and everything has equal claim to being morally right? What about Yąnomamö men who routinely offer their wives to others, and react violently to women who allegedly commit some social impropriety? Sometimes, Chagnon reports, this goes as far as men shooting women with arrows or otherwise mutilating them. Even in the unlikely event that Yąnomamö women accept this sort of treatment, should we adopt the culturally relative view that such practices are morally right simply because the Yąnomamö themselves accept them?

As members of one human species, we might as-

head to capture everyone's attention, is poked and taunted to provoke its full viciousness. Suddenly, the snake's head is punctured by a hook suspended from the ceiling and—as it continues to flash back and forth in anguish—the man tears the skin from the snake's body, handing it to members of the audience. Then, using skills learned from hundreds of such displays, the master of ceremonies squeezes venom from the body of the snake into a small glass. Paying for the prize, a spectator promptly chugs the fluid like so much whiskey as the crowd cheers. The process is repeated.

Looking away from this display, the traveler's eyes settle on a small monkey caged at the back of the stall. The observer soon stiffens as the monkey is snatched from the cage and thrust into the center of attention. "Pay to see him die!" the man shrieks. "See *real* blood now!" More cash is passed forward. One's mind whirls in disbe-

lief. Can he mean it? Would he really kill the monkey? Before the observer can regain wits enough to respond, the monkey is struck dead. Although a few turn and deliberately walk off, others continue to shout their approval, encouraging more of the same.

Snake Alley, an arena where cultural values collide, illustrates what might be called "the traveler's dilemma." On the one hand, ethnocentrism closes off insight and understanding by leading us to judge others quickly, simplistically, and thus unfairly. On the other hand, cultural relativism suggests that right and wrong are just a simple matter of convention so that, in the end, morality fades into the realm of arbitrary and meaningless posturing.

Is there a way to resolve "the traveler's dilemma?" Here are some guidelines. First, try to resist making judgments so that you can confront the unfamiliar with an open mind. We learn by being re-

ceptive to others' ways of living. Second, try to imagine events from the standpoint of *them* rather than *us*. Witnessing the events of the night market, for instance, one might wonder if animals have a different significance in a society in which human poverty, hunger, and suffering are commonplace. Third, after a period of careful and critical thinking, we can and should try to make some judgment of the cultural practice. After all, a world in which everyone passively accepted their surroundings would be frightening. But, in making an evaluation, bear in mind that we can never experience the world as others do. Fourth, and finally, try to evaluate realistically our own way of life in light of others' cultural practices. Would an experience in the night market of Taipei change an American's view of fox hunts or boxing in the United States?

SOURCE: Based on the author's personal experiences in Taipei.

In outdoor markets throughout the southern region of the People's Republic of China, dogs are a prized food. To a North American observer, selecting a puppy for dinner may seem cruel and unnatural. From the Chinese point of view, however, our common practice of drinking milk provokes disgust.

sume there would be some universal standards of proper conduct for people everywhere. But what are they? How can we avoid applying our own standards of fair play to everyone else? Sociologists have reached no consensus on this question, yet in a world in which societies confront each other amid ever-present problems such as hunger and war, this issue deserves careful thought.

The tension between ethnocentrism and cultural relativism often poses difficult problems for those who venture abroad. The box on pages 82–83 looks more closely at "the traveler's dilemma."

## Theoretical Analysis of Culture

Culture allows us to understand ourselves and the world around us. Sociologists and anthropologists, however, have the special task of understanding culture. To understand something this complex requires several theoretical approaches.

### Structural-Functional Analysis

Recall from Chapter 1 ("The Sociological Perspective") that structural-functional analysis sees society as a relatively stable system of integrated parts devised to meet human needs. Thus various cultural traits each help to maintain the overall operation of society.

The stability of cultural systems is rooted in core values, like the American values noted earlier (Parsons, 1964; Williams, 1970). In this way, structural-functionalism draws on the philosophical doctrine of *idealism*, the assertion that ideas (rather than, say, patterns of material production) are the basis of human reality. Expressed in a wide range of everyday activities, core values serve to bind all members of a society together.

Using a structural-functional approach, let us reconsider the Amish farmer plowing hundreds of acres with a team of horses. Within the Amish cultural system, rejecting tractors, automobiles, and electricity makes sense because it ensures that there is plenty of hard work. Continuous labor—usually outside the home for men and inside for women—functions to maintain the Amish value of discipline, which shapes their way of life. Long days of work, along with meals and recreation at home, define Amish culture and bind family members together. Their rejection of modern technology also has the function of making the Amish self-sufficient (Hostetler, 1980).

Of course, cultural traits have both functional and dysfunctional consequences. The Amish trait of "shunning," by which people cease social contact with anyone judged to have violated Amish mores, generates conformity but also provokes tension and, at the extreme, can cause a serious rift in the community.

Because cultures are strategies to meet human needs, we would expect that cultures the world over would have some elements in common since they were all devised by members of the same species. The term **cultural universals** refers to *traits found in every culture of the world*. Comparing hundreds of cultures, George Murdock (1945) found dozens of traits common to them all. One cultural universal is the family, which functions everywhere to control sexual reproduction and to oversee the care and upbringing of children. Another cultural universal, funeral rites, serves as a tellingly human response to the reality of death. Jokes, too, are found in all cultures, acting as a relatively safe means of releasing social tensions.

*Critical evaluation.* To its credit, the structural-functional paradigm explains culture as an organized system for meeting human needs. This approach allows researchers to grasp both cultural universals and cultural diversity. One limitation of the structural-functional paradigm, however, is its tendency to see cultural values as bridging social divisions. Often the cultural patterns favored by powerful people dominate a society, while shunting others to the margins. There is typically far more culture-based conflict in a society than structural-functional analysis suggests. Similarly, this paradigm emphasizes cultural stability, downplaying the extent of change.

## Social-Conflict Analysis

The social-conflict paradigm views culture in a very different light. To social-conflict theorists, culture forms a dynamic arena of conflict generated by social inequality. This paradigm draws attention to the ways in which cultural traits serve the needs of some members of society at the expense of others.

Social-conflict analysis critically questions why certain values dominate in a society. What forces generate one set of values rather than another? Who benefits from these social arrangements? Many using this paradigm, especially sociologists influenced by Karl Marx, argue that values are shaped by a society's system of economic production. "It is not the consciousness of men that determines their existence," Marx asserted, "it is their social existence that determines their consciousness" (1977:4; orig. 1859). This shows the social-conflict paradigm's link to the philosophical doctrine of *materialism*, the assertion that how people fashion their material world (for example, the capitalist economy

Funerals are often defined as a form of respect for the deceased. The social function of funerals, however, has much more to do with the living. For survivors, funerals reaffirm their sense of unity and continuity in the face of separation and disruption.

in the United States) has a powerful effect on other dimensions of their culture. Such a materialist approach contrasts with the idealist leanings of structural-functionalism.

Social-conflict analysis, then, would suggest that the competitive and individualistic values of this society reflect our capitalist economy, and thus serve the interests of those who own factories and other productive enterprises. The culture of capitalism further teaches us to believe that the rich and powerful have more talent and discipline than others and therefore deserve their wealth and privileges. Viewing capitalism as somehow "natural," then, leads people to distrust efforts to lessen the economic disparity found in the United States.

From a social-conflict point of view, however, strains fostered by social inequality exert continuous pressure toward change. The civil rights movement and the women's movement exemplify the drive for change supported by disadvantaged segments of the U.S. population. Both, too, have encountered opposition from defenders of the status quo.

*Critical evaluation.* The strength of the social-conflict paradigm lies in showing that, if cultural systems address human needs, they do so unequally. Put otherwise, this orientation holds that cultural elements "function" to maintain the dominance of some people over others. This inequity, in turn, promotes change. Because the social-conflict paradigm stresses the divisiveness of culture, however, this approach understates the ways in which cultural patterns integrate all members of society. Thus we should consider both social-conflict and structural-functional insights to gain a fuller understanding of culture.

## Cultural Ecology

A third theoretical paradigm is derived from ecology, the natural science that delves into the relationship between a living organism and its environment. **Cultural ecology,** then, amounts to *a theoretical paradigm that explores the relationship of human culture and the physical environment.* This paradigm investigates how climate and the availability of food, water, and other natural resources shape cultural patterns.

Consider the case of India. This nation contends with widespread hunger and malnutrition, yet has cultural norms that prohibit the killing of cows. According to Hindu belief, cows are defined as sacred animals. To North Americans who enjoy so much beef, this is puzzling. Why should Indians not consume beef to supplement their diet?

Investigating India's ecology, Marvin Harris (1975) concluded that the importance of cows greatly exceeds their value as a food source. Harris points out that cows cost little to raise, since they consume grasses of no interest to humans. And cows produce two valuable resources: oxen (the neutered offspring of cows) and manure. Unable to afford expensive farm machinery, Indian farmers rely on oxen to power their plows. For Indians, killing cows would be as clever as farmers in the United States destroying factories that build tractors. Furthermore, each year millions of tons of cow manure are processed into building material and burned as fuel (India has little oil, coal, or wood). To kill cows, then, would deprive Indians of homes and a source of heat. In short, there are sound ecological reasons to culturally protect the cow.

*Critical evaluation.* Cultural ecology expands our understanding of culture by highlighting its interplay with the environment. This approach reveals how cultural patterns arise among human beings in response to particular natural conditions. However, this paradigm has several limitations. First, we can only rarely draw simple or direct connections between the environment and culture because cultural and physical forces interact in subtle and complex ways. Further, this approach has less application to technologically sophisticated societies that extensively manipulate the natural world.

## Sociobiology

Since its origin in the nineteenth century, sociology has had a rather uneasy relationship with biology. In part, there is rivalry because the two disciplines both study human life. In addition, however, sociology played a role in challenging early biological notions about society—for example, that some categories of people were inherently "better" than others—as expressions of racism and ethnocentrism rather than legitimate science.

By the middle of this century, sociologists and anthropologists had convincingly demonstrated that culture rather than biology is the major force shaping human lives. But does this mean that biology has *nothing* to do with how we live? Providing an answer to this question is the focus of **sociobiology,** *a theoretical paradigm that studies ways in which biological forces affect human culture.* Some sociologists are skeptical about this new paradigm, but others think that it may offer useful insights into human culture.

### Sociobiology and Human Evolution

The scientific view of how life developed on earth is based on the theory of evolution. In his book *The Origin of Species,* Charles Darwin (1859) asserted that living organisms change over long periods of time as a result of the process of *natural selection,* a matter of four simple principles. First, all living things live and reproduce within a natural environment. Second, each species displays some random variability in genes, basic units of life that carry traits from one generation to the next. Darwin considered this variation as the way a species "tries out" new life patterns in a particular environment. Third, based on this variation, some organisms endure better than others. Survivors pass on their advantageous genetic variation to offspring. Fourth and finally, over thousands of generations the traits that promote survival and reproduction in a species grow dominant while traits that decrease the propensity for survival disappear. Naturally selected traits form the "nature" of a species, and they become pronounced as the species *adapts* to its environment.

### Sociobiology and Human Culture

Darwin's insights revolutionized the study of biology. But in applying his ideas to human behavior a number of problems arise. Simply put, nonhuman behavior is largely regulated by encoded genetic programs so that all ants or bees, for example, behave much the same. These insects interact in complex ways and thus form "societies." But they are unable to creatively fashion their lives as humans can, making them prisoners of their own biology (Berger, 1967). Freed from biological instinct, humans thrive in diverse and changing cultures.

But sociobiologists correctly note that the world's cultures are not nearly as different as they *could be*, as evidenced by cultural universals. In other words, because human beings all belong to a single species, people everywhere develop many of the same cultural patterns. Perhaps our common evolutionary history is somehow imprinted on the cultures we create.

Humans delightfully consume foods with sucrose, calling them "sweet." By contrast, people avoid foods that are "sour." Why? According to sociobiologist David Barash, the riddle of "sweetness" is rooted in human evolution:

Debate continues about the role of biology in shaping human behavior. The truth is that scientists are only beginning to "map" genetic factors that guide physical development. Present evidence suggests that our biology does have some subtle influence on how individuals think and act. But in the bigger picture, our human nature demands that we create culture, and we learn this way of life through social experience.

> Just as beauty is in the eye of the beholder, sweetness is in the mouth of the taster. To anteaters, ants are "sweet"; anteaters may even find sugar bitter—certainly they don't like it as much as we do. The reason is clear enough: we are primates, and some of our ancestors spent a great deal of time in trees, where they ate a great deal of fruit. Ripe fruit is more nutritious than unripe, and one thing about ripe fruit is that it contains sugars. It doesn't take much imagination to reconstruct the evolutionary sequence that selected for a strong preference among our distant ancestors for the taste that characterized ripe fruit. Genes that influenced their carriers to eat ripe fruit and reject the unripe ultimately made more copies of themselves than did those that were less discriminating. (1981:39)

Sociobiologists extend this argument to other human behavior. Sex, for example, is certainly "sweet" to human beings, as it is to all forms of life. From a sociobiological standpoint, sex feels good because it is vital to reproducing our genes in the next generation. Further, we are all aware of what has long been called the "double standard" by which males engage in sexual activity more freely than females do. As sex researcher Alfred Kinsey put it, "Among all people everywhere in the world, the male is more likely than the female to desire sex with a variety of partners" (cited in Barash, 1981:49).

Speaking sociobiologically, nature has assigned the sexes very different roles in the reproductive process. We all know that children are the product of joining a woman's egg with a man's sperm. But these resources have a very different reproductive value. For a healthy man, sperm is a "renewable resource" produced by the testes through most of his life. A man releases hundreds of millions of sperm in a single ejaculation—technically speaking, enough "to fertilize every woman in North America" (Barash, 1981:47). A woman, however, carries from birth in her ovaries a limited allotment of follicles or immature eggs. She generally releases just one mature egg cell each month. Thus men are biologically capable of fathering thousands of offspring, while women can bear only a relatively small number of children.

From a strictly biological point of view, men reproduce their genes most efficiently through a strategy of sexual promiscuity. But this strategy violates the reproductive interests of women. Each of a woman's relatively few pregnancies demands that she carry the child for the duration of the pregnancy, give birth, and perhaps nurse the child afterward. Thus, her most efficient reproductive strategy is selectively to seek a man whose own qualities (including the willingness to remain by her side after conception) will contribute to her child's survival and successful reproduction (Remoff, 1984). No one doubts that the double standard also reflects the historical domination of women by men (Barry, 1983). But sociobiology suggests that this cultural pattern, like many others, has an underlying bio-logic. Simply put, the double standard emerged worldwide because men and women benefit from different reproductive strategies.

***Critical evaluation.*** A relative newcomer on the sociological scene, sociobiology has not yet established itself as a significant force in the field. Potentially, sociobiology offers insights about the biological roots of some cultural patterns—especially cultural universals. At present, however, it remains controversial for several reasons.

First, because so-called biological facts have historically been used (or more precisely, *mis*used) to justify oppression of one race or sex, some people suspect sociobiology of having the same agenda. Defenders respond, however, that sociobiology has no connection to the past pseudo-science of racial superiority. Quite the contrary, sociobiology stresses that humans of all cultures share but one evolutionary history, and thus have much in common.

The assertion that men are inherently superior to women also has no part in sociobiological thinking. Sociobiology does maintain that, from a biological standpoint, men and women differ in ways that no culture will ever completely eliminate—if, in fact, any culture intended to. As Barash points out, rather than asserting that males are somehow more worthy than females, this approach emphasizes that both sexes are equally vital to reproducing the human species.

A second issue raised by sociobiology's critics focuses on the lack of scientific proof for its claims. Edward O. Wilson (1975, 1978), generally considered to be the founder of this field of study, maintains that through future research sociobiologists will find clear evidence of the biological roots of human culture. Yet a generation of work by sociobiologists has yet to realize this ambitious goal. Further, it is highly doubtful that biological forces will ever be shown to *determine* human behavior in any direct sense. More likely, the value of sociobiology will lie in showing that biological forces make some cultural patterns more widely adopted than others. But even so, the biological forces Barash calls "whisperings within" definitely respond to cultural influences. The development of birth control techniques, for example, has allowed people in many cultures to separate sexual intercourse from reproduction and therefore to develop sexual attitudes very different from those that prevailed in the past.

The final value of both cultural ecology and sociobiology lies in reminding us that humans are physical creatures who create their culture in a physical environment. In this view, the forces of nature and the forces of culture are more intertwined than in opposition. Sociological and naturalist interpretations of human culture are not irreconcilable, nor inconsistent. Each provides a partial analysis of our symbolic world, and we increase our understanding by drawing on them both.

# Culture and Human Freedom

We have introduced the elements of human culture, considered culture's complexity, and examined several approaches to cultural analysis. Now we turn to how culture affects the individual. Does culture enhance or inhibit our capacity to think critically and to make choices?

## Culture as Constraint

Over the long course of human evolution, culture became our strategy for survival. But though we can hardly live without it, culture does have some negative consequences. By experiencing the world through symbols and meaning, we become detached, susceptible to the experience of alienation unknown to other life forms. Further, established cultural systems sometimes impose a form of social inertia on our lives, driving us to relive troubling patterns from the past. Extensive social inequal-

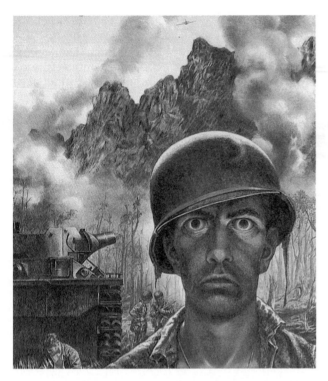

Although culture is the key to realizing our human potential, we sometimes experience our way of life as threatening and overwhelming. This alienation is evident in Tom Lea's portrayal of a marine caught up in the agony of World War II.

ity is supported by American culture, for example, by which some enjoy great privilege while others struggle simply to get by. Women of all social classes have often felt powerless in the face of cultural patterns that reflect the dominance of men.

Similarly, our cultural insistence on competitive achievement encourages us to strive for excellence, yet cultural patterns also isolate us from one another. Material comforts improve our lives in many ways, yet foster a preoccupation with objects that diverts us from the security and satisfaction of close relationships or strong religious faith. Our emphasis on personal freedom affords us privacy and autonomy, yet our culture often denies us the support of a human community in which to share the problems of life (Slater, 1976; Bellah et al., 1986). Thus while culture is as vital to humans as biological instinct is to other forms of life, it poses special problems for us.

## Culture as Freedom

Human beings may appear to be prisoners of culture, just as other animals are prisoners of biology. But careful thought about the ideas presented in this chapter suggests a crucial difference. Over millions of years of human evolution, the unfolding of culture gradually took our species from a world shaped largely by biology to a world we shape for ourselves.

Therefore, although culture seems at times to circumscribe our lives, it embodies the human capacity for hope and creative choice. The evidence that supports this conclusion lies all around us. Fascinating cultural diversity exists in our own society, and even greater variety is found around the world. Furthermore, far from static, culture is ever-changing. And although it sometimes functions as a constraint, culture also presents a continuous source of human opportunity. The more we discover about the operation of our culture, the greater our ability to use the freedom it offers us.

## Summary

1. Culture refers to patterned ways of human life. Although several species have simple forms of culture, only human beings rely on culture for survival.

2. Culture emerged over the long course of human evolution as the brain gradually enlarged. Basic elements of culture appeared some 2 million years ago; the complex culture that we call civilization emerged during the last 12,000 years.

3. Through symbols, which are the basis of culture, we attach meaning to objects and action. Language is the symbolic means with which we transmit culture from generation to generation.

4. Values are cultural elements that shape our orientation to the world around us.

5. Cultural norms guide human behavior. Mores consist of norms of great moral significance; folkways

are norms of lesser moral significance in which greater individual discretion is allowed.

6. Values and norms are expressions of ideal culture; in practice, real culture varies considerably from these standards.

7. Material creations reflect cultural values as well as a society's technology.

8. Culture involves not only common patterns but social diversity. Subcultures are distinctive cultural forms that characterize a segment of society; countercultures are strongly at odds with widely accepted cultural patterns. Multiculturalism refers to efforts to enhance awareness and appreciation of cultural diversity.

9. Culture is never static: invention, discovery, and diffusion all generate cultural change. Not all parts of a cultural system change at the same rate, however; this produces cultural lag.

10. Having learned the standards of one culture, we often evaluate other cultures ethnocentrically. The alternative to ethnocentrism, called cultural relativism, means judging different cultures according to their own standards.

11. The structural-functional paradigm views culture as a relatively stable system built on core values. Specific cultural traits are understood in terms of their function in maintaining the entire cultural system.

12. The social-conflict paradigm envisions cultural systems as dynamic arenas of social inequality and conflict. Cultural patterns typically benefit some categories of people more than others.

13. The cultural-ecology paradigm explores ways in which human culture is shaped by the natural environment.

14. Sociobiology studies the influence of humanity's evolutionary past on present patterns of culture.

15. Culture can constrain human needs and ambitions; yet as cultural creatures we have the capacity to shape and reshape the world to meet our needs and pursue our dreams.

## Key Concepts

**Afrocentrism** highlighting the viewpoint of people of African descent

**counterculture** social patterns that strongly oppose popular culture

**cultural ecology** a theoretical paradigm that explores the relationship of human culture and the physical environment

**cultural integration** the close relationship among various parts of a cultural system

**cultural lag** disruption in a cultural system resulting from the unequal rates at which different cultural elements change

**cultural relativism** the practice of judging a culture by its own standards

**cultural transmission** the process by which one generation passes culture to the next

**cultural universals** traits found in every culture

**culture** the beliefs, values, behavior, and material objects shared by a particular people

**culture shock** personal disorientation that accompanies exposure to an unfamiliar way of life

**ethnocentrism** the practice of judging another culture by the standards of one's own culture

**Eurocentrism** the dominance of European (especially English) culture

**folkways** norms that have little moral significance

**ideal culture** social patterns consistent with cultural values and norms

**language** a system of symbols that allows members of a society to communicate with one another

**material culture** tangible elements of culture such as clothing and cities

**mores** norms that have great moral significance

**multiculturalism** an educational program seeking to recognize the past and present cultural diversity of American society and to promote the equality of cultural traditions

**nonmaterial culture** intangible elements of culture such as values and norms

**norms** rules and expectations by which a society guides the behavior of its members

**real culture** actual social patterns that typically only approximate cultural values and norms

**Sapir-Whorf hypothesis** the assertion that people perceive the world only in terms of the symbols provided by their language

**social control** the process by which members of a society encourage conformity to cultural norms

**sociobiology** a theoretical paradigm that studies ways in which biological forces affect human culture

**subculture** cultural patterns that distinguish some segment of a society's population

**symbol** anything that carries a particular meaning recognized by members of a culture

**technology** the application of cultural knowledge to the task of living in a physical environment

**values** culturally defined standards of desirability, goodness, and beauty that serve as broad guidelines for social life

## Suggested Readings

Napoleon Chagnon's account of the Yąnomamö offers fascinating insights into a culture very different from our own. It is also a compelling tale of carrying out fieldwork in an unfamiliar world.

> Napoleon A. Chagnon. *Yąnomamö: The Fierce People.* 3rd ed. New York: Holt, Rinehart and Winston, 1983.

Twelve essays by an important contributor to black studies demonstrate the centrality of African-American culture to the United States.

> Sidney Kaplan. *American Studies in Black and White: Selected Essays, 1949–1989.* Allan D. Austin, ed. Amherst, MA: University of Massachusetts Press, 1991.

Cannibalism is a practice almost impossible for Westerners to comprehend. Yet, as this book explains, this consuming passion is quite acceptable to some cultures.

> Peggy Reeves Sanday. *Divine Hunger: Cannibalism as a Cultural System.* Cambridge, UK: Cambridge University Press, 1986.

Here are two views of the Amish, a fascinating North American counterculture.

> Sue Bender. *Plain and Simple: A Woman's Journey to the Amish.* San Francisco: Harper & Row, 1989.

> John A. Hostetler, ed. *Amish Roots: A Treasury of History, Wisdom, and Lore.* Baltimore: Johns Hopkins Press, 1989.

This book examines campus culture in the United States, its central assumptions and goals, as well as its cultural diversity.

> Michael Moffat. *Coming of Age in New Jersey: College and American Culture.* New Brunswick, NJ: Rutgers University Press, 1989.

These two books comment on our national way of life. The first argues that core cultural values like freedom and democracy are betrayed by our social institutions. The second compares the cultures of the two largest societies in North America.

> Frances Moore Lappé. *Rediscovering America's Values.* New York: Ballantine Books, 1989.

> Seymour Martin Lipset. *Continental Divide: The Values and Institutions of the United States and Canada.* New York: Routledge, 1990.

Since language is the key to culture, this history of the English language in the United States—in all its variety—helps to explain the interaction of various cultural forces in our history. The second book also traces the development of English, and explains why it is becoming the global language.

> J. L. Dillard. *Toward a Social History of American English* (with a chapter on Appalachian English by Linda L. Blanton). New York: Mouton Publishers, 1985.

> Bill Bryson. *The Mother Tongue.* New York: William Morrow, 1990.

Marvin Harris uses the cultural-ecology paradigm to explain many puzzling cultural practices.

> Marvin Harris. *Good to Eat: Riddles of Food and Culture.* New York: Simon and Schuster, 1985.

Although specialists carefully keep track of economic inflation, the United States has no measure of symbolic inflation. One result is that hype and other inflations of language continuously make traditional standards obsolete, as this book explains.

> Orrin E. Klapp. *Inflation of Symbols: Loss of Values in American Culture.* New Brunswick, NJ: Transaction, 1991.

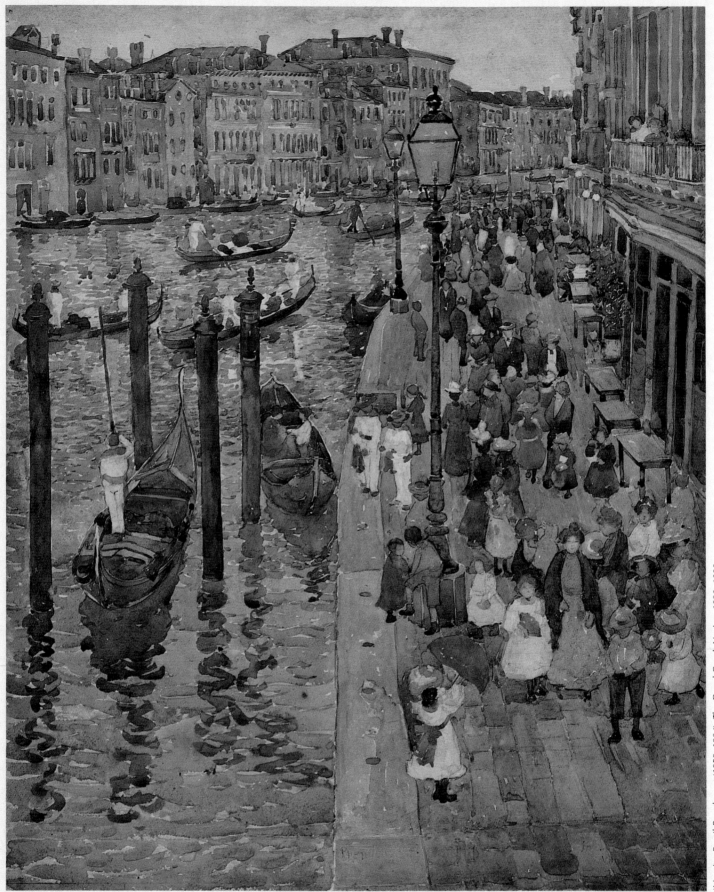

(Maurice Brazil Prendergast (1858–1924). The Grand Canal, Venice, 1898–1899.
Watercolor and pencil on paper. Daniel J. Terra Collection, 29. 1980.
Terra Museum of American Art, Chicago.)

# Society

The space program in the United States has sent astronauts to the moon, probed the clouds of Venus, mapped the craters of Mars, and carried video cameras hundreds of millions of miles to the edge of the solar system. The achievements that many people now take for granted, our ancestors surely would have found almost incomprehensible. Through most of the millennia of human history, the greatest distance people could put between themselves and the earth was the reach of a tall tree. And, until the proliferation of steam locomotives in the nineteenth century, human beings could travel no faster than about thirty miles per hour—the speed of a swift horse. Many subsequent train travelers were terrified as locomotives reached fifty miles per hour, fearing that, at such speeds, the breath would be sucked from their bodies. Today, by contrast, space shuttle passengers confidently rocket from earth at speeds of 18,000 miles per hour and settle into an orbit almost 300 miles above our planet's surface.

The National Aeronautics and Space Administration (NASA), at the forefront of space exploration in the United States, recently has turned its attention from probing the universe to healing environmental damage to the earth. During the 1990s, the agency intends to launch a program called Mission to Planet Earth, in which a number of satellites will be used to investigate global warming, the loss of the earth's forests, and the spread of our planet's deserts. This effort reveals an important truth about humankind: as our species has gained technological power, we have both improved our lives and simultaneously threatened our very existence.

To understand how we have come to this point, we need to explore the changes to the nature of society wrought by technological advances. This chapter begins with an historical survey of the development of technology and its effects on societies—expanding our capabilities, changing the ways in which we organize our lives, and forcing us to confront new and unexpected problems. The chapter continues by exploring other dimensions of society—social conflict, changing patterns of human ideas, and social integration—that are both cause and effect of technological development.

The concept **society** refers to *people who interact within a limited territory and who share a culture.* This deceptively simple term will be explored from four vantage points, each of which has broadened the scope of sociology and will be used in later chapters.

**Gerhard and Jean Lenski** describe the changing character of human society over the last ten thousand years. Focusing on how *technology* shapes social life, their analysis shows that a technological breakthrough often has revolutionary consequences for society as a whole. The remainder of the chapter presents classic visions of society developed by three of sociology's founders. Like the Lenskis, **Karl Marx** also understood human history as a long and complex process of social change.

For Marx, however, the story of society spins around *social conflict*, which results from inequality rooted in how people produce material goods. **Max Weber** recognized the importance of productive forces as well, but he sought to demonstrate the power of *human ideas* to shape society. Weber believed that modern society turns on human rationality, a world view that encourages change. Finally, **Emile Durkheim** investigated patterns of *social integration*, that is, how societies are held together. Identifying various sources of solidarity, Durkheim explored what makes modern societies distinctive.

All four visions of society address important questions: How do societies of the past and present differ from one another? How and why do societies change? What forces divide a society? What forces hold a society together? Are societies improving the human condition or making it worse? The theorists included in this chapter all investigated these questions, although they disagree on the answers. Thus, similarities and differences will be highlighted as we proceed.

# Gerhard and Jean Lenski: Society and Technology

For hundreds of years, a small society called the Ona lived at the southernmost tip of South America. As they gathered vegetation and hunted game, the Ona may well have observed the Portuguese explorer Ferdinand Magellan sail in 1520 through the straits that now bear his name. Although the Ona endured for centuries with little change, the encroachment of people with more complex technology gradually reduced their land holdings. Many Ona fell victim to foreign diseases; others simply gave up the old ways. The death of the last full-blooded member of the Ona was recorded in 1975 (Lenski & Lenski, 1987:127–29).

As members of the industrialized world, accustomed to rapid transportation and global communication, we might regard the Ona merely as a curious vestige of the past. But the story of the Ona tells us much about our own past, and helps us to better understand how we live today. Gerhard and Jean Lenski, introduced in the box, have chronicled the great differences among societies that have flourished and declined throughout human history. They explain how technologically simple people like the Ona—the only type of human society

until about ten thousand years ago—have now all but disappeared as the world evolves, driven by powerful industrial technology.

The Lenskis call the focus of their research **sociocultural evolution,** *the process of social change that results from gaining new cultural information, particularly technology* (Lenski, Lenski, & Nolan 1991:65). This approach draws on the biological concept of evolution to explore how societies, like living organisms, change over time as they gain greater ability to manipulate their physical environments. The Lenskis see technology as vital to defining other cultural patterns. Societies with rudimentary technology can support only a small number of people who adopt a simple way of life. Technologically complex societies—while not necessarily "better" in many respects—develop large populations engaged in highly diverse activities.

The Lenskis also explain that the amount of technological information a society has in its grasp affects the rate at which it changes. Because of their simple technology, societies like the Ona evolve very slowly. In striking contrast, highly industrialized societies, with access to much more technological information, change so quickly that people witness dramatic transformations during their lifetimes. Consider some familiar elements of North American culture that would probably puzzle, or even alarm, people who lived just a few generations ago: laser surgery, test-tube babies, genetic engineering, the threat of nuclear holocaust, computers, smart bombs, electronic surveillance, transsexualism, space shuttles, and artificial hearts (Lenski & Lenski, 1982:3).

As a society extends its technological reach, the effects ripple through the cultural system causing many more changes. A single innovation (say, harnessing the power of the wind) can be applied to many existing cultural elements (to produce windmills, kites, sailing ships, and eventually airplanes). Consider, as more recent examples, the many ways modern life has been changed by the computer or unleashing the power of the atom.

Drawing on the Lenskis' work, we will describe four general types of societies distinguished by their level of technology: hunting and gathering societies, horticultural and pastoral societies, agrarian societies, and industrial societies.[1]

---

[1] This account examines only the major types of societies described by the Lenskis.

# Gerhard Lenski and Jean Lenski

Gerhard Lenski is a contemporary American sociologist known for his research on religion, social inequality, and history. Jean Lenski, a writer and poet, has collaborated with her husband on sociological research projects. Together, they have brought to the attention of their colleagues in the field of sociology a wide range of research on the role of technology in human societies.

The Lenskis' approach to understanding society has much in common with that of Marvin Harris, the cultural ecologist described in Chapter 3 ("Culture"). Recall that cultural ecology focuses on how specific practices help a society to survive in a particular natural environment. The Lenskis highlight the role of technology in channeling the power of a society to produce and process material resources from their surroundings.

Cultural ecology and sociocultural evolution differ, however, in one important respect. While both emphasize that the natural environment shapes cultural patterns, the Lenskis' analysis explains why this is true of some societies more than others. With little ability to manipulate nature, technologically simple societies are influenced the most by their surroundings. Technologically sophisticated societies, by contrast, bring greater technological resources to their interaction with the physical world, even recasting nature according to their own designs. Therefore, technologically simple societies tend to resemble one another, with minor variations that reflect different natural environments. More technologically complex societies, on the other hand, reveal the striking cultural diversity described in Chapter 3.

## Hunting and Gathering Societies

**Hunting and gathering** refers to *simple technology to hunt animals and gather vegetation*. From the emergence of our species until about ten thousand years ago, all humans were hunters and gatherers. Although hunting and gathering societies were common several centuries ago, only a few persist today including the Pygmies of central Africa, the Bushmen of southwestern Africa, the Aborigines of Australia, the Kaska Indians of northwest Canada, and the Tasaday of the Philippines.

Food production is inefficient at this early stage of sociocultural evolution so that the people's primary task involves searching for game and edible plants. In harsh environments, this work goes on continually; in areas where food is plentiful, however, hunters and gatherers may enjoy considerable leisure. In any case, food production requires a large amount of land, so hunting and gathering societies are scattered at some distance from one another and are limited to several dozen people. They are also typically nomadic, moving on as they deplete vegetation in one area, or in pursuit of migratory animals. Although periodically returning to earlier sites, they rarely form permanent settlements.

Hunting and gathering societies are organized as family groups. The family obtains and distributes food, teaches necessary skills to children, and protects its members. While most activities are shared by everyone and center on seeking their next meal, some specialization occurs by age and sex. The very young and the very old are expected to contribute only what they can, while healthy adults secure most of the food. The gathering of vegetation—the more reliable food source—is typically the work of women, while men do the less certain work of hunting. Therefore, although the two sexes have somewhat different responsibilities, most hunters and gatherers probably viewed men and women as having comparable social importance (Leacock, 1978).

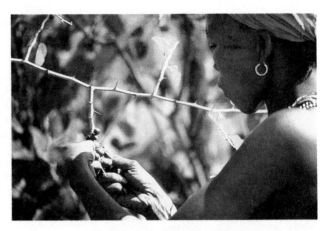

In technologically simple societies, successful hunting wins men great praise. However, the gathering of vegetation by women is a more abundant and dependable source of nutrition.

Hunting and gathering societies have few formal leaders. Most recognize a *shaman*, or spiritual leader, who enjoys high prestige but no greater material rewards. Because of the society's limited technology, even the shaman must help procure food. Men who hunt with exceptional skills are admired, as are women who are unusually productive in gathering vegetation. But, overall, the social organization of hunters and gatherers is relatively simple and egalitarian.

Hunting and gathering societies rarely use their handcrafted weapons—the spear, the bow and arrow, and the stone knife—to wage war. Although peaceful toward each other, they are often ravaged by the forces of nature. Storms and droughts can easily destroy their food supply, and their simple skills leave them vulnerable to accident and disease. Continual risks encourage cooperative activities and sharing of food, strategies that increase everyone's odds of survival. Nonetheless, many die in childhood, and perhaps half perish before the age of twenty (Lenski, Lenski, & Nolan 1991:91).

During this century, technologically complex societies have slowly closed in on the remaining hunters and gatherers, so that these simple societies face depletion of game and vegetation. The Lenskis predict that the 1990s may well see the end of hunting and gathering societies on earth. Their plight is tragic. Fortunately, study of this way of life has already produced valuable information about human history and our fundamental ties to the natural world.

## Horticultural and Pastoral Societies

Ten to twelve thousand years ago, a new technology began to change many hunting and gathering societies. **Horticulture** is *a technology based on using hand tools to cultivate plants.* The most important tools of horticulturalists are the hoe to work the soil and the digging stick to punch holes in the ground for seeds. These tools were first developed in fertile regions of the Middle East and Southeast Asia and were carried by cultural diffusion as far as Western Europe and China by about six thousand years ago. In Central and South America, the cultivation of plants emerged independently about nine thousand years ago, although horticulture was less efficient there because of the rocky soil and mountainous terrain.

Not all societies were quick to abandon hunting and gathering in favor of horticulture. Hunters and gatherers living amid plentiful vegetation and game probably had little reason to embrace the new technology (Fisher, 1979). The Yanomamö, described in Chapter 3 ("Culture"), illustrate the common practice of combining horticulture with more traditional hunting and gathering

(Chagnon, 1983). Then, too, in particularly arid regions, horticulture was of relatively little value. People in such regions developed **pastoralism,** *technology that supports the domestication of animals.* Some societies combined horticulture and pastoralism to produce more varied foods. Today, many horticultural-pastoral societies are found in South America, Africa, the Middle East, and Asia.

The domestication of plants and animals transformed societies in various ways. First, producing more food enabled societies to grow, and populations climbed into the hundreds. Societies that emphasized pastoralism remained nomadic, leading their herds to fresh grazing lands. Those that adopted horticulture as their primary technology formed settlements of several hundred people, relocating only when they depleted the soil. As such

settlements were joined by trade, they formed multicentered societies with overall populations often exceeding five thousand.

Domesticating plants and animals increased efficiency to the point of generating a *material surplus,* more resources than necessary to sustain day-to-day living. At this point, not everyone had to produce food, so some people could fashion crafts, engage in trade, or serve as full-time priests. In comparison to hunting and gathering societies, horticultural and pastoral societies display far more specialized and complex social arrangements.

The religious beliefs of hunters and gatherers recognize numerous spirits inhabiting the world. Horticulture, however, encourages the emergence of ancestor worship and a conception of God as Creator. Pastoral societies

Pastoralism has historically been common in arid regions of the world where little can be grown. Pastoral people still flourish today in Northern Africa, living much as they did a thousand years ago.

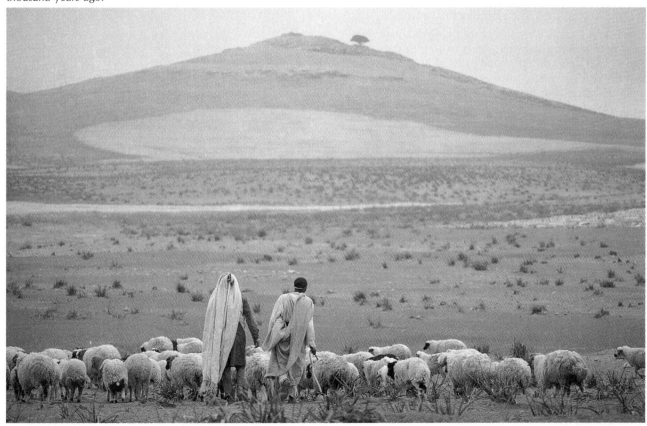

carry this belief further, perceiving God as directly involved in the well-being of the entire world. This view of God ("The Lord is my shepherd . . . ," Psalm 23) is widespread among Americans because both Christianity and Judaism were originally pastoral religions.

Expanding productive technology also intensifies social inequality. As some families produce more food than others, they assume positions of relative privilege and power and form alliances with other privileged families, so that social advantages persist over many generations. From the power of such elites, rudimentary government emerges. However, technology also limits this power. Without the ability to communicate or travel quickly, a ruler can control only a small number of people. Furthermore, the exercise of power often breeds opposition, and there is evidence of frequent revolts and other forms of political conflict in these societies.

The domestication of plants and animals enabled societies to become much more productive than was possible relying on hunting and gathering. But advancing technology is never entirely beneficial. The Lenskis suggest that technological progress is sometimes accompanied by ethical regression. Throughout history, greater production has paralleled a rise in social inequality, with privileged members of society less willing to share their resources. Horticulturalists and pastoralists also stand out as more warlike, just as they may engage in slavery and, in some cases, cannibalism.

## Agrarian Societies

About five thousand years ago, another technological revolution surrounded **agriculture,** *the technology of large-scale farming using plows powered by animals or advanced energy.* Agrarian technology first appeared in the Middle East, and gradually diffused throughout the world. The Lenskis assert that the profound social significance of the animal-drawn plow, along with other technological innovations of the period—including irrigation, the wheel, writing, numbers, and the expanding use of metals—clearly qualifies this era as "the dawn of civilization" (1991:160).

Animal-drawn plows cultivated vast fields in contrast to the garden-sized plots worked by horticulturalists. Plows have the additional advantage of turning, and thereby aerating, the soil to increase fertility. Agrarian people can thus farm the same land for decades, encouraging permanent settlements. Large food surpluses, transported on animal-powered wagons, allowed agrarian soci-

Of Egypt's 130 pyramids, the Great Pyramids at Giza are the largest. Each of the three major structures stands more than forty stories high and is composed of three million massive stones. They are the product of the efforts of tens of thousands of people, who labored so that one man, the pharaoh, might have a god-like monument for his tomb. Clearly social inequality in this agrarian society, some 4,500 years ago, was striking.

eties to expand to unprecedented size both in terms of population and land area. As an extreme case, the Roman Empire at its height (about 100 C.E.) boasted a population of 70 million spread over some 2 million square miles (Stavrianos, 1983; Lenski, Lenski, & Nolan, 1991).

As always, greater surplus means more specialization. Tasks once performed by everyone, such as clearing land, building, and processing food, became distinct occupations. Money emerged around this time as a universal standard of value which, unlike the older barter system, could forge countless, specialized activities into an expanding economy. Trade further sparked the growth of cities. Ancient Rome reached 1 million people, and cities in modern agrarian societies such as India and Egypt are now many times that size. As population increased, social life became steadily more individualistic and impersonal.

Agrarian societies exhibit dramatic social inequality. In many cases—including the United States early in its history—a whole segment of the population is relegated to slavery or serfdom—and a life of labor for elites. Freed from the need to work, elites engage in the study of philosophy, art, and literature. This explains the historical link between "high culture" and social privilege.

In horticultural societies, women gain prestige because they produce much of the food. Agricultural technology, however, seems to have propelled men into a position of clear social dominance (Boulding, 1976; Fisher, 1979). The box looks more closely at the declining position of women at this point in the course of sociocultural evolution.

Religion plays an important role in reinforcing the power of agricultural elites. Religious doctrine typically propounds the idea that people are morally obligated to perform their tasks according to their place in the social order. Chinese emperors could mobilize their people to build the Great Wall (still the only human creation visible from space), the Forbidden City, and other massive public works only because they were defined as gods with virtually absolute power.

In agrarian societies, then, the elites gain unparalleled power. To maintain control of large empires, leaders require the services of a wide range of administrators. Along with the growing economy, then, the political system becomes established as a distinct part of society.

In relation to societies described so far, the Lenskis conclude that agrarian societies have greater internal diversity and social inequality. And unlike horticultural and pastoral societies, agrarian societies exhibit distinct characteristics from one another because advancing technology gives them increasing control over the natural world.

## Industrial Societies

**Industrialism**, as found in the United States, Canada, and much of the northern hemisphere, is *the technology that powers sophisticated machinery with advanced fuels.*

---

SOCIAL DIVERSITY

# Technology and the Changing Status of Women

In technologically simple societies of the past, women produced more food than men did. Hunters and gatherers valued meat highly, but men's hunting was not a dependable source of nourishment. Thus vegetation gathered by women was the primary means of ensuring survival. Similarly, tools and seeds used in horticulture developed under the control of women, who already had primary responsibility for providing and preparing food. With women handling the cultivation of plants for food, men typically engaged in trade and tended herds of animals. Only at harvest time did everyone pitch in and work together.

About five thousand years ago, societies discovered how to mold metals. Metal tools spread by cultural diffusion, primarily along trade networks made up of men. Thus men invented the metal plow and, since they already managed animals, soon devised the notion of hitching the device to cattle. This initiated the transition from horticulture to agriculture and thrust men for the first time into a dominant position in the production of food. Elise Boulding explains how this technological breakthrough undermined the social position of women:

The shift of the status of the woman farmer may have happened quite rapidly, once there were two male specializations relating to agriculture: plowing and the care of cattle. This situation left women with all the subsidiary tasks, including weeding and carrying water to the fields. The new fields were larger, so women had to work just as many hours as they did before, but now they worked at more secondary tasks. . . . This would contribute further to the erosion of the status of women.

SOURCES: Based on Boulding (1976) and Fisher (1979).

**Figure 4–1** The Increasing Rate of Technological Innovation

This figure illustrates the increasing rate of technological innovation in Western Europe after the beginning of the Industrial Revolution in the mid-eighteenth century. Technological innovation occurs at an accelerating rate because each innovation combines with existing cultural elements to produce many further innovations.

(Lenski, Lenski, & Nolan, 1991:57)

Before the industrial era, the major source of energy was the muscle power of humans and other animals. At the dawning of the Industrial Revolution, about 1750, flowing water and then steam were used to power ever-larger and more efficient machinery.

Once industrial technology appeared, change increased exponentially, as shown in Figure 4–1. Industrial societies transformed themselves more in a century than they had in thousands of years before. As explained in Chapter 1 ("The Sociological Perspective"), this stunning change stimulated the birth of sociology itself. During the nineteenth century, railroads and steamships revolutionized transportation, and steel-framed skyscrapers recast the urban landscape, dwarfing the cathedrals that symbolized an age gone by.

Early in the twentieth century, automobiles further reshaped Western societies, and electricity was fast becoming a part of everyday life. Electronic communication, including the telephone, radio, and television, were gradually making a large world seem smaller and smaller. More recently, transportation technology has given humanity the capacity to fly faster than sound and even

to break entirely the bonds of earth. Nuclear power, used for destruction ten years before it generated electricity, has also forever changed the world. During the last generation, computers have ushered in an "information revolution," dramatically increasing humanity's capacity to process information.

In agrarian societies, most men and women work in the home. Industrial machinery, however, led to the creation of factories, a far less personal setting for work. Lost in the process were not just close ties but many of the traditional values, beliefs, and customs that had guided agrarian life for centuries.

Industrialism engendered societies of unparalleled prosperity. Although health in industrial cities was initially poor, a rising standard of living and advancing health-related technology gradually controlled diseases that had for centuries killed both children and adults. Consequently, life expectancy increased, fueling rapid population growth. Industrialization also concentrated the increasing population. Agrarian people were dispersed over the land, with perhaps one in ten living in cities. In industrial societies, however, a majority of the population (now more than 75 percent in the United States) clusters in cities.

Occupational specialization, which expanded over the long course of sociocultural evolution, has become more pronounced than ever. Industrial people often identify one another in terms of their jobs, rather than according to their family background (the common practice in technologically simple societies, where kinship is paramount). Rapid change and movement from place to place also prompt cultural diversity, leading to the emergence of numerous subcultures and countercultures, as described in Chapter 3 ("Culture").

The family, too, has been reshaped by industrial technology, with far less of its traditional significance as the center of social life. No longer does the family serve as the primary setting for economic production, learning, and religious worship. And so-called "traditional" families have given way to increasing numbers of single people, divorced people, single-parent families, and stepfamilies. These new family variations also reflect technological advance, as Chapter 15 ("Family") describes in detail.

The Lenskis suggest that early industrialization concentrated the benefits of advancing technology on only a small segment of the population, with the majority living in poverty. In time, however, the material products of industrial progress have been extended to more of the population. Poverty remains a very serious problem in industrial societies, but compared to the situation a century ago, the standard of living has risen, and economic, social, and political inequality has diminished. Some social leveling, detailed in Chapter 9 ("Social Stratification"), occurs because industrial societies require a literate and skilled labor force. In contrast to the dramatic social inequality common to agrarian societies, industrial societies gradually provided some schooling and extended political rights to almost everyone. In global perspective, industrialization has also intensified demands for political participation among the people of South Korea, Taiwan, the People's Republic of China, the former Soviet Union, and the societies of Eastern Europe.

A summary of how technology shapes societies is presented in Table 4–1 on pages 102–3. Sociocultural evolution continues apace. We will explore the emerging *postindustrial* society in later chapters.

## The Limits of Technology

The technological might of industrial societies is unparalleled in human history. However, technology offers no "quick fix" for many social problems. Poverty remains the plight of millions of women and men in this country (detailed in Chapter 10, "Social Class in the United States") and of 1 billion people worldwide (Chapter 11, "Global Inequality"). Moreover, the capacity to reshape the world has created new problems that our ancestors could hardly have imagined. Industrial societies confer greater personal freedom, yet this often comes at the expense of the sense of community that characterized agrarian life. Furthermore, our ability to manipulate nature, coupled with our failure to restrain human greed, has wrought a staggering problem of global pollution. Perhaps most important, although industrial societies

Technology can threaten as well as serve humanity, a lesson symbolized by the utter destruction of Hiroshima by the armed forces of the United States at the end of World War II using a single, "primitive" atomic bomb. Weeks after the blast, heavily radiated people walked about the city—many aimlessly—due to their illness and the disorientation caused by losing their homes, families, and social routines.

**Table 4–1** SOCIOCULTURAL EVOLUTION: A SUMMARY

| Type of Society | Historical Period | Productive Technology | Population Size |
|---|---|---|---|
| **Hunting and Gathering Societies** | Only type of society until about 10,000 years ago; still common several centuries ago; the few examples remaining today are threatened by extinction | Primitive weapons | 25–40 people |
| **Horticultural and Pastoral Societies** | From about 10,000 years ago, with decreasing numbers after about 3000 B.C.E. | Horticultural societies use hand tools for cultivating plants; pastoral societies are based on the domestication of animals | Settlements of several hundred people, interconnected to form societies of several thousand people |
| **Agrarian Societies** | From about 5,000 years ago, with large but decreasing numbers today | Animal-drawn plow | Millions of people |
| **Industrial Societies** | From about 1750 to the present | Advanced sources of energy; mechanized production | Millions of people |

engage in warfare far less frequently than their technologically simpler counterparts, war now poses unimaginable horrors. Should nations ever unleash the present generation of nuclear weapons, human society would almost certainly regress to a technologically primitive state if, indeed, we survived at all. In some respects, technological advances have brought the world's people closer, creating a "global village." Yet in the wake of technological progress lie daunting problems of establishing peace and justice—problems that technology alone can never solve.

## Karl Marx: Society and Conflict

The first of our classical visions of society comes from Karl Marx. Few observed the industrial transformation of Europe as keenly as he did. Marx spent most of his adult life in London, then the capital of the vast British Empire, and a city that symbolized the wealth and power of the new social order. He was awed by the productive power of industry; not only were European societies producing more goods than ever before, but resources from around the world were being funneled through their factories at a dizzying rate.

Beyond the new technology, Marx was also keenly aware of the concentration of industry's riches in the hands of a few. A walk almost anywhere in London revealed dramatic extremes of affluence and squalor. A handful of aristocrats and industrialists lived in massive mansions well staffed by servants, where they enjoyed luxury and privileges barely imaginable to most of their fellow Londoners. The majority, however, labored long hours for low wages, living in slums or even in the streets, where many eventually succumbed to poor nutrition and disease.

Marx was both saddened and angered by the social inequities he saw around him. The technological miracles of industrialization had finally made possible human society without want. Instead, however, industry had done little to improve the lives of most people. To Marx, this represented a fundamental contradiction: in a society so rich, how could so many be so poor? Just as important, Marx asked, how can this situation be changed? Many

| Type of Society | Settlement Pattern | Social Organization | Examples |
|---|---|---|---|
| **Hunting and Gathering Societies** | Nomadic | Family-centered; specialization limited to age and sex; little social inequality | Pygmies of central Africa<br>Bushmen of southwest Africa<br>Aborigines of Australia<br>Tasaday of the Philippines<br>Kaska Indians of Canada |
| **Horticultural and Pastoral Societies** | Horticulturalists form relatively small permanent settlements; pastoralists are nomadic | Family-centered; religious system begins to develop; moderate specialization; increased social inequality | Middle Eastern societies about 5,000 B.C.E<br>Various societies today in New Guinea and other Pacific islands<br>Yanomanö today in South America |
| **Agrarian Societies** | Cities become common, though they generally contain only a small proportion of the population | Family loses significance as distinctive religious, political, and economic systems emerge; extensive specialization; increased social inequality | Egypt during construction of the Great Pyramids<br>Medieval Europe<br>Numerous nonindustrial societies of the world today |
| **Industrial Societies** | Cities now contain most of the population | Distinct religious, political, economic, educational, and family systems; highly specialized; marked social inequality persists, diminishing somewhat over time | Most societies today in Europe and North America<br>Japan |

people, no doubt, think of Karl Marx as a man determined to tear societies apart. But he was motivated by compassion for humanity and sought to help a society already badly divided to forge a new and just social order.

The key to Marx's thinking lies in the concept of **social conflict**, *struggle between segments of society over valued resources*. Social conflict can, of course, take many forms: individuals may quarrel, some colleges have long-standing rivalries, and nations sometimes go to war. For Marx, however, the most significant form of social conflict arises from the way a society produces material goods.

## Society and Production

The nineteenth-century societies Marx observed had industrial-capitalist economies, similar to those found today in North America, Western Europe, and elsewhere. Analyzing capitalist society, Marx designated a small part of the population as **capitalists**, *people who own factories and other productive enterprises*. A capitalist's goal is

profit, which is made by marketing a product for more than it costs to produce. The vast majority of the population fell into the category of industrial workers that Marx termed the **proletariat**, *people who provide labor necessary to operate factories and other productive enterprises*. Workers sell their labor for the wages needed to live. To Marx, an inevitable conflict between capitalists and workers stems from the productive process itself. To maximize profits, capitalists try to minimize wages, generally their single greatest expense. Workers, however, want wages to be as high as possible. Since profits and wages come from the same pool of funds, ongoing conflict occurs. Marx argued that this conflict could be resolved only by fundamentally changing the capitalist system. This revolutionary economic upheaval, he believed, would eventually come to pass.

Marx's analysis of society draws on the philosophical approach called *materialism*, which asserts that the production of material goods shapes all aspects of society. Marx did not think that, once established, an economic system neatly or simplistically determines cultural values, politics, and family patterns. But just as the Lenskis

# Karl Marx (1818–1883)

Few names evoke a response as strong as Karl Marx. Some consider him a genius and a prophet, others see only evil in his ideas. Everyone agrees that Marx stands among the social thinkers who have had the greatest impact on the world's people. Today, more than one-fifth of all humanity live in societies that consider themselves Marxist.

Controversy surrounded Marx even during his own lifetime. Born in the German city of Trier, he earned a doctorate in 1841 and began working as a newspaper editor. But because of his relentless social criticism, he clashed with government authorities and was driven out of Germany to Paris. Soon he was forced from France as well and he spent the rest of his life in London.

Along with Max Weber and Emile Durkheim, Marx was a major figure in the development of sociology, as we saw in Chapter 1 ("The Sociological Perspective"). However, his ideas received relatively little attention in the United States until the 1960s. Why? The answer lies in Marx's explicit criticism of industrial-capitalist society. Early American sociologists dismissed his ideas as mere "politics" rather than serious scholarship. For Marx, though, scholarship *was* politics. While most sociologists heeded Max Weber's call for value-free research by attempting to minimize or conceal their own values (see Chapter 2, "Sociological Investigation"), Marx's work was explicitly value-laden. Marx did not merely observe society; he offered a rousing prescription for profound social change. As we in North America have come to recognize the extent to which values shape all ideas, Marx's social analysis has finally gained the attention it deserves as an important part of sociology.

SOURCE: Based, in part, on Ritzer (1983).

---

argue the fundamental importance of technology, so Marx contended that the economic system exerts a key influence in every society:

> [T]he economic structure of society [is] the real foundation . . . . The mode of production in material life determines the general character of the social, political, and spiritual processes of life. (1959:43; orig. 1859)

Marx therefore viewed the economic system as the social *infrastructure* ("infra" is Latin meaning "below"). Other social institutions, including the family, the political system, and religion, are built on this foundation, becoming society's *superstructure*. These institutions extend economic principles and patterns into other areas of life, as illustrated in Figure 4–2 on page 106. In practical terms, social institutions reinforce the domination of the capitalists, by legally protecting their wealth, for example, and transmitting property from one generation to the next through the family.

Generally speaking, most members of industrial-capitalist societies do not view their legal or family systems as hotbeds of social conflict. On the contrary, individual rights to private property come to be defined as "natural." To illustrate, people in the United States tend to believe that individuals live in poor-quality housing because they cannot afford something better. And no one expects a business to provide better housing unless doing so would be profitable. Similarly, we find it easy to characterize people who are out of work as lacking the skills or motivation to become employed. Marx challenged this kind of reasoning, asserting that it stemmed from a social system—preoccupied with the "bottom line"—that treats human well-being as a market commodity. Poor housing

All societies use art to convey political ideas. This fact is most evident in socialist countries where, following Marx's thinking, people are expected to apply the lessons of economic revolution to all dimensions of social life. Stephan Carpov's hopeful painting *Friendship of the People* (1924) represents the vision of a new human race that shined brightly at the dawning of socialism.

and unemployment are not inevitable; nor is it true that some people "simply don't deserve more." Substandard housing and chronic unemployment merely constitute one set of human possibilities generated by capitalism (Cuff & Payne, 1979).

This realization led Marx to claim that capitalism promotes **false consciousness,** *any belief suggesting that the shortcomings of individuals, rather than society, are responsible for widespread social problems.* Marx was saying, in effect, that industrial capitalism itself was responsible for many of the social problems he saw all around him. False consciousness, he maintained, not only victimizes people, it obscures the real cause of their problems.

## Conflict in History

Marx believed that the power of ideas lies in action. He studied how societies have historically changed, noting that often a shift occurred gradually, following an evolutionary pattern; yet sometimes it happened rapidly, in revolutionary fashion. Marx observed (as do the Len-

skis) that change is partly prompted by technological advance. But he steadfastly held that conflict underlies all transformations in society.

In Marx's terms, the earliest hunters and gatherers formed primitive communist societies. The word *communism* means, simply, that the production of food and other material goods involves a common effort shared more or less equally by all members of society. Because the resources of nature were available to all hunters and gatherers (rather than privately owned), and because everyone performed similar tasks (rather than dividing the labor into specialized pursuits), there was little possibility for social conflict.

Marx noted that horticulture introduced significant social inequality. Among horticultural, pastoral, and early agrarian societies—which Marx lumped together as the "ancient world"—frequent warfare produced military captives who typically became slaves. A small elite (the "masters") used the labor of slaves to generate riches for themselves. From earliest civilizations, then, masters and slaves were locked into an irreconcilable pattern of social conflict (Zeitlin, 1981).

Agriculture brought still more wealth to members

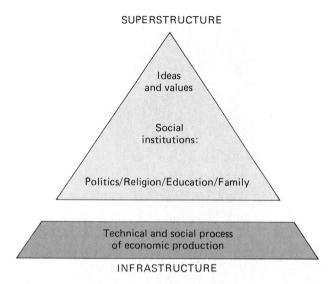

SUPERSTRUCTURE

Ideas
and values

Social
institutions:

Politics/Religion/Education/Family

Technical and social process
of economic production

INFRASTRUCTURE

**Figure 4–2** Karl Marx's Model of Society

This diagram illustrates Marx's materialist approach: that the process of economic production shapes the entire society. Economic production involves both technology (industry, in the case of capitalism) and social relationships (for capitalism, the relationship between the capitalists, who control the process, and the workers, who are simply a source of labor). Upon this infrastructure, or economic foundation, are built the major social institutions, as well as core cultural values and ideas. Taken together, these additional social elements represent the society's superstructure. Marx maintained that all the other parts of the society are likely to operate in a manner consistent with the economic system.

of the elite, fueling further social conflict. Agrarian serfs, occupying the lowest reaches of European feudalism from about the twelfth to the eighteenth centuries, were only slightly better off than slaves. In Marx's view, the power of both church and state defended and legitimized agrarian inequality by declaring that the existing social order embodied God's will. Thus, Marx viewed feudalism as little more than "exploitation, veiled by religious and political illusions" (Marx & Engels, 1972:337; orig. 1848).

Gradually, new productive forces undermined the feudal order. Commerce grew steadily throughout the Middle Ages, mostly carried out by peasants who had settled in the cities to escape feudal obligations to the nobility. Such people formed a new social category,

the *bourgeoisie* (a French word meaning "of the town"). Profits earned in the expanding market brought the bourgeoisie increasing wealth. After the mid-eighteenth century, with factories at their command, the bourgeoisie became true capitalists with power rivaling that of the landed nobility. While the nobility regarded this upstart class of men and women "of commerce" with disdain, the capitalists firmly took control of the emerging industrial-capitalist societies of Europe. Following Marx's analysis, then, technological change powered only part of the Industrial Revolution. More important, the agrarian economy, with its elite class of nobles, was overthrown from below by capitalists who presided over the emerging industrial economy.

Industrialization also fostered the development of the proletariat. English capitalists converted fields once tilled by serfs into grazing land for sheep, because these animals provided wool for the prospering textile industry. As serfs migrated to the cities to work in factories, they took their place among the burgeoning industrial proletariat. Marx believed that these workers would one day join together to form a unified class, setting the stage for historic confrontation, this time between capitalists and the exploited workers.

Much of Marx's analysis centers on the destructive aspects of industrial capitalism—especially how it promotes class conflict and alienation. In examining his views on each of these topics, we come to understand why he advocated the overthrow of this type of society.

## Capitalism and Class Conflict

"The history of all hitherto existing society is the history of class struggles." With this observation, Marx and his collaborator Friedrich Engels began their best-known work, the "Manifesto of the Communist Party" (1972:335; orig. 1848). The idea of social class lies at the heart of Marx's critique of capitalist society. Industrial capitalism, like earlier types of society, encompasses two major social classes, reflecting positions people hold in the productive system. Capitalists and proletarians are the historical descendants of dominant and oppressed classes in earlier societies: masters and slaves in the ancient world, nobility and serfs in feudal systems. In each case, one class controls the other, as productive property. Marx used the term **class conflict** (and sometimes *class*

Fildes's painting *Awaiting Admission to the Casual Ward* shows the numbing poverty commonplace among immigrants to cities that grew rapidly soon after the Industrial Revolution began. Marx saw in such suffering a fundamental contradiction of modern society: industrial technology promised material plenty for all, yet capitalism concentrated wealth in the hands of a few.

*struggle*) to refer to *the struggle between social classes over the distribution of wealth and power in society.*

Class conflict, then, dates back to civilizations long dead. What distinguishes the conflict in capitalism, however, is oppression that is obvious to all. In feudal societies, tradition and mutual obligations bound serfs and nobles together. Industrial capitalism dissolved those ties, so that people confronted each other merely in terms of "naked self-interest" and "callous cash payment." With no personal ties to their oppressors, Marx concluded, the proletariat had little reason to tolerate their suffering.

Even though industrial capitalism had brought class conflict out in the open, Marx realized that fundamental social change would require several key steps. First, he claimed, workers must *become aware* of their shared oppression and its true cause (industrial capitalism). Second, they must *organize and act* to address their problems. In other words, they must recognize that they suffer not from personal failings (as capitalist beliefs suggest), nor because other workers compete for their jobs. Rather, their suffering arises from the structure and workings of capitalism itself. In short, workers must adopt a Marxist version of the sociological perspective to replace false consciousness with **class consciousness,** *the recognition by workers of their unity as a class in opposition to capitalists and, ultimately, to capitalism itself.* Because the inhumanity of early capitalism seemed so obvious to Marx, he firmly believed that industrial workers would inevitably rise up en masse to destroy industrial capitalism. In doing so, they would cease to

# Alienation and Industrial Capitalism

These excerpts from the book *Working* by Studs Terkel illustrate how men and women may experience social alienation in their jobs.

Phil Stallings is a twenty-seven-year-old auto worker in a Ford Motor Company assembly plant in Chicago.

I start the automobile, the first welds. From there it goes to another line, where the floor's put on, the roof, the trunk, the hood, the doors. Then it's put on a frame. There is hundreds of lines. . . . I stand in one spot, about two- or three-feet area, all night. The only time a person stops is when the line stops. We do about thirty-two jobs per car, per unit. Forty-eight units an hour, eight hours a day. Thirty-two times forty-eight times eight. Figure it out. That's how many times I push that button.

The noise, oh it's tremendous. You open your mouth and you're liable to get a mouthful of sparks. (Shows his arms) That's a burn, these are burns. You don't compete against the noise. You go to yell and at the same time you're straining to maneuver the gun to where you have to weld.

You got some guys that are uptight, and they're not sociable. It's too rough. You pretty much stay to yourself. You get involved with yourself. You dream, you think of things you've done. I drift back continuously to when I was a kid and what me and my brothers did. The things you love most are what you drift back into.

Lots of times I worked from the time I started to the time of the break and I never realized I had even worked. When you dream, you reduce the chances of friction with the foreman or the next guy.

It don't stop. It just goes and goes and goes. I bet there's men who have lived and died out there, never seen the end of the line. And they never will—because it's endless. It's like a serpent. It's just all body, no tail. It can do things to you. . . .

Twenty-four-year-old Sharon Atkins is a college graduate working as a telephone receptionist for a large midwestern business.

I don't have much contact with people. You can't see them. You don't know if they're laughing, if they're being satirical or being kind. So your conversations become very abrupt. I notice that in talking to people. My conversation would be very short and clipped, in short sentences, the way I talk to people all day on the telephone. . . .

You try to fill up your time with trying to think about other things: what you're going to do on the weekend or about your family. You have to use your imagination. If you don't have a very good one and you bore easily, you're in trouble. Just to fill in time, I write real bad poetry or letters to myself and to other people and never mail them. The letters are fantasies, sort of rambling, how I feel, how depressed I am.

. . . I never answer the phone at home.

SOURCE: Terkel (1974).

---

be merely a social class *in* themselves and become a social class acting *for* themselves.

And what of their adversaries, the capitalists? The formidable wealth and power of capitalists, protected by the institutions of society, might seem invulnerable. But Marx saw a weakness in the capitalist armor. Motivated by a desire for personal gain, capitalists fear the competition of other capitalists. Thus Marx thought that capitalists would be reluctant to band together, even though they, too, share common interests. Furthermore, he reasoned, by competing with one another, capitalists keep wages low; this strategy further bolsters the resolve of workers to forge an alliance against them. In the long run, Marx claimed, capitalists could only contribute to their own undoing.

## Capitalism and Alienation

Marx also condemned capitalism for producing widespread **alienation**, *the experience of separation resulting from powerlessness*. Dominated by capitalists and dehumanized by their jobs (especially monotonous and repetitive factory work), workers find little satisfaction and feel individually powerless to improve their situation. Capitalist society itself gives rise to a major contradiction, observed Marx: as human beings have acquired and used technology to gain power over the world, the productive process itself has increasingly exerted power over human beings.

The basic problem here is that workers find industrial-capitalist work unsatisfying. They view themselves merely as a commodity, a source of labor, bought by capitalists and discarded when they are no longer needed. Marx cited four ways in which industrial capitalism alienates workers.

1. **Alienation from the act of working.** Ideally, people work both to meet their immediate needs and to develop their long-range potential. Capitalism, however, denies workers a voice in the fruits of production or the productive process itself. Further, work is often tedious, involving countless repetitions of routine tasks. The modern-day replacement of human labor by machines would hardly have surprised Marx; as far as he was concerned, capitalism had turned human beings into machines long ago.

2. **Alienation from the products of work.** The product of work belongs not to workers but to capitalists, who dispose of it in exchange for profits. Thus, Marx reasoned, the more workers invest of themselves in the products of their labor, the more they lose.

3. **Alienation from other workers.** Marx celebrated work as the productive affirmation of human community. Industrial capitalism, however, makes work competitive rather than cooperative. As the box illustrates, work often provides little chance even for human companionship.

4. **Alienation from humanity.** Industrial capitalism alienates workers from their own human potential. Marx argued that a worker "does not fulfill himself in his work but denies himself, has a feeling of misery rather than well-being, does not freely develop his physical and mental energies, but is physically exhausted and mentally debased. The worker, therefore, feels himself to be at home only during his leisure time, whereas at work he feels homeless" (1964a:124–25; orig. 1844). In short, industrial capitalism distorts an activity that should bring out the best qualities in human beings into a dull and dehumanizing experience.

Marx viewed alienation, in its various forms, as a barrier to social change. But he hoped that industrial workers eventually would overcome their alienation as they united into a true social class, aware of the cause of their problems, and galvanized to transform society.

## Revolution

The only way out of the trap of capitalism, contended Marx, was to refashion society. He envisioned a more humane and egalitarian productive system, which he termed *socialism*. Marx knew well the obstacles to a socialist revolution; even so, he was disappointed that workers in England did not overthrow industrial capitalism during his lifetime. Still, convinced of the basic immorality of capitalist society, he was sure that, in time, the working majority would realize they held the key to a better future in their own hands. This transformation would certainly be revolutionary, and perhaps even violent. The end product, however, would be a cooperative socialist society that would meet the needs of all.

The discussion of social inequality in Chapter 9 ("Social Stratification") reveals more about changes in

Marxism, one of the world's most influential social movements, has shaped the economic and political life of one-fifth of the world's people. For years, the conventional wisdom in the United States was that, once established, socialism stifled its opposition, making its overthrow impossible. But that notion collapsed along with the governments of Eastern Europe and the former Soviet Union. The political transformation of this world region is symbolized by the removal of statues of Vladimir Lenin (1870–1924), architect of Soviet Marxism, in city after city during the last few years.

industrial-capitalist societies since Marx's time, and why the revolution he longed for has not taken place. Later chapters also suggest why people in the societies of Eastern Europe and the former Soviet Union recently revolted against established socialist governments. Marx, however, looked toward the future with hope (1972:362; orig. 1848): "The proletarians have nothing to lose but their chains. They have a world to win."

# Max Weber: The Rationalization of Society

With a broad understanding of law, economics, religion, and history, Max Weber produced what many regard as the greatest individual contribution to sociology. Weber's ideas span such a wide range that they are difficult to summarize. The present discussion focuses on Weber's vision of modern society and how our world differs from earlier societies.

Weber's analysis of society reflects the philosophical approach called *idealism*, which emphasizes how human ideas shape society. Weber understood the power of technology, and he shared many of Marx's ideas about social conflict. But he departed from Marx's materialist views, arguing that societies differ from one another primarily in terms of how human beings think about the world. For Weber, human consciousness—ideas, beliefs, and values—was a transforming force. Thus he saw modern society as the result of not just new technology and new means of production but new ways of thinking as well. An emphasis on ideas, in contrast to Marx's focus on material production, has led scholars to characterize Weber's work as "a debate with the ghost of Karl Marx" (Cuff & Payne, 1979:73–74).

Weber conducted his research comparatively, contrasting social patterns in different times and places. To facilitate comparisons, he used the **ideal type,** *an abstract statement of the essential characteristics of any social phenomenon.* He explored religion through constructing ideal types of "Protestants," "Jews," "Hindus," and "Buddhists," even though no individual may precisely conform to the models. Similarly, we have already described entire societies in ideal terms, comparing "hunters and gatherers" to "industrial people." An ideal type has much in common with the more familiar idea of stereotype, in that both are abstract conceptualizations. Unlike a stereotype, however, an ideal type is essentially factual and emotionally neutral rather than being infused with unfair positive or negative connotations (Theodorson & Theodorson, 1969). Finally, Weber's use of the word *ideal* does not imply that something is "good" or "the best"; "criminals" as well as "priests" can be analyzed as ideal types.

## Rationality and Industrial Capitalism

Rather than categorizing societies in terms of technology or productive systems, Max Weber highlighted differences in the ways people view the world. In simple terms, Weber concluded that members of preindustrial societies embrace *tradition*, while industrial capitalism fosters *rationality*.

By **tradition,** Weber meant *sentiments and beliefs passed from generation to generation.* Thus social patterns in traditional societies are guided by the past. People evaluate particular actions as right and proper precisely because they have been accepted for so long.

Modern society takes a different approach, according to Weber, encouraging **rationality,** *deliberate, matter-of-fact calculation of the most efficient means to accomplish any particular goal.* Sentiment has no place in a rational world view, which is largely indifferent to the past. Ideally speaking, Weber continued, modern people treat tradition simply as a form of information with no special claim on them. We choose to think and act on the basis of present and future consequences, evaluating jobs, schooling, and even relationships in terms of what we contribute to them and what we expect to receive in return.

Weber viewed both the Industrial Revolution and the rise of capitalism as evidence of a historical surge in rationality. He used the phrase **rationalization of society** to denote *the historical change from tradition to rationality as the dominant mode of human thought.* Modern society, therefore, has been "disenchanted" as scientific thinking and technology have swept away sentimental ties to the past.

To conceptualize the impact of rationalization on the modern world, Global Map 4–1 on page 112 shows expenditures on the sciences for the world's nations. The Commonwealth of Independent States and the United States spend a great deal on scientific projects. Many of the more traditional societies in Latin America, Africa, and Asia devote far less of their resources to scientific pursuits.

Weber's comparative perspective—and the data found in the map—suggest that societies value technolog-

# Max Weber (1864–1920)

To be called merely a "sociologist" would probably have offended Max Weber. Not that he was indifferent to the study of society; in fact, he spent most of his life exploring the intricacies of our social arrangements. But Weber's contribution to understanding humanity is so broad and rich that no single discipline can properly claim him.

The product of a prosperous German family, Weber completed law school and set off on a legal career. But he soon felt confined by the constraints of legal practice. Continuing his studies, he became a college professor. His curiosity racing across the entire human condition, he integrated many approaches into his rich scholarship.

Throughout his life, Weber's family ties continued to influence his work. His mother's devout Calvinism no doubt prompted Weber's study of world religions and the link between Calvinism and the rise of industrial capitalism. From his father, a notable politician, Weber clearly gained insights into the workings of bureaucracy and political life.

Weber flirted with politics, and his wife Marianne was a leading feminist of her time. But Weber found politics to be incompatible with his work as a scholar. Politics, he claimed, demands action and strong personal conviction, while scholarship requires impartiality and patient reflection. Late in his life, Weber began urging his colleagues to become involved in politics as citizens outside the classroom, while striving for scientific neutrality in their professional work.

For many reasons, Weber's life was far from happy. He did not get along well with his father, and soon after his father's death Weber began to suffer from psychological problems. Illness sharply limited his ability to work during the remainder of his life. Even so, the exceptional number of major studies he conducted has led many to call him the most brilliant sociologist in history.

---

ical achievements differently. What one society might herald as a technological breakthrough, another might deem unimportant, and a third might strongly oppose as a threat to an established way of life. Elites in ancient Greece, for instance, devised many surprisingly elaborate mechanical devices to perform household tasks. Well served by slaves, however, they viewed their inventions as merely entertaining. In the United States today, the Amish are guided by their traditions to staunchly oppose modern technology.

In Weber's view, then, technological innovation is encouraged or hindered by the way people understand their world. He concluded that many societies in history held the technological keys to industry, but only in the supportive cultural climate of Western Europe did the Industrial Revolution actually take root (1958; orig. 1904–5).

Here we note another crucial difference between two great sociologists. Weber considered industrial capitalism as the essence of rationality, since capitalists pursue profit in eminently rational ways. Marx dismissed capitalism as the antithesis of rationality, claiming that this economic system failed to meet the basic needs of most of the people (Gerth & Mills, 1946:49).

## The Roots of Rationality

Weber elaborated on his analysis of modern rationality by noting that industrial capitalism actually developed in the wake of Calvinism—a Christian religious movement spawned by the Protestant Reformation. Weber knew that Calvinists, as an ideal type, approached life in a highly disciplined and rational way. But how did a religion spark the development of a new economy?

Central to the doctrine of John Calvin (1509–1564)

**Global Map 4–1**  Spending on Science in Global Perspective
In general, industrial societies spend relatively more of their gross national product (the value of all goods and services produced annually) on scientific pursuits than less industrialized societies do. From Weber's point of view, such expenditures are an indicator of a society's world view: less industrialized societies embrace tradition while more industrialized nations espouse rationality as a source of meaning.

is *predestination*, the idea that an all-powerful God has selected some people for salvation and others for eternal damnation. With everyone's fate predestined before birth, Calvinists were taught that people could do nothing to alter their destiny. Nor could they even know what their fate was. The only certainty was what hung in the balance: heavenly glory or hellfire for all of eternity.

The lives of Calvinists, then, were framed by visions of salvation or damnation. For such people, the anxiety of not knowing one's fate can only be imagined. Calvinists gradually came to a resolution of sorts: those chosen for glory in the next world, they concluded, should see signs of divine favor in *this* world as well. This conclusion prompted Calvinists to interpret worldly prosperity as a sign of God's grace. Anxious to acquire this reassurance, Calvinists threw themselves into a quest for success, applying rationality, discipline, and hard work to their tasks. This pursuit of riches was not for its own sake, however, since self-indulgently spending money was clearly sinful. Calvinists also were little moved to share their wealth with the poor because poverty was seen as a sign of God's rejection. Their ever-present purpose was to carry out what they held to be their personal *calling* from God as effectively as possible.

All the same, Calvinists built the foundation of capitalism as they reinvested their profits for greater success. Their deliberate and pious plan was to use wealth to generate more wealth, to practice personal thrift, and to eagerly embrace the technological advances that accompanied the Industrial Revolution.

These traits, Weber explained, distinguished Calvinism from other world religions. Catholicism, the traditional religion in most of Europe, encouraged an "other-worldly" acceptance of life as it was in hopes of greater rewards in the life to come. For Catholics, material wealth had none of the spiritual significance that so motivated the Calvinists. And so it was, Weber concluded, that industrial capitalism became established primarily in areas of Europe where Calvinism held sway.

Weber's study of Calvinism provides striking evidence of the power of ideas (which Marx considered merely a reflection of the productive process) to shape all of society. Weber's analysis does not imply, however, that something as complex as industrial capitalism sprang full blown from a single source. On the contrary, such simplicity would have offended Weber, whose work was partly in response to what he saw as Marx's narrow explanation of modern society in terms of economics. Later in his career, in fact, Weber (1961; orig. 1920) stressed that the development of industrial capitalism stemmed from a complex web of factors, including both economic and legal considerations as well as a distinctive world view (Collins, 1986).

But Weber never wavered in his contention that the defining characteristic of the modern world was rationality. As religious fervor diminished among later generations of Calvinists, he noted, success-seeking personal discipline remained. A *religious* ethic became simply a "*work* ethic," in pursuit of profit rather than the glory of God. From this point of view, industrial capitalism appears as "disenchanted" religion, with wealth now valued for its own sake. It is revealing that *accounting*, by which early Calvinists meant a daily record of moral deeds, now refers simply to money.

## Rationality and Modern Society

Weber contended that rationality, which had spawned the Industrial Revolution and the development of capitalism, had defined the character of modern society. Rationality influences modern social life in various ways.

1. **Distinctive social institutions.** Rationality promotes the emergence of distinctive **social institutions,** defined as *the major spheres of social life organized to meet basic human needs.* Among hunters and gatherers, the family was the center of virtually all activities. Gradually, however, other social institutions, including religious, political, and economic systems, emerged separate from the family. In modern societies, institutions of formal education and health care have also appeared. These social institutions—each detailed in a later chapter—are rational strategies for more efficiently addressing human needs.

2. **Specialization.** Distinctive social institutions encourage the pursuit of specialized activities. In traditional societies, everyone shares in carrying out many of the same tasks. Modern rationality, however, guides people into narrow pursuits like biological research, welding, or driving a taxi.

3. **Personal discipline.** Modern society puts a premium on adopting a disciplined approach to achieving life goals. For early Calvinists, of course, discipline was rooted in religious belief. Although now distanced from its religious origin, discipline is still encouraged by cultural values such as achievement, success, and efficiency.

4. **Awareness of time.** Central to a rational world view is a keen awareness of time. In modern societies, the traditional rhythm of sun and seasons gives way to scheduling according to the precise hour and minute. In addition, rationality turns people's attention from the past to the present and to the future, as they seek to improve their lives.

5. **Technical competence.** Members of traditional societies evaluate one another largely on the basis of *who* they are—how they are connected to others in the web of kinship. Modern rationality, in contrast, encourages us to judge people according to *what* they are—that is, their technical skills and personal abilities.

6. **Impersonality.** Because technical competence takes priority over personal relationships in a ra-

tional society, the world becomes more and more anonymous. Modern society increasingly turns on the interplay of specialists concerned with particular tasks, rather than the interaction of people sensitive to human feelings. Weber explained that we tend to devalue personal feelings and emotions as "irrational" because they sometimes run counter to rational principles.

7. **Large-scale organizations.** Finally, modern rationality is exemplified in the expansion of large-scale organizations. As early as the horticultural era, organizations deliberately administered activities like religious celebrations, public works, and warfare. As societies became larger and more complex, so did their organizations. In medieval Europe, the Catholic Church had become an enormous organization with thousands of officials; today's federal government has millions of employees.

### Rational Organization: Bureaucracy

Weber argued that rationality did not fully characterize the medieval church because its purpose was largely to preserve tradition. Truly rational organizations, in which tradition has been subsumed by efficiency, emerged only in the last few centuries in Western societies. The organizational type Weber termed *bureaucracy* accompanied capitalism as an expression of rationality.

Bureaucracy, the organizing principle of modern businesses, government agencies, labor unions, and universities, is explored in depth in Chapter 7 ("Groups and Organizations"). For now, it is important to recognize that Weber viewed bureaucracy as the clearest expression of a rational world view because its organizational elements—offices, duties, and policies—all are designed to achieve specific goals as efficiently as possible. In addition, any part of the organization is subject to modification to increase organizational efficiency. By contrast, traditional social organization places little emphasis on efficiency and is typically hostile to change. Weber asserted that bureaucracy had done for society as a whole what industrialization had done for the production of material goods:

> The decisive reason for the advance of bureaucratic organization has always been its purely technical superiority over any other form of organization. The fully developed bureaucratic apparatus compares with other organizations exactly as does the machine with the nonmechanical modes of production. (1978:973; orig. 1921)

Rational bureaucracy, Weber explained, also has a natural affinity to capitalism:

> Today, it is primarily the capitalist market economy which demands that the official business of public administration be discharged precisely, unambiguously, continuously, and

Max Weber agreed with Karl Marx that modern society is alienating, but the two thinkers saw different causes for this estrangement. For Marx, economic inequality is the culprit; for Weber, the issue is pervasive and dehumanizing bureaucracy. George Tooker's painting *Landscape* echoes Weber's sentiments.

Max Weber's pessimism about the future of human society lay in his conviction that technology, while enriching life in some respects, impoverishes it in others. In Weber's lifetime, the factory enhanced material production but often transformed workers into machines. In the decades to come, what are the implications of the expanding use of computers and robotics for the quality of our lives?

with as much speed as possible. Normally, the very large capitalist enterprises are themselves unequaled models of strict bureaucratic organization. (1978:974; orig. 1921)

### Rationality and Alienation

So far, we have emphasized the unparalleled efficiency of modern society. Worth remembering, however, is that Karl Marx reached much the same conclusion, at least as far as the productive efficiency of capitalism was concerned. But Marx ultimately rejected this type of society because of widespread alienation and other destructive consequences of economic inequality inherent in industrial-capitalist systems.

Weber, too, criticized modern society, but for different reasons. For him, the primary problem was not the economic inequality that so troubled Marx. Rather, the price of rational efficiency appeared to be alienation and dehumanization—people stifled by bureaucratic impersonality and regulation.

Large-scale organizations, Weber observed, tend to treat people as cases rather than as individuals. In addition, much of modern society's highly specialized work involves tedious repetition. Perhaps most important, Weber feared that the human spirit was being extinguished by rational formality. In the end, Weber envisioned modern society as a vast and growing system of rules and regulations that sought to direct virtually every human endeavor. In this way, he observed, human beings were becoming alienated from their own spontaneity and creativity.

An irony found in the work of Marx appears once again in Weber's analysis: rather than serving humanity, modern society turns on its creators and enslaves them. In language reminiscent of Marx's description of the human toll of industrial capitalism, Weber portrayed the modern individual as "only a small cog in a ceaselessly moving mechanism which prescribes to him an endlessly fixed routine of march" (1978:988; orig. 1921).

Despite obvious advantages of modern society over earlier types of societies, Weber ended his life deeply pessimistic. More and more, the modern world was coming to resemble a vast "machine," which, he worried, "chained" people to their work despite their efforts to "squirm free." Weber wondered if the logical conclusion of the rationalization of society would be to reduce people to mere robots.

## Emile Durkheim: Society and Function

"To love society is to love something beyond us and something in ourselves." These are the words of Emile Durkheim, another architect of sociology, introduced in the box. In this curious phrase[2] we find one more influential vision of human society.

---

[2] *Sociology and Philosophy*, 1974:55; orig. 1924.

# Emile Durkheim (1858–1917)

Why would wanting to be a sociology professor be controversial? Because there *weren't* any, at least not in France, until Emile Durk-

heim became the first in 1887. Up to this time, researchers studied human behavior almost exclusively in terms of biology and psychology. But Durkheim argued that one cannot comprehend humanity by looking at the individual. Instead, he maintained, understanding individuals demands examining their society.

In Chapter 1 ("The Sociological Perspective"), we encountered persuasive evidence of society's power to shape people's lives. By studying suicide, among the most personal and individualistic of actions, Durkheim showed that where people are embedded in society—as women or men, rich or

poor, and as followers of various religions—affects their suicide rates.

Durkheim is introduced here because his work, like that of Marx and Weber, is referred to extensively in later chapters. Durkheim's contributions to the understanding of crime are especially significant and figure prominently in Chapter 8 ("Deviance"). He also spent much of his life investigating religion, and we include his ideas on this subject in Chapter 17 ("Religion"). Just as important, Durkheim is one of the major architects of the structural-functional paradigm, which is used in almost every chapter that follows.

## Social Fact: Society Beyond Ourselves

The starting point for understanding the work of Emile Durkheim is the concept of **social fact,** *any social pattern that people confront as an objective reality beyond themselves.* Familiar examples of social facts include cultural norms and values, described in the last chapter ("Culture"), or the degree of social integration that Durkheim found to influence suicide rates, as explained in Chapter 1 ("The Sociological Perspective").

Durkheim's concept of social fact becomes clearer with three additional observations. First, society has *structure* because social patterns exist in orderly relation to one another. Second, because the social world surrounds us, such patterns shape our thoughts and actions. Third, social patterns constitute "facts" because they have an objective existence apart from any individual's subjective experience of them.

For Durkheim, then, society is more than the sum of its parts. He envisioned society as an elaborate, collective organism, with a certain life and momentum of its own. Society confronts its creators, demanding a measure of obedience, and we experience society as we feel the urge of morality. A first-grade classroom, a family having

dinner, and a country auction are commonplace situations that have an existence apart from any particular individual who has ever participated in them. These patterns not only shape behavior, but affect our thoughts and feelings as well. In Durkheim's view, society precedes us, makes claims on us while we are here, and continues after we are gone.

## Function: Society in Action

The next step in understanding Durkheim's vision of society involves the concept of *function.* Along with Herbert Spencer, introduced in Chapter 1, Durkheim helped to formulate what we now call the "structural-functional paradigm" in sociology. Durkheim argued that we discern the function of social facts not in the experience of individuals, but in their contribution to the general life of society itself.

Without sociological insight, Durkheim reasoned, common sense leads us to misunderstand events solely in terms of ourselves or other individuals. Crime, for example, brings to mind harm that offenders inflict on their victims. For Durkheim, though, the function of crime has little to do with particular people but involves society as a system. As Chapter 8 ("Deviance") explains, the way people identify and respond to particular acts as criminal vitalizes society as a moral system. Thus most people never recognize the social function of crime: to sustain the moral power of society. For this reason, Durkheim rejected the common view of crime as "pathological." On the contrary, he concluded, crime is quite "normal" for the most basic of reasons: no society could exist without it (1964a, orig. 1895; 1964b, orig. 1893).

## The Individual: Society in Ourselves

Durkheim contended that, while society is "beyond us," it is simultaneously "something in ourselves." Individuals, in other words, build personality by internalizing social facts. Through society and the social restraints we learn growing up, we nurture our humanity. That is, the moral education of society—through norms and values—regulates the natural insatiability of human beings. We are in danger of being overpowered by desire, Durkheim observed, because "the more one has, the more one wants, since satisfactions received only stimulate instead of filling needs" (1966; orig. 1897). Society, then, must necessarily instill restraints in each of us.

The need for societal regulation is illustrated by Durkheim's study of suicide (1966; orig. 1897), detailed in Chapter 1. In nineteenth-century France, as well as in the United States today, it is precisely the *least* regulated categories of people that suffer the *highest* rates of suicide. The greater autonomy afforded to men, for example, yields a suicide rate four times higher than that among women (U.S. Bureau of the Census, 1991).

Modern societies, however, have less of a hold on us. While Durkheim found some reasons to praise individualism, he warned of a rise in **anomie,** *a condition in which society provides individuals with little moral guidance.* The familiar—if uncommon—image of people leaping from office buildings during a stock-market crash exemplifies the extreme case of anomic suicide. Here, a radical collapse of the social environment disrupts society's support and regulation of the individual, sometimes with fatal results. Interestingly, sudden affluence does much the same thing, tearing individuals out of established social patterns and overwhelming them with unregulated free choice. The record of reckless behavior leading to accidental death among rock performers of recent decades who experienced sudden stardom clearly reveals the danger of self-destructiveness in extreme individualism.

Although he was an outspoken defender of individual rights, Durkheim never doubted that the needs of the individual must be balanced by the claims and guidance of society. Nowhere has this balance become more precarious than in the modern world.

## Evolving Societies: The Division of Labor

Like Marx and Weber, Durkheim experienced first-hand the rapid social changes that were transforming European societies during the nineteenth century. Durkheim saw in these changes new forms of social organization.

Historical study led Durkheim to conclude that societies with simple technology have strong traditions, and operate as powerful moral systems demanding unbending conformity. The *collective conscience* of traditional societies is so strong that the community moves quickly to punish any person who dares to differ very much from accepted ways of life. Durkheim called this intense moral consensus **mechanical solidarity,** meaning *social bonds, common to preindustrial societies, based on shared moral sentiments.* In horticultural and agrarian societies, for example, social solidarity is *based on likeness,* or shared experiences, since everyone acts and thinks mostly the same. Durkheim called such solidarity "mechanical" because people feel a more or less automatic sense of belonging.

The decline of mechanical solidarity marked the emergence of modern society. But, continued Durkheim, a new type of solidarity emerged to fill some of the void left by vanished traditions. This new social integration Durkheim dubbed **organic solidarity,** defined as *social bonds, common to industrial societies, based on specialization.* Social solidarity, *based on difference,* arises among people who, although conforming less in moral terms, find that specialization makes them need one another. Therefore, Durkheim summed up this entire historical process as a growing **division of labor,** or *specialized economic activity.* As we have already seen in Max Weber's analysis, modern societies rationally promote efficiency through specialization. From Durkheim's point of view, the result is a complex web of functional interdependence by which each person relies on tens of thousands of others—most complete strangers—who help produce the products and provide the services we use every day.

Modern organic solidarity, then, shares with traditional mechanical solidarity the function of maintaining the unified operation of society. But while the former

Historically, most members of human societies have engaged in the same basic activities: building shelters and obtaining food. Modern societies, claimed Durkheim, have a rapidly expanding division of labor. Increasing specialization is evident on the streets of societies beginning to industrialize: providing people with their weight is the livelihood of this man in Istanbul, Turkey; on a Bombay street in India, another earns a small fee for cleaning ears.

system is grounded in morality, the latter owes its force to practicality. Thus members of modern societies depend more and more on people we trust less and less. Why, after all, should we trust people we hardly know? And people whose beliefs probably differ from our own? Durkheim's answer: "because we can't live without them." But he knew that trust comes hard in a world that has lost much of its moral foundation. This prompts what we might call "Durkheim's Dilemma": that the positive benefits of modern society, including technological advance and greater personal freedom, are achieved at the cost of undermining morality and unleashing the ever-present danger of anomie.

Durkheim certainly found much to celebrate in modern society, especially individualism, privacy, and freedom of choice. Like Marx and Weber, though, he had misgivings about the direction society was taking. Still, of the three, Durkheim was the most optimistic. Confidence in the future sprang from his hope that we could enjoy greater freedom while creating for ourselves the moral regulation that had once been forced on us by tradition.

## Critical Evaluation: Four Visions of Society

This chapter opened with several important questions about human societies. We will conclude by probing how these questions are answered in light of the four visions of society we have examined.

### How Have Societies Changed?

According to the model of sociocultural evolution spelled out by the Lenskis, societies throughout history differ primarily in terms of their *technology*. Modern society is distinctive essentially because of its large-scale industrial productivity. Karl Marx, who also stressed historical differences in the productive system, was more concerned with demonstrating that material production in all historical societies (except perhaps for simple hunters and gatherers) generates social conflict. For Marx, modern society stands out only in that social conflict has become more obvious. In contrast to Marx, Max Weber distinguished societies in terms of characteristic modes of human thought. Preindustrial societies, he claimed, were traditional, while modern societies embrace a rational view of the world. Finally, for Emile Durkheim, societies differ in how they are bound together. Preindustrial mechanical solidarity is based on likeness; this gives way in industrial societies to organic solidarity based on difference.

## Why Do Societies Change?

Here again, the visions we have considered bring to bear different insights. The Lenskis see social change primarily as a matter of technological innovation that, over time, can transform an entire society. Marx pointed to the struggle between classes as the "engine of history," pushing societies toward revolutionary reorganization. Weber's idealist approach complemented Marx's materialism, showing that particular modes of thought also contribute to social change. He demonstrated how the rational underpinnings of Calvinism bolstered the Industrial Revolution, which, in turn, reshaped much of modern society. Finally, Durkheim believed that an expanding division of labor was propelling the increasing complexity of human societies.

## How Are Societies United and Divided?

The Lenskis hold that all societies are united by cultural patterns, although these patterns change according to a society's level of technological development. They note, too, that inequality tends to intensify as technology becomes more complex, although diminishing somewhat with the onset of industrialization. Marx argued that material production has drawn classes into conflict with one another throughout history. From his point of view, a unified and just social order could only emerge if production became a truly cooperative enterprise. Without denying the importance of economic rifts, Weber claimed that members of a society share a distinctive world view. Just as tradition has fused people together in the past, so rational, large-scale organizations now link the lives of modern individuals. Guided by the structural-functional paradigm, Durkheim focused on social integration. He contrasted the mechanical solidarity of preindustrial societies with modern society's organic solidarity, a change he explained in terms of an increasing division of labor. Durkheim's analysis also helps to clarify

the modern tolerance (and sometimes encouragement) of individuals cultivating a distinctive personality.

## Are Societies Improving?

The visions presented in this chapter differ on the question of human progress. From their survey of history, the Lenskis conclude that industrial societies provide important advantages, such as a higher standard of living and a longer life span. But the potential threat to our planet posed by advancing technology—through war or environmental pollution—makes it problematic to equate technological advance with improved quality of life. Without passing judgment on all the consequences of technological advances, the Lenskis predict that change will continue to be rapid, and perhaps more dramatic than ever.

Marx applauded the power of advancing technology, but he concluded that only the few would enjoy its benefits until society underwent a radical restructuring. He looked to the future for a final resolution of historical class conflict as socialism placed the productive system under the control of all the people.

Weber found little comfort in Marx's vision, fearing that socialist revolution would only intensify the power of large-scale organizations to dominate the lives of individuals. As explained in Chapter 19 ("The Economy and Work"), Weber's forecast that state control of everyday life would expand—especially under socialism—helps to explain the recent overthrow of governments in Eastern Europe and the former Soviet Union. Despite the successes of these systems in promoting economic equality, in other words, they sharply limited political participation. Recognizing that the expansion of organizations would take on global proportions made Weber's view of the course of human society the most pessimistic of all.

Durkheim, by contrast, holds the most optimistic view. He saw in the twilight of tradition the possibility for greater freedom than individuals had ever known. Individualism has its dangers, however, as Durkheim's concern with anomie suggests. Despite this reservation, Durkheim comes closest to applauding the history of human societies as a march of genuine "progress."

The significant differences among these four approaches do not mean that any one of them is, in an absolute sense, right or wrong. Society is exceedingly complex, and we shall return to each of these visions in later chapters.

# Summary

### Gerhard and Jean Lenski

1. The Lenskis' model of sociocultural evolution explores the societal consequences of technological advance.
2. The earliest and most simple societies, based on hunting and gathering, are composed of a small number of family-centered nomads. These societies are rapidly vanishing from the world.
3. Horticulture emerged about ten thousand years ago, with the invention of hand tools for cultivation. Pastoral societies are nomadic, domesticating animals and engaging in extensive trade.
4. Agriculture, which appeared some five thousand years ago, involves large-scale cultivation using animal-drawn plows. This technology allows societies to grow into vast empires with more productivity, specialization, and inequality.
5. Industrialization began only 250 years ago in Europe, as sophisticated machinery was powered with advanced sources of energy. In industrial societies, change typically happens quickly. Most people live in cities, and highly specialized activities take place separate from the family.

### Karl Marx

6. Marx pointed up the conflict between social classes. Classes are production-based, making Marx's analysis a materialist one.
7. Social conflict has characterized human history. Conflict in "ancient" societies involved masters and slaves; in agrarian societies, nobility and serfs; in industrial-capitalist societies, the bourgeoisie and the proletariat.
8. Industrial capitalism alienates workers in four ways: from the act of working, from the products of their labor, from other workers, and from human potential.
9. Marx believed that workers could overcome elites and their own false consciousness to overthrow the industrial-capitalist system.

### Max Weber

10. The idealist approach of Max Weber reveals that ways of thinking have a powerful effect on society.
11. The rationality of modern society contrasts with the tradition that directed feudal society; Weber described the historical process that brings us to modern-day life as the rationalization of society.
12. Weber feared that rationality, embodied in anonymous organizations, would stifle human creativity.

### Emile Durkheim

13. Durkheim characterized the way society confronts individuals as external, objective facts.
14. His approach relates social elements to the larger society through their functions.
15. Societies require solidarity; mechanical solidarity is based on traditional likeness, while organic solidarity is based on the division of labor, or productive specialization.

# Key Concepts

**agriculture** the technology of large-scale farming using plows powered by animals or advanced energy

**alienation** the experience of separation resulting from powerlessness

**anomie** Durkheim's designation of a condition in which society provides individuals with little moral guidance

**capitalists** people who own factories and other productive enterprises

**class conflict** Marx's term for the struggle between social classes over the distribution of wealth and power in society

**class consciousness** Marx's term for the recognition by workers of their unity as a social class in opposition to capitalists and to capitalism itself

**division of labor** specialized economic activity

**false consciousness** Marx's description of any belief suggesting that the shortcomings of individuals, rather than society, are responsible for widespread social problems

**horticulture** technology based on using hand tools to cultivate plants

**hunting and gathering** simple technology to hunt animals and gather vegetation

**ideal type** an abstract statement of the essential characteristics of any social phenomenon

**industrialism** technology that powers sophisticated machinery with advanced fuels

**mechanical solidarity** Durkheim's term for social bonds, common to preindustrial societies, based on shared moral sentiments

**organic solidarity** Durkheim's designation of social bonds, common to industrial societies, based on specialization

**pastoralism** technology that supports the domestication of animals

**proletariat** people who provide labor necessary for the operation of factories and other productive enterprises

**rationality** deliberate, matter-of-fact calculation of the most efficient means to accomplish any particular goal

**rationalization of society** Weber's characterization of the historical change from tradition to rationality as the dominant mode of human thought

**social conflict** struggle between segments of society over valued resources

**social fact** Durkheim's term for any social pattern that people confront as an objective reality beyond themselves

**social institution** a major sphere of social life organized to meet a basic human need

**society** people who interact in a limited territory and share a culture

**sociocultural evolution** the Lenskis' term for the process of social change that results from gaining new cultural information, particularly technology

**tradition** sentiments and beliefs passed from generation to generation

## Suggested Readings

A comprehensive account of Gerhard and Jean Lenski's analysis of human societies is found in the following textbook.

> Gerhard Lenski, Jean Lenski, and Patrick Nolan. *Human Society: An Introduction to Macrosociology.* 6th ed. New York: McGraw-Hill, 1991.

These essays, in two volumes, point out various misconceptions about our human ancestors.

> Tim Ingold, David Riches, and James Woodburn, eds. *Hunters and Gatherers 1: History, Evolution and Social Change,* and *Hunters and Gatherers 2: Property, Power and Ideology.* New York: Berg, 1988.

This book highlights the distinctive ways in which women are defined, with particular attention to virginity, motherhood, and other expressions of sexuality.

> Shirley Ardener, ed. *Defining Females: The Nature of Women in Society.* New York: Berg, 1991.

Using the thinkers included in this chapter, as well as literary figures, this book examines the emergence of sociology amid the changes of the nineteenth century.

> Bruce Mazlish. *A New Science: The Breakdown of Connections and the Birth of Sociology.* New York: Oxford University Press, 1989.

This is one of the best sources of essays by Karl Marx and Friedrich Engels.

> Robert C. Tucker, ed. *The Marx-Engels Reader.* 2nd ed. New York: W. W. Norton, 1978.

Perhaps Max Weber's best-known study is his analysis of Protestantism and capitalism.

> Max Weber. *The Protestant Ethic and the Spirit of Capitalism.* New York: Charles Scribner's Sons, 1958 (orig. 1904–5).

This collection of essays demonstrates the multifaceted ways in which Max Weber incorporated history, politics, and social criticism into his work.

> Wolfgang J. Mommsen. *The Political and Social Theory of Max Weber: Collected Essays.* Chicago: University of Chicago Press, 1989.

This is one of the most thorough studies of Emile Durkheim and his pioneering work in sociology.

> Steven Lukes. *Emile Durkheim, His Life and Work: A Historical and Critical Study.* New York: Harper & Row, 1972.

Sociological theory has yet to respond adequately to the large number of women who entered sociology in recent decades. This book takes a step in that direction.

> Ruth A. Wallace, ed. *Feminism and Sociological Theory.* Newbury Park, CA: Sage Publications, 1989.

# Socialization

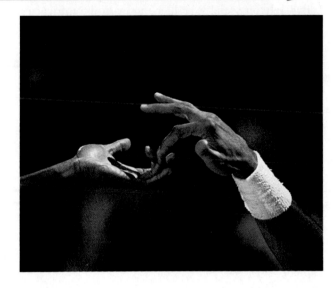

On a cold winter day in 1938, a social worker walked anxiously to the door of a farmhouse in rural Pennsylvania. Investigating possible child abuse, the social worker soon discovered a five-year-old girl hidden in a second-floor storage room. The child, whose name was Anna, was wedged into an old chair with her arms tied above her head so that she could not move. She was dressed in a few filthy garments, and her arms and legs were like matchsticks—so thin and frail that she could not use them (Davis, 1940:554).

Anna's situation was both moving and tragic. She was born in 1932 to an unmarried and mentally impaired woman of twenty-six who lived with her father. Enraged by his daughter's "illegitimate" motherhood, the grandfather initially refused to even allow the child in his house. Anna therefore spent the first six months of her life in various institutions. Finally, because her mother was unable to pay for such care, Anna was forced to live with her mother and grandfather.

At this point, her ordeal intensified. To avoid the grandfather's hostility, Anna's mother moved her to a room that resembled an attic, where she received little attention and just enough milk to keep her alive. There she stayed, with essentially no human contact, for five years.

Upon learning of the discovery of Anna, sociologist Kingsley Davis traveled immediately to see the child, who had been transported by local authorities to a county home for children. He was appalled by her condition. Anna was emaciated, devoid of strength, and she displayed virtually no human qualities. She could not laugh, smile, speak, or even show anger. She was completely unresponsive, as if the world around her did not even exist. Not surprisingly, people initially thought she was deaf and blind (Davis, 1940).

## The Importance of Social Experience

Here is a deplorable but instructive case of a human being deprived of virtually all social contact. Although Anna was physically alive, she had none of the capacities associated with full humanity. Her plight revealed that, without social experience, an individual develops little or no capacity for thought, emotion, and meaningful behavior. In short, an individual who has no social interaction is likely to remain an *object* rather than to become a *person*.

This chapter explores what Anna was deprived of—the means by which we become fully human. We call this process **socialization,** *lifelong social experience by which individuals develop human potential and learn the patterns of their culture.* Unlike other living species

123

for which behavior is determined biologically, human beings rely on social experience to learn the intricacies of their culture in order to survive. Social experience is also the foundation of **personality,** which refers to *a person's fairly consistent pattern of thinking, feeling, and acting.* Personality is constructed from our social surroundings and how we learn to respond to them. As personality develops, we simultaneously become distinctive individuals and share a culture. In the absence of social experience, as the case of Anna shows, personality simply does not develop.

Social experience is obviously as vital for society as it is for individuals. A society extends both forward and backward in time, far beyond the life span of any person. As explained in Chapters 3 ("Culture") and 4 ("Society"), every society teaches something of its past way of life to its new members. The complex and lifelong process of socialization is the way in which society transmits culture from one generation to another (Elkin & Handel, 1984).

## Human Development: Nature and Nurture

Virtually helpless at birth, the human infant needs others to provide for its care and nourishment. A child also relies on others to teach patterns of culture. Although Anna's experience makes these facts very clear, a century ago most people mistakenly believed that human behavior was the product of biology.

Chapter 3 ("Culture") described Charles Darwin's ground-breaking work in the mid-nineteenth century. In brief, Darwin's theory of evolution held that a species gradually changes over thousands of generations as genetic variations promote more successful survival and reproduction. As Darwin's influence grew, others applied his ideas to the understanding of human behavior. By the end of the nineteenth century, most people spoke of human behavior as if it were instinctive, part of the "nature" of the human species.

Such notions are still with us. People sometimes claim, for example, that our economic system reflects "instinctive human competitiveness," that some people are "born criminals," or that women are more emotional while men are more rational (Witkin-Lanoil, 1984). The term *human nature* is often used to mean personality traits that people are supposedly born with, just as we are born with five senses. More accurately, however,

human nature involves the creation and learning of cultural traits, as we shall see.

Darwin's thinking was also misconstrued by people trying to explain how societies varied from one another. Centuries of world exploration and empire building brought Western Europeans into contact with people who behaved quite differently than they did. They attributed such contrasts to biological differences rather than to cultural diversity. Thus Europeans and North Americans viewed the members of technologically simple societies as biologically less evolved, and, therefore, less human. This self-serving and ethnocentric view helped them justify their colonial practices. It is easy to enter another society, exploit its resources, and perhaps enslave its people if you believe they are not truly human in the same sense that you are.

In the twentieth century, naturalistic explanations of human behavior came under fire. Psychologist John B. Watson (1878–1958) devised an approach called *behaviorism,* which held that specific patterns of behavior are not instinctive but learned. Arguing that all of the world's cultures have the same biological foundation, Watson rejected the idea that cultural variations reflect any evolutionary distinctions. To Watson, human behavior was malleable, open to the influence of any imaginable environment:

> Give me a dozen healthy infants . . . and my own specified world to bring them up in, and I will guarantee to take any one at random and train him to become any type of specialist that I might select—doctor, lawyer, artist, merchant-chief, and yes, even beggar-man and thief—regardless of his talents, penchants, tendencies, abilities, vocations, and race of his ancestors. (1930:104)

Watson was aware that he was overstating his case, but he was convinced that linking human behavior to biology was fundamentally wrong and that nurture—or learning—was far more influential than "nature."

Watson's assertions were supported by the research of anthropologists that showed variable cultural patterns, even among societies with similar technology. An outspoken proponent of the "nurture" view, anthropologist Margaret Mead summed up the evidence: "The differences between individuals who are members of different cultures, like the differences between individuals within a culture, are almost entirely to be laid to differences in conditioning, especially during early childhood, and this conditioning is culturally determined" (1963:280; orig. 1935).

Human infants display various reflexes, biologically based behavioral patterns that enhance survival. The sucking reflex, which actually begins before birth, enables the infant to obtain nourishment. The grasping reflex, triggered by placing a finger on the infant's palm, causes the hand to close. This response helps the infant to maintain contact with a parent and, later on, to grasp objects. The Moro reflex, which occurs when an infant is startled, causes the infant to swing both arms outward and then bring them together on the chest. This action, which disappears during the first months of life, probably developed among our evolutionary ancestors so that a falling baby could grasp the body hair of a parent.

Today, social scientists are cautious about describing any type of behavior as instinctive. Even sociobiology, discussed in Chapter 3, does not challenge the assertion that human behavior is primarily guided by the surrounding culture. This does not mean that biology plays *no* part in human behavior. Human life, after all, depends on the functioning of the human body. We also know that children share some biological traits with their parents, especially physical characteristics such as height, weight, hair and eye color, and facial features. Intelligence and personality characteristics (for example, how one reacts to stimulation) have some genetic component, as does the potential to excel in such activities as art and music (Herrnstein, 1973). But whether or not a person develops any inherited potential depends on the opportunities associated with social position (Plomin & Foch, 1980; Goldsmith, 1983). Overall, clear evidence supports the conclusion that nurture is far more important

than nature in shaping human behavior. Finally, bear in mind, as suggested in Chapter 3, that what we call human nature is the creation, learning, and modification of culture. Thus, nature and nurture stand not so much in opposition as intertwined.

## Social Isolation

For obvious ethical reasons, researchers cannot subject human beings to experimental isolation. Consequently, much of what we know about this issue comes from rare cases of children subjected to abuse like Anna. Even then, researchers typically enter the picture at the end of an ordeal and have to piece together what happened over a period of years. Researchers have, however, studied the effects of social isolation on animals.

### Effects of Social Isolation on Nonhuman Primates

A classic investigation of the effects of social isolation on nonhuman primates was conducted by psychologists Harry and Margaret Harlow (1962). The Harlows placed rhesus monkeys—whose behavior is in some ways surprisingly similar to that of humans—in various conditions of isolation to observe the consequences.

They found that complete social isolation for a period of even six months (with adequate nutrition) seriously disturbed the monkeys' development. When isolated monkeys subsequently encountered others of their kind, they were fearful and unable to defend themselves against aggression.

The Harlows modified their experiment, isolating infant rhesus monkeys in cages but with an artificial "mother" of wire mesh with a wooden head and the nipple of a feeding tube where the breast would be. These monkeys survived physically, but they, too, were subsequently unable to interact with other monkeys. A further variation of the research, however, showed that when the artificial mother was covered with soft terry cloth, the infant monkeys clung to it and apparently derived emotional benefit from the closeness. These monkeys later displayed less emotional distress. The Har-

lows thus concluded that normal emotional development requires affectionate cradling as part of mother-infant interaction.

The Harlows also made two other discoveries. First, as long as they were surrounded by other infants, monkeys were not adversely affected by the absence of a mother. This suggests that deprivation of social experience, rather than the specific absence of maternal contact, has devastating effects. Second, the Harlows found that, when socially isolated for shorter periods of time (about three months), infant monkeys eventually regained normal emotional patterns after rejoining others. The damage of short-term isolation, then, can be overcome; longer-term isolation, however, appears to inflict on monkeys irreversible emotional and behavioral damage.

### Effects of Social Isolation on Children

The case of Anna, described at the beginning of this chapter, is the best-known instance of the long-term social isolation of a human infant. After her discovery, however, Anna benefited from extensive social contact and she soon showed some improvement. When Kingsley Davis (1940) visited her in the county home after ten

The personalities we develop depend largely on the environment in which we live. When a child's world is shredded by violence, the damage can be profound and lasting. This drawing was made by a four-year-old living in a low-income neighborhood of Washington, D.C. What are the likely effects of such an environment on a child's self-confidence and capacity to form trusting ties to others?

days, he noted that she was more alert and showed some human expression, even smiling with obvious pleasure. During the next year, Anna made slow but steady progress, as she experienced the humanizing effects of socialization, showing greater interest in other people and gradually learning to walk. After a year and a half, she could feed herself, walk alone for short distances, and play with toys.

Consistent with the observations of the Harlows, however, it was becoming apparent that Anna's five years of social isolation had left her permanently damaged. At the age of eight her mental and social development was still less than that of a two-year-old. Not until she was almost ten did she show the first signs of using language. Complicating the problem is the fact that Anna's mother was mentally retarded, so that Anna may have been similarly disadvantaged. The puzzle was never untangled, because Anna died at age ten from a blood disorder, possibly related to her long years of abuse (Davis, 1940).

A second, quite similar case reveals more about the long-range effects of social isolation. At about the same time that Anna was discovered, another girl of about the same age was found under strikingly similar circumstances. After more than six years of virtual isolation, this girl—known as Isabelle—showed the same lack of human responsiveness as Anna (Davis, 1947). Unlike Anna, though, Isabelle benefited from an intensive program by psychologists to aid her development. Within a week, Isabelle was attempting to speak, and a year and a half later, her vocabulary was nearly two thousand words. The psychologists concluded that Isabelle had progressed through what is normally about six years of development with two years of intensive effort. By the time she was fourteen, Isabelle was attending sixth-grade classes in school, apparently well on her way to at least an approximately normal life.

A final case of childhood isolation involves a thirteen-year-old girl in California isolated in a small room from the age of about two. For years Genie had been victimized by her parents in a host of ways, including being deprived of social contact. Upon discovery, her condition was similar to that of the two other children we have described. Genie was emaciated (weighing only fifty-nine pounds) and had the mental development of a one-year-old. She was given intensive treatment by specialists and is alive today. Yet even after years of care, her ability to use language is little better than that of a young child (Curtiss, 1977; Pines, 1981).

All the evidence points to the crucial role of social experience in personality development. Human beings are resilient creatures, sometimes able to recover from even the crushing experience of prolonged isolation. But there is a point—precisely when is unclear from the limited number of cases—at which social isolation in infancy results in irreparable developmental damage.

# Understanding the Socialization Process

Socialization is a highly complex process, and no one researcher to date has fully explained how we gain our humanity. The following sections introduce several thinkers who have made important contributions to our understanding of social development.

## Sigmund Freud: The Elements of Personality

Sigmund Freud (1856–1939) lived in Vienna at a time when most Europeans linked human behavior to biological forces. Freud himself was trained in the natural sciences and began his career as a physician. His importance today, however, is based on his ground-breaking analysis of personality from which he developed his theory of psychoanalysis. Many aspects of this work have direct bearing on understanding socialization.

### Basic Human Needs

Freud contended that biology plays an important part in personality development, although he never reduced human behavior to simple biological instinct. For Freud, instinct meant general human needs or drives. Freud ultimately decided that two human drives underlie all others. First, he claimed, humans have a basic need for bonding, which he described as the life instinct, or *eros* (from the Greek god of love). In Freud's view, this life instinct manifests itself in the pursuit of sensory pleasure, including sex. Second, opposing this need, he asserted that people also have an aggressive drive, which he called the death instinct, or *thanatos* (from Greek meaning "death"). Freud postulated that these opposing forces generate tension in the personality, even though we are not necessarily conscious of this interplay of forces.

Sigmund Freud stands among the pioneers who charted the human personality. His daughter Anna Freud, also shown here in a 1913 family photograph, further developed her father's theory of psychoanalysis.

Together, he maintained, these drives form the foundation of the human drama.

### Freud's Model of Personality

Freud incorporated both basic drives and the influence of society into a broader model of personality with three parts: id, ego, and superego. The **id** represents *the human being's basic drives*, which are unconscious and demand immediate gratification. (The word *id* is simply Latin for "it," suggesting the tentative way in which Freud explored the unconscious mind.) Rooted in our biology, the id is present at birth so that, from a Freudian point of view, a newborn is basically a bundle of needs that demands attention, touching, and food. Since society opposes such a self-centered orientation, the id's desires inevitably encounter resistance. This is why the first word a child learns is often "no." To avoid frustration, the child learns to approach the world realistically. This is accomplished through the ego, the second component of the personality, which gradually emerges from the id. The **ego** (Latin for "I") represents *a person's conscious efforts to balance innate pleasure-seeking drives with the demands of society*. The ego arises as we gain awareness of our distinct existence; it develops as we face up to the fact that we cannot have everything we want. Finally, the human personality develops the **superego** (Latin meaning "above" or "beyond" the ego), which is *the presence of culture within the individual*. In this intriguing overlay of personality, we see *why* we cannot have everything we want. The superego consists of the internalized values and norms of our culture, and takes the form of conscience. First expressed as the recognition of parental control, the superego eventually matures as the child learns that parental control is itself a reflection of the moral demands of the larger culture.

From a child's point of view, the world first appears as a bewildering array of physical sensations and need satisfactions. With the gradual development of the superego, however, the child's comprehension extends beyond pleasure and pain to the moral concepts of right and wrong. In other words, initially a child can feel good only in the physical sense. Later, though, a child feels good for behaving in culturally appropriate ways and feels bad (the experience of guilt) for failing to do so.

In a well-adjusted personality, the ego successfully manages the opposing forces of the id and the superego. If conflicts are not successfully resolved, personality disorders result. Freud viewed childhood as the critical period in the formation of an individual's basic personality, and he regarded conflicts experienced during this stage of life as an unconscious source of personality problems later on.

Freud called society's efforts to control human drives *repression*. In his view, some repression is inevitable, since people must be coerced into looking beyond themselves. Often, the competing demands are resolved through compromise, so that basic needs are redirected into socially approved forms. This process, which Freud named *sublimation*, transforms fundamentally selfish drives into socially acceptable activities. For example, sexual urges may lead to marriage, and aggression can be expressed in a sports stadium.

*Critical evaluation.* Freud's work sparked controversy in his own lifetime and some of that controversy still smolders today. The world he knew vigorously repressed human sexuality, and few of his contemporaries were inclined to concede that sex was a basic human need. Recently, Freud has drawn fire for his depictions of humanity in allegedly male terms, thereby distorting the lives of women (Donovan & Littenberg, 1982). But Freud provided a foundation that influenced virtually everyone who later studied the human personality. Of special importance to sociology is his notion that we internalize social norms, and that childhood experiences have lasting importance to socialization.

## Jean Piaget: Cognitive Development

Jean Piaget (1896–1980) also stands among the foremost psychologists of the century. Much of his work centered on human *cognition*—how people think and understand. Early in his career, Piaget was fascinated by the behavior of his three children, wondering not only what they knew, but *how* they understood the world. Systematic observations led him to conclude that children's conceptions of the world vary with age. Piaget identified four stages of cognitive development, each a product of biological maturation and increasing social experience.

### The Sensorimotor Stage

The first step in human development, according to Piaget, is the **sensorimotor stage,** *the level of human development in which people experience the world only through sensory contact.* In this stage, which corresponds roughly to the first two years of life, the infant explores the world by touching, looking, sucking, and listening. By about four months of age, children learn to distinguish their own bodies from their surroundings. Nearing the end of this stage, children comprehend what Piaget called *object permanence*, realizing that objects continue to exist even if the youngster cannot sense them directly. Young infants, for example, may think that an adult leaving the room actually has ceased to exist (and respond accordingly).

Children gain skill at imitating the actions or sounds of others during the sensorimotor stage, but they have no comprehension of symbols. Thus, very young children do not think; they know the world only in terms of direct physical experience.

### The Preoperational Stage

The second level in Piaget's account of development is the **preoperational stage**, *the level of human development in which individuals first use language and other symbols.* Typically, this stage extends from age two to seven. Using symbols, children can now engage the world mentally—that is, they are able to think about things they cannot sense directly. As they begin to attach meaning to the world, they learn to distinguish between ideas and objective reality. At this age, children realize that their dreams are not real, and they appreciate the element of fantasy in fairy tales (Kohlberg & Gilligan, 1971; Skolnick, 1986). Unlike adults, however, they identify the names and meanings only of specific things. A child at this stage who takes pleasure in describing a favorite toy, for example, will be unable to describe the qualities of toys in general.

Without a grasp of general concepts, a child cannot abstractly conceive of size, weight, and volume. In one of his best-known experiments, focusing on a principle Piaget called *conservation of matter*, the researcher placed two identical glasses containing equal volumes of water on a table. He then asked several children aged five and six if the amount in each glass was the same. They nodded that it was. The children then watched Piaget take one of the glasses and pour its contents into a taller, narrower glass, raising the level of the water. He asked again if each glass held the same amount. The typical five- and six-year-old now insisted that the taller glass held more water. But children over the age of seven, who are able to think more abstractly, could usually comprehend that the amount of water remained the same.

During the preoperational stage, children still have a very egocentric view of the world (Damon, 1983). For example, we have all seen young children place their hands in front of their faces and exclaim, "You can't see me!" They assume that if they cannot see you, then you are unable to see them. This illustrates that they perceive the world only from their own vantage point and have yet to learn that a situation may appear different to another person.

### The Concrete Operational Stage

Next, in Piaget's model, comes the **concrete operational stage,** *the level of development at which individuals first use logic to understand their surroundings.* At this point, typically between seven and eleven, children make significant strides in comprehending and manipulating their environment. Having gained the capacity for logical thought, they now connect what they experience in terms of cause and effect. In addition, girls and boys can attach more than one symbol to a particular event or object. For instance, if you say to a girl of six, "Today is Wednesday," she might respond, "No, it's my birthday!" belying the limitation of being able to use but one symbol at a time. Within a few years, however, she would be able to respond, "Yes, this Wednesday is my birthday!"

However, during the concrete operational stage, the thinking of children remains focused on concrete objects and events. They may understand that hitting brothers without provocation will bring punishment, but children still cannot conceive of situations in which hitting a brother would be fair or why parents punish. In a final development during the concrete operational stage, children transcend their earlier egocentrism, imagining themselves in the position of another person. As we shall explain shortly, perceiving a situation from another's point of view is the foundation of complex social activities, such as games.

### The Formal Operational Stage

The fourth level in Piaget's model, the **formal operational stage,** refers to *the level of human development at which people use highly abstract thought and are able to imagine alternatives to reality.* By about the age of twelve, children begin to reason using abstract qualities rather than thinking only of concrete situations. If, for example, you were to ask a child of seven or eight, "What would you like to be when you grow up?" you might prompt a concrete response, such as "A teacher." Once the final stage of cognitive development is attained, however,

In a well-known experiment, Jean Piaget demonstrated that children over the age of seven entered the concrete operational stage of development as they came to recognize that the quantity of liquid remained the same when poured from a wide beaker into a tall one.

the child is capable of responding abstractly, "I would like a job that is exciting." At this point, the child has acquired the marvelous human quality of imagination, which frees us from the immediate bounds of our lives. Children capable of formal operations often display a keen interest in imaginative literature like science fiction (Skolnick, 1986). They also are able to comprehend metaphors. Hearing the phrase "A penny for your thoughts" might lead a younger child to think of money, but the older child will recognize a gentle invitation to intimacy.

***Critical evaluation.*** If Freud envisioned humanity torn by the opposing forces of biology and society, Piaget believed the human mind to be active and creative, so that children soon learn to shape their own social world, an achievement that is well documented by other research (Corsaro & Rizzo, 1988). His contribution to understanding socialization lies in showing that this capacity unfolds gradually as the result of biological maturation and growing social experience.

In global perspective, there is some question as to whether people in every culture progress through Piaget's stages, and do so in the same time frame. For instance, living in a society that changes very slowly is likely to inhibit the ability to imagine the world being very different. In addition, Carol Gilligan (1982) has suggested that we have yet to examine adequately how gender affects the process of social development. She claims that boys and girls take a somewhat different approach to moral reasoning, with boys embracing abstract standards of right and wrong while girls morally evaluate events according to how they affect others. Finally, among both women and men, as many as 30 percent of American thirty-year-olds appear not to reach the formal operational stage at all (Kohlberg & Gilligan, 1971). This finding again underscores the importance of social experience in the development of personality. Regardless of biological maturity, people who are not exposed to highly creative and imaginative thinking are less likely to develop this capacity in themselves.

## George Herbert Mead: The Social Self[1]

What exactly is social experience? How does it enhance our humanity? These fundamental questions guided the work of George Herbert Mead, who is introduced in

---

[1] This section reflects suggestions by Howard Sacks of Kenyon College.

# George Herbert Mead (1863–1931)

Few people were surprised that George Herbert Mead became a college professor. He was born to a Massachusetts family with a strong intellectual tradition, and both his parents were academics. His mother served for ten years as president of Mount Holyoke College, and his father was both a preacher and teacher at a number of colleges.

But Mead also had a hand in shaping his own life, and in some unexpected ways. Early on, he rebelled against the strongly religious atmosphere of his home and community. After completing college, he traveled around the Pacific Northwest, surveying for the railroad and reading as much as he could. Restless about his future, he gradually settled on the idea of studying philosophy, which he did at Harvard and abroad.

Mead took a teaching position at the new University of Chicago. But his outlook still veered far from the conventional. For one thing, he rarely published, an activity expected of many academics. Mead's fame spread after his death when colleagues and former students published a collection of his lecture notes. For another, Mead drew together ideas from a wide range of disciplines to generate

new and fascinating insights that helped launch the new field of social psychology. Finally, never content with life as it was, Mead was an active reformer, often championing controversial causes. His firm belief in the human capacity for change gave him confidence that society could overcome its problems. In addition to teaching, then, Mead labored to improve the lives of the city's disadvantaged.

George Herbert Mead envisioned both an individual life and the course of an entire society as unpredictable and ongoing. His own life exemplifies the themes of his work: the power of society to shape individuals and the power of people to shape society.

SOURCES: Based, in part, on Coser (1977) and Schellenberg (1978).

---

the box. Among sociologists, Mead is widely regarded as having made the greatest contribution to explaining the process of socialization.

Mead's approach (1962; orig. 1934) has often been described as *social behaviorism*, suggesting a connection to the thinking of psychologist John B. Watson, described earlier. Mead agreed with Watson that environment influences human behavior, but he saw a basic error in Watson's approach. By focusing on behavior itself, Mead reasoned, Watson ignored mental processes—the key to our humanity—and treated the behavior of humans and other animals as essentially the same. Mead conceded to Watson the difficulty of studying the human mind, but he pressed ahead, certain that the key to social experience lay not in how humans act but in how we think.

## The Self

Mead's central concept is the **self**, *a dimension of personality composed of an individual's self-conception*. Mead's genius lay in seeing that the self is inseparable from society, a connection explained in a series of steps.

First, Mead asserted, *the self emerges from social experience*. The self is not biological, it is not the same as any part of the body, and it does not exist at birth. Mead rejected the notion that personality is guided by biological drives (as asserted by Freud) or biological maturation (as Piaget claimed). For Mead, the self simply develops through social experience and *only* through social experience. In the absence of social interaction, as we see from the cases of isolated children, the body may grow but no self will emerge.

George Herbert Mead wrote: "No hard-and-fast line can be drawn between our own selves and the selves of others." The impressionist art of French painter Georges Seurat (*Untitled*, 1883) conveys this idea. The painting suggests that, although we tend to think of ourselves as distinct from others, there are no hard boundaries between the personalities of people in regular interaction.

*(Georges-Pierre Seurat, L'Echo drawing. Yale University Art Gallery. Bequest of Edith M. K. Wetmore.)*

Second, Mead explained, *social experience is based on the exchange of symbols.* By using symbols, people create meaning in their interaction. People use words, a wave of the hand, and a smile symbolically. Thus, while Mead agreed with Watson that human behavior can be shaped by manipulating rewards and punishments, he maintained that this ignores distinctively human characteristics in our behavior. We can train a dog, after all, to respond to a command, but the dog attaches no meaning to its action. Human beings, by contrast, search for meanings as we infer intention as well as observe action. In short, a dog responds to *what you do*; a human responds to *what you have in mind* as you do it.

Return to our friendly dog for a moment. Using reward and punishment, you can train a dog to walk to the porch and return with an umbrella. But the dog grasps no meaning in the act, no intention behind the command. Thus, if the dog cannot find the umbrella, it is incapable of the *human* response: to look for a raincoat instead. Human beings do this because we understand actions in terms of meanings.

The third step in Mead's analysis is the assertion that *understanding someone's intentions requires imagining the situation from that person's point of view.* Our symbolic capacity empowers us to imaginatively place ourselves in another person's shoes, and to see ourselves as that person does. Intentional social action depends on being able to envision how others will respond to us even before we act. Even the simplest act of tossing a ball requires stepping outside of ourselves to imagine how another will respond to our throw. Social interaction, then, involves seeing ourselves as others see us— a process that Mead termed *"taking the role of the other."*

### The Looking-Glass Self

How we think about ourselves is inseparable from how others think of us. Charles Horton Cooley (1864–1929), one of Mead's colleagues, suggested that others represent a mirror or looking glass in which we perceive ourselves as they see us. Cooley (1964; orig. 1902) used the phrase **looking-glass self** to capture *the idea that the self is based on how others respond to us.* Whether we think of ourselves as clever or clumsy, worthy or worthless, handsome or homely, depends in large measure on what we think others think of us.

### The I and the Me

The notion that "the self thinks about itself" suggests an important dualism. First, *the self is subject,* a point brought home as humans initiate social action. Mead claimed humans are innately active and spontaneous. For simplicity, he dubbed this subjective element of the self the *I* (the subjective form of the first-person pronoun). Second, *the self is object,* that is, how we imagine ourselves from the perspective of someone else. Mead called this objective element of the self the *me* (the objective form of the first-person pronoun). Social experience begins as a person initiates action (the I-phase of the self) and then guides the action (the me-phase of the self) by reflectively taking the role of the other. All social experience involves a continuous interplay of the I and the me: our actions are spontaneous yet guided by how others respond to us.

Mead stressed that thinking, too, has a social dimension. Our thoughts are partly creative (representing the I), but in thought we also become objects to ourselves (representing the me), as we imagine how others would respond to our ideas.

## Development of the Self

According to Mead, the self develops by gaining sophistication in taking the role of the other. Like Freud and Piaget, Mead regarded early childhood as crucial to this process. However, he did not think the development of the self was rigidly linked to age. Both Freud and Piaget emphasized the role of biology in personality development, but Mead consistently minimized the importance of biological forces. Thus Mead thought that the self emerged over time due simply to more and more social experience.

Mead declared that infants with limited social experience respond to others only in terms of *imitation*. They mimic behavior but do not understand underlying intentions. Without symbolic interaction, Mead concluded, no self exists.

As children learn to use language and other symbols, the self becomes evident in the form of *play*. Children begin to experience the complex behavior they observe around them by role playing. At first, they model themselves on significant people—such as parents—sometimes called *significant others*. Playing "Mommy and Daddy," for example, helps children imagine the world from their parents' point of view.

Gradually, children learn to take the roles of several others simultaneously. In other words, the developing self is able to initiate distinctive actions in response to various others. This is the key to moving from simple play involving one role to more complex *games* involving many roles at once. Doing so, a person's self becomes more complex, based now on numerous "looking-glasses." The box applies Mead's analysis of play and games to several familiar activities.

A final step in the development of the self involves acquiring the ability to see ourselves as society in general does. Figure 5–1 on page 134 shows how this constitutes an extension of play and games. Even in a game, the others involved are limited. Going a step further, we eventually learn to take the role of virtually anyone in any situation. This depends on recognizing that people throughout society share cultural norms and values. As they incorporate general cultural patterns into the self, children begin to respond to themselves as they imagine anyone might. Mead used the term **generalized other** to refer to *widespread cultural norms and values we use as a reference in evaluating ourselves*.

## SOCIOLOGY OF EVERYDAY LIFE

# Play and Games: Taking the Roles of Others

Playing at being mother, father, doctor, or athlete is the first way in which a child takes the role of another. Often two or more children play together, perhaps as doctor and patient. Whatever else they may learn, they begin the vital human process of seeing themselves as others do.

Games take place in a single setting in which a person takes the role of many others. An avid baseball fan, Mead often turned to his favorite sport to illustrate his ideas. Place yourself, then, in the role of shortstop in a baseball game. With one out and a runner on first base, the batter hits a sizzling ground ball to you, setting up the classic double-play. In order to respond, you have to take the role of several players at once. The fielder at first base normally does not expect you to throw the ball there; but the fielder at second base is hustling toward the bag awaiting your throw, and as quickly as possible. But the final choice of where to throw depends on viewing this process through the eyes of yet another person, the runner moving toward second base. If this player will beat the throw, the ball goes to first instead. But even that choice is contingent on a fourth person—the batter who is closing in on first base.

Children of four or five usually have had enough social experience to play "catch" with one other person. But because baseball requires the ability to simultaneously take the role of many others, young children must gain further social experience before they are capable of complex games.

Finally, the socialization process does not end with the emergence of the self. Quite the contrary: Mead claimed that socialization continues as long as we have social experience. Furthermore, changing social circumstances can reshape who we are. The self may change, for example, if someone becomes rich, divorced, or disabled. But we are not pawns, simply moved by others. Mead steadfastly maintained that social experience is based on interaction, so that society shapes us, but we also act back on society. In short, as active and creative beings, we play a large part in our own socialization.

*Critical evaluation.* George Herbert Mead's contribution to the understanding of socialization lies in exploring social experience itself. He succeeded in showing how symbolic interaction underlies the self as well as society.

Mead's view is sometimes criticized for being radically social—meaning that it recognizes no biological element in the emergence of the self. In this, he stands apart from Freud (who identified general drives within the human organism) and Piaget (whose stages of development are tied to biological maturation).

Mead's concepts of the I and the me are often confused with Freud's concepts of the id and the superego. One difference is that Freud rooted the id in the biological organism, while Mead rejected any link between the self and biology (although he never specified the origin of the I). Freud's concept of the superego and Mead's concept of the me both reflect the power of society to shape personality. But for Freud, superego and id are locked in continual combat. Mead, however, understood the I and the me as working closely and cooperatively together (Meltzer, 1978).

# Agents of Socialization

We are affected in at least some small way by every social experience we have. In modern industrial societies, however, several agents of socialization have pronounced importance.

## The Family

The family is the most important agent of socialization. As we have seen, infants are dependent on others to meet their needs, and this responsibility almost always falls on parents and other family members. Typically, the family stands as a child's entire social world, at least until the onset of schooling, and it remains central to social experiences throughout the life course (Riley, Foner, & Waring, 1988). The family also plays a crucial part in transmitting culture from one generation to the next. Through countless family activities, children are taught to reproduce social patterns familiar to adults.

Family-based socialization is not all intentional. Children learn continuously from the kind of environment that adults create. Whether children learn to think of themselves as strong or weak, smart or stupid, loved or simply tolerated, and whether they believe the world to be trustworthy or dangerous, largely stem from this early environment.

Although parents do not solely determine the course of their children's development, many attitudes, interests, goals, beliefs, and prejudices are acquired in the family. Also, from infancy boys and girls receive both conscious and unconscious guidance from family members in how to be "masculine" and "feminine" (Tavris & Wade, 1984; Witkin-Lanoil, 1984). In sum, much

**Figure 5–1**   Building on Social Experience
George Herbert Mead described the development of self as the process of gaining social experience. This is largely a matter of taking the role of the other with increasing sophistication.

of what we consider to be innate in ourselves actually comes from patterns of socialization learned in the family.

Parenting styles vary from home to home, but research points to the importance of *attention*, paid by parents to children, in the social development of children. Physical contact, verbal stimulation, and responsiveness from parents have all been shown to foster intellectual growth (Belsky, Lerner, & Spanier, 1984).

Another crucial function of the family is providing children with a social position. In other words, parents not only bring children into the physical world, they also place them in society in terms of social class, religion, race, and ethnicity. In time, all these elements of social identity become part of a child's self-concept. Of course, this social placement may change in at least some respects, but it affects us throughout our lives.

Investigating the importance of social class to socialization, Melvin Kohn (1977) interviewed working-class and middle-class parents in the United States. He found that working-class parents tend to stress behavioral conformity in rearing their children. Middle-class parents, however, typically tolerate a wider range of behavior and show greater concern for the intentions and motivations that underlie their children's actions. Kohn explained this difference in terms of the education and occupations common to parents in each category. Working-class parents usually lack higher education and often have jobs in which they are closely supervised and expected to do as they are told. This leads them to foster similar obedience and conformity in their children. By contrast, with more schooling, middle-class parents typically have jobs that provide greater autonomy and encourage the use of imagination. These parents are therefore likely to inspire the same qualities in their children. Such differences in socialization have long-term effects on children's ambitions, partly explaining why middle-class children are more likely than working-class children to go to college themselves and are generally more confident of success in college and in later careers (Wilson, 1959; Ballantine, 1989). In many ways, then, parents teach children to follow in their footsteps, and to adapt to the constraints or privileges of their inherited social positions.

## Schooling

Schooling introduces children to new people and experiences. In school, children learn to interact with others who are initially strangers and who may have social backgrounds that differ from their own. As children consider social diversity, they are also likely to become self-conscious of their own social identities and respond to others accordingly. For example, one study of kindergarten children documented the tendency for blacks and whites to form same-race play groups (Finkelstein & Haskins, 1983). Similarly, boys and girls tend to form distinct play groups, grasping more of the importance that our culture attaches to sex (Lever, 1978).

Formally, schooling teaches children a wide range of knowledge and skills. The early grades are devoted to basic abilities like reading, writing, and arithmetic. Secondary schools and colleges subsequently convey more specialized material needed to perform various occupational roles. But what children learn in school goes far beyond the official curriculum. What is often called the *hidden curriculum* teaches them important cultural values. Activities such as spelling bees and sports encourage children to be competitive and to value success. Children also receive countless subtle messages that their society's way of life is morally good.

Children's value in the family is based on personal relationships: they are loved because of *who they are*. Thus school presents a new experience for children, with evaluations of skills like reading based on impersonal, standardized tests. Here, the emphasis shifts from who they are to *how they perform*. As such evaluations define personal abilities, they greatly affect how children come to view themselves. At the same time, the confidence or anxiety that children develop at home can have a significant effect on how well they perform in school (Belsky, Lerner, & Spanier, 1984). Finally, the school gives most children their first experience with rigid formality. The school day is organized according to a strict time schedule, subjecting children to impersonal regimentation and fostering traits such as punctuality that will be expected by many large organizations later in life.

Finally, schools further socialize children into culturally approved sex roles. As Raphaela Best (1983) points out, instructional activities for boys and girls often differ, so that boys engage in more physical activities and spend more time outdoors, while girls tend to be more sedentary, sometimes even helping the teacher with various housekeeping chores. Such gender distinctions continue through the college years. College women encounter pressure to select majors in the arts, humanities, or social sciences, while men are steered toward the physical sciences. Further, the informal campus culture provides more support for the academic achievement of men,

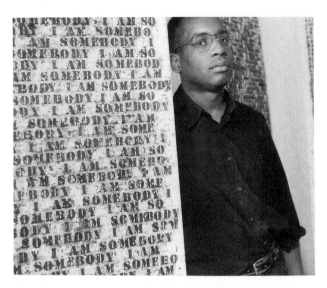

A young person of color in a predominantly white society often finds the task of forging a positive self-image to be difficult. Amid negative racial messages from their environment, many young people grapple with the notion that *they are important*. The art *I Am Somebody* expresses this struggle in the life of the artist, Glen Ligon.

while making romantic life a central concern of women (Holland & Eisenhart, 1990).

Overall, schooling plays a vital part in guiding child development. Schools help children adjust to living in a large, impersonal world and also teach them the knowledge and skills necessary to successfully perform adult roles. All this is done without disturbing larger patterns of social inequality. As Chapter 16 ("Education") explains, schooling perpetuates social inequality by linking the extent and type of education that children receive to gender and social class.

## Peer Groups

By the start of school, children have discovered another new setting for social activity in the **peer group**, *a social group whose members have interests, social position, and age in common.* A young child's peer group generally consists of neighborhood playmates; later, peer groups are composed of friends from school or other activities.

The peer group differs from the family and the school because it affords an escape from the direct supervision of adults. Of course, this constitutes much of the attraction of peer groups in the first place. With considerable independence, peer groups offer individuals valuable experience in forging social relationships on their own and developing a sense of themselves apart from their families. Peer groups also provide the opportunity to discuss interests that may not be shared by adults (such as styles of dress and popular music) as well as topics young people may wish to avoid in the presence of parents and teachers (such as drugs and sex).

The ever-present possibility of activity not condoned by adults is, no doubt, the reason parents have long expressed concern about who their children's friends are. Especially in a society that is changing rapidly, peer groups often rival parents in influence. This is simply because the interests and attitudes of parents and children may differ considerably—as suggested by the familiar phrase "the generation gap." The importance of peer groups typically peaks during adolescence, when young people begin to break away from their families and think of themselves as responsible adults. It is during this stage of life that individuals typically draw the greatest identity from peer groups, and they are often anxious in their efforts to conform. The reward of belonging to a peer group eases some of the uneasiness provoked by breaking away from the family.

The conflict between parents and peers may be more apparent than real, however, for even during adolescence children remain strongly influenced by their families. While the peer group may guide such short-term concerns as style of dress and musical taste, parents retain more sway over the long-term aspirations of their children. For example, one study found that parents had more influence than even best friends on young people's educational aspirations (Davies & Kandel, 1981).

Finally, a neighborhood or school forms a social mosaic of many peer groups. As we will see in Chapter 7 ("Groups and Organizations"), members tend to perceive their own peer group in positive terms while discrediting others. Therefore, *many* peer groups are important to the socialization process as individuals conform to their own groups while forming an identity in opposition to others. In some cases, too, people are strongly influenced by peer groups they would like to join. For example, upon entering a new school, a young man with a desire to excel at basketball may wish to become part of the basketball players' social crowd. He is likely to adopt what he sees as the social patterns of this group in the hope of eventual acceptance. This represents what sociologists call **anticipatory socialization,** *the process* of social learning directed toward gaining a desired position. Later in life, jobs are likely to prompt further anticipatory socialization. For instance, a young lawyer who hopes to eventually become a partner in her law firm may conform to the attitudes and behavior of other partners to encourage her inclusion into this rarefied group.

## The Mass Media

The **mass media** are *impersonal communications directed to a vast audience.* The term "media" is derived from Latin meaning "middle," so that media function to connect people. In large industrial societies, media take on a mass scale so that television, radio, newspapers, and magazines link tens of millions of people. In the United States, the mass media have an enormous impact on our attitudes and behavior. For this reason, we need to critically consider the content of the media. Often media sources claim to present world events in a factual manner. Some sociologists, however, argue that the media tend to support the *status quo,* while portraying people who challenge the system in negative terms (Gans, 1980; Parenti, 1986).

Introduced in 1939, television rapidly became part of the U.S. scene after 1950. At that time, only about 9 percent of all households had one or more television sets. By 1990, this proportion had soared to 98 percent (while only 93 percent had telephones). Video cassette recorders (VCRs), the fastest-growing appliance in history, are already found in 63 percent of homes, up from 1 percent in 1980. One-fourth of all households also have video-game equipment (U.S. Bureau of the Census, 1991). Clearly, "the tube" now has profound significance for socialization.

The latest statistics show that the average household in the United States has a television turned on for seven hours a day (U.S. Bureau of the Census, 1990). Before most children learn to read, watching television has become a regular routine, and young girls and boys actually spend more hours in front of a television than they do in school (Anderson & Lorch, 1983; Singer, 1983). Indeed, television may very well consume more of children's time than interacting with parents. Overall, television is now the most powerful mass medium (Singer & Singer, 1983).

There is almost one television set for every person in the United States, but television is far from common in many other countries. Global Map 5–1 on page 138 provides a look at where in the world this medium is found.

Television does more than provide entertainment; it programs many of our attitudes and beliefs. For example, television has traditionally portrayed men and women according to cultural stereotypes, showing, for instance, men in positions of power and women as mothers or subordinates (Cantor & Pingree, 1983; Ang, 1985). As Chapter 13 ("Sex and Gender") describes in detail, advertising in the mass media contributes to gender stereotyping (Courtney & Whipple, 1983). Similarly, television shows have long presented affluent people in favorable terms, while suggesting that less affluent people (Archie Bunker is the classic example) are ignorant and wrongheaded (Gans, 1980). In addition, although racial and ethnic minorities tend to watch more television than others, they have until recently been all but absent from programming. The successful 1950s comedy *I Love Lucy,* for example, was initially shunned by major television producers because it featured Desi Arnaz—a Hispanic— in a starring role. Even today, television often portrays minorities in ways that are attractive and non-threatening to white middle-class people (as in the affluent African-American family on *The Cosby Show*). The number of people of African and Hispanic descent making appearances in all the mass media has increased mainly because

Joe Camel, the debonair dromedary, has sent the sales of Camel cigarettes soaring. Since this ad campaign began, the proportion of Camels sold to minors, in violation of the law, has risen to one-fourth. The increase attests to the marketing power of the mass media, but also raises ethical questions about how the public should regulate this power.

**Global Map 5–1** Television Ownership in Global Perspective

The mass media have the greatest influence in industrialized societies like the United States and Canada. In less technologically complex societies, people are more likely to communicate in the traditional manner, through face-to-face talk. This pattern is evident in the number of television sets per thousand people: in the United States there is roughly one set for every woman, man, and child in the country.

advertisers recognize the marketing advantages of appealing to these large segments of our society (Wilson & Gutierrez, 1985). The box offers a critical look at how mass media advertising has traditionally portrayed minorities in terms of negative stereotypes.

One dimension of television in which significant change has taken place is news reporting. Recognition of social diversity today is now far greater than it was

even a decade ago. In large measure, this stems from deliberate personnel policies. Women now fill one-third of all television reporting jobs, almost double the proportion found a generation ago. In addition, 8 percent of television reporters are African Americans, an increase from less than 1 percent in 1970 (Hess, 1991).

Still, television continues to influence us through what it ignores, such as the lives of the poor and the large homosexual minority in the United States. In this way, television sends the message that these categories of people do not matter or—even more incorrectly—that they do not exist at all.

Television has unquestionably enriched the United States in many respects, bringing into our homes a wide range of entertaining and educational programming. Furthermore, this "window on the world" has increased our awareness of diverse cultures and provided a means of addressing current public issues. At the same time, the power of television has made this medium controversial, and especially to the extent that it supports traditional stereotypes.

## Public Opinion

**Public opinion** is defined as *the attitudes of people throughout a society about one or more controversial issues*. Although family and peer groups have the greatest impact on socialization, our attitudes and behavior are also influenced by what we perceive to be the opinions of other members of our society. As discussed in Chapter 6 ("Social Interaction in Everyday Life"), people often conform to the attitudes of others—even complete strangers—to avoid being singled out as different. The mass media track the latest trends, and there is little doubt that both adults and children mimic these patterns. For

---

**SOCIAL DIVERSITY**

# When Advertising Offends: Another Look at Aunt Jemima

Commercial advertisers want to sell products. However, some ad campaigns offend rather than persuade their audience by portraying particular categories of people in inaccurate and unfair ways.

A century ago, the vast majority of consumers in the United States were white, and many were uneasy with the growing racial and cultural diversity of American society. Businesses commonly exploited this discomfort by depicting various categories of people in ways that were clearly condescending. In 1889, for example, a pancake mix first appeared featuring a servant mammy named "Aunt Jemima." Although recently modified, this logo is widely seen in the mass media, largely because the product continues to have a commanding share of the market. Likewise, the hot cereal "Cream of Wheat" is still symbolized by the black chef Rastus, and "Uncle Ben" is familiar to millions of people as a brand name for rice. To many Americans, use of such caricatures—which, after all, originally depicted the black slaves of white people—is racially insensitive at best.

Changes in advertising have occurred in recent decades in all the mass media. The stereotypical Frito Bandito, long familiar to older television viewers, was abandoned in 1971 by Frito-Lay (a company, ironically, whose first product was a corn chip invented by a Hispanic in San Antonio). The characteriza-tion of Hispanics as bandits or outlaws, embodied in the bumbling cartoon figure of Frito Bandito, discredited an entire segment of the population. A host of other such images has also disappeared as businesses in this country confront a new reality: the growing voice and financial power of minorities, who represent a market worth half a trillion dollars a year. Taken together, Americans of African, Hispanic, and Asian descent comprise 20 percent of the population, and will constitute a majority of the U.S. population by the middle of the next century.

Many of today's minorities are immigrants, people who rely heavily on television to learn about their new society. This makes them especially susceptible to advertising. For reasons of fairness, as well as good business sense, products should not be marketed at the expense of human dignity.

SOURCE: Based on Westerman (1989).

example, the clothing industry's success in marketing new fashions several times a year illustrates people's tendency to adopt, within their budgets, what the trend makers define as desirable.

Public opinion sometimes exaggerates the degree of conformity in the United States. We have all heard "people say" that homosexuals are "weird," that noncompetitive men "lack character," and that women who are assertive are "pushy." But it is worth remembering that our culture is highly diverse, and no one ever conforms completely to so-called dominant values and norms. Even people who publicly conform to these notions are apt to experience private anxiety about their failure to live up to unrealistic cultural expectations.

Beyond the agents of socialization we have described, other spheres of life play a part in social learning as well. For most people, these include religious organizations, the workplace, the military, and social clubs. As a result, socialization inevitably involves inconsistencies as we learn different information from various kinds of social experiences. In the end, socialization is not a simple learning process; it is a complex balancing act in which we encounter a wide range of ideas as we try to forge our own distinctive personalities and world views.

# Socialization and the Life Course

Although discussions of socialization focus on childhood, this process continues throughout our lives. Members of all societies organize social experience according to age to produce distinctive stages of the life course; in industrial nations, these are commonly understood to include childhood, adolescence, adulthood, and, as a final phase of adulthood, old age. Socialization has characteristic traits during each stage.

## Childhood

Charles Dickens's classic novel *Oliver Twist* is set in London early in the nineteenth century, when the Industrial Revolution was bringing sweeping changes to English society. Oliver's mother died in childbirth and, barely surviving himself, he began life as an indigent orphan, "buffeted through the world—despised by all, and pitied by none" (Dickens, 1886:36; orig. 1837–1839).

Knowing little pleasure in his early years, Oliver Twist began a life of toil and drudgery in a workhouse, laboring long hours to pay for filthy shelter and meager food.

In our present culture, *childhood*—roughly the first twelve years of life—is a time of freedom from the burdens of the adult world. But during the Middle Ages in Europe—and, as Oliver Twist testifies, long afterward—children's lives mirrored those of adults. Historian Philippe Ariès (1965) explains that medieval Europeans did not share our conception of childhood; as soon as children were able to survive without constant care, they took their place in the world as adults. This meant that poor children worked long hours, just as most adults did. Although "child labor" is now scorned in the United States, this pattern persists in preindustrial societies throughout Latin America, Africa, and Asia. Global Map 5–2 shows that work is commonplace for children in poor societies of the world.

The notion of young children working long hours may be startling because our common sense suggests that youngsters are very different from adults—inexperienced in the ways of the world and biologically immature. But much of this difference is rooted in society and culture. Because technologically complex societies are more affluent, everyone does not need to work. In addition, such societies extend childhood to allow time for learning many complex skills required for adult activities. These facts encourage us to define children and adults in contrasting ways, with "irresponsible" children looked after by "responsible" adults (Benedict, 1938). In global perspective, however, this pattern is far from an inevitable consequence of biological maturation. Many characteristics of childhood—and even whether it exists at all—are highly variable among the world's cultures. The box on page 142 provides an example.

Recently, sociologists and psychologists have found evidence that childhood is changing yet again, this time becoming shorter. Especially among affluent families, children are subjected to mounting pressures to dress, speak, and act like adults (Elkind, 1981; Winn, 1983). Evidence of what is called the "hurried child" pattern includes ten-year-old boys in designer jeans, and girls of the same age adorned with jewelry, makeup, and perfume. The mass media now interject into a child's world sexuality, violence, and a host of other issues that were considered only a generation ago to be strictly adult topics. Young children may routinely watch films that graphically depict violence and listen to rock music that contains sexually explicit lyrics. Pressure to grow up quickly is also exerted in the home because greater num-

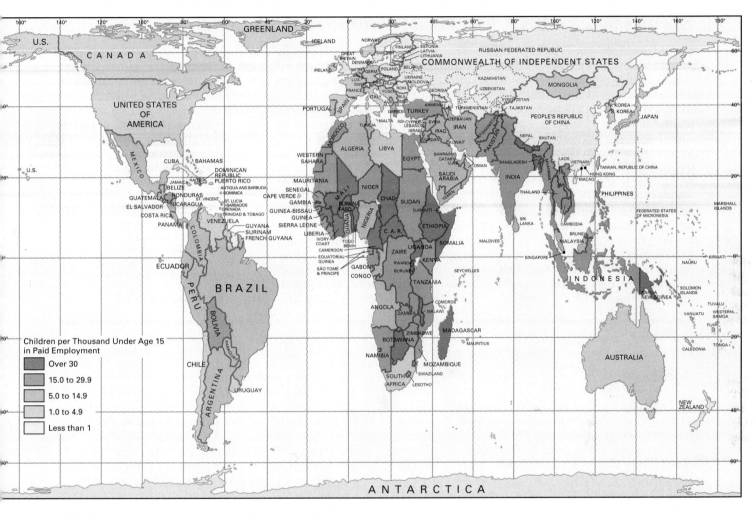

**Global Map 5–2** Child Labor in Global Perspective

Industrialization has the effect of prolonging childhood and discouraging children from engaging in work and other activities deemed suitable only for adults. Thus child labor is relatively uncommon in the United States and other industrial societies. In less industrialized nations of the world, however, children form a vital economic asset and they typically begin working as soon as they are able.

bers of mothers work, requiring children to fend more for themselves. Furthermore, today's parents are often delighted if their children can read, spell, or discuss world events before their peers can, believing that this indicates greater intelligence. Schools also encourage rapid maturation by emphasizing achievement, which

reflects positively on both parents and teachers. In the view of child psychologist David Elkind (1981), the "hurried child" pattern is a detrimental change in our society's conception of childhood because children are confronting issues that they lack the experience to understand, let alone successfully resolve.

# Sex among Children? The Social Construction of Childhood

Should children be sexual? Most people in the United States find sexual activity among children to be disturbing and unnatural. Anthropologist Ruth Benedict explains that the Zuni—a Native American society of New Mexico—also discourage childhood sexuality, but not for the same reason. According to Zuni culture, sex is simply a means of reproduction, so the activity has little significance before reaching puberty, when reproduction is possible. Among the Melanesian cultures of Southeast New Guinea, Benedict found easy acceptance of sexual activity among children. Rather than re-

acting with alarm as we commonly would, adults in this society typically laugh it off, believing that no harm can result.

Certainly, the reproductive immaturity of children is a biological reality (although puberty now occurs earlier in life due to social changes). But the significance of being young extends far beyond biology to culture.

How do comparisons of this kind help us to better understand our own way of life? Ruth Benedict suggests that, unlike many other cultures, our culture defines childhood and adulthood *in opposition*. Thus socialization cannot be

a simple matter of accumulating information as we grow. On the contrary, to learn to be adults in the United States, we must *unlearn* many of the proscriptions imposed in childhood. Perhaps, observed Benedict, this may offer some insight into the widespread sexual anxieties among adults in our culture:

> The adult in our culture has often failed to unlearn the wickedness or the dangerousness of sex, a lesson that was impressed upon [the child] strongly during [the] most formative years. (1938:165)

SOURCE: Benedict (1938).

## Adolescence

As childhood emerged as a distinct stage of life in industrial societies, adolescence came into focus as a buffer stage between childhood and adulthood, corresponding roughly to the teenage years. This stage of life offers time to learn various specialized skills required for adult life.

We generally associate adolescence with emotional and social turmoil; young people experience conflict with their parents and struggle to develop their own, separate identities. Since adolescence generally occurs at the same time as the onset of puberty, we often attribute much of the social and emotional turmoil of this stage of life to physiological changes. However, thinking sociologically, the instability of adolescence also reflects inconsistencies in socialization. For example, adults expect adolescents to be increasingly self-reliant and responsible for themselves, yet adults view teenagers as unequipped for the occupations that would give them financial independence. The adult world also gives adolescents mixed messages about sexuality; sexual activity is often encouraged by the mass media, while parents urge restraint. Consider, too, that an eighteen-year-old male may face

the adult responsibility of going to war, while simultaneously being denied the right to drink alcohol.

Definitions of adolescence also evolve and change. In 1971, the Twenty-sixth Amendment to the United States Constitution gave eighteen-year-olds of both sexes the right to vote. But by 1990, all the states had raised the drinking age to twenty-one. Without minimizing the role of biological forces in adolescence, this is a time of social contradictions when people are no longer children but not yet adults.

As is true of all stages of life, the experience of adolescence varies according to social background. Young people from working-class families often move directly into the adult world of work and parenthood after completing high school. Those from wealthier families, however, have the resources to attend college and perhaps graduate school, which may extend adolescence into the later twenties and even the thirties (Skolnick, 1992). Poverty, too, can extend adolescence. Especially in the inner cities, many young minorities cannot attain full adult standing because jobs are not available or accessible.

Cross-cultural research offers further evidence that adolescence is not simply a matter of biological maturation. When anthropologist Margaret Mead studied the culture of the Samoan Islands in the 1920s, she found that boys and girls were simply defined as adults when they reached their mid-teens. In the Samoan culture, unlike our own, childhood and adulthood did not differ radically from each other, so the transition between the two stages of life was not dramatic (M. Mead, 1961; orig. 1928).

## Adulthood

At the age of thirty-five, Eleanor Roosevelt, one of our nation's most widely admired women, wrote in her diary: "I do not think I have ever felt so strangely as in the past year . . . all my self confidence is gone and I am on the edge, though I never was better physically I feel sure" (cited in Sheehy, 1976:260). What explains Eleanor Roosevelt's self-doubt? Perhaps she was troubled by the attention her husband was paying to another, younger woman; perhaps as she looked into the future, she could not see what challenges or accomplishments might bring further satisfaction to her life. But as she struggled with what we might today call a "midlife crisis," there was much that she could not foresee. Her husband, Franklin Delano Roosevelt, was shortly to become disabled by poliomyelitis, although his rising political career would lead ultimately to thirteen consecutive years as his country's president. And Eleanor herself would become perhaps the most active and influential of all First Ladies. After her husband's death, she would remain outspoken and serve as a delegate to the United Nations.

Eleanor Roosevelt's life illustrates two major characteristics of the stage of life we call *adulthood*, which our culture defines as beginning in the twenties. First, adulthood is the period during which most of life's accomplishments typically occur. In other words, having been socialized into society's conception of adulthood, people embark on careers and raise families of their own. Second, especially in later adulthood, people reflect on what they have accomplished, feeling great satisfaction or perhaps coming to the sobering realization that many of the idealistic dreams of their youth will never come true.

### Early Adulthood

Personalities are largely formed by the start of adulthood. Even so, a marked shift in an individual's life situation—brought on by dislocations such as unemployment, di-

vorce, or serious illness—may result in significant change to the self (Dannefer, 1984). Early adulthood—until about the age of forty—is generally a time of working toward many goals set earlier in life.

Young adults learn to manage for themselves a host of day-to-day responsibilities that had been handled by parents or others. Beginning a family, people draw on the experience of having lived in the family of their parents, although as children they may have perceived little of adult life. In addition, young adults typically try to master patterns of intimate living with another person who may have just as much to learn. Early adulthood also involves juggling conflicting priorities: parents, spouse, children, and work (Levinson et al., 1978). Women, especially, face up to the difficulty of "doing it all," since our culture confers on them primary responsibility for child rearing and household chores, even if they have demanding occupations outside the home (Hochschild, 1989). In short, women today are often caught between traditional femin*ine* ideals learned as children and the more contemporary femin*ist* ideals learned as adults (Sexton, 1980; cited in Giele, 1982:121).

### Middle Adulthood

Young adults usually cope optimistically with such tensions. But in middle adulthood—roughly the years between the ages of forty and sixty—people begin to sense that marked improvements in life circumstances are less likely. Greater reflection characterizes middle adulthood, as people assess their achievements in light of earlier expectations. They become more aware of the fragility of health, which is typically taken for granted by the young. Women who have already spent many years raising a family can find middle adulthood especially trying. Children grow up and require less attention, husbands become absorbed in their careers, leaving some women with spaces in their lives that are difficult to fill. Women who divorce during middle adulthood may experience serious financial problems (Weitzman, 1985). For all these reasons, many women mark middle adulthood by returning to school and beginning new careers. Neither education nor a career is easy after several decades of working primarily in the home. But, since 1970, women between twenty-five and forty-four years of age have been the fastest-growing segment of the U.S. labor force (U.S. Bureau of the Census, 1991).

The traditional conception of femininity also stresses the importance of physical attractiveness. Both older men and older women face the reality of physical decline, but our society's traditional socialization of women has made good looks crucial, so that wrinkles, weight gain, and loss of hair are more traumatic for women than for men. Men, of course, experience their own particular difficulties. Some confront limited achievement, knowing that their careers are unlikely to change for the better. Others, realizing that the price of career success has been neglect of family or personal health, harbor deep uncertainties about their self-worth even as they bask in the praise of others (Farrell & Rosenberg, 1981). Women, too, who devote themselves single-mindedly to careers in early adulthood, may experience regrets about what they have given up in pursuit of occupational success.

Eleanor Roosevelt's midlife crisis may well have involved some of the personal transitions we have described. But her story also illustrates that the greatest productivity and personal satisfaction may occur after the middle of life. Socialization in our youth-oriented culture has convinced many people that life ends at forty. As average life expectancy in the United States has increased, however, such limiting notions about growing older have begun to change. Major transformations may become less likely, but the potential for learning and new beginnings continues all the same.

## Old Age and Dying

*Old age* comprises the later years of adulthood and the final stage of life itself, beginning about the mid-sixties. Here again, societies attach different meanings to a particular time of life. Among preindustrial people, advancing age typically affords great influence and respect. As noted in Chapter 14 ("Aging and the Elderly"), this stems from two main sources: in traditional societies, the elderly usually control land and other wealth, and in societies that change slowly, elders amass a lifetime of wisdom (Sheehan, 1976; Hareven, 1982).

In industrial societies, however, younger people typically work apart from the family, lessening the influence of the elderly. Also, rapid change promotes a definition of what is older as marginal or even obsolete. To younger people, the elderly are unaware of new trends and fashions, and their knowledge and experience often seem irrelevant. As we have already observed, the youth orientation in the United States tends to rate everyone by the standards of physical beauty, activities, and attitudes of the young.

No doubt, however, this youth orientation will

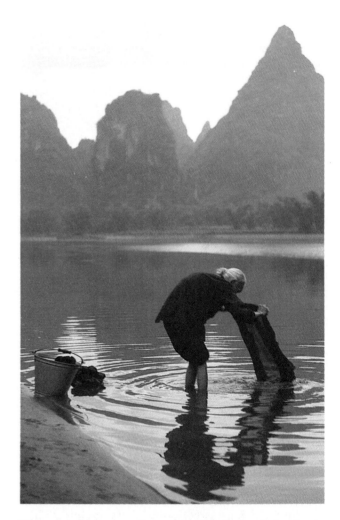

The sociological perspective suggests that, far from being simple expressions of our biology, stages of the life course are shaped by society. In industrial societies, elderly people are deemed ready for "retirement," which often means finishing their lives with little meaningful activity. In preindustrial societies, including the People's Republic of China, older people are a vital resource. Thus their productive work continues as long as they are able.

diminish as the proportion of older people steadily increases. The percentage of those in the United States over the age of sixty-five has almost tripled since the beginning of this century, so that today more men and women are elderly than in their teens. Moreover, life expectancy is still increasing, so more and more individuals will live well past the age of sixty-five. Looking to the next century, the Census Bureau (1988) predicts that the fastest-growing segment of our population will be those over eighty-five. It is projected that there will be almost six times as many people over that age a century from now as there are today.

At present, the final phase of socialization differs in an important way from learning earlier in life. For the young, advancing age typically means entering new roles and assuming new responsibilities. Old age, however, involves the opposite process: leaving roles that have long infused life with social identity and meaningful activity. Retirement is one clear example. Although retirement sometimes fits the common image of being a period of restful activity, it often means the loss of familiar routines, and sometimes outright boredom. Like any life transition, retirement demands that a person learn new and different ways of living while simultaneously *un*learning patterns and routines that guided earlier stages in life. A comparable transition is required of the nonworking wife or husband who must change routines to accommodate a spouse now spending more time at home.

Today most people assume that death occurs in old age. Historically, however, death was caused by disease or accident during any stage of life, because living standards were lower and medical technology was primitive. By contrast, in industrial societies, although death can still occur at any time (especially among the poor), almost 85 percent of people in the United States die after the age of fifty-five (U.S. Bureau of the Census, 1991). More and more men and women reaching old age can look forward to decades of life, but patterns of socialization in this stage of the life course cannot be separated from the realization of impending death.

After observing many dying people, Elisabeth Kübler-Ross (1969) described death as an orderly transition involving five distinct stages. Because our culture tends to ignore the reality of death, a person's first reaction to the prospect of dying is usually *denial* and avoiding contact with anything that might suggest the inevitability of death. The second stage is *anger*: here the person has begun to accept the idea of dying but views it as a gross injustice. In the third stage, anger gives way to *negotiation*, the attitude that death may not be inevitable and that a bargain might be struck with God to allow life to continue. The fourth stage, *resignation*, is often accompanied by psychological depression. Finally, adjustment to death is completed in the fifth stage, *acceptance*. At this point, rather than being paralyzed by fear and anxiety, the person sets out to use constructively whatever time remains.

As the proportion of women and men in old age increases, we can expect our culture to become more comfortable with the idea of death. Today, for example, death is more widely discussed than it was earlier in this century, and many people view death as preferable to months or even years of suffering and social isolation in hospitals and rest homes. In addition, married couples are more likely to anticipate their own deaths in discussions and estate planning. This may ease somewhat the disorientation that usually accompanies the death of a spouse—a greater problem for women, who usually outlive their husbands.

This brief examination of the life course leads to two general conclusions. First and most important, although linked to the biological process of aging, the essential characteristics of each stage of life are socially constructed. For this reason, a stage of life may be experienced differently by people in other cultures. Second, each period of the life course presents characteristic problems and transitions that involve learning something new and, in many cases, unlearning what has become familiar.

Two additional points are worth noting. Just because social experience is organized according to age in every society, this in no way negates the effects of other social forces, such as social background, race, ethnicity, and gender. Thus, the general patterns we have described are all subject to further modification as they apply to various categories of people. Finally, people's typical life experiences vary depending on when, in the history of the society, they were born. A **cohort** is *a category of people with a common characteristic, usually their age*. Age-cohorts are likely to have similar reactions to particular issues to the extent that they were influenced by the same major events (Riley, Foner, & Waring, 1988). Women and men born early in this century, for example, were influenced by two world wars and an economic depression unknown to many of their children. In this sense, too, general patterns pertaining to the life course will vary.

## Resocialization: Total Institutions

This chapter has focused on socialization as experienced by the vast majority of individuals in countless familiar settings. Almost 1 million people in the United States, however, experience a different type of socialization—

often against their will—in prisons or mental hospitals where they are confined. This is the special world of a **total institution,** *a setting in which people are isolated from the rest of society and manipulated by an administrative staff.*

According to Erving Goffman (1961), total institutions have three distinctive characteristics. First, staff members supervise all spheres of daily life, including where residents (often called "inmates") eat, sleep, and work. Second, a rigid routine subjects inmates to standardized food, sleeping quarters, and activities. Third, formal rules govern how inmates behave in every setting, from how they dress to when and where they may smoke.

Total institutions impose such regimented routines with the goal of **resocialization,** *deliberate control of an environment to radically alter an inmate's personality.* The power of a total institution to do this lies in depriving people of any other source of social experience. An inmate's isolation is achieved through physical barriers such as walls and fences (usually with barbed wire and guard towers), barred windows, and locked doors. Cut off in this way, the inmate's entire world can be manipulated by the administrative staff to produce lasting change—or at least immediate compliance—in the inmate.

Resocialization is a two-part process. First, the staff attempts to erode the new inmate's established identity. This involves a series of experiences that Goffman describes as "abasements, degradations, humiliations, and profanations of self" (1961:14). For example, inmates are required to surrender personal possessions, including clothing and grooming articles normally used to maintain a person's distinctive appearance. In their place, inmates receive standard-issue items that make everyone alike. In addition, inmates are given standard haircuts, so that, once again, what was personalized becomes uniform. The staff also processes new inmates by searching, weighing, fingerprinting, and photographing them, and by issuing them a serial number. Once inside the walls, individuals surrender the right to privacy: guards often demand that inmates undress publicly as part of the admission procedure, and guards routinely conduct surveillance and searches of inmates' living quarters. These "mortifications of self" undermine the identity and autonomy that inmates bring to the total institution from the outside world.

The second part of the resocialization process turns on efforts to systematically build a different self. The staff manipulates inmate behavior through a system of rewards and punishments. The privilege of keeping a book or receiving extra cigarettes may seem trivial from the vantage point of outsiders, but, in the rigid environment of the total institution, they can be powerful motivations toward conformity. Noncompliance carries the threat that privileges will be withdrawn or, in more serious cases, that the inmate will suffer physical pain or isolation, even from other inmates. The duration of confinement in a prison or mental hospital also has to do with policy, which is related to the degree of cooperation with the staff an inmate displays. Goffman emphasized that conformity in a total institution must reflect both inward motivation as well as outward behavior. Even a person who does not outwardly violate the rules, in other words, may still be punished for having "an attitude problem."

Resocialization in a total institution can considerably change a human being. The rebuilding of the self is extremely difficult, however, and no two people are likely to respond to any such program in precisely the same way (Irwin, 1980). Some inmates may experience "rehabilitation" or "recovery" (meaning change that is officially approved), while others may gradually sink into an embittered state because of the perceived injustice of their incarceration. Furthermore, over a considerable period of time, the rigidly controlled environment of a total institution may render people completely *institutionalized,* incapable of the independence required for living in the outside world.

## Socialization and Human Freedom

Through socialization, society shapes how we think, feel, and act. If society has this power over us, in what sense are we free? This chapter ends with a closer look at this important question.

Children and adults throughout North America delight in watching the Muppets, stars of television and film. Observing the expressive antics of Kermit the Frog, Miss Piggy, and the rest of the troupe, one almost believes that these puppets are real rather than mere objects animated by movement that originates backstage. The sociological perspective suggests that human beings are like puppets in that we, too, respond to the backstage guidance of society. Indeed, more so, in that society affects not just our outward behavior but our innermost thoughts and feelings.

But our analysis of socialization also reveals where

the puppet analogy ultimately breaks down. Viewing human beings as the puppets of society leads into the trap that Dennis Wrong (1961) has called an "oversocialized" conception of the human being. In part, Wrong wishes to remind us that we are biological as well as social creatures, a point emphasized by Sigmund Freud, who identified general human drives. To the extent that any biological force affects our being, we can never be entirely shaped by society.

The fact that human beings may be subject to *both* biological and social influences, however, hardly advances the banner of human freedom. Here is where the ideas of George Herbert Mead are of crucial importance. Mead recognized the power of society to act on human beings, but he argued that human spontaneity and creativity (conceptualized in the I) empower us to continually *act back* on society. Thus the process of socialization affirms the human capacity for choice as we reflect, evaluate, and act. Therefore, although the process of socialization may initially suggest that we respond like puppets to forces beyond our control, Peter Berger points out that "unlike the puppets, we have the possibility of stopping in our movements, looking up and perceiving the machinery by which we have been moved" (1963:176). Doing this, we can act to change society by, so to speak, pulling back on the strings. And, Berger adds, the more we utilize the sociological perspective to study how the machinery of our society works, the freer we are.

## Summary

1. Socialization is a process through which social experience confers on the individual the qualities we associate with being fully human. For society as a whole, socialization is the means of transmitting culture to each new generation.

2. A century ago, people thought most human behavior was grounded in biological instinct. Today, we understand human behavior to be mostly a product of nurture rather than nature. So-called "human nature," then, is the capacity to create variable cultural patterns.

3. The damaging effects of social isolation reveal the importance of social experience to human development.

4. Sigmund Freud envisioned the human personality as composed of three parts. The id represents general human drives (the life and death instincts), which Freud claimed were innate. The superego represents cultural values and norms internalized by individuals. Competition between the needs of the id and the restraints of the superego are mediated by the ego.

5. Jean Piaget believed that human development reflects both biological maturation and increasing social experience. He asserted that socialization involves four major stages of development: sensorimotor, preoperational, concrete operational, and formal operational.

6. To George Herbert Mead, socialization is based on the emergence of the self, which he viewed as partly autonomous (the I) and partly guided by society (the me).

7. Charles Horton Cooley used the term looking-glass self to underscore that the self is influenced by perceptions of how others respond to us.

8. Commonly the first setting of socialization, the family has the greatest influence in shaping a child's attitudes and behavior.

9. School exposes children to greater social diversity and introduces the experience of being evaluated according to impersonal, universal standards of performance. In addition to formal lessons, the hidden curriculum teaches cultural lessons about race and gender.

10. Members of youthful peer groups are subject to adult supervision less than in the family or in school. Peer groups take on increasing significance in adolescence.

11. The mass media, especially television, have a considerable impact on the socialization process. The average child in the United States now spends more time watching television than attending school.

12. Public opinion plays a key role in the socialization process because popular attitudes and widespread values influence how we think and act.

13. As is true of each phase of the life course, the characteristics of childhood are socially constructed. During the Middle Ages, European societies scarcely recognized childhood as a stage of life. In industrial societies such as the United States, we define childhood as much different from adulthood.

14. Members of our society consider adolescence, the transition between childhood and adulthood, to be a difficult period. However, this is not the case in all societies.

15. During early adulthood, socialization involves settling into careers and raising families. Later adulthood is marked by considerable reflection about earlier goals in light of actual achievements.

16. In old age, people make many transitions, including retirement and establishing new patterns of social life. While the elderly typically enjoy high prestige in preindustrial societies, industrial societies are more youth-oriented.

17. Members of industrial societies typically fend off death until old age. Adjustment to the death of a spouse (an experience more common to women) and acceptance of the inevitability of one's own death are part of socialization for the elderly.

18. Total institutions such as prisons and mental hospitals have the goal of resocialization—radically changing the inmate's personality.

19. Socialization demonstrates the power of society to shape our thoughts, feelings, and actions. Yet, as George Herbert Mead pointed out, the relationship between the self and society is a two-way process: each shapes the other through social interaction.

# Key Concepts

**anticipatory socialization** the process of social learning directed toward gaining a desired position

**cohort** a category of people with a common characteristic, usually their age

**concrete operational stage** Piaget's term for the level of development at which people first use logic to understand their surroundings

**ego** Freud's designation of a person's conscious attempt to balance pleasure-seeking drives with the demands of society

**formal operational stage** Piaget's term for the level of human development at which people use highly abstract thought and are able to imagine alternatives to reality

**generalized other** George Herbert Mead's term for widespread cultural norms and values we use as a reference in evaluating ourselves

**id** Freud's designation of the human being's basic drives

**looking-glass self** Cooley's assertion that the self is based on how others respond to us

**mass media** impersonal communications directed toward a vast audience

**peer group** people who interact regularly, usually with common interests, social position, and age

**personality** a person's fairly consistent pattern of thinking, feeling, and acting

**preoperational stage** Piaget's term for the level of human development in which the individual first uses language and other symbols

**public opinion** the attitudes of people throughout a society about one or more controversial issues

**resocialization** deliberate control of an environment intended to radically alter an inmate's personality

**self** George Herbert Mead's term for a dimension of personality encompassing an individual's self-conception

**sensorimotor stage** Piaget's term for the level of human development in which people experience the world only through sensory contact

**socialization** lifelong social experience by which individuals develop human potential and learn patterns of their culture

**superego** Freud's designation of the presence of culture within the individual in the form of internalized values and norms

**total institution** a setting in which people are isolated from the rest of society and manipulated by an administrative staff

# Suggested Readings

Many dimensions of socialization are covered in these two books. The first focuses on infancy, the second encompasses the entire life course.

> Judith Rich Harris and Robert Liebert. *Infancy and the Child*. Englewood Cliffs, NJ: Prentice Hall, 1992.

> Grace Craig. *Human Development*. 6th ed. Englewood Cliffs, NJ: Prentice Hall, 1992.

This analysis of Freud's theories and research examines the implications of his work for a broad range of social issues.

> Paul Roazen. *Encountering Freud: The Politics and Histories of Psychoanalysis*. New Brunswick, NJ: Transaction Books, 1989.

George Herbert Mead's analysis of the development of the self is presented in this paperback, compiled after Mead's death by many of his students.

> George Herbert Mead. *Mind, Self, and Society from the Standpoint of a Social Behaviorist*. Charles W. Morris, ed. Chicago: The University of Chicago Press, 1962; orig. 1934.

The first of these two books is a classic study of the history of the family, exploring changing conceptions of childhood. The second book describes the recent development of the "hurried child" pattern in the United States.

> Philippe Ariès. *Centuries of Childhood: A Social History of Family Life*. New York: Vintage Books, 1965.

> David Elkind. *The Hurried Child: Growing Up Too Fast Too Soon*. Reading, MA: Addison-Wesley, 1981.

An overview of what is known about adolescent stress, these essays include evidence about which intervention programs have proved useful for practitioners.

> Mary Ellen Colton and Susan Gore, eds. *Adolescent Stress: Causes and Consequences*. Hawthorne, NY: Aldine de Gruyter, 1991.

This book, a compilation of fourteen essays on how people organize their lives by age in various societies, offers historical and cross-cultural material on the links between age, power, and retirement.

> David I. Kertzer and K. Warner Schaie, eds. *Age Structuring in Comparative Perspective*. Hillsdale, NJ: Lawrence Erlbaum, 1989.

This collection of fourteen essays explores the distinctive elements of socialization among African-American children.

> Harriette Pipes McAdoo and John Lewis McAdoo, eds. *Black Children: Social, Educational, and Parental Environments*. Beverly Hills, CA: Sage Publications, 1985.

Gay people are deprived of many of the social supports that heterosexuals take for granted. As a result, a gay folklore has emerged that is influential in the social development of millions of Americans. This book examines the growing folklife of the gay subculture.

> Joseph P. Goodwin. *More Man than You'll Ever Be: Gay Folklore and Acculturation in Middle America*. Bloomington, IN: Indiana University Press, 1989.

Reviewing decades of research about children and television, this researcher concludes that we still have much to learn.

> Carmen Luke. *Constructing the Child Viewer: A History of the American Discourse on Television and Children, 1950–1980*. New York: Greenwood, 1990.

How have the mass media shaped the way whites perceive minorities? This book spotlights images of African Americans, Hispanic Americans, Native Americans, and Asian Americans, as presented by the mass media.

> Clinty C. Wilson II and Félix Gutiérrez. *Minorities and Media: Diversity and the End of Mass Communication*. Beverly Hills, CA: Sage, 1985.

The following two books examine the role of gender in socialization.

> Ray Raphael. *The Men from the Boys: Rites of Passage in Male America*. Lincoln: University of Nebraska Press, 1988.

> Dorothy C. Holland and Margaret A. Eisenhart. *Educated in Romance: Women, Achievement, and College Culture*. Chicago: The University of Chicago Press, 1990.

Personality is shaped to some extent by the particular times in which we live. How the 1960s influenced a generation of men and women is suggested by this historical look at a turbulent decade.

> Joan Morrison and Robert K. Morrison. *The Sixties Experience: Sights and Sounds of the Decade of Change in the Words of Those Who Lived It*. New York: Times Books, 1987.

# 6

# Social Interaction in Everyday Life

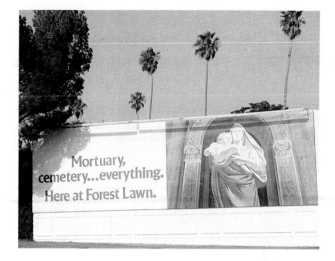

If you stop to think about it, a cemetery has a hard time selling its product. Brochures—like the one that just arrived in the mail—announce "limited-time offers"; in this case, $395 will buy two burial spaces in the "Garden of the Praying Hands." But isn't there something wrong with trying to sell burial plots as if they were cars, even if many people (sooner or later) need them? For one thing, someone opening the morning mail still might be grieving over the death of a family member, and hardly needs to be reminded of the loss. More generally, social rules demand that we treat death with a special respect. People selling cemetery plots must be as dignified and low key as possible, acting quite differently from dealers who hawk automobiles. Consider, as examples, some of the following lines common to the car business that you will *never* read in cemetery advertising:[1]

1. We're dealing.
2. How do we keep prices low? Volume.
3. Doing business at the same location for years.
4. Our customers never go anywhere else.
5. We're having a midnight madness sale.
6. The boss says everything must go.
7. Push it, pull it, tow it in.

Such contrasts are among the fascinating patterns that compose everyday life, the topic of this chapter. The chapter begins by presenting many of the building blocks of our common experiences, continues by exploring the almost magical way in which face-to-face interaction generates reality, and concludes with a look at humor and what our jokes tell us about ourselves.

The key concept throughout is **social interaction,** *the process by which people act and react in relation to others.* Social interaction is the key to creating the reality we perceive. We interact, moreover, according to particular social guidelines.

## Social Structure: A Guide to Everyday Living

Earlier chapters have described social life as an organized system. Chapter 3 ("Culture") examined the symbolic web that unites members of society into a culture, directing everyday interaction with norms and values. Chapter 4 ("Society") explained that the social world is shaped by its technological development, its economic system,

---

[1] This opening is adapted from a news feature by Mike Harden (1989).

and its particular world view and moral beliefs. Chapter 5 ("Socialization") showed how individuals gain humanity only as they engage others in society.

Although we have encountered ample evidence of the power of society, the notion that our behavior is socially patterned often provokes some initial resistance. Living in a culture that prizes self-reliance, few of us will readily admit to being part of any kind of system. Instead, we emphasize personal responsibility for behavior and highlight the unique elements of our personalities. But behaving in patterned ways does not threaten our individuality. Quite the contrary: social structure in everyday life actually serves to promote our individuality.

Social structure enhances our lives in two key ways. First, becoming fully human is possible only through social life, as Chapter 5 ("Socialization") explained. Human development occurs as we blend our unique qualities with the values and norms of the larger culture to produce distinct personalities. Second, in the absence of social structure, we would have no way of making sense out of any social situation. The social world can be disorienting, even frightening, when behavioral guidelines are unclear. Entering an unfamiliar setting generally inhibits us from freely expressing ourselves. Stepping onto a college campus for the first time, for example, we feel understandable anxiety at not knowing quite what to expect. Therefore, we look to others for clues about what sort of behavior is appropriate. Only after we understand the behavioral standards that apply to the situation are we likely to feel comfortable enough to "act like ourselves."

This is not to deny that social structure places some constraints on everyday life: established social patterns inevitably discourage the unconventional. Traditional values and norms in North America, for example, still reflect the expectation that males will be dominant and assertive in social situations and that females will adopt a subordinate and supportive stance. By pressuring each of us to fit neatly into "feminine" or "masculine" categories, social structure gives us identity but at the cost of limiting individual freedom to think and act according to personal preference.

Keep in mind, however, that social structure *guides* human behavior, rather than *rigidly determining* it. A saxophone is designed to make only certain kinds of sounds just as "fatherhood" encompasses specific patterns of behavior. Like musical instruments, however, any social arrangement can be "played" creatively in a wide range of ways.

# Status

Among the most important components of social interaction is **status,** which refers to *a recognized social position that an individual occupies.* The sociological meaning of the term "status" differs markedly from its everyday meaning of "prestige." In common usage, a bank president has more "status" than a bank teller. Sociologically, however, both "bank president" and "bank teller" are statuses because they represent socially defined positions, even though one does confer more power and prestige than the other.

Every status involves various rights, duties, and expectations. The statuses people occupy therefore guide the way they act in any setting. In the college classroom, for example, professors and students have different and well-defined rights and duties. Similarly, family interaction turns on the interplay of mother, father, daughters, and sons (and sometimes members of extended families). In all these situations, statuses define people in terms of each other, thereby forging relationships among individuals. A status, then, also defines who and what we are in relation to specific others.

We all simultaneously hold many statuses. The term **status set** refers to *all the statuses a person holds at a given time.* A girl may be a *daughter* to her parents, a *sister* to her siblings, a *friend* to members of her social circle, and a *goalie* to others on her hockey team. Just as status sets branch out in different directions, they also change over the life course. A child grows into an adult, a student becomes a lawyer, and people marry to become husbands and wives, sometimes becoming single again as a result of divorce or death. Joining an organization or finding a job enlarges our status set; retirement or withdrawing from activities diminishes it. Individuals gain and lose dozens of statuses over a lifetime.

Status plays an important part in how we define ourselves. Occupational status, for example, forms a major part of most peoples' self-concept. Even after retirement, for instance, a man may still think of himself as a professor and be similarly defined by others.

## Ascribed and Achieved Status

Sociologists use a helpful distinction to describe how people obtain various statuses. An **ascribed status** is *a social position that is received at birth or involuntarily* *assumed later in the life course.* Examples of ascribed statuses include being a daughter, a Latino, a teenager, or a widower. Ascribed statuses are matters about which people have little or no choice.

By contrast, an **achieved status** refers to *a social position that is assumed voluntarily and that reflects a significant measure of personal ability and effort.* Among achieved statuses in the United States are being an honors student, an Olympic athlete, a wife, a computer programmer, or a thief. In each case, the individual has a definite choice in the matter.

Most statuses actually involve a combination of ascription and achievement. That is, people's ascribed statuses influence the statuses they are likely to achieve. Children cannot be lawyers until they become adults. Moreover, the adults who earn a law degree are likely to have another ascribed trait in common: being born into relatively privileged families. More generally, any person of a privileged gender, race, ethnicity, or age has far more opportunity to achieve desirable statuses than does someone without such advantages. By the same token, many less desirable statuses, such as criminal, welfare recipient, or drug addict are more easily "achieved" by people disadvantaged by ascription.

## Master Status

Among the many statuses a person holds at any time, one often overshadows all the others. A **master status** is *a status that has exceptional importance for social identity, often shaping a person's entire life.* In our society, a person's occupation—largely due to achievement—often ranks as a master status. This is because occupation conveys so much information, including some idea of a person's education, income, and family background. No doubt, this is why adults typically introduce themselves by stating their occupations along with their names. Other master statuses, however, are based on ascription. For a Rockefeller or a Kennedy, family name stands out in the minds of others. Similarly, people of color know that race can sometimes overshadow personal achievements.

Serious disease can also underlie a master status. Sometimes even lifelong friends avoid cancer patients. For persons with acquired immune deficiency syndrome (AIDS), disease may result in social isolation. Most societies of the world limit the opportunities of women, whatever their abilities, so that sex, too, can serve as a master status. Additionally, the physically disabled can

In any rigidly ranked setting, no interaction can proceed until people assess each other's social standing. In traditional Indian society, each individual wears a caste mark on the forehead, which serves as a master status guiding subsequent behavior.

be made to feel dehumanized by people who perceive them only in terms of their handicaps. In the box on page 154, several people with physical disabilities describe this problem.

# Role

Besides status, a second major component of social interaction is **role,** *patterns of expected behavior attached to a particular status.* Ralph Linton (1937) described a

## Physical Disability as Master Status

Now in his late thirties, David Clark was stricken with polio when he was ten months old. He lives and works in Corning, New York. Being defined as different or incomplete has clearly affected how he sees himself.

> All the stares you get from the public used to really bother me when I was younger. But either it doesn't happen as much nowadays, or parents have taught their children better about disabilities, or else I'm older and more immune to it, I don't know. It doesn't bother me now like it used to; it used to really bother me. But I really think people are better educated now about disabilities and they don't look as much and make you feel like you're a freak, which is the way I felt when I was younger and they were looking at you like you didn't belong there, what's your problem?

Donna Finch is twenty-nine years old, holds a master's degree in social work, and lives with her husband and son in Muskogee, Oklahoma. She is also blind.

> Most people don't expect handicapped people to grow up, they are always supposed to be children. . . . [Y]ou aren't supposed to date, you aren't supposed to have a job, somehow you're just supposed to disappear. I'm not saying this is true of anyone else, but in my own case I think I was more intellectually mature than most children, and more emotionally immature. I'd say that not until the last four or five years have I felt really whole.

Rose Helman is an elderly woman living near New York City. She suffers from spinal meningitis and is also blind.

You ask me if people are really different today than in the '20s and '30s. Not too much. They are still fearful of the handicapped. I don't know if fearful is the right word, but uncomfortable at least. But I can understand it somewhat; it happened to me. I once asked a man to tell me which staircase to use to get from the subway out to the street. He started giving me directions that were confusing, and I said, "Do you mind taking me?" He said, "Not at all." He grabbed me on the side with my dog on it, so I asked him to take my other arm. And he said, "I'm sorry, I have no other arm." And I said, "That's all right, I'll hold onto the jacket." It felt funny hanging onto the sleeve without the arm in it.

SOURCE: Orlansky and Heward (1981).

role as the dynamic expression of a status. The various obligations and privileges attached to a status, in other words, call out a particular role. The student role, for example, involves responsibility to professors and other students, as well as the privilege of being able to devote much of one's time to personal enrichment through academic study. Thus, individuals *hold* a status, and *perform* a role. Cultural norms suggest how a person holding a particular status ought to act, which is often called a *role expectation*. As noted in Chapter 3 ("Culture"), however, real culture only approximates ideal culture, so that actual role performance varies according to an individual's unique personality. In addition, cultural diversity in a society ensures that people will perform comparable roles quite differently.

Like a status, a role is *relational*, organizing our behavior toward some other person. The parent's role, for example, centers on responsibilities toward a child. Correspondingly, the role of daughter or son consists largely of obligations toward a parent. Other examples of such role pairs include wives and husbands, baseball pitchers and catchers, physicians and patients, and performers and members of an audience.

Because individuals occupy many statuses simultaneously—a status set—they perform multiple roles. The total number of roles usually exceeds the number of statuses because each status can require an individual to carry out several roles in relation to various other people. Robert Merton (1968) introduced the term **role set** to identify *a number of roles attached to a single status*. Figure 6–1 illustrates the status set and corresponding role sets of one individual. Four statuses are presented, each linked to a different role set. First, this woman occupies the status of "wife," with corresponding roles toward her husband ("conjugal roles" such as confidant and sexual partner), with whom she would share a "domestic role" toward the household. Second, she also holds the status of "mother," with routine responsibilities toward her children (the "maternal role") and activities in various organizations such as the PTA (the "civic role"). Third, as a professor, she interacts with students (the "teaching role") as well as with other academics (the "colleague role"). Fourth, her work in a laboratory (the "researcher role") provides the data she uses in her publications (the "author role"). Of course, Figure 6–1 lists only some of this person's status and role sets, since anyone generally occupies dozens of statuses at one time, each linked to a role set.

## Role Conflict and Role Strain

The personal performances required by an array of role sets often make heavy demands on an individual's time and energy. This holds especially true for members of industrial societies in which people routinely assume many statuses and an even greater number of roles. As mothers working outside the home can testify, carrying out the role of parent as well as the role of breadwinner taxes both their physical and emotional strength. Sociologists define such **role conflict** as *incompatibility among roles corresponding to two or more different statuses.*

We experience role conflict when we find ourselves pulled in various directions while trying to respond to the many statuses we hold. National political officials, for example, sometimes decide not to run for the presidency because the demands of such a campaign would impoverish family life; in other cases, ambitious people sometimes defer having children or choose to remain childless in order to build their careers as quickly as possible.

Even the many roles linked to a single status may make competing demands on us. The concept of **role strain** refers to *incompatibility among roles corresponding to a single status.* A plant supervisor may wish to be a good friend and confidant to other workers. At the same time, however, a supervisor's responsibility for everyone's performance may require maintaining some measure of personal distance. In short, performing the roles attached to even one status may involve a "balancing act" of trying to fulfill various duties and obligations.

Individuals handle problems associated with conflicting roles in a number of ways. One simple strategy for reducing role conflict is to define some roles as more important than others. A new mother, for instance, might devote most of her efforts to parenting and put her career on hold, at least for the present. Resolving role conflict in this way, however, depends on being able to afford not to work—an option unavailable to many mothers.

Setting priorities also reduces the strain among roles linked to a single status. Adopting this approach, a person concentrates on one particular role (from among the many tied to a status), while downplaying another with which it conflicts. A father, for example, may decide that maintaining a close and trusting relationship with his child is more important than enforcing cultural norms as a disciplinarian.

Another strategy for minimizing role conflict is "insulating" roles from one another (Merton, 1968). Instead of downplaying a particular role, people "compartmentalize" their lives so that they perform roles linked to one status in one place for part of the day, while roles corresponding to another status dominate activity elsewhere or at some other time. For example, people usually try to leave their jobs behind them when they go home to assume the responsibilities of spouse or parent.

**Figure 6–1**   Status Set and Role Set

We learn from what we see. Thus each of us selects others as *role models*, people whose behavior we wish to emulate. The behavior we wish to model can be as simple as that of Rosa Parks, a woman of color and seamstress who boarded a public bus on December 1, 1955 in Montgomery, Alabama. Although she took her place in the section reserved for blacks, the driver ordered her to give up her seat to a white man. When she courageously refused, police arrested her. The episode led to the Montgomery Bus Boycott, which lasted for a year, and finally brought an end to racial segregation on that city's buses.

## Role Exit

Recent research has focused on *role exit*, the process by which people disengage from social roles that have been central to their lives. Helen Rose Fuchs Ebaugh (1988) began to study this issue as she herself left the life of Catholic nun to become a university sociologist. Studying a range of "exes," including ex-nuns, ex-doctors, ex-husbands, and ex-alcoholics, Ebaugh found many common elements to the process of "becoming an ex."

According to Ebaugh, people considering role exit typically begin by reflecting critically on their existing lives, raising doubts about their ability or willingness to carry out that role. As they focus on alternative roles, they may ultimately reach a turning point and decide to pursue a new life. In the subsequent "ex-role," they disengage from the previous situation, building a new sense of self, which emerges through changes in outward appearance and behavior (an ex-nun, for example, begins

to wear stylish clothing and make-up). "Exes" must also grapple with changing responses from those who may have known them in their earlier role, as well as those who do not realize how new and unfamiliar their present role may be. Forming new relationships is especially challenging for an "ex," since many new social skills must be learned. Ebaugh reports, for example, that nuns who begin dating after decades in the church are often startled to learn that sexual norms are now vastly different from those they knew as teenagers.

In modern society, fewer and fewer people expect to spend their entire lives in one job or one marriage. The study of role exit, therefore, promises to attract greater attention.

## The Social Construction of Reality

Over fifty years ago, the Italian playwright Luigi Pirandello skillfully applied the sociological perspective to social interaction. In *The Pleasure of Honesty*, Angelo Baldovino—a brilliant man with a rather checkered past—enters the fashionable home of the Renni family and introduces himself in a most peculiar way:

> Inevitably we construct ourselves. Let me explain. I enter this house and immediately I become what I have to become, what I can become: I construct myself. That is, I present myself to you in a form suitable to the relationship I wish to achieve with you. And, of course, you do the same with me. . . . (1962:157–158)

This curious statement suggests that, while social interaction is guided by status and role, each human being has considerable ability to shape what happens moment to moment. "Reality," then, is not as fixed as we may think. The social world does have an objective existence, of course; it existed long before we were born, affects us throughout our lives, and will continue long after we die. But, in everyday terms, society is nothing more than the behavior of countless people. If society affects individuals, then individuals creatively shape society (Berger & Luckmann, 1967).

The phrase **social construction of reality** refers to *the process by which individuals creatively shape reality through social interaction.* This idea stands at the foundation of the symbolic-interaction paradigm in sociology, as described in earlier chapters. In this context, Angelo Baldovino's remark suggests that, especially in an unfa-

Ambiguity and awkwardness are the outstanding characteristics of this scene in which a white woman pays a call on her former slaves. Notice the stiffness of the figures and the space that separates the people of each color. Winslow Homer's *A Visit From the Old Mistress*, painted in 1876, depicts a time of transition in race relations in the United States. Although formal slavery had been abolished, both whites and African Americans were taking their first, uncertain steps towards social equality in which race would no longer guide their interaction. The artist leaves little doubt that, however long the road ahead, the abolition of slavery has transformed the United States fundamentally and forever.

*A Visit from the Old Mistress, 1876. Oil on canvas, 18 x 24⅛ (45.7 x 61.3). Unsigned. National Museum of American Art, Smithsonian Institution. Gift of William T. Evans.*

miliar situation, quite a bit of "reality" remains unclear in everyone's mind. Pirandello's character will simply use his ability to "present himself" in terms that he thinks suit his purposes. As others do the same, a complex reality emerges, although few people are so "up front" about their deliberate efforts to foster an impression.

Social interaction, then, amounts to a process of negotiating reality. Usually, interaction results in at least some agreement about how to define a situation. But participants rarely share precisely the same perception of events. Subjective realities vary because social interaction brings together people with different purposes, interests, and hidden agendas, each of whom is seeking a somewhat different shaping of reality.

Steering reality in this way is sometimes referred to as "street smarts." In his biography *Down These Mean Streets*, Piri Thomas recalls moving to a new apartment in New York City's Spanish Harlem, which placed him squarely on the turf of the local street gang. Returning home one evening, young Piri found himself cut off by Waneko, the gang's leader, who was flanked by a dozen others.

"Whatta ya say, Mr. Johnny Gringo," drawled Waneko.

*Think man,* I told myself, *think your way out of a stomping. Make it good.* "I hear you 104th street coolies are supposed to have heart," I said. "I don't know this for sure. You know there's a lot of streets where a whole 'click' is made

out of punks who can't fight one guy unless they all jump him for the stomp." I hoped this would push Waneko into giving me a fair one. His expression didn't change.

"Maybe we don't look at it that way."

*Crazy, man. I cheer inwardly, the* cabron *is falling into my setup.* . . . "I wasn't talking to you," I said. "Where I come from, the pres is president 'cause he got heart when it comes to dealing."

Waneko was starting to look uneasy. He had bit on my worm and felt like a sucker fish. His boys were now light on me. They were no longer so much interested in stomping me as seeing the outcome between Waneko and me. "Yeah," was his reply. . . .

I knew I'd won. Sure, I'd have to fight; but one guy, not ten or fifteen. If I lost, I might still get stomped, and if I won I might get stomped. I took care of this with my next sentence. "I don't know you or your boys," I said, "but they look cool to me. They don't feature as punks."

I had left him out purposely when I said "they." Now his boys were in a separate class. I had cut him off. He would have to fight me on his own, to prove his heart to himself, to his boys, and most important, to his turf. He got away from the stoop and asked, "Fair one, Gringo?" (1967:56–57)

This situation reveals the drama—sometimes subtle, sometimes savage—by which human beings creatively build reality. There are limits, of course, to what even the most skillful and persuasive personality can achieve. Should a police officer have come upon the fight that ensued between Piri and Waneko, both young men might well have ended up in jail. Not everyone enters a social negotiation with equal standing; the police officer would probably have the last word simply because of a status that holds greater power than that of the two key players (Molotch & Boden, 1985).

## The Thomas Theorem

Piri Thomas won acceptance that evening. Having been defined as worthy, he was now one of the group, and from that moment his social identity was changed. W. I. Thomas (1966:301; orig. 1931) succinctly expressed this insight in what has come to be known as the **Thomas theorem**: *situations that are defined as real are real in their consequences.* Applied to social interaction, his observation means that although reality is initially "soft" or fluid, as it is fashioned, it can become "hard" in its effects. In the case of Piri Thomas (no relation to W. I. Thomas for whom the Thomas theorem is named), because he succeeded in defining himself as worthy, he *was* now worthy in the eyes of his new comrades.

## Reality-Building in Global Perspective

Of course, people do not construct everyday experience "out of thin air." Rather, we creatively manipulate elements in the surrounding culture. For this reason, residents of Spanish Harlem build somewhat different realities than people living on the affluent East Side of Manhattan. In global perspective, reality varies even more, so that social experiences common to, say, women in Saudi Arabia would seem unreal to many women in the United States. Similarly, social reality changes over time. People living in ancient Japan forged social worlds that were very different from those typical of the Japanese today.

Because social reality is grounded in the surrounding culture, any object or action is subject to different interpretations, depending on the cultural context. The meanings people attach to the two sexes, to stages of the life course, or even to the days of the week vary from culture to culture. Supporting this conclusion, Wendy Griswold (1987) asked people from different societies—the West Indies, Great Britain, and the United States—to interpret several novels. She found that the messages her respondents drew from what they read differed and, furthermore, were consistent with the basic "blueprint" of their culture. What people see in a book—or anything else—is guided by their social world.

Cultures frame reality differently. This man lay on the street in Bombay, India, for several hours and then quietly died. In the United States, such an event would probably have provoked someone to call the rescue squad. In a poor society in which death on the streets is a fact of everyday life, however, many Indians responded not with alarm but with simple decency by stopping to place incense on his body before continuing on their way.

This variability of human experience leads to an interesting question: since people everywhere are members of a single species, don't we all share many of the same basic feelings? A number of researchers have conducted cross-cultural investigations of human emotions. The answer to the question is yes—and no—as the box on pages 160–61 explains.

## Ethnomethodology

It is hardly surprising that human beings take for granted most of the reality they create. After all, what would social life be like if we questioned every situation we experienced? For some sociologists, however, challenging the patterns of conventional behavior yields rich insights into the organization of everyday life.

*Ethnomethodology* is a specialized approach within the symbolic-interaction paradigm. The term itself has two parts: the Greek *ethno* refers to understandings of cultural surroundings that people share, and "methodology" designates a system of methods or principles. Combining them makes **ethnomethodology,** *the study of the everyday, common-sense understandings that people have of the world.*

Ethnomethodology was devised in the 1950s by Harold Garfinkel, a sociologist dissatisfied with the then-widespread view of society as a broad "system" with a life of its own (recall the approach of Emile Durkheim, described in Chapter 4, "Society"). Garfinkel wanted to explore how we create rules and expectations in countless familiar, everyday situations (Heritage, 1984). For example, people readily expect certain behavior when sitting down to dinner in a restaurant, when beginning to take a final examination, or when driving onto a freeway. As important as such conventional understandings may be, Garfinkel (1967) maintained that few of us ever think much about them.

In the rebellious social climate of the 1960s, Garfinkel developed a distinctive technique for exposing the unacknowledged patterns of everyday life: *break the rules.* In other words, a good way to tease out the conventional realities is to deliberately ignore them.

In a series of experiments, Garfinkel (1967) and his students mapped everyday life by refusing to "play the game." Some entered stores and insisted on bargaining for standard-priced items, others recruited people into simple games (like tic-tac-toe) only to intentionally flout the rules, still others initiated conversations and slowly moved closer and closer until they were almost nose to nose with their quarry. At the very least, this rule violation was met with bewilderment; often "victims" responded with anger. One of Garfinkel's students reported, for example, the following exchange (1967:44):

> Acquaintance: "How are you?"
> Student: "How am I in regard to what? My health, my finances, my school work, my peace of mind, my . . ."
> Acquaintance (now red in the face and suddenly out of control): "Look! I was just trying to be polite. Frankly, I don't give a damn how you are."

This deliberate lack of social cooperation allows the researcher to see more clearly the unspoken rules of everyday life. One measure of the importance of these rules is that people find their violation unpleasant, even threatening.

Because of its provocative character and its focus on commonplace experiences, ethnomethodology has gained a reputation as less-than-serious research. Even so, ethnomethodology has succeeded in heightening awareness of many unnoticed patterns of everyday life.

# Dramaturgical Analysis: "The Presentation of Self"

Erving Goffman (1922–1982) shared with Garfinkel an interest in the patterned character of everyday life. Goffman argued that people socially constructing reality have much in common with actors performing on a stage. Calling to mind a director scrutinizing the action in a theater, Goffman termed his approach **dramaturgical analysis,** *the investigation of social interaction in terms of theatrical performance.*

Dramaturgical analysis offers a fresh look at two now-familiar concepts. In this theoretical scheme, a status mirrors a part in a play, and a role serves as a script, supplying dialogue and action for each of the characters. In any setting, then, each of us plays a role, like an actor, and also forms part of the audience. Goffman called the intricate interaction that makes up everyday life the **presentation of self,** *ways in which individuals, in various settings, try to create specific impressions in the minds of others.* This process, sometimes termed *impression management,* contains several distinctive elements (Goffman, 1959, 1967).

## Human Emotions in Global Perspective

On a New York sidewalk, a woman reacts angrily to the skateboarder who hurtles past her. Apart from a few choice words, her facial expression broadcasts a strong emotion that any American can recognize. But would an observer from New Guinea be able to interpret her emotion? In other words, do people everywhere share similar emotions, and do they express them in the same way?

Paul Ekman (1980) and his colleagues have studied emotions around the world and even among members of a small society in New Guinea. Their conclusion is that people everywhere feel the same basic emotions—including anger, fear, happiness, disgust, surprise, and sadness. Moreover, people all over the globe recognize that these feelings are expressed by the same distinctive facial gestures. To Ekman, this commonality suggests that much of our emotional life is universal—rather than culturally specific—with the display of emotion biologically programmed in our facial features, muscles, and central nervous system.

But the reality of emotions is only partly rooted in our biology. Ekman and others have noted three ways in which emotional life differs significantly in global perspective. First, what *triggers* an emotional response is highly variable from one culture to another. Whether a particular situation is defined as an insult (causing anger), a loss (calling out sadness), or a mystical event (provoking surprise and awe) depends on the cultural surroundings of the individual. Second, people *display* emotions according to the norms of their culture. Every society has certain rules about when, where, and to whom people may exhibit certain emotions. People in the United States typically approve of emotional expression among family members, but consider such behavior out of place at work. Similarly, we expect children to express emotions to parents, although parents are taught to guard their emotions in front of children. Third, cultures differ in terms of how people *cope* with emotions. Some societies encourage the expression of feelings, while others belittle emotions and demand that their members suppress them. Societies also display significant gender differences in this regard: in the United States, people tend to regard emotional expression as feminine, expected of women but a sign of weakness among men. In other societies, however, this sex-typing of emotions is less pronounced or even reversed.

In sum, emotional life in cross-cultural perspective has both common and variable dimensions. People around the world experience many of the same human feelings. But what sparks a particular emotion, how a person expresses feelings, and what people think about emotions in general are variable products of social learning. In global perspective, therefore, everyday life differs not only in terms of how people think and act, but how they infuse their lives with feeling.

SOURCES: Ekman (1980a, 1980b), Lutz & White (1986), and Lutz (1988).

## Performances

As we present ourselves to others, we convey information—consciously and unconsciously—about how we wish to be understood. Goffman called these efforts, taken together, a *performance*. Dress (costume), the objects people carry with them (props), and our tone of voice and gestures (manner) are all part of a performance. In addition, everyone takes account of the setting in crafting a performance. People may joke loudly on a sidewalk, for instance, but assume a more reverent manner when they enter a church. Equally important, individuals often design settings, such as their home or office, to invoke desired reactions in others. A setting, then, is a stage that enhances a person's performance by providing numerous specific pieces of information.

Consider, for example, how a physician's office guides social interaction and conveys appropriate information to an audience of patients. Physicians enjoy considerable prestige and power in the United States, which is evident to patients immediately upon entering the doctor's office. First, the physician is nowhere to be

Would people anywhere in the world see in these facial expressions anger, fear, happiness, disgust, surprise, and sadness? Research supports the conclusion that all human beings experience the same basic emotions and display them to others in ways characteristic of our species. Culture plays a central part, however, in setting the range of situations that triggers one or another emotion.

seen. Instead, in what Goffman describes as the "front region" of the setting, the patient encounters a receptionist who functions as a gatekeeper, deciding if and when the patient can meet the physician. A simple survey of the doctor's waiting room, with patients (often impatiently) waiting to gain entry to the inner sanctum, leaves little doubt that the medical team controls events.

The physician's private office and examination room constitute the "back region" of the setting. Here the patient confronts a wide range of props, such as medical books and framed degrees, that reinforce the impression that the physician, and not the patient, has the specialized knowledge necessary to guide their interaction. In the office, the physician usually remains seated behind a desk—the larger, the greater the statement of power—while the patient is provided with only a chair.

The physician's appearance and manner convey still more information. The usual costume of white lab coat may have the practical function of keeping clothes from becoming soiled, but its primary function is to let others know at a glance the physician's status. A stethoscope around the neck or a black medical bag in hand has the same purpose. A doctor's highly technical terminology—occasionally necessary, but frequently mystifying—also emphasizes the hierarchy in the situation. The use of the title "Doctor" by patients who, in turn, are frequently addressed only by their first names also underscores the physician's dominant position. The overall message of a doctor's performance is clear: "I can help you, but you must allow me to take charge."

## Nonverbal Communication

Novelist William Sansom describes a fictional Mr. Preedy, an English vacationer on a beach in Spain:

He took care to avoid catching anyone's eye. First, he had to make it clear to those potential companions of his holiday that they were of no concern to him whatsoever. He stared through them, round them, over them—eyes lost in space. The beach might have been empty. If by chance a ball was thrown his way, he looked surprised; then let a smile of amusement light his face [Kindly Preedy], looked around dazed to see that there were people on the beach, tossed it back with a smile to himself and not a smile *at* the people. . . .

. . . [He] then gathered together his beach-wrap and bag into a neat sand-resistant pile [Methodical and Sensible Preedy], rose slowly to stretch his huge frame [Big-Cat Preedy], and tossed aside his sandals [Carefree Preedy, after all]. (1956; cited in Goffman, 1959:4–5)

# Telling Lies: Clues to Deceit

On September 15, 1938, Germany's chancellor Adolf Hitler and Britain's prime minister Neville Chamberlain met for the first time, as the world looked on in hopes of avoiding war. Although his plans for war were already well under way, Hitler assured Chamberlain that peace could be preserved. Chamberlain believed what he heard, writing soon afterward, "In spite of the hardness and ruthlessness I thought I saw in his face, I got the impression that here was a man who could be relied upon when he had given his word" (Ekman, 1985:15–16). In retrospect, we can see that Chamberlain should have paid less attention to the message Hitler *gave* and more to the contradictory nonverbal signals he *gave off*.

Detecting lies is a difficult task, because no bodily gesture directly indicates deceit as, for example, a smile indicates pleasure. Even so, because each performance involves so many expressions, few people can confidently lie without allowing some piece of contradictory information to arouse the suspicions of a careful observer. The key, therefore, to identifying deceit is to scan a complete performance with an eye for any discrepancies in the information that is conveyed.

Specifically, Ekman suggests scrutinizing four types of informa-

Telling lies is no easy task because most people lack the ability to manipulate correctly their facial muscles. Looking at the three faces below, the expression of grief in Figure A is probably genuine, since few people can deliberately lift the upper eyelids and inner corners of the eyebrows in this way. Likewise, the apprehension shown in Figure B also appears authentic, since intentionally raising the eyebrows and pulling them together is nearly impossible. People who fake emotions usually do a poor job of it, illustrated by the phony expression of pleasure shown in Figure C. Genuine delight, for most people, would produce a balanced smile.

**Figure A**          **Figure B**          **Figure C**

Through his conduct, Mr. Preedy offers a great deal of information about himself to anyone caring to observe him. Notice that he does so without uttering a single word. This illustrates the process of **nonverbal communication,** *communication using body movements, gestures, and facial expressions rather than speech.*

Through nonverbal communication, we use the body to convey information to others, as suggested by the more common phrase *body language.* Facial expressions form the most significant element of nonverbal communication. As noted earlier, smiling and other facial gestures constitute an almost universal language to express basic emotions like pleasure, surprise, and anger. Further, people express particular shades of meaning with their faces according to the demands of the situation. We distinguish, for example, between the casual, light-hearted smile of Kindly Preedy on the beach, a smile of embarrassment, and a full, unrestrained smile of self-satisfaction we often associate with the "cat who ate the canary."

Eye contact is another important element of nonverbal communication. Generally, we use eye contact to initiate social interaction. Someone across the room "catches our eye," for example, sparking a conversation. Avoiding the eyes of another, by contrast, discourages communication. Hands, too, speak for us. Common hand gestures in our culture convey, among other things, an insult, a request for a ride, an invitation for someone

tion provided by a performer—words, voice, body language, and facial expression. *Language* serves as the major channel of communication in social interaction. But a liar can manipulate words with relative ease by mentally rehearsing what will be said. One clue to deceit, however, is a simple slip of the tongue—something the performer did not mean to say in quite that way. For example, a young man who is deceiving his parents by claiming that his roommate is a male friend rather than a female lover might inadvertently use the word *she* rather than *he* in a conversation about his living arrangements. The more complicated the deception, the more likely a performer is to make a revealing mistake.

*Voice,* meaning the qualities of speech other than words, also contains clues to deception. Tone and patterns of speech are especially important because they are hard to control. A person trying to hide a powerful emotion, for example, cannot easily prevent the voice from trembling or breaking. Similarly, the individual may speak quickly (suggesting anger) or slowly (indicating sadness). Nervous laughter, inappropriate pauses between words, or non-words, such as *ah* and *ummm,* also hint at discomfort.

A "leak" of *body language* that a performer is unable to conceal may tip off an observer to deception as well. Subtle body movements, for example, give the impression of nervousness, as do sudden swallowing or rapid breathing. These are especially good clues to deception because few people can control them. Sometimes, *not* using the body in the expected way to enhance words—as when a person tries to fake excitement—also suggests deception.

Uncontrollable *facial expressions* may give away a phony performance. A sad person feigning happiness, for example, generally "flashes" momentary frowns through a crooked smile. In this case, the concealed emotion "leaks" through the deliberate facade. A signal of fear or worry is raising and drawing together the eyebrows, a movement virtually impossible for most people to make voluntarily. Crossing the face of a person who is supposedly at ease, this expression sounds the alarm of deception.

In sum, lies are detectable, but the ability to notice relevant clues usually requires training. Knowing the other person well makes detecting deception much easier; parents, for example, can usually spot deception in their children. Clues to deception are also more evident if a person is trying to contain strong emotions. Even so, some have (or develop) the ability to carefully manage their verbal and nonverbal performances. There are, in short, both good and bad liars.

SOURCE: Ekman (1985).

to join us, or a demand that others stop in their tracks. Gestures also supplement spoken words. Pointing in a menacing way at someone, for example, intensifies a word of warning, as shrugging the shoulders adds an air of indifference to the phrase "I don't know," and rapidly waving the arms lends urgency to the single word "Hurry!"

Most nonverbal communication is culture-specific. Hand gestures and body movements have different meanings from place to place, so that many gestures significant to North Americans mean nothing—or something very different—to members of other societies, as explained in Chapter 3 ("Culture"). For instance, what many of us call the "A-Okay" gesture with thumb touching forefinger means "You're a zero" to the French, and conveys a crude word for "rectum" to many Italians (Ekman, Friesen, & Bear, 1984).

Individuals deliberately express many elements of nonverbal communication. Sometimes, however, the information we unintentionally give off contradicts our intended performance. Listening to her teenage son's explanation for returning home at a late hour, for example, a mother begins to doubt his words because he avoids her eyes. The guest on a television talk show claims that her recent divorce is "the best thing that ever happened to me," but the nervous swing of her leg suggests otherwise. Such nonverbal communication may provide clues to deception, in much the same way that a lie detector measures subtle physical changes in breathing, pulse rate, perspiration, and blood pressure that signal the stress of telling lies. Does this mean that careful observers can detect dishonesty in someone else's performance? Paul Ekman believes they can, as the box on pages 162–63 explains.

## Gender and Personal Performances

Because women are socialized to be more assertive than men, they tend to be especially sensitive to nonverbal communication. In fact, *gender*—which involves distinct social expectations for females and males—is a central element in personal performances. In other words, because women and men are subject to different cultural norms and have unequal social power, the members of each sex typically behave differently in most settings. Based on the work of Nancy Henley, Mykol Hamilton, and Barrie Thorne (1992), we can extend the conventional analysis of personal performances to spotlight the importance of gender.

### Demeanor

Goffman (1967) links *demeanor*—general conduct or deportment—to social power. Simply put, people in positions of power have far greater personal discretion in how they act; those subject to supervision act more formally and self-consciously. Office behavior such as swearing, removing shoes, or putting feet up on the desk may well be considered acceptable for the boss, but not for subordinates (Henley, Hamilton, & Thorne, 1992). Similarly, people in positions of dominance can interrupt the performances of others with impunity, while those subject to their power are expected to display deference by becoming silent (Smith-Lovin & Brody, 1989).

For women, who generally occupy positions of low power, demeanor is a matter of particular concern. As Chapter 13 ("Sex and Gender") explains, about half of all working women in the United States hold clerical or service jobs that place them under the control of supervisors, who are usually men. Women, then, must craft their personal performances more formally than men, and display a greater degree of deference in everyday interaction.

### Use of Space

How much space does a personal performance require? Here again, power plays a key role, since using more space conveys a nonverbal message of personal importance. According to Henley, Hamilton, and Thorne (1992), men use significantly more space than women do. Typically, men command more space when they stand before a convention audience making a presentation or even when they lounge casually about the beach on vacation. Why? Because our society traditionally has measured femininity by how little space women occupy (the standard of "daintiness"), while men enhance their masculinity by controlling as much territory as possible (the standard of "turf").

The concept of **personal space** refers to *the surrounding area over which a person makes some claim to privacy.* In the United States, we typically remain at least several feet from others, maintaining somewhat greater personal space than people in more densely populated societies such as Japan. But this distance varies significantly by sex. In daily life, men readily intrude on the personal space of women. A woman's intrusion into a man's personal space, however, is likely to be construed as a sexual overture. Here again, women have less power to define a specific reality than men do.

Women and men use space in different ways. Because controlling space is a measure of power, men typically take up as much space as they can—even while relaxing—while women try to use as little as possible.

## Staring, Smiling, and Touching

Eye contact encourages interaction. Women more than men actively maintain interaction, generally sustaining eye contact longer. One exception is *staring*. Men often make women the objects of stares, which reflects both the dominance of men in the United States and their tendency to define women as sexual objects.

Although frequently conveying pleasure, *smiling* can also project a wide range of meaning. In a male-dominated world, women often smile to indicate appeasement, or acceptance of submission. For this reason, Henley, Hamilton, and Thorne maintain, women smile more than men; in extreme cases, smiling may reach the level of nervous habit.

Finally, *touching* constitutes an intriguing social pattern. Mutual touching generally conveys intimacy and caring. Apart from close relationships, however, touching is generally something men do to women. A male physician touches the shoulder of his female nurse as they examine a report, a young man who has just begun dating touches the back of his woman friend as he guides her across the street, or a male skiing instructor excessively and unnecessarily touches his female students. In these examples—as well as many others—the touching may evoke little response, so common is it in everyday life. But it amounts to a subtle ritual by which

men express their dominant position in an assumed hierarchy that subordinates women.

## Idealization

Complex motives underlie all human behavior. Even so, Goffman suggests, performances tend to *idealize* our intentions. That is, we try to convince others that what we do reflects ideal cultural standards rather than less virtuous motives.

Idealization is easily illustrated by returning to the world of physicians and patients. In a hospital, physicians engage in a performance commonly described as "making rounds." Entering the room of a patient, the physician often stops at the foot of the bed and silently examines the patient's chart. Afterwards, physician and patient briefly converse. In ideal terms, this routine involves a physician making a personal visit to inquire about a patient's condition.

In reality, something less exemplary is usually going on. A physician who sees perhaps thirty-five patients a day may remember little about most of them. Reading the chart gives the physician the opportunity to rediscover the patient's identity and medical problems. Openly revealing the actual impersonality of much medical care would undermine the culturally ideal perception of the physician as deeply concerned about the welfare of others. Idealizing the behavior of physicians also encourages patients to "follow doctor's orders," which, they assume, are in their own best interest. No doubt this is often the case. But, as Chapter 20 ("Health and Medicine") explains, physicians often prescribe drugs, order tests, admit patients to hospitals, and perform surgery with a keen awareness of what's in it for themselves (Kaplan et al., 1985).

Idealization is woven into the fabric of everyday life in countless ways. Physicians and other professionals typically idealize their motives for entering their chosen careers. They describe their work as "making a contribution to science," perhaps "answering a calling from God," or "serving the community." Rarely do such people concede the less honorable, although common, motives of seeking the high income, power, and prestige these occupations confer. More generally, we all smile and make polite remarks to people we do not like. Such small hypocrisies ease our way through social interactions. Even when we suspect that others are putting on an act, we are unlikely to openly challenge their performance, for reasons that we shall explain next.

## Embarrassment and Tact

The presidential candidate enters the room and stumbles over the rug; the eminent professor consistently mispronounces a simple word; the visiting dignitary rises from the table to speak, unaware of the napkin that still clings to her dress. As carefully as individuals may craft their performances, slipups of this kind frequently occur. The result is *embarrassment*, which in a dramaturgical analysis means the discomfort that follows a spoiled performance. Goffman describes embarrassment simply as "losing face."

Embarrassment looms as an ever-present danger because, first, idealized performances typically contain some deception. Second, most performances involve a complex array of elements, any one of which if badly done can shatter the intended impression.

Curiously, an audience often overlooks flaws in a performance, thereby allowing the individual to avoid embarrassment. We discreetly inform a man that his zipper is open (creating limited embarrassment) only to help him avoid an even greater loss of face. In Hans Christian Andersen's classic fable "The Emperor's New Clothes," the child who blurts out that the emperor is naked tells the truth, but is scolded for being rude.

Members of an audience not only ignore flaws in a performance, Goffman explains, they often help the performer recover from them. *Tact* is an effort to help another person "save face." After hearing an educated person make an embarrassingly crude remark, for example, people may handle the situation in a variety of tactful ways. No response at all may signal the pretense that the statement was never made. Mild laughter may indicate they wish to dismiss what they have heard as a joke. Or a listener may simply respond, "I'm sure you didn't mean that," suggesting that the statement will not be allowed to destroy the actor's overall performance.

Why is tact such a common response? Simply because embarrassment provokes discomfort not only for one person but for *everyone*. Just as members of a theater audience feel uneasy when an actor forgets a line, people who observe a poor performance are reminded of how fragile their own performances often are. Socially constructed reality thus functions like a dam holding back a sea of chaotic possibility. Should one person's performance spring a leak, others tactfully assist in making repairs. Everyone, after all, is engaged in jointly building reality, and no one wants it to be suddenly swept away.

Goffman's research shows that although individuals interact with a considerable degree of individuality and spontaneity, everyone's social interactions are constructed out of similar, patterned elements. Almost four hundred years ago, Shakespeare wrote:

*All the world's a stage,*
*And all the men and women merely players.*
*They have their exits and their entrances,*
*And one man in his time plays many parts.*
*(As You Like It, V)*

Hand gestures vary widely from one culture to another. Yet a chuckle, grin, or smirk in response to someone's performance is universally defined as not taking the person seriously. Therefore, the world over, people who cannot restrain their mirth tactfully cover their faces.

Of course, human behavior is never as rigidly scripted as a stage performance. In a lifetime, though, each individual does assume many roles in ways that combine social structure with expressions of a unique personality. But although human behavior does not simply consist of stage and script, Shakespeare's observation still contains a good measure of truth.

# Interaction in Everyday Life: Two Illustrations

We have now examined a number of dimensions of social interaction. The final sections of this chapter illustrate these lessons by focusing on two important, yet quite different, elements of everyday life.

## Language: The Gender Issue

As explained in Chapter 3 ("Culture"), language is the thread with which members of a society weave the symbolic web we call culture. In everyday life, language conveys meaning on more than one level. Besides the *manifest* content, or what is explicitly stated, the *latent* content conveys various additional assumptions about reality. One latent message involves gender. Language defines men and women differently in at least three ways (Henley, Hamilton, & Thorne, 1992).[2]

### The Control Function of Language

A young man drives into the gas station, eager to display his new motorcycle, and proudly says, "Isn't she a beauty?" On the surface, the question has little to do with females and males. Yet, curiously, a common linguistic pattern confers the female "she," rather than male "he," on the man's prized possession.

Men often use language to establish control over their surroundings. That is, a man attaches a female pronoun to a motorcycle, car, yacht, or other object because it reflects *ownership*. Conversely, for a man or a woman to use a male pronoun in such cases sounds awkward.

---

[2] The following sections draw primarily on Henley, Hamilton, & Thorne, 1992. Additional material comes from Thorne, Kramarae, & Henley, 1983; MacKay, 1983; and others as noted.

A more obvious control function of language relates to people's names. Traditionally in the United States, and in many other parts of the world, a woman takes the family name of the man she marries. While few today consider this an explicit statement of a man's ownership of a woman, it certainly reflects historical male dominance. For this reason, an increasing proportion of women have retained their own name (more precisely, the family name obtained from their father) or merged two family names.

### The Value Function of Language

Language usually attaches greater value, force, or significance to what is defined as masculine. This pattern is deeply rooted in the English language, in ways that probably few men or women realize. For instance, the laudatory adjective "virtuous," meaning "morally worthy" or. "excellent," is derived from the Latin word *vir* meaning "man." By contrast, the pejorative adjective "hysterical" is derived from the Greek word *hyster*, meaning "uterus."

In numerous, more familiar ways, language also confers different value on the two sexes. Traditional masculine terms such as "king" or "lord" have retained their positive meaning, while comparable terms, such as "queen," "madam," or "dame" have acquired negative connotations in contemporary usage. Language thus both mirrors social attitudes and helps to perpetuate them.

Similarly, use of the suffixes "ette" and "ess" to denote femininity generally devalues the words to which they are added. For example, a *major* has higher standing than a *majorette*, as does a *host* in relation to a *hostess*. And, certainly, men's groups with names such as the Los Angeles Rams carry more stature than women's groups with names like the Radio City Music Hall Rockettes.

### The Attention Function of Language

Language also shapes reality by directing greater attention to masculine endeavors. The most obvious example is our use of personal pronouns. In the English language, the plural pronoun "they" is neutral in referring to both sexes. But the corresponding singular pronouns "he" and "she" are sex linked. According to traditional grammatical practice, "he" along with the possessive "his" and objective "him" are used to refer to *all people*. Thus, we assume that the masculine pronoun in the bit of wisdom "He who hesitates is lost" refers to women as well as to men. But this practice also reflects the traditional cultural pattern of ignoring the lives of women. Some research suggests that people continue to respond to allegedly inclusive or generic male pronouns as if only males were involved (Martyna, 1978, 1980; MacKay 1983). To many women, especially those who embrace feminism, encountering male pronouns sends a disconcerting message that women are of peripheral importance (MacKay, 1983).

For a century, advocates of gender equality have urged creation of a gender-neutral, third-person singular personal pronoun. In 1884, one language critic offered the new word "thon" (from "that" + "one") to solve the pronoun problem, as in "the successful person is thon who is well-prepared" (Converse, 1884; cited in Kramarae, Thorne, & Henley, 1983:175). The awkward sound of this phrasing suggests how firmly established traditional patterns are in our everyday lives. More recently, the plural pronoun "they" has gained currency as a singular pronoun ("*Everyone* should do as *they* please"). This usage remains controversial because it violates grammatical rules. Yet, in an age of growing concern over gender-linked bias, the English language may eventually evolve to accept this construction.

## Humor: Playing with Reality

Humor plays a vital part in our everyday lives. Comedians are among our favorite entertainers, most newspapers contain cartoon pages, and even professors and the clergy incorporate humor in their performances. Like many aspects of everyday life, humor is largely taken for granted. While everyone laughs at a joke, few people think about what makes something funny or why humor is found among humans everywhere in the world. Many of the ideas developed in this chapter provide insights into the character of humor, as we shall now see.[3]

### The Foundation of Humor

Humor stems from the contrast between two incongruous realities. Generally, one socially constructed reality can be termed *conventional* because it describes what people expect in a specific setting. The other reality, dubbed *unconventional*, represents a significant violation of cultural patterns. Humor, therefore, arises from contradic-

tion, ambiguity, and "double meanings" generated by two differing definitions of the same situation. Note how this principle works in these simple pieces of humor:

> Steve Martin muses: "I like a woman with a head on her shoulders. *I hate necks!*"

> A car pulls alongside the steaming wreck and the driver calls out: "Have an accident?"

> "No thanks," comes the reply. "*Just had one!*"

In each of these examples, the first sentence represents a conventional reality. A man seeks a woman who is sensible and intelligent. One driver offers help to another. There is nothing startling here. The second sentence in each example, however, provides an unconventional meaning that collides with what we take for granted. In the Steve Martin joke, the assertion "I hate necks!" suddenly transforms the entire statement into an unexpectedly grotesque image. Similarly, the motorist who replies, "Just had one," absurdly transforms an offer of help into an invitation to further injury. All humor is grounded in such contrasting realities.

The same simple pattern characterizes the humor of other well-known comedians:

> Groucho Marx, trying to sound manly: "This morning, I shot a lion in my pajamas." He then turns to the camera and adds, "What the lion was doing in my pajamas I'll *never* know . . ."

> On the television show "M*A*S*H", Hawkeye Pierce observes Colonel Henry Blake gallivanting around with a young woman half his age and dryly responds, "There's an age problem there; she's twenty-two and his wife's forty-eight."

Like the other two examples, each of these jokes contains two major elements, a conventional assertion followed by an unconventional one. The greater the opposition, or incongruity, between the two definitions of reality, the greater the potential for humor. The humor that opens this chapter flows from contrasting the hucksterism of car dealers with the formality and dignity expected of those who provide funeral services.

When telling jokes, people can strengthen this opposition in various ways. One technique, often used by Groucho Marx, George Burns, Gracie Allen, and other comedians of the screen, is to present the first, or conventional, remark in conversation with another actor, then to turn toward the audience (or the camera)

---

[3] The ideas contained in this discussion are those of the author (1987), except as otherwise noted. The general approach draws on work presented earlier in this chapter, especially on the ideas of Erving Goffman.

Because humor is based on incongruous definitions of reality, the most common format for comedy is "funny person-straight person." Here, one comic disrupts social conventions to the consternation of the other. The Smothers Brothers are among the many comedians to generate laughter in this way, with Tommy playing the fool to Dicky's dismay.

when delivering the second, or unconventional, line. This "shift of channel" underscores the incongruity of the two parts. To fashion the strongest contrast, comedians must pay careful attention to their performances—the precise words they use, as well as the timing of each part of the delivery. A joke is "well told" if the comic creates the sharpest possible opposition between the realities, just as humor falls flat in a careless performance. Since the key to humor lies in the opposition of realities, it is not surprising that the climax of a joke is called the *punch line*.

## The Dynamics of Humor: *"Getting It"*

Someone who does not understand both the conventional and unconventional realities embedded in a joke offers the typical complaint: "I don't get it." To "get" humor,

members of an audience must understand the two realities involved well enough to perceive their incongruity.

But there is something more to getting a joke, because some of the information listeners must grasp is usually left unstated. The audience, therefore, must pay attention to the stated elements of the joke and then inferentially complete the joke in their own minds. Consider the following exchange, from the well-known television show "Cheers":

Sam: "Diane, you're drunk."

Diane: "Yes, Sam, and you're stupid, but I'll be sober in the morning."

In this case, "getting" the joke depends on following the logic well enough to mentally complete Diane's line with the words ". . . and you'll *still* be stupid."

A more complex joke was written on the wall of a college restroom:

Dyslexics of the World, Untie!

This joke demands much more of the audience. One must know, first, that dyslexia is a condition in which people routinely reverse letters; second, one must identify the line as an adaptation of Karl Marx's call to the world's workers to unite; third and finally, one must recognize "untie" as an anagram of "unite," as one might imagine a disgruntled dyslexic person would write it.

Why would an audience be required to make this sort of effort in order to understand a joke? Simply because our reaction to a joke is heightened by the pleasure of having completed the puzzle necessary to "get it." This pleasure partly derives from satisfaction at our mental abilities. Additionally, "getting" the joke confers a favored status as an "insider" in the larger audience. These insights also explain the frustration that accompanies not getting a joke: the fear of mental inadequacy coupled with a sense of being socially excluded from a pleasure shared by others. Not surprisingly, "outsiders" in such a situation may fake "getting" the joke; others may tactfully explain a joke to them to end their sense of being left out.

But, as the old saying goes, if a joke has to be explained, it couldn't be very funny. Besides taking the edge off the language and timing on which the *punch* depends, an explanation completely relieves the audience of any mental involvement, substantially reducing their pleasure.

## The Topics of Humor

People throughout the world smile and laugh, providing ample evidence that humor is a universal human trait. But because people live in diverse cultures, they differ in what they find funny. Musicians frequently travel to perform for receptive audiences around the world, suggesting that music may be the "common language" of humanity. Comedians rarely do this, demonstrating that humor does not travel well.

What is humorous to the Chinese, then, may be lost on people in the United States. To some degree, too, the social diversity of our society means that people will find humor in different situations. New Englanders, southerners, and westerners have their own brands of humor, as do Hispanics and Anglos, fifteen- and forty-year-olds, bankers and construction workers.

For everyone, however, humor deals with topics that lend themselves to double meanings or *controversy*. For example, the first jokes many of us learned as children concerned what our culture defines as a childhood taboo: sex. The mere mention of "unmentionable acts" or even certain parts of the body can dissolve young faces in laughter.

The controversy inherent in humor often walks a fine line between what is funny and what is considered "sick." During the Middle Ages, the word *humors* (derived from the Latin *humidus*, meaning "moist") referred to a balance of bodily fluids that determined a person's degree of health. Most cultures value the ability to take conventional definitions of reality lightly (in other words, having a "sense of humor"). In fact, empirical evidence supports the old saying "Laughter is the best medicine": maintaining a sense of humor does contribute to a person's physical health partly by decreasing stress (Robinson, 1983; Haig, 1988). At the extreme, however, people who always take conventional reality lightly risk being defined as deviant or even mentally ill (mental hospitals have long been dubbed "funny farms").

Every social group considers some topics too sensitive for humorous treatment. A violation may result in the comedian being admonished for telling a "sick" joke, one that pokes fun at a situation that is expected to be handled with reverence. Some topics, in other words, are "off limits," because people expect them to be understood in only one way. People's religious beliefs, tragic accidents, or appalling crimes are the stuff of "sick" jokes.

## The Functions of Humor

As a widespread means of communication, humor has survival value for any society and for the entire human species. A structural-functional analysis suggests that humor has a valuable function as a social "safety valve," allowing people to release potentially disruptive sentiments with little consequence. Put another way, jokes express ideas that might be dangerous if taken seriously, as in the case of racial and ethnic jokes. Called to account for a remark that could be defined as offensive, a person may defuse the situation by simply stating, "I didn't mean anything by what I said—it was just a joke!" Likewise, rather than taking offense at another's behavior, a person might use humor as a form of tact, smiling, as if to say, "I could be angry at this, but I'll assume you were only kidding."

Like theater and art, humor also allows a society to challenge orthodox ideas and to explore alternatives to the status quo. Sometimes, in fact, humor may actually promote social change by loosening the hold of convention.

## Humor and Conflict

If humor holds the potential to liberate, it can also be used for subjugation. Men who tell jokes about feminists, for example, typically are voicing some measure of hostility to the interests of women (Benokraitis & Feagin, 1986; Powell & Paton, 1988). Similarly, jokes at the expense of homosexuals reveal the tensions surrounding sexual orientation in the United States.

"Put-down" jokes, which make one category of people feel good at the expense of another, are common around the globe. After collecting and analyzing jokes from many societies, Christie Davies (1990) concluded that conflict among ethnic groups is a driving force behind humor virtually everywhere. Typically, jokes label some disadvantaged category of people as stupid or ridiculous, thereby imputing greater wisdom and skills to those who share the humor. In the United States, Poles have long been the "butt" of jokes, as have Newfoundlanders ("Newfies") in eastern Canada, the Irish in Scotland, the Sikhs in India, the Hausas in Nigeria, the Tasmanians in Australia, and the Kurds in Iraq.

Disadvantaged people, of course, also make fun

Because humor involves challenging conventional definitions of a situation, outsiders—particularly ethnic and racial minorities—have always been disporportionately represented among our society's comedians.

of the powerful. Women in the United States have long joked about men, just as African Americans portray whites in humorous ways, and poor people poke fun at the rich. Throughout the world, people target their leaders with humor, and officials in some countries take such jokes seriously enough to vigorously repress them.

The significance of humor is therefore much greater than first impressions suggest. Michael Flaherty (1984, 1990) points out that socially constructing reality is constant and demanding work. Furthermore, the reality that emerges may suffer by comparison to what we are able to imagine. As long as we maintain a sense of humor, however, we are never prisoners of the present. Rather, in laughter we assert our freedom. And, in doing so, we change the world and ourselves just a little.

Although quite different, the impact of gender in our language and the way humor plays with reality are both important dimensions of everyday life. Each demonstrates our power to socially construct a world of meaning and then to react to what we have made. Each also demonstrates the value of the sociological perspective for understanding—and more actively participating in—this process.

## Summary

1. Social life is patterned in various ways. By guiding behavior within culturally approved bounds, social structure helps to make situations more understandable and predictable.

2. A major component of social structure is status. Within an entire status set, a master status has particular significance.

3. Ascribed statuses are essentially involuntary, while achieved statuses are largely earned. In practice, however, many statuses incorporate elements of both ascription and achievement.

4. Role is the dynamic expression of a status. Like statuses, roles are relational, guiding people as they interact.

5. When roles corresponding to two or more statuses are incompatible, role conflict results. Likewise, incompatibility among various roles linked to a single status (the role set) can generate role strain.

6. The phrase "social construction of reality" conveys the important idea that people build the social world as they interact.

7. The Thomas theorem states, "situations defined as real are real in their consequences."

8. People build social reality using elements of their culture and according to their available social resources.

9. Ethnomethodology refers to a means of exploring the structure of everyday social situations by violating patterns of expected behavior.

10. Dramaturgical analysis explores how people construct personal performances. This approach views everyday life in terms of theatrical performances.

11. People speak, use body language, and fashion physical settings to assist their performances. Often these performances attempt to idealize underlying intentions.

12. Women and men craft their situational behavior differently based on their different relative social power.
13. Social behavior carries the ever-present danger of embarrassment. Tact is a common response to a "loss of face" by others.
14. Language constitutes a major element in forming social reality. In various ways, language defines females and males differently, generally to the advantage of males.
15. Humor stems from the contrast between conventional and unconventional social realities. Because comedy is framed by the specific culture, people throughout the world find humor in very different situations.

## Key Concepts

**achieved status** a social position that is assumed voluntarily and that reflects a significant measure of personal ability and effort

**ascribed status** a social position that is received at birth or involuntarily assumed later in the life course

**dramaturgical analysis** the investigation of social interaction in terms of theatrical performance

**ethnomethodology** the study of the everyday, common-sense understandings that people have of the world

**master status** a status that has exceptional importance for social identity, often shaping a person's entire life

**nonverbal communication** communication using body movements, gestures, and facial expressions rather than speech

**personal space** the surrounding area over which a person makes some claim to privacy

**presentation of self** the ways in which individuals, in various settings, try to create specific impressions in the minds of others

**role** patterns of expected behavior attached to a particular status

**role conflict** incompatibility among the roles corresponding to two or more different statuses

**role set** a number of roles attached to a single status

**role strain** incompatibility among roles corresponding to a single status

**social construction of reality** the process by which individuals creatively shape reality through social interaction

**social interaction** the process by which people act and react in relation to others

**status** a recognized social position that an individual occupies

**status set** all the statuses a person holds at a given time

**Thomas theorem** the assertion that situations that are defined as real are real in their consequences

## Suggested Readings

Drawing on the sociological perspective, this paperback provides many rich insights into everyday life.

David A. Karp and William C. Yoels. *Sociology and Everyday Life*. Itasca, IL: Peacock, 1986.

These two readable classics in sociology are readily available in paperback.

Erving Goffman. *The Presentation of Self in Everyday Life*. Garden City, NY: Doubleday Anchor Books, 1959.

Peter L. Berger and Thomas Luckmann. *The Social Construction of Reality: A Treatise in the Sociology of Knowledge*. Garden City, NY: Doubleday Anchor Books, 1967.

Fiske offers an intriguing, multidisciplinary thesis that all interaction can be reduced to basic social forms.

Alan Paige Fiske. *Structures of Social Life: The Four Elementary Forms of Human Relations*. New York: The Free Press, 1991.

Television is central to everyday lives in the United States. This book brings together thirteen essays that explore television and women from a feminist perspective.

Mary Ellen Brown, ed. *Television and Women's Culture: The Politics of the Popular*. Newbury Park, CA: Sage, 1990.

A fascinating study of role conflict, this account delves into the lives of gay men who became Roman Catholic priests.

James G. Wolf. *Gay Priests*. San Francisco: Harper & Row, 1989.

The everyday lives of women—especially women of color—in our society have long been overlooked. This paperback offers an oral history of one African-American woman's life as told to her sociologist granddaughter.

Mamie Garvin Fields with Karen Fields. *Lemon Swamp and Other Places*. New York: The Free Press, 1985.

A crucial aspect of personal performances is their believability. This book explores persuasiveness in face-to-face interaction, in the mass media, and in large organizations.

Kathleen Kelley Readron. *Persuasion in Practice*. Newbury Park, CA: Sage, 1991.

Here is a recent book by an analyst of deceit whose ideas were noted in this chapter.

Paul Ekman. *Why Kids Lie: How to Encourage Truthfulness*. New York: Charles Scribner's Sons, 1989.

This sociological study explores the process of *leaving* roles.

Helen Rose Fuchs Ebaugh. *Becoming an EX: The Process of Role Exit*. Chicago: University of Chicago Press, 1988.

Physical attractiveness is a topic of growing interest in social science. This book offers a good introduction to the issue.

Elaine Hatfield and Susan Sprecher. *Mirror, Mirror . . . The Importance of Looks in Everyday Life*. Albany, NY: SUNY Press, 1986.

The centrality of gender to language and everyday reality is explored in this collection of essays; the editors also provide a comprehensive and annotated bibliography.

Barrie Thorne, Cheris Kramarae, and Nancy Henley. *Language, Gender and Society*. Cambridge: Newbury House, 1983.

As the negative tone of the phrase "woman driver" suggests, our culture has traditionally denied women the mobility it afforded to men. In this book, Virginia Scharff examines the gradual process by which women entered the automobile age.

Virginia Scharff. *Taking the Wheel: Women and the Coming of the Motor Age*. New York: The Free Press, 1991.

This report of research on a Pacific island suggests ways in which emotions, and how people think about them, are culturally variable.

Catherine A. Lutz. *Unnatural Emotions: Everyday Sentiments on a Micronesian Atoll and Their Challenge to Western Theory*. Chicago: University of Chicago Press, 1988.

Relatively little attention has been paid to the sociological analysis of humor. The following two books introduce various approaches.

Marvin R. Koller. *Humor and Society: Explorations in the Sociology of Humor*. Houston: Cap and Gown Press, 1988.

Christie Davies. *Ethnic Humor Around the World: A Comparative Analysis*. Bloomington: Indiana University Press, 1990.

This account of one of the most popular radio and television programs in history provides keen insights into race relations in the United States.

Melvin Patrick Ely. *The Adventures of Amos 'n' Andy: A Social History of an American Phenomenon*. New York: The Free Press, 1991.

# 7

# Groups
and
Organizations

Nine-year-old Alicia Martin was playing in front of her New Hampshire home when her ball rolled into the next yard. Annoyed at the child's carelessness, her eighty-eight-year-old neighbor refused to return the ball. Alicia's parents then did the properly American thing: they *sued* their neighbor, winning a court judgment for $30.20.

Although far from typical, this story of neighborhood relations points to an emerging trend in the United States: the increasing use of lawyers and the courts to settle issues that once were resolved with some hasty apologies and a handshake. The number of lawyers in the United States is fast approaching 1 million; already there is one lawyer for every 300 people in the country. Every year, some 18 million lawsuits are filed in state and federal courts, roughly one for every ten adults.

No wonder that many contemporary commentators have raised questions about whether the United States has too many lawyers. Vice-president Dan Quayle (himself an attorney who is married to an attorney) pointedly asked the American Bar Association if the United States really needs 70 percent of the world's lawyers. In fact, most of the world's societies have few lawyers; some have none at all. Even among industrial nations, the United States has produced attorneys at more than twice the rate of Great Britain, more than three times the rate of Germany, and more than twenty-five times the rate of Japan (Cohn, 1991; Johnson, 1991).

Our country's reliance on formal litigation, of course, has a number of causes beyond the large number of attorneys. As a nation, we embrace the notion of individual rights as much as any on earth, and this belief makes people quick to perceive infringements on their rights and interests. More broadly, the United States has become a vast, complex, and impersonal society, in which many traditional social clusters like neighborhoods (and perhaps even families) play a smaller role in our lives than in the past. Across the country, individuals recognize fewer obligations to their neighbors and, in many cases, do not even want to know them. A telling fact about our desire for privacy is that more than one-fourth of all households in the United States have unlisted telephone numbers. In a number of cities, including Los Angeles, the proportion rises to two-thirds.

This chapter examines the importance of *social groups*, the clusters of people with whom we interact during our daily lives. As we shall explain, the scope of group life has expanded during this century, from the small and personal families and neighborhoods of the past to the vast and anonymous bureaucracies and businesses that sociologists describe as *formal organizations*. We now turn to explaining how groups and organizations operate, and assessing the impact they have on our lives.

# Social Groups

Virtually everyone moves through life with a sense of belonging; that is the experience of group life. A **social group** is defined as *two or more people who identify with one another and have a distinctive pattern of interaction.* As human beings, we continually come together to form couples, families, circles of friends, neighborhoods, churches, businesses, clubs, and numerous large organizations. Whatever the form, groups encompass people with shared experiences, loyalties, and interests. In short, while maintaining their individuality, the members of social groups also think of themselves as a special "we."

## Groups, Aggregates, and Categories

Not every collection of people constitutes a social group. The term *aggregate* refers to people who are in the same place at the same time but who interact little, if at all, and have no sense of belonging together. People riding together on a subway, for example, form an aggregate, not a social group.

People who have some status in common, such as "mother," "sergeant," "homeowner," or "Roman Catholic" are considered a *category*. They do not constitute a social group because, while they may be aware of others like themselves, most are strangers who never socially interact.

People in some aggregates and categories *could* fuse into a social group, if the right circumstances gave them a shared identity and produced interaction over a period of time. When a subway train recently crashed beneath the streets of New York City, for example, passengers facing a common plight developed a sense of group awareness and helped each other. Similarly, a house fire or other tragic event often renews a neighborhood's community spirit as people pitch in to assist the family in need.

## Primary and Secondary Groups

People frequently greet one another with a smile and the simple phrase, "Hi! How are you?" The response is usually a well-scripted, "Just fine, thanks. How about you?" This answer, of course, is often far from truthful: in most cases, providing a detailed account of how you

Around the world, families are the most significant primary group. Weddings are one example of various rituals that reaffirm the primary bonds of family life, linking the generations with ties of identification and duty. Here members of a wedding party in Monrovia, Liberia commemorate their celebration through a family photograph.

*really* are doing would prompt the other person to beat a hasty and awkward exit.

Social groups fall into two types according to the degree of personal concern members display toward each other. According to Charles Horton Cooley, who is introduced in the box on page 178, a **primary group** refers to *a small social group in which relationships are both personal and enduring.* Bound together by strong and lasting loyalties that Cooley termed *primary relationships,* people in primary groups share many activities, spend a great deal of time together, and feel they know one another well. As a result, they typically display genuine concern for each other's welfare. The family is the most important primary group in any society.

Cooley called personal and tightly integrated groups *primary* because they are among the first groups we experience in life. In addition, the family and peer groups hold primary importance in the socialization process, shaping personal attitudes and behavior. We look to members of our primary groups for clues to our social identity as well, which is why members of any primary group almost always think of themselves in the first-person plural, as "we."

The strength of primary relationships gives many individuals considerable comfort and security. In the familiar social circles of family or friends, people feel they can "be themselves" without constantly worrying about the impressions they are making.

Members of primary groups generally provide one another with personal, financial, and emotional support. Even so, people generally think of a primary group as an end in itself rather than as a means to other ends. For example, we readily call on family members or close friends to help us move into a new apartment, without expecting to pay for their services. And we would do the same for them. For this reason, a friend who never returns a favor leaves us feeling "used" and questioning the depth of the friendship.

Members of a primary group look at fellow members as unique individuals rather than interchangeable, faceless functionaries. We usually do not care who cashes our check at the bank or pumps gasoline for our car at the corner service station. Yet in primary groups—especially the family—we are bound to others by deep ties of emotion and loyalty. Although brothers and sisters experience periodic conflict, they always remain siblings.

In contrast to the primary group, the **secondary group** is *a large and impersonal social group based on a specific interest or activity.* Secondary groups are typically larger than primary groups. For example, people who work together in an office, enroll in the same college course, live in the same city neighborhood, or belong to a particular political organization form secondary groups.

In most respects, secondary groups have precisely the opposite characteristics of primary groups. *Secondary relationships* usually involve little personal knowledge of one another and weak emotional ties. Groups built on such ties vary in duration, but they are frequently of short term, beginning and ending without particular significance. Students in a college course, for instance, who may not see one another after the semester ends, exemplify the secondary group. Because secondary groups focus on a particular interest or activity, members have little chance to develop a deep concern for one another's overall welfare. In some cases, such as co-workers who share an office, relationships are transformed from secondary to primary with the passing of time. People in a secondary group sometimes think of themselves as "we," but the boundary that distinguishes members from nonmembers is usually far less clear than in primary groups.

While secondary relationships are not particularly intense, people depend on them to achieve specific ends. Primary relationships have a *personal orientation*, then, while secondary relationships have a *goal orientation*. This does not mean that secondary ties need be formal and unemotional. On the contrary, social interactions among students, co-workers, and business associates can be enjoyable even if they are rather impersonal.

In primary groups, members define each other according to *who* they are; members of secondary groups look to one another for *what* they are, that is, what they can do. In secondary groups, in other words, we are always mindful of what we offer others and what we receive in return. This "scorekeeping" comes through most clearly in business relationships. Likewise, neighbors typically expect that a neighborly favor will be reciprocated.

The goal orientation of secondary groups encourages members to carefully craft their behavior. In these roles, then, we remain characteristically impersonal and polite. The secondary relationship, therefore, is one in which the question "How are you?" may be asked without really wanting a truthful answer.

The characteristics of primary and secondary groups are summarized in Table 7–1. As the figure sug-

**Table 7–1  PRIMARY GROUPS AND SECONDARY GROUPS: A SUMMARY**

|  | Primary Group | Secondary Group |
|---|---|---|
| *Quality of relationships* | Personal orientation | Goal orientation |
| *Duration of relationships* | Usually long-term | Variable; often short term |
| *Breadth of relationships* | Broad; usually involving many activities | Narrow; usually involving few activities |
| *Subjective perception of relationships* | As an end in itself | As a means to an end |
| *Typical examples* | Families; close friendships | Co-workers; political organizations |

## Charles Horton Cooley (1864–1929)

Many men and women fear that the world is becoming so fast paced and impersonal that people are losing touch with one another. This is nothing new: Charles Horton Cooley shared this concern a century ago as he grew up in a small town and witnessed rapid change across the United States.

Cooley's home was in Ann Arbor, Michigan, where he spent his childhood and returned to teach, serving on the faculty of the University of Michigan from 1892 until his death. His major contribution to sociology was exploring the character of the primary group. Cooley noted a disturbing trend: as the United States became more a nation of cities and factories, people seemed to become ever more individualistic and competitive, displaying less concern for the traditional family and local neighborhood. This transformation made Cooley uneasy because he was convinced of the crucial importance of small, cooperative social groups to human life. Without them, he wondered, how could people experience a feeling of belonging and develop a sense of fairness and compassion?

Cooley hoped that calling attention to the importance of primary groups would encourage the preservation of traditional values and a socially cohesive way of life. Certainly, the United States has continued to change since Cooley's lifetime, and not entirely in ways he would have wished. But, as a testament to the value of his insights, many of Cooley's social concerns are with us still.

SOURCES: Rieff (1962) and Coser (1977).

gests, we have described these two types of social groups in ideal terms; neither one precisely describes actual groups in our lives. But placing these concepts at opposite ends of a continuum provides a helpful shorthand for describing and analyzing group life.

By spotlighting primary and secondary ties, we can track changes in society itself. In general, primary relationships dominate in preindustrial societies, as people live and work within families and local villages. Strangers stand out in the social landscape. By contrast, secondary ties take precedence in modern, industrial societies, where people assume highly specialized social roles. In today's world, we all routinely engage in impersonal, secondary contacts with virtual strangers—people about whom we know very little and may never meet again (Wirth, 1938).

### Group Leadership

Social groups vary in the extent to which members recognize leaders—people charged with the responsibility for directing the group's activities. Some friendship groups grant someone the clear status of leader; others do not. Within families, parents have leadership roles, although husband and wife may disagree about who is really in charge. In secondary groups like corporations, leadership is likely to involve a formal chain of command with clearly defined duties.

Leaders are generally thought to possess extraordinary personal abilities, but decades of research have failed to produce convincing evidence of so-called "natural leaders." No particular individual traits seem to qualify a person as a leader; rather, the needs of the group itself dictate the type of leader who will be most effective (Ridgeway, 1983; Ridgeway & Diekema, 1989).

Two different leadership roles commonly emerge in groups (Bales, 1953; Bales & Slater, 1955). **Instrumental leadership** refers to *group leadership that emphasizes the completion of tasks*. Members look to instrumental leaders to "get things done." **Expressive leadership,** by contrast, *emphasizes collective well-being*. Expressive leaders take less of an interest in the performance goals of a group than with providing emotional support to group members and minimizing tension and conflict among them.

Because they concentrate on performance, instrumental leaders usually forge secondary relationships with other group members. Instrumental leaders give orders or punish people according to their contribution to the group's efforts. Expressive leaders, however, cultivate more primary relationships. They offer sympathy to a member having a tough time, work to keep the group united, and lighten serious moments with humor. While successful instrumental leaders gain a more distant *respect* from group members, expressive leaders generally enjoy more personal *affection*.

In the past, this differentiation of leadership has been linked to gender. In the traditional American family, cultural norms bestow instrumental leadership on men. As fathers and husbands, they assume primary responsibility for providing family income, making major family decisions, and disciplining children. By contrast, expressive leadership has traditionally been the purview of women. Mothers and wives historically have been expected to lend emotional support and to maintain peaceful relationships among all family members (Parsons & Bales, 1955). This division of labor partly explains why many children have greater respect for their fathers, but closer personal ties with their mothers (Macionis, 1978). Changes in family gender roles have blurred the gender-linked distinction between instrumental and expressive leadership. In other group settings, women and men are both assuming leadership roles.

Decision-making styles also distinguish types of leaders. *Authoritarian leaders* focus on instrumental concerns, make decisions on their own, and demand strict compliance from subordinates. Although this leadership style wins little affection from group members, they may praise an authoritarian leader in a crisis situation requiring immediate decisions and strong group discipline. *Democratic leaders* are more expressive, and try to include everyone in the decision-making process. Although less successful during crises, when there is little time for discussion, democratic leaders can otherwise draw on the ideas of all members to forge reflective and imaginative responses to the tasks at hand. *Laissez-faire leaders* (from the French phrase meaning roughly "to leave alone") downplay their position and power, allowing the group to function more or less on its own. Laissez-faire leaders generally are least effective in promoting group goals. Leadership style in a particular case depends, in large part, on the traits and needs of the group itself (White & Lippitt, 1953; Ridgeway, 1983).

## Group Conformity

Groups influence the behavior of their members, often promoting conformity. Some amount of group conformity provides a secure feeling of belonging; group pressure, however, can be considerable and unpleasant. Even interaction with strangers can promote conformity, as a classic experiment by Solomon Asch (1952) showed.

### Asch's Research

Asch formed groups of six to eight people, allegedly to study visual perception. He arranged with all but one member of the group to create a situation in which the remaining subject would be pressured to accept conclusions that were quite unreasonable. Sitting around a table, group members were asked one at a time to match a "standard" line, as shown in Figure 7–1 on "Card 1," to one of three lines on "Card 2." Anyone with normal vision could easily see that the line marked "A" on the right card would be the correct choice. Initially, everyone gave correct answers. Then Asch's secret accomplices began answering incorrectly, causing the naive subject to become bewildered and uncomfortable. Asch found that more than one-third of all subjects placed in such an awkward situation chose to conform to the others by answering incorrectly. Many of us are apparently willing to compromise our own judgment to avoid

**Figure 7–1**   The Cards Used in Asch's Experiment in Group Conformity
*(Asch, 1952:452–53)*

the discomfort of being different from others, even from people we do not know.

## Milgram's Research

In the early 1960s, Stanley Milgram—a one-time student of Solomon Asch—conducted a controversial conformity experiment of his own. In Milgram's initial study (1963, 1965; Miller, 1986), a researcher explained to pairs of participants that they were about to engage in a study of memory. One took the role of "teacher" and the other—who was an insider to the study—became the "learner."

The learner sat in a forbidding contraption resembling an electric chair with electrodes attached to one arm. The researcher then instructed the teacher to read aloud pairs of words. In subsequent trials, the teacher repeated the first word of each pair and asked the learner to recall the corresponding second word. As mistakes occurred, the researcher instructed the teacher to administer a shock to the learner using a "shock generator," marked to regulate electric current ranging from 15 volts (labeled "mild shock") to 300 volts (marked "intense shock") to 450 volts (marked "Danger: Severe Shock" and "XXX"). Beginning at the lowest level, the researcher instructed teachers to increase the shock by 15 volts every time the learner made a mistake. The experimenter explained to the teacher that the shocks would become "extremely painful" but cause "no permanent tissue damage."

The results provided striking evidence of the ability of leaders to obtain compliance. None of forty subjects assigned in the role of teacher during the initial research even questioned the procedure before 300 volts had been applied, and twenty-six of the subjects—almost two-thirds—went all the way to 450 volts.

In later research, although the proportion of subjects who applied the maximum shock varied, Milgram's subjects administered shocks to people who verbally objected, people who protested that they had heart conditions, and many even turned up the voltage as individuals screamed and then feigned unconsciousness. Understandably, many subjects found the experiment extremely stressful, the source of controversy ever since. No less disturbing is the implication of Milgram's research that people who commit atrocities against fellow human beings—as did hundreds of German soldiers during the Nazi regime—are more or less ordinary people who are "just following orders."

Milgram (1964) then modified his research to see if Solomon Asch had found a high degree of group conformity only because the task of matching lines seemed trivial. What if groups pressured people to administer electrical shocks? To investigate, he varied the experiment so that a group of three "teachers," two of whom were his accomplices, made decisions jointly. Milgram's rule was that each of the three teachers would suggest a shock level when the learner made an error, and the shock actually given would be the *lowest* of the three suggestions. This gave the naive subject the power to lessen the shock level regardless of what the other two "teachers" suggested. The accomplices recommended increasing the shock level with each error, placing group pressure on the third member to do the same. Responding to this pressure, subjects applied voltages three to four times higher than in experiments when they were acting alone. Thus Milgram's research suggests that people are surprisingly likely to follow not only the directions of "legitimate authority figures," but also groups of "ordinary individuals."

Social organization depends on some measure of obedience and conformity. But who we recognize as legitimate leaders and the extent to which we respect them depend on a host of political factors that vary from situation to situation.

Reference groups are important not only for making specific evaluations; they also serve as role models, guiding the personality development of a society's young people.

### Janis's Research

Even the experts succumb to pressure for group conformity, according to Irving L. Janis (1972, 1989). Janis contends that a number of foreign policy errors made by the United States, including the failure to foresee the Japanese attack on Pearl Harbor in World War II, the disastrous U.S. invasion of Cuba's Bay of Pigs in 1961, and our ill-fated involvement in the Vietnam War, may have been the result of group conformity among our highest-ranking political leaders.

We often think that a group's "brainstorming" will improve decision making. However, Janis argues that group decision making sometimes backfires. First, rather than examining a problem from many points of view, groups often seek consensus, thereby *narrowing* the range of options. Second, groups may develop a distinctive language, adopting terms that favor a single interpretation of events. Third, having settled on a position, members of the group may come to see anyone with another view as the "opposition." Janis called this process **"groupthink,"** *a limited understanding of some issue due to group conformity.*

Janis claims that "groupthink" led the Kennedy administration to invade Cuba—a plan that failed and provoked international criticism of the United States. Arthur Schlesinger, Jr., former adviser to President John Kennedy, confessed guilt "for having kept so quiet during those crucial discussions in the Cabinet Room," but added that the group discouraged anyone from challenging what, in retrospect, appeared to be "nonsense" (Janis, 1972:30, 40).

Of course, U.S. officials are not the only leaders who can be blinded by group consensus. In 1991, a group of eight top government officials carried out a short-lived seizure of power in the Soviet Union. From their point of view, their actions did not constitute an illegal "coup" but a necessary and patriotic act to save their country from reform that had slipped out of control. Despite access to vast amounts of information through government agencies, however, these leaders failed to accurately anticipate the reaction of their opponents, foreign governments, and even their own people to their power grab.

## Reference Groups

How do we know if a particular decision is a good one? Frequently, we evaluate our views in relation to those of others, often using some **reference group,** *a social group that serves as a point of reference for people making evaluations or decisions.*

A young man who imagines his family's response to a woman he is dating is using his family as a reference group. Similarly, a banker who assesses her colleagues' reactions to a new loan policy is using her co-workers as a standard of reference. As these examples suggest, reference groups can be primary or secondary. And because we are often strongly motivated to conform to a group, the attitudes of group members can greatly affect personal evaluations.

Groups of which we are *not* members also can

be used for reference. People preparing for job interviews typically anticipate how those in the company dress and act, and they adjust their personal performances accordingly. The use of groups by nonmembers illustrates the process of *anticipatory socialization*, described in Chapter 5 ("Socialization"). By conforming, individuals hope to win acceptance to the group.

### Stouffer's Research

Samuel A. Stouffer (1949) and his associates conducted a classic study of reference group dynamics during World War II. In a survey, researchers asked soldiers to evaluate the chances of promotion for a competent soldier in their branch of the service. Common sense suggests that soldiers serving in outfits with a relatively high promotion rate would be optimistic about their future advancement. Yet survey results revealed just the opposite: soldiers in branches of the service with low promotion rates were actually more optimistic about their own chances for advancement.

The key to this paradox lies in recognizing the groups against which the soldiers measured their progress. Those in branches with lower promotion rates compared their advancement with people like themselves; typically, they had not been promoted, but neither had many others, so they did not feel deprived and expressed favorable attitudes about their chances for promotion. Soldiers in a service branch with a higher promotion rate, however, could easily think of people who had been promoted sooner or more often than they had. Using these people as a reference group, even soldiers who had been promoted were likely to feel they had come up short. These were the soldiers who voiced more negative attitudes in their evaluations.

Stouffer's research demonstrates that we do not make judgments about ourselves in isolation, nor do we compare ourselves with just anyone. Instead, we use specific social groups as standards in developing individual attitudes. Regardless of our situation in *absolute* terms, then, we perceive well-being subjectively, *relative* to some specific reference group (Merton, 1968; Mirowsky, 1987).

## Ingroups and Outgroups

Differences among groups, in political outlook, social prestige, even manner of dress, may lead us to embrace one while avoiding others. Across the United States,

Ingroups and outgroups are often based on dimensions of inequality. In Joseph Decker's painting, *Our Gang* (1886), the artist shows how readily race can lead some people to experience social marginality. The African-American boy has his back against a wall covered with weathered posters that seem to point to him like a finger of accusation (Decker originally named this painting *The Accused*). The reality of race in the United States is that people of color often find themselves cast in the role of an outgroup.

*Our Gang, 1886. Oil on canvas, 10¾ × 20 (27.3 × 50.8). Signed in lower right corner: J. Decker (illegible). Private Collection.*

for example, students wear high-school jackets and place school decals on car windows to indicate that, to them, school serves as an important social group. Students attending another school may become the targets of derision simply because they belong to a rival group.

This illustrates an important process of group dynamics: the opposition of ingroups and outgroups. An **ingroup** is *a social group commanding a member's esteem and loyalty.* An ingroup exists in relation to an **outgroup,** *a social group toward which one feels competition or opposition.* Many social groups follow this pattern. A sports team, for example, is both an ingroup to its members and an outgroup for members of opposing teams. A town's Democrats generally think of themselves as an ingroup in relation to the local Republicans. All ingroups and outgroups work on the principle that "we" have valued characteristics that "they" lack.

Tensions among groups often help to sharpen their boundaries and to give people a clearer social identity. However, distinguishing groups in this way promotes self-serving distortions of reality. Research has shown that the members of ingroups hold overly positive views of themselves and unfairly negative views of various outgroups (Tajfel, 1982). Ethnocentrism, for example, grows out of the tendency to overvalue one's own "group," while undervaluing other cultures as outgroups.

When an ingroup has greater social power than an outgroup it opposes, serious personal and social problems may result. For example, whites have historically viewed people of color in negative terms and subjected them to certain social, political, and economic disadvantages. Internalizing these negative attitudes, people of African, Hispanic, Asian, and Native-American descent often struggle to overcome negative self-images based on stereotypes held by the larger society. The operation of particular ingroups and outgroups often mirrors patterns of social inequality in the larger society. Clarifying group boundaries, then, may foster both loyalty (to the ingroup) as well as social tension and conflict (with the outgroup).

## Group Size

If you are the first person to arrive at a party, you can observe a fascinating process in group dynamics. Until about six people enter the room, everyone generally shares a single conversation. But as more people arrive, the group soon divides into two or more smaller clusters. It is apparent that size plays a crucial role in how group members interact.

To understand why, consider the mathematical connection between the number of people in a social group and the number of relationships among them, as shown in Figure 7–2. Two people form a single relationship; adding a third person generates three relationships; a fourth person yields six. Adding people one at a time—a process mathematicians describe as an *arithmetic progression*—rapidly increases the number of relationships in a *geometric progression*. By the time six people join one conversation, fifteen different relationships connect them, so the group usually divides at this point.

German sociologist Georg Simmel (1858–1918) explored the social dynamics in the smallest social groups. Simmel (1950; orig. 1902) used the term **dyad** to designate *a social group with two members*. In the United States, love affairs, marriages, and the closest friendships are dyadic. Simmel identified two special qualities of the dyad. First, they are typically less stable than groups with many members. Both members of a dyad must actively participate in the relationship; if either withdraws, the group collapses. Because the stability of marriages is important to society, this dyad is supported with legal and often religious ties. In contrast, a large group is inherently more stable. A volunteer fire company, for example, does not dissolve even if a few members drop out.

Second, social interaction in a dyad is typically more intense than in other groups. In such a one-to-one relationship, neither member shares the other's attention with anyone else. For this reason, dyads also have the potential to be the most meaningful social bonds we ever experience. Because marriage in our culture is dyadic, powerful emotional ties generally unite husbands and wives. As we shall see in Chapter 15 ("Family"), however, marriage in other societies can involve more than two people. In that case, the marriage is more stable although the many marital relationships, viewed individually, are typically less strong.

Simmel also probed the **triad**, *a social group with three members*. A triad encompasses three relationships, each uniting two of the three people. Two can form a coalition to press their views on the third, or two may

**Figure 7–2**  Group Size and Relationships

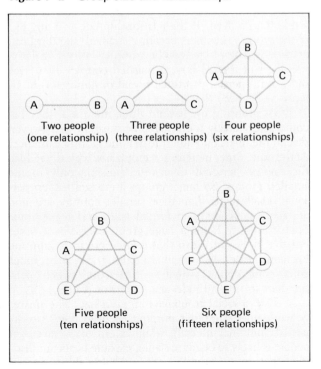

Two people
(one relationship)

Three people
(three relationships)

Four people
(six relationships)

Five people
(ten relationships)

Six people
(fifteen relationships)

A distinctive characteristic of a triad is that the social bond that joins two members can intensify, to the exclusion of the third.

intensify their relationship, leaving the other feeling like a "third wheel." For example, the members of a triad, two of whom develop a romantic interest in each other, are likely to understand the old saying "Two's company, three's a crowd."

Despite characteristic problems, a triad is more stable than a dyad. If the relationship between any two of the group's members becomes strained, the third can act as a mediator to restore the group's vitality. Similarly, members of a dyad (say, a married couple) often seek out a third person (a trusted friend or counselor) to air tensions between them.

As groups grow beyond three members, they become progressively more stable because the loss of even several members does not threaten the group's existence. At the same time, increases in group size typically reduce the intense personal interaction possible only in the smallest groups. So larger groups are based less on personal attachments than their smaller counterparts and are more dependent on formal rules and regulations. Such formality helps a large group persist over time, but that does not mean that a large group is immune to change. After all, numerous members give large groups considerable contact with the outside world, which opens the door to new attitudes and behavior (Carley, 1991).

Does a social group have an ideal size? The answer depends on the group's purpose. A dyad offers unsurpassed emotional intensity, while a group of several dozen people is likely to be more stable, capable of accomplishing larger, more complex tasks, and better able to assimilate new members or ideas. People typically find more personal *pleasure* in smaller groups, while deriving greater *satisfaction* from accomplishing tasks in larger organizations (Slater, 1958; Ridgeway, 1983; Carley, 1991).

## Social Diversity

Social diversity also affects the behavior of group members, especially the likelihood that they will interact with someone of another group. Peter Blau (1977, 1982; South & Messner, 1986) points out four ways in which the structure of social groups regulates intergroup association.

First, extending Simmel's analysis, Blau identifies a further consequence of group size. The larger a group, he claims, the more likely any individual member is to maintain relationships exclusively within the group; the smaller the group, by contrast, the greater the odds that members will reach beyond their immediate social circle. To illustrate, increasing the number of international students on a campus may well have the effect of enabling these students to maintain their own distinctive social group. Thus intentional efforts to promote social diversity may well have the unintended effect of limiting contact between international students and others. As a broader example, members of smaller communities (say, based on ethnicity) are more likely to marry out of their group than members of larger communities (Gurak & Fitzpatrick, 1982).

Second, Blau argues that the more internally heterogeneous groups are, the more likely members of one group are to interact with members of another group. We would expect, for example, that campus groups that recruit members of both sexes and of various ethnic and geographic backgrounds, would promote more intergroup contact than those who choose members of one social type.

Third, Blau asserts that the greater the overall social parity within a setting, the more likely it is that people of diverse backgrounds will mingle and form social ties. In socially diverse settings, then, members typically forge social ties that transcend their own cultural, ethnic, or racial categories. By contrast, members of socially exclusive groups are less likely to establish friendships or other ties with people whose backgrounds differ markedly from their own.

Fourth, Blau contends that physical space affects the chances of contacts among groups. To the extent that a social group is physically segregated from others (by having its own dorm or dining area, for example), its members are less apt to engage other people.

## Networks

Not all social interaction takes place within well-defined groups. A **network** is *a web of social ties that links people who may have little common identity and interaction.* A network resembles a social group in that it joins people in relationships. But unlike people in groups, network members typically feel little sense of membership and rarely have direct contact with one another. The boundaries of networks are thus less clear cut than those of groups. If we think of a group as a "circle of friends," we might describe a network as a "social web" expanding outward, with most members connected indirectly through others.

Network ties may be close, as among college friends who years later keep in touch by mail and telephone. More commonly, however, a network includes people we *know of*—or who *know of us*—but with whom we interact infrequently, if at all. As one woman with a widespread reputation as a community organizer explains, "I get calls at home, someone says, 'Are you Roseann Navarro? Somebody told me to call you. I have this problem . . .'" (Kaminer, 1984:94). For this reason, social networks have been described as "clusters of weak ties" (Granovetter, 1973).

Network ties may be weak, but they can serve as a significant resource. For example, many people rely on their networks to find jobs. Even the scientific genius Albert Einstein needed a hand in landing his first job. After a year of unsuccessful interviewing, he obtained employment only when the father of one of his classmates put him in touch with an office manager who hired him (Clark, 1971; cited in Fischer, 1977:19). As the saying goes, *who you know* is often just as important as *what you know.*

A survey by Nan Lin (1981) determined that almost 60 percent of 399 men in one city in the United States had found a job through networks. Lin concluded that networks were the greatest single occupational resource, but he also found that networks do not provide equal advantages to everyone. The sons of men with important occupational positions gained the greatest advantages from networks. This finding supports the notion that networks link people of similar social background, thereby perpetuating social privilege.

Peter Marsden (1987) discovered that the most ex-

Today's college campuses value social diversity. One of the challenges of multiculturalism is ensuring that all categories of students are integrated into campus life. But as the number of minority students increases, according to Blau's theory of group dynamics, these individuals are able to form a group unto themselves, perhaps interacting less with others.

tensive social networks are maintained by people who are young, well educated, and living in urban areas. The networks of men and women tend to be the same size, although women include more relatives in their networks while those of men encompass more co-workers (Moore, 1990). Women's networks, therefore, may not carry the clout that the "old-boy" networks do. In response, many women have begun to pay more attention to building networks in the world of work. Women's networks provide the support, camaraderie, and business contacts that women might otherwise lack (Speizer, 1983; Coppock, 1987).

## Formal Organizations

A century ago, social life was centered in small groups— the family, friendship and working groups, and the local neighborhood. Today, our lives revolve far more around **formal organizations,** *large, secondary groups that are organized to facilitate achieving their goals efficiently.* Formal organizations, such as corporations or branches of government, differ from small family or friendship groups in more than simply the size of their membership. Their greater size renders social relationships less personal, and also fosters a planned or formal atmosphere. People design formal organizations to accomplish specific tasks, rather than to meet personal needs.

With a population exceeding 250 million, the United States performs countless, complicated tasks ranging from educating expectant parents to delivering the mail. Most of these responsibilities are carried out by large, formal organizations. The United States government, the nation's largest formal organization, employs more than 5 million people in various agencies and the armed forces. Each government division includes an array of smaller organizations with specific goals. Such large groups develop lives and cultures of their own, so that as members come and go, the statuses they fill and the roles they perform remain unchanged over the years.

## Types of Formal Organizations

Amitai Etzioni (1975) has identified three types of formal organizations, distinguished by the type of member affiliation—normative organizations, coercive organizations, and utilitarian organizations.

### Normative Organizations

People join *normative organizations* to pursue goals they consider morally worthwhile, and derive personal satisfaction, perhaps social prestige, but no monetary reward for their efforts. Sometimes called *voluntary associations*, these include community service groups (such as the PTA, the Lions Club, the League of Women Voters, Red Cross, and Kiwanis), political parties, religious organizations, and numerous other confederations concerned with specific social issues. Because women have historically been excluded from much of the paid labor force, they have played a greater part than men in civic and charitable organizations.

### Coercive Organizations

In Etzioni's typology, *coercive organizations* are distinguished by involuntary membership. That is, people are forced to join the organization as a form of punishment (prisons) or treatment (psychiatric hospitals). Coercive organizations have extraordinary physical features, such as locked doors, barred windows, and security personnel (Goffman, 1961). They are designed to segregate people as "inmates" or "patients" for a period of time, and sometimes radically alter people's attitudes and behavior. Recall from Chapter 5 ("Socialization") the power of coercive total institutions to transform a human being's overall sense of self.

### Utilitarian Organizations

According to Etzioni, people join *utilitarian organizations* in pursuit of material rewards. Large business enterprises, for example, generate profits for their owners and income in the form of salaries and wages for their employees. Joining utilitarian organizations is usually a matter of individual choice, although, obviously, most people must join one utilitarian organization or another to make a living. While utilitarian organizations certainly offer greater individual freedom than coercive organizations, they provide less autonomy than normative organizations. This is because most people have little choice but to spend something approaching half of their waking hours at work, and because most workers have only limited control over their jobs.

From differing vantage points, any particular organization may fall into *all* of these categories. A psychiatric hospital, for example, serves as a coercive organization for a patient, a utilitarian organization for a psychiatrist, and a normative organization to a part-time hospital volunteer.

## Origins of Bureaucracy

Formal organizations date back thousands of years. Religious and political administrations extended the power of elites over millions of people living in vast areas. Formal organization also allowed rulers to collect taxes, undertake military campaigns, and construct monumental structures such as the Great Wall of China.

The effectiveness of these early organizations was limited, however. This was not because the elites lacked grandiose ambition; rather it was due to the traditional character of preindustrial societies. Long-established cultural patterns placed greater importance on "God's will" than on organizational efficiency. Only in the last few centuries did there emerge what Max Weber called a "rational world view," as described in Chapter 4 ("Society"). In the wake of the Industrial Revolution, the organizational structure called *bureaucracy* became commonplace in Europe and North America.

Although formal organization is vital to modern, industrial societies, it is far from new. Twenty-five centuries ago, the Chinese philosopher and teacher K'ung Fu-Tzu (known to Westerners as Confucius) endorsed the idea that government offices should be filled by the most talented young men. This led to one of the world's first systems of civil service examinations. Here, would-be bureaucrats compose essays to demonstrate their knowledge of Confucian texts.

**Bureaucracy** is *an organizational model rationally designed to perform complex tasks efficiently.* Through bureaucratic organization, officials deliberately enact and revise policy to make the organization as efficient as possible. To appreciate the power and scope of bureaucratic organization, consider the telephone system in the United States. Each of more than 160 million telephones can be used to reach any other telephone in homes, businesses, and automobiles within seconds. This major organizational feat reaches far beyond the imagination of the ancient world. Of course, the telephone system depends on technological developments such as electric-

ity. But neither could the system exist without the organizational capacity to keep track of every telephone call—noting which phone was used to call which other phone, when, and for how long—and presenting all this information to millions of telephone users in the form of monthly bills.

In global context, the availability of telephones and other forms of electronic communication is one indicator of the extent of bureaucratic organization. As shown in Global Map 7–1 on page 188, facsimile (fax) machines and other devices for data transmission are most common in the United States and Canada, Western

**Global Map 7–1**  Data Transmission in Global Perspective

The expansion of formal organization depends partly on available technology. Facsimile (fax) machines and other devices for transmitting data are most widespread in economically developed regions of the world, including the United States, Canada, Western Europe, Japan, and Australia. In poor societies, such devices are all but unknown. Note, too, that the wealthy elite in small nations like Kuwait make use of advanced technology to support their global business operations.

Europe, Japan, and Australia and New Zealand. In most nations of the world, however, such devices are limited to government officials, large businesses, and urban elites. Thus the proliferation of bureaucracy is closely tied to economic development.

## Characteristics of Bureaucracy

What are the characteristics of an efficient organization? Max Weber (1978; orig. 1921) argued that six key elements define the ideal bureaucratic organization.

1. **Specialization.** Through most of human history, all people's lives centered on securing food and shelter. Bureaucracy embodies a whole different set of imperatives by assigning people highly specialized tasks that correspond to organizational offices.
2. **Hierarchy of offices.** Bureaucracies arrange offices vertically to form a hierarchy, according to each official's responsibilities. Each employee is thus supervised by "higher-ups" in the organization while, in turn, supervising others in lower positions.
3. **Rules and regulations.** Tradition holds scant sway in bureaucracy. Instead, operations are guided by rationally enacted rules and regulations. These rules guide not only the organization's own functioning but, as much as possible, its larger environment. Ideally, a bureaucracy seeks to operate in a completely predictable fashion.
4. **Technical competence.** Bureaucratic officials are expected to have the technical competence to carry out the duties of their offices. Bureaucracies typically evaluate new staff members according to specified criteria and subsequently monitor their performance. This practice of impersonal evaluation based on performance contrasts sharply with the custom, followed through most of human history, of favoring relatives—whatever their talents—over strangers.
5. **Impersonality.** In bureaucratic organizations, rules take precedence over personal feelings. Ideally, this ensures uniform treatment for each client, supervisor, or subordinate. From this detached approach stems the notion of the "faceless bureaucrat."
6. **Formal, written communications.** Certainly, some truth lies in the adage that the heart of bureaucracy is not people but paperwork. Rather than casual, verbal communication, bureaucracy demands formal, written letters, memos, and reports. Over time, this correspondence accumulates into vast *files.* Such documents guide an organization in roughly the same way that personality guides the individual.

## Bureaucracy Versus Small Groups

In small groups, especially primary groups like the family, people are valued for who they *are,* that is, for the personal relationships they maintain. By contrast, the value of bureaucratic organizations lies in what they *do.* As a path to efficient performance, then, bureaucracy serves as a means to an end.

Bureaucratic organization promotes efficiency by carefully recruiting personnel and limiting the variable and unpredictable effects of personal tastes and opinions. In smaller, informal groups, members have considerable discretion in their behavior, they respond to each other personally, and consider one another more or less equal in rank. Weber believed, however, that such traits compromised organizational efficiency. He concluded that a rigid and impersonal organizational system maximizes performance, but does not necessarily enhance the personal satisfaction of members. Table 7–2 on page 190 summarizes the differences between small social groups and large formal organizations.

## The Informal Side of Bureaucracy

In Weber's ideal bureaucracy, every activity is deliberately regulated. In actual organizations, however, human behavior often diverges from bureaucratic blueprints. Sometimes informality helps to meet a legitimate need overlooked by formal regulations. In other situations, such as cutting corners in one's job, informal behavior clearly violates official rules (Scott, 1981).

Personality, for example, greatly affects patterns of organizational leadership. Formally, power resides in offices, not with the people who occupy them. Studies of corporations in the United States reveal, however,

**Table 7–2    SMALL GROUPS AND FORMAL ORGANIZATIONS: A COMPARISON**

|  | Small Groups | Formal Organizations |
|---|---|---|
| *Activities* | Members typically engage in many of the same activities | Members typically engage in various highly specialized activities |
| *Hierarchy* | Often informal or nonexistent | Clearly defined, corresponding to offices |
| *Norms* | Informal application of general norms | Clearly defined rules and regulations |
| *Criteria for membership* | Variable, often based on personal affection or kinship | Technical competence to carry out assigned tasks |
| *Relationships* | Variable; typically primary | Typically secondary, with selective primary ties |
| *Communications* | Typically casual and face to face | Typically formal and in writing |
| *Focus* | Person oriented | Task oriented |

that the qualities and quirks of individuals—including their charisma or skill in interpersonal relations—have a tremendous impact on organizational outcomes (Halberstam, 1986). Among the many leaders of the former Soviet Union, the exceptional leadership skills of Mikhail Gorbachev and Boris Yeltsin have played a central part in the continuing reorganization of Soviet society.

Authoritarian, democratic, and laissez-faire types of leadership—described earlier in this chapter—also reflect individual personality as much as any organizational plan. Then, too, decision making within an organization does not always conform to official regulations. As the recent savings and loan scandal reveals, officials and their friends may personally benefit through abuse of organizational power. In the "real world" of organizational life, officials who attempt to operate strictly by the book may even find themselves denied the promotions and power that are based on informal alliances. In some organizations, too, people in leadership positions rely on subordinates to handle much of their own work. Many secretaries, for example, have more authority and responsibility than their official job titles and salaries suggest.

Communication offers another example of how informality creeps into large organizations. Formally, memos and other written communications disseminate information through the hierarchy. Typically, however, individuals cultivate informal networks or "grapevines" that spread information much faster, if not always as accurately. Grapevines are particularly significant to subordinates because executives often attempt to conceal important information from them.

Sometimes employees modify or ignore rigid bureaucratic structures to advance their own interests. A classic study of the Western Electric factory in Chicago revealed that few employees reported fellow workers who violated rules, as they were required to (Roethlisberger & Dickson, 1939). On the contrary, those who *did* were socially isolated, labeled by other workers as "squealers" who could not be trusted. Although the company formally set productivity standards, workers informally created their own definition of a fair day's work, criticizing those who exceeded it as "rate-busters" and others who fell short as "chiselers."

Such informal social structures suggest that people often resist the dehumanizing aspects of bureaucracy. Organizational informality also reveals that human beings have the creative capacity to personalize even rigidly defined social situations.

## Limitations of Bureaucracy

Weber touted the ideal bureaucracy as a model of efficiency. Still, real-life formal organizations certainly have their limitations, even when it comes to the performance of specific tasks. Anyone who has ever tried to replace a lost driver's license, return defective merchandise to a discount chain store, or change an address on a magazine subscription knows that large organizations can be maddeningly unresponsive to individual needs.

Of course, no organizational system will ever eradicate human failings. Moreover, some problems occur because organizations are *not* truly bureaucratic. But, as Weber himself recognized, even the pure form of bureaucracy has inherent limitations. Perhaps the most serious limitation of bureaucracy is its potential to *dehumanize* those it purports to serve. To operate efficiently, each client must be treated impersonally as a standard "case." In other words, in striving for efficiency, organization members lose the ability to personally know their clients or customers and to provide individual attention.

Weber also feared that bureaucratic impersonality would *alienate* those who worked in large organizations. A human being in a formal organization, he claimed, was often reduced to "a small cog in a ceaselessly moving mechanism" (1978:988; orig. 1921). Although formal organizations are intended to serve humanity, Weber worried that humanity would eventually end up serving formal organizations.

The ambivalence of many people toward bureaucracy, then, is understandable. On the one hand, formal organizations advance many of our deeply held cultural values (see Chapter 3, "Culture"), including efficiency, practicality, and achievement. On the other hand, bureaucracies threaten the cherished ideals of democracy and individual freedom. In addition, the growth of formal organizations has prompted a decline in individual privacy (Long, 1967; Smith, 1979). The box on page 192 provides details.

### Bureaucratic Waste and Incompetence

*"Work expands to fill the time available for its completion."* Enough truth underlies C. Northcote Parkinson's (1957) tongue-in-cheek assertion that it is known today as Parkinson's Law.

To illustrate, assume that a bureaucrat processes fifty applications in an average day. If one day this worker had only twenty-five applications to examine, how much time would the task require? The logical answer is half a day. But Parkinson's Law suggests that if a full day is available to complete the work, a full day is how long it will take. Because organizational employees have little personal involvement in their work, few are likely to seek extra work to fill their spare time. Bureaucrats strive to *appear* busy, however, prompting organizations to take on more employees. The added time and expense required to hire, train, supervise, and evaluate a larger staff makes everyone busier still, setting in motion a vicious cycle that results in *bureaucratic bloat*. Ironically, the larger organization may accomplish no more real work than it did in its leaner incarnation.

Laurence J. Peter (Peter & Hull, 1969) devised the Peter Principle, which states that *bureaucrats are promoted to their level of incompetence*. The logic here is simple: employees competent at any level of the organizational hierarchy are likely to be promoted to higher positions. Eventually, however, when they reach a posi-

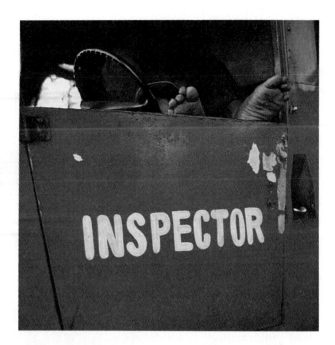

According to Max Weber, bureaucracy is an organizational strategy that promotes efficiency. Impersonality, however, also fosters alienation among employees, who may become indifferent to the formal goals of the organization. The behavior of this municipal employee in Bombay, India is understandable to members of formal organizations almost anywhere in the world.

tion where they are in over their heads and perform poorly, they are no longer eligible for promotion. They are thereby doomed to a future of inefficiency. Adding to the problem, by this time they have almost certainly acquired enough power to protect their interests, avoiding demotion or dismissal by hiding behind rules and regulations and taking credit for work actually performed by their more competent subordinates.

### Bureaucratic Ritualism

For many of us, the concept *bureaucracy* conjures up images of *red tape* (derived from the red tape used by eighteenth-century English officials to wrap official parcels and records; Shipley, 1985). Red tape refers to a tedious concern with organizational procedures. In Robert Merton's view (1968), red tape amounts to a type of group conformity. He coined the term **bureaucratic ritualism** to signify *a preoccupation with rules and regula-*

# Bureaucracy and the Information Revolution: A Threat to Privacy?

A century ago, people who wanted personal privacy built a fence around their houses and hung "Beware of Dog" signs on the gates. Today, however, fences and dogs do little to protect people in the United States from some kinds of intrusions. More people now have access to more information about each one of us than ever before.

Why? Because of the growth of formal organizations. Without a doubt, bureaucracy is essential to a vast and complex society, but the cost is ever-larger banks of personal information. Automobile drivers must be licensed, but doing so requires gathering information about everyone who legally operates a vehicle. Similarly, the Internal Revenue Service, the Social Security Administration, and programs that benefit veterans, students, the poor, and unemployed people must each collect extensive information.

The explosive growth of credit in the country's economy has also fueled the drive for information. In the past, local merchants offered credit to customers with no more paperwork than an I.O.U. Today, people in the United States carry almost 1 billion credit cards, enabling them to obtain credit from total strangers.

This information revolution has

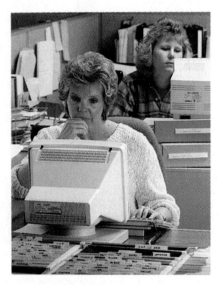

The Information Revolution—the ability to process and store information efficiently—has transformed organizational life in the United States. At the center of this transformation is the computer. While improving our lives in various ways, computers also amass a vast amount of data about each of us, thus generating an unprecedented threat to personal privacy.

spawned a new growth industry: maintaining files about people's place of residence, marital status, employment, income, debts, and history of paying their bills on time. Further eroding our privacy, computers now disseminate this information more widely and more

rapidly than ever before. Because addresses are easily added to mailing lists, we are now deluged by so-called junk mail, which makes up half of all correspondence. Of greater concern, information circulates from organization to organization, generally without the knowledge or consent of the people in question.

In response, many states have adopted laws recognizing the right of citizens to examine records about themselves kept by employers, banks, and credit bureaus. The U.S. Privacy Act of 1974 also places limitations on the exchange of information about individuals among government agencies. Additionally, citizens now have the right to examine the information contained in most government files, and they may offer corrections that become part of the record. Additional legislation is now being devised, since some existing laws give the public access to conventional paper files, but not more recent computer data bases.

Existing laws have slowed the erosion of personal privacy, but even expanded legislation is unlikely to reverse this trend. The price of relying on formal organizations may be the sacrifice of much personal privacy.

SOURCES: Smith (1979) and Miller (1991).

George Tooker's painting *Government Bureau* is a powerful statement about the human costs of bureaucracy. The artist depicts members of the public in monotonous similitude—reduced from human beings to mere "cases" to be disposed of as quickly as possible. Set apart from others by their positions, officials are "faceless bureaucrats" concerned more with numbers than with providing genuine assistance.

Government Bureau, 1956. Egg tempera on gesso panel. 19⅝ x 29⅝ inches. The Metropolitan Museum of Art, George A. Hearn Fund, 1956. (56.78)

*tions as ends in themselves rather than as the means to organizational goals.*

Bureaucratic ritualism occurs when people become so intent on conforming to rules that they thwart the goals of the organization. Besides reducing individual and organizational performance, ritualism stifles creativity and imagination, robbing the organization of the talents, ideas, and innovations necessary to operate more efficiently as circumstances change (Whyte, 1957; Merton, 1968). In bureaucratic ritualism, we see one form of the alienation that Max Weber feared would arise from bureaucratic rigidity.

## Bureaucratic Inertia

Weber noted that "once fully established, bureaucracy is among the social structures which are hardest to destroy" (1978:987; orig. 1921). Through **bureaucratic inertia,** *the tendency of bureaucratic organizations to persist over time,* formal organizations take on a life of their own and perpetuate themselves. Occasionally, a formal organization that meets its organizational goals will simply disband—as the anti-British Sons of Liberty did after the Revolutionary War. More commonly, an organization redefines its goals so that it can continue to provide a livelihood for its members. The National Association for Infantile Paralysis, the sponsor of the well-known March of Dimes, was created to help find a cure for polio. They succeeded with the development of the Salk vaccine in the early 1950s. But the organization did not then dissolve; it simply redirected its efforts toward other medical problems such as birth defects (Sills, 1969). It still exists today.

Once created, then, formal organizations may remain in operation whether or not they have any meaningful purpose. "Sunset laws," widely enacted in the United States, require government agencies that cannot justify their existence to be terminated. In Illinois, for example, officials who reviewed the qualifications of people who shoe horses were finally relieved of their duties decades after their usefulness had ceased. Despite such examples, bureaucratic inertia usually leads formal organizations to devise justifications for themselves long after they have outlived their originally intended purpose.

## Oligarchy

Early in this century, Robert Michels (1876–1936) pointed out that one of the consequences of bureaucracy is **oligarchy,** *the rule of the many by the few* (1949; orig. 1911). The earliest human societies did not possess the organizational means for even the most power-hungry ruler to control everyone. The development of formal

The notion that organizations can muster vast resources to perpetuate themselves is called into question by the rapid and sweeping changes in Eastern Europe and the former Soviet Union. Oligarchies, it turns out, are more vulnerable to popular opposition than the thinking of Robert Michels suggests they are.

organizations, however, enhanced the opportunities for a small elite to dominate society. According to what Michels called "the iron law of oligarchy," the pyramid-like structure of bureaucracy places a few leaders in charge of vast and powerful government organizations.

Weber credited bureaucracy's strict hierarchy of responsibility for increasing organizational efficiency. Applying Weber's thesis to the organization of government, Michels added that this hierarchical structure discourages democracy. While government leaders are expected to subordinate personal interests to organizational goals, people who occupy powerful positions can—and often do—use their access to information and the media and numerous other advantages to promote their personal interests. Oligarchy, then, thrives in the hierarchical structure of bureaucracy, and undermines people's control over their elected leaders.

Political competition and checks and balances in this nation's system of government prevent the flagrant oligarchy found in some societies. In 1974, for example, Richard Nixon was forced to resign as president of the United States. Even so, among national office-holders, incumbents enjoy enormous advantages of power and funding over challengers. In 1990, all but one incumbent senator was returned to office by the voters. But even the most entrenched oligarchs are not immune to forces of political change. In recent years, popular uprisings have toppled Communist regimes in Eastern Europe; in 1991, many long-time officials were sent packing by the people of the Soviet Union as that nation continues on its road to a new political form.

## Gender and Race in Organizations

Rosabeth Moss Kanter, introduced in the box, has analyzed how ascribed statuses such as gender and race figure in the power structure of bureaucratic hierarchies. To the extent that an organization has a dominant social composition, the gender- or race-based ingroup enjoys greater social acceptance, respect, credibility, and access to informal social networks. In American society, the most powerful positions are generally held by well-to-do white men. By contrast, women, people of color, and those from economically disadvantaged backgrounds sometimes feel like members of socially isolated outgroups. Often uncomfortably visible, they are taken less seriously and have lower chances of promotion than others. Understandably, these people generally believe they must work twice as hard as those in dominant categories to maintain their present positions, let alone advance to higher positions (Kanter, 1977; Kanter & Stein, 1979:137).

Kanter (1977) finds that providing more opportunities for some members of corporations and not others has important consequences for everyone's on-the-job performance. Beyond the popular wisdom that being smart and "hustling" helps people get ahead, her research indicates that an organization's policies greatly influence employee performance. According to Kanter, organizations that offer everyone a chance for promotion typically motivate employees to become "fast-trackers," with higher aspirations, greater self-esteem, and a stronger commitment to the organization. By contrast, companies made up of "dead-end" jobs encourage a "just-get-by" attitude among workers, who have little aspiration, poor self-concept, and minimal loyalty to the organization.

Kanter adds that widely shared responsibility and opportunity also promote flexible leadership and heighten

# Rosabeth Moss Kanter

How did a woman who began her career studying communes and other utopian settlements end up shaping the real-world decisions of some of the most successful corporations in the United States? Timing had a lot to do with it; many ideas about organizations originally advanced in the 1960s have now found a receptive audience in the 1990s. Rosabeth Moss Kanter, a professor of business admin-

istration at Harvard University, has shown businesses how their organizational patterns can influence productivity, performance, and profits. For her work, Kanter has been awarded numerous honorary doctoral degrees and has been the subject of feature stories in national publications. Her achievements rank her among the most influential women in our society.

Kanter's career is divided between academic duties and Goodmeasure, Inc., a corporate consulting firm she and her husband founded. She is the author of several widely read books that apply sociological insights to the task of making corporations more effective. What lessons does Kanter offer corporate executives that warrant fees as high as $15,000 for a single appearance? She challenges conventional organizational wisdom by demonstrating that *people*—not technology or machinery—are a corporation's most

important resource. In the long run, she maintains, an organizational environment that develops human potential will ensure success. Reflecting on her career, Kanter explains:

> I remember when participation was what was being talked about on college campuses by Vietnam war protesters or people looking for student power. Now it's a respectable concept in corporate America, and now very large companies are figuring out how to divide themselves into small units. Many ideas and values of the '60s have been translated into the workplace. Take, for example, the right of workers to free expression, the desirability of participation and teamwork, the idea that authority should not be obeyed unquestioningly, the idea that smaller can be better because it can create ownership and family feeling. All of these are mainstream ideas.

SOURCES: Murray (1984) and McHenry (1985).

concern among officials for the morale of subordinates. Leaders in positions of little real power often jealously guard what privileges they do have, and rigidly supervise subordinates. Table 7–3 on page 196 summarizes Kanter's findings. In her view, organizations must "humanize" their structure to bring out the best in their employees and improve the "bottom line."

## Humanizing Bureaucracy

**Humanizing bureaucracy** means *fostering an organizational environment that develops human resources.* Research by Kanter (1977, 1983, 1989; Kanter & Stein, 1980) and others (cf. Peters & Waterman, Jr., 1982) shows that humanizing bureaucracy produces both hap-

pier employees and healthier profits. Based on the discussion so far, we can identify three paths to a more humane organizational structure.

1. **Social inclusiveness.** The social composition of the organization should, ideally, make no one feel "out of place" because of gender, race, or ethnicity. The performance of all employees will improve to the extent that no one is subject to social exclusion.

2. **Sharing of responsibilities.** Humanizing bureaucracy means reducing rigid, oligarchical structures by spreading power and responsibility more widely. Managers cannot benefit from the ideas of employees who have no channels for expressing their opin-

**Table 7–3** KANTER'S RESEARCH: A SUMMARY

| | Advantaged Employees | Disadvantaged Employees |
|---|---|---|
| *Social composition* | Being represented in high proportions helps employees to more easily fit in and to enjoy greater credibility; they experience less stress, and are usually candidates for promotion | Being represented in low proportions puts employees visibly "on display" and results in their not being taken seriously; they tend to fear making mistakes and losing ground rather than optimistically looking toward advancement |
| *Power* | In powerful positions, employees contribute to high morale and support subordinates; such employees tend to be more democratic leaders | In positions of low power, employees tend to foster low morale and restrict opportunities for subordinates to advance; they tend to be more authoritarian leaders |
| *Opportunity* | High opportunity encourages optimism and high aspirations, loyalty to organization, use of higher-ups as reference groups, and constructive responses to problems | Low opportunity encourages pessimism and low aspirations, weak attachment to the job, use of peers as reference groups, and ineffective griping in response to problems |

SOURCE: Based on Rosabeth Moss Kanter, *Men and Women of the Corporation* (New York: Basic Books, 1977), pp. 246–49.

ions. Knowing that superiors are open to suggestions encourages all employees to think creatively, increasing organizational effectiveness.

3. **Expanding opportunities for advancement.** Expanding opportunity reduces the number of employees stuck in routine, dead-end jobs with little motivation to perform well. Employees at all levels, therefore, should be encouraged to share ideas and to try new approaches, and no position should be ruled out as the start of an upward career path.

*Critical evaluation.* Kanter's work takes a fresh look at the concept of bureaucracy and its application to business organizations. Perhaps rigid formality may have made sense in the past, when uneducated workers were hired primarily as a source of physical labor. But today, employees can contribute a wealth of ideas to bolster organizational efficiency if the organization encourages and rewards innovation.

Kanter's suggested changes may encounter resistance, however, since they mandate a redistribution of power. Interestingly, some research suggests women leaders are especially likely to embrace the kinds of changes Kanter advocates; if so, we might expect organizations to evolve as women gradually fill more executive positions traditionally held by men (Helgesen, 1990). But whether leaders are women or men, Kanter maintains, loosening up rigid organization is the key to improved performance. Comparing forty-seven companies with strictly bureaucratic structures to competitors of similar size but with

more flexible approaches, Kanter (1983) found that flexibility increased profits. She argues, therefore, that bureaucratic structure limits an organization's success to the extent that it treats employees as a group to be controlled rather than as a resource to be developed. Thus, while the basic bureaucratic model may still promote efficiency, productivity is enhanced by flexible management styles, coupled with efforts to spread power and opportunity throughout the organization (Kanter, 1985).

## Organizational Environment

How any organization operates depends on more than its internal structure. Recently, researchers have stressed the importance of the **organizational environment,** *a range of factors outside an organization that affect its operation.* Such factors include technology, politics, the economy, population patterns, and other organizations.

*Technology* is an especially important factor in an organizational environment. As we have already suggested, modern organizations could not exist without the technical capacity to communicate provided by telephone systems and facsimile (fax) machines, and the ability to process and store information afforded by copiers and computers. Technological changes currently under way are likely to have two, somewhat contradictory, consequences for organizational structure. On the one hand, the proliferation of personal computers and facsimile machines gives individuals throughout an organization access to more information than ever before; this may produce some leveling in the traditional hierarchy that concentrates information and decision making at the top of an organizational pyramid. On the other hand, however, computer technology also enables organizational leaders to monitor the activities of workers more than ever before in Big Brother–like fashion; this is likely to enhance the concentration of power in the executive suite (Markoff, 1991).

A second key dimension of the organizational environment is *politics*. Changes in law often have dramatic consequences for the operation of an organization, as many industries have learned in the face of new environmental standards. In global perspective, a dramatic change like the reorganization of the Soviet government in 1991 rippled throughout virtually every organization in that country.

Third, the state of the *economy* has obvious importance for an organization's well-being. Businesses in the United States expand or contract along with cycles in the overall economy. Even people's ability to get an organization off the ground depends on the availability of funds, which varies according to economic trends and banking policies (Pennings, 1982).

Fourth, *population patterns*—such as the size and composition of the surrounding populace—also affect organizations. The average age, typical education, and social diversity of a local community shapes both the available work force and the market for an organization's products or services.

Fifth, *other organizations* also form part of the organizational environment. The people who operate a hospital, for example, must be responsive to organizations of doctors, nurses' associations, and unions of other hospital workers. Similarly, to stay competitive, a hospital must keep abreast of the kinds of equipment and procedures available at other health-care facilities. And what happens in hospitals everywhere reflects policies in the insurance industry (Fennell, 1980).

In short, no organization operates in a social vacuum. On the contrary, organizations are linked in many ways to the surrounding society. This is especially evident when comparing organizations in other societies.

## Formal Organizations in Japan

Because of Japan's extraordinary success, Japanese corporations have captured the attention of people around the world and sparked many debates about organizational structure. Since the end of World War II, Japan's economy has surged ahead five times faster than our own. Although geographically no larger than the state of Montana, Japan's gross national product in 1990 was more than one-third that of the United States.

Businesses in Japan have a distinctive organizational environment: a culture rooted in strong collective identity and solidarity. While most members of our society prize rugged individualism, the Japanese maintain traditions of cooperation. This cohesiveness results in relatively low levels of social problems—such as alcoholism, violence, and drug abuse—compared to more root-

Japan is a fascinating blend of the old and the new. Traditional loyalties and patterns of deference—of the young toward the old and women toward men—are still evident in modern, corporate life.

# The Japanese Model: Will It Work in the United States?

What the company wants is for us to work like the Japanese. Everybody go out and do jumping jacks in the morning and kiss each other when they go home at night. You work as a team, rat on each other, and lose control of your destiny. That's not going to work in this country.

John Brodie
President, United Paperworkers
Local 448
Chester, Pennsylvania

Who can argue with the economic success of the Japanese? Economic competition from Asia (and, increasingly, from Europe) is forcing companies in the United States to reconsider long-held notions about how corporate organizations should operate, from the assembly line right up to the board room. Among the most interesting examples of new organizations are Japanese manufacturing plants

built here in this country. By and large, these "transplant-organizations" have been quite successful in terms of productivity, demonstrating the ability of organizations to both adapt to and modify a new environment. Yet some voices in industry—including workers, union leaders, and managers—are speaking as bitterly about transplanting Japanese organizational techniques as they are about importing Japanese cars.

Manufacturing plants operated in the United States by Honda, Nissan, and Toyota employ more than 250,000 people and have achieved the same degree of efficiency and quality that have won these companies praise in Japan. However, these organizations have struggled to win the support of many Americans for some traditional Japanese practices, especially the idea of

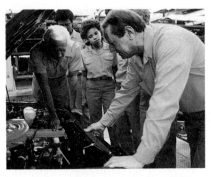

To a large extent, organizational life reflects the surrounding culture. But, stirred by the economic power of Japanese corporations, more and more companies in the United States are employing some of Japan's organizational techniques, such as quality control groups. However, few experts think that organizational patterns can be transplanted easily from one society to another.

broad worker participation. Our corporate culture, with its rigid hierarchy, its heritage of individual-

less and competitive societies like the United States (Ouchi, 1981). Japanese cities also lack the abject poverty and crime found in much of urban America. Even late at night, a person can walk safely through downtown Tokyo. Japanese solidarity also underlies the remarkable small number of lawyers in that society. Among the Japanese, obligations and disputes are typically settled according to traditional norms rather than by resorting to formal legal procedures.

Because of Japan's social cohesiveness, formal organizations in that country contradict the conventional wisdom of our society; they appear to be extremely large primary groups. In the United States, although many companies have experimented with Japanese organizational principles, even humanized bureaucracy has many more secondary relationships. William Ouchi (1981) highlights five distinctions between formal organizations in Japan and their counterparts in industrial societies

of the West. In each case, the Japanese organization reflects that society's more collective orientation.

1. **Hiring and advancement.** Organizations in the United States hold out promotions and raises in salary as prizes won through individual competition. In Japanese organizations, however, companies hire new graduates together and all employees in a particular age cohort receive the same salary and responsibilities. As one employee moves ahead, so do they all. Only after several years is anyone likely to be singled out for special advancement. This corporate approach generates a common identity among employees of the same age.

2. **Lifetime security.** Employees in the United States rarely remain with one company for their entire careers; rather, we expect to move from one company to another in pursuit of personal goals. For

ism, and its history of labor-management conflict makes proposals to enhance worker participation highly controversial.

Many workers in this country dislike the concept of worker participation because they see it as increasing their personal workload. While still responsible for building cars, for instance, workers are now asked to worry about quality control, unit costs, and overall company efficiency—tasks traditionally shouldered by management. At the extreme, Japanese-style policies require workers to learn about the operation of the entire company. Moreover, some employees in the United States do not want to move from job to job, since learning new skills is both demanding and threatening. Many union leaders are also suspicious of new plans formulated by management, even those purporting to share power. Labor unions themselves introduced the idea of worker participation in decision making more than fifty years ago. Today, though, union leaders are wary that an alliance between workers and managers under the banner of "worker participation" may undermine union strength, which has been declining steadily in recent decades (see Chapter 19, "The Economy and Work"). Some managers, too, have been slow to adopt worker participation programs. Sharing with lower-level employees the power to procure supplies, direct production, and even schedule their own vacations does not come easily in light of past practices. Finally, in an age of corporate takeovers and short-term profits, those who control corporations may not wish to invest the time and money in restructuring the organization.

Nonetheless, worker-participation programs are changing the U.S. workplace. A recent government survey found that, despite reservations and some outright resistance, about 70 percent of large businesses in the United States had initiated at least some programs of this kind. The advantages go right to the bottom line: productivity and profits are usually higher when workers have a say in decision making. And most employees in worker-participation programs—even those who may not want to sign up for morning jumping jacks—seem significantly happier about their jobs. Workers who have long used only their bodies are now enjoying the opportunity to use their minds as well.

SOURCES: Hoerr (1989) and Florida & Kenney (1991).

their part, companies are quick to lay off employees when economic setbacks strike. By contrast, Japanese companies typically hire employees for life, fostering strong, mutual loyalties among members of an organization. Japanese companies avoid layoffs by providing workers with other jobs in the organization, along with any necessary retraining.

3. **Holistic involvement.** In the United States, work and private lives are usually distinct. Japanese organizations differ by playing a broad role in their employees' lives, to the point of being described as "welfare corporations" (Lincoln & Kalleberg, 1985). Companies often provide dormitory housing or mortgages for the purchase of homes, sponsor recreational activities, and schedule a wide range of social events in which every worker participates. Employee interaction outside the workplace strengthens collective identity, while offering the respectful Japanese worker an opportunity to more readily voice suggestions and criticisms in a neutral setting.

4. **Nonspecialized training.** Bureaucratic organization in the United States is based on specialization; many people spend an entire career at a single task. From the outset, a Japanese organization trains employees in all phases of its operation, again with the idea that employees will remain with the organization for life. Ideally, nonspecialized training helps workers understand how each job relates to the organization's overall operation. As a result, Japanese workers generally have more technical knowledge than their U.S. counterparts (Sengoku, 1985). Broad training also enables the company to move employees from job to job more easily as circumstances dictate.

5. **Collective decision making.** In the United States, most organizational decisions are made by a handful of executives. This cultural pattern is evident in the well-known sign on the desk of President Harry Truman: "The buck stops here." Although leaders of Japanese organizations also take responsibility for their company's performance, they involve workers in any decision that affects them. A closer working relationship is also encouraged by greater economic equality between management and workers: the salary differential between executives and the lower-ranking employees is about half that found in the United States. Additionally, Japanese companies typically encompass many semi-autonomous working groups, called "quality circles." Instead of responding simply to the directives of superiors, all employees in Japan share managerial responsibilities. This trait of Japanese organizations and some of the pitfalls of applying it to the U.S. workplace are discussed in the box.

These characteristics give the Japanese a strong sense of organizational loyalty. The cultural emphasis on *individual* achievement in our society finds its parallel in Japanese *groupism*. By tying their personal interests to those of their company, workers realize their ambitions through the organization.

Finally, internal solidarity allows Japanese organizations to map long-term strategies. Akio Morita, a founder of the SONY corporation, quipped that Japanese businesses operate by looking ten years ahead, while U.S. corporations think ahead only about the next ten minutes. The kernel of truth in this exaggeration is that top-heavy management and pursuit of short-term profits have hurt the global competitiveness of U.S. businesses.

# Groups and Organizations in Global Perspective

In recent years, the emphasis in the study of formal organizations has shifted from the organizations themselves to the environment in which they operate. In part, this change stems from a growing global focus on organizational research, which shows that the structure and performance of organizations reflect a host of broad societal factors.

Despite Weber's depiction of bureaucracy as a singular organizational form, formal organizations actually developed quite differently in various world regions. Several centuries ago, most businesses in Europe and the United States were small family enterprises. But as Western societies were rocked by the Industrial Revolution, the rational world view, described by Max Weber, came to the fore. Primary relationships were defined as a barrier to organizational efficiency. Thus, Western organizational tradition scorns nepotism (favoritism shown to a family member) or other forms of personal bias. This helps to explain why Weber's model of bureaucracy—widely embraced by organizations in Europe and North America—maintains that the key to efficiency is impersonal, secondary relationships based on technical specialization and impartiality.

The development of formal organizations in Japan followed a different route. Historically, that society was even more socially cohesive, organized according to family-based loyalties. As Japan industrialized, people there did not see primary relationships as a threat to efficiency, as Westerners did. On the contrary, the Japanese modeled their large businesses on the family and, as that nation modernized, traditional family loyalties were transferred to corporations. From our point of view, then, the Japanese seem to be simultaneously modern and traditional as they promote organizational efficiency by cultivating personal ties. Perhaps Japanese workers are now becoming more individualistic; the startling economic success of the Japanese is prompting some to leave the big industrial corporations in search of higher salaries offered by newer financial organizations. Yet the Japanese model still demonstrates a basic truth: organizational life need not be impersonal.

Economically challenged as never before, businesses in the United States are taking a closer look at organizational patterns elsewhere, especially in Japan. In fact, many efforts to humanize bureaucracy in this country are clear attempts to mimic the Japanese way of doing things.

Beyond the benefits for U.S. businesses there is another reason to study the Japanese approach carefully. Our society is less socially cohesive now than the more family-based society Weber knew. A rigidly bureaucratic form of organization only atomizes society further. Perhaps by following the lead of the Japanese, our own formal organizations can promote—rather than diminish—a sense of collective identity and responsibility.

Beyond Japan, organizations throughout the world are developing distinctive structures based on their distinctive environments. Businesses in Poland are gaining vitality as that country establishes a convertible currency and opens its markets to global trade. European nations are forging a new and promising multinational economic system. The Communist party in the People's Republic of China has clamped down on organizations throughout the country. In the former Soviet Union, associations of all kinds are coming out from under rigid political control for the first time in three-quarters of a century. Each of these developments will have an effect on organizational patterns in the United States.

As some analysts point out, organizations in our society are still the envy of the world for their productive efficiency; after all, there are few places on earth where telephones are as reliable and where the mail arrives as quickly and dependably as in the United States (Wilson, 1991). But absolute truths about formal organizations elude us in the face of global diversity and change. To seize the opportunities inherent in the changes sweeping the world, we must maintain a sense of openness and curiosity about the possibilities for reorganizing our future.

# Summary

1. Social groups are important building blocks of societies, fostering common identity and distinctive patterns of interaction.

2. Primary groups tend to be small and person-oriented; secondary groups are typically large and goal-oriented.

3. Leadership often involves two distinctive roles. Instrumental leaders are concerned with a group's goals; expressive leaders focus on the collective well-being of members.

4. The process of group conformity is well documented by researchers. Because members often seek consensus, groups do not necessarily generate a wider range of ideas than do individuals working alone.

5. Individuals use reference groups—both ingroups and outgroups—to make decisions and evaluations.

6. Georg Simmel argued that dyads have a distinctive intensity but lack stability because of the effort necessary to maintain them. A triad can easily dissolve into a dyad by excluding one member.

7. Peter Blau has shown that structural characteristics of groups—including size, internal homogeneity, relative social parity, and physical segregation—all affect the behavior of group members.

8. Social networks are grouplike relational webs that link people who typically have little common identity and uncertain interaction.

9. Formal organizations are large, secondary groups that seek to perform complex tasks efficiently. Depending on their members' reasons for joining, formal organizations can be classified as normative, coercive, or utilitarian.

10. Bureaucratic organization expands in modern societies and allows the efficient performance of many complex tasks. Bureaucracy is based on specialization, hierarchy, rules and regulations, technical competence, impersonal interaction, and formal, written communications.

11. Limitations of bureaucracy include the inability to deal efficiently with special cases, depersonalizing of the workplace, and the fostering of ritualism among some employees. Further, as Max Weber recognized, bureaucracy resists change.

12. Formal organizations are often oligarchies. Rosabeth Moss Kanter's research has shown that the concentration of power and opportunity in U.S. corporations can compromise organizational effectiveness.

13. Humanizing bureaucracy means recognizing that people are an organization's greatest resource. To develop human resources, organizations must not allow people of any one gender or race to dominate decision making; rather, responsibility and opportunity should be available to everyone at all levels.

14. Recently, researchers have shifted attention from organizations themselves to the organizational environment. Technology, politics, the economy, population patterns, and other organizations are among the external factors that influence organizations.

15. Formal organization in Japan differs from the Western, bureaucratic model because of the collective spirit of Japanese culture. Formal organizations in Japan are based on more personal ties than are their counterparts in the United States.

# Key Concepts

**bureaucracy** an organizational model rationally designed to perform complex tasks efficiently

**bureaucratic inertia** the tendency of bureaucratic organizations to persist over time

**bureaucratic ritualism** a preoccupation with organizational rules and regulations as ends in themselves rather than as the means to organizational goals

**dyad** a social group with two members

**expressive leadership** group leadership that emphasizes collective well-being

**formal organization** a large secondary group that is formally organized to facilitate achieving its goals efficiently

**"groupthink"** a limited understanding of some issue due to group conformity

**humanizing bureaucracy** fostering an organizational environment that develops human resources

**ingroup** a social group commanding a member's esteem and loyalty

**instrumental leadership** group leadership that emphasizes the completion of tasks

**network** a web of social ties that links people who may have little common identity and interaction

**oligarchy** the rule of the many by the few

**organizational environment** a range of factors outside an organization that affect its operation

**outgroup** a social group toward which one feels competition or opposition

**primary group** a small social group in which relationships are both personal and enduring

**reference group** a social group that serves as a point of reference for people making evaluations or decisions

**secondary group** a large and impersonal social group based on some special interest or activity

**social group** two or more people who identify with one another and have a distinctive pattern of interaction

**triad** a social group with three members

# Suggested Readings

These two books delve into many of the issues addressed in this chapter.

> Richard H. Hall. *Organizations: Structures, Processes, and Outcomes.* Englewood Cliffs, NJ: Prentice Hall, 1991.
>
> Cecilia L. Ridgeway. *The Dynamics of Small Groups.* New York: St. Martin's Press, 1983.

Controversy has dogged the obedience experiments of Stanley Milgram for more than thirty years. This book reviews Milgram's work and related studies, and tackles broad ethical questions such research raises.

> Arthur G. Miller. *The Obedience Experiments: A Case Study of Controversy in Social Science.* New York: Praeger, 1986.

This book, by the originator of the term "groupthink," examines organizational leadership.

> Irving L. Janis. *Crucial Decisions: Leadership in Policymaking and Crisis Management.* New York: The Free Press, 1989.

This intriguing book argues that women typically adopt a more humanized leadership style in managerial positions that works to the advantage of corporations.

> Sally Helgesen. *The Female Advantage: Women's Ways of Leadership.* New York: Doubleday, 1990.

Throughout the world, women have played a large part in voluntary associations. The first of these two books investigates the unpaid work of U.S. women outside the home. The second analyzes women's associations in the context of national politics in India.

> Arlene Kaplan Daniels. *Invisible Careers: Women Civic Leaders from the Volunteer World.* Chicago: University of Chicago Press, 1988.
>
> Patricia Caplan. *Class and Gender in India: Women and Their Organizations in a South Indian City.* New York: Tavistock, 1985.

This brief book spells out strategies for effectively organizing people into task groups.

> Carl E. Larson and Frank M. J. LaFasto. *Teamwork: What Must Go Right/What Can Go Wrong.* Newbury Park, CA: Sage, 1989.

The first of these books challenges the conventional belief that traditional social patterns run counter to bureaucracy, revealing how both are shaped by the same cultural forces. The second, by a renowned organizational researcher, brings together essays showing that government bureaucracies are far more varied than Weber's model suggests.

> Michael Herzfeld. *The Social Production of Indifference:*

*Exploring the Roots of Western Bureaucracy.* New York: Berg, 1991.

James Q. Wilson. *Bureaucracy: What Government Agencies Do and Why They Do It.* New York: Basic Books, 1989.

These two books exemplify the growing trend of applying sociological analysis to problems of corporate management. The first, by one of the best-known sociologists in the field of formal organizations, examines the future of corporate organization. The second, by a noted futurist, argues that simply "doing more of the same" in a changing society will surely lead to declining business.

Rosabeth Moss Kanter. *When Giants Learn to Dance: Mastering the Challenges of Strategy, Management, and Careers in the 1990s.* New York: Simon and Schuster, 1989.

Alvin Toffler. *The Adaptive Corporation.* New York: McGraw-Hill, 1985.

This collection of essays spotlights the power of large organizations in American society. Corporations and government agencies, which are often linked by formal and informal networks, affect our nation's politics at the national and local levels.

Robert Perrucci and Harry R. Potter, eds. *Networks of Power: Organizational Actors at the National, Corporate, and Community Levels.* Hawthorne, NY: Aldine de Gruyter, 1989.

This is one of the better books contrasting formal organizations in the United States with those in Japan.

Boye De Mente. *Japanese Etiquette and Ethics in Business.* 5th ed. Lincolnwood, IL: NTC Business Books, 1987.

Challenging the notion that formal organizations are based on cool-headed, rational behavior, some organizations deliberately foster emotional intensity among their members. This study highlights companies such as Mary Kay cosmetics and Amway products that have used emotional, motivational techniques successfully.

Nicole Woolsey Biggart. *Charismatic Capitalism: Direct Selling Organizations in America.* Chicago: The University of Chicago Press, 1989.

# 8

# Deviance

Sirens sliced through the night as police cruisers joined in angry pursuit of the 1988 Hyundai through a suburban neighborhood in Los Angeles. As the black-and-white cars closed in on their quarry, a helicopter chattered overhead, its powerful floodlight bathing the surreal scene in a shimmering brilliance.

Twenty-five-year-old Rodney Glen King, the lone occupant of the Hyundai, brought his car to a halt, opened his door, and stumbled into the street. In an instant, police swarmed around him, and a sergeant lunged forward, staggering King with the discharge of a 50,000-volt Taser stun gun. Unarmed and now helpless, King fell to the pavement. As a group of eleven police officers looked on, three officers took turns kicking King and striking him with their clubs as he tried in vain to protect himself. By the time the beating ended, King had sustained a crushed cheekbone, a broken ankle, damage to his skull, a burn on his chest, and internal injuries.

The capture and beating of an unemployed construction worker by police might have attracted little public notice except for one extraordinary coincidence: the resident of a nearby apartment building had observed the event through the eyepiece of his videocamera. In a matter of hours, the flagrant abuse of power was being replayed on television screens across the United States.

The King incident touched off a firestorm of public debate over the operation of police departments in Los Angeles and elsewhere. In Washington, DC, the attorney general ordered a national investigation of the extent of police misconduct. To some critics, the scene was all too familiar: a black man being brutalized by white police for little or no reason. Sociologist and law professor Jerome Skolnick explained the need for caution in asserting that the case was racially motivated. But, he concluded, "racist police are more likely to be brutal and brutal police are more likely to be racist." Other critics declared that the King episode was notable only because the Los Angeles police had been caught in the act; during the previous year, that city's police department had paid $10 million to compensate citizens who claimed they, too, had been victims of abuse.

The officers involved in the King incident soon stood charged with assault with a deadly weapon and use of excessive force. But many people could not help but wonder if police are being asked to perform an almost impossible task: maintaining some semblance of order in cities seething with crime, drugs, and poverty. Typically for little pay, police routinely risk personal harm as they try to hold back the rising tide of violence, often feeling that they have little support from the courts, little understanding from the public, and little chance for success. In short, many police see themselves embroiled in an actual war on crime, in which atrocities are committed by people on both sides.[1]

---

[1] This account is based on Lacayo (1991) and Morrow (1991).

Every society struggles to establish standards of justice, to reward people who play by the rules, and to punish those who do not conform. But, as the Rodney King incident so vividly demonstrates, the line that separates good and evil is no simple matter of black and white. This chapter investigates many of the questions that underlie this case: How do societies create a moral code in the first place? Is deviance inevitable, or can it be checked? Why are some people more likely than others to be charged with offenses? How has the scope of the crime problem changed in recent decades? And what are the legitimate purposes of the criminal justice system? We shall begin by defining several basic concepts.

## What Is Deviance?

**Deviance** is *the recognized violation of cultural norms.* Norms guide virtually all human activities; the concept of deviance covers a correspondingly broad spectrum. One distinctive category of deviance is **crime,** *the violation of norms formally enacted into criminal law.* Even criminal deviance spans a wide range, from minor traffic violations to serious offenses such as rape and murder. A subcategory of crime, **juvenile delinquency,** refers to *the violation of legal standards by the young.*

Some instances of deviance barely raise eyebrows; other cases command greater attention, and some demand a swift and severe response. People in the United States may pay little notice to mild nonconformity like left-handedness or boastfulness, but we take a dimmer view of a Mohawk hairstyle or a child flunking out of school. The vast majority define an act like violent rape as most serious, demanding a response by the police.

Not all deviance involves action or even choice. For some categories of individuals, just *existing* may be sufficient to provoke condemnation from others. To whites, who are in the majority, the mere presence of people of color may cause some discomfort. Similarly, many people of all races consider the poor disreputable, because they understandably cannot conform to some conventional middle-class standards. Gay men and lesbians also confront derision and even hostility from those who are intolerant of their sexual orientation.

Examples of nonconformity that come readily to mind—swimming in the nude, neglecting a pet, driving while intoxicated—involve overtly breaking some rule. But since we all have shortcomings, we sometimes define especially righteous people—those who *never* raise their

Each and every normative pattern creates the possibility for deviance. Many societies retain traditional norms that women should be soft and submissive; in this context, women who develop their physical strength—or those who are assertive—may be viewed as deviant.

voices or who are enthusiastic about paying their taxes—as deviant, even if we accord them a measure of respect (Huls, 1987). Deviant actions or attitudes, then, can be negative or positive. In either case, however, deviance stems from *difference* that causes us to react to another person as an "outsider" (Becker, 1966).

Finally, Edwin Schur (1984) argues that women—who have less social power than men—become entangled in deviance more readily than men. Although, as we shall see presently, men are more likely than women to be formally convicted of crime, virtually every society in the world subjects women to more stringent normative controls in their daily lives. Historically, our society has limited the roles of women largely to the home. Even today, in the United States and many other societies, women are banned from combat positions in the armed forces; in Saudi Arabia, women cannot legally operate motor vehicles; in Iran, women who dare to expose their hair or wear make-up in public can be whipped.

## Social Control

Members of every society are subject to *social control,* attempts by society to regulate the behavior of individuals. Like norms, social control takes many forms. Socialization, discussed in Chapter 5, constitutes a complex process of social control in which family, peer groups, and the mass media influence people's attitudes and behavior. Through social control, people earn a positive response for conforming and a negative response for deviant attitudes or actions. Praise from parents, high grades in school, and positive recognition from people in the community encourage conformity to conventional patterns of thought and behavior.

Many instances of deviance provoke only informal responses, such as a scowl or a bit of friendly criticism. Charges of more serious deviance, however, may propel an individual into the **criminal justice system,** *a formal system that responds to alleged violations of law using police, courts, and punishment.*

In sum, although we think of deviance simply in terms of individual choice or personal failings, society actually shapes the world of good and evil. *How* a society defines deviance, *who* is targeted as deviant, and *what* people decide to do about nonconformity are all issues of social organization. Only gradually, however, have people recognized this essential truth, as we shall now explain.

## The Biological Context

Chapter 5 ("Socialization") noted that human behavior was understood—or, more correctly, misunderstood—during the nineteenth century as an expression of biological instincts. Understandably, then, early interest in criminality emphasized biological causes.

### Early Research

In 1876 Caesare Lombroso (1835–1909), an Italian physician who worked in prisons, suggested that criminals had distinctive physical features—low foreheads, prominent jaws and cheekbones, protruding ears, hairiness, and unusually long arms that made them resemble human beings' apelike ancestors. In essence, Lombroso viewed criminals as evolutionary throwbacks to lower forms of life. Toward the end of his career he acknowledged the importance of social forces in criminality, but his early assertion that some people were literally

On May 4, 1970, Ohio National Guard troops trained their weapons on students who had gathered for an antiwar demonstration at Kent State University. A minute of gunfire left four students dead and nine wounded. Widespread opinion held that the shootings were justified, although regrettable, as a firm response to the disruptive campus protests that were taking place at the time. No criminal prosecution of any soldier occurred in the wake of this tragic event.

"born criminals" gained currency among powerful people who dismissed the idea that failings in social arrangements might account, in part, for criminal deviance (Jones, 1986).

Although popular for a time, Lombroso's research was flawed. He failed to realize that the physical features he noted among prisoners appeared to the same degree in the population as a whole. Several decades later the British psychiatrist Charles Buckman Goring (1870–1919) probed the matter more carefully, comparing thousands of convicts and noncriminals. He found great physical variation within both categories, but no overall physical differences, of the kind suggested by Lombroso, distinguishing criminals from noncriminals (1972; orig. 1913).

### Delinquency and Body Structure

Although Lombroso's work had been discredited, others continued to search for alleged biological explanations of criminality. William Sheldon (1949) suggested that body structure was significant. He described three general types of body structure: *ectomorphs*, who are tall, thin, and fragile; *endomorphs*, who are short and fat; and *mesomorphs*, who are muscular and athletic. After analyzing the body structure and criminal history of hundreds of young men, Sheldon found criminality to be more common among men with the mesomorphic body type. Criminality, according to Sheldon, is linked to a muscular, athletic build.

Sheldon and Eleanor Glueck (1950) agreed with William Sheldon. However, the Gluecks cautioned that a powerful build is not necessarily a *cause* of criminality. Mesomorphic men, they suggested, were somewhat less likely to be raised with affection and understanding from family members; consequently, they showed less sensitivity toward others and tended to react aggressively to frustration. Young, muscular men also have the physical capacity to become the "bullies on the block" (Gibbons, 1981). Moreover, expecting muscular and athletic boys to be more physically aggressive than others, people may treat them accordingly, thereby provoking aggressive behavior in a self-fulfilling prophesy.

### Recent Research

Since the 1960s, increasing knowledge of genetics has rekindled interest in the biological origins of criminality. Some investigators have focused on unusual genetic patterns that may engender criminality in some people (Vold & Bernard, 1986). The sex of human beings is determined by chromosomes: females have two X chromosomes and males have one X and one Y. Perhaps once in a thousand cases, a genetic mutation yields a male with an extra Y chromosome, an XYY pattern. Such men seem more likely than others to end up in prisons or mental institutions. Initially, researchers thought the XYY pattern triggered criminal violence, but it appears now that such men are only taller and perhaps less intelligent than average. Probably whatever greater criminality occurs among XYY men is the result of a tendency by others to define them as threatening and less capable, which is a social barrier to acceptance and a good job (Hook, 1973; Suzuki & Knudtson, 1989).

As of now, there is no convincing evidence that criminality stems from any specific genetic flaw. However, there is support for the notion that overall genetic composition, in combination with social influences, can account for some criminality. In other words, biological factors probably have a small but real effect on whether or not individuals engage in criminal activity (Rowe, 1983; Rowe & Osgood, 1984; Wilson & Herrnstein, 1985; Jencks, 1987). The new field of sociobiology (see Chapter 3, "Culture") is tackling a number of intriguing questions relating to deviance such as why men engage in violence more than women, and why parents are more likely to abuse disabled or foster children than healthy or natural children (Daly & Wilson, 1988).

***Critical evaluation.*** Most biological theories have tried to explain crime in terms of people's physical traits. Early research focused on rare and abnormal cases, which, under any circumstances, could explain only a small proportion of all crimes. More recent sociobiological research suggests that specific biological traits may be related to criminality but, as yet, too little is understood about the links between genetics and human behavior to warrant causal connections. In any case, an individualistic biological approach cannot address the issue of how some kinds of behaviors come to be defined as deviant in the first place. Therefore, although there is much to be learned about how human biology may affect behavior, research currently places far greater emphasis on social influences on human behavior (Gibbons & Krohn, 1986; Liska, 1991).

## Personality Factors

Like biological theories, psychological explanations of deviance spotlight the individual, focusing on abnormalities in the individual personality. Though some abnormalities are hereditary, psychologists believe that most result from social experience. According to this view, deviance is thought to be the result of "unsuccessful" socialization.

The research of Walter Reckless and Simon Dinitz (1967) illustrates a psychological approach to explaining juvenile delinquency. They claimed that the odds of young boys engaging in delinquency are reduced to the extent that they develop strong moral values and a positive self-image. Reckless and Dinitz called their analysis *containment theory*.

They began their research by asking teachers to identify boys about age twelve who seemed likely to engage in delinquent acts and to pick out those who were not. Interviews with both categories of boys and their mothers provided information on each boy's self-concept—how he viewed himself and how he related to the world around him. The "good boys" displayed a strong conscience (or *superego*, in Sigmund Freud's terminology), coped well with frustration, and identified positively with cultural norms and values. The "bad boys" had a weaker conscience, had little tolerance for frustration, and identified less strongly with conventional culture. Over a four-year period, the researchers found that the "good boys" did indeed have fewer contacts with the police than the "bad boys." Since all the boys studied lived in areas where delinquency was widespread, the researchers concluded that boys who managed to stay out of trouble had a strong conscience and a positive self-concept that, taken together, served as "an internal buffer which protects people against [violation] of the social and legal norms" (Reckless, 1970:401).

*Critical evaluation.* Psychological research has demonstrated that personality patterns have some relationship to delinquency and other types of deviance. Nevertheless, the vast majority of serious crimes are committed by people whose psychological profiles are normal. This finding limits the value of the psychological approach. Also, because this analysis focuses on individuals, it ignores how definitions of what is "normal" and "abnormal" vary from society to society. Finally, psychological research sheds little light on why, among people who behave in the same manner, some are defined as deviant while others are not.

Both biological and psychological approaches view deviance as an individual attribute without exploring how conceptions of right and wrong initially arise and without investigating the deviant person's place in the larger society. We now address these issues by delving into sociological explanations of deviance.

## The Social Foundations of Deviance

Americans have long viewed deviance in terms of the free choice or personal failings of individuals. But all behavior—deviance as well as conformity—is shaped by society. Three *social* foundations of deviance are identified below; they will be detailed in the following sections of the chapter.

1. *Deviance varies according to cultural norms.* No thought or action is inherently deviant; it becomes deviant only in relation to particular norms. The life patterns of rural Vermonters, small-town Texans, and southern Californians differ in some significant ways; for this reason, what each category prizes or scorns varies also. Laws, too, differ from place to place. Texans, for example, can legally consume alcohol in a car, a practice that draws the attention of police in most other states. Casinos thrive in Atlantic City, New Jersey, and Las Vegas, Nevada, although such gambling is illegal every-

The arts allow members of a society to explore alternatives to conventional ideas and social arrangements. For this reason, we have long celebrated artists, but labeled them with a mildly deviant identity. Some provocative art has recently sparked controversy as to whether a nation should fund, or even permit, *any* type of artistic presentation. When officials tried to prevent the display of photographs by the late Robert Mapplethorpe in Cincinnati, artists marched in outspoken defense of their freedom of expression.

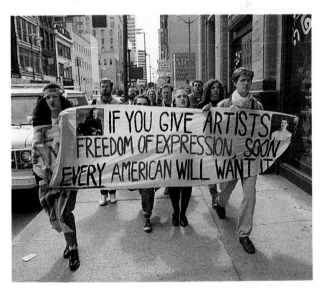

where else in the United States. Further, most cities and towns have rarely enforced statutes not found elsewhere: only in Seattle, for example, is a person subject to arrest for appearing in public while suffering from the flu.

In global context, deviance is even more diverse. Albania outlaws any public display of religious faith, such as "crossing" oneself; Cubans can be prosecuted for "consorting with foreigners"; U.S. citizens risk arrest by our own government if they travel to Libya or Iraq.

2. *People become deviant as others define them that way.* Even within a particular setting, people selectively apply cultural norms. Everyone violates norms from time to time, even to the extent of breaking the law. For example, most of us have at some point walked around talking to ourselves or "borrowed" supplies such as pens and paper from the workplace. Others may or may not take note of our actions; even if they do, they may or may not define what they see as mental illness or theft. In short, deviance is a product of the perceptions, definitions, and responses of others.

3. *Both rule-making and rule-breaking involve social power.* As explained later in this chapter, Karl Marx considered norms, and especially laws, as devices to protect the interests of powerful people. For example, the owners of an unprofitable factory have a legal right to close their business, even if doing so puts thousands of people out of work. If workers commit an act of vandalism that closes the same factory for a single day, however, they are likely to be defined as criminal. Also, poor people may be looked upon as deviant for exactly the same behavior that powerful people engage in with impunity. A homeless person who stands on a street corner denouncing the city government risks arrest for disturbing the peace; a mayoral candidate can do the same thing while receiving extensive police protection. In short, norms and their application are linked to social inequality.

## Structural-Functional Analysis

Deviance is inherent in the operation of society. The structural-functional paradigm examines how deviance makes important contributions to a social system.

## Emile Durkheim: The Functions of Deviance

A pioneering study of deviance was carried out by Emile Durkheim, whose vision of society is outlined in Chapter 4 ("Society"). In Durkheim's day, as now, most people thought that deviance meant destruction; crime, for example, causes some $15 billion in losses annually in the United States today, and death or personal injury to hundreds of thousands of people. Durkheim conceded that the costs of deviance are great, but he argued that the positive functions of deviance are even greater. In fact, he concluded, in the absence of deviance, society could not exist at all. Durkheim (1964a, orig. 1895; 1964b, orig. 1893) cited four major functions of deviance.

1. *Deviance affirms cultural values and norms.* Culture turns on moral choices: people must prefer some attitudes and behaviors to others. Conceptions of what is morally right exist only in antithesis to notions of what is wrong. For example, respect for law is strengthened as a society condemns those who violate legal standards. Deviance, therefore, is indispensable to the process of generating and sustaining cultural values.

2. *Responding to deviance clarifies moral boundaries.* In defining people as deviant, a society sets the boundary between right and wrong. For example, a college marks the line between academic honesty and dishonesty through disciplinary procedures that declare some behavior as intolerable plagiarism.

3. *Responding to deviance promotes social unity.* People typically react to serious deviance with collective outrage. In doing so, Durkheim explained, they reaffirm the moral ties that bind them. For example, many people in our society joined in a surge of patriotism as we condemned the invasion of Kuwait by the Iraqi military in 1990.

4. *Deviance encourages social change.* People who push society's moral boundaries are able to suggest alternatives to the status quo, thereby provoking change. Today's deviance, Durkheim noted, may well become tomorrow's morality (1964a:71). For example, in the 1950s, most Americans denounced rock and roll music as a threat to the morals of youth and an affront to traditional musical tastes. Since then, however, rock and roll has been swept up in the musical mainstream, perhaps more "all-American" than apple pie, and certainly more profitable, as the box explains.

# Rock and Roll: From Deviance to Big Business

Rock and roll exploded onto our national scene in the early 1950s, bursting with energy and inciting controversy. With roots in the rhythm and blues of African Americans, rock was initially taboo, a musical style that few white-owned record companies or radio stations were willing to promote. To make matters worse, rock and roll had long been synonymous with sex; the phrase originally referred to sexual intercourse. Little wonder that rock and roll soon became the anthem of rebellion among members of the emerging youth subculture, who delighted in flouting parental authority. By the 1960s, protest music and drug-based psychedelic rock urged listeners to challenge parents, police, and anyone else linked to "the system." In short, rock and roll seemed to oppose everything our culture valued, and to advocate attitudes and actions our way of life had long condemned.

Representing the conventional musical tastes of the 1950s, singers like Perry Como and Doris Day were upstaged by the gyrating Elvis Presley—the first superstar of rock and roll. Although dismissed by

critics as vulgar and lacking talent, Presley started rock and roll on a ride that has accelerated ever since. But there was strong resistance to the new music. Especially in the South, church groups campaigned to suppress rock and roll, burning records and condemning the antics of singers as sexually suggestive and their lyrics (mild by today's standards) as obscene.

Gradually, however, our culture embraced rock and roll. Why? For one compelling reason: there was so much money to be made from it. By the early 1960s, the Beatles were not only selling millions of records but had discovered a vast market for side-line products, con-

cert tours, and successful films. Coca-Cola jumped on the bandwagon and for the first time used rock music in advertising.

Rock music is now bigger business than anyone two generations ago could have imagined. From 5 percent of record sales in 1955, rock is now a multibillion-dollar industry, accounting for more than 80 percent of sales of all recorded music. Promoter Dick Clark had it right when he quipped, "I don't make culture, I sell it" (cited in Chapple & Garofalo, 1977:305).

SOURCES: Chapple & Garofalo (1977) and Gillett (1983).

## An Illustration: The Puritans of Massachusetts Bay

Durkheim's functional analysis of deviance is supported by Kai Erikson's (1966) historical research about the early Puritans of Massachusetts Bay. This highly religious "society of saints," Erikson discovered, created deviance in order to clarify moral boundaries. Durkheim could well have had the Puritans in mind when he asked us to

imagine a society of saints, a perfect cloister of exemplary individuals. Crimes, properly so called, will there be un-

known; but faults which appear [insignificant] to the layman will create there the same scandal that the ordinary offense does in ordinary consciousness. . . . For the same reason, the perfect and upright man judges his smallest failings with a severity that the majority reserve for acts more truly in the nature of an offense. (1964a:68–69)

Deviance, in short, is inevitable in society, however righteous individuals may be.

The kind of deviance the Puritans created changed over time, depending on the moral questions they confronted. Whether or not they could continue their tradi-

No social class stands apart from others as being criminal or free from criminality. According to various sociologists, however, people with less stake in society and their own future typically exhibit less resistance to some kinds of deviance. Photographer Stephen Shames captured this scene in the Bronx, New York, in 1983.

the observation that financial success stands as a widespread *goal* in the United States. We expect people to pursue financial success according to certain approved *means*, such as schooling and hard work, and not through theft or other dishonest activities. Therefore, to the extent that people are willing and able to seek success according to such rules, *conformity* should result.

But not everyone who desires success has the opportunity to achieve it legitimately. Moreover, even successful people may be lured by the promise of further gain to violate cultural norms. Corporate executives, for example, may engage in dishonest business practices or embezzle company funds; many wealthy men and women misrepresent their income to the Internal Revenue Service. Merton called this type of deviance *innovation*—attempting to achieve culturally approved goals using unconventional means. Table 8–1 shows that innovation involves accepting the goal of success while rejecting conventional means to that goal.

According to Merton, innovation grows out of "strain" between the value of success and the limited opportunity to become successful in approved ways. The poor, especially, experience this strain as their aspirations are frustrated by a lack of educational and job opportunities. To alleviate this strain, people may resort to making their own rules, stealing, selling illegal drugs, or engaging in other kinds of street hustling and racketeering. The box, highlighting the life of mobster Al Capone, explains why Merton's "innovation" has been historically attractive to people at the margins of our society.

tion of lively dissent, how they should respond to outsiders who joined them, and what their religious goals should be—all such questions were answered through celebrating some members while defining others as deviant.

Finally, Erikson discovered that although the reasons for deviance changed, the proportion of Puritans declared to be deviant remained stable over time. To Erikson, this fact supported Durkheim's idea that deviants serve as moral markers, outlining the changing boundaries of conventional attitudes and behavior for a society. By constantly defining a small portion of their members as deviant, Puritan society ensured that the social functions of deviance were carried out.

## Merton's Strain Theory

Robert Merton (1938, 1968) has amplified Durkheim's structural-functional analysis by linking deviance to certain societal imbalances. Merton's theory begins with

**Table 8–1  MERTON'S STRAIN THEORY OF DEVIANCE**

| Individual Responses to Dominant Cultural Patterns | Cultural Goals | Cultural Means |
|---|---|---|
| Nondeviant response | | |
| Conformity | Accept | Accept |
| Deviant responses | | |
| Innovation | Accept | Reject |
| Ritualism | Reject | Accept |
| Retreatism | Reject | Reject |
| Rebellion | Reject current goals but promote new ones | Reject current means but promote new ones |

SOURCE: Based on Robert K. Merton, *Social Theory and Social Structure* (New York: Free Press, 1968), pp. 230–46.

## Al Capone: Crime and Social Marginality

At the onset of Prohibition, which outlawed alcoholic beverages in the United States between 1920 and 1933, Al Capone seized the opportunity to build a vast criminal empire. For someone willing to take the risk, there was a lot of money to be made in bootlegging.

Capone rose to power and wealth during an era when U.S. cities bustled with millions of European immigrants, most poor but eager to share in the American Dream of success. Defined by their backgrounds, their languages, and their religions as second-class citizens, immigrants collided time and again against the barriers of prejudice and discrimination. The vast majority nonetheless patiently remained "conformists," in Merton's terminology. But some saw in organized crime a means to achieve their most cherished goals. So it was that Al Capone—a man of personal genius and ambition, yet socially handicapped by having been born in Naples, Italy, and having grown up in an Italian slum of New York City—came to dominate one of the largest criminal empires of our history.

Capone exemplifies Merton's "innovator," an individual who pursues the culturally approved goal of success according to unconventional means. For people like Al Capone, this type of deviance is a product of ambition coupled with a lack of legitimate opportunity. In the words of one analyst of the criminal underworld:

The typical criminal of the Capone era was a boy who had . . . seen what was rated as success in the society he had been thrust into—the Cadillac, the big bank-roll, the elegant apartment. How could he acquire that kind of recognizable status? He was almost always a boy of outstanding initiative, imagination, and ability; he was the kind of boy who, under different conditions, would have been a captain of industry or a key political figure of his time. But he hadn't the opportunity of going to Yale and becoming a banker or broker; there was no passage for him to a law degree from Harvard. There was, however, a relatively easy way of acquiring these goods that he was incessantly told were available to him as an American citizen, and without which he had begun to feel he could not properly count himself as an American citizen. He could become a gangster. (Allsop, 1961:236)

Even the few gangsters who did manage to garner wealth and power found that they were denied the prestige accorded to members of more "respectable" families. To overcome this marginality, some tried to distance themselves from their ethnic origins by changing their names, among other things. Capone's first employer, for example, was a fellow immigrant who started calling himself Mr. Frankie Yale. A reputed mafia boss, Yale operated an establishment on Coney Island that he named the Harvard Inn. After he had become a leader of the Chicago rackets, Capone demanded that others address him only as Anthony Brown, and according to an associate, he never hired men who displayed any of the ethnic traits he sought to leave behind.

The Big Fellow hires nothing but gentlemen. They have to be well dressed at all times and have to have cultured accents. They always have to say "Yes, Sir" and "No, Sir" to him. (Allsop, 1961:249)

Capone even displayed the public generosity favored by many upper-class people when, during the Depression, he provided food to Chicago's poor. Later he enrolled his son Anthony at Yale University, and subsequently he celebrated the young man's wedding to a well-to-do woman from Nashville.

Although one of the most notorious criminals of the twentieth century, Al Capone's hopes for himself and his family were modeled on the American Dream. His deviance—which brings to mind that of thousands of young people dealing drugs in today's cities—has a distinctly American cast: it is motivated by the hunger for success amid limited opportunity.

SOURCES: Allsop (1961) and Baltzell (1964).

The inability to become successful by normative means may also prompt what Merton calls *ritualism* (see Table 8–1). Ritualists resolve the strain of not having realized their goals by abandoning them in favor of compulsively conforming to cultural norms as a means of seeking respectability. Ritualism, Merton suggests, is common among people of modest social standing who have little opportunity to gain more in life but fear risking what they have through innovation. Consider the "bureaucratic ritualist," described in Chapter 7 ("Groups and Organizations"): the lower-level official, obsessed with rules, who loses sight of their overall purpose. In Merton's view, such deviance stems from giving up the pursuit of success; however, ritualists may gain the reputation of being "good citizens" because they rigidly adhere to the rules.

A third response to the inability to succeed is *retreatism*—the rejection of both the goals and the norms of one's culture. Retreatists are society's dropouts. They include some alcoholics and drug addicts, and some of the street people common to U.S. cities. The deviance of retreatists lies in their unconventional way of life and, perhaps more seriously, their acceptance of their situation.

The fourth response to failure is *rebellion*. Like retreatists, rebels reject both the cultural definition of success and the normative means of achieving it. Rebels, however, go further by advocating radical alternatives to the existing social order. They may promote unconventional values and norms through political revolution or zealous religious activity. Either way, rebels withdraw from established society, forming a counterculture.

## Deviant Subcultures

Richard Cloward and Lloyd Ohlin (1966) extended Merton's theory in their investigation of delinquent youths. They maintain that criminal deviance results not simply from limited legitimate opportunity but also from accessible illegitimate opportunity. In short, some patterns of deviance and conformity can be explained in terms of the *relative opportunity structure* various categories of young people face in their lives.

The life of Al Capone, described earlier, illustrates this idea. As a poor immigrant, Capone was denied legitimate paths to success, such as a college education. Yet his world did provide illegitimate opportunity for success as a bootlegger. Where relative opportunity favors what Merton might call "organized innovation," Cloward and Ohlin predict the development of *criminal subcultures*. These subcultures offer the knowledge, skills, and other resources people need to succeed in unconventional ways.

But in many poor and highly transient neighborhoods, organized innovation may be lacking. Here, delinquency is likely to surface in the form of *conflict subcultures* where violence explodes as an expression of frustration and a claim to territorial supremacy. Finally, among those who fail to achieve success, even using criminal means, *retreatist subcultures* may arise. Consistent with Merton's analysis, such subcultures comprise dropouts who may use alcohol or other drugs.

Albert Cohen (1971) suggests that delinquency is most pronounced among lower-class youths because society offers them little opportunity to achieve success in conventional ways. Because conventional definitions of success call for acquiring wealth and all its trappings, they find little basis for self-respect in their impoverished condition. In response, they may create a delinquent subculture that defines them in more favorable terms. These subcultures, Cohen says, "define as meritorious the characteristics [these youths] *do* possess, the kinds of conduct of which they *are* capable" (1971:66). For example, because the dominant culture values the calculated pursuit of wealth, a delinquent subculture may extol stealing "for the hell of it." In short, members of a delinquent subculture publicly flout conventional norms while carefully conforming to their own standards.

Walter Miller (1970) agrees that delinquent subcultures are most likely to develop in the lower classes where society provides the least legitimate opportunity. He describes six focal concerns of delinquent subcultures: (1) *trouble*, arising from frequent conflict with teachers and police; (2) *toughness*, the value placed on physical size, strength, and athletic skills, especially among males; (3) *smartness*, the ability to succeed on the streets, to outthink or "con" others, and to avoid being similarly taken advantage of; (4) *excitement*, the search for thrills, risk, or danger to gain needed release from a daily routine that is predictable and unsatisfying; (5) a concern with *fate*, derived from the lack of control these youths feel over their own lives; and (6) *autonomy*, a desire for freedom often expressed as resentment toward figures of authority.

## Hirschi's Control Theory

A final argument that builds on Durkheim's analysis of deviance is Travis Hirschi's (1969) *control theory*. Hirschi assumes that everyone finds at least some deviance tempting. What requires explanation, then, is not deviance, but *conformity*. He suggests that conformity arises from four types of social controls.

1. **Attachment.** Strong social attachments to others encourage conformity; weak relationships in the family, peer group, and school leave people freer to engage in deviance.
2. **Commitment.** The higher one's commitment to legitimate opportunity, the greater the advantages of conformity. A young person bound for college, with good career prospects, has a high stake in conformity. In contrast, someone with little confidence in future success has a low investment in conformity and is more likely to follow a deviant path.
3. **Involvement.** Extensive involvement in legitimate activities, such as holding a job, going to school and completing homework, or pursuing hobbies, inhibits deviance. People with little legitimate involvement—who simply "hang out" waiting for something to happen—have time and energy for deviant activity.
4. **Belief.** Strong beliefs in conventional morality and respect for authority figures also restrain tendencies toward deviance; people with weak beliefs are more vulnerable to whatever temptation deviance presents.

Hirschi's analysis explains many kinds of deviant behavior, and it has gained support from subsequent research (Wiatrowski, Griswold, & Roberts, 1981; Sampson & Laub, 1990). Here, again, a person's social ranking is crucial in generating a stake in conformity or allowing everyday temptations to cross the line into actual deviance.

***Critical evaluation.*** Durkheim's pioneering work in the functions of deviance remains central to sociological thinking. Even so, recent critics point out that a community does not always come together in reaction to crime; sometimes fear of crime has a chilling effect on interaction (Liska & Warner, 1991).

Various structural-functional theories derived from Durkheim's analysis—especially Merton's strain theory—have also enjoyed widespread support. Merton's theory has much credibility, but it also has several limitations. First, no evidence shows precisely how deviance is caused by societal "strain." After all, most people who cannot realize their dreams keep playing by the rules all the same. Second, Merton offers only a few

clues as to which categories of people would choose one response to strain over another. Third, Merton's approach explains some kinds of deviance (theft, for example) far better than others (such as crimes of passion or mental illness). Fourth, we should recognize that not everyone seeks success in conventional terms of wealth, as strain theory implies. As explained in Chapter 3 ("Culture"), members of our society embrace many different cultural values and are motivated by various notions of personal success.

The general argument of Cloward and Ohlin, Cohen, Miller, and Hirschi—that deviance reflects the opportunity structure of society—has been confirmed by subsequent research (cf. Allan & Steffensmeier, 1989). However, these theories fall short in assuming that people use a single cultural standard for determining which attitudes and behavior are legitimate and illegitimate. Our society upholds various, sometimes competing, ideas of what is and is not deviant. A second problem lies in our defining deviance in terms that focus most attention on poor people. If crime is defined to include stock fraud as well as street theft, criminals are more likely to come from the ranks of well-integrated, affluent individuals. A third problem with this approach is that structural-functional theories imply that everyone who violates conventional cultural standards will be defined as deviant. Defining particular actions or attitudes as deviant, however, actually involves a highly complex process, as the next section explains.

# Symbolic-Interaction Analysis

The symbolic-interaction paradigm directs attention to how people construct reality as they interact in countless everyday situations. In the early 1950s, sociologists began to apply this theoretical orientation to the study of deviance. Their work revealed that surprising flexibility underscores definitions of deviance and conformity.

## Labeling Theory

The central contribution of symbolic-interaction analysis is **labeling theory**, *the assertion that deviance and conformity result from the response of others.* Labeling theory stresses the relativity of deviance, meaning the same behavior may be defined in any number of ways. Howard S. Becker therefore claims that deviance is nothing more than "behavior that people so label" (1966:9). Consider these situations: a woman takes an article of clothing from a roommate; a married man at a convention in a distant city has sex with a prostitute; a member of Congress drives home intoxicated after a party. The reality of each of these situations depends on the response of others. The first could be defined as borrowing or as theft. The consequences of the second situation depend largely on whether news of the man's indiscretion follows him back home. In the third situation, the official might be defined as either an active socialite or a dangerous drunk. In the social construction of reality, then, a highly variable process of detection, definition, and response comes into play.

People sometimes contend with deviant labels for involvement in situations completely beyond their control. For example, victims of violent rape may be labeled as deviants because of the misguided assumption that they must have provoked the offender. Similarly, people with a serious disease may be viewed as deviant by others who cannot cope with the illness. Employers, friends, and even family members, for instance, sometimes shun people with Acquired Immune Deficiency Syndrome (AIDS).

## Primary and Secondary Deviance

Edwin Lemert (1951, 1972) explains that being labeled as deviant can affect a person's subsequent behavior. Lemert calls activity that is initially defined as deviant *primary deviance*. What Lemert terms *secondary deviance* may follow if the deviant label becomes part of the person's self-concept and social identity. Initial labeling, then, can start someone down the road to fulfilling the expectations of others.

## Stigma

The onset of secondary deviance marks the emergence of what Erving Goffman (1963) called a *deviant career*. Typically, this occurs as a consequence of acquiring a **stigma,** *a powerfully negative social label that radically changes a person's self-concept and social identity*. Stigma, then, operates as a master status (see Chapter 6, "Social Interaction in Everyday Life"), overpowering other dimensions of social identity so that an individual is "reduced in our minds from a whole and usual person to a tainted, discounted one" (1963:3). The person who is stigmatized may become socially isolated, allegedly because of personal failings.

Sometimes the condemnation of an entire community is conveyed formally through what Harold Garfinkel (1956) calls a *degradation ceremony*. A criminal prosecution, for example, is much like a high-school graduation, except that people stand before others to be formally labeled in a negative rather than positive way.

More casually, adults socialize children to devalue stigmatized categories of people. Those stigmatized may include not only lawbreakers but also people of certain races and social classes, as well as those who are physically disabled or unconventional in a host of other respects. For some children, the most emotionally wrenching experience comes from realizing that a particular stigma applies to them personally. Confronted with bigotry, for example, an African-American child learns that, in the eyes of some people, being different means being ignored or even hated. Understandably, then, many people with physical limitations, gay people, and members of racial minorities have come together to counter stigma by recognizing and emphasizing their positive personal qualities.

### Retrospective Labeling

Once stigmatized, a person may be subject to **retrospective labeling,** *the interpretation of someone's past consistent with present deviance* (Scheff, 1984). For example, after discovering that a man who has worked for years with the Boy Scouts has sexually molested a child, others rethink his past, perhaps musing, "He always did want to be around young children." Clearly, retrospective labeling involves a highly selective and prejudicial view of a person's past, guided more by the present stigma than by any attempt to be fair. But this process may nonetheless deepen a person's deviant identity.

### Labeling and Mental Illness

Generally speaking, psychiatrists believe that mental disorders have a concrete reality that parallels diseases of the body. Factors such as heredity, diet, stress, and chemical imbalances in the body do account, in part, for some mental disturbances. However, much of what we label as "mental illness" is actually a matter of social definition (Thoits, 1985). Sometimes defining and treating the "mentally ill" boils down to an attempt to enforce conformity to conventional standards.

If a woman believes that Jesus accompanies her as she rides the bus to work each day, is she seriously

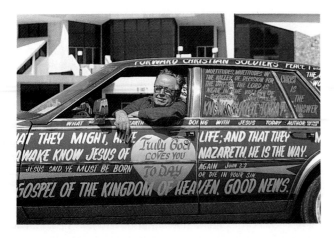

The world is full of people who are unusual in one way or another. This man spends his days driving the streets of New York with a religious message. Should his opinions, and his unconventional way of expressing them, be defined as simple eccentricity or are they evidence of mental illness?

deluded or merely expressing her religious faith in a graphic way? If a man refuses to bathe or observe common etiquette, much to the dismay of his family, is he insane or simply choosing a unconventional way of life? Is a homeless person loudly denouncing the city government while shivering on a street corner mentally ill or expressing justifiable anger?

According to psychiatrist Thomas Szasz, the label of insanity is widely applied to behavior that is merely "different." Therefore, Szasz concludes, the notion of mental illness should be abandoned (1961, 1970; Vatz & Weinberg, 1983). Illness, he asserts, afflicts only the body. Disease can ravage the brain; however, mental illness per se is a myth. Being different in thought or action may irritate others, but it does not justify labeling someone as sick. To do so, Szasz claims, simply enforces conformity to the standards of people powerful enough to get their way. Thus, for decades political dissidents in the Soviet Union reportedly were sent to mental hospitals for "rehabilitation"; similarly, homeless people in New York may be hospitalized for refusing an offer of a bed in a city shelter when outdoor temperatures fall below freezing.

Szasz's views are controversial; many of his colleagues reject the idea that all mental illness is a fiction. Others have hailed his work, however, for pointing to the danger of abusing medical practice in the interest of conformity.

Erving Goffman (1961) has also criticized the label of mental illness. He pointed out that commitment to a mental institution may reflect the desires of others as much as the needs of the patient. Forcible commitment, says Goffman, is often triggered by contingencies that have no direct bearing on the patient's mental condition:

> . . . a psychotic man is tolerated by his wife until she finds herself a boyfriend, or by his adult children until they move from a house to an apartment; an alcoholic is sent to a mental hospital because the jail is full, and a drug addict because he declines to avail himself of psychiatric treatment on the outside; a rebellious adolescent daughter can no longer be managed at home because she now threatens to have an open affair with an unsuitable companion. . . . One could say that mental patients distinctively suffer not from mental illness, but from contingencies. (1961:135)

The stigma of mental illness can transform a person's life, and should not be applied lightly. After all, most of us have experienced periods of extreme stress or other mental disability. Such episodes, although upsetting, are usually of passing importance. If, however, others use the occasion to attach a powerful label to us, they may initiate a self-fulfilling prophecy (Scheff, 1984).

## The Medicalization of Deviance

Labeling theory, particularly the ideas of Szasz and Goffman, helps to explain an important shift in the way we understand deviance. Over the last fifty years, the growing influence of psychiatry and medicine in the United States has encouraged the **medicalization of deviance**, *the transformation of moral and legal issues into medical matters.* In essence, this amounts to a change in labels. Conventional moral judgment designates people or their behavior as "bad" or "good." However, the scientific objectivity of medicine passes no moral judgment; instead, science applies morally neutral diagnoses such as "sick" and "well."

Changing views on alcoholism illustrate this process. Until the middle of this century, alcoholics were generally considered morally deficient, easily tempted by the pleasure of drink. Gradually, however, specialists redefined alcoholism as a medical problem. Now most people view alcoholism as a disease, affecting people who are "sick" rather than "bad." Similarly, obesity, drug addiction, child abuse, and other behaviors that used to provoke cries of moral outrage are today widely defined as illnesses for which the people deserve help rather than punishment.

There are various kinds of deviant labels, and which ones we apply determine how we respond to a situation. If we think of this woman as simply a "drunk," we subject her to moral condemnation and perhaps arrest. This response assumes that her behavior is a matter of at least some choice. If we view the same drinking as evidence of alcoholism, however, we conclude that she is ill and in need of treatment. No longer responsible for her condition, she will not be morally criticized, but she may be subjected to treatment whether she wants it or not.

In some complex cases, moral and medical views alternate over time. For centuries, most women and men in the United States considered homosexuality as a moral issue, a straightforward example of being "bad" as measured against a heterosexual standard of "good." But the growing influence of psychiatry gradually led to the inclusion of homosexuality among medical conditions; in 1952, the American Psychiatric Association (APA) officially declared homosexuality as a "sociopathic personality disturbance." Such a pronouncement by medical authorities had a powerful influence on public opinion and, by 1970, some two-thirds of American adults agreed that homosexuality was a "sickness that could be cured."

More recently, however, yet another view has emerged: homosexual and bisexual people may be *different* without being *deviant*. Supporters of this view point to the lack of success in "curing" homosexuality and to the growing evidence that sexual orientation is not a matter of personal choice. In 1974, the APA switched again, redefining homosexuality as simply a "form of sexual behavior" (Conrad & Schneider, 1980:193–209).

In the wake of this shift to a more neutral view of homosexuality, many gay and straight people have countered traditional prejudices by labeling unwarranted hostility toward homosexuals as "homophobia." This strategy attempts to turn the tables on those who denounce gays by suggesting that deviance may lie in "conventional" people and not those they victimize.

Whether we define deviance as a moral or a medical issue has a number of profound consequences. First, consider *who responds* to deviance. An offense against common morality typically provokes a response by members of the community or police. Applying medical labels, however, places the situation under the control of clinical specialists, including counselors, psychiatrists, and physicians. A second difference is *how people respond* to a deviant. A moral approach defines the deviant as an "offender" subject to punishment; medically, however, "patients" cry out for treatment. Therefore, while punishment is designed to fit the crime, treatment programs are tailored to the patient and may involve virtually any therapy that might prevent future deviance (von Hirsh, 1986). Third, and most important, the two labels differ on the issue of *the personal competence of the deviant person*. Morally, people must take responsibility for their own behavior; they may do wrong, but they understand what they are doing and must face the consequences. Medically, sick people are not considered responsible for what they do. Defined as personally incompetent and unaware of what is in their own best interest, they become vulnerable to more intense, often involuntary, treatment. For this reason alone, attempts to define deviance in medical terms should be made only with extreme caution.

## Sutherland's Differential Association Theory

Related to the issue of how we view others' behavior is how we learn to define our own. Edwin Sutherland (1940) suggested that social patterns, including deviance, are learned through association with others, especially in primary groups. Because of the complexity of socialization, people are exposed to forces encouraging criminality as well as those supporting conformity. The likelihood that a person will engage in criminal activity depends on the frequency of association with those who encourage norm violation compared with those who encourage conformity. This is Sutherland's theory of *differential association*.

Sutherland's theory is illustrated by a study of drug and alcohol use among young adults in the United States (Akers et al., 1979). Analyzing responses to a questionnaire completed by junior and senior high-school students, researchers found that the extent of alcohol and drug use among the respondents varied according to the degree to which peer groups encouraged such activity. The researchers concluded that young people adopt delinquent patterns if they receive praise and other rewards for doing so, defining deviance rather than conformity in positive terms.

A learning approach to deviance also helps to explain the persistence of juvenile delinquency in specific neighborhoods (Shaw & McKay, 1972; orig. 1942). Once established in delinquent subcultures, older youths transmit skills and attitudes promoting deviance to younger boys and girls. The result of this cultural transmission is that delinquency takes on a life of its own, sometimes spanning decades.

***Critical evaluation.*** Labeling theory links deviance not to *action* but to the *reaction* of others. Thus some people are defined as deviant while others who think or behave in the same way are not. The concepts of stigma, secondary deviance, and deviant career demonstrate how the label of deviance can be incorporated into a lasting self-concept.

Yet labeling theory has several limitations. First, because this theory takes a highly relative view of deviance, it glosses over how some kinds of behavior, such as murder, are almost universally condemned (Wellford, 1980). Labeling theory is thus most usefully applied to less serious deviance, such as certain kinds of sexual behavior and mental illness. Second, the consequences of deviant labeling remain unclear. Labeling sometimes promotes subsequent deviance, but it can also discourage people from engaging in further violations (Smith & Gartin, 1989). Thus questions remain as to when and how deviant labeling launches deviant careers. Third, labeling theory assumes that people resist the label of deviance. Probably most do, but some may seek to be defined as deviant (Vold & Bernard, 1986). For example, civil disobedience leading to arrest is a deliberate strategy for calling attention to social injustice. Fourth, we still have much to learn about how people respond to those who are labeled as deviant. One recent study found that the stigma of being a former mental patient resulted in social rejection only in cases when an individual was considered dangerous (Link et al., 1987).

Although Sutherland's differential association theory has exerted considerable influence in sociology, it overlooks instances of deviance that are impulsive rather than planned. Many deviant acts, such as shoplifting or cheating on an examination, may happen spontaneously, rather than signaling the onset of a deviant career. Put otherwise, young people sometimes drift into and out of deviant episodes, many of which are not serious (Matza, 1964; Elliot & Ageton, 1980). Furthermore, differential association theory offers little insight into why society's norms and laws define certain kinds of activities as deviant in the first place. This important question is addressed by social-conflict analysis, described in the next section.

## Social-Conflict Analysis

The social-conflict paradigm links deviance to social inequality. This approach suggests that who or what is labeled as deviant depends on the relative power of categories of people.

Why, Alexander Liazos (1972) asks, does the term "deviance" bring to mind "nuts, sluts, and 'preverts'?" The answer, he suggests, is that such terms identify powerless people. In the power hierarchy, then, deviants inhabit the lowest levels. Bag ladies (not tax evaders) and unemployed men on street corners (not those who profit from wars) contend with the burden of deviance. Similarly, we tend to define the peer groups of poor youths as "street gangs," while those of affluent young people are simply called "cliques."

Social-conflict theory explains this pattern in three ways. First, the norms—including laws—of any society generally reflect the interests of the rich and powerful. People who threaten the wealthy, either by taking their property or by advocating a more egalitarian society, may be readily defined as "thieves" or "political radicals." As was noted in Chapter 4 ("Society"), Karl Marx argued that all social institutions tend to support the capitalist economic system and protect the interests of the rich, capitalist class. Richard Quinney makes the point succinctly: "Capitalist justice is by the capitalist class, for the capitalist class, and against the working class" (1977:3).

Second, even if their behavior is called into question, the powerful have the resources to resist deviant labels. Corporate executives who might order or condone the dumping of hazardous wastes are rarely held personally accountable for these acts. While such mischief poses dangers for all of society, it is not necessarily viewed as criminal.

Artist Frank Romero painted *The Closing of Whittier Boulevard* based on a recollection of his youth in East Los Angeles. To many young Hispanics, identified here by their distinctive "low-rider" cars, police represent a hostile Anglo culture likely to use heavy-handed tactics to discourage them from venturing out of their neighborhood.

Third, the widespread belief that norms and laws are natural and good obscures their political character. For this reason, we may condemn the *unequal application* of the law but give little thought to whether the *laws themselves* are inherently fair (Quinney, 1977).

## Deviance and Capitalism

Steven Spitzer (1980) claims that the people who run the risk of being labeled as deviant are those who impede the operation of capitalism. First, capitalism is based on private control of property, so people who threaten the property of others—especially the poor who steal from the rich—are prime candidates for labeling as deviant. Conversely, the rich who exploit the poor are unlikely to be defined as deviant. Landlords, for example, who charge poor tenants unreasonably high rents, refuse to make repairs on their buildings, and evict those who cannot pay are not officially considered a threat to society: they are simply "doing business."

Second, because capitalism depends on productive labor, those who cannot or will not work risk deviant labeling. We commonly think of people who are out of work—even those unemployed through no fault of their own—as somehow personally inadequate.

Third, capitalism depends on respect for figures of authority, so those who resist society's leaders are likely to be labeled as deviant. Consider the deviant labels that attach to children who skip school or talk back to parents and teachers, adults who do not cooperate with employers or police, and anyone who opposes "the system."

Fourth, capitalism, like all economic systems, rests on the widespread acceptance of the status quo. Those who challenge or undermine the capitalist system, therefore, are subject to deviant labeling. In this category fall antiwar activists, environmentalists, labor organizers, and anyone who supports an alternative economic system.

By contrast, whatever enhances the operation of capitalism attracts positive labels. Athletes, for example, are praised because sports express the values of individual achievement and competition vital to capitalism. Additionally, Spitzer notes, we define the use of drugs for escape (marijuana, psychedelics, heroin, and crack) as deviant, while we endorse consuming drugs that promote adjustment to the status quo (such as caffeine).

Deviant individuals, Spitzer continues, fall into one of two general categories. The system defines people who are a "costly yet relatively harmless burden" to capitalism as *social junk* (1980:184). People devalued in this way do not support themselves by working, typically depending on others or the government for their well-being. Such nonproductive, but nonthreatening, members of society include Robert Merton's retreatists (for example, those addicted to alcohol or other drugs) and the elderly, physically disabled, mentally retarded, or mentally ill. Defined as moderately deviant, these people are typically subject to control by social welfare agencies.

People who threaten capitalism, meanwhile, are labeled as *social dynamite*. Those in this second category range from members of the inner-city "underclass," to alienated youths, radicals, and revolutionaries—in Merton's terms, society's innovators and rebels. To the extent that they become threatening, such people are subject to control by the criminal justice system and, in times of crisis, by military forces such as the National Guard.

Following Marx's lead, Spitzer claims that capitalism itself produces both "social junk" and "social dynamite." The unemployment and poverty that overwhelm much of these populations stem from the workings of the capitalist system. Having created these categories of people, capitalism must also control them—through the social welfare system and the criminal justice system. In the process of doing so, both systems apply deviant labels that place responsibility for social problems on the people themselves. Those who receive welfare because they have no other source of income are considered unworthy; poor people who vent their rage at being deprived of a secure life are labeled as rioters; anyone who actively challenges the government is called a radical or a communist; and those who attempt to gain illegally what they cannot otherwise acquire are called common thieves.

## White-Collar Crime

Until 1989, few people other than Wall Street stockbrokers had ever heard of Michael Milken. Yet Milken had accomplished a stunning feat, becoming the highest paid U.S. worker in half a century. With salary and bonuses in 1987 totaling $550 million—*about $1.5 million a day*—Milken ranks behind only Al Capone, whose earnings in 1927 reportedly reached $600 million in current dollars (Swartz, 1989). Milken has something else in common with Capone: the government accused him of one hundred violations of securities and exchange laws.

Such activities exemplify **white-collar crime**, defined by Edwin Sutherland in 1940 as *crimes committed by persons of high social position in the course of their occupations* (Sutherland & Cressey, 1978:44). As the Milken case suggests, white-collar crime rarely involves uniformed police converging on a scene with drawn guns. Thus it does not refer to crimes such as murder, assault, or rape that happen to be carried out by people of high social position. Instead, white-collar crimes are acts by powerful people making use of their occupational positions to enrich themselves or others illegally, often causing significant public harm in the process (Hagan

Marijuana use is not illegal simply because it is harmful. In fact, smoking tobacco is far more dangerous since it contributes to more than 300,000 premature deaths each year. The legal standing of a drug depends on many factors, including whether it promotes social adjustment or encourages escape and what potential profit it represents for businesses.

& Parker, 1985; Vold & Bernard, 1986). In short, white-collar offenses that occur in government offices and corporate board rooms are commonly dubbed *crime in the suites* rather than *crime in the streets*.

The public harm wreaked by false advertising, marketing of unsafe products, embezzlement, and bribery of public officials extends far beyond what most people realize. Some researchers contend that white-collar crime causes greater public harm than the more visible "street crime" (Reiman, 1990). Estimates of the economic costs of business-related crimes range up to several hundred billion dollars a year—an amount far exceeding the economic loss of common theft (Reid, 1982; Reiman, 1984; U.S. Department of Justice, 1987).

At the time Sutherland (1940) conducted his research, he claimed that all the largest U.S. businesses had broken the law, causing considerable social harm. Yet only about one case in ten was officially defined as the criminal action of a specific person. Rather, as is still the case, violations by corporations or government agencies are far more likely to end up as part of a civil dispute than in a criminal court.

*Civil law* refers to the regulation of economic losses between private parties, while *criminal law* encompasses specific laws that define every individual's moral responsibility to society. Civil settlements involve restitution for damage or injury, but no party in a civil complaint is defined as a criminal. Further, since corporations have the legal standing of persons, allegations of white-collar offenses commonly involve the organization, thereby sparing particular individuals. Today, as at the time of Sutherland's research, elite deviance rarely results in criminal labeling of powerful people (Simon & Eitzen, 1990).

Although the recent savings and loan scandal may end up costing U.S. taxpayers some $600 billion dollars—$2,500 for every adult and child in the country—authorities have prosecuted only a handful of individuals. Much the same pattern is currently unfolding as investigators bring to light mischief—including drug-dealing, illegal arms sales, and influence-peddling in more than seventy countries—carried out by officers of the Bank of Commerce and Credit International (BCCI). In this case, too, extensive public harm is evident, yet it is far from certain that officials will be prosecuted. And when white-collar criminals do face the music, the odds are they will not go to jail. In 1987, fewer than three in ten embezzlers convicted in the U.S. District Court system spent a single day in prison; most were placed on probation (U.S. Bureau of Justice Statistics, 1989).

White-collar polluters also have reason to scoff at the law: only ninety people were jailed for all federal environmental crimes between 1986 and 1991 (Gold, 1991).

Sutherland also noted that the public voices less concern about white-collar crime than about street crime, partly because corporate crime victimizes everyone—and no one. White-collar criminals don't stick a gun in anyone's ribs, and the economic costs are usually spread throughout the population.

As the "backbone of capitalism," corporations have immense power, influencing both the mass media and the political process. High corporate officials are frequently graduates of prestigious universities and professional schools, belong to exclusive social clubs, and have well-developed networks linking them to other powerful people in all walks of life. Many government officials, drawn from the ranks of corporate executives, regulate the very corporate enterprises in which they have spent most of their working lives. Not surprisingly, then, serious episodes of white-collar crime only make headlines from time to time.

***Critical evaluation.*** According to social-conflict theory, the inequality in wealth and power that pervades our way of life also guides the creation and application of laws and other norms. This approach suggests that the criminal justice and social welfare systems act as political agents, controlling categories of people who threaten the capitalist system.

Like others approaches to deviance, however, social-conflict theory has its critics. First, this approach assumes that laws and other cultural norms are created directly by the rich and powerful. This is certainly an oversimplification, since many segments of our society influence, and benefit from, the political process. For example, laws also protect workers, consumers, and the environment, sometimes in opposition to the interests of capitalists. A second criticism holds that while social-conflict theory points to the social injury caused by the powerful, the average individual in the United States remains far more concerned about street crime. Third, this approach implies that criminality springs up only to the extent that a society treats its members unequally. However, according to Durkheim, all societies generate deviance, and crime is well known in societies far more socially and economically egalitarian than our own.

We have presented various sociological explanations for crime and other types of deviance. Table 8–2 presents a summary of the contributions of each approach.

**Table 8–2** SOCIOLOGICAL EXPLANATIONS OF DEVIANCE: A SUMMARY

| Theoretical Paradigm | Major Contribution |
|---|---|
| Structural-functional analysis | While what is deviant may vary, deviance itself is found in all societies; deviance and the social response it provokes serve to maintain the moral foundation of society; deviance can also direct social change |
| Symbolic-interation analysis | Nothing is inherently deviant but may become defined as such through the response of others; the reactions of others are highly variable; the label of deviance can lead to the emergence of secondary deviance and deviant careers |
| Social-conflict analysis | Laws and other norms reflect the interests of powerful members of society; those who threaten the status quo are likely to be defined as deviant; social injury caused by powerful people is less likely to be defined as criminal than social injury caused by people who have little social power |

## Deviance and Gender

Anne Campbell (1991) points out that no variable is related to deviance more than gender: her own research shows that the vast majority of gang members are men. Curiously, however, analysis of gang behavior and other types of deviance rarely takes gender into account. Let us now examine how gender figures in to some of the theories we have already discussed.

Robert Merton's strain theory, for example, defines cultural goals in terms of financial success. Traditionally, however, this preoccupation with material things has dominated the thinking of men while women have been socialized to define success in terms of relationships, particularly marriage and motherhood (Leonard, 1982). Only recently have women and men come to recognize the "strain" caused by cultural ideals of equality clashing with the reality of gender-based inequality.

Labeling theory, the major approach in symbolic-interaction analysis, offers some insights into ways in which gender influences how we define deviance. Since the behavior of females and males is judged by different standards, the very process of labeling stems from sex-linked biases. Further, Edwin Schur (1983) explains that because society generally places men in positions of power over women, men often escape direct responsibility for actions that victimize women. Frequently, men who engage in sexual harassment or other assaults against women are tagged with only mildly deviant labels; sometimes, they suffer no adverse consequences and, in some quarters, they may even gain social approval for their actions. By contrast, women who are victimized may have to convince an unsympathetic audience that they are not to blame for what happened. Research confirms an important truth: whether people define a situation as deviance—and, if so, whose deviance it is—depends on the sex of both the audience and the actors (King & Clayson, 1988). The box on pages 224–25 takes a closer look at the issue of date rape, in which many women and men are standing up for an end to a double standard that has long threatened the well-being of women.

Finally, a notable irony is that social-conflict analysis—despite its focus on social inequality—has neglected the importance of gender. If, as this approach asserts, economic oppression is a primary cause of crime, why do women (whose economic position is much worse than that of men) commit far *fewer* crimes than men do? The next section, in which we examine crime rates in the United States, answers this question.

## Crime

Speak of crime and people immediately conjure up images of unsavory characters ducking into alleyways, waiting to prey on unsuspecting victims. But crime covers a surprisingly wide range of behaviors, including activities that in one time or place provoke a swift response while in another barely merit a raised eyebrow. In centuries past, a commoner who simply looked at the Chinese emperor in public was accused of a serious crime. Today a citizen of the People's Republic of China who expressed support for the nation's historic monarchy would likely face criminal charges. The judicial system in the United

# Date Rape: Exposing Dangerous Myths

Completing a day of work during a business trip to the courthouse in Tampa, Florida, thirty-two-year-old Sandra Abbott* pondered how she would return to her hotel. An attorney with whom she had been working—a pleasant enough man—made a kind offer of a lift. As his car threaded its way through the late afternoon traffic, their conversation was animated. "He was saying all the right things," Abbott recalled, "so I started to trust him." He wondered if she would join him for dinner; she happily accepted. After lingering over an enjoyable meal, they walked together to the door of her hotel room. The new acquaintance angled for an invitation to come in, apparently eager to continue their conversation. Abbott hesitated. Sensing that he might have something more on his mind, she explained that she took an old-fashioned view when it came to relationships. He could come in, she finally agreed, but only for a little while, and with the understanding that talk was *all* they would do.

Sitting on the couch in the room, soon Abbott was overcome with drowsiness. Feeling comfort-

The 1992 rape conviction of heavyweight boxing champion Mike Tyson suggested that our society is taking the problem of sexual violence against women more seriously.

able in the presence of her new friend, she let her head fall gently onto his shoulder and, before she knew it, she fell asleep. That's when the attack began. Abbott was startled back to consciousness as the man thrust himself sexually upon her. She shouted "No!" but he paid no heed. Abbott describes what happened next:

> I didn't scream or run. All I could think of was my business contacts and what if they saw me run out of my room screaming rape. I thought it was my fault. I felt so filthy, I washed myself over and

over in hot water. Did he rape me?, I kept asking myself. I didn't consent. But who's gonna believe me? I had a man in my hotel room after midnight. (Gibbs, 1991a:50)

Abbott knew that she had said "No!" and thus had been raped. She notified the police, who conducted an investigation and turned their findings over to the state attorney's office. But the authorities backed away from Abbott. In the absence of evidence like bruises, a medical examination, and torn clothes, they responded, there was little point in prosecuting.

The case of Sandra Abbott is all too typical. Even today, in most incidences of sexual attack, a victim files no police report, and no offender is arrested. The woman faces the bitter reality of simply trying as best she can to put a traumatic experience behind her.

The reason for such appalling inaction is that many people have a misguided understanding of rape. Three inaccurate notions about rape are so common in the United States that they might be called "rape myths." A first myth is that rape involves strangers. A sexual attack brings to mind young men who lurk in the shadows and suddenly spring on their unsuspecting victims, much like the gang of young New Yorkers who attacked the Central Park jogger

_____
* A pseudonym; the facts of this case are from Gibbs (1991a).

States has also undergone sweeping changes, from first supporting slavery to eventually condemning racial discrimination.

All societies have a formal means of dealing with perceived violations of law. Generally, then, crime

amounts to a violation of the criminal law enacted by the local, state, or national government. Because jurisdictions define legal standards differently, what is a crime in one time and place may or may not be so at another. Technically, however, all crimes are constructed of two as described at the beginning of Chapter 1 ("The Sociological Perspective"). But this pattern is the exception rather than the rule: experts report that only one in five rapes involves strangers. For this reason, people have begun to speak more realistically about *acquaintance rape* or, more simply, *date rape*. A rape—legally speaking, the carnal knowledge of a female forcibly and against her will—is typically committed by a man who is known to, and even trusted by, his victim. But common sense dictates that being a "friend" (or even a husband) does not prevent a man from committing murder, assault, or rape.

A second myth about rape is that women provoke their attackers. Surely, many people think, a woman claiming to have been raped must have done *something* to encourage the man, to lead him on, to make him think that she really wanted to have sex. In the case described above, didn't Sandra Abbott agree to have dinner with the man? Didn't she willingly admit him to her room? Such thinking often paralyzes victims; women themselves often experience self-doubt about their actions after having been raped. But having dinner with a man—or even inviting him into her hotel room—is hardly a woman's statement of consent to have sex with him any more than

it is an invitation to have him beat her with a club.

A third myth is the notion that rape is simply sex. If there is no knife held to a woman's throat, or if she is not bound and gagged, then how can sex be a crime? The answer is simply that *forcing a woman to have sex without her consent is rape*. To accept the idea that rape is sex we would also have to see no difference between brutal combat and playful wrestling. In the absence of consent, as Susan Brownmiller (1975) explains, rape is not sex but violence. "Having sex" implies intimacy, caring, and communication—none of which is present in cases of rape. Beyond the brutality of being physically violated, date rape also undermines a victim's sense of trust.

The more people believe these myths about rape—that offenders are strangers, that victims provoke their attackers, and that rape is just spirited sex—the more women will become victims of sexual violence. The ancient Babylonians stoned married women who became victims of rape, claiming that the women had committed adultery. To a startling extent, ideas about rape have not changed over thousands of years, which helps explain why, even today, most rapes go unreported to police and, even when authorities are notified, prosecutions and convictions are

rare. At present, perhaps one in twenty rapes results in an offender being sent to jail.

Nowhere has the issue of date rape been more widely discussed than at colleges and universities. The campus is distinctive in several respects: students have easy access to one another, the collegiate setting encourages trust, and young people often have much to learn about relationships and about themselves. While this open environment encourages communication, it also allows for an alarming level of sexual violence. Studies estimate that one in six college women will be raped before she graduates.

To eliminate sexual violence we must begin by exposing the myths about rape. In addition, the campus must be transformed so that women and men interact with dignity and equality. Serious questions surround the role of alcohol in campus social life and the effect of traditional cultural patterns that define sex as a sport. To address the crisis of date rape, everyone needs to understand two simple truths: forcing sex without a woman's consent constitutes rape, and when a woman says "no," she means just that.

SOURCES: Gibbs (1991a, 1991b).

distinct elements: the *act* itself (or, in some cases, the failure to do what the law requires) and *criminal intent* (in legal terminology, *mens rea*, or "guilty mind"). Intent is a matter of degree, ranging from a deliberate action to negligence in which a person acts (or fails to act) in a manner that may reasonably be expected to cause harm. Juries weigh the degree of intent in determining whether, for example, someone who kills another is guilty of first-degree murder, second-degree murder, or negligent manslaughter (Reid, 1991).

## Types of Crime

In the United States, the Federal Bureau of Investigation gathers information on criminal offenses and regularly reports the results in a publication called *Crime in the United States.* Two major types of offenses are used to generate the "crime index."

**Crimes against the person** constitute *crimes against people that involve violence or the threat of violence.* Such "violent crimes" include murder and manslaughter (legally defined as "the willful killing of one human being by another"), aggravated assault ("an unlawful attack by one person on another for the purpose of inflicting severe or aggravated bodily injury"), forcible rape ("the carnal knowledge of a female forcibly and against her will"), and robbery ("taking or attempting to take anything of value from the care, custody, or control of a person or persons by force or threat of force or violence and/ or putting the victim in fear").

**Crimes against property** encompass *crimes that involve theft of property belonging to others.* "Property crimes" range from burglary ("the unlawful entry of a structure to commit a [serious crime] or a theft"), to larceny-theft ("the unlawful taking, carrying, leading, or riding away of property from the possession of another"), auto theft ("the theft or attempted theft of a motor vehicle"), and arson ("any willful or malicious burning or attempt to burn the personal property of another").

A third category of offenses, not incorporated into major crime indexes, is **victimless crimes**, *violations of law in which there are no readily apparent victims.* So-called "crimes without complaint" include illegal drug use, prostitution, and gambling. However, "victimless crime" is often a misnomer. How victimless is a crime when young people purchasing drugs may be embarking on a life of crime to support a drug habit? How victimless is a crime if a young pregnant woman smoking crack causes the death or permanent injury of her baby? How victimless is a crime when a young runaway is lured into prostitution and then brainwashed into thinking that's her only way to live? And how victimless is the crime when a gambler falls so deeply into debt that he cannot make the mortgage payments or afford food for his family? In truth, the people who commit such crime can themselves be both offenders and victims.

Because public opinion about such activities varies considerably, the laws regulating victimless crimes differ from place to place. In the United States, gambling is legal only in Nevada and part of New Jersey; prostitution is legal only in part of Nevada; homosexual (and some heterosexual) behavior is still legally restricted in about half the states. Where such laws do exist, enforcement is generally uneven.

## Criminal Statistics

Statistics gathered by the Federal Bureau of Investigation show that crime rates increased dramatically during the 1970s, declined during the early 1980s, and rose again after 1984. During the 1980s, overall violent crime rose by 23 percent; property crime was off a modest 3 percent (U.S. Federal Bureau of Investigation, 1991). Figure 8–1 illustrates the relative frequency and the trend for various serious crimes.

Crime statistics should be read with caution, however, since they include only certain offenses, which are sometimes tagged "index" crimes. The official record also includes only crimes known to the police. Police learn about almost all homicides, but assaults—especially among acquaintances—are far less likely to be reported. Police records include even a smaller proportion of property crimes that are committed, especially those involving items of little value. Some victims may not realize that a crime has occurred, or they may assume they have little chance of recovering their property even if they notify the police.

As already noted in the box, rape statistics reflect less than half of all such assaults (cf. Harlow, 1991). Because of the traditional stigma attached to innocent victims, many women choose to remain silent after being attacked. However, in recent years improved public support for rape victims—including the establishment of rape crisis centers, and increased sensitivity to the trauma on the part of police officers and hospital personnel—has prompted more victims to come forward. This change is reflected in the 25-percent increase in the number of forcible rapes reported to police during the 1980s.

One way to evaluate crime statistics is through a *victimization survey*, in which a representative sample of people is asked about being victimized. According to these surveys, actual criminality occurs at a rate about three times higher than what official reports indicate.

## The "Street" Criminal: A Profile

Government statistics paint a broad-brush picture of people arrested for violent and property crimes. We now examine the breakdown of these arrest statistics by age, gender, social class, and race.

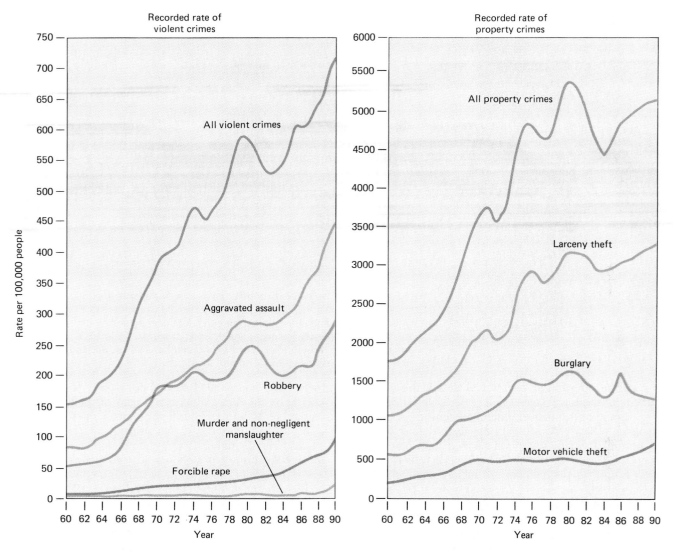

**Figure 8–1** Crime Rates in the United States, 1960–1990
(*U.S. Federal Bureau of Investigation, 1991*)

### Age

Official crime rates rise sharply during adolescence and the early twenties, falling thereafter (Hirschi & Gottfredson, 1983; Krisberg & Schwartz, 1983). Although people between the ages of fifteen and twenty-four represent only 15 percent of the U.S. population, they accounted for 45 percent of all arrests for serious crimes in 1990: 42.9 percent for violent crimes and 46.2 percent for property crimes (U.S. Federal Bureau of Investigation, 1991).

### Gender

Official statistics suggest that the vast majority of crime is committed by males. Although each sex constitutes roughly half the population, males were about three times more likely than females to be arrested for serious crimes in 1990: 74.7 percent of property crime arrests were of males; 25.3 percent, females. For violent crimes, the disparity was even greater: 88.7 percent of arrests involved males and 11.3 percent females. Although some research suggests that the criminal disparity between the

In Saudi Arabia, women cannot vote, drive a car, or appear in public without being veiled. Given this rigid regulation, crimes by women are rare. In the United States, women have much more freedom over what they do and how they dress. This greater freedom is reflected in crime rates that are steadily moving closer to those of men. Even so, women have less power and remain subject to more extensive social control than men.

sexes diminishes in the lower social classes, this general pattern is striking (Hagan, Gillis, & Simpson, 1985).

Some of this gender difference stems from the reluctance of law enforcement officials to define women as criminals. Even so, the arrest rate for women has been moving closer to that of men, perhaps because of increasing sexual equality in our society. Between 1981 and 1990, the *increase* in arrests of women was greater (48.4 percent) than that for men (27.4 percent) (U.S. Federal Bureau of Investigation, 1991). In addition, girls and boys display comparable patterns of delinquency in families where females and males are treated with relative equality (Hagan, Simpson, & Gillis, 1987). Finally, research confirms that the greatest difference in crime rates between the two sexes appears in societies that most limit the social opportunities of women (Blum & Fisher, 1980).

### Social Class

People in the United States associate criminality with poverty. Sociological research suggests, however, that rich and poor alike commit crimes, albeit somewhat different *kinds* of offenses.

People arrested for violent and property crimes in the United States and elsewhere disproportionately have low social standing (Wolfgang, Figlio, & Sellin, 1972; Clinard & Abbott, 1973; Elliott & Ageton, 1980; Braithwaite, 1981; Thornberry & Farnsworth, 1982; Wolfgang, Thornberry, & Figlio, 1987). Here the difference partly reflects the historical tendency to view poor people as less worthy than those whose wealth and power confers on them "respectability" (Tittle & Villemez, 1977; Tittle, Villemez, & Smith, 1978; Elias, 1986). Some contend that this bias in the criminal justice system has gradually diminished, with criminality among various segments of the population becoming more equal. Evidence also suggests that street crime disproportionately *victimizes* people of lower social position.

Crime—especially violence—is commonplace among the small number of chronically poor people living in inner-city neighborhoods. But only a small proportion of less advantaged people are ever convicted of crimes; most crimes are committed by relatively few hard-core offenders (Wolfgang, Figlio, & Sellin, 1972; Elliott & Ageton, 1980; Wolfgang, Thornberry, & Figlio, 1987; Harries, 1990). Additionally, as John Braithwaite notes, the connection between social standing and criminality "depends entirely on what form of crime one is talking about" (1981:47). If the definition of crime is expanded beyond street crime to include white-collar crime, the average "common criminal" has a much higher social position.

### Race

Probing the relationship between race and criminality, we confront a raft of complex issues. Official statistics indicate that 69.2 percent of arrests for index crimes in 1990 involved whites. However, African Americans were arrested more often than whites in proportion to their numbers, representing about 12 percent of the population and 34.4 percent of index crime arrests. Blacks comprised 29.9 percent of arrests for property crimes (versus 68.3 percent for whites) and 44.1 percent of arrests for violent crimes (as opposed to 54.4 percent for whites) (U.S. Federal Bureau of Investigation, 1991).

Just as most people have long considered criminality the province of the poor, they have also associated crime with people of color (and, particularly, young, black males). This despite clear evidence that most crimes are committed by whites.

We can draw no simple conclusions about crime for three key reasons. First, arrest records do not qualify as statements of proven guilt. To the degree that prejudice related to color prompts police to arrest blacks more readily than whites, and leads white citizens more readily to report blacks to police as potential offenders, African Americans are overly criminalized. The same prejudices may work in the courtroom. In the long run, even small biases by law enforcement officials and the public substantially distort the official link between race and crime (Liska & Tausig, 1979; Unnever, Frazier, & Henretta, 1980; Smith & Visher, 1981).

Second, race in the United States closely relates to social standing, which, as we have already shown, affects the likelihood of engaging in street crimes. Several researchers claim that membership in lower-class gangs promotes criminality. Judith and Peter Blau (1982) take a different tack, suggesting that criminality—especially violent crime—is promoted by income disparity. That is, the Blaus argue that criminality is caused less by deviant subcultures than by the sting of poverty in the midst of affluence. Suffering the hardships of poverty in a rich society encourages people to perceive society as unjust and to disregard its laws. Because unemployment among African-American adults is two to three times higher than among whites, and because *almost half* of black children grow up in poverty (in contrast to about one in six white children), we should expect proportionately higher crime rates for African Americans

(Sampson, 1987). Research suggests that rigid systems of social inequality in other societies generate similar patterns of criminality (Messner, 1989).

Third, as noted earlier, white-collar crimes are excluded from the official crime index. Clearly, this omission contributes to the view of the typical criminal as not simply poor but a person of color. If our definition of crime were broadened to include insider stock trading, toxic-waste dumping, embezzlement, bribery, and cheating on income tax returns, the proportion of white criminals would rise dramatically.

## Crime in Global Perspective

By world standards, the United States has a lot of crime. Marshall Clinard (1978) observes that in Switzerland murders are relatively rare, even in the largest cities. New York City, by contrast, led all U.S. cities with 2,245 murders in 1990. Hardly a day passes with no murder in New York; typically more New Yorkers are hit by stray bullets than are gunned down deliberately in cities elsewhere in the world.

Although crime rates rose in Europe more than in the United States during the 1980s, crime pervades our society to a much greater extent than it does European countries. Global comparisons fall short because nations define crimes differently and not every country collects data with care. But rough comparisons suggest that the homicide rate in the United States stands five times higher than that in Europe, the rape rate seven times higher, and the rate of property crime twice as high. Figure 8–2 on page 230 graphically illustrates global comparisons for rape and robbery. Although the patterns differ for each crime, we can conclude from these figures that the United States contends with more crime than virtually any other country in the world (Kalish, 1988).

Elliot Currie (1985) suggests that crime stems from our culture's emphasis on individual economic success, frequently at the expense of family and community cohesion. Currie also notes that, unlike European nations, the United States neither guarantees families a minimum income nor publicly funds childcare programs. Such public policy decisions, he claims, erode the fabric of our society, fuel frustration among society's have-nots, and thus encourage criminal behavior. Furthermore, Currie asserts that the high level of unemployment and underemployment tolerated in the United States (and increasingly in Europe) helps create a category of perpetually poor people whose opportunities to make money are often limited to criminal pursuits. The key to reducing

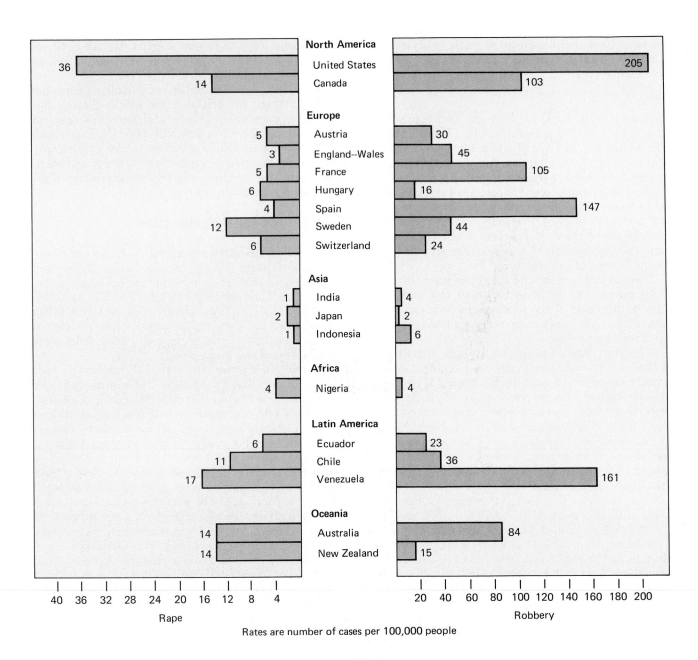

**Figure 8–2** Global Comparisons: Rates for Rape and Robbery
(*Interpol data, as reported by Kalish, 1988*)

crime, then, lies in *social change*, not in hiring more police and building more prisons.

Another contributing factor to the relatively high level of violence in the United States is widespread private ownership of guns. About 60 percent of the 20,000 mur-

der victims annually in the United States are killed by guns. In recent years, the proliferation of high-powered, military-type weaponry has prompted police organizations and citizens' groups to press for gun control. Public support propelled the passage in 1991 of the so-called

230    Chapter 8    Deviance

Brady Bill, named for James Brady, President Reagan's press secretary who was shot along with the president in 1981. The law requires a seven-day waiting period for the purchase of handguns. No one thinks reining in the gun trade will end crime in the United States. There are already about as many guns in the hands of private individuals as there are people in the United States. Further, Elliot Currie argues that the causes of violence go far beyond the availability of guns. He notes that the number of Californians killed each year by knives alone exceeds the number of Canadians killed by weapons of all kinds. Most experts do think, however, that gun control would curb the level of violence.

Available evidence indicates that crime rates are skyrocketing in the largest cities of the world—cities like Sao Paulo, Brazil, where the population is soaring and most people are desperately poor. By and large, however, crime rates in less developed societies are lower than in the United States. Some countries have high rates of violence (Colombia's recent drug war stands out), but the rate of property crime in the United States dwarfs that of most poor nations. This lower crime rate reflects

There are enough guns in the United States to arm every woman, man, and child; about half of all households contain one or more weapons of this kind. Guns are not the key to our country's high crime rate, since unarmed criminality in the United States is also high by world standards. But the ready availability of guns does contribute to accidental shootings—especially by children—and it also raises the risk that interpersonal violence will be deadly.

the traditional character of nonindustrial societies; there, strong families and cohesive residential neighborhoods informally control crime (Clinard & Abbott, 1973; *Der Spiegel*, 1989). By the same token, however, traditional social patterns promote a crime like prostitution by sharply limiting the opportunities available to women. Global Map 8–1 on page 232 shows the extent of prostitution in various world regions.

## The Criminal Justice System

Through the criminal justice system, society formally responds to crime. We shall briefly introduce the key elements of this system: police, the courts, and the punishment of convicted offenders.

### Police

The police generally serve as the point of contact between the public and the criminal justice system. In principle, the police maintain public order by uniformly enforcing the law. In reality, 650,000 full-time police officers in the United States (in 1990) cannot effectively monitor the activities of 250 million people. As a result, the police exercise considerable discretion about which situations warrant their attention and how to handle them.

Police discretion is a two-edged sword. On the one hand, police officers must have a good deal of latitude in decision making because of the magnitude of police responsibilities. On the other hand, however, the ability of police to pursue a situation as they see fit also fosters unequal treatment of some categories of people, as suggested by the Rodney King incident in Los Angeles, described at the beginning of this chapter. Professional police work involves using the power of the job to enhance rather than undermine public well-being.

How, then, do police carry out their duties? In a study of police behavior in five cities, Douglas Smith and Christy Visher (1981; Smith, 1987) concluded that, because they must often act quickly, police rely on external cues to guide their actions. These researchers identified six factors that affect police when confronted with apparent crime. First, the more serious they perceive the situation to be, the more likely they are to make an arrest. Second, police assess the victim's preference as to how the matter should be handled. If a victim demands that police make an arrest, they are likely to

**Global Map 8–1**   Prostitution in Global Perspective

Roughly speaking, prostitution is widespread in societies of the world where women have low social standing in relation to men. Officially, at least, the now defunct socialist regimes in Eastern Europe and the Soviet Union, as well as the People's Republic of China, boasted of gender equality, including the elimination of "vice" such as prostitution. By contrast, in much of Latin America, a region of pronounced patriarchy, prostitution is commonplace. In many Islamic societies, where patriarchy is also strong, religious forces temper this practice. Western, industrial societies also display a moderate amount of prostitution.

do so. Third, police more often arrest suspects who appear uncooperative. Fourth, they are more likely to arrest suspects with whom they have had prior contact, presumably because this suggests guilt. Fifth, the presence of bystanders increases the likelihood of arrest. According to Smith and Visher, the presence of observers prompts police to act assertively because they want to appear in control of the situation, and also because an arrest moves the interaction from the street (the suspect's turf) to the police department (where law officers have the edge).

Sixth, all else being equal, police are more likely to arrest people of color than whites. Smith and Visher concluded that police generally consider people of African or Hispanic descent as either more dangerous or more likely to be guilty. In the researchers' view, this perception contributes to the disproportionately high arrest rates among these categories of people.

Finally, the greatest number of police relative to population is found in cities with two key characteristics: high concentrations of minorities and large income disparities between rich and poor (Jacobs, 1979). This finding squares with Judith and Peter Blau's (1982) conclusion that striking inequality promotes criminal violence. Thus police form an imposing presence where a volatile mix of social forces encourages social disruption.

## Courts

After arrest, a suspect's guilt or innocence is determined by a court. In principle, our courts rely on an adversarial process involving attorneys—who represent the defendant on the one side and the state on the other—in the presence of a judge who monitors adherence to legal procedures. In practice, however, about 90 percent of criminal cases are resolved prior to court appearance through **plea bargaining,** *a legal negotiation in which the prosecution reduces a defendant's charge in exchange for a guilty plea.* For example, a defendant charged with burglary may agree to plead guilty to the lesser charge of possession of burglary tools; another charged with selling cocaine may go along with pleading guilty to mere possession.

Plea bargaining has gained widespread acceptance because it spares the judicial system the time and expense of court trials. A trial is usually unnecessary if there is little disagreement as to the facts of the case. By selectively trying only a small proportion of the cases, the courts can also channel their resources into those deemed most important (Reid, 1991).

But in the process, defendants (who are presumed innocent) are pressured to plead guilty. A person can exercise the right to a trial, but only at the risk of receiving a more severe sentence if found guilty. In essence, then, plea bargaining undercuts the right of defendants as it circumvents the adversarial process. According to Abraham Blumberg (1970), defendants who have little understanding of the criminal justice system, as well as those unable to afford a good lawyer, are likely to suffer from this system of "bargain-counter justice."

## Punishment

In 1831 the officials in an English town hanged a nine-year-old boy who was found guilty of the crime of setting fire to a house (Kittrie, 1971:103). The history of the United States records 281 youths executed for crimes committed as juveniles, most recently a young man in Texas for a murder committed when he was seventeen. Twenty-seven other juveniles are currently on death row, waiting for the Supreme Court to decide whether their age should preclude their execution (Rosenbaum, 1989).

Dutch painter Vincent Van Gogh (1853–1890) strongly identified with suffering people that he found around him. Perhaps this is why he included his own likeness in this portrait of the dungeon-like prisons of the nineteenth century. Since then, the stark isolation and numbing depersonalization of prison life has changed little. Prisons are still custodial institutions in which officials make few efforts at rehabilitation.
*Vincent Van Gogh, 1853–1890.* Prisoners' Round. *Dutch. Pushkin State Museum, Moscow.*

Such cases spark controversy because, in the United States, young people are widely regarded as having *diminished capacity* for crime. In addition, the issue of juvenile crime raises the general question of why societies punish in the first place. Four justifications of punishment are commonly advanced.

## Retribution

The celebrated justice of the Supreme Court, Oliver Wendell Holmes, stated that "The first requirement of a sound body of law is that it should correspond with the actual feelings and demands of the community." Because people react to crime with a passion for revenge, Holmes continued, "the law has no choice but to satisfy [that] craving" (cited in Carlson, 1976).

From this point of view, punishment satisfies a society's need for **retribution,** *an act of moral vengeance by which society subjects an offender to suffering comparable to that caused by the offense.* Retribution is based on a view of society as a system of moral balance. When criminality upsets this balance, punishment exacted in comparable measure restores the moral order, as suggested in the biblical dictum "An eye for an eye."

Retribution stands as the oldest justification for punishment. During the Middle Ages, crime was widely viewed as sin—an offense against God as well as society—therefore warranting harsh punishment. Although sometimes criticized today because it overlooks the issue of reforming the offender, retribution remains a strong justification for punishment.

## Deterrence

A second justification for punishment, **deterrence,** amounts to *the attempt to discourage criminality through punishment.* Deterrence is based on the Enlightenment notion that humans are calculating and rational creatures. From this point of view, people engage in deviance for personal gain, but if they think that the pain of punishment outweighs the pleasure of mischief, they will forgo temptation.

Initially, deterrence was instituted to reform a system of excessive punishments based on retribution. Why put someone to death for stealing, for example, if that crime could be discouraged with a prison sentence? As the concept of deterrence became better accepted, execution and physical mutilation of criminals were replaced by milder forms of punishment such as incarceration.

Punishment may deter in two ways. *Specific deterrence* demonstrates to an individual offender that crime does not pay. Through *general deterrence,* the punishment of one person serves as an example to others.

## Rehabilitation

The third justification for punishment, **rehabilitation,** involves *reforming the offender to preclude subsequent offenses.* Rehabilitation paralleled the development of the social sciences in the nineteenth century. According to early social analysts, crime and other deviance sprang from an unfavorable social environment, one pervaded by poverty or a lack of parental supervision, for example. Defenders of rehabilitation argued that, just as offenders learn to be deviant, they learn to obey the rules if placed in the right setting. *Reformatories* or *houses of correction,* therefore, afforded offenders a controlled environment that might help them learn proper behavior (recall the description of total institutions in Chapter 5, "Socialization").

Rehabilitation resembles deterrence because it motivates the offender to conform to societal norms. But rehabilitation emphasizes constructive improvement while deterrence and retribution simply make the offender suffer. In addition, while retribution demands that the punishment fit the crime, rehabilitation focuses on the distinctive problems of each offender. Thus identical offenses might prompt similar acts of retribution, but different programs of rehabilitation.

## Social Protection

A final justification for punishment, **social protection,** refers to *rendering an offender incapable of further offenses either temporarily during a period of incarceration or permanently by execution.* Like deterrence, social protection is a rational approach to punishment and seeks to protect society from crime.

Table 8–3 summarizes these four justifications of punishment.

*Critical evaluation.* We have identified four aims of punishment. Assessing the actual consequences of punishment, however, is no simple task.

The value of retribution relates to Durkheim's ideas about the functions of deviance, presented earlier in this chapter. Recall that Durkheim believed that responding to deviance increases people's awareness of shared

**Table 8–3   FOUR JUSTIFICATIONS OF PUNISHMENT: A SUMMARY**

| | |
|---|---|
| Retribution | The oldest justification of punishment that remains important today. Punishment is atonement for a moral wrong by an individual; in principle, punishment should be comparable in severity to the deviance itself. |
| Deterrence | An early modern approach, deviance is viewed as social disruption, which society acts to control. People are viewed as rational and self-interested, so that deterrence requires that the pains of punishment outweigh the pleasures of deviance. |
| Rehabilitation | A modern approach linked to the development of the social sciences, deviance is viewed as the product of social problems (such as poverty) or of personal problems (such as mental illness). Social conditions are improved and offenders subjected to intervention appropriate to their condition. |
| Social protection | A modern approach easier to effect than rehabilitation. If society is unable or unwilling to improve offenders or reform social conditions, protection from further deviance is afforded by incarceration or execution. |

morality. Punishing a person for a moral offense, moreover, draws together disparate members of society by reinforcing a shared sense of justice. For this reason punishment was traditionally carried out in public. Public executions occurred in England until 1868; the last public execution in the United States took place in Kentucky in 1936. Today the mass media ensure public awareness of executions carried out inside prison walls (Kittrie, 1971). Nonetheless, it is difficult to prove scientifically that punishment upholds social morality. Often it advances one conception of social morality at the expense of another, as when people who object to military service are imprisoned.

To some degree, punishment serves as a specific deterrent. Yet our society also has a high rate of **criminal recidivism,** *subsequent offenses by people previously convicted of crimes.* A recent study of people released from prison found that within three years 63 percent had been rearrested and 41 percent had been returned to jail (U.S.

Bureau of Justice Statistics, 1989). Such a high rate of recidivism raises questions about the extent to which punishment actually deters crime. In addition, only about one-third of all crimes are reported to police, and of these, only about one in five results in an arrest. The old adage that "crime doesn't pay" rings rather hollow when we consider that only a small proportion of offenses ever result in punishment.

General deterrence is even more difficult to investigate scientifically, since we have no way of knowing how people might act if they were unaware of punishments meted out to others. In the debate over capital punishment, now permitted in thirty-six states, critics of the practice point to research suggesting that the death penalty has limited value as a general deterrent in the United States, which is the only Western, industrial society that routinely executes serious offenders (Sellin, 1980; van den Haag & Conrad, 1983; Lester, 1987; Archer & Gartner, 1987; Bailey & Peterson, 1989; Bailey, 1990; Bohm, 1991).

Efforts at rehabilitation have sparked controversy as well. Prisons accomplish short-term social protection by keeping offenders off the streets, but they do very little to reshape attitudes or behavior in the long term. For this reason, penologists concede that prisons do not rehabilitate inmates (Carlson, 1976). Perhaps this is to be expected, since according to Sutherland's theory of differential association, placing a person among criminals for a long period of time should simply strengthen criminal attitudes and skills. Prisons also tolerate a destructive level of physical and sexual violence. And because incarceration severs whatever social ties an inmate may have in the outside world, individuals may be prone to further crime upon their release, consistent with Hirschi's control theory. Finally, inmates returning to the surrounding world contend with the stigma of being ex-convicts, often an obstacle to successful integration in the larger society. One study of young offenders in Philadelphia found that boys who were sentenced to long prison terms, and were therefore more likely to acquire a criminal stigma, later committed both more crimes and more serious ones (Wolfgang, Figlio, & Sellin, 1972).

Ultimately, we should never assume that the criminal justice system—including the police, courts, and prisons—can ever eliminate crime. The reason, echoed throughout this chapter, is simple: crime—in fact, all kinds of deviance—is more than simply the acts of "bad people"; it is inextricably bound up in the operation of society itself.

# Summary

1. Deviance refers to norm violations that span a wide range, from mild breaches of etiquette to serious violence.

2. Biological explanations of crime, from Lombroso's research in the nineteenth century to developing research in human genetics, has yet to produce much insight into the causes of crime.

3. Psychological explanations of deviance focus on abnormalities in the individual personality, which arise from either biological origins or the social environment. Psychological theories help to explain some kinds of deviance.

4. Social forces produce nonconformity because deviance (1) exists in relation to cultural norms, (2) involves a process of social definition, and (3) is shaped by the distribution of social power.

5. Sociology links deviance to the operation of society rather than the deficiencies of individuals. Using the structural-functional paradigm, Durkheim identified several functions of deviance for society as a whole.

6. The symbolic-interaction paradigm is the basis of labeling theory, which holds that deviance arises in the reaction of some audience to a person's behavior. Labeling theory focuses on secondary deviance and deviant careers, which result from acquiring the stigma of deviance.

7. Social-conflict theory directs attention to the relationship between deviance and patterns of social inequality. Following the approach of Karl Marx, this paradigm holds that laws and other norms reflect the interests of the most powerful people in society. Social-conflict theory also spotlights white-collar crimes that cause extensive social harm, although the offenders are rarely defined as criminals.

8. Official statistics indicate that arrest rates peak in adolescence, then drop steadily with advancing age. Males are arrested about 3.5 times as often as females for serious street crimes. Three-fourths of property crime arrests are of males, as are almost nine of ten arrests for violent crimes.

9. People of lower social position tend to commit more street crime than those with greater social privilege. When white-collar crimes are included among criminal offenses, however, this disparity in overall criminal activity diminishes.

10. More whites than African Americans are arrested for street crimes. However, African Americans are arrested more often than whites in proportion to their respective populations. Eliminating racial bias from the criminal justice system would lessen this disparity.

11. The police exercise considerable discretion in their work. Research suggests that factors such as the seriousness of the offense, the presence of bystanders, and the accused being male and African American make arrest more likely.

12. Although ideally an adversarial system, U.S. courts predominantly resolve cases through plea bargaining. An efficient method of handling cases where the facts are not in dispute, plea bargaining nevertheless places less powerful people at a disadvantage.

13. Punishment has been justified in terms of retribution, deterrence, rehabilitation, and social protection. Because its consequences are difficult to evaluate scientifically, punishment—like deviance itself—sparks considerable controversy among sociologists and the public as a whole.

# Key Concepts

**crime** the violation of norms formally enacted into criminal law

**crimes against the person** (violent crimes) crimes against people that involve violence or the threat of violence

**crimes against property** (property crimes) crimes that involve theft of property belonging to others

**criminal justice system** a formal system that responds to alleged violations of the law using police, courts, and punishment

**criminal recidivism** subsequent offenses by people previously convicted of crimes

**deterrence** the attempt to discourage criminality through punishment

**deviance** the recognized violation of cultural norms

**juvenile delinquency** the violation of legal standards by the young

**labeling theory** the assertion that deviance and conformity result from the response of others

**medicalization of deviance** the transformation of moral and legal issues into medical matters

**plea bargaining** a legal negotiation in which the prosecution reduces a defendant's charge in exchange for a guilty plea

**rehabilitation** reforming the offender to preclude subsequent offenses

**retribution** an act of moral vengeance by which society subjects an offender to suffering comparable to that caused by the offense

**retrospective labeling** the interpretation of someone's past consistent with present deviance

**social protection** rendering an offender incapable of further offenses either temporarily during a period of incarceration or permanently by execution

**stigma** a powerfully negative social label that radically changes a person's self-concept and social identity

**victimless crimes** violations of law in which there are no readily apparent victims

**white-collar crime** crimes committed by people of high social position in the course of their occupations

# Suggested Readings

The first of these books surveys many issues raised in this chapter. The second provides a critical account of how the United States falls short of the ideal of equal justice under the law.

Allen E. Liska. *Perspectives in Deviance*. 3rd ed. Englewood Cliffs, NJ: Prentice Hall, 1991.

Sally Engle Merry. *Getting Justice and Getting Even: Legal Consciousness Among Working-Class Americans*. Chicago: University of Chicago Press, 1990.

These two books are valuable efforts to incorporate gender into the study of deviance. The first explains how women have virtually been ignored up to the present in studies of crime; the second applies labeling theory to gender issues.

Eileen B. Leonard. *Women, Crime and Society: A Critique of Theoretical Criminology*. New York: Longman, 1982.

Edwin M. Schur. *Labeling Women Deviant: Gender, Stigma, and Social Control*. Philadelphia: Temple University Press, 1983.

These two books present the history and many contemporary controversies surrounding punishment in the United States.

Charles W. Thomas. *Corrections in America: Problems of the Past and the Present*. Newbury Park, CA: Sage, 1987.

Larry E. Sullivan. *The Prison Reform Movement: Forlorn Hope*. Boston: Twayne Publishers/G.K. Hall & Co., 1990.

Focusing on the death penalty, the first of these two books provides a gripping account of a researcher's personal investigation of the ultimate penalty; the second offers eight essays that summarize current research on the topic.

Robert Johnson. *Death Work: A Study of the Modern Execution Process*. Pacific Grove, CA: Brooks/Cole, 1990.

Robert M. Bohm. *The Death Penalty in America: Current Research*. Cincinnati, OH: Anderson Publishing, 1991.

This sociological account of mental illness delves into who in the United States is affected by such conditions and the social role of the mental patient.

Bernard J. Gallagher III. *The Sociology of Mental Illness*. 3rd ed. Englewood Cliffs, NJ: Prentice Hall, 1991.

Most research about youth gangs in the United States is by and about men. Anne Campbell provides a rare and insightful account of young women in New York street gangs.

Anne Campbell. *The Girls in the Gang*. 2nd ed. Cambridge, MA: Basil Blackwell, 1991.

A critical review of the case linking the XYY chromosome to crime is found in Chapter 6 of this study of the ethical consequences of human biology.

David Suzuki and Peter Knudtson. *Genethics: The Clash Between the New Genetics and Human Values*. Cambridge, MA: Harvard University Press, 1989.

These books offer a broad overview of murder in the United States and include discussions of drugs, punishment, public policy, assassination, and social diversity as they figure into the national problem of violence.

Gerhard Falk. *Murder: An Analysis of Its Forms, Conditions, and Causes*. Jefferson, NC: McFarland, 1990.

Keith D. Harries. *Serious Violence: Patterns of Homicide and Assault in America*. Springfield, IL: Charles C Thomas, 1990.

# Social Stratification

On April 10, 1912, the ocean liner *Titanic* left the docks of Southampton, England, on its maiden voyage across the North Atlantic to New York. A proud symbol of the new industrial age, the towering ship carried 2,300 passengers, some enjoying more luxury than most travelers today could imagine. Crowded into the lower decks, however, were poor immigrants, journeying to what they hoped would be a better life in the United States.

On April 14, the crew received reports of icebergs in the area but paid little notice. Then, near midnight, as the ship steamed swiftly and silently westward, a lookout was stunned to see a massive shape rising out of the dark ocean directly ahead. Moments later, the ship collided with a huge iceberg, almost as tall as the *Titanic* itself, which opened the starboard side of the ship as if it were a giant tin can. Sea water exploded into the vessel's lower levels, and within twenty-five minutes people were crowding into the lifeboats. By 2 A.M. the bow of the *Titanic* was submerged and the stern reared high above the water. There on the deck, silently observed by those in the lifeboats, stood hundreds of helpless passengers solemnly passing their final minutes before the ship disappeared into the frigid Atlantic (Lord, 1976).

The tragic loss of more than 1,600 lives shocked the world. Looking back dispassionately at this terrible incident with a sociological eye, however, we see that some categories of passengers had much better odds of survival than others. Of those holding first-class tickets, more than 60 percent were saved, primarily because they were on the upper decks, where warnings were sounded first and lifeboats were accessible. Only 36 percent of the second-class passengers survived, and of the third-class passengers on the lower decks, only 24 percent escaped drowning. On board the *Titanic*, class turned out to mean much more than the quality of accommodations: it was truly a matter of life or death.

The fate of the *Titanic* dramatically illustrates the consequences of social inequality for the ways people live—and sometimes whether they live at all. This chapter introduces a number of sociological ideas concerning social stratification. Chapter 10 continues the story by examining social inequality in the United States, and Chapter 11 explores where our society fits into a global system of wealth and poverty.

## What Is Social Stratification?

For tens of thousands of years, all of humanity was divided into small hunting and gathering societies. Although one person might enjoy praise from others for being swifter, stronger, or more skillful in collecting food, everyone had more or less the same social standing. As societies became more complex—a process detailed

Human beings feel directly and personally the effects of triumph or failure. This idea is captured in this haunting photograph, a universal portrait of suffering, by Sebastiao Salgado. The essential sociological insight is that, however strongly individuals feel its effects, social standing is largely a consequence of the way in which a society (or a world of societies) structures opportunity and reward. In short, we are all the products of social stratification.

in Chapter 4 ("Society")—a monumental change came about. Entire *categories* of people came to enjoy more money, schooling, health, and power than others.

Such social inequality is not simply due to the varying abilities and efforts of people themselves. Rather, sociologists document that patterns of this kind reflect how societies produce and distribute valued resources. Sociologists use the concept **social stratification** to refer to *a system by which a society ranks categories of people in a hierarchy*. Social stratification is a matter of four fundamental principles.

1. *Social stratification is a characteristic of society, not simply a function of individual differences.* Social inequality stands as a basic dimension of how a society is organized. Sociologists try to identify ways people are unequal and to measure how unequal they are. Further, basic patterns of inequality—whether societies are divided into peasants and landlords, whether most people believe they share in a society's bounty, or whether the poor are few in number or legion—differ according to time and place. How people understand their social position also varies. In some societies, people attribute their standing simply to their birth; in others, individuals speak of social position as their

"achievement," thought to reflect personal efforts and abilities. A focus on achievement characterizes industrial societies such as the United States, although people typically exaggerate its importance.

Did a higher percentage of the first-class passengers on the *Titanic* survive because they were smarter or better swimmers than second- and third-class passengers? Hardly. They fared better because of their privileged position on the ship. Similarly, children born into wealthy families are more likely than those born into poverty to enjoy health, achieve academically, succeed in their life's work, and to live well into old age. Neither rich nor poor people are responsible for creating social stratification, yet this system shapes the lives of them all.

2. *Social stratification persists over generations.* To understand that stratification stems from society rather than growing out of individual differences, note how it persists over time. Social position is closely linked to the family, so that children assume the social positions of their parents. In agrarian societies, the vast majority of people spend their entire lives at one social level, as their children do after them. In industrial societies, too, social position is initially ascribed, although it sometimes changes over time as a result of personal efforts or, occasionally, by sheer chance.

The concept of **social mobility** refers to *changes in people's positions in a system of social stratification.* Social mobility may be *upward* or *downward*. Our society celebrates the achievements of a Roseanne Arnold or a Bill Cosby, both of whom rose to prominence from modest beginnings. People may also move downward socially as a result of business setbacks, unemployment, or illness. Nevertheless, as explained in Chapter 10 ("Social Class in the United States"), dramatic changes in social position are uncommon: for most people, social standing remains much the same over a lifetime. Somewhat more common is *horizontal* social mobility by which people move from one occupation to another that is comparable.

3. *Social stratification is universal but variable.* Social stratification is found everywhere. At the same time, its character and extent vary widely from one society to another. Among the members of technologically primitive societies, social differentiation is minimal and based mostly on age and sex. As societies develop sophisticated technology

for growing food, they also forge complex and more rigid systems for distributing what they produce. Industrialization has the effect of increasing social mobility, and of reducing at least some kinds of social inequality.

4. *Social stratification involves not just inequality but beliefs.* Any system of inequality not only confers more resources on some people than on others, but it also defines these arrangements as fair. Just as *what* is unequal differs from society to society, then, so does the justification for inequality—the explanation of *why* people should be unequal. Virtually everywhere, however, people with the greatest social privileges express the strongest support for their society's system of social stratification, while those with fewer social resources are more likely to challenge the system.

# Caste and Class Systems

In describing social stratification in particular societies, sociologists often use two opposing standards: "closed" systems that allow little change in social position, and "open" systems that permit considerable social mobility (Tumin, 1985).

## The Caste System

A **caste system** amounts to *social stratification based on ascription.* A pure caste system, in other words, is closed, with no social mobility at all; birth alone determines one's destiny. People living in caste systems usually define their precise social standing simply by indicating the category to which they belong.

### Illustrations: India and South Africa

A number of the world's societies approximate caste systems, including traditional village life in India and South Africa's system of racial apartheid. In the Indian caste system, a person is born into one of several thousand subcaste groups, which rank people in relation to others in countless local communities. Race is the key to social ranking in South Africa. Of a total population of some 40 million, roughly one South African in eight (about 5 million people) is of European ancestry, approximately the same proportion as people of African descent in the United States. Yet this white minority commands an overwhelming share of wealth and power. Representing three-fourths of South Africans, 30 million blacks have far fewer rights and privileges. In a middle position are another 3 million South Africans, known as "coloreds," who are of mixed race, along with about 1 million Asians. The box on pages 242–43 explores the current state of South African apartheid.

In a caste system, birth determines the fundamental shape of people's lives in three crucial respects. First, traditional caste groups are linked to occupation so that families in each ranking perform one type of work from generation to generation. Although some occupations (such as farming) are open to all, castes are socially identified with the work their members do (priests, barbers, leather workers, and so on). In South Africa, whites hold almost all the desirable jobs, while the black majority is primarily consigned to manual labor and other work in service to whites.

Second, a rigid system of social stratification would break down quickly if people married outside their own castes. In such cases, what rank would their children hold? To keep the hierarchy clear, then, caste systems mandate that people marry others of the same social ranking. Sociologists call this pattern *endogamous* marriage (*endo* stems from the Greek, meaning "within"). Tradition in India directs parents to select their children's marriage partners, often when the children are quite young. Among such families, instances of cross-caste marriage are rare; when they do occur, a female typically marries a male of a higher position (Srinivas, 1971). In South Africa, sexual relationships and marriage between the races have been banned by law; although these regulations were eased in 1985, interracial marriage remains relatively rare since racial categories continue to live in separate areas.

Third, powerful cultural beliefs underlie caste systems. In India, Hindu traditions define acceptance of one's social position and fate as a moral duty; therefore, people must carry out their life's work, whatever it may be. Caste systems are typical of agrarian societies, because such beliefs foster the habits of diligence and discipline that agriculture demands. The same logic helps explain why caste systems break down as societies industrialize. Much of the intense pressure to end the racial caste system in South Africa stems from the inconsistency of categorical ranking with a more talent-based industrial economy.

Members of various castes are also constrained in

# South Africa: Race as Caste

At the southern tip of the African continent lies South Africa, a territory about the size of Alaska, with a population of almost 40 million. Long inhabited by people of African descent, the region was colonized by Dutch traders in the mid-seventeenth century. Early in the nineteenth century, the descendants of these settlers from the Netherlands were pushed inland by a new wave of British colonization. By the beginning of this century, the British had gained control of the country, calling it the Union of South Africa. In 1961 the Republic of South Africa formally severed ties with the United Kingdom and became politically independent.

But freedom was a reality only for the white minority. To ensure their political control, the whites developed the policy of *apartheid*, or separation of the races. A common practice for many years, apartheid was enshrined in law in 1948 so that whites could deny the black majority South African citizenship, ownership of land, and any formal voice in the government. Under this policy, blacks became a subordinate caste, receiving only the ed-

ucation needed to perform the low-paying jobs deemed inappropriate for whites. In this racial caste system, even white housewives of limited means became accustomed to having a black household servant. Under such conditions, blacks were able to earn, on average, only one-fourth of what whites received. A final plank in the platform of apartheid was the forcible resettlement of millions of blacks to so-called homelands, dirt-poor districts set aside by whites to confine and control blacks. The overall effect was devastating on the black majority. In a land rich with natural resources, most blacks lived close to abject poverty.

The prosperous white minority has traditionally defended its privileges by viewing blacks as social inferiors. Increasingly, however, whites have been forced to rely on a system of brutal military repression to maintain their power. Without formal rights, blacks suspected of opposing white rule have been subject to arbitrary arrest and indefinite detention.

Despite its severity, this repression has not kept blacks—and a growing number of sympathetic whites—from challenging apart-

heid. Violent confrontations have been frequent, especially among younger blacks impatient for political and economic opportunity. By the end of the 1980s, some 200 U.S. corporations had also severed direct economic ties with South Africa. This foreign divestment has staggered the South African economy, hurting both blacks and whites in the process. But it has accomplished its primary objective: to pressure the Pretoria regime to make significant reforms and begin dismantling apartheid.

In 1984, South Africans of mixed race and Asians were granted a limited voice in government. Blacks have also won the right to form labor unions, and are now permitted to enter a number of occupations once restricted to whites, resulting in economic gains for some workers. The government has also extended property rights to all people. Additionally, officials have abolished a host of "petty apartheid" regulations that segregated blacks and whites in public places, including beaches and hospitals. In 1990, the release from prison of Nelson Mandela and the legalization of the anti-apartheid African National Congress opened the political system and raised the hope

their social ties by traditional beliefs. Hindu thought defines higher caste groups in India as ritually "pure," while lower caste groups are deemed "polluted." The ingrained belief that a member of a higher caste is defiled by contact with a member of a lower caste forces the two to keep their distance in all routine activities. In the same way, many white South Africans support apartheid claiming they are morally superior to the black

majority and, thus, justly dominate them.

Since the Industrial Revolution, beliefs that rank entire categories of people as "better" or "worse" than others have gradually lost their force. In India, for example, the Hindu caste system now holds little significance for most people in large cities as people exercise greater choice about their marriage partners and their work (Bahl, 1991). As later chapters explain, such traditional atti-

South African performer John Clegg has blended familiar rock and roll with traditional African music and dancing. For his efforts, the apartheid government banned him on the grounds that his work brought the races together. In the currently more liberal climate, however, Clegg has enjoyed unprecedented popularity.

for more basic change. And, in 1992, a majority of white voters in a national referendum endorsed the principle of bringing apartheid to an end.

The reforms to date have enraged traditionalists who charge the government is selling out white interests. But despite many significant changes, the basic structure of apartheid remains intact. Win-

ning the legal right to own property means little to millions of blacks who barely make enough money to survive; opening hospitals to South Africans of every race amounts to an empty gesture for nonwhites who cannot afford to pay for medical care; opening the ranks of the professions to blacks offers little real opportunity to men and women with minimal schooling. The harsh reality is that more than one-third of all black adults cannot find any work at all and, by the government's own estimate, half of all blacks live in desperate conditions.

The worst off are those called *ukuhleleleka* in the Xhosa language, which means the marginal people. Some 7 million blacks fall into this category, living on the edge of society and on the edge of life itself. In Soweto-by-the-Sea, an idyllic-sounding community, thousands of people live crammed into shacks built of discarded material like packing cases, corrugated metal, cardboard, sheetrock, and pieces of pipe. There is no electricity for lights or refrigeration; without plumbing, people use buckets to haul sewage; women line up awaiting their turn at a single tap that provides water

for more than a thousand people. Jobs are hard to come by, partly because Ford and General Motors have closed their factories in nearby Port Elizabeth, and partly because people keep migrating to the town from regions where life is even worse. Those who can find work are lucky to earn $200 a month.

To those who struggle simply to survive, the pace of change is agonizingly slow. Defenders of government reforms, however, urge patience, and remind people in the United States that our nation, too, had a racial caste system, one that even today casts a long shadow over the relative social standing of blacks and whites.

South Africa has made some real progress toward breaking down apartheid, and expressed its determination to do more. Under discussion now are plans for eventual power sharing among all people. Yet until traditional notions about race are finally dispelled, and until the underlying problem of intense and persistent poverty is addressed, South Africa will remain a society divided.

SOURCES: Fredrickson (1981), Wren (1991), Contreras (1992), and various news reports.

tudes, now cast as various "isms"—racism, sexism, ageism—are increasingly denounced as unjust. Sixty years ago, India outlawed its caste system, although it remains deeply embedded in village life even today. And in South Africa, the gradual erosion of apartheid is under way—albeit at a pace that many find excruciatingly slow—in the face of condemnation of that system by almost every other industrial society in the world.

## The Class System

A caste system bolsters stable, agrarian life; industrial societies, by contrast, depend on individual initiative and the development of specialized talents. Industrialization does not abolish social inequality, but it does change its character, from a caste system to a **class system**, *social stratification based on individual achievement.*

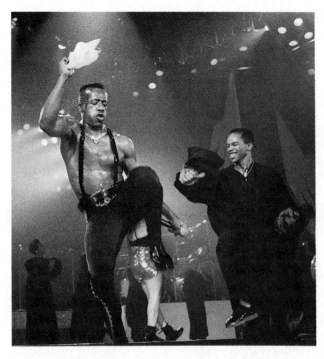

The success of entertainers such as Hammer—whose talents transformed a young man of modest background into a superstar—encourages us to think that personal merit is the key to social standing.

Social "classes" are not as rigidly defined as castes. As people gain schooling and develop their individual talents, they are likely to experience at least some social mobility in relation to their parents and siblings, blurring class distinctions. Social categories also break down as people immigrate from abroad or move from rural areas to industrialized cities, lured by better jobs, greater opportunities for education, and the promise of a brighter future (Lipset & Bendix, 1967; Cutright, 1968; Treiman, 1970). Movement of this kind not only contributes to social diversity in industrial societies, but it also stimulates social mobility as newcomers take low-paying jobs, typically pushing others up the social ladder (Tyree, Semyonov, & Hodge, 1979). Furthermore, industrial societies generally extend political rights more broadly (Glass, 1954; Blau & Duncan, 1967). In other words, while castes each have distinctive privileges and duties, everyone in a class system—in principle, at least—stands equal before the law.

Class systems stand on a relatively new conception of fairness: that talent and effort, rather than birth, should determine social position. People tend to think of their careers as matters of individual achievement and choice, rather than a duty passed from generation to generation as members of caste systems do. Greater individuality also translates into more freedom in marriage, with parents and cultural traditions playing a lesser role in children's selections of their mates.

Greater freedom and mobility confer on members of class systems characteristically lower **status consistency,** *consistent standing across various dimensions of social inequality.* Linking social ranking to birth (as in caste systems) generates high status consistency, meaning that an individual has the same relative standing with regard to wealth, prestige, power, ritual purity, or other dimensions of difference. Class systems, with their greater social mobility, offer less status consistency. In the United States, some people with prestigious occupations (such as priests or professors) accumulate little wealth and wield only moderate social power. Such inconsistencies make class boundaries less clear than those separating castes.

## Caste and Class Together: Great Britain

There are no pure caste or class systems; in every society, social stratification involves some combination of these two forms. The mix of caste and class is most pronounced in societies in which centuries of agriculture have recently given way to industrialization. A case in point is England, a nation that weaves together traditional caste distinctions and modern class differences.

### The Estate System

In the Middle Ages, social stratification in England (which, together with Wales, Scotland, and Northern Ireland, comprise today's United Kingdom of Great Britain and Northern Ireland) took the form of a caste-like system of three *estates.* A hereditary nobility, or *first estate,* accounted for only 5 percent of the population. These nobles maintained wealth and power through the ownership of land (Laslett, 1984). Typically, they had no occupation at all, for to be "engaged in trade" or any other type of work for income was deemed "beneath" them. Well tended by servants, nobles used their extensive leisure time to cultivate refined tastes in art, music, and literature.

Vast landholdings were preserved from generation to generation by the practice of *primogeniture* (from Latin meaning "first born"). This law mandated that property be passed to only the eldest son rather than divided among all children. Under this system, however, younger sons fared less well; typically, they were forced to find other ways to support themselves. Thus many nobles entered the clergy—the *second estate*—where spiritual power was supplemented by the church's extensive land-holdings. Others became military officers, lawyers, or took up work that has come down to us today as "honor-able" callings for "gentlemen." In an age when few women could expect to earn a living on their own, a daughter of the nobility depended for her security on marrying well.

Below the nobility and the clergy, the vast majority of men and women formed the *third estate*, or common-ers. With little property, most commoners or serfs worked parcels of land belonging to nobles. The phrase "one's *lot* in life" literally describes the daily plight of common-ers during the Middle Ages. Unlike the nobility and the clergy, commoners had little access to schooling, so most remained illiterate.

As the Industrial Revolution gradually transformed England's economy in the nineteenth century, some commoners, especially those who made their way to cities, gained wealth and power that rivaled and some-times surpassed that of the nobility. This economic ex-pansion, along with the extension of education and legal rights to more people, soon blurred traditional social rankings as a class system emerged. In a pointed illustra-tion of how far the pendulum has swung, a descendant of nobility, now making a living as a writer, was asked in a press interview if England's caste-like estates had finally broken down. Playfully she retorted, "Of course they have, or *I* wouldn't be here talking to someone like *you!*" (*New Haven Journal-Courier*, Nov. 27, 1986).

### Great Britain Today

While individual achievement does have an impact on social stratification in Great Britain, today's class system retains the mark of a long, feudal past. The great wealth enjoyed by some people in contemporary Great Britain is achieved through their own efforts. Others, descendants of traditional nobility, still maintain inherited wealth, savor the highest prestige, attend expensive, elite universi-ties, and wield considerable power to shape British soci-ety. A traditional monarch remains as Britain's head of state, and Parliament's House of Lords is composed of "peers," almost all of whom are of noble birth. Actual control of government, however, resides in the House of Commons, comprising commoners who are more

likely to have achieved their positions through individual effort than through ascription.

Below the upper class, roughly one-fourth of the British population falls into the "middle class." Some are moderately wealthy, with high incomes from profes-sions and business. These richer "commoners," along with members of the upper class, make up the 10 percent of Britons with significant financial holdings in the form of stocks and bonds (Sherrid, 1986). Most members of the British middle class, however, earn too little to accu-mulate substantial wealth.

Under the middle class, across a boundary that cannot be precisely defined, lie roughly half of all Britons known as the "working class." As in the United States, members of the working class earn modest incomes, generally doing manual labor. Although the British econ-omy expanded during the 1980s, traditional industries such as coal mining and steel production declined, sub-jecting many working-class families to unemployment. Some slipped into poverty, joining the remaining one-fourth of Britons who are socially and economically deprived. Lower-class people—or, more simply, "the poor"—are heavily concentrated in northern and western regions of the country plagued by economic decay.

Today Great Britain displays typical class-system traits: unequally distributed wealth, power, and prestige, but with some opportunity for significant movement up and down in the overall hierarchy. In one legacy of the estate system, however, movement between social classes occurs less frequently than in the United States (Kerckhoff, Campbell, & Winfield-Laird, 1985). Com-pared with people in the United States, therefore, Britons are more resigned to remaining in the social position to which they were born (Snowman, 1977). The greater rigidity of British stratification is exemplified in the im-portance attached to accent as a mark of social position. Distinctive patterns of speech develop in a society as categories of people are segregated from one another over long periods. In Great Britain, families of long-standing affluence and those living in chronic poverty speak so differently that they seem to be, as the saying goes, a single people divided by a common language.

## Another Example: Japan

Social stratification in Japan also mixes the traditional and the contemporary. As in Great Britain, a modern emphasis on individual achievement has reshaped an ancient hierarchy of rank by birth.

Hereditary nobles, in principle at least, become enshrined in the traditions of their country. For this reason, Japan's Emperor Akihito enjoys the highest prestige and widespread popularity, especially among older people in his nation. Japan's transformation into the more egalitarian culture of an industrial society, however, has eroded the emperor's standing, shifting political power to a popularly elected prime minister.

## Feudal Japan

For centuries, Japan was an agrarian society composed of nobles and commoners in one of the most rigidly stratified societies the world has ever known. This system dates back to the fifth century C.E., when an imperial family, claiming divine right to rule, formally presided over the country. More accurately, however, the imperial family maintained often uneasy alliances with a network of regional nobility. These nobles were men who excelled in military combat; such warlords—called *shoguns*—routinely fought among themselves, as did their counterparts in medieval England.

Below the nobility stood the *samurai*, or warrior caste. This second rank of Japanese society cultivated elaborate martial skills, often in highly ritualized form. Although not nobles themselves, the *samurai's* role as defenders of the nobility placed them clearly above the common people. Like all Japanese of that time, the *samurai* dressed and behaved according to their rank, as demanded by traditional codes of honor.

As in England, the majority of people in Japan at this time in history were commoners, who labored for a lifetime to eke out only a bare subsistence for themselves and their families. Feudal society in Japan afforded commoners no political voice, just as European serfs had little political power. Unlike their European counterparts, however, Japanese commoners were not the lowest in rank. The *burakumin*, or "outcasts," stood further down on that country's hierarchy; such people were shunned as unworthy by even "common" Japanese. Much like the lowest caste groups in India, "outcasts" lived apart from others, engaged in the most distasteful occupations, and, like everyone else, had no opportunity to change their standing.

## Japan Today

Important changes in nineteenth-century Japan—industrialization, the growth of cities, and the opening of Japanese society to outside influences—combined to weaken the traditional caste structure. In 1871 the Japanese legally banned the social category of "outcast," although even today people look down on women and men who trace their lineage to this rank. After Japan's defeat in World War II, the nobility too lost their legal standing, and since then fewer and fewer Japanese are willing to accept the notion that their emperor rules by divine right. Thus social stratification in contemporary Japan is a far cry from the rigid caste system in force centuries ago. Today, analysts identify a range of social gradations, including "upper," "upper-middle," "lower-middle," and "lower," but they disagree about what proportion of the population falls in each.

Although Japanese society now displays many of the traits of a class system, this nation's fascinating ability to combine the traditional with the modern still comes through in patterns of social inequality. Because many Japanese people revere past practices, family background is never far from the surface in assessing someone's social standing. Therefore, despite legal reforms that grant all people equal standing before the law, and a modern culture that stresses individual achievement, the Japanese continue to perceive each other through the centuries-old lens of caste.

This dynamic mix echoes from the campus to corporate board rooms. The most prestigious universities—now gateways to success in the industrial world—admit students with outstanding scores on rigorous entrance examinations, a process detailed in Chapter 16 ("Education"). Still, the highest achievers and business leaders in Japan are products of privilege, with *samurai* or noble background. At the other extreme, "outcasts" continue to live in isolated communities cut off from opportunities to better themselves (Hiroshi, 1974; Norbeck, 1983).

Finally, traditional ideas about gender shape Japanese society to this day. Despite legal reforms that confer formal equality on the sexes, women are clearly subordinate to men in many important respects. More than twice the proportion of Japanese parents (73 percent) express the desire to send a son to college compared to a daughter (29 percent) and, predictably enough, women in Japan are far less likely than men to receive a university education (Brinton, 1988). As a consequence, women predominate in lower-level support positions in the corporate world, only rarely assuming leadership roles. In this sense, too, individual achievement in Japan's modern class system operates in the shadow of centuries of traditional privileges.

## The Former Soviet Union

During the last decade, the new Commonwealth of Independent States—the former Union of Soviet Socialist Republics (USSR)—has experienced changes so dramatic that many observers have heralded a second Russian revolution. The history of this military superpower has been a grand experiment, first, to eliminate class differences and, more recently, to reintroduce some aspects of the Western market economy that will further transform social stratification in the world's largest country.

### A Classless Society?

The current Soviet federation was born out of a revolution in 1917 that brought an abrupt end to a feudal estate system ruled by a hereditary nobility. The Russian Revolution transferred most farms, factories, and other productive property from private ownership to control by the state. This transformation was guided by the ideas of Karl Marx, who asserted that private ownership of productive property is the basis of social classes (see Chapter 4, "Society"). As the state gained control of the economy, the Soviet Union boasted of reaching a milestone in human history by becoming a classless society.

Analysts outside the Soviet Union were always skeptical of this claim, pointing out that Soviet society remained clearly stratified (Lane, 1984). The occupations of the Soviet people are clustered into four major categories, listed here in descending order of income, prestige,

and power: (1) high government officials, also known as *apparatchiks*; (2) the intelligentsia, including lower government officials and professional workers—engineers, scientists, college professors, and physicians; (3) manual workers in state-controlled industries; and (4) the rural peasantry. This ranking of categories of people illustrates that the Soviet Union neither eliminated social classes nor eradicated social inequality. At the same time, however, a more modest claim can be advanced: because factories, farms, colleges, and hospitals were collectively owned and operated, the Soviet Union had less economic inequality than capitalist societies such as the United States.

### The Second Soviet Revolution

Economic reforms were accelerated by Mikhail Gorbachev when he came to power in the Soviet Union in 1985. His economic program, popularly known as *perestroika*, meaning "restructuring," was put in place in response to a dire economic problem: while the Soviet system had succeeded in minimizing economic inequality, the overall standard of living lagged far behind that of other industrial nations. Gorbachev's program was designed to stimulate economic expansion by reducing inefficient centralized control of the economy.

Few Soviet people were satisfied with their living standards when Gorbachev began his campaign and, by most accounts, economic conditions today have plummeted even further. Economic reform has been complicated by a host of factors, including the need to acquire advanced technology and to cut military spending. But perhaps most important is the popular reform movement that swept through many socialist societies. First in the countries of Eastern Europe and then in the Soviet Union itself, demands for wholesale change reached a fever pitch, spurred by shortages of consumer goods as well as a growing recognition that the ideal of a classless society is far from reality in socialist nations. Thus people blamed their plight and powerlessness on the small ruling classes of Communist party officials. After the Soviet Union was formed in 1917, the Communist party retained a monopoly of power, often brutally repressing any opposition. Until its hold over Soviet society was broken in 1991, some 18 million party members (about 6 percent of the Soviet people) not only made all the decisions about Soviet life, but also enjoyed privileges unknown to the vast majority of the population. These privileges included vacation homes, chauffeured automobiles, access to prized consumer goods, and elite educations for their children (Zaslavsky, 1982; Shipler, 1984; Theen, 1984). The second Soviet revolution, then, mirrors the first in one important respect: the goal is nothing less than the overthrow of the ruling class. By the winter of 1991, the Soviet Union had dissolved into a new federation of republics. Because the nation remains in flux, its future cannot be predicted. But it seems likely that the enormous political power held by a handful of party officials has come to an end.

The case of the Soviet Union demonstrates that social inequality involves more than simply economic resources. While Soviet society lacked the extremes of wealth and poverty found in Great Britain and the United States, elite standing in that nation was based on *power* rather than wealth. Thus, neither Mikhail Gorbachev nor Boris Yeltsin, despite their awesome power, ever earned more than an average worker in the United States, and neither man has anywhere near the personal fortune of U.S. president George Bush.

And what about social mobility in the Soviet Union? Evidence suggests that during this century there has been more upward social mobility in the Soviet Union than in Great Britain, Japan, or even the United States. This is partly because Soviet society lacks the concentrations of wealth passed from generation to generation in other societies. Even more important, the Soviet Union's rapid industrialization and bureaucratization during this century pushed a large proportion of the working class and rural peasantry upward to occupations in industry and government. In the last few decades, however, Soviet society experienced decreasing social mobility. Most analysts contend that the country's earlier high rate of upward mobility stemmed from industrial development more than socialism (Dobson, 1977; Lane, 1984; Shipler, 1984).

The close link between societal transformation and personal changes in social standing exemplifies what sociologists call **structural social mobility,** *a shift in the social position of large numbers of people due more to changes in society itself than to individual efforts.* Half a century ago, industrialization created a vast number of new jobs that drew the Soviet people to cities from rural farming villages. Similarly, the growth of bureaucracy propelled countless Soviet citizens from the fields into the offices. Now, with the recent introduction of private property into the economy and new laws sanctioning individual ownership of business enterprises, further structural social mobility is likely, perhaps including greater economic inequality. But the hope is that everyone will enjoy a higher standard of living.

## Ideology

Considering the extent of social inequality everywhere in the world, how do stratified societies persist without distributing their resources more equally? The caste systems of Great Britain and Japan lasted for centuries, placing most wealth and power in the hands of several hundred families. Even more striking, for two thousand years most people in India accepted the idea that their lives should be privileged or poor because of the accident of birth. One reason for the remarkable persistence of social hierarchies is that they are bolstered by **ideology,** *cultural beliefs that reflect and support the interests of certain categories of people.* Any cultural pattern—an idea or an action—is ideological to the extent that its consequences favor some people over others.

The ancient Greek philosopher Plato (427–347 B.C.E.) claimed that justice was primarily a matter of agreement about who should have what. To generate a high level of agreement about inequality, most people in a society are socialized to view their system as basically "fair." From Plato's point of view, then, cultural beliefs are necessary to legitimate any social hierarchy.

Karl Marx, too, understood this process, although he was far more skeptical about claims of fairness than Plato was. In Marx's view, the economy channels wealth and power into the hands of a few, defining the process as simply "the laws of the marketplace." Further, the legal system defends the right to own private property as a basic human freedom, just as family members are merely "looking out for their own" when they funnel money and privileges from generation to generation. In short, Marx concluded, both resources and ideas come under the control of a society's elite, which helps to explain why social stratification is so difficult to change.

Though Plato looked more favorably on social hierarchy than Marx did, both thinkers recognized the essential role of ideology in maintaining social inequality. Ideology is rarely a simple matter of privileged people conspiring to generate self-serving ideas about social inequality. Typically, ideology takes the form of evolving cultural patterns that directly and indirectly justify according a disproportionate share of resources and privileges to certain categories of people. Through socialization, the primary means by which ideology is transmitted over time, most people learn to embrace their society's system of social hierarchy. As a result of learning certain conceptions of fairness, people who challenge the system generally question not the system itself but simply their own position in it.

# Ideology: When Is Inequality Unjust?

Inequality may or may not be unjust: Such judgments depend on cultural definitions of fairness. As a cultural issue, justifications for social stratification vary, displaying marked variety across history and from place to place.

A millennium ago, the feudal estate system was taking root in Europe. This rigidly stratified social order drew strength from the teachings of the church, which claimed social arrangements on earth reflected the will of God. As the expression of a divine plan, religious leaders asserted, God had assigned people on earth to distinctive stations. The majority of people endured a harsh life of serfdom, driving the feudal economy with their muscles. Most people born to such a life knew nothing else, but even imagining an alternative risked challenging not only the nobility but also the church and, ultimately, God. Although their lives were framed with far more comforts, the nobility fit into the same plan; their various duties of defending the realm and maintaining law and order were imbued with a sense of divine purpose. The religious justification that cloaked the entire medieval estate system, and which helped to sustain this form of inequality for centuries, is clearly expressed in the following lines from an old hymn sung by members of the official church of the realm, the Church of England:

> The rich man in his castle,
> The poor man at his gate,
> He made them high and lowly
> And ordered their estate.
> All things bright and beautiful . . .

During the Industrial Revolution, newly rich industrialists gradually toppled the feudal nobility, advancing a new ideology in the process. Capitalists scorned the notion that social hierarchy should rest on the accident of birth; a view that had been compelling to hundreds of generations living under feudalism soon became ludicrous once the economy had been reorganized. If there was a natural order to the world, the new thinking went, it was that society should be dominated by the most talented and hard-working individuals. Early industrialists like John D. Rockefeller (1839–1937), who made a vast fortune in oil, was fond of defending the wealth and power of his class as the product of personal effort and initiative, which, he asserted, was consistent with the laws of nature and the will of God. The poor, who in feudal societies had been the objects of charitable assistance (since, after all, being poor was not their own fault but part of a divine plan), were redefined as lacking ambition and ability and, consequently, scorned. The ideological shift from birth to individual achievement as the basis of social inequality was evident to the early nineteenth-century German writer Johann Wolfgang von Goethe, who quipped:

> Really to own
> What you inherit,
> You first must earn it
> With your merit.

Clearly, medieval and modern justifications of inequality differ dramatically—what an earlier era defined as just, a later one rejected as wrongheaded. Yet both cases illustrate the role of culture in defining a particular form of hierarchy as fair and beyond the power of society itself to change.

Further, actual rewards—especially income—may have little to do with an individual's functional importance to society. Speaker of the House Thomas "Tip" O'Neill, who retired from Congress in 1988, subsequently appeared in television commercials for a motel chain, a credit card organization, and a beer company. Making ads, O'Neill earned in a day the $100,000 or so he received in salary for an entire year as a lawmaker. Or consider that the money garnered by Mike Tyson for one of his heavyweight championship bouts was one hundred times what George Bush is paid annually to perform the duties of President of the United States. Would anyone argue that a few minutes in a boxing ring measures up in societal significance to the tasks of the presidency? The box on page 253 takes a critical look at the link between pay and societal importance.

A second charge made by Tumin is that the Davis–Moore thesis exaggerates the consequences of social stratification when it comes to developing individual talents.

Our society does reward individual achievement, but families also follow the caste-like practice of transferring wealth and power from generation to generation regardless of talent. Additionally, for women, people of color, and others with limited opportunities, the social hierarchy stands as a barrier to personal accomplishment. In practice, concludes Tumin, social stratification in the United States functions to develop some people's abilities to the fullest while guaranteeing that others will *never* reach their potential.

Third, by suggesting that social stratification benefits all of society, the Davis–Moore thesis ignores how social inequality promotes conflict and even outright revolution. This assertion leads us to the social-conflict paradigm, which provides a very different explanation for the persistence of social hierarchy.

# Stratification and Conflict

Social-conflict analysis argues that, rather than benefiting society as a whole, social stratification ensures that some people gain advantages at the expense of others. This analysis draws heavily on the ideas of Karl Marx; additional contributions were made by Max Weber.

## Marx's View of Social Class

Karl Marx, whose approach to understanding social inequality was detailed in Chapter 4 ("Society"), argued that the two major social classes correspond to the two basic relationships people have to the means of production: individuals can own productive property or they can labor for others. In medieval Europe, the nobility and clergy owned the productive land on which peasants toiled. Similarly, in industrial class systems, the *capitalists* (or the bourgeoisie) control factories, which utilize the labor of *workers* (the proletariat). So great are the disparities in wealth and power that arise from this productive system, Marx contended, that conflict between these two classes is inevitable. In time, he believed, oppression and misery would drive the working majority to organize and ultimately overthrow capitalism once and for all.

Marx's analysis was inspired by his observations of capitalism early in the nineteenth century, a time at which society seemed irrevocably divided into contending classes. This was the era during which wealthy capitalists like Andrew Carnegie, J. P. Morgan, and John Jacob Astor (one of the few very rich passengers to perish on the *Titanic*) lived in fabulous mansions filled with priceless art and staffed by dozens of servants. Their fortunes

John George Brown made a fortune a century ago as a painter who portrayed the world as most people wanted to see it. Others, including photographer Jacob Riis, found far less fame by capturing something closer to the truth. This is Riis's well-known image of "street arabs" who survived as best they could on the mean streets of the growing industrial cities.

# Salaries: Are the Rich Worth What They Earn?

For an hour of work, a Los Angeles priest earns about $4, a bus driver in San Francisco makes about $15, and a Detroit auto worker earns roughly $20. John McEnroe garners about $400 an hour playing tournament tennis; actor Burt Reynolds receives about $5,000 for every hour he spends making movies; singer and actress Dolly Parton is paid about $25,000 for every hour she performs in Las Vegas nightclubs. Bill Cosby commands about $100,000 an hour to take the stage, and boxer Mike Tyson earned about $1 million per minute to throw punches in heavyweight title bouts.

According to the Davis–Moore thesis, rewards reflect an occupation's value to society. But is Oprah Winfrey, who hosts talk shows for some $25 million annually, worth twice as much to our society as all one hundred United States senators? In short, do earnings reflect the social importance of work?

Salaries in industrial-capitalist societies like the United States are a product of market forces. Defenders of the laws of supply and demand claim that the market impartially evaluates worth, rewarding each worker according to the supply of the talent in question and the public demand for it. According to this view, movie stars, top athletes, skilled professionals, and many business executives have rare talents that are much in demand; thus they may earn hundreds of times more than the typical worker in the United States. But are the highest-earning half of one percent of our number really worth the mega-million dollar incomes they pull down each year?

Some critics claim that the market is not a good evaluator of occupational importance. First, critics maintain, the U.S. economy is dominated by a small proportion of people who manipulate the system for their own benefit. Corporate executives, for example, pay themselves salaries and bonuses that have an uncertain connection to how well their companies perform. In 1990, for example, Steven J. Ross was the highest paid corporate leader in the United States, receiving $39 million in salary, bonuses, and one-time stock options, despite the fact that his company—Time Warner—actually fared below average for large corporations. Looking across the board, chief executive officers of all the biggest companies in the United States gave themselves a pay raise of almost 10 percent in 1990 (to an average of $2.5 million annually) even though the average price of their stocks *dropped* almost the same percentage (Crystal, 1991). In global perspective, Japanese executives earn far less than their counterparts in this country; this despite the fact that most Japanese corporations have handily outperformed their rivals in the United States.

A second problem with the idea that the market measures people's value to society is that many people who make clear and significant contributions receive surprisingly little money. Tens of thousands of teachers, counselors, and health-care workers enhance the welfare of others every day for little salary, partly because many people do not think of income as the best measure of the value of their work. In 1987, the notorious "junk-bond" king Michael Milken earned $550 million dealing on Wall Street; in the process, he enriched a small number of investors other than himself while weakening the nation's economy, according to Wall Street analysts. During the same year, Rachel Stuart counseled thirty-five poor women in rural Louisiana who were preparing to give birth. Her work helped them to deliver healthy babies. Since the cost of neonatal care for a single premature baby runs as high as $200,000, Stuart probably saved the public millions; yet she is paid $4,000 a year for her work (Werman, 1989).

Using salary to measure social worth, then, only works to the extent that market forces actually gauge peoples' societal contribution. Some people view market forces as the most accurate measure of occupational worth. Others contend that lucrative activities may or may not be socially valuable. From this standpoint, the market system amounts to a closed game in which only a handful of people have the money to play.

were staggering: the wealth of John Jacob Astor is estimated at $25 million; Andrew Carnegie reportedly earned more than $20 million in a single year as the new century began (worth perhaps $80 million in today's dollars); all this at a time when the wages paid to the average worker totaled roughly $500 a year (Baltzell, 1964; Pessen, 1990).

Throughout the course of capitalist development, Marx claimed, the economy stands out as the social institution with the greatest influence on the rest of society. Other institutions serve, in general, to support the operation of the economy. This means, for example, that the family enables wealthy people to pass their accumulated savings and property from generation to generation, and the legal system defends this process through inheritance law. Similarly, exclusive schools bring children of the elite together, training them in the ways of their class, and encouraging the informal social ties that will benefit them throughout their lives. Overall, from Marx's point of view, the operation of capitalist society contributes to the *reproduction of the class structure*, meaning that class divisions are perpetuated over time.

***Critical evaluation.*** By exploring how the capitalist economic system generates conflict between classes, Marx's analysis of social stratification has had an enormous influence on sociological thinking in recent decades. Because it is revolutionary—at least in a capitalist society—Marxism is also controversial.

One of the strongest criticisms of the Marxist approach is that it denies one of the central elements of the Davis–Moore thesis: that motivating people to perform various social roles requires some system of unequal rewards. Marx separated reward from performance, endorsing an egalitarian system based on the principle of "from each according to ability; to each according to need" (1972:388). Critics argue that severing rewards from performance goes a long way toward explaining the low productivity that has been characteristic of the former Soviet Union and other socialist economies around the world, and the recent efforts by these nations to reform their economies by introducing market elements. However, it is important to recognize that considerable evidence supports the view of humanity that underlies the Marxist position: that people are inherently social rather than unflinchingly selfish and individualistic (Clark, 1991; Fiske, 1991). Therefore, we should not assume that individual rewards (much less *monetary* compensation alone) constitute the only way to motivate people to perform their social roles.

Second, although capitalist society does perpetuate poverty and privilege from generation to generation, the revolutionary developments Marx considered inevitable have failed to materialize. Here lies a second major critique of his ideas. The next section explores why the socialist revolution Marx predicted and promoted has not occurred, at least in advanced capitalist societies.

## Why No Marxist Revolution?

Despite Marx's prediction to the contrary, capitalism is still thriving. Even so, as we shall see, Western capitalism has evolved in some of the ways Marx anticipated.

Why have workers in the United States not overthrown capitalism? Ralf Dahrendorf (1959) has suggested four overarching reasons. First, in the century since Marx's death, the capitalist class in the United States has grown fragmented. Nineteenth-century companies were typically owned by *families*; today they are owned by numerous *stockholders*. Further, a large managerial class, whose members may or may not own a significant share of the companies they manage, has also emerged. The overall effect is that an increasing number of people have a direct stake in preserving the capitalist system.

Second, Marx's industrial proletariat has also been transformed by the so-called white-collar revolution. As Chapter 19 ("The Economy and Work") details, a century ago the vast majority of workers in the United States filled the ranks of **blue-collar occupations,** *work involving mostly manual labor*, in factories or on farms. Today, most of the labor force holds **white-collar occupations,** *higher-prestige work involving mostly mental activity*. These jobs include positions in sales, management, and other service work, frequently in large, bureaucratic organizations. While these white-collar workers have much in common with the industrial working class described by Marx, evidence suggests that most do not think of themselves in those terms. For much of this century, then, the white-collar revolution has prompted many people to perceive their social positions as higher than those held by their parents and grandparents. Just as important, the overall standard of living of workers in the United States has risen over the course of the century about four-fold in dollars adjusted for inflation. As a result of this rising tide of upward social mobility, our society seems less sharply divided between the rich and poor than it did to people during Marx's lifetime (Edwards, 1979; Gagliani, 1981; Wright & Martin, 1987).

Third, the plight of workers is not as desperate

This cartoon, entitled "Capital and Labor," appeared in the English press in 1843, when the ideas of Karl Marx were first gaining attention. It links the plight of that country's coal miners to the privileges enjoyed by those who owned coal-fired factories.

today as it was a century ago. Despite setbacks for many workers during the 1980s, the overall quality of life in Western societies has improved significantly since Marx's time. Moreover, workers have won the right to organize into labor unions that can make demands of management backed by threats of work slowdowns and strikes. Recently union membership has been declining, but research suggests that well-established unions continue to enhance the economic standing of the workers they represent (Rubin, 1986). Further, labor and management now regularly engage in contract negotiations. If not always peaceful, worker-management disputes are now institutionalized.

Fourth, legal protection has been widely extended during the last century. Laws now protect workers' rights and mandate safe working conditions, and workers have greater access to the courts for redressing grievances. Government programs such as unemployment insurance, disability protection, and Social Security also provide workers with substantially greater financial resources than the capitalists of the last century were willing to grant them.

Taken together, these developments suggest that despite persistent and marked stratification, many of capitalism's rough edges have been smoothed out. Conse-

quently, social conflict today is less intense than it was a century ago. Nonetheless, many sociologists continue to find value in Marx's analysis, often in modified form (Miliband 1969; Edwards, 1979; Giddens, 1982; Domhoff, 1983; Stephens, 1986).

Advocates of social-conflict analysis respond with four key points of their own. First, wealth in the United States remains highly concentrated, just as Marx contended: about half of all privately controlled corporate stock is owned by just 1 percent of individuals, who persist as a capitalist class. Second, the jobs generated by the white-collar revolution offer income and security no greater (and often less) than factory jobs did a century ago. In addition, much white-collar work is as monotonous and routine as factory work, especially the low-level clerical jobs commonly held by women. Third, they suggest, although labor organizations have certainly advanced the interests of workers over the last half century, regular negotiation between workers and management does not signal the end of social conflict. Many of the concessions workers have won came about precisely through the class conflict Marx described. Moreover, workers still struggle to gain concessions from capitalists and, in the 1990s, to hold on to the advances they have already made. Even today, for instance, half of workers in the United States have no employer pension program. Fourth, workers may have gained some legal protections, but the law has not changed the overall distribution of wealth in our society, nor can "average" men and women use the legal system to the same advantage as the rich do.

Therefore, social-conflict theorists conclude, the fact that no socialist revolution has taken place in the United States hardly invalidates Marx's analysis of capitalism. This nation's cultural values, emphasizing individualism and competition, may have curbed revolutionary aspirations in this country, but, as we shall see in Chapter 10 ("Social Class in the United States"), pronounced social inequality persists in our society, as does social conflict—albeit less overtly and violently than in the nineteenth century.

Finally, some defenders of capitalist, free-market economics contend that the collapse of communist regimes in Eastern Europe and the Soviet Union validates their long-standing arguments in favor of capitalism. To be fair, however, analysis of socialist and capitalist systems (detailed in Chapter 19, "The Economy and Work") are separate issues. Without denying the difficulties that have overwhelmed socialist societies in some parts of the world, many analysts claim that capitalism in the United States has yet to demonstrate its ability to address problems of poor public education and desperation among members of the urban underclass (Uchitelle, 1991). Table 9–1 summarizes the contributions of the two contrasting sociological approaches to these problems.

## Max Weber: Class, Status, and Power

Max Weber, whose approach to social analysis is described in Chapter 4 ("Society"), agreed with Karl Marx that social stratification sparks social conflict, but he differed with Marx in several important respects.

Weber considered Marx's model of two social classes simplistic. Instead, he viewed social stratification as the interplay of three distinct dimensions. First is economic inequality—the issue so vital to Marx—which Weber termed *class* position. Weber's use of "class" refers not to crude categories, but to a continuum on which anyone can be ranked from high to low. Second is *status*, meaning level of social prestige. This, too, forms a continuum. Third, Weber noted the importance of *power*, yet another dimension of social hierarchy.

Marx believed that social prestige and power stemmed from the same factor: economic position. Thus, he saw no reason to treat them as distinct dimensions of social inequality. Weber disagreed, asserting that stratification in industrial societies has characteristically low status consistency, meaning that a person might have a high standing on one dimension of inequality while having a lower position on another. For example, bureau-cratic officials might wield considerable power yet have little wealth or social prestige. So while Marx viewed social inequality in terms of two clearly defined classes, Weber saw something more subtle at work in the social stratification in industrial societies. Weber's key contribution in this area, then, lies in identifying rankings along a multidimensional hierarchy. Sociologists often use the term **socioeconomic status** to refer to *a composite ranking based on various dimensions of social inequality.*

A population that varies widely in class, status, and power—Weber's three dimensions of inequality—creates a virtually infinite array of social groupings, all of which pursue their own interests. Thus, unlike Marx, who saw a clear conflict between two classes, Weber considered social conflict as a highly variable and complex process.

Weber also suggested that each of his three dimensions of social inequality stands out at different points in the history of human societies. Agrarian societies, he maintained, emphasize status or social prestige, typically in the form of honor or symbolic purity. Members of these societies gain such status by conforming to cultural norms corresponding to their rank. Industrialization and the development of capitalism level traditional rankings based on birth but generate striking financial disparities in the population; thus, Weber argued, the crucial difference among people lies in the economic dimension of class. Mature industrial societies, especially socialist societies, witness a surging growth of the bureaucratic state and accord tremendous power to high-ranking officials.

---

**Table 9–1** TWO EXPLANATIONS OF SOCIAL STRATIFICATION: A SUMMARY

| Structural-Functional Paradigm | Social-Conflict Paradigm |
| --- | --- |
| 1. Social stratification keeps society operating. The linkage of greater rewards to more important social positions benefits society as a whole. | Social stratification is the result of social conflict. Differences in social resources serve the interests of some and harm the interests of others. |
| 2. Social stratification encourages a matching of talents and abilities to appropriate positions. | Social stratification ensures that much talent and ability within the society will not be utilized at all. |
| 3. Social stratification is both useful and inevitable. | Social stratification is useful to only some people; it is not inevitable. |
| 4. The values and beliefs that legitimate social inequality are widely shared throughout society. | Values and beliefs tend to be ideological; they reflect the interests of the more powerful members of society. |
| 5. Because systems of social stratification are useful to society and are supported by cultural values and beliefs, they are usually stable over time. | Because systems of social stratification reflect the interests of only part of the society, they are unlikely to remain stable over time. |

SOURCE: Adapted in part from Authur L. Stinchcombe, "Some Empirical Consequences of the Davis-Moore Theory of Stratification," *American Sociological Review,* Vol. 28, No. 5 (October 1963): 808.

Finally, recall from Chapter 4 ("Society") Weber's disagreement with Marx about the future of industrial-capitalist societies. Marx, who focused almost exclusively on economics, believed that most social stratification could be eliminated by abolishing private ownership of productive property. Weber doubted that overthrowing capitalism would significantly diminish social stratification in modern societies because of the rising significance of power based on positions in formal organizations. In fact, Weber imagined that a socialist revolution might actually increase social inequality by expanding government and concentrating power in the hands of a political elite. Recent popular uprisings against entrenched bureaucracies in Eastern Europe and the Soviet Union lend support to Weber's position.

***Critical evaluation.*** Weber's multidimensional analysis of social stratification retains enormous influence among sociologists, especially in the United States. Some analysts (particularly those influenced by Marx's ideas) argue that while social class boundaries have become less pronounced, striking patterns of social inequality persist in our own society as they do elsewhere in the industrial world.

As we shall see in Chapter 10 ("Social Class in the United States"), the enormous wealth of the most privileged Americans contrasts sharply with the grinding poverty of millions of people who are barely able to meet their day-to-day needs. The upward social mobility that historically blurred class lines in the United States ceased in the 1970s; during the 1980s, the extent of economic inequality in this country actually increased. Against this backdrop of economic polarization, the 1990s may well see a renewed emphasis on "classes" in conflict rather than on the subtle shadings of a "multidimensional hierarchy."

# Stratification and Technology in Global Perspective

We can weave together a number of observations made in this chapter by considering the relationship between a society's technology and its type of social stratification. Gerhard and Jean Lenski's model of sociocultural evolution, examined in Chapter 4 ("Society"), puts social stratification in historical perspective, and also helps us to understand the varying degrees of inequality found around the world today (Lenski, 1966; Lenski, Lenski, & Nolan, 1991).

Simple technology limits the production of hunting and gathering societies to only what is necessary for day-to-day living. No doubt, some individuals are more successful hunters or gatherers than others, but the group's survival depends on everyone sharing what they have. With little or no surplus, therefore, no categories of people emerge as better off than others. Thus social stratification among hunters and gatherers, based on age and sex, is less pronounced than among societies with more complex technologies.

Technological advances historically generate a productive surplus, while intensifying social inequality. In horticultural and pastoral societies, a small elite controls most of the surplus. Agrarian technology based on large-scale farming generates vastly greater abundance, which is unequally shared. In agrarian societies, then, various categories of people lead strikingly different lives. In one sense, agrarian societies seem egalitarian, since the vast majority of people are poor and work the land as peasants. However, the social distance between the favored strata—hereditary nobility—and the serfs looms as large as at any time in human history. In most cases, nobles wield godlike power over the masses.

In industrial societies, social inequality diminishes to some degree. The eclipse of tradition and the need to develop individual talents gradually erode caste rankings in favor of greater individual opportunity. The increasing productivity of industrial technology steadily raises the living standards of the historically poor majority. Specialized, technical work also encourages the expansion of schooling, sharply reducing illiteracy. A literate population, in turn, tends to press for a greater voice in political decision making, further diminishing social inequality. And, as already noted, additional technological advances transform much blue-collar labor into higher-prestige white-collar work. All these transformations help to explain why Marxist revolutions have occurred in agrarian societies—such as the Soviet Union (in 1917), Cuba (1959), and Nicaragua (1979)—where social inequality is most pronounced, rather than in industrial societies, as Marx predicted more than a century ago.

Initially, industrialization appears to increase the concentration of wealth—the pattern so troublesome to Marx. In time, however, the share of all property in the hands of the very rich declines somewhat. Estimates suggest the proportion of all wealth controlled by the richest one percent of U.S. families, for example, peaked at about 36 percent just before the stock market crash in 1929; during the 1980s, this economic elite owned

**Figure 9–1**  Social Stratification and Technological Development: The Kuznets Curve

The Kuznets Curve suggests that greater technological sophistication is generally accompanied by greater intensity of social stratification. The trend reverses itself, however, as industrial societies gradually become more egalitarian. Rigid caste-like distinctions are relaxed in favor of greater opportunity and equality before the law. Political rights are more widely extended, and there is even some leveling of economic differences. The Kuznets Curve may also be applied to the relative social standing of the two sexes.

between 20 and 25 percent of all wealth (Williamson and Lindert, 1980; Beeghley, 1989).

Finally, industrialization lessens the domination of women by men, which is generally strongest in agrarian societies. The movement toward social parity for the sexes derives from the industrial economy's need to cultivate individual talent as well as a growing belief in basic human equality.

In short, reducing the intensity of social stratification is actually functional for industrial societies. This historical pattern, recognized by Nobel Prize–winning economist Simon Kuznets (1955, 1966), is illustrated by the "Kuznets Curve," shown in Figure 9–1.[1]

Current patterns of social inequality in global perspective generally accord with the Kuznets Curve. As shown in Global Map 9–1, industrialized societies of

---

[1] The ideas of Simon Kuznets are discussed by Peter Berger (1986:43–46), whose interpretations are reflected in what appears here.

the world have somewhat less income inequality—one important measure of social stratification—than nations that remain predominantly agrarian. Specifically, mature industrial societies such as the United States and the nations of Western Europe exhibit less income inequality than many of the less industrialized societies of Latin America, Africa, and Asia. The pattern, however, is far from perfectly consistent: income disparity reflects a host of factors beyond technology, especially political and economic priorities. Societies that have operated as socialist economic systems (including the People's Republic of China, the former Soviet Union, and the nations of Eastern Europe) display relatively little income inequality. Keep in mind, however, that an egalitarian society like the People's Republic of China has an average income level that is quite low by world standards; further, this society has pronounced social inequality on noneconomic dimensions such as political power.

Finally, even if the general global patterns suggested by Kuznets appear to hold, his analysis does not necessarily mean that industrial societies will gradually become less and less stratified. In the abstract, the principle of equal opportunity for all is widely endorsed in the United States; even so, this goal has not—and may never—become a reality. The objective of social equality, like all concepts related to social stratification, is controversial, as the final section of this chapter explains.

## Social Stratification: Facts and Values

> The year was 2081 and everybody was finally equal. They weren't only equal before God and the law. They were equal every which way. Nobody was smarter than anybody else. Nobody was better looking than anybody else. Nobody was stronger or quicker than anybody else. All this equality was due to the 211th, 212th, and 213th Amendments to the Constitution and the unceasing vigilance of agents of the Handicapper General. . . .

With these words, novelist Kurt Vonnegut, Jr. (1961) opens the story of "Harrison Bergeron," an imaginary account of a future United States in which social inequality has been totally abolished. Although the ideal of equality may be appealing in principle, Vonnegut is not celebrating this achievement in practice. Far from it: He describes a social nightmare in which every individual talent that makes one person different from another

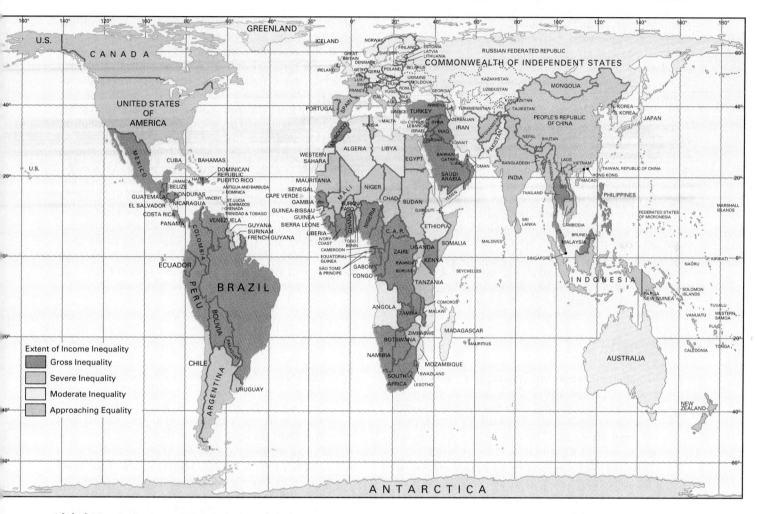

**Global Map 9–1**   Income Disparity In Global Perspective

Societies of the world differ in the rigidity and intensity of social stratification as well as in their overall standard of living. This map highlights income inequality. Generally speaking, countries that have had centralized, socialist economies (including the People's Republic of China, the former Soviet Union, and Cuba) display the least income inequality, although their standard of living has been relatively low. Industrial societies with predominantly capitalist economies, including the United States and most of Western Europe, have higher overall living standards, accompanied by severe income disparity. The less industrialized societies in Latin America and Africa (including Mexico, Brazil, and Zaire) exhibit the most pronounced inequality of income.

has been systematically neutralized by agents of the government. The most physically attractive people are required to wear masks that render them average-looking, intelligent people wear earphones that send distracting shrieks of noise every few seconds, and the legs of the best dancers are precisely fitted with weights to make their movements just as cumbersome as everyone else's. In short, although we may imagine that social equality would liberate people to make the most of their talents, Vonnegut suggests that more likely everyone would be reduced to a lowest common denominator.

All accounts of hierarchy and equality involve such value judgments. The Davis–Moore thesis argues that social stratification is necessary to social life because some occupational roles have greater importance than others. Social inequality, from this point of view, reflects both variation in human abilities and the variable tasks of society. Just as important, how could absolute social equality be achieved in a world of human diversity? Vonnegut fears that it could only occur through the relentless efforts of officials like the agents of his fictitious "Handicapper General."

Social-conflict analysis, advocated by Karl Marx, also mixes facts and values. Marx rejected the argument that stratification serves human societies, condemning social hierarchy as a product of greed that favors the few at the expense of the many. Guided by egalitarian values, he opposed any social arrangements that prevented everyone from sharing equally in important resources. Rather than undermining the quality of life, Marx maintained that equality would enhance humanity, and could be realized if the corrupting effects of capitalism were eradicated.

The next chapter ("Social Class in the United States") takes a close look at inequality in our own society. But even people who agree on the basic facts often interpret them quite differently. The same holds true for Chapter 11 ("Global Inequality"); there, we shall examine not only how much inequality exists among societies of the world, but why this hierarchy of nations exists. These chapters also reveal global links by which events and trends in the United States affect people elsewhere, just as changes in the larger world affect us.

## Summary

1. Social stratification involves ranking categories of people in a hierarchy. Such inequality is (1) a characteristic of society, not something that simply arises from individual differences; (2) universal, yet variable in form; (3) persistent over many generations; and (4) supported by cultural beliefs.

2. Caste systems, common in agrarian societies, are based on ascription and permit little or no social mobility. Caste hierarchy, which is supported by strong moral beliefs, shapes a person's entire life, including occupation and marriage.

3. Class systems, typical of industrial societies, reflect a greater measure of individual achievement. The emphasis on achievement allows for social mobility, so classes are less clearly defined than castes.

4. Socialist societies have historically claimed to be classless because of public ownership of productive property. Such societies, however, are unquestionably stratified, especially with regard to power.

5. Social stratification persists over time because of support from various social institutions and the power of ideology to define inequality as just, natural, or the expression of divine will.

6. The Davis–Moore thesis states that social stratification is universal because it contributes to the operation of society. In class systems, unequal rewards motivate the most able people to perform the most important occupational positions.

7. Critics of the Davis–Moore thesis note that (1) it is difficult to determine objectively the functional importance of any occupational position; (2) stratification prevents many people from developing their abilities; and (3) social stratification often generates social conflict.

8. Karl Marx's social-conflict analysis has had an enormous influence on the sociological debate over social stratification. Marx recognized two major social classes in industrial societies: the capitalists, or *bourgeoisie*, who own the means of production and seek profits; and the *proletariat*, who provide labor in exchange for wages.

9. The socialist revolution that Marx predicted has not occurred in industrial societies like the United States. While some sociologists cite this fact as evidence that Marx's analysis was flawed, others point out that our society is still marked by pro-

nounced social inequality and substantial class conflict.

10. Max Weber identified three distinct dimensions of social inequality: economic class, social status or prestige, and power. Taken together, these three dimensions form a complex hierarchy of socioeconomic standing.

11. Gerhard and Jean Lenski observe that, historically, technological advances have been associated with more pronounced social stratification. A limited reversal of this trend occurs in advanced industrial societies, as represented by the "Kuznets Curve."

12. Social stratification is a complex and controversial area of research because it deals not only with facts but with values that suggest how society should be organized.

# Key Concepts

**blue-collar occupations** work involving mostly manual labor

**caste system** a system of social stratification based on ascription

**class system** a system of social stratification based on individual achievement

**ideology** cultural beliefs that reflect and support the interests of certain categories of people

**meritocracy** a system of social stratification based entirely on personal merit

**social mobility** changes in people's positions in a system of social stratification

**social stratification** a system by which society ranks categories of people in a hierarchy

**socioeconomic status** a composite ranking based on various dimensions of social inequality

**status consistency** consistent standing across various dimensions of social inequality

**structural social mobility** a shift in the social position of large numbers of people due more to changes in society itself than to individual efforts

**white-collar occupations** higher-prestige work involving mostly mental activity

# Suggested Readings

The first of these two books explores a number of issues raised in this chapter. The second, a historical account, traces how sociology has grappled with the study of social stratification.

Charles E. Hurst. *Social Inequality: Forms, Causes, and Consequences.* Needham Heights, MA: Allyn & Bacon, 1992.

Michael D. Grimes. *Class in Twentieth-Century American Sociology: An Analysis of Theories and Measurement Strategies.* New York: Praeger, 1991.

This recent collection of essays brings together a number of influential points of view concerning social diversity and hierarchy.

David B. Grusky, ed. *Social Stratification: Class, Race, and Gender in Sociological Perspective.* Boulder, CO: Westview, 1992.

Based on interviews with twenty-one African-American domestics and the white women who employed them, this book offers powerful insights into the barriers and bridges between racial castes in the Deep South.

Susan Tucker. *Telling Memories Among Southern Women: Domestic Workers and their Employers in the Segregated South.* New York: Schocken, 1991.

This historical study of social stratification takes exception to the widespread notion that, prior to the Civil War, the United States was a more or less egalitarian society.

Edward Pessen. *Riches, Class, and Power: America Before the Civil War.* New Brunswick, NJ: Transaction, 1990.

This analysis of social stratification in Sweden points up the role of culture and national politics in the creation of this nation's extensive welfare system.

Sven E. Olsson. *Social Policy and Welfare State in Sweden.* Lund, Sweden: Arkiv, 1990.

This book compares social equality in three distinctive societies.

Sidney Verba with Steven Kelman, Gary R. Orren, Ichiro Miyake, Joji Watanuki, Ikuo Kabashima, and G. Donald Ferree, Jr. *Elites and the Idea of Equality: A Comparison of Japan, Sweden, and the United States.* Cambridge, MA: Harvard University Press, 1987.

Discussions about social hierarchy often revolve around the thorny question of whether, by nature, individuals are selfish or altruistic. This collection of a dozen essays presents comparative evidence of the existence of altruism in every culture.

Margaret S. Clark, ed. *Prosocial Behavior.* Newbury Park, CA: Sage, 1991.

# Social Class in the United States

As John Coleman[1] stepped from the door of Penn Station into the streets of New York City, frigid, mid-January air whipped him in the face. The sting was enough to make him wonder at the wisdom of what he was about to do. But, determined to begin his adventure, he raised his coat collar and pulled down his cap to shield himself from the wind.

Coleman had just joined the legions of homeless people found in cities across the United States. Yet his case was far from typical, for he had *chosen* to live on the streets. Why would a man who had spent a decade as a college president, a man with a lovely home and money in the bank, decide to become homeless? The answer lies in one individual's insatiable curiosity about the lives of the disadvantaged: Coleman wanted to find out for himself what it is like to be "down and out" in the richest city in the world.

Before the morning of his first day on the streets was over, Coleman had learned his first lesson: *To the average person, the poor are second-class citizens.* He was used to being acknowledged by others, to being *somebody.* But the change in his status could be read in the faces of those passing by. To some, he was a puzzle; to most, he was not even there. Those he gently asked for directions or for the time became uneasy, evi-

dently wishing he would simply go away. Entering a coffee shop, for example, he became flushed with self-consciousness as the man at the counter scrutinized him. Cautiously, he sat down. The counterman finally spoke: Coleman could eat, the man allowed, but only if he paid in advance.

On the second day, Coleman learned his next lesson: *Becoming poor changes how you see yourself.* As a homeless person, he was already walking more slowly, no longer dashing ahead to beat a traffic light, or rushing to be first through a revolving door. Habit still directed his eyes to his wrist, where he normally wore a watch, but his skin was bare. It hardly mattered: Coleman was much more concerned about temperature than time.

For ten days, John Coleman walked the streets of New York. He slept on sidewalk vents where there was heat, encountered the indifference of employment agencies, and ducked the hostility of social service workers. Even this brief time as a homeless person was sufficient to reveal the trap of poverty. Coleman felt himself pulled into a self-defeating, downward spiral. Describing one of his final experiences, he writes:

> Early this afternoon, I went again to [a] restaurant where I had eaten five times before. I didn't recognize the man at the cash register.
>
> "Get out," he said.
>
> "But I have money."

---

[1] This opening is a selective adaptation of Coleman's (1992) description of his urban adventure.

263

"You heard me. Get out." His voice was stronger.

"That man knows me," I said, looking toward the owner in the back of the restaurant.

The owner nodded, and the man at the register said, "Okay, but sit in the back."

If this life on the streets had been real, I'd have gone out the door at the first "Get out." And the assessment of me as not worthy would have been self-fulfilling: I'd have lost so much respect for myself that I wouldn't have been worthy of being served the next time. The downward spiral would have begun. (1992:89–90)

John Coleman's experiences teach us about more than homelessness; they help us see that social inequality involves not only money and power but human value: whether a person is deemed worthy or deficient. In short, the story of social class in the United States is partly about what we have and partly about who we are.

## Dimensions of Social Inequality

We have long considered our society to be responsive to individual initiative. Unlike Japan or most countries in Europe, the United States has never had a feudal aristocracy. With the significant exception of our racial history, our nation has never known a caste system that rigidly ranks categories of people.

Even so, U.S. society is highly stratified. The rich not only control most of the money, but they also benefit from more schooling, they enjoy better health, and they consume a greater share of almost all goods and services than others do. Such privilege contrasts sharply with the poverty of millions of poor women and men who struggle from day to day simply to survive. This chapter will explain that the popular portrayal of the United States as a "middle-class society" does not square with many important facts.

There are several reasons that we underestimate the extent of stratification in our society. First, founded in the wake of the Enlightenment, the United States formally embraced the ideal of equal standing under the law for all people, although, in reality, some people have been "more equal" than others. Second, our cultural emphasis on individual autonomy and achievement promotes the notion that people create their own social positions. This kind of thinking, although not entirely wrong, obscures the fact that birth confers on some people

advantages and opportunities that others who are less fortunate could never imagine. Third, people cannot easily recognize the extent of social inequality in the United States because our primary groups—including family, neighbors, and friends—typically have the same social standing as we do. Most of our daily lives, then, involves interaction within a narrow stratum of society, with only brief and impersonal encounters with people very different from ourselves. Fourth, and finally, as Chapter 11 ("Global Inequality") explains, the overall standard of living in the United States is extremely high in global perspective. We tend, therefore, to see everyone in this country as at least fairly well off.

When people do acknowledge their differences, they often speak of a "ladder of social class" as if inequality were determined by a single factor such as money. More accurately, however, social class in the United States has several dimensions. *Socioeconomic status* (SES), discussed in Chapter 9 ("Social Stratification"), amounts to a composite measure of social position that encompasses not only money but power, occupational prestige, and schooling.

### Income and Wealth

One important dimension of inequality involves **income,** *occupational wages or salaries and earnings from investments.* The Bureau of the Census reports that the median U.S. family income[2] in 1990 was $33,500. Figure 10–1 shows the distribution of income among all families in the country. The 20 percent of families with the highest earnings received 46.6 percent of all income, while the bottom 20 percent make only about 3.9 percent. At the very top, the highest paid 5 percent of families (who earn at least $80,000 per year) secured 17 percent of all income, more than the earnings of the lowest-paid 40 percent. In short, the bulk of the nation's income is earned by a small proportion of families, while the rest of the population makes do with far less.

This income disparity increased during the 1980s as a result of changes in the economy, new tax policies, and cuts in social programs that assist low-income people (Levy, 1987; Reich, 1989). The real income (controlled for inflation) of the top fifth of all families rose by almost

---

[2] Reported for households rather than families, median income is somewhat lower: $29,943 in 1990. Most of the difference is due to size: 1990 households included an average of 2.63 people compared to an average of 3.17 for families.

$18,000. The *very* rich—the highest-earning 1 percent of families—saw their pre-tax incomes just about double to more than $600,000. Families near the middle of the income distribution fared about the same throughout the 1980s, while the income of the typical family in the lowest fifth of the income scale actually dropped $650. Later in this chapter, we shall explore some of the recent changes in the economy of the United States that underlie this trend and present details about changing income inequality during the 1980s. For now, we can simply point out that the 1990s began with the income gap between rich and poor in the United States greater than at any time since the end of World War II (Jaeger & Greenstein, 1989; DeParle, 1991b).

Income is but one component of the broader economic factor of **wealth**, *the total amount of money and valuable goods that a person or family controls.* Wealth— in the form of stocks, bonds, real estate, and other privately owned property—is distributed even less equally than income is. Figure 10–2 shows the approximate

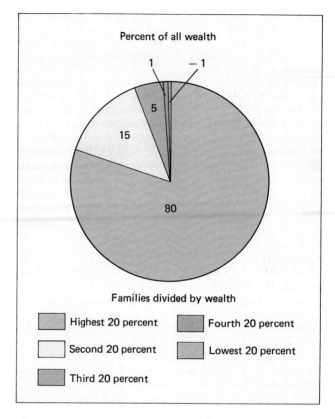

**Figure 10–2**  Distribution of Wealth in the United States, 1990

*(Based on sources cited in footnote 3)*

distribution of wealth in the United States in 1990.[3] The richest 20 percent of U.S. families own roughly four-fifths of the country's entire wealth. High up in this privileged category are the wealthiest 5 percent of families—the "super-rich," who control over half the nation's property. Richer still—with wealth into the tens of millions of dollars—one half of one percent of families possess about one-third of our nation's privately held resources. And at the very top of the wealth pyramid,

**Figure 10–1**  Distribution of Income in the United States, 1990

*(U.S. Bureau of the Census, 1991)*

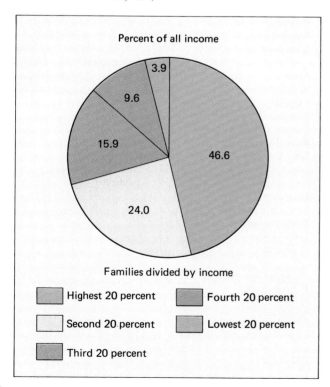

---

[3] This distribution is based on data from the Office of Management and the Budget (*Social Indicators*, 1973) and the Joint Economic Committee (1986), modified by the author on the basis of the Survey of Consumer Finances carried out in 1983 and 1989–90 by the Federal Reserve Board (cf. Kennickell & Shack-Marquez, 1992). Worth noting is the relative ease with which social scientists may obtain income data from the government and the frustrating difficulty of securing data about wealth.

the *three* richest families have a combined wealth totaling some $12 billion, which equals the total property of half a million "average" adults (enough people to fill the city of Boston) (Joint Economic Committee, 1986; *Forbes*, 1991).

The wealth of more typical U.S. families—in the second and third fifths of Figure 10–2—lies in the range of the median annual income for all families, or about $35,000 (*1991 Green Book*). Lesser wealth is also different in *kind*: the richest people have most of their property in the form of stocks and other income-producing investments. The wealth of average people resides primarily in property that generates no income, such as a home. When financial liabilities are balanced against assets for the least affluent 40 percent of U.S. families, wealth simply does not exist. The negative percentage shown in the figure for the wealth of the lowest 20 percent of the population means that people in this bottom fifth actually live in debt.

## Power

In American society, as elsewhere, wealth stands as an important source of power. People who own substantial shares of corporations, for example, make decisions that create jobs for ordinary people or scale back operations, putting men and women out of work.

For this reason, the small proportion of families who own most of the property in the United States typically set the agenda in the American political system. Thomas Jefferson (1953; orig. 1785), the third U.S. president and a large landholder himself, cautioned that democracy depends on "subdividing property" among the people. Chapter 18 ("Politics and Government") raises a question that has engaged sociologists for decades: Can a society maintain a political democracy if a small share of the population controls most of the wealth? Some analysts maintain that, while the rich may have some advantages, they do not dominate the political process.

**Table 10–1**  THE RELATIVE SOCIAL PRESTIGE OF SELECTED OCCUPATIONS IN THE UNITED STATES

| White-collar Occupations | Prestige Score | Blue-collar Occupations | White-collar Occupations | Prestige Score | Blue-collar Occupations |
|---|---|---|---|---|---|
| Physician | 86 | | Computer programmer | 61 | |
| Lawyer | 75 | | Sociologist | 61 | |
| College/university professor | 74 | | Editor/reporter | 60 | |
| Architect | 73 | | | 60 | Police officer |
| Chemist | 73 | | Actor | 58 | |
| Physicist/astronomer | 73 | | Radiologic technician | 58 | |
| Aerospace engineer | 72 | | Dietician | 56 | |
| Dentist | 72 | | Statistician | 56 | |
| Geologist | 70 | | Forester and conservationist | 55 | |
| Clergy | 69 | | Radio/TV announcer | 55 | |
| Psychologist | 69 | | Librarian | 54 | |
| Pharmacist | 68 | | | 53 | Aircraft mechanic |
| Optometrist | 67 | | | 53 | Firefighter |
| Registered nurse | 66 | | Postmaster | 53 | |
| Secondary-school teacher | 66 | | Dental hygienist | 52 | |
| Accountant | 65 | | Painter/sculptor | 52 | |
| Air traffic controller | 65 | | Social worker | 52 | |
| Athlete | 65 | | Draftsman | 51 | |
| Electrical engineer | 64 | | | 51 | Electrician |
| Elementary-school teacher | 64 | | Computer operator | 50 | |
| Mechanical engineer | 64 | | Funeral director | 49 | |
| Economist | 63 | | Realtor | 49 | |
| Industrial engineer | 62 | | Bookkeeper | 47 | |
| Veterinarian | 62 | | | 47 | Machinist |
| Airplane pilot | 61 | | | 47 | Mail carrier |

SOURCE:  Adapted from *General Social Surveys, 1972–1991: Cumulative Codebook* (Chicago: National Opinion Research Center, 1991), pp. 827–35.

Others argue that, in general, the political system operates to serve the interests of the "super-rich."

## Occupational Prestige

Occupation is a major determinant of income, wealth, and power. In addition, it is an important source of social prestige. Americans commonly evaluate others according to the kind of work they do, envying and respecting some, shunning and looking down on others.

For more than half a century, sociologists have measured the relative social prestige of various occupations (Counts, 1925; Hodge, Treiman, & Rossi, 1966; N.O.R.C., 1991). Table 10–1 presents the results of a recent survey involving a random sample of adults in the United States. The listing indicates that high-prestige occupations—such as physicians, lawyers, engineers—are generally those that provide high income. This pres-

tige reflects more than just high pay, however, since these occupations also typically require considerable ability, education, and training. By contrast, less prestigious work—as a cashier or janitor, for example—not only pays less, but usually requires less ability and schooling. In global perspective, occupational prestige rankings tend to be roughly the same in all industrial societies (Ma, 1987).

White-collar work that involves mental activity free from extensive supervision by superiors confers greater prestige than blue-collar occupations that require supervised, manual labor. There are exceptions to this pattern, however. As the table shows, for example, a blue-collar police officer enjoys greater social prestige than a white-collar bank teller.

In any society, the most privileged categories of people tend to have occupations that provide the greatest prestige. Starting from the beginning of Table 10–1, one passes at least a dozen occupations before finding

| White-collar Occupations | Prestige Score | Blue-collar Occupations | White-collar Occupations | Prestige Score | Blue-collar Occupations |
|---|---|---|---|---|---|
| Musician/composer | 47 | | | 34 | Bulldozer operator |
| | 46 | Secretary | | 34 | Meter reader |
| Insurance agent | 45 | | | 32 | Bus driver |
| Photographer | 45 | | | 32 | Hotel clerk |
| Bank teller | 43 | | | 31 | Auto body repairperson |
| Buyer, farm products | 42 | | Apparel retail salesperson | 30 | |
| | 42 | Tailor | | 30 | Truck driver |
| | 42 | Welder | Cashier | 29 | |
| | 41 | Apprentice electrician | | 28 | Elevator operator |
| | 41 | Locomotive engineer | | 28 | Garbage collector |
| | 40 | Farmer | | 28 | Taxi driver |
| | 40 | Telephone operator | | 28 | Waiter/waitress |
| Auctioneer | 39 | | | 27 | Bellhop |
| | 39 | Carpenter | | 27 | Freight handler |
| | 39 | Furniture finisher | | 25 | Bartender |
| | 38 | Mining explosives worker | | 23 | Farm laborer |
| | 38 | TV repairperson | | 23 | Household servant |
| | 37 | Security guard | | 23 | Midwife |
| | 36 | Brick/stone mason | | 22 | Door-to-door salesperson |
| | 36 | Child care worker | | 22 | Janitor |
| File clerk | 36 | | | 19 | Car washer |
| | 36 | Hairdresser | | 19 | News vendor |
| | 35 | Baker | | 09 | Shoe shiner |
| | 35 | Upholsterer | | | |

one in which a significant number of workers are women. Not until reaching "registered nurse" do we find an occupation in which *most* workers are women. As Jessie Bernard (1981) explains, women are highly concentrated in a small number of so-called *pink-collar jobs*. Most are service occupations—including secretaries, waitresses, and beauticians—that provide little income and fall near the bottom of the prestige hierarchy. Chapter 13 ("Sex and Gender") examines the link between gender and work more closely.

Similarly, reading the table in reverse order, beginning at the end, shows how many jobs that provide the least amount of prestige (and income) are commonly performed by people of color. In short, social diversity typically is not found at the extremes of the occupational hierarchy; rather, favored categories of people (men and whites) dominate the high-prestige occupations, while less powerful people (women and minorities) are concentrated at the bottom.

## Schooling

Industrial societies generally define schooling as everyone's right; even so, the opportunity for formal education is far from equal in the United States or elsewhere. Table 10–2 indicates how much formal education women and men aged twenty-five and over had acquired in 1990. According to the table, more than three-fourths had completed high school, although roughly one-fifth of women and one-fourth of men were college graduates.

Schooling promotes not just personal development but also affects an individual's occupation and income. Most (but not all) of the better paying, white-collar jobs shown in Table 10–1 require a college degree or other

advanced study. Similarly, most of the blue-collar occupations that offer less income and social prestige are held by people with limited schooling.

# Ascription and Social Stratification

To some degree, the class system in the United States rewards individual talent and effort. But, as explained in Chapter 9 ("Social Stratification"), class systems still rest on ascription. Who we are at birth, then, greatly influences what we become later in life.

## Ancestry

Nothing affects most Americans' social standing as much as our birth into a particular family, an event over which we have no control. Ancestry, or what we commonly call *social background*, determines our point of entry into the system of social inequality. Some families in the United States, including duPonts, Rockefellers, Roosevelts, and Kennedys, are known around the world. On a more modest scale, certain families in practically every community in North America have wealth and power that have become well established over several generations.

Being born to privilege or poverty sets the stage for our future schooling, occupation, and income. Research suggests that about half of the richest individuals—those with hundreds of millions of dollars in wealth—derived their fortunes primarily from inheritance (Thurow, 1987; Queenan, 1989). By the same token, the "inheritance" of poverty and the lack of opportunity that goes with it just as surely shapes the future for those in need. The family, which transmits property, power, and possibilities from one generation to the next, accounts, more than any other single factor, for the persistence of social stratification.

## Race and Ethnicity

Race is strongly related to social position in the United States. Overall, whites have higher occupational standing than blacks, and also receive more schooling. These differences are reflected in median income: African-American families earned on average $21,423 in 1990, which was about 58 percent of the $36,915 earned by

**Table 10–2** SCHOOLING OF U.S. ADULTS, 1990 (AGED 25 AND OVER)

|  | Women | Men |
| --- | --- | --- |
| Not a high-school graduate | 21.7% | 21.5% |
| 8 years or less | 10.3 | 11.0 |
| 9–11 years | 11.4 | 10.5 |
| High-school graduate | 78.3 | 78.5 |
| High school only | 41.0 | 36.0 |
| 1–3 years college | 18.5 | 18.2 |
| College graduate or more | 18.8 | 24.3 |

SOURCE: U.S. Bureau of the Census, 1991.

the average white family (U.S. Bureau of the Census, 1991). Differences in family patterns account for some of this income disparity. Comparing only families that include married couples, the racial disparity is far smaller, with African-American families earning 84 percent of what white families earn.

Over time, this income differential creates a considerable "wealth gap," with average wealth among African Americans (about $4,100) only about 10 percent of that found among whites ($43,300) (O'Hare, 1989; *1991 Green Book*). Finally, the effects of race are significant even among affluent families; the box takes a closer look at this issue.

As in the case of race, ethnic background also relates to social stratification in the United States (Hirschman & Wong, 1984). Throughout our nation's history, people of English ancestry have acquired the most wealth and the greatest power. The rapidly growing Hispanic population in the United States, by contrast, has long been relatively disadvantaged. In 1990, median family income among all Hispanics was $23,431, about 63 percent of the comparable figure for all whites. A detailed examination of how race and ethnicity affect social standing is presented later, in Chapter 12 ("Race and Ethnicity").

## SOCIAL DIVERSITY

# Two Colors of Affluence: Do Blacks and Whites Differ?

The typical African-American family has only about 58 percent of the income of the average white family. This creates a strong link between race and poverty. But there is another side to black America—an affluent side—that expanded dramatically during the 1980s.

The number of affluent African-American families—those with annual incomes over $50,000—is increasing rapidly. In 1990, more than 1 million black families were financially privileged; adjusted for inflation, this represents a five-fold increase over two decades before. Today, almost 15 percent of African-American families—more than 2 million adults and their children—are affluent. About 15 percent of Hispanic families rank as affluent, too, although twice as many non-Hispanic white families (30 percent) have this much income.

Black and white affluence differs in several key respects. First, well-off people of African descent

are not *as rich* as affluent whites. Almost 40 percent of affluent white families (about 8 percent of all white families) earn more than $75,000 a year; only 26 percent of affluent African-American families (not quite 3 percent of all black families) reach this level of income. Second, blacks are more likely than whites to achieve affluence through multiple incomes—from two employed spouses, or

employed parents and children. Third, affluent blacks generally *earn* their income rather than deriving it from investments. Three-fourths of affluent white families had unearned investment income, compared to only one-half of affluent African-American families.

Beyond differences in income, affluent blacks still contend with social barriers based on color. Even African Americans with the money to purchase a home, for example, may find they are unwelcome as neighbors. For this reason, affluent black families are more likely to live in central-city areas (56 percent) than in the suburbs (40 percent). Affluent whites, by contrast, are much more likely (61 percent) to have a suburban address.

Affluent Americans come in all colors. Yet, race exerts a powerful influence on the lives of affluent people, just as it does on all of us.

SOURCES: O'Hare (1989) and U.S. Bureau of the Census (1991).

## Gender

Societies also place men and women in different social positions. Of course, people of both sexes are born into families at every social level. Women born into families of high social standing, therefore, draw on many more social resources than men born into disadvantaged families. Yet, women earn less income, accumulate less wealth, enjoy less occupational prestige, and place lower in some aspects of educational achievement when compared to men (Bernard, 1981; Lengermann & Wallace, 1985). Perhaps most important, as we shall explain presently, households headed by women are ten times more likely to be poor than those headed by men. Chapter 13 ("Sex and Gender") further examines the link between gender and social stratification.

## Religion

Religion, too, has a bearing on social standing in the United States. Among Protestant denominations, with which almost two-thirds of individuals identify, Episcopalians and Presbyterians have significantly higher social standing, on average, than Lutherans and Baptists. In recent decades, Jews have gained high social standing, while Roman Catholics hold a more modest position (Roof, 1979; Gallup, 1981). Even John Fitzgerald Kennedy—a member of one of this country's wealthiest and most powerful families—became our first Catholic president just three decades ago, and only by overcoming opposition directed against him because he belonged to a religious minority. Understandably, then, throughout our history many upwardly mobile Americans have converted to a higher-ranking religion (Baltzell, 1979). Chapter 17 ("Religion") offers a closer look at the role of religion in the U.S. class system.

# Social Classes in the United States

As Chapter 9 ("Social Stratification") explained, people living in rigid caste systems consider relative social rankings to be clear and obvious to everyone. Defining the social categories in a more fluid class system, however, poses a number of challenges.

Consider the joke about the fellow who orders a pizza, asking that it be cut into six slices because he isn't hungry enough to eat eight. While all sociologists acknowledge extensive social inequality in the United States, they have long debated precisely how to divide up this social hierarchy. Some who follow Karl Marx's thinking about classes contend that there are two major categories; other sociologists suggest that our society breaks down into as many as six classes (Warner & Lunt, 1941) or even seven (Coleman & Rainwater, 1978). Still others endorse Max Weber's contention that there are no clear classes at all; rather, Weber argued, people have different positions on various dimensions of social inequality. From this point of view, the United States does not contain clear classes but rather a complex status hierarchy.

The task of defining classes would be far less difficult were it not for the relatively low level of status consistency in the United States. Especially toward the middle of the class system, an individual's social standing on one dimension often contradicts that person's position on another (Gilbert & Kahl, 1987). A government official, for example, may control a multimillion-dollar budget yet earn a modest income. Similarly, members of the clergy typically enjoy ample prestige while possessing only moderate power and little property. Or consider a lucky professional gambler who accumulates considerable wealth yet has little power or prestige.

Finally, the social mobility typical of class systems—again, most pronounced near the middle—means that social position often changes over the life course. This further blurs the lines between social classes.

Despite these problems of definition, we can identify four general social classes in the United States: the upper class, the middle class, the working class, and the lower class. As we shall explain, however, some categories are more clear-cut than others.

## The Upper Class

The upper class encompasses 3 or 4 percent of the population. The yearly income of upper-class families is at least $100,000 and can exceed ten times that much. Typically, much of this income is derived from inherited wealth, in the form of stocks and bonds, real estate, and other investments. In 1991, *Forbes* magazine profiled the richest four hundred people in the United States, estimating their combined wealth at $273 billion. These richest Americans had a *minimum* net worth of $260 million, and included sixty-six billionaires. The upper class thus comprises what Karl Marx termed "capitalists," those who own most of the nation's productive property.

A popular distinction in the United States and elsewhere sets off the "new rich" from people with "old money." Men and women who suddenly begin to earn high incomes tend toward public extravagance perhaps because they enjoy the new thrill of high-roller living and want others to know of their success. Those who grow up surrounded by wealth, by contrast, are more used to their privileges and more quiet about them. In short, the "conspicuous consumption" of the lower-upper class differs from the more private pursuits and characteristic understatement of the upper-upper class.

Besides their immense wealth, many members of the upper class work as top executives in large corporations and as senior government officials, further enhancing their power to shape events in the nation and, increasingly, the entire world. Members of the upper class also attain the highest levels of education, typically in the most expensive and highly regarded schools and colleges. Historically, though less so today, the upper class has been composed of white Anglo-Saxon Protestants (WASPs) (Baltzell, 1964, 1976, 1988).

A useful distinction is sometimes made between the "upper-upper class" and the "lower-upper class." The *upper-upper class*, often described as "society" or "bluebloods," includes just 1 percent of the U.S. population (Warner & Lunt, 1941; Coleman & Neugarten, 1971; Rossides, 1990). Membership is almost always the result of ascription or birth, as suggested by the old quip that the easiest way to become an "upper-upper" is to be born one. These families possess enormous wealth, primarily inherited rather than earned. For this reason, members of the upper-upper class are said to have *old money*. Noting the favor accorded to this segment of our society, C. Wright Mills commented that "prestige is the shadow of money and power" (1956:83).

Set apart by their wealth, members of the upper-upper class live in a world of exclusive affiliations. They inhabit elite neighborhoods, such as Beacon Hill in Boston, the Rittenhouse Square area or the Main Line in Philadelphia, the Gold Coast of Chicago, and Nob Hill in San Francisco. Schools and colleges extend this privileged environment. Their children typically attend private secondary schools with others of similar background, completing their formal education at high-prestige colleges and universities. In the historical pattern of European aristocrats, they study liberal arts rather than vocationally directed subjects. Women of the upper-upper class often maintain a full schedule of volunteer work for charitable organizations. For example, women from the Main Line were responsible for establishing the Philadelphia Museum of Art, and old-money families continue to support the organization, offering their time as well as funds. While helping the larger community, these activities are not entirely altruistic; Susan Ostrander (1980, 1984) explains that volunteer work is a means by which women forge networks that identify them as members of the city's elite.

The remaining 2 or 3 percent of the population that makes up the upper class falls into the *lower-upper*

# Caste and Class in America: *The Social Register* and *Who's Who*

The upper-upper class is small and exclusive; this level of the U.S. class structure comes closest of all to being a social group. There is even a listing of these privileged Americans: the *Social Register*, first published in 1887 as industrial fortunes were being made. Various versions of the *Social Register*, prepared for particular urban areas across the country, note those who fall within the ranks of "old money."

Because membership in the upper-upper class is typically based on birth, this level of our society operates much like a caste. You are either "in" or "out"; and, with tradition as a guide, young women and men are urged to seek out one of their own kind as a partner, thus perpetuating the class into another generation. Family is thus crucial to the upper-upper class, as it is to all caste systems. This is evident just by looking at the *Social Register*: listings are made by family rather than by individuals.

The listing for David Rockefeller, a member of one of the most socially prominent families in the United States, indicates (1) the family's address and home telephone number; (2) Mrs. Rockefeller's maiden name; (3) the names of the Rockefeller children, noting the boarding schools and colleges they are attending; and (4) exclusive social clubs to which the family belongs. Echoing the practice of aristocrats of a past age, listings in the *Social Register* make no mention of occupation or place of business; nor do they cite any mark of individual achievement.

The lower-upper class, by contrast, is an elite built on achievement. This larger category of "newly rich" individuals has no clear boundaries, and its members do not engage in formal rituals (like debutante balls) the way "old-money" families often do. There is a listing—roughly speaking—of people at this class level: the national edition of *Who's Who in America*. Here, instead of "established" families, we find individuals distinguished for high achievement in various pursuits: outstanding athletes, the most successful business people, college presidents, Nobel Prize winners, and famous entertainers.

Some *Social Register* families include men and women, such as David Rockefeller, who are also listed in *Who's Who*, but the information offered in the two listings differs markedly. David Rockefeller's entry in *Who's Who* includes a brief biography (date of birth, schooling, and honorary degrees), a list of accomplishments (military decorations, government service, books authored), and—most important—his position as chairman of the board of Chase Manhattan Bank. The address provided in *Who's Who* is his place of business.

Comparing the two listings suggests that there are two kinds of elites in the United States. The castelike *Social Register* lists high-prestige families according to *who they are*. The more classlike *Who's Who* lists individuals on the basis of *what they have done*. But, as the dual listings of David Rockefeller suggest, social privilege and personal achievement frequently overlap.

*class.* From the point of view of most Americans, such people seem every bit as privileged as the upper-upper class. The major difference, however, is that "lower-uppers" depend on earnings rather than wealth as the primary source of their income. Few people in this category inherit a vast fortune from their parents, although the majority do inherit some wealth. Especially in the eyes of members of "society," the lower-upper class constitutes the "new rich," people who can never savor the highest levels of prestige enjoyed by those with rich and famous grandparents. Thus, while the "new rich" typically live in expensive homes, they often find themselves excluded from the most prestigious clubs and associations maintained by "old-money" families.

Historically, the American dream of great success has meant joining the ranks of the lower-upper class through exceptional accomplishment. The young author whose novel is made into a popular Hollywood movie; the athlete who accepts a million-dollar contract to play in the big leagues; the clever computer whiz who designs a new program that sets a standard for the industry—these are the lucky and talented achievers who reach the level of the lower-upper class. Their success stories fascinate most of us because this kind of upward social mobility has long stood as a cultural goal. No doubt this is why Americans display little interest in the upper-upper class, who move in rarefied circles far from most people's everyday reality, while we simultaneously aspire to the "lifestyles of the rich and famous." The box examines the distinctions between "society" and the people we see on television shows like *Dallas* and *Dynasty*—those who seem just like the rest of us except that they have made a lot of money.

## The Middle Class

The middle class includes 40 to 45 percent of the U.S. population. Because it is so large and represents the aspirations of many more people, the middle class exerts tremendous influence on patterns of American culture. Television and other mass media usually portray middle-class people, and most commercial advertising is directed at these "average" consumers. The middle class encompasses far more racial and ethnic diversity than the upper class. While many upper-class people (especially "upper-uppers") know each other personally, such exclusiveness and familiarity do not characterize the middle class.

The top half of this category is often termed the *upper*-middle class, based on above-average income in the range of $50,000 to $100,000 a year. Family income may be even greater if both wife and husband work. High income allows upper-middle-class families gradually to accumulate considerable property—a comfortable house in a fairly expensive area, several automobiles, and some investments. Virtually all upper-middle-class people receive college educations, and postgraduate degrees are common. Many work in white-collar fields such as medicine, engineering, and law, or as business executives. Lacking the power of the upper class to influence national or international events, the upper-middle class often plays an important role in local political affairs.

The rest of the middle class typically works in less prestigious white-collar occupations (as bank tellers, middle managers, and sales clerks) or in highly skilled blue-collar jobs (including electrical work and carpentry). Commonly, family income is between $30,000 and $50,000 a year. This roughly equals the median family income in the United States ($33,500 in 1990) and provides a secure, if modest, standard of living. Middle-class people generally accumulate a small amount of wealth over the course of their working lives, and most eventually own a house. Middle-class men and women are likely to be high-school graduates, but only some

will be able to send their children to college. And limited income means that young people in this class who do go to college generally attend state-supported schools.

## The Working Class

Including about one-third of the population, the working class refers to people who have lower incomes than those in the middle class and virtually no accumulated wealth. In Marxist terms, the working class forms the core of the industrial proletariat. The blue-collar occupations of the working class generally yield a family income of between $15,000 and $30,000 a year, somewhat below

Television programming in the United States has typically portrayed people in a relatively narrow range of the class structure, from middle class to lower-upper class. In the last decade or so, however, an increasing number of shows have featured working-class families—belated recognition of the fact that at least one-third of all families in this country think of themselves in these terms. Roseanne Arnold, herself from a working-class family, is the star of one of the most popular shows on television.

the national average. Working-class families thus find themselves vulnerable to financial problems brought on by unemployment or illness.

Besides generating less income than the occupations of the middle class, working-class jobs typically provide less personal satisfaction. Tasks tend to be routine, requiring discipline rather than imagination, and workers are usually subject to continual supervision by superiors (Edwards, 1979). Such jobs also provide fewer benefits such as medical insurance and pension programs. About half of working-class families own their homes, usually in lower-cost neighborhoods. College is an expense that few working-class people can afford for themselves or their children.

As these facts suggest, working-class people lack the power to shape events, leading many to cultivate a sense of fatalism about their lives. Families live in modest neighborhoods because they cannot afford better housing. They want their children to attend college but lack the money to send them. While they find little satisfaction in their jobs, opportunities for upward mobility are scarce. Still, many working-class families express a great deal of pride in the possessions they have and compare themselves favorably to those who are not working at all.

## The Lower Class

The remaining 20 percent of our population make up the lower class. A lack of income renders their lives unstable and insecure. In 1990, some 33 million people (13.5 percent of the population) were classified by the federal government as poor. Millions more—the so-called "working poor"—are only marginally better off. Most lower-class people in the United States are white; however, people of African or Hispanic descent and members of other minorities are disproportionately represented at the low end of the socioeconomic scale.

The poor typically work in low-prestige jobs that provide minimal income and little intrinsic satisfaction. Only some manage to complete high school; a college degree is usually out of reach. Many lower-class men and women are functionally illiterate.

Society segregates the lower class into particular neighborhoods and schools, especially when the poor belong to racial or ethnic minorities. Such segregation appears most starkly in cities where large numbers of poor people live in deteriorating areas, in rental housing shunned by the other social classes.

Lower-class children learn early on the harsh reality that many people consider them only marginal members of society. Observing their parents and other lower-class adults, they may conclude that their own future holds little hope for breaking the cycle of poverty. Lower-class life, then, often generates self-defeating resignation, as these people are cut off from the resources of an affluent society (Jacob, 1986).

Some may simply give up. Most poor people, however, work desperately—often at two or three jobs—to make ends meet. In a study conducted in a northern city, Carol Stack (1975) discovered that, far from lacking initiative and responsibility, many poor people devise ingenious means to survive. They do so, she concluded, because they simply have no other choice.

# The Difference Class Makes

Stratification affects nearly every dimension of social life. We will briefly examine some of the ways social standing is linked to our health, values, politics, and family life.

## Class and Health

Health is one of the most important correlates of social standing. Children born into poor families are several times more likely to die—from disease, accidents, or violence—during their first year of life than children born into more privileged families (Gortmaker, 1979; Children's Defense Fund, 1991). Among adults, people with above-average incomes are twice as likely to describe their health as excellent as are low-income people. Conversely, only 4 percent of better-paid people complain that their health is merely fair or poor, although this assessment is made by 23 percent of low-income individuals (Adams & Benson, 1990). This general pattern holds in Great Britain and in virtually every other industrial society (Doyal, 1981).

Adequate income buys many things that ensure a long life. Nutritious foods, a safe environment, and medical care all promote well-being for those who can afford them. Medical costs have risen sharply in recent years to an average exceeding $1,500 annually per person in the United States. Such costs are simply out of reach for a family of four with an annual income of, say,

$15,000. Thus categories of people who suffer greater poverty also do not live as long as others. African-American children, for example, are three times more likely to be poor than white children and can expect to live about seventy years, while whites have an average life expectancy of more than seventy-five years (U.S. Bureau of the Census, 1991).

Men and women in the lower social classes also live and work in more dangerous environments than privileged people. Factories and mines contain greater threats to health than office buildings, just as the neighborhoods of the poor are all-too-often plagued by drugs and crime. People with fewer privileges also suffer from more problems of mental health (Link, Dohrenwend, & Skodol, 1986; Mirowsky & Ross, 1989). As one study concluded, "Lower class people are exposed to more of the stressful events and situations that can lead to emotional distress than their middle and upper class counterparts" (Kessler & Cleary, 1980:476). Moreover, when problems do arise, people with greater social resources respond more effectively because they can afford professional help. As a result, they recover more quickly, avoiding the stigma of mental illness.

## Class and Values

Cultural values also vary somewhat from class to class. Women and men with the highest social standing have an unusually strong sense of family history since their social position is based on wealth and social prestige passed down from generation to generation (Baltzell, 1979). Many others, by contrast, do not know the full names of even their four grandparents. Because their privileges are guaranteed as a birthright, the "old rich" also tend to be understated in their manners and tastes, as if to say, "I know who I am and I don't have to prove anything to anyone else."

Below the upper class, patterns of consumption take on greater importance as class boundaries start to blur. Houses, clothes, and cars are often viewed as *status symbols* that "make a statement" about their owners. Perhaps this is why designer clothing—avoided by members of "society"—is nonetheless prized by those directly below them in class.

Because of their greater personal and financial security, financially comfortable people in the middle class are more tolerant than their working-class counterparts of controversial behavior such as premarital sexual activity and homosexuality (Humphries, 1984). As Chapter

Life expectancy is closely related to social-class position. Poor people—especially males—who struggle to get by in our cities have a strikingly high rate of death and injury from illness, accident, and violence. To some extent, this reflects their dangerous environment; in addition, it may indicate that people caught up in poverty have little reason to think that the future will be brighter than the present.

5 ("Socialization") explained, working-class people grow up in an atmosphere of greater supervision and discipline which prefigures their experience on the job as adults. In raising their children, then, they encourage greater conformity to conventional beliefs and practices (Kohn, 1977).

Even the meaning of time varies according to social class. Generations of wealth give upper-class families a strong sense of pride in the past. Middle-class people, especially those who are upwardly mobile, look optimistically to the future for a better life. By contrast, the drive for daily survival focuses the attention of lower-class people on the moment. Such a present-time orientation often reflects the limited opportunities for advancement open to the lower class (Liebow, 1967; Lamar, Jr., 1985; Jacob, 1986).

## Class and Politics

Political attitudes also tend to follow class lines. More privileged people in the United States support the Republican Party, while less advantaged people favor the Democrats (Wolfinger, Shapiro, & Greenstein, 1980). A desire to protect their wealth prompts people who are well off to take a more conservative approach to economic issues. Thus, members of the higher social classes—often men and women who own or manage businesses—favor a free-market economy unregulated by government. On social issues, such as support for the Equal Rights Amendment, abortion, and other feminist concerns, however, affluent people tend to be more liberal. People of lower social standing display the opposite pattern, favoring liberal policies on economic issues and conservative social goals (Nunn, Crockett, & Williams, 1978; Erikson, Luttberg, & Tedin, 1980; Syzmanski, 1983; Humphries, 1984).

Individuals with higher incomes, more schooling, and white-collar jobs are more likely to vote and to support various political groups and associations (Hyman & Wright, 1971; Wolfinger & Rosenstone, 1980). This is probably because people of higher social positions also are better served by the political system.

## Class, Family, and Gender

Finally, family life is closely related to social class. At all social levels, in the United States, women and men typically marry someone of comparable social position. Thus distinctive family patterns emerge at each level. Family size is one case in point: in general, lower-class parents have more children than middle-class parents do. This is because less affluent people marry earlier in life and make less use of birth control. Upper-class families, too, have more children, partly because they can afford the added child-rearing expenses.

Child-rearing practices also reveal the effect of social position. Working-class parents encourage children to conform to conventional norms and display obedience and respect to authority figures. By contrast, parents of higher social standing motivate children to express their individuality and to use their imagination more freely. This difference reflects parents' expectations about their children's future: the odds are that less privileged children will take jobs demanding close adherence to specified rules, while more advantaged children will probably enter fields that call for greater creativity (Kohn, 1977). And it stands to reason that the more social resources a family has, the better able parents will be to develop their children's talents and abilities. In this way, society reproduces the class structure from generation to generation.

How spouses relate to one another is also shaped by social class. Elizabeth Bott (1971) documented that working-class couples maintain a more rigid division of responsibilities so that husband and wife may spend little time together. Middle-class marriages, she found, are more egalitarian, with greater sharing and interpersonal intimacy. This insight helps to explain why divorce is more common among disadvantaged couples, whose limited communication skills are sometimes overwhelmed by the stresses of low income and unemployment (Kitson & Raschke, 1981; Fergusson, Horwood, & Shannon, 1984).

Finally, as Chapter 15 ("Family") explains, the number of families headed by women increased rapidly during the 1980s. This fact looms large because women raising children without the support of husbands are at high risk of poverty. This risk is most pronounced among African Americans, although more and more women in all categories are grappling with the economic burdens of single parenthood.

# Social Mobility

Ours is a dynamic society marked by a significant measure of social mobility. As we noted in the last chapter, social mobility involves individuals moving upward or downward in the stratification system. Earning a college degree, securing a higher-paying job, or succeeding in a business endeavor contributes to *upward social mobility*, while dropping out of school, losing a job, or having a business enterprise fail may signal the onset of *downward social mobility*.

Social mobility is not just a matter of the changing fortune of individuals. Changes in society itself account for most social mobility, at least over long periods. During the first half of this century, for example, industrialization expanded the economy, dramatically raising living standards for millions of people in the United States. Even without being very good swimmers, so to speak, people were able to "ride a rising tide of prosperity." As explained presently, *structural social mobility* in a downward direction has more recently dealt many people economic setbacks.

In studying social mobility, sociologists distinguish between changes within a single generation and shifts between generations of a family. **Intragenerational social mobility** refers to *a change in social position occurring during a person's lifetime.* Sociologists pay even greater attention to **intergenerational social mobility,** *upward or downward social mobility of children in relation to their parents.* Social mobility across generations reflects changes in society that affect virtually everyone.

## Social Mobility: Myth and Reality

In few societies do people dwell on social mobility as much as in the United States: historically, moving ahead has been central to the American Dream. To a large degree, U.S. social stratification rests on the belief that people have the opportunity to realize their individual potential (Kleugel & Smith, 1986).

Precisely how much social mobility does takes place in the United States? Using the broad categories of blue-collar and white-collar jobs, studies of intergenerational mobility (that, unfortunately, have focused almost exclusively on men) show that almost 40 percent of the sons of blue-collar workers attain white-collar jobs and almost 30 percent of sons born into white-collar families end up doing blue-collar work. Changes from occupation to occupation, of course, are quite common, with about 80 percent of sons showing some social mobility in relation to their fathers (Blau & Duncan, 1967; Featherman & Hauser, 1978).

Among the population of the United States, several patterns of social mobility emerge clearly. First, mobility for men has been fairly high, as we would expect in a class system. Second, with the significant exception of the last twenty years, the trend in social mobility has been upward rather than downward. This structural social mobility resulted from better-paying white-collar jobs steadily replacing the blue-collar and farming work more common several generations ago. Third, although significant changes appear over many generations, social mobility within a single generation is usually incremental rather than dramatic. This means that individuals rarely move "from rags to riches," or the other way around. Social mobility typically involves subtle changes *within* the social classes rather than dramatic changes *between* classes.

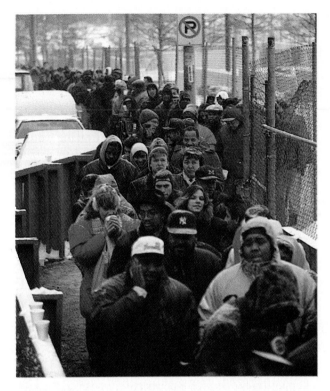

Thousands of people recently lined up in the freezing cold hoping to land one of the new jobs created by the opening of a Chicago hotel. The queue stretched for blocks despite the fact that most of the jobs paid only minimum wage. Such sights are an increasingly common part of the postindustrial economy. While the 1980s were a boom time for the wealthiest people in the United States, they brought no gains to most families, and a slight drop in living standards for the poor.

Any analysis of mobility, however, must take account of social diversity. African Americans have traditionally experienced less upward social mobility than whites, especially in recent years (Featherman & Hauser, 1978; Pomer, 1986). Although the United States enjoyed a sustained economic recovery during the 1980s, African Americans lost ground before 1985, made some gains after that, but ended up the decade with no overall improvement. In comparison to whites, blacks fell further behind: African-American families earned 65 percent of what white families did in 1980, sliding to about 58 percent of white income by 1990 (Jacob, 1986; DeParle, 1991b). Hispanic families also suffered economically during the 1980s, although not quite as much. Hispanics began the decade earning about 73 percent as much as (non-Hispanic) whites, but ended up with 66 percent of whites' income. For Americans of African and Hispanic descent, structural downward mobility stemmed from falling wage rates coupled with persistent discrimination.

Historically, women have had less opportunity for upward mobility than men. As we shall see in Chapter 13 ("Sex and Gender"), the majority of working women hold clerical positions (such as secretaries) and low-paying service jobs (such as waitresses). These jobs offer little chance for advancement, creating barriers to upward social or economic movement. Divorce also commonly results in downward social mobility for women—but not men—as Chapter 15 ("Family") explains. Data reflecting income change during the 1980s reveal a narrowing of the gap between the earnings of women and men. Among full-time workers in 1980, women earned 60 percent as much as men, with the proportion rising to an all-time high of 72 percent in 1990. Much of this change was due to a *drop* in men's earnings at the end of the 1980s, however, while the income of women remained about the same (U.S. Bureau of the Census, 1991).

The United States has long been called a "land of opportunity." In global perspective, however, the rates of social mobility in this country have been about the same as those of other industrial societies. As the economies of the world become more interrelated, we can expect that the structural shifts—both upward and downward—that occur in Europe and Japan will mirror those we experience in the United States (Lipset & Bendix, 1967; McRoberts & Selbee, 1981; Kaelble, 1986).

## The "Middle-Class Slide"

The assumption that everyone has a shot at upward social mobility is deeply rooted in American culture and our national consciousness. For much of our history, economic expansion has fulfilled the promise of prosperity by raising the overall standard of living. Beginning about 1970, however, this upward trend ended, prompting some sociologists to declare that the United States has entered an "age of decline" (Pampel, Land, & Felson, 1977; Blumberg, 1981; Levy, 1987). Income data confirm this prognosis. According to economist Frank Levy, the annual income of a fifty-year-old man working full time rose by half between 1958 and 1973 (from about $21,000 to $32,000 in 1990 dollars adjusted for inflation).

Between 1973 and 1990, however, this worker's income stagnated, even as the cost of necessities like housing and medical care rose sharply (DeParle, 1991a). Understandably, then, a large proportion of people in the United States now concentrate on simply holding on to what they have, while many find that the economic security long associated with middle-class living is slipping away.

The factor underlying what has been widely described as *the middle-class slide* is change in the economy. The brisk pace of economic expansion, long taken for granted, has now slowed for a generation. Figure 10–3 shows median U.S. family income between 1950 and 1990 in constant 1990 dollars. Between 1950 and 1973, median family income grew by almost 65 percent; however, it has remained roughly stable since then (U.S. Bureau of the Census, 1991).

Earlier in this century, the rapid surge in white-collar positions drew millions of workers from blue-collar and farming jobs, encouraging optimistic projections that the United States was becoming predominantly a middle-class society (Kerckhoff, Campbell, & Winfield-Laird, 1985). Since 1970, however, new jobs in the U.S. economy have typically paid *less* than in the past. This accounts for the shift in social mobility in the *downward* direction. Between 1960 and about 1973, almost half of all new jobs provided workers with high income (paying at least $30,000 annually in 1990 dollars). Through the remainder of the 1970s, most new jobs paid in the middle-income range (between about $15,000 and $30,000). During the 1980s, the number of new high– and middle–income jobs fell even further. Simultaneously, the proportion of low-income jobs (paying less than $15,000 annually) jumped sharply. Simply stated, this means that many "average" families in the middle class and working class have had to settle for lower incomes, causing them to suffer an economic decline.

## The U.S. Class Structure in Global Perspective

Underlying the middle-class slide is a global economic transformation. Much of the industrial production that offered U.S. workers high-paying jobs a generation ago has been transferred overseas, while a growing proportion of new jobs in the United States falls into the category of so-called "service work," requiring little skill and providing minimal income (Blumberg, 1981; Rosen, 1987; Thurow, 1987). The United States now serves as a vast

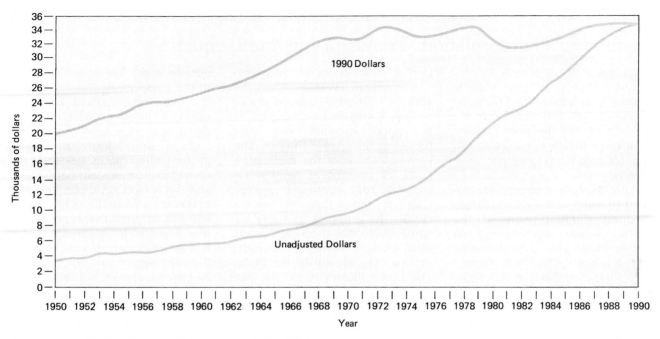

**Figure 10–3** Median Income, U.S. Families, 1950–1990
(*U.S. Bureau of the Census*)

market for industrial goods—such as cars, and popular items, like stereos and cameras—produced in Japan, Korea, and other countries. At home, traditionally high-paying corporations like USX (formerly United States Steel) have fallen on such hard times that they now employ fewer people than McDonald's. Echoing this shift toward low-paying work, one study predicts that the fastest-growing job categories in the 1990s will be cashiers, nurses, janitors, waiters, and truck drivers (Howe & Strauss, 1991). The expansion of global corporations has sparked upward social mobility for the small number of rich men and women who manage and invest in multinational companies. But this process has hurt many individuals of more moderate income whose factory jobs have been "exported" overseas (Reich, 1989, 1991).

What has been called "the deindustrialization of America" has hurt the standard of living and shaken the confidence of many people. Compared to a generation ago, far fewer now expect to improve their social position, and a growing number worry about being able to maintain the way of life they knew as children in

their parents' home. Even home ownership—long a key component of the American Dream—has slipped in recent years (from 66 percent to 64 percent during the 1980s). The standard of living in the United States has stopped rising even though women and men are working harder than ever: half of today's families have two or more people in the labor force, double the proportion in 1950.

Not surprisingly, in light of the mixed performance of the U.S. economy, the 1980s generated intense controversy and debate. The box on page 280 delves into how the 1980s affected various segments of our population. With these patterns in mind, we shall turn our attention to the growing problem of poverty in the United States.

## Poverty in the United States

Social stratification simultaneously creates "haves" and "have-nots." Poverty, therefore, inevitably grows within all systems of social inequality. The concept of poverty,

# Economic Transformation: Trends in Income Inequality

Were the 1980s a decade of economic recovery, as some analysts suggest? Or a time when transformations in the economy made the rich richer and the poor poorer? As is often the case, each side can point to some facts to support their claims.

First, as we have noted, the standard of living in the United States stopped climbing early in the 1970s, when skyrocketing oil prices threw the U.S. economy into a tailspin. The 1980s opened with little promise that this situation would improve; in the first few years of the decade, the average family actually lost ground in terms of income. But the trend soon turned around. Average income bottomed out in 1982, and then slowly rebounded for the rest of the decade. In 1990, median family income topped $33,000, an all-time high, even when adjusted for inflation. Such overall improvement in average family income supports the conclusion that during the 1980s the United States experienced an economic recovery.

But overall averages mask the strikingly different experiences of various categories of people. At the upper extreme, the 1980s brought a bonanza to the rich. The earnings share of the highest-income 20 percent of families increased from about 44 percent (1980) to more than 46 percent (1990). The proportion of total income received by the lowest three-fifths of U.S. families, however, dropped slightly during the 1980s. The figure illustrates this change by showing income dollars through the decade. The highest-income 20 percent of American families enjoyed a rapid rise in annual income from about $64,600 in 1980 to $82,300 in 1990, an increase of 27 percent. Families in the second 20 percent, on average, showed a modest 6 percent upturn, gaining $2,000 in income over the decade. For the remaining 60 percent, the 1980s brought an income decline of about $600, which amounted to a 9 percent loss for

people in the lowest-income fifth of the population.

Notice an apparent paradox: during a decade in which the nationwide average family income increased, the majority of families in the United States saw their income fall. Both actually happened, and the reason is simple. The rise in income among the richest families was so great that it pulled up the average for everyone. The highest-paid one percent of families—the uppermost tip of the top 20 percent shown in the figure—had median earnings of $325,000 in 1980; by 1990, however, the income of this economic elite had doubled to $650,000 (in dollars controlled for inflation).

Changes in the U.S. tax structure during the 1980s amplified the effect of changes in the economy, further increasing the income disparity. Total taxes on income dropped 5 percent for the highest-income fifth, while rising 15 percent for the fifth with the lowest income. All things considered,

---

however, is used in two different ways. **Relative poverty,** the universal societal trait, refers to *the deprivation of some people in relation to those who have more.* Even a rich society has some members who live in relative poverty. Much more serious is **absolute poverty,** or *a deprivation of resources that is life threatening.* Defined in this way, poverty is a pressing, but solvable, human problem.

As the next chapter ("Global Inequality") explains, the global dimensions of absolute poverty place the lives of perhaps 1 billion people—one in five of the earth's entire population—at risk. Even in the affluent United States, however, the wrenching reality of poverty results in hunger, inadequate housing, and poor health for millions.

## The Extent of U.S. Poverty

As part of its "war on poverty," the United States government began counting the poor in 1964. The *poverty threshold* is an annual income level below which a person or family is defined as poor and, therefore, entitled to certain benefits. In creating the poverty threshold, the government's intention was to determine how many people were living close to absolute poverty. Mollie Orshansky (1969:38), one of its original architects, claimed that the poverty threshold reflects the income needed "to purchase a nutritionally adequate diet on the assumption that no more than a third of the family income is used for food." In simple terms, then, the poverty threshold

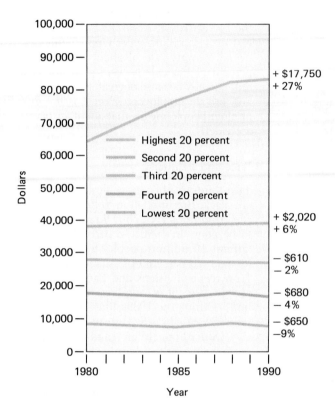

100,000 —
90,000 —
80,000 —    + $17,750
           + 27%
70,000 —

Dollars

60,000 —    ▬▬ Highest 20 percent
            ▬▬ Second 20 percent
50,000 —    ▬▬ Third 20 percent
            ▬▬ Fourth 20 percent
40,000 —    ▬▬ Lowest 20 percent    + $2,020
                                     + 6%
30,000 —                            − $610
                                     − 2%
20,000 —                            − $680
                                     − 4%
10,000 —                            − $650
                                     −9%
0 —

1980          1985          1990

Year

**Median After-Tax Income, U.S. Families, 1980–1990 (in estimated 1992 dollars, adjusted for inflation)**

(*Congressional Budget Office*)

Americans who were affluent when the decade began prospered during the 1980s. The next tier of families with above-average incomes also made gains, but far smaller than those of the rich. But for most families, the 1980s saw a gradual slide downward, with income falling slightly as the cost of living and tax rates rose. For the poor, those least able to absorb an economic setback, the 1980s hit the hardest. This trend dashed hopes—for the present, at least—that the problem of poverty would be routed in the United States any time soon. But the increasing income disparity of the 1980s did boost public awareness of the many problems linked to low income. People across the country began talking about homeless families; the term "underclass" became rooted in our national vocabulary; and social scientists and public officials launched investigations into poverty with a renewed sense of urgency.

is three times what the government estimates people must spend to eat. The government keys the exact dollar amount to family size and adjusts it annually to reflect the changing cost of living.

Figure 10–4 on page 282 shows the official poverty rate calculated for each year, beginning in 1960. The long-term trend is downward, although the poverty rate rose early in the 1980s and jumped again in 1989 as more than 2 million people were added to the ranks of the poor. As the 1990s began, a total of 33 million men, women, and children—13.5 percent of the population—were officially living in poverty. Another 12 million people were supported by incomes above this level but within 25 percent of the poverty threshold; these

people are termed the *marginally poor*.

For two adults and two children living in an urban area in 1990, the poverty threshold was $13,359. The income of the typical poor family, however, is about $4,000 *below* the poverty threshold. The *poorest of the poor* struggle to get by earning no more than half the amount constituting the poverty threshold. One recent study concluded that almost 40 percent of the poor fall within this most disadvantaged category (Littman, 1989; Children's Defense Fund, 1991).

Poverty means hunger. Estimates suggest that some 20 million people in the United States experience daily hunger (Schwartz-Nobel, 1981; Physician Task Force on Hunger, 1987). Estimates by the Children's Defense

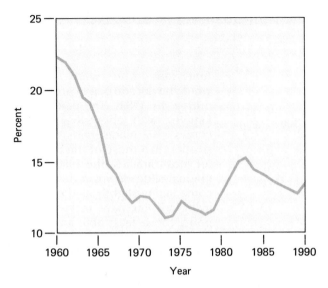

**Figure 10–4**   The Poverty Rate in the United States, 1960–1990

(*U.S. Bureau of the Census*)

Fund (1991) suggest that ten thousand children may die each year for various reasons stemming from poverty, making low income the leading cause of death among the youngest members of our society. We have the resources to eradicate poverty among children in the United States; the Children's Defense Fund claims that the $28 billion needed annually to end child poverty roughly equals what the country has been spending each year to bail out the savings and loan industry and is far less than the additional income received in 1990 alone by the richest one percent of families as a result of tax reforms carried out in recent years.

## Who Are the Poor?

Although no single description covers all poor people, poverty is pronounced among certain categories of our population. Children, people of color, women, and those who live in rural areas are all at higher risk of being poor. Where these categories overlap, the problem of poverty is especially serious.

### Age

The burden of poverty falls most heavily on children. In 1990, 20.6 percent of people under age eighteen (almost 13 million children) were officially classified as poor. From another perspective, four in ten poor Americans are children under the age of eighteen.

A generation ago, the elderly were at greatest risk for poverty. The poverty rate for women and men over the age of sixty-five was 12.2 percent in 1990 (yielding just over 3 million elderly poor); this rate is below the overall poverty rate of about 13 percent. In 1967, 30 percent of the elderly were poor; the figure has fallen dramatically because of greater support from government and private employers. Even so, the growing number of older people means that about 11 percent of the poor are elderly.

### Race and Ethnicity

Two-thirds of all poor people are white; about 30 percent are black. But in relation to their overall numbers, African Americans are about three times as likely as whites to be poor. In 1990, 32 percent of African Americans (almost 10 million people) lived in poverty, compared to about 28 percent of Hispanics (more than 6 million), 14 percent of Asians and Pacific Islanders (1 million), and 11 percent of non-Hispanic whites (about 17 million). During the 1980s, the "poverty gap" between the races increased (U.S. Bureau of the Census, 1991).

Since both children and people of color are disproportionately poor, minority children are especially likely to live in poverty. About 20 percent of all boys and girls under the age of eighteen were poor in 1990; this included 15 percent of white children, 36 percent of young Hispanics, and 44 percent of black youth.

### Gender and Family Patterns

Of all poor people over age eighteen, 63 percent are women and 37 percent are men. This disparity reflects the fact that women who head households bear the brunt of poverty. On their shoulders falls the financial burden of raising children, which makes working for income difficult. For those able to work, low-paying jobs are the norm. Of all poor families, 53 percent are headed by women with no husband present. In marked contrast, only 5 percent of poor families are headed by single men.

Because of the link between single-parent families and poverty, divorce typically threatens the economic security of children. Andrew Cherlin (1990) concludes that the income of single-parent families typically plummets by more than a third within several months of divorce or separation. Mothers living alone with their

A widespread stereotype links poverty to people of color in the inner cities of the United States. Although minorities are more likely to be disadvantaged, most poor people in the United States are white. Furthermore, although inner cities have the greatest concentration of poverty, rural people are actually at higher risk of poverty than their urban counterparts.

children face a disproportionate measure of economic hardship.

Sociologists investigating women's increased risk of poverty describe a process called the **feminization of poverty,** *the trend by which women represent an increasing proportion of the poor.* The box on page 284 takes a closer look at this phenomenon.

### Area of Residence

The highest poverty rate is found among people who live in central cities: about 18 percent in 1990. For all of urban America, however, the poverty rate was 13 percent—actually lower than the 16 percent found in rural areas. Generally speaking, living in cities raises living standards because job opportunities and social services are concentrated there. This is true even though urban areas encompass the largest pockets of poverty. Suburban areas, too, have their share of poverty, but less so (8 percent) than the inner cities.

## Explaining Poverty

The presence of tens of millions of poor people in one of the world's most affluent societies raises serious social and moral concerns. But it also sparks considerable controversy, as noted in Figure 10–5. The figure presents the results of a recent survey that asked a representative sample of adults in the United States whether they expect the government or poor people themselves to take the lead in combating poverty. The results suggest that people are divided on this issue, and many more are of two minds. One-third of respondents thought the government should do more, but more than one-fifth countered that people should take responsibility for themselves. Note, further, that more than 40 percent agreed with both contentions. We now turn to arguments underlying each of these two approaches to the problem of low income, which together frame a lively and pressing political debate.

Proponents of one side of the issue hold the following view: *The poor are primarily responsible for their own poverty.* Throughout our history, Americans have

**Figure 10–5** Government or People: Who Is Responsible for Poverty?

*(General Social Surveys, 1972–1991: Cumulative Codebook. Chicago: National Opinion Research Center, 1991:324)*

Question: "Some people think that the government in Washington should do everything possible to improve the living standards of all poor Americans [they are at point 1 below]. Other people think it is not the government's responsibility, and that each person should take care of himself [they are at point 5 below]. Where would you place yourself on this scale, or haven't you made up your mind on this?"

| 1 | 2 | 3 | 4 | 5 | Don't know, no answer |
|---|---|---|---|---|---|
| 16.8 | 16.1 | 42.8 | 13.0 | 8.1 | 3.2 |
| I strongly agree the government should improve living standards | | I agree with both answers | | I strongly agree that people should take care of themselves | |

# Why Poverty Is a Women's Issue

In 1978, Diana Pearce first coined the term *feminization of poverty* to designate the correlation between gender and low income. This idea has been widely used by sociologists ever since. What, exactly, does it mean?

To answer this question, we must carefully examine the changing profile of the poor in the United States. Gender can be linked to poverty in two ways. First, we could start by examining *all families headed by women,* and determine what percentage of them are poor. Conversely, we might begin with *all poor families,* and see what proportion are headed by women. Using government data, very different pictures emerge from the two approaches.

First, we shall investigate what proportion of families headed by women are poor. In 1960, more than 40 percent of families with a female head of household were poor; the figure fell to almost 30 percent by 1980, and rose during the last decade to about 32 percent in 1990. The green line in the accompanying figure represents this trend. Based on this approach, the conclusion is clear: *The proportion of all families headed by women that are in poverty has generally declined since 1960.* This trend *cannot* be described as the "feminization of poverty."

The second relationship turns out to be what we are looking for. In 1960, about 25 percent of all poor families were headed by women; most of the remainder had both wives and husbands present. By 1990, however, the propor-

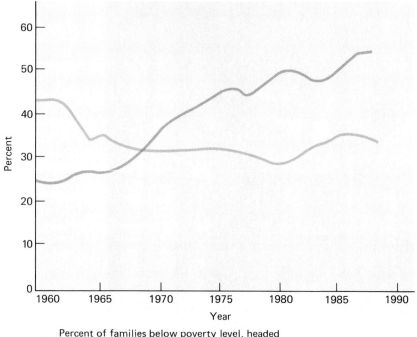

Percent of families below poverty level, headed by a female with no husband present.

Percent of female-headed families, with no husband present, below the poverty level.

**Poverty and Gender, 1960–1990**

(*U.S. Bureau of the Census*)

tion of poor families with no husband present had increased to more than 50 percent. The purple line in the figure represents this process. Thus the "feminization of poverty" emerges when we consider the following point: *The proportion of poor families that are headed by women (with no husband present) has increased over time.*

The number of families headed by women in the United States—including all income levels—roughly doubled between 1960 and 1990. Interestingly, the number of families headed by relatively affluent women is actually increasing faster than the number of families headed by poor women. But women who head households remain at great risk of being poor, and these women and their children represent an increasing share of our country's poor. The "feminization of poverty," then, designates the fact that a rising proportion of poor families are headed by women.

embraced the notion that people are largely responsible for their own social standing. This approach assumes that our society offers considerable opportunity for anyone able and willing to take advantage of it. The poor, then, are those with fewer skills, less schooling, lower motivation, or, perhaps, a debilitating drug addiction—in sum, people who are somehow undeserving. This view is expressed, in various degrees, on the right side of the continuum in Figure 10–5.

Anthropologist Oscar Lewis (1961) illustrates this approach in his studies of Latin American poverty. Lewis claims that the poor become entrapped in a *culture of poverty* that fosters resignation to one's plight as a matter of fate. Socialized in this environment, children come to believe that there is little point to aspiring to a better life. The result is a self-perpetuating cycle of poverty, at least as long as people tolerate their condition.

Edward Banfield (1974) adds the contention that, especially in areas of intense poverty such as the inner cities, there exists a distinctive lower-class subculture that denigrates and erodes personal achievement. One element of this subculture, a present-time orientation, encourages living for the moment rather than looking toward the future by engaging in hard work, saving, and other behavior likely to promote upward social mobility. In Banfield's view, poor people who live largely for the moment perpetuate their own poverty; he defines this kind of behavior as basically irresponsible, and he concludes that the poor reap more or less what they deserve.

The other view of the issue follows this reasoning: *Society is primarily responsible for poverty*. This alternative position, argued by William Ryan (1976), holds that society—not the poor—is responsible for poverty because of the way it distributes resources. Looking at this problem in global context, societies that distribute wealth very unequally (including the United States) face a significant poverty problem; societies that strive for more equality (such as Sweden and Japan) lack such extremes in income.

Poverty, Ryan insists, is not inevitable; this problem is simply a matter of low incomes, not personal deficiencies. Ryan interprets any lack of ambition on the part of poor people as a *consequence* rather than a *cause* of their lack of opportunity. He therefore dismisses Banfield's analysis as little more than "blaming the victims" for their own suffering. In Ryan's view, social policies that empower the poor would give them real economic opportunity, and this should yield greater equality. In Figure 10–5, the positions on the left side of the continuum express support for action by the government to reduce poverty.

African-American artist Henry O. Tanner (1859–1937) captured the humility and humanity of the impoverished people in his painting *Thankful Poor*. This insight is important in a society that tends to dismiss poor people as morally unworthy and deserving of their bitter plight.

(*Henry O. Tanner,* Thankful Poor. *1894. Oil on canvas. 35 x 44". William H. and Camille O. Cosby Collection.*)

*Critical evaluation.* Each of these explanations of poverty has won its share of public support, and each has advocates among government policy makers. As Banfield sees it, society should strive to encourage equality of opportunity, but should otherwise adopt a laissez-faire attitude toward the poor. Ryan holds that society should actively reduce poverty by redistributing income in a more equitable manner. This could be accomplished through programs like a comprehensive child-care package that would allow poor mothers to gain skills necessary to maintain jobs or a guaranteed minimum income for every family.

Little hard evidence conclusively validates either of these approaches; most research about the poor is subject to various interpretations. But data reflecting patterns of work among the poor are suggestive. Banfield's position gains support from government data showing that half the heads of poor families did not work at all during 1990. In fact, only one in five heads of families in poverty worked steadily (at least fifty weeks) during that year (U.S. Bureau of the Census, 1991). From this point of view, then, the major cause of poverty is *not holding a job.*

But the *reasons* that people do not work seem more consistent with Ryan's position. Most women who are poor claim they cannot work because they need to care for their children. In the United States, few employers provide child-care programs for workers, and few low-paid workers can afford to obtain child care on their own. Most poor men report that either there are no jobs to be found, illness or disability has sidelined them, or, in the case of the elderly, they have retired. Overall, poor adults in the United States feel they have few options and alternatives (Popkin, 1990).

But not all poor people are jobless. The 20 percent of poor heads of families (1.4 million people) who work full time are included in the *working poor*; these men and women labor for at least fifty weeks of the year and yet cannot escape poverty. Another 25 percent of these heads of families (1.5 million people) remained poor despite working between 26 and 29 weeks, and an additional 4 percent (about 300,000 people) worked 25 weeks or less (U.S. Bureau of the Census, 1991). Such "working poverty" places the poor in a bind: their jobs provide low wages that barely allow them to make ends meet, but consume the time and energy needed to obtain training or schooling that might open new doors. Most are reluctant to risk the job they do have in hopes of finding something better (Levitan & Shapiro, 1987). For most of the 1980s, the minimum wage remained at $3.35; it rose to $4.25 in 1991. Even at this higher level, a full-time worker could not support a family above the official poverty line.

Clearly, individual ability and initiative play a part in shaping everyone's social position. On balance, though, evidence points to society—not individual character traits—as the primary source of poverty. Some poor people do lack ambition. Overall, however, the poor are *categories* of people—women heads of families, minorities, people isolated from the larger society in inner-city areas—without the same opportunities as others.

## Homelessness

Many low-income people in the United States lack the resources to support even basic housing; as a society, we have failed to ensure an adequate supply of affordable housing. In light of the enormous wealth of the United States and its commitment to providing opportunity for everyone, homelessness may be fairly described as a scar on our society that demands an effective response (Schutt, 1989).

There is no precise count of homeless people. The Census Bureau carried out a tally of the homeless during the night of March 20, 1991; they found 178,828 people at shelters and 49,793 on the streets in neighborhoods where homeless people are known to live. Officials stressed that this was not intended as an enumeration of homeless people; it merely helped the Census Bureau more accurately estimate the entire population of the United States (U.S. Bureau of the Census, 1991). One limitation of such estimates is that homelessness is not just an urban problem; homeless families can be found in rural counties across the United States, even if the greatest concentrations of the homeless are in cities. One recent study concluded that there are some 20,000 homeless people in rural areas just in the state of Ohio (Toomey, First, & Rife, 1990). If the numbers could be tallied, experts suggest, we would find that about 500,000 people are homeless *on any given night* and three times this number—1.5 million Americans—are homeless *for some time during the course of any year* (Kozol, 1988; Wright, 1989).

The familiar stereotypes of homeless people—men sleeping in doorways and women carrying everything they own in a shopping bag—have recently been undermined by the reality of the "new homeless," those thrown out of work because of plant closings, people forced out of apartments by rising rents or condominium conversions, and others unable to meet mortgage or rent payments because they must work for low wages. Today, no stereotype of the homeless paints a complete picture because such people are now a highly varied segment of our society.

But virtually all homeless people have one status in common: *poverty.* For that reason, the approaches already used in explaining poverty also apply to homelessness. One side of the debate places responsibility on *personal* traits of the homeless themselves. Perhaps one-third of homeless people are mentally ill; others are addicted to alcohol or other drugs. Some, for whatever reason, seem unable to cope in a complex and highly competitive society (Bassuk, 1984; Whitman, 1989). On the other side of the debate, advocates assert that homelessness results from *societal* factors, including a lack of low-income housing in the United States and the economic transition toward low-paying jobs described earlier (Kozol, 1988; Shutt, 1989). Advocates of this position are quick to point out that fully one-third of all homeless people are now entire families, and children are the fastest growing category of the homeless. A minister living in a Pennsylvania town that has lost hundreds of industrial jobs due to plant closings describes the real-life effects of economic recession:

> Yes, there are new jobs. There's a new McDonald's and a Burger King. You can take home $450 in a month from jobs like that. That might barely pay the rent. What do you do if someone gets sick? What do you do for food and clothes? These may be good jobs for a teenager. Can you ask a thirty-year-old man who's worked for GM since he was eighteen to keep his wife and kids alive on jobs like that? There are jobs cleaning rooms in the hotel . . . Can you expect a single mother with three kids to hold her life together with that kind of work? (Kozol, 1988:6)

No one disputes that a large proportion of homeless people are personally impaired to some degree, although how much is cause and how much effect is difficult to untangle. But structural changes in the U.S. economy, sliding incomes among the poor segments of the population during the 1980s, and government policies that reduced support for lower-income people have all contributed to homelessness.

A comprehensive response to homelessness must consider both personal and societal dimensions of the problem. Increasing the supply of low-income housing (other than shelters) is one important step. Additionally, low-income people must have the opportunity to earn the income necessary to pay for housing. Homelessness,

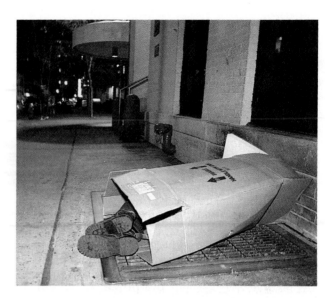

The increase in homelessness during the 1980s intensified the controversy over poverty in the United States. Some homeless people have personal problems that render them unable to cope with a demanding world. But how much of this is cause and how much is effect remains a hotly contested issue. What is clear is that major causes of rising homelessness include economic stagnation, a declining stock of low-income housing, and cutbacks in social service programs.

however, is not only a housing problem; it is also a *human* problem. People who endure months or years of insecure living come to need various types of social services. John Coleman, the college president whose experience as a homeless man was described at the beginning of this chapter, identified the personal injury caused by even short-term homelessness. His experience illustrates that solving the problem of homelessness also means coming to terms with the social damage inflicted by poverty.

## Class and Welfare, Politics and Values

This chapter has presented a great many facts about social class in the United States. In the end, however, our understanding of what it means to be wealthy and privileged or poor and perhaps homeless also turns on politics and values. Understandably, support for the notion that social standing reflects personal merit is strongest among people who are well-off. The idea that society should distribute wealth and other resources more equally finds greatest favor among those with relatively few advantages (Rytina, Form, & Pease, 1970; N.O.R.C., 1991).

The perceptions of *everyone* are shaped by cultural values that hold people responsible for their own life circumstances. When a random sample of adults was asked, "How important is hard work for getting ahead in life?" almost 90 percent responded that it was "essential" or "very important" (N.O.R.C., 1991:549). Such cultural values encourage us to see successful people as personally meritorious and the poor as personally deficient. Richard Sennett and Jonathan Cobb (1973) called this judgment, applied to the poor, the *hidden injury of class.* In other words, poverty significantly lowers the self-image of disadvantaged people, while others display their affluence as a personal "badge of ability." Values supporting individual responsibility also contribute to the historically negative view of social welfare programs and those who receive public assistance in the United States (Waxman, 1983; Handler & Hasenfeld, 1991). While advocates for the poor defend welfare programs as necessary for millions of people lacking opportunities and advantages, our cultural values promote the view that social welfare programs undermine initiative. Accepting assistance of this kind thus becomes personally demeaning, which helps explain why half the people eligible for various forms of needed assistance do not apply for it (U.S. Bureau of the Census, 1991).

Curiously, this same value system paints a more positive picture of government benefits provided to allegedly "deserving" well-to-do men and women. Current tax law, for example, allows homeowners to deduct from their taxable income interest paid on home mortgages as well as real estate tax payments. The tax savings realized from this policy—which, of course, goes into the pockets of people affluent enough to own their own homes—amounts to more than $40 billion annually, over *five times* the amount the government spends to help house the poor. Our cultural tendency to equate privilege with personal merit leads us to wink at "wealthfare" while denouncing welfare for the poor. Such attitudes guide government policy, aggravating rather than minimizing social inequality.

Finally, the drama of social stratification extends far beyond the borders of the United States. The most striking social disparities are found not by looking inside one country but by comparing living standards in various parts of the world. In Chapter 11, we broaden our investigation of social stratification, focusing on global inequality.

## Summary

1. Social inequality in the United States involves disparities in a host of variables, including income, wealth, and power.

2. White-collar occupations generally confer more prestige and higher incomes than blue-collar jobs. The pink-collar occupations typically held by women offer little social prestige or income.

3. Schooling is also a resource that is distributed unequally. About three-fourths of people over age twenty-five have completed high school, but only one-fifth are college graduates.

4. Ascription exerts a powerful effect on stratification in the United States; ancestry, race and ethnicity, gender, and religion are all related to social position.

5. The upper class, which is small (about 4 percent), includes the richest and most powerful families. Members of the upper-upper class, or the old rich, derive their wealth through inheritance over several generations; those in the lower-upper class, or the new rich, depend on earned income as their primary source of wealth.

6. The middle class encompasses 40 to 45 percent of the population. The upper-middle class may be distinguished on the basis of higher income, higher-prestige occupations, and more schooling.

7. The working class comprises about one-third of our population. With below-average income, working-class families have less financial security than those in the middle class. Few working-class Americans attain more than a high-school education, and they commonly work in blue-collar or lower white-collar jobs.

8. About one-fifth of the population belong to the lower class. Most live near or below the official poverty threshold. People of African and Hispanic descent, and all women, are disproportionately represented in the lower class.

9. Social class affects nearly all aspects of life, beginning with health and life expectancy, and encompassing a wide range of attitudes and patterns of family living.

10. Social mobility is common in the United States, as it is in other industrial societies; typically, however, only small changes occur from one generation to the next.

11. Since the early 1970s, changes in the U.S. economy have reduced the standard of living for low- and moderate-income families. In one important trend, manufacturing industries have declined in the United States, paralleling growth in low-paying service-sector jobs.

12. Some 33 million people in the United States are officially classified as poor. About 40 percent of the poor are children under the age of eighteen. Two-thirds of the poor are white, but African Americans and Hispanic Americans are disproportionately represented among low-income people. A growing share of poor families are headed by women.

13. Oscar Lewis and Edward Banfield advanced the "culture of poverty" thesis, suggesting how poverty can be perpetuated by the social patterns of the poor themselves. Opposing this view, William Ryan argues that poverty is caused by the unequal distribution of wealth in society. Although Banfield's view is consistent with our society's cultural pattern of personalizing social position, Ryan's view is supported by more evidence.

## Key Concepts

**absolute poverty** a deprivation of resources that is life threatening

**feminization of poverty** the trend by which women represent an increasing proportion of the poor

**income** occupational wages or salaries and earnings from investments

**intergenerational social mobility** upward or downward social mobility of children in relation to their parents

**intragenerational social mobility** a change in social position occurring during a person's lifetime

**relative poverty** the deprivation of some people in relation to those who have more

**wealth** the total amount of money and valuable goods that any person or family controls

## Suggested Readings

This text explores in detail many of the issues raised in this chapter.

Michael D. Grimes. *Class in Twentieth-Century American Sociology: An Analysis of Theories and Measurement Strategies.* New York: Praeger, 1991.

The first of these books explains how the lives of privileged women differ from those of privileged men; the second argues that elite class standing does not override the significance of race in the United States.

Susan A. Ostrander. *Women of the Upper Class.* Philadelphia: Temple University Press, 1984.

Lois Benjamin. *The Black Elite: Facing the Color Line in the Twilight of the Twentieth Century.* Chicago: Nelson-Hall, 1991.

These readable and insightful books probe middle America during a time of economic decline.

Barbara Ehrenreich. *Fear of Falling: The Inner Life of the Middle Class.* New York: HarperCollins, 1990.

Reeve Vanneman and Lynn Weber Cannon. *The American Perception of Class.* Philadelphia: Temple University Press, 1987.

The first of these books on the American welfare system examines the history and theoretical underpinnings of current welfare policy. The second analyzes public assistance programs from a feminist point of view.

Joel F. Handler and Yeheskel Hasenfeld. *The Moral Construction of Poverty: Welfare Reform in America.* Newbury Park, CA: Sage, 1991.

Dorothy C. Miller. *Women and Social Welfare: A Feminist Analysis.* New York: Praeger, 1990.

This report by an advocacy group concerned with the well-being of children in the United States probes the growing problem of child poverty and proposes an agenda for change.

*Child Poverty in America.* Washington, DC: Children's Defense Fund, 1991.

# Global Inequality

Half an hour from the center of Cairo, Egypt's capital city, the bus turned onto a dirt road and jerked to a stop. It was not quite dawn, and the Mo'edhdhins would soon climb the minarets of Cairo's many mosques to call the Islamic faithful to morning prayers. The driver turned, genuinely bewildered, to the busload of students from the United States and their instructor. "Why," he said, mixing English with some Arabic, "do you want to be *here*? And in the middle of the night?"

Why, indeed? No sooner had we left the bus than smoke and stench, the likes of which we had never before encountered, overcame us. Eyes squinting, handkerchiefs pressed against noses and mouths, we moved slowly uphill along the path ascending mountains of trash and garbage that extended for miles. We had reached the Cairo Dump, where the fifteen million people of one of the world's largest cities deposit their trash and garbage.[1] We walked stiffly and with great care, since only a scattering of light came from small fires smoldering around us. Suddenly, spectral shapes appeared out of the shadows. After a moment, we identified them as dogs peering curiously through the curtain of haze. As startled as we were, they quickly turned and

vanished into the thick air. Ahead of us, we could see blazing piles of trash encircled by people seeking warmth and companionship.

Human beings actually inhabit this inhuman place, creating a surreal scene, like the aftermath of the next war. As we approached, the fires cast an eerie light on their faces. We stopped some distance from them, separated by a vast chasm of culture and circumstances. But smiles eased the tension, and soon we were sharing the comfort of their fire. At that moment, the melodious call to prayer sounded across the city.

The people of the Cairo Dump, called the Zebaleen, belong to a religious minority—Coptic Christians—in a predominantly Muslim society. Barred by religious discrimination from many jobs, the Zebaleen use donkey-carts and small trucks to pick up refuse throughout the city and bring it here. The night-long routine reaches a climax at dawn when the hundreds of Zebaleen gather at the dump, swarming over the new piles in search of anything of value. That morning, we watched men, women, and children accumulate bits of metal and ribbon, examine scraps of discarded food, and slowly fill their baskets with what would get them through another day. Every now and then, someone gleefully displayed a "precious" find that would bring the equivalent of a few dollars in the city. Watching in silence, we became keenly aware of our sturdy shoes and warm clothing, and self-conscious that our watches and cameras repre-

---

[1] This portrayal is based on the author's visit to the Cairo Dump in 1988 with more than 100 students. It also draws on the discussion found in Spates & Macionis, 1987, and conversations with James L. Spates, who has also traveled to the Cairo Dump.

291

sented more money than most of the Zebaleen earn in a year.

Although unfamiliar to most North Americans, the Zebaleen of the Cairo Dump are hardly unique. Their counterparts live in almost every country of the world. In poor societies around the globe, as we shall see, poverty is not only more widespread than in the United States, but also far more severe.

# The Importance of Global Perspective

Why should we study unfamiliar parts of the world, especially in a course primarily concerned with North America? Earlier chapters have explained that our society shapes how we behave, what we think, and even molds our self-image. Taken one step further, the same logic applies to the relationship of the United States to other nations. To understand our own society, we must explore how our part of the world fits into the larger global order. Extending the sociological perspective in this way is particularly important today, as political changes sweep through Latin America, Eastern Europe, the former Soviet Union (now the Commonwealth of Independent States), the Middle East, and South Africa, and rapid economic development reshapes many countries in Eastern Asia. All these global realignments affect the United States and the lives of each one of us.

This chapter highlights an important theme of the text: that our world has grown increasingly interdependent. St. Augustine, a scholar of the early Christian era, once described the world as a book, noting that those who concentrate only on their own society read just a single page. Beyond academic arguments, there is also a very practical reason to learn more about the larger world: success, for most workers of the twenty-first century, will depend on being "globally competent." No future investment banker in New York will be able to neglect what happens on the trading floor of the Tokyo stock exchange, just as no midwestern farmer will dare to ignore wheat production in Ukraine or Georgia. One-fifth of all economic activity in the United States now involves international trade, a proportion that has doubled since 1960. Looking ahead, analysts predict that 80 percent of new jobs in the United States will have an international component. The competitiveness of the U.S. economy depends on imbuing the workforce with

a global vision (Macionis, 1991). More broadly, making sound decisions about the future of our nation also depends on understanding the various roles the United States can play in the larger world order. For all these reasons—and with much of the contemporary world seized by political and economic change—looking beyond our own borders has never been more important than it is today.

# The Three Worlds

Just as Chapter 3 ("Culture") emphasized the need to recognize cultural variation in the world, this chapter focuses on the character, causes, and consequences of global inequality. While pronounced social stratification divides members of our society, the United States stands among the richest nations in the world. Because the average U.S. family is very well off by world standards, even most people living below our government's poverty threshold enjoy a much higher standard of living than the majority of those in the poorest nations on earth. We begin our study of global inequality by dividing the world's societies into three broad categories or "worlds."

First, however, a word of caution. There are roughly 180 nations on earth (the precise number changes frequently in response to political events). To sort them all into only three sweeping categories ignores striking differences in their ways of life. The societies in each category have rich and varied histories, speak dozens of languages, and encompass diverse peoples whose cultural distinctiveness serves as a source of pride. However, the three broad categories that follow are widely used to group societies together based on (1) their level of technological development and (2) their political and economic systems.

## The First World

The term **First World** refers to *industrial societies that have predominantly capitalist economies*. They are not called "first" because they are "better" or "more important" than other countries, but rather because the Industrial Revolution came first to these nations, beginning two centuries ago. Chapter 4 ("Society") explained that industrialization increases a society's productive capacity one hundred-fold, which greatly raises living standards.

Japan represents the First World, in which industrial technology and economic expansion have produced material prosperity. The presence of market forces is evident in this view of downtown Tokyo. The Commonwealth of Independent States is the leading nation in the Second World. Industrial development has been slower in the former Soviet Union, as socialist economies performed sluggishly. Residents of Moscow, for example, chafe at having to wait in long lines for their daily needs. The hope is that the introduction of a market system will raise living standards, although it probably will also increase economic disparity. Bangladesh represents the Third World. As this photograph suggests, these nations have limited economic development and rapidly increasing populations. The result is widespread poverty.

In historical context, the economic activity surrounding the care of household pets in the United States today exceeds the economic enterprise of all of Europe during the Middle Ages.

Global Map 11–1 on page 294 identifies nations of the First World. Shown in blue, this region includes the nations of Western Europe such as the United Kingdom (made up of England, Scotland, Wales, and Northern Ireland). It was in southeastern England that industrialization began about 1775. Also part of the First World are the United States and Canada in North America, where the Industrial Revolution got under way around 1850. On the African continent, the advanced economic development of South Africa places this country (more precisely, its *white minority*) in the First World. Israel stands alone in the Middle East as a First-World nation. Also ranking in the First World is Japan, the most economically powerful nation in Asia. And, in the world region known as Oceania, Australia and New Zealand belong to the First World.

Collectively, the First World covers roughly 25 percent of the earth's land area, includes parts of five continents, and lies mostly in the northern hemisphere. In 1992, the population of the First World was approaching 800 million, just over 15 percent of the earth's people. By global standards, the First World is not densely populated.

Despite significant cultural differences, First-World nations now share an industrial capacity that generates, on average, a rich material life for their people. The world's income is concentrated among the minority of humanity living in the First World. The economies of these nations are predominantly capitalist, so that a market system (or "private enterprise"), rather than government, controls most production. Since World War I, the United States has been the dominant nation (often

**Global Map 11–1** The Three Worlds

termed a "superpower") of the First World. Because the United States and Western Europe are linked by political and economic alliances, the First World is sometimes referred to as "the West."

## The Second World

The **Second World** is composed of *industrial societies that are currently transforming their socialist economies.* Industrialization took hold in much of this broad region of the world only in the twentieth century. This accounts,

in part, for the lesser economic strength of the Second World in relation to the First World. Second-World nations have less powerful industrial capacities: proportionately more of their people live in rural areas and remain in agricultural production. (Chapter 19, "The Economy and Work," compares the performance of capitalist and socialist economies.)

In Global Map 11–1, the Second World appears in red stripes. During this century, the dominant nation in the Second World was the Union of Soviet Socialist Republics (U.S.S.R.), which, in 1992, was recast as the Commonwealth of Independent States. The former

Soviet Union's military strength rivaled that of the United States, giving it "superpower" status. After World War II, the Soviet Union took control of most of Eastern Europe, including the Baltic countries, Poland, the German Democratic Republic (East Germany), Czechoslovakia, Hungary, Romania, and Bulgaria. In 1989, most of Eastern Europe was transformed by the popular overthrow of established socialist governments, the opening of borders to the West, and the call for Western-style market systems. Within a year, the "two Germanys" were rejoined, so that the united Germany is shown on the map as part of the First World. In 1991, change accelerated in the Soviet Union as well, as leaders ended the historic monopoly on power enjoyed by that nation's communist party. After the Baltic republics of Estonia, Latvia, and Lithuania won their independence, the remaining republics of the old Soviet Union formed the current new federation. Reform toward a market economy is currently underway throughout the new Commonwealth of Independent States. The future course of the Second World is unclear; perhaps the concept of a "second world" may soon be obsolete. For the present, the Soviet-led alliance that was long called the "Eastern bloc" appears to have disintegrated. In the future, no doubt, the political systems of these countries will continue to evolve.

The Second World spans roughly 15 percent of the earth's land area. Most of it lies in the Commonwealth of Independent States, which, stretching from Europe to Asia, is geographically the largest nation on earth. Roughly 500 million people or 10 percent of humanity live in the Second World. Like the First World, this region is not densely populated by global standards.

## The Third World

The **Third World** encompasses *primarily agrarian societies, in which most people are poor*. In these countries, economic activity centers on farming; in fact, slightly more than half of the world's people are rural peasants. Many are staunchly traditional, following the folkways of their ancestors. Industrial technology plays a limited role in the lives of such people; its impact is evident mostly in Third-World cities. With more simple technology, Third-World societies are less productive by world standards. This pattern holds true even though some Third-World countries—notably the oil-rich nations of the Middle East—have an extremely high average standard of living due to the great wealth of *some* of their people. Global Map 11–1 indicates that the Third World, shown in green, spans most of the globe. In our hemisphere, Third-World countries range from the poor, but industrializing, nation of Mexico, on the southern border

When natural disasters strike rich societies, property loss is great but loss of life is low; in poor societies, the converse is true. A cyclone recently devastated coastal Bangladesh, killing tens of thousands of people who had little choice but to live in regions prone to flooding. Tragically, most of those who survived remained there, hoping against the odds to escape future catastrophe.

of the United States, to all the nations of Central America and South America. Moving across the Atlantic Ocean, the continent of Africa (except for South Africa) falls into the Third World. Included, too, is the Middle East except Israel, and all of Asia except Japan.

The Third World represents about 60 percent of our planet's land area including most of the countries near and below the equator. More significantly, 77 percent of the world's 5.5 billion people live in the Third World. Population density is very high, ten times higher in India, for instance, than in the United States. Because of its large and rapidly increasing population, coupled with low economic productivity, the Third World faces poverty on a massive scale. Hunger, unsafe housing, and high rates of disease all plague Third-World nations.

Although they share poverty, less-developed societies have no single economic system in common. Some poor countries, such as the People's Republic of China (with 1.2 billion people, the world's most populous nation), maintain a predominantly socialist economy. Other nations, like India and Egypt, blend elements of government socialism and market capitalism. Still others, including Brazil and much of Latin America, have adopted a capitalist approach. We shall examine some of the consequences of the form of economic system a country embraces both in this chapter and in later chapters concerned with politics and economics. For now, we must recognize that all Third-World societies share a common plight: devastating poverty.

This identification of "three worlds" is the foundation for understanding the problem of global inequality. For people living in an affluent nation such as the United States, the scope of the problem is difficult to grasp. From time to time, televised scenes of famine in the poorest countries of the world, including Ethiopia and Bangladesh, give people in the United States a shocking glance at the absolute poverty that makes daily living a life-and-death struggle for so many. Behind these images lie cultural, historical, and economic forces that we shall explore in the remainder of this chapter.

## Third-World Poverty

Poverty always means suffering. Third-World poverty, however, typically involves more severe hardship than poverty in this country (see Chapter 10, "Social Class in the United States"). This does not mean, of course,

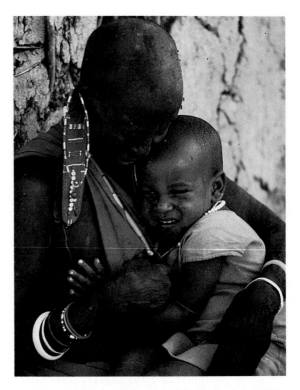

In all regions of the world, poverty falls hardest on children because they are vulnerable. But the ordeal of child poverty is especially severe in poor societies of the Third World for two additional reasons. First, children represent a larger share of the population; in many poor nations, 60 percent of the people are no older than their teens. Second, Third-World children have only a small share of the resources that most of us took for granted when we were at that stage of life.

that deprivation among Americans constitutes only a minor issue. Especially in a rich society, the lack of food, housing, and health care for tens of millions of people—many of them children—amounts to a national tragedy. Yet, in global perspective, poverty in the Third World is *more severe* and *more extensive* than in the United States.

### The Severity of Poverty

*Poverty in the Third World is more severe than it is in rich societies such as the United States.* The data in Table 11–1 suggest why. The first column of figures shows, for selected countries, the gross domestic product

**Table 11–1**   WEALTH AND WELL-BEING
IN GLOBAL PERSPECTIVE, 1990

| Country | Gross Domestic Product ($ billion) | Per-Person Income ($) | Quality of Life Index |
|---|---|---|---|
| **First World** | | | |
| Japan | 2,818 | 23,810 | .993 |
| Canada | 488 | 19,030 | .983 |
| Sweden | 167 | 21,570 | .982 |
| United States | 5,156 | 20,910 | .976 |
| United Kingdom | 717 | 14,610 | .967 |
| Germany | 1,189 | 20,440 | .959 |
| **Second World** | | | |
| Czechoslovakia | 50 | 9,709 | .920 |
| Hungary | 29 | 8,260 | .911 |
| Soviet Union | 2,000 | 8,662 | .908 |
| Bulgaria | 16 | 2,320 | .899 |
| Poland | 68 | 6,879 | .863 |
| **Third World** | | | |
| *Latin America* | | | |
| Argentina | 200 | 2,160 | .854 |
| Mexico | 400 | 2,010 | .838 |
| Brazil | 319 | 2,540 | .759 |
| Colombia | 39 | 1,200 | .757 |
| Nicaragua | 3 | 850 | .612 |
| El Salvador | 6 | 1,070 | .524 |
| Bolivia | 5 | 620 | .416 |
| *Africa/Middle East* | | | |
| Saudi Arabia | 80 | 6,020 | .697 |
| Lebanon | 3 | 1,150 | .592 |
| Iran | 150 | 3,200 | .577 |
| Egypt | 32 | 640 | .394 |
| Cameroon | 11 | 1,000 | .328 |
| Zaire | 10 | 260 | .299 |
| Nigeria | 29 | 250 | .242 |
| Burkina Faso | 2 | 350 | .081 |
| Sierra Leone | 220 | 890 | .048 |
| *Asia* | | | |
| Hong Kong | 53 | 10,300 | .934 |
| South Korea | 211 | 4,400 | .884 |
| Thailand | 69 | 1,220 | .713 |
| P. R. of China | 417 | 350 | .614 |
| Pakistan | 36 | 370 | .311 |
| India | 235 | 340 | .308 |
| Bangladesh | 20 | 180 | .186 |

SOURCES: United Nations Development Programme, *Human Development Report 1991*, New York: Oxford University Press, 1991; The World Bank, *World Development Report 1991: The Challenge of Development*, New York: Oxford University Press, 1991.

(GDP).[2] Industrial societies typically have a high economic output due mainly to their productive industrial technology. A large, First-World nation like the United States had a 1990 GDP of more than $5 trillion; the GDP of the former Soviet Union, the largest Second-World country, stood at about $2 trillion. The rest of the table shows that Third-World countries around the globe, with little industrial technology, had far lower GDPs.

The second column of figures in Table 11–1 indicates "per-person income" for these countries, calculated by dividing the country's economic output by the total population. The resulting figures for First-World nations are relatively high—topping $20,000 for the United States, for example. Income levels in Second-World societies are significantly lower than those in the First World. But the most dramatic difference involves the Third World. In many poor societies, per-person income is below $1,000 a year. At roughly $180, per-capita income in Bangladesh amounts to less than 1 percent of that found in the United States. In simple terms, this means that the typical person in this poor Asian nation labors all year to make what the average worker in the United States earns in several days.[3]

The third column of Table 11–1 provides a measure of the quality of life in the various nations. Income is obviously one important component of well-being, although certainly not the only one. The index used here, calculated by the United Nations, reflects not only income but education (adult literacy and average years of schooling) and longevity (how long people typically live). Index values are decimals that fall between hypothetical extremes of 1 (highest) and zero (lowest). Japan has the highest rating of world societies (.993), and the African nation of Sierra Leone has the lowest (.048). The United

---

[2] Gross domestic product refers to all the goods and services produced by a society's economy in a given year. Income earned abroad by individuals or corporations is excluded from this measure, differentiating GDP from gross national product (GNP), which includes foreign earnings. For countries that invest heavily abroad (Kuwait, for example) GDP is considerably less than GNP; for countries in which other nations invest heavily (Hong Kong), GDP is considerably higher than GNP. For societies that both invest heavily abroad and have considerable foreign investment (including the United States), the two measures are comparable. For the present purpose, simply notice the striking differences in the power of the various world economies.

[3] The per-person income figures for the poorest of the world's societies are understated to the extent that they exclude products grown for home consumption or bartered with others. But even if the figures were doubled to neutralize this bias, per-capita income of Third-World societies remains well below that of rich nations.

States has a quality of life index of .976, placing us ninth in the world (United Nations Development Programme, 1991).

One key reason that quality of life differs so dramatically among the societies of the world is that economic productivity is lowest in precisely the regions of the globe where population is highest. Figure 11–1 shows the division of global income and population for each of the "three worlds." The First World is by far the most advantaged: here two-thirds of the world's income is spread among only 15 percent of the world's people. The people of the Second World are less well off, but they, too, claim a disproportionately large share of global income. In the Third World, 20 percent of global income supports a full 75 percent of humanity. Factoring together income and population, for every dollar received by a Third-World worker, a person in the Second World takes home five dollars and a worker in the First World earns sixteen dollars.

Bear in mind that, beyond overarching global patterns, each society is *internally* stratified. As a result, affluent Americans live worlds apart from the most disadvantaged people on our planet, such as Cairo's Zebaleen, described in the chapter opening.

**Figure 11–1**  The Relative Share of Global Income by World Region

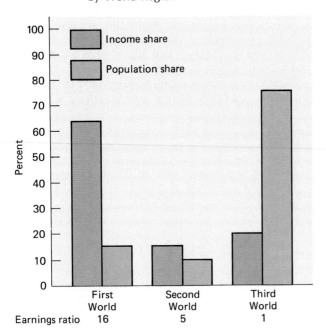

Earnings ratio   16        5        1

**Relative Versus Absolute Poverty**

A distinction made in the last chapter has an important application to global inequality. The members of rich societies typically focus on the *relative poverty* of some of their members, highlighting how some people lack resources that are taken for granted by others. Relative poverty, by definition, exists in every society, even in the First World. But especially important in a global context is the concept of *absolute poverty*, a lack of resources that is life threatening. Commonly, human beings living in absolute poverty lack the nutrition necessary for health and long-term survival.

In a rich society like the United States, most people described as poor are deprived in the relative sense. That is, women, men, and children fall short of the standard of living that we like to think is the birthright of everyone in our society. But absolute poverty, too, exists in the United States. Inadequate nutrition that leaves children or elderly people vulnerable to illness and even outright starvation a stark and tragic reality. By global standards, however, immediately life-threatening poverty in the United States strikes only a small proportion of the population. Third-World societies face a severe problem of absolute poverty, involving one-fifth of the population—1 billion people—who lack nutrition adequate for a safe and productive life.

## The Extent of Poverty

*Poverty in the Third World is more extensive than it is in the United States.* Chapter 10 ("Social Class in the United States") indicated that 13.5 percent of the U.S. population is officially classified as poor. In the societies of the Third World, however, *most* people live no better than the poor in our country, and at any given time, about 20 percent of Third-World people are near absolute poverty. In some parts of the world (such as East Asia), the extent of absolute poverty is not so great; in other regions (rural areas in Central America and Africa, for example), half the population is malnourished. In the world as a whole, 100 million people have no shelter and approximately 1 billion people do not eat enough to allow them to work regularly. Of these, at least 800 million are at risk for their lives (Sivard, 1988; Helmuth, 1989; United Nations Development Programme, 1991).

Global Map 11–2 on page 300 illustrates nutritional resources in various world regions. If anything, the problem in the First World is too much nutrition: on average,

The United States enjoys a large share of the world's wealth. Even so, the standard of living of the poorest of our people is little better than that of the poor throughout the Third World. The plight of some children growing up in New York's Harlem (left) is remarkably similar to that of many children in Nicaragua.

a person living in the First World consumes more than 3,500 calories daily, which contributes to obesity and related health problems. People in much of the Third World, by contrast, do not have adequate nutrition. Especially in parts of central Africa, the problem of hunger regularly reaches crisis proportions.

Simply stated, in many parts of the world, people die every minute of every day from lack of basic nutrition. In the ten minutes it takes to read through this section of the chapter, about three hundred people in the world will die of starvation. This amounts to more than 40,000 people a day, or 15 million people each year. Even more than in the United States, the burden of poverty in the Third World falls on children. Across the Third World, about one child in four dies before reaching the age of five.

Two further comparisons suggest the human toll of global poverty. First, at the end of World War II, the United States obliterated the Japanese city of Hiroshima with an atomic bomb. The worldwide loss of life from starvation reaches the Hiroshima death toll *every three days*. Second, the death toll from hunger in just the last five years equals the number of deaths from war, revolution, and murder during the last 150 years (Burch, 1983). Given the magnitude of this problem, easing world hunger is one of the most serious responsibilities facing humanity today.

## Third-World Women: Work and Poverty

Even more than in rich societies, in the Third World women are disproportionately the poorest of the poor. In societies poor to begin with, the opportunities for women are sharply limited by traditions that accord them primary responsibility for child rearing and maintaining the household.

Especially in rural regions of the Third World, women have historically worked long hours—typically twelve hours a day for women compared to about eight hours for men (House of Representatives, 1988). Much of women's work—cleaning and repairing the home, gathering firewood, traveling to and from the market, tending to the needs of children, and preparing meals for the family—remains "invisible" to those who monitor the labor force. In comparison to rich societies, in the Third World more of women's work is not paid, making the economic position of women correspondingly weaker.

Even Third-World women who work for pay are at a greater disadvantage than their counterparts in rich societies. As Chapter 13 ("Sex and Gender") details, in the United States and the rest of the industrialized world, women receive less income for their efforts than men do. In the largely agrarian societies of the Third World, traditional subordination of women to men is more pro-

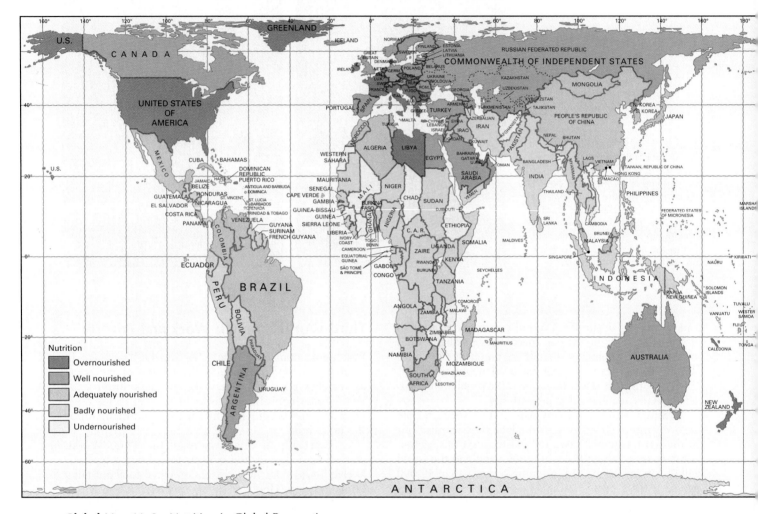

**Global Map 11–2** Nutrition in Global Perspective

To remain healthy, an average, active adult requires 2,500 to 3,000 calories a day in food energy. Women and men in many poor societies are not well nourished: hundreds of millions of people survive on fewer than 2,000 calories daily despite engaging in extensive physical labor. By contrast, members of rich societies are typically overnourished—consuming in excess of 3,500 calories each day—just as they are less active physically. Although not as immediately life threatening as undernourishment, overconsumption contributes to obesity and a host of longer-term health problems.

Life for both women and men throughout the Third World is more often than not a matter of continual labor to meet basic needs. But because social inequality between the sexes is pronounced in agrarian societies, the relative disadvantages endured by women are greater than for women living in industrial societies.

nounced, making the gender differences in salary even greater. Third-World women have less access to education than men have, a pattern that has diminished in industrial societies (United Nations, 1988). Lacking education, Third-World women have far fewer choices about their lives.

Finally, the United Nations estimates that roughly 90 percent of land in the Third World is formally owned by men (in rich societies, men control a lesser proportion of wealth). In reality, wives and mothers exert considerable control over property that formally belongs to husbands and sons. Nevertheless, strong traditions reinforced by law give men ultimate control of the land, the chief source of wealth in agrarian societies.

Overall, then, Third-World poverty is both severe and extensive. The burden of poverty is heavy, and it is not shared equally; women are generally among the most disadvantaged.

## Correlates of Third-World Poverty

What accounts for severe and extensive poverty in the Third World? The rest of this chapter weaves together explanations from the following facts about poor societies.

1. **Technology.** The Third World is largely agrarian, lacking the productive power of industrial technol-ogy. Energy from human muscles or beasts of burden falls far short of the force from steam, oil, or nuclear fuels; this technological disparity limits the use of complex machinery. Moreover, the focus in agrarian societies on farming, rather than on specialized production, limits the need to develop human skills and abilities.

2. **Population growth.** As Chapter 21 ("Population and Urbanization") explains in detail, Third-World societies have the highest birth rates in the world. Despite high death rates from poverty, the populations of poor societies in Africa, for example, double every twenty-five years. In such countries, more than half the people are not yet through their teens so that they are just entering their childbearing years. Future population growth, therefore, looms large. Even a developing economy would not be able to support the inevitable surges in population. Typically, then, economic growth is overwhelmed by population growth, resulting in little or no real increase in people's standard of living.

3. **Cultural patterns.** Societies yet to industrialize usually embrace tradition. Families and community groups pass down folkways and mores from generation to generation. Adhering to long-established ways of life, such people resist innovations—even those that promise a richer material life.

# India: A Different Kind of Poverty

Most North Americans know that India is one of the poorest societies on earth: typical personal income in this Asian nation stands at only $340 a year (see Table 11–1). Hunger pervades this vast society, where one-third of the world's starving people can be found. But few members of our society fully comprehend the reality of poverty in India. Most of the country's 750 million people live in conditions far worse than those of us who are labeled as "poor." A traveler's first experience of Indian life is sobering and sometimes shocking; in time, however, the outsider learns that, in India, people understand poverty differently than we do.

Arriving in Madras, one of India's largest cities, a visitor immediately recoils from the smell of human sewage, which hangs over the city like a malodorous cloud. Untreated sewage also renders much of the region's water unsafe to drink. The sights and sounds of Madras are strange and intense—streets are choked by motorbikes, trucks, carts pulled by oxen, and waves of people. Along the roads, vendors sitting on burlap cloth hawk fruits, vegetables, and prepared foods. Seemingly oblivious to the urban chaos all around them, people work, talk, bathe, and sleep in the streets. Tens of millions of homeless people fill the cities of India.

Madras is also dotted by more than a thousand shanty settle-

Third-World societies may be poor, but strong traditions and vital families place everyone in a network of social support. Thus people endure poverty with the help of their kin, which contrasts to the often isolating poverty in the United States.

ments, home to roughly half a million people, many of whom converge on the city from traditional rural villages in search of a better life. Shantytowns are clusters of huts constructed of branches, leaves, and discarded material. These dwellings offer little privacy and no refrigeration, running water, or bathrooms. The visitor from the United States understandably feels uneasy entering such a community, since the poorest sections of our inner cities abound with frustration and, oftentimes, out-

right violence. But here, too, India offers a sharp contrast. No angry young people hang out at the corner, no drugs pervade the area, and there is surprisingly little danger. Instead, the social units of shantytowns are strong families—children, parents, and sometimes elderly grandparents—who extend a smile and a welcome. In traditional societies like India, ways of life change little, even over many generations. Moreover, the lives of traditional Indians are shaped by *dharma*—the Hindu concept of duty and destiny—that presses people to accept their fate, whatever it may be. Mother Teresa, who has won praise for her work among the poorest of India's people, goes to the heart of the cultural differences: "Americans have angry poverty," she explains. "In India, there is worse poverty, but it is a happy poverty."

No one who lives on the edge of survival can be called truly "happy." The deadly horror of poverty in India, however, is eased by the strength of families and traditional communities, a sense of purpose to life, and a world view that encourages each person to accept whatever society offers. As a result, the visitor comes away from the first encounter with Indian poverty in confusion: "How can people be so poor, and yet apparently content, vibrant, and so *alive*?"

SOURCE: Based on the author's research in Madras, India, November, 1988.

The members of poor societies often accept their fate, although it may be bleak, in order to maintain a sense of family vitality and cultural heritage. Although such attitudes discourage development, they bolster strong social bonds. The box explains why traditional people in India respond to their poverty differently than poor people in the United States generally do.

4. **Social stratification.** The modest wealth of Third-World societies is distributed very unequally among their people. Chapter 9 ("Social Stratification") explained that social inequality is more pronounced in agrarian societies, where land is a vital resource, than in industrial societies. In the farming regions of Bangladesh in Central Asia, for example, 10 percent of all landowners own more than half the land, while almost half of farming families possess little or no land of their own (Hartmann & Boyce, 1982). According to another estimate, the richest 10 percent of landowners in Central America control more than three-fourths of the region's land (Barry, 1983). Such concentrations of land and wealth have prompted widespread demands for land reform in many agrarian societies.

5. **Global power relationships.** A final cause of global poverty lies in the relationships among the nations of the world. Much of the wealth of the Third World has enriched the First World. Historically, this stems from **colonialism,** *the process by which some nations enrich themselves through political and economic control of other countries.* The societies of Western Europe colonized and maintained control over much of Latin America for more than 300 years; much of Africa endured a century of colonization; parts of Asia were also under domination by colonial powers for long periods. Some analysts claim that this global exploitation spurred certain nations to *develop* economically at the expense of others that were systematically *underdeveloped.*

During the twentieth century, about 130 former colonies gained their independence, leaving only a small number of countries as formal colonies today (Strang, 1990). As we shall see, however, a continuing pattern of domination has emerged. **Neocolonialism** (*neo* comes from Greek, meaning "new") amounts to *a new form of international, economic exploitation that involves not direct political control but the operation of multinational corporations.* **Multinational corporations,** in turn, are simply *large corporations that operate in many different countries.* As Chapter 19 ("The Economy and Work") explains, multinational corporations historically developed through rapid corporate growth and mergers. These corporations now wield such vast economic power that corporate decision makers can—and often do—manipulate the political systems in countries where they do business.

# Global Inequality: Theoretical Analysis

There are two major explanations for the unequal distribution of the world's wealth and power—*modernization theory* and *dependency theory.* Each suggests not only why so many of the world's people are poor, but why we as North Americans enjoy such comparative advantages.

The two explanations overlap to some extent. Both acknowledge enormous inequality on our planet, and they agree that changes are needed to guarantee the future security of humanity, rich and poor alike. Yet, emphasizing different factors, each reaches a different conclusion about where responsibility lies for global poverty.

## Modernization Theory

**Modernization theory** is *a model of economic and social change that explains global inequality in terms of differing levels of technological development among societies.* Modernization theory developed in the 1950s, a period of fascination with technology in the United States and a time of hostility to U.S. interests in much of the Third World. Socialist nations of the Second World were gaining influence in the Third World by asserting that Third-World countries simply could not make economic progress under the sway of the capitalist First World. In response, U.S. policy makers framed a broad defense of the First World and its free-market economy that has shaped official foreign policy toward poor nations ever since.[4]

---

[4] The following discussion of modernization theory draws primarily on Rostow (1960, 1978), Bauer (1981), and Berger (1986).

### Historical Perspective

According to modernization theorists, the *entire world* was poor as recently as several centuries ago. Because poverty has been the norm throughout human history, *affluence*—not deprivation—demands an explanation.

Affluence came within reach of a small segment of humanity during the twilight of the Middle Ages as economic activity expanded in Western Europe. Initially, this economic growth involved trade within cities. By the beginning of the sixteenth century, exploration of other parts of the world revealed vast commercial potential. Then, the Industrial Revolution in the eighteenth and nineteenth centuries transformed Western Europe and, soon after, North America. Industrial technology and the innovations of countless entrepreneurs created new wealth on a grand scale. At the outset, modernization theorists concede, this new wealth benefited only a few. Yet industrial technology was so productive that gradually the standard of living of even the poorest people began to rise. The specter of absolute poverty, which had cast a menacing shadow over humanity for its entire history, was finally being routed.

During the last century, the standard of living in the First World—the regions where the Industrial Revolution first began—has continued to improve. Today, industrialization confers unprecedented affluence on First-World societies and, to a lesser extent, on nations of the Second World. But without industrial technology, Third-World countries contend with the same low productivity they have endured throughout history.

### The Importance of Culture

Why didn't people the world over share in the Industrial Revolution so that they, too, could enjoy material plenty? Modernization theory holds that people may or may not seek out and utilize new technology depending on whether their *cultural environment* emphasizes tradition or touts the benefits of innovation and greater productivity.

In a word, then, the greatest barrier to economic development is *traditionalism*. In societies that celebrate strong family systems and revere the past, ancient ways offer powerful guides to understanding the present and shaping the future. Predictably, this creates a form of "cultural inertia" that discourages societies from adopting

Early in the nineteenth century, exhausting and dangerous work was a fact of childhood in England. An unknown artist portrayed the perilous coal mines of Britain in this 1844 painting. Initially, the Industrial Revolution did little to improve the lives of children, who had historically labored just as adults did. Gradually, however, as machinery reduced the need for labor, the role of children was transformed so that they left the mines and factories for schools.

technological advances that would boost their material standard of living. For example, Western innovations and technological advances have encountered fierce resistance in Iran because they threaten traditional Islamic family relationships, customs, and religious beliefs.

Max Weber (1958; orig. 1904–1905) explained that, at the end of the Middle Ages, Western Europe developed a distinctive cultural environment that favored change. As detailed in Chapter 4 ("Society"), the Protestant Reformation's attack on traditional Catholicism created a progress-oriented culture. Material affluence—regarded with suspicion by the Catholic Church—became a personal virtue, and individualism steadily eroded the long-standing emphasis on kinship and community. Taken together, these changing cultural patterns nurtured the Industrial Revolution, which allowed one segment of humanity to prosper.

### Rostow's Stages of Modernization

Modernization theory does not condemn poverty-stricken regions of the globe to a future as poor as their past. As technological advances diffuse around the world, all societies are gradually converging on one general form: the industrial model. According to W. W. Rostow (1960, 1978), the process of modernization follows four overarching stages.

1.  **Traditional stage.** Initially, cultural traditions are strong, so poor societies resist technological innovation. Socialized to venerate the past, people in traditional societies cannot easily imagine how life could be different. They build their lives around their families and local communities, granting little individual freedom to one another, which, of course, inhibits change. Life in such communities is often spiritually rich, but lacking in material abundance.

    A century ago, much of the world was in this initial stage of economic development. And because societies like Bangladesh in central Asia and Burkina Faso in central Africa are still at the traditional stage, they remain impoverished to this day.

2.  **Take-off stage.** Reaching this point, a society experiences a weakening of tradition, and the economy begins to grow. A limited market emerges as people produce goods not just for their own consumption but to profitably trade with others. Paralleling these developments, greater individualism and a stronger

achievement orientation take hold, often at the expense of family ties and long-standing norms and values.

Great Britain reached the take-off stage by about 1800; the United States began take-off around 1820. Developing nations of the Third World, including Thailand in eastern Asia, are now at this stage.

Rostow stresses that economic "take-off" in Third-World societies depends on progressive influences—including foreign aid, the availability of advanced technology and investment capital, and schooling abroad—that only rich nations can provide.

3.  **Drive to technological maturity.** By this time, a society is in full pursuit of a higher standard of living. An active, diversified economy is driven by a population eager to enjoy the benefits of industrial technology. At the same time, however, people begin to realize (and sometimes lament) that industrialization is eroding traditional life in families and local communities. Great Britain reached this point by about 1840, the United States by about 1860. Today, Mexico and the People's Republic of China are among the nations driving to technological maturity.

    At this stage of economic development, absolute poverty has greatly declined. Cities swell with people drawn from the rural hinterlands in search of economic opportunity; occupational specialization renders relationships less personal; and heightened individualism often sparks movements for expanded political rights. Societies approaching technological maturity also provide basic schooling for all their people, with advanced training for some. Increasingly, tradition falls into disrepute, propelling the drive for rapid social change. The social position of women steadily becomes more equal to that of men. At least initially, however, the process of development subjects women to new and unanticipated problems, as the box on page 306 explains.

4.  **High mass consumption.** Economic development through industrial technology steadily raises living standards. This occurs, Rostow explains, as mass production stimulates mass consumption. Put more simply, people soon learn to "need" the expanding array of goods that is being produced. The United States reached the mass-consumption stage by the beginning of the twentieth century.

# Modernization and Women: What Are the Drawbacks?

In global perspective, gender inequality is greatest where people are poorest. Economic development, then, weakens traditional male domination and gives women opportunities to work outside the home. Birth control emancipates women from a continual routine of childbearing, which allows them to benefit from schooling and to enter the paid workforce.

Even as living standards rise, however, economic development has drawbacks for women. Investigating a poor, rural district of Bangladesh, Sultana Alam (1985) identified several problems women face as a result of modernization.

First, economic opportunity draws men from rural areas to cities in search of work, leaving women and children to fend for themselves. Men sometimes sell their land and simply abandon their wives, who are left with nothing but their children.

Second, the eroding strength of the family and neighborhood leaves women who are deserted in this way with few sources of assistance. The same holds true for women who become single through divorce or the death of a spouse. In the past, Alam reports, kin or neighbors readily took in a Bangladeshi woman who found herself alone. Today, as Bangladesh struggles to advance economically, the number of poor households headed by women is increasing. Rather than enhancing women's autonomy, Alam argues, this spirit of individualism has actually lowered the social standing of women.

Third, economic development undermines women's traditional roles as wives, sisters, and mothers, while redefining women as objects of men's sexual attention. Today, especially under the influence of the Western mass media, a modern emphasis on sexuality encourages men to desert aging spouses for women who are younger and more physically attractive.

Modernization, then, does not affect the world's women and men in the same ways. In the long run, the evidence suggests, modernization does give the sexes more equal standing. In the short run, however, the economic position of many women actually declines, and women are also forced to contend with new problems that were virtually unknown in traditional societies.

One consequence of modernization in Third-World societies might be termed "the sexualization of women." Rather than being defined in terms of traditional kinship roles, men increasingly value women for their sexual attractiveness. It is noteworthy that many of the growing number of prostitutes in Third-World cities have discarded traditional dress for Western styles of clothing.

SOURCES: Based on Alam (1985) and Mink (1989).

---

Other First-World societies were not far behind. For example, Japan became a military power early in this century. After recovering from the destruction of World War II, the Japanese enjoyed high mass consumption, and Japan now rivals the United States as the world's leading economic power. The former Soviet Union claimed to be entering this stage in 1950, although the sluggish economy in the new Commonwealth of Independent States still limits the availability of many goods and services. Closing in on this level of economic development are some of the most prosperous Third-World societies in East Asia: South Korea, Taiwan, Hong Kong, and Singapore.

### The Role of Rich Nations

Modernization theory claims that the First World plays a crucial role in global economic development. Far from being the *cause* of the abject poverty that afflicts much of humanity, rich societies hold the key to *solving* global inequality in the following ways:

1. **Assisting in population control.** As we have already noted, population growth is greatest in the poorest societies of the world. Rising population easily overtakes economic advances, lowering the standard of living. Curbing global population, therefore, is crucial to combating poverty. First-World nations can help control population growth by exporting birth control technology and helping to promote its use. Once economic development is under way and women's lives are no longer circumscribed by household and child-rearing chores, birth rates should decline as they have in industrialized societies.

2. **Increasing food production.** Modernization theory asserts that "high-tech" farming methods, exported from rich societies to poor nations, will raise agricultural yields. Such techniques, collectively referred to as the *green revolution*, encompass the use of new hybrid seeds, modern irrigation methods, chemical fertilizers, and pesticides for insect control.

3. **Introducing industrial technology.** Technological transfers should involve industry as well as agriculture. Rich nations can accelerate economic growth in poor societies by introducing machinery and computer technology. Such cultural diffusion helps to transform the labor force of poor countries from lower-skill agricultural work to higher-skill industrial and service work, improving the society's productivity.

4. **Instituting programs of foreign aid.** Investment capital from rich nations can boost the prospects of poor societies striving to reach the "take-off" stage. Developing countries can spend the money to purchase high technology—fertilizers and irrigation projects to raise agricultural productivity and power plants and factories to improve industrial output.

*Critical evaluation.* Modernization theory, which identifies how industrialization affects other dimensions of social life, has influential supporters among social scientists (Parsons, 1966; W. Moore, 1977, 1979; Bauer, 1981; Berger, 1986). Modernization theory has shaped the foreign policy of the United States and other First-World nations for decades. Proponents maintain that a number of poor societies have made impressive strides with the assistance of rich countries. For instance, the Asian nations of South Korea, Taiwan, the former British colony of Singapore, and the current British colony of Hong Kong each receive extensive First-World assistance, and each has an impressive record of economic development. Similarly, concerted efforts to modernize by nations like Turkey have greatly improved national living standards.

From the outset, however, modernization theory has come under fire from nations of the Second World as a thinly veiled defense of capitalism. By the 1960s, a growing number of critics in First-World societies were also citing flaws in this approach. Perhaps the most serious failing, according to critics, is that modernization theory has failed by its own standards. Instead of making the industrial model widely accessible, only limited modernization has occurred. Critics maintain that global inequality remains as striking as ever.

A second criticism lodged against modernization theory holds that this view tends to ignore historical global changes by suggesting that the same opportunities for growth that were available to First-World nations several centuries ago are still accessible to poor, Third-World nations today. (Indeed, modernization theorists claim that the road to development is, in some ways, *easier* today since rich nations can offer assistance to the Third World.) However, critics claim, self-interested rich nations in today's world stand as a barrier to the development of poor nations, ensuring the perpetuation of global poverty. In essence, they argue, the First World industrialized from a position of global *strength*; the Third World cannot be expected to modernize from a position of global *weakness*.

Third, critics charge that, by treating rich and poor societies as worlds unto themselves, modernization theory offers little insight into how global development continues to affect First-World societies. As suggested in Chapter 10 ("Social Class in the United States"), the expansion of multinational corporations around the globe has brought a windfall to wealthy people in this country; at the same time, the production of industrial goods abroad has weakened many traditional U.S. industries such as steel and automobiles, eroding the economic security of rank-and-file workers.

Fourth, critics contend that modernization theory holds up the First World as the standard by which the rest of humanity should be judged, thus betraying an ethnocentric bias. As Chapter 23 ("Social Change and Modernity") explains, "progress" thus translates into reducing the cultural diversity of our world by promoting a materialistic, Western way of life around the globe.

Fifth, and finally, modernization theory draws criticism for suggesting that the causes of global poverty lie almost entirely in the poor societies themselves. This amounts to "blaming the victims" for their own plight. Instead, critics argue, an analysis of global inequality should focus as much attention on the behavior of *rich* nations as that of poor nations (Wiarda, 1987).

From all these concerns has emerged a second major approach to understanding global inequality: dependency theory.

## Dependency Theory

**Dependency theory** is *a model of economic and social development that explains global inequality in terms of the historical exploitation of poor societies by rich societies.* Dependency theory offers a dramatically different analysis of global inequality than modernization theory, placing primary responsibility for global poverty on rich nations. Dependency theory holds that the First World has systematically impoverished the Third World so that today poor nations are *dependent* on richer ones. That is, while modernization theory contends that poverty is a condition that precedes development, dependency theory maintains that global poverty is caused by development (Berger, 1986). This destructive process, which continues today, extends back several centuries.

### Historical Perspective

Before the Industrial Revolution, there was little of the affluence present in some of the world today. Dependency theory asserts, however, that most of the people living in what we now call the Third World were actually better off economically in the past than they are now. André Gunder Frank (1975), a noted proponent of this approach, argues that the *development* of rich societies paralleled the *underdevelopment* of poor societies:

> Underdevelopment is not just the lack of development. Before there was development there was no underdevelopment. . . . Development and underdevelopment are . . . related through the common historical process that they have shared during the past several centuries. . . . (1975:1)

Dependency theory hinges on the crucial insight that the economic positions of the rich and poor nations of the world are linked and cannot be understood correctly in isolation from one another. Modernization theory, its critics argue, errs by suggesting that poor societies are lagging behind rich ones on a single "path of progress." According to dependency theory, the increasing prosperity of the First World has come largely at the expense of the Third World. In short, *some nations have grown rich only because other nations have become poor.* This complex process, which began centuries ago with the onset of global commerce, continues in much of the world today.

### The Importance of Colonialism

Half a millennium has passed since Europeans set out to explore the "New World" of North America to the west, the massive continent of Africa to the south, and Asia to the east. Across the United States, 1992 marked the quincentennial of the voyage of Christopher Columbus, who ventured from Spain believing that he could reach the Orient by sailing west. The unintended outcome of Columbus's voyage—what Europeans called "the discovery of the New World"—has long been celebrated as a stunning achievement. In recent decades, however, historians have provided a more complete understanding of this fateful collision of two worlds, as the box on page 310 explains.

What Europeans dubbed "the age of exploration" is more accurately described as an era of conquest. Colonial efforts by adventurers such as Christopher Columbus brought vast wealth to First-World nations, whose economic fortunes began to rise. By the late fifteenth century, the Third World was systematically falling under the control of European governments. Spain and Portugal colonized nearly all of Latin America. By the beginning of the twentieth century, Great Britain had colonies around the world and boasted that "The sun never sets on the British Empire." The United States, itself originally a British colony, colonized the Virgin Islands, Haiti, Puerto Rico, and part of Cuba in the Western hemisphere, and Guam and the Philippines in Asia.

Overt colonialism has largely disappeared from the world. Most Latin American nations achieved political independence during the first half of the nineteenth century, and most African and Asian colonies gained their freedom during this century. However, according to dependency theory, *political* liberation has not translated into *economic* autonomy. Far from it: poor societies of the Third World maintain economic relationships with rich nations that reproduce the colonial pattern. This neocolonialism is fueled by a capitalist world economy.

One side of the "Christopher Columbus controversy" is illustrated by artist Diego Rivera in his mural *Colonial Domination*. As this painting expresses in graphic detail, the arrival of Europeans to this hemisphere initiated considerable conflict and violence, placing the Americas under the political control of European nations for more than 300 years.

## Wallerstein's Capitalist World Economy

Immanuel Wallerstein (1974, 1979, 1983, 1984) developed a model of the "capitalist world economy" to explain the origins of contemporary global inequality.[5] Wallerstein's term *world economy* suggests that production in various nations is linked through a global economic network. He argues that this global economy results from economic expansion rooted in the First World that has steadily spilled beyond national boundaries over the last five hundred years. The dominant character of the world economy is capitalist.

Wallerstein terms the nations of the First World the *core* of the world economy. Colonialism established this core as raw materials, funneled to Western Europe from the rest of the world, fueled the Industrial Revolution. Today, multinational corporations operate profitably around the globe, drawing wealth to North America, Western Europe, and Japan. By contrast, the Third World encompasses countries at the *periphery* of the

world economy. Originally drawn into the world economy by colonial exploitation, these poor countries continue to support industrial societies by providing inexpensive labor and serving as a vast market for First-World products.

According to Wallerstein, the world economy benefits the First World (in terms of profits) and harms the Third World (by perpetuating poverty). The world economy thus imposes a state of dependency on poor nations, which remain under the control of rich ones. This dependency arises from the following three factors:

1. **Narrow, export-oriented economies.** Unlike the economies of core nations, production in Third-World countries is not diversified. Historically, colonial powers forced farmers to stop growing a variety of traditional crops for local consumption in favor of producing just a few products for export. Thus, most colonial economies export a limited number of products—mostly raw materials. Coffee and fruits from Latin American nations, oil from Nigeria, hardwoods from the Philippines, and palm oil from Malaysia are some of the key products central to the economies of these poor societies.

---

[5] While based mostly on Wallerstein's ideas, this section also draws ideas from the work of Frank (1980, 1981), Delacroix & Ragin (1981), and Bergesen (1983).

# When Worlds Collide: The Christopher Columbus Controversy

For generations, teachers across the United States told young people that the Italian explorer Christopher Columbus (1446–1505) "discovered" a "New World." Conventional accounts held that Columbus forged a link between Europe and the Americas [two continents whose names honor Amerigo Vespucci (1452–1512), who accompanied Columbus on his fateful voyage], introducing "civilization" to a land that had never known Christianity and bringing "enlightened" political and scientific ideas to replace backwardness. In short, according to conventional history, Columbus tamed a savage wilderness with the tools and thinking of a progressive culture, and set the New World on the path to economic development.

As Americans throughout the hemisphere observe the five-hundred-year anniversary of Columbus's voyage, spirited controversy surrounds this historical figure and his legacy. Against the backdrop of conventional history, the story of Columbus and his expedition is literally being rewritten by scholars informed by multicultural perspectives. These critics challenge the heroic stature of Columbus on a number of counts. First, although Columbus's discovery had enormous consequences, it was nonetheless quite accidental. Columbus sailed from Spain thinking that Asia was only three thousand miles to the west. Contrary to popular opinion, most educated people in the late fifteenth century knew that the world was round, but the planet's size was much in doubt. The

westward route from Europe to Asia is three times what Columbus imagined, with the American continents in between. Thus when Columbus and the crews of his three wooden ships stumbled onto the Bahamian Islands at the eastern edge of the Americas, they were actually quite lost.

Second, critics point out, this world was "new" only to the Europeans; the Americas had been inhabited for tens of thousands of years by a host of distinctive societies that originated in Asia. The notion that Europeans "discovered" the "New World" illustrates how, from the outset, our history has recorded contact between various cultures from the point of view of only one of them. To critics of conventional history, this amounts to a clear case of Eurocentrism—evaluating facts from a European perspective (see Chapter 3, "Culture"). The anniversary of Columbus's voyage serves as an appropriate occasion to correct such distortions.

Third, the consequences of contact between Europeans and the indigenous cultures of the Americas were strikingly one-sided. Columbus represented a way of life that aggressively pursued wealth; from the outset, he expected his voyage to bring him riches and power. In comparison to the Europeans, the people who received Columbus maintained a more gentle way of life. Their society, too, was hierarchical, but they lived peacefully and, typical of those with simple technology, they displayed a reverence for nature. Columbus enforced his rule with

determination and brutality. Setting a pattern for later colonizers, he looted gold and silver from the lands he controlled, subjugating native peoples for labor. Even more tragically, Europeans unintentionally introduced to the Americas diseases against which native peoples had no natural defenses. Taken together, violence and disease took a severe toll, decimating indigenous populations within several generations. Columbus's show of brute force to bend native peoples to his will foreshadowed another disastrous collision of different worlds: the slave trade by which Europeans and Africans transported human beings from Africa to the Americas to be sold into bondage.

The European conquest forever changed the course of life in the Americas. In at least some respects, the clash of two worlds in 1492 had long-term positive consequences. Useful instances of cultural diffusion resulted, including the introduction of horses from Europe to the Americas and the exchange of Native American–grown corn and potatoes (and also tobacco) that soon became popular in Europe. Further, in time, entire new societies—including the United States—emerged as a product of European settlement. But, from the point of view of the original inhabitants of the Americas, contact with Europeans initiated a five-hundred-year nightmare: a loss of traditional culture, centuries of oppressive colonization, and the virtual obliteration of many societies.

SOURCES: Sale (1990) and Gray (1991).

Multinational corporations maintain this pattern today as they purchase raw materials cheaply in poor societies and transport them to core societies where they can be processed and profitably sold. Corporations have also increased their land-holdings in Third-World nations, transforming traditional farmers into low-paid laborers in for-eign-owned industries. This pattern prevents Third-World societies from developing industries of their own.

2. **Lack of industrial capacity.** Without an industrial base, poor societies face a double bind: they rely on rich nations to buy their inexpensive raw materi-als, and they depend on rich nations to sell them whatever expensive manufactured goods they can afford. In a classic example of this double depen-dency, British colonialists allowed the people of India to raise cotton, but prohibited them from manufacturing their own cloth. Instead, Indian cotton was shipped to the textile mills of Birming-ham and Manchester in England, woven into cloth, and shipped back for profitable sale in India.

   Dependency theorists also blast the *green rev-olution*, widely praised by modernization theory. To promote agricultural productivity, poor coun-tries must purchase expensive fertilizers, pesticides, and mechanical equipment from core nations. Typically, rich countries profit more from "high-tech" farming than poor societies do.

3. **Foreign debt.** Such unequal trade patterns have plunged Third-World countries deeper and deeper in debt to industrialized nations. Collectively, the Third World owes First-World countries roughly $1 trillion, including hundreds of billions of dollars owed to the United States. This staggering debt is a financial burden few poor societies can bear. Excessive debt—which drains the resources of any society—can destabilize a Third-World country's economy, making matters worse for poor nations already reeling from high unemployment and ram-pant inflation, and sparking widespread social un-rest (Walton & Ragin, 1990). Moreover, the Third-World debt crisis requires continuous transfers of wealth from poor to rich societies—roughly $50 billion annually (United Nations Development Programme, 1991)—further impoverishing periph-eral societies and increasing their dependence on rich nations. According to dependency theorists, this results in a vicious circle that makes rich na-tions richer and poor nations poorer.

   Seeing no way out of the "debt trap," some Third-World countries have simply stopped mak-ing payments. Cuba, for example, refused to make further payments on its $7 billion foreign debt in 1986. Because failure to repay loans threatens the economic growth of rich nations, the United States and other First-World countries oppose such ac-tions, and have proposed various ways to refinance these debts.

Struggling under massive foreign debt, the economy of Argentina has been dev-astated by raging inflation. This eco-nomic calamity has propelled tens of thousands of Argentinos into the streets to demand change. The problem is stated simply on the banner, which reads "Argentinos Are Hungry."

## The Role of Rich Nations

Nowhere is the difference between modernization theory and dependency theory sharper than in the role they assign to rich nations. Modernization theory holds that the *production of wealth* determines whether a nation is rich or poor. From this point of view, First-World societies create new wealth through technological innovation. Their success in this regard does not impoverish other nations. According to modernization theory, productive technology needs to be more widely adopted; as Third-World nations modernize, their level of poverty will decrease. By contrast, dependency theory casts global inequality in terms of the *distribution of wealth*. This approach asserts that rich societies have unjustly seized the wealth of the world for their own purposes. That is, the *over*development of some parts of the globe is directly tied to the *under*development of the rest of it.

Dependency theorists dismiss the idea that First-World programs of population control, agricultural and industrial technology, and foreign aid help poor societies. Instead, they contend that rich nations act simply in pursuit of profit. Selling technology makes money, and foreign aid typically goes to ruling elites (rather than the poor majority) in exchange for maintaining a favorable "business climate" for multinational corporations (Lappé, Collins, & Kinley, 1981).

Hunger activists Frances Moore Lappé and Joseph Collins (1986) claim that the capitalist culture of the United States encourages people to think of poverty as somehow natural. Following this line of reasoning, poverty results from having (too many) children and disasters such as droughts. But, they insist, there is nothing inevitable about global hunger. Lappé and Collins point out that the world produces enough grain so every man, woman, and child could consume 3,600 calories a day, sufficient to make everyone on the planet overweight! Even most of the poorest societies grow enough to feed all their people. The problem, however, is that many people cannot afford to buy food. Therefore, while several hundred million people in India suffer from malnutrition, that nation *exports* beef, wheat, and rice. Similarly, millions of children go hungry in Africa, a vast continent whose agricultural abundance also makes it a net food exporter.

According to Lappé and Collins, the contradiction of poverty amid plenty stems from a deliberate First-World policy of producing food for profit, not people. Rich nations cooperate with elites in the Third World to grow and export profitable crops, which eat into the production of food for local consumption. As an example, coffee, grown in much of Latin America as a crop for export, simultaneously reduces production of corn and beans, which are consumed by local people. Governments of poor societies often support the practice of growing for export rather than local consumption because food profits help to repay massive foreign debt. The problem is complex, but at its core, according to Lappé and Collins, lies the capitalist corporate structure of the First World.

***Critical evaluation.*** The central contribution of dependency theory—that no society develops (or fails to develop) in isolation—points up how the system of global inequality shapes the destiny of all nations. Citing Latin America and other Third-World areas, dependency theorists claim that development simply cannot proceed under the constraints presently imposed by the First World. Addressing global poverty, they conclude, demands more than internal change within poor societies. Rather, these theorists call for reform of the entire world economy so it operates in the interests of the majority of people.

Critics of the dependency approach identify some important weaknesses in the theory. First, critics charge, dependency theory wrongly contends that the wealth of the First World resulted from stealing resources from poor societies. Farmers, small-business owners, and industrialists can and do create new wealth through their imagination and drive. Wealth is not a zero-sum resource by which some gain only at the expense of others. The entire world's wealth has grown during this century, largely due to technological advances and other innovations.

Second, critics reason, if dependency theory were correct in condemning the First World for creating global poverty, then nations with the strongest ties to rich societies would be among the poorest. However, the most impoverished nations of the world (such as Ethiopia and other countries in Central Africa) have had little contact with rich societies. Similarly, critics continue, a long history of trade with rich countries has dramatically improved the economies of a number of nations including Singapore, South Korea, Japan, and Hong Kong (which became a British colony in 1841 and will remain so until 1997). On the other hand, many nations historically active as colonizers (Portugal and Spain, for example) are far from "superpowers" today.

Third, critics contend that dependency theory simplistically points the finger at a single factor—world capitalism—as the sole cause of global inequality. By directing attention to forces *outside* poor societies, dependency theory views poor societies as victims, ignoring factors

Hong Kong, an economic marketplace that operates as freely as any in the world, is a monument to the power of capitalism to generate wealth. Land values in Hong Kong are among the highest anywhere, and many of the British colony's people enjoy a lavish lifestyle. At the same time, however, there is a striking contrast between the rich and the poor. In Aberdeen, shown here, thousands of Chinese people reside in a floating neighborhood with poor sanitation and few chances for improving their lives.

*inside* these countries that may contribute to their economic plight. Sociologists have long recognized the vital role of culture in shaping human behavior. Cultural patterns vary greatly around the world; some societies embrace change readily while others staunchly resist economic development. As we noted earlier, for example, Iran's fundamentalist form of Islam deliberately discourages economic ties with other countries. Capitalist societies can hardly be blamed for Iran's resulting economic stagnation. Nor can rich societies be saddled with responsibility for the reckless and self-serving behavior of certain foreign leaders. Governments of poor societies must assume some measure of blame for widespread poverty when leaders engage in far-reaching corruption and militaristic campaigns to enhance their own power (examples include the regimes of Marcos in the Philippines, Duvalier in Haiti, Noriega in Panama, and Saddam Hussein in Iraq). Governments may even use food supplies as a weapon in internal political struggles; this occurred in

Ethiopia and the Sudan in Africa. Other regimes, including many in Latin America and Africa, fail to support programs to improve the status of women or control population growth.

Fourth, critics chide dependency theorists for downplaying the economic dependency fostered by the former Soviet Union. The Soviet army seized control of most of Eastern Europe during World War II and subsequently dominated these nations politically and economically. Critics of dependency theory see the popular uprisings against Soviet-installed governments, beginning in 1989, as rebellions against Soviet domination and the resulting economic dependency. Eastern European nations were forced to buy Soviet-manufactured goods and Soviet-produced energy, and prevented from trading more profitably on the world market. The Soviets did not broadly colonize the Third World, but until recently they supported regimes in Cuba and Angola that remain highly dependent on this foreign aid.

A fifth criticism is that the policy implications of dependency theory are inherently vague. Most dependency theorists urge poor societies to sever economic ties to the First World, and to nationalize foreign-owned industries. On a broader scale, dependency theory implies that global poverty could be eliminated by a world-wide overthrow of international capitalism. What form emerging economies would take, and whether they would be capable of meeting the economic needs of a growing world population (in light of the historic shortcomings of socialist societies) remains unclear.

## The Future of Global Inequality

People in the United States, sociologists included, are discovering many ways in which global trends are linked to our lives at home. The U.S. economy is playing a pivotal role in an unfolding global drama, as corporations based in the United States invest abroad, and business interests around the world gain control of properties here. As Chapter 10 ("Social Class in the United States") explained, this process is reshaping inequality in this country. Profitable investments, especially in poor nations, and lucrative sales of U.S. companies to foreign inter-

ests, have brought greater affluence to those who already have substantial wealth. At the same time, increasing industrial production abroad has cut factory jobs in this country, exerting downward pressure on wages. The net result: a gradual economic polarization in the United States.

As this chapter has noted, however, social inequality is far more striking in global context. The concentration of wealth among First-World countries, coupled with the grinding poverty in the Third World, may well constitute the most important dilemma facing humanity in the twenty-first century. To some analysts, rich nations are the key to ending world hunger; to others, rich nations are the cause of this tragic problem. Faced with these two, radically different approaches to understanding global inequality, we might wonder which one is "right." As with many controversies in sociology, each view has some merit as well as inherent limitations. Table 11–2 summarizes key arguments made by advocates of each approach.

In searching for truth, we must consider empirical evidence. In some regions of the world, such as the "Pacific Rim" of Eastern Asia, the market forces endorsed by modernization theory are raising living standards rapidly and substantially. At the same time, other societies of the Third World, especially in Latin America, are

**Table 11–2**  MODERNIZATION THEORY AND DEPENDENCY THEORY: A SUMMARY

|  | Modernization Theory | Dependency Theory |
|---|---|---|
| Historical pattern | The entire world was poor just two centuries ago; the Industrial Revolution brought affluence to the First World; as industrialization gradually transforms the Third World, all societies are likely to become more equal and alike. | Global parity was disrupted by colonialism, which developed the First World and simultaneously underdeveloped the Third World; barring change in the world capitalist system, rich nations will grow richer and poor nations will become poorer. |
| Primary causes of global poverty | Characteristics of Third-World societies cause poverty, including lack of industrial technology, traditional cultural patterns that discourage innovation, and rapid population growth. | Global economic relations—historical colonialism and the operation of multinational corporations—have enriched the First World while placing the Third World in a state of economic dependency. |
| Role of rich nations | First-World countries can and do assist Third-World nations through programs of population control, technology transfers that increase food production and stimulate industrial development, and by providing investment capital in the form of foreign aid. | First-World countries have concentrated global resources, advantaging themselves while producing massive foreign debt in the Third World; rich nations represent a barrier to economic development in the Third World. |

experiencing economic turmoil that frustrates hopes for market-based development.

The Third-World societies that have surged ahead economically have two factors in common. First, they are relatively small.[6] Combined, the Asian nations of South Korea, Taiwan, Hong Kong, Singapore, and Japan encompass only about one-fifth of the land area and population of India. The economic problems smaller countries face are more manageable; consequently, small societies more effectively administer programs of development. Second, these "best case" societies have cultural traits in common, especially traditions emphasizing individual achievement and economic success. In other areas of the world, where powerful societal forces inhibit change and squelch individualism, even smaller nations have failed to turn development opportunities to their advantage.

The picture now emerging calls into question key arguments put forward by both approaches. Theorists in both camps, for instance, are revising their views on the major "paths to development." On the one hand, few societies seeking economic growth now favor a market economy completely free of government control. This view challenges orthodox modernization theory, which endorses a free-market approach over government-directed development. Also, as recent upheavals in the former Soviet Union and in Eastern Europe demonstrate, a global reevaluation of socialism is currently under way. These events, following decades of poor economic per-formance and political repression, make many Third-World societies reluctant to consider this path to development. Because dependency theory has historically supported socialist economic systems, changes in world socialism will surely generate new thinking here as well.

In the immediate future, no strategy for development is likely to significantly reduce the overwhelming problems of world hunger and rapid population growth. Looking to the next century, however, there are reasons for hope. The approaches described in this chapter identify the two keys to combating global inequality. One, revealed by modernization theory, is that world hunger is partly a *problem of technology*. A higher standard of living for a surging world population depends on raising agricultural and industrial productivity. The second, derived from dependency theory, is that global inequality is also a *political issue*. Even with higher productivity, crucial questions concerning how resources are distributed—both within societies and around the globe—must be addressed.

As debate over global inequality continues, people are coming to recognize that the security of everyone in the world depends on reducing the destabilizing extremes of contemporary global poverty. We can only hope that, as the Cold War between the superpowers winds down, energy and resources will be redirected to the needs of the vast majority of humanity, many of whom are trapped in a desperate struggle for survival.

## Summary

1. Adopting a global perspective, we can discern a system of social stratification that involves all of humanity. This inequality is best perceived by dividing the globe into "three worlds," based on patterns of economic development. The First World encompasses industrialized, capitalist societies including the United States; the Second World is composed largely of industrialized societies with socialist economies in transition, including the former Soviet Union; the Third World represents the remaining poor societies that have yet to industrialize.

2. In addition to relative poverty, the Third World grapples with widespread, absolute poverty. The typical member of a Third-World society struggles to survive on an income far below that of the average person in the United States.

3. Poverty places about 20 percent of the Third-World population—at least 800 million people—at serious risk. Some 15 million people, many of them children, die of starvation every year.

4. Women are more likely than men to be poor nearly everywhere in the world. In poor, agrarian societies, women's relative and absolute disadvantages are greater than they are in industrial societies such as the United States.

---

[6] This argument was suggested by Professor Alan Frishman of Hobart College.

5. The poverty of Third-World societies is a complex problem whose roots lie in limited industrial technology, rapid population growth, traditional cultural patterns, internal social stratification, and barriers to development in the form of global power relationships.

6. Modernization theory maintains that acquiring advanced productive technology is crucial to economic development. Traditional cultural patterns that value kinship ties over individual achievement are viewed as a barrier to modernization.

7. Modernization theorist W. W. Rostow identifies four stages of development: traditional, take-off, drive to technological maturity, and high mass consumption.

8. Arguing that rich societies hold the keys to creating wealth, modernization theory cites four ways rich nations can assist poor nations: by bolstering population control strategies, food-producing technologies, industrial development, and investment and other foreign aid.

9. Critics of modernization theory maintain that this approach has produced limited economic development in the world, while ethnocentrically assuming that poor societies can follow the path to development taken by rich nations centuries ago.

10. Dependency theory claims global wealth and poverty are directly linked to the historical operation of the capitalist world economy.

11. The dependency of Third-World countries is rooted in colonialism. In this century, neocolonialism continues the historic exploitation of politically independent societies of the Third World through the operation of multinational corporations.

12. Immanuel Wallerstein views the First World as the advantaged "core" of the capitalist world economy; poor societies of the Third World form the global "periphery."

13. Three key factors—export-oriented economies, a lack of industrial capacity, and foreign debt—perpetuate Third-World dependency on rich nations.

14. Critics of dependency theory argue that this approach overlooks the success of some nations in creating new wealth. Contrary to the implications of dependency theory, these critics maintain, the poorest societies are not those with the strongest ties to the First World.

15. Both modernization and dependency approaches offer useful insights into the operation of global inequality. Some evidence supports each view. Less controversial is the urgent need to address the various problems brought on by worldwide poverty.

## Key Concepts

**colonialism** the process by which some nations enrich themselves through political and economic control of other countries

**dependency theory** a model of economic and social development that explains global inequality in terms of the historical exploitation of poor societies by rich ones

**First World** industrial societies that have predominantly capitalist economies

**modernization theory** a model of economic and social change that explains global inequality in terms of differing levels of technological development among world societies

**multinational corporation** a large corporation that operates in many different countries

**neocolonialism** a new form of international, economic exploitation that involves not direct political control but the operation of multinational corporations

**Second World** industrial societies that are currently transforming their socialist economies

**Third World** primarily agrarian societies, in which most people are poor

# Suggested Readings

This classic statement concerning global inequality sets a radical agenda.

Frantz Fanon. *The Wretched of the Earth*. New York: Grove Press, 1963.

The following publications contain recent data on the state of the global economy, and explore contrasts between the rich and poor societies of the world.

United Nations Development Programme. *Human Development Report 1991*. New York: Oxford University Press, 1991.

The World Bank. *World Development Report 1991: The Challenge of Development*. New York: Oxford University Press, 1991.

This recent analysis of social inequality in the United States includes an enlightening chapter (5) on global economic changes.

Kevin Phillips. *The Politics of Rich and Poor: Wealth and the American Electorate in the Reagan Aftermath*. New York: Random House, 1990.

Robert Reich is one of the leading contemporary analysts who traces the causes and consequences of global developments in the United States.

Robert B. Reich. *The Work of Nations: Preparing Ourselves for 21st-Century Capitalism*. New York: Knopf, 1991.

This useful, short paperback offers a readable introduction to the growing economic disparity between rich and poor societies.

Peter Donaldson. *Worlds Apart: The Development Gap and What It Means*. 2nd ed. New York: Penguin, 1986.

This collection of essays focuses on the frequency of revolution in the world and the global trends that underlie insurgency.

Terry Boswell, ed. *Revolution in the World-System*. New York: Greenwood Press, 1989.

These books provide a solid overview of the issue of hunger.

Arthur Simon. *Bread for the World*. Rev. ed. New York: Paulist Press, 1984; Grand Rapids: Wm. B. Erdmans Publishing Co., 1984.

Frances Moore Lappé and Joseph Collins. *World Hunger: Twelve Myths*. New York: Grove Press/Food First Books, 1986.

The first two of these books present the modernization model of development; the second pair examine and evaluate dependency theory.

W. W. Rostow. *The World Economy: History & Prospect*. Austin and London: University of Texas Press, 1978.

P. T. Bauer. *Equality, the Third World and Economic Delusion*. Cambridge, MA: Harvard University Press, 1981.

Thomas Richard Shannon. *An Introduction to the World-System Perspective*. Boulder, CO: Westview Press, 1989.

Tom Barry. *Roots of Rebellion: Land and Hunger in Central America*. Boston: South End Press, 1987.

In chapters 6 through 8 of this book, Peter Berger presents evidence in support of modernization theory.

Peter Berger. *The Capitalist Revolution: Fifty Propositions about Prosperity, Equality, and Liberty*. New York: Basic Books, 1986.

This recent collection of essays offers a comparative analysis of capitalist economies, especially in the United States and East Asia.

Stewart R. Clegg and Gordon Redding, eds., assisted by Monica Cartner. *Capitalism in Contrasting Cultures*. Hawthorne, NY: Aldine de Gruyter, 1990.

An economic crisis of capitalism is causing decline in rich and poor societies alike, according to this collection of essays.

Richard Peet, ed. *International Capitalism and Industrial Restructuring: A Critical Analysis*. Boston: Allyn & Unwin, 1987.

Among the most popular—and controversial—of recent books concerned with global inequality is this account of the Columbus expedition and its consequences.

Fitzpatrick Sale. *The Conquest of Paradise: Christopher Columbus and the Columbian Legacy*. New York: Knopf, 1990.

# Race
# and Ethnicity

*Hey Adam,*

*Sociology Blows!*

*— Adam —*

Sitting around the kitchen table, a Croatian farmer recounts a tale of horror he has heard in the village.[1] His wife and neighbors look on silently, nodding from time to time to signal agreement. The farmer explains that a band of Serbs attacked a bus full of Croats on their way to Zagreb; they blocked the road, forcing the vehicle to stop, and then pulled the Croats from the bus one by one, beating and kicking them. An old woman was clubbed to death—the farmer pauses, shuddering with anger—and no Serb moved to help her. Such brutality, he storms, shows that the Serbs are not people but animals. The man collapses into his chair. Others in the small kitchen murmur that the fighting in Yugoslavia must continue until the Serbs are driven from the region. Or until all the Serbs are dead.

Curiously, not one person in the room has actually observed the barbarity being described. In fact, no one has ever seen a Serb commit an act of violence against a Croat, or anyone else for that matter. Some listening to the sordid tale, if isolated from the others, would even admit that most of the Serbs who live nearby are people very much like themselves, except for different religious beliefs and some distinctive customs.

Here we see the power of ethnicity to divide humanity, to fuel anger and to provoke animosity, in much

of the world today. Stories such as this one—true or not—are passed from house to house, and from generation to generation, until they become real to those who believe them. Across Eastern Europe, as the heavy hand of government control was lifted, blood feuds that have pitted categories of people against one another for centuries broke out once again. In the former republic of Yugoslavia, Croats and Serbs fell into civil war and declared their independence; throughout the former Soviet Union, Ukrainians, Moldavians, Azerbaijanis, and a host of other ethnic peoples struggled to recover their cultural identity after decades of subjugation by the Russian majority. In the Middle East, efforts continue to bring an end to decades of conflict between Arabs and Jews. In South Africa, democratic government struggles to emerge after centuries of racial separation. Throughout the Americas, the five-hundredth anniversary of the initial contact between native people and Europeans offers an opportunity to confront and try to resolve old wounds.

All over the world, human beings are set apart— and sometimes come together viciously—based on their culture, color, and social heritage. In one of the greatest ironies of the human condition, those characteristics that most define us are often the very traits that underlie our hatred and violence toward others.

In the United States, as elsewhere, race and ethnicity trumpet personal identity and group pride while sometimes provoking conflict. This chapter examines the

---

[1] This chapter opening is adapted from an account by Celestine Bohlen (1991).

319

meaning of race and ethnicity, delves into how these social constructs have shaped our history, and explains why they continue to play such a central part—for better or worse—in the world today.

## The Social Significance of Race and Ethnicity

People in the United States and elsewhere in the world frequently use the terms "race" and "ethnicity" imprecisely and interchangeably. For this reason, we begin with important definitions.

### Race

A **race** is *a category composed of men and women who share biologically transmitted traits deemed socially significant*. Races are commonly distinguished by physical characteristics such as skin color, hair texture, facial features, and body shape. All humans are members of a single biological species, but the biological variations we describe as "racial characteristics" have resulted from living for thousands of generations in different geographical regions of the world (Molnar, 1983). In regions of intense heat, for example, humans developed darker skin (from the natural pigment, melanin) that offers protection from the sun; in regions with moderate climates, people have lighter skin.

Over the course of history, migration encouraged intermarriage, so that many genetic characteristics once common to a single region have spread through much of the world. In regions that historically have been "crossroads" of human migration, like the Middle East, people display striking racial variation. Among more isolated people, such as the Japanese, we find greater uniformity of racial characteristics. No society, however, lacks genetic mixture, and increasing contact among the world's people will enhance racial blending in the future.

Trying to make sense of what can be bewildering human variety, nineteenth-century biologists developed

The range of biological variation in human beings is far greater than any system of racial classification allows. This fact is made obvious by trying to place all of the people pictured here into simple racial categories.

a three-part scheme of racial classifications: they labeled people with relatively light skin and fine hair as *Caucasian*; they called those with darker skin and coarser, curlier hair *Negroid*; and they described people with yellow or brown skin and distinctive folds on the eyelids as *Mongoloid*. Such categories are misleading, however, because we now know there are no biologically pure races. In fact, the world traveler notices gradual and subtle racial variations from region to region all around the globe. The people conventionally called "Caucasians" or "whites" actually display skin color that ranges from very light to very dark, and the same variation occurs among so-called "Negroids" and "Mongoloids." Some "whites" (such as the Caucasians of southern India) actually have darker skin and hair than some "blacks" (including the blond Negroid aborigines of Australia).

Although we readily distinguish between "black" and "white" people, research confirms that people in the United States are genetically mixed. Over many generations, the genetic traits of Negroid Africans, Caucasian Europeans, and Mongoloid Native Americans (historic descendants of people from Asia) have spread widely through the Americas. Many "black" people, therefore, have a large proportion of Caucasian genes, and many "white" people have at least some Negroid genes. In short, race is not a black-and-white issue.

Despite the reality of biological mixing, however, people around the world place each other into racial classifications and rank these categories in systems of social inequality. In some cases, they defend this racial hierarchy by claiming that physical traits are signs of innate intelligence and other mental abilities, although there is no scientific foundation for such beliefs. With so much at stake, no wonder societies strive to make social rankings clear and enforceable. Earlier in this century, for example, many states in the South legally defined as "colored" anyone who had at least one thirty-second African ancestry (that is, one African-American great-great grandparent or any closer ancestor). Today, with race less of a caste distinction in the United States, the law enables parents to declare the race of a child.

## Ethnicity

**Ethnicity** is *a shared cultural heritage*. Members of an *ethnic category* may have common ancestors, language, and religion which, together, confer a distinctive social identity. The forebears of Polish, Hispanic, and Chinese Americans, for example, lived in particular areas of the world. Millions of people in the United States speak Spanish, Italian, German, French, or other languages in their homes. The United States and Canada are predominantly Protestant societies, but most Americans and Canadians of Spanish, Italian, and Polish ancestry are Roman Catholic, while others of Greek, Ukrainian, and Russian ancestry are members of the Eastern Orthodox Church. More than 6 million Jewish Americans (with ancestral ties to various nations) share a common religious history. Similarly, several million women and men in the United States have a Muslim heritage.

Race and ethnicity, then, are quite different: one is biological, the other cultural. But the two sometimes go hand in hand. Japanese Americans, for example, have distinctive physical traits and—for those who maintain a traditional way of life—cultural attributes as well. But ethnic distinctiveness should not be viewed as racial. For example, Jews are sometimes described as a race although they are distinctive only in their religious beliefs as well as their history of persecution (Goldsby, 1977). Finally, people can change their ethnicity by adopting a different way of life. Polish immigrants who discard their cultural background over time may cease to have a particular ethnicity. Assuming people mate with others like themselves, however, the physical traits of race persist for generations.

## Minorities

A racial or ethnic **minority**[2] is *a category of people, distinguished by physical or cultural traits, who are socially disadvantaged*. Minorities are of many kinds, including people with physical disabilities and (as Chapter 13, "Sex and Gender," suggests) women. Table 12–1 on page 324 presents the broad sweep of racial and ethnic minorities in the United States as recorded by the 1990 census. Whites of non-Hispanic background continue to predominate in the United States numerically: about 80 percent of the national population falls into this broad category. But the absolute numbers and share of population for virtually every minority in the United States grew rapidly during the 1980s. As the box on pages 322–23 explains, the time is approaching when various *minorities*, taken together, will form a *majority* of people in the United States.

---

[2] We use the term "minority" rather than the commonly used "minority group" because, as explained in Chapter 7 ("Groups and Organizations"), minorities are categories, not groups.

# The Coming Minority-Majority

During the 1980s, Manhattan, the central borough of New York City, gained a "minority-majority." This means that people of African, Asian, and Hispanic descent, together with other minorities, became a majority of the population. The same transformation is now taking place in St. Louis and Fresno, California, as well as 186 counties across the United States—about 6 percent of the total. By 2060, projections suggest, minorities will be a majority in the United States as a whole.

The table shows the entire population of the United States increased by almost 10 percent during the 1980s. The rate of increase for non-Hispanic whites, however, stood below this average, at 6 percent. The population of Asians or Pacific Islanders grew the fastest, more than doubling; the Hispanic population swelled by more than half, and the number of Native Americans increased by more than one-third. The number of African Americans increased by 13 percent.

Population growth in the United States during the 1980s was highly

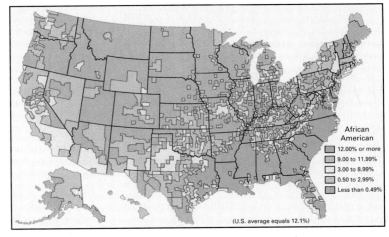

Percent African American, Hispanic American, and Asian American, by County, 1990

(*American Demographics Desk Reference Series, No. 1, June 1991, pp. 8, 14, 16*)

concentrated. More than half the increase took place in just three states: California, Florida, and Texas. As the maps show, these states and others surrounding them have large minority populations: 1990 census data show that counties with high proportions of African Americans are in the southeast, while Hispanics are concentrated in the southwest, and Asian Americans on the west coast.

As the twentieth century began, most people in the United States thought of "minorities" as people of German, Irish, or Italian descent. Ironically, during the twenty-first century, people of European ancestry (other than Hispanics) will again become minorities as a host of others—those often termed *people of color*—emerge as the majority in the United States.

---

Minorities have two major characteristics. First, they share a *distinctive identity*. Because race is highly visible (and virtually impossible for a person to change), people of African descent in the United States or those of Chinese descent in South Africa typically have a keen awareness of their race. The significance of ethnicity (which can be changed) is more variable. Throughout U.S. history, some people (many Reform Jews among them) have downplayed their historic ethnicity, while others (including many Orthodox Jews) have maintained

their cultural traditions and lived in distinctive ethnic neighborhoods.

A second characteristic of minorities is *subordination*. Chapter 10 ("Social Class in the United States") explained that U.S. minorities typically have lower incomes and less occupational prestige and formal education. But not all members of any such category are disadvantaged. Some Hispanics, for example, are quite wealthy, certain Chinese Americans are celebrated business leaders, and African Americans are included among

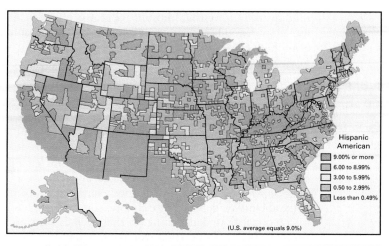

Hispanic
American

■ 9.00% or more
▨ 6.00 to 8.99%
□ 3.00 to 5.99%
□ 0.50 to 2.99%
▨ Less than 0.49%

(U.S. average equals 9.0%)

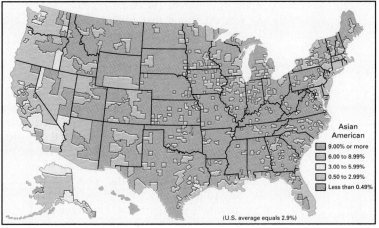

Asian
American

■ 9.00% or more
▨ 6.00 to 8.99%
□ 3.00 to 5.99%
□ 0.50 to 2.99%
▨ Less than 0.49%

(U.S. average equals 2.9%)

| Percent Change in Population by Racial and Ethnic Category, 1980–1990 | |
| --- | --- |
| Category | 1980–1990 Increase |
| Asian or Pacific Islander | 107.8% |
| Hispanic | 53.0% |
| American Indian, Eskimo, or Aleut | 37.9% |
| African American | 13.2% |
| All other minorities | 45.1% |
| White (non-Hispanic) | 6.0% |
| Entire U.S. population | 9.8% |
| SOURCE: U.S. Bureau of the Census, 1991. | |

our nation's leading scholars. But even the most successful individuals may be viewed negatively on the basis of their minority standing. Race or ethnicity often serves as a master status (as described in Chapter 6, "Social Interaction in Everyday Life") that overshadows personal accomplishments.

Minorities usually constitute a small proportion of a society's population, but there are exceptions. For example, blacks form a numerical majority in South Africa although they are grossly deprived of economic and political power by whites. In the United States, women represent slightly more than half the population but are still struggling to gain opportunities and privileges enjoyed by men.

As this chapter's opening vignette suggests, social conflict between minorities and the majority is common around the world. Categories of people—African Americans in the United States, Kurds in Iraq, Christians in Egypt, Sikhs in India, Azerbaijanis in the former Soviet Union—are struggling to win rights formally guaranteed

## Table 12–1 RACIAL AND ETHNIC CATEGORIES IN THE UNITED STATES, 1990

| Racial or Ethnic Classification | Approximate U.S. Population | Percent of Total Population |
|---|---|---|
| African descent | 29,986,060 | 12.1 |
| Hispanic descent* | 22,354,059 | 9.0 |
| Mexican | 13,495,938 | 5.4 |
| Puerto Rican | 2,727,754 | 1.1 |
| Cuban | 1,043,932 | 0.4 |
| Other Hispanic | 5,086,435 | 2.1 |
| Native-American descent | 1,959,234 | 0.8 |
| American Indian | 1,878,285 | 0.8 |
| Eskimo | 57,152 | < |
| Aleut | 23,797 | < |
| Asian or Pacific Islander descent | 7,273,662 | 2.9 |
| Chinese | 1,645,472 | 0.7 |
| Filipino | 1,406,770 | 0.6 |
| Japanese | 847,562 | 0.3 |
| Asian Indian | 815,447 | 0.3 |
| Korean | 798,849 | 0.3 |
| Vietnamese | 614,547 | 0.2 |
| Hawaiian | 211,014 | < |
| Samoan | 62,964 | < |
| Guamanian | 49,345 | < |
| Other Asian or Pacific Islander | 821,692 | 0.3 |
| White | 199,686,070 | 80.3 |

* People of Hispanic descent can be of any race.
< Indicates less than $1/10$ of one percent.
SOURCE: U.S. Bureau of the Census, 1991.

by law. Malaysia represents an unusual and interesting case: a society in which ethnic minorities are *unequal* under the law. The box provides details.

## Prejudice

**Prejudice** amounts to *a rigid and irrational generalization about an entire category of people*. Prejudice is irrational insofar as people hold inflexible attitudes that are supported by little or no direct evidence. Prejudice can be directed toward individuals of a particular social class, sex, sexual orientation, age, political affiliation, race, or ethnicity. Prejudices are prejudgments that can be positive or negative, and most people hold some of each

type. With positive prejudices, we tend to exaggerate the virtues of people like ourselves, while our negative prejudices condemn those who differ from us. Negative prejudice also runs along a continuum, ranging from mild aversion to outright hostility. Because attitudes are rooted in our culture, everyone has at least some measure of prejudice.

## Stereotypes

A common form of prejudice is the **stereotype** (*stereo* is derived from Greek meaning "hard" or "solid"), *a set of prejudices concerning some category of people*. Because stereotypes often involve emotions like love (generally toward members of ingroups) or hate and fear (toward outgroups), they are hard to change even in the face of contradictory evidence. For example, some people have a stereotypical understanding of the poor as lazy and irresponsible freeloaders who would rather rely on welfare than support themselves (Waxman, 1983; N.O.R.C., 1991). As was explained in Chapter 10 ("Social Class in the United States"), this stereotype distorts reality: more than half of poor people in our nation are children, working adults, and elderly people.

Stereotypes have been devised for virtually every racial and ethnic minority, and such attitudes may become deeply rooted in a society's culture. As the opening to this chapter illustrates, conflict between Serbs and Croats has long been fueled by stereotypes. In the United States, many white people stereotype African Americans as lacking motivation to improve their own lives, just as wealthy people stereotype the poor (N.O.R.C., 1991:286). Such attitudes assume that social disadvantage stems from personal deficiency. This stereotypical view ignores some key facts: that most poor people in the United States are white and that most African Americans work as hard as anyone else and are *not* poor. In this case the bit of truth in the stereotype is that blacks are more likely than whites to be poor. But by building a rigid attitude out of a few selected facts, stereotypes grossly distort reality.

## Racism

A powerful and destructive form of prejudice, **racism** refers to *the belief that one racial category is innately superior or inferior to another*. Racism has pervaded world history. The ancient Greeks, various peoples of India,

## Unequal Under the Law: Race and Ethnicity in Malaysia

Almost 20 million Malaysian people live in a nation roughly the size of New Mexico. This society, on the southeast tip of Asia, also includes the northern part of the island of Borneo. As a Third-World nation, Malaysia is still poor in comparison to the United States, but its standard of living is rising.

Race and ethnicity are fundamental to Malaysian society. The earliest inhabitants of the region, called Malays, make up just over half the population. People of Chinese ancestry account for one-third of the population, while an additional 10 percent are Indians whose ancestors came to work on agricultural plantations. Combinations of Malay, Chinese, English, and Indian tongues form the various languages of this nation; despite this linguistic complexity, most Malaysians manage to communicate with one another.

Social differences among Malaysians generate controversy and conflict. The Chinese, who tend to be wealthy and concentrated in large cities, control the most prosperous businesses and live in ex-pensive neighborhoods. Indians, too, live in urban areas, but most own small businesses or work for wages. The typical Indian Malaysian earns only about two-thirds as much as a Chinese Malaysian. Ironically, the Malays, the region's first inhabitants, are the poorest. Most are rural farm laborers earning about half what Chinese Malaysians do.

These disparities erupted into violence in 1969, leading to years of martial law. Determined to help the Malay majority advance socially, the government enacted policies granting Malays special privileges. The growing government bureaucracy now gives hiring preference to Malays. A quota system requires state-supported universities to admit applicants according to their proportion in the population as a whole; thus, half the places in the universities are reserved for Malays, regardless of academic performance. Similarly, most government licenses to operate small businesses, such as taxi services, are given to Malays. The government also encourages the practice of traditional Malay customs.

Malaysia defends such unequal and categorical treatment of its people as necessary to help the Malays catch up to the wealthy Chinese. But many Malays—and Indians—still feel disadvantaged and resentful, and some critics contend that the programs have done little to promote their social standing. The Chinese community, too, is embittered by what it sees as an official policy of favoritism for the Malays. Many Chinese complain, for instance, that the quota system forces them to send their children abroad for a college education.

Most world societies are composed of distinctive races and ethnicities, which usually have different social standing. Malaysia is one of only a few societies in which special treatment for racial and ethnic categories is enshrined in the constitution. Unlike the apartheid system under attack in South Africa, however, this policy is intended not to create but to eliminate social disparities. Whether it will accomplish its goals—and at what cost—remains to be seen.

SOURCES: Based on information provided by Professor Steven Chee, University of Malaysia, and travel by the author in Malaysia.

and many Asian societies viewed anyone unlike themselves as inferior. Racism has also been widespread in the United States; for centuries the enslavement of people of African descent was supported by notions of their innate inferiority. Today, overt racism in this country has been weakened by a more egalitarian culture. Yet racism still persists, though in less open and direct forms; research continues to document the injury and humiliation that racism causes to people of color (Feagin, 1991).

Historically, the assertion that certain categories of people are *innately* inferior has provided a powerful justification for subjecting others to *social* inferiority. By the end of the last century, Great Britain, France, Spain, and the United States had forged colonial empires throughout the Third World. Colonial exploitation often took the form of ruthless oppression, which was defended by the argument that the subjugated people were inferior beings. Similarly, European colonizers alleged the innate

In an effort to improve the social standing of the lowest castes, Indian law reserves half of all government jobs for particular castes deemed to be disadvantaged. Because the government is the largest employer, higher-caste students fear they will be shut out of employment when they graduate from college. So intense are these concerns that recently eleven students killed themselves—five by fire—in public protest over this controversial policy.

inferiority of Native Americans, whose land they proceeded to seize.

In this century, racism was central to the Nazi regime in Germany. Nazi racial doctrine proclaimed a so-called "Aryan race" of blond-haired, blue-eyed Caucasians that was allegedly superior to all others and destined to rule the world. This racist ideology was used to justify the murder of anyone deemed inferior, including some 6 million European Jews and millions of Poles, gypsies, homosexuals, and people with physical and mental disabilities.

More recently, racial conflict has intensified in European societies as whites confront millions of immigrants from former colonies (Glenn & Kennedy-Keel, 1986). Similarly, in the United States the 1980s was marked by increasing racial tensions in cities and on college campuses across the country. Racism—in thought and deed—remains a serious social problem here and elsewhere.

## Individual Versus Institutional Racism

Stokely Carmichael and Charles Hamilton (1967) point out that we typically think of racism in terms of the acts of specific individuals who hatefully and violently strike out at people they deem inferior. This, argue Carmichael and Hamilton, constitutes *individual racism*, and such actions—for example, whites who prevent a black family from moving into their neighborhood— are typically denounced by the public at large.

But even greater harm can be done by *institutional racism*, which refers to racism that guides the operation of schools, hospitals, the police force, and the workplace. For example, the beating of Rodney King by police officers in Los Angeles (described at the beginning of Chapter 8, "Deviance") appeared to some as an isolated case of brutality; for others, however, it epitomized a wide-ranging, systematic program of police violence directed at the city's black community. According to Carmichael and King, the public is less likely to condemn or even to recognize institutional racism because it often involves "established and respected" authority figures. Yet this kind of pervasive racism is typically more damaging.

## Theories of Prejudice

If prejudice has little basis in a rational assessment of facts, what are its origins? Social scientists have offered various answers to this vexing question, citing the importance of frustration, personality, culture, and social conflict.

### Scapegoat Theory of Prejudice

*Scapegoat theory* holds that prejudice springs from frustration. Such attitudes are common among people who are themselves disadvantaged (Dollard, 1939). A white woman earning low wages in a textile factory, for example, might understandably be unhappy with her situation. But she is less likely to direct her hostility at the powerful people who operate the textile plant than at powerless minority coworkers. Prejudice of this kind will not go far toward improving the woman's situation in the factory, but it serves as a relatively safe way to vent anger and it may give her the comforting feeling that at least she is superior to someone.

A **scapegoat** is thus *a person (or category of people), typically with little power, who is unfairly blamed for the troubles of others.* Because they often are "safe targets," minorities are frequently used as scapegoats. The Nazis painted the Jews as responsible for all of Germany's ills fifty years ago. A less extreme example of the same kind is the practice among British people of attributing their nation's troubles today to the presence of Pakistani and Indian immigrants.

## Authoritarian Personality Theory

T. W. Adorno (1950) and others claim that extreme prejudice forms a personality trait in certain individuals. This conclusion is supported by research showing that people who display strong prejudice against one minority are usually intolerant of all minorities. Such people exhibit *authoritarian personalities*, rigidly conforming to conventional cultural values, envisioning moral issues as clear-cut matters of right and wrong, and advocating strongly ethnocentric views. People with authoritarian personalities also look on society as naturally competitive and hierarchical, with "better" people (like themselves) inevitably dominating those who are weaker.

By contrast, Adorno found, people tolerant toward one minority are likely to be accepting of all. They tend to be more flexible in their moral judgments and believe that, ideally, society should be relatively egalitarian. They feel uncomfortable in situations in which some people exercise excessive and damaging power over others.

According to these researchers, authoritarian personalities tend to develop in people with little education and harsh and demanding parents. Raised by cold and insistent authority figures, they theorized, children may become angry and anxious, and ultimately, as adults,

The efforts of these four women advanced the United States toward the goal of equal opportunity regardless of a person's color. Sojourner Truth (1797–1883) (right), born a slave, became an influential preacher and later directed her charisma to the abolitionist cause. Near the end of the Civil War, President Abraham Lincoln honored her at the White House. Harriet Tubman (1820–1913) (bottom left), after escaping from slavery, masterminded the flight from bondage of hundreds of African-American men and women. She was one of the most successful participants in what came to be known as the "Underground Railroad." Ida Wells-Barnett (1862–1931) (bottom middle), born to slave parents, was outspoken in pursuit of social equality in the ante-bellum era. After becoming a partner in a Memphis newspaper, she was a tireless crusader against the practice of lynching that terrorized people of color throughout the United States. Marian Anderson (bottom right), born in 1902, has an exceptional voice, which became part of her church choir when she was six years old. For years, Anderson's career was restrained by racial prejudice. Thus, when she sang in the White House (1936), and on the steps of the Lincoln Memorial to a crowd of almost 100,000 people (1939), she symbolically broke an important "color line."

hostile and aggressive toward scapegoats—others they view as their social inferiors.

### Cultural Theory of Prejudice

A third approach suggests that, while extreme prejudice may characterize particular people, a certain measure of prejudice is embedded in cultural values. As noted in Chapter 3 ("Culture"), the social superiority of some categories of people stands as a core American value. Recent multicultural research echoes this idea, calling for educational initiatives to broaden the traditionally Eurocentric attitudes of people in the United States by promoting appreciation of the culture and contributions of those of non-European backgrounds (Asante, 1987, 1988).

Emory Bogardus (1968) studied the effects of culturally rooted prejudices on interpersonal relationships for more than forty years. He devised the concept of *social distance* to assess how close or distant people feel in relation to members of various racial and ethnic categories. His research reveals that people in the United States share many of the same assessments of various groups, suggesting that such attitudes are normative in our culture. We hold the most positive views toward people of English, Canadian, and Scottish background, Bogardus explains, and welcome close relationships, including marriage, with them. Attitudes are somewhat less favorable toward the French, Germans, Swedes, and Dutch. According to Bogardus, the most negative prejudices target people of African and Asian descent; our culture discourages cultivating close social ties with them.

With prejudice so widespread, according to Bogardus's findings, intolerance cannot be dismissed merely as a trait of a handful of abnormal people, the implication of Adorno's research. Rather, it is routinely expressed by people well adjusted to a "culture of prejudice."

### Conflict Theory of Prejudice

A fourth approach views prejudice as the product of social conflict among various categories of people. According to this theory, an ideology of prejudice is used to justify the oppression of minorities. People are encouraged to denigrate illegal Hispanic immigrants in the Southwest, for example, because doing so justifies paying these people low wages for hard work.

Conflict theories of prejudice take various forms. One argument, based on Marxist theory, holds that elites foster prejudice as a strategy to divide workers. Our na-

tion's history chronicles numerous cases of white workers using minority coworkers as scapegoats; this process serves the interests of capitalists insofar as such conflict decreases the chances that *all* workers will join together to advance their common interests (Geschwender, 1978; Olzak, 1989).

A different argument, recently propounded by Shelby Steele (1990), is that minorities themselves spark conflict to the extent that they encourage a climate of *race consciousness*, a political strategy to gain power and privileges for themselves. Race consciousness, Steele explains, amounts to the claim that historically disadvantaged people are now entitled to special considerations because of their race. While this may yield short-term gains for minorities, he cautions, such policies are likely to spark a backlash from whites who see "special treatment" on the basis of race or ethnicity as unfair.

# Discrimination

Closely related to prejudice is the concept of **discrimination,** *treating various categories of people unequally.* While prejudice refers to attitudes, discrimination is a matter of action. Like prejudice, discrimination can be either positive (providing special advantages) or negative (subjecting categories of people to obstacles). Discrimination also varies in intensity, ranging from subtle to blatant.

**Figure 12–1**  Patterns of Prejudice and Discrimination
*(Merton, 1976)*

| | | Does the person discriminate? | |
|---|---|---|---|
| | | **Yes** | **No** |
| Is the person prejudiced? | **Yes** | Active Bigot (prejudiced person who discriminates) | Timid Bigot (prejudiced person who does not discriminate) |
| | **No** | Fair-Weather Liberal (nonprejudiced person who discriminates) | All-Weather Liberal (nonprejudiced person who does not discriminate) |

Prejudice and discrimination often occur together. A personnel manager prejudiced against members of a particular minority may refuse to hire them. Robert Merton (1976) describes such a person as an *active bigot* (see Figure 12–1). Fearing legal action, however, a prejudiced personnel manager may not discriminate, thereby becoming a *timid bigot*. What Merton calls *fair-weather liberals* may discriminate without being prejudiced, perhaps in the case of a manager discriminating only because a superior demands it. Finally, Merton's *all-weather liberal* is free of both prejudice and discrimination.

## Institutional Discrimination

Like prejudice, discrimination involves both individual action and the structure of society. **Institutional discrimination** refers to *discrimination that is a normative and routine part of the economy, the educational system, or some other social institution*. As minorities in the United States have learned through painful experience, traditional ideas of people's "place" are sometimes deeply entrenched in the operation of the workplace, the courts, and the schools.

Until 1954, for example, the principle of "separate but equal" justified the practice of educating black and white children separately in different schools. While the education of African-American children lagged far behind that of whites, the law upheld this educational caste system. This example of institutional discrimination was formally banned by the Supreme Court in the landmark decision *Brown* v. *The Board of Education of Topeka*. Racial discrimination has proven difficult to end in the United States, however; almost forty years after the 1954 *Brown* ruling, many young people still attend racially imbalanced schools.

## Prejudice and Discrimination: The Vicious Cycle

Prejudice and discrimination persist because they tend to reinforce each other. W. I. Thomas offered a simple explanation of this fact, noted in Chapter 6 ("Social Interaction in Everyday Life"). The Thomas theorem states: *If situations are defined as real, they are real in their consequences* (1966:301; orig. 1931).

Thomas recognized that reality is a matter of how people define situations. Stereotypes become real to those who believe them, sometimes even to those who are victimized by them. Categories of people with considerable social power can enforce their prejudices to the detriment of others. Prejudice on the part of whites toward people of color, for example, does not produce *innate* inferiority but it can produce *social* inferiority, consigning minorities to poverty, low-prestige occupations, and poor housing in racially segregated neighborhoods. If whites interpret this disadvantage as evidence that minorities do not measure up to their standards, a new round of prejudice and discrimination is unleashed. Prejudice and discrimination thereby form a *vicious cycle*—each perpetuating the other over time, even from generation to generation, as illustrated in Figure 12–2.

**Figure 12–2** Prejudice and Discrimination—The Vicious Cycle

Prejudice and discrimination can form a vicious cycle, perpetuating themselves, as explained below.

Stage 1: Prejudice and discrimination begin, often as an expression of ethnocentrism or an attempt to justify economic exploitation.

Stage 2: As a result of prejudice and discrimination, a minority group is socially disadvantaged, occupying a low position in the system of social stratification.

Stage 3: This social disadvantage is then interpreted not as the result of earlier prejudice and discrimination but as evidence that the minority group is innately inferior.

Stage 4: This unleashes renewed prejudice and discrimination, and the cycle repeats itself.

# Majority and Minority: Patterns of Interaction

Patterns of interaction between minorities and more privileged members of a society can be described in terms of four models: pluralism, assimilation, segregation, and genocide.

## Pluralism

**Pluralism** is *a state in which racial and ethnic minorities are distinct but have social parity.* This means that, although categories of people are different, they are not treated in a grossly unequal manner.

Social diversity has long been a source of pride in the United States. Large cities encompass countless "ethnic villages" where people proudly maintain the cultural traditions of their immigrant ancestors (Greeley, 1971; Gans, 1982). In New York these include Harlem and Spanish Harlem, Little Italy, and Chinatown; in Philadelphia, Polish Kensington and Italian "South Philly"; in Chicago, Vietnamese "Little Saigon"; and in Los Angeles, Hispanic East Los Angeles.

Nevertheless, the United States is far from pluralistic for three reasons. First, while most people appreciate their cultural heritage, only a small proportion want their race or ethnicity to set them clearly apart from others and to live only with their "own kind" (N.O.R.C., 1991). Second, our tolerance for social diversity has its limits. One reaction to the growing proportion of minorities in the United States, for example, has been a social movement seeking to establish English as this country's official language. Third, racial and ethnic identity sometimes is forced on people by others. For example, many communities in the Appalachian Mountains of the eastern United States remain culturally distinctive because their members are snubbed as "hillbillies" and subjected to discrimination that perpetuates their poverty (Sacks, 1986).

In global perspective, Switzerland presents a much sharper example of pluralism. In this European nation of more than 6 million people, strong German, French, and Italian cultural traditions run deep. The relative success of the Swiss in maintaining pluralism (albeit involving little difference in skin color) is evident in its official recognition of the languages of the three ethnicities. Just as important, no category is subjected to economic disadvantage (Simpson & Yinger, 1972).

The ritual of Kwanza, devised in 1968, has gained popularity in recent decades as a celebration of African-American heritage. Observed soon after Chanukah and Christmas, Kwanza combines Christian and Jewish elements in a distinctly African ritual that builds the strength of families and communities.

## Assimilation

**Assimilation** is *the process by which minorities gradually adopt patterns of the dominant culture.* Assimilation involves changing modes of dress, values, religion, language, or friends.

Many men and women have traditionally viewed the United States as a "melting pot" in which various nationalities fused into an entirely new way of life. This perception is beautifully expressed in the following description by one European immigrant at the turn of the century:

> America is God's Crucible, the great melting-pot where all races of Europe are melting and reforming. Here you stand, good folks, think I, when I see them at Ellis Island [historical entry point for many immigrants in New York], here you stand with your fifty groups, with your fifty languages and histories, and your fifty blood-hatreds and rivalries. But you won't be long like that, brothers, for these are the fires of God . . . Germans and Frenchmen, Irishmen and Englishmen, Jews and Russians, into the Crucible with you all! God is making an American! (Zangwill, 1921:33; orig. 1909)

The melting-pot characterization of the United States is misleading, however. Rather than "melting" into some new cultural pattern, many minorities have adopted the traits (the dress, the accent, and sometimes even the names) of the dominant English culture established by the earliest settlers. They did so to improve their social position and to escape the prejudice and discrimination directed against them (Newman, 1973). This is not to deny the rich contributions to our culture made by various minorities; cultural contact, however, generally means more change by less powerful minorities than by members of the dominant category.

While assimilation certainly has occurred in U.S. history (witness the "melting" of many European immigrant neighborhoods over the course of this century), ethnic enclaves remain—and others are now forming—suggesting that race and ethnicity endure as building blocks of our society (Glazer & Moynihan, 1970; Alba, 1985).

As a cultural process, assimilation involves changes in ethnicity but not in race. For example, many Americans of Japanese descent have discarded their traditional way of life but still have their racial identity. However, distinguishing racial traits may diminish over generations as the result of **miscegenation,** *the biological process of interbreeding among racial categories.* Although resistance to such biological mixing remains strong, miscegenation (often outside of marriage) has occurred throughout U.S. history.

## Segregation

**Segregation** refers to *the physical and social separation of categories of people.* Sometimes minorities, especially religious orders like the Amish, voluntarily segregate themselves. Usually, however, minorities are involuntarily segregated by others who exclude them. Various degrees of segregation characterize residential neighborhoods, schools, workplaces, hospitals, and even cemeteries. While pluralism fosters distinctiveness without disadvantage, segregation enforces separation to the detriment of a minority.

South Africa's system of apartheid (described in Chapter 9, "Social Stratification") exemplifies racial segregation of a rigid and pervasive nature. Alien to the cultures of Africa, apartheid was created by the European minority it favors, and it has historically been enforced through the use of brutal power (Fredrickson, 1981). Apartheid is currently being eroded in South Africa by widespread opposition among blacks and a growing number of whites. But the basic racial structure of South Africa has yet to change; it remains essentially two different societies that interact only when blacks provide services for whites.

In the United States, too, racial segregation has a long history. Centuries of slavery gave way to racially separated lodging, schooling, and transportation. Decisions such as the 1954 *Brown* case have reduced overt and *de jure* (Latin meaning "by law") discrimination in the United States. However, *de facto* ("in fact") segregation continues today. In the 1960s, Karl and Alma Taeuber (1965) measured the degree of residential segregation of blacks and whites in more than two hundred cities in the United States. On a numerical scale ranging from zero (a mixing of races in all neighborhoods) to 100 (total racial segregation), they calculated an *average* segregation score of 86.2. In the decades since, segregation has decreased little, even for African Americans with substantial economic resources who would prefer to live in racially integrated neighborhoods (Van Valey, Roof, & Wilcox, 1977; Hwang et al., 1985; Calmore, 1986; N.O.R.C., 1991; Saltman, 1991; Wilson, 1991).

Recent research by Douglas Massey and Nancy Denton (1989) reveals that segregation involves more than neighborhood composition. These researchers dis-

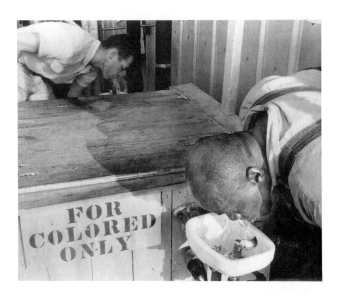

After more than two centuries of slavery in the United States, laws continued to separate the people of European and African ancestry in virtually every public accommodation. This system of "Jim Crow" laws segregated hotels, restaurants, parks, buses, and even drinking fountains. During the 1950s and 1960s, most of these laws were abolished. Even so, forcible segregation in housing and schooling remains a reality for millions of people of color in the United States.

covered a pattern of racial isolation by which residents of black neighborhoods in inner cities have little social contact with the outside world. Such *hypersegregation* is more common among African Americans, they determined, than among any other minority in the United States. Another study concluded that about one-fifth of poor blacks live in such ghettos, compared to only 2 percent of poor (non-Hispanic) whites (Jgarowsky & Bane, 1990).

Segregation and resulting second-class citizenship are understandably opposed by minorities. Sometimes the action of even a single individual can have lasting consequences. On December 1, 1955, Rosa Parks was riding a bus in Montgomery, Alabama, sitting in a section designated by law for African Americans. When a crowd of white passengers boarded the bus, the driver asked four blacks to give up their seats to whites. Three did so, but Rosa Parks refused. The driver left the bus and returned with police, who arrested her for violating the racial segregation laws. She was later convicted in court and fined $14. However, her action touched off a boycott

of city buses by the black community of Montgomery, which ultimately brought an end to this form of segregation (King, 1969).

## Genocide

**Genocide** is *the systematic annihilation of one category of people by another.* This brutal form of racism and ethnocentrism violates nearly every recognized moral standard; nonetheless, it has recurred time and again in human history.

Genocide has figured prominently in centuries of contact between Europeans and the original inhabitants of the Americas. From the sixteenth century on, the Spanish, Portuguese, English, French, and Dutch forcibly established vast colonial empires. The native populations of North and South America were decimated after colonization began, and Europeans moved to gain control of their wealth. Some were victims of calculated killing sprees; most succumbed to diseases brought by Europeans and to which native peoples had no natural defenses (Cottrell, 1979; Butterworth & Chance, 1981; Matthiessen, 1984; Sale, 1990).

Genocide has also occurred in the twentieth century. Unimaginable horror befell European Jews in the 1930s and 1940s, as the Nazi regime seized control of much of Europe. During Adolf Hitler's reign of terror, known as the Holocaust, the Nazis exterminated more than 6 million Jewish men, women, and children. Between 1975 and 1980 the Communist regime of Pol Pot in Cambodia slaughtered anyone thought to represent capitalist cultural influences. Condemned to death were people able to speak any Western language and even those who wore eyeglasses, viewed as a symbol of capitalist culture. In the "killing fields" of Cambodia, 2 million people (one-fourth of the population) perished (Shawcross, 1979).

These four patterns of minority-majority interaction exist together in a society. For example, we proudly point to patterns of pluralism and assimilation but only reluctantly acknowledge the degree to which our society has been built on segregation (of African Americans, for example) and genocide (of Native Americans). The remainder of this chapter explores how these four types of minority-majority contact have shaped the history and present social standing of major racial and ethnic categories in the United States.

# Race and Ethnicity in the United States

*Give me your tired, your poor,*
*Your huddled masses yearning to breathe free,*
*The wretched refuse of your teeming shore,*
*Send these, the homeless, tempest-tossed to me:*
*I lift my lamp beside the golden door.*

These words by the poet Emma Lazarus, inscribed on the Statue of Liberty, express American ideals of human dignity, personal freedom, and opportunity. But our nation's golden door has opened more widely for some than for others. Social inequality, entrenched in U.S. society since its beginnings, is clearly evident in the history of this country's racial and ethnic minorities.

## Native Americans

The term *Native Americans* refers to the hundreds of distinct societies—including Aleuts, Eskimos, Cherokee, Zuni, Sioux, Mohawk, Aztec, and Inca—who were the original inhabitants of the Americas. Thousands of years ago, migrating peoples crossed a land bridge from Asia to North America where the Bering Strait (off the coast of Alaska) lies today, and over the centuries they spread throughout the Western hemisphere. When Christopher Columbus and other European explorers arrived late in the fifteenth century, Native Americans numbered in the millions and had a thirty-thousand-year history in this hemisphere (Dobyns, 1966).

As explained in Chapter 11 ("Global Inequality"), contact with Europeans was disastrous for Native Americans. What some Europeans ethnocentrically called "taming the wilderness" actually amounted to the destruction of many ancient civilizations. Exposure to European diseases took a terrible toll among Native Americans, and tens of thousands more fell victim to violence at the hands of Europeans seeking wealth and land. By the beginning of the twentieth century, the "vanishing Americans" numbered a mere 250,000 (Tyler, 1973).

Native Americans were first referred to as *Indians* by Christopher Columbus, who landed in the Bahama Islands in the Caribbean while searching for India. Columbus found indigenous Americans to be passive and peaceful (Matthiessen, 1984; Sale, 1990). Such attitudes clashed with those of Europeans, whose way of life was more competitive and aggressive. Even as Europeans seized the land of Native Americans, the invaders demeaned their victims as thieves and murderers in an attempt to justify their actions (Unruh, 1979; Josephy, 1982).

After the Revolutionary War, the new United States government adopted a pluralistic approach to Native-American societies, seeking to gain more land through treaties. Payment for land was far from fair, however, and when Native Americans resisted demands to surrender their homelands, superior military power was brought in to evict them. Thousands of Cherokees, for example, died on a forced march—the Trail of Tears—from their homes in the southeastern United States to segregated reservations in the Midwest. By the early 1800s, few Native Americans remained east of the Mississippi River.

After 1871, the United States made Native Americans wards of the government and tried to resolve "the Indian problem" through forced assimilation. Native Americans continued to lose their land, and were well on their way to losing their culture as well. Reservation

A century to the day after the December 29, 1890 killing of almost 300 Native American men, women, and children at Wounded Knee, South Dakota, by members of the 7th Cavalry, members of the Sioux braved a sub-zero wind chill to retrace the path taken by their ancestors. The Wounded Knee massacre marked the end of Native-American resistance to white settlement in the United States, and it has come to symbolize the tragic and shameful victimization of Native Americans at the hands of European settlers.

life fostered dependency, teaching English in place of ancestral languages and eroding traditional religion in favor of Christianity. Many children were taken from their parents and placed in boarding schools, operated by the Bureau of Indian Affairs, to be resocialized as "Americans." Local control of reservations was placed in the hands of the few Native Americans who supported government policies, and reservation land—traditionally held collectively—was distributed as the private property of individual families (Tyler, 1973). In the process, some whites managed to grab still more land for themselves.

Not until 1924 were Native Americans entitled to U.S. citizenship. Since then, the government has encouraged their migration from reservations. Some have adopted mainstream cultural patterns and married non–Native Americans. Many large cities now have sizable Native-American populations. As is shown in Table 12–2, however, median family income for Native Americans was far below average in the United States in 1980, and Native Americans were much less likely to earn a college degree (7.7 percent) than Americans as a whole (17.1 percent).

From in-depth interviews with Native Americans in a western city, Joan Albon (1971) concluded that many were disadvantaged by little education, few marketable skills, less than perfect English, and dark skin that provokes prejudice and discrimination. Additionally, she noted, Native Americans often lacked the pointed individualism and driving competitiveness that contribute to success in the United States. This passivity stemmed from both traditional values and long dependence on government assistance.

Like other racial and ethnic minorities in the United States, Native Americans have recently reasserted pride in their cultural heritage. As the 1990s began, Native-American organizations were reporting a surge of new membership applications from people who had long ignored their heritage (Johnson, 1991). These organizations not only promote the self-esteem of Native Americans, they also pursue greater rights and opportunities for their members. In lawsuits against the federal government, they have pressed for return of lands forcibly seized in the past, and they have sought democratic control of reservation lands by Native Americans themselves. In some instances, violent confrontations with federal officials have erupted. Few Native Americans support violence as a way to address grievances, but the vast majority share a profound sense of the injustice endured at the hands of whites (Josephy, 1982; Matthiessen, 1983).

## White Anglo-Saxon Protestants

White Anglo-Saxon Protestants (WASPs) were not the first people to inhabit the United States, but they came to dominate this nation once European settlement began. Not until the nineteenth century, in fact, did substantial migration of non-WASPs begin. Most WASPs are of English background, but Scots and Welsh are also included. With more than 50 million Americans of English ancestry, roughly one in five of our people can claim some WASP background.

Historically, WASP immigrants were highly skilled and motivated toward achievement by what we now call the Protestant work ethic. Also, because their numbers placed them in the majority among Europeans, WASPs were not subject to the prejudice and discrimination experienced by other categories of immigrants. The historical dominance of WASPs has been so great that, as noted earlier, assimilation into U.S. society has meant becoming more like the WASPs (Gordon, 1964).

Many WASPs responded to growing social diversity in the nineteenth century by directing prejudice and discrimination toward the new arrivals they deemed "undesirable foreigners." Nativist political movements promoted laws to limit the rapid surges in immigration. Those with substantial resources devised a personal solution to the "problem" by sheltering themselves in exclusive suburbs and restrictive clubs. Thus the 1880s—the

**Table 12–2** THE SOCIAL STANDING OF NATIVE AMERICANS, 1980*

| | Native Americans | Entire United States |
|---|---|---|
| Median family income | $16,672 | $19,917 |
| Proportion in poverty | 27.5% | 12.4% |
| Median education (years; age 25 and over) | 12.2 | 12.5 |
| Completion of four or more years of college (age 25 and over) | 7.7% | 17.1% |

* Although the rest of this chapter's data are from the 1990 census, the Census Bureau did not release its 1990 statistical profile of Native Americans until early 1993, too late for publication. Thus 1980 data are retained here.

SOURCE: U.S. Bureau of the Census.

decade in which the Statue of Liberty first welcomed immigrants to the United States—also saw the founding of the first all-WASP country club. Soon afterward, WASPs began publishing the *Social Register* (1887), a listing of members of "society," and established various genealogical organizations such as the Daughters of the American Revolution (1890) and the Society of Mayflower Descendants (1894). These efforts further insulated wealthy WASPs from newly arrived immigrants (Baltzell, 1964).

By about 1930, the growing wealth of other categories of people and more egalitarian values undermined the WASPs' commanding privileges in the United States (Baltzell, 1964, 1976, 1988). Exemplifying this shift was the 1960 election of John Fitzgerald Kennedy as the first non-WASP (Irish-Catholic) president of the United States. Even so, WASPs continue to exert great influence; with extensive schooling, they work in high-prestige occupations, enjoy above-average incomes, and still make up most of the upper-upper class (Greeley, 1974; Baltzell, 1979; Roof, 1981; Neidert & Farley, 1985).

Although it is now being challenged by multicultural educational initiatives, the WASP cultural legacy persists. English remains the dominant language of the United States, and Protestantism is the majority religion. Our legal system, too, reflects its English origins. The historical dominance of WASPs is most evident in the widespread use of the terms "race" and "ethnicity" to describe everyone but them.

## African Americans

Although African Americans accompanied Spanish explorers to the New World in the fifteenth century, accounts of black history in the United States usually begin in 1619, when a Dutch trading ship brought twenty Africans to Jamestown, Virginia (Holt, 1980). Whether these people arrived as slaves or as indentured servants, obligated to perform labor for a specified period in return for passage across the Atlantic Ocean, being of African descent on these shores soon became virtually synonymous with being a slave. In 1661 the first law recognizing slavery was passed in Virginia (Sowell, 1981).

In the colonies' agrarian economy, slavery became the foundation of the plantation system. Whites prospered as plantation owners, and as slave traders—a business legal until 1808. Some 10 million Africans were forcibly brought to various countries in the Americas; about 400,000 entered the United States (Sowell, 1981).

Hundreds of slaves were chained on board small sailing ships as human cargo during a voyage of several weeks across the Atlantic Ocean. Filth and disease killed many; others were driven to suicide. Overall, perhaps half died en route (Tannenbaum, 1946; Franklin, 1967).

Surviving the journey was a mixed blessing, as these people endured a life of servitude as the property of white owners. Most slaves engaged in farming, although some worked in cities at a variety of trades (Franklin, 1967). Work usually lasted from daybreak until sunset, and for up to twenty hours a day during the harvest. The law allowed slave owners to impose whatever disciplinary measures they deemed necessary to ensure that slaves labored continuously. Even the killing of a slave by an owner rarely prompted legal action. Owners also divided slave families at public auctions where human beings were bought and sold as pieces of property. Unschooled and dependent on their owners for all their basic needs, slaves had little control over their destinies (Sowell, 1981).

There were, however, free persons of color in both the North and the South, small-scale farmers, skilled workers, and small-business owners (Murray, 1978). But the lives of most African Americans stood in glaring contradiction to the principles of equality and freedom on which the United States was founded. The Declaration of Independence states:

> We hold these Truths to be self-evident, that all Men are created equal, that they are endowed by their Creator with certain unalienable Rights, that among these are Life, Liberty, and the Pursuit of Happiness. . . .

Most whites, however, did not apply these ideals to blacks. In the Dred Scott case in 1857, the U.S. Supreme Court addressed the question, "Are blacks citizens?" and answered, "We think they are not, and that they are not included, and were not intended to be included, under the word 'citizens' in the Constitution, and can therefore claim none of the rights and privileges which that instrument provides for and secures for citizens of the United States" (Blaustein & Zangrando, 1968:160). Thus arose what Swedish sociologist Gunnar Myrdal (1944) termed the *American dilemma*: the denial of basic rights and freedoms to an entire category of people. To resolve this dilemma, many whites simply defined blacks as innately inferior.

In 1865 the Thirteenth Amendment to the Constitution outlawed slavery. Three years later the Fourteenth Amendment reversed the Dred Scott ruling, giving citi-

The message of the Civil Rights movement was never stated more simply or clearly than it is here. The claim "I Am a Man"—regardless of color or class—is a bold challenge to the racism that continues to compromise the basic humanity of millions of women and men in the United States.

zenship to all people born in the United States. The Fifteenth Amendment, ratified in 1870, stated that neither race nor previous condition of servitude should deprive anyone of the right to vote. However, so-called Jim Crow laws, which enshrined discrimination and segregation in the legal code, still divided U.S. society into two racial castes (Woodward, 1974). Especially in the South, whites beat and lynched blacks (and some whites) who challenged the racial hierarchy.

The twentieth century has wrought dramatic changes for African Americans. In the decades after World War I, tens of thousands left the rural South for jobs in northern factories. While they did find more economic opportunity up North, they did not escape racial prejudice and discrimination, which set them apart from white immigrants arriving from Europe at the same time (Lieberson, 1980). In the 1950s and 1960s, blacks and sympathetic whites launched a wide-ranging attack on racism in the United States that grew into a national civil rights movement. During this period, landmark judicial decisions outlawed racially segregated schools and overt racial discrimination in employment and public accommodations. In addition, the "black power movement" gave African Americans a renewed sense of pride and purpose, which is now being reinforced through Afrocentric education, described in Chapter 3 ("Culture"). This educational initiative spotlights Africa and

people of African descent. While such programs are controversial, many African Americans herald them as a welcome counterbalance to Eurocentric programs that place blacks in the shadow of white culture.

Gains notwithstanding, people of African descent continue to occupy a subordinate position in the United States, as shown in Table 12–3. The median income of black families in 1990 ($21,423) was 58 percent of that earned by white families ($36,915)[3] and substantially below average for all families in the United States ($33,500). Black families are also three times as likely as white families to be poor. In general, African Americans made significant economic gains from the 1940s through the 1960s; the 1970s brought economic stagnation, and while the 1980s saw a rise in affluence for some, more endured a slight decline in income (Jacob, 1986; Jaynes, David, & Williams, 1989; Littman, 1989; Welniak & Littman, 1989). One clear indicator of the growing economic problems for blacks: the National Center for Health Statistics recently reported that life expectancy for African Americans actually *fell* slightly in the late 1980s.

---

[3] Part of this difference is due to a higher proportion of one-parent families among blacks than whites; comparing only families headed by a married couple, black families earn 84 percent of what white families earn.

The declining fortunes of African Americans reflect changes in the U.S. economy, described in Chapter 10 ("Social Class in the United States"). During the 1980s, millions of factory jobs—vital to residents of inner cities—were lost to other countries, where labor costs are substantially lower. Thus black unemployment stands at more than twice the level found among whites; among African-American teenagers in many cities, the figure exceeds 40 percent (Wilson, 1984; Jacob, 1986; Lichter, 1989; U.S. Bureau of the Census, 1991).

In 1960, the median schooling for women and men over the age of 25 was 8.2 years for blacks compared to 10.9 years for whites. By 1990 this gap had almost closed: the respective figures were 12.4 years and 12.7 years. But racial differences remain in college attendance. Table 12–3 shows that African Americans are still only about half as likely as whites to complete four years of college. During the 1980s, the number of African Americans enrolling in college and graduate schools actually fell slightly, with about one-fourth of high-school graduates entering college compared to about one-third a decade earlier (American Council on Education, 1987; *Black Issues in Higher Education*, 1987; U.S. Bureau of the Census, 1991).

Further concern springs from evidence that schooling sparks less upward mobility among blacks than among whites (Blau & Duncan, 1967; Tienda & Lii, 1987). Achievement among African Americans has been significant. In 1990, about one in four families was securely ensconced in the middle class with an annual income of at least $35,000—a 50 percent jump during the 1980s; and one in ten African-American families is affluent, with an income exceeding $50,000. But these gains stand out against the persistent poverty of upwards of one million African Americans—mostly single women and children—who are part of an economically desperate underclass (Wilson, 1984; O'Hare, 1989; Patterson, 1991).

The political clout of African Americans has increased in recent years, paralleling a surge in the number of black registered voters and elected officials. Black migration to cities, along with white movement to the suburbs, has resulted in black majorities in many large cities; by 1990 half of this country's ten largest cities had elected black mayors. In 1989, Virginia elected Douglas Wilder (a grandson of slaves) as the first black governor in U.S. history; in 1992, Wilder briefly threw his hat in the ring as a Democratic Party candidate for the presidency. Among national officials, however, only 1 percent of elected leaders are people of color. After the 1990 elections, 26 blacks (of 435) sat in the House of Representatives and no black person (of 100) was in the Senate.

In sum, for more than 350 years, people of African ancestry in the United States have struggled for social equality. As a nation, we can certainly take pride in how far we have come in pursuit of racial equality. Fifty years after slavery was outlawed, W.E.B. DuBois chronicled many notable achievements of African Americans (1992; orig. 1913). In recent decades, most forms of overt discrimination have been legally banned. Much research suggests that our society is moving along a path of long-term decline in antiblack prejudice as we come to see racial justice as a matter of basic fairness (Firebaugh & Davis, 1988). During the 1970s, for example, about 60 percent of adults in the United States supported the right of a white person to sell a home only to someone who was white; by 1991 that proportion had dropped below 35 percent (N.O.R.C., 1991:179).

In his 1913 assessment of African Americans, DuBois cited grounds for optimism, but he also cautioned that racial caste remained strong in the United States. Clearly, this is still the case today. One response to persistent bigotry is the government policy of affirmative action, or preferential treatment for categories of people historically subjected to prejudice and discrimination. The box on pages 338–39 examines this controversial policy.

## Asian Americans

Although Asian Americans share racial traits, enormous cultural diversity marks this category of people. The 1990 census placed their number at more than 7 million—approaching 3 percent of the population. As noted earlier

**Table 12–3    THE SOCIAL STANDING OF AFRICAN AMERICANS, 1990**

|  | African Americans | Entire United States |
|---|---|---|
| Median family income | $21,423 | $33,500 |
| Proportion in poverty | 31.9% | 10.7% |
| Median education (years; age 25 and over) | 12.4 | 12.7 |
| Completion of four or more years of college (age 25 and over) | 11.3% | 21.4% |

SOURCE:   U.S. Bureau of the Census.

(in the "Minority-Majority" box), the Asian and Pacific Islander population more than doubled during the 1980s. The largest category within the Asian-American population is people of Chinese ancestry (1.6 million), followed by those of Filipino (1.4 million), Japanese (847,000), and Asian-Indian (815,000) background. In 1990, most Asian Americans lived in the western United States; 39 percent of the total lived in California.

Migration from China and Japan to the United States began over a century ago. More recent immigrants from Asia include Filipinos, Asian Indians, Koreans, Vietnamese, Samoans, and Guamanians. As this country's fastest-growing minority, Asian Americans account for almost half of all immigration to the United States (Winnick, 1990).

Asian immigrants—especially young people—have commanded both attention and respect as high achievers. Young Asian Americans are disproportionately represented among students at the best colleges and universities in the country (Brand, 1987). Many of their elders have also made significant economic and social gains in recent years. Yet some people have expressed attitudes ranging from aloofness to outright hostility in their relations with Asian Americans despite this record of achievement. Moreover, as we shall see, the "model minority" image that Asian Americans have cultivated obscures the poverty of some among their ranks. We now focus on the history and current standing of Chinese Americans and Japanese Americans, the longest-established Asian-American minorities.

**CRITICAL THINKING**

## Affirmative Action: Problem or Solution?

After World War II, the government of the United States funded higher education for veterans of all races. At the time, the G.I. Bill held special promise for African Americans, people with notable economic disadvantages. By the 1960s, some 350,000 blacks had gone to college with government funding, but these men and women were not finding the kinds of jobs for which they qualified. In short, *educational* opportunity was not translating into the kind of *economic* opportunity the government thought it would.

Against this backdrop originated a program that came to be known as "affirmative action." In the early 1960s, the Kennedy Administration initiated affirmative action as a means of finding qualified minorities that the government knew were out there—a process of throwing a broader "net of opportunity."

Affirmative action did help thousands of women and men of color gain the kinds of jobs for which they were qualified. For this, the program won many supporters. But it also drew criticism because, by the early 1970s, affirmative action was coming to mean "group preferences" for minorities.

In practice, affirmative action calls on employers and colleges to encourage applications from people of all races and ethnicities, and to carefully monitor hiring and promotion or admissions policies to eliminate discrimination—even unintentional discrimination—against minorities. Initially, the government set a clear goal for affirmative action: to enable talented people to enter various occupations and educational programs without regard to their race.

Many people reasonably assumed that talent was spread throughout the population; therefore, they concluded, minorities should be present in jobs or universities in proportion to their numbers in the larger population. This line of argument propelled affirmative action toward the controversial idea of a "quota system." Under a quota system, a fixed number of minority members are guaranteed favorable treatment regardless of how they stack up against other applicants. In effect, an employer is required to find the best minority member, rather than the best person, for the job. Rigid quota systems have been rejected by U.S. courts, but the law supports preferences based on race and ethnicity as a means of increasing the proportion of minorities in settings that have historically excluded them.

Advocates applaud affirmative action as a fair and necessary corrective for historical discrimination. Everybody alive today, they argue, has been affected by privileges accorded or denied to their

## Chinese Americans

Chinese immigration to the United States began when the California Gold Rush of 1849 sparked an economic boom in the West. As new towns and businesses sprang up virtually overnight, entrepreneurs met the pressing need for cheap labor in the decades that followed by bringing to this country about 100,000 Chinese immigrants. Most were hard-working young men willing to take lower-status jobs shunned by whites (Ling, 1971). When the economy soured in the 1870s, desperate whites began competing with the Chinese for jobs. Suddenly the industriousness of the Chinese and their willingness to work for low wages posed a threat. Repeating a well-known pattern, economic hard times led to mounting prejudice and discrimination (Boswell, 1986).

Soon, laws barred the Chinese from many occupations. Courts also withdrew legal protections, encouraging whites to initiate vicious campaigns against the so-called "Yellow Peril" (Sowell, 1981). Everyone seemed to line up against the Chinese, and the saying that a person didn't have "a Chinaman's chance" gained currency (Sung, 1967:56).

In 1882, the U.S. government passed the first of several laws curtailing Chinese immigration. This action created great domestic hardship because, of the Chinese already in the United States, men outnumbered women by almost twenty to one (Hsu, 1971; Lai, 1980). This sex imbalance caused the Chinese population to fall to about 60,000 by 1920. Chinese women already in the United States benefited from the situation, however; in high demand, they soon became far less submissive to men (Sowell, 1981).

---

parents and grandparents. "Special treatment," then, is nothing new and is necessary for those denied opportunity through no fault of their own. Only in this way, advocates claim, can we break the vicious cycle of prejudice and discrimination.

Opponents of affirmative action agree that minorities have historically suffered from discrimination, but they see affirmative action as *reverse discrimination*. Why should whites today—many of whom are far from privileged—be penalized for past discrimination for which they were in no way responsible? Opponents also claim that minorities have largely overcome historical barriers to opportunity and that those who have made the greatest efforts have had the most success—which is as it should be. Giving entire categories of people special treatment inevitably compromises standards, opponents insist, fosters race-consciousness and a hostile backlash from whites, and undermines the real accomplishments of minorities. Moreover, critics point out, affirmative action typically helps minorities who have already acquired more schooling (presumably those who least need help) while doing little for the persistently poor who need assistance the most.

When affirmative action policies are applied to African Americans, adults in the United States tend to oppose such policies, as the following survey item indicates:

> Some people think that blacks have been discriminated against for so long that the government has a special obligation to help improve their living standards. Others believe that the government should not be giving special treatment to blacks. (N.O.R.C., 1991:327)

The numbers 1 through 5 show the range of opinion in relation to the three responses.

| I strongly agree that the government is obligated to help blacks. | | I agree with both answers. | | I strongly agree that the government shouldn't give blacks special treatment. | |
|---|---|---|---|---|---|
| 1 | 2 | 3 | | 4 | 5 |
| 10.2% | 11.1% | 30.6% | | 18.6% | 26.0% |

No Response = 3.5%          Total = 1,017 respondents

SOURCE: Survey data from N.O.R.C., *General Social Surveys* (Chicago: National Opinion Research Center, 1991), p. 327.

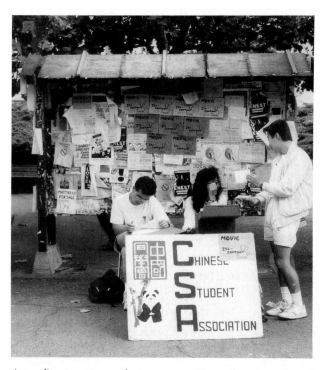

According to some analysts, communities gather strength and people gain social confidence through emphasizing racial and ethnic identity. From another point of view, however, these processes heighten divisions within our society and fuel social conflict. Resolving the tension between appreciating our distinctive heritage and respecting our common humanity will continue to challenge us into the next century.

Responding to their plight, some Chinese moved eastward; many more sought the relative safety of urban Chinatowns (Wong, 1971). There Chinese traditions flourished, and kinship networks, called *clans*, gave financial assistance to individuals and served as political organizations representing the interests of all. With the help of the clans, Chinese immigrants obtained loans to start businesses and find jobs. At the same time, however, those living in a Chinatown had little incentive to learn the English language or pursue cultural assimilation.

With the onset of World War II, a renewed need for labor increased the opportunities of the Chinese (Lai, 1980). In 1943 President Roosevelt ended the ban on Chinese immigration and extended the rights of citizenship to Chinese Americans born abroad. Many responded by moving out of Chinatowns and seeking cultural assimilation. In turn-of-the-century Honolulu, for example,

70 percent of the Chinese people lived in Chinatown; by 1980, only 20 percent did (Lai, 1980).

By 1950, many Chinese Americans were enjoying considerable upward social mobility. Today, Americans of Chinese ancestry are no longer restricted to self-employment in laundries and restaurants; many now work in high-prestige occupations. Their achievement has been outstanding in science and technology, fields in which many Chinese Americans—including several Nobel Prize winners—have excelled (Sowell, 1981). As shown in Table 12–4, the median family income of all Asian Americans in 1990 ($42,240) was above the national average ($33,500). Chinese Americans also have above-average incomes, although not to the extent that Japanese Americans do. Note, however, that the higher income of Chinese Americans, as well as that of other categories of Asian Americans, reflects a larger number of family members working, on average. Chinese Americans have also built a remarkable record of educational achievement: the proportion of Chinese-American college graduates is twice the national average.

Despite this overall record of success, many Chinese Americans still grapple with serious problems. Overt prejudice and discrimination have diminished, but racial hostility persists. Poverty among Chinese Americans stands above the national average, especially among those who remain in the protective circle of Chinatowns. At the beginning of the 1980s, the poverty level of New York's Chinatown was twice as high as that of the city as a whole, with half of all Chinese men working in restaurants and three-fourths of Chinese women stuck in low-paying jobs in the garment industry (Sowell, 1981). This mixed economic picture has prompted a debate over whether racial and ethnic enclaves exploit or economically assist their residents (Portes & Jensen, 1989; Zhou & Logan, 1989).

### Japanese Americans

Japanese immigration to the United States began slowly in the 1860s, reaching only 3,000 by 1890. Japanese immigrants were welcomed to the Hawaiian Islands (a state since 1959) as a source of cheap labor on sugar plantations. Early in this century, however, as Japanese immigration rose along with demands for better pay, whites sought to curb their immigration (Daniels, 1971). In 1908 the United States signed an agreement with

Japan limiting immigration of men, who were deemed the greater economic threat, while allowing Japanese women to immigrate to ease the sex-ratio imbalance. By the early 1920s, in California and elsewhere, new laws mandated segregation and prohibited interracial marriage, virtually ending Japanese immigration. The United States denied foreign-born Japanese citizenship until 1952.

Japanese immigrants differed from the Chinese in three ways. First, the number of Japanese immigrants was smaller, which allowed them to escape some of the hostility directed at the more numerous Chinese immigrants. Second, the Japanese knew more than the Chinese about the United States before migrating; this encouraged assimilation and eased racial conflict (Sowell, 1981). Third, fewer Japanese immigrants clustered in cities, instead favoring rural farming.

Whites reacted swiftly to Japanese purchases of farmland in California. In 1913, no noncitizen was permitted to own farmland. Such laws were principally motivated by economic considerations, but they also reflected a measure of racial hostility as suggested by this comment from the state's attorney general:

> The fundamental basis of all legislation has been, and is, race undesirability. It seeks to limit [the Japanese] presence by curtailing the privileges which they may enjoy here, for they will not come here in large numbers and abide with us if they may not acquire land. (Kitano, 1980:563)

Foreign-born Japanese (called the *Issei*) responded by placing farmland in the names of their U.S.-born children (*Nisei*), who were automatically citizens under the Constitution. Others leased farmland with great success.

Japanese Americans faced their greatest struggle after December 7, 1941, when the nation of Japan destroyed much of the U.S. naval fleet at Hawaii's Pearl Harbor. Rage toward Japan was directed at the Japanese living in the United States. Some feared the Japanese here would commit acts of espionage and sabotage on behalf of Japan. Within a year, President Roosevelt had signed Executive Order 9066, an unprecedented act intended to protect this nation's security. Areas of the West Coast were designated as military zones from which anyone considered likely to be disloyal would be relocated inland to remote military reservations. Ninety percent of Americans of Japanese ancestry—110,000 in all—were forcibly interned in security camps.

While concern about national security always rises in times of war, this policy was criticized, first, because it targeted an entire category of people, not one of whom was ever convicted of any disloyal act. Second, roughly two-thirds of those imprisoned were Nisei American, citizens by birth. But racism is often stronger than concern for the rights of U.S. citizens, and the cry "The Japs must go" was raised by liberals and conservatives alike (Kitano, 1985:244). Third, the United States was also at war with Germany and Italy, yet no such action was taken against whites of German or Italian ancestry.

Relocation meant selling homes, furnishings, and businesses on short notice for whatever price could be obtained. As a result, almost the entire Japanese-American population was devastated economically. In the military prison camps—surrounded by barbed wire and armed soldiers—families suffered greatly as they were crowded into single rooms, often in buildings that had previously been used for livestock (Fujimoto, 1971; Bloom, 1980). The internment ended in 1944, when the policy was declared unconstitutional by the Supreme Court. In 1988 Congress awarded $20,000 as compensation to each victim of this policy—token recognition of the economic loss and personal suffering endured by Japanese Americans.

After World War II, Japanese Americans staged a dramatic recovery. Having lost their traditional businesses, they entered a wide range of new occupations. Because their culture places a high value on education and hard work, Japanese Americans have enjoyed remarkable success. The median income of Japanese-American households has remained very high—even by Asian-American standards—being more than 30 percent above the national average. And the rate of poverty among Japanese Americans is half that for the United States as a whole.

**Table 12–4  THE SOCIAL STANDING OF ASIAN AMERICANS, 1990**

| | Asian Americans | Entire United States |
|---|---|---|
| Median family income | $42,240 | $33,500 |
| Percent in poverty | 12.2% | 10.7% |
| Median education (years; age 25 and over) | 13.7 | 12.7 |
| Completion of four or more years of college (age 25 and over) | 39.0% | 21.4% |

SOURCE:  U.S. Bureau of the Census.

The U.S. government defended the internment of Japanese Americans during World War II as necessary to ensure national security. But this policy also expressed the racial hostility that whites commonly directed toward people of Asian ancestry at this time in the western United States.

Upward social mobility has encouraged cultural assimilation. The third and fourth generations of Japanese Americans (the *Sansei* and *Yonsei*) rarely live in residential enclaves, as many Chinese Americans still do, and a significant number have married non–Japanese Americans. In the process, many have abandoned their traditions, including the ability to speak Japanese. Yet a high proportion of Japanese Americans do participate in ethnic associations as a way of maintaining some ethnic identity (Fugita & O'Brien, 1985). Drawn one way by their roots and another by their aspirations for success, some appear to be caught between two worlds, belonging to neither. As one Japanese-American man claims, "I never considered myself 100 percent American because of obvious physical differences. Nor did I think of myself as Japanese" (Okimoto, 1971:14).

## Hispanic Americans

In 1990, there were at least 22 million Hispanics, representing one in twelve people in the United States. Although some Hispanics are of purely Spanish descent,

most combine Spanish, African, and Native-American ancestry. Hispanics also represent a variety of cultures. More than half (at least 13 million) are Mexican Americans, commonly called *Chicanos*. Puerto Ricans are next in population size (3 million), followed by Cuban Americans (1 million). Many other societies of Latin America are represented in smaller numbers (totaling 5 million). Because of a high birth rate, the Hispanic-American population is currently increasing by almost a million a year. If this trend continues, Hispanics may outnumber African Americans in the United States early in the next century (Moore & Pachon, 1985).

The social standing of Hispanics improved in some respects during the 1980s. One researcher reports that between 1984 and 1988 the number of Hispanic men in managerial and professional occupations jumped 42 percent; among Hispanic women, the increase was a remarkable 61 percent (Schwartz, 1989). Another calculation shows that the number of Hispanic households with at least $50,000 in annual income more than tripled (to 638,000) between 1972 and 1988 (O'Hare, 1990). Nevertheless Hispanic family income—about $23,000 in 1990—represents only a slight increase in real purchasing power during the 1980s. Furthermore, as the following sections reveal, some categories of Hispanics have fared better than others.

### Mexican Americans

Some Mexican Americans are descendants of people living in a part of Mexico annexed by the United States after the Mexican-American War (1846–1848). Most, however, are recent immigrants. Between 1970 and 1990, more immigrants came to the United States from Mexico than from any other nation. Most of the official total of more than 13 million Mexican Americans live in the West and Southwest (as shown earlier on page 323). The actual number could be far higher, of course, because large numbers of Mexican Americans enter the United States illegally and have not been counted by the Census Bureau.

Mexican Americans play an important role in the economy of the United States, yet they derive only meager benefits from their work. Many provide inexpensive labor, especially as farm workers; many more hold other low-paying jobs. Table 12–5 shows that in 1990 the median family income for Mexican Americans was $23,240, about 69 percent of the comparable national figure of $33,500. This disparity increased during the 1980s; at the beginning of the decade Mexican Americans earned 74 percent of the median income for the country. In 1990, one-fourth of Chicano families were classified as poor—more than twice the national average, but less than the proportion of blacks living in poverty. Finally, despite notable improvement since 1980, Mexican Americans have acquired significantly less education than U.S. adults as a whole.

## Puerto Ricans

Puerto Rico has been a possession of the United States since the end of the Spanish-American War in 1898. In 1917, islanders became U.S. citizens, and Puerto Ricans now move freely to and from the mainland (Fitzpatrick, 1980).

New York City is the center of Puerto Rican life in the continental United States. From about 500 in 1910, the number of Puerto Ricans living in New York reached 70,000 by 1940. But it was the start of regular airline service between New York City and San Juan, the capital of Puerto Rico, that sparked a surge in migration; by 1950, New York's Puerto Rican population had soared to 187,000 (Glazer & Moynihan, 1970).

Life in New York has not met the expectations of many Puerto Ricans. By the mid-1960s, half the Puerto Ricans in New York were living in poverty (Moore & Pachon, 1985). Today, half of the more than 2 million Puerto Ricans in the continental United States live in New York's Spanish Harlem, and more than one-third are severely disadvantaged. Adjusting to cultural patterns on the mainland—including, for many, learning English—is a major challenge; Puerto Ricans with darker skin encounter especially strong prejudice and discrimination. As a result, about as many Puerto Ricans return to Puerto Rico each year as arrive from the island.

This "revolving door" pattern has hampered cultural assimilation. About three-fourths of Puerto Rican families in the United States continue to speak Spanish at home, compared with about half of Mexican-American families (Sowell, 1981; Stevens & Swicegood, 1987). Speaking only Spanish helps maintain a strong ethnic identity but it may also limit economic opportunity. Puerto Ricans have a higher incidence of female-headed households than do other Hispanics, which raises the risk of poverty (Reimers, 1984). Table 12–5 shows that in 1990 the median household income for Puerto Ricans was $18,008—51 percent of the national average. Throughout the 1980s, therefore, Puerto Ricans were the most socially disadvantaged Hispanic minority.

## Cuban Americans

Large numbers of Cubans came to the United States after the 1959 Marxist revolution led by Fidel Castro. By 1972, aided by special legislation, 400,000 Cubans had immigrated (Perez, 1980). Most settled in Miami, although the Cuban community in New York now numbers over 50,000. Those who fled Castro's Cuba were generally not the "huddled masses" described on the Statue of Liberty, but highly educated business and professional people. They wasted little time building much the same success in the United States that they had enjoyed in their homeland (Fallows, 1983). Table 12–5 shows that the median household income for Cuban Americans in 1990 was $31,439—well above that of other Hispanics although still below the national standard. Poverty among Cuban Americans is substantially higher than average.

Cuban Americans have managed a delicate balancing act—achieving success in the larger society while retaining much of their traditional culture. Of the categories of Hispanics we have considered, they are the most

---

Table 12–5  THE SOCIAL STANDING OF HISPANIC AMERICANS, 1990

| | All Hispanics | Mexican Americans | Puerto Ricans | Cuban Americans | Entire United States |
|---|---|---|---|---|---|
| Median family income | $23,431 | $23,240 | $18,008 | $31,439 | $33,500 |
| Proportion in poverty | 25.0% | 25.0% | 37.5% | 13.8% | 10.7% |
| Median education (years; age 25 and over) | 12.0 | 10.8 | 12.0 | 12.4 | 12.7 |
| Completion of four or more years of college (age 25 and over) | 9.2% | 6.2% | 10.1% | 18.5% | 21.4% |

SOURCE:  U.S. Bureau of the Census.

likely to speak Spanish in their homes; eight out of ten Cuban families do (Sowell, 1981). However, cultural distinctiveness and living in highly visible communities, like Miami's Little Havana district, provoke hostility from some whites. While some whites in Miami applaud the economic and social strengths of the city's Cuban community, others angrily denounce the Cubans as outsiders who are taking over their domain. As a bumper sticker states bluntly, "Will the last American to leave Miami remember to bring the flag?"

The 1990 census placed the total number of Cuban Americans at more than one million. Substantial population growth during the 1980s followed the so-called Mariel boat lift, the influx of 125,000 refugees from Mariel Harbor in Cuba. Several thousand of these "boat people" had been released from Cuban prisons and mental hospitals, and they became the focus of mass-media accounts fueling prejudice against Cuban Americans (Clark, Lasaga, & Regue, 1981; Portes, 1984).

About 90,000 of this second wave of Cuban immigrants settled in the Miami area while others—especially those with darker skin—entered cities in the Northeast (Perez, 1980). Typically poorer and less educated than those who arrived a generation earlier, these recent immigrants clashed with the more established Cuban community in Miami (Fallows, 1983). But they too are quickly putting down roots. Soon after their arrival, most applied for resident status so that their relatives abroad could also be admitted to the United States.

## White Ethnic Americans

In the 1960s, the term *white ethnics* was coined in recognition of the visible ethnic heritage of many whites. The term conveys a quasi-minority standing: members of the white majority who are not of privileged WASP ancestry. Thus white ethnics have some non-English European background, with some ancestors coming from Germany, Ireland, France, Italy, or other countries. Overall, more than half the women and men in the United States fall into some white ethnic category.

Unprecedented immigration from Europe during the nineteenth century greatly increased social diversity in the United States. Initially, the Germans and Irish predominated. Italians, and Jews from many European countries, soon followed. Despite cultural differences, all shared the hope that the United States would offer greater political freedom and economic opportunity than they had known in their homelands. The fanciful belief

that the streets of their new land were paved with gold contrasted sharply with the harsh reality of life for the vast majority of immigrants. Jobs were not always easy to find, and most demanded hard labor for low wages.

Economic problems were aggravated by prejudice and discrimination, which rose with the increasing tide of immigration. Nativist organizations opposed the entry of non-WASP Europeans to the United States and denounced those already here. Newspaper ads seeking workers in the mid-nineteenth century often carried a warning to new arrivals: "None need apply but Americans" (Handlin, 1941:67).

Some of this prejudice and discrimination was based on class rather than ethnicity, since immigrants with little command of English were typically poor as well. But even distinguished achievers faced hostility. Fiorello La Guardia, the son of immigrants, half Italian and half Jewish, served as mayor of New York between 1933 and 1945 despite being rebuked by President Herbert Hoover in words that reveal unambiguous ethnic hatred:

> You should go back where you belong and advise Mussolini how to make good honest citizens in Italy. The Italians are preponderantly our murderers and bootleggers. . . . Like a lot of other foreign spawn, you do not appreciate the country that supports and tolerates you. (Mann, 1959, cited in Baltzell, 1964:30)

Nativists were finally victorious. In 1921 the government enacted legislation that limited immigration by imposing a quota from each foreign country; this quota system remained in effect until 1968. The most severe restrictions were placed on southern and eastern Europeans—people likely to have darker skin and to differ culturally from the dominant WASPs (Fallows, 1983).

In response to widespread bigotry, many white ethnics followed the pattern of forming supportive residential enclaves. Some also gained footholds in specialized trades: Italian Americans entered the construction industry; Irish Americans worked in various building trades and civil service jobs; Jews predominated in the garment industry; many Greeks (like the Chinese) worked in the retail food business (Newman, 1973).

White ethnics who prospered were more easily assimilated into the larger society. Many working-class "ethnics," however, still live in traditional neighborhoods. Despite continuing problems, white ethnics have achieved considerable success over the course of this century. Many descendants of immigrants who labored in sweatshops and lived in overcrowded tenements now hold respectable positions—both socially and economically. As a result, ethnic heritage now serves as a source of pride to many white Americans.

## U.S. Minorities: A Hundred-Year Perspective

The United States has been—and will remain—a land of immigrants. Immigration has generated striking cultural diversity, as well as tales of hope and struggle, told in hundreds of tongues.

For most who came to this country in the first wave of immigration that peaked in 1910, the next two generations brought gradual economic gains and at least some cultural assimilation. The United States also granted basic freedoms where they had earlier been denied: citizenship was extended to Native Americans (1924) and to foreign-born Chinese Americans (1943) and Japanese Americans (1952). In the 1950s, African Americans organized the civil rights movement in response to centuries of oppression.

As Figure 12–3 indicates, a second wave of immigration began after World War II. During the 1980s, about 400,000 people came to the United States each year, about the same number that entered during the "Great Immigration" a century ago (although newcomers now enter a country with five times as many people). A change in U.S. immigration law in 1990 allows the annual number of immigrants to reach 750,000. Today most immigrants come not from Europe but from Latin America and Asia, with Mexicans, Filipinos, and Koreans arriving in the largest numbers. Rather than entering on the "European" side of the United States, most new immigrants are bringing profound cultural changes to the South and West.

New arrivals face much of the same prejudice and discrimination experienced by those who came before them. Also, like European immigrants of the past, many now struggle to enter the "golden door" of U.S. society without abandoning their traditional culture. Some have built racial and ethnic enclaves: the Little Havana and Little Saigon of today stand alongside the Little Italy and Germantown of the past. New Americans also share the hope that racial and ethnic diversity, while a dimension of difference, will not become a badge of inferiority.

**Figure 12–3**  Immigration to the United States, by Decade
(*U.S. Immigration and Naturalization Service*)

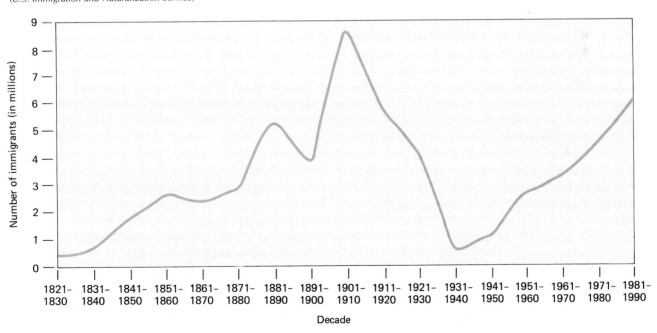

# Summary

1. Race involves a cluster of biological traits that form three broad, overarching categories: Caucasians, Mongoloids, and Negroids. There are, however, no pure races. Ethnicity is based on shared cultural heritage. Minorities are categories of people who are socially distinctive—including those of certain races and ethnicities—and who have a subordinate social position.

2. A prejudice is an inflexible and distorted generalization about a category of people. Racism, a powerful form of prejudice, is any assertion that one race is innately superior or inferior to another.

3. Discrimination is a pattern of action by which a person treats various categories of people differently.

4. Pluralism refers to a state in which racial and ethnic categories, although distinct, have equal social standing. Assimilation is a process by which minorities gradually adopt the patterns of the dominant culture. Segregation means the physical and social separation of categories of people. Most segregation of minorities is involuntary. Genocide is the annihilation of a category of people.

5. Native Americans—the original inhabitants of the Americas—have endured genocide, segregation, and forced assimilation. Today the social standing of Native Americans is well below the national average.

6. WASPs, who predominated among the original European settlers of the United States, continue to enjoy a high social position today.

7. African Americans lived for two centuries as slaves. Emancipation in 1865 led to rigid segregation by law. Despite formal equality under the law, blacks are still relatively disadvantaged today.

8. Chinese and Japanese Americans historically have suffered due to both racial and ethnic differences. Today, however, both categories have above-average income and education.

9. Hispanic Americans represent many ethnicities rooted in Spanish culture. Mexican Americans, the largest Hispanic minority, are concentrated in the Southwest. Puerto Ricans, most of whom live in New York, are poorer. Cubans, concentrated in Miami, are the most affluent category of Hispanics.

10. White ethnic Americans include non-WASPs of European ancestry. While making gains during the last century, many white ethnics are still struggling for economic security.

11. Immigration has increased in recent years. No longer primarily from Europe, immigrants now come mostly from Latin America and Asia.

# Key Concepts

**assimilation** the process by which minorities gradually adopt patterns of the dominant culture

**discrimination** treating various categories of people unequally

**ethnicity** a shared cultural heritage

**genocide** the systematic annihilation of one category of people by another

**institutional discrimination** discrimination that is a normative and routine part of the economy, the educational system, or some other social institution

**minority** a category of people, distinguished by physical or cultural traits, who are socially disadvantaged

**miscegenation** the biological process of interbreeding among racial categories

**pluralism** a state in which racial and ethnic minorities are distinct but have social parity

**prejudice** a rigid and irrational generalization about a category of people

**race** a category composed of men and women who share biologically transmitted traits deemed socially significant

**racism** the belief that one racial category is innately superior or inferior to another

**scapegoat** a person (or category of people), typically with little power, who is unfairly blamed for the troubles of others

**segregation** the physical and social separation of categories of people

**stereotype** a set of prejudices concerning some category of people

## Suggested Readings

This paperback text delves into the issues raised in this chapter.

Harry H. L. Kitano. *Race Relations*. 4th ed. Englewood Cliffs, NJ: Prentice Hall, 1990.

This collection of essays spotlights the centrality of race to social stratification in the United States.

Vincent N. Parrillo, ed. *Rethinking Today's Minorities*. Westport, CT: Greenwood, 1991.

This well-illustrated account of militant, white, racist organizations details both their history in the United States and current agenda.

James Ridgeway. *Blood in the Face: The Ku Klux Klan, Aryan Nations, Nazi Skinheads, and the Rise of a New White Culture*. New York: Thunder's Mouth Press, 1990.

This detailed analysis explores prejudice and discrimination in the United States.

Joe R. Feagin and Clairece Booher Feagin. *Discrimination American Style: Institutional Racism and Sexism*. 2nd ed. Malabar, FL: Kreiger, 1986.

If cultural patterns can build community, they can also turn people against one another. Nowhere has this been truer than in the Middle East. The first book examines how ethnicity stands at the core of Middle Eastern social structure. The second book, by a noted foreign correspondent who lived in Jerusalem for five years, explores how stereotypes carry hatred into the lives of each new generation.

Milton J. Esman and Itamar Rabinovich, eds. *Ethnicity, Pluralism, and the State in the Middle East*. Ithaca, NY and London: Cornell University Press, 1988.

David K. Shipler. *Arab and Jew: Wounded Spirits in a Promised Land*. New York: Times Books, 1986.

An increasing amount of research investigates issues of interest to African Americans. This book provides a "medical history" of the black community.

David McBride. *From TB to AIDS: Epidemics Among Urban Blacks Since 1900*. Albany, NY: SUNY Press, 1990.

These two recent volumes review the social standing of African Americans.

Gerald David Jaynes and Robin M. Williams, eds. *A Common Destiny: Blacks and American Society*. Washington, DC: National Academy Press, 1989.

Janet Dewart, ed. *The State of Black America, 1991*. 16th ed. New York: National Urban League, 1991.

This book traces the history of Hispanic cultures in the United States.

Lewis H. Gann and Peter J. Duignan. *The Hispanics in the United States: A History*. Boulder, CO: Westview, 1986.

These books investigate the social dynamics of race and ethnicity in two societies that have great importance to the United States.

John Solomos. *Race and Racism in Contemporary Britain*. London: Macmillan, 1989.

Edward N. Herberg. *Ethnic Groups in Canada: Adaptations and Transitions*. Scarborough, Ontario: Nelson Canada, 1989.

Do immigrants bring innovation and economic vitality to a society or merely raise unemployment? This book paints a multidimensional portrait of newcomers to the United States and assesses the economic consequences of immigration.

George J. Borgas. *Friends or Strangers: The Impact of Immigrants on the U.S. Economy*. New York: Basic Books, 1990.

This liberal analysis of race and ethnicity critiques conservative policies that have dominated the 1980s and 1990s.

Gary Orfield and Carole Ashkinaze. *The Closing Door: Conservative Policy and Black Opportunity*. Chicago: University of Chicago Press, 1991.

This global analysis explores the experiences of Jews, Scots, Chinese, and other ethnic categories that have marginal standing in various societies.

Walter P. Zenner. *Minorities in the Middle: A Cross-Cultural Analysis*. Albany, NY: SUNY Press, 1991.

These personal accounts chronicle the experiences of some of the more than 1 million Asian refugees that have come to the United States in recent decades.

Lucy Nguyen-Hong-Nhiem and Joel M. Halpern, eds. *The Far East Comes Near: Autobiographical Accounts of Southeast Asian Students in America*. Amherst, MA: University of Massachusetts Press, 1989.

This history of racial preferences examines the complex consequences of affirmative action with regard to race relations.

Herman Belz. *Equality Transformed: A Quarter-Century of Affirmative Action*. New Brunswick, NJ: Transaction, 1991.

# Sex
# and Gender

Unity Dow smiled at her friends and supporters as the judge announced the court's decision; there were hugs and handshakes all around. Dow, a thirty-two-year-old lawyer and citizen of the African nation of Botswana, has won the first round in her efforts to overturn the laws by which, she maintains, her country defines women as second-class citizens.

The law that sparked Unity Dow's suit against her government regulates how citizenship is extended to children. Traditionally in Botswana, family membership is traced through men—that is, children are part of their father's family line, but not their mother's. The nation's citizenship law, which also follows the *patrilineal* model, has special significance for anyone who marries a citizen of another country as Unity Dow did. Under the law, a child of a Botswanan man and a woman of another country would be a citizen of Botswana, since legal standing passes through the father. By the same token, however, the child of a Botswanan woman and a foreign man is denied citizenship. Because she is married to a man from the United States, Unity Dow's children had no rights as citizens in the country where they were born.

The significance of the Dow case goes far beyond citizenship to the foundation of unequal legal standing of the two sexes. In rendering the decision in Dow's favor, High Court Judge Martin Horwitz declared, "The time that women were treated as chattels or were there to obey the whims and wishes of males is long past." In support of his decision, Horwitz pointed to the constitution of Botswana, which guarantees fundamental rights and freedoms to women as well as men. But not everyone agreed. Arguing the government's case against Dow, Ian Kirby, a deputy attorney general, claimed that the Botswanan constitution does allow a legal distinction between women and men. He readily conceded that the citizenship laws—and a host of other statutes—favor men, but, he added, this pattern is consistent with Botswanan culture, which has long given men power over women. To challenge such traditions in the name of Western feminism, he continued, was nothing more than cultural imperialism by which some people seek to subvert their own way of life by advancing foreign notions popular elsewhere.

Women from many African nations attended the hearing of the Dow case, some traveling great distances to bear witness to what they considered to be historic change. The case is complex and will be debated for years to come. Undoubtedly, this will be the first of many similar lawsuits—in various African societies—with the goal of establishing social equality between the sexes (Dow, 1990; Shapiro, 1991).

To many people in the United States, the Dow case may seem strange, since the notion that men and women are entitled to equal rights and privileges is widely endorsed here. But, as this chapter will explain, in our

349

own society the two sexes are far from equal in many respects. In fact, it is the United States, and not Botswana, that has no constitutional guarantee of equal standing under the law for women and men.

# Sex and Gender

Many people think that differences in the social standing of men and women simply reflect innate differences between the sexes. As this chapter will explain, however, the different social experiences of women and men are more a creation of society than biology. To begin, we shall explore the key concepts of sex and gender.

## Sex: A Biological Distinction

**Sex** refers to *the division of humanity into biological categories of female and male.* Sex is determined at the moment a child is conceived through sexual intercourse. The female ovum and the male sperm, which join to form a fertilized embryo, each contain twenty-three pairs of chromosomes—biological codes that guide physical development. One of these chromosome pairs determines the child's sex. The mother always contributes an X chromosome; the father contributes either an X or a Y. A second X from the father produces a female (XX) embryo; a Y from the father yields a male (XY) embryo.

Within six weeks of conception, the sex of an embryo begins to guide its development. If the embryo is male, testicular tissues begin producing testosterone, a hormone that stimulates the development of the male genitals. Without testosterone, the embryo develops female genitals. About 105 boys are born for every 100 girls in the United States, but a higher death rate among males renders females a slight majority by the time people reach their mid-thirties (U.S. National Center for Health Statistics, 1990).

At birth, females and males are distinguished by **primary sex characteristics,** *the genitals, used to reproduce the human species.* Further sex differentiation occurs years later when children reach puberty and their reproductive systems become fully operational. At this point, humans exhibit **secondary sex characteristics,** *physical traits, other than the genitals, that distinguish physiologically mature females and males.* To accommodate pregnancy, childbirth, and the nurturing of infants, adolescent females develop wider hips, breasts, and soft fatty

Sex is a biological distinction that develops prior to birth. Gender is the meaning that a society attaches to being female or male. That is, the range of human feelings, thoughts, and behavior is divided into what is defined as feminine or masculine. Moreover, gender differences are also a matter of power, as what is masculine typically has social priority over what is feminine. Gender differences are not evident among infants, of course, but the ways in which we think of boys and girls set in motion patterns that will continue for a lifetime.

tissue, providing a reserve supply of nutrition for pregnancy and breast-feeding (Brownmiller, 1984). Usually slightly taller and heavier than females from birth, adolescent males typically develop more muscles in the upper body, more extensive body hair, and voices deeper in tone. These are only general differences, however. Many males are smaller and lighter than many females; some males have less body hair than some females; and some males speak in a higher tone than some females.

Sex is not always a clear-cut matter. In rare cases, a hormone imbalance before birth produces a **hermaphrodite** (a word derived from Hermaphroditus, the offspring of the mythological Greek gods Hermes and Aphrodite, who embodied both sexes), *a human being* *with some combination of female and male internal and external genitalia.* Because our culture is anxious about sexual ambiguity, we generally regard hermaphrodites with confusion and even disgust. By contrast, the Pokot of Eastern Africa are indifferent to what they define as a simple biological error, and the Navajo look on hermaphrodites with awe, viewing them as the embodiment of the full potential of both the female and the male (Geertz, 1975).

Further complicating the issue, some people deliberately choose to change their sex. Hermaphrodites may have their genitals surgically altered to gain the appearance (and occasionally the function) of a sexually normal man or woman. Surgery is also commonly considered by **transsexuals,** *people who feel they are one sex though biologically they are the other.* Some 20,000 transsexuals in the United States have medically altered their genitals to escape the sense of being "trapped in the wrong body" (Restak, 1979, cited in Offir, 1982:146).

## Sexual Orientation

**Sexual orientation** is *the manner in which people experience sexual arousal and achieve sexual pleasure.* For most living things, sexuality is biologically programmed. In humans, however, sexuality is bound up in the complex web of culture. The norm in all industrial societies is *heterosexuality* (*hetero* is a Greek word meaning "the other of two"), by which a person is sexually attracted to the opposite sex. However, *homosexuality* (*homo* is the Greek word for "the same"), by which a person is sexually attracted to people of the same sex, is not uncommon.

More broadly, all cultures endorse heterosexuality, although many tolerate—and some even encourage—homosexuality. Among the ancient Greeks, for instance, elite intellectual men celebrated homosexuality as the highest form of relationship, while devaluing relations with women, whom they considered to be their intellectual inferiors. In this light, heterosexuality was seen as little more than a reproductive necessity, and men who did not engage in homosexuality were defined as deviant. But because homosexual relations do not permit reproduction, no record exists of a society that has favored homosexuality to the exclusion of heterosexuality (Kluckhohn, 1948; Ford & Beach, 1951; Greenberg, 1988).

By the 1960s, homosexuals became more outspoken in opposition to heterosexual norms, and they adopted the label *gay* to describe themselves. This new terminology allowed gays to express satisfaction with their sexual orientation, amid a culture that broadly condemns homosexuality. Although stereotypes of homosexuals abound, the personalities of gay people vary as much as those of "straights."

Tolerance of gay people has increased during this century. In 1974 the American Psychiatric Association removed homosexuality from its listing of mental disorders. Gays were subject to increasing prejudice, discrimination, and violence during the 1980s, however, when the deadly disease AIDS became publicly identified with homosexual men. Today, 70 percent of adults in the United States continue to view homosexuality as morally wrong, but the same majority thinks our society should allow gays and straights equal opportunities in the workplace (Salholz, 1990; N.O.R.C., 1991:257).

Until our society becomes truly accepting of homosexuality, some gay people will understandably choose to remain "in the closet," fearfully avoiding public disclosure of their sexual orientation. Heterosexuals can begin to understand what this secrecy means by imagining never speaking about their romances to parents, roommates, or anyone else (Offir, 1982:216). For their part, many organizations of gay people are struggling to overcome the stereotypes applied to gay men and gay women (commonly called *lesbians*). In the late 1960s, a new term took hold: *homophobia* (with Greek roots meaning "fear of sameness") refers to an irrational fear of gay people (Weinberg, 1973). Instead of asking "What's wrong with gay people?" in other words, this label casts the spotlight on society itself, implying "What's wrong with people who can't accept this sexual orientation?"

The pioneering research by Alfred Kinsey (1948, 1953) suggested that about 4 percent of males and roughly 2 percent of females have an exclusively same-sex orientation. Nevertheless, roughly 10 percent of people in the United States—between 15 and 20 million adults—have a strong enough homosexual orientation to designate themselves as "gay" (Kirk & Madsen, 1989). In the broadest terms, at least twice this number have had at least one erotic experience with someone of the same sex. Sexual orientations, then, are not mutually exclusive; some people have a *bisexual* (combining homosexual and heterosexual) preference.

How does a person develop a particular sexual orientation? There is growing evidence that sexual orientation is rooted in biological factors present at birth and is further reinforced by the hormone balance in the body as we grow (Gladue, Green, & Hellman, 1984; Weinrich, 1987; Isay, 1989). Still other research points to the importance of the social environment in promoting particular sexual attitudes and behaviors (Troiden, 1988). According to these researchers, humans are born with the capacity and desire to be sexual, but *how* we express our sexuality is learned as our personality develops in society. Most likely, both nature and nurture play a part. To complicate matters further, sexual orientation is not established in precisely the same way for everyone. One influential study concluded that a complete explanation for sexual orientation simply does not exist at present (Bell, Weinberg, & Kiefer-Hammersmith, 1981).

## Gender: A Cultural Distinction

**Gender** refers to *society's division of humanity, based on sex, into two distinctive categories.* Gender guides how females and males think about themselves, how they interact with others, and what positions they occupy in society as a whole.

Gender deals not only with difference—how a society constructs feminine and masculine people—but also with how society confers power on each of the sexes. Thus, gender also operates as a dimension of social inequality. This inequality, which has historically favored males, is no simple matter of biological differences between the two sexes. Females and males do, of course, differ biologically, but these disparities are complex and inconsistent. Beyond the primary and secondary sex characteristics already noted, males have more muscle in the arms and shoulders, so the average man can lift more weight than the average woman can. Furthermore, males can sustain greater strength over short periods of time. Yet, females can outperform males in some tests of long-term endurance because they can draw on the energy derived from greater body fat. Females also outperform males in life itself. According to the Bureau of the Census (1991), the average life expectancy for men is now 71.8 years, while women can expect to live 78.5 years.

Adolescent males exhibit greater mathematical ability, while adolescent females outperform males in verbal skills, differences that certainly reflect different patterns of socialization and, as recent research suggests, may have some basis in biology (Maccoby & Jacklin, 1974; Baker et al., 1980; Lengermann & Wallace, 1985; Nash, 1991). In any case, however, research indicates no difference in overall intelligence between males and females.

Biologically, then, only limited differences distinguish females from males, with neither sex naturally superior. Nevertheless, the deeply rooted *cultural* notion of male superiority may seem so natural that we assume that it stems from sex itself. But society, much more than biology, is at work here, as several kinds of research reveal.

### An Unusual Case Study

In 1963 a physician was performing a routine penis circumcision on seven-month-old identical twins. While using electrocautery (surgery employing a heated needle), the physician accidentally burned off the penis of one boy. Understandably, the parents were horrified. After months of medical consultation, they decided to employ further surgery to change the boy's sex and to raise him as a girl.

The child was dressed as a girl, her hair grew long, and she was treated according to cultural definitions of femininity. Meanwhile, the brother—born an exact biological copy—was raised as a boy.

Because of their different socialization, each child learned a distinctive **gender identity**, *traits that females and males, guided by their culture, incorporate into their personalities.* In this example, one child learned to think of himself in terms that our culture defines as masculine, while the other child—despite beginning life as a male—soon began to think of herself as feminine. As the twins' mother observed:

> One thing that really amazes me is that (my daughter) is so feminine. I've never seen a little girl so neat and tidy. . . . She is very proud of herself, when she puts on a new dress, or I set her hair. She just loves to have her hair set; she could sit under the dryer all day long to have her hair set. She just loves it. . . . (My daughter) likes for me to wipe her face. She doesn't like to be dirty, and yet my son is quite different. I can't wash his face for anything. . . . She seems to be daintier. (Money & Ehrhardt, 1972:124)

However, the girl's development did not proceed smoothly, suggesting that some biological forces were coming into play. While feminine in many respects, the researchers reported that she also displayed some masculine traits, including a desire to gain dominance among her peers. Later, researchers following the case reported that, by the time she was reaching adolescence, she was showing signs of resisting her feminine gender identity (Diamond, 1982). This complex case raises a question about whether environment can completely overcome any and all biological factors. But it also demonstrates that gender can be socially constructed to a greater degree than most people would imagine.

## The Israeli Kibbutzim

Further evidence of society's power to generate gender differences is found in studies of collective settlements in Israel called *kibbutzim*. The *kibbutz* (the singular form) is important for gender research because its members historically have embraced the ideal of social equality, with men and women sharing in required work and decision making.

Both sexes in the kibbutzim typically perform all kinds of work including child care, building repair, cooking, and cleaning. Boys and girls are raised in the same way and, from the first weeks of life, live in dormitories under the care of specially trained personnel. To members of kibbutzim, then, gender is barely relevant to much of everyday life.

Here, again, we find reason for caution about completely discounting biological forces. Some observers noted that women in the kibbutzim resisted spending much of the day away from their own children; as a result, many of these organizations have returned to more traditional social roles. Sociobiologists (see Chapter 3, "Culture") who have studied the kibbutzim attribute this reemergence of conventional social patterns to subtle but persistent biological dispositions. A close examination of kibbutz life suggests that nature may undermine efforts to achieve complete gender equality (Tiger & Shepher, 1975). But even if this were so—and this research has its critics—the kibbutzim certainly stand as evidence of wide cultural latitude in defining what is feminine and masculine. They also exemplify how, through conscious efforts, a society can pursue the goal of sexual equality just as it can encourage the domination of one sex by the other.

## Cross-Cultural Research

Another way to determine whether gender reflects culture or some inborn imperative is to take a broad view of how the two sexes interact in many different cultures. To the extent that gender reflects the biological facts of sex, the human traits defined as feminine and masculine should be the same everywhere; if gender responds to cultural influences, these conceptions should vary.

The best-known research of this kind is a study

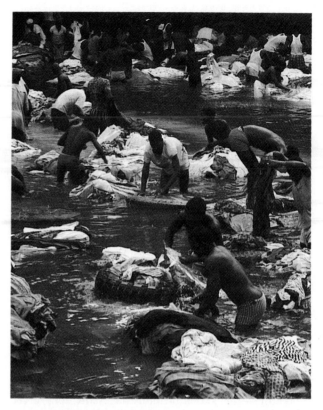

In every society, people assume some tasks are "naturally" feminine while others are just as obviously masculine. But, in global perspective, we see remarkable variety in such social definitions. These men of Africa's Ivory Coast are engaged in what they think of as the masculine routine of "washing day."

of gender in three societies of New Guinea by anthropologist Margaret Mead (1963; orig. 1935). High in the mountains of New Guinea, Mead observed the Arapesh, whose men and women displayed remarkably similar attitudes and behavior. Both sexes, she reported, were cooperative and sensitive to others. They were, in short, what our culture would term "feminine."

Moving south, Mead then observed the Mundugumor, whose culture of head-hunting and cannibalism stood in striking contrast to the gentle ways of the Arapesh. Here, Mead reported, females and males were again alike, although they were startlingly different from the Arapesh. Both Mundugumor females and males were typically selfish and aggressive, traits defined as more "masculine" in the United States.

Finally, traveling west to observe the Tchambuli, Mead discovered a culture that, like our own, defined females and males differently. Yet the Tchambuli *reversed* many of our notions of gender: females were dominant and rational, while males were submissive, emotional, and nurturing toward children.

Based on her observations, Mead concluded that cultures can exaggerate or minimize social distinctions based on sex. Additionally, where differences are pronounced, what one culture defines as masculine may be considered feminine by another. Mead's research, therefore, strongly supports the conclusion that gender is a variable creation of society.

A broader study of more than two hundred preindustrial societies by George Murdock (1937) revealed some general agreement about which tasks tend to be viewed as feminine or masculine. Hunting and warfare, Murdock found, generally fall to males, while home-centered chores such as cooking and child care tend to be defined as female tasks. With only simple technology, preindustrial societies apparently adopt this strategy to benefit from men's greater size and short-term strength; because women bear children, their activities are likely to be more domestic.

But within these general patterns, Murdock found significant variation. Just as many societies considered agriculture—the core of preindustrial production—to be feminine as masculine. For most, in fact, farming responsibilities were shouldered by both women and men. When it came to many other tasks—from building shelters to tattooing the body—Murdock observed that societies of the world were as likely to turn to one sex as the other.

In global perspective, then, only a few specific activities are consistently defined as feminine or masculine. And as societies industrialize, with a resulting decrease in the significance of muscle power, even these distinctions are minimized (Lenski, Lenski, & Nolan, 1991). Gender, therefore, is simply too variable across cultures to be considered a simple expression of the biological categories of sex. Instead, as with many other elements of culture, what it means to be female and male is mostly a creation of society.

## Patriarchy and Sexism

Although conceptions of gender do vary, one universal pattern characterizes all societies to some degree: **patriarchy** (literally, "the rule of fathers"), *a form of social organization in which males dominate females*. Despite mythical tales of societies dominated by female "Amazons," the pattern of **matriarchy**, *a form of social organization in which females dominate males*, is not at present part of the human record (Gough, 1971; Harris, 1977; Kipp, 1980; Lengermann & Wallace, 1985). While a tendency toward patriarchy may be universal, however, world societies reveal significant variation in the relative power and privilege of females and males.

**Sexism,** *the belief that one sex is innately superior to the other*, stands as an important ideological underpinning of patriarchy. Historically, patriarchy has been supported by a belief in the innate superiority of males who, therefore, legitimately dominate females. As Table 13–1 shows, sexism has much in common with racism, which was covered in Chapter 12 ("Race and Ethnicity"). Just as racism constitutes an ideology supporting white domination of people of color, so sexism is an ideology justifying the domination of (allegedly inferior) females by (allegedly superior) males.

Also like racism, sexism is more than a matter of individual attitudes. The notion that one sex is superior to the other is built into various institutions of our society. As we shall see presently, *institutional sexism* pervades the operation of the economy, with women highly concentrated in jobs that are less challenging and offer relatively low pay. In another example of institutional sexism, the legal system has historically minimized or overlooked entirely violence against women, especially violence perpetrated by boyfriends, husbands, and fathers (Landers, 1990).

Sexism—especially when it is institutionalized—has clear costs to women, who stand at increased risk of poverty and sexual violence. But society as a whole also pays a high price for maintaining sexism. Limiting the opportunities available to women ensures that the full talents and abilities of half the population will never be developed. And men, too, are hurt by sexism. Without denying that sexism confers on men a disproportionate share of wealth and power, this privilege comes at a high price. As Marilyn French (1985) argues, patriarchy compels men to relentlessly seek control—not only of women, but of themselves and the entire world. The consequences include far higher rates of death from suicide, violence, accidents, stress, heart attacks, and other diseases related to lifestyle. The so-called Type A personality—characterized by chronic impatience, driving ambition, competitiveness, and free-floating hostility—is known to be linked to heart disease and is precisely the behavior that our culture defines as masculine (Ehren-

**Table 13–1  SEXISM: ECHOES OF RACIAL STEREOTYPES**

| | Women | African Americans |
|---|---|---|
| Link to highly visible personal traits | Secondary sex characteristics. | Skin color. |
| Assertion of innate inferiority | Women are mentally inferior. Women are irresponsible, unreliable, and emotional. | Blacks are mentally inferior. Blacks are irresponsible, unreliable, and pleasure-seeking. |
| Assertion that those who are disadvantaged are content with their "proper place" in society | "A woman's place is in the home." All women really enjoy being treated "like a woman." | "Blacks should remain in their place." Blacks are content living just as they do. |
| Assertion that victims are under the protection of their oppressors | "Men put women on a pedestal." | Whites "take care of" blacks. |
| Coping strategies on the part of victims | Behavior flattering to men; letting men think they are better even when they are not. Hiding one's real feelings. Attempting to outwit men. | Deferential behavior toward whites; letting whites think they are better even when they are not. Hiding one's real feelings. Attempting to outwit whites. |
| Barriers to opportunity | Women don't need an education. Confined to "women's work." Women should stay out of politics. | Blacks don't need an education. Confined to "black occupations." Blacks should stay out of politics. |
| Criticism of those who do not "stay in their place" | Assertive women are "pushy." Ambitious women are trying to be like men. Women as traditional targets of violence by men. | Assertive blacks are "uppity." Ambitious blacks are trying to be like whites. Blacks as traditional targets of violence by whites. |

SOURCE:   Adapted from Helen Mayer Hacker, "Women as a Minority Group," *Social Forces*, Vol. 30 (October 1951): 60–69; and "Women as a Minority Group: Twenty Years Later," in Florence Denmark, ed., *Who Discriminates Against Women?* (Beverly Hills, CA: Sage, 1974), pp. 124–34.

reich, 1983). Furthermore, insofar as men seek control over others, they lose the ability to experience intimacy and trust (French, 1985). One recent study concluded that although competition is supposed to separate "the men from the boys," in practice it separates men from men, and from everyone else (Raphael, 1988).

Overall, when human feelings, thoughts, and actions are rigidly scripted according to a culture's conceptions of gender, people cannot develop and freely express the full range of their humanity. Males are strongly pressured to be assertive, competitive, and in control, a weighty burden for many to bear. Females are constrained to be submissive, dependent, and self-effacing, regardless of their individual talents and personalities.

## Is Patriarchy Inevitable?

In technologically simple societies, patriarchy stems from individuals having little control over the natural differences of sex. Pregnancy and childbirth limit the scope of women's lives, while men's greater height and strength typically allow them to overpower women. Technological advances, however, give members of industrial societies a wider range of choices in how the two sexes interact. Contraception has given women greater control over pregnancy, just as industrial machinery has diminished the primacy of muscle power in everyday life. Today, then, biological differences provide little justification for patriarchy.

Categorical social inequality—whether based on race, ethnicity, or sex—comes under attack in the more egalitarian culture of industrial societies. In many industrial nations, laws mandate equal employment opportunities for women and men and equal pay for equal efforts. Nonetheless, in all industrial societies, the two sexes continue to hold different jobs and receive unequal pay, as we will explain presently.

Another indicator of patriarchy is housework; the more unequal the social standing of the two sexes, the greater the proportion of housework assigned to women. Global Map 13–1 puts housework in world perspective: although members of industrial societies share housework more than people in agrarian societies do, nowhere is housework shared equally.

Do the facts that women retain primary responsibility for the household while men control most wealth and power mean that patriarchy is inevitable? Some researchers claim that biological factors imprint different behaviors and motivations on the two sexes, making the complete eradication of patriarchy difficult, if not impossible (Goldberg, 1974, 1987). Many sociologists acknowledge that biological differences between the sexes have *some* effect on human behavior (Rossi, 1985). But virtually all sociologists believe that gender is primarily a social construction. As such, it is subject to change. Simply because no society has yet eliminated patriarchy, then, does not mean that we are prisoners of the past.

**Table 13–2  TRADITIONAL NOTIONS OF GENDER IDENTITY**

| Feminine Traits | Masculine Traits |
| --- | --- |
| Submissive | Dominant |
| Dependent | Independent |
| Unintelligent and incapable | Intelligent and competent |
| Emotional | Rational |
| Receptive | Assertive |
| Intuitive | Analytical |
| Weak | Strong |
| Timid | Brave |
| Content | Ambitious |
| Passive | Active |
| Cooperative | Competitive |
| Sensitive | Insensitive |
| Sex object | Sexually aggressive |
| Attractive because of physical appearance | Attractive because of achievement |

To understand the persistence of patriarchy, we now examine how gender is rooted and reproduced in society, a process that spans the way we learn to think of ourselves as children to how sexual inequality affects us as adults.

# Gender and Socialization

From birth until death, human feelings, thoughts, and actions reflect social definitions of the sexes. As children gain their first social experience, they quickly learn that their society defines females and males as different kinds of human beings; by about the age of three or four, they begin to apply gender standards to themselves (Kohlberg, 1966, cited in Lengermann & Wallace, 1985:37; Bem, 1981). Table 13–2 lists some of the traits that people in the United States traditionally have used to define females and males. Consider the overall pattern: not only do we tend to distinguish between the two sexes but we also define them in *opposing* terms. Polarizing humanity in terms of gender is still widespread in this country as it is elsewhere, although research suggests that most young people in the United States do not develop consistently "feminine" or "masculine" personalities (L. Bernard, 1980).

Just as socialization incorporates gender into personal identity, so it teaches us to *act* according to cultural conceptions of what is feminine and masculine. **Gender roles** (or sex roles) are *attitudes and activities that a culture links to each sex.* Gender roles are the active expression of gender identity. In other words, insofar as our culture defines males as ambitious and competitive, we expect them to engage in team sports and seek out positions of leadership. To the extent that females are defined as deferential and emotional, we expect them to be good listeners and supportive observers.

## Gender and the Family

The first question people usually ask about a newborn child—"Is it a boy or a girl?"—looms so large because the answer involves more than the infant's sex; it carries a great deal of significance for the child's entire life.

Sociologist Jessie Bernard, introduced in the box on page 358, suggests that females and males live in different worlds within a single society, and that the "pink world" of girls contrasts in many respects to the "blue world" of boys (1981). In fact, gender is at work

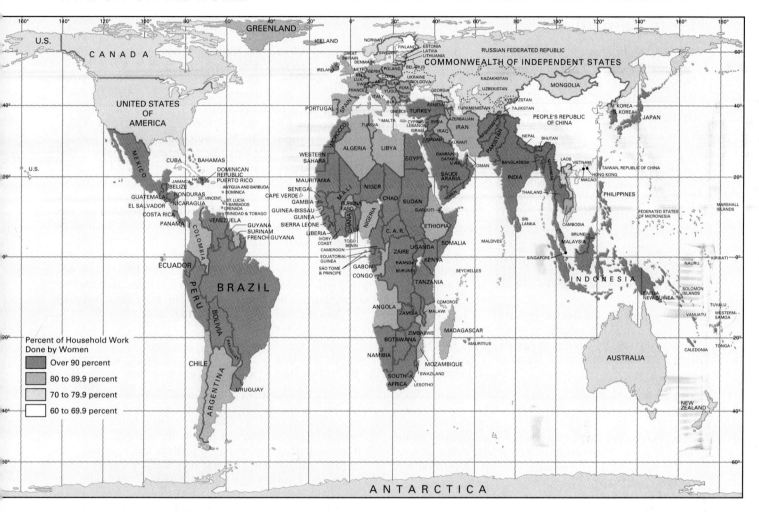

**Global Map 13–1** Housework in Global Perspective

Housework—made up of necessary, although tiring and repetitive, tasks—is one good indicator of how societies construct gender. To the extent that housework is carried out by only one sex, a society differentiates its members in terms of gender. In general, the greater the proportion of housework that women perform, the greater the social dominance of men. Housework is most rigidly assigned to women in poor societies of the Third World, although in Japan and many European societies as well women do almost all these tasks. The United States is more egalitarian with regard to housework than most of the world. The People's Republic of China appears to divide housework most equally, the result of deliberate socialist policies. Even there, however, men dominate women in a host of ways.

# Jessie Bernard

Now in her eighties, Jessie Bernard continues to make valuable contributions to the discipline of sociology. Her work has long focused on gender.

Bernard urges her colleagues to include women as well as men in their work. In the past, sociologists—even those critical of the status quo—have tended to disregard women. Karl Marx, for instance, paid almost no attention to women in his writings. One reason for not giving balanced attention to females and males, Bernard suggests, is that sociology, like other disciplines, has developed largely under the control of men. Many familiar sociological issues and concepts thus betray a built-in male bias.

Consider the topic of social stratification. As was explained in Chapter 10 ("Social Class in the United States"), to be a member of the upper class, a man must have considerable wealth. But this definition neglects the other half of humanity, since a woman's social class position is traditionally derived from *men*: initially from her father and subsequently from her husband. Further, in ranking the prestige of occupations (Table 10–1), sociologists usually ignore housework—conventionally the most common activity of women. By defining the concept of occupational prestige so that it applies primarily to men, sociologists exclude women from sociological research.

In sum, sociologists must use care to ensure that their work addresses both females and males; otherwise, the discipline investigates only half of society.

SOURCES: Based on Jessie Bernard (1981) and personal communication.

---

even before the birth of a child: more parents in the United States (45 percent in one study) claim to want a boy than a girl (20 percent) (cited in Lengermann & Wallace, 1985:61).

In global perspective, the preference for boys is even more pronounced. Societies that are strongly patriarchal place far greater value on males than on females. Many of these societies also face enormous population pressure. These two facts, taken together, set the stage for **female infanticide**, *the practice of aborting female fetuses and neglecting, or even actively killing, infant girls by parents who would prefer to raise boys.* In North Africa and most of Asia, life-threatening discrimination against females is commonplace. Researchers know that, assuming equal social treatment, a society should have about 106 females for every 100 males—a disparity that reflects the generally hardier physical condition of females. In the People's Republic of China, however, there are only 94 females for every 100 males. This means that roughly 12 percent of the females that we

would expect to find are not in the records. Some of this shortfall is explained by parents not reporting the birth of a daughter. The rest may well be due to active biases by families against daughters. Worldwide, researchers estimate, perhaps 100 million females are "missing," and many presumably have fallen victim to deadly discrimination (United Nations Development Programme, 1991).

As children grow, families continue to shape the lives of girls and boys differently. Research on parental attitudes suggests that fathers and mothers want sons who are strong, aggressive achievers while they expect daughters to be delicate, sensitive, and less assertive (Witkin-Lanoil, 1984). Parents may unconsciously convey these expectations in the way they handle their children. A researcher at an English university presented an infant dressed as either a boy or a girl to a number of women. By and large, the women handled the "female" child tenderly, with frequent hugs and caresses, while treating the "male" child more aggressively, often lifting him up high in the air or bouncing him on the knee (Bonner, 1984). Other research shows that mothers have more overall physical contact with infant boys than with infant girls (Major, 1981). The message is clear: the female world revolves around passivity and emotion, while the male world involves substantial independence and action.

## Gender and the Peer Group

As children reach school age, they interact more outside the family, especially with others their own age. Peer groups further distinguish the pink and blue worlds of girls and boys. The box explains how play groups shaped one young boy's sense of himself as masculine.

Janet Lever (1978), who spent a year observing fifth graders at play, concluded that female and male peer groups provide girls and boys with distinctive socialization. Boys, Lever reported, engage more in team sports—such as baseball and football—that involve many roles, complex rules, and clear objectives like scoring a run or making a touchdown. These games are nearly always competitive, separating winners from losers. Male peer activities reinforce masculine traits of aggression and maintaining control.

By contrast, girls in peer groups play hopscotch or jumprope, or simply talk, sing, or dance together. Spontaneous activities with few formal rules are commonplace, and this play rarely has "victory" as its ultimate goal so that girls are unlikely to oppose one another. Instead of teaching girls to be competitive, Lever explains, female peer groups promote interpersonal skills of communication and cooperation—presumably the basis for family life.

Carol Gilligan (1982) reports similar results in research concerning how children engage in moral reasoning. Boys learn to reason according to abstract principles. For them, "rightness" consists largely of "playing by the rules." In the female world, by contrast, morality is more a matter of responsibility to other people. Girls learn that "rightness" lies in maintaining close relationships with others. In a host of ways, then, boys and girls draw different lessons from their peer groups.

## Gender and Schooling

Even before children enter school, their reading tends to promote gender distinctions. A generation ago, a group of researchers examined books read by parents to pre–elementary school children (Weitzman et al., 1972). Males were the focus of attention in most of these books. For example, the researchers calculated the ratio of males to females in illustrations to be about ten to one. Similarly, three times as many book titles mentioned males as females. The researchers concluded that children "are bound to receive the impression that girls are not very important because no one has bothered to write books about them" (1972:1129).

**SOCIOLOGY OF EVERYDAY LIFE**

# Masculinity as Contest

By the time I was ten, the central fact in my life was the demand that I become a man. By then, the most important relationships by which I was taught to define myself were those I had with other boys. I already knew that I must see every encounter with another boy as a contest in which I must win or at least hold my own. . . . The same lesson continued (in school), after school, even in Sunday School. My parents, relatives, teachers, the books I read, movies I saw, all taught me that my self-worth depended on my manliness, my willingness to stand up to the other boys. This usually didn't mean a physical fight, though the willingness to stand up and "fight like a man" always remained a final test. But the relationships between us usually had the character of an armed truce. Girls weren't part of this social world at all yet, just because they weren't part of this contest. They didn't have to be bluffed, no credit was gained by cowing them, so they were more or less ignored. Sometimes when there were no grownups around we would let each other know that we liked each other, but most of the time we did as we were taught.

SOURCE: Silverstein (1977).

The books also presented the lives of females and males in stereotypical ways: females usually stayed home while males engaged in diverse and interesting activities. Here females displayed obvious concern with pleasing males: girls courted the favor of fathers and brothers, as women endeavored to please their husbands. More like dolls than living beings, the researchers argued, the girls in these books were by and large attractive and compliant objects, sources of support and pleasure to males.

In the last decade, the growing awareness among authors, teachers, and readers that childhood learning shapes people's lives as adults has prompted changes in children's literature. Recent research suggests that today's books for children portray females and males in a more balanced way, although some sex-stereotyping persists (Purcell & Stewart, 1990).

In addition to the formal lessons of school, what Raphaela Best (1983) calls "the second curriculum"—the informal messages and experiences of school life—encourages children to embrace traditional gender patterns. By the time children reach high school, topics of study reflect the different roles females and males are expected to assume as adults. Instruction in home-centered skills such as nutrition, cooking, and sewing has long been provided to classes composed almost entirely of females. Classes in woodworking and auto mechanics, conversely, still attract a nearly all-male enrollment.

In college, males and females follow this same pattern, tending toward different majors. Traditionally, the natural sciences—including physics, chemistry, biology, and mathematics—have been defined as part of the male province. Women have been encouraged to major in the humanities (such as English), the fine arts (painting, music, dance, and drama), or the social sciences (including anthropology and sociology). New areas of study also become linked to one sex or the other. Computer science, for example, with its grounding in engineering, logic, and abstract mathematics, predominantly appeals to men (Klein, 1984); courses in gender studies, by contrast, tend to enroll women.

Extracurricular activities also segregate the two sexes. Athletics and other activities for men benefit from more attention and greater funding. In additions, mass media coverage of men's athletics far outstrips coverage devoted to women's sports. This male dominance signals to women that they should assume supportive roles, as observers or cheerleaders, rather than excelling in their own right.

## Gender and the Mass Media

Chapter 5 ("Socialization") explained that the mass media exert a powerful influence on the socialization process. Films, magazines, and television significantly affect how we think and act.

Since it first captured the public imagination in the 1950s, television has placed the dominant segment of our population—white males—at center stage. Racial and ethnic minorities were all but absent from television until the early 1970s, and only in the last decade have a number of programs featured women in prominent roles.

Even when both sexes appear on camera, men

Some recent advertising reverses traditional gender definitions by portraying men as the submissive sex objects of successful women. Although the reversal is new, the use of gender stereotypes to sell consumer products is very old indeed.

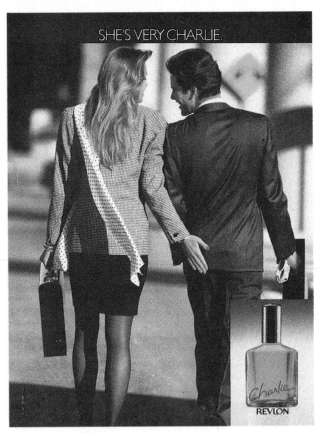

SHE'S VERY CHARLIE.

Charlie
REVLON

tend to play the brilliant detectives, fearless explorers, and skilled surgeons. Men take charge, give orders, and exude competence. Women, by contrast, generally rely on men, are portrayed as less capable, and are more often the targets of comedy (Busby, 1975). Women, who have also been traditionally valued for their sexual attractiveness, are spotlighted in shows that deal with romance. Such stereotypes have persisted into the 1990s, although more programming now involves interesting and responsible roles for women.

Change has come more slowly to advertising. Advertising, after all, sells products most successfully by conforming to widely established cultural patterns. Historically, television and magazine advertising has presented women in the home, rather than in the workplace, to sell household items such as cleaning products, food, clothing, and appliances. Men, on the other hand, predominate in ads for cars, travel, financial services, industrial companies, and alcoholic beverages. The authoritative "voiceover"—the faceless voice that describes some product in television and radio advertising—is almost always male (Busby, 1975; Courtney & Whipple, 1983).

Despite vigorous efforts by proponents of gender equality to combat sex-based stereotyping, women are still used in advertising simply as sex objects. The controversial "Swedish bikini team" television ad campaign in 1991, in which scantily clad women descend out of nowhere to entertain beer-drinking men, would simply be impossible for viewers to imagine if the sexes were reversed.

In a systematic study of magazine and newspaper ads, Erving Goffman (1979) found other, more subtle biases. Men, he concluded, are photographed to appear taller than women, implying male superiority. Women are more frequently presented lying down (on sofas and beds) or, like children, seated on the floor. In their expressions and gestures, men exude competence and authority, whereas women are more likely to appear in childlike poses. While men tend to focus on the products being advertised, the attention of women is generally directed toward men, conveying their supportive and submissive role.

Advertising tries to persuade us that embracing traditional notions of femininity and masculinity ensures our personal and professional success. With that groundwork in place, advertising then dictates what we should consume. For example, the masculine man drives the "right" car and vacations at the "in" place. The truly feminine woman, according to the $20-billion-a-year cosmetics industry, needs a plethora of beauty aids to help her look younger and more attractive to men (Wolf, 1990).

## Gender and Adult Socialization

Reinforced in so many ways by the surrounding culture, gender identity and gender roles typically come to feel "natural" well before we reach adulthood. As a result, the attitudes and behavior of adults commonly follow feminine and masculine patterns (Spender, 1980; Kramarae, 1981).

In a simple but revealing bit of research, Pamela Fishman (1977, 1978) tape-recorded two weeks of conversations by three young, white, middle-class, married couples in their homes. Even casual exchanges, she discovered, reinforce male dominance. For example, when the men began a conversation, the women usually kept it going; yet when the women initiated a conversation, the men frequently allowed it to founder. This suggests that what men have to say is considered more important. Similarly, women—but rarely men—opened conversations with remarks like "This is interesting" or "Do you know what?" This pattern, also common to the speech of children, is women's way of finding out if men really want to hear what they have to say. Starting a conversation with "This is interesting," for example, cues the listener to pay attention to what follows. Opening with "Do you know what?" amounts to stating, "I have something to say; are you willing to listen?"

The women in this research also asked many more questions than the men did, a further indication of deference to their partners. Both the men and women used a wide range of "minimal responses" (such as "yeah," "umm," and "huh"), but they used them in different ways. For the men, such responses expressed minimal interest, as if to say, "I guess I'll continue to listen if you insist on speaking." For the women, however, minimal responses more often took the form of "support work," inserted continually to show their interest in the conversation.

Years of gender-based socialization set the foundation for marriages between men and women who inhabit different social worlds. Not surprisingly, husbands and wives may have considerable difficulty simply communicating with each other. Studies of verbal interaction in marriage confirm that not talking openly—or sometimes not talking at all—is a problem common to spouses (Komarovsky, 1967; Rubin, 1976, 1983; Fitzpatrick, 1988; Tannen, 1990).

# Gender and Social Stratification

Gender implies more than how people think and act. The concept of **gender stratification** refers to *a society's unequal distribution of wealth, power, and privilege between the two sexes*. Specifically, societies allocate fewer valued resources to women than to men. This can be seen, first, in the world of work.

## Working Men and Women

In 1991, 66.4 percent of people in the United States over the age of fifteen were working for income; the labor force includes 76.2 percent of men and 57.4 percent of women (U.S. Bureau of Labor Statistics, 1991). In 1900, only about one-fifth of women were in the labor force; as is shown in Figure 13–1, that proportion has increased steadily in recent decades. Furthermore, 76.2 percent of women in the labor force in 1991 were working full time. The traditional view that earning an income is "man's work" thus no longer holds true.

Among the key factors altering the composition of the labor force are the growth of cities, declining family size, more flexible norms regarding appropriate roles for women, and, more recently, the increasing number of service jobs. In addition, because economic decline reduced the income of many families in the United States during the last fifteen years (see Chapter 10, "Social Class in the United States"), an increasing proportion of families require more than one income to maintain a comfortable standard of living. In 1991, about 60 percent of married couples relied on two incomes.

A common misconception holds that women in the labor force are single or, if married, without children. Of all married women, 58 percent work outside the home, and the proportion stays the same for married women with children under six. Among married women with children between six and seventeen years of age, 73 percent are employed. For divorced women with children, the comparable figures are higher still: 70 percent of women with younger children and 85 percent of women with older children (U.S. Bureau of the Census, 1991). A gradual increase in employer-sponsored child-care programs is giving more women and men the opportunity to combine the responsibilities of working and parenting, a trend that is especially important for divorced mothers.

**Figure 13–1**  Men and Women in the U.S. Labor Force
*(U.S. Bureau of Labor Statistics)*

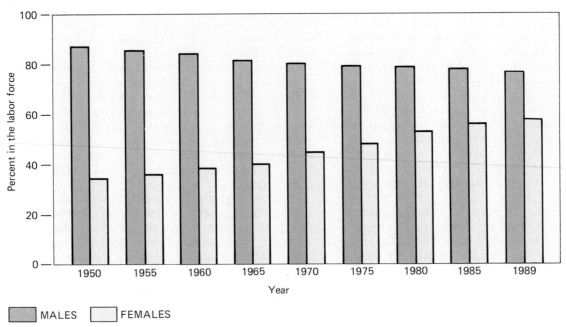

## Gender and Occupations

While the proportions of men and women in the labor force have been converging—especially since 1970—the work done by the two sexes remains distinct. According to the U.S. Bureau of Labor Statistics (1991), women enter a narrow range of occupations, with almost half of working women holding two types of jobs. Administrative support work, the first of these two, draws 28 percent of all working women. In this category fall clerical workers (secretaries, typists, stenographers, and the like) and other workers whose efforts typically support the work of men. Of all such "pink-collar" jobholders, not surprisingly, 80 percent are women. The second broad category is service work, performed by 18 percent of employed women. This includes waitressing and other food-service work as well as health-care positions. Both categories of jobs lie at the low end of the pay scale and offer limited opportunities for advancement.

Table 13–3 shows the ten occupations with the highest concentrations of women in 1990. Although increasing numbers of women, both married and single, are working, women remain highly segregated in the labor force because our society continues to link work to gender (Roos, 1983; Kemp & Coverman, 1989; U.S. Bureau of Labor Statistics, 1991).

Men predominate in most job categories beyond the ten occupations noted in the table. The highest proportion of men work in the trades: 99.5 percent of brickmasons, stonemasons, structural metal workers, and heavy-equipment mechanics are men. Men also hold the lion's share of positions that provide a great deal of income, prestige, and power. For example, more than 92 percent of engineers, 80 percent of lawyers and judges, 80 percent of physicians, 70 percent of corporate managers, and 65 percent of computer specialists are men (U.S. Department of Labor, 1991). Only a few women appear as the top executives of the largest corporations in the United States. Even where men and women do much the same work, titles (and consequently pay) confer greater benefits on men. A "special assistant to the president," for example, is likely to be a man, while an "executive secretary" is nearly always a woman.

There is one notable exception to this pattern, however: an increasing proportion of small businesses are now owned and operated by women. Women now run 30 percent of all firms in the United States, and the number of women-owned companies jumped by more than 50 percent during the 1980s. Most of these businesses are small; 90 percent are sole proprietorships with

**Table 13–3** JOBS WITH THE HIGHEST CONCENTRATIONS OF WOMEN, 1990

| Occupation | Number of Women Employed | Percent in Occupation Who Are Women |
|---|---|---|
| 1. Dental hygienist | 86,217 | 99.1% |
| 2. Secretary | 3,916,440 | 99.0% |
| 3. Dental assistant | 184,569 | 98.7% |
| 4. Prekindergarten and kindergarten teachers | 448,704 | 98.4% |
| 5. Private household child-care worker | 307,406 | 97.9% |
| 6. Child-care worker | 872,030 | 97.0% |
| 7. Receptionist | 825,470 | 97.0% |
| 8. Dress maker | 107,968 | 96.4% |
| 9. Licensed practical nurse | 426,609 | 96.3% |
| 10. Typist | 611,200 | 95.5% |

SOURCE: U.S. Bureau of Labor Statistics, *Employment and Earnings*, Vol. 38, No. 1, January 1991, pp. 185–90.

a single employee (Ando, 1990; U.S. Bureau of the Census, 1990; O'Hare & Larson, 1991). Even so, the success of these talented entrepreneurs demonstrates that women have the power, incentive, and drive to create opportunities for themselves, and many find the rewards of working for themselves far greater than those offered by larger, male-dominated companies.

Overall, then, gender stratification permeates the workplace, where men tend to hold occupational positions that confer more wealth and power than those typically held by women. This gender-based hierarchy is ever present in the job setting: male physicians are assisted by female nurses, male executives have female secretaries, and male airline pilots work with female flight attendants. In any occupation, the greater a job's income and prestige, the more likely it is that the position will be held by a man. Among teachers, for example, women make up 98 percent working at the kindergarten level; 85 percent in the elementary grades; and 53 percent at the secondary school level. But only 38 percent of professors in colleges and universities are women (U.S. Bureau of Labor Statistics, 1991). At the top of the pyramid of higher education, just 12 percent of college and university presidents are women, and these usually preside over smaller institutions, many that enroll only women (American Council on Education, 1984).

African-American artist Jacob Lawrence (1917– ) painted *Ironers* (1943) to depict the daily lives of women in his working-class neighborhood in New York's Harlem. The painting suggests that the work women perform in the labor force often parallels the tasks women perform in the home.

*Jacob Lawrence, Ironers. 1943. Gouache on paper, 21½ x 29½ (54.6 x 74.9). Signed in the bottom right: J. Lawrence 43. Private Collection.*

## Housework: Women's "Second Shift"

As we have already seen, housework—maintaining the home and caring for children—is the province of women throughout the world. In the United States, housework has always embodied a cultural contradiction: touted on the one hand as essential to an orderly life, carrying little reward or social prestige on the other (J. Bernard, 1981).

Surprisingly, women's rapid entry into the labor force has prompted little change in the pattern of responsibility for housework. One estimate indicates that the hours of housework performed by women declined only slightly in recent decades and the proportion of housework shared by men remained the same (Fuchs, 1986). Typically, couples in the United States share the disciplining of children and managing finances, but few other tasks. Men routinely perform home repairs and mow the lawn; women see to the daily shopping, cooking, and cleaning. Thus women commonly return from the workplace to face a "second shift" of unpaid work on the home front (Schooler et al., 1984; Benokraitis & Feagin, 1986; Hochschild, 1989).

Underlying changes in the workplace in recent decades is a set of contradictory attitudes. Men support the idea of women in the labor force, and many men depend on the income women earn; yet men resist modifying their own behavior to ease the pressure on women of juggling responsibilities at home and on the job (Komarovsky, 1973). Only in rare cases, such as the Israeli kibbutzim, is housework shared to any great extent. Even in Sweden—a society with a strong belief in the social equality of the sexes—only one in five couples shares housework equitably (Haas, 1981).

## Gender, Income, and Wealth

Because women predominate in clerical and service jobs while men hold most business and professional positions, women earn less than men. Thus, income—a major measure of self-worth and a source of power—reinforces women's disadvantaged position in the occupational and social hierarchy.

In 1990, the median earnings for women working full time were $19,822, while men working full time earned $27,678. Stated more simply, for every dollar earned by men, women earned about 72 cents. Women thus cluster in low-paying positions, while men tend to rank among the more affluent. Of all full-time workers, 72 percent of working women earned less than $25,000 in 1990, whereas just over half of men earned more. At the other extreme, men were six times more likely than women (4.5 percent versus 0.7 percent) to earn more than $75,000 (U.S. Bureau of the Census, 1991).

In global perspective, research shows that income

disparity due to gender is greater in the United States than in many other industrial nations, including Australia, Canada, Norway, and Sweden, but not Japan (Rosenfeld & Kalleberg, 1990; United Nations Development Programme, 1991). In historical context, however, differences in earnings between men and women in the United States have gradually declined in recent decades. Some of this change is due to increasing opportunities for working women; mostly, however, it reflects a *decline* in the earnings of men.

This earning disparity stems primarily from the different jobs held by men and women. Taking a closer look, we discover a close link between jobs and gender: jobs with less clout are considered "women's work," and, turning the argument around, jobs have less value to the extent that they are performed by women (Parcel, Mueller, & Cuvelier, 1986). During the 1980s, this disparity was challenged by people who advocated a policy of "comparable worth," the concept that women and men should be paid not according to historical double standards but rather based on the worth of what they do. Thus women should receive equal pay for work that has equal, or comparable, worth. Several countries (including Great Britain and Australia) have national comparable worth laws, and some areas of the United States have passed legislation of this kind. Still, critics argue, women in this country are losing as much as $1 billion annually based on their sex.

A second cause of this gender-based income disparity has to do with the family. Both men and women have children, of course, but parenthood is more of a barrier to the careers of women than it is to the advancement of men. Pregnancy, childbirth, and rearing small children keep some younger women out of the labor force altogether at a time when men of the same age stand to make significant occupational gains. As a result, women workers have less job seniority than their male counterparts (Fuchs, 1986). Moreover, women who choose to have children may be reluctant or unable to maintain fast-paced jobs that demand evening and weekend work. Career women with children may seek jobs that offer a shorter commuting distance, flexible hours, and child-care services (Schwartz, 1989). The box on pages 366-67 examines a recent—and controversial—proposal to benefit corporate women.

The two factors noted so far—type of work and family responsibilities—account for roughly two-thirds of the earnings disparity between women and men. Researchers assume that a third factor—discrimination against women—accounts for the remainder (Pear,

1987). Because discrimination is illegal, it is often practiced in subtle ways, but it remains a major cause of economic disadvantage for working women (Benokraitis & Feagin, 1986). Corporate women often encounter a "glass ceiling," a barrier that, while formally denied by high company officials, effectively prevents women from rising above middle management. The traditional dominance of men at the highest corporate levels excludes women from "old boys' networks" that support many younger men on the way up. Then, too, some men are threatened by talented and ambitious women just as some are uneasy about interacting with colleagues whom they find sexually attractive.

For a variety of reasons, then, women earn less than men even within a single occupational category. As shown in Table 13–4, this disparity varies according

**Table 13–4  EARNINGS OF FULL-TIME U.S. WORKERS, BY SEX, 1990\***

| Selected Occupational Categories | Median Income (dollars) Men | Median Income (dollars) Women | Women's Income as a Percentage of Men's |
|---|---|---|---|
| Executives, administrators, and managers | $40,103 | $24,589 | 61% |
| Professional specialties | $39,449 | $27,933 | 71% |
| Technical workers | $31,371 | $21,768 | 69% |
| Sales | $29,676 | $16,057 | 54% |
| Precision production, craft, and repair workers | $26,499 | $17,457 | 66% |
| Clerical and other administrative support workers | $25,138 | $17,517 | 70% |
| Transportation workers | $23,612 | $16,288 | 69% |
| Machine operators and tenders | $22,343 | $14,463 | 65% |
| Service workers | $18,903 | $11,669 | 62% |
| Farming, forestry, and fishing workers | $13,885 | $11,305 | 63% |
| All occupations listed above | $27,430 | $18,778 | 68% |

\* Workers aged 15 and over.

SOURCE: U.S. Bureau of the Census, *Current Population Reports*, Series P-60, No. 168, Washington, DC: U.S. Government Printing Office, 1991.

## Corporate Women: The "Mommy-Track" Controversy

The facts of corporate life are changing. Once the preserve of male executives and female support workers, management positions are now being occupied by women in record numbers. This is good news for corporations, because women are among the top college and business school graduates in the United States. The end of the post–World War II baby boom has reduced the supply of corporate workers, while the rapid growth in administrative positions in the new "information economy" has increased the demand for talented people. Overall, there are no longer enough men (and even fewer *good* men) to fill all the positions. Speaking purely in terms of the bottom line, U.S. corporations need women.

At the same time, the corporate world is decidedly unfriendly to women. Felice N. Schwartz—founder and president of Catalyst, an organization that promotes the

careers of women—explains the problem this way: by trying to make women equal to men in the workplace, we now ignore *maternity*, the most crucial difference between the two sexes. Many young adults want to divide their time and energy between a career and young children. Currently,

Schwartz claims, doing this is easy for men, but almost impossible for women. As evidence, she points out that, by age forty, 90 percent of executive men have children, but only 35 percent of executive women do. Men, in other words, do not face a conflict between family and career, as long as their wives take responsibility for child care.

Businesses have long been uneasy about women employees having children because, under current policies, motherhood takes women away from their jobs. Professional women usually start thinking about having children in their early thirties, after corporations have invested almost a decade in training them. Paradoxically, when a corporate woman becomes a mother, her company is likely to pressure her to decide between the company and her family. But forcing such a choice is unfair because women usually want *both*

to type of work, but in only two of these selected job classifications do women earn more than 70 percent of what men do.

Finally, perhaps because women typically outlive men, many people in the United States think that women own most of the country's wealth. Government statistics tell a different story: 57 percent of individuals with $1 million or more in assets were men, although widows were highly represented. The distribution is the same (57 percent men, 43 percent women) among people with more modest wealth (between $250,000 and $1 million) (U.S. Bureau of the Census, 1991). Looking at the handful of richest people in the United States, estimates prepared by *Forbes* magazine in 1991 listed

only sixty-one women (15 percent) among our country's four hundred richest individuals.

### Gender and Education

Women have traditionally been discouraged, and sometimes formally excluded, from higher education because advanced schooling was thought to be unnecessary for homemakers. In 1990, however, 54 percent of all associate's and bachelor's degrees were earned by women, with the remaining 46 percent earned by men (National Center for Education Statistics, 1991).

As noted earlier, men and women still tend to

career and family. Currently, however, many mothers end up leaving their careers; when that occurs, both the corporations and the women themselves lose out.

The solution to the problem, Schwartz suggests, is for corporations to develop two tracks for women executives, a "career track" and a "career and family track." Women who wish to put their careers first (even if they have children) should be identified early and given as much opportunity and encouragement as the best and most ambitious men.

"Career and family women" —the majority of women, in Schwartz's view—value their occupations, but are willing to forgo some professional advancement so they can care for their children. These women can be a vital asset to a company, Schwartz continues, especially in the middle-management positions currently staffed by less competent men. By creating positions of moderate responsibility, with part-time, flex-time, or job-sharing options, corporations would allow women to combine career and child rearing. Women often bring much-needed creativity and enthusiasm to jobs traditionally held by men who have stalled in their careers. Finally, a "career and family" option should never rule out women returning to the "career track" at a later time. Whatever women eventually decide to do, a twin-track program allows corporations to recover their investment from past training and gain future benefits from loyal workers whose personal needs are being met.

Schwartz's proposal has generated a heated controversy. Some critics fear that creating a "mommy track" would embolden those who claim that women have a weaker attachment to their careers, thereby undermining women's gains in the workplace. And because such a plan is unlikely to apply to men, critics charge, it may reinforce the traditional notion that women are simply unsuited to management. Thus, critics conclude, Schwartz's proposal will compromise women's position in the corporate workplace rather than bolstering it.

Schwartz disagrees. Women, she claims, have demonstrated that they are the equal of men in any kind of work. Because roughly 40 percent of management positions are now held by women, corporations have an unprecedented responsibility to give women more choices about how they do their jobs. By expanding the range of choices open to women, corporations will defuse the conflict between careers and children. In the process, corporations will benefit from more productive and satisfied employees.

SOURCE: Schwartz (1989).

---

pursue different courses of study in college, although less so than in the past. In 1970, for example, only 17 percent of the bachelor's degrees in natural sciences, computer science, and engineering were awarded to women; by 1990 the proportion had almost doubled, nearing one-third.

Women now enjoy more opportunities for postgraduate education, often a springboard to high-prestige jobs. Today, when all areas of study are counted, women earn more master's degrees (51.1 percent of the total) than men do (48.9 percent). Furthermore, a growing number of women are pursuing academic programs that were until recently virtually all male. For example, in 1970 only a few hundred women received a Master of Business Administration (M.B.A.) degree; in 1980 the number reached 12,000 (25 percent of such degrees); by 1990, the number exceeded 23,000 (34 percent of degrees) (Kaufman, 1982; National Center for Education Statistics, 1991).

However, men still outnumber women in many professional fields. In 1990, men received two-thirds of doctorates (although women earned 52 percent of Ph.D.s in sociology). Men also earned 60 percent of law degrees (LL.B. and J.D.), 66 percent of medical degrees (M.D.), and 74 percent of dental degrees (D.D.S. and D.M.D.) (National Center for Education Statistics, 1991). In a culture that still defines high-paying professions (and the drive and competitiveness needed to succeed in them) as masculine, women may be discouraged from completing professional education after they begin their postgraduate studies (Fiorentine, 1987). Nonetheless, the proportion of women in professional schools and the professions is rising steadily.

## Gender and Politics

A century ago, virtually no women held elected office in the United States. Women were legally barred from voting in national elections in the United States until 1920 (until 1917 in Canada). A few women were candidates for political office, however, even before they could vote. The Equal Rights Party supported Victoria Woodhull for the U.S. presidency in 1872; perhaps it was a sign of the times that she spent election day in a New York City jail. Table 13–5 cites milestones in women's gradual movement into political life.

Today, thousands of women serve as mayors of cities and towns across the United States, and tens of thousands more hold responsible administrative posts in the federal government (Mashek & Avery, 1983; Schreiner, 1984). At the state level, women comprised a mere 6 percent of legislators in 1970; by 1991, the proportion had more than tripled to 21 percent. Less change has occurred at the highest levels of politics, although a majority of people claim that they would support a woman for any office, including the presidency. In 1992 (prior to national elections), 3 of the 50 state governors were women (6 percent); in Congress, 29 of 435 members of the House of Representatives (6 percent) and 2 of 100 senators (2 percent) were women.

## Minority Women

If minorities (see Chapter 12, "Race and Ethnicity") are socially disadvantaged, are minority women doubly so? Generally speaking, yes. First, there is the disadvantage associated with race and ethnicity. For example, in 1990, median annual earnings for African-American women working full time were $18,518—88.9 percent as much as the $20,840 earned by white women. Hispanic women earned $16,186, which was 77.7 percent as much as their white (non-Hispanic) counterparts. Second, there is the obstacle associated with sex. Thus, African-American women earned 86.0 percent as much as African-American men, while Hispanic women earned about 83.8 percent as much as Hispanic men.

**Table 13–5  SIGNIFICANT "FIRSTS" FOR WOMEN IN U.S. POLITICS**

1872  First woman to run for the presidency (Victoria Woodhull) represents the Equal Rights Party.

1917  First woman elected to the House of Representatives (Jeannette Rankin of Montana).

1924  First women elected state governors (Nellie Tyloe Ross of Wyoming and Miriam Ferguson of Texas); both followed their husbands into office.
First woman to have her name placed in nomination for the vice presidency at the convention of a major political party (Lena Jones Spring).

1931  First woman to serve in the Senate (Hattie Caraway of Arkansas); completed the term of her husband upon his death and was reelected in 1932.

1932  First woman appointed to a presidential cabinet (Frances Perkins, Secretary of Labor); as of 1990, only eight women have been so appointed.

1964  First woman to have her name placed in nomination for the presidency at the convention of a major political party (Margaret Chase Smith).

1972  First black woman to have her name placed in nomination for the presidency at the convention of a major political party (Shirley Chisholm).

1981  First woman appointed to the U.S. Supreme Court (Sandra Day O'Connor).

1984  First woman to be successfully nominated for the vice presidency (Geraldine Ferraro).

1988  First woman chief executive to be elected to consecutive third term (Madeleine Kunin, governor of Vermont).

SOURCE:  Adapted from Sandra Salmans, "Women Ran for Office Before They Could Vote," *New York Times,* July 13, 1984, p. A 11.

Combining these disadvantages, African-American women earned 61.3 percent as much as white men and Hispanic women earned 53.6 percent as much (U.S. Bureau of the Census, 1991).

The reduced income of minority women reflects their lower position on the occupational ladder in comparison to white women. Women of color tend to be more concentrated in lower-paying jobs (Bonilla-Santiago, 1990). Further, whenever the economy sags, as it has in recent years, minority women are especially likely to experience declining income and unemployment.

Chapter 10 ("Social Class in the United States") noted that women are becoming a larger proportion of this nation's poor. The primary reason for this trend is that more families are headed by women, and this pattern puts families at risk of poverty. In 1990, 53.1 percent of poor families were headed by women, in contrast to

4.9 percent headed by men. The link between poverty and families headed by women is especially dramatic among African Americans: families headed by women comprised 75.1 percent of all African-American families in poverty; the comparable proportions for Hispanics was 46.1 percent, and for whites, 43.5 percent.

## Are Women a Minority?

In Chapter 12 ("Race and Ethnicity") a minority was defined as a category of people both socially disadvantaged and identifiable by physical or cultural traits. In a patriarchal society, women fit this definition, since they contend with a number of social barriers because of their sex, as we have explained.

Even so, most white women do *not* think of themselves as members of a minority (Hacker, 1951; Lengermann & Wallace, 1985). This is partly because, more than racial and ethnic minorities, white women belong to families at higher social levels. Yet, within every social class, women typically have less income, wealth, and power than men do. In fact, patriarchy makes women dependent for their social standing on men—first their fathers and later their husbands (J. Bernard, 1981).

Another reason that women may not consider themselves a minority is that they have been socialized to accept their situation as natural. A woman taught conventional ideas about gender believes that she should be deferential to men.

In sum, women—especially the relatively privileged—may not think of themselves as a minority. Yet as a category of people in the United States, women have both a distinctive identity and social disadvantages just as other minorities do.

## Violence Against Women

Perhaps the most wrenching kind of suffering that our society imposes on women is violence. As we explained in Chapter 8 ("Deviance"), official statistics reveal that criminal violence has an overwhelmingly male cast. This is not surprising since aggressiveness is a trait our culture defines as masculine. (What, for example, makes a man a "wimp" according to our norms and values? What, by contrast, makes him a "real man?") Furthermore, a great deal of "manly" violence is directed against women, which might also be expected since much of what is culturally defined as feminine is devalued and even despised.

Because violence is commonplace in our society, and closely linked to gender, it arises most often where men and women interact most intensively. Richard Gelles (cited in Roesch, 1984) argues that, with the exception of the police and the military, the family is the most violent group in the United States. Individuals are more likely to be attacked at home, Gelles continues, than they are in any other setting. Both sexes suffer from family violence although, by and large, women sustain more serious injuries than men do (Straus & Gelles, 1986; Schwartz, 1987; Gelles & Cornell, 1990). Chapter 15 ("Family") examines family violence in more detail.

Violence against women also occurs in casual relationships. As Chapter 8 ("Deviance") explained, the notion that sexual violence involves strangers is a myth; most rapes, for instance, are perpetrated by men known (and sometimes even trusted) by women. A tendency toward sexual violence, in other words, is built into our way of life. Dianne F. Herman (1992) argues that all forms of violence against women—from the wolf whistles that intimidate women on city streets to a pinch in a crowded subway to physical assaults that occur at home—are expressions of a "rape culture." By this, Herman means that violence is used by men as a means to dominate women. Sexual violence, then, is fundamentally about *power* rather than sex; that is why it is properly studied as a dimension of gender stratification (Griffin, 1982). Moreover, Herman argues, it is not primarily "weirdos" and misfits who engage in violence against women. Because our patriarchal way of life defines the control of women as normative, men who exercise power in this way are actually well adjusted to their surroundings. To these men, sexual violence forms a strategy to generate fear—and, ultimately, compliance—among women. No wonder surveys indicate that women are several times more likely than men to be afraid even when walking in their own neighborhoods (N.O.R.C., 1991).

### Sexual Harassment

The 1991 Senate hearings that led to the confirmation of Supreme Court Justice Clarence Thomas drew national attention to the issue of **sexual harassment,** which can be defined as *comments, gestures, or physical contact of a sexual nature that is deliberate, repeated, and unwelcome.* Anita Hill, a law professor and former colleague,

Although allegations of sexual harassment made by Anita Hill against Clarence Thomas did not prevent his appointment to the Supreme Court, the incident brought this issue to the attention of the entire nation. Just as important, mass media coverage of the case made all too clear that national power in the United States is in the hands of men.

alleged that Thomas harassed her during the time they worked together for the federal government. The Senate never clearly resolved the specific allegations made by Hill and vigorously denied by Thomas; however, people across the United States lined up on one side or the other as the episode touched off a national debate that promises to significantly redefine the norms of workplace interaction between the sexes.

Both men and women can be victims of sexual harassment. For two reasons, however, the victims of harassment are typically women. First, because our culture encourages men to be sexually assertive and to view women in sexual terms, sexuality can easily find its way into social interaction in the workplace, on the campus, and elsewhere. Second, most individuals in positions of power—including business executives, physicians, bureau chiefs, assembly line supervisors, professors, and military officers—are men who typically oversee the work of women. Surveys carried out in widely different work settings confirm that women find the problem of sexual harassment to be widespread; generally, more than half of respondents report receiving some form of recent unwanted sexual attention (Loy & Stewart, 1984; Paul, 1991). In one study of colleges, one-third of women students reported unwanted sexual advances from their male teachers (Dziech & Weiner, 1984).

Sexual harassment is sometimes blatant and direct, as when a supervisor solicits sexual favors from a subordi-

nate coupled with threats of reprisals if the advances are refused. Behavior of this kind—which not only undermines the dignity of an individual but prevents her from earning a living—is widely condemned. Courts have declared such *quid pro quo* sexual harassment (the Latin phrase means "one thing in return for another") to be illegal and a form of discrimination that violates civil rights.

However, the problem of harassment frequently involves subtle behavior—sexual teasing, innuendos, off-color jokes, pin-ups displayed in the workplace—none of which any individual may intend to be harassing to a specific subordinate or coworker. In effect, however, such actions may create a *hostile environment* that is interpreted as sexual harassment (Cohen, 1991; Paul, 1991). Sexual harassment of this kind is inherently ambiguous, with each party seeing the behavior in question in a different light. For example, a man may think that showing romantic interest in a coworker is paying the woman a compliment; she, on the other hand, may find his behavior offensive and a hindrance to her job performance.

Many women have long chafed at subtle forms of harassment. Untangling precisely what constitutes a hostile working environment, however, demands clearer standards of proper conduct than those we have now. Creating such guidelines—and educating the public to embrace them—is likely to take some time, since it means defining new forms of deviance (Cohen, 1991; Majka, 1991). In the end, courts (and, ultimately, the court of public opinion) will have to draw the line between what amounts to "reasonable friendliness" and behavior that is "unwarranted harassment."

As we have already explained, the entrance of women into the workplace has accelerated in recent decades. But merely having the two sexes working side by side does not in itself ensure that people will treat each other equally and with respect. Defining new moral and legal codes that will condemn and discourage sexual harassment will not be easy, as the controversy over the Thomas hearing revealed. But doing so is a necessary step toward protecting the rights of everyone in the workplace.

### Pornography

*Pornography* underlies sexual violence as well. Defining pornography, however, has long been a vexing question, and the Supreme Court has been unable to formulate a single, specific standard to distinguish what is, and what is not, pornographic. Current law requires local cities and counties to decide for themselves what violates "community standards" of decency and lacks any redeeming social value. There is little doubt, however, that pornography (loosely defined) has a large following in the United States: X-rated videos, 900 telephone numbers providing sexual conversation, and a host of sexually explicit magazines together constitute a $7-billion-dollar-a-year industry.

Traditionally, pornography was not tied to sexual violence at all. Rather, it was cast as a *moral* issue, a violation of cultural norms about how people should express their sexuality. National survey data show that pornography is still widely viewed in moral terms: 60 percent of adults in the United States endorse the statement that "sexual materials lead to a breakdown of morals" (N.O.R.C., 1991:258).

More recently, however, pornography has come under attack for fostering a social climate that demeans women. From this point of view, pornography is framed as a *political* issue because pornographic material graphically underscores the notion that men should control both sexuality and women. Catherine MacKinnon (1987) has denounced pornography as one foundation of male dominance in the United States because it dehumanizes women as the subservient playthings of men. Worth noting, in this context, is that the term pornography is derived from the Greek word *porne*, meaning a harlot who acts as a man's sexual slave.

A related charge asserts that pornography promotes specific acts of violence against women. Certainly anyone who has viewed recent "hard-core" videos can understand this assertion. Yet, using strict scientific standards, it is difficult to demonstrate a clear cause-and-effect relationship between what people look at and how they act. However, research does bear out the conclusion that pornography encourages men to think of women as objects rather than as people (Mallamuth & Donnerstein, 1984; Attorney General's Commission on Pornography, 1986). The public as a whole also shares a concern about the behavioral effects of pornography, with 55 percent of adults supporting the contention that pornography "leads people to commit rape" (N.O.R.C., 1991:258).

Like sexual harassment, the pornography issue raises complex and sometimes conflicting concerns. Certainly most people object to material they find offensive, but most also endorse the right of free speech and wish to safeguard artistic expression. But pressure to restrict this kind of material is building as the result of an unlikely coalition of conservatives (who oppose pornography on moral grounds) and progressives (who condemn it for political reasons).

# Theoretical Analysis of Gender

Both the structural-functional and social-conflict paradigms point up the importance of gender to social organization.

## Structural-Functional Analysis

The structural-functional paradigm views society as a complex system of many separate but integrated parts. In this view, every social structure contributes to the overall operation of society.

As explained in Chapter 3 ("Culture"), the earliest hunting and gathering societies had limited ability to challenge biological facts and forces. Lacking effective birth control, women experienced frequent pregnancies, and the responsibilities of child care kept them close to home more or less continually (Lengermann & Wallace, 1985). As a result, social norms encouraged women to center their lives around home and children. Likewise, based on their greater short-term strength, norms guided men to the pursuit of game and other tasks away from the home. This sexual division of labor created feminine and masculine worlds.

As long as technology remains simple, the biological facts of sex and the cultural facts of gender closely intertwine. This is not a matter of biological imperative so much as a cultural strategy that preindustrial societies adopt to survive. Over many generations, the sex-based division of labor becomes institutionalized, built into the structure of society and taken for granted.

Industrial technology opens up a vastly greater range of cultural possibilities. The muscles of humans and other animals no longer serve as the primary sources of energy, so the physical strength of men loses much of its earlier significance. At the same time, the ability to control reproduction gives women greater choice in shaping their lives. At this level of technological development, societies can unlock considerable amounts of talent by eroding traditional conceptions of gender. Yet change comes slowly, because gender-based assumptions about behavior are deeply embedded in social mores.

### Talcott Parsons: Gender and Complementarity

In addition, as Talcott Parsons (1942, 1951, 1954) explained, gender differences form a social fabric that integrates society—at least in its traditional form. Gender lies at the heart of Parsons's theory of *complementary roles* by which men and women join together to form family units that, in turn, carry out other functions vital to the operation of society. Women are charged with maintaining the internal cohesion of the family, managing the household, and taking primary responsibility for raising children; men connect the family to the larger world, primarily by participating in the labor force. From this point of view, one would expect the increasing participation of women in the labor force to transform the traditional family.

Parsons further argued that the two sexes are exposed to distinctive patterns of socialization in order to prepare them for their respective adult roles. Boys and girls learn their appropriate gender identity and acquire skills and attitudes deemed appropriate to their sex. This explains the earlier observation that, destined for the labor force, boys are taught to be rational, self-assured, and competitive—a complex of traits that Parsons described as *instrumental*. To prepare girls for child rearing, their socialization stresses what Parsons called *expressive*

qualities, such as emotional responsiveness and sensitivity to others.

Finally, according to Parsons, society promotes gender-linked behavior through various means of social control. This social guidance is partly internal: people who violate gender norms may experience guilt. It is also partly external, with the failure to display the normative gender traits provoking criticism from others. One notable method of fostering conformity, according to Parsons, is teaching each person that straying too far from accepted gender roles courts rejection by members of the opposite sex. In simple terms, women learn to view nonmasculine men as sexually unattractive, while unfeminine women risk rejection by men.

***Critical evaluation.*** Structural-functionalism highlights the traditional complementarity of gender roles. From this point of view, gender integrates society both structurally (in terms of what people do) and morally (in terms of what people believe). This approach was very influential during mid-century; however, for several reasons it is rarely used today by researchers exploring the impact of gender on society.

First, critics charge that this analysis supports a vision of society that is less and less consistent with how people actually live. For example, many women have traditionally worked outside the home out of economic necessity, and the proportion doing so is rising steadily. Another problem, in the eyes of critics, is that Parsons's analysis minimizes the personal strains and social costs produced by rigid, traditional gender roles (Giele, 1988). Finally, to those whose goals include equality for the two sexes, this approach is patently unappealing. From this perspective, what Parsons describes as gender complementarity simply amounts to male domination.

## Social-Conflict Analysis

From a social-conflict point of view, gender involves not just differences in action but disparities in power. Conventional gender patterns historically have benefited men while subjecting women to prejudice and discrimination comparable to that experienced by racial and ethnic minorities (Hacker, 1951, 1974; Collins, 1971; Lengermann & Wallace, 1985). Thus gender inequality promotes not cohesion but tension and conflict as men seek to protect their privileges while women challenge the status quo.

A social-conflict analysis of gender also places *sex-*

**"Hire him. He's got great legs."**

SEX DISCRIMINATION ISN'T FUNNY.
SUPPORT THE NATIONAL ORGANIZATION FOR WOMEN
28 EAST 56 STREET N.Y.C. 10022

For generations, the evaluation of women in terms of physical appearance instead of job performance contributed to unequal occupational opportunities. By turning the tables, this educational poster helps people to see how grossly unfair this practice really is.

*ism* at center stage. A web of notions about female inferiority that justify depriving women of opportunities and subjecting them to manipulation and violence, sexism supports lower pay for women in the workplace, the exclusion of women from positions of power in national affairs, and the subordination of women in the home.

As noted in earlier chapters, the social-conflict paradigm draws heavily on the ideas of Karl Marx. Ironically, in light of his other criticisms of society, Marx paid little attention to gender, focusing his work almost exclusively on men. His friend and collaborator Friedrich Engels, however, did develop a conflict analysis of gender

that brings to bear on this issue Marx's general ideas about social classes (1902; orig. 1884).

### Friedrich Engels: Gender and Class

Engels suggested that, although they were different, the activities of women and men in hunting and gathering societies had comparable importance. A successful hunt may have brought men great prestige, but the vegetation gathered by women constituted most of a society's food supply (Leacock, 1978). As technological advances led to a productive surplus, however, social equality and communal sharing gave way to the notion of private property and, ultimately, to stratified social classes. At this point, men gained pronounced power over women. With surplus wealth to dispose of, men of the upper class took a keen interest in their progeny, who would inherit their estates. In Engels's view, this control of property encouraged the creation of monogamous marriage and the family. Ideally, then, men could be certain of paternity and, by identifying their offspring—especially sons—they could plan for their wealth to be passed on to the next generation of males. For their part, women built their lives around bearing and raising children.

Engels contended that capitalism intensified this male domination. First, capitalism created more wealth, which conferred greater privilege on men as the owners of property, the heirs of property, and the primary wage earners. Second, an expanding capitalist economy depended on defining people—especially women—as consumers and encouraging them to seek personal fulfillment through buying and owning products. Third, to support men working in factories, women were assigned the task of maintaining the home. The double exploitation of capitalism, then, lies in paying low wages for male labor and *no* wages for female work (Eisenstein, 1979; Barry, 1983; Jagger, 1983; Vogel, 1983).

*Critical evaluation.* The social-conflict paradigm stresses inequality; thus any social-conflict analysis of gender must highlight how societies place the sexes in differential positions with regard to privilege, prestige, and power. As a result, conflict approaches are decidedly critical of conventional gender roles.

Social-conflict analysis, too, has critics who cite its weaknesses. One problem, voiced by people with traditional attitudes, is that social-conflict analysis casts conventional families—historically defined by traditionalists as morally positive—as a source of social evil. Second, from a more practical point of view, social-conflict analysis minimizes the extent to which women and men live together cooperatively, and often quite happily, in families. A third problem with this approach, at least for some critics, is its contention that capitalism stands at the root of gender stratification. Societies with socialist economic systems—including the People's Republic of China and the former Soviet Union—have also been strongly patriarchal.

# Feminism

**Feminism** is *the advocacy of social equality for the sexes, in opposition to patriarchy and sexism.* Feminism is not new to the United States. In the 1840s, a number of women brought together by their common opposition to racial slavery formed a "first wave" of feminism. Elizabeth Cady Stanton and Lucretia Mott, two feminist pioneers, drew parallels between the oppression of people of color and the oppression of women (Randall, 1982). The primary objective of the early women's movement was securing the right to vote, but after suffrage for women was achieved in 1920, other disadvantages persisted. As a response, a "second wave" of feminism (sometimes termed the "New Women's Movement") swelled in the 1960s and continues to reshape our society today.

## Basic Feminist Ideas

Feminism embraces a wide range of thinking about women and men; there are many issues on which people who consider themselves feminists disagree. Generally, though, all feminists share the view that our personal experiences are significantly linked to gender. How we think of ourselves (gender identity), how we act (gender roles), and our privilege or deprivation relative to the opposite sex (gender stratification) are all derived from how our society attaches meaning and social standing to the two sexes. Here are five ideas widely considered to be central to feminism.

1. **The importance of change.** First and foremost, feminism, which is critical of the status quo, advocates equitable social standing for women and men. Thus feminism calls not only for sociological thinking but also for political action. A basic feminist contention holds that "the personal is political." A feminist perspective on human thought and in-

teraction demands that we consider how culture defines masculinity in terms of power over others while constructing femininity as a model of altruism.

2. **Expanding human choice.** Feminists argue that cultural conceptions of gender divide the full range of human qualities into two distinct and limited spheres: the female world of emotions and cooperation, and the male world of rationality and competition. As an alternative, feminists pursue a "reintegration of humanity" (French, 1985). Feminism holds that every human being is capable of developing *all* human traits. Through a process of feminist resocialization, then, all people can pursue their human potential without limits based on gender.

3. **Eliminating gender stratification.** Feminism seeks an end to laws and cultural norms that confer privilege on men while simultaneously limiting the opportunities of women to gain education, income, and prestige from the widest range of work. Supporters of the women's movement oppose the historical pattern by which the female half of the population has been subject to decisions made by the male half—whether in the privacy of the home or in the public world of national politics. For this reason, feminists have long advocated passage of the Equal Rights Amendment (ERA) to the U.S. Constitution, which states simply:

   > Equality of rights under the law shall not be denied or abridged by the United States or any State on account of sex.

   The ERA, first proposed in Congress in 1923, has the support of two-thirds of adults in the United States (N.O.R.C. 1991:279). Even so, it has yet to become law. This disparity between public opinion and public policy probably reflects the opposition of the men who dominate state legislatures around the country.

4. **Ending sexual violence.** A major objective of the New Women's Movement is eliminating sexual violence. In a patriarchal society, sexual relationships between men and women often mirror power relationships between the sexes in the larger society (Millet, 1970; J. Bernard, 1973; Dworkin, 1987). Feminists assert that men's more powerful position in society leads to the violent subordination of women, in the form of rape, domestic abuse, sexual harassment, and the degradation of women through pornography. Thus feminism actively campaigns

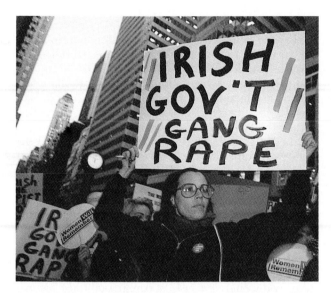

Ireland is one of the few industrial societies in the world in which abortion is constitutionally banned. Irish law forbids physicians even from giving out information about how to obtain an abortion abroad. When fourteen-year-old Ann Lovett became pregnant—as the result of rape—the government initially denied her request to travel to England to terminate the pregnancy. International protest eventually drove officials to relent, and Lovett did receive the abortion she sought.

against all violence directed against women by working to transform the basic power relationship between the sexes.

5. **Promoting sexual autonomy.** Finally, feminism seeks to ensure that women have control of their own sexuality and decisions involving reproduction. Feminists advocate the right of women to obtain birth control information—something that was illegal in some states as recently as the 1960s. In addition, most feminists support a woman's right to choose whether to bear children or to terminate a pregnancy. Feminism as an ideology does not favor abortion, but it holds that the decision to bear children should be made by women themselves rather than by men—such as husbands, physicians, and legislators. Many feminists also support gay peoples' drive to overcome prejudice and discrimination in a culture dominated by heterosexuality. More than gay men, lesbians suffer distinct social disadvantages because they violate both the cultural norm of heterosexuality and the norm that

men should control the sexuality of women (Deckard, 1979; Barry, 1983; Jagger, 1983).

## Variations within Feminism

Because the goal of sexual equality means different things to different people, and because there are various ways to promote a more equitable society, more than one kind of feminism exists today. Although the distinctions among them are far from clear-cut, three general types of feminist thinking will be described briefly (Barry, 1983; Jagger, 1983; Stacey, 1983; Vogel, 1983; Hansen & Philipson, 1990).

### Liberal Feminism

*Liberal feminism* is rooted in classic liberal thinking that individuals should be free to develop their own abilities and pursue their own interests. Liberal feminists accept the basic organization of our society but hold that women do not yet share the same rights as men. If people are to be evaluated on their personal merits rather than according to their race or sex, in other words, the sexes must have the same opportunities to shape their lives (Jagger, 1983). To that end, much as liberals endorse the civil rights movement in support of African Americans, liberal feminists endorse the Equal Rights Amendment and oppose prejudice and discrimination that have historically limited women's opportunities.

Those supporting this approach advocate reproductive freedom for all women. Only if women can choose whether to bear children, and only if both parents share the responsibilities of child rearing, can women and men have equal opportunities in their working lives. For the same reason, liberal feminism advocates the right of women to maternity leave and child care. Although more than one hundred nations guarantee all working women maternity leave, liberal feminists point out, the United States has no such public policy (Hewlett, 1986).

Finally, liberal feminists support the family as a social institution, but they point out that families may need to change in order to accommodate the ambitions of both women and men. With their strong belief in the rights of individuals, liberal feminists do not see all women as a single entity, thinking that all women must advance for some to advance. The key to women's liberation (and that of men) lies primarily in ending legal and cultural constraints that prevent individuals from realizing their personal goals.

## Socialist Feminism

*Socialist feminism* evolved from Marxist conflict analysis, but largely as a criticism of this approach's inattention to gender issues. As noted earlier, Engels placed Marx's general approach in a feminist context as he claimed that the root of patriarchy is private property. Furthermore, explained Engels, although capitalism did not create patriarchy, it has intensified this form of domination by concentrating wealth and power in the hands of a small number of men.

The family, an institution basically acceptable to liberal feminists, is targeted for change by socialist feminists. The "bourgeois family," fostered by capitalism, oppresses women by keeping them in the home where they work without wages and remain economically dependent on men. In addition, this family form effectively prevents women from politically organizing with other women and men, and restricts opportunities so that women derive little personal satisfaction from any endeavors other than consuming products. In place of this family system, which Engels dismissed as "domestic slavery," socialist feminism advocates a state-centered society, which frees women by collectively performing tasks like cooking and child care. This implies that a class revolution is the prerequisite for a gender revolution.

Clearly, socialist feminists conclude that the reforms sought by liberal feminism are, by themselves, insufficient to produce equality of the sexes. Only through a socialist revolution—which simultaneously banishes private property and reorganizes life in a cooperative manner—can women and men be freed from historic oppression. Since sweeping changes are required to approach this goal, women and men must pursue their personal liberation together, rather than individually, as liberal feminists maintain. (Further discussion of socialism is found elsewhere, especially in Chapter 19, "The Economy and Work.")

## Radical Feminism

*Radical feminism* argues that the root of sexual oppression is the concept of gender itself. The historical foundation of gender, radical feminism maintains, lies in the biological differences of sex by which women carry and bear children. The family, from this point of view, does not constitute merely an economic arrangement as Engels conceived it, but rather a system that institutionalizes heterosexual relations and inevitably confines women to the monotonous burdens of child care.

What is the alternative? Until recently, options were few because the biological process of reproduction was beyond human control. But now advancing technology has made conventional heterosexual parenting—and thus the historical family—unnecessary. So radical feminism envisions a revolution more radical than that sought by Marxists. New reproductive technology (see Chapter 15, "Family"), which already allows conception outside the body, holds the promise of separating women's bodies from the process of childbearing. With the demise of motherhood, radical feminists reason, the entire family system could be left behind, liberating the two sexes from the tyranny of gender itself.

For the radical feminist vision to be realized, four other objectives must be achieved. First, similar to the argument made by socialist feminism, technology must ensure a level of production that meets all human needs so that no one is economically dependent on anyone else. Second, responsibilities for raising children cannot fall on individuals; the tasks of parenthood must become the responsibility of society as a whole. Third, since no woman should have to bear children nor conform to conventional definitions of motherhood (or men contend with fatherhood), historical definitions of children as dependent on parents and families must be revised. Thus radical feminism advocates a program of children's rights (Jagger, 1983). Fourth, conventional thinking about sexuality itself—including norms that favor heterosexuality over homosexuality or demand that sex take place only within certain relational forms like marriage—must be abandoned (Dworkin, 1987).

If this radical feminist agenda were put in place, the resulting society would be vastly different from any known to date. From this point of view, society would evolve toward the goal of eliminating all social distinctions based on sex: that is, toward the elimination of gender.

## Resistance to Feminism

Feminism has encountered resistance from both men and women who embrace dominant cultural ideas about gender. Some men oppose feminism for the same reasons that many whites have historically resisted drives for social equality for people of color: they want to preserve privileges linked to their social position. Other men, including those who are neither rich nor powerful, distrust a social movement (especially its more radical expressions) that advocates socialism or seeks to abolish traditional marriage, family, and parenthood. Further, for some men, feminism threatens an important basis of their status

Has there been a "feminist backlash" in the United States? Many feminists think so, and point to various kinds of evidence to support their contention. The popular television program *thirtysomething* portrayed women as seeking happiness through boyfriends, husbands, and children rather than from work or other personal pursuits as men do.

and self-respect: their masculinity. Men who have been socialized to value strength and dominance understandably feel uneasy about the feminist notion that they can also be gentle and warm (Doyle, 1983).

Some women, as well, shy away from feminism. For example, women who center their lives around their husbands and children may consider feminism a threat to their most cherished values. From this point of view, feminism amounts to an effort to revise the law, the workplace, and the family—in short, to remake all of society—according to the radical political agenda of a few. Feminists, then, would dispose of the traditional values that have guided life and protected individual liberties in the United States for centuries. Additionally, some women believe that, in the process of recasting the conventional "feminine" spheres of life, including the home and the family, women will lose rather than gain power and personal identity (Marshall, 1985).

A final area of resistance to feminism involves *how* women's social standing should be improved. Although a large majority of people in the United States believe women should have equal rights, most also maintain that women should advance individually, according to their abilities. In a national survey, 70 percent of respondents claimed that women should expect to get ahead on the basis of their own training and qualifications; only 10 percent thought women's rights groups repre-

sented the best approach (N.O.R.C., 1991:387). Thus it appears that, at present, resistance to feminism is primarily directed at its socialist and radical variants; by contrast, there is widespread support for the principles that underlie liberal feminism.

## Gender in the Twenty-First Century

Predictions about the future are, at best, informed speculation. Just as economists disagree about the likely inflation rate a year from now, sociologists differ in their views on the future of our society. Yet we can venture some general observations about gender, today and in the future.

To begin, change has been remarkable. The position of women in the United States a century ago was one of clear and striking subordination. Husbands controlled property in marriage, women were barred from most areas of the labor force, and no woman could vote. Although women remain socially disadvantaged, the movement toward greater equality has been dramatic. Perhaps nowhere is this change more evident than in the workplace. A century ago, women were defined as unsuitable for paid work; today's economy, by contrast, *depends* on the earnings of women (Hewlett, 1990). This economic trend will continue: two-thirds of people entering the workforce during the 1990s will be women.

Many factors have contributed to this transformation. Perhaps most important, industrialization both broadened the range of human activity and shifted the nature of work from physically demanding tasks that favored male strength to jobs that require human thought and imagination, placing the talents of women and men on an even footing. Additionally, medical technology has given us control over reproduction, so women's lives are less circumscribed by unwanted pregnancies.

Many women and men have also made deliberate efforts in pursuit of social equality. Feminism seeks to end constraints imposed on people by a society that assigns activities and channels self-expression on the basis of sex. As these efforts continue, the social changes in the twenty-first century may be even greater than those we have already witnessed.

In the midst of change, strong opposition to feminism persists. Many feminists are fearful of legal changes that will undercut women's reproductive options, setting back a generation of hard-won gains. On a broader front, gender still forms an important foundation of personal identity and of family life, and it is deeply woven into the moral fabric of our society. Therefore, attempts to change cultural ideas about the two sexes will no doubt continue to provoke considerable opposition.

On balance, while dramatic and radical change in the way we understand gender may not occur in the short run, the movement toward a society in which women and men enjoy equal rights and opportunities seems certain to gain strength.

# Summary

1.  Sex is a biological concept; a human fetus is female or male from the moment of conception. People with the rare condition of hermaphroditism combine the biological traits of both sexes. Transsexuals are people who deliberately choose to surgically alter their sex.

2.  Heterosexuality is the dominant sexual orientation in virtually every society in the world. Homosexuals make up a small but significant proportion of the population of the United States. Sexual orientation is not always clear-cut; many people are bisexual.

3.  Gender refers to human traits that a culture attaches to each sex. Gender varies historically and across cultures.

4.  Some degree of patriarchy exists in every society. The ideology of sexism justifies male dominance, just as racism supports racial dominance.

5.  The socialization process links gender to personal identity (gender identity) and distinctive activities (gender roles). The major agents of socialization— the family, peer groups, schools, and the mass media—reinforce cultural definitions of what is masculine and feminine.

6.  Gender stratification entails numerous social disadvantages for women. Although most women are now in the paid labor force, a majority of working women hold clerical or service jobs. Unpaid housework also remains predominantly a task performed by women.

7.  On average, women earn about 72 percent as much as men do. This disparity is due to differences in jobs, family patterns, and discrimination.

8.  Historically excluded from higher education, women now form a slight majority of all college students and receive half of all master's degrees. Men still earn a majority of doctorates and professional degrees.

9.  The number of women in politics—especially on the local level—has increased sharply in recent decades. Still, the vast majority of national political officials are men.

10. Minority women have greater social disadvantages than white women. Overall, minority women earn only half as much as white men, and almost half the households headed by minority women are poor.

11. On the basis of their distinctive identity and social disadvantages, all women can be considered members of a social minority.

12. Structural-functional analysis suggests that distinctive roles for males and females constitute a survival strategy in preindustrial societies. In industrial societies, extensive gender inequality becomes dysfunctional, yet long-established cultural norms related to gender change slowly. According to Talcott Parsons, complementary gender roles serve to integrate the family and the larger society.

13. Social-conflict analysis, which views gender in terms of economic inequality and social conflict, links gender stratification to the development of private property. Friedrich Engels claimed that capitalism intensified male dominance by devaluing women as homemakers working for no pay.

14. Feminism supports the social equality of the sexes and actively opposes patriarchy and sexism. Feminism advocates a shift toward greater choice for women and men, eliminating gender stratification, ending sexual violence against women, and promoting women's control over their own sexuality.

15. There are three main variants of feminist thinking. Liberal feminism seeks equal opportunity for both sexes within the current institutional arrangements; socialist feminism advocates abolishing private property as the means to forging gender equality; radical feminism proposes ending all social distinctions based on sex to create a gender-free society.

16. Because gender distinctions stand at the core of our way of life, feminism has encountered strong

resistance. Although two-thirds of adults in the United States express support for the Equal Rights Amendment, this legislation has yet to become part of the U.S. Constitution.

# Key Concepts

**female infanticide** the practice of aborting female fetuses and neglecting, or even actively killing, infant girls by parents who would prefer to raise boys

**feminism** the advocacy of social equality for the sexes, in opposition to patriarchy and sexism

**gender** society's division of humanity, based on sex, into two distinctive categories

**gender identity** traits that females and males, guided by their culture, incorporate into their personalities

**gender roles** (sex roles) attitudes and activities that a culture links to each sex

**gender stratification** a society's unequal distribution of wealth, power, and privilege between the two sexes

**hermaphrodite** a human being with some combination of female and male internal and external genitalia

**matriarchy** a form of social organization in which females dominate males

**patriarchy** a form of social organization in which males dominate females

**primary sex characteristics** the genitals, used to reproduce the human species

**secondary sex characteristics** physical traits, other than the genitals, that distinguish physiologically mature females and males

**sex** the division of humanity into biological categories of female and male

**sexism** the belief that one sex is innately superior to the other

**sexual harassment** comments, gestures, or physical contact of a sexual nature that is deliberate, repeated, and unwelcome

**sexual orientation** the manner in which people experience sexual arousal and achieve sexual pleasure

**transsexuals** people who feel they are one sex though biologically they are the other

# Suggested Readings

These three books delve into various issues raised in this chapter.

Joyce McCarl Nielsen. *Sex and Gender in Society: Perspectives on Stratification.* 2nd ed. Prospect Heights, IL: Waveland Press, 1991.

Linda L. Lindsey. *Gender Roles: A Sociological Perspective.* Englewood Cliffs, NJ: Prentice Hall, 1990.

Sara E. Rix, ed. *The American Woman 1990–91: A Status Report.* New York: W. W. Norton, 1990.

This useful source examines the sexual lives of young people in our culture.

Jules H. Masserman and Victor M. Uribe. *Adolescent Sexuality.* New York: Charles C. Thomas, 1990.

Here are two books about homosexuality. The first takes a sociological look at sexual orientation. The second sketches the fascinating historical context for the current debate about gays and the military.

David F. Greenberg. *The Construction of Homosexuality.* Chicago: The University of Chicago Press, 1988.

Allan Berube. *Coming Out Under Fire: The History of Gay Men and Women in World War Two.* New York: The Free Press, 1990.

Here the earning disparity between women and men is analyzed in historical perspective.

Claudia Goldin. *Understanding the Gender Gap: An Economic History of American Women.* New York: Oxford University Press, 1990.

This multinational research focuses on how social changes in various global regions have affected women's work and social standing.

Setenyi Shami, Lucine Taminian, Soheir A. Morsy, Zeinab Bashir El-Bakri, and El-Wathig Kameir. *Women in Arab Society: Work Patterns and Gender Relations in Egypt, Jordan, and Sudan.* New York: Berg, 1991.

Donald Meyer. *Sex and Power: The Rise of Women in America, Russia, Sweden, and Italy.* 2nd ed. Middletown, CT: Wesleyan University Press, 1989.

One notion about gender that has changed little over the years is the importance of physical beauty for women. This book argues that our culture sets up unrealistic and destructive standards of feminine attractiveness.

Naomi Wolf. *The Beauty Myth: How Beauty Images are Used Against Women.* New York: William Morrow, 1990.

# Aging
# and the Elderly

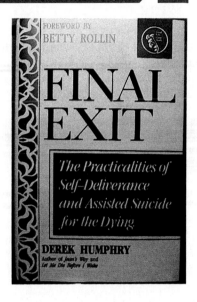

FOREWORD BY
BETTY ROLLIN

FINAL
EXIT

*The Practicalities of
Self-Deliverance
and Assisted Suicide
for the Dying*

**DEREK HUMPHRY**
Author of *Jean's Way* and
*Let Me Die Before I Wake*

The book *Final Exit* shot to the top of the best seller list in 1991. This is a book about dying—not about the death of a famous person, or a philosophical treatise about death, but rather a "how-to" manual that tells people how to commit suicide. *Final Exit* gives readers specific instructions on how to kill themselves in a host of ways, including taking sleeping pills, through self-starvation, and by causing suffocation with a plastic bag.

The author of *Final Exit* is Derek Humphrey, a founder and executive director of The Hemlock Society. This organization, founded in 1980, offers support and practical assistance to people who wish to die. Humphrey explains that the time has come for people in the United States to have access to a straightforward manual on how people can end their own lives. The immediate and remarkable popularity of *Final Exit*—especially among the elderly—suggests that millions of people agree with him.

Not surprisingly, *Final Exit* has sparked controversy. While some people applaud the book as a humane effort to assist people who are painfully and terminally ill, others claim that it has encouraged suicide by people who are experiencing only temporary depression (Angelo, 1991). A legal battle is also underway as laws that prohibit physicians from assisting in the death of a patient are being tested.

But the appearance of *Final Exit* also raises broader questions that are no less disturbing and controversial. As we shall explain in this chapter, the ranks of the elderly are swelling rapidly as more and more men and women live longer and longer. As a result, people are uneasy about their responsibilities toward aging parents. Officials worry that the health-care system is unable to meet the needs of older people, or can do so only by shortchanging the needs of younger people. And older people themselves are, on the one hand, fearful of not being able to afford medical care they may need and, on the other hand, alarmed at the prospect of losing control of their lives to a medical establishment that often seeks to prolong life at any cost.

In the 1990s, many issues relating to aging and the elderly will command the attention of policy makers, just as they will generate intense discussion among everyone else in the United States. In some respects, growing old in the United States has never been more inviting; poverty, confronted by many elderly a generation ago, has been greatly reduced. But many stubborn problems persist: older people, for example, continue to grapple with prejudice and discrimination. And, as unprecedented numbers of women and men in our society enter old age, new and daunting problems of aging loom on the horizon.

# The Graying of the United States

A quiet but powerful revolution is reshaping the United States: the number of elderly people—women and men aged sixty-five and over—is increasing more than twice as fast as the population as a whole. Put another way, the *elderly* population of the United States is increasing at a higher rate than the *overall* population of India. The effects of this "graying of the United States" promise to be profound.

Some comparative statistics bring this change into sharp focus. In 1900, half of our population was under twenty-three years of age and only one in twenty-five people had reached sixty-five. As shown in Figure 14–1, however, the median age in this country is steadily rising. In 1980, the median age of the U.S. population reached thirty, and about 11 percent of all people were over sixty-five. By the mid-1980s, elderly people outnum-bered teenagers. By 1990, the median age had jumped again to thirty-three, with the elderly accounting for more than one in eight. By the year 2050—within the lifetimes of many readers of this book—the median age of people in the United States will be about forty-five years and one in four people will be over sixty-five (Spencer, 1989). Put in other terms, between 1990 and 2020, the population of the United States over the age of fifty will increase by 75 percent; during that time, the number of people under the age of fifty will rise by only 2 percent (Wolfe, 1991).

What is prompting the aging of our society? Two factors stand out. The first is the baby boom that began in the late 1940s. After World War II, men and women enthusiastically settled into family life and, before this era ended in 1965, some 75 million babies had been born. This enormous cohort of baby boomers first gained attention by forging the youth culture of the 1960s. They are setting trends as middle-aged people in the 1990s,

**Figure 14–1**  The Graying of U.S. Society
*(Spencer, 1989; U.S. Bureau of the Census, 1991)*

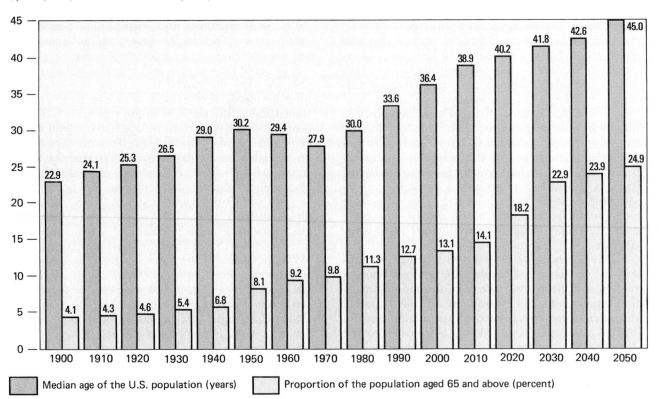

Median age of the U.S. population (years)    Proportion of the population aged 65 and above (percent)

During this century a remarkable change has occurred; today's youngsters have a greater chance of living beyond age sixty-five than infants born in 1900 had of reaching their first birthday. As a result, women and men over the age of sixty-five already outnumber teenagers and will account for one-fifth of the U.S. population by 2030.

and their numbers alone ensure that they will influence our society as they reach old age. The birth rate then took a sharp turn downward after 1965 (the so-called "baby bust"), so that our population is becoming increasingly "top-heavy" in the coming decades.

The second cause of the aging of our society is increasing life expectancy. Females born in 1900 lived, on average, only about forty-eight years; males, only forty-six years. By contrast, women born in 1990 can expect to live 79.0 years; for men, life expectancy has stretched to 72.1 years (U.S. Bureau of the Census, 1991). This striking increase reflects medical advances that have virtually eliminated infectious diseases such as smallpox, diphtheria, and measles, which killed many young people in the past, as well as more recent medical strides in combating cancer and heart disease, afflictions common to the elderly (Wall, 1980). In addition, a rising standard of living during this century has promoted the health of people of all ages. One clear indication of this change is that the fastest-growing segment of the entire population is people over eighty-five, who are already more than twenty times more numerous than they were at the beginning of this century. These "older old" now number 3.3 million (about 1.3 percent of the total population). Projections place their number at 15.3 million (about 5 percent of the total) by the year 2050 (Spencer, 1989; Kaufman, 1990; Harbert & Ginsberg, 1991).

We can only begin to imagine the consequences of this transformation. Assuming that people over sixty-five continue to retire from the labor force, the proportion of nonemployed adults—already about ten times greater than in 1900—will soar even higher. This, in turn, will generate ever-greater demands for social resources and programs providing support for the nonworking elderly. During this century, the share of federal spending supporting people over sixty-five has more than doubled from 15 percent to nearly 33 percent (Callahan, 1987).

The elderly also draw heavily on the health-care system, accounting for one-fourth of all medical expenditures. Older people make the greatest use of physicians, hospitals, and prescription drugs. As Chapter 20 ("Health and Medicine") explains, the costs of medical care have skyrocketed in recent years, a trend that shows little evidence of slowing. Unless steps are taken to meet the medical needs of tens of millions of additional older people—at prices that average people can *afford*—our society will face a monumental health care crisis in the next century.

Perhaps most important, in the coming decades interacting with elderly people will become commonplace. People in the United States are now accustomed to a considerable degree of age segregation. Young people rarely mingle in familiar settings with old people, so that most of the young know little about aging. In the twenty-first century, when the size of the elderly population of the United States stands at twice what it is now, those who are not elderly will have extensive daily contact with people who are.

As the proportion of older people rises, adult children will have an unprecedented responsibility to care for aging parents. As the box on pages 384–85 explains, many middle-aged adults already think of themselves as the "sandwich generation."

## Growing Old: Biology and Culture

The graying of the United States has prompted the development of a relatively new field of social science. **Gerontology** (derived from the Greek word *geron*, meaning "an old person"), is *the study of aging and the elderly*. Gerontology encompasses the biological processes of aging, a psychological focus on personality, and a more sociological look at how individual cultures define this stage of life.

# The Sandwich Generation: Who Should Care for Aging Parents?

How can anyone deny that parents who have toiled for their children in their youth, have lost many a good night's sleep when they were ill, have washed their diapers long before they could talk and have spent about a quarter of a century bringing them up and fitting them for life, have the right to be fed by them and respected when they are old?

So asked the ancient Chinese philosopher Lin Yutang. This perennial question is taking on new meaning in the United States as the current baby boomers become the first generation in our nation's history destined to spend as much time caring for elderly parents as for their young children. This challenge has earned them the title of the "sandwich generation," because they are facing the demands of their children, on the one hand, and those of their aging parents on the other.

Why are people nearing midlife the first generation to be squeezed in this way? There are three major reasons. The first reason is *there are now more elderly people*. An explosion of the elderly population is now under way making for more older people, who will live longer and require greater support and assistance. The second factor is *adults are now having fewer children*. The number of young children in the United States actually began falling about 1960 as the baby boom came to an end. This downturn in birth rates means that the increasing number of old people will have fewer children to care for them.

Researchers estimate that a couple now have living parents for a far greater share of the life course than they have dependent children under age twenty (Preston, 1984). Further, as couples age, their caregiving responsibilities no longer come to an end; they merely shift from young children to old parents.

A third factor that places more demands on today's families is that *more women are in the labor force*. The typical married couple in the United States comprises two people who work. Dual-career couples sometimes fear that they shortchange their own children; now they are also facing demands for time and attention from their aging parents. Historically, caring for the elderly has fallen to women (in their roles as daughters and daughters-in-law). Women now have less time and energy available to do this.

Who should support the elderly? An ongoing debate raises three possibilities: the elderly themselves, the elderly's adult children, and the government.

The elderly in the United States have always taken primary responsibility for their own welfare. People learn early in life that they are

## Biological Changes

As we age, the body undergoes a series of gradual, yet continual, changes. How we think about these changes—whether we celebrate our maturity or bemoan our physical decline—depends largely on whether our society labels such changes as positive or negative. The culture of the United States is youth-oriented, so we tend to consider biological changes that occur early in life as positive. Growing children and adolescents approaching adulthood gain greater measures of responsibility and look forward to additional legal rights.

At the same time, our culture views biological changes that unfold later in life with a negative eye. Few people are congratulated for getting old. We commiserate with those entering old age, and make jokes about aging to avoid the harsh conclusion that the elderly are sliding down a slope of physical and mental decline. We assume, in short, that at roughly the mid-point of the life course, people cease growing *up* and begin growing *down*.

Physical problems generally complicate old age. Yet, many people in our society exaggerate the physical differences between the elderly and younger people (Harris, 1976). Research in gerontology helps to separate the facts of aging from cultural stereotypes.

Gray hair, wrinkles, loss of height and weight, and an overall decline in strength and physical mobility—these all characterize the aging process that begins in middle age (Colloway & Dollevoet, 1977). After about the age of fifty, bones become more brittle; falls that would be of little consequence earlier in life can result expected to save for their old age. But the costs of growing old (inflated by soaring medical expenses and added years of life) even threaten the security of older women and men who have tried to be self-reliant.

The extent to which adult children should be responsible for their elderly parents' care is not easily defined. Advocates of a larger role for adult children, echoing the sentiments of Lin Yutang, point out that family ties involve reciprocity and obligation; if people do not feel some obligation to care for their own parents, this argument continues, they are simply too self-centered. Furthermore, the family seems properly suited to provide the emotional support that older people require. Daniel Callahan states the case simply:

In a world of strangers or fleeting casual acquaintances, of distant government agencies and a society beyond their control, elderly parents can see in their children their only hope for someone who ought to care for them.

But not everyone is convinced that caring for aging parents is a family matter. This opposing view has roots in our culture. While our way of life stresses the duties of parents toward their young children, the obligations of children to aging parents are not clearly spelled out. Moreover, the growth of government social programs (especially Social Security and Medicare) during the last fifty years has weakened our sense of family responsibility toward the elderly. Additionally, many adult children simply do not have the resources—financial or emotional—to do as much as they would like.

A significant proportion of adults do a great deal for older parents. Research suggests that about one-fourth (mostly women) spend five hours or more every day caring for their aging parents. Further, with only one in twenty elderly people in a rest home, family members step in to perform roughly 80 percent of all home health care for elderly people who are disabled.

In the future, most elderly people will be able to care for themselves—as they have in the past—without a great deal of help from anyone. But the graying of the United States means that the costs and responsibilities of supporting the elderly population will rise dramatically. With fewer adult children to meet this need, the inescapable conclusion is that government involvement in elderly care will have to expand. Deciding precisely how to assign responsibility for meeting the needs of the elderly will command national attention for decades.

SOURCES: Based on the Institute for Philosophy and Public Policy (1988); also Gelman (1985); Callahan (1987); and Stone, Cafferata, & Sangl (1987).

in disabling injuries. Broken bones also take longer to heal as we get older. In addition, a substantial proportion of the elderly suffer from chronic illnesses like arthritis and diabetes, which limit physical activity, and with the passing years more people contend with life-threatening conditions such as heart disease and cancer. Alzheimer's disease is a devastating disability that afflicts some 3 million elderly people in the United States, about 10 percent of the population over sixty-five. This condition—which involves slow deterioration of the nerve fibers in the brain—is especially taxing on family members who must provide more and more care as they endure the gradual loss of a loved one.

The sensory abilities—taste, sight, touch, smell, and especially hearing—tend to diminish with age. While only about 5 percent of middle-aged people are visually impaired, 10 percent of the elderly are. Hearing problems are more common, increasing in frequency from about 15 percent of middle-aged people to almost 30 percent of the elderly. Both impairments affect men more than women (National Center for Health Statistics, 1990). A declining ability to taste and smell can adversely affect eating habits, creating other health problems related to poor nutrition (Eckholm, 1985).

Without denying that health becomes more fragile with advancing age, the vast majority of older people are neither discouraged nor disabled by their physical condition. Only about one in ten reports trouble walking, and just one in twenty requires intensive care in a hospital or nursing home. No more than 1 percent of the elderly are bedridden. Overall, about 70 percent of people over the age of sixty-five assess their health as "good" or "excel-

To many of her family, the idea seemed silly if not dangerous, but ninety-seven-year-old Beatrice Ferguson mastered the art of the hula hoop and made others rethink some of their assumptions about the elderly.

lent," while 30 percent characterize their overall condition as "fair" or "poor" (National Center for Health Statistics, 1990).

Bear in mind, of course, that these patterns vary greatly within the elderly population. Generally speaking, elderly men tend to fare better than elderly women. Women live longer, on average, than men do, but they also spend more of their lives suffering from chronic disabilities like arthritis than men. In addition, as Chapter 10 ("Social Class in the United States") explained, physical health varies among the different social classes. Stated simply, this means that people who live and work in a healthful and safe environment and who can afford extensive preventive medical care have an easier time aging than those with fewer resources. This pattern emerges clearly from self-reports of elderly people: over 80 percent of those with incomes exceeding $35,000 assess their own health as "excellent" or "good," while only 60 percent of people with incomes under $10,000 do. Income disparity also explains why about three-fourths of elderly

whites consider their health "good" or "excellent," in contrast to only half of older people of color (U.S. Department of Health and Human Services, 1991).

## Psychological Changes

Just as we tend to overstate the physical problems of aging, so it is easy to exaggerate the psychological changes that accompany growing old. Samuel Johnson, the famous eighteenth-century observer of British society, once reflected:

> There is a wicked inclination in most people to suppose an old man decayed in his intellect. If a young or middle-aged man, when leaving a company, does not recollect where he laid his hat, it is nothing; but if the same inattention is discovered in an old man, people will shrug their shoulders and say, "His memory is going" (cited in Berger, 1983:544).

Cultural assumptions about the various stages of life shape everyone's perceptions of human behavior; this can be true of psychologists, too. Until recently, most psychologists contended that changes in intelligence over the life course followed a simple rule: "What goes up must come down" (Baltes & Schaie, 1974). According to some research, mental decline actually begins as early as twenty-five (Wechsler, 1972). In recent years, psychologists have reassessed changes in mental capacity brought on by aging, and few would now argue that growing old means enduring an inevitable loss in intellectual acuity. Some researchers now argue that several aspects of intelligence actually grow stronger in later years.

To clarify this matter, we need to precisely operationalize the concept of intelligence. Sensorimotor coordination, including the ability to arrange objects to match a drawing, declines steadily after midlife. Similarly, the facility to learn new material and to think quickly appear to subside among people over the age of seventy (Schaie, 1980). But the ability to use familiar ideas does not diminish with age, and verbal and mathematical skills often improve with advancing years (Baltes & Schaie, 1974). Again, education and social class affect all these capacities, and they may actually have a greater impact on intelligence than aging does (Botwinick, 1977; Riegel, 1977).

Most people wonder if they will think or feel differently when they are older. Psychologists assure us, for better or worse, that the answer is no. Personality changes little as we grow old, except that most men and women become somewhat more introverted as they age—more engaged with their own thoughts and emotions. In short, two elderly people who knew each other as children would recognize in each other many of the same personality traits that distinguished them as youngsters (Neugarten, 1971, 1972, 1977).

## Aging and Culture

Sociology offers the following valuable insight: whatever changes age brings to our minds and bodies, the *significance* of growing old is very much a matter of cultural definitions.

In global perspective, one factor that shapes the meaning of aging is life expectancy, which is closely linked to a society's overall standard of living and medical technology. Throughout most of human history, people's lives were—as English philosopher Thomas Hobbes (1588–1679) put it—"nasty, brutish, and short" (although Hobbes himself managed to reach the age of ninety-one). Most people of his day married and had children in their teens, were middle-aged in their twenties, and succumbed to illnesses by their thirties or forties. It took several more centuries before a rising standard of living and technological advances began to curb infectious diseases that killed people of all ages. These factors eventually made surviving the ordeal of birth and living to, say, age forty or fifty commonplace by the beginning of this century (Mahler, 1980; Cox, 1984).

Global Map 14–1 on page 388 provides a comparative look at life expectancy. In the poorest nations of the Third World, including much of central Africa, the average lifespan is about fifty years. This is only slightly more than life expectancy in Europe during the Middle Ages. In the industrial societies of the world, including the United States, life expectancy is half again longer: about seventy-five years. In First-World societies, people are not thought to be "old" until the mid-sixties or even later.

Reports from Abkhasia, a republic of the former Soviet Union, indicate that a surprisingly large number of people live well beyond what even we in the United States consider to be a ripe old age: to one hundred and even older. Many individuals may exaggerate their age to researchers; but, even so, Abkhasian society illustrates the important lesson that social relationships—perhaps even more than technological advances—are the key to a rich and long life. The box on pages 390–91 provides details about a society in which people are reputed to live a century or even longer.

## Aging and Social Stratification

Like race, ethnicity, and gender, age is one basis for socially ranking individuals. **Age stratification,** then, is defined as *the unequal distribution of wealth, power, and privileges among people of different ages.* Like other dimensions of social hierarchy, age stratification varies from one society to another.

As explained in Chapter 4 ("Society"), hunters and gatherers lack the technology to produce a surplus of food and are nomadic. Thus, they value physical strength and stamina, since these traits contribute to their survival. As people age, productivity declines along with strength and energy. Members of these societies, therefore, consider the elderly (who may actually be only thirty) as an economic burden (Sheehan, 1976).

Pastoral, horticultural, and agrarian societies have the technology to produce a material surplus; consequently, individuals may accumulate considerable wealth over a lifetime. Older people in these societies generally become richer and more powerful, so these societies tend toward **gerontocracy,** *a form of social organization in which the elderly have the most wealth, power, and privileges.* Old people, particularly the men, are honored (and sometimes feared) by their families and, as in the case of the Abkhasians, they remain active leaders of society until they die.

Additionally, the rich folk life in preindustrial societies fosters respect for the elderly, since it is they who serve as guardians of traditional wisdom and rituals—from how to plant crops to homemaking skills to marking the entry of the young into the adult community. This veneration of elders also explains the widespread practice of ancestor worship among members of agrarian societies.

Industrialization and advances in medical technology gradually increase life expectancy, but these forces also erode the power and prestige of the elderly. In part, this is because the prime source of wealth shifts from land (typically controlled by the oldest members of society) to factories and other new forms of production (often owned or managed by younger people). The growth of urban centers also divides families and forces children to depend less on their parents and more on their own earning power. Furthermore, advanced technology accelerates social change, so many of the skills, traditions, and life experiences that served the old have less relevance to the young. Over the long term, these factors transform old people from *elders* (a term with positive connotations) to the *elderly* (commanding far less prestige). Finally, the tremendous productivity of industrial societies makes

**Global Map 14–1** Life Expectancy in Global Perspective

Life expectancy has shot upward over the course of this century in industrial societies including Canada, the United States, the nations of Europe, Japan, and Australia. A newborn in the United States can expect to live about seventy-five years, and our life expectancy would be greater still were it not for the high risk of death among infants born into poverty. Since poverty is the rule in much of the world, lives are correspondingly shorter, especially in parts of Africa and Asia where life expectancy may be as low as forty years.

the labor of everyone unnecessary; as a result, the very old and the very young often occupy nonproductive roles (Cohn, 1982).

In mature industrial societies such as the United States and Canada, economic and political leaders are generally middle-aged rather than elderly people because people at midlife usually combine experience with up-to-date skills. In rapidly changing sectors of the economy—the various high-tech fields—key executives are frequently much younger, sometimes just out of college. Older people are often consigned to marginal positions in the economy because they lack the knowledge and training demanded by a fast-changing marketplace. Certainly some elderly men and women remain at the helm of businesses they own but, more commonly, older people predominate in traditional occupations (such as barbers, tailors, and seamstresses) and jobs that involve minimal activity (night security guards, for instance) (Kaufman & Spilerman, 1982).

Industrialization also changes the relationships among the generations that make up families. Preindustrial societies favor *extended families*, with more than two generations living together, so that young and old remain in close contact. Industrial societies, as Chapter 15 ("Family") explains, promote *nuclear families* composed of just parents and their dependent children. This pattern separates the old and the young; only in 20 percent of homes in the United States do adults live with their parents. But this multigenerational pattern seems to be gaining in popularity, perhaps because of the sagging economy. About 45 percent of adults in the United States now say that, in principle, older people sharing a home with their grown children is a good idea (N.O.R.C., 1991:224). But multigenerational living does not restore the historic prestige of the elderly. In such homes, adult children—rather than elderly parents—are usually defined as the heads of the household, reversing the pattern common at the beginning of this century (Dahlin, 1980).

In a few industrial societies—notably Japan—traditional cultural values and religious beliefs are still strong enough to confer high social standing on the oldest citizens. Most aged people in Japan live with an adult son or daughter and they continue to play a significant part in family life. The elderly in Japan are also more likely than their counterparts in the United States to remain in the labor force, and in many Japanese corporations the oldest employees receive the greatest respect. But even Japan is steadily becoming more like other industrial societies, in which growing old means giving up a large

measure of social importance (Harlan, 1968; Cowgill & Holmes, 1972; Treas, 1979; Palmore, 1982; Yates, 1986).

# Transitions and Problems of Aging

Chapter 5 ("Socialization") explained that we confront change at each stage of the life course. People must unlearn self-concepts and social patterns that no longer apply to their lives and simultaneously learn to cope with new circumstances. Of all stages of the life course, however, old age presents the greatest personal challenges.

Although physical decline in old age is less serious than most younger people think, this change can cause emotional stress among the elderly. Older people endure more pain, become resigned to limited activities, adjust to greater dependence on others, and see in the deaths of friends and relatives frequent reminders of their own mortality. Also, because our culture places such a high value on youth, physical vitality, and good looks, signs of aging may give rise to frustration, fear, and self-doubt in older people (Hamel, 1990). As one retired psychologist recently said of his old age: "Don't let the current hype about the joys of retirement fool you. They are not the best of times. It's just that the alternative is even worse" (Rubenstein, 1991:13).

Erik Erikson (1963, 1980) suggests that elderly people must resolve a tension of "integrity versus despair." No matter how much they may still be learning and achieving, older people must recognize that their lives are nearing an end. Elderly people spend much time reflecting on their past accomplishments and disappointments. To shore up their personal integrity, Erikson explains, older women and men must accept past mistakes as well as successes. Otherwise, this period may turn into a time of despair—a dead end with little positive meaning.

Research suggests that people who find satisfaction and meaning in earlier stages of life are likely to achieve personal well-being in old age. In a study of people in their seventies, Bernice Neugarten (1971) identified four distinct personality types whose responses to old age differ markedly.

The worst off are the small number of people with *disintegrated and disorganized personalities*. These individuals find it nearly impossible to come to terms with old age. Despair forms a common thread in their lives,

# Growing (Very) Old in Abkhasia

Anthropologist Sula Benet was sharing wine and conversation with a man in Tamish, a small village in the Republic of Abkhasia in the southwest corner of the Commonwealth of Independent States. Judging the man to be about seventy, she raised her glass and offered a toast to his long life. "May you live as long as Moses," she exclaimed. The gesture of goodwill fell flat: Moses lived to 120, but Benet's companion was already 119.

An outsider—even open-minded anthropologists who study many of the world's mysteries—should be skeptical about the longevity claims made by the Abkhasians. In one village of twelve hundred visited by Benet, for example, almost two hundred people declared they were more than eighty years old, and many said they were far older than that. Research suggests that Abkhasia may well have

Cultural patterns appear to be the secret of the remarkable longevity of the Abkhasians, many of whom claim to live well beyond what is common in the United States.

six times more people over the age of ninety as the United States.

To her surprise, Benet discovered that some Abkhasians actually understate their age. For example, after one man claimed to be ninety-five, his daughter (herself, eighty-one) produced a birth certificate stating his actual age as 108. Why the deception? In this instance, because the man was soon to be married. As another man (of 104) explained with a wink of his eye, "A man is a man until he is 100, you know what I mean. After that, well, he is getting old."

What accounts for the Abkhasians's remarkable longevity? The answer certainly is not the advanced medical technology in which people in the United States place so much faith; many Abkhasians have never seen a physician or a hospital. Nonetheless, their vigor and health are exceptional by our standards.

One possible explanation involves genetics: natural selection,

often making them dependent on help from others. Some may become passive residents of hospitals or nursing homes.

People with *passive-dependent personalities* are only slightly better off. With little confidence in their abilities to cope with daily events, they often seek help, whether or not they actually need it. Always in danger of social withdrawal, their level of life-satisfaction is relatively low.

People with *defended personalities* live independently but nonetheless fear advancing age. As best they can, they try to shield themselves from the reality of old age by fighting to stay youthful and physically fit. While concerns about health are certainly positive, setting unrealistic standards breeds stress and disappointment.

Most of Neugarten's subjects fared far better, drawing strength from what she termed *integrated personali-*

*ties.* As the key to successful aging, such a personality orientation displays a high level of dignity, self-confidence, and optimism in the face of growing old.

Curiously, most younger adults in the United States think that the elderly are unhappy: one national survey found that just 1 percent of people under age sixty-five thought that the best years of their lives awaited them in old age (Harris, 1976). As we have seen, some elderly people share this dim view, but most have a more positive outlook. Overall, research suggests that, while personal adjustments are necessary, the experience of growing old in the United States often provides much cause for joy. However, a person's view does vary based on individual personality, family circumstances, social class, and financial position. People who adapt successfully to changes earlier in life can confidently look forward to deriving satisfaction and meaning from their lives later on (Neugarten, 1971; Palmore, 1979a).

over many centuries of grueling warfare, has probably favored those with robust physical traits. But no clear evidence supports this hypothesis. A more likely answer has to do with lifestyle, including diet and physical activity. Abkhasians eat little saturated fat (which is linked to heart disease), use no sugar, drink no coffee or tea, and few Abkhasians smoke or chew tobacco. They do consume large amounts of healthful fruits and vegetables, and drink lots of buttermilk and low-alcohol wine. Additionally, Abkhasians maintain active lives built around regular physical work for people of all ages.

Beyond diet and lifestyle, Abkhasian culture may hold another key to long life. A clear and consistent set of traditional values and norms characterizes Abkhasian society. This gives all Abkhasians a strong sense of belonging and imbues their lives with purpose. This is especially true of the elderly, whose active lives and accumulated experience are highly valued, in marked contrast to our own practice of pushing old people to the margins of social life. As Benet explains: "The old (in the United States), when they do not simply vegetate, out of view and out of mind, keep themselves 'busy' with bingo and shuffleboard." For their part, the Abkhasians do not even have a word for old people or have a notion of retirement. Furthermore, younger people accord their elders great prestige and respect since, in their minds, advanced age confers the greatest wisdom. It is the old, rather than the young, whom people look to for decisions and guidance in everyday life. According to Benet:

The extraordinary attitude of the Abkhasians—to feel needed at 99 or 110—is not an artificial, self-protective one; it is a natural expression, in old age, of a consistent outlook that begins in childhood. . . .

Because their society is organized to accord the greatest respect to individuals who have lived the longest, Abkhasians expect to lead long and useful lives, and have good reason to look forward to old age. Their society values its traditions highly, and the old are viewed as indispensable guardians of culture. The elders preside at important ceremonial occasions, and they transmit their knowledge to the young. They feel needed because, in their own minds and everyone else's, they are. Rather than being a burden, they are the center of society.

SOURCE: Based on Benet (1971).

## Social Isolation

Although being alone can provoke anxiety among people of any age, this problem is most common among elderly people. Retirement closes off one source of social interaction, physical problems may limit the ability to move about, and many older people in the United States prefer not to share a home with their adult children. Then, too, negative stereotypes that depict the elderly as "over the hill" may discourage younger people from close social contact with their elders.

The greatest cause of social isolation, however, is the inevitable death of significant others. Few human experiences affect people as profoundly as the death of a spouse. One study found almost three-fourths of widows and widowers cited loneliness as their most serious problem (Lund, 1989). Widows and widowers must rebuild their lives in the glaring absence of people with whom, in many instances, they spent most of their adult lives. Some survivors choose not to live at all: one study of elderly men noted a sharp increase in the incidence of mortality, sometimes by suicide, in the months following the death of their wives (Benjamin & Wallis, 1963).

The problem of social isolation falls most heavily on women, who typically outlive their husbands. Table 14–1 on page 392 shows that three-fourths of elderly men live with spouses, while only half of elderly women do. About 42 percent of older women live alone, compared to almost 16 percent of older men. The more pronounced isolation among elderly women may well account for research findings that their mental health is not as strong as that of elderly men in the United States (Chappell & Havens, 1980).

For most older people, families provide the primary source of social support. In one study, Ethel Shanas (1979) found that more than half of older people lived

The painting *Willis Avenue Bridge* (1940) by Ben Shahn (1901–1969) conveys the social marginality that often accompanies growing older, especially for people of color in the cities of the United States.

less than ten minutes away from at least one adult child, and over three-fourths said they had seen one or more of their children during the preceding week. Only 10 percent reported that they had not visited with an adult child during the past month. Women (especially daughters and daughters-in-law) are more likely than men to care for aging people (Stone, Cafferata, & Sangl, 1987). Overall, then, social activity diminishes in old age, but families lessen the sting of social isolation.

## Retirement

Work not only provides us with a source of income, it also figures prominently in our personal identity. Retirement from paid work, therefore, generally entails some reduction in income, diminished social prestige, and a loss of purpose in life (Chown, 1977).

Organizations may help individuals striving to ease this transition. Colleges and universities, for example, confer the title of "professor emeritus" (from Latin, meaning "fully earned") on some retired faculty members, giving them library, parking, and mail privileges. These honored retirees may, if they wish, attend faculty meetings, and some colleges make office space available so they can pursue research.

For many older people, new activities and new interests minimize the personal disruption and loss of prestige brought on by retirement (Rose, 1968). Volunteer work can be personally rewarding, allowing individuals to apply their career skills to new challenges and opportunities. The American Association of Retired Persons (AARP), with more than 15 million members over the age of fifty and more than three thousand local chapters across the United States, lists a wide range of volunteer opportunities for these "experienced Americans."

Although the notion of retirement is familiar enough to us, it is actually a recent social creation, becoming widely adopted only during the last century

**Table 14–1   LIVING ARRANGEMENTS OF THE ELDERLY, 1990**

|  | Men | Women |
|---|---|---|
| Living alone | 15.7% | 42.0% |
| Living with spouse | 74.3 | 39.7 |
| Living with other relatives | 7.7 | 16.1 |
| Living with nonrelatives | 2.3 | 2.2 |
| Living in nursing home | 1.3 | 1.7 |

SOURCE:   U.S. Bureau of the Census.

and only in industrial societies (Atchley, 1982). Advancing technology reduces the need for everyone to work, as well as placing a premium on up-to-date skills. Retirement permits younger workers, who presumably have the most current knowledge and training, to predominate in the labor force. In poor societies of the Third World, by contrast, most people work until they are incapacitated because everyone's labor is vital to a family's survival.

People in the United States generally consider sixty-five to be the proper age for retirement. In global context, however, retirement age varies significantly: some societies (including the Japanese) approve of retirement in the mid-fifties while others have no practice of retirement at all (Kii, 1979; Palmore, 1982). Not long ago, retirement was rarely an option in the United States. Before the Social Security system was established in the 1930s, few people could afford to retire, whatever their age. As Social Security and other pension programs bolstered the financial security of older people, they also promoted the idea that people *should* retire, taking life easy in the later years.

In light of diverse practices in the world and over time, one might wonder if a society should formally designate any specific age for retirement. Vast differences in the interests and capacities of older people also make the notion of fixed retirement controversial. As a result, Congress began phasing out mandatory retirement policies in 1970, and ended the practice for most occupations by 1987. Statistically, however, most workers in the United States still choose to retire by age sixty-five. In

fact, the trend in recent decades has been toward "early" retirement.

In the United States, men more than women have traditionally faced the transition of retirement. Elderly women who spend their lives as homemakers do not retire per se, although the departure of the last child from home serves as a rough parallel. But even lifelong homemakers must adjust to their husband's retirement and presence at home; this has been tagged the "husband underfoot syndrome" (Mitchell, 1972). But in adjusting to their husbands' retirement, women may also find new joys, joining their husbands in activities they previously had little time for (Keating & Cole, 1980). As the proportion of women in the labor force continues to rise, of course, both women and men will confront the changes brought on by retirement.

## Aging and Poverty

For most people in the United States, retirement leads to a significant decline in income. For many, home mortgages and children's college expenses are paid; yet the expenses for medical care, household help, and home utilities typically rise. Many elderly people do not have sufficient savings or pension benefits to be self-supporting; for this reason, Social Security is their greatest source of income. Because many will live with fixed incomes as they face rising costs, poverty rates rise somewhat as people enter old age (see Figure 14–2). As noted in

**Figure 14–2** Poverty and the Life Course, 1990
*(U.S. Bureau of the Census)*

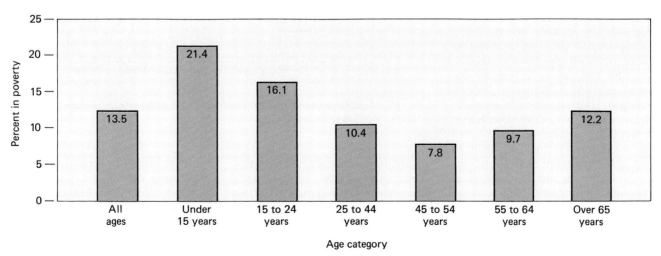

Chapter 10 ("Social Class in the United States"), children are the age category most at risk of poverty, with the incidence of poverty declining until about age fifty-five.

Over time, the rate of poverty among the elderly has gone downward. From about 35 percent in 1960, the official poverty rate for elderly people in the United States stood at 12.2 percent in 1990 (U.S. Bureau of the Census, 1970, 1991). Since 1982, in fact, poverty has been lower among the elderly than among the non-elderly (Stone, 1986). This downward trend in poverty among elderly men and women became pronounced during the last decade as a result of various government programs, as the box explains.

In every age category, members of racial and ethnic minorities face special economic disadvantages; the elderly are no exception. Although, overall, the elderly have never been better off financially in the United States, the poverty rate among Hispanics over sixty-five in 1990 (22.5 percent) was twice the rate for their white counterparts (10.1 percent); elderly African Americans (33.8 percent) had three times the white risk of poverty.

Table 14–2 shows the median income for elderly

## A DECADE OF CHANGE

# The Elderly: A Financial Windfall

A generation ago, the elderly were at high risk of poverty; today, people over sixty-five are less likely to be poor than are children. There are various reasons for this change, including better health that boosts earnings among older people, better pension programs from employers, and stock market values that tripled during the 1980s. But government policies also play a big part and, during the 1980s, federal programs favored the old over the young as never before.

During the 1980s, federal spending on all programs (including Social Security) that directly benefit the elderly soared by a whopping 50 percent to about 47 percent of all government spending. By 1990, as spending for defense eased, helping the elderly became our single greatest national expense. On the other hand, spending for children actually fell by 4 percent during the 1980s to roughly 11 percent of all spending.

Not surprisingly, median household income fell among young people, as shown in the figure. The general pattern is clear: advancing age meant income gains during the 1980s, with elderly households gaining most of all. As the proportion of our population over the age of sixty-five rises, this trend is likely to continue. But a reasonable question is, can we afford to neglect the youngest members of our society in favor of the oldest?

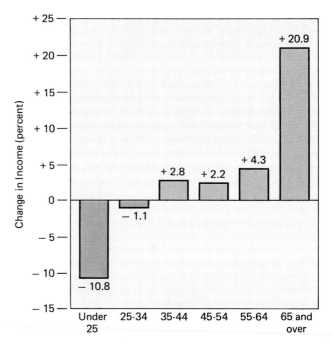

Change in Median Household Income 1980–1990, by Age
*(U.S. Bureau of the Census)*

**Table 14–2** EARNINGS AND TOTAL INCOME OF ELDERLY MEN AND WOMEN, 1990

| | Median Annual Income from Full-time Work (workers only) | Median Total Income for All Elderly (working and nonworking) |
|---|---|---|
| Men, 65 and over | $35,520 | $12,450 |
| Women, 65 and over | $22,866 | $ 8,044 |

SOURCE: U.S. Bureau of the Census.

women and men, based on wages and salaries, Social Security, pensions, and investment income. Looking only at full-time workers, women over sixty-five had median earnings of $22,866 in 1990; comparable men earned $35,520. A quick calculation shows that the income disparity between women and men *intensifies* with advancing age. In 1990, comparing full-time workers of all ages, women earned 72 percent as much as men. However, among workers aged 65 and above the disparity widens, with women earning only 64 percent as much as men. Of course most elderly people do not work full time. Broadening the picture to include the entire elderly population—nonworking as well as working—median income falls to $8,044 for women and $12,450 for men. Although income drops for both sexes when nonworkers are included, the income ratio remains the same with women receiving 64 percent as much as men.

In the United States, growing old means a growing risk of poverty, especially among people of color and women. The privation of the elderly, however, is often hidden from view. Because of personal pride and a desire to maintain the dignity of independent living—values taught to members of our society from childhood—elderly people may conceal financial problems even from their own families. It is often difficult for people who have supported their children for years to admit that they can no longer provide for themselves, even though it may be through no fault of their own.

## Abuse of the Elderly

In the United States, we seem to awaken to the problems of personal violence in stages: child abuse was first discussed in the 1960s, spouse abuse came to the fore in the 1970s, and abuse of the elderly was publicly acknowledged in the 1980s. Abuse of older people takes many forms, from passive neglect to active torment, and includes verbal, emotional, financial, and physical harm. Most elderly people suffer from none of these things; but government data suggest that some 1 million elderly people (3 percent of the total) endure serious maltreatment each year (Pillemer, 1988). Perhaps three times as many elderly people sustain abuse at some point in time (Clark, 1986). Like violence against children or women in the home, it is difficult to determine how widespread abuse of the elderly is because victims are understandably reluctant to talk about their plight. But the trend is disturbing: as the proportion of elderly people rises, so does the incidence of abuse (Bruno, 1985).

What motivates people to abuse the elderly? Often, as suggested earlier, the cause lies in the stress of caring—financially and emotionally—for aging parents. This is especially true today because adult daughters as well as sons are now likely to be holding down jobs as well as caring for children of their own. Even in Japan—where tradition demands that adult children care for aging parents at home—more and more people find themselves unable to cope with the situation (Yates, 1986). Abuse appears to be most common where the stresses are greatest: in families with a very old person suffering from serious health problems, and where the relationship between parent and child has historically been poor. Here, family life may be grossly distorted by demands and tensions that people simply cannot endure, even if their intentions are good (Douglass, 1983; Gelman, 1985).

In sum, growing old involves serious problems and transitions. Some are brought on by physical decline. But others—including social isolation, adjustment to retirement, risk of poverty, and abuse from family members—are social problems. In the next section, we bring to bear various theoretical perspectives on how society shapes the lives of the elderly.

## Theoretical Analysis of Aging

Various theories—developed from the major theoretical paradigms in sociology—help to shed light on the process of aging in the United States. We examine them each in turn.

## Structural-Functional Analysis: Aging and Disengagement

Based on the ideas of Talcott Parsons—an architect of the structural-functional paradigm—Elaine Cumming and William Henry (1961) argue that aging inevitably brings on biological decline and, eventually, death. How is society to minimize the enormous disruption caused by the loss of its members? In their view, a social system ensures that tasks are performed without interruption through a gradual and orderly transfer of various statuses and roles from the old to the young. Continual turmoil would ensue if only incompetence or death brought about a changing of the guard. But a society heads off this outcome if the elderly disengage from productive roles while they are still able to perform them. Such disengagement by the elderly is also functional because, in a rapidly changing society, younger workers typically have skills and training that are more up-to-date. Formally, then, **disengagement theory** is *an analysis linking disengagement by elderly people from positions of social responsibility to the orderly operation of society.*

Disengagement may benefit elderly people as well as their society. Aging individuals with diminishing capacities presumably look forward to relinquishing some of the pressures of their jobs in favor of new pursuits of their own choosing (Palmore, 1979b). Society also grants older people greater freedom of behavior so that unusual actions on their part are construed as harmless eccentricity rather than dangerous deviance.

*Critical evaluation.* In delineating one strategy societies pursue to deal with the human decline brought on by aging—by transferring responsibilities from older to younger people—disengagement theory also suggests why our society tends to define elderly people as marginal.

There are several limitations to this approach. First, workers cannot disengage from paid work unless they have sufficient financial security to fall back on. Most elderly people in the United States have had access to such resources only in recent decades, and some still do not. Second, many elderly people do not wish to disengage from their productive roles. Disengagement, after all, has high personal costs, including loss of social prestige, social isolation, and reduced income. Third, there is no clear evidence that the societal benefits of disengagement outweigh its costs, which include the loss of human resources and the need to care for people who might otherwise be able to fend better for themselves. Then, too, any useful system of disengagement would have to take account of widely differing abilities of the elderly themselves.

## Symbolic-Interaction Analysis: Aging and Activity

One critical rebuttal to disengagement theory draws heavily on the symbolic-interaction paradigm. **Activity theory** is *an analysis linking personal satisfaction in old age to a high level of activity.* Because individuals build their social identity from statuses and roles, this theory notes that disengagement in old age has the dysfunction of eroding the satisfaction and meaning many elderly people find in their lives. Therefore, what elderly people need is a source of activity beyond retirement.

Activity theory proposes that the elderly substitute new roles and responsibilities for the ones they leave behind. After all, as members of a society that values productive activity, the elderly are likely to find the prospect of disengagement as unsatisfying as a younger person would. Another problem with disengagement theory is its tendency to see old people as a monolithic category. Activity theory stresses, more accurately, that older people have distinctive needs, interests, and physical abilities that guide their activities and attitudes about aging.

Research supports the conclusion that elderly people who maintain high activity levels are the most satisfied with their lives (Friedman & Havighurst, 1954; Havighurst, Neugarten, & Tobin, 1968; Neugarten, 1977; Palmore, 1979a). But no single conclusions should be applied to the socially diverse population of elderly women and men. Many aging people find satisfaction in high levels of activity; for some older people, however, a less active schedule—or, in some cases, uninterrupted leisure—brings the greatest happiness.

*Critical evaluation.* Focusing on the elderly themselves rather than on the needs of society, activity theory provides a useful counterpoint to disengagement theory. Activity theory also highlights the social diversity among elderly people, an important consideration in formulating any government policy. Further, activity theory's assertion that the elderly generally enhance their personal satisfaction by leading active lives is well supported by research.

One limitation of this approach, from a structural-functionalist point of view, is a tendency to exaggerate the well-being and competence of the elderly. Do we want active elderly people serving as physicians or airline pilots, for example? From another perspective, activity theory falls short by overlooking how many of the problems that beset older people have more to do with how well their *society* (rather than *they*) operate. We turn now to that point of view, social-conflict theory.

## Social-Conflict Analysis: Aging and Inequality

The social-conflict approach spotlights the fact that different age categories compete for scarce social resources. Various stages in the life course, therefore, form the basis of age stratification. In the past, middle-aged people in the United States have enjoyed the greatest social privileges, while the elderly (like children in many respects) had less power and prestige and ran a higher risk of poverty. Employers have been likely to push elderly workers aside in favor of men and women who are younger because less-senior workers typically command lower wages. The end result has been turning older people into second-class citizens (Atchley, 1982; Phillipson, 1982).

The roots of this age-based hierarchy reach into the operation of industrial-capitalist society. Following the ideas of Karl Marx, Steven Spitzer (1980) points out that, because our society has an overriding concern with profit, we devalue those categories of people who are economically unproductive. Thus, Spitzer reasons, most of the elderly have a mildly deviant status and are easily ignored. Old people are destined to be marginal members of a society consumed by material gain.

Social-conflict analysis also draws attention to social diversity in the elderly population. Differences of class, race, ethnicity, and gender divide older people as they do everyone else. Thus the fortunate seniors in higher social classes have far more economic security, greater access to top-flight medical care, and more options for personal satisfaction in old age than those with fewer privileges. Likewise, elderly WASPs typically enjoy a host of advantages denied to older people of color. And women—who represent an increasing majority of the elderly population with advancing age—suffer the social and economic disadvantages of sexism.

***Critical evaluation.*** Social-conflict theory adds further to our understanding of the aging process by underscoring age-based inequality and focusing on ways that capitalism devalues elderly people who are less productive. The implication of this analysis is that the aged fare better

in noncapitalist societies, a view validated by some research (Treas, 1979).

One shortcoming of this approach goes right to its core contention: rather than blaming *capitalism* for the lower social standing of elderly people, critics hold that *industrialization* is the true culprit, so that socialism might provide no improvement in the situation. Furthermore, the notion that capitalism dooms the elderly to economic distress is challenged by the significant rise in the income of elderly people in the United States. As we have explained, the elderly now enjoy the greatest government benefits. Future conflict seems likely to pit younger people (especially children) against the elderly in pursuit of economic security.

# Ageism

In earlier chapters, we explained how ideology—including racism and sexism—seeks to justify the social disadvantages of minorities. Sociologists use a parallel term, **ageism,** to designate *prejudice and discrimination against the elderly.*

Like racism and sexism, ageism can be blatant (as when individuals deny elderly women or men a job or access to housing simply because of their age) or subtle (as when people speak to the elderly with a condescending tone as if they were children) (Kalish, 1979). Also like racism and sexism, ageism builds physical traits into stereotypes; in the case of the elderly, graying hair, wrinkled skin, and stooped posture may be viewed as badges of personal incompetence. Negative stereotypes picture the aged as helpless, confused, resistant to change, and generally unhappy (Butler, 1975). Even supposedly positive stereotypes of older people can deny them the full range of their humanity. Sentimental depictions of sweet little old ladies and charmingly eccentric old gentlemen ignore the fact that old people are complex individuals with distinct personalities and long years of experience and accomplishment.

Ageism, like other forms of prejudice, may have some foundation in reality. Statistically speaking, old people are more likely than young people to be mentally and physically impaired. But we slip into ageism when we make unwarranted generalizations about an entire category of people, most of whom do not conform to any stereotypes. As explained earlier in this chapter, most elderly people do not suffer from significant disabilities, and most have the same needs, feelings, and diversity of views as people who are younger. Finally, despite prejudices suggesting that anyone with gray hair and wrinkles lacks sex appeal, elderly people in good health are quite capable of maintaining satisfying sexual relationships.

Media-watchers have long criticized the exclusion of the aged, and especially elderly women, from programming and advertising. Research suggests that the media do not stereotype the elderly as extensively as they do women, but television and the print media have contributed to ageism in the United States (Kubey, 1980; Buchholz & Bynum, 1982). In recent years, television and films have featured more elderly people—many in a positive light. Estimates suggest that people aged fifty and over now purchase almost half of all consumer goods, and this fact is not lost on marketing executives and media moguls (Hoyt, 1985).

On a hopeful note, some research indicates that negative stereotypes about the elderly are disappearing. Perhaps we are not as preoccupied with work as we were in the past, and are therefore less likely to devalue elderly people as nonproductive. Older men and women have also gained political clout through organizations like the American Association of Retired Persons and because of their rising affluence. But, most important, older people themselves are dispelling the negative stereotypes. Remaining active and maintaining a positive view of their lives, older people exude self-confidence, which acts as a powerful force to undermine negative social images (Tibbitts, 1979).

## The Elderly: A Minority?

The evidence is clear that, as a category of people in this country, the elderly do face social disadvantages. But sociologists differ as to whether the aged form a minority in the same way as, say, people of color or women. By briefly outlining key arguments in this debate, we will point up the similarities and differences between the elderly and other categories of people that are widely known as minorities.

Three decades ago, Leonard Breen (1960) pronounced the elderly a minority. He defended this assertion by noting that, first, older people have a clear social identity based on the ascribed status of being old and, second, they are subject to prejudice and discrimination. In addition, as we have explained, the elderly are often socially isolated, denied equal opportunity for jobs, and

more likely than middle-aged Americans to be poor (Eitzen, 1980; Levin & Levin, 1980; Barrow & Smith, 1983).

Other sociologists, however, were not convinced and made the counterargument that the elderly do not qualify as a minority. Gordon Streib (1968) responded that minority status is usually both permanent and exclusive. That is, a person is African American, of Asian descent, or a woman *for life*, and any such standing precludes being part of the dominant category of white males. But being elderly, Streib continued, is an *open* status because people are elderly for only part of their lives. Further, he added, everyone who has the good fortune to live long enough grows old.

The elderly are marked by social diversity more than members of any sex, race, ethnicity, or social class. Not surprisingly, then, they are unlikely to define themselves collectively as old people. On the contrary, although aware of their age, the elderly commonly think of themselves in terms of other social categories.

Streib made one further point. The social disadvantages faced by the elderly are less substantial than those experienced by the minorities described in earlier chapters. For example, old people have never been deprived of the right to own property, to vote, or to hold office, as people of color and women have. In fact, older men—and, to a lesser extent, older women—exercise considerable political influence in the United States, and their risk of poverty is only slightly greater than average. Some elderly people, Streib conceded, do suffer economic disadvantages, but these do not stem primarily from old age. Instead, most of the aged poor fall into categories of people likely to be poor at any age. Streib concludes that "the poor grow old," *not* that "the old grow poor."

For all the reasons delineated here, old people do not form a minority in the same sense as other categories of people do. Nor do they even have enough characteristics in common to be called a subculture, as some have suggested (Rose, 1968). Perhaps the best way to describe the elderly is simply as a *distinctive segment* of the population of the United States.

# Death and Dying

*To every thing there is a season,*
*And a time for every matter under heaven:*
*A time to be born and a time to die . . .*

These well-known lines from the Book of Ecclesiastes in the Bible convey two basic truths about human exis-

Paintings provide a dramatic record of how common death was to everyday experience in the medieval era. *The Triumph of Death,* by sixteenth-century Flemish artist Pieter Breughel, makes this point with chilling realism.

tence: the fact of birth and the inevitability of death. Just as life varies in striking ways across history and around the world, so does death. We conclude this chapter with a brief look at the changing character of death—the final stage in the process of growing old.

## Historical Patterns of Death

Throughout most of human history, death was a familiar fact of life. In technologically simple hunting and gathering societies, no one dared to assume that a newborn child would live for long. This uncertainty was so great, in fact, that parents often did not name children until they reached several years of age (Herty, 1960). Surviving infancy was an achievement and a matter of good luck; but thereafter illness brought on by poor nutrition, accidents, and natural catastrophes such as drought or famine combined to make life uncertain, at best. Sometimes death was deliberate, a strategy that emerges in societies that lack the resources to feed their people. Typically, the least productive people were killed so that others could live. In some cases, societies resorted to *infanticide,* the killing of newborn infants; in others, *geronticide,* the killing of the elderly.

Agricultural technology provided far more food,

which enabled societies to grow in size and establish permanent settlements. But still death remained part of the common experience. Herds of animals in close proximity to villages spread infectious disease. Larger towns devised few effective means to dispose of human waste, resulting in poor sanitation. Until about the seventeenth century, plagues brought on and spread by unsanitary conditions sometimes wiped out a town's entire population.

In sum, most of our human ancestors regarded death as an integral part of life. In medieval Europe, Christianity offered the consolation that death fit into the divine plan for human existence. To illustrate, historian Philippe Ariès describes how Sir Lancelot, one of King Arthur's fearless Knights of the Round Table, prepared for his own death when he believed himself mortally wounded:

> His gestures were fixed by old customs, ritual gestures which must be carried out when one is about to die. He removed his weapons and lay quietly upon the ground. . . . He spread his arms out, his body forming a cross . . . in such a way that his head faced east toward Jerusalem. (1974:7–8)

As societies gradually gained control over many causes of death, attitudes began to change. Death became less and less an everyday experience: fewer children died at birth, and accidents and disease took a smaller toll among adults. Except in times of war or other catastrophes, people came to view dying as quite *extra*ordinary, except among the very old. In 1900, about one-third of all deaths in the United States occurred before the age of five, another third occurred before the age of fifty-five, and the remaining one-third of men and women died in what was then defined as old age. By 1990, 85 percent of Americans died *after* the age of fifty-five. Thus old age and death have become fused in our culture.

## The Modern Separation of Life and Death

Less a part of everyday experience, death is now looked on as something unnatural. Religious beliefs that place both life and death in a divine scheme have been eroded by the growing ability of medical technology to overcome disease and slow the physical deterioration that accompanies aging. If social conditions prepared our ancestors to accept their deaths, modern society has fostered a desire for immortality, or eternal youth. In this sense, death has become separated from life.

This denial of death, coupled with the rapid increase in the elderly population of the United States, has forced our society to confront difficult ethical questions. Should life be extended as long as technologically possible? Should we commit an increasing share of medical resources to the task of prolonging life? Medical ethicist Daniel Callahan addresses these questions, arguing that society will have to devise limits on longevity, as the box explains.

Death is also *physically* removed from the rest of life. The clearest evidence of this is that many of us have never seen a person die. While our ancestors typically died at home in the presence of family and friends, death today often occurs in unfamiliar and impersonal settings such as hospitals and nursing homes (Ariès, 1974). Even hospitals commonly relegate dying patients to a special part of the building, and hospital morgues are located well out of sight of patients and visitors alike (Sudnow, 1967).

Perhaps it is no wonder that, while our ancestors accepted death as part of life, we confront the prospect of dying with fear and anxiety. No doubt, this fearful attitude has propelled the rapid increase in medical research aimed as prolonging the life of the elderly. How-

ever, we may be on the verge of forging a new norm relating to death and dying. As the opening to this chapter suggests, many aging people are less terrified of death than they are at the prospect of being kept alive at all costs. In other words, medical technology now threatens personal autonomy because doctors and hospitals rather than dying individuals are deciding a course of action. The surprising popularity of the book *Final Exit* demonstrates that people want control over their deaths no less than they seek control over their lives.

Consequently, patients and families are now taking the initiative, oftentimes choosing not to make use of available medical technology to prolong life. After long deliberation, patients, families, and doctors may decide to forgo any "heroic measures" to resuscitate a person who is dying. Living Wills—statements of what medical

The infancy of photography in the 1840s was also a time of deadly epidemics in the United States, with between one-third and one-half of children dying before the age of ten. Many grieving parents rushed to capture their dead children on film. The post-mortem photograph, in most cases the only picture ever taken of someone, suggests a far greater acceptance of death during the nineteenth century. In this century, death became rare among the young so that dying is separated from life as a grim reality that people do their best to deny.

# Setting Limits: How Much Old Age Can We Afford?

For most of human history, the question "Can people live *too long*?" would have been absurd. In recent decades, however, a surge in the elderly population, widespread support for using technology to prolong life, and a dizzying increase in funding for medical research directed toward diseases of old age have prompted people in the United States to grapple with this question.

The graying of our society, Daniel Callahan warns, will eventually force us to look critically at what proportion of limited resources should be allocated for the needs of older people. To even raise this issue, he concedes, smacks of a lack of caring. But ignoring it poses a serious threat to the well-being of everyone.

The $80 billion spent on health care for the elderly in 1981 will soar beyond $200 billion by the end of the 1990s. This dramatic boost reflects a policy that channels a growing proportion of medical resources—both in research and treatment—toward diseases and disabilities common to old age.

Callahan argues, first, that if we continue to increase spending on behalf of the elderly we will have to spend less on others, including children. At some point, this trend will be intolerable, forcing policy makers to set limits. Although difficult to devise, we are fast approaching the day when such a policy will become a fiscal and moral imperative.

Second, Callahan urges us to recognize that while medical technology produces *longer* life, it does not necessarily make for *better* life. Costs aside, does expensive and stressful heart surgery that may prolong the life of an eighty-four-year-old woman for two years truly improve the quality of her life? Costs considered, would those resources yield more "quality of life" if used, say, to transplant a kidney into a ten-year-old boy?

Third, Callahan urges all of us to reconsider our notion of death. Today many people rage against death as an enemy to be conquered at all costs. Yet, he suggests, a sensible health-care program in an aging society must recognize death as a natural end to the life course. If we cannot make peace with death for our own well-being, limited resources demand that we do so for the benefit of others.

In short, Callahan concludes, the aging of our society should provoke critical thinking about death, life, and old age, leading to

an understanding of the process of aging and death that looks to our obligations to the young and to the future, that sees old age as a source of knowledge and insight of value to other age groups, that recognizes the necessity of limits and the acceptance of decline and death, and that values the old for their age and not their continuing youthful vitality. (1987:223)

SOURCE: Callahan (1987).

procedures an individual wants and does not want under specific conditions—are becoming widely accepted. Certainly, there are dangers in this practice. Family members may exert subtle pressure on a failing parent to refuse medical care, for example, because others wish to be spared emotional stress or a financial burden. Patients and family members will face difficult decisions that are as much moral as they are medical; to assist them, hospitals now offer the services of biomedical ethics committees, composed of physicians, social service professionals, and members of the clergy. The trend seems clear: if decline and death remain inevitable, at least people can make their own choices about when and where and perhaps even how they will die.

## Bereavement

In Chapter 5 ("Socialization"), we described the stages by which people usually confront their own death. Elizabeth Kübler-Ross (1969) claims that individuals initially react with *denial*, followed by *anger*, efforts toward *negotiation* of divine intervention, gradual *resignation* and, finally, *acceptance*. But it is not only the dying person who must adjust to the approaching death but also those who will experience bereavement through the loss of a significant person.

According to some researchers, bereavement is a process that parallels the stages of dying described by Kübler-Ross. Those close to a dying person, for instance, may initially deny the reality of impending death, reaching the point of acceptance only with time. Other researchers question the use of linear stage theories, arguing that bereavement may not follow any rigid schedule (Lund, Caserta, and Diamond, 1986; Lund, 1989). But all the experts agree that how others view a death influences the attitudes of the person who is dying. That is, if family and friends accept the reality of approaching death, it helps the dying person do the same; conversely, a dying person may have difficulty accepting death if surrounded by loved ones who deny the reality of the situation. Such denial also serves to emotionally isolate the dying person, who is unable to share feelings and experiences with others who refuse to accept that death is imminent.

One recent development intended to provide support to dying people is the *hospice* movement. Unlike a hospital that is designed to cure disease, a hospice helps people have a good death. These care centers for dying people work to minimize pain and suffering, and encourage family members to remain close to the patient. Hospices also help dying people avoid the social isolation that commonly accompanies terminal illness by removing obstacles for patients who wish to return home to die in familiar surroundings. In every case, the hospice staff strives to enhance the comfort and dignity of the dying person as well as family members (Stoddard, 1978).

Even under the most favorable circumstances, bereavement may persist for some time. Besides profound grief, many survivors experience social disorientation because the dead person served as a point of reference in their lives. As we suggested earlier, among the elderly—especially older women—the loss of a spouse is both common and difficult.

Research teaches us that bereavement is less intense among people who, themselves, have high self-esteem, and who understand and accept the death of a loved one (Lund et al., 1985). And survivors who feel their relationship with the dying person has reached a satisfactory resolution experience shorter and less painful grieving. By taking the opportunity to bring an appropriate closure to their relationship with a dying person, in other words, family and friends are better able to comfort and support one another after the death finally occurs (Atchley, 1983).

This chapter has described a number of consequences of the "graying of the United States." As the ranks of the elderly increase, they will become a more visible and vocal part of everyday life. Gerontology, the study of the elderly, will also gain in stature, paralleling an expansion in medical care directed toward old people. As part of this transformation, we can also expect changes in the way we view death. The growing presence of the elderly in everyday settings will almost certainly shift our perception of death from a social taboo to a natural part of the life course. Both young and old alike may benefit.

## Summary

1. From 4 percent of the population in 1900 and over 12 percent today, the elderly will represent 25 percent of the population of the United States by the middle of the next century.

2. Gerontology, the study of aging and the elderly, focuses on biological and psychological changes in old age, as well as how aging is defined in a culture.

3. Growing old is accompanied by a rising incidence of disease and disability. Younger people commonly exaggerate the extent of disability among the elderly, however.

4. Psychological research confirms that growing old does not bring about an overall loss in intelligence or great changes in individual personality.

5. The age at which people are defined as old has varied historically: until several centuries ago, old age began as early as thirty. In poorer societies today, life expectancy is substantially lower than in North America.

6. In global perspective, industrialization fosters a decline in the social standing of elderly people.

7. As people age, they commonly experience social isolation brought on by retirement, physical disability, and the death of friends or spouse. Even so, most elderly people find that family members provide considerable social support.

8. Retirement forces people to make various social adjustments. Although traditionally a problem faced only by men, retirement will become a con-

cern of both sexes because of the increasing participation of women in the labor force.

9. Since 1960, poverty among the elderly has dropped significantly. Elderly women and elderly people of color are especially likely to be poor.

10. Disengagement theory—based on structural-functional analysis—suggests that the elderly disengage from positions of social responsibility before the onset of disability or death. In this way, a society transfers statuses and roles from the old to the young in an orderly way.

11. Activity theory, based on symbolic-interaction analysis, claims that a high level of activity affords people greater personal satisfaction in old age.

12. Age stratification is a focus of social-conflict analysis. According to this paradigm, the emphasis on economic productivity in capitalist societies leads to a devaluing of those who are less productive,

including the elderly. The growing affluence of the elderly—coupled to their rising numbers—underlines a trend toward older people dominating the national agenda.

13. Ageism—prejudice and discrimination against old people—serves to justify age stratification.

14. Although many old people are socially disadvantaged, the elderly encompass people of both sexes and all races, ethnicities, and social classes. Thus older people do not constitute a minority.

15. Death is no longer part of everyday life, prompting personal discomfort with the subject of death. Today most people in our society die only after reaching old age. In our attempt to isolate death from life, we have segregated dying people. Recent trends suggest that people are confronting death more directly and seeking control over the process of dying.

## Key Concepts

**activity theory** an analysis of aging linking personal satisfaction in old age to a high level of activity

**ageism** prejudice and discrimination against the elderly

**age stratification** the unequal distribution of wealth, power, and privileges among people of different ages

**disengagement theory** an analysis of aging linking disengagement by elderly people from positions of social responsibility to the orderly operation of society

**gerontocracy** a form of social organization in which the elderly have the most wealth, power, and privileges

**gerontology** the study of aging and the elderly

## Suggested Readings

These two texts examine a number of issues related to aging, the elderly, and the life course.

Harold Cox. *Later Life: The Realities of Aging*. 3rd ed. Englewood Cliffs, NJ: Prentice Hall, 1993.

Eric R. Kingson, Barbara A. Hirshorn, and John M. Cornman. *Ties That Bind: The Interdependence of Generations*. Washington, DC: Seven Locks Press, 1986.

The first of these books is a Pulitzer Prize–winner, first published in 1975, criticizing America's approach to aging. The second offers a more recent assessment of the issue.

Robert N. Butler. *Why Survive? Being Old in America*. New York: Harper and Row, 1985.

Richard J. Margolis. *Risking Old Age in America*. Boulder, CO: Westview, 1989.

This fascinating and richly illustrated analysis of aging highlights the treatment of the elderly in Western societies over the last one thousand years.

Herbert C. Covey. *Images of Older People in Western Art and Society*. Westport, CT: Greenwood Publishers, 1991.

A psychological approach guides this study of the adjustments to growing old.

George Thorman. *Emotional Problems of Aging*. New York: Charles C Thomas, 1989.

This government study examines the timely issue of poverty among older women.

Robyn Stone. *The Feminization of Poverty and Older Women*. Washington, DC: U.S. Department of Health and Human Services, 1986.

(Faith Ringgold, The Wedding: Lover's Quilt #1, 1986. Oil on canvas, tie-dyed, printed, pieced fabric. 77½ × 58". Collection of Marilyn Lanfear, Texas. Photograph courtesy Bernice Steinbaum Gallery, New York City.)

# Family

Twins were born in 1991 to Arlette Schweitzer, a forty-two-year-old librarian in the town of Aberdeen, South Dakota. While having twins is not extraordinary, the Schweitzer children made medical history as *the first case of a woman giving birth to her own grandchildren*.

Arlette Schweitzer agreed to carry and bear a child for her daughter—a woman born without a uterus and thus unable to have children on her own. Medical specialists removed eggs from the daughter's ovaries, placed them in a laboratory dish where they were fertilized with sperm from the daughter's husband, and then implanted the embryos in Arlette Schweitzer's womb (Kolata, 1991). When the twins—a girl and a boy—were born to Ms. Schweitzer, her daughter was at her side, tears of joy streaming down her face as she witnessed what would have been impossible a generation ago.

Cases of *surrogacy* like this one—in which one woman bears children using an egg from another woman—are becoming increasingly common throughout the world. In effect, new reproductive technology is bending what were once regarded as the "rules" of family life, including the idea that only couples have children. In addition, such techniques are blurring conventional kinship relations: what, for example, is Arlette Schweitzer's relation to the children she bore?

Surrogacy is only one of many ways in which the traditional notion of family has changed in recent decades. Not long ago, the cultural ideal of the family was a working husband, a homemaker wife, and their children. This pattern still exists, of course, but now it represents barely one in ten households in the United States. If a single set of characteristics ever accurately described our society's families, it simply does not today. This chapter will examine family life in the United States and elsewhere in the world, explore how families have changed over time, and explain why this important social group displays so much diversity today.

In all its forms, the family remains a major social institution in the United States, as it is in every other society. Recall from Chapter 4 ("Society") that social institutions are organizational systems a society uses to address one or more of its basic needs. Other social institutions, including schools, religion, politics, and the economy, are discussed in subsequent chapters of this book. We will see that each social institution is complex and has many consequences—negative as well as positive—for the operation of a society.

## The Family: Basic Concepts

**Kinship** refers to *social ties based on blood, marriage, or adoption*. We develop emotional bonds toward people to whom we are "related," and kin meet many of an individual's needs. Especially in small preindustrial societies, most people cooperate with kin to secure their food and maintain their shelter. The functional significance of kinship declines somewhat in industrial societies: here people distinguish between close relatives, who interact regularly and typically live together, and distant relatives, among whom there is often little social contact.

Definitions of the family vary considerably around the world and change over time. Generally, the **family** is defined as *a relatively permanent social group of two or more people related by blood, marriage, or adoption, and who usually live together.* Family life tends to be cooperative. As the most important of our primary groups, families encourage members to share economic resources and day-to-day responsibilities. In industrial societies, people live first in a **family of orientation,** *the family into which a person is born and receives early socialization.* Later in life, a person may live in a **family of procreation,** *a family in which people have or adopt children of their own.* In most societies of the world, families are formed by **marriage,** *a socially approved relationship, involving economic cooperation and allowing sexual activity and childbearing, that is expected to be relatively enduring.*

As we shall explain, although U.S. law only recognizes marriage as the formal union of one male and one female, marital patterns show striking variation in global perspective. The significance of marriage as the basis for procreation is evident in the traditional attachment of the label of *illegitimacy* to children born out of wedlock, and in the word *matrimony,* which is derived from Latin meaning "the condition of motherhood." This norm linking childbearing to marriage has weakened considerably, however, as the proportion of children born to unmarried women has increased.

Yet even these few generalizations cannot be applied to every family in the United States today. For example, many people object to defining as "families" only married couples and children. Thus traditional families have been increasingly complemented by various *families of affinity:* groups whose members are drawn together and who think of themselves as a family. For example, some communal groups of unrelated people who choose to live together for a period of time and share resources regard themselves as families. Similarly, an unmarried couple and their children may live as a family, even if this pattern provokes disapproval in some quarters. Many gay and lesbian couples, some residing with children of one or both partners, also consider themselves family units.

Others, however, argue that because the family is central to our society, social approval should not be extended to any relationship simply because those involved wish to be defined as a family (Dedrick, 1990). What does or does not constitute a family, then, is now a matter of political debate. Courts play a part in this controversy: in some parts of the country, the law now recognizes the partnership of two people of one sex (although legal marriage remains restricted to heterosexual couples). Courts have more widely declared that unmarried partners may make claims on each other's property in the event that the relationship dissolves. Such rulings suggest that the concept of family—legally as well as socially—is taking on a broader meaning.

## The Family in Cross-Cultural Perspective

Virtually all societies recognize families (Murdock, 1945), yet families are subject to significant cross-cultural variation.

As was noted in earlier chapters, industrial societies recognize the **nuclear family,** *a social unit composed of one or, more commonly, two parents and children.* Typically based on marriage, the nuclear family is also often called the *conjugal family.* In preindustrial societies, however, the **extended family,** *a social unit including parents, children, and other kin,* predominates. This is also called the *consanguine family,* meaning that it is based on blood ties. Extended families frequently include grandparents, aunts, uncles, and other kin. In the United States, extended families are not typical, but they are common among some ethnic categories, especially Americans of Hispanic ancestry. In addition, about one in seven elderly people lives with a relative other than a spouse, thereby forming an extended family.

Although many members of our society live in extended families, the nuclear family has been the predominant form in the United States (Laslett, 1978; Degler, 1980). Industrialization intensifies the nuclear family pattern by moving productive work away from the home so that children grow up in one family (of orientation) only to leave in order to pursue their careers and form a new family (of procreation). Both geographical and social mobility can tug at kinship ties, distancing members of extended families from one another.

What does the future hold for families? Sweden is considered a very progressive society by most social

In modern industrial societies, the members of extended families usually live apart from one another. However, they may assemble for rituals such as weddings, funerals, and family reunions.

analysts; therefore, looking to the Swedes may point up some likely patterns in our own future. Sociologist David Popenoe (1991) has examined the state of the Swedish family and, as the box on pages 408–9 explains, he concludes that this nation may have the weakest families in the entire world.

## Marriage Patterns

Cultural norms, often in the form of law, regulate whom a person may marry. These norms distinguish categories of people who *are* suitable mates from those who are *not*. One pattern that results from such norms is **endogamy**, *marriage between people of the same social group or category*. Every society has norms of endogamy that endorse marriage between people of the same age, tribe, race, religion, or social class. Some religions in the United States—especially Judaism and Catholicism—actively encourage endogamous marriage. The second pattern, also found in every society, is **exogamy**, *marriage between people of different social groups or categories*. The prohibition against gay marriage in the United States

and most other societies is the most obvious form of exogamy.

All societies, then, endorse some combination of endogamy and exogamy. Traditional villagers in India, for example, require a young person to marry someone from the same caste category but also from a different village. By uniting people of similar backgrounds, endogamy encourages group solidarity and helps to maintain traditional values and norms. At the same time, exogamy helps to forge useful alliances and encourages cultural diffusion.

In every industrial society, both law and cultural norms prescribe a form of marriage called **monogamy** (from Greek meaning "one union"), *marriage that joins one female and one male*. However, because divorce and remarriage occur frequently in our society, *serial monogamy*, that is, a series of monogamous marriages, more accurately describes the most prevalent pattern of matrimony in the United States. Global Map 15–1 on page 410 shows that monogamy is legally prescribed throughout the Americas, in Europe, and in much of Asia.

Most marriages in the rest of the world are also monogamous. But, as Global Map 15–1 shows, many preindustrial societies—especially in Africa and southern Asia—permit **polygamy** (from Greek meaning "many unions"), *marriage that unites three or more people*. In polygamous marriage two or more nuclear families are combined to form an extended family. Polygamy takes two forms. By far the more common is **polygyny** (from the Greek, meaning "many women" or "many wives"), *marriage that joins one male with more than one female*. Islamic societies in southern Asia and Africa, for example, allow men to have up to four wives. In societies that endorse polygyny, most families are nonetheless monogamous because great wealth is required to support several wives and even more children. In our own history, polygyny was officially sanctioned by the Mormon church (formally known as the Church of Jesus Christ of Latter-Day Saints) based in Utah. In 1890, however, the Mormons banned what they termed "plural marriage" in order to win statehood for Utah from the federal government. Even today, informal estimates suggest that between ten thousand and thirty thousand Mormons live in plural marriages—one legal marriage and others performed by a local church.

**Polyandry** (from the Greek, meaning "many men" or "many husbands") is *marriage that joins one female with more than one male*. This pattern is extremely rare, appearing only in a few settings, such as among Tibetan Buddhists. Polyandry discourages the division of land

# Sweden: The Weakest Families on Earth?

Sweden, one of the Scandinavian countries of northern Europe, has managed to avoid many of the social problems that plague the United States. In its cities, violent crimes are rare, and the nightmare of drug abuse rarely touches the lives of its people. There is little evidence of the grinding poverty that has blighted whole regions of urban America. To many observers, Sweden fulfills the promise of the modern welfare state, a society in which an extensive and professional government bureaucracy sees to virtually all human needs.

According to David Popenoe, however, Sweden has another, more dubious, distinction: it has what are arguably the weakest families on earth. For one thing, people in Sweden are less likely to marry than in any other industrialized society; the country also has the highest proportion of adults living alone (20 percent versus about 13 percent in the United States). For another, a larger share of couples live together outside of

marriage (25 percent versus about 5 percent in the United States) than anywhere else, and half of all Swedish children (compared to about one in five in the United States) are born to unmarried parents. Average household size is also the smallest in the world (2.2 persons versus 2.6 in the United States). Finally, families (based on marriages or consensual unions) are more likely to dissolve than in any other country. Reviewing the evidence, Popenoe concludes that the family

has probably become weaker in Sweden than anywhere else—certainly among advanced Western nations. Individual family members are the most autonomous and least bound by the group, and the group as a whole is least cohesive. (1991:69)

This is a new development in Sweden, one that has become pronounced only since the 1960s. It is worthy of study because many of the trends that have transformed Swedish society are also at work in the United States. Pope-

noe claims that a developing culture of individualism and self-fulfillment and the declining influence of religion have both served to undermine Swedish families. In addition, Sweden has the lowest proportion of women who are homemakers (10 percent versus about 25 percent in the United States) and the highest percentage of women in the labor force (77 percent versus 58 percent in the United States). But even more important in the erosion of the family than these social forces, Popenoe contends, is the expansion of the welfare state.

Government programs provide for human needs in every industrial society. The United States stands out as having perhaps the least developed social-welfare system. Sweden, by contrast, enshrined in law the most far-reaching scheme of its kind. All Swedes are issued a national registration number at birth, and their citizenship entitles them to a lifetime of services (and high taxes). For example, they can count on the government to deliver their children, to educate them, to sustain their

---

into parcels too small to support a family and divides the burdensome costs of supporting a wife among many men. Polyandry has also been associated with female infanticide, the aborting of female fetuses or killing of female infants. This practice reduces the female population so that men must share women.

In sum, the historical record shows that in the majority of world societies monogamy has been just one of several approved marital patterns; yet, most marriages throughout the world have been monogamous (Murdock, 1965). This cultural preference for monogamy stems

from two common-sense factors: first, the financial burden of supporting multiple spouses is onerous, and second, the rough numerical parity of the sexes limits the possibility for polygamy.

## Residential Patterns

Just as societies guide the process of mate selection, so they have norms that designate where a couple should reside. Most industrial societies favor **neolocality** (from income, to give them jobs, to ensure their health care, and, when the time comes, to pay for their funeral.

Many Swedes supported the creation of this welfare apparatus in the 1960s, Popenoe explains, as a means of *strengthening* families. But with the benefit of hindsight, he concludes, we can see that proliferating government programs have actually been *replacing* families. This has happened because members of Swedish families no longer view the family as an economic unit. Historically, families the world over have been fused by economic interdependence. In contemporary Sweden, people look to the government for financial security, and with growing indifference to their families.

Put differently, Swedish government policies discourage families from looking out for their own. If a person does not want to tend to an aging parent at home, the government will do it at a community facility—at no direct cost to that individual. Government child-care centers are available for all working parents; but no compara-

ble subsidy is provided for those who wish to care for their own children at home.

During the last several generations, then, Swedes have relaxed their family ties as they have become more dependent on their government. But if this system has apparently solved so many social problems, why should anyone be concerned about the erosion of family life? For two reasons, Popenoe suggests. First, government programs to entirely replace the family would be astronomically expensive. As family responsibilities have diminished, the welfare state has grown larger and larger. Already a majority of Swedes consider their government too big and funding such a comprehensive welfare system beyond their means. If government policies further undermine families, the government will have to take over even more services formerly provided by family members to one another—eventually bankrupting the society. The second reason to protect what remains of the Swedish family is concern for children. Government programs have

greatly relieved adults of the responsibilities and financial burden of raising the young. But what of children, who are increasingly growing up in large, impersonal care centers rather than in homes imbued with parental love? Small, intimate groups may well be able to accomplish some human tasks far better than formal organizations can.

While Popenoe thinks the Swedes have gone too far in delegating family responsibilities to government, he also cautions that we in the United States may not have gone far enough. Programs allowing time off from the workplace for new parents is a case in point. Sweden provides eighteen months' leave for one or the other parent at 90 percent of salary; the United States has no national program of this kind. By helping parents to meet the conflicting demands of earning a living and caring for children, the U.S. government might actually *strengthen* families.

SOURCES: Popenoe (1991); also Herrstrom (1990).

the Greek, meaning "new place"), *a pattern in which a married couple establishes a new residence apart from their parents.* Although newlyweds may live with the parents of one spouse—especially if finances do not permit their setting up a new home—our cultural norm appears to be "Honor thy mother and father—but get away from them" (Blumstein & Schwartz, 1983:26).

In preindustrial societies, newlyweds often gain economic assistance and personal security by residing with one set of parents or the other. **Patrilocality** (Greek for "place of the father") is *a residential pattern in which*

*a married couple lives with or near the husband's family.* In global perspective, this is the most prevalent pattern (Murdock, 1965). Less common in the world is **matrilocality** (meaning "place of the mother"), *a residential pattern in which a married couple lives with or near the wife's family.* Evidence suggests that patterns of locality have much to do with warfare; in bellicose societies, families favor keeping married sons at home. In addition, whether a society is matrilocal or patrilocal depends on whether daughters or sons are thought to be greater economic assets (Ember & Ember, 1971, 1991).

**Global Map 15–1** Marital Form in Global Perspective

Monogamy is the legally prescribed form of marriage in all industrial societies, and throughout the Western hemisphere. In most African nations, as well as in south Asia, however, polygamy is permitted by law. In the majority of cases, this reflects the historic influence of Islam, a religion that allows a man to have no more than four wives. Even so, most marriages in these societies are also monogamous.

## Patterns of Descent

**Descent** refers to *the system by which members of a society trace kinship over generations*. In simple terms, descent is the system of defining relatives. Industrial societies like our own recognize a pattern of **bilateral descent** ("two-sided descent"), *a system tracing kinship through both females and males*. In a bilateral society, children are linked by kinship to the families of both parents.

Most preindustrial societies, however, trace kinship only through one parent or the other. **Patrilineal descent,** *a system tracing kinship through males*, predominates in these societies. This means that the father's side of the family—but not the mother's—is defined as kin;

practically speaking, in patrilineal schemes only males can inherit property. Less common is **matrilineal descent,** *a system tracing kinship through females.* Here, only the mother's side of the family is considered kin, and property passes from mothers to daughters. Patrilineal descent is common among pastoral and agrarian societies, in which men produce the most valued resources. Matrilineal descent characterizes most horticultural societies, in which women are the primary breadwinners (Haviland, 1985).

Laws regarding citizenship often reflect traditional patterns of descent. As explained in the opening to Chapter 13 ("Sex and Gender"), laws in the southern African nation of Botswana until recently extended citizenship to children born to a Botswanan man and a foreign woman, but denied citizenship to the offspring of a Botswanan woman and a foreign man. This pattern was overturned in 1991 by a lawsuit brought by a woman in just such a situation; it is likely to be the first of many challenges to laws based in traditional patriarchy throughout the African continent (Shapiro, 1991).

## Patterns of Authority

The predominance of polygyny, patrilocality, and patrilineal descent in the world reflects the ubiquity of some degree of patriarchy. In industrial societies such as the United States, households containing a married couple are usually headed by a man, just as men dominate most areas of social life. More egalitarian family patterns are gradually evolving, especially as increasing numbers of women enter the labor force, but the social status of wife remains lower than that of husband. Parents in the United States also still prefer boys to girls, and most children are given their father's last name.

# Theoretical Analysis of the Family

As in earlier chapters, several theoretical approaches will be used to provide various insights about the family.

## Functions of the Family

The structural-functional paradigm holds that the family performs several of any society's basic tasks. This explains why the family is sometimes described as "the backbone of society."

## Socialization

As explained in Chapter 5 ("Socialization"), the family is the first agent in the socialization process, typically exerting more influence than peer groups, schools, churches, and the mass media. The personalities of each new generation take shape within the family, so that, ideally, adults guide children to become well-integrated and contributing members of the larger society. Early functionalists argued that the two sexes were socialized differently because the adult responsibilities of husbands (as breadwinners) and wives (as caregivers) were quite different (Parsons, 1954; Parsons & Bales, 1955). Within families of orientation, in short, boys and girls learn many of the attitudes and skills that will serve them as they establish families of procreation later on.

## Regulation of Sexual Activity

Every culture restricts sexual activity because human reproduction is central to kinship organization and property rights. One universal regulation is the **incest taboo,** *a cultural norm forbidding sexual relations or marriage between certain kin.* Although the incest taboo is found throughout the world, precisely which kin are regulated in this way varies from one culture to another. The Navajo, for example, forbid their members to marry any relative of one's mother. Most people in the United States apply the incest taboo to both sides of the family but limit it to close relatives, including parents, grandparents, siblings, aunts, and uncles. But even here norms are not consistent. Catholics in the United States reject marriage between first cousins, for example, while Jews do not (Murphy, 1979). Legally, as many states prohibit first-cousin marriages as allow them.

Interestingly, the sexual relations that most members of our society view as immoral and unnatural have been condoned, or even encouraged, in some other cultures. Brother-sister marriages, for example, were common among the ancient Babylonian, Egyptian, Incan, and Hawaiian nobility, and reports suggest that male nobles of the Azande in eastern Africa married their daughters (Murdock, 1965; Masserman & Uribe, 1989).

The significance of the incest taboo lies primarily in social rather than biological imperatives. While sexual activity between close relatives can adversely affect the mental and physical health of offspring, this outcome, in and of itself, does not explain why the incest taboo is observed by only one form of life: human beings. As Robert Murphy (1979) suggests, it is society more than nature that punishes incest. Why? Because the incest taboo supports family life in several ways. First, by restricting legitimate sexual activity to spouses, the incest taboo minimizes sexual competition and resulting conflict within families. Second, it forces people to marry outside their immediate family; this produces political and economic ties throughout the society. Third, in every society kinship forms an important system that determines people's rights and obligations toward one another. Allowing close relatives to reproduce would erode kinship and threaten relational chaos. It is for this reason that our society has moved cautiously to allow surrogate parenting of the kind described at the beginning of this chapter.

### Social Placement

Although families are not *biologically* required for reproduction, they do provide for the *social* placement of children. Most social statuses—including race, ethnicity, religion, and social class—are ascribed at birth through the family. This fact explains the historical concern that children be born of socially sanctioned marriages. So-called "legitimate" birth—especially when parents are of similar social position—allows for the stable transmission of property and other dimensions of social standing from parents to children.

### Material and Emotional Security

People turn to family members for physical protection as well as emotional and financial support. Because the family is a person's most important primary group, kin generally have intense and enduring relationships. Such personal concern seems to engender a sense of self-worth and security, two emotional elements that bolster strong physical health. Significantly, people living in families tend to be healthier than those living alone.

*Critical evaluation.* Structural-functional analysis identifies a number of the family's major functions. From this point of view, it is easy to see that society as we know it could not exist without families.

However, this approach has several limitations. First, in implying support for the traditional family, the structural-functional view minimizes how other institutions (like government, for example) could meet at least some of these human needs. This paradigm also overlooks

The "family resemblance" of Martin and Charlie Sheen means more than sharing physical features. The range of any child's opportunities and interests depends on the social position of parents. As sociologists have discovered, the family actually serves to reproduce the class structure, a fact suggested by the way in which children typically "follow in the footsteps" of the older generation.

the great diversity of family life in the United States. Finally, by highlighting the social cohesion that families can engender, structural-functionalism focuses little attention on the conflict and problems of family life. For example, while many families do provide emotional support to their members, violence is also common in families, with the dysfunctional effect of undermining people's self-confidence and well-being.

## Social Inequality and the Family

Like the structural-functional approach, the social-conflict paradigm also links the family to the operations of society, but conflict theorists investigate how the family perpetuates patterns of social inequality. Still another "function" of the family, in other words, is to maintain the social dominance of certain categories of people at the expense of others.

## The Family, Class, and Race

As noted in Chapter 13 ("Sex and Gender"), Friedrich Engels (1902; orig. 1884) traced the origin of the family to the historical development of private property. In brief, Engels argued that families emerged so individuals—at least those of the higher classes—could identify their heirs, ensuring that wealth would be passed from generation to generation. In this view, families concentrate wealth in the hands of a small proportion of the population and privilege their offspring (Mare, 1991). In industrial societies, then, the family shores up social inequality and also restrains individual social mobility. Following Engels's lead, then, the family is part and parcel of capitalism.

Moreover, racial and ethnic inequality, described in Chapter 12 ("Race and Ethnicity"), is also perpetuated through the operation of the family. Norms of endogamy guide people at each social level to marry others in the same category—for example, only about four in one thousand marriages in the United States join blacks and whites (N.O.R.C., cited in Wilkerson, 1991). As a result, social inequality persists across the generations.

## The Family and Patriarchy

The family, Engels explained, also reflects and perpetuates patriarchy. The only way for men to clearly identify their progeny is by controlling the sexuality of women. Moreover, Engels continued, families turn women into both the sexual and economic property of men. A century ago in the United States the earnings of wives typically belonged to their husbands as heads of the household. Although this practice is no longer upheld by law, other examples of husbands' domination of their wives remain. Women still bear major responsibility for childrearing and housework, a pattern that has changed little even as women have entered the paid work force (Haas, 1981; Schooler et al., 1984; Fuchs, 1986). Although patriarchal families offer considerable benefits to men, they too are disadvantaged by having less opportunity to share in the human satisfaction and personal growth derived from interaction with children.

Later in this chapter, we will explore how the link between the traditional family and social inequality relates to a number of conflicts and changes, such as violence against women, divorce, and the trend of women choosing to raise children outside of marriage.

*Critical evaluation.* Social-conflict analysis reveals another side of the family: its significant role in maintaining various kinds of social inequality. As later sections explain, inequality also shapes the family, so that various classes, races, and even the two genders experience family life in significantly different ways.

The greatest limitation of the approach taken by Engels is that even societies that have rejected the capitalist economy have families all the same. The family and social inequality are deeply intertwined, as Engels maintained, but the family appears to carry out various societal functions that are not easily accomplished by other means.

## Other Theoretical Analyses

Both structural-functional and social-conflict analyses view the family in broad terms as a central structure of society. More micro-level approaches, by contrast, explore individual experiences of family life.

### The Social Construction of Family Life

Chapter 6 ("Social Interaction in Everyday Life") explores the process by which people in interaction construct the reality they perceive. Applying this insight to the family, symbolic-interaction analysis argues that the reality of living in a particular household is likely to be quite different for various family members. Research supports the conclusion that women and men view their marriages very differently (Bernard, 1982). Similarly, a child and parent may share a home but understand little of each other's lives. For example, children usually think of their parents only as fathers and mothers, with little appreciation that these adults are also lovers.

Furthermore, the experiences and perceptions of parents and children alike change over time. Two people's expectations as they exchange their wedding vows usually evolve considerably as they confront the daily realities of married life. A change in the role of one spouse, such as a wife entering law school, may also alter the roles of other family members. And, of course, the arrival of a first child rewrites the rules of life for many couples. Thus the symbolic-interaction approach addresses the inadequacy of describing marriage and the family in terms of any rigid characteristics.

### Social-Exchange Analysis

Social-exchange analysis is an insightful approach that casts courtship and marriage as a negotiation in which people offer each other socially valued resources and advantages (Blau, 1964). In courtship, each person assesses the likely advantages and disadvantages of taking the other as a spouse. Physical attractiveness is one critical dimension of exchange. In patriarchal societies around the world, beauty has long been a commodity offered by women on the marriage market. The social value assigned to beauty explains women's traditional concern with physical appearance and their sensitivity about revealing their age. Men, by contrast, often showcase their financial resources so that less physically attractive men may succeed in marrying attractive women if they can offer them a high income (Melville, 1983). Dimensions of social exchange are converging for the two sexes as more women enter the labor force and become less dependent on men to support them and their children.

***Critical evaluation.*** Micro-level analysis provides a useful counterbalance to structural-functional and social-conflict visions of the family as one of society's institutional systems. Adopting an interactional viewpoint, we gain a better sense of the individual experiences of family members, who creatively shape reality as they engage others in various ways.

The prime limitation of this approach is that the family *is*, in important respects, a system, one shaped by economic and cultural forces and traditions. Further, families in the United States do vary according to key social dimensions such as class and ethnicity and, as the next section explains, they evolve through typical stages linked to the life course.

# Stages of Family Life

The family is dynamic, experiencing marked changes across the life course. Typically, family life begins with courtship, followed by settling into the realities of married life. Next, for most couples at least, is raising children, leading to the later years of marriage after children have left home to form families of their own. We will look briefly at each of these stages.

## Courtship

Because family ties are vital economic assets, the members of preindustrial societies consider courtship too important to leave to prospective spouses (Stone, 1977;

Haviland, 1985). *Arranged marriages* represent an alliance between two extended families that affects the social standing of both. Parents spend considerable time and effort investigating possibilities for marriage and, given the right opportunity, they make arrangements for marriage when their child is very young. A century ago in India, for example, children were married as early as five years of age, and half the females were married by the age of fifteen (Mayo, 1927; Mace & Mace, 1960). Today, such early marriages are less common, but still occur in traditional villages.

Arranged marriages fit into Emile Durkheim's scheme of "mechanical solidarity" (see Chapter 4, "Society"). In homogeneous traditional societies, almost any member of the opposite sex is a suitable marriage partner because all children are socialized in similar fashion to perform that society's roles of spouse and parent. While we think of marriage as joining two individuals who are *personally* compatible, in short, members of internally homogeneous societies consider that virtually any couple will be *culturally* compatible.

With industrialization, the declining importance of extended families fosters growing individuality and more personal choice in courtship. Therefore young people need to gain extensive experience in courtship because they will have a greater say in selecting their partner. The duration of courtship depends on the age at which people first marry; this, in turn, has much to do with economic security (Landale & Tolnay, 1991). Through much of this century, economic prosperity pushed down the age of first marriage, as shown in Figure 15–1. By mid-century, the typical first marriage for women occurred at age twenty (down two years from the beginning of the century) and for men at about age twenty-two (some four years earlier than at the turn of the century). Since 1970, however, real income has stalled and more women have entered the labor force to shore up their families' standard of living. In this uncertain economic climate, women and men are delaying marriage once again as they pursue schooling or save money before beginning family life. Notice one continuing trend: the two sexes are closer in age at first marriage now than they were a century ago.

Despite some variation, marriage concludes a long period of dating. Courtship generally begins as group dating, in which several girls and boys interact together. In time, group dating gives way to couple dating. In the United States today, courtship frequently involves a period of sexual experimentation; couples may also live together before deciding to marry.

Industrial societies such as our own elevate *romantic love*—the experience of affection and sexual passion toward another person—as the basis for marriage. The distaste for arranged marriages certainly reflects this exaltation of romantic love. For most people in the United States, marriage without love is difficult to imagine, and the mass media—from traditional fairy tales like "Cinderella" to contemporary paperback romance novels—present romantic love as the keystone of successful matrimony.

Romantic love was well established among the nobility early in the Middle Ages. Courtly love (like the term "courtship," derived from the noble courts of this earlier era) was not, however, grounds for marriage: more practical considerations of social standing held sway in the choice of a marital partner. The notion of romance was more a feudal ideal by which knights pledged themselves in service to noblewomen whom they revered from a distance but were ineligible to marry. Such love was never destined to develop into even personal intimacy. The most knights could hope to win for themselves through displays of bravery and dedication was a noblewoman's praise and respect (Beigel, 1951).

Over the centuries, romantic love grew in importance as the basis of marriage. In our more individualistic society, romantic love now functions to encourage an individual to leave the original family of orientation to form a new family of procreation. As an incentive to forming new families, romantic love is usually most intense when people first marry, sometimes helping to carry a newly married couple through the difficult adjustments to the realities of married life (Goode, 1959). Yet, the modern emphasis on romantic love also presents problems. Because it rests on feelings that may change, romantic love is a less stable foundation for marriage than social and economic considerations. Furthermore, as "Cinderella" and other folk tales suggest, romantic love can draw together people of different social backgrounds. Although social pressures discourage such pairings, they are increasing. Thus, romantic love can be a truly revolutionary force as marriages guided solely by the heart challenge racial, ethnic, religious, and social class boundaries.

Sociologists have long recognized that Cupid's arrow is aimed by society more than individualistic Americans like to believe. Even today, most married couples are about the same age and of the same race, religion, and social class. This pattern is called **homogamy** (literally, "like marrying like"), *marriage between people who are socially alike.*

Homogamy is common, first, because people of one social background tend to interact in the same neigh-

**Figure 15–1**  Median Age at First Marriage, by Sex: 1890–1990

(*U.S. Bureau of the Census. Current Population Reports, Special Studies, Series P-23, No. 173. Washington, DC: U. S. Government Printing Office,  1991, p. 8.*)

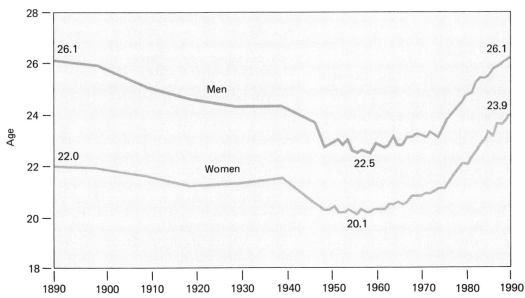

borhoods, attend the same schools, and frequent the same recreational settings. Second, a common socialization encourages similar tastes and interests, so that we are likely to be attracted to people with the same social backgrounds as we have. Third, parents and peers often discourage marrying an "outsider." In some cases, this influence is subtle; in others, it is quite heavy-handed. Traditional Jews, for example, strongly oppose the marriage of their children to non-Jews. If a son or daughter should marry out of the religion, parents may "sit shiva," observing a ritual to lament the loss of a loved one. While usually done following a death, here sitting shiva signifies that by marrying an outsider the child has undergone social death and may no longer be considered a member of the family.

"Falling in love," then, may induce strong personal feelings, but the process of courtship is guided by a host of social forces. Perhaps we exaggerate the importance of romantic love to reassure ourselves that even in the midst of society we are capable of making personal choices.

## Settling In: Ideal and Real Marriage

In light of the social importance of marriage, we can understand why socialization often instills highly idealized images of matrimony. Consider the following account of a thirty-one-year-old woman, married eleven years and the mother of three children:

> When I got married, I suppose I must have loved him, but at the time, I was busy planning the wedding and I wasn't thinking about anything else. I was just thinking about this big white wedding and all the trimmings, and how I was going to be a beautiful bride, and how I would finally have my own house. I never thought about problems we might have or anything like that. I don't know even if I ever thought much about him. Oh, I wanted to make a nice home for Glen, but I wasn't thinking about how anyone did that or whether I loved him enough to live with him the rest of my life. I was too busy with my dreams and thinking about how they were finally coming true. (Rubin, 1976:69)

We do not have to read between the lines to see that for this woman family life has fallen short of earlier expectations. Idealizing marriage and the family often amounts to courting disappointment. Especially for women—who, more than men, are socialized to view marriage as the key to future happiness—marital pleas-

*The Wedding Portrait* (1434), by Flemish artist Jan Van Eyck (1390–1441), is a masterpiece of its time. Here we see a young couple solemnly reciting their wedding vows—a statement of the reverence with which people of that age approached marriage. The single candle in the chandelier above their heads symbolizes Christ, and the couple's removal of their shoes indicates that they are engaged in a holy ritual.

*(Jan Van Eyck, Giovanni Arnolfini and His Bride, 1434. Oil on wood. 33 × 22½". The National Gallery, London.)*

ures often give way to disenchantment. Courtship brings couples together for limited periods, so they may see each other only at their best. Moreover, research suggests that romantic love involves a good deal of fantasy: people fall in love with others, not necessarily as they are, but as they want them to be (Berscheid & Hatfield, 1983). Within marriage, however, spouses confront each other regularly and realistically, for better and for worse. And only after marriage do many couples face the day-to-day challenges of maintaining a household. Sobering responsibilities include paying monthly bills, managing relations with in-laws, and performing mundane tasks such as shopping, cooking, and cleaning. Therefore, a great deal about marriage and one's spouse is learned only *after* the wedding.

Newly married couples may also have to make sexual adjustments. Several generations ago, cultural norms in the United States endorsed sexual activity only after marriage and, no doubt, some people married simply for this reason. By the end of the 1980s, however, most nineteen-year-olds—88 percent of men and 81 percent of women—reported having had sexual intercourse (U.S. Congress, 1989).

But earlier experiences do not prevent sex from proving a disappointment in marriage. In the romantic haze of falling in love, people may anticipate marriage as an extended erotic honeymoon only to find that, in time, sex becomes less than an all-consuming passion. One important study of marital sex found that 70 percent of married respondents claimed to be satisfied with the sexual dimension of their marriage, but documented a decline in sexual activity over time, as Table 15–1 shows (Blumstein & Schwartz, 1983).

Research also suggests that couples with the most satisfying sexual relationships have the greatest overall satisfaction with their marriages. While this does not mean that sex ensures marital bliss, good sex and good relationships apparently go together (Hunt, 1974; Tavris & Sadd, 1977; Blumstein & Schwartz, 1983).

Infidelity—sexual activity outside marriage—is another area in which the reality of marriage does not coincide with our cultural ideal. Most people claim to endorse traditional marriage vows "to forsake all others": in a recent survey, 74 percent of U.S. adults claimed that sex outside of marriage is "always wrong," compared to 15 percent who said that it is "not wrong at all," with the remainder taking a middle position (N.O.R.C., 1991:257). Despite such support for fidelity, many married people in the United States do engage in extramarital sex. Some forty years ago Alfred Kinsey and his associates (1948, 1953) estimated that about half of married men and one-fourth of married women had engaged in extramarital sex. Subsequent research suggests that this percentage has remained stable for men while increasing somewhat for women, especially younger wives who experience more contact with other men in the workplace (Hunt, 1974; Offir, 1982; Saunders & Edwards, 1984; Thompson, 1984). During the 1980s, public disapproval of extramarital sex showed a modest increase, partly because of the AIDS crisis. Thus we should bear in mind that sexual behavior involves not only moral concerns

**Table 15–1  FREQUENCY OF SEXUAL ACTIVITY AMONG MARRIED COUPLES**

| Years Together | Sexual Frequency (times per month) | | | |
|---|---|---|---|---|
| | 1 or less | 1–4 | 4–12 | 12 or more |
| 0–2 | 6% | 11% | 38% | 45% |
| 2–10 | 6 | 21 | 46 | 27 |
| 10 or more | 16 | 22 | 45 | 18 |

SOURCE: Adapted from Philip Blumstein and Pepper Schwartz, *American Couples* (New York: William Morrow, 1983), p. 196.

but practical fears of contracting sexually transmitted diseases.

## Child Rearing

The birth of a child changes marriage significantly as new demands are made on each spouse's attention, time, and energy. One thirty-year-old father described how the birth of his son had disrupted his marriage:

> Those first two years were almost perfect. . . . But when the baby was born everything began to change; it sort of all fell apart. It seemed [my wife] was busy with him all the time. And I felt like I didn't count anymore . . . and I got resentful of Danny, then I felt terrible. What kind of father am I to feel resentful at a little kid like that? But I couldn't help how I felt. (Rubin, 1983:61)

Although some people may be ambivalent about children, Table 15–2 on page 418 shows that almost all adults in the United States include at least one child in their conception of the ideal family. Two children is the overwhelming preference, and few people today desire four or more children—a change from two centuries ago, when *eight* children was the norm (Newman & Matzke, 1984).

In preindustrial societies, production depends on human labor, so adults view children as an economic asset. Then, too, having children was also regarded as a wife's duty. Birth control technology was crude and unreliable, so women frequently became pregnant whether they wanted to or not. Finally, having many babies did not necessarily mean raising a large family: as late as 1900, about one-third of children born in the United States died before reaching adolescence (Wall, 1980).

**Table 15–2**  THE IDEAL NUMBER OF CHILDREN
FOR AMERICANS, 1990

| Number of Children | Proportion of Respondents |
|---|---|
| 0 | 1.1 |
| 1 | 2.7 |
| 2 | 52.4 |
| 3 | 21.6 |
| 4 | 10.1 |
| 5 | 1.4 |
| 6 or more | 0.7 |
| As many as you want | 6.0 |
| No response | 3.9 |

SOURCE: N.O.R.C., *General Social Surveys, 1972–1991* (Chicago: National Opinion Research Center, 1991), p. 252.

With industrialization, the economic equation changes drastically when it comes to children. Children today rarely become financially independent until at least age eighteen (and sometimes not until their mid-twenties), and the expense of raising them can be staggering. One estimate projected the cost of rearing a child to age eighteen at over $100,000, which would double if the child goes to college (*Family Economics Review*, 1989).

The rising proportion of women in the labor force also delays marriage and reduces childbearing. Technology is also at work here, since birth control is now effective, simple to use, and easy to obtain, reducing the number of unplanned pregnancies. Abortion was legally declared to be a woman's choice in 1973; roughly 1.5 million abortions are performed each year in the United States, further suppressing family size. Finally, a significant reduction in infant mortality has also lessened parents' need to have many children because the vast majority of infants now survive to adulthood. Taken together, these factors explain the steadily declining birth rate over the course of this century to roughly two children per family today.

This low rate of childbirth stands in sharp contrast to that in poor societies of the world. Having four or five children is typical for women in much of Latin America and Asia; in most countries of Africa, the number is closer to six. The reason for such high birth rates is that Third World women have few alternatives to bearing and raising children, and families depend on the labor of offspring to survive.

In much of the world, child rearing is a cooperative task performed by the extended family. In the United States, a nuclear family system makes the care of children the primary responsibility of parents, people who may have little preparation for this vital role. Nor does our society demand competence before men and women become parents: the privilege of driving a car requires a person to demonstrate necessary skills, but there is no comparable measure of fitness for parenthood. While we acquire many useful lessons from our parents, we often learn little about family life from their point of view (Macionis, 1978; Pollak & Wise, 1979). Thus new parents learn "on the job" from their own successes and mistakes.

As explained in Chapter 13 ("Sex and Gender"), the entry of women into the labor force in the United States has been dramatic. In 1991, 57.4 percent of women over the age of fifteen were in the workforce; moreover, two out of three women with children under eighteen worked for income (U.S. Bureau of the Census, 1991). But while women and men are sharing the burdens of earning an income, contemporary women still bear the traditional responsibility for raising children and doing a variety of tasks at home. Although some men in our society eagerly embrace parenting chores, most continue to resist accepting responsibility for household tasks that our culture has historically defined as feminine (Radin, 1982).

As more women join men in the labor force, public attention has focused on what are called *latchkey kids*—children whose working parents leave them to fend for themselves for a good part of the day. There are 7 million such children in the United States today; half of all nine-year-olds look after themselves after school (U.S. Women's Bureau, 1989). Defenders of traditional family values such as Phyllis Schlafly (1984) contend that many working mothers are neglecting their responsibilities to children. Husbands and fathers are rarely subject to this criticism because their income is assumed to be necessary to support their families. But the same now holds true for most mothers working outside the home (Keniston, 1985). This new reality underlies growing support for programs of childcare sponsored either by private employers or, more equitably, by the government.

Because parenting competes with other personal interests and, increasingly, the need to earn a living, more couples are choosing to delay childbirth or to remain childless. In 1960, almost 90 percent of women between twenty-five and twenty-nine who had ever been married had at least one child; by 1990 this proportion had dropped to 70 percent (U.S. Bureau of the Census,

1991). One recent survey indicated that about two-thirds of parents in the United States would like to be able to devote far more time to child rearing (Snell, 1990). But unless we are willing to endure a decline in our material standard of living, economic realities demand that both parents pursue careers outside the home. The child rearing patterns we have described fundamentally reflect how people are coming to terms with economic change.

## The Family in Later Life

Increasing life expectancy in the United States means that, barring divorce, couples are likely to remain married for a long time. By about age fifty, most have completed the major task of raising children. The remaining years of marriage are commonly described as the "empty nest" period because, as at the beginning of marriage, couples usually have no children living in their households. This phase has been delayed (or interrupted) in recent years due to economic pressures (and sometimes divorce) that keep increasing numbers of young people living with their parents. In 1990, of single people between twenty-five and thirty-four, one-third of men and one-fifth of women were living in the home of their parents (U.S. Bureau of the Census, 1991).

Like the birth of children, their eventual departure causes important changes in a family. Couples must make serious adjustments to losing a common focus of daily routines. Even so, spouses frequently grow closer and the marital relationship often becomes more satisfying at this point in life (Kalish, 1982). A healthy marriage at this stage of life is generally characterized by companionship. Years of living together may have diminished a couple's sexual passion for each other, but mutual understanding and commitment are likely to have grown stronger.

Personal contact with children usually continues, since most older adults live a short distance from at least one of their children (Shanas, 1979). People's incomes peak in late middle age, as the expenses of child rearing diminish. Thus at this stage in family life, parenting may involve helping children make large purchases (a car or a house) and, of course, periodically babysitting for grandchildren.

As explained in Chapter 14 ("Aging and the Elderly"), more adults in midlife face the challenge of caring for aging parents. The "empty nest" may not be filled by a parent coming to live in the home, but many adults find that parents living into their late seventies and beyond make practical, emotional, and financial demands that cannot always be met. The oldest of the "baby boomers"—now in their mid-forties—are being touted as the "sandwich generation" because they will spend as many years caring for their aging parents as they did raising their own children.

Retirement, also discussed in Chapter 14 ("Aging and the Elderly"), represents another change in family life. Traditionally, the man retired from the labor force to spend much more time at home. Although the husband's presence was often a source of pleasure to both, it sometimes undermined wives' established routines. The presence of a retired husband was little more than an intrusion to one woman, who bluntly stated: "I may have married him for better or worse, but not for lunch" (Kalish, 1982:96). Because retirement is becoming a common experience for both spouses, this final stage of family life will provide the opportunity for wives and husbands to enjoy many new activities together.

The final and surely the most difficult transition in married life comes with the death of a spouse. Wives typically outlive their husbands because of their longer life expectancy and also because women usually marry men who are several years older than they are. Wives can thus expect to spend a significant period of their lives as widows. The bereavement and loneliness accompanying the death of a spouse can pose serious challenges. This experience may be even more difficult when the tables are turned: widowers usually have fewer friends than widows do, and men who have spent their lives in traditional masculine roles must adjust to the unfamiliar responsibility of housework (Berardo, 1970).

# Varieties of Family Life

Social class, race and ethnicity, and gender are powerful forces that shape the lives of people in all settings and situations. Together, they generate considerable variation in marriage and family life.

## Social Class

As was described in Chapter 10 ("Social Class in the United States"), social class accounts for vast differences in standard of living. A family's class position affects its financial resources and range of opportunities, as well as patterns of interaction in the home.

Affluence is no guarantee of personal happiness, nor does it ensure a successful family life. But economic advantages do permit a greater sense of security in an uncertain world. In a study of working-class families, Lillian Rubin reports the following observations of a working-class housewife:

> I guess I can't complain. He's a steady worker; he doesn't drink; he doesn't hit me. That's a lot more than my mother had, and she didn't sit around complaining and feeling sorry for herself, so I sure haven't got the right. (1976:33)

Being a steady worker, not drinking excessively, and refraining from violence, Rubin discovered, were the three attributes most frequently mentioned by working-class women as positive qualities in a husband. By contrast, Rubin found, these attributes were almost never mentioned by middle-class women evaluating their marriages. More privileged women were concerned with intimacy, sharing, and communication with their husbands. Of course, working-class women value these things, too, but they simply recognize that issues of relational quality are secondary to the basic need for economic and physical security.

Social scientists have also documented the negative effects of unemployment on family life (Brenner, 1976). The loss of a job is more common among people of lower social standing, who have fewer resources to begin with. For those who contend with daily economic uncertainty, unemployment sharply heightens fears and anxieties, which can erode family life. A thirty-year-old man recalls the turmoil caused by the loss of his job:

> Right after our first kid was born, I got laid off . . . and I didn't have much in the way of skills to get another job with. My unemployment [payments] ran out pretty quick, and Sue Ann couldn't work because of the baby . . . so we moved in with my folks. We lived there for about a year. What a mess. My mom and Sue Ann just didn't get along. (Rubin, 1976:73)

While money cannot buy happiness, as the saying goes, its absence certainly introduces strains and pressures into the lives of parents and children.

Social class also affects the relationship between spouses. Men and women of higher social class tend to be more open and expressive with each other (Komarovsky, 1967; Rubin, 1976; Fitzpatrick, 1988). This is because people of higher social standing have more schooling, and most hold jobs that emphasize verbal skills. Additionally, each social class has a distinctive pattern of socialization. As was noted in Chapter 5 ("Socialization"), working-class parents, more than their middle-class counterparts, teach their children to embrace conventional gender roles and to follow rules. By contrast, middle-class parents stress the importance of imagination and self-expression (Rubin, 1976; Kohn, 1977).

Rigid adherence to gender roles creates a rift between husbands and wives, who end up leading very different lives and sharing fewer interests. Lillian Rubin (1976) explains that men who grew up with conventional notions about masculine self-control and the need to stifle emotional expressiveness tend to be tight-lipped about their personal feelings. Women socialized to be feminine find it easier to express themselves more openly. As a result, husbands and wives may speak different languages, seeking out members of their own sex as confidants because they experience frustration in trying to simply talk to one another.

## Ethnicity and Race

As Chapter 12 ("Race and Ethnicity") indicated, ethnicity and race exert powerful influences in our lives. The effects of both surface in family life.

### Hispanic Families

Many people of Hispanic ancestry in the United States maintain extended families based on strong loyalties and mutual support. Hispanic parents have historically exercised considerable control over their children's courtship, viewing marriage as an alliance between two extended families rather than a union based on romantic love. Traditionally, too, Hispanic families stress adherence to conventional gender roles. *Machismo*—masculine strength, daring, and sexual prowess—is especially pronounced in Hispanic culture. Women, on the other hand, are closely supervised; those who resist such controls are likely to be stigmatized as immoral and "loose." The result is a double standard, by which men are encouraged to engage in sexual activities outside marriage while women are expected to marry as virgins and remain faithful to their husbands.

Assimilation into the larger culture is gradually softening these traditional patterns. Puerto Ricans who have moved to New York, for example, rarely maintain the strong extended families they knew in Puerto Rico. Especially among affluent Hispanic families—whose

Hispanic cultures traditionally have maintained strong kinship ties. Carmen Lomas Garza's painting, *Family Pictures*, portrays the extended family pattern that has historically been common to Hispanics.

(*Carmen Lomas Garza*, Tamalda, *1988. Oil/ linen mounted on wood. 24 × 32".* Laguna Gloria Art Museum, Austin, TX.)

number has tripled in the last twenty years—the traditional authority of men over women has diminished (Fitzpatrick, 1971; Moore & Pachon, 1985; O'Hare, 1990).

Other researchers warn of the danger of exaggerating the role of machismo in Hispanic families. It is easy to assume, they argue, that Hispanic men try to compensate for their relative powerlessness by bullying their wives and children. But, they continue, the typical Hispanic family is more egalitarian than such accounts suggest. Just as important, the traditional concept of machismo is not merely the expression of power, it is also a matter of honoring and respecting the dignity of women and other family members (Ybarra, 1977; Staples & Mirande, 1980; Nielsen, 1990).

There is less controversy surrounding the economic disadvantages endured by Hispanics, whose numbers in the United States grew by more than half during the 1980s. But despite the prosperity of some, the overall economic standing of this category remains about the same: the typical Hispanic family has an annual income of about $23,000, which is two-thirds that of the nation as a whole (U.S. Bureau of the Census, 1991). Not surprisingly, then, Hispanic families contend with the stress of unemployment and other problems that accompany low income.

### African-American Families

Analysis of African-American families must begin with the stark reality of economic disadvantage: as explained in earlier chapters, the typical African-American family earned $21,423 in 1990, 64 percent of the income for all families in the United States. People of African ancestry are three times as likely as whites to be poor so that their family patterns are shaped by unemployment, underemployment, and, in many cases, a physical environment replete with crime and drug abuse.

Under these circumstances, maintaining stable family ties is difficult. One study found that 25 percent of African-American women born in the early 1950s never married, compared with about 10 percent of comparable white women (Bennett, Bloom, & Craig, 1989). This means that women—often with children—are likely to be heads of households without husbands. As Figure 15–2 on page 422 shows, women headed 43.8 percent of all African-American families in 1990, compared with 23.1 percent of Hispanic families, 12.3 percent of Asian or Pacific Islander families, and 12.9 percent of white families (U.S. Bureau of the Census, 1991).

Among all these categories of the population, female-headed families have increased in recent decades. Such families are at high risk of poverty: about one-

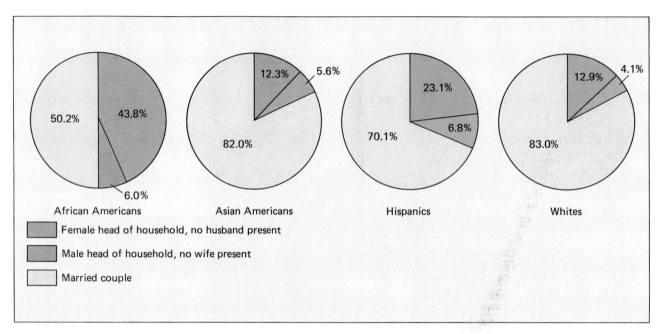

**Figure 15–2** Family Composition, 1990
(*U.S. Bureau of the Census*)

third of families headed by white women are poor, and the proportion is closer to half among minorities. African-American families with both wife and husband in the home—which represents half the total—earn about 85 percent as much as comparable white families; these run a far lower risk of poverty. However, two-thirds of all African-American children are born to women who are unmarried, which means that, among this category of people in the United States, childhood poverty is the greatest burden (Hogan & Kitagawa, 1985; U.S. Bureau of the Census, 1991).

A generation ago Daniel Patrick Moynihan (1965), now a U.S. Senator, published a controversial report claiming the black family was in crisis. In over 20 percent of African-American households in 1960, Moynihan reported, no man served as husband and father, a situation found in only 5 percent of white households. Absent husbands, he suggested, encouraged a raft of social problems, including poverty, welfare dependency, crime, and births to single mothers. He predicted that this crisis would escalate as financially and culturally deprived children grew up to form "broken" families of their own. In short, a *cycle of poverty* was being unleashed in the black community that would pass disadvantage from one generation to the next.

In the liberal climate of the 1960s, Moynihan's conclusions were hotly contested. Moynihan downplayed the fact that most African-American families then (as now) included a married couple. And his description of female-headed black families as a "tangle of pathology" struck critics as an expression of prejudice against women and people of color. African-American novelist and social critic Toni Morrison recently refuted Moynihan's position stating, "I don't think a female running a house is a problem. It is perceived as one because of the notion that a 'head' is a man" (Angelo, 1989:120).

Moynihan was also criticized for implying that a single-parent family was at least partly the *cause*—rather than the *consequence*—of poverty and other problems. William Ryan (1976) denounced the contention that the black family itself was a cause of poverty; that view, he asserted, amounts to simply blaming poor people for their own victimization. The one-parent pattern is more common among African-Americans than among whites, in Ryan's view, because of greater prejudice, discrimination, and poverty.

In addition, Moynihan contended that the instability of African-American families was one legacy of slavery, a cruel system that forcibly separated kin from one another. More recent research challenges this conclusion, however. New data show that the growing proportion of families headed by women emerged during black migration to cities after 1940. At that point, half of all African Americans lived in cities; by 1990, the proportion exceeded 80 percent. Many migrants, who entered cities with few industrial skills, were further disadvantaged by racial prejudice and discrimination. Predictably, African Americans were soon caught up in an economic crisis of monumental proportions. Forced to work in low-paying, unskilled jobs and constantly in danger of unemployment, many poor men and women could not attain the financial security necessary to maintain a family. Therefore, some scholars conclude that the transformation of the African-American family has its roots not in slavery, as Moynihan contended, but in enormous economic disadvantages and persistent racism (Gutman, 1976; Wilson, 1984).

To make matters worse, the decline of traditional industries during the 1980s hit African Americans especially hard. During a decade of prosperity for some people, poor families became poorer, and some black families' hold on middle-class standing became tenuous (Updegrave, 1989). A black underclass now exists in cities across the United States, increasingly cut off from opportunity and hope. Amid despair, violence has become a way of life, and the use of crack and other dangerous drugs reached epidemic proportions by the beginning of the 1990s. The tragic reality is that about 45 percent of African-American children in this country now grow up in poverty. This fact, coupled with the rise in motherhood among poor teenagers, fulfills the bitter prediction made by Moynihan of an expanding cycle of poverty among women and their children (Ladner, 1986; Furstenberg, Brooks-Gunn, & Morgan, 1987).

In light of overwhelming problems, disadvantaged African-American families display remarkable resilience. Members of the extended family, one great source of strength, often provide emotional and financial assistance to kin in need. For example, government data indicate that 13 percent of African-American children (1.2 million boys and girls) live with a grandparent, compared to 6 percent of Hispanic children and 4 percent of white children. More broadly, men and women generate mutual dependence networks composed of people who take on kin-like roles (a substitute "aunt," for instance). Such resourcefulness has allowed people confronting tremendous barriers to care for children and meet their daily needs (Stack, 1975; Cherlin & Furstenberg, 1983; Leslie & Korman, 1989).

## Gender

For people of any social class, ethnicity, and race, cultural definitions of femininity and masculinity affect marriage and the family. Jessie Bernard (1982) puts the matter simply, stating that each union is actually *two* different marriages: a female marriage and a male marriage.

During the last century the extent of male domination of family life has diminished to some degree, but even today few marriages are composed of socially equal partners. When Mirra Komarovsky (1973, 1976) asked college seniors to describe an ideal marriage, most—of both sexes—painted the man as dominant. The reason lies in the socialization of women to defer to men, which encourages a woman to think of her husband as superior. Similarly, few men—and even those who espouse a belief in sexual equality—wanted to marry a woman who might upstage them. Such patterns underlie our expectation that men will be older as well as taller than the women they marry. And after the wedding, even when both spouses work, most people assume that the husband's career is more important (McRae, 1986).

Surprisingly, in light of this male dominance, our culture promotes the idea that marriage benefits women more than men (Bernard, 1982). At bridal showers, women congratulate one of their own on her impending marriage; at bachelor parties, men sing a different song, bemoaning the loss of one of their number to his new wife. The same contrast appears in the positive stereotype of a carefree bachelor as opposed to the negative image of the lonely spinster. All this adds up to a simple conclusion: we imagine that women eagerly pursue husbands, while husbands savor their freedom until they reluctantly settle down.

The notion that marriage favors women is rooted in their historical exclusion from the labor force. A woman's financial security, that is, depended on her finding a husband. But in most respects, Jessie Bernard claims, marriage has never been beneficial for women. In comparison to single women, she notes, married women have poorer mental health, more passive attitudes toward life, and report greater unhappiness. Therefore, she concludes, *men* are the real beneficiaries of marriage. Married men generally live longer than single men, have better mental health, and report greater happiness. Bernard suggests that this also explains why, after divorce, women more than men report greater happiness, and men more than women eagerly look for a new partner. There is no better guarantor of long life, health, and happiness for a man, Bernard concludes, than a woman well socialized to perform the "duties of a wife" by devoting her life to caring for him and providing the security of a well-ordered home (see also Gove, 1972, 1979).

Bernard argues that marriage need not stifle the aspirations and happiness of women. The problem, she asserts, lies in the "anachronistic way in which marriage is structured today": husbands dominating wives and constraining them to tedious work in the home. Under these circumstances, men reap considerable advantages from marriage while women have reason to spearhead the drive to reform marital patterns.

Recent research based on a random sample of couples in the United States sorts out the connections between gender, power, and mental health in marriage (Ross, Mirowsky, & Huber, 1983; Mirowsky & Ross, 1984). Four types of marriage, the investigators found, yield different levels of depression for men and women.

Type I marriages have a traditional pattern by which only the husband is employed and the wife does all housework and child rearing. Further, both partners willingly embrace conventional gender roles. Figure 15–3 shows that this arrangement appears to favor the husband, who derives income and prestige from his work. Wives in this situation, however, have higher levels of depression, presumably because their status as homemaker carries little social prestige, even though this is her preferred role.

In Type II marriages, both spouses work, although the wife performs a "second shift" by doing all the housework and child rearing. Here the wife works out of economic necessity, although she and her husband would prefer that she stay home. This arrangement, as Figure 15–3 shows, places emotional burdens on both partners: depression is high for the wife but higher still for the husband. The wife has two demanding jobs, one (or both) of which she does not want. The husband is frustrated by his own low-income job and the fact that he cannot support his family as he thinks he should. This is the only marital pattern in which husbands have poorer mental health than wives.

In Type III marriages, husband and wife are happy that the wife has a job, which provides psychological benefits for her; however, she is still responsible for all the housework. The husband benefits even more: the greater family income reduces the chance that his unemployment or any other unexpected setback will cause financial hardship for the family.

A Type IV marriage pattern has both husband

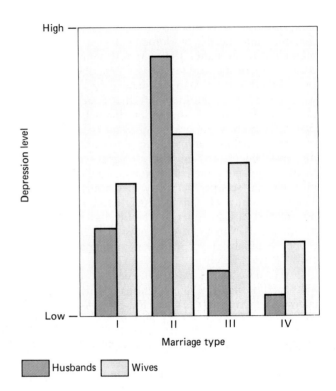

**Figure 15–3** Depression in Four Types of Marriage
(Ross, Mirowsky, & Huber, 1983)

and wife happily working outside the home but also sharing most family and household responsibilities. This pattern is linked to the lowest depression levels of the four types for both husbands and wives because sharing household responsibilities reduces tensions that arise when a working wife is expected to take sole responsibility for housework and children. This pattern is gradually becoming more common in our society, although it is still relatively rare.

These findings support the conclusions by Jessie Bernard (1982) and others that more egalitarian marriages tend to be happier for husbands as well as wives. Such evidence may make us wonder why conventional and unequal marriages persist. The answer is that conventional ideas about gender are deeply rooted in our way of life; changing them involves a difficult and slow process despite evidence that both men and women benefit from doing so.

# Transition and Problems in Family Life

Ann Landers, one of the best-known observers of the U.S. scene, summed up what she had learned from thousands of letters from wives and husbands about their marriages: "One marriage out of twenty is wonderful, four are good, ten are tolerable, and five are pure hell" (Landers, 1984). We have already explained that the reality of family life often falls short of the ideal. In some cases, however, problems are serious enough to undermine families and threaten family members.

## Divorce

Over the course of the last century, as Figure 15–4 illustrates, the divorce rate has grown ten-fold in the United States. By about 1980, half of marriages in the United States were ending in divorce (for African Americans, about two-thirds); since then, these rates have stabilized. In global context, the U.S. divorce rate is second to none. Couples still proclaim "'til death us do part," but the reality is that marriages are now as likely to be ended by divorce as by death (Cherlin, 1981; Kitson & Raschke, 1981; Weitzman, 1985).

One reason that divorce rates are so high in the United States is that nowhere else are people as likely to marry: about nine out of ten adults eventually do so. During the last century, however, the marriage rate has remained stable while the divorce rate has soared upward. Researchers have identified seven major reasons for the rising risk of divorce (Huber & Spitze, 1980; Kitson & Raschke, 1981). First, people in the United States used to spend more of their time in family activities. Today parents and children work and play together less often; they are more active individually in schools, workplaces, and various recreational settings. We have also become more individualistic, seemingly more concerned with personal happiness than committed to the well-being of families. Second, as was noted earlier, our culture bases marriage on romantic love. Because sexual passion usually subsides with time, spouses may end a marriage in favor of a relationship that renews excitement and romance. Third, increasing participation in the labor force has reduced women's financial dependence on husbands. The growing economic strength of women also may strain conventional marriages as it gives women options to remaining in an unhappy relationship. Fourth, when both parents work outside the home, child rearing adds a considerable burden. Children do stabilize some marriages (Waite, Haggstrom, & Kanouse, 1985), but divorce is most common during the early years of marriage when many couples have young children. Fifth, divorce no longer carries the powerful negative stigma it did a century ago. Sixth, in today's transient society, marriages receive less support from extended family members and neighbors than was typical in the past (Thornton, 1985; Gerstel, 1987).

The seventh reason for our high divorce rate is that, legally speaking, marriages have become easier to dissolve. In the past, courts required divorcing couples to demonstrate that one or both were guilty of behavior such as adultery or physical abuse. Today most states allow divorce simply because a couple thinks their marriage has failed. National survey data show that 48.1 percent of adults in the United States think divorce is too easy to obtain, 27.7 percent think divorce procedures are too difficult, 19.3 percent approve of current standards, and the remainder offered no opinion (N.O.R.C., 1991:255).

**Figure 15–4** The Divorce Rate for the United States, 1890–1990

(*U.S. Bureau of the Census*)

As Ed Kain (1990) points out, we tend to exaggerate the stability of marriage in the past—death ended as many marriages a century ago as divorce does now. But just as the dissolution of marriage was once due to forces beyond people's control, marriages are now much more likely to end simply because people want to be single—or married to somebody else.

## Who Divorces?

People who marry young are the most likely to divorce. Teens who marry usually had a brief courtship and typically have less financial stability and emotional maturity. People in lower social classes, too, are more likely to divorce because of financial strains. At all social levels, the risk of divorce rises if a couple marries in response to an unexpected pregnancy, and when one or both partners have alcohol or other substance-abuse problems. Dissimilar social backgrounds, too, may introduce tensions that are difficult to resolve, and lead to marital breakup. Divorce also is more common among women who have successful careers, sometimes because of the strains of a two-career marriage and sometimes because financially independent women do not feel compelled to remain in an unhappy marriage. In addition, people who move far away from family and friends have higher rates of divorce. Finally, men and women who divorce once are more likely to divorce again because problems tend to follow them from one marriage to another (Booth & White, 1980; Yoder & Nichols, 1980; Glenn & Shelton, 1985).

## Problems of Divorce

Divorce itself is not necessarily a problem; it may merely constitute a transition that benefits each party. Even in the best case, however, ending a marriage brings as much change as beginning one.

Paul Bohannan (1970) suggests that people who divorce must make six distinct adjustments. First, there is the *emotional divorce*. A deteriorating marriage is often fraught with disappointment and frustration, if not outright hostility. Second is the formal, *legal divorce*, which involves various legal procedures and may embroil couples in complicated financial disputes. Bohannan describes a third transition as *psychic divorce*. Divorced people may experience a sense of personal failure, loneliness, and a need for personal repair. Fourth, *community*

Because the family is an important primary group, divorce can be a lesson in conflict and hostility for children. This four-year-old, the object of a guardianship battle between his parents, bluntly expresses his opinion as the judge awarded custody to his mother.

*divorce* refers to the need to reorganize friendships ("Were they really *my* friends or my spouse's?") and to adjust relations with parents and other family members who are accustomed to seeing someone as part of a couple.

A fifth problem, especially for women, is the *economic divorce*. Recent no-fault divorce laws have reduced the amount of alimony and child support paid by men to their former wives. Divorce courts are now likely to require that homes be sold so that marital assets can be evenly divided. These legal changes, claim researchers, have hurt women financially. Studies suggest that, in the year following divorce, women suffer a one-third reduction in their living standard while men experience a 10 to 15 percent rise in theirs (Faludi, 1991). For the woman, especially one who does not work, this loss usually means a marked reduction in housing quality. Ex-wives often lose other forms of financial security as well, such as insurance policies, pension programs, and credit, all of which typically remain with ex-husbands. Older women who have not been in the labor force contend with economic problems that are even more severe, since they generally lack job skills (Weitzman, 1985).

A sixth and final adjustment noted by Bohannan is *parental divorce*, in which parents must resolve the difficult issues surrounding custody of children. More than half of divorcing partners have children under eighteen, and about half of children under eighteen experience the divorce of their parents (Bumpass, 1984; Weitzman, 1985; Leslie & Korman, 1989). The conventional practice of awarding custody to mothers is based on the notion that women are better parents than men are. Recently, however, a growing number of fathers have sought to gain custody of their children. As a result, the trend is toward joint custody, with children having a primary home with one parent but regularly spending time with the other, or dividing their lives more or less evenly between the two parents. Although joint custody is difficult if the divorced parents live far apart or do not get along, it does have the advantage of keeping children in regular contact with both parents (Roman & Haddad, 1978; Cherlin & Furstenberg, 1983).

Because mothers usually have custody of children but fathers typically earn more income, the well-being of children often depends on fathers making court-ordered child-support payments. Yet about half of children of divorced parents do not receive the financial support to which they are entitled by law. What has been called "an epidemic of nonsupport" has led to federal legislation mandating that parents who fail to fulfill this obligation will have the payments withheld from their earnings (Weitzman, 1985).

Conventional wisdom suggests that divorce is hardest on children. Divorce tears young people from familiar surroundings and may distance them from a parent they love. Moreover, in their own minds, children may saddle themselves with responsibility for the divorce of their parents. There is little doubt, however, that children who experience family breakup fare better than those who remain in a family racked by tension or violence (Goetting, 1981; Zill, 1984). Ideally, of course, children thrive in the absence of both family conflict and divorce.

## Remarriage

Despite the rising divorce rate, marriage—and especially remarriage—remain as popular as ever. Four out of five people who divorce remarry, most within five years. Men, who derive greater benefits from marriage, are more likely to remarry than women are. This is especially true of older men who receive cultural approval for marrying younger women. For their part, because women are expected to "marry up," the older a woman is, the more education she has, and the better her job, the more difficulty she has in finding a suitable husband (Leslie & Korman, 1989).

Common sense suggests that what people learned from failed first marriages should make their subsequent marriages more successful. Yet remarriages are even more likely to end in divorce. For one thing, people who have already been through a divorce have demonstrated their willingness to end an unsatisfactory marriage. Additionally, the first divorce may have been caused by attitudes or behavior that will undermine a subsequent marriage.

The same transitions that Paul Bohannan links to divorce are present in remarriage. According to Ann Goetting (1982), *emotional remarriage* involves reestablishing a bond based on attraction, commitment, and trust. *Legal remarriage* follows, including various agreements about property and a decision about where to reside. *Psychic remarriage* suggests the need to reforge personal identity as part of a couple: often individuals must relinquish the autonomy and privacy gained after a divorce. *Community remarriage* means altering relationships with friends and family based on, once again, being married. *Economic remarriage* generally increases a couple's standard of living, since two incomes now maintain only one residence. When there are children, the more complex issue of establishing and managing child-support payments arises. Child support might flow both to and from the new household. As noted earlier, such payments are often sporadic, making economic planning difficult.

Where there are children, *parental remarriage* consists of establishing relationships with the children of the spouse, a task that often demands a huge measure of sensitivity, skill, finesse, and patience. Remarriage often gives rise to the *blended family*, composed of biological parents and stepparents. In any particular household, then, children may have two, one, or no parents in common. Since many children of blended families have one biological parent living elsewhere, the adults in their world must make special efforts to clarify who is defined as part of the child's nuclear family (Furstenberg, 1984). Children of blended families are also subject to new relationships: an only child, for example, may suddenly find she has two older brothers. For these reasons, stress and conflict multiply in remarriages involving children, adding to the risk of another divorce (Kalmuss & Seltzer, 1984).

## Family Violence

The ideal family serves as a safe haven from the dangers of an unfamiliar world. The disturbing reality of many homes, however, is **family violence**, *emotional, physical, or sexual abuse of one family member by another.* According to sociologist Richard J. Gelles,

> The family is the most violent group in society with the exception of the police and the military. You are more likely to get killed, injured, or physically attacked in your home by someone you are related to than in any other social context. In fact, if violence were a communicable disease, the government would consider it an epidemic. (Cited in Roesch, 1984:75)

Such facts are chilling, and in some cases, almost incredible. Public awareness is the first step toward solving this problem, which victimizes millions of adults and children.

### Violence Against Women

> I guess the first time he hit me was when we had been married about eight years. I'd gone to my music lesson and had arranged for a babysitter to take the children to a school fair. When my husband got home from work the house was dark and no one was there. This enraged him, and in the driveway when I arrived, he greeted me with a punch in the kidneys. I doubled over. I didn't even know what I'd done. We never talked afterward. I swallowed my pain and tried to forget.

This incident took place in a fashionable suburb of Philadelphia in a family with plenty of money, beautiful children—and a lot of violence (Saline, 1984).

The common stereotype of a violent partner is a lower-class man who now and then drinks too much, loses control, and beats up his wife. In reality, although financial problems and unemployment do make the problem worse, violence against women in the home is perpetrated by men of all social classes, races, and ethnicities. Furthermore, as the example above suggests, this violence often occurs at random. Family brutality frequently goes unreported to police, but researchers estimate that some 9 million couples—or one in six—endure at least some violence each year. Between 1 and 2 million of these couples experience serious incidents of violence, including kicking, biting, and punching.

Not all family turmoil involves violence by men against women. But two crucial gender-based patterns have been established by research. First, women suffer most of the serious injuries. Second, men initiate most family violence so that violence against men by women often takes the form of retaliation and self-defense (Straus & Gelles, 1986; Schwartz, 1987).

Government statistics show that almost 30 percent of women who are murdered—as opposed to 6 percent of men—are killed by spouses, ex-spouses, or unmarried partners. Nationwide, the death toll from family violence is four thousand women each year. Further, women are more likely to be injured by a family member than they are to be mugged or raped by a stranger or injured in an automobile accident.

*Marital rape* has attracted growing attention in recent years. Historically, the law declared wives to be the property of their husbands, so that no man could be charged with raping his wife. By 1990, however, all but ten states had outlawed rape by husbands although, in some cases, a marital rape charge can be pursued only under specific circumstances such as after legal separation (Russell, 1982; O'Reilly, 1983; Margolick, 1984; Goetting, 1989).

Physically abused women have traditionally had few options. They may want to leave home, but many—especially those with children and without much money—have nowhere to go. Most wives are also committed to their marriages and believe (however unrealistically) that they can help abusive husbands to change. Some, unable to understand their husbands' violence, blame themselves. Others, raised in violent families, consider assault to be part of family life. Most abused women see no way out of the family violence that makes fear the centerpiece of their lives. In one study, researchers found that one-fourth of women who had entered a metropolitan hospital after attempting suicide had been victims of family violence (Stark & Flitcraft, 1979).

In the past, the law regarded domestic violence as a private concern of families. Now, even without filing for separation or divorce, a woman can obtain court protection from an abusive spouse. Medical personnel are also more aware today of the telltale signs of spouse violence and are likely to report such cases to police.

Communities across North America are establishing shelters that provide counseling as well as temporary housing for women and children driven from their homes by violence. The first one was established in Pasadena, California, in 1964, and almost a thousand such shelters now exist (although this number is fewer than the 3,000 animal shelters in the United States). Some men and women who abuse their partners are also joining self-help groups in an effort to understand and control their own behavior. In various ways, then, our society is beginning to mobilize against this serious problem.

### Violence Against Children

Kelly, now an adult, will never be able to forget the sexual abuse she suffered as a child. Her stepfather regularly separated her from other members of the family and, often in a parked car, forced her to have oral sex with him. Her mother was sick at the time, and the stepfather warned Kelly that telling of their sexual relationship would cause her mother to die. "I believed him," she recalls. "I thought my mother would die and I would be left with this man" (Watson, 1984).

The vicious nature of child abuse lies in adults' use of power and trust to victimize children. Child abuse therefore inflicts both *physical* and *emotional* harm, undermining the core of family life. It is difficult to establish the extent of child abuse because, like violence against women, most instances are never reported to anyone. Estimates suggest that upwards of 2 million children—especially the very young—are victimized each year including several thousand who die as a result. In proportional terms, this amounts to perhaps one in five girls and one in ten boys (Finkelhor, 1984; Straus & Gelles, 1986; U.S. House of Representatives, 1987).

Many abused children suffer in silence, believing throughout their formative years that they are to blame for their own victimization. The initial abuse, compounded by years of guilt, can leave lasting emotional scars that prevent people abused as children from forming healthy relationships as adults.

About 90 percent of child abusers are men, but they conform to no simple stereotype. As one man who entered a therapy group reported, "I kept waiting for all the guys with raincoats and greasy hair to show up. But everyone looked like regular middle-class people" (Lubenow, 1984). One trait common to abusers, however, is a history of having been abused as children, leading to the conclusion that violent behavior in personal relationships is learned (Gwartney-Gibbs, Stockard, & Bohmer, 1987). Treatment programs, then, coupled with legal protection for victims, offer some hope of restraining offenders.

Nations, as well as parents, can abuse children. Prior to the fall of the Ceausescu regime in 1989, the Romanian government denied women any form of birth control and banned abortion. Tens of thousands of unwanted children were the result, many of whom remain warehoused in orphanages like this one.

## Alternative Family Forms

In recent decades, our society has displayed greater social diversity in family life. While more traditional forms are still preferred by most, marriage and the family now represent a range of legitimate lifestyles.

## One-Parent Families

Figure 15–5 indicates that, in 1970, 87.1 percent of families with children under eighteen years of age had two parents in the household. By 1990, this proportion had fallen to 71.9 percent. Thus the proportion of *one-parent families* is growing rapidly, and almost one-third of children in the United States now live in these families. Single parenthood—four times more common among women than among men—may result from divorce, the inability to find a suitable husband, or the desire to have a child without marriage (Kantrowitz, 1985). Now that most women are in the labor force, they have the financial resources to become single parents. Single parenthood—when the parent is a woman—greatly increases the risks of poverty, however, because many mothers can find only low-paying jobs or are unable to work at all. This is especially true among young women. Child-care options are also limited, making full-time employment for single parents problematic as well. Estimates suggest that at least one-third of women in the United States become pregnant as teenagers, and many decide to raise their children (Wallis, 1985). These young women with children—especially if they have the additional disadvantage of being minorities—form the core of the rising problem of child poverty in the United States.

As was shown earlier in Figure 15–2, the proportion of families with one parent is highest—about half—among African Americans: 43.8 percent with a mother only and 6.0 percent with only a father. Single-parent families are less common among Hispanics (29.9 percent), among Asian Americans (17.9 percent), and among non-Hispanic whites (17.0 percent) (U.S. Bureau of the Census, 1991).

While the negative stigma attached to being born out of wedlock has certainly declined, conventional ideas about parenthood are still echoed by a majority of adults in the United States. Public opinion holds that a woman should not become pregnant if she does not plan to raise the child with its biological father (Kelley, 1984).

Most research suggests that growing up in a one-parent family can, but does not necessarily, have negative effects on children. Divorce is stressful for children, and many contend with emotional scars years later (Wallerstein & Blakeslee, 1989). Some studies link growing up in a single-parent family to low educational achievement, low income, and having children out of wedlock. But other research argues that the problems faced by families with one parent—especially if that parent is a

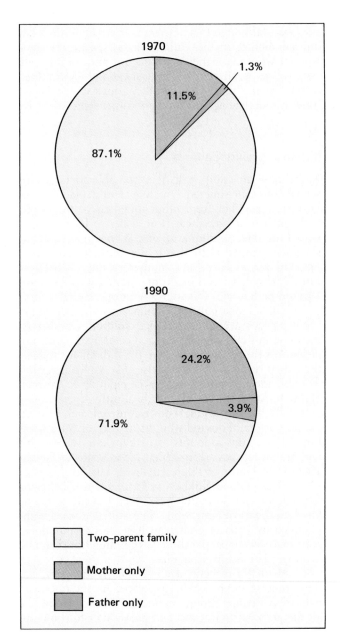

**Figure 15–5**  Single-Parent Families in the United States, 1970 and 1990

*(U.S. Bureau of the Census)*

woman—are caused by poverty rather than the absence of a second parent. Such inconsistent results show the need for continuing research about this emerging family form (Mueller & Cooper, 1984; McLanahan, 1985; Weisner & Eiduson, 1986; Astone & McLanahan, 1991).

## Cohabitation

**Cohabitation** is *the sharing of a household by an unmarried couple.* A generation ago, widespread use of terms such as "shacking up" and "living in sin" indicated that cohabitation was viewed as deviant. Yet the number of cohabiting couples in the United States has increased sharply, from about 500,000 in 1970 to almost 3 million by 1990 (U.S. Bureau of the Census, 1991). Although such couples still represent only 5 percent of all couples, cohabiting is especially common on college and university campuses, where perhaps one-fourth of students cohabit for some period of time.

The national impact of cohabiting is unclear. One study of Lane County, Oregon, found that the proportion of married couples who had previously cohabited had increased from about one in eight in 1970 to over one-half by 1980 (Gwartney-Gibbs, 1986). These findings suggest that cohabiting often precedes marriage, as a way of testing a serious relationship. But most cohabitation still does not lead to marriage and, in many cases, it merely serves as an intentionally temporary arrangement or one that saves money for the individuals involved. Most cases of cohabitation last several years; at that point, about 40 percent of couples marry, and the remainder split up (Blumstein & Schwartz, 1983; Macklin, 1983). As we have already explained, in Sweden cohabitation is sometimes a prelude to marriage, but for many it is a lifelong relational alternative (Popenoe, 1991).

Cohabitation, then, typically lacks the commitment (and the degree of sexual fidelity) that characterizes marriage. One twenty-four-year-old woman who married her live-in partner of five years expressed the difference between cohabitation and marriage this way: "For me, [marriage] was deciding to make a real commitment. When we were living together I felt I could walk out at any time" (Clancy & Oberst, 1985). Another clue that cohabitation is not as binding on partners as marriage is that cohabiting couples rarely have children.

However cohabiting partners define their relationship, court decisions state that individuals who live together can make claims on each other's property. In other words, as cohabitation has gained in popularity, the legal distinction between this pattern and marriage is beginning to blur.

Finally, cohabitation takes various forms. Although this relational form is most common among younger adults who are sexual partners, many elderly people with no sexual motives also choose to live together. For them, cohabitation provides some needed economic assistance or a source of companionship.

## Gay and Lesbian Couples

In 1989, Denmark became the first country to formally recognize homosexual marriages, thereby extending to gay and lesbian couples the legal advantages for inheritance, taxation, and joint property ownership. Danish law, however, stops short of allowing such couples to adopt children. In the United States, recent laws in San Francisco, New York, and elsewhere confer some of the legal benefits of marriage on gay and lesbian couples. In addition, while gay and lesbian couples have long raised children from previous marriages, a growing number are now adopting children as well.

Even though they are barred from legal marriage, many gay men and lesbians form long-term, committed partnerships and families (Bell, Weinberg, & Kiefer-Hammersmith, 1981; Gross, 1991). This is especially true of lesbian couples, who are more likely than gay couples to remain sexually exclusive (Blumstein & Schwartz, 1983).

Like heterosexual couples, gays and lesbians enter relationships with romantic ideals and then adjust to day-to-day realities; they share the strains of financial and household responsibilities. In addition, they must deal with conventional cultural values that favor masculine attributes more than feminine traits. Some homosexual couples also raise children, usually from previous heterosexual relationships, but sometimes from adoption. Artificial insemination, furthermore, now provides women with the option of having children without a male partner.

Although remaining "in the closet" is less common today than years ago, many gay men and lesbians still feel compelled to keep their relationships secret—even from other family members—to minimize prejudice and discrimination. Partners must therefore turn to each other for all the emotional, spiritual, and material support that heterosexual couples can find elsewhere. This places great strains on the gay or lesbian relationship. Yet, despite these disadvantages, many partnerships between lesbians and between gay men are strong, resilient, and long-lasting.

## Singlehood

Because nine out of ten people in the United States marry, singlehood is often seen as simply a transitory stage of life that ends with marriage. In recent decades, however, more women and men have deliberately chosen the freedom and independence of living alone, remaining both single and childless.

The increase in one-person households is shown in Figure 15–6. In 1950 only about one household in ten contained a single person. By 1990 this proportion was approaching one in four: a total of 23 million single adults. Most will marry at some point in their lives, but an increasing number will deliberately choose to remain single.

Perhaps the greatest change in marital status is evident among young women. In 1960 about one in four women aged twenty to twenty-four were single; by 1990 the proportion was nearing two-thirds. The key to this trend is greater participation in the labor force: women who are economically secure view a husband as a matter of choice rather than a financial necessity.

By midlife, however, women who have not married confront a lack of available men. Because our culture discourages women from marrying partners much young-er than they are (while encouraging men to do so), middle-aged women who do wish to marry find the odds rising against them. In 1990, there were 83 unmarried men aged forty to forty-four for every 100 unmarried women of the same age (U.S. Bureau of the Census, 1991).

# New Reproductive Technology and the Family

The case of Arlette Schweitzer, the first woman on record to bear her own grandchildren, illustrates how *new reproductive technology* has created new choices—and sparked new controversies—for families. The benefits of this rapidly developing technology are exciting, but its use raises daunting ethical questions about the creation and manipulation of life itself.

## *In Vitro* Fertilization

It was only a generation ago that Louise Brown, an English woman, became the world's first "test-tube" baby. Since then, thousands of people have been conceived in this way. Early in the next century, 2 or 3 percent of the population of industrial societies may be the result of "new birth technologies" (Vines, 1986; Ostling, 1987).

Technically speaking, test-tube babies result from *in vitro fertilization*: a union of the male sperm and the female ovum "in glass" rather than in a woman's body. In this complex medical procedure, drugs stimulate the production of more than one egg in each ovary during a woman's reproductive cycle. Then doctors surgically "harvest" eggs from the ovaries and combine them with sperm in a laboratory dish. The successful fusion of eggs and sperm produces embryos, which are placed in the womb of a woman who is to bear the child. The embryos may also be frozen for use at a later time.

The benefits of *in vitro* fertilization are twofold. First, many couples cannot conceive children normally; one-fifth of these couples can be helped through this process. Second, looking to the future, many medical experts believe that new birth technologies will reduce the incidence of birth defects. In other words, by genetically screening sperm and eggs, medical specialists can increase the odds for the birth of a healthy baby (Vines, 1986).

**Figure 15–6** One-Person Households in the United States, 1950–1990

*(U.S. Bureau of the Census)*

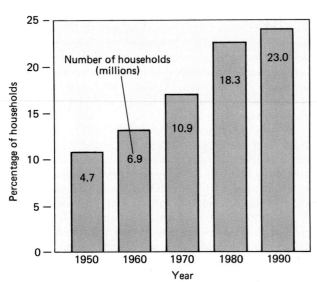

432    Chapter 15    Family

# Are New Reproductive Technologies Immoral? The Catholic Church's View

Most people in our society hail technological advances. This confidence in science extends to new reproductive technologies, including *in vitro* fertilization and genetic research, which allow women, previously unable to conceive, to have children, and promise to drastically reduce birth defects.

The Catholic Church takes a very different view, condemning this technology as a moral danger to humanity. No child, concludes a recent report, should be "conceived as the product of an intervention of medical or biological techniques" because such techniques treat human life as an object of research and manipulation. Church officials remind us that, during the 1930s and 1940s, the Nazis conducted genetic experiments with the stated goal of improving the health of children, although these experiments were actually designed to genetically engineer a race of "superhumans."

Many scientists in the United States believe that new reproductive technology can reduce many maladies of infancy, but the Church counters that nothing can justify manipulating an embryo— a human life—in a laboratory. The

Church doesn't stand alone on this issue; half the states currently restrict such practices, as do many European countries.

Less popular is the Church's opposition to using new reproductive technologies to help infertile couples have children. *In vitro* fertilization, the Church maintains, separates the act of procreation from the loving union of two parents. Catholics will recognize this argument as an extension of the Church's long-time prohibition against artificial contraception. Once separated from human sex-

uality, church officials fear, reproduction may quickly become as much a business as a family concern.

The popular view—even among Catholics—is that sexual intercourse between husband and wife is not the only moral way to conceive children. Since certain loving couples cannot conceive at all, they argue, artificial insemination (in which a husband's sperm is used to fertilize an ovum directly in the wife's womb) or *in vitro* fertilization has obvious value. Moreover, some Catholics complain that this prohibition strikes hardest at those people who accept the Church's view that Catholic families are incomplete without children.

Many Catholics will ignore the Church's recent pronouncements, just as many have overlooked prohibitions against artificial birth control in the past. But few people—whether Catholics or not—can easily dismiss the Church's concern that what is technologically possible may not always be morally desirable.

SOURCES: Based on Congregation for the Doctrine of the Faith (1987), Ostling (1987), and Woodward (1987).

## Ethical Issues

New reproductive technology has sparked heated debate. Simply put, medical technology now provides control over life itself that would have been unthinkable only a few decades ago. The result is a classic example of "cultural lag" (see Chapter 3, "Culture"), in which soci-

ety has to catch up to the moral implications of this new technological power.

Moral quandaries abound. As with most cases of technological advance, benefits are expensive and available only to those who can afford them. A cost exceeding $5,000 for a single attempt at *in vitro* fertilization ensures that only a small fraction of infertile couples can even consider this procedure. A second problem surrounds guidelines that limit this technology to proper "families." In most cases, doctors and hospitals have been willing to apply *in vitro* fertilization only to women who are under forty years of age and are part of a heterosexual couple. Single women, older women, and lesbian couples have so far been widely excluded from this opportunity.

A third ethical problem concerns *surrogate motherhood*, in which one woman bears a child for another. Surrogate motherhood can take one of two forms. In the first type—illustrated by the case of Arlette Schweitzer—the ovum and sperm produced by a couple are joined, and the resulting embryo is implanted into the body of another woman—the surrogate—who gives birth to the child. In the second type—illustrated by the "Baby M case" several years ago—a couple contracts with a woman to bear a child for them by having the woman's own ovum artificially fertilized by the man's sperm.

Both types of surrogate motherhood raise daunting questions about who a baby's parents are. In some situations, lengthy and emotionally wrenching legal battles have been needed to resolve issues of parenthood. Until society generates moral and legal standards to clarify such cases, surrogate motherhood will remain highly controversial.

An outspoken party in controversies surrounding new reproductive technologies is the Catholic Church. As the box on page 433 explains, this church has condemned all new reproductive technology as reducing human life to a manipulated object. However, many practicing Catholics do not share their Church's position.

## The Family in the Twenty-First Century

Family life in the United States has changed significantly in recent decades, and new reproductive technology will surely prompt further change in the future. This possibility has led some to wonder if the family may eventually disappear entirely. Locked in debate are advocates of traditional family values, on the one hand, and proponents of new family forms and greater personal choice on the other (Berger & Berger, 1983).

We will close this chapter with five general assertions about the family with an eye toward the next century. First, divorce has become an accepted—if regret-table—element of family life. This does not mean that couples are less durable today than they were a century ago, since it was not long ago that death took a heavy toll on parents. But more couples now *choose* to end their marriages, so that the traditional view that marriage lasts " 'til death do us part" no longer holds true. Although the divorce rate has recently stabilized, it is unlikely that marriage will regain the durability characteristic of the 1950s. One major reason is that increasing numbers of women are able to support themselves, and traditional marriages appeal to fewer of them. Men, as well, are seeking more satisfying relationships. The higher divorce rate of the last several decades should probably be viewed less as a threat to families than as a sign of change in family form. After all, most divorces still lead to remarriage, casting doubt on the notion that marriage itself is becoming discredited. As women's and men's roles change, new forms of family life will emerge that may prove more stable and more fulfilling.

Second, family life in the twenty-first century will be highly variable. We have noted an increasing number of cohabiting couples, one-parent families, gay and lesbian families, and blended families created from remarriage after divorce. Each family arrangement makes for its own set of problems and satisfactions. Some alternatives, such as singlehood and childless marriage, are unlikely to be chosen by a majority of the population. Taken together, however, they represent growing social diversity and a conception of family life as a matter of choice.

Third, in most families men play a limited role in child rearing. This process was well under way in the 1950s, a decade many people see as the "golden age" of families (Snell, 1990). Then, fathers left home each day for work, leaving the children in the care of mothers. A counter-trend has been evident for some time as many fathers—now older, on average, and more established in their careers—try to become more involved in child care. But the increasing number of women raising children outside of marriage, the rising divorce rate, and the surge in single motherhood all combine toward the same result: more and more children are growing up without social ties to their fathers. Most research suggests that the absence of fathers is not directly and significantly detrimental to children, but there is little doubt that the absence of husbands and fathers from families figures in the feminization of poverty in the United States.

Fourth, changes in the economy are affecting marriage and the family. The economic reality for most couples is that both partners must work if they are to acquire a measure of financial security. As Arlie Hochschild (1989) points out, economic changes reshape society in ways that people *feel* in family life. Marriage today is often the interaction of weary men and women; adults try their best to raise children, yet contend with suspicions that popular ideas like "quality time" are little more than ways to justify minimal parenthood (Dizard & Gadlin, 1990). Two-career couples may advance the goal of gender equality, but the long-term effects on families are likely to be mixed.

Fifth, and finally, new reproductive technology will shape families of the twenty-first century. Opposition may limit such developments, but it seems very likely that new forms of reproduction will alter traditional meanings of parenthood. At the very least, we can be sure, new technology will direct a continued focus on family life.

Despite social changes that have buffeted the family in the United States and elsewhere, most people still report being happy as partners and as parents (Cherlin & Furstenberg, 1983). Marriage and family life have always given rise to controversy and conflicting views, and as the family evolves, this will certainly continue. But both marriage and family life will still remain the foundation of our society.

## Summary

1.  Societies are built on kinship; in industrial societies, the family is composed of close relatives. Family forms vary considerably across cultures, as they have across history.

2.  Nuclear families have historically predominated in the United States. As in other industrial nations, marriage in our society is monogamous. Many preindustrial societies, however, allow polygamy, of which there are two types: polygyny and polyandry.

3.  Cross-culturally, families differ in residential patterns. Industrial societies favor neolocality; patrilocality is more common throughout the world, and a few cultures have matrilocal households. Industrial societies recognize bilateral descent, while preindustrial societies tend to be either patrilineal or matrilineal.

4.  Structural-functional analysis points to four major functions of the family: socialization of the young, regulation of sexual activity, social placement, and provision of emotional support.

5.  Social-conflict theory draws attention to how the family perpetuates social inequality by strengthening social classes, ethnic and racial divisions, and gender distinctions.

6.  Symbolic-interaction analysis highlights the dynamic nature of family life. This approach also explains that various family members may experience their families quite differently. The social-exchange approach highlights how people evaluate potential mates in terms of what they bring to a relationship.

7.  Families originate in the process of courtship. Unlike the United States, most societies limit the role of romantic love in the choice of a mate. Even among members of our society, romantic love tends to join people with similar social backgrounds.

8.  The reality of marriage usually falls short of the cultural ideal. New spouses frequently discover that they have much to learn about each other as well as about married life. A majority of married men and a sizeable minority of married women engage in sexual infidelity, although doing so still violates cultural norms.

9.  Although the vast majority of married couples have children, family size has decreased over time. At the root of this trend lies industrialization, which transforms children into economic liabilities, encourages women to join the labor force, and reduces infant mortality.

10. In later life, marriage changes as children leave home to form families of their own. Couples are likely to spend more time caring for aging parents, however. Retirement may affect the relationship between spouses. The final stage of marriage begins with the death of one spouse, usually the husband.

11. Social class shapes family life by providing some families with more options and financial security than others.

12. Hispanics are more likely to maintain extended families and adhere to conventional gender roles. African-American families are three times more likely to be headed by women than white families; thus, two-thirds of first children are born to black women who are unmarried. Many African-American families contend with poverty through extended kinship and network systems of economic support.

13. Gender affects family dynamics. Husbands continue to dominate the vast majority of families. Research suggests that marriage provides more benefits to men than to women.

14. The divorce rate today is ten times higher than it was a century ago; almost one-half of current marriages will end in divorce. Most people who divorce—especially men—remarry. Remarriage can create blended families that include children from previous marriages.

15. Violence against women and children remained major public issues in the 1980s. Both problems are widespread and underreported to authorities. Commonly, adults who abuse family members were themselves abused as children.

16. Family life in the United States has become more varied. Cohabitation and one-parent families have proliferated in recent years. Gay men and lesbians cannot legally marry but typically form long-lasting relationships. Singlehood—by chance or choice—is also increasingly common.

17. Based on current research, close to half of all marriages will end in divorce, family life will continue to take many diverse forms, the family will have to come to terms with unprecedented career demands, new reproductive technology may alter patterns of parenting, and fathers are likely to have limited importance in child rearing because of their absence from many families.

## Key Concepts

**bilateral descent** a system tracing kinship through both females and males

**cohabitation** the sharing of a household by an unmarried couple

**descent** the system by which members of a society trace kinship over generations

**endogamy** marriage between people of the same social group or category

**exogamy** marriage between people of different social groups or categories

**extended family** (consanguine family) a social unit including parents, children, and other kin

**family** a relatively permanent social group of two or more people, who are related by blood, marriage, or adoption and who usually live together

**family of orientation** the family into which a person is born and receives early socialization

**family of procreation** a family in which people have or adopt children of their own

**family violence** emotional, physical, or sexual abuse of one family member by another

**homogamy** marriage between people who are socially alike

**incest taboo** a cultural norm forbidding sexual relations or marriage between certain kin

**kinship** social ties based on blood, marriage, or adoption

**marriage** a socially approved relationship, involving economic cooperation and allowing sexual activity and childbearing, that is expected to be relatively enduring

**matrilineal descent** a system tracing kinship through females

**matrilocality** a residential pattern in which a married couple lives with or near the wife's family

**monogamy** a form of marriage that joins one female and one male

**neolocality** a residential pattern in which a married couple lives apart from the parents of both spouses

**nuclear family** (conjugal family) a social unit composed of one or, more commonly, two parents and children

**patrilineal descent** a system tracing kinship through males

**patrilocality** a residential pattern in which a married couple lives with or near the husband's family

**polyandry** a form of marriage that joins one female with more than one male

**polygamy** a form of marriage that unites three or more people

**polygyny** a form of marriage that joins one male with more than one female

# Suggested Readings

This new textbook offers a detailed look at marriage and the family.

> Nijole V. Benokraitis. *The Family*. Englewood Cliffs, NJ: Prentice Hall, 1993.

This historical study of families in the United States challenges the notion that families are in decline.

> Edward L. Kain. *The Myth of Family Decline: Understanding Families in a World of Rapid Social Change*. Lexington, MA: Lexington Books, 1990.

This recent best seller argues that feminism has suffered setbacks over the last decade.

> Susan Faludi. *Backlash: The Undeclared War Against American Women*. New York: Crown, 1991.

The first book, an account of several working-class families in California's Silicon Valley, highlights the effects of class, religion, and feminism to domestic patterns. The second explores changes in class and ethnicity over several generations.

> Judith Stacey. *Brave New Families: Stories of Domestic Upheaval in Late Twentieth-Century America*. New York: Basic Books, 1990.

> Corinne Azen Krause. *Grandmothers, Mothers, and Daughters: Oral Histories of Three Generations of Ethnic American Women*. Boston: Twayne Publishers/G.K. Hall & Co., 1991.

Economics exerts a strong influence inside families. The first book analyzes how making money, spending it, and giving it away affects relations among family members. The second book looks at dual-career couples—now the norm in the United States—and shows how clout in a marriage relates to economic power. The third book is a fascinating account of marriages in which women have more economic power than their husbands.

> Marcia Millman. *Warm Hearts and Cold Cash: The Intimate Dynamics of Families and Money*. New York: The Free Press, 1991.

> Rosanna Hertz. *More Equal Than Others: Women and Men in Dual-Career Marriages*. Berkeley: University of California Press, 1986.

> Susan McRae. *Cross-Class Families: A Study of Wives' Occupational Superiority*. New York: Oxford University Press, 1986.

This collection consists of cross-cultural essays on childbearing and family life.

> W. Penn Handwerker, ed. *Births and Power: The Politics of Reproduction*. Boulder, CO: Westview Press, 1989.

How does family life evolve among partners of different religious backgrounds? This volume takes an insightful look at the challenges of interfaith marriages.

> Susan Weidman Schneider. *Intermarriage: The Challenge of Living with Differences Between Christians and Jews*. New York: The Free Press, 1989.

The first book is one of the most influential studies of the history of the African-American family in the United States. The second is a collection of essays on the current state of black families.

> Herbert G. Gutman. *The Black Family in Slavery and Freedom: 1750–1925*. New York: Pantheon Books, 1976.

> Harold E. Cheatham and James B. Stewart, eds. *Black Families: Interdisciplinary Perspectives*. New Brunswick, NJ: Transaction Books, 1989.

Despite our idealized vision of the family as a haven from trouble, troubled families are common in the United States. These books are recent additions to the growing literature on violence in families.

> Suzanne M. Retzinger. *Violent Emotions: Shame and Rage in Marital Quarrels*. Newbury Park, CA: Sage, 1991.

> Richard J. Gelles and Claire Pedrick Cornell. *Intimate Violence in Families*. Newbury Park, CA: Sage, 1990.

This book takes a look at the dynamics of living in a so-called "blended family."

> Anne C. Bernstein. *Yours, Mine, and Ours: How Families Change When Remarried Parents Have a Child Together*. New York: Charles Scribner's Sons, 1989.

Conventional wisdom holds that families should be self-sufficient units that provide for their members. These researchers claim that families are being hard pressed in an age when both parents work while they try to manage a home and raise children. The book considers both positive and negative consequences of this trend.

> Jan E. Dizard and Howard Gadlin. *The Minimal Family*. Amherst: The University of Massachusetts Press, 1990.

Adults are also delaying childbirth while pursuing a career or the right relationship. This study outlines the likely effects of being a "latecomer" child.

> Andrew L. Yarrow. *Latecomers: Children of Parents over 35*. New York: The Free Press, 1991.

The first of these two books examines recent changes in divorce law in the United States; the second reports on a decade-long study of divorced couples and their children.

> Herbert Jacob. *Silent Revolution: The Transformation of Divorce Law in the United States*. Chicago: University of Chicago Press, 1988.

> Judith S. Wallerstein and Sandra Blakeslee. *Second Chances: Men, Women, and Children a Decade After Divorce*. New York: Ticknor & Fields, 1989.

Many of the reasons that husbands and wives often communicate poorly are explored in this book.

> Mary Anne Fitzpatrick. *Between Husbands and Wives: Communication in Marriage*. Newbury Park, CA: Sage, 1988.

# Education

Thirteen-year-old Naoko Masuo has just returned from school to her home in a suburb of Yokohama, Japan. She does not drop off books and head off for an afternoon of fun, as is the norm in the United States. Instead, she immediately settles into her homework. Several hours later, her mother reminds her of the time and she gathers her books once again and departs for the *juku* or "cram school" that Naoko attends for three hours three afternoons a week. Mother and daughter travel four stops on the subway to downtown Yokohama and climb to the second floor of an office building where Naoko joins dozens of other girls and boys for intensive training in Japanese, English, math, and science. Tuition at the *juku* consumes several hundred dollars of the Masuo family's monthly income. But they know well the realities of the Japanese educational system, and consider this investment in extra schooling a necessity.

The extra hours in the classroom will soon pay off when Naoko takes the national examination for children her age—a high score is the key to being admitted to a better school. Three years hence, Naoko will face another hurdle—the high-school examination—that, once again, will determine the quality of her education. Then will come the greatest challenge of all: earning admission to an exclusive national university. Only the one-third of Japanese students who perform best on the college entrance examination enter this elite category. Once accepted to the university, a young person in Japan is virtually guaranteed a high-paying career with a prestigious company. Stumbling in the race that is Naoko's next five years will mean learning to settle for less. Like most other Japanese families, the Masuos are convinced that one cannot work too hard or begin too early in preparation for university admission (Simons, 1989).

Education has become increasingly valuable in Japan's complex and changing society, as it has in other industrial nations. **Education** refers to *the various ways in which a society transmits knowledge—including factual information and occupational skills as well as cultural norms and values—to its members.* In industrial societies, education centers on **schooling,** which is *formal instruction under the direction of specially trained teachers.* Schooling or formal education is one of the major social institutions in industrial societies.

## Education: A Global Survey

Like people in Japan, we in the United States expect that children will spend much of their first eighteen years of life in school. Only a century ago, however, schooling in the United States was a privilege restricted to a small elite. In Third-World societies, even today, the vast majority of people receive little or no schooling.

439

Chapter 4 ("Society") explained that most people who have inhabited this planet have lived in technologically simple hunting and gathering societies. In such societies, the family was the central social institution; just as there were no governments or churches, so there was no formal system of education. Necessary knowledge and skills were simply taught to children by adults, generally within the family (Lenski, Lenski, and Nolan, 1991).

In more technologically complex agrarian societies—common in much of the world today—people routinely teach others specialized crafts and trading skills. This kind of learning is directed toward immediate needs; the opportunity to study literature, art, history, or science in schools is a privilege generally available only to wealthy people. The English word *school* is, in fact, derived from the Greek word for "leisure." In ancient Greece, renowned teachers such as Socrates, Plato, and Aristotle concentrated their efforts on a small circle of aristocratic men. Similarly, in ancient China the famous philosopher K'ung-Fu-tzu (Confucius) also taught a select few (Rohlen, 1983).

During the Middle Ages, the church expanded schooling as it established the first colleges and universities (Ballantine, 1989). But as has always been the rule in agrarian societies, schooling remained primarily a privilege of the ruling elites in both Western Europe and North America.

Dramatic change in education followed the Industrial Revolution. In the nineteenth century, the United States was among the first nations to embrace the principle of mass education. In part, schooling served to forge a literate citizenry capable of playing a part in political life. Operating the new factories also required that workers have at least basic skills of reading, writing, and arithmetic. In the twentieth century the steady growth of bureaucracy ushered in an economy based on paperwork more than machines, making schooling even more important.

In 1850 about half the U.S. population between the ages of five and nineteen were enrolled in school. By 1918, every state had a **mandatory education law,** *the legal requirement that children receive a minimum of formal education* (typically to the age of sixteen or completion of the eighth grade). These laws recast the social roles of children, who left farms and factories for classrooms across the country. Table 16–1 shows that a milestone was reached in the mid-1960s when a majority of adults had completed high school. In 1991, almost four out of five adults in the United States had

**Table 16–1   EDUCATIONAL ACHIEVEMENT IN THE UNITED STATES, 1910–1991***

| Year | High-School Graduates | College Graduates | Median Years of Schooling |
|---|---|---|---|
| 1910 | 13.5% | 2.7% | 8.1 |
| 1920 | 16.4 | 3.3 | 8.2 |
| 1930 | 19.1 | 3.9 | 8.4 |
| 1940 | 24.1 | 4.6 | 8.6 |
| 1950 | 33.4 | 6.0 | 9.3 |
| 1960 | 41.1 | 7.7 | 10.5 |
| 1970 | 55.2 | 11.0 | 12.2 |
| 1980 | 68.7 | 17.0 | 12.5 |
| 1991 | 78.4 | 21.4 | 12.7 |

* For persons twenty-five years of age and over.

SOURCE:   U.S. Bureau of the Census, 1992.

a high-school education and more than one in five had completed four years of college.

Today, officially at least, only a small fraction of people are illiterate in the United States as well as in Japan, Great Britain, and the Russian-led Commonwealth of Independent States. As shown in Global Map 16–1, this is not the case in agrarian societies. Illiteracy is considerably higher in the Americas to our south, and, in the nations of Africa and Asia, *most* people neither read nor write. The reason, as Chapter 11 ("Global Inequality") explained in detail, is that agrarian societies are terribly poor, with families earning only about 5 percent of the income enjoyed by typical families in the United States. Faced with the need simply to survive, people in the Third World can spare little in the way of financial resources and human energy in pursuit of schooling. Except for a small number of high-quality schools that cater to privileged elites, formal education is mostly of low quality, so children learn substantially less than their peers in richer societies (Hayneman & Loxley, 1983).

Yet, striking educational successes have been documented. Before the 1960 revolution that brought the Castro regime to power, schooling in Cuba was limited to a small upper class. While Castro has made little progress in reducing poverty, Cuba has widely expanded formal education and claims now to have virtually eradicated illiteracy. Such cases suggest that educational achievement is possible even in poor societies if the government defines it as a high social priority.

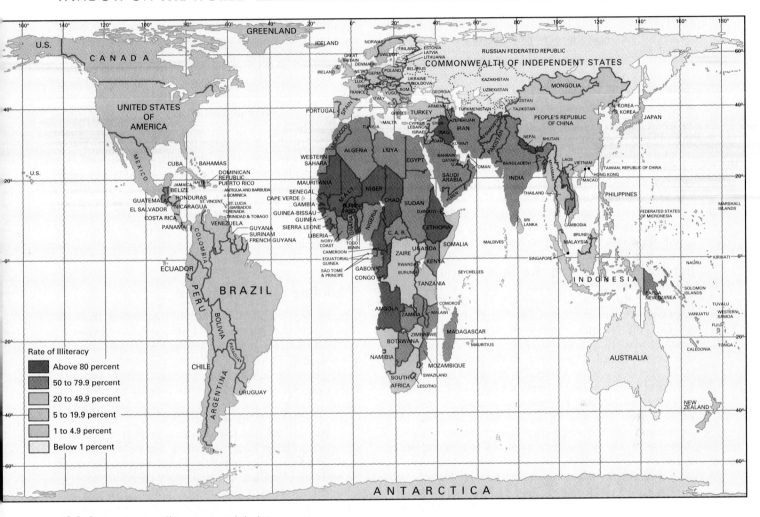

**Global Map 16–1**  Illiteracy in Global Perspective

Reading and writing skills are widespread in every industrial society, with illiteracy rates generally below 5 percent. Throughout Latin America, however, illiteracy is more common-place—one consequence of limited economic development. In about a dozen nations of the world—many of them in Africa—illiteracy is the rule rather than the exception. In such societies, people rely on what sociologists call "the oral tradition" of face-to-face communication rather than communicating through the written word.

Industrial societies provide extensive schooling for their people, but each does so in a distinctive way, as the following brief descriptions of schooling in Japan, Great Britain, and the new Russian-led confederation demonstrate.

## Schooling in Japan

Before industrialization brought mandatory education to Japan in 1872, only a privileged few received schooling. The contemporary Japanese educational system is unique in all the world, reflecting the historical influence of China, Western Europe, the United States (which occupied Japan after World War II), and Japan's own strong traditions (Rohlen, 1983).

In the early grades, schools foster the cultural values long central to Japanese life, including obligation to family (Benedict, 1974). In their early teens, as illustrated by the account of Naoko Masuo at the beginning of this chapter, students encounter Japan's system of rigorous and competitive examinations. Written evaluations, much like the Scholastic Aptitude Test (SAT) college admissions officers rely on in the United States, are used to place the brightest students in the best schools. In terms of schooling, Japan is more of a meritocracy than the United States. Here, even students with low SAT scores can expect to be admitted to some college; a bigger barrier to advanced education is the high cost involved. In Japan, by contrast, government support covers most of the financial cost of higher education; however, the performance of individuals on achievement tests literally makes or breaks the college aspirations of rich and poor alike.

More men and women in Japan (about 90 percent) graduate from high school than in the United States (about 78 percent). But competitive examinations steadily cut down the number of college-bound Japanese youths, so that only about 30 percent of high-school graduates end up entering college—half the figure for our society (Simons, 1989). Understandably, then, Japanese students view entrance examinations with the utmost seriousness, and families send about half of all students to *juku* "cram schools" to give them an extra edge when they take their examinations.

Japanese women take such an active interest in their children's schooling that they have been dubbed *koiku mamas* (a mixture of Japanese and English that means "education mothers"). This maternal role reflects the stark reality that acceptance or rejection by a university shapes a student's career. In addition, most Japanese

women are still not in the labor force, and many Japanese men work late into the evening. Thus mothers have the time and energy to devote themselves to the future success of their sons and, to a lesser extent, their daughters (Brinton, 1988; Simons, 1989). The payoff—or disappointment—after years of effort on the part of mother and child comes as they anxiously await the results of university examinations. So high is the suspense that observing the outcome has become something of a national pastime.

Although the Japanese educational system places considerable pressure on adolescents, the results are impressive. Especially in mathematics and science, Japanese students outperform students of every other industrial country, including the United States (Hayneman & Loxley, 1983; Rohlen, 1983). Japanese cultural traditions of hard work and loyalty to family, as well as the highly competitive examination system, appear to be a strongly motivating combination.

## Schooling in Great Britain

Chapter 9 ("Social Stratification") explained that the legacy of Great Britain's feudal history is evident in British society today. During the Middle Ages, schooling was a privilege of the nobility. Young men and women of noble station studied classical subjects since they had little need for the practical skills related to earning a living. Those in schools and colleges, then, usually shared much the same elite background.

As the Industrial Revolution created a need for an educated labor force, schooling was expanded to include a greater proportion of the British people. Demands by working-class families that their children, too, be schooled accelerated this process. Today, every British child is required by law to attend school until the age of sixteen.

Traditional social distinctions, however, continue to shape British education. Many wealthy families send their children to what the British call *public schools*, the equivalent of private boarding schools in the United States. Elite public schools in Britain do more than teach academic subjects; they also socialize children from wealthy families into a distinctive way of life. Patterns of speech, mannerisms, and social graces are learned in the educational setting; together, these distinguish members of the upper class from everyone else. Since public schools are beyond their financial reach, most British parents send their children to state-supported day schools, just as most families do in our country.

Wealth and power in Great Britain has long been linked to "public" schools—actually privately funded boarding schools for young men and, to a lesser extent, women. The most elite of these schools transmit the way of life of the upper class not so much in the classroom as on the playing fields, in the dining halls, and in the dormitories where informal socialization goes on continuously. Elite boarding schools are especially important to new-rich families; parents with modest backgrounds and large bank accounts send their children to these schools to mix with and learn from the offspring of "old-money" families.

The 1960s and 1970s saw a marked expansion in the British university system (Sampson, 1982). In order to lessen the influence of social background on schooling, British children now must compete for places in universities by taking examinations during their high-school years. In stark contrast to the United States, in Britain the government generally pays tuition and living expenses of those who are successful. Compared with the Japanese system, the British examinations are less crucial, evident in the fact that a disproportionate number of well-to-do children still manage to attend Oxford (alma mater for eighteen British prime ministers) and Cambridge, the most prestigious British universities, which are

roughly comparable to Yale, Harvard, and Princeton in the United States. Graduates of "Oxbridge" form a national elite with top positions in business and government.

## Schooling in the Commonwealth of Independent States

Schooling has changed considerably in the new Russian-led commonwealth over the course of the last century. Before the socialist revolution of 1917, Russia was an agrarian society with schooling reserved primarily for nobles. By the 1930s, the Soviet Union adopted mandatory education laws and had embarked on a program to make education universal in the new socialist society. In the next two decades, political unrest and the costs and social disruption of World War II slowed educational progress, but by the end of the 1940s half the young people in the Soviet Union were attending school. In forging a national educational system, the Soviets had to contend with striking cultural diversity—still making news today—in the geographically largest country in the world. By 1975 the Soviets began to boast of having achieved virtually universal schooling (Matthews, 1983; Ballantine, 1989).

According to official Soviet policy, children of both sexes and every ethnic background had broad educational opportunities. This goal was partially realized, but Soviet women have long been overly represented in areas of study (such as education and medicine) with relatively low social prestige in that society, while men have dominated higher-prestige fields like agriculture and engineering. Similarly, although considerable strides have been made toward providing equal access to higher education for diverse ethnic groups, the Russian majority still fares better than others (Avis, 1983).

Schooling in the former Soviet Union reflects and reinforces important cultural values, just as it does in every society. Besides helping the country become an industrial power, Soviet education had important political purposes. Although changes are now under way as this society sheds its socialist past (see Chapters 18 and 19), the Soviet educational system was highly standardized under the direction of the central government so that schools taught norms and values of socialist living (Matthews, 1983; Tomiak, 1983). As in Japan and Great Britain, competitive examinations have long characterized the Commonwealth of Independent States, identifying the most academically able students who are admitted to higher education. Further, as Chapter 9 ("Social Stratification") notes, disparity of wealth was far less pronounced in the Soviet Union than in the United States, and the government paid most educational costs. This economic parity has gone a long way toward creating a level playing field for young people in the Commonwealth of Independent States—much more so than in our society. During the heyday of the Communist party, however, being the daughter or son of an important official factored in significantly when it came to either going to a selective university or simply learning a trade (Avis, 1983; Matthews, 1983; Ballantine, 1989).

This brief comparison illustrates a basic truth: education is shaped by other institutions and social forces. Societies generally adopt mandatory education laws in response to industrialization and growing political democracy. Also, schools show the influence of surrounding cultural patterns (such as the achievement orientation and intense competition of Japan), historical forces (seen in centuries of inequality in British schooling), and the political system (evident in decades of socialist education in the former Soviet Union).

## Schooling in the United States

The educational system in the United States, too, has been shaped by the larger society. Compared with our mother country—Great Britain—the United States has a stronger tradition of widespread political participation. Such democratic ideals demand formal education so that, as Thomas Jefferson once put it, the people can "read and understand what is going on in the world" (cited in Honeywell, 1931:13). In practice, political rights were long restricted to white men, and, even today, some are withheld from women, gay people, and other minorities. However imperfect the application of its democratic ideals, the United States can boast that a larger proportion of its people attend colleges and universities than any other industrial society (Rubinson, 1986).

Formal education in the United States is shaped by the professed cultural value of *equal opportunity*. National surveys show that the vast majority of people in this country view schooling as crucial to personal success (Gallup, 1982; N.O.R.C., 1991). Just eight of the forty-one men who have reached the presidency of the United States did not graduate from college; this has been true of only four presidents since the Civil War and only one in this century (Harry Truman).

More than a century ago, the United States initiated a policy of universal primary and secondary schooling financed by public taxes. Since then, an increasing amount of public funds have been earmarked for support of state colleges and universities. Such expenditures are made with the intention of giving everyone the opportunity to achieve as much as their individual talents and efforts allow. Most people think our society does well in this regard; various surveys show that about two-thirds of respondents endorse the notion that people get an education consistent with their abilities (N.O.R.C., 1991). While this reflects our cultural ideals, it exaggerates the historical record. Women were effectively excluded from higher education until this century, and even today only among the higher social classes do a majority of young people attend college.

Besides trying to make schooling more widely accessible, our society has long favored *practical* learning, that is, education that has a direct bearing on people's lives, and especially their occupations. The educational philosopher John Dewey (1859–1952) advanced the idea that children would readily learn information and skills they found useful. Rejecting the traditionalist emphasis on teaching a fixed body of knowledge to each generation of students, Dewey (1968; orig. 1938) endorsed *progressive education* that reflected people's changing concerns and needs.

George Herbert Mead, the architect of the symbolic-interaction paradigm in sociology, echoed the sentiments of his friend John Dewey, claiming that "any education that is worthy of the name [provides] the solution to problems that we all carry with us" (1938:52). By contrast, Mead argued, "whatever is stored up, without immediate need, for later occasion, for display, or to pass examinations is mere information [with] no enduring place in the mind" (1906:395). Reflecting this practical emphasis, today's college students select major areas of study with an eye toward future jobs. The box takes a closer look at the changing interests of college students during the 1980s.

## The Functions of Schooling

Structural-functional analysis directs attention to ways in which formal education enhances the operation and stability of society. Central to the socialization process, schooling serves as one cultural lifeline linking the generations.

# Following the Jobs: Trends in Bachelor's Degrees

College attendance in the United States has never been higher, and the 1980s showed a pronounced increase in the number of bachelor's degrees earned by women. For both sexes, however, higher education remained practical, meaning people are pursuing degrees in areas where the economy is expanding.

Corresponding to economic trends, the figure shows considerable change in the distribution of bachelor's degrees between 1978 and 1988. The greatest increase—reflecting the Information Revolution—was in computer science degrees, which soared almost five-fold. The number of degrees in law and communications, both central to the postindustrial economy, also doubled during this decade. Business, management, and accounting—which throughout the time period remained the most popular fields for college study—also made gains.

By and large, declines in degrees earned by college and university students appeared in disciplines where the demand for workers has stabilized or fallen. Library science heads the list of fields posting reductions, followed by agriculture, education, biology, and foreign languages. Notice, too, that during the 1980s there was a modest decline in the number of bachelor's degrees earned

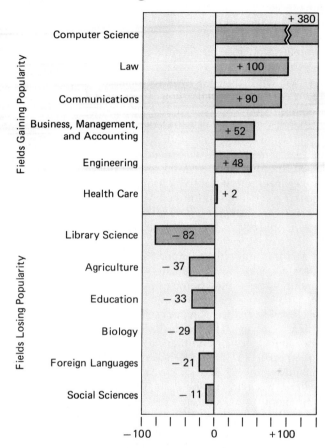

Percentage Changes in Bachelor's Degrees Earned, 1987–1988 Compared with 1977–1978

(*National Center for Education Statistics, 1980, 1991*)

in the social sciences. Happily, however, this trend has turned: other data suggest that these disciplines (including sociology) have enjoyed an upswing that began in the late 1980s.

SOURCE: National Center for Education Statistics (1991).

## Socialization

Every society employs various strategies to transmit its way of life from one generation to the next. In technologically simple societies, most of this cultural transmission is handled by the family. As societies become more technologically complex, young people need to acquire rapidly expanding information and new skills, beyond the grasp of family members themselves, so other social institutions play a greater role in socialization. In industrial societies, schooling requires specially trained personnel to efficiently teach a wide range of knowledge.

At the primary-school level, children learn basic language and mathematical skills. Secondary school steadily builds on this foundation and, for some, college allows further specialization. Because industrial societies change so rapidly, schooling not only conveys specific information (which may become obsolete) but also, at its best, empowers students to teach themselves so that they will be able to adapt to future changes.

Schools also transmit cultural values and norms. Civics classes, for example, provide students with explicit instruction in our ways of life. Sometimes important cultural lessons are learned in subtle ways, as students experience the operation of the classroom itself. Teachers give children in U.S. schools a great deal of individual responsibility for their behavior and their tasks; spelling bees and classroom drill also foster a keen sense of competitive individualism.

As elsewhere, schooling in the United States has a political component. It has already been noted how the former Soviet Union utilized formal education to teach socialist principles. Although dominant political values in the United States are different from those in the Commonwealth of Independent States, the same process occurs here. Our political system and our way of doing business are commonly championed in the classroom, just as rituals such as saluting the flag and singing "The Star-Spangled Banner" foster patriotism.

## Cultural Innovation

Educational systems create as well as transmit culture. Schools stimulate intellectual inquiry and critical thinking, which lead to the development of new ideas.

Today, for example, many college professors not only teach but engage in research that yields discoveries and innovations. Research in the humanities, the social sciences, and the natural sciences is changing attitudes

Schooling is a way of teaching the values and attitudes that a society deems important. It is also a means favored by political regimes to instill conformity and compliance into children. These children in Taiwan are receiving a lesson in "political correctness."

and patterns of life throughout the United States and the larger world. Medical research, carried on mainly at major universities, has helped to increase life expectancy, just as research by sociologists and psychologists has encouraged us to take advantage of this longevity.

## Social Integration

Schooling helps to forge a mass of people into a unified whole. This function is especially important in nations characterized by great social diversity, where various cultures are indifferent or even hostile to one another. The Soviet Union and Yugoslavia relied on schools to tie their disparate peoples together—without ultimately succeeding—and similar strains are emerging in the United States.

Societies in the Americas, Africa, and Asia, encompassing dozens of ethnic categories, all strive to foster social integration. Schools meet this challenge, first, by establishing a common language to encourage broad communication and forge a national identity. Of course, some ethnic minorities resist state-sponsored schooling precisely for this reason. In the Commonwealth of Independent States, for example, Lithuanians, Ukrainians, Azerbaijanis, and others long chafed at having to learn Russian, which they saw as emblematic of their domination by outsiders and a threat to their own traditions.

Similarly, the Amish, a culturally distinctive people in the United States, refuse to have their children taught in conventional public schools.

Despite resistance to schooling by certain segments of the population, the striking cultural diversity of the United States makes formal education a key path to social integration. A century ago, mandatory education laws coincided with the arrival of millions of immigrants. Even today, formal education plays a major role in integrating disparate groups, as people from Latin America and Asia blend their traditions with the existing cultural mix. By 1990, racial and ethnic minorities had formed a majority of the students in many of the largest school districts in the country and, across the nation, a debate over multicultural education (highlighted in Chapter 3, "Culture") was under way.

## Social Placement

Formal education helps young people assume culturally approved statuses and perform roles that contribute to the ongoing life of society. To accomplish this, schooling operates as a screening process that identifies and develops people's various aptitudes and abilities. Ideally, schools evaluate students' performance in terms of achievement while downplaying their social background. In this ideal scheme, the "best and the brightest" are encouraged to pursue the most challenging and advanced studies, while students of more pedestrian abilities are guided into educational programs and occupations suited to their talents. Schooling, in short, enhances meritocracy, linking social position to personal merit.

Meritocracy has always had special significance to people who begin life with social disadvantages based on ascribed traits such as sex, race, ethnicity, and social class. For this reason, schooling has historically been the major avenue of upward social mobility in the United States (Hurn, 1978).

## Latent Functions of Schooling

Besides these purposeful, manifest functions of formal education, a number of latent functions are less obvious and less widely recognized. One is child care. As the number of one-parent families and two-career marriages rises, schools have become vital to relieving parents of some child-care duties. Among teenagers, too, schooling

consumes much time and considerable energy, in many cases fostering conformity to conventional social norms at a time of life when the likelihood of unlawful behavior is high. And because many students attend school well into their twenties, education usefully engages thousands of young people for whom few jobs may be available.

Another latent function of schools is to establish social relationships and networks. High schools, colleges, and universities bring together people of marriageable age, many of whom meet their future spouse as a result. Affiliation with a particular school also forms the basis of social ties that provide not only friendship, but also valuable career opportunities and resources later on in life.

***Critical evaluation.*** Structural-functional analysis of formal education stresses the various ways in which this social institution supports the operation of an industrial society. This paradigm has usefully identified various manifest and latent functions of schooling.

One key limitation of functionalism is that it overlooks how the quality of schooling is far greater for some than for others. In the next section, social-conflict analysis places the spotlight squarely on this issue.

# Schooling and Social Inequality

Social-conflict analysis links formal education to patterns of social inequality. To some extent, schooling does seek to develop people's individual talents and abilities. But schools are hardly indifferent to social background, and actually perpetuate social inequality based on sex, race, ethnicity, and social class.

Throughout the world, people traditionally have thought that schooling is more important for males than for females. Chapter 13 ("Sex and Gender") explained that the education gap between women and men has been closing in recent decades, but many females and males still typically study conventionally feminine and masculine subjects. And by stressing the experiences of certain types of people (say, European men) while ignoring the lives of others in the same society, schools tend to reinforce the values and importance of dominant racial and cultural categories, to the detriment of minorities. As we shall see, too, affluent people in the United States have much more educational opportunity than their poorer counterparts.

From a functionalist point of view, schooling provides children with the information and skills they will need as adults. A conflict analysis adds that schooling also instills discipline and respect for authority, thereby molding the children of today into the docile labor force of tomorrow.

## Social Control

Social-conflict analysis suggests that schooling acts as a means of social control, encouraging acceptance of the status quo with its inherent inequities. In various, often subtle ways, schools serve to reproduce the status hierarchy, although this process is not always evident to students or even to teachers.

Samuel Bowles and Herbert Gintis (1976) point out that public education grew exponentially in the late nineteenth century when capitalists in the United States were seeking a docile, disciplined, and moderately educated work force. Mandatory education laws ensured that schools would teach immigrants with diverse cultural backgrounds the English language as well as cultural values supportive of capitalism. Compliance, punctuality, and discipline were—and still are—part of what is called the **hidden curriculum**, *ideas and behavior that support the status quo, taught in subtle ways to students.*

## Testing and Social Inequality

Here is a question of the kind traditionally used to measure the intelligence and academic ability of school-age children in the United States:

*Painter is to painting as ___ is to sonnet.*

*Answers:*    *(a) driver*
           *(b) poet*
           *(c) priest*
           *(d) carpenter*

The correct answer is (b) *poet*: a painter creates a painting as a poet creates a sonnet. This question purports to measure logical reasoning, but demonstrating this skill depends entirely on knowing what each term means. Unless students have been exposed to sonnets as a form of written verse, they are unlikely to answer the question correctly. An upper-middle-class student of European descent is likely to have more of the experiences rewarded by such tests. The same person, however, might not score as well on an intelligence test devised by the Native American Hopi of the Southwest! Controversy now surrounds the standardized tests used in the United States. Critics charge that such tests reflect our society's dominant culture, thereby placing people of color or other minorities at a disadvantage. Defenders acknowledge that the problem did exist, but maintain that it is now far less pronounced than in the past.

Ironically, intelligence tests were developed at the beginning of this century with the intention of fairly evaluating the innate ability of individuals, whatever their social background. In recent years, organizations that create these tests have carefully studied test results to eliminate the kinds of questions that seem to discriminate against certain categories of people. Any question that is found to discriminate on the basis of racial or ethnic background is deleted from future tests. Furthermore, The College Board—the organization that prepares the Scholastic Aptitude Test (SAT)—plans to supplement its traditional multiple-choice questions with open-ended tasks that it is hoped will provide a fairer measure of student ability. But some critics continue to charge that any standardized test will have questionable validity because scores will inevitably reflect a subject's cultural environment (Owen, 1985; Crouse & Trusheim, 1988; Putka, 1990).

## Tracking and Social Inequality

Despite the deficiencies of standardized tests, many schools in the United States use them as the basis for **tracking,** *the categorical assignment of students to different types of educational programs.* Tracking is also a common practice in many other industrial societies, including Great Britain, France, and Japan.

The educational justification for tracking is to give students the kind of schooling appropriate to their individual aptitude. For a variety of reasons, including innate ability and level of motivation, some students are capable of more challenging work than others are. Also, interests differ among students, with some seeking college preparatory classes, while others simply wish to acquire a general high-school education, and still others want to pursue job-related technical training. Thus a single program for all students would actually serve few of them well.

According to critics, however, tracking actually works to perpetuate privilege rather than to encourage or reward achievement. They point to research revealing social background has as much to do with tracking as individual merit (Bowles & Gintis, 1976; Persell, 1977; Davis & Haller, 1981; Oakes, 1982; Kilgore, 1991). Almost all students have the capacity to succeed in any educational program, asserts Jeannie Oakes (1985), but tracking—based on "scientific" testing—defines half of all students as below average. In practice, students from affluent families (who in the United States are disproportionately white) typically expect to be placed in college-bound tracks while those from modest backgrounds (the poor and people of color) are likely to end up learning a trade. Because students forge friendships with their classmates, tracking effectively socially segregates the advantaged from the disadvantaged (Hallinan & Williams, 1989).

Boys and girls in higher tracks benefit from teachers who put more effort into lessons, show their young charges more respect, and encourage them to think creatively and take an active role in class. By contrast, students in lower tracks contend with greater memorization, classroom drill, and other unstimulating teaching techniques. Lower tracks also emphasize regimentation, punctuality, and respect for authority figures.

In light of these criticisms, many schools across the United States are now cautious about making tracking assignments, and some schools have moved away from the practice entirely. Without tracking, however, less gifted children may be unable to compete with some of their classmates, and teachers face the difficult task of teaching students of differing abilities in one class. But these problems are not insurmountable; tracking, on the other hand, has a clear and strong impact on students' self-concept. Young people who spend years in higher tracks tend to see themselves as bright and able, whereas those in lower tracks develop lower ambition and self-esteem (Bowles & Gintis, 1976; Persell, 1977; Rosenbaum, 1980; Oakes, 1982, 1985).

## Inequality Among Schools

Just as students are treated differently within schools, entire schools vary among themselves. Private schools differ in many ways from public schools; public schools also vary from place to place.

### Public and Private Schools

In 1990 almost 90 percent of the 65 million students at the primary and secondary level in the United States attended state-funded public schools. The remainder were in private schools.

A majority of private-school students attend one of more than 8,000 *parochial schools* (from the Latin meaning "of the parish") operated by the Catholic Church. The Catholic school system grew rapidly late in the nineteenth century when cities swelled with millions of Catholic immigrants and their children. These schools helped the new arrivals maintain their religious heritage in the midst of a predominantly Protestant society. Today, after decades of flight from the city by whites, many parochial schools enroll non-Catholics, including a growing number of young African Americans whose families jump at this alternative to the neighborhood public school. Protestants, too, have private schools or Christian academies, but these are a more recent development among fundamentalist denominations. Both kinds of Christian schools are favored by parents who want their children to receive religious instruction or those who believe that these parochial schools hold students to higher academic and disciplinary standards (Zigli, 1984). Some parents have less honorable motives—a desire to maintain a racially homogeneous environment in the face of recent school desegregation mandates. This strategy has been especially strong among whites in the South, as government policies have significantly reduced public-school segregation (James, 1989).

Additionally, some 1,500 nonreligious private schools in the United States enroll students mostly from the upper classes. These prestigious and expensive preparatory schools are favored by families with established wealth, as well as "new money" parents eager for their daughters and sons to rub elbows with children of the "old rich." These institutions—many modeled on boarding schools in Great Britain—are academically outstanding and send a large share of their graduates to equally prestigious and expensive private universities. Prep schools, then, provide a strong academic program and also inculcate the mannerisms, attitudes, and social graces of the socially prominent. "Preppies" are likely to maintain lifelong social networks with other graduates of their school that provide numerous social advantages.

Private schools, research suggests, teach students more effectively than public schools do. Two influential reports (Coleman, Hoffer, & Kilgore, 1981; Coleman & Hoffer, 1987) indicate that students in private schools show higher rates of academic achievement than public-school students with similar social backgrounds. Private schools seem to generate greater interest in learning than do public schools, at least in schools with smaller class size and more extensive student-teacher contact. Furthermore, private schools are more academically demanding and enforce stringent disciplinary policies resulting in a safer, more orderly environment. By and large, graduates of private schools are more likely than public-school graduates to complete college and subsequently enter high-paying occupations. Some of this superlative achievement can be traced to advantages these children had to begin with, but it also reflects the high quality of elite education in the United States.

## Inequality in Public Schooling

Funds allocated to public schools across the United States vary considerably. Affluent communities spend more per pupil than poor ones do because they can afford to. Winnetka, Illinois—one of the richest areas in the United States—spends more than $8,000 annually per student compared to less than $3,000 spent in Socorro, Texas, one of the poorest. Although some of this disparity is offset by cost-of-living differences, it reflects the stark reality of unequal educational opportunities among the nation's 15,000 school districts (Carroll, 1990).

In 1966 a team of researchers headed by James Coleman completed an influential survey of educational inequality. They investigated 4,000 public schools across the United States and gathered survey data from 645,000 students. One clear pattern involved race: the researchers documented that the vast majority of students in this country attended racially segregated schools. They found racial segregation especially strong at the primary level, because the racial composition of schools mirrors that of their neighborhoods, which are typically racially homogeneous.

The Coleman report prompted the policy of *busing*—transporting students of one race to schools attended primarily by students of another race. This policy to equalize educational opportunities has been controversial ever since, although it directly affects only about 5 percent of all schoolchildren. Advocates assert that busing overcomes the educational effects of urban segregation. Only if more affluent white children attend schools across the entire city, the thinking goes, will adequate funds be available to schools in poorer neighborhoods. Critics point to the high cost of busing, the long periods of time students spend on buses, and claim that the policy undermines the concept of neighborhood schools. Additionally, any effective busing plan would have to span both the cities (where people of color are concentrated) and their suburbs (which are overwhelmingly white). Central cities, by themselves, simply lack the number of white students needed to make much difference in racial composition, with or without a busing program. Broad-based political resistance to busing has been strong enough to prevent the implementation of busing programs on a larger scale.

The Coleman report found that whites and blacks were schooled not only apart but unequally. Predominantly white schools were better funded, so there were fewer students per class, more science laboratories, foreign-language instruction, extensive libraries, and varied extracurricular programs. Steeped in this richer environment, white students showed significantly higher academic achievement than minority students did.

Coleman, however, argued that available funding was far from the key to high-quality education. In his view, other factors—the attitudes of teachers, the involvement of parents, and the orientation of peer groups—had a greater impact on academic achievement. He claimed that schools do not account primarily for the low academic performance of a significant segment of minority children, in other words, but rather the fault lies with a broad spectrum of economic and cultural disadvantages. Supporting this position, Christopher Jencks (1972) maintained that even if *educational* opportunity were equalized for all students in this country, academic performance would still be markedly unequal because some students have many more *social* advantages than others.

One conclusion is clear: schools alone cannot overcome the broad patterns of social inequality in the United States. Educational reform, therefore, will never by itself be sufficient to provide all young people with equal academic opportunities. The changes required are more sweeping, and would certainly provoke strong resistance. But the troubling reality is that the costs of ignoring the educational needs of poor minority children are going up because these young men and women represent a steadily increasing share of our nation's work force (Cohen, 1989). The interests of our entire society would be served by wide-ranging social reforms that boost educational opportunity for those historically denied this vital experience.

## Unequal Access to Higher Education

In the United States, people regard higher education as a path to occupational achievement. Not surprisingly, the vast majority of parents would send their children to college if they could (Gallup, 1982). While the proportion of people attending college has risen steadily during this century, it still falls far below our national aspirations. Currently, only 60 percent of high-school graduates enroll in college the following fall (U.S. Department of Education, 1991), and, as noted earlier, only about one-fifth of the population over twenty-five are college graduates.

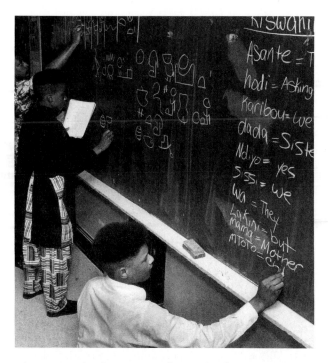

Afrocentric schooling is currently a topic of controversy in the United States. Proponents of this policy argue that teaching children African cultures—such as Egyptian hieroglyphics and Swahili vocabulary—will raise their self-esteem and strengthen their interest in learning. Critics respond that Afrocentrism promotes racial separation, precisely the problem that our nation has long struggled to overcome.

There are many reasons that most people in the United States do not graduate from college. Some high-school students want to enter the labor force right away; others simply do not wish to continue going to school despite parental encouragement. The intellectual demands of the college curriculum may also dissuade some students with limited talents. Yet most of our children would like to attend college, and doing so is certainly within the academic ability of the vast majority.

In the United States, the most crucial factor affecting access to higher education is money. Unlike primary and secondary schooling, which is supported by public funds, higher education must be purchased privately. The price is high and rapidly rising. Even at state colleges and universities (which do have government support), tuition is usually at least several thousand dollars a year, and in 1992 the annual costs at the most expensive private colleges and universities topped $20,000. Additionally, students face the extra costs of books, supplies, and travel. Against this backdrop of high prices, government cuts in student aid programs during the 1980s made college attendance for people with modest financial means less likely.

In some respects, we have moved closer to the goal of equal access to higher education in the United States. Chapter 13 ("Sex and Gender") noted that women and men now attend college in equal numbers. Low or moderate family income, however, remains a formidable barrier to both men and women who wish to enroll (Mare, 1981). Figure 16–1 shows, for different income levels, the proportion of families with young people aged eighteen to twenty-four who have one or more of these children in college. Almost two-thirds of such families earning more than $75,000 a year had a child on campus; by contrast, only 20 percent of those families earning under $10,000 a year managed to send a child to college (U.S. Bureau of the Census, 1991). Most colleges offer needy students some financial aid; but, even with a scholarship, many people still cannot afford the remaining costs. This problem worsened during the 1980s, a decade when real income declined for many families while college costs soared at a rate of approximately 8 percent annually (Evangelauf, 1987).

One result of these rising costs is that people of color—more of whom have below-average family incomes—have greater difficulty attending college. Figure 16–2 shows that whites are more likely than minorities to complete high school, and the disparity widens with each level upward in the educational system. During the 1980s, Hispanics made notable strides in higher education, with the number of students in college rising by roughly 50 percent. During this decade, however, the number of African-American students on campus remained steady (U.S. Bureau of the Census, 1991).

Even among those privileged enough to commence higher education, not everyone receives the same type and quality of schooling. People of limited financial means generally attend less expensive public community colleges and other government-supported schools. Certainly many students receive an excellent education in these public institutions. Community colleges also have some clear advantages, including a faculty whose primary concern is teaching rather than research. Private colleges and universities, supported by high tuition and endowments, allow for smaller classes and expose students to professors who may have national reputations. Also, a degree from a private college or university typically confers greater social prestige and admission to networks of more powerful people than one from a state-supported institution (cf. Monk-Turner, 1990).

**Figure 16–1** College Attendance and Family Income, 1990

*(U.S. Bureau of the Census, 1991)*

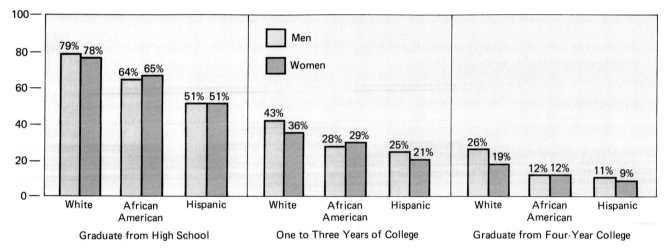

**Figure 16–2** Educational Achievement for Various Categories of People

(*U.S. Bureau of the Census, 1991*)

The most prestigious private universities are the eight Ivy League schools—Harvard, Yale, Princeton, Pennsylvania, Dartmouth, Cornell, Columbia, and Brown. A degree from any of these is likely to impress prospective employers and provide entree to social networks of influential people. In general, those who attend private institutions gain higher-prestige and higher-paying occupational positions than those who attend state schools (Monk-Turner, 1983; Useem & Karabel, 1986).

Before World War II, the majority of students in private colleges and universities were wealthy, white men. This was often a matter of policy, since some of these schools formally excluded women and limited the number of other minorities. Today equal-opportunity policies and financial aid have opened these institutions to a broader cross-section of the U.S. population. Socially advantaged students still predominate at private colleges and universities, but for decades now most have weighed individual talent more in relation to social background (Baltzell, 1976).

Whatever kind of college someone attends, higher education expands career opportunities and increases earnings. Table 16–2 shows median income for full-time workers age twenty-five and over according to their educational achievement. Women with an eighth-grade education typically earn $12,251 annually; income rises above $18,000 for high-school graduates and exceeds $28,000 for college graduates. The numbers in parentheses are ratios, showing that a woman with at least some graduate-school education earns 2.8 times as much

as her counterpart with only an eighth-grade education. While more schooling boosts income for men at the same rate, notice that men earn about 40 percent more than women do at every education level.

Certainly many people find schooling to be its own reward, opening minds to the fascinating world around us. The income figures shown here indicate that schooling is also a sound investment in financial terms, increasing income by hundreds of thousands of dollars over a person's working life. Bear in mind, of course, that the higher earnings of more educated people stem

**Table 16–2  MEDIAN INCOME BY SEX AND YEARS OF SCHOOLING***

| Schooling | Men | Women |
|---|---|---|
| Graduate school | $49,304 (2.8) | $33,750 (2.8) |
| College graduate | 39,238 (2.3) | 28,017 (2.3) |
| 1–3 years college | 31,734 (1.8) | 22,227 (1.8) |
| High-school graduate | 26,653 (1.5) | 18,319 (1.5) |
| 9–12 years | 20,902 (1.2) | 14,429 (1.2) |
| 8 years or less | 17,394 (1.0) | 12,251 (1.0) |

* Persons age twenty-five years and over, working full time, 1990. The earnings ratio, in parentheses, indicates how many times the lowest income level is earned by an individual with additional schooling.

SOURCE:  U.S. Bureau of the Census, 1991.

from more than schooling. As we have seen, college graduates are likely to come from relatively well-to-do families and to enjoy social and economic advantages that made college possible in the first place.

## Credentialism

Sociologist Randall Collins (1979) has dubbed the United States a *credential society*, suggesting that we take diplomas and degrees as evidence that a person can perform some specialized occupational role. As modern societies have become more technologically advanced, culturally diverse, and socially mobile, credentials have assumed some of the significance once attached to family background. That is, instead of sizing people up by asking who their parents are, we now check their resumes and count their degrees.

**Credentialism,** then, is *the requirement that a person hold some particular diploma or degree as a condition of employment.* Structural-functional analysis suggests that credentialism is simply the way our technologically complex society goes about ensuring that important jobs are filled by well-trained people. By contrast, social-conflict analysis holds that credentials often bear little relation to the skills and responsibilities of a specific job. Employers in an insurance agency, for example, may expect applicants for managerial positions to have a college degree, but they really do not expect them to know much about the insurance business—management trainees will go through the company's own training program.

Then why are degrees so important? Collins (1979) argues that they have a latent function of allowing in only the kind of people who will fit into the corporate world, with the manners and attitudes desirable for high-prestige occupations. Credentials, in short, work as a gate-keeping strategy that restricts powerful and lucrative occupations to a small segment of the population.

Finally, this emphasis on credentials in the United States has encouraged **overeducation,** *a situation in which workers have more formal education than the performance of their occupations requires.* Many new and specialized jobs obviously demand advanced schooling. Research indicates, however, that educational achievement has actually outpaced the demands of the labor market (Berg, 1970; Rumberger, 1981). This does not negate the intellectual value of schooling; rather, it simply points up the inconsistency between more and more schooling for our population and the expansion of low-skill service jobs over the last few decades, a trend described in Chapter 10 ("Social Class in the United States"). Why are we intent on gaining more education if available jobs do not require it? Val Burris (1983) suggests that if we define credentials as the key to getting a job, we will invest in schooling whether or not jobs demand it. One-fifth of the U.S. labor force, Burris estimates, is overly educated. This excessive schooling may make some dissatisfied with their jobs, but it does improve their chances of achieving better jobs and gaining access to a host of other opportunities for social advancement (Shockey, 1989).

## Privilege and Personal Merit

One of the themes of social-conflict analysis deserves to be highlighted: *schooling turns social privilege into personal merit.* Attending college, in other words, is more or less a right of passage for men and women from well-to-do families, and a real challenge for young people from families with fewer financial resources and whose parents have little experience with the world of higher education.

But our cultural emphasis on individualism pushes us to see credentials as "badges of ability" as Richard Sennett and Jonathan Cobb (1973) put it, rather than as symbols of family affluence. While some people certainly rise from modest beginnings by studying long and hard, we need to recognize that when we congratulate the typical new graduate, we usually overlook the social resources that made this achievement possible. In the same way, we are quick to condemn the high-school dropout as personally deficient with little thought to the social circumstances that surround that person's life. The box illustrates the process of transforming social disadvantage into personal deficiency in the life of one bright but disillusioned boy.

***Critical evaluation.*** Social-conflict analysis explores formal education in terms of social inequality. Thus we see that schooling is unequal for different categories of people; schooling can also serve to transform privilege into personal ability and social disadvantage into personal deficiency.

Social-conflict analysis can be criticized for ignoring how different kinds of schooling may actually meet the needs of socially and individually diverse students. This approach also minimizes the extent to which schooling develops everyone's talents and abilities. Finally, without denying that personal ability and privilege are

# "Cooling Out" the Poor: Transforming Disadvantage into Deficiency

Thomas J. Cottle gives voice to the struggle of one young man to establish a positive self-image in the face of negative labeling by his school's system of tracking.

Disadvantaged students are often labeled as "dumb" in school, and, over time, some even come to accept the notion that they are personally deficient. This process of "cooling out" aspirations for themselves sets in motion a self-fulfilling prophecy by which they seem to deserve no more than

what society handed them when they were born. Eleven-year-old Ollie Taylor describes his situation in these words:

> The only thing that matters in my life is school and there they think I'm dumb and always will be. I'm starting to think they're right. Hell, I know they put all the black kids together in one group if they can, but that doesn't make any difference either. I'm still dumb. Even if I look around and know that I'm the smartest in my group, all that

means is that I'm the smartest of the dumbest, so I haven't got anywhere at all, have I? I'm right where I always was. Every word those teachers tell me, even the ones I like most, I can hear in their voice that what they're really saying is "All right you dumb kids. I'll make it as easy as I can, and if you don't get it then, you'll never get it. Ever." That's what I hear every day, man. From every one of them. Even the other kids talk that way to me too.

SOURCE: Cottle (1974):22–24.

closely linked, there has always been considerable meritocracy in our educational system, and the historical record shows that schooling has led to upward social mobility for many talented women and men.

## Problems in the Schools

The 1980s was a decade of intense debate about schooling in the United States. Attitudes about our public schools were mixed, as shown in Table 16–3. Few people believe that public schools are doing an excellent job; about half of survey respondents gave the public schools a grade of C or below (Elam, Rose, & Gallup, 1991). Certainly, violence and lack of discipline pose serious problems in many schools. In addition, many students tend to be passive, displaying little interest in learning. Taking a longer view, the record indicates that academic standards at all levels of formal education have declined in recent decades.

### School Discipline

Adults in the United States overwhelmingly think that schools should inculcate personal discipline (N.O.R.C., 1991:490). But many suspect that the job is not being

done properly. This suspicion is supported by some disturbing facts. The government estimates that several hundred thousand students and at least one thousand teachers are physically assaulted on school grounds every year. About one-fourth of students attending school in central cities voice a fear of being attacked going to or from school; roughly the same proportion claim they fear phys-

**Table 16–3  GRADING PUBLIC SCHOOLS IN THE UNITED STATES**

| Rating | Proportion of Respondents |
|--------|---------------------------|
| A | 10% |
| B | 32 |
| C | 33 |
| D | 10 |
| FAIL | 5 |
| Don't know | 10 |

These figures reflect the responses of a national sample of U.S. adults to the question: Students are often given the grades A, B, C, D, and FAIL to denote the quality of their work. Suppose the public schools themselves, in this community, were graded in the same way. What grade would you give the public schools here—A, B, C, D, or FAIL?

SOURCE: Stanley M. Elam, Lowell C. Rose, and Alec M. Gallup, "The 23rd Annual Gallup Poll of the Public's Attitudes Toward Public Schools," *Phi Delta Kappan*, Vol. 73 (September 1991):54.

ical attack *while in school*. The National Education Association reports that three-fourths of their members consider discipline to be a major problem in their classrooms (McGrath, 1984; U.S. Bureau of Justice Statistics, 1991).

Such disorder is not necessarily the fault of the schools: the classroom is only a small part of a larger—and often violent—society. As Chapter 8 ("Deviance") explained, our nation is among the most violent in the world, and disorder is epidemic in communities of the desperately poor. In large cities like Chicago, for example, more than half the children who attend public schools live in households below the poverty line. Inevitably, much violence spills over into the schools. Nevertheless, schools do have the power to effect change for the better.

Early in the 1980s, for example, Thomas Jefferson High School in Los Angeles was plagued by violence, drug abuse, and vandalism. In 1982 Francis Nakano became principal and set out to instill discipline and improve the school's view of itself. Officials refurbished the building to improve its physical appearance, and Nakano and his staff held students personally responsible for any disorder. Gang leaders, at the center of much of the disruption, were informed that violence would be suppressed by all means necessary. These changes brought a remarkable turnaround: Jefferson High is now getting on with the business of education (McGrath, 1984).

Examples of such constructive change can be found throughout the country. The key to success appears to lie in firm disciplinary policies, supported by parents and, when necessary, law enforcement officials (Burns, 1985). Schools are unlikely to solve problems of violence and drug abuse that have roots deep in society itself (Reed, 1983), but they can broaden their power to control violence by forming alliances with parents and community leaders.

## Bureaucracy and Student Passivity

A problem more specific to schools themselves is pervasive *student passivity*. Most young women and men do not take an active role in their own learning. This problem is not confined to any particular type of school: it can be found in private as well as public schools and at all grade levels (Coleman, Hoffer, & Kilgore, 1981).

Schooling is a wonderful opportunity, and one that is rare in human history. In medieval Europe, children assumed many adult responsibilities before they

In some cities of the United States, the level of violence has escalated to the point that parents fear for their children not only while traveling to and from school but also while *in* school. These two brothers, aged 4 and 5, set off for school in New York City wearing bulletproof jackets.

were teenagers; a century ago, children in the United States worked long hours for little pay in factories, on farms, and in coal mines. Today, by contrast, the major task facing young people is to study their human heritage—to learn the effective use of language, master the manipulation of numbers, and acquire knowledge and skills that will enhance their comprehension, enjoyment, and participation in the surrounding world.

Yet many students perceive schooling less as a privilege than as a series of hurdles to be mechanically cleared in pursuit of credentials. In short, students are bored. Some of the blame must be placed on students themselves and on other factors like television, which now consumes more of young people's time than school does. Even so, pervasive student passivity is also a product of our educational system.

In the nineteenth century, most children lived in small communities where they were taught in one-room schoolhouses. As the United States became more urbanized and the costs of schooling rose, and as state governments began to oversee the educational process, many local schools were dissolved in favor of large regional schools. Such schools have reduced per-student costs through economies of scale and fostered greater curricular uniformity, but they have also generated numbing impersonality. For better and worse, then, schools at all levels now reflect the bureaucratic organization that typifies our entire society.

After studying high schools across the United States, Theodore Sizer (1984) acknowledged that the bureaucratic structure of schools is necessary to meet the massive educational demands of our vast and complex society. Yet he found that a bureaucratic educational system fosters five serious problems (1984:207–9).

First, *bureaucratic uniformity* ignores the social diversity of the United States. It takes schools out of the local community and places them under the control of outside "specialists" who may have little understanding of the everyday lives of students.

Second, bureaucratic schools define success in terms of *numerical performance ratings*. School officials focus on attendance rates, dropout rates, and achievement test scores. In doing so, they overlook dimensions of schooling that are difficult to quantify, such as the creativity of students and the energy and enthusiasm of teachers. Bureaucratic school systems tend to define an adequate education in terms of the number of days (or even minutes) per year that students spend inside a school building rather than probing the school's contribution to students' personal development.

Third, bureaucratic schools have *rigid expectations* of all students. For example, fifteen-year-olds are thought to belong in the tenth grade, and eleventh-grade students are expected to score at a certain level on a standardized verbal achievement test. The high-school diploma thus rewards a student for going through the proper sequence of educational activities in the proper amount of time. Rarely are exceptionally bright and motivated students allowed to graduate early. Likewise, the system tends to push along students who learn little in school—even some who are illiterate in high school—so they graduate with their class.

Fourth, the school's bureaucratic *division of labor* requires specialized personnel. High-school students learn Spanish from one teacher, receive guidance from another, and are coached in sports by others. No school official comes to know and appreciate the "whole" student as a complex human being. Students experience this division of labor as a continual shuffling among rigidly divided fifty-minute periods throughout the school day.

Fifth, the highly bureaucratic school system gives students *little personal responsibility* for learning. Similarly, teachers have little latitude in what and how they teach their classes; they dare not teach algebra to eighth-graders if the school considers this a tenth-grade skill. Any attempt to accelerate learning risks punishment for

disrupting "the system." Such standardized policies render many teachers as passive and unimaginative as their students.

Several factors have contributed to the expansion and entrenchment of school bureaucracy. Formal organization, Sizer claims, was needed to meet the needs of the rapid influx of immigrant children during the last century, and the numbers have continued to grow since then. The student population of New York City alone, for example, now exceeds that of the entire United States in 1900. Cultural values are also at work: Americans tend to believe that the most effective way to accomplish any task is to formulate a system, and for better or worse, that is precisely what formal education in the United States has become.

But by discouraging initiative and creativity bureaucracy sets the stage for student passivity. One solution, described in Chapter 7 ("Groups and Organizations"), is to *humanize bureaucracy* or, in this case, to humanize schools. Sizer recommends eliminating rigid class schedules, reducing class size, and training teachers more broadly to enable them to become more fully involved in the lives of their students. His most radical suggestion is that graduation from high school should depend on what a student has learned rather than simply on the length of time spent in school.

## College: The Silent Classroom[1]

Here are the observations of a bright and highly motivated first-year student at a high-quality four-year college. Do they strike a familiar chord?

> I have been disappointed in my first year at college. Too many students do as little work as they can get away with, take courses that are recommended by other students as being "gut" classes, and never challenge themselves past what is absolutely necessary. It's almost like thinking that we don't watch professors but we watch television. (Forrest, 1984:10)

As this student observes, passivity is also common in colleges and universities. Sociologists have done little research on the college classroom—a curious fact considering how much time they spend there. One study carried out by David Karp and William Yoels (1976) shows

---

[1] The phrase "silent classroom" was coined by Martha E. Gimenez (1989).

that patterns of interaction in the college classroom are remarkably predictable, involving little student initiative and minimal creative thinking.

Karp and Yoels conducted a survey of students and systematically observed classes at a coeducational university. They attended seminars as well as lectures. Although the small classes had slightly more student participation, in most cases only four or five students made more than one comment during a class period, which amounted to three-fourths of the interaction in the class. In larger classes, only two or three students took an active role, generating more than half the discussion. In short, Karp and Yoels found that passivity is a classroom norm; students themselves become irritated when one of their number is especially talkative.

Gender also affects classroom dynamics. Karp and Yoels note that, in coeducational classes taught by a man, male students initiated and participated in most class discussion. With women as instructors, however, the two sexes were more equal in terms of active participation. Many women are apparently more comfortable in a class taught by a woman. Why? Perhaps because women instructors directed questions to women students as frequently as to men, while male teachers favored their male students.

Students offered various explanations for classroom passivity; these are listed in Table 16–4. Note that they saw passivity as mostly their own fault, which is, to some degree, a case of the victims of bureaucratic schooling blaming themselves. Long before reaching college,

Karp and Yoels explain, students are taught to view instructors as "experts" who serve up "truth." Thus they find little value in classroom discussion or debate and perceive their proper role as quietly listening and taking notes. This explains the finding of Karp and Yoels that only 10 percent of class time is devoted to discussion.

Students also know that instructors generally come to class ready to deliver a prepared lecture. The lecture format allows instructors to present a great deal of material in each class, so in their view, student questions or comments merely distract from the planned material (Boyer, 1987). Faculty lectures, then, are designed to accommodate only a few questions in class. Early in each course a handful of students are recognized by everyone as the ones ready and able to provide whatever limited responses instructors desire. Taken together, these facts have a single consequence: passivity on the part of the majority of college students.

## Dropping Out

If many students are passive in class, others are not there at all. The problem of *dropping out*—quitting school before completing a high-school diploma—leaves young people (many of whom are disadvantaged to begin with) ill-equipped for the world of work and at high risk for poverty.

The dropout rate has eased slightly in recent decades. In 1970, 12.2 percent of people between the ages

**Table 16–4** STUDENT EXPLANATIONS OF CLASSROOM PASSIVITY

|  | Men | | Women | |
|---|---|---|---|---|
|  | Percent | Rank | Percent | Rank |
| I had not done the reading assignment | 80.9 | 1 | 76.3 | 2 |
| The feeling that I didn't know enough about the subject matter | 79.6 | 2 | 84.8 | 1 |
| The large size of the class | 70.4 | 3 | 68.9 | 4 |
| The feeling that my ideas were not well enough formulated | 69.8 | 4 | 71.1 | 3 |
| The course simply isn't meaningful to me | 67.3 | 5 | 65.1 | 5 |
| The chance that I would appear unintelligent in the eyes of the teacher | 43.2 | 6 | 41.4 | 7 |
| The chance that I would appear unintelligent in the eyes of other students | 42.9 | 7 | 45.4 | 6 |
| The small size of the class | 31.0 | 8 | 33.6 | 8 |
| The possibility that my comments might negatively affect my grade | 29.6 | 9 | 24.3 | 9 |
| The possibility that other students might not respect my point of view | 16.7 | 10 | 12.5 | 11 |
| The possibility that the teacher might not respect my point of view | 12.3 | 11 | 12.5 | 10 |

SOURCE: David A. Karp and William C. Yoels, "The College Classroom: Some Observations on the Meaning of Student Participation," *Sociology and Social Research*, Vol. 60, No. 4 (July 1976), 108.

of 14 and 24 had left school; in 1990, the comparable figure was 10.7 percent. There has been modest improvement, but our schools still fail to engage the interest of more than 4 million young people enough to keep them in the classroom. The problem of dropping out is least pronounced among whites (10.5 percent), slightly greater among African Americans (11.4 percent), and the most serious among Hispanics (27.9 percent) (U.S. Bureau of the Census, 1991).

On the surface, dropping out of school stems from low academic achievement, but there are many reasons students reach this point. For many Spanish-speaking students, a limited ability to speak English—and, therefore, to comprehend the material being taught—is the basic problem (Suro, 1990). For women of all racial and ethnic categories, becoming pregnant can transform school into an insurmountable barrier. For both women and men who are poor, the need to work sometimes crowds out the time and energy needed to do homework and go to class. Disproportionately, young people who drop out of school have parents with little schooling themselves. Thus, low educational achievement often takes the form of a multi-generational cycle of disadvantage.

For young people who drop out of school in a credential-based society, the risks of unemployment or becoming stuck in a low-paying job are easy to imagine. Faced with this reality, approximately one-third of those who leave school return to the classroom at a later time.

## Academic Standards and Educational Quality

Because classroom passivity has become the norm in the United States, it is not a problem that alarms many students or troubles the public at large. More controversial is the general decline in student academic performance.

A comprehensive report on the quality of education in the United States was issued in 1983 by the National Commission on Excellence in Education. The title, A Nation at Risk, suggests the intensity of the problem, and the researchers begin with strong language:

> If an unfriendly foreign power had attempted to impose on America the mediocre educational performance that exists today, we might well have viewed it as an act of war. As it stands, we have allowed this to happen to ourselves. (1983:5)

Numerous facts support this conclusion. The average scores on standardized achievement tests, including the Scholastic Aptitude Test (SAT), began to decline in the early 1960s. Then, average scores for students in this country stood at about 500 on the mathematical test and 480 on the verbal test; by 1991, the averages had slipped to 474 and 422. Educators have advanced various explanations for this disturbing trend, including the fact that a broader segment of students—some of whom are less well prepared—now take the college boards (Owen, 1985). Whatever the reasons, few doubt that schooling has suffered a setback.

A Nation at Risk also notes with alarm the extent of **functional illiteracy**, *reading and writing skills insufficient for everyday living.* Roughly one in eight children in the United States completes secondary school without learning to read or write very well. For young people of color, the report continued, the proportion is more than one in three. The box on page 460 provides a closer look at this serious national problem.

As important as basic skills are, schools must also develop the capacity for abstract and critical thinking. Yet the report of the National Commission on Excellence in Education claims that "nearly 40 percent of seventeen-year-olds cannot draw inferences from written material; only one-fifth can write a persuasive essay; and only one-third can solve mathematical problems requiring several steps" (1983:9).

A Nation at Risk recommends drastic changes in our schools. First it calls for more rigorous requirements: schools must ensure that every student take several years of English, mathematics, social studies, general science, and computer science courses. Second, schools at all levels must raise their academic standards and cease tolerating a failure to teach. Third, schools should keep students as long as necessary to teach basic skills. Fourth, communities must raise teachers' salaries to attract better people to this profession, and improve teacher training by supporting those who enrich their own education through further study and research. A Nation at Risk concludes that educators must ensure that schools meet all these goals, and the public must be willing to provide resources sufficient to support good schools.

A final concern is the low performance of U.S. students in global context. The poor showing can be traced to all the issues already raised, but it may also reflect the fact that children spend fewer days in school each year in the United States than they do in almost every other industrial country. As Figure 16–3 illustrates, European countries require up to 30 more days of school-

## Functional Illiteracy: Must We Rethink Education?

Imagine being unable to read labels on cans of food, instructions for assembling a child's toy, the dosage on a medicine bottle, or even the information on your own paycheck. These are some of the debilitating experiences of *functional illiteracy*, reading and writing skills inadequate for carrying out everyday responsibilities.

As schooling became universal in the United States, the U.S. government confidently concluded that illiteracy has been all but eliminated. The truth of the matter—now acknowledged by the government—is that some 25 million adults read and write at no more than a fourth-grade level, and another 25 million have only eighth-grade language skills. Overall, about one in four adults in the United States is functionally illiterate, and the proportion is higher among the elderly and minorities.

Functional illiteracy is a complex social problem. It is caused partly by an educational system that passes children from one grade to the next whether they learn or not. Another cause is community indifference to local schools that prevents parents and teachers from working together to improve children's learning. Still another cause is that millions of children grow up with illiterate parents who offer little encouragement to learn language skills.

Functional illiteracy costs our society more than $100 billion a year. This cost includes decreased productivity (by workers who perform their jobs improperly) and increased accidents (by people unable to understand written

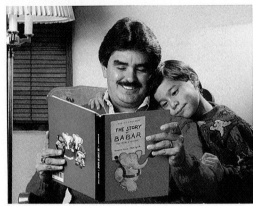

## Paco learned to read last year. So did Dad.

Literacy
Volunteers
of America, Inc.

The problem of illiteracy in the United States is most serious among Hispanics. In part this is due to a dropout rate among fourteen- to twenty-four-year-olds of almost 30 percent, which is three times the rate among whites or African Americans. The broader issue is that schools fail to teach many Spanish-speaking people to read and write any language very well.

instructions). It also reflects the costs of supporting those unable to read and write well enough to find work and end up receiving public assistance or in prison.

Correcting this national problem requires one approach for young people and another for adults. To stop functional illiteracy before it happens, the public must demand that children not be graduated from school until they have learned basic language skills. For adults, the answer begins with diagnosis—a difficult task since many feel shame at their plight and avoid disclosing their need for help. Once such people are identified, however, adult education programs must be provided.

Our society is one of the richest and most powerful nations on earth, yet more than a dozen other countries have a more literate population than we do. For those living in a world of incomprehensible symbols, functional illiteracy is a personal disaster; for all of us, it is an urgent national problem.

SOURCE: Based on Kozol (1980, 1985).

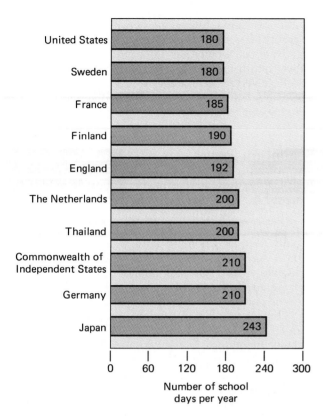

**Figure 16–3**  Length of the School Year by Country
(*Education Commission of the States*)

ing each year than we do; in Japan, youngsters spend 60 more days in school.

# Recent Issues in U.S. Education

Our nation's schools must continuously respond to changing demands, new challenges, and technological innovation. We will conclude this chapter with a brief look at several recent and significant educational issues.

## Magnet Schools

One response to the educational problems we have described is the concept of **magnet schools,** *schools that attract students through special facilities and programs promoting educational excellence.* Magnet schools, first begun in the 1970s, enrich educational opportunities by improving school buildings and providing intensive

learning in subjects like computer science, foreign languages, or science and mathematics. There are now over a thousand magnet schools throughout the country.

One goal of magnet schools is better learning, and the record here is positive. Better facilities and the expectation of higher achievement have helped magnet schools raise the academic achievement of their students. In some cases, schools plagued by high drop-out rates now find students eagerly coming to class and regularly completing homework assignments.

Proponents of magnet schools also hoped that they would enhance racial integration by making inner-city schools more attractive to more affluent people—especially whites—likely to send their children to private schools. Magnet schools thus formed the centerpiece of a strategy for voluntary integration, making court-ordered busing unnecessary. But the performance of magnet schools in this respect has been mixed. Some cities have reported reductions in segregation since whites and blacks alike are drawn to quality schools. But this is the exception more than the rule. In 1989, for example, Kansas City concluded that there were simply not enough white students left to allow racial balance in schools. To meet court orders for racial balance in their magnet schools, therefore, the city had to limit enrollment of African Americans to roughly the available number of whites (King, 1989). While magnet schools are a promising development, then, they are unlikely to solve the deeply entrenched problem of racial segregation in our educational system.

## Schooling the Disabled

Mandatory education laws not only require children to attend school, they also symbolize our national obligation to provide a basic education for everyone. Nevertheless, millions of young people with mental and physical disabilities receive little or no schooling. A highly bureaucratized system of mass education does not meet the needs of many children with disabilities and too often dismisses them as simply uneducable.

Providing an education for disabled children unquestionably poses a challenge. Some children with physical disabilities have difficulty getting to and from school, and those who use crutches or wheelchairs cannot negotiate stairs and other obstacles inside school buildings. Children with developmental disabilities like mental retardation, and those who suffer from emotional problems, require extensive personal attention from teachers with specialized training. As a result, many children with mental and physical disabilities have received a public education only after persistent efforts by parents and other concerned citizens. In 1990, about 5 million children, with a wide range of disabilities, were attending school in the United States.

About one-fourth of these children are schooled in special facilities. Recently, however, more educators have been advocating a policy of **mainstreaming**, *integrating students with disabilities into the educational program as a whole*. Mainstreaming, an alternative to segregated "special education" classes containing only disabled students, varies depending on students' disabilities. Some mainstreamed students receive quite a bit of extra attention in the classroom, while others are treated just like everyone else. Mainstreaming works best for students with physical disabilities who have no difficulty keeping up academically with the rest of the class. These students benefit from the broadest educational experiences within the limits of their abilities. Moreover, in a mainstreamed setting children with disabilities learn how to interact with other children and, just as important, other children learn how to interact with them.

Mainstreaming is less feasible for students with serious mental, developmental, or emotional disabilities, however. These individuals may have great difficulty matching the performance of other students, and they may simultaneously be deprived of special education appropriate to their needs. Under any circumstance, mainstreaming is an expensive undertaking, requiring changes in physical facilities and the hiring of teachers capable of meeting the needs of children with disabilities.

## Adult Education

Many people think that schooling affects only children and adolescents. In recent decades, however, a growing proportion of the adult population has enrolled in school, some returning after a considerable period of time.

By 1990, almost 25 million adults—more than ever before—were enrolled in some type of school. The women and men range in age from the twenties to well past sixty-five; some are taking an art class at a local community center, while others are attending college full time.

What prompts adults to return to school? There are as many reasons as there are students, but usually the motivation is work-related. Many pursue areas of study directly linked to their careers. Almost 25 percent

of adult education students are studying business; another 25 percent are enrolled in courses in health and engineering (National Center for Education Statistics, 1989). Others return to school to earn a high-school diploma or college degree because they recognize its occupational advantages. Still others go back to school simply in search of intellectual stimulation.

## School for Profit

Betty Castor, the Commissioner of Education in Florida, proposed in 1991 that one of her state's school systems be turned over to private companies to be operated as a profit-making business. Because our society has traditionally viewed schooling as a public responsibility, "school for profit" has provoked controversy. But the approach—which has been publicly endorsed by President George Bush—is gaining favor as frustration mounts over the currently weak state of public education.

Private schooling is nothing new, of course; more than 10,000 schools are operated by private organizations and religious groups. In addition, preschooling and vocational training have long been offered by profit-seeking companies. What is new is that private companies are now beginning to provide mass education that some people think will be of higher quality than established public school systems.

The debate over schools for profit is part of the larger *"educational choice"* movement, which emerged during the 1980s. In essence, supporters of educational choice argue that public schools perform inefficiently because they have no competition. Some proponents of this view seek tax credits or cash from the government for parents to spend on the school of their choice; Milwaukee began a similar plan in 1990. Under such a system, the thinking goes, public schools would be forced to perform better in order to win the confidence of families. Another direction being pursued by enterprising educators is to open schools for profit and hope that enough parents are willing to pay tuition over and above their school taxes. Chris Whittle, head of a large media corporation that includes a commercial television channel for the classroom, has taken the lead in this area with plans to open some 200 schools for profit in the next five years.

Few would argue that many public school systems suffer from bureaucratic bloat that forces costs up and holds performance down. Proponents of school for profit think they have found the answer to both these problems by creating an educational marketplace. In addition, they add, such a plan gives parents a financial incentive to monitor the academic performance of their children's school. But critics of the school-for-profit idea worry, first, that this trend will allow commercialism to subvert the educational process and, second, that it will also result in a two-tier educational system, with affluent children enjoying far better schooling while poor children are left further behind (Putka, 1991; Toch, 1991).

## Schooling, Computers, and the Future

Oblivious to the final bell that has already rung at Benjamin Franklin Junior High in Ridgewood, New Jersey, some students remain engrossed in their work. This reaction may sound unusual, and it is. The explanation for such intense student interest is Benjamin Franklin's computer science program. George Mamunes is completing a program that will graphically display every part of the human heart; Pam Miller is developing a simulation of a nuclear reactor; Meilin Wong is debugging a business management system; Jim McGuire is enjoying a video game he created on his own. Teacher Bob Muller explains this schoolroom scene: "No one told [the students] they have to be here. They're not usually doing assignments. They're experimenting. They're letting their imaginations run free" (Golden, 1982:51).

Just as the Industrial Revolution had a major impact on schooling in the nineteenth century, formal education is now being transformed by computers and the Information Revolution. Computers are already used in virtually every occupation; therefore, this new information technology is now a mainstay of the school curriculum. By 1990, more than 95 percent of schools reported having instructional computers and, across the country, there was one computer for every sixteen students. Currently, government data indicate that about 44 percent of boys and 42 percent of girls use computers in school, although the proportion rises and falls with the income level typical of any given school. Among affluent children with annual household incomes over $80,000, half use computers

in the classroom; among those with incomes of only $15,000, the figure slips to 38 percent. White children are the most likely to use computers (46 percent), while this opportunity is less available to Hispanic (43 percent) and African-American (33 percent) children (U.S. Bureau of the Census, 1991).

Computers can help students learn more than job-related skills; they can improve the overall quality of learning. More and more, students and computers are interacting with one another, which has the advantage of making students more active learners as well as allowing them to progress at their own pace. For disabled students unable to write with pencil and paper, computers permit easier self-expression. The introduction of computers into schools—in some cases, as early as kindergarten—appears to significantly increase learning speed and retention of information (Fantini, 1986).

The enthusiasm sparked by computers should not blind us to their limitations, however. Computers will never bring to the educational process the personal insight into the needs of individual students that a qualified and motivated human teacher will. Also a computer is of little value in many areas of traditional education. As one educator notes, "There's a whole world of real problems, of human problems, which is essentially being ignored." Another teacher fears that students will be "out of touch with certain springs of human identity and creativity, which belong to the full use of language rather than mathematical and symbolical codes" (Golden, 1982:56).

Some analysts point out that, while the number of computers in schools across the United States has doubled since 1985, they have yet to change teaching and learning in any fundamental sense or to replace the traditional blackboard (Berger, 1991; Elmer-Dewitt, 1991). Moreover, the introduction of computers into the educational system will not solve many of the problems that plague our schools. Yet the evidence suggests that teachers and students using this new technology are steadily exploring new ways to engage in learning. There seems little doubt that computers will significantly shape the classrooms of the twenty-first century.

## Summary

1. Education is a major social institution for transmitting knowledge and skills, as well as teaching cultural norms and values, to young people. In preindustrial societies, education occurs informally within the family; industrial societies are characterized by formal schooling.

2. The United States was among the first countries to embrace compulsory mass education, reflecting

both democratic political ideals and the needs of the industrial-capitalist economy. The educational system has also been shaped by cultural values such as practicality, efficiency, and competitive individualism.

3. Structural-functional analysis, which highlights the role of schooling in socialization, delves into how formal education promotes social integration, places people in the social hierarchy, and encourages cultural innovation. Latent functions of schooling include child care and forging lasting personal relationships.

4. Social-conflict analysis points out that the opportunity for formal education is unequally distributed across the population. This approach also explains that schooling acts as a means of social control, instilling the value of discipline that produces compliant adult workers.

5. Critics have charged that standardized intelligence tests are culturally biased in favor of some categories of people while placing others at a disadvantage.

6. Allegedly based on individual talents, tracking is also strongly related to students' social background. Tracking confers greater educational resources on more privileged students, thereby perpetuating social inequality and transforming social privilege into personal merit.

7. The great majority of girls and boys in the United States attend state-funded public schools. Most privately funded schools are affiliated with religious organizations. A very small proportion of young people—generally of privileged social background—attend private preparatory schools.

8. School districts across the United States vary in the resources allocated to each student. Although research shows that spending money is no guarantee of educational quality, schools in affluent settings typically offer a richer, more well-rounded education than those in poorer areas.

9. Today one-fifth of the U.S. population over the age of twenty-five are college graduates. Most attended state-funded institutions; private colleges and universities are usually much more expensive and enroll students from wealthier families. A college degree greatly increases lifetime earnings.

10. The United States is a "credential society." By requiring degrees for higher-paying occupations, employers ensure that workers have learned norms and attitudes appropriate to the business setting. Since degrees are expensive, those able to afford higher education are also more likely, ultimately, to obtain the most desirable occupational positions.

11. Many people are critical of public schools. School violence is a highly visible problem, especially in poor neighborhoods. The bureaucratic character of our schools has also fostered widespread student passivity. In addition, millions of young women and men drop out of school; this places them at high risk of unemployment and poverty.

12. Declining academic standards, a major educational problem in the United States, are reflected in lower average scores on academic achievement tests and functional illiteracy among a significant proportion of high-school graduates.

13. The magnet school, a recent innovation, has improved education in some cities. These schools, however, have not significantly lessened racial segregation in our educational system.

14. Children with physical, mental, and developmental disabilities traditionally have been schooled in special classes or not at all. In recent years, mainstreaming has afforded these students greater educational opportunities.

15. Adults represent a growing proportion of students in the United States. Most of these older learners are engaged in job-related study.

16. As part of the educational choice movement, profit-making schools are beginning to spring up in the United States. Proponents hope they will make established school systems more competitive; critics fear they will generate greater educational inequality.

17. As an educational tool, computers can be highly effective, but they are not suitable for teaching every subject.

## Key Concepts

**credentialism** the requirement that a person hold an advanced degree as a condition of employment

**education** the various ways in which knowledge—including factual information and occupational skills as well as cultural norms and values—is transmitted to members of a society

**functional illiteracy** the lack of basic reading and writing skills needed for everyday life

**hidden curriculum** ideas and behavior that support the status quo, taught in subtle ways to students

**magnet schools** schools that attract students through special facilities and programs promoting educational excellence

**mainstreaming** the integration of students with disabilities into the educational program as a whole

**mandatory education laws** legal requirements that chil-

dren receive a minimum of formal education

**overeducation** a situation in which workers have more formal education than the performance of their occupations requires

**schooling** formal instruction under the direction of specially trained teachers

**tracking** categorically assigning students to different types of educational programs

## Suggested Readings

This textbook is a good resource for the sociological analysis of education.

Jeanne H. Ballantine. *The Sociology of Education.* 2nd ed. Englewood Cliffs, NJ: Prentice Hall, 1989.

The first of the following books on schooling and gender examines how academia is being transformed by feminist thinking. The second book, based on the lives of sixty-two women, asserts that women continue to have a marginal existence in the academic world.

Carol S. Pearson, Donna L. Shavik, and Judith G. Touchton. *Educating the Majority: Women Challenge Tradition in Higher Education.* New York: Macmillan, 1989.

Nadya Aisenberg and Mona Harrington. *Women of Academe: Outsiders in the Sacred Grove.* Amherst: The University of Massachusetts Press, 1988.

The computer is not the only example of technology changing the classroom. Television is being utilized in more and more ways in college classes, as this book explains.

James Zigerell. *The Uses of Television in American Higher Education.* New York: Greenwood Press, 1991.

The first of these books is a best-seller that helped launch the current debate over "political correctness" on the college campus. The second echoes these conservative sentiments, indicting "PC" for undermining higher education.

Allan Bloom. *The Closing of the American Mind: How Higher Education Has Failed Democracy and Impoverished the Souls of Today's Students.* New York: Simon & Schuster, 1987.

Dinesh D'Souza. *Illiberal Education: The Politics of Race and Sex on Campus.* New York: The Free Press, 1991.

These researchers investigate how a "culture of romance" erodes the career aspirations of women on the college campus.

Dorothy C. Holland and Margaret A. Eisenhart. *Educated in Romance: Women, Achievement, and College Culture.* Chicago: University of Chicago Press, 1990.

In recent years the educational system of the United States has been the subject of considerable criticism and debate. The first book listed below is a comprehensive government report on schooling that framed debate during the 1980s; the second offers a critical appraisal by a man who has spent his

life in administrative positions in many levels of schools; the third is the critical report of the Carnegie Foundation on higher education in the United States.

The National Commission on Excellence in Education. *A Nation at Risk: The Full Account.* Cambridge, MA: USA Research, 1984.

Theodore R. Sizer. *Horace's Compromise: The Dilemma of the American High School.* Boston: Houghton Mifflin, 1984.

Ernest L. Boyer. *College: The Undergraduate Experience in America.* Prepared by the Carnegie Foundation for the Advancement of Teaching. New York: Harper & Row, 1987.

This collection of essays asks why so few African Americans have entered scientific fields and makes suggestions for increasing the numbers.

Willie Pearson, Jr. and H. Kenneth Bechtel, eds. *Blacks, Science, and American Education.* New Brunswick, NJ: Rutgers University Press, 1989.

The following two books are well-known accounts of how and why schooling in the United States perpetuates social inequality.

Samuel Bowles and Herbert Gintis. *Schooling in Capitalist America: Educational Reform and the Contradictions of Economic Life.* New York: Basic Books, 1976.

Jeannie Oakes. *Keeping Track: How High Schools Structure Inequality.* New Haven, CT: Yale University Press, 1985.

Here are two books that offer insightful and critical impressions of what goes on in classrooms today.

Samuel G. Freedman. *Small Victories: The Real World of a Teacher, Her Students, and Their School.* New York: Harper & Row, 1990.

Susan Moore Johnson. *Teachers at Work: Achieving Success in Our Schools.* New York: Basic Books, 1990.

Schooling boys and girls separately was common in Europe until recently; how and why did the United States develop the policy of coeducation?

David Tyack and Elisabeth Hansot. *Learning Together: A History of Coeducation in America.* New Haven: Yale University Press, 1990.

# Religion

David Van Horn found himself facing a jail term in 1990 for simply doing his job—at least, that's the way he saw it. Van Horn works as a contract archaeologist for developers, who are legally required to investigate a site for scientifically valuable artifacts before building on it. Digging on a desolate stretch of prairie near the southern California town of Indian Wells, Van Horn came upon a handful of bone chips. Following routine scientific procedures, he sent the fragments to a laboratory for analysis. His hunch—later confirmed by tests—was that they were human remains charred by cremation, which dated back centuries before Europeans inhabited the region.

But David Van Horn got some other news as well: officials notified him that he had run afoul of state law. A California statute requires anyone who unearths human remains to report the discovery—and to turn over what is found—to the local coroner. California enacted this law in response to leaders of the Native American community, who claim that perhaps a million of their ancestors have been unearthed by scientists like Van Horn or, worse still, by simple "grave robbers" looking for anything of value to sell to local souvenir shops (Mydans, 1991).

For their part, scientists like David Van Horn have no desire to offend anyone. On the contrary, they see their work as helping us to understand and appreciate the ways of life of people who inhabited our lands long ago. From this point of view, the remains unearthed by Van Horn provide important evidence about the diets, diseases, and standard of living of people who lived centuries ago. To Native Americans, however, this work constitutes sacrilege. From this perspective, excavating another people's burial place amounts to defiling sacred ground and transforming revered ancestors into laboratory specimens or mere trinkets.

Almost half the states have now passed laws forbidding people from disturbing Native American burial sites, and a number of museums and universities have returned skeletal remains to Native American groups for reburial. This confrontation between scientists and Native Americans illustrates a dynamic dimension of social life that guides this chapter: what one person defines as an everyday article, another may view as a sacred object commanding reverence and respect. As we shall explain, this distinction between the otherworldly and the ordinary lies at the heart of *religion*, a major social institution.

## Religion: Basic Concepts

The scientific point of view takes a matter-of-fact approach to investigating human society as well as the natural world. Although many members of our society

Every religion distinguishes the sacred from the secular. Followers of Islam reverently remove their shoes—which touch the profane ground—before entering this sacred mosque in the Persian Gulf nation of Brunei.

defined as extraordinary, inspiring a sense of awe, reverence, and even fear. Throughout human history, distinguishing between the profane and the sacred has been the key to all religious belief. In brief, then, **religion** is *a system of beliefs and practices based on recognizing the sacred.*

Because religion deals with ideas that transcend everyday experience, neither common sense nor science can establish religious truth. Religion is a matter of **faith,** *belief anchored in conviction rather than scientific evidence.* In the New Testament of the Bible, Christians are said to "walk by faith, not by sight" (II Corinthians 5:7), and faith is described as "the conviction of things not seen" (Hebrews 11:1).

In global perspective, matters of faith vary greatly. Nothing is placed in the category of sacred or profane by everyone on earth; anything may become one or the other depending on how a community of people defines it. In the United States, for example, we view most books as profane or secular, but the Torah (the first five books of the Hebrew Bible, or Old Testament) is defined as sacred by Jews, as is the entire Bible by Christians and the Qur'an (Koran) by Muslims. Similarly, most cities fall within the profane world, but Jerusalem is considered sacred by members of all three of these religions.

Durkheim (1965:62) explained that we understand profane things in terms of their everyday usefulness; we sit down at a computer or turn the key of a car to accomplish various jobs. What is defined as sacred, however, we separate from everyday life and denote as "set apart and forbidden" so that it evokes a reverent and submissive response. For instance, followers of Islam demand that people remove their shoes before entering a mosque—a sacred place of worship that is not to be symbolically defiled by shoes that have touched the profane ground outside.

As this example suggests, the sacred is addressed through **ritual,** *formal, ceremonial behavior.* Holy communion is the central ritual for most Christians; the wafer and wine consumed during communion are never defined as food—they are sacred symbols of the body and blood of Jesus Christ.

consider scientific inquiry to be an expression of human curiosity, for most of our history on earth, human beings living in small societies attributed birth, death, and whatever happened in between to the operation of supernatural forces. At the time of the Industrial Revolution, for example, most Europeans framed their life experiences as expressions of divine will. Gradually, however, science emerged as an alternative world view, one that seeks to explain our surroundings through systematic observation.

Sometimes, as the archaeological incident described at the beginning of this chapter illustrates, science and traditional beliefs collide. More broadly, however, science and our human fascination with the supernatural often go hand in hand since, as our scientific knowledge advances, the universe seems all the more awesome and mysterious.

French sociologist Emile Durkheim, whose ideas we explored in detail in Chapter 4 ("Society"), claimed that religions the world over share a focus on "all sorts of things that surpass the limits of our knowledge" (1965:62; orig. 1915). Human beings, Durkheim explained, define any idea, object, event, or experience in one of two ways. Most things we consider **profane** (from the Latin for "outside the temple"), meaning *ordinary elements of everyday life.* But some things, Durkheim continued, are set apart as **sacred,** *that which is*

## Religion and Sociology

Some people with strong religious beliefs are disturbed by the thought of sociologists, archaeologists, or other scientists studying what they hold to be sacred. In truth, however, the sociological study of religion carries no threat to anyone's faith. Because sociologists recognize that religion is central to virtually every culture on earth, they seek to understand how religious beliefs and practices guide human societies.

In doing this, sociology does not pass judgment on religion, nor does it make any claim about whether any specific matter of faith is right or wrong. As a science, sociological analysis is concerned with the social consequences of religious activity. Therefore, while sociologists can explain how religion is tied to other dimensions of social life, science offers no insights at all about the properly religious matters of the *meaning and purpose* of human existence. While some sociologists have interpreted the *consequences* of religion as positive, others as negative, and still others in a neutral manner, sociological analysis can never assess the *validity* of religious doctrine, which is a matter of faith rather than empirical evidence. Sociologists, like other people, may have one or another religious orientation: some are not believers, while others participate fully in their religions.

# Theoretical Analysis of Religion

Whatever their personal religious beliefs, sociologists agree that religion is a major social institution that must be understood in the context of society. Each of the major theoretical paradigms explores how religion affects social life.

## The Functions of Religion

Emile Durkheim believed that each one of us confronts the power of society every day. Society, he claimed, has an existence of its own that goes beyond the life of any individual. Thus society itself is "godlike"; unlike individuals, society does not die, it has the power to shape the lives of all of us, and it evokes a sense of reverence and awe. Then, too, society demands that individuals submit to its values and norms. According to Durkheim (1965; orig. 1915), then, the sacred lies at the heart of society: as people develop religious beliefs, they celebrate the awesome power of their society.

This explains why, in every society, people transform certain everyday objects into sacred symbols. The sacred represents the collective immortality of individual mortal beings. The members of technologically simple societies, Durkheim explained, exemplify the power of their society by a **totem,** *an object in the natural world*

*that is imbued with sacred qualities.* The totem—perhaps an animal or an elaborate work of art—becomes the centerpiece of ritual, symbolizing the power of society to transform individuals into a well-integrated collectivity.

In the modern world, the apparent weakening of traditional religion led Durkheim to fear the erosion of society itself. His concept of *anomie* or normlessness captures the idea that modern society, steeped in science and rational skepticism, cannot duplicate religion's historical power to imbue our lives with meaning and unite us into a human community. Thus, reasoned Durkheim, we moderns are left to celebrate a profane world, becoming caught up in the individualistic pursuit of money and possessions, often at the expense of our concern for spiritual values, our neighbors, or even our families.

Note that Durkheim's analysis of the parallel between the sacred and society ignores the question of whether a divine power exists or not. Either way, he concluded, religious beliefs and practices arise to reflect the power of society in all our lives. From this general beginning, Durkheim went on to identify several specific functions of religion for the operation of society.

### Social Cohesion

Religion promotes social cohesion by uniting members of a society through shared symbolism, values, and norms. In simple societies, the visible expression of this unity is the totem. Complex societies, too, foster cohesion with such symbolism. In the United States, the American eagle is a quasi-religious totem. In addition, placing the inscription "In God We Trust" on all currency implies a national bond of religious belief. Local communities across the United States also gain a sense of unity through totem-like symbolism attached to sports teams: from the New England "Patriots" to the Ohio State University "Buckeyes" to the Los Angeles "Rams."

### Social Control

Every society tries to promote some degree of social conformity. To do this, cultural norms, especially those that deal with reproduction, birth, marriage, and death, are imbued with religious meaning. More broadly, religion also confers legitimacy on the political system. In medieval Europe, this process was quite explicit as monarchs claimed to rule by divine right. Few of today's political leaders would claim to be picked by God, but many publicly ask for divine blessing and guidance, implying to the rest of us that their efforts are right and just.

**Providing Meaning and Purpose**

In the face of human failings, disease, and death, life can seem hopelessly chaotic. Religious beliefs offer the comforting sense that the vulnerable human condition serves some greater purpose. Strengthened by such convictions, people are less likely to collapse with despair when confronted by life's uncertainties and calamities. Major life transitions—including birth, marriage, and death—are usually marked by religious observances that place these events in a context of meaning. To many people, religion also figures in the vital human dimension of *love*, the emotional and spiritual connection to others (Wright & D'Antonio, 1980). Religion, then, addresses ultimate issues of life, death, and attachment that transcend both common sense and science.

*Critical evaluation.* Durkheim's work provides the foundation of the structural-functional analysis of religion. This approach emphasizes that the sharing of religious beliefs—whatever they may be—produces social cohesion and stability, and enhances a sense of meaning and purpose.

The major weakness of this approach is in downplaying the dysfunctions of religion—especially the capacity of strong beliefs to generate destructive social conflict. During the early Middle Ages, for example, religious faith was used to justify the Crusades, in which European Christians waged a military campaign against Muslims in the Middle East. Muslims, in turn, were driven by moral duty to fight the invading Christians. Conflict among Muslims, Jews, and Christians has been a source of political instability in various parts of the world ever since, as it is in the Middle East today. Social divisions in Northern Ireland, too, turn partly on conflict between Protestant and Catholic religious beliefs, while Dutch Calvinism historically supported apartheid in South Africa (Renick, 1991). Religious conflict also continues to divide India, Sri Lanka, Malaysia, Yugoslavia, and other nations. Ironically, in light of our assumption that religion is a force for good in the world, differences in faith have provoked more violence in the world than differences of social class.

## The Social Construction of the Sacred

The symbolic-interaction paradigm views all of society as a human construction. "Society," asserts Peter Berger (1967:3) "is a human product and nothing but a human product, that yet continuously acts back upon its producer." Once formed through social interaction, then, society shapes the existence of its creators.

Religion, in Berger's view, is also a social construction (although perhaps inspired by divine forces). Various religious practices, from everyday rituals like saying grace before meals to periodic religious services, teach individuals what their society defines as sacred.

Why should societies construct the sacred? Echoing Durkheim's insights, Berger explains that the sacred legitimizes and stabilizes social life. As a human creation, society is inherently precarious and subject to disruption. Placing everyday events within a "cosmic frame of reference" confers on the fallible, transitory creations of human beings "the semblance of ultimate security and permanence" (1967:35–36).

Marriage is a good example. If it is seen only as a contract between two people, marriage can be ended as easily as it is begun. But if two people negotiate a relationship defined as *holy matrimony*, this bond has far greater claims on both of them. In the same way, cultural norms that regulate sexual activity are made stronger if violations are viewed as *sin*. When humans confront uncertainty and life-threatening situations—such as illness, war, and natural disaster—sacred symbols come to the fore. Even people who are otherwise not very religious may pray as loved ones are dying, just as soldiers have traditionally gone to war "with God on their side." In short, the social construction of the sacred lifts humanity above the ultimate reality of death, so that society—if not its individual members—becomes immortal.

*Critical evaluation.* The symbolic-interaction approach suggests that, as we negotiate the life course, we place many natural experiences and events under a "sacred canopy" of meaning (Berger, 1967). But, as Berger points out, the sacred can only legitimize and stabilize society if the socially constructed character of the sacred goes unrecognized or people attribute the process to divine inspiration. The conception of holy matrimony is less compelling if we think of it merely as a social strategy to shore up relationships. Faced with life-threatening disaster, human beings could also derive little strength from sacred beliefs they viewed simply as devices for coping with tragedy. This reminds us again of the reason many people are uncomfortable with the sociological study of religion: it may be disconcerting to think that we have constructed the sacred in the same manner as we have created the rest of society.

## Religion and Social Inequality

The social-conflict paradigm offers additional insights about religion by focusing on how religion supports social inequality. Religion, according to Karl Marx, amounts to an ideology that serves ruling elites by legitimizing the status quo and diverting people's attention from social inequities.

In Great Britain, the monarch has traditionally been crowned by the head of the Church of England, illustrating the close alliance between religious and political elites. In practical terms, working for political change may well mean opposing the church—and, by implication, God. Moreover, when religious leaders declare that existing social arrangements are morally just, it weakens people's drive to change a system marred by a grossly unequal distribution of social resources, with privileges allocated for the few at the expense of the many. Religion, Marx continued, encourages people to look hopefully to a "better world to come," patiently enduring social problems of *this* world. In one of his best-known statements, Marx offered a stinging criticism of religion as "the sigh of the oppressed creature, the sentiment of a heartless world, and the soul of soulless conditions. It is the opium of the people" (1964:27; orig 1848).

An additional link between religion and social inequality involves gender. Virtually all the world's major religions have reflected and encouraged male dominance of social life, as the box on page 472 explains.

During Marx's lifetime, powerful Christian nations of Western Europe used the "conversion of heathens" as one justification for colonial exploitation of societies in Africa, Asia, and throughout the Americas. In the United States, major churches in the South declared the enslavement of African Americans to be consistent with God's will. Until well into this century, many churches actively supported segregation and other forms of racial inequality. Some religious organizations still do so today.

But religion has another side—one that promotes change, sometimes on a grand scale. Consider the analysis of nineteenth-century European society by Max Weber (1958; orig. 1904–1905). As Chapter 4 ("Society") explains in detail, Weber viewed industrial-capitalist societies as the product not of social conflict, but of the rational world view embodied by early Calvinism. In Weber's terms, the "Protestant ethic"—an approach to life based on discipline, thrift, and a desire to carry out God's will on earth—worked as an engine of change.

One way that religions support social inequality is by restricting leaders to certain categories of people. Historically, this has meant the dominance of white men, but this pattern has eroded in recent years. In 1989, for example, Barbara Harris became the first woman of color to be ordained as a bishop in the Episcopal Church.

From this religious ethic evolved the "spirit" of capitalism, a way of thinking and acting that eventually transformed much of Western Europe. Weber's analysis of the social consequences of Calvinism helps us to see that religion does not always support established hierarchies and the status quo.

***Critical evaluation.*** Social-conflict analysis shows that the power of religion can legitimize social inequality. This has been true in the United States as elsewhere.

Yet critics of religion's conservative face, Marx included, minimize ways in which religion has promoted not only change but social equality. Nineteenth-century religious groups in the United States played a key role in the abolition of slavery. During the 1950s and 1960s, the heart of the civil-rights movement in this country was found in the black church; the most compelling leader in this movement was Martin Luther King, Jr., a minister. During the 1960s and 1970s, many clergy actively opposed the Vietnam War and, as explained presently, some now support revolutionary change in Latin America and elsewhere. Churches in the United States have also offered asylum to refugees from El Salvador, Nicaragua, Guatemala, and other politically unsta-

# Religion and Patriarchy: Does God Favor Males?

Most people in the United States envision God as male (N.O.R.C., 1991:156). Because we link attributes like wisdom and power to men, it is not surprising that we think of God in masculine terms. By and large, organized religions also favor males, as seen in passages from many of the sacred writings of major world religions.

The Qur'an (Koran)—the sacred text of Islam—asserts that men are to have social dominance over women:

> Men are in charge of women. . . . Hence good women are obedient. . . . As for those whose rebelliousness you fear, admonish them, banish them from your bed, and scourge them. (cited in Kaufman, 1976:163)

Christianity—the dominant religion of the Western world—has also supported patriarchy. While Christians do revere Mary, the mother of Jesus, the New Testament also includes the following passages:

> A man . . . is the image and glory of God; but woman is the glory of man. For man was not made from woman, but woman from man. Neither was man created for woman, but woman for man. (I Corinthians 11:7–9)

> As in all the churches of the saints, the women should keep silence in the churches. For they are not permitted to speak, but should be subordinate, as even the law says. If there is anything they desire to know, let them ask their husbands at home. For it is shameful for a woman to speak in church. (I Corinthians 14:33–35)

> Wives, be subject to your husbands, as to the Lord. For the husband is the head of the wife as Christ is the head of the church. . . . As the church is subject to Christ, so let wives also be subject in everything to their husbands. (Ephesians 5:22–24)

Judaism, too, has traditionally supported patriarchy. Male Orthodox Jews include the following words in daily prayer:

> Blessed art thou, O Lord our God, King of the Universe, that I was not born a gentile. Blessed art thou, O Lord our God, King of the Universe, that I was not born a slave. Blessed art thou, O Lord our God, King of the Universe, that I was not born a woman.

In another dimension of religious patriarchy, the major religions have long excluded women from the clergy, although this is now being widely challenged. Islam continues to exclude women from such positions, as does the Roman Catholic Church. A growing number of Protestant denominations, however, have overturned historical practices and now ordain women. While Orthodox Judaism still upholds the traditional prohibition against women serving as rabbis, Reform Judaism has long elevated women to this role (and is the largest denomination of the major religions to ordain gay and lesbian people). In 1985, the first woman became a rabbi in the Conservative branch of Judaism. The proportion of women among students in seminary schools across the United States has never been higher (now roughly one-third), so that further change is only a matter of time.

Challenges to the patriarchal structure of organized religion—from women entering the clergy to revisions in the language in hymns and prayers—spark heated controversy, delighting progressives while outraging traditionalists. Propelling these developments is a lively strain of feminism within most religious communities today. According to feminist Christians, for example, patriarchy in the church stands in stark contrast to the largely feminine image of Jesus Christ in the Scriptures as "nonaggressive, noncompetitive, meek and humble of heart, a nurturer of the weak and a friend of the outcast" (Sandra Schneiders, cited in Woodward, 1989:61). Moreover, they argue, unless traditional notions of gender are removed from our understanding of God, women will never share equally with men in the church. Theologian Mary Daly puts the matter bluntly: "If God is male, then male is God" (cited in Woodward, 1989:58).

ble countries to our south. In global context, much the same pattern emerges: in South Africa, for example, some of the strongest voices for dismantling the system of racial apartheid come from inside churches. Marx apparently underestimated the extent to which religion would promote social change in the twentieth century.

## Liberation Theology

Significantly, religion has mixed with the sociological thinking of Karl Marx to form a recipe for change called *liberation theology*. Christianity shares with many world religions a longstanding concern for the suffering of poor and oppressed people. Traditionally, the Christian response has been to strengthen the faith of the believer in a better life to come. In recent decades, however, some church leaders and theologians have embraced Karl Marx's pursuit of social equality in *this* world.

Formally, **liberation theology** is *a fusion of Christian principles with political activism, often Marxist in character*. This social movement developed in the late 1960s within Latin America's Roman Catholic Church. Liberation theology begins with the Church's established teaching that Christianity offers liberation from human sin. What is new—and controversial—is the assertion that the church cannot be content with addressing people's spiritual needs; it must also help people liberate themselves from the abysmal poverty of the Third World, as described in Chapter 11 ("Global Inequality").

Although they disagree among themselves on many issues, advocates of liberation theology embrace three general principles. First, human suffering in the world is tragic and beyond the imagination of most secure, comfortable people in the United States. Second, this massive anguish runs counter to Christian morality, by threatening the survival of a large share of humanity. Third, global poverty is preventable and, as an expression of faith and conscience, Christians must act to reduce this suffering. Many—but not all—clergy who support this kind of change see in Marxism a path toward a better future for those who have endured a lifetime of suffering.

A growing number of Catholic men and women have allied themselves with the poor in a political struggle against the ruling powers in some Latin American societies. The costs of opposition have been high. Church members have been killed in the violence that engulfs much of that region. In 1980, Oscar Arnulfo Romero, the archbishop of San Salvador (the capital of El Salvador) and an outspoken advocate of the poor, was gunned down inside his church while celebrating mass. In 1989, during the continuing civil unrest in El Salvador, six Jesuit priests were murdered in their home by government troops.

The radicalization of the Latin American church has attracted some additional support from the people of the region (Neuhouser, 1989). But it has also polarized the Catholic community. With strong advocates on one side, liberation theology also has powerful adversaries, among them Pope John Paul II, who condemns this movement for tainting traditional church doctrine with politics. The Vatican claims that liberation theology endangers the Catholic faith by diverting attention from the otherworldly concerns of Christianity, and embroiling the church in political controversy. Thus, the pope has forbidden church officials to participate in political conflicts. Nonetheless, the liberation theology movement is gaining strength in Latin America—especially El Salvador and Brazil—fueled by the belief that Christian faith and a sense of basic human justice demand efforts to mitigate the plight of the world's poor (Boff, 1984).

# Types of Religious Organization

Because there are hundreds of different religious organizations in the United States, sociologists have developed schemes to categorize them. The most widely used model takes the form of a continuum with "churches" on one pole and "sects" on the other. We can describe any actual religious organization, then, in relation to these two ideal types by locating it on the church–sect continuum.

## Church and Sect

Max Weber deserves the credit for drawing the general distinction between church and sect—and his student Ernst Troeltsch (1931) elaborated on this polar model. A **church**, described in ideal terms, is *a type of religious organization that readily seeks accommodation with the larger society*. Church-like organizations are well established, typically persisting for centuries and usually including all members of a particular family over many generations. Churches favor formality in their organization, with extensive bureaucratic regulations and an approved program of training leading to the ordination of officials.

As they address the realm of the sacred, Troeltsch explained, churches strive to broaden their appeal. Thus they conceive of God in highly intellectualized terms (for example, as a force for good in the world), and generally favor abstract moral standards (such as "do unto others as you would have them do unto you") over specific codes that guide actual day-to-day behavior.

Troeltsch pointed out that in their drive for universality, churches not only develop an intellectualized vision of God but also seek accommodation and compromise with their secular surroundings. By teaching morality in safely abstract terms, churches can wink at specific social arrangements that run counter to their principles. For example, a church may pronounce all human beings brothers and sisters, but raise no objection to laws that deny equal rights to people of one race or sexual orientation. Similarly, churches urge their members to pursue moral righteousness, but usually shy away from specifics when it comes to which behaviors (regarding sex, for instance) should be praised or condemned. Such generality simultaneously gives these religious organizations wide appeal and minimizes conflict between the church and the political state (Troeltsch, 1931; O'Dea & Aviad, 1983).

Some church-like organizations are tied to the government. An **ecclesia** is *a church that is formally allied with the state.* Ecclesias have been common in human history: the Catholic Church was for centuries allied with the Roman Empire; the Anglican Church is now the official Church of England; Confucianism was the state religion in China until early in this century; and Islam is today the official religion of Pakistan and Iran. Empowered by the state, ecclesias claim all people in a society as members. Membership in the official church, then, is usually required by law, virtually eliminating religious freedom of choice. Because church and state are fused, an ecclesia most clearly exemplifies religious acceptance of political arrangements in the larger society.

A second type of church is a **denomination,** *a church, not linked to the state, in a society that recognizes religious pluralism.* The United States has never had an official religion. The first amendment to the U. S. Constitution forbids Congress from giving legal support to any religion, so that our society favors the denominational model in which many church-like organizations coexist with one another. Ours is a nation of religious diversity, with dozens of church-like Christian denominations—including Catholics, Baptists, Methodists, and Lutherans—as well as denominations within Judaism and other religious traditions. While members of any denomination hold certain religious beliefs, they recognize the right of others to disagree.

A second general religious form is the **sect,** *a type of religious organization that resists accommodation with the larger society.* Simply stated, sect members place their religious convictions ahead of what others around them may hold to be true. In extreme cases, members of a sect may withdraw completely in order to practice their religion without interference from outsiders. The Amish, described in Chapter 3 ("Culture"), are one North American sect that has long sought isolation from outsiders (Hostetler, 1980). More commonly, however, members of sects participate in the world more or less as other people do; the difference is that sect members typically try to allow their religious principles to guide their thoughts and deeds. In a society like ours that affords individuals considerable moral autonomy and holds up tolerance as a virtue, members of sects are more likely than most people to view their beliefs as the only true religion, which puts them at odds with the doctrine of religious pluralism. For this reason, members of church-like organizations sometimes perceive sectarians as dogmatic in their insistence that their religious community represents "authentic" faith in contrast to those who have made too many compromises with the world (Stark & Bainbridge, 1979).

In organizational terms, many sects shun the rigid formality of established churches. They do so in order to rejoice in the personal experience of God's presence, again in contrast to churches, which practice more subdued and formal ritual. Thus members of sects often exude a spontaneity and emotional fervor as they worship, while members of churches tend to be passive and attentive to the formal leader. Put otherwise, sects reject the intellectualized approach of churches, stressing instead the fundamental experience of a divine power. We can pinpoint this distinction in patterns of prayer, as Rodney Stark (1985:314) points out: the sense of a distant God, found in "church" prayer—"Our Father, who art in Heaven"—contrasts sharply with the image of a more immediate God typical of sects—"Lord, bless this poor sinner kneeling before you now."

A further distinction between church and sect turns on patterns of leadership. The more church-like a religious organization is, the more likely that its leaders are formal officials with approved training, such as priests, rabbis, and ministers. Because more sect-like organiza-

In global perspective, the range of human religious activity is truly astonishing. Members of one Christian cult in the Latin American nation of Guatemala observe Good Friday by vaulting over fire, an expression of their faith that God will protect them.

tions celebrate the personal presence of God, members expect their leaders to embody divine inspiration in the form of **charisma,** which, in religious context, means *evidence of God's favor in the behavior of an individual.* This term has Greek roots meaning "divine favor." A charismatic leader, then, is presumably endowed with divine inspiration that awakens feelings of spiritual joy in an audience, infusing followers with the emotional experience that sects value so highly.

Traditionally, many sects relied heavily on outsiders joining their ranks. This underlies the practice of actively recruiting, or *proselytizing,* outsiders. Sects tout the experience of **conversion,** *a personal transformation resulting from adopting new religious beliefs.* Members of Jehovah's Witnesses, for example, have long encouraged the faithful to share their beliefs with others. But proselytizing often does more to increase the commitment of those who already believe than to actually attract new members.

Troeltsch and later researchers have noted that churches and sects differ in their social composition. Generally speaking, people of high social standing favor well-established churches. This is not surprising, since privileged people accommodate the larger society most comfortably. By contrast, sects attract people of lower social position. A sect's openness to new members and promise of salvation and personal fulfillment holds special appeal to people who perceive themselves as social outsiders. However, as we shall explain presently, many of the more established churches in the United States have lost membership in recent decades. As a consequence, sects now find themselves with more affluent members.

Sects usually form as breakaway groups from established churches or other religious organizations; sects, in short, emerge from religious schism (Stark & Bainbridge, 1979). In some cases, as a religious organization becomes more established by accommodating the secular world, some members (especially those of lower social position) may defect to create a new organization that better meets their spiritual needs. The psychic intensity and lack of formal structure characteristic of sects make them less stable than churches; some sects, therefore, blossom only to disappear soon after. By and large, sects that endure become more and more like churches, losing religious fervor as they become more bureaucratic, established, and respectable. Both the Puritan and the Quaker colonists who came to the United States from England were members of breakaway sects. Each of these sects has subsequently evolved into an established church, although further schism leading to the creation of new sects has also occurred. In sum, the concepts of church and sect are opposite ends of a dynamic continuum on which religious organizations may move over time.

## Cult

A **cult** is *a religious organization with roots outside the dominant religious traditions of a society.* Whereas a sect emerges from division and reform within a conventional religious organization, a cult represents something almost entirely new. Because some cult principles or practices seem unconventional to members of a particular society, the popular view of cults pictures them as deviant or even evil. In recent decades, negative media publicity given to a few cults has raised suspicion about any unfamiliar religious organization. Thus, some scholars note, to call a religious community a cult amounts to declaring it to be unworthy (Richardson, 1990).

This is unfortunate because there is nothing intrinsically wrong with this kind of religious organization; many long-standing religions—Christianity, Islam, and Judaism included—began as cults. The product of religious *innovation* or cultural *diffusion,* a cult may become popular, but most do not. Cults formed through innovation typically center around a highly charismatic leader who offers a new and unprecedented message. This was the case when Jesus of Nazareth began attracting followers in a remote part of the Roman Empire two millennia ago. More recently, Joseph Smith founded the Church of Jesus Christ of Latter-Day Saints (the Mormons) in New York State in 1830. Smith accepted many established Christian principles—cults are rarely entirely novel—but he distinguished early Mormonism with several unconventional religious ideas, including the practice of polygamy or plural marriage. In the following 150 years, Mormons became steadily more church-like, abandoning unorthodox practices. Spurred by a doctrine of proselytizing, Mormonism is now one of the fastest-growing religious organizations in the United States (Stark, 1984).

Cultural diffusion produces a cult as religious ideas from one society (where they are conventional) are carried to another society (where they are not). Transcendental Meditation (TM) developed in the United States when Maharishi Mahesh Yogi introduced Hindu principles and practices to our society in the late 1950s. During the 1970s, TM became widely popular, attracting some 500,000 followers. Since then, however, its fortunes have faded and TM has relatively few followers in the United States today (Bainbridge & Jackson, 1981).

To the extent that they are novel, cults may be at odds with conventional society, even more than sects are. Some cults demand that members not only adopt distinctive religious beliefs but also embrace an entire *lifestyle* involving a radical change in self-identity. It is cases of this kind that have sparked popular press reports of cult leaders brainwashing new members into renouncing their past lives. While this has happened, it is not very common.

In a complex and changing world, cults arise regularly. They gain importance when people are anxious about their lives, disenchanted with established religions, and thus are ready to embrace new answers. But, in most cases, cults arise only to quickly fade. Many cults actively proselytize, but usually with little success. Most people show only a passing interest in cults and do not join; those who do may or may not remain members for long, and only rarely is anyone psychologically harmed from such an experience. Of course some cults have considerable success in attracting and retaining members. By and large, however, cults that flourish tend to become more church-like over time (Barker, 1981; Kilbourne, 1983).

# Religion in History

Religion shapes every society of the world. And, like other social institutions, religion shows considerable variation historically and cross-culturally.

## Religion in Preindustrial Societies

Religion extends further back in the human record than written history. How do we know? Because archaeologists have collected evidence that our human ancestors routinely engaged in religious rituals at least forty thousand years ago.

Among early hunters and gatherers, religion took the form of **animism** (from Latin meaning "the breath of life"), *the belief that elements of the natural world are conscious forms of life that affect humanity.* Animistic people may view forests, oceans, mountains, or the wind as spiritual forces responsible for shaping human experience. Many Native American societies that flourished throughout the Americas have been animistic, which accounts for their deeply respectful view of the natural environment. For such people, religion is not a distinctive sphere of life; hunting and gathering societies carry out religious activity entirely within the family. They may look to a *shaman* or religious leader, but shamanism is not a full-time, specialized activity.

Belief in a single divine power responsible for creating the world evolved more recently, roughly coinciding with the development of horticulture and agriculture. As single-deity religions take root, religious life starts to reach beyond the family; at this stage, religion is often fused with politics. To illustrate, ancient leaders such as the Egyptian pharaoh and the early Chinese emperor ruled as both kings and priests.

In agrarian societies, religion stands alone as a powerful social institution; the centrality of the church in medieval Europe exemplifies this supremacy. The physical design of the medieval city even casts this dominance in stone, with the cathedral rising above all other structures.

## Religion in Industrial Societies

The Industrial Revolution ushered in a growing emphasis on science, diminishing the scope of religious thinking. Increasingly, people in distress looked to physicians and other practitioners of science for the comfort they had earlier sought from religious leaders.

Yet religion continues to thrive in a scientific world, largely because science is powerless to address issues of ultimate meaning in human life. In other words, learning *how* the world works falls to scientific investigators; but *why* we and the surrounding universe exist at all constitutes both a more important question and one about which scientists have nothing to say. Therefore, many traditional religions have endured during the twentieth century, and new religions have also emerged. Whatever the benefits of science to our material lives, then, religion has a unique capacity to address the spiritual dimension of human existence.

Because religion and science represent powerful but distinct ways of viewing the universe, the two sometimes fall into an uneasy relationship. In recent decades, controversy has continued over the origin of humanity. As the box on pages 478–79 explains, this debate puts scientific "facts" about human evolution in opposition to religious "beliefs" commonly called *creationism*.

# World Religions

Religion is found virtually everywhere on our planet and, remarkably, the diversity of religious expression is almost as wide-ranging as culture itself. Many of the thousands of different religions are highly localized with few followers. A few may be termed *world religions* because they have millions of adherents and are known throughout the world. We shall briefly describe six world religions, which together claim the support of 3.8 billion people—almost three-fourths of humanity. Clearly, the societies of our world remain significantly tied to religion.

## Christianity

Christianity is the most widespread religion, with 1.7 billion adherents, which amounts to roughly one-third of humanity. Most Christians live in Europe or throughout the Americas; more than 85 percent of the people in the United States and Canada identify with Christianity. As shown in Global Map 17–1 on page 480, however, Christians represent a significant share of the population in many other world regions, with the notable exceptions of Northern Africa and Asia. This pattern reflects the diffusion of Christianity by European colonizers during the last 500 years. The dominant influence of Christianity in the Western Hemisphere is evident in the Western practice of numbering years on the calendar beginning with the birth of Christ.

The roots of Christianity lie in Middle-Eastern Judaism. Christianity originated as a cult, although it retained many of the teachings and practices of Judaism, which dates back much further. Like many cults, Christianity was propelled by the personal charisma of a leader, Jesus of Nazareth, who preached a message of personal, spiritual salvation. From a sociological point of view, one reason for the success of this new religion was that Jesus did not seek to antagonize the political powers-that-be; rather he accepted edicts from the Roman Empire, calling on his followers to "Render therefore to Caesar things that are Caesar's" (Matthew 22:21). Yet, from a moral standpoint, Jesus' message was quite revolutionary, offering the promise of human triumph over sin and death through faith. Jesus preached a universal message that all people should join in spiritual love.

Christianity is one example of **monotheism**, *belief in a single divine power*. This new religion challenged the Roman Empire's traditional **polytheism**, *belief in many gods*. Yet Christianity has a unique vision of the Supreme Being as a sacred Trinity: God the Creator; Jesus Christ, Son of God and Redeemer; and the Holy Spirit, a Christian's personal experience of God's presence.

The claim that Jesus was imbued with divinity rests on accounts of his final days on earth. Tried and sentenced to death in Jerusalem, by officials who sensed that his ideas were a threat to established political leaders, Jesus endured a cruel execution by crucifixion, which transformed the cross into a sacred Christian symbol. According to Christian belief, Jesus was resurrected—that is, he rose from the dead—showing that he was the Son of God.

At the time, the Roman Empire imposed a broad peace in the Mediterranean region. This so-called Pax Romana allowed the Apostle Paul and others to travel safely, spreading Christianity widely. Although the Romans initially persecuted Christians, by the fourth century Christianity became an ecclesia—the official religion of the Roman Empire. What had begun as a cult four centuries before had been transformed into an established church.

Soon afterward, Rome declined, but the eastern part of the empire, based in the city of Constantinople

# The Creation Debate: Does Science Threaten Religion?

"In the beginning God created the heavens and the earth." So begins the book of Genesis in the Bible, the sacred text for millions of Christians and Jews. Read literally, Genesis states that life on earth began on the third day when God created vegetation; on the fifth and sixth days, God created animal life including human beings, fashioned in God's own image.

The stage was set for controversy over the Genesis account of creation when, in 1859, the English scientist Charles Darwin published *On the Origin of Species*, a biological explanation of human origins. Darwin's theory of evolution maintained that the world at creation was a far cry from what we find today; rather, life on the planet changed over time due to biological evolution (described in Chapter 3, "Culture"). From this point of view, human beings first walked the earth not days after the creation but only after a billion years of evolution had produced our species from lower forms of animal life.

In a largely Christian society, many people objected loudly to Darwin's theory. While some considered the theory a great contribution to science, others saw it as an all-out attack against centuries-old sacred beliefs. On the surface, Darwin's scientific analysis certainly seems to contradict biblical creation: after all, if human beings took a billion years to evolve, they could hardly have been the final act of creation. This discrepancy stands at the center of the *creation debate*.

As public schooling expanded, with biology teachers propagating evolutionary thinking around the country, the creationist debate intensified. A major event in the course of this controversy unfolded in 1925 in the little town of Dayton, Tennessee. Wanting to blunt any attack by scientists on religious beliefs, legislators in Tennessee enacted a law forbidding educators to teach students "any theory that denies the story of the Divine Creation of man as taught in the Bible," and especially the notion that "man descended from a lower order of animals." One afternoon, as the locals gathered in Doc Robinson's drugstore to talk, John Thomas Scopes, a science teacher in the local high school, conceded that, yes, on occasion, he had taught evolution in the Dayton high school. As a means of challenging the law, Scopes agreed to stand trial for defying it.

Dubbed the "Scopes monkey trial" (because of Darwin's contention that humans descended from lower primates), the proceeding drew intense public interest, which was heightened by the presence of two of the greatest trial lawyers of the day. William Jennings Bryan (three times a presidential candidate) was a fundamentalist Christian leading a national campaign against evolutionary science; he weighed in to prosecute the case. Clarence Darrow, the most renowned criminal lawyer in the country, made an equally enthusiastic advocate for the defense.

(now Istanbul, Turkey), flourished until the fifteenth century. A religious division in the eleventh century resulted in twin centers of Christianity: the Roman Catholic Church (based in Rome) and the Orthodox Church centered in Constantinople.

Further divisions splintered Christianity toward the end of the Middle Ages, when religious leaders such as Martin Luther (1483–1546) protested established church doctrine. The Reformation in Europe spawned numerous Protestant organizations and ushered in a period of religious pluralism. More than a dozen denominations—the Baptists and Methodists are the two largest—now command sizable followings in the United States.

While not the oldest of the world religions, Christianity has most influenced Western civilization. Through division, diffusion, and innovation, we now see Christian organizations that resemble churches, sects, and cults. What they all share is the belief that a historical figure named Jesus of Nazareth was sent by God to provide salvation from sin, and that he still offers everlasting life to those who accept him as their personal savior (Smart, 1969; Kaufman, 1976; Stavrianos, 1983).

## Islam

Islam, has almost 1 billion followers (18 percent of humanity) who are called Muslims (or Moslems). A majority

During the eleven-day trial, Darrow gave one of his finest performances, while Bryan, aging, ill, and only days from death, did little to advance the creationist cause. Yet many in the community applauded when Scopes was found guilty and fined $100. The state reversed the conviction on appeal, however, perhaps to prevent the case from reaching the U.S. Supreme Court. Thus the Tennessee law forbidding the teaching of evolution remained in place until 1967. The following year, the U.S. Supreme Court struck down all such laws, arguing that they violated the constitutional prohibition against government-supported religion.

Creationists fumed at what they saw as the court's hostility to religion. To sidestep the ruling, they adopted a new line of attack: if evolution was going to be taught in schools, so should creationism, to provide needed balance. Creationism, stripped of its most blatant religious overtones, became *creation science*.

Essentially, creation science seeks to advance scientific support for a literal reading of Genesis. This approach found favor in many communities, and some state legislatures soon required that creation science be included in school curricula. But again the Court stepped in, rejecting these laws in 1985 as violating the constitutional separation of church and state.

This time, however, the Court went even further, declaring creation science itself to be invalid *as science*. The decision rests on the assertion that science, by definition, has a provisional character so that any theory must change as new empirical evidence emerges. The scientific theory of evolution *has* changed as new facts are discovered, but creation science has resisted any revision, leading the judges to rule that it is religion rather than science.

Despite the Court's ruling, many people in the United States continue to view the biblical account of creation as literal truth. In a recent national survey, just over one-third of adults said they take the Bible literally as the actual word of God (N.O.R.C., 1991:168). Many others, who think of evolution as a scientific fact, believe that it proceeded with divine direction.

The creation debate, therefore, continues to rage. Many church leaders have tried to defuse the confrontation, pointing out that science and religion need not be in conflict at all. John S. Spong, the Episcopal bishop of Newark, New Jersey, states that scientists and biblical scholars alike must accept the "enormous amount of evidence" that humanity did evolve over a billion years. Even so, he continues, science only investigates *how* the natural world operates; it is left for religion to address *why* we exist and to point up God's role in this process. In the end, the story of human creation will rest on both scientific fact and religious faith.

SOURCES: Based on Gould (1981); Numbers (1982); and Nelson & Jermain (1985). Professor J. Kenneth Smail, Kenyon College, also contributed ideas to this section.

of people in the Middle East are Muslims, which explains the tendency of people in the United States to link Islam to Arabs in that region of the world. But most Muslims are not Arabs; Global Map 17–2 on page 480 shows that a majority of people throughout Northern Africa and Western Asia are Muslims. Moreover, significant concentrations of Muslims are found in Pakistan, India, Bangladesh, Indonesia, and the southern republics of the Commonwealth of Independent States. Although representing only a tiny share of the population, estimates place the Muslim population of North America at roughly 5 million, and the number is rapidly growing (Roudi, 1988; Weeks, 1988).

Islam is the word of God as revealed to the prophet Muhammad, who was born in the city of Mecca (in western Saudi Arabia) about the year 570. To Muslims, Muhammad was a prophet, not a divine being as Christians define Jesus. The Qur'an (Koran), sacred to Muslims, is the word of God—in Arabic, Allah—as transmitted through Muhammad, God's messenger. In Arabic, the word Islam means both "submission" and "peace," and the Qur'an urges submission to Allah as the path to inner peace. Muslims express this spiritual devotion in a daily ritual of five prayers.

Islam spread rapidly after the death of Muhammad, although divisions arose as they did within Christianity. All Muslims, however, accept the Five Pillars of Islam: (1) recognizing Allah as the one, true God, and Muham-

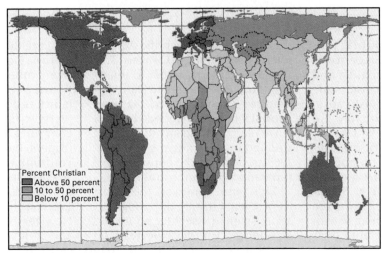

Percent Christian
■ Above 50 percent
▦ 10 to 50 percent
□ Below 10 percent

**Global Map 17–1**   Christianity in Global Perspective

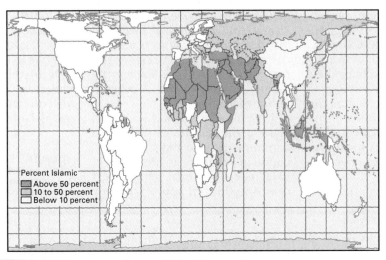

Percent Islamic
▦ Above 50 percent
▨ 10 to 50 percent
□ Below 10 percent

**Global Map 17–2**   Islam in Global Perspective

mad as God's messenger; (2) ritual prayer; (3) giving alms to the poor; (4) fasting during the month of Ramadan; and (5) making a pilgrimage once to the Sacred House of Allah in Mecca (Weeks, 1988; El-Attar, 1991). Like many religions, Islam holds people accountable to God for their deeds on earth. Those who live obediently will be rewarded in heaven, while nonbelievers will suffer unending punishment.

Muslims are also obligated to defend their faith. Sometimes this tenet has justified holy wars against non-

believers (in roughly the same way that medieval Christians joined the Crusades to recapture the Holy Land from the Muslims). In recent decades, especially in Iran, Muslims have sought to rid their societies of Western social influences they regard as morally compromising (Martin, 1982; Arjomand, 1988).

Like most religions, Islam is linked to the domination of women by men. Westerners often view Muslim women as among the most socially oppressed people on earth. Muslim women do lack many of the personal freedoms enjoyed by Muslim men, yet patriarchy was already well established in the Middle East at the time of Muhammad's birth. Some defenders argue that Islam actually improved the social position of women by demanding that husbands deal justly with their wives. Further, although Islam permits a man to have up to four wives, it warns men to have only one wife if more than one will encourage him to treat these women unjustly (Qur'an, "The Women," Verse 3).

## Hinduism

Hinduism is the oldest of all the world religions, originating in the Indus River Valley some 4,500 years ago. Hindus number some 700 million (13 percent of humanity). Global Map 17–3 on page 482 shows that Hinduism remains the predominant religion of Pakistan and India today; in addition, a significant Hindu population is found in a few societies of southern Africa and in Indonesia. Over the centuries, Hinduism and Indian culture have become intertwined, so that now one is not easily described apart from the other. Because of this intermingling of culture and religion, Hinduism, unlike Christianity and Islam, has experienced relatively little diffusion (Schmidt, 1980). However, an estimated 1 million adherents in the United States makes Hinduism a significant part of the religious diversity of our country.

Hinduism also differs from Christianity and Islam in several other key ways. First, it is not linked to the life of any single person. Second, it has no sacred writings comparable to the Bible or the Qur'an. Third, Hinduism does not even envision God as a specific entity. For this reason, Hinduism—like other Asian religions, as we shall see—is sometimes thought of as an "ethical religion." Hindu beliefs and practices vary widely, but all Hindus recognize that the moral force of our universe confronts everyone with responsibilities known as *dharma*. One traditional example of dharma is the duty to act in concert with the traditional caste system, described in Chapter 9 ("Social Stratification").

A second Hindu principle, called *karma*, refers to the belief in the spiritual progress of the human soul. To a Hindu, every action we take has a spiritual consequence; proper living enhances moral development, while improper living results in moral decline. Karma works through *reincarnation*, a cycle of new birth following death, so that the individual is reborn into a spiritual state corresponding to the moral quality of a previous life. Unlike Christianity and Islam, Hinduism proclaims

This page from a Persian manuscript, dated about 1540, depicts *The Ascent of the Prophet Mohammed to Heaven*. Rising from earth through a host of angels, the prophet Mohammed is about to enter Paradise in the presence of Allah. Note that the prophet's face is blank—apparently because the artist deemed it sacred and unsuitable for reproduction.
(Ascent of the Prophet Mohammed to Heaven. *British Library, London*.)

no ultimate justice at the hands of a supreme god, although in the cycle of rebirth, each person reaps exactly what is sown. The sublime state of *nirvana* represents spiritual perfection; when a soul reaches this rarefied existence, it is spared further rebirth.

Looking at Hinduism, we realize that not all religions can be neatly labeled monotheistic or polytheistic. Hinduism may be described as monotheistic because it envisions the universe as a single moral system; yet Hindus see evidence of this moral order in every element of nature. While central to a Hindu's life, rituals are also quite variable. Such variety stems from weaving religion into daily lives in countless Indian villages over

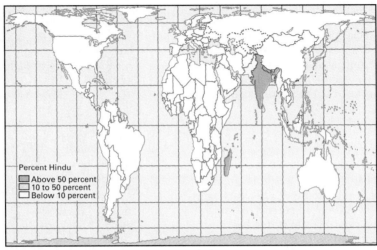

**Global Map 17–3** Hinduism in Global Perspective

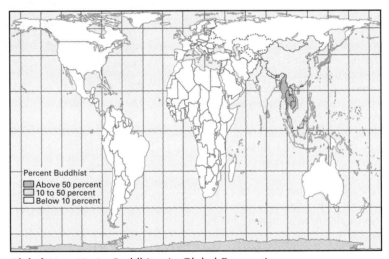

**Global Map 17–4** Buddhism in Global Perspective

thousands of years. Most Hindus, however, practice private devotions, including, for example, ritual cleansing following contact with a person of lower caste position. Many also participate in massive public events, such as the Kumbh Mela, which occurs every twelve years. At this time, millions of Hindus make a pilgrimage to the sacred Ganges River to bathe in its ritually purifying waters.

While elements of Hindu thought have characterized some cults in the United States over the years, Hinduism is still unfamiliar to most Westerners. But,

like religions more well known to us, Hinduism is a powerful force offering both explanation and guidance in life (Pitt, 1955; Sen, 1961; Embree, 1972; Kaufman, 1976; Schmidt, 1980).

## Buddhism

India also gave rise to Buddhism, a religion that emerged about 2,500 years ago. Today more than 300 million people (6 percent of humanity) embrace Buddhism, and almost all are Asians. As shown in Global Map 17–4, adherents to Buddhism represent over half the populations of Myanmar, Thailand, Cambodia, and Japan; Buddhism is also widespread in India and the People's Republic of China. Of the world religions considered so far, Buddhism most resembles Hinduism in doctrine, but, like Christianity, its inspiration springs from the life of one individual.

Siddhartha Gautama was born to a high-caste Indian family about 563 B.C.E. As a young man, he was preoccupied with spiritual matters. At the age of twenty-nine, he underwent a radical personal transformation. Setting off for years of travel and meditation, he finally achieved what Buddhists describe as *bodhi*, or enlightenment. Understanding the essence of life, Gautama became a Buddha.

Energized by Buddha's personal charisma, followers spread his teachings—the *dhamma*—across India. During the third century B.C.E., the ruler of India joined the ranks of Buddhism, and subsequently sent missionaries throughout Asia, elevating Buddhism to the status of a world religion.

Central to Buddhist belief is the notion that human existence involves suffering. Buddhism does not forbid pleasure, but rather holds that such experience is transitory. This belief stems from Buddha's own travels throughout a society rife with poverty. But Buddhism rejects wealth as a solution to suffering; on the contrary, in this world view materialism inhibits spiritual development. Buddhism's response to world problems is for individuals to pursue personal, spiritual transformation.

Buddhism closely parallels Hinduism in its belief in reincarnation; here again, only full enlightenment ends the cycle of death and rebirth, thereby liberating a person from the suffering of the world. Also like Hinduism, Buddhism recognizes no god of judgment, but, rather, sees spiritual consequences in each daily action.

Like Christianity, Buddhism originated in the life of a charismatic teacher. However, its conception of a moral universe in which spiritual development occurs over many lifetimes places Buddhism closer to Hinduism overall (Schumann, 1974; Thomas, 1975).

## Confucianism

From about 200 B.C.E. until the beginning of this century, Confucianism was an ecclesia—the official religion of China. Following the 1949 revolution, religion was suppressed by the Communist government of the People's Republic of China. Hundreds of millions of Chinese are influenced by Confucianism, although the government provides little in the way of official data to establish more precise numbers. Almost all adherents of Confucianism live in the People's Republic of China, but cultural diffusion and Chinese immigration have introduced this religion to other societies in Southeast Asia. Estimates hold that 100,000 followers of Confucianism live throughout North America.

This religion was founded by K'ung-Fu-tzu, known to Westerners as Confucius, who lived between 551 and 479 B.C.E. Confucius shared with Buddha a deep concern for the problems and suffering of the world. Buddha encouraged a more sect-like spiritual withdrawal from the world; Confucius, however, instructed his followers to engage the world but to do so with correct moral conduct. Thus, Confucianism became fused with the traditional culture of China. Here we see a second example of what might be called a "national religion": as Hinduism has remained largely synonymous with Indian culture, Confucianism is enshrined in the Chinese way of life.

A central concept of Confucianism is *jen*, meaning humaneness. In practice, this means that self-interest must always be subordinated to moral concerns. In the family, the individual must display loyalty and consideration for others. Likewise, families must remain mindful

A general trait of most Eastern religions is that they recognize no god of judgment; rather, they provide a model for spiritually healthful everyday living.

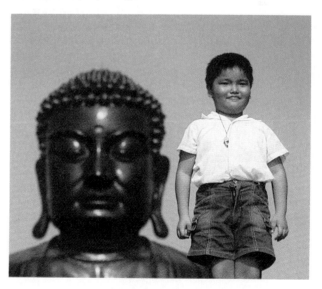

of their duties toward the larger community. In this way, an overarching morality integrates society as a whole: personal loyalty builds strong families; strong families form wholesome communities, and so on. Unlike Jesus and Buddha, then, Confucius directed attention *to* the world, not *away from* it; he also sought guidance in the past for actions in the present, while Christianity and Buddhism look more to the future for salvation and spiritual fulfillment.

Most of all, Confucianism stands out because it lacks a clear sense of the sacred. We could view Confucianism as the celebration of society itself as sacred, in the sense that Durkheim described that process. Alternatively, we might argue that Confucianism is less a religion than a model for leading a disciplined life based on Chinese traditions. Certainly the historical dominance of Confucianism helps to explain why Chinese culture has long taken a skeptical attitude toward the supernatural. If we conclude that Confucianism is best thought of as a disciplined and scholarly way of life, we must also recognize that it shares with religion a body of beliefs and practices that have as their goals goodness and the promotion of social unity (Kaufman, 1976; Schmidt, 1980; McGuire, 1987).

## Judaism

Speaking purely in numerical terms, Judaism is less a world religion than any of the others we have considered, with about 17 million adherents (0.3 percent of humanity). Only in Israel is Judaism a majority religion. But Judaism has special significance to our society because the largest concentration of Jews (some 7 million people) live in North America. Followers of Judaism are also found in every other region of the world, with most of the remainder living in Europe and the Middle East.

Like Confucianism, Judaism has deep roots: Jews look to the past as a source of guidance in the present and for the future. Jewish history extends back some 4,000 years before the birth of Christ to the ancient cultures of Mesopotamia. At that time, Jews were animistic, but this belief was to change after Jacob—grandson of Abraham, the earliest great ancestor—led his people to Egypt.

Under Egyptian rule, Jews endured centuries of slavery. In the thirteenth century B.C.E., a turning point came as Moses, the adopted son of an Egyptian princess, was called by God to lead the Jews from bondage. This exodus (the word's Latin and Greek roots mean "a marching out") from Egypt is commemorated by Jews today in the celebration of Passover. As a result of the Jews' liberation from bondage, Judaism became monotheistic, recognizing a single, all-powerful God.

A distinctive concept of Judaism is the *covenant*, a special relationship with God by which Jews became a "chosen people." The covenant also implies a duty to observe God's law, especially the Ten Commandments as revealed to Moses on Mt. Sinai. Jews regard the Bible (or, in Christian terms, the Old Testament) as both a record of their history and a statement of the general obligations of Jewish life. Of special importance are the first five books of the Bible (Genesis, Exodus, Leviticus, Numbers, and Deuteronomy), designated as the *Torah* (a word roughly meaning "teaching" and "law"). In contrast to Christianity's central concern with personal salvation, Judaism (not unlike Confucianism) emphasizes moral behavior in this world.

Judaism is composed of various denominations distinguished by interpretations of doctrine. Orthodox Jews (including more than 1 million people in the United States) strictly observe traditional beliefs and practices,

Chanukah is an important Jewish ritual of commemoration that serves to teach young people their long and rich history.

including historical forms of dress, segregation of men and women at religious services, and consumption of only kosher foods. Such distinctive practices set off Orthodox Jews as the most sect-like. In the mid-nineteenth century, many Jews sought greater accommodation to the larger society, leading to the formation of the more church-like Reform Judaism (now including more than 1.3 million people in this country). More recently, a third segment—Conservative Judaism (with about 2 million adherents in the United States)—has established a middle ground between the other two denominations.

All Jews, however, share a keen awareness of their cultural history, which has included considerable prejudice and discrimination. A collective memory of centuries of slavery in Egypt, conquest by Rome, and persecution in Europe has shaped Jewish awareness and identity. Interestingly, the urban ghetto (derived from the Italian word *borghetto*, meaning settlement outside the city walls) was first home to Jews in medieval Italy; this form of residential segregation soon spread to other parts of Europe.

Jewish emigration to the United States began in the mid-1600s. Many early immigrants prospered and many were also assimilated into largely-Christian communities. But as more and more Jews joined the Great Immigration during the final decades of the nineteenth century, prejudice and discrimination against them—commonly termed *anti-Semitism*—increased. During this century, anti-Semitism reached a vicious peak when Jews experienced the most horrific persecution in modern times. During the Holocaust, the Nazi regime in Germany systematically annihilated some 6 million people during the 1930s and 1940s. The killing was so extensive and methodical that many in the United States and Europe initially did not comprehend the scope of this genocide (Abzug, 1985).

Despite its historical themes, Judaism has changed considerably over thousands of years. Like Christianity and Islam, Judaism recognizes a single God; like Hinduism and Confucianism, it emphasizes moral directives in this world rather than hope for salvation in a world to come. The history of Judaism also points up a tragic dimension of the human record—the extent to which religious minorities have been the target of hatred and even slaughter (Bedell, Sandon, & Wellborn, 1975; Holm, 1977; Schmidt, 1980; Seltzer, 1980; B. Wilson, 1982; Eisen, 1983).

# Religion in the United States

The United States has experienced remarkable changes over the past 350 years, with transformation in all social institutions including religion. Some wonder if the Industrial Revolution, the establishment of universal schooling, and the advancing role of science and technology together have undermined traditional religion. Yet the evidence shows that religion continues to play a central role in our way of life (Collins, 1982; Greeley, 1989; Woodward, 1992).

## Religious Affiliation

National surveys reveal that about 90 percent of adults in the United States identify with a particular religion (N.O.R.C., 1991:140–41). Table 17–1 records survey results showing that Protestants make up almost two-thirds of the population, Catholicism is embraced by one-fourth of respondents, and 2 percent identify with Judaism. Only about 7 percent claim to have no religious affiliation.

About two-thirds of adults in the United States report that they attend religious instruction classes more or less regularly, and 60 percent consider themselves to be a member of some religious organization (N.O.R.C., 1991:398–99). A comparison of survey data over the last fifty years shows that religious affiliation has remained relatively stable in the United States.

**Table 17–1   RELIGIOUS IDENTIFICATION IN THE UNITED STATES, 1991**

| Religion | | Proportion Indicating Preference |
|---|---|---|
| Protestant denominations | | 63.7% |
| Baptist | 20.1 | |
| Methodist | 9.0 | |
| Lutheran | 6.7 | |
| Presbyterian | 4.9 | |
| Episcopalian | 2.1 | |
| All others or no denomination | 20.9 | |
| Catholic | | 25.4 |
| Jewish | | 2.1 |
| Other or no answer | | 2.1 |
| No religious preference | | 6.7 |

Our society has no official religion; as we have already explained, the separation of church and state is enshrined in the First Amendment. The population of the United States is also more religiously diverse than that of virtually any other country on earth—one result of our historically high level of immigration.

Figure 17–1 shows the dominant religious affiliation of the United States by state and county, based on 1990 census data. In the vast majority of counties, at least 25 percent of people who report having a religious affiliation are members of the same religious group. In New England, urban areas of the Midwest, the Southwest, and southern Florida, the most common religious affiliation is Catholic. The southern states are overwhelmingly Baptist, while Lutherans stand out in the northern Plains states. Members of the Church of Jesus Christ of Latter-Day Saints (Mormons) are heavily concentrated in and around Utah.

## Religiosity

**Religiosity** is a general concept that refers to *the importance of religion in a person's life*. North Americans are a comparatively religious people, more so, for example, than Europeans or the Japanese. Quantitative measures of religiosity in the United States, however, vary depending on exactly how this concept is operationalized. Years ago, Charles Glock (1959, 1962) identified five distinct dimensions of religiosity. *Experiential* religiosity refers to the strength of a person's emotional tie to a religion. *Ritualistic* religiosity deals with frequency of

**Figure 17–1** Major Denominations by Counties of the United States, 1990
*(Glenmary Research Center, Atlanta, Georgia)*

Heaven and hell were never portrayed more vividly than by Jan Van Eyck (1390–1441) in his painting *The Last Judgment* (c. 1420). Notice how heaven is a setting of calm and order while earth and the underworld of hell are scenes of torment and despair. In our more secular world, many people may doubt the reality of Van Eyck's vision, but two out of three adults in the United States claim to believe in a life after death.

(Jan Van Eyck, The Last Judgment. *The Metropolitan Museum of Art, New York. Fletcher Fund, 1933.*)

ritual activity such as prayer and church attendance. *Ideological* religiosity concerns an individual's degree of belief in religious doctrine. *Consequential* religiosity has to do with how much religious beliefs influence a person's daily behavior. Finally, *intellectual* religiosity refers to a person's knowledge of the history and doctrines of a particular religion. Anyone is likely to be more religious on some dimensions than on others; this inconsistency compounds the difficulty of measuring the concept of religiosity.

How religious, then, are members of our society? Almost everyone in the United States (95 percent) claims to believe in a divine power of some kind, although only about 65 percent claim to "know that God exists and have no doubts about it" (N.O.R.C., 1991:401). We have already noted that 90 percent of adults identify with a specific religion. Asked "How close do you feel to God most of the time?", half of respondents said "somewhat close" while another third reported feeling "extremely close" (N.O.R.C., 1991:152). In terms of experiential religiosity, then, people in the United States do seem to be notably religious.

But on other dimensions of religiosity, the pattern changes markedly. In ideological terms, the United States appears to be a less religious nation: only about 70 percent, for example, voice a belief in a life after death. On dimensions of ritualistic religiosity, the numbers drop even lower. For example, only half of adults claim to pray at least once a day, and just one-third attend religious services on a weekly or almost-weekly basis (N.O.R.C., 1991:144, 150, 142).

The question "How religious are we?" thus yields no easy answers. Keep in mind, too, that belief in God is normative in our culture so that people may make such a claim simply to conform. Similarly, we should not assume that everyone who attends services does so for religious reasons; a synagogue, mosque, or church can provide a sense of identity and belonging, a means of satisfying family members, a way to serve the community, or a source of social prestige. Our general conclusion, then, is that most people in the United States are at least somewhat religious, and a large minority deeply so. This estimation squares with what adults in the United States say about themselves when asked to describe the strength of their religious beliefs, as illustrated in Figure 17–2.

Religiosity also varies among different religious organizations. In a classic study of religious diversity, Rodney Stark and Charles Glock (1968) found Catholics to be generally more religious than Protestants. And mem-

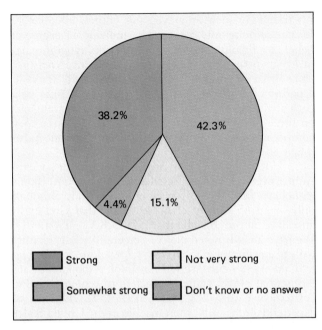

**Figure 17–2** The Strength of Religious Beliefs in the United States, 1991

*(National Opinion Research Center, 1991:144)*

bers of sects, they concluded, are typically more religious than members of Catholic or Protestant churches.

## Correlates of Religious Affiliation

Sociologists study religion not only to comprehend how people address the sacred but because religious affiliation is related to a host of familiar social patterns.

### Social Class

Religious organizations are socially stratified. Wade Roof (1979) found that Jews and certain Protestant denominations (Episcopalians and Presbyterians) had the highest overall social standing in the United States. In a middle position were other Protestant denominations, including Congregationalists and Methodists. Somewhat lower social standing was found among Catholics, Lutherans, and Baptists. As noted earlier in this chapter, members of sect-like organizations typically have a lower social

position than that of more church-like religious communities.

Protestant denominations with the highest social position are those whose membership is mainly of Northern European background, including many families whose ancestors came to the United States more than a century ago. They encountered little prejudice and discrimination and have had the most time to establish themselves socially. Roman Catholics, more recent immigrants to the United States, have contended with greater social barriers based on being a minority religion.

Jews have unexpectedly high social standing considering that many are fairly recent immigrants who confronted anti-Semitism from some members of the Christian majority. A common stereotype links Jewish success to working in banks and other financial positions. This notion is not true, however: in New York, for example, Jews represent half of the city's college graduates, but only 2 percent of its banking officials (Schaefer, 1979). A more plausible explanation is cultural. Jewish traditions place great value on achievement and education. Although a large proportion of Jews immigrated to the United States in poverty, an intense desire for learning led parents to ensure that their children were extensively schooled. As a result, the social position of many Jews—although certainly not all—rose in subsequent generations.

### Ethnicity and Race

Around the world, religion is strongly linked to ethnicity. Many religions predominate in a geographical region, sometimes in a single society. The vast majority of Muslims, for example, live in the Eastern Hemisphere; Hinduism is virtually synonymous with the culture of India, as is Confucianism with the culture of China.

Religion is also fused with national identity in the United States. The social diversity of our society, for example, includes *Anglo-Saxon* Protestants, *Irish* Catholics, *Russian* Jews, and *Greek* Orthodox. This linking of nation and creed results from the influx of immigrants to the United States from societies with a single major religion. Beyond these broad patterns, however, nearly every ethnic group in this country displays at least some religious diversity. People of English ancestry, for instance, include members of many Protestant denominations, Roman Catholics, Jews, and adherents of other religions.

The church has historically been a central element in the lives of African Americans. After arrival in the

Western Hemisphere, most people of African descent became Christians—the dominant religion in the Americas—but they blended Christian belief and practice with elements of African religions. Guided by this religious mix, many Christian people of color embraced ritual that was—by European standards—highly emotional and spontaneous. These expressive qualities persist in many African-American religious organizations today (Frazier, 1965; Roberts, 1980).

Christian fellowship notwithstanding, racial segregation has historically been a fact of religious life. Among adults who are regular church-goers, about 55 percent report that their congregations include only members of their own race. White religious organizations are somewhat more likely to be racially exclusive than those with a primarily black or Hispanic membership; similarly, religious groups with low social standing tend to be more exclusive than those that include more affluent and well-educated members (N.O.R.C., 1991:184).

Religious organizations have long been central to meeting the various needs of African Americans. After emancipation, as people of color migrated from the rural South to the industrial cities of the North, religious groups devised strategies to address problems of dislocation, poverty, and prejudice. For a category of people often cut off from the larger society, churches also provided opportunity for talented men and women to distinguish themselves as leaders. Ralph Abernathy, Martin Luther King, Jr., and Jesse Jackson each gained national and world recognition for leadership while serving as ministers in primarily African-Americans religious organizations.

### Political Attitudes

On most issues, Protestants in the United States take more conservative stands than Catholics. Protestants are more likely to support the (more conservative) Republican Party, while Catholics have historically been (more liberal) Democrats. Jews, too, have traditionally voted with the Democratic Party (J. Wilson, 1978; Gallup, 1982). Political orientations are complex, however, as explained in Chapter 18 ("Politics and Government"). Because Protestants have higher overall social standing than, say, Catholics, they are more conservative about economic issues (to protect their wealth), while at the same time holding liberal social attitudes (reflecting their greater education). Thus Protestants are much more likely to take a pro-choice stand on the abortion controversy or to endorse gay rights than Catholics are (Davis, 1987).

# Religion in a Changing Society

Every society changes over time, which implies a transformation of social institutions. Just as family life and schooling have changed over the course of this century, so has our society's religious life.

## Secularization

One of the most important and controversial patterns of social change is **secularization,** *a historical trend away from the supernatural and the sacred.* For society as a whole, secularization points to a declining influence of religion in everyday life. For religious organizations, becoming more secular means that they direct attention less to otherworldly issues (like life after death) and more to worldly affairs (like whether women or gay people should be ordained as clergy).

Secularization, a concept derived from a Latin word meaning "the present age," is generally associated with modern, technologically advanced societies (Cox, 1971; O'Dea & Aviad, 1983). Conventional wisdom holds that secularization is one result of the increasing importance of science to human understanding. Imagine the early scientist Sir Isaac Newton (1642–1727) sitting under a tree observing an apple falling to the ground. Had he thought the way most Europeans did during the Middle Ages, Newton might have taken an otherworldly view of the event, concluding that apples grow and fall according to the will of God. But living in an age when human beings were adopting the logic of science to understand the natural world, his observation led him to formulate the far more worldly law of gravity.

Evidence of contemporary secularization can be seen in the fact that, since mid-century, public schools have taught children less and less about religion. More broadly, adults perceive birth, illness, and death less as the work of a divine power than as natural stages in the life course that are now more likely to occur in the presence of physicians (whose knowledge is based on science) than religious leaders (whose knowledge is based on faith). Theologian Harvey Cox comments on the diminishing sphere of religion:

> The world looks less and less to religious rules and rituals for its morality or its meanings. For some, religion provides a hobby, for others a mark of national or ethnic identification, for still others an aesthetic delight. For fewer and fewer does it provide an inclusive and commanding system of personal and cosmic values and explanations. (1971:3)

The painting *Arts of the South* by Thomas Hart Benton (1889–1975) suggests that religious fundamentalism is strongly integrated into the community life of rural people in the southern United States.

*(Thomas Hart Benton, Arts of the South. Tempera with oil glaze, 8 × 13 feet. 1953.20. From the collection of the New Britain Museum of American Art, Connecticut. Harriet Russell Stanley Fund.)*

If Cox is correct, one might wonder if religion will some day completely disappear. But this is not the consensus among sociologists (Hammond, 1985; McGuire, 1987). Recall that the vast majority of people in the United States continue to profess a belief in God, and two-thirds are affiliated with a religious organization. We might also bear in mind that people in the United States are as likely to pray every day as they are to vote. Further, we should not assume that all dimensions of religiosity were much higher years ago. Religious affiliation today is actually twice as likely as it was in 1900 and four times as high as in 1850 (Hout & Greeley, 1987). As explained presently, our society has also recently experienced a swell of religious innovation.

Secularization, therefore, does not signal the impending death of religion. More accurately, secularization is an uneven process of change in which a decline in some dimensions of religiosity parallels an increase in others. Similarly, while some religious organizations have lost significant membership in recent decades, others are rapidly gaining in popularity. Finally, in global perspective we see that while religion is declining in importance in some world regions (the Scandinavian countries, for example), religious fervor is rising in others (like Algeria) (Cox, 1990).

Given the complexity of secularization, public attitudes concerning its merits vary significantly. Some people lament secularization as the loss of traditional American values. More secular religious organizations, these critics fear, are no longer addressing otherworldly needs and are preaching instead a doctrine of greater permissiveness in behavior, even sanctioning actions previously viewed as deviant. But others celebrate secularization, touting this drive as a liberation from the all-encompassing beliefs of the past and a way for people to assume greater responsibility for what they choose to believe. Further, secularization has brought the practices of many religious organizations in line with widespread social attitudes. As an example, more women are becoming religious leaders.

## Civil Religion

The inconsistent character of secularization is illustrated in what Robert Bellah (1975) has called **civil religion,** *a quasi-religious loyalty binding individuals in a basically secular society.* The term *civil* refers to the ordinary life of citizens of a political state; patriotism and various national rituals, in other words, have the power to evoke religious feelings. The ascendancy of civil rites offset, at least to some degree, the declining prominence of religion.

Just as religion presents a blueprint for leading a good life, a vast majority of people in the United States believe that our political and economic systems exemplify what is good and that our nation's involvement in world affairs benefits other countries. By contrast, most think of communism as an evil system (N.O.R.C., 1991). Thus the collapse of communist governments in much of the world in recent years has been widely perceived as a moral triumph for the United States. Bear in mind, however, that the social diversity of the United States allows for no single vision of our moral purpose or destiny; various political movements—liberal and conservative alike—draw strength from civil religion (Williams & Demerath, 1991).

Civil religion also encompasses a wide range of rituals. Before the opening of sporting events, spectators rise respectfully for the playing of the national anthem. Public parades held regularly during the year (including New Year's Day, Memorial Day, the Fourth of July, Labor Day, Thanksgiving Day, and Christmas) foster patriotism and build social unity. Roughly like the cross to Christians and the Star of David to Jews, the flag serves as a sacred symbol of our national identity that we expect to be treated with reverence. We object to using a flag like any other piece of cloth, or even allowing it to touch the ground. Patriotism and more traditional religious experiences also evoke a similar sense of wonder and awe. The explanation lies in Emile Durkheim's insight that all ritual allows us to experience our collective identity—the power of society.

Civil religion is not a specific religious doctrine, of course. But civil religion does incorporate many elements of traditional religion into the political system of a secular society. The belief shared by most people in the United States that their society stands as a force for good in the world (based more on faith than on clear and convincing evidence) amounts to one vital religious expression in a modern, secular society.

## Religious Revival

We have already noted that, overall, religiosity in the United States has been stable in recent decades. But a great deal of change is going on inside the world of organized religion. Membership in established, "mainstream" churches like the Episcopalian and Presbyterian denominations has plummeted by almost 50 percent in the last three decades. During this same period, membership in other religious organizations (including the Mormons, Seventh-Day Adventists, and especially Christian sects) has increased just as dramatically or even

more so. This suggests that secularization is a self-limiting process. In other words, as the most church-like organizations become more worldly in their orientation, people abandon them in favor of other, more sect-like religious communities that better address their spiritual concerns (Stark & Bainbridge, 1981; Roof & McKinney, 1987; Jacquet & Jones, 1991).

### Religious Fundamentalism

A significant element in this change is the growth of **religious fundamentalism,** *a conservative religious doctrine that opposes intellectualism and worldly accommodation in favor of restoring a traditional otherworldly focus.* In the United States, fundamentalism has made the biggest inroads among Protestants; a look back at Figure 17–1 leaves little doubt that Southern Baptists now form the largest denomination of any Protestant organization in the United States. But fundamentalism has proliferated beyond Protestants denominations; it is also gaining popularity among Roman Catholics and Jews.

While fundamentalism is hardly new, its influence has steadily increased during this century (Bromley & Shupe, 1984). In the nineteenth century, fundamentalism fueled opposition to the teaching of evolution in schools and promoted later efforts to keep religious instruction in the classroom. To many people in the United States, however, fundamentalism emerged as a key political and social force when conservative Christian organizations publicly supported Ronald Reagan's candidacy for president in 1980 and his conservative social agenda.

Throughout its history, religious fundamentalism has defended traditional beliefs against the tide of change in the United States. During the nineteenth century, our country was in the throes of rapid change as schooling was becoming universal and science was gaining ground on traditional religious thinking. Compounding this transformation, immigrants were streaming into the country in increasing numbers, and industrial cities soon eclipsed in size and productive power the farms and villages familiar to earlier generations.

In times of tumultuous social change, such as the nineteenth century when greater social diversity was eroding traditions and fostering secularization, religious conservatives respond by trying to restore what followers hold to be *fundamental* religious practices and beliefs (Hunter, 1983, 1985, 1987, 1989; Wilcox, 1989). Four fundamentalist tenets stand out. First, fundamentalists *literally interpret Scripture.* They charge that worldly accommodation and increasing intellectualism lead more liberal religious organizations to lose sight of God's message. In the creationism debate described earlier, for example, fundamentalists accept the idea that God created the world precisely as described in Genesis. Second, fundamentalists *reject religious diversity* on the grounds that tolerance and relativism water down personal faith. Third, members of fundamentalist organizations *pursue the personal experience of God's presence.* In contrast to the worldliness and intellectualism of other religious organizations, fundamentalism seeks to propagate "good old-time religion" and spiritual revival. To fundamentalist Christians, the experience of being "born again," meaning they establish a personal relationship with Jesus, is expected to translate clearly into their everyday life. Fourth, fundamentalism *opposes worldly accommodation* because the broader society is viewed as a dangerous source of "secular humanism" that undermines religious conviction. Taken together, these traits suggest why some people consider fundamentalism to be somewhat rigid and self-righteous. At the same time, this brief sketch helps us understand why others find in fundamentalism—with its greater religious certainty and its emphasis on personally experiencing God's presence—an appealing alternative to the more intellectual, tolerant, and worldly "mainstream" denominations.

The label "fundamentalist" applies better to some religious organizations than to others. Generally, the term is used by conservative Christian organizations in the evangelical tradition, including Pentecostals, Southern Baptists, Seventh-Day Adventists, and the Assembly of God. When asked in the *General Social Survey* to describe their religious upbringing, "fundamentalist" was selected by 33 percent of respondents, "moderate" by 42 percent, and "liberal" by the remaining 25 percent (N.O.R.C., 1991:161). This squares exactly with the proportion of respondents—one-third—who claim to interpret the Bible literally (N.O.R.C., 1991:168).

Although Christian fundamentalism has typically shunned worldly concerns, in 1980 it took on a decidedly political character; it emerged as the *New Christian Right* (Viguerie, 1981; Hunter, 1983; Speer, 1984; Ostling, 1985). Jerry Falwell, a fundamentalist preacher, led what he labeled the "Moral Majority" through most of the 1980s. His target was what he termed the nation's "liberal agenda," including the Equal Rights Amendment, abortion as a matter of choice, the civil rights of gay people, and the widespread availability of pornography. Moral Majority members also sought to bring back prayer in public schools, which they view as bastions of permissiveness and secular humanism. To a certain extent, their efforts were successful; they helped launch the "Reagan revolution" and a decade of conservative policies. Falwell disbanded his Moral Majority in 1989, however, partly due to his successes and partly to a diminishing audience.

## The Electronic Church

Finally, conservative religious organizations have received a boost through skillful use of the mass media to generate religious excitement and gain converts. In contrast to small village congregations of years past, "gatherings" now take the form of radio and television audiences who support what is commonly called the *electronic church* dominated by "prime-time preachers" (Hadden & Swain, 1981). Although many members of more liberal churches contend that "prime-time preaching" undermines religion with emotional simplicity, millions of people have become regular participants in this new form of religious activity.

At the beginning of the 1980s, electronic religion was unique to the United States and included approximately 1,400 radio stations and sixty television stations (including many cable television channels). Aided by their electronic churches, religious leaders such as Oral Roberts, Robert Schuller, and Jim and Tammy Bakker have become better known than all but a few clergy in the past. Estimates hold that about 5 percent of the national television audience (about 10 million people) regularly tune in to religious television, while some 20 percent (about 40 million) watch at least some religious programming every week (Martin, 1981; Gallup, 1982; N.O.R.C., 1991).

Sending religious messages via the mass media prompted two notable developments during the 1980s. On the one hand, regular solicitation of contributions brought a financial windfall to some religious organizations. Broadcasting with 3,200 stations in half the countries in the world, for example, Jimmy Swaggart received $180 million in contributions in 1986 alone. On the other hand, some media-based ministries were corrupted by the power of money. In 1989, Jim Bakker (who, with his ex-wife Tammy, began his television career in 1965 hosting a children's puppet show) was jailed following a conviction for defrauding contributors. Such cases, although few in number, attracted enormous national attention and eroded public support as people began to wonder whether television preachers were more interested in raising cash or moral standards.

## The Future of Religion

The popularity of media ministries, the rapid growth of religious fundamentalism, religious innovation and cult formation, and the continued adherence of millions more people to the "mainstream" churches all clearly demonstrate that secularization is not squeezing the religion from our society (Stark & Bainbridge, 1981; Bateson & Ventis, 1982; Hunter, 1985). The world is becoming more complex, with rapid changes almost outstripping our capacity to keep pace. But rather than undermining religion, these processes end up firing the religious imagination of people everywhere who, more than ever, long for a sense of religious community, meaning, and purpose. Science is simply unable to address these central human needs and questions. Moreover, four in ten adults in the United States are troubled that science makes the world change too quickly, breaking down our sense of right and wrong (N.O.R.C., 1991:388). Against this backdrop of uncertainty, it is little wonder that many people turn to their faith for assurance and hope (Cox, 1977; Barker, 1981).

## Summary

1.  Religion is a major social institution based on distinguishing the sacred from the profane. Religion is a matter of faith, not scientific evidence, which people express through various rituals.

2.  Sociology analyzes the social consequences and correlates of religion, but makes no claims as to the ultimate truth or falsity of any religious belief.

3.  Emile Durkheim argued that religion expresses the power of society over individuals. His structural-functional analysis suggests that religion promotes social cohesion, enhances social control, and confers meaning and purpose on life.

4.  Using the symbolic-interaction paradigm, Peter Berger explains that religious beliefs are socially constructed. These beliefs provide a vital source of individual meaning and security, just as religious rituals overlay relationships like marriage, and major life events from birth to death with sacred significance.

5.  Using the social-conflict paradigm, Karl Marx linked religion to social inequality. While religion does perpetuate inequality in some respects, religious ideals also motivate people to seek greater social equality.

6.  A church is one kind of religious organization that seeks accommodation with the larger society. A further distinction among churches is made between an ecclesia, or state-sponsored church, and a denomination, which recognizes religious pluralism.

7.  A sect, another type of religious organization, resists accommodation with the larger society. Sects emerge as a result of religious division and often have charismatic leadership.

8.  Cults are religious organizations that embrace beliefs and practices that are unconventional from the point of view of the surrounding society. By making distinctions among churches, sects, and cults, sociologists do not judge one type of religious organization as more valid or worthy than another.

9.  Technologically simple human societies were generally animistic; in more complex societies, religion emerges as a distinct social institution.

10. Followers of six world religions—Christianity, Islam, Hinduism, Buddhism, Confucianism, and Judaism—represent three-fourths of all humanity.

11. Almost all adults in the United States identify with a religion; about 60 percent have a formal religious affiliation, with the largest number belonging to various Protestant denominations.

12. How religious our nation is depends on how religiosity is operationalized. The vast majority of people claim to believe in God, but only two-thirds confess no doubts about it. About half engage in daily prayer and just about one-third regularly attend religious services.

13. The United States has considerable religious diversity, with affiliation linked to social class, ethnicity, and race.

14. Secularization, an important dimension of social change, involves declining attention to the supernatural and the sacred. Religious organizations become more secular (church-like) as they become more intellectual and conceive of God in more

distant terms. Some people view secularization as a breakdown of traditional morality; others perceive it as a form of liberation and a source of greater tolerance.

15. Membership in more liberal "mainstream" churches has declined sharply in recent decades; however, more conservative religious organizations (notably Christian sects) have been surging in popularity. These parallel trends suggest that secularization will not result in the demise of religion.

16. Civil religion is a quasi-religious belief by which people profess loyalty to their society, often in the form of patriotism.

17. Fundamentalism opposes religious accommodation to the world and stresses a more otherworldly

focus. Fundamentalist Christianity also stresses literal interpretation of the Bible, rejects religious diversity, and pursues the personal experience of God's presence. During the 1980s, some fundamentalist Christian organizations actively supported conservative political goals in the United States.

18. Despite the historical process of secularization, the shifting of support toward fundamentalist organizations and the continued expression of religious beliefs by people in the United States casts doubt on the notion that religion is eroding. Rather, evidence abounds that religion still addresses many timeless questions about human experiences and needs.

## Key Concepts

**animism** the belief that natural objects are conscious forms of life that can affect humanity

**charisma** in religious terms, evidence of God's favor in the behavior of an individual

**church** a type of religious organization that readily seeks accommodation with the larger society

**civil religion** a quasi-religious loyalty binding individuals in a basically secular society

**conversion** a personal transformation resulting from adopting new religious beliefs

**cult** a religious organization with roots outside the dominant religious traditions of a society

**denomination** a church, not linked to the state, in a society that recognizes religious pluralism

**ecclesia** a church that is formally allied with the state

**faith** belief that is anchored in conviction rather than scientific evidence

**liberation theology** a fusion of Christian principles with political activism, often Marxist in character

**monotheism** belief in a single divine power

**polytheism** belief in many gods

**profane** that which is defined as an ordinary element of everyday life

**religion** a system of beliefs and practices based on recognizing the sacred

**religiosity** the importance of religion in a person's life

**religious fundamentalism** a conservative religious doctrine that opposes intellectualism and worldly accommodation in favor of restoring a traditional otherworldly focus

**ritual** formal, ceremonial behavior

**sacred** that which is defined as extraordinary, inspiring a sense of awe, reverence, and even fear

**sect** a type of religious organization that resists accommodation with the larger society

**secularization** a historical trend away from the supernatural and the sacred

**totem** an object in the natural world that is imbued with sacred qualities

## Suggested Readings

This text provides a sweeping, sociological analysis of religion.
   Meredith B. McGuire. *Religion: The Social Context.* 3rd ed. Belmont, CA: Wadsworth, 1991.

This historical account of American religious life before the Civil War asserts that our society's religious habits and beliefs were far more varied and complex than most people imagine.

Jon Butler. *Awash in a Sea of Faith: Christianizing the American People*. Cambridge, MA: Harvard University Press, 1990.

Focusing on the life of St. Paul, the first of these books argues that charisma is not merely a personal trait but a collective phenomenon generated in response to a social need. The second, an intellectual history of the concept of charisma, draws on the work of Weber, Durkheim, and Freud.

Anthony J. Blasi. *Making Charisma: The Social Construction of Paul's Public Image*. New Brunswick, NJ: Transaction, 1991.

Charles Lindholm. *Charisma*. Cambridge, MA: Basil Blackwell, 1990.

The state of religion in the United States is explored in the first of the following books. The second comprises nine essays that survey religion in global perspective.

Thomas Robbins and Dick Anthony. *In Gods We Trust: New Patterns of Religious Pluralism in America*. New Brunswick, NJ: Transaction, 1989.

James A. Beckford and Thomas Luckmann, eds. *The Changing Face of Religion*. Newbury Park, CA: Sage, 1989.

These two books focus on the Catholic church. The first, a personal exploration of "charismatic Catholics," reveals that Catholicism is not always highly formal and ritualized. The second, challenging the view that the Catholic Church is a conservative force in the world, shows the progressive agenda of the church in Brazil.

Mary Jo Neitz. *Charisma and Community: A Study of Religious Commitment Within the Charismatic Renewal*. New Brunswick, NJ: Transaction, 1987.

Scott Mainwaring. *The Catholic Church and Politics in Brazil, 1916–1985*. Palo Alto, CA: Stanford University Press, 1986.

The first of these books documents the genocide of European Jews during World War II, and explains how the enormity of the Holocaust was difficult for many in the United States to grasp. The second, written by a sociologist who survived the Holocaust, attempts to explain why some Christians risked their lives to save Jews.

Robert H. Abzug. *Inside the Vicious Heart: Americans and the Liberation of Nazi Concentration Camps*. New York: Oxford University Press, 1985.

Nechama Tec. *When Light Pierced the Darkness: Christian Rescue of Jews in Nazi-Occupied Poland*. New York: Oxford University Press, 1986.

This book examines life in five Islamic communities in the United States, shedding light on a religion about which many Americans know little.

Yvonne Yazbeck Haddad and Adair T. Lummis. *Islamic Values in the United States: A Comparative Study*. New York: Oxford University Press, 1987.

Religion has long played a major role in the social relations between the sexes. This collection of ten essays examines both the ideal and the real social position of women in Islamic societies.

Freda Hussain, ed. *Muslim Women*. New York: St. Martin's Press, 1984.

This book traces the history of religions embraced by African Americans, especially those promising "deliverance" to people suffering oppression.

Wilson Jeremiah Moses. *Black Messiahs and Uncle Toms: Social and Literary Manipulations of a Religious Myth*. University Park, PA: The Pennsylvania State University Press, 1986.

Based on personal exploration of a fundamentalist Christian church in New England, this study explains how and why one sect resists accommodation with the surrounding society.

Nancy Tatum Ammerman. *Bible Believers: Fundamentalists in the Modern World*. New Brunswick, NJ: Transaction, 1988.

This collection of essays delves into the process of secularization.

Philip E. Hammond, ed. *The Sacred in a Secular Age: Toward Revision in the Scientific Study of Religion*. Berkeley, CA: University of California Press, 1985.

# Politics and Government

One thousand years ago, halfway around the world, a man stood by the side of the road, surveying his homeland in the wake of war. As the cold wind swirled around him, he could see that the soldiers had left, but the graves of those who were not so lucky seemed to be everywhere. He noticed oxen-drawn carts weighted down with crops grinding slowly toward the distant city; he knew that they would soon return with other goods, just as they had before the fighting began. He watched families nervously looking about as they hunched over in the fields, scavenging for food. He heard people trying to assure themselves that life was returning to normal. But, as the man walked to his house, he knew that all was not the same. He sat and wrote the following lines (Chang Pin, "Lament for Ten Thousand Men's Graves"):

> The war ended on the Huan border,
> And the trading roads are open again;
> Stray crows come and go,
> Cawing in the wintry sky.
> Alas for the white bones,
> Heaped together in desolate graves;
> All had sought military honors for their leader.

Chang Pin's poem raises a number of timeless points: how power is distributed within a society; why people often feel that they have little control over their lives; and why the many sometimes die in service to the few. His thoughts also draw us to the broader question

of why nations fall into conflict. The sobering fact is that warfare has been present—at least somewhere in the world—continually virtually without end from long before Chang Pin's lifetime right down to our own.

At several levels, this chapter investigates the dynamics of power in and between societies. A central concept of this inquiry is **politics,** *the institutionalized system by which a society distributes power and makes decisions.* We shall begin by examining the role of power in social organization, survey political systems around the world and examine the operation of government in the United States, and conclude the chapter with a look at the military, asking why nations go to war and how they might, instead, pursue peace.

## Power and Authority

Political life fuels disagreement and often ignites conflict. Early in this century, Max Weber (1978; orig. 1921) recognized these facts when he defined **power** as *the ability to achieve desired ends despite possible resistance from others.* History shows that *force*—physical might or psychological coercion—constitutes the most basic form of power. But no society exists for long if its power derives solely from force, because people will break rules they do not respect at the first opportunity. Coercing

497

Leaders want to have legitimacy in the eyes of the people they rule because such acceptance affords stability to a government. Becoming established in this way, however, is no easy task; a look at many nations of the world reveals that a thin line separates political authority from military power.

people's compliance through terror is both difficult and limited in effectiveness. By contrast, durable social organization depends on significant agreement about proper goals (cultural values) and the suitable means of attaining them (cultural norms). But in what circumstances do members of a society define the use of power as just? Weber viewed power with justice as the essence of the concept of **authority,** which he defined as *power people perceive as legitimate rather than coercive.*

Whether people perceive power as legitimate or coercive depends on the social context. To illustrate, consider the power of teachers to assign term papers to their classes. Although students may greet such assignments with groans, they usually do the work according to their teacher's directions. Students complete the task for the same reason that the teacher assigns it in the first place: the ritual of assigning a paper is built on the roles we expect people to follow in the classroom. In short, power used in a normative fashion is transformed into authority.

On the other side of the coin, a teacher who threatens a student with a poor grade in order to obtain sexual favors violates cultural norms as well as college regulations. Such behavior constitutes coercive power rather than legitimate authority. So while power and authority both produce compliance, they differ in the meanings people attach to the actions involved. Notice, too, that when authority is at work those who command are bound by cultural norms just as much as those who obey.

What, then, are the roots of authority? Max Weber

identified three, which come together in many everyday experiences of power.

## Traditional Authority

**Traditional authority,** claimed Weber, is *power legitimized by respect for long-established cultural patterns.* Traditional authority pervades preindustrial societies in which change happens slowly. People come to think of traditional social patterns—their society's collective memory—as nearly sacred. In ancient China, the power of the emperor rested on tradition, as did the rule of monarchs in medieval Europe. Traditional authority is commonly exercised by families whose members may reign for centuries. The near-sacred character of traditional authority gives many traditional leaders a god-like standing; some even claim to rule by divine right.

As a society industrializes, tradition no longer holds sway as a means of legitimizing power. Hannah Arendt (1963) explains that traditional authority is compelling only so long as everyone in a society shares one historical world view; this form of authority, then, is undermined by the cultural diversity that accompanies immigration. Because ours is a nation of immigrants, national leaders in the United States rely little on traditional authority—no president, for example, would claim to rule by grace of God. At the same time, as E. Digby Baltzell (1964) points out, some well-established upper-class families—such as the Roosevelts, Kennedys, and Rockefellers—

have occupied a privileged position for long enough to enjoy some measure of traditional authority. In many European societies that have historically experienced less immigration, a royal family still exists although the more democratic culture of today's world has shifted real power to commoners popularly elected to office.

If traditional authority plays a smaller part in politics, it continues to be present in many dimensions of everyday life. Patriarchy, the traditional domination of women by men, is still widespread, although increasingly challenged, in the United States. Less controversial is the traditional authority parents exert over their young children. Family life also shows us that traditional authority enables some people to direct the actions of others based on their status rather than the wisdom of their commands. To children who ask *why* they should obey, parents have long retorted, "Because I said so!" To debate the merits of a command would, after all, place parent and child on the same level.

## Rational-Legal Authority

As explained in Chapter 7 ("Groups and Organizations"), Weber viewed bureaucracy as the organizational backbone of industrial societies. Bureaucracy is one expression of our modern, rational view of the world, an outlook that erodes traditional customs and practices. Rather than venerating the past, members of industrial societies typically build their lives around formal rules, often in the form of law. But rational law, like tradition, serves to legitimize power. Thus Weber defined **rational-legal authority** (sometimes called *bureaucratic authority*) as *power legitimized by legally enacted rules and regulations*. Rational-legal authority is closely linked to **government**, *formal organizations that direct the political life of a society*.

Rationally enacted rules not only guide government in the United States, they also underlie much of our everyday life. The authority of classroom teachers, for example, rests primarily on their official status in bureaucratic colleges and universities. Likewise, officers of the law strive to maintain the public peace. In such cases, authority flows, not from family background, but from offices in formal organizations. In other words, what is important today is less the person and more the office so that, while a queen is always a queen, a president accepts and relinquishes power as given by law to the office itself. To put the matter in different terms, traditional authority is transmitted by ascription, while bureaucratic authority follows achievement. A modern of-ficeholder exercises rational-legal authority not on the basis of birth but rather based on talent and special training.

## Charismatic Authority

Max Weber was intrigued by charisma—exceptional personal qualities, as discussed in Chapter 17 ("Religion"). Broadening this religious concept to take account of all kinds of leadership, Weber defined **charismatic authority** as *power legitimized through extraordinary personal abilities that inspire devotion and obedience*. Charisma, therefore, provides a third way in which power can be transformed into authority. But unlike tradition and rational law, charisma is less a quality of social organization than a dimension of individual personality.

Members of every society regard some of their number as especially forceful, creative, and magnetic. In modern societies, these may include famous artists, entertainers, and political leaders. In traditional societies, Weber noted, charisma can enhance the stature of a traditional leader, but it can also empower an individual to challenge tradition, leading others away from established beliefs and practices. Likewise, the prospects of would-be politicians in the United States rise or fall according to their degree of personal charisma. Some of our more charismatic presidents have embraced traditional views (President Ronald Reagan, for example) or changed the direction of our nation's government (as President Franklin Roosevelt did when he launched the "New Deal").

For Weber, charismatic authority was most clearly expressed in founding new ways of life. By motivating an audience to follow their lead, charismatics often are able to make their own rules, as if drawing on some higher power. Driven by individual visions for radical change, some charismatics have left their mark on global politics. Vladimir Lenin guided the former Soviet Union's overthrow of feudal monarchy, Mahatma Gandhi inspired the struggle to free India from British colonialism, and Martin Luther King, Jr., galvanized the civil rights movement in the United States.

Charisma may arise from personality, but it also reflects a society's expectations about what kind of people emerge as leaders. Patriarchy encourages us to tap men as our national leaders, while steering charismatic women more toward the arts, the family, and other social contexts traditionally defined as feminine. Yet, in recent years, charismatic women—including Indira Gandhi of India,

Neoclassical artist Jacques Louis David (1748–1825) painted *The Death of Socrates* (1787) to memorialize that Greek philosopher as he was about to drink the cup of hemlock that would end his life. Like Christ, the artist suggests, Socrates is being put to death by a society that fails to understand his message—note that he is surrounded by twelve disciples as he defends virtue even at the cost of his own life. To many thinkers of this age, the eighteenth century promised a triumph of reason over numbing tradition.

*(Jacques Louis David, The Death of Socrates. 1787. Oil on canvas. 59 × 78". The Metropolitan Museum of Art. New York. Wolfe Fund, 1931. Catharine Lorillard Wolfe Collection.)*

Benazir Bhutto of Pakistan, and Margaret Thatcher of the United Kingdom—gained national political prominence.

Because charismatic authority emanates from a single individual, any charismatic movement—whether religious or political—faces a crisis of survival upon the death of its leader. The persistence of a charismatic movement, Max Weber reasoned, requires **routinization of charisma,** *the transformation of charismatic authority into some combination of traditional and bureaucratic authority.* Christianity, for example, began as a cult driven by the personal charisma of Jesus of Nazareth. After the death of Jesus, the Roman Catholic Church gradually emerged on the twin foundations of tradition and bureaucracy, and it continues to flourish today, 2,000 years later. Oftentimes, however, there is no routinization of charisma; most charismatic movements simply disintegrate upon the departure of the inspirational leader. One example is the nineteenth-century Christian sect founded by cleric John Humphrey Noyes, which settled in the Oneida region of upstate New York. Although the Oneida community thrived under Noyes's leadership, it floundered after its aging leader left the community.

## Politics in Global Perspective

Like most other dimensions of social life, politics varies significantly from one society to another. To survey this diversity, we begin with a look back in time; then we turn to political systems in today's world.

## Politics in History

Glancing back over human history, we see that politics has not always been a major social institution. With few specialized roles and minimal material wealth, technologically simple hunting and gathering societies operated like a large family. In general, members recognized as their leader a man with unusual strength, hunting skill, or personal charisma. But such leaders exercised little power over others, since they had few resources to reward supporters or to punish challengers. In simple societies, then, leaders were barely discernible from everyone else, and politics as a sphere of life remained on the fringe (Lenski, Lenski, & Nolan, 1991).

Agrarian societies, which are larger and more complex, benefit from more specialized activity and a plentiful material surplus. In these societies, hierarchy becomes increasingly pronounced, as wealth and power are concentrated among a small elite. Such inequality thrusts politics outside the family so that it becomes a social institution in its own right. Elites whose families have maintained their privileged position for generations may acquire traditional authority, sometimes claiming divine right to rule. These leaders may benefit further from Weber's rational-legal authority to the extent that they are served by a bureaucratic political administration and a system of law.

As politics expands in scope, societal power eventually takes the form of a **political state,** *a formal government claiming the legitimate use of coercion to support its rule.* Governments claim authority, in other words, based on some combination of tradition, law, and charismatic leadership. But governments rarely stand as the sole source of power in a society. Political revolutions, after all, have occurred throughout human history.

Historically, the political state has developed slowly because the power of government depends on technology; only a few centuries ago, communication over even short distances was uncertain and the transportation of armies and supplies was slow and cumbersome. Thus governments could confidently control only limited areas. Even early political empires—such as Mesopotamia in the Middle East about 5,000 years ago—constituted a collection of small *city-states* rather than a single nation (Stavrianos, 1983). The greatest political power in the ancient world was Rome, the center of a far-reaching empire for some 500 years beginning in the first century B.C.E. By today's standards, the government of the Roman Empire seems as inefficient and unwieldy as the weapons used by the Roman armies. Unable to effectively control its vast empire, Rome eventually collapsed.

In the modern world, political organization has evolved toward *nation-states*. Currently, the world has roughly 185 independent nation-states, which differ in countless ways including culture, technology, and political system. In industrial societies, the political state is most broadly involved in the everyday lives of the population, providing a host of services ranging from income assistance and schooling to enforcing safety standards in the workplace.

## Contemporary Political Systems

Four types of political systems manage the affairs of contemporary nation-states. Despite significant differences, all types of government strive to legitimize their power by winning the hearts and minds of the population.

### Monarchy

**Monarchy** (a word with Latin and Greek roots meaning "ruling alone") is *a type of political system in which power is passed from generation to generation in a single family*. Monarchy dates back very far as a form of government; great kings and queens even take center stage in the Bible. In Weber's terms, monarchy is legitimized primarily by tradition. In Great Britain, the royal family (as well as many members of the traditional aristocracy) trace their ancestry back through centuries of nobility. Typically, a monarch enjoyed the support of a governmental organization; sometimes the power of a monarch was enhanced by personal charisma. But the core of royal authority lies in deeply rooted tradition.

Not all monarchs wield unlimited power. During the medieval era, *absolute monarchy*, in which hereditary rulers claimed a virtual monopoly of power based on divine right, flourished from England to China and in some parts of the Americas. Monarchy remained widespread even early in this century. On a spring morning in 1910, seventy national leaders assembled in London for the funeral of King Edward VII; of these rulers, more than fifty were hereditary monarchs (Baltzell, 1964).

Over the course of this century, monarchs have gradually given way to elected officials. In European nations that have retained their royalty—including Great Britain, Spain, Norway, Sweden, Belgium, Denmark, and the Netherlands—these families now preside over *constitutional monarchies* in which monarchs are little more than symbolic heads of state. Actual governing is now the responsibility of elected officials, led by a prime minister, and guided by a constitution. In these countries, then, the nobility may reign, but elected officials actually rule (Roskin, 1982).

### Democracy

The historical trend in the modern world has favored **democracy**, *a political system in which power is exercised by the people as a whole*. The members of democratic societies rarely participate directly in routine decision making; numbers alone make this an impossibility. In a system more precisely termed *representative democracy*, citizens place authority in the hands of elected leaders, who must answer to the people for their performance in office. Legitimacy, then, is based on popular support, measured by lawful elections. In most societies that think of themselves as democratic, many eligible voters never go to the polls. In the 1988 presidential election, for example, only 57 percent of eligible voters in the United States cast a ballot.

Democratic political systems are common in First-World industrial societies that are relatively rich by world standards (Hannan & Carroll, 1981). Economic development and democratic government go together because both depend on a motivated and literate populace. A monarchy derives legitimacy from a strong sense of tradition and little desire for change—a condition common to agrarian societies but one that dissipates in the winds of industrialization. A democratic political system is based on rational-legal authority that functions by means of a rational election process. Elections place leaders in offices that confer authority limited by law. Thus democracy and rational-legal authority are linked just as monarchy and traditional authority are.

But modern political systems consist not just of leaders and followers; they are built on extensive bureaucracy. Formal organization is necessary to carry out the increasing range of government activities found in democratic societies; yet, democracy and bureaucracy exist in uneasy alliance. The federal government of the United States, for example, employs more than 3 million people (excluding the armed forces), placing it among the largest bureaucracies in the world. Another 14 million people work in some 80,000 local governments. The great majority of these bureaucrats were never elected and are unknown to the public they purport to serve. To elect them would be impractical given their numbers and the need for highly specialized training. So, ironically, while the public focuses attention on elected leaders, most everyday decision making is carried out by career bureaucrats who are not directly accountable to the people (Scaff, 1981; Edwards, 1985; Etzioni-Halevy, 1985).

### Democracy and Freedom: Contrasting Approaches

Virtually all industrialized nations have claimed to be democratic and politically free, even though they have forged very different political systems. This curious fact prompts us to take a closer look at what it means to be "free" in various societies.

The United States, Canada, and the nations of Western Europe—together known as "the West"—are societies shaped by the free-market principles of capitalism. The operation of a market system requires that individuals enjoy a high measure of personal freedom to pursue whatever goals advance their self-interest. Thus, the Western tradition of political freedom means personal *liberty*. Liberty is the *freedom to* vote for one's preferred leader or otherwise act with minimal interference from government.

As Chapter 19 ("The Economy and Work") explains, however, capitalism fosters considerable inequality of wealth, which has fueled criticism of Western societies as neither free nor democratic because wealth gives some people the power to impose their will on others. From this standpoint, popular elections are unlikely to change the capitalist system, so political rituals have little practical importance or impact. Whoever is elected presides over a society that permits some to enjoy lavish housing, extensive education, and abundant health care while necessities are denied to others.

For most of this century, the Soviet Union and the nations of Eastern Europe had centralized, government-controlled economies. Socialist governments in these societies demanded that individuals act in ways that officials deemed socially responsible, and leaders monitored social life in order to provide every citizen with a job, housing, schooling, and medical care. The socialist governments of the Eastern Bloc defended these policies on the basis that they created a more or less equal standard of living for everyone. Thus the Soviet socialist tradition defined "freedom" quite differently from countries in the West: as *freedom from* basic want. By Western standards, at least, these societies lacked the basic elements of democracy, in that their people had no right to elect political leaders, to form opposition parties, or to freely act in their own interests. But officials called theirs a democratic system because government was responsive to the needs of people.

In light of the changes in the socialist world, however, it may be reasonable to ask if economic equality and political liberty are compatible. To foster economic equality, socialism—and the heavy hand of government—infringed on individual initiative. But, by the same token, as these nations have moved toward Western-style political liberty, they are encountering far greater economic inequality.

The political transformation of much of the socialist world has led many analysts in our own society to trumpet the expansion of democracy. The box on pages 504-5, which reviews global political shifts during the last decade, explains that an unprecedented share of the world's people now have sufficient political rights and civil liberties to be called "free." A graphic illustration of this transformation appears in Global Map 18–1.

### Authoritarianism and Totalitarianism

Despite evidence of a trend toward democracy in some parts of the world, not all nations try to involve their people in politics. **Authoritarianism** refers to *any political system that denies popular participation in government.* As we have already explained, no society involves all its citizens in the daily activities of government, so every political system is authoritarian to some degree. Therefore, we should reserve this term for political systems that are broadly indifferent to people's lives, in which leaders cannot be legally removed from office, and that provide the people with little or no way to voice their

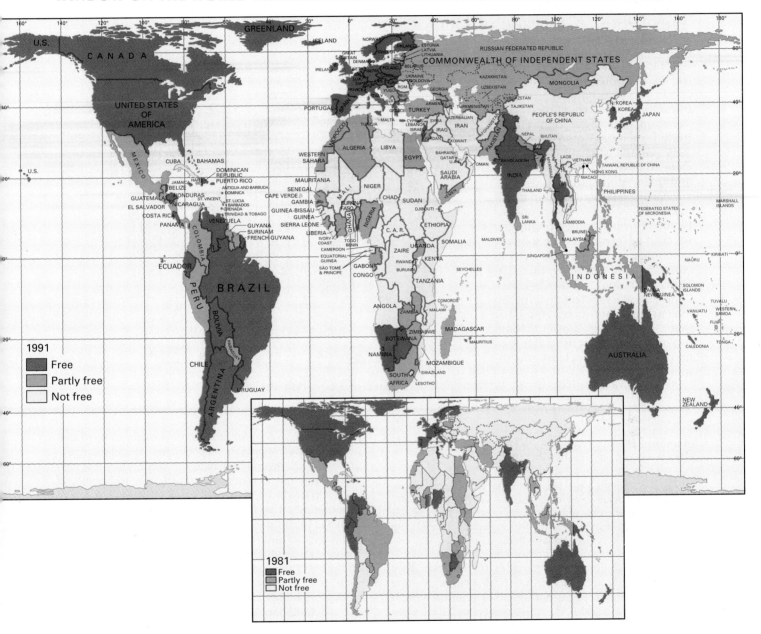

**Global Map 18–1**   Political Freedom in Global Perspective

In 1991, sixty-seven of the world's nations that contained almost 40 percent of all people were politically "free." Another fifty nations that included almost 30 percent of the world's people were "partly free." The remaining thirty nations with about one-third of humanity remained "not free." Comparing the two maps shows that, during the 1980s, democratic gains were made in Eastern Europe, the former Soviet Union, and South America. Political rights are most extensive in the rich nations of the world and least extensive in poorer countries of Africa and Asia.

# The 1980s: A Decade of Democracy

Beginning with the rise of the Polish trade union Solidarity in the late 1970s, popular opposition to socialist governments swelled throughout Eastern Europe. The "opening" of these tightly controlled societies intensified after 1985 when Mikhail Gorbachev came to power in the Soviet Union and initiated his program of *perestroika* or "restructuring." In the final months of 1989, the people of Eastern Europe toppled unpopular socialist governments like so many dominoes first in Poland, then in Hungary, East Germany, Bulgaria, Czechoslovakia, and Romania. Long-time dissatisfaction erupted into action when it became clear that the former Soviet Union lacked the power or the will to sustain their existing socialist governments.

The future of political life in

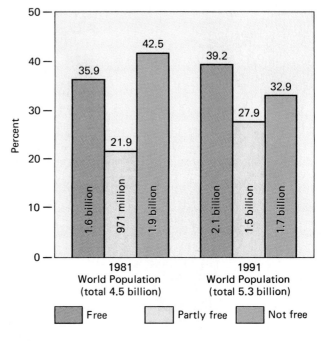

Global Democracy, 1981 and 1991

opinions. Polish sociologist Wlodzimierz Wesolowski (1990:435) puts the matter this way:

> [In a democracy,] the self-organizing principle of society takes precedence over the organizing activity of the state, so that society is the ultimate source of power. The authoritarian philosophy argues for the supremacy of the state [over other] organized social activity.

Although absolute monarchies are now rare, they illustrate highly authoritarian political systems. A more common example of an authoritarian political system in the modern world is the military dictatorship. Examples include the regime of Juan and Eva Peron in Argentina during the 1940s and 1950s, and the military juntas that have ruled Chile, the Philippines, Haiti, and Panama. Here, again, we can point to nations that have become more democratic in recent years.

The greatest measure of political control of a society by government is termed **totalitarianism,** *a political sys-*

*tem that denies popular participation in government and also extensively regulates people's lives.* Totalitarian governments are relatively new to the world; they emerged within the last century along with the technological means to rigidly regulate the lives of citizens. The Soviet government as well as the Nazi regime in Germany both had the military power and the electronic technology to broadly monitor the lives of their people. Still more sophisticated equipment for electronic surveillance and computers that store vast amounts of information have increased the potential for government manipulation of a large population.

Totalitarian leaders sometimes claim to embody the will of the people, but more accurately they try to bend people to the will of the government. Such governments form *total* concentrations of power, permitting no organized opposition. Denying the populace the right to assemble for political purposes, totalitarian regimes thrive in an environment of fear and social atomization. Such governments also limit the access of citizens to these countries is far from clear, as they struggle to gain a greater measure of economic security. What seems all but certain, however, is that political *pluralism*—meaning many political parties competing for popular support—is replacing the monopoly of power held by Communist parties since World War II.

In 1991, the Communist Party's historic monopoly on power also came to an end in the Soviet Union. The former Baltic republics—Latvia, Estonia, and Lithuania—won their independence (lost during World War II when the Soviet armies moved westward), and, in 1992, most of the remaining republics formed a new Commonwealth of Independent States.

While Eastern Europe and the former Soviet Union have made dramatic strides toward political freedom, democratic forces are making gains elsewhere as well. Multiple parties are more in evidence now across the continent of Africa; Latin America continues a struggle to recover democratic institutions; and South Asian nations grapple to sustain a drive toward democracy. There are also new threats to democratic institutions—especially the reemergence of nationalism and ethnicity, which has turned people against one another from Ireland to the former Soviet Union to the dividing nation of Yugoslavia and politically tense India. But, on balance, the 1990s opened with greater prospects for political democracy in the world than have existed in recent memory.

According to Freedom House, a New York-based organization that tracks global political trends, almost 40 percent of the world's people—more than 2 billion out of a total of 5.3 billion—are now living in "free" societies with extensive political rights and civil liberties. As shown in the figure, another 28 percent (1.5 billion) people are "partially free," with more limited rights and liberties. The final one-third of the world's people remain in countries where government sharply restricts individual initiative. Comparing these figures with the percentages a decade ago, the trend toward democracy is unmistakable. Additionally, in 1991—for the first time on record—*more of the world's people lived in "free" societies than in nations deemed "not free."*

SOURCES: Based on Mathews (1991) and McColm et al. (1991).

information: in the former Soviet Union, for example, the mass media have only recently begun to act independently of the government. Further, that totalitarian state weakened the public capacity for collective action by restricting access to items such as telephone directories, accurate city maps, and copying machines. Another typical tactic of totalitarian governments is to encourage citizens to disclose the allegedly unpatriotic activities of other people—a sure recipe for widespread terror. After the 1989 crackdown on the Beijing democracy movement in the People's Republic of China, for example, officials demanded that citizens report anyone—even their own family members—who had challenged the government.

Because totalitarian governments demand not only outward conformity but inward commitment to their rule, socialization in such societies is intensely political. Schools and the mass media are government controlled, presenting only official versions of events. In North Korea, among the most totalitarian states in the modern world, political banners and pictures of leaders are found everywhere, and pedestrians rarely gain respite from partisan slogans that blare over loudspeakers. These messages serve as constant reminders that the government expects and commands the total support of each citizen. Government indoctrination is especially intense whenever political opposition surfaces. In the aftermath of the pro-democracy movement, for example, Chinese officials subjected students at the sixty-seven Beijing universities to mandatory political "refresher" courses (Arendt, 1958; Kornhauser, 1959; Friedrich & Brzezinski, 1965; Nisbet, 1966; Goldfarb, 1989).

Although they always coerce a population toward conformity with the party line, totalitarian governments span the political spectrum from the far right (Nazi Germany) to the far left (North Korea and Albania). Many people in the United States view socialist societies as totalitarian by definition, because they involve extensive government regulation of the economy. Yet socialism (an economic system) is not synonymous with totalitar-

The concept of political liberty burned in the minds of many European thinkers during the eighteenth and nineteenth centuries; authoritarian regimes were often just as intent on stamping out dissent. In *The Third of May, 1808*, the Spanish painter Francisco Goya (1746–1828) commemorates the death of Madrid citizens at the hands of faceless soldiers. The martyrs shown here are dying not for religious salvation, as in so much medieval art, but for the modern principle of political freedom.

ianism (a political system). Socialism generally means pervasive government involvement in everyday life. But limited socialism—as it exists in Sweden, for example—meshes with political democracy. Then, too, some societies with capitalist economies, including Chile and South Africa, exercise totalitarian control over the lives of most of their citizens.

A century and a half ago, in his famous book *Democracy in America* (1969; orig. 1834–1840), the brilliant French thinker Alexis de Tocqueville warned that *all* modern governments were growing in size and scope, thereby gaining the potential for totalitarian control. Tocqueville believed that citizens could counteract this danger by organizing among themselves, forging wide-ranging voluntary associations that enhanced democracy as they diffused power throughout the society.

## Politics in the United States

The founding of the United States was one of the boldest political experiments in human history. Settled as part of a colonial empire, the new nation emerged from a revolutionary war against Great Britain. George Washington was elected the first president in 1789, and Congress met for the first time in New York—the nation's first capital.

Early political leaders rejected the British model of monarchy in favor of a more democratic political system. Over more than two centuries, the commitment of our population to democratic principles has persisted, even as the political system has grown vastly larger and more complex. The U.S. version of democracy is also distinctive, shaped by our particular history, economy, and cultural traditions.

## Culture, Economics, and Politics

The culture of the United States has traditionally celebrated hardy individualists—strong, self-reliant, and competitive people who pursue success commensurate with their abilities and effort. The Bill of Rights, the first ten amendments to the U.S. Constitution, guarantee the personal freedoms that underlie such individualism.

Embracing this tradition of personal liberty, many people in the United States no doubt would nod in support of the sentiment of nineteenth-century philosopher and poet Ralph Waldo Emerson: "The government that governs best is the government that governs least." Yet few of us would actually want to do away with government entirely because almost everyone thinks that it is necessary for some purposes, including national defense, managing our schools, or maintaining public law and order. As the United States has become more populous and more complex, the list of government responsibilities

**Table 18–1  THE GROWTH OF UNITED STATES GOVERNMENT SPENDING**

| Year | Federal Government Expenditure (in Millions of Dollars; Unadjusted for Inflation) | Government Expenditure as Proportion of Gross National Product |
|------|------|------|
| 1795 | 6 | |
| 1800 | 11 | |
| 1810 | 9 | |
| 1820 | 18 | |
| 1830 | 25 | |
| 1840 | 20 | |
| 1850 | 44 | |
| 1860 | 56 | |
| 1870 | 411 | |
| 1880 | 334 | 2.4 |
| 1890 | 403 | 2.4 |
| 1900 | 567 | 2.8 |
| 1910 | 676 | 2.0 |
| 1920 | 6,649 | 6.9 |
| 1930 | 4,058 | 3.7 |
| 1940 | 6,361 | 9.1 |
| 1950 | 39,485 | 13.9 |
| 1960 | 92,492 | 18.3 |
| 1970 | 195,600 | 19.8 |
| 1980 | 590,900 | 22.1 |
| 1990 | 1,251,700 | 23.2 |

SOURCE:  U.S. Bureau of the Census and U.S. Bureau of Economic Analysis.

has expanded dramatically, a trend that has continued regardless of the political party in power.

As shown in Table 18–1, the first federal budget in 1789 was a mere $4.5 million; by 1990 the federal budget had soared well past the $1 trillion mark. In more meaningful terms, during the first year of our nation's life the federal government spent about $1.50 for each person in the country. In 1990, federal expenditure surpassed $5,000 per person. Government has become so extensive—and expensive—that even our leaders have trouble grasping its scope. The late U.S. Senator Everett Dirksen once quipped, as he observed the workings of Congress, that spending "a billion here and a billion there soon adds up to a lot of money."

Early in the nineteenth century, one federal government employee served every 1,800 people; today, the corresponding ratio is one official for every seventy-nine people. If state and local governments are included, there is one official for every thirteen Americans (U.S. Bureau of the Census, 1991). As this century opened,

communities across the United States saw no evidence of the federal government, except, perhaps, for a local post office. Today, universal schooling, civil rights legislation, safety standards that protect consumers and workers, financial support for a majority of people including students, veterans, and the elderly, and a vast system of national defense exemplify a new truth: our lives now depend on the operation of government (Caplow et al., 1982; Devine, 1985).

Data from the General Social Survey indicate that adults in the United States are divided about the proper role of government. More than one-fourth of respondents think that government should do more to address social problems, but almost as many people claim the government is already doing too much. Most of the remainder express support for both views. People of color, those who are poor, and younger adults across the board favor a more activist government; whites, those who are more affluent, and older people approve of more modest government programs (Davis, 1987; *CHIP1 Social Survey* software, 1991).

## Political Parties

Since the beginning of the nineteenth century, people in the United States have banded together into **political parties,** *organizations operating within the political system that seek control of the government.* Although most of us take political parties for granted, our nation's founders hotly debated whether they should exist at all. Some, such as Thomas Jefferson, supported political parties, reasoning that various organized groups would enhance political pluralism. Others, including George Washington and Benjamin Franklin, feared that parties—or political "factions" as they were known back then—could potentially tear the new nation apart. Because they were so controversial, political parties are not mentioned at all in the U.S. Constitution (Hilsman, 1985).

Yet, political parties were born, and many came and went in the early years of the republic. The two major parties we know today—the Democrats and the Republicans—were established on the eve of the Civil War (Burnham, 1983). The two-party system still exists, although minor parties sometimes gain significant support. In the 1968 presidential election, the American Independent Party led by George Wallace received 13 percent of the popular vote; Ross Perot made a dramatic entrance into the political scene as an independent candidate in 1992. Presidential elections typically rally candidates representing a wide range of "third" parties, including the Libertarian Party, the Populist Party, the Communist Party, the Workers League, and the Prohibition Party.

### Functions of Political Parties

Political parties in the United States have key societal functions.

1. **Promoting political pluralism.** Political parties create centers of power independent of the government. This is why totalitarian governments routinely quash all political parties, save their own.

2. **Increasing political involvement.** Parties draw people into the political process by articulating various points of view about controversial issues. They function as reference groups that help people shape their individual opinions. Political campaigns encourage public debate, helping to make government more responsive to the people.

3. **Selection of political candidates.** Political parties nominate candidates to run for office. Through primary elections in each party, people hear a variety of positions and can voice support for candidates whose views most closely mirror their own.

4. **Forging political coalitions.** While parties can divide a society, they often forge broad coalitions among people interested in various, specific issues. Party platforms usually incorporate a wide range of proposals so that the party will appeal to many people, making victory at the polls more likely. Many nations have dozens of narrowly based political parties; the United States, by contrast, has two major parties, both of which seek majority support.

5. **Maintaining political stability.** By maintaining relatively consistent positions on a number of issues, parties promote political stability. For the same reason, of course, those who seek radical change in the United States may lambaste political parties—neither of which mentions class conflict, for example—for bolstering the status quo (Wolfinger, Shapiro, & Greenstein, 1980; Irish, Prothro, & Richardson, 1981; Burnham, 1983).

## The Political Spectrum

People commonly label their political views in terms of the *political spectrum*, a continuum ranging from extreme liberalism on the left to extreme conservatism on the right. Historically, the Republican Party has endorsed more conservative stances while the Democratic Party has taken a more liberal approach. Within each party, however, there are conservative and liberal wings so that the difference between a liberal Republican and a conservative Democrat is more a matter of symbols than substance.

Table 18–2 shows how adults in the United States describe themselves in terms of the political spectrum. Slightly more than one-fourth of the respondents fall into one of the liberal categories, and about one-third describe themselves as some stripe of conservative. But an even larger share (38.5 percent) avoid any such labels by claiming to be "middle of the roaders" (N.O.R.C., 1991:103).

One reason so many people describe themselves as moderates is that they simultaneously hold conservative positions on some issues and liberal views on others. In other words, for at least half the adults in the United States, there is not one political spectrum but *two* (Barone

---

**Table 18–2**   THE POLITICAL SPECTRUM: A NATIONAL SURVEY, 1991

QUESTION: We hear a lot of talk these days about liberals and conservatives. I'm going to show you a seven-point scale on which the political views people might hold are arranged from extremely liberal—point 1—to extremely conservative—point 7. Where would you place yourself on this scale?

| Extremely liberal | Liberal | Slightly liberal | Middle of the road | Slightly conservative | Conservative | Extremely conservative |
|---|---|---|---|---|---|---|
| 2.4% | 10.2% | 14.1% | 38.5% | 14.4% | 14.0% | 2.6% |
| 1 | 2 | 3 | 4 | 5 | 6 | 7 |

Don't know, no answer: 3.8%

SOURCE:   N.O.R.C., *General Social Surveys*, 1972–1991 (Chicago: National Opinion Research Center, 1991), p. 103.

& Ujifusa, 1981; McBroom & Reed, 1991). *Economic issues* focus on economic inequality and the opportunity available for all categories of people. *Social issues* refer to moral concerns about how people live.

## Economic Issues

The industrialization of the United States after the Civil War generated enormous wealth, but much of it ended up in the pockets of a small elite. By the time of the Great Depression in 1929, mounting evidence suggested that, despite the undeniable productivity of our capitalist economy, many people had little financial security. The New Deal programs of Franklin Delano Roosevelt, the Democrat elected president in 1932, responded to this dilemma by greatly expanding the role of government in promoting social welfare. In short, the federal government took an unprecedented step and injected itself directly into the U.S. economy. Agencies regulated the stock market, guaranteed the savings people had entrusted to banks, expanded pension programs for the elderly, and in numerous other ways increased the financial security of the people.

Today, both political parties support a large and active federal government, although they disagree about the kinds of things that should and should not concern government. Generally, the Democratic Party supports extensive government involvement in the economy, while the Republican Party favors allowing the economy to operate free of government regulation. Economic liberals (on the Democratic side of the fence) think that the health of the economy and ensuring the supply of jobs are primary government responsibilities. Economic conservatives (likely to be Republicans) argue that government should interfere little with the operation of the economy since federal regulations tend to hamper economic productivity (Burnham, 1983).

## Social Issues

Social issues encompass moral judgments spanning a wide range, from reproductive issues to the death penalty to the legal standing of gay couples. Social liberals tend to express views broadly tolerant of individual choice in what they see as matters of lifestyle, and support equal rights and opportunities for all segments of our society. They usually oppose policies, like the death penalty, that historically have been unfairly applied to minorities. Moving to the right on the political spectrum, social conservatives endorse traditional ideas about gender and

oppose affirmative action and other "special programs" for minorities that, from this point of view, reward group membership rather than individual initiative. Social conservatives·generally condemn abortion as morally wrong and favor the death penalty as an appropriate response to outrageous crimes.

The more socially liberal Democratic Party looks to government to fashion greater justice in our society; the Republican Party, which takes a more socially conservative position, leans toward the idea that traditional values serve as a better guide to national virtue than government mandates. But this simple distinction masks the fact that both parties favor active government involvement when it advances their own aims. Socially liberal Democrats, for instance, support the Equal Rights Amendment (ERA) to the Constitution, believing it will reduce traditional patriarchy. Socially conservative Republicans oppose this change, arguing that existing laws provide adequate protection for women's rights and that the government should not be in the business of aggressively undermining traditional conceptions of gender. Socially conservative Republicans, however, *do* want government to enact legislation forbidding abortion, a practice they condemn as morally wrong. Socially liberal Democrats strongly object to the intrusion of government into what they see as one of the most personal decisions a woman ever makes.

## Mixed Positions

Pegging the political views of individuals is difficult because most people do not hold consistent positions on these two kinds of issues. With wealth to protect, well-to-do men and women tend to express conservative views on economic issues. Yet the rich typically voice liberal positions when it comes to social issues. Generally speaking, their affluence has provided them with extensive schooling, travel, and other broadening experiences. Further, the rich are socially secure, with little to fear from granting more opportunities to those with lower social standing.

People who think of themselves as working class or lower-middle class evince the opposite pattern: they tend to take liberal stances on economic issues while adopting conservative positions on social questions. Less well educated and more bound by tradition, these men and women seek greater economic opportunity because they need it, but they take pride in conforming to conventional cultural patterns. Thus, they commonly disparage people—such as gay or cohabiting couples—who do not adhere to traditional cultural mores (Nunn, Crocket, & Williams, 1978; Erikson, Luttbeg, & Tedin, 1980; Syzmanski, 1983; Humphries, 1984).

Political attitudes also vary according to race and ethnicity. African Americans, with significantly less income than whites, are more liberal on economic issues and, since the New Deal era of the 1930s, have been overwhelmingly Democratic. On many social issues (including reproductive rights for women), disadvantaged blacks and whites both lean toward a liberal stance. But when the social issue involves race or ethnicity (like busing schoolchildren or increasing government spending to assist minorities), people of African or Hispanic descent are more liberal than whites, and more liberal than their class position might suggest (N.O.R.C., 1991).

Because African Americans overwhelmingly express liberal views on the economy and broadly support government activism on racial issues, we might infer that the black community has a single mind when it comes to politics. This is not the case, however. In fact, as the box explains, a number of outspoken African Americans take decidedly conservative positions that challenge what others see as the conventional political wisdom.

### Party Identification

If so many people are not consistently liberal or conservative, in their views, it should come as no surprise that party identification is weak in the United States. In this respect, our society differs from most Western European democracies, where people usually adhere strongly to one or another political party (Wolfinger, Shapiro, & Greenstein, 1980). The general pattern here is that more well-to-do people tend to support the Republican Party, while the less privileged lean toward the Democratic Party. But while people do "vote their pocketbooks," neither of our major political parties confidently commands the loyalty of a majority of the population.

Table 18–3 shows the results of a national survey of party identification among adults. About 44 percent identified themselves—to some degree—as Democrats and about 42 percent favored the Republicans. Twelve percent declared themselves to be independents, with no preference for either major party. These data point to three conclusions: first, the two major political parties in the United States have rough parity in terms of public identification; second, a large majority of people identify with some political party; but, third, only one-fourth of adults are strongly committed to their party. From

time to time, then, a large share of voters may "swing" from one party to another.

One reason for this political vacillation is that the two major parties have much in common. For example, both organizations support the capitalist economic system, both favor a strong national defense, and both embrace the basic principles of the U.S. Constitution.

The similarity between the two major parties, including their support for the status quo, forces people seeking radical change to move outside the relatively narrow political mainstream. Some people, politically on the far left, advocate a socialist economy with increased government intervention; others, on the far right, favor a market economy completely free from government regulation. Because such views fall toward the extremes of the nation's political spectrum, they do not form part of the political platform of either major political party.

Most other democracies have a larger number of political parties that represent a wider range of positions. In Great Britain, the Labour party (on the left) and the Conservative Party (on the right) are further apart politically than are the two major parties in the United States. Sweden, the Netherlands, Switzerland, Belgium, and Israel are among the nations with three or more major political parties. These societies offer their people a broader array of political choices than do our own parties (Roskin, 1982).

**Table 18–3  POLITICAL PARTY IDENTIFICATION IN THE UNITED STATES, 1991**

| Party Identification | Proportion of Respondents |
| --- | --- |
| Democrat | 44.4% |
|   Strong Democrat | 14.8 |
|   Not very strong Democrat | 21.0 |
|   Independent, close to Democrat | 8.6 |
| Republican | 41.8 |
|   Strong Republican | 11.9 |
|   Not very strong Republican | 18.8 |
|   Independent, close to Republican | 11.1 |
| Independent | 12.4 |
| Other party, no response | 1.3 |

SOURCE: N.O.R.C., *General Social Surveys, 1972–1991* (Chicago: National Opinion Research Center, 1991), p. 96.

# African-American Conservatives: Some New Thinking on Old Issues

On the face of it, the numbers suggest a high level of political consensus among African Americans. About three-fourths of adults identify with the Democratic Party, with another 20 to 25 percent claiming to be independent. Only about one in twenty black women and men say they are Republicans. The party affiliation of African-American political leaders is even more one-sided: of 436 state legislators across the United States, Republicans can claim only three.

Perhaps this is not surprising: after all, why would any person of color opt for conservatism, when traditional social patterns in the United States have largely promoted disadvantage and outright oppression? The answer is that, while virtually all African Americans seek change, a lively debate has emerged about the best strategy for improving the social position of the black community.

The conventional wisdom in the civil rights community has been that government activism and support is crucial to bettering the lives of African Americans. But a growing number of black thinkers are taking a different approach, one emphasizing *self-help*. The concept of self-help is hardly new to the black community—the idea was widely praised by Booker T. Washington (1856–1915), and was also featured in the otherwise very different ideas of Malcolm X (1925–1965). The surging importance of the self-reliance movement in the last decade stems from two disparate forces. On the one hand, the lives of some African Americans have improved greatly (see the box, "Two Colors of Affluence," in Chapter 10). With expanding wealth and ownership of businesses, many of these men and women are convinced that talent, coupled with hard work, can and will pay off. On the other hand, after decades of expanded government programs, many other African Americans—especially in our country's inner cities—are still mired in poverty, leading to frustration and despair.

Considering the questionable results of government programs, conservatives—black as well as white—are now asking if government benefits like public assistance promise a cure for the ills of the black underclass or merely a continuing curse. Thomas Sowell, for example, argues that government largesse fosters dependency among minorities rather than giving people the tools to help themselves. Clarence Thomas, recently appointed to the U.S. Supreme Court, has cited his own life experience as evidence of the fruits of hard work and self-reliance. Shelby Steele (1990) criticizes the current civil rights establishment for heightening the significance of race rather than judging people of all colors, as Martin Luther King, Jr., urged, by the "content of their character." Whites who learn to feel guilty and blacks who are taught self-doubt, Steele continues, come together (especially on the college campus) and place African Americans in the passive role of "victims," rather than encouraging blacks to embrace a positive identity grounded in the aspirations and abilities of people eager to make positive changes in their own lives.

From the point of view of African-American conservatives, government action remains crucial to ensure a relentless attack on racial discrimination and other barriers to opportunity. At the same time, they add, people must never expect government to do for them what they are unwilling to do for themselves.

In the ongoing debate about how government should address the problems of African Americans, some people will take strength in the notion of self-reliance while others condemn what they see as a shift away from the larger black community. This discussion itself shows that no single political group should claim to speak for the entire black community. Or as Yale Law School's Stephen Carter puts it, when it comes to politics, "There is no one way to be black."

SOURCES: Steele (1990), Carter (1991), and Lane (1991).

## Special-Interest Groups

In 1992, President Bush proposed repealing the luxury tax on expensive boats. The boating industry, which had complained strenuously that this regulation was choking their business, applauded loudly. No doubt, too, affluent Americans contemplating the six-figure purchase of a boat were also pleased. Some others took a less charitable view, commenting that there is nothing wrong with expecting the rich to pay a greater share of the tax burden.

The boating industry, associations of elderly people, and women's organizations are each an example of a **special-interest group**, *a political alliance among people who share an interest in some economic or social issue.* Many voluntary associations (described in Chapter 7, "Groups and Organizations") are special-interest groups to the extent that they seek to shape political events. Interestingly, special-interest groups tend to flourish in societies (such as the United States) where political parties are relatively weak (Burnham, 1983). Our society contains a vast array of special-interest groups, representing various businesses and professions, religions, recreational and leisure activities, as well as women and men of particular races or ethnicities. Alexis de Tocqueville (1969; orig. 1834–1840) described the United States as a nation of joiners: in no other society, he correctly predicted, would special-interest groups be so numerous.

Many special-interest groups employ *lobbyists* who earn their living by advocating for one group or another on the political scene. The number of registered lobbyists in the United States—now well into the thousands—has increased rapidly in recent decades, and research suggests that special-interest groups do realize many of their political goals (Sheler, 1985; Durden, Shogren, & Silberman, 1991).

### The Agenda of Special-Interest Groups

The most powerful special-interest groups in the United States deal with economic issues. Big business, with its tremendous wealth, exerts vast power in the political arena. Representing some 20 million workers, labor unions, too, exert plenty of political clout (Goldfield, 1987). The American Federation of Labor–Congress of Industrial Organizations (AFL–CIO) is the nation's largest labor union and can draw on the talents and resources of some 14 million members. While big business directs financial support primarily to the Republican Party, the AFL–CIO channels most of its money to Democrats.

Other special-interest groups focus on social issues.

Examples of socially oriented special-interest groups are the National Organization of Women (NOW), numerous consumer-protection organizations, environmentalist groups such as the Sierra Club, and the American Civil Liberties Union (ACLU). There is a special-interest group representing virtually every social issue on our political agenda; such organizations are spread all across the political spectrum. The ACLU, which often champions the interests of disadvantaged people, is generally liberal. The National Rifle Association is a socially conservative organization whose primary concern is opposing any legislation that would restrict the private ownership of firearms.

Religious organizations, too, try to influence public opinion and government policy on a variety of social issues, including abortion and school prayer. Although the most established churches tend to maintain a low political profile, many fundamentalist sects are active and outspoken conservatives.

### Political Action Committees

Many special-interest groups work outside the framework of political parties to target their efforts on particular issues or for specific candidates. A **political action committee** (PAC) is *an organization formed by a special-interest group, independent of political parties, to pursue political aims by raising and spending money.* Typically, political action committees channel their funds directly to candidates likely to support their interests.

The first PACs were labor organizations formed during the early years of the Franklin Delano Roosevelt administration in the 1930s. In the 1970s, the number and influence of PACs grew rapidly as legal reforms limited direct contributions to candidates. Then, some 600 PACs were operating; by 1990, the number exceeded 4,000 (Sabato, 1984; Jones & Miller, 1985; U.S. Federal Election Commission, 1989a; U.S. Bureau of the Census, 1991).

The success of PACs correlates directly with their ability to raise money (Walker, 1983). The largest spenders—meaning the most powerful—are PACs that focus on economic issues, and support Republicans more than Democrats. Special-interest groups concerned with social issues also form PACs: the National Organization of Women (NOW) attempts to advance the social equality of women, while the National Conservative Political Action Committee (NCPAC) opposes abortion and advocates a return to traditional values in the United States.

Because of the rapid increase in the cost of political

campaigns, most candidates eagerly accept financial support from political action committees. More than half of all senators have received more than $1 million apiece from PACs, and these organizations now provide over one-third of all Congressional campaign funding (U.S. Federal Election Commission, 1989b).

Their power to shape the nation's political agenda has made political action committees controversial. On one side of the issue, supporters maintain that PACs represent the interests of many citizens—most of whom are not rich—whose businesses, unions, or churches support candidates and causes they believe in. According to this view, PACs amount to a positive reform in the political system because now many average people can gain a louder voice by joining together. The election law that expanded the role of PACs also limits direct contributions to candidates by the wealthiest organizations and individuals, and rich families now cannot use their wealth directly to influence the political process (Allen & Broyles, 1991). In short, from this point of view, PACs disperse power more broadly. On the other side of the issue, critics point out that any organization that supplies cash to politicians expects to be treated favorably in return. In essence, critics conclude, PACs try to buy political influence and advance positions that may or may not be in the broad public interest (Sabato, 1984).

Whether PACs are good or not, they have certainly spotlighted the importance of money in our political system. Rising campaign spending clearly favors incumbents, who have better access to PACs. Outspending their challengers by about three to one in 1990, 96 percent of all Congressional candidates seeking reelection in 1990 were returned to office. Such a state of affairs certainly undermines democracy; in fact, the membership of Congress as the 1990s began was more stable than that of the British House of Lords, whose members depart that division of Parliament only upon their death. In response to the sense that our political leaders have lost touch with the people, a political tide against incumbents surged during the 1992 campaign.

## Politics and the Individual

The U.S. political system, in principle, responds to the needs and judgments of the electorate. But how do people acquire political attitudes in the first place? And to what extent do we use our right to participate in the political system?

### Political Socialization

John F. Kennedy was the only president in this century to raise young children in the White House. From time to time, Kennedy referred to his children as "good little Democrats" knowing, of course, that no one is born with any particular political orientation. Like other elements of culture, we learn political attitudes through the socialization process. As noted in Chapter 5 ("Socialization"), the family, the schools, and the mass media work as instruments of socialization, which also shape political views.

The family is a powerful agent of socialization; not surprisingly, then, children typically come to share many opinions held by their parents. Because people of the same race and social class cluster together in neighborhoods, a child's initial peer groups are likely to reinforce ideas about the world learned at home. By the time children reach elementary school, most consciously identify with their parents' political party (Knoke & Felson, 1974; Burnham, 1983).

As described in Chapter 16 ("Education"), schools teach the culture's dominant political values. In rituals such as reciting the Pledge of Allegiance, students affirm support of their country ("I pledge allegiance to the flag of the United States of America . . .") and come to believe that its political system is good (". . . one nation, under God, indivisible, with liberty and justice for all"). Schools also foster discipline and respect for those in positions of authority, thereby strengthening patriotism (Bowles & Gintis, 1976). The mass media, too, convey values and opinions. Conservative people sometimes charge the media with having a "liberal agenda"; liberal critics of the media often claim that what is packaged as "news" really amounts to support for the status quo (Gans, 1980).

Socialization does not increase everyone's political involvement or enthusiasm for our system of government; on the contrary, a significant segment of our population learns that the political system responds little, if at all, to their needs. Indifference—or even hostility—toward the political system is evident especially among the poor, those unable to find employment, and people who believe that society has failed to offer them a fair shake (Zipp, 1985; Pinderhughes, 1986).

### Voter Apathy

In light of the courageous desire of people around the world to gain a greater voice in government—sometimes at the cost of their lives—we may be compelled to wonder why so many men and women in the United States seem to take their political rights for granted. The record shows that Americans are less likely to vote today than they were a century ago. The problem of *voter apathy* may well be worse in the United States than in most other industrialized democracies (Harvard/ABC News Symposium, cited in Piven & Cloward, 1988). In the 1988 presidential election, only 57 percent of eligible voters went to the polls.

Who is and is not likely to vote? After gaining the right to vote in 1920, women have cast ballots in lower proportions than men. This trend shifted in 1988, however, as women outpolled men, with 58.3 percent versus 56.5 percent, respectively, voting. A long-standing pattern holds that the likelihood of voting increases sharply with age. Of eligible voters between eighteen and twenty-four years of age in 1988, 36.2 percent voted, while 68.8 percent of people over sixty-five did so. Voting was also more likely among whites (59.1 percent) than among African Americans (51.5 percent). The voices of Hispanics (28.8 percent) are notably underrepresented in elections. In terms of class position, people with higher incomes, more prestigious occupations, and more schooling vote in the greatest numbers (Wolfinger & Rosenstone, 1980; Bennett, 1991; U.S. Bureau of the Census, 1991).

What underlies voter apathy? That question itself has sparked a political debate. To begin, some inactivity of this kind in inevitable, due to illness, travel away from home, or failure to register after moving to a new neighborhood. Then, too, registration and voting require the ability to read and write, which no doubt discourages millions of functionally illiterate people.

But the problem of voter apathy goes far beyond these factors. Conservatives make the case that voter apathy amounts to *indifference* to politics, which only shows that most people are by and large content with their lives. Along with a high standard of living in the United States, in other words, comes political complacency. This explains low rates of voting despite extending the franchise through elimination of literacy tests and poll taxes and, in 1971, dropping the voting age from twenty-one to eighteen.

Liberals take a very different view of voter apathy, countering that many people are so deeply dissatisfied with our way of life that they doubt elections will significantly change anything for the better. From this perspective, voter apathy signifies *alienation* from politics or, at least, from routine elections. But a desire for meaningful change emerges in commonplace political activity such as protests, strikes, and work stoppages (Piven & Cloward, 1988).

Each explanation contains some measure of truth. There are also two additional factors worth considering. First, many people may not see elections as important because well-heeled incumbents, at least until recently, have almost always remained in office. In addition, people may become apathetic because they perceive few differences between our two major parties. In global perspective, countries with multiple parties representing a

African-American artist Thomas Waterman Wood painted *American Citizens (To the Polls)* in 1867 to commemorate the new right of black men to vote. We see an affluent Yankee, a working-class Irishman, a Dutch transportation worker, and an African American, whose clothing provides little clue as to his occupation or his social standing. Despite differences of class, ethnicity, and race, in other words, Wood was optimistic that our political system would forge a representative, democratic government.

(*T. W. Wood*, American Citizens (To the Polls). *1867. Watercolor on paper, 17½ × 35½ (44.5 × 90.2). Signed and dated in the lower left corner: T. W. Wood/1867. T. W. Wood Art Gallery.*)

wider spectrum of political opinion generally have much higher rates of voting than we have in the United States (Zipp & Smith, 1982; Zipp, 1985).

# Theoretical Analysis of Power in Society

For most of this century, sociologists and political scientists have debated the answers to some basic questions about power in our society: How is power distributed? Who makes the decisions? Whose interests does government serve?

Power is among the most difficult topics of scientific research because decision making is complex and often occurs behind closed doors. Moreover, as Plato recognized more than 2,000 years ago, theories about power are difficult to separate from the beliefs and interests of social thinkers themselves. From this mix of facts and values, two competing models of power in the United States have emerged.

## The Pluralist Model

Formally, the **pluralist model** is *an analysis of politics in which power is dispersed among many competing interest groups.* The pluralist model is linked to the structural-functional paradigm in sociology; from this point of view, the political system responds to the needs of various constituencies that make up the society, trying to fashion agreements and to strike compromises.

Pluralists claim, first, that politics is an arena of negotiation. There are thousands of interest groups in the United States, most of which seek rather narrow goals. The American Association of University Professors, for example, responds to issues that affect college and university faculty, leaving to others debates over health policy or gun control. But even with limited objectives, no organization holds sufficient power to realize all its goals. As a result, organizations often operate as *veto groups*, realizing some success while keeping competitors from achieving all their goals. The political process, then, relies heavily on negotiating alliances and compromises that bridge differences among various interest groups and produce policies that have wide support (Dahl, 1961, 1982).

Government officials play a key role in transform-ing special interests into popular public policy. They do so by taking account of lobbying efforts on the part of organizations, as well as monitoring election results. Officials of the federal government also must coordinate their efforts with those of state and local governments, which, in turn, are influenced by still more interest groups. In sum, pluralists see power as widely dispersed throughout our society.

A second pluralist assertion holds that power has many sources—including wealth, political office, social prestige, and personal charisma. Only in exceptional cases do all these sources of power fall into the same hands. Here, again, we conclude that power is diffused across a wide spectrum.

### Research Results

The pluralist model is grounded in several well-known studies of power in local areas. Investigating the power structure of New Haven, Connecticut, Nelson Polsby (1959) found that key decisions on various issues—including urban renewal, nominations of political candidates, and school policies—were made by different groups. Polsby also noted that few members of the New Haven upper class—people listed in that city's *Social Register*—had major positions of economic leadership. Thus, Polsby concluded, no one segment of society was all-powerful.

Echoing Polsby's conclusions, Robert Dahl (1961) looked at New Haven's history. He found that the city's politics had once been dominated by a small number of families but, over the generations, power had increasingly become dispersed. Summing up his sense of New Haven politics, he stated "no one, and certainly no group of more than a few individuals, is entirely lacking in [power]" (1961:228).

The implication of this research is that the United States is more or less democratic and fair, granting at least some power to everyone. Pluralists assert that not even the most influential people always get their way, and even the most disadvantaged are able to band together to ensure that at least some of their political interests are addressed.

## The Power-Elite Model

The **power-elite model** is *an analysis of politics holding that power is concentrated among the rich.* This second approach is closely allied with the social-conflict paradigm in sociology.

The term *power elite* is a lasting contribution of C. Wright Mills (1956), who argued that the upper class (described in Chapter 10, "Social Class in the United States") holds the bulk of society's wealth, enjoys most of its prestige, and exercises the lion's share of power. The power elite are this country's "super-rich," families who forge alliances primarily with one another—in corporate boardrooms and at the altar. In this way, Mills noted, a handful of families perpetuate their privileges and ensure that their priorities become the national agenda.

Mills did not mean that our national elite forms an anti-American conspiracy; he simply meant that there is a coalition of families that has historically dominated the three major sectors of our society—the economy, the government, and the military. According to Mills, individual men and women circulate from one sector to another, consolidating their power as they go. Alexander Haig, for example, has held top positions in private business, was secretary of state under Ronald Reagan as well as a 1988 presidential candidate, and is a retired army officer holding the rank of general. Haig is far from the only case of this kind: a majority of national political leaders enter public life from powerful and highly paid positions in business—and return to the corporate world later on (Brownstein & Easton, 1983).

The power-elite model blasts claims that the United States is a political democracy; the concentration of wealth and power, from this point of view, is simply too great for the average person's voice to be heard. Rejecting pluralist assertions that various centers of power serve as checks and balances on one another, the power-elite model maintains that those at the top have no real opposition.

## Research Results

Supporting the power-elite model, Robert and Helen Lynd (1937) studied Muncie, Indiana (which they called "Middletown" to suggest that it was a typical city). They documented the fortune amassed by a single family—the Balls—from their business that manufactures glass canning jars, and showed how the Ball family dominated many dimensions of life in Muncie. This point was driven home, the Lynds explained, by the fact that the family name appeared on a local bank, a university, a hospital, and a department store. A closer look also showed that the Balls had financial interests in dozens of other businesses and charities. In Muncie, according

to the Lynds, the power elite more or less boiled down to a single family.

Floyd Hunter's (1963) more recent study of Atlanta, Georgia, provided further support for the power-elite model. Atlanta, concluded Hunter, had no one dominant family, but there were no more than about forty people who held all the top positions in the city's businesses and controlled the city's politics.

*Critical evaluation.*  These two models of power, summarized in Table 18–4, present vastly different analyses and reach opposing conclusions about the nature of contemporary U.S. politics. The view of politics emerging from the research in New Haven bears little resemblance to that based on the Muncie and Atlanta studies. Perhaps the politics of U.S. cities varies from place to place. More likely, researchers come to different conclusions because they ask different questions and interpret their results from different points of view. For example, G. William Domhoff, an advocate of the power-elite model (1967, 1971, 1979), reexamined the New Haven data of Robert Dahl (1961) and took issue with many of Dahl's earlier conclusions (Domhoff, 1983). From Domhoff's point of view, cities are not politically pluralistic at all; they behave more like "growth machines" in which wealthy landowners dominate the political system in pursuit of the economic growth that enhances their personal fortunes.

Reviewing all the research on this issue, there is probably greater support for the power-elite model. Even Robert Dahl (1982)—one of the stalwart supporters of the concept of pluralism—concedes that the marked concentration of wealth, as well as the barriers to equal opportunity faced by minorities, are basic flaws in our nation's quest for a truly pluralist democracy.

Does this mean that the pluralist model is entirely wrong? No, but it does suggest that our political system is not as democratic as most people think it is. Although each adult has the right to vote, the choices we make in elections usually are limited to positions acceptable to the most powerful segments of our society (Bachrach & Baratz, 1970). Republican and Democratic leaders may offer different approaches to helping the poor, for example, but no major-party politician has suggested radically redistributing wealth or abolishing the capitalist system.

Still, even the most powerful members of our society do not always get their way. As long as ordinary people continue to form political associations, our society will retain some pluralism. Domhoff reports that, in

**Table 18–4** THE PLURALIST AND POWER-ELITE MODELS: A COMPARISON

|  | Pluralist Model | Power-Elite Model |
|---|---|---|
| How is power distributed in the United States? | Highly dispersed. | Highly concentrated. |
| How many centers of power are there? | Many, each with a limited scope. | Few, with power that extends to many areas. |
| How do centers of power relate to one another? | They represent different political interests and thus provide checks on one another. | They represent the same political interests and face little opposition. |
| What is the relation between power and the system of social stratification? | Some people have more power than others, but even minority groups can organize to gain power.<br><br>Wealth, social prestige, and political office rarely overlap. | Most people have little power, and the upper class dominates society.<br><br>Wealth, social prestige, and political office commonly overlap. |
| What is the importance of voting? | Voting provides the public as a whole with a political voice. | Voting cannot promote significant political change. |
| What, then, is the most accurate description of the U.S. political system? | A pluralist democracy. | An oligarchy—rule by the wealthy few. |

his own city of Santa Cruz, California, local residents and university students have joined forces to successfully oppose business interests in nearly every major decision affecting urban development (Domhoff, 1984).

Both the pluralist and the power-elite models of social power offer insights into our country's political system. We can take pride in the fact that our political system does afford each person basic rights and offers every segment of the population a political voice. Marked social inequality, however, ensures that some people have more power than others.

## Power Beyond the Rules

Politics is always a matter of disagreement about goals and the means to achieve them. Yet a political system tries to resolve controversy within a system of rules. The basic precepts of the U.S. political system are enunciated in the Constitution and its twenty-six amendments. Countless other regulations guide the hand of every political official from the president to the county tax assessor.

But political activity sometimes exceeds—or tries to do away with—established practices.

## Revolution

As we have already explained, political stability depends on transforming power into legitimate authority. Sometimes political systems that lose legitimacy make way for radical alternatives. **Political revolution** is *the overthrow of one political system in favor of another.*

Political revolution is more profound than mere reform. Reform involves change *within* the system's rules; revolution implies change *of the system itself.* Moreover, reform may spark conflict, but it rarely escalates into violence. The extreme case of reform is the overthrow of one leader by another—a *coup d'état* (in French, literally "stroke concerning the state"), which typically involves violence on a limited scale. By contrast, revolution often produces widespread violence. The 1989 prodemocracy movement in the People's Republic of China was revolutionary because participants envisioned a new and more open political system. The government recognized the threat and responded brutally, causing thousands of deaths before the uprising was ended. In the successful week-long revolution against Romanian dictator Nicolae Ceauçescu in 1989, thousands of citizens perished, victims of attacks by state soldiers on unarmed crowds. But revolution can sometimes occur nonviolently. In other Eastern European countries, the sweeping transformations of the late 1980s took place with little or no bloodshed.

No type of political system is immune to revolution; nor does revolution invariably produce any one kind of government. The American Revolution ended the colonial control of the British monarchy and produced a democratic government. French revolutionaries in 1789 also overthrew a monarch, summarily executing members of the feudal aristocracy only to observe, within a decade, the return of monarchy in the person of Napoleon. In 1917, the Russian Revolution replaced the czarist monarchy with a socialist government built on the ideas of Karl Marx. In 1992, the Soviet Union formally came to an end, launching revolutionary change toward political democracy and a market system.

Despite their striking variety, analysts of revolution have pointed out several common patterns (Tocqueville, 1955, orig. 1856; Davies, 1962; Brinton, 1965; Skocpol, 1979; Lewis, 1984).

1. **Rising expectations.** Common sense suggests that revolution would be more likely in bad times than good, but history shows that political upheaval usually takes place when people's lives are improving. Extreme deprivation can be paralyzing, while a rising standard of living stimulates the desire for an even better life so that expectations may outpace reality. Crane Brinton explains that revolutions are typically "not started by down-and-outers, by starving, miserable people," but are "born of hope and their philosophies are formally optimistic" (1965:250).

2. **Deprivation and social conflict.** Revolutionary aspiration is propelled by a sense of injustice. The appeal of insurgency rises to the extent that people think they deserve more than they have while seeing little chance for improving their lot within the confines of the prevailing political system (Griffin & Griffin, 1989).

3. **Nonresponsiveness of the old government.** Revolutions gain momentum if a political regime is unable or unwilling to reform, especially when demands for change are made by large numbers of people or powerful segments of society (Tilly,

1986). The Ceauçescu regime in Romania, for example, defied popular calls for economic and political reforms, making revolution increasingly likely.

4. **Radical leadership by intellectuals.** The English philosopher Thomas Hobbes (1588–1679) observed that political rebellion in seventeenth-century England often was centered at the universities. This pattern has been repeated at other times and places. During the 1960s in the United States, student demonstrations touched off the political unrest that marked that tumultuous decade. More recently, it was students who initiated the pro-democracy movement in the People's Republic of China. Students stand at the forefront of so many of these insurrections because intellectuals formulate the principles that justify radical change.

5. **Establishing a new legitimacy.** The overthrow of a political system is rarely easy, but more difficult still is ensuring a revolution's long-term success. Revolutionary movements are sometimes unified by hatred of the past government. After the first taste of success, divisions within a revolutionary movement may intensify. A political regime also faces the task of legitimizing its newly won power, and it must guard against counterrevolution as past leaders maneuver to regain control. This explains the speed and ruthlessness with which victorious revolutionaries typically dispose of past leaders.

Scientific research cannot pronounce the effects of revolution as good or bad; the full consequences of such upheaval depend on one's values and, in any case, become evident only after many years. In hindsight, we can see that revolutions have propelled nations—including the United States—to world prominence. In the wake of recent revolutions, the Commonwealth of Independent States and the nations of Eastern Europe remain unsettled, their long-term development uncertain.

## Terrorism

The 1980s was a decade characterized by heightened concern over **terrorism,** *violence or threat of violence employed by an individual or a group as a political strategy.* Like revolution, terrorism is a political act entirely beyond the rules of the established political system. Paul

Johnson (1981) links terrorism to concepts introduced earlier in this chapter.

First, explains Johnson, terrorists try to paint violence as a legitimate political tactic. Terrorists generally have difficulty winning the support of their audience since violent intimidation is condemned as immoral by virtually every culture. Terrorists also set themselves up for criticism as they reject established channels of political negotiation. But from the terrorist's point of view, the political system under attack is both inherently unjust and unresponsive. More practically speaking, terrorism can greatly enhance the power of a small number of individuals. Those who held the U.S. hostages in the Middle East until 1991 may have been morally wrong to do so, but they did accomplish two key goals: embarrassing the United States and directing the world's attention to problems in that region of the world. To counter their claims of legitimacy, established governments typically refuse to negotiate publicly with terrorists.

Second, Johnson continues, terrorism is not only a tactic employed by groups, it is also a strategy used by governments against their own people. **State terrorism** refers to *the use of violence, generally without support of law, against individuals or groups by a government or its agents.* While inconsistent with democratic political systems, state terrorism may be formal and lawful within authoritarian and totalitarian governments, which survive by inciting fear and intimidation. The left-wing Stalinist regime in the Soviet Union and the right-wing Nazi regime in Germany each employed widespread terror. More recently, government-backed "death squads" have sought to eliminate opposition to military governments in Latin America, and terror campaigns are periodically used by the government of the People's Republic of China to quell dissent.

Third, although democratic systems reject state terrorism, democratic societies are especially vulnerable to terrorism by individuals. This is the case, Johnson explains, because they afford extensive civil liberties to their people and have minimal police networks. This susceptibility helps to explain the tendency of democratic governments to suspend civil liberties if officials think themselves under attack. After the Japanese attack on Pearl Harbor at the outset of World War II, the U.S. government responded to widespread fears that Japanese Americans might engage in terrorism by imprisoning more than 100,000 Japanese-American citizens for the duration of the war.

During the 1980s, global terrorism increased in frequency and severity. Terrorists seized embassies and

Because governments can direct military force at their people, the most destructive form of terrorism is directed by the state. During 1992, the government of Thailand called out troops to crush a popular opposition to an undemocratic prime minister, which resulted in a week of violence and scores of deaths as soldiers fired into crowds of demonstrators on the streets of Bangkok.

consulates of more than fifty nations; they also kidnapped (and sometimes murdered) hundreds of political officials, business leaders, teachers, and Olympic athletes, as well as several world leaders (Jenkins, 1982). Even the pope was a victim of a terrorist attack in 1981. Citizens of the United States have been the targets of about one in four terrorist incidents worldwide. The most notable events included the 1983 bombing of the U.S. embassy and marine barracks in Beirut, Lebanon, killing 258 people; the 1985 terrorist seizure of a U.S. airliner departing from Athens, in which one U.S. soldier was killed; and the 1988 terrorist bombing of Pan Am flight 103 over Lockerbie, Scotland, which killed all 270 people on board, including 189 Americans. For all but nine months of the 1980s, U.S. citizens were held hostage by terrorists somewhere in the world (Jenkins, 1990).

How should governments respond to terrorist acts? For the U.S. government, the immediate problem has usually been identifying those responsible. Because terrorist groups are nearly always shadowy organizations with no formal connection to any established state, targeting reprisals may be impossible. Yet, terrorism expert Brian Jenkins warns, "Threats of retaliation that aren't carried out create unfulfilled expectations that lead to the conclusion that America is impotent. It also encourages other terrorist groups, who begin to realize that this can be a pretty cheap way to wage war on the United States" (cited in Whitaker, 1985:29). The dilemma posed by terrorism, then, is the urge on the one hand to respond—in some way—to violent attack, and the fear on the other hand of broadening the conflict and confronting other governments.

A final dimension of terrorism involves political definitions. In any society, the state claims to rule justly and asserts its right to employ violence to maintain "law and order." Further, the state generally has the power to convince much of the population of the rightness of its actions, even when they are violent. Thus governments use force to "uphold the law," while their opponents who use violence are branded as "terrorists." Similarly, given political differences in a society and around the world, one person's "terrorist" may be another's "freedom fighter."

# War and Peace

We conclude our discussion with a look at what is perhaps the most critical political issue of all, war. Formally defined, **war** is *armed conflict among the people of various societies, directed by their governments.* As we suggested at the beginning of this chapter, war is as old as humanity. But if the presence of violent conflict remains the same, understanding it now takes on a new urgency. Because we have the technological capacity to destroy ourselves, war poses unprecedented danger to the entire planet. Most scholarly investigation of war has as its ultimate aim promoting **peace,** which is *the absence of war,* although not necessarily the lack of all conflict.

Although many people think of war as extraordinary, rather than a common element of life, global peace is actually what is rare, existing only for brief periods throughout this century. In our nation's short history, we have participated in ten large-scale wars, as noted in Figure 18–1, which resulted in the deaths of more than 1.3 million of our men and women and caused injury to many times that number (Vinovskis, 1989). Thousands more died in "undeclared wars" and limited

military actions, in countries like the Dominican Republic, Lebanon, Grenada, and Panama.

As for the future, national survey data show that a majority of adults in the United States think our country will continue to be involved in conventional ground wars, although most people conclude that all-out nuclear war is unlikely (N.O.R.C., 1991:317–18). Presumably, recent changes in the former Soviet Union have further reduced the perceived threat of nuclear annihilation.

## The Causes of War

The frequency of war in human affairs might imply that there is something "natural" about armed confrontation. Certainly members of every culture come to embrace certain symbols and principles—such as patriotism and freedom—to the point that they are willing to fight to defend (or extend) them. But while evidence supports the conclusion that some animals are naturally aggressive (Lorenz, 1966), research provides no basis for concluding that human beings inevitably go to war under any particular circumstances. As Ashley Montagu (1976) reminds us, governments around the world must resort to considerable coercion in order to enlist the support of their people for wars. Moreover, armies are deliberately constructed of small social groups in which soldiers are motivated to fight in order to protect close companions as well as themselves. Loyalty to small groups, rather than allegiance to abstract principles, stands at the heart of war as it is experienced on the battlefield (Hruschka, 1990).

Like all forms of social behavior, warfare is one product of *society* that varies in frequency and purpose from culture to culture. The Tasaday in the Philippines, among the most peace-loving of the world's people, rarely resort to violence. In contrast, the Yąnomamö, described in Chapter 3 ("Culture"), are quick to wage war with others. These patterns follow from social arrangements: Napoleon Chagnon (1988) explains that the ferocity of Yąnomamö men stems from a system of rewards that confers prestige and the society's most desirable women on successful warriors.

If society holds the key to war or peace, under what circumstances *do* humans engage in warfare? Based on the work of Quincy Wright (1987), we can identify five factors that promote war.

1. **Perceived threats.** Societies mobilize their members when leaders perceive a threat to people, terri-

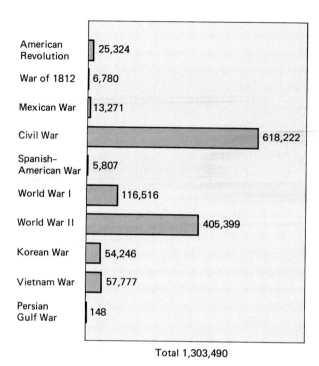

| | |
|---|---|
| American Revolution | 25,324 |
| War of 1812 | 6,780 |
| Mexican War | 13,271 |
| Civil War | 618,222 |
| Spanish-American War | 5,807 |
| World War I | 116,516 |
| World War II | 405,399 |
| Korean War | 54,246 |
| Vietnam War | 57,777 |
| Persian Gulf War | 148 |

Total 1,303,490

**Figure 18–1** Deaths of Americans in Ten U.S. Wars
(*Compiled from various sources by Maris A. Vinovskis, 1989:37*)

tory, or culture. On the other hand, the likelihood of peace increases in the absence of such threats. The chance of armed conflict with the former Soviet Union has subsided to the extent that our nation now defines that country as less of a danger to us.

2. **Social problems.** Internal problems that generate widespread frustration encourage a society's leaders to become aggressive toward their neighbors. Sometimes, in effect, enemies are "socially constructed" as a form of scapegoating. Political leaders are well aware that warfare tends to raise their popularity, just as it turns attention away from troublesome domestic problems. The lack of economic development in the People's Republic of China, for example, has sparked that nation's hostility toward Vietnam, Tibet, and the former Soviet Union.

3. **Political objectives.** Leaders sometimes settle on war as a desirable political strategy. Poor societies, such as Vietnam, have fought wars to end foreign domination. For powerful societies like the United States, a periodic "show of force" (such as the invasions of Grenada and Panama, and the Gulf War) may enhance global political objectives. A deliberate decision to escalate conflict may also win concessions from an opponent unwilling or unable to do the same (Patchen, 1987).

4. **Moral objectives.** Rarely do populations support going to war simply for tangible rewards, such as territory or wealth. Recognizing this, leaders infuse military campaigns with moral urgency, inspiring people to fight for causes like "freedom," "making the world safe for democracy," or the "fatherland." Leaders often paint an enemy as wicked, as Ronald Reagan did when he characterized the former Soviet Union as an "evil empire," or as Iranian officials did when they tagged the United States as the "great Satan," or as President George Bush did when he rallied the United States to war against Iraq by casting that country's leader, Saddam Hussein, as a modern-day Adolf Hitler.

5. **The absence of alternatives.** A fifth factor that encourages armed conflict is the absence of other means to resolve international disputes. Societies establish political systems partly to reduce conflict through the rule of law. Article 1 of the United Nations's Charter defines that organization's task as "maintaining international peace." Its ability to resolve tensions among strongly nationalistic societies, while at times significant, has been limited.

## Militarism and the Arms Race

Most people accept the idea that there are "just wars," armed conflicts that are necessary to oppose evil. But there is no doubt that the costs of wars and the militarism that sustains them is high indeed. These costs extend considerably beyond those of actual fighting. Together, the world's community of nations spends more than $5 billion annually on militarism. In addition to these direct expenditures, additional indirect costs include the diverting of resources that might otherwise be used in the struggle for survival by millions of desperately poor people throughout the world (see Chapter 11, "Global Inequality"). Assuming the will and the political wisdom of doing so, there is little doubt that resources currently spent on militarism could be used to eradicate global poverty. A large proportion of the world's top scientists also direct their talents toward military research; this is another vital resource that is siphoned away from other activity that might benefit humanity.

Although the armies of some countries stand out as far larger than others, every nation on earth has some military power. The former Soviet Union had the world's largest armed forces in terms of men and women in uniform, with some 5 million soldiers. The United States, which has the world's mightiest military capacity based on nuclear bombs and other high technology weapons, historically has allocated more money to defense than to any other single purpose—currently about 25 percent of all government spending. In 1990, this amounted to $328 billion, or $1,300 for every man, woman, and child in the United States. Proposals now being made call for significant cuts in the military budget during the 1990s in response to the dissolution of the Soviet Union; yet the costs of waging war and maintaining the peace will remain staggeringly high.

The extraordinary expense of militarism is largely due to the **arms race,** *a mutually reinforcing escalation of military might*, which for decades involved the two military "superpowers," the United States and the Soviet Union. The United States became a superpower as this nation emerged victorious from World War II with newly developed nuclear weapons. The atomic bomb was first used in war by U.S. forces to crush Japan in 1945. But the Soviet Union exploded a bomb of its own in 1949 unleashing the "cold war," so that each superpower leader became convinced that the other was committed to military superiority. For the next four decades, both nations aggressively developed more and more powerful nuclear weaponry, and more efficient means to deliver a rain of death on their enemy.

The irony—and the tragedy—of the arms race is that the United States and the Soviet Union pursued a policy that neither nation wanted nor could afford. The dissolution of the Soviet Union in 1992 has produced, at first glance at least, the possibility that each of these two military superpowers may no longer view the other as an adversary. This warming of relations, coupled with serious economic problems that have turned the attention of both nations homeward, offers what is probably the best chance yet for an end to the arms race.

But turning this tide will not be easy. The world remains a dangerous place, and the conventional wisdom holds that military strength ensures the peace. Furthermore, the arms race has had several positive consequences. Sam Marullo (1987) points out that the arms race has provided wages to tens of thousands of workers, swelled the profits of hundreds of corporations, and re-

sulted in research discoveries that led to new civilian products. Even so, he concludes, the enormous resources allocated for the arms race would probably be better spent for our people if invested in conventional industries.

C. Wright Mills (1956, 1958) took a more narrow view of militarism, linking the arms race to the interests of the power elite. Drawing on the ideas of Karl Marx, Mills viewed the expanding of the military-industrial complex as highly profitable for the small number of capitalists who control the economy. From Mills's point of view, military expenditures are antithetical to the interests of the population as a whole, but enrich the capitalist class.

Ironically, another argument against growing militarism was advanced by a decorated army general who went on to become president. In his last official speech as president in 1961, Dwight Eisenhower warned of the increasing power of the **military-industrial complex,** *the close association between the federal government and defense industries*. In rough agreement with the contention of C. Wright Mills, Eisenhower claimed that a power elite dominating both the economy and defense establishment had acquired unparalleled control over this nation's government. The military-industrial complex, he observed, had the potential to undermine democracy as it became less and less responsive to the American people.

## Nuclear Weapons and War

Technological advance has made warfare more deadly than ever. The typical warhead on one of today's MX missiles is far more destructive than the relatively "puny" atomic device that obliterated the Japanese city of Hiroshima nearly fifty years ago.

Not only are nuclear weapons more powerful, but there are many more of them. As the 1990s began, the world contained some 50,000 nuclear weapons, representing a destructive power roughly equivalent to five tons of TNT for every human being on the planet. This level of "overkill" means that, should even a fraction of this arsenal be consumed in war, life as we know it would cease to exist on much of the earth. Albert Einstein, whose genius contributed to the development of nuclear weapons, reflected on this achievement with these sobering words: "The unleashed power of the atom has changed everything *save our modes of thinking*, and we thus drift toward unparalleled catastrophe." In short, nuclear weapons have rendered unrestrained war unthinkable in a world not yet capable of peace.

At present, the vast majority of nuclear weapons

are held by the United States and Russia. Three other nations—Great Britain, France, and the People's Republic of China—have a substantial nuclear arsenal. Even as superpower tensions are diminished, the danger of catastrophic war increases with **nuclear proliferation,** *the acquisition of nuclear weapons by more and more societies.* Most analysts agree that several additional nations (including Israel, India, Pakistan, and South Africa) already possess nuclear weapons. Evidence exists that still more countries (including Algeria, Argentina, Brazil, Iraq, Libya, North Korea, Syria, and Taiwan) have been or currently are developing nuclear technology that could lead to weapons. By the end of this decade, estimates suggest, between twenty-five and fifty nations will have the ability to engage in nuclear war. Because many of these countries have long-standing conflicts with their neighbors, nuclear proliferation places the entire world at risk (Spector, 1988).

## Social Diversity and the Military

Debate about our country's military does not focus solely on halting nuclear proliferation or curbing the arms race. In recent years, many critics have raised questions about barriers that limit opportunity in the U.S. military for women and about the military's formal exclusion of gay people.

Women were part of this country's armed forces during the Revolutionary War, even before the United States became an independent nation. Today, about twelve percent of Coast Guard, Army, Navy, Air Force, and Marine Corps personnel are women. In the 1991 war in the Persian Gulf, 35,000 women represented 6.5 percent of a total deployment of 540,000 U.S. troops. Five of the 148 Gulf War casualties were women.

The reasons for the historical underrepresentation of women in the military have to do with views about gender. Women, conventional wisdom holds, are suitable for some—but not all—military assignments. Figure 18–2 shows that the extent of gender-based exclusion varies by branch of the service: while all jobs in the Coast Guard are open to women, only 20 percent of positions in the Marine Corps are so defined.

In all branches of the military, women have historically been excluded from combat roles. Defenders of this policy argue that, on average, women lack the physical strength of men. Proponents of women gaining parity in the military point out that military women score higher on intelligence tests and are better educated than their

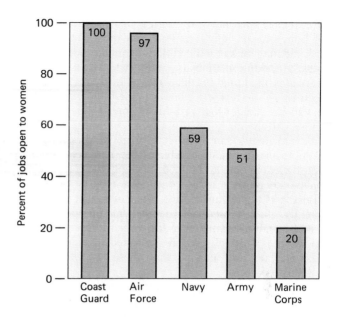

**Figure 18–2** Proportion of Assignments Open to Women by Branch of Armed Forces
*(U.S. Department of Defense, 1991)*

male counterparts. The heart of the issue, however, turns on the fact that our society has long defined women as *nurturers*—people who give life and help others. This view clashes intolerably with the image of women as professional killers.

Still, women are moving into more and more military assignments. One reason is a change in the law: in 1991, for example, Congress acted to allow (but not require) women to operate combat aircraft in all branches of the armed forces. More broadly, the technology of war has undermined traditional distinctions between combat and non-combat personnel. A combat pilot often fires missiles at a radar-screen target miles away; nonfighting medical evacuation teams regularly enter the immediate heat of battle (Moskos, 1985; Stiehm, 1989; May, 1991; McNeil, Jr., 1991).

All military services formally bar homosexual men and women. This does not mean that gay and lesbian people have not served their country in this way, but admitting a homosexual orientation or even activity that raises suspicion of being homosexual can result in discharge. In recent years, roughly 1,400 men and women have been expelled annually from the armed forces because of their sexual orientation.

The official reason for this policy is that soldiers

live in close quarters with minimal privacy; the presence of homosexuals, the argument goes, puts discipline at risk and may undercut the military's morale and effectiveness. In addition, officials worry that gay people who were identified might be blackmailed into compromising security. More recently a new argument has been added to the list: danger that gays might spread the virus that causes AIDS.

As in the case of military women, policies have more to do with traditional stereotypes than facts. Studies conducted by the military document that gay people have had commendable performance records. Research also shows that homosexuals—most of whom remained silently "in the closet"—have long made significant contributions to all branches of the armed forces. Furthermore, the rights of gays are protected in civilian jobs that are far more sensitive than those of rank and file soldiers.

Although change is slow, the exclusion of gay men and women from the military will probably end. Already a majority of the U.S. population disapproves of current policy. The policy is also coming under attack more and more in the courts (Bérubé, 1990; Miller, 1991).

## The Pursuit of Peace

The final question to consider in completing this survey of war and the military is how the world might reduce the dangers of war. We shall sketch out several approaches to promoting peace.

1. **Maintaining the status quo.** The logic of the present arms race suggests that security is derived from a balance of terror between the superpowers. A policy that has been tagged *mutually assured destruction* (MAD) states that either superpower launching a first-strike nuclear attack against the other would itself suffer massive retaliation. The strength of this notion of deterrence is that it appears to have kept the peace for forty years. But it does have three flaws. First, by encouraging the arms race, deterrence burdens the economies of the United States and the Commonwealth of Independent States. Second, as military technology becomes more complex—as missiles deliver their warheads more quickly and computers have less time to react to an apparent attack—the risks of unintended war increase. Third, deterrence cannot control nuclear proliferation which, as we have already

explained, will only increase in the future. For the long term, an alternative strategy is obviously needed.

2. **High-technology defense.** One alternative to deterrence that emerged during the 1980s is the *strategic defense initiative* (SDI). Under this proposal, initiated by the Reagan administration, a complex system of satellites and ground installations would provide a protective shield against enemy attack. In principle, the system detects enemy missiles soon after launch and destroys them with lasers and particle beams before they can reenter the atmosphere. If perfected, advocates argue, the "star wars" defense will render nuclear weapons obsolete.

The SDI proposal has prompted heated controversy. Some claim that such a program, even after years and trillions of dollars have been spent on research and development, would produce at best a leaky umbrella in the event of war. Just as serious, leaders of the former Soviet Union viewed SDI as an offensive system, able to assist the United States in making a first strike on them. For this reason, its development and deployment would likely provoke our adversaries to adopt countermeasures, with both sides taking one more costly step in the arms race (Kurtz, 1988).

3. **Diplomacy and disarmament.** Still another approach views peace as a diplomatic challenge rather than a technological problem (Dedrick & Yinger, 1990). If diplomacy can ease nations toward disarmament, both military costs and stockpiles of weapons will decrease. The idea behind disarmament is simple: a build-up of weapons in the past can lead to a mutual process of build-*down* in the future.

Disarmament also has limitations. No country wants to increase its vulnerability by reducing its defenses. Successful diplomacy, then, depends not on allowing "soft" concessions or making "hard" demands, but on everyone involved sharing responsibility for a common problem (Fisher & Ury, 1988). Disarmament proceeds best in a climate of mutual trust, but self-interest alone should motivate nations to seriously consider this approach to peace.

The leaders of the United States and the former Soviet Union recorded modest success in negotiating arms-control agreements. Given the rising costs of the arms race, the pressing domestic social problems of the two superpowers, and the easing of the cold war in the 1990s, we may look toward significant disarmament with guarded optimism.

4. **Resolving underlying conflict.** In the end, success in reducing the dangers of nuclear war will depend on resolving deep-rooted conflicts that have fueled the arms race. Even with rapid transformation in the former Soviet Union, political differences between the superpowers will surely keep the two sides wary. Yet these political changes have made nuclear war less likely now than at any time since World War II.

But sources of world conflict are found all around the globe. Despite the improving relations between Washington and Moscow, regional conflicts continue unabated in Latin America, Africa, the Middle East, and Asia. According to one estimate, the world currently spends 3,000 times as much money on militarism as it does on peacekeeping efforts (Sivard, 1988). In some cases, superpowers can assist efforts to reach fair and reasonable settlements of regional problems. The United States is currently taking such a role in the Middle East. In other situations, powerful nations need to recognize their part in creating these problems. The United States, for example, has helped fuel conflict in several Latin American countries by supporting repressive regimes and even by covertly destabilizing governments unfriendly to U.S. interests.

The danger of war remains great: scattered around the globe are vast stockpiles of weapons, we see a growing proliferation of nuclear technology, and we face a powerful military-industrial establishment at home. Forces working for peace also marshall great resources and the power of imagination: organizations such as the United Nations are promoting stability in the world, we see international cooperation in expanding trade worldwide, and improving superpower relations are lessening the threat of global annihilation. Perhaps most crucial is the growing realization that the aspirations of billions of people for a better life depend on a nonviolent solution to the age-old problem of war.

## Summary

1. Politics is a major social institution by which a society distributes power and organizes decision making. Any political system seeks legitimacy. Max Weber explained that three social contexts transform power into authority: tradition, rationally enacted rules and regulations, and the personal charisma of a leader.

2. Traditional authority predominates in preindustrial societies; industrial societies legitimize power through bureaucratic organizations and law. Charismatic authority arises in every society and—if organizations founded by charismatic leaders are to endure—they must become routinized into traditional or rational-legal authority.

3. All members of technologically simple societies have roughly the same amount of power, and they engage in no distinct political life. Political systems separate from family life arise only as societies generate a material surplus.

4. Monarchy is based on traditional authority and is common in preindustrial societies. As industrialization introduces egalitarian forces, including widespread individual rights and schooling, politics becomes more democratic and is based on rational-legal authority and extensive bureaucracy.

5. Democracy is a type of political system in which the population as a whole has considerable power. At the beginning of the 1990s, most of the world's nations were democratic for the first time in human history.

6. Authoritarian political systems prevent popular participation in government, and display indifference to the aspirations and initiatives of the population. Totalitarian political regimes also involve little popular participation, but exert extensive control over the everyday lives of the people.

7. The government of the United States has grown dramatically during the past two centuries, reflecting population increase but also wider government involvement in society.

8. The United States has two major political parties: the Republican Party is more conservative, and the Democratic Party more liberal.

9. Although we often speak of a single political spectrum, from extreme liberalism on the left to extreme conservatism on the right, many people hold different attitudes on economic issues and social issues. Economic issues concern the degree of economic inequality and the extent to which government should regulate the economy. Social issues deal with moral questions about how people ought to live and the rights and opportunities available to various segments of the population.

10. Special-interest groups employ lobbyists in their efforts to influence the political process on behalf of various segments of the population.

11. In recent decades, special-interest groups have formed more and more political action committees to fund political campaigns. This development has paralleled a decline in the power of political parties.

12. Many people in the United States do not readily describe themselves in political terms, nor are they strongly allied with one political party. Moreover, only about half of those eligible actually vote.

13. The pluralist model holds that political power is widely dispersed in the United States; the power-elite model takes an opposing view, arguing that power is concentrated in a small, wealthy segment of the population.

14. Revolution brings radical transformation to a political system. Efforts at revolutions aim at different political objectives and meet with varied degrees of success.

15. Terrorism is the use of violence in pursuit of political goals. Although attention has long focused on group terrorism, state terrorism is potentially far more powerful.

16. War is armed conflict between governments. The development of nuclear weapons, and their proliferation, has increased the possibility for global catastrophe. Enhancing world peace ultimately depends on resolving social problems and the conflicts that underlie militarism.

## Key Concepts

**arms race** a mutually reinforcing escalation of military might

**authoritarianism** any political system that denies popular participation in government

**authority** power that people perceive as legitimate rather than coercive

**charismatic authority** power legitimized through extraordinary personal abilities that inspire devotion and obedience

**democracy** a type of political system in which power is exercised by the people as a whole

**government** formal organizations that direct the political life of a society

**military-industrial complex** the close association between the federal government and defense industries

**monarchy** a type of political system in which power is passed from generation to generation in a single family

**nuclear proliferation** the acquisition of nuclear-weapons technology by more and more societies

**peace** the absence of war

**pluralist model** an analysis of politics in which power is dispersed among many competing interest groups

**political action committee** (PAC) an organization formed by a special-interest group, independent of political parties, to pursue specific aims by raising and spending money

**political parties** organizations operating within the political system that seek control of government

**political revolution** the overthrow of one political system in order to establish another

**political state** a formal government claiming the legitimate use of coercion to support its rule

**politics** the institutionalized system by which a society distributes power and makes decisions

**power** the ability to achieve desired ends despite possible resistance from others

**power-elite model** an analysis of politics holding that power is concentrated among the rich

**rational-legal authority** (also bureaucratic authority) power legitimized by legally enacted rules and regulations

**routinization of charisma** the transformation of charismatic authority into some combination of traditional and bureaucratic authority

**special-interest group** a political alliance of people who share an interest in some economic or social issue

**state terrorism** the use of violence, generally without support of law, against individuals or groups by a government or its agents

**terrorism** violence or the threat of violence employed by an individual or group as a political strategy

**totalitarianism** a political system that denies popular participation in government and extensively regulates people's lives

**traditional authority** power that is legitimized through respect for long-established cultural patterns

**war** armed conflict among the people of various societies, directed by their governments

# Suggested Readings

Here is a general text dealing with politics and society.

Anthony M. Orum. *Introduction to Political Sociology: The Social Anatomy of the Body Politic*. 3rd ed. Englewood Cliffs, NJ: Prentice Hall, 1988.

The exercise of power goes beyond government to the way we interact in countless everyday situations. This analysis explores social life in terms of three types of power: exploitation, negotiation, and cooperation.

Kenneth E. Boulding. *Three Faces of Power*. Newbury Park, CA: Sage, 1989.

Law is deeply shaped by gender. In sixteen essays, this feminist legal scholar explains why many issues we often think of as moral and criminal—including rape, pornography, and sex discrimination—are also thoroughly political.

Catherine A. MacKinnon. *Feminism Unmodified: Discourses on Life and Law*. Cambridge: Harvard University Press, 1987.

This analysis of the contemporary political scene investigates recent trends and probes the consequences of proliferating individual "rights."

Mary Ann Glendon. *Rights Talk: The Impoverishment of Political Discourse*. New York: The Free Press, 1991.

Another current debate surrounds the effects of the press—with its increasingly aggressive investigation and reporting—on our political system.

Larry J. Sabato. *Feeding Frenzy: How Attack Journalism Has Transformed American Politics*. New York: The Free Press, 1991.

This classic analysis of politics and society is based on a journey through the United States made by a brilliant French aristocrat in the early 1830s. Many of Tocqueville's insights about this country's political system remain as fresh and valuable today as when he wrote them.

Alexis de Tocqueville. *Democracy in America*. Garden City, NY: Doubleday-Anchor Books, 1969 (orig. 1834–1840).

These essays examine dimensions of political life among African Americans in the United States.

Lucius J. Barker, ed. *Black Electoral Politics: Participation, Performance, Promise*. New Brunswick, NJ: Transaction, 1990.

Here are the two classics that frame much of political sociology. The power-elite thesis of C. Wright Mills and the pluralist democratic vision of Robert A. Dahl offer divergent and stimulating visions of our nation's political system.

C. Wright Mills. *The Power Elite*. New York: Oxford University Press, 1956.

Robert A. Dahl. *Who Governs?* New Haven, CT: Yale University Press, 1961.

Burlington, Vermont, stands out among cities in the United States because of its history of left-wing political leadership.

W. J. Conroy. *Challenging the Boundaries of Reform: Socialism in Burlington*. Philadelphia: Temple University Press, 1990.

A provocative account of the controversial trial and execution of two Italian working-class immigrants for bank robbery and murder, this book stresses the anarchistic social movement that framed the lives of new immigrants early in this century.

Paul Avrich. *Sacco and Vanzetti: The Anarchist Background*. Princeton: Princeton University Press, 1991.

Starting with the recognition that millions of people in the United States seem politically apathetic, these authors cite various barriers to voting.

Frances Fox Piven and Richard A. Cloward. *Why Americans Don't Vote*. New York: Pantheon, 1988.

This analysis of war surveys the four major wars involving the United States in this century, and also investigates religious and ethnic warfare in the Middle East and Asia.

John G. Stoessinger. *Why Nations Go to War*. 5th ed. New York: St. Martin's Press, 1990.

This anthology of almost thirty articles brings together some of the most timely and convincing arguments on the topic of international terrorism.

Charles W. Kegley, Jr., ed. *International Terrorism: Characteristics, Causes, Controls*. New York: St. Martin's Press, 1990.

This books surveys the standing of women in the American armed services.

Judith Hicks Stiehm. *Arms and the Enlisted Woman*. Philadelphia: Temple University Press, 1989.

# 19

# The Economy and Work

"We must do something to help the economy here at home!" concluded the town council of Greece, New York, an upstate community outside of Rochester. "It's time to buy American." On top of the dismal economic news—recession, rising unemployment, and deepening federal deficit—a Japanese official had just suggested that U.S. workers had lost their competitive edge, demanding fat paychecks regardless of product quality or factory efficiency. Council members decided that enough was enough and, early in 1992, they voted to cancel their purchase of a $40,000 piece of excavating equipment from Japan's Komatsu corporation and to give the business to U.S. manufacturer John Deere, even at a higher price.

The action prompted applause from many corners of the land, reflecting the rising national anxiety that our country is slipping from its traditional place as the world's economic superpower. But the council's symbolic protest only ended up revealing how complicated today's global economy really is. The Komatsu model, it turns out, is actually built in the United States, while the John Deere is powered by an engine—you guessed it—made in Japan.

This chapter examines the economy as a social institution, explores the character of work in today's world, and explains some of the consequences of the emerging global marketplace for people in the United States. We will see—as did the town council members—that a good deal of the conventional wisdom about economic life no longer applies in the face of sweeping changes in the United States and around the world.

## The Economy: Historical Overview

The **economy** is *the institutionalized system for production, distribution, and consumption of goods and services.* The range of economic activity is immense, involving any material object or human activity that has value. *Goods* range from necessities (such as food, clothing, and shelter) to luxury items (such as automobiles, yachts, and swimming pools). *Services* include all the things people do that benefit others (such as the work of religious leaders, physicians, police officers, and telephone operators).

We value goods and services because they ensure survival or because they make life easier, more interesting, or more aesthetically pleasing. What we produce and the things we consume are also important for our self-concepts and social identities. How goods and services are distributed, then, shapes the lives of everyone in basic ways.

The complex economies that mark modern industrial societies are themselves the product of centuries of technological innovation and social change. As Chapter 4 ("Society") explained, technologically simple societies of the past produced only what they immediately consumed. These small nomadic groups lived off the land—hunting game, gathering vegetation, and fashioning rudimentary clothing, tools, and shelters. Production, distribution, and consumption were all part of family life.

## The Agricultural Revolution

Agriculture emerged as human inventiveness harnessed plows to animal power. Agrarian societies are ten to twenty times more productive than hunting and gathering societies, so they produce a significant surplus and establish permanent settlements. Because producing food no longer consumes the time and energy of all, individuals assume specialized economic roles, producing crafts, designing tools, and constructing dwellings. Trading networks link more and more towns, facilitating the exchange of food, animals, and other goods (Jacobs, 1970). These four factors—agricultural technology, productive specialization, permanent settlements, and trade—were the keys to a revolutionary expansion of the economy.

As noted in previous chapters, this economic expansion also increases social inequality. In contrast to relatively egalitarian hunters and gatherers, agrarian elites control most of the land—the primary productive resource. Greater productivity, therefore, does not necessarily enhance the standard of living of everyone.

In agrarian societies, the economy becomes a social institution distinct from family life, although people's work is typically done close to home. In medieval Europe, for instance, most people farmed nearby fields. City dwellers often worked in their homes—a pattern called *cottage industry*. What they produced they sold in regularly scheduled outdoor markets (the historical origin of contemporary "flea markets," suggesting that not everything was of the highest quality).

In London three centuries ago, for example, a home may have included several rooms used for baking, under the direction of the husband, who held the status of master baker. His wife could expect to be no more than his lifelong assistant, due to the pronounced patriarchy of the times. In addition, the household usually included several younger male apprentices working for wages as they developed their skills, and perhaps a young man or woman working as a servant (Laslett, 1984).

## The Industrial Revolution

Beginning in mid-eighteenth-century England, industrialization introduced five revolutionary changes to the economies of Western societies.

1.  **New forms of energy.** Since the earliest hunting and gathering societies, energy had been produced by the muscles of human beings and animals. At the dawn of industrialization in 1765, James Watt pioneered the application of steam power to machinery. Surpassing muscle power a hundred-fold, steam engines soon made production far more efficient than ever before.

2.  **The spread of factories.** Steam-driven machinery soon rendered cottage industries uncompetitive and thus obsolete. Factories—centralized workplaces apart from the home—spread rapidly. Although more productive, factory work lacked the personal feeling and close ties that had characterized family-based cottage industries.

3.  **Manufacturing and mass production.** Before the Industrial Revolution, most work involved propagating raw materials, such as crops, wool, and wood. The industrial economy shifted that focus to manufacturing raw materials into a wide range of salable products. For example, factories mass-produced clothing from wool and transformed lumber into furniture.

4.  **Specialization.** A worker in a cottage industry fashioned a product from beginning to end based on skill acquired from years of apprenticeship. Factory work, by contrast, is highly specialized; laborers repeat a single task, making only a small contribution to the finished product. Thus factories raised productivity, but they also lowered the skill level required of the average worker (Warner & Low, 1947).

5.  **Wage labor.** Instead of working for themselves or joining with other members of a household in a productive enterprise, industrial workers became wage laborers. In essence, they sold their labor to strangers who often cared less about them than about the machines they operated. Supervision of workers became routine and intense.

The impact of the Industrial Revolution gradually rippled outward from the factories to transform all of society. Greater productivity steadily raised the standard of living as countless new products and services filled an expanding economy. Especially at the outset, these benefits were shared very unequally. Some factory owners made vast fortunes, while the majority of industrial workers remained perilously close to poverty. Children were soon working as wage laborers in factories and deep in coal mines for pennies a day. Women factory workers were among the lowest paid of all and endured special problems, as the box explains.

## The Postindustrial Society

Industrialization is an ongoing process. In Europe and North America, workers gradually organized into labor unions in opposition to factory owners. During this century, governments outlawed child labor, forced wages upward, improved workplace safety, and extended schooling and political rights to a larger segment of the population.

By the mid-twentieth century, the United States was becoming a **postindustrial economy,** *a productive system based on service work and high technology.* Com-

---

**SOCIAL DIVERSITY**

# Women in the Factories of Lowell, Massachusetts

The U.S. textile industry began in 1822 in the Massachusetts town of Lowell, named for Francis Cabot Lowell, ancestor of two prominent Boston families, the Cabots and the Lowells, who brought plans for a textile factory from England.

About 75 percent of Lowell workers were women. The factory owners preferred women because, at about $2 to $3 a week, they earned half the wages men did. In addition, prejudiced factory owners favored native New England women over newly arriving male immigrants, who were also willing to work for low wages.

Recruiters drove wagons throughout New England, encouraging parents to send their daughters to learn skills and discipline in the factories. The offer appealed to many families that could not provide for their children. Then, too, the few occupations open to women at that time, such as teaching and household service, paid even less than factory work.

The Lowell factory provided dormitory-type housing and meals, at a cost of one-third a worker's wages. Women were subject to a curfew and, as a condition of employment, attended church regularly. Any morally questionable conduct (such as bringing men to their rooms) brought firm disciplinary action against offenders. Owners enforced these strict policies for more than reasons of morality; closely supervised

women could not organize among themselves. Working almost thirteen hours a day, six days a week, the Lowell employees had good reason to seek improvements in their working conditions. Yet any open criticism of the factory, or even the possession of "radical" literature, could cost a worker her job.

SOURCE: Based on Eisler (1977).

---

puterized machinery has reduced the role of human labor in production. Simultaneously, bureaucracy has expanded the ranks of clerical workers and managers. Robert Heilbroner (1985) points out that, a century ago, managers accounted for only one in fourteen workers; now they represent one in three employees. Service industries—such as public relations, advertising, banking, and sales—now employ most of our country's labor force. Distinguishing the postindustrial era, then, is a shift by workers from industrial production to service jobs.

The crucial technology of a postindustrial age concerns information. The computer stands at the center of an *Information Revolution* in the United States and elsewhere in the industrial world, generating a host of new, specialized occupations. Just as gaining technical skills was the key to success in the past, now women and men must enhance their literacy skills. People unable to speak, write, or otherwise communicate effectively face less and less economic opportunity.

The postindustrial society also brings further change in the location of work. Industrialization initially centralized the workforce in factories where enormous machinery and energy sources were situated. Today, however, computers, facsimile (fax) machines, and other new information technologies allow workers to perform many jobs at home or even while driving in their cars. More educated and skilled workers also no longer require—and often do not tolerate—the close supervision that marked yesterday's factories.

## Sectors of the Modern Economy

In line with the broad historical changes just described, we can see a shifting balance among three sectors of a society's economy. The **primary sector** is *the part of the economy that generates raw materials directly from the natural environment.* The primary sector, which includes agriculture, animal husbandry, fishing, forestry, and mining, dominates economies of preindustrial, agrarian societies. Early in our nation's history, for example, most work involved agriculture and other primary-sector activities. Today, by contrast, just 3 percent of the labor force is employed in the primary sector.

Globally, the economies of developing nations of the world such as India and the People's Republic of China are still dominated by the primary sector. Global Map 19–1 illustrates the importance of the primary sector in the world's economies.

The **secondary sector** is *the part of the economy*

*that transforms raw materials into manufactured goods.* This sector gains prominence as societies industrialize; manufacturing grew rapidly in the United States during the first half of this century. Secondary-sector production includes refining petroleum, and manufacturing tools, building materials, and automobiles. In societies that are still industrializing—such as Yugoslavia and Greece—the secondary sector of the economy has grown to roughly the same size as the primary sector.

Global Map 19–2 illustrates the share of the economy claimed by industrial production around the world. The map is essentially a reverse image of Global Map 19–1: First-World economies with the smallest primary sectors have the largest industrial sectors.

As industrial societies mature, the secondary sector peaks and eventually declines. From a peak of almost half the workforce about fifty years ago, the secondary sector now includes only one-fourth of all workers in the United States. In place of manufacturing, growth has occurred in the **tertiary sector,** *the part of the economy that generates services rather than goods.* Accounting for only a tiny share of work in preindustrial economies, the tertiary sector grows with industrialization and becomes the dominant economic sector in postindustrial societies. About 70 percent of the U.S. labor force is employed in a wide range of service occupations, including secretarial and clerical work and positions in food service, sales, law, advertising, and teaching (U.S. Department of Labor, 1992).

# Comparative Economic Systems

Two overarching models—capitalism and socialism—have dominated analysis of economic systems during this century. No society has an economy that is purely capitalist or purely socialist; these models represent two ends of a continuum on which an actual economy can be placed. Further, societies toward each end of the continuum have undergone extensive change.

## Capitalism

**Capitalism** is *an economic system in which productive resources are privately owned.* Ideally, a capitalist economy has three distinctive features.

**Global Map 19–1**   Agricultural Employment in Global Perspective

The primary sector of the economy predominates in societies with the least economic development. Thus, in the poor countries of Africa and Asia, half, or even three-fourths, of all workers are farmers. The picture is altogether different among First-World nations—including the United States, Canada, Great Britain, and Australia—which have less than 10 percent of their workforce in agriculture.

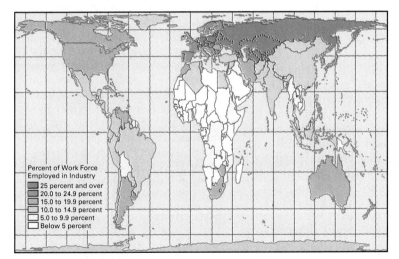

**Global Map 19–2**   Industrial Employment in Global Perspective

The Third World, by and large, has yet to industrialize. For this reason, in the countries of Latin America, Africa, and Asia, a small proportion of the labor force engages in industrial work. The industrial nations of the Second World—including the Commonwealth of Independent States—have the largest share of their workers in industry. In the First World, we see a reverse of this trend, with more and more workers moving from industrial jobs to service work. Thus, the postindustrial economy of the United States now has about the same share of workers in industrial jobs as the much poorer nation of Argentina.

1. **Private ownership of property.** A capitalist economy supports the right of individuals to own almost anything, from forests and other natural resources to factories and retail businesses. While all societies permit individuals to have personal possessions, the more capitalist an economy is, the more private ownership extends to wealth-producing property.

2. **Pursuit of personal profit.** A capitalist society encourages the accumulation of private property and defines a self-centered, profit-minded orientation as natural and simply a matter of "doing business." In practical terms, according to Scottish economist Adam Smith (1723–1790), when individuals pursue their own self-interest, the entire society benefits from greater "wealth and prosperity" (1937:508; orig. 1776).

3. **Free competition and consumer sovereignty.** A purely capitalist economy would operate without interference from the government. The state thereby assumes a *laissez-faire* (a French expression meaning "to leave alone") approach to the marketplace. Adam Smith claimed that a freely competitive economy regulates itself by the "invisible hand" of the laws of supply and demand.

   According to Smith, whose *An Inquiry into the Nature and Causes of the Wealth of Nations* (1776) became the bible of the free-trade movement, the market system is dominated by consumers who compare quality and price, buying those goods and services that provide the greatest value. Producers compete with one another to offer the highest-quality goods and services at the lowest possible price. And prodded by competition to be as efficient as possible, producers readily embrace technological innovations that end up benefiting consumers even more. Although both producers and consumers are motivated by personal gain, the overall economy grows as production becomes more efficient, technology advances, and consumers enjoy ever-increasing value. Smith's time-honored maxim holds that from narrow self-interest comes the greatest good for the greatest number of people.

   If we were to think of an economy as a vast and complex ship, Smith's argument suggests that the self-interested actions of individual crew members with no single captain would ensure that the ship remains on course (Albrecht, 1983:47). From another perspective, Smith argued that government control of an economy would inevitably upset the complex market system, sapping producer motivation, diminishing the quality of goods produced, and thereby shortchanging consumers.

The United States is the leading capitalist society, yet even here the guiding hand of government plays an extensive role in economic affairs. Through various regulatory agencies, government policies affect what is produced, the quality and costs of production, what is imported and exported, and how the country develops or conserves natural resources. The federal government also owns and operates a host of productive organizations; the U.S. Postal Service, the Amtrak railroad system, the Tennessee Valley Authority (a large electrical utility company), and the Nuclear Regulatory Commission (which conducts atomic research and produces nuclear materials) are all branches of the federal government. The entire U.S. military is operated by the federal government as well. Federal officials also act to prevent the collapse of businesses, as in the "bailout" of Amtrak, Chrysler Corporation, and the savings and loan industry. State and local governments operate numerous large businesses also, including the Port Authority of New York and New Jersey, the Los Angeles Department of Water and Power, and San Francisco's Bay Area Rapid Transit (BART) system (Herman, 1981). Government agencies set minimum wage levels, enact safety standards for the workplace, enforce antitrust regulations that limit mergers of large corporations, set price supports that affect farm products, and maintain various programs including Social Security, public assistance, student loans, and veterans' benefits that together provide regular financial support for most people in the United States. Finally, the local, state, and federal governments, taken together, are our country's biggest employer, providing jobs for about 15 percent of the U.S. labor force (U.S. Department of Labor, 1992).

## Socialism

**Socialism** is *an economic system in which productive resources are collectively owned.* In its ideal form, a socialist economy opposes each of the three characteristics of capitalism just described.

1. **Collective ownership of property.** An economy is socialist to the extent that it limits the rights to private property, especially property used in producing goods and services. Socialist economies di-

rect the production of food, clothing, and other goods and services toward meeting the needs of the population as a whole, not just those of some privileged segment of society. A socialist society, for example, defines housing as a right of all instead of a private commodity to be traded in the marketplace for profit.

Karl Marx asserted that private ownership of productive property spawns social classes and invariably generates a powerful economic elite. Because socialism regards such classes as opposing the interests of the broader population, socialist law prevents class formation by forbidding the private ownership of property.

2. **Pursuit of collective goals.** The individualistic pursuit of profit also stands at odds with the collective orientation of socialism. Cultural values and norms in socialist societies define as illegal what capitalists call the entrepreneurial spirit. For this reason, private trading is branded as illegal "black market" activity.

3. **Government control of the economy.** Socialism rejects the idea that a free-market economy regulates itself. Instead of a laissez-faire approach, socialist societies place the economy under government control. Thus, socialism creates a *centrally controlled economy.* From a socialist point of view, individuals acting on the basis of narrow self-interest—Adam Smith's ship without a captain—should flounder or, worse still, destroy themselves on the rocks. In the absence of the guiding hand of government, the economy will endure spasms of growth and recession, inflation and unemployment, that adversely affect everyone.

Socialism rejects the contention that consumers guide capitalist production through their purchases. Marx maintained that consumers often lack the information necessary to evaluate the performance and potential dangers of various products. Nor is advertising much help; from this point of view, ads manipulate people to buy what is profitable rather than what they genuinely need. Commercial advertising thus plays a small role in a socialist economy.

## Socialism and Communism

Most people equate the terms *socialism* and *communism.* More precisely, as the realization of the ideal spirit of socialism, **communism** is *a hypothetical economic and political system in which all members of society have economic and social equality.* Karl Marx viewed socialism as a transitory stage on the path toward the ideal of a communist society devoid of all class divisions and conflict. In many socialist societies today, the dominant political party describes itself as communist, but nowhere has the communist goal been achieved.

Why? For one thing, social stratification involves differences of power as well as wealth. Socialist societies have generally succeeded in reducing disparities in income and wealth only through expanding government bureaucracies, giving officials extensive power over the people. In the process, government has not "withered away" as Karl Marx imagined. On the contrary, during this century political elites have gained enormous power and privilege in socialist societies.

Marx would have been the first to agree that a communist society is a *utopia* (from Greek words meaning "not a place"). His writings provide only a vague description of true communism. Yet Marx considered communism a worthy goal, and would probably have disparaged existing "Marxist" societies like the People's Republic of China and Cuba for falling far short of his communist ideal.

## Democratic Socialism in Europe

Leaders of socialist societies have discovered that a state powerful enough to regulate the economy also has the capacity to limit individual liberties. But socialist economic policies do not necessarily imply the stifling of democracy. In fact, many of the nations of Western Europe combine socialist economic policies with a democratic political system. This hybrid is called **democratic socialism,** *an economic and political system that combines significant government intervention in the economy with free elections.*

In most countries of this kind, the government owns at least many of the largest industries and services, such as mining, transportation, utilities, the mass media, education, and health care. Private industry also exists, but it is subject to extensive regulation. High taxation (aimed especially at the rich) transfers wealth, through various social welfare programs, to less advantaged members of society.

In Great Britain, about 15 percent of the economy is nationalized. In Sweden, Italy, and France, roughly 12 percent of production is state-controlled. In all these

The productivity of capitalist Hong Kong is evident in the fact that streets are choked with advertising and shoppers. Socialist Beijing, by contrast, is dominated by government buildings rather than a central business district. Here bicyclists glide past the Great Hall of the People.

European countries, public support for social welfare programs is far stronger than it is in the United States. Therefore, basic health care, housing, and child care are each treated as a right of all citizens rather than as a commodity available only according to what people can afford in a free-market system (Roskin, 1982; Gregory & Stuart, 1985; Pedersen, 1990).

Democratic-socialist societies recognize advantages in both the market economy and government regulation. They also embrace open political contests and typically have a far greater share of their citizens casting votes than is the case in the United States.

## Relative Advantages of Capitalism and Socialism

The recent economic changes that are reshaping many societies of the world sparked debate over the relative advantages of capitalism and socialism. Assessing these economic models is difficult because nowhere do they exist in their pure states. Societies mix capitalism and socialism to varying degrees, and each also has distinctive cultural attitudes toward work, unequal natural resources, different levels of technological development, and disparate patterns of trade. Finally, the destructive effects of war burden some societies more than others

(Gregory & Stuart, 1985). Despite these complicating factors, some crude comparisons seem possible.

### Productivity

Table 19–1 compares economic performance in a number of societies, divided into those with predominantly capitalist economies and those that, until recently, were predominantly socialist. "Gross Domestic Product" (GDP) is the total value of all goods and services produced annually within the country's borders; "per capita" (or per person) GDP allows us to compare societies of different size. Because each country uses its own currency system, the table presents per capita GDP in 1990 U.S. dollars.

Among the societies with predominantly capitalist economies (collectively termed the First World), the United States had the highest per capita GDP ($17,615), closely followed by Canada ($16,375) and the former Federal German Republic (West Germany) ($14,730). Greece had the lowest per capita GDP ($5,500). There is considerable variation in GDP among these countries, due to complicating factors already noted. But, by world standards, per capita GDP in these eleven predominantly capitalist societies is high, with an unweighted average (ignoring the unequal population size) of $13,345. This average figure is a rough measure of the value of goods and services produced annually per person in predominantly capitalist societies.

Looking at the former Soviet Union and the nations of Eastern Europe just before their upheavals at the end of the last decade, the German Democratic Republic (East Germany prior to German reunification) had the highest economic output per person ($8,000), while Albania had the lowest ($2,000). Overall, these socialist economies produced considerably less than their capitalist counterparts. The unweighted average is $5,000 or 37 percent of the figure for capitalist societies. The comparison between what were West and East Germany is especially interesting, because this is a case of a single society divided at the end of World War II into two

**Table 19–1  ECONOMIC PERFORMANCE OF CAPITALIST AND SOCIALIST ECONOMIES, 1988**

| | Per Capita GDP (U.S. dollars) |
|---|---|
| Predominantly Capitalist Economies | |
| Austria | 12,386 |
| Belgium | 13,140 |
| Canada | 16,375 |
| Federal Republic of Germany (the former West Germany) | 14,730 |
| France | 13,961 |
| Great Britain | 12,270 |
| Greece | 5,500 |
| Hong Kong | 13,900 |
| Japan | 13,135 |
| Sweden | 13,780 |
| United States | 17,615 |
| Unweighted average | 13,345 |
| Predominantly Socialist Economies | |
| Albania | 2,000 |
| Bulgaria | 4,750 |
| Czechoslovakia | 7,750 |
| German Democratic Republic (the former East Germany) | 8,000 |
| Hungary | 4,500 |
| Poland | 4,000 |
| Romania | 3,000 |
| Sovier Union | 6,000 |
| Yugoslavia | 5,000 |
| Unweighted average | 5,000 |

SOURCE: United Nations Development Programme. *Human Development Report 1990.* New York: Oxford University Press, 1990, p. 129.

**Table 19–2  DISTRIBUTION OF INCOME IN CAPITALIST AND SOCIALIST ECONOMIES**

| | Income Ratio |
|---|---|
| Predominantly Capitalist Economies | |
| United States (1968) | 12.7 |
| Canada (1971) | 12.0 |
| Italy (1969) | 11.2 |
| Sweden (1971) | 5.5 |
| Great Britain (1969) | 5.0 |
| Unweighted average | 9.3 |
| Predominantly Socialist Economies | |
| Soviet Union (1966) | 5.7 |
| Czechoslovakia (1965) | 4.3 |
| Hungary (1964) | 4.0 |
| Bulgaria (1963–1965) | 3.8 |
| Unweighted average | 4.5 |

SOURCE: Adapted from P. J. D. Wiles, *Economic Institutions Compared* (New York: Halsted Press, 1977), as cited in Paul R. Gregory and Robert C. Stuart, *Comparative Economic Systems,* 2nd ed. (Boston: Houghton Mifflin, 1985), p. 503.

parts—one capitalist and one socialist. In the late 1980s, per capita GDP in the socialist German Democratic Republic was about 54 percent that of the capitalist Federal Republic of Germany.

### Distribution of Income

How income is distributed is also important in comparing capitalist and socialist economies. Table 19–2 gives an idea of the extent of income inequality in several societies with predominantly capitalist and predominantly socialist economies during the 1960s and 1970s. The income ratios indicate how many times more income was received by highly paid people than was earned by poorly paid people.[1]

Of the five primarily capitalist societies listed in Table 19–2, the United States had the greatest income inequality, with a rich person earning almost thirteen times more than a poor person. The income ratios of Canada (12.0) and Italy (11.2) were only slightly lower. Both Sweden (5.5) and Great Britain (5.0) had much

---

[1] Specifically, income ratio is derived by dividing the 95th percentile income by the 5th percentile income. The author is unaware of more recent data on global income inequality.

less income inequality because they incorporate socialist principles into traditionally capitalist economies. The unweighted average shows that a rich person earned more than nine times as much as a poor person in predominantly capitalist societies.

With an unweighted average of 4.5, these formerly socialist societies had about half as much income inequality. This comparison of economic performance supports the conclusion that *capitalist economies are relatively more productive but they also generate greater social inequality; socialist economies produce greater social equality, but with a lower standard of living.*

Chapter 18 ("Politics and Government") explained that a society's economic and political systems are closely linked. Capitalism depends on the freedom of producers and consumers to interact in a market setting without extensive interference from the state. Thus economic capitalism is linked to extensive civil liberties and political freedom. Socialist societies strive to maximize economic and social equality. This requires considerable state intervention in the economy, limiting the personal liberty of citizens.

## Changes in Socialist Countries

During the last decade, a profound transformation has taken place in many socialist countries of the world. Beginning in the shipyards of Poland's port city of Gdansk in 1980, workers began organizing in opposition to their socialist government. Despite struggle and setback, the Solidarity movement—with backing from the U.S. government and the Vatican—eventually succeeded in dislodging the Soviet-backed party officials, electing their own leader, Lech Walesa, as national president. The Poles are now in the process of introducing market principles to their economy.

Other countries of Eastern Europe, all of which fell under the political control of the former Soviet Union at the end of World War II, also shook off socialist regimes during 1989 and 1990. These nations—including the German Democratic Republic, Czechoslovakia, Hungary, Romania, and Bulgaria—have likewise introduced capitalist elements into what had for decades been centrally controlled economies. In 1992, the Soviet Union itself formally dissolved, a process that, along the way, liberated the Baltic states of Estonia, Latvia, and Lithuania and forged a loose federation out of most of the remaining republics, now called the Commonwealth of Independent States.

The reasons for the sweeping changes in what Chapter 11 ("Global Inequality") described as Second-World socialism are many and complex. In light of earlier discussions, however, two factors stand out. First, these predominantly socialist economies have not been as productive as their capitalist counterparts. As we have explained, they were successful in achieving economic equality; living standards for everyone, however, were low compared to those in Western European countries. Second, the brand of socialism that was imprinted on Eastern Europe by the former Soviet Union encouraged heavy-handed and unresponsive government that rigidly controlled the media as well as the ability of individuals to move about, even in their own countries. Put in other words, the socialist revolutions in these nations *did* do away with economic elites (as Karl Marx predicted); but, as Max Weber might have foreseen, they *expanded* the clout of political elites as party bureaucracies grew massive.

Now that the expansive party apparatus has been all but dismantled and these countries are moving toward market systems, what can we expect in the future? In light of the unexpected twists and turns in this region of the world, few people are confident about what lies ahead. What we can say, at this early stage, is that the consequences of market reforms are uneven, with some nations faring better than others. Further, for the short term at least, the introduction of market forces has sparked rapid price increases, which have further eroded living standards. In the long term, officials in these nations contend, this change will raise everyone's standard of living through greater productivity. At the same time, to the extent that these countries gradually come to resemble their neighbors farther to the West, a rising standard of living will be accompanied by increasing economic disparity.

# Work in the Postindustrial Economy

Change is not restricted to the socialist world; the economy of the United States has also changed dramatically during the last century. The Industrial Revolution transformed the U.S. work force a century ago; further changes are taking place today.

In 1991, 125 million people were in the labor force, representing two-thirds of those over the age of sixteen. As shown in Table 19–3, a larger proportion of men (75.5 percent) than women (57.3 percent) hold income-producing jobs. As noted in Chapter 13 ("Sex and Gender"), this gap has diminished in recent decades. Among men, the proportion of people of African descent in the labor force (69.5%) is somewhat less than the proportion of whites (76.4%); among women, about the same share of African Americans (57.0%) and whites (57.4%) are gainfully employed.

Age also affects labor force participation. Figure 19–1 shows that both women and men join the work force in their teens and early twenties. During the child-bearing years, women's participation levels off. After about the age of forty-five, the working profiles of the two sexes again become similar, with a marked withdrawal from the labor force as people approach age sixty-five. After that point in life, only a small proportion of each sex continues to work.

## The Decline of Agricultural Work

At the beginning of this century, the United States was still largely rural, with almost 40 percent of the labor force engaged in farming. By 1950, this proportion had fallen to almost 10 percent, and by 1991 to less than 3 percent. Figure 19–2 graphically illustrates this rapid decline, which reflects the diminished role of the primary sector in the U.S. economy. Still, because today's agriculture involves more machinery and fewer people, it is more productive than ever. A century ago, a typical farmer could feed five people; today, a farmer now grows

**Figure 19–1**  Participation in the Labor Force by Age and Sex, 1991

(U.S. Department of Labor, 1992)

food for seventy-five. This dramatic rise in productivity also reflects new types of crops, pesticides that promote higher yields, greater energy consumption, and other advances in farming techniques. The average U.S. farm has also doubled in size since 1950 to about 465 acres today. This process signals the eclipse of "family farms," which are declining in number and produce only a small part of our agricultural yield; more and more production is carried out by *corporate agribusinesses*. But, more productive or not, this transformation has wrought painful adjustments for farming communities across the country, as a way of life is lost. And, all of us are indirectly affected by this change: prices have generally been kept low by the rising productivity of agribusiness, although a growing proportion of people are concerned about the effect of widespread use of pesticides and chemicals on crops.

## From Factory Work to Service Work

Industrialization swelled the ranks of blue-collar workers early in this century. As shown in Figure 19–2, by 1900 more than 40 percent of working people in the United

**Table 19–3**  PARTICIPATION IN THE LABOR FORCE BY SEX AND RACE, 1991

| | In the Labor Force | |
| Category of the Population | Number (millions) | Percent |
| --- | --- | --- |
| Men (aged 16 and over) | 68.4 | 75.5 |
| White | 59.3 | 76.4 |
| Black | 6.8 | 69.5 |
| Women (aged 16 and over) | 56.9 | 57.3 |
| White | 48.2 | 57.4 |
| Black | 6.8 | 57.0 |

SOURCE:  U.S. Department of Labor. *Employment and Earnings*, Vol. 39, No. 1 (January 1992), pp. 164–66.

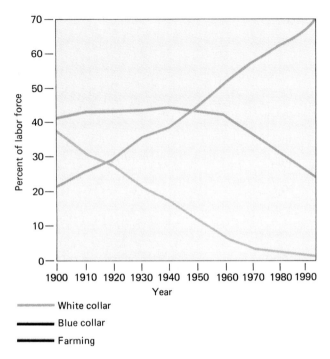

**Figure 19–2** The Changing Pattern of Work in the United States, 1900–1990

*(U.S. Department of Labor)*

## The Dual Labor Market

We can also describe the change from factory work to service jobs in terms of a shifting balance between two different *labor markets* (Edwards, 1979). The **primary labor market** includes *occupations that provide extensive benefits to workers.* This segment of the labor market encompasses the traditional white-collar professions and high management positions. These are jobs that people think of as *careers*: work in the primary labor market provides high income and job security and is also personally challenging and intrinsically satisfying. Such occupations require a broad education rather than specialized training, and they offer solid opportunity for advancement.

But few of these advantages apply to work in the **secondary labor market,** *jobs providing minimal benefits to workers.* This segment of the labor force consists of low-skill, blue-collar work like routine assembly-line operations, and low-level white-collar jobs including clerical positions. The secondary labor market offers workers much lower income, affords little job security, and most positions are non-unionized. Even if workers attain more schooling, they face little opportunity for advancement. In truth, many of these jobs are dead ends, often lacking even the benefits of a seniority system. Not surprisingly, then, workers in the secondary labor market are most likely to experience alienation and dissatisfaction (Mottaz, 1981; Kohn & Schooler, 1982). These problems are especially serious for women and other minorities, who tend to be overly represented in this segment of the labor force (Kemp & Coverman, 1989).

A growing proportion of the jobs being created in the emerging postindustrial economy fall within the secondary labor market. Like manufacturing jobs in factories a century ago, these positions require workers to perform unchallenging tasks, for low wages, under poor working conditions (Edwards, 1979; Gruenberg, 1980). In the box, a traditional factory worker and a new service worker describe their jobs in very similar terms, echoing Karl Marx's concept of worker alienation, described in Chapter 4 ("Society").

Finally, for people with low-paying, service-sector jobs, getting by in the present postindustrial economy depends on working more hours. For this reason the work week has been getting longer in recent years, and it now averages almost forty-nine hours (Hunnicutt, 1988, 1990).

States had blue-collar jobs—surpassing the share employed in agriculture. By mid-century, another transformation had occurred, as the white-collar revolution carried a majority of workers into service occupations. By 1991, more than two-thirds of employed men and women held white-collar jobs, and blue-collar work had slipped to encompass about one-fourth of the labor force.

Looking back, the growth of white-collar occupations is one reason for the widespread—if misleading—description of the United States as a middle-class society. As explained in Chapter 10 ("Social Class in the United States"), much so-called "white-collar" work is more accurately termed "service work," including sales positions, secretarial jobs, and employment in fast-food restaurants. Such work yields little of the income, prestige, and other benefits of traditional white-collar occupations. Therefore, more and more of the jobs being created in this postindustrial era provide only a modest standard of living.

# Factory and Service Jobs: The More Things Change . . .

Mike Lefevre works in a Chicago steel mill. He is aware that jobs such as his are becoming rare in the United States. But he also knows that this work provides little personal satisfaction.

I'm a dying breed. A laborer. Strictly muscle work . . . pick it up, put it down, pick it up, put it down. We handle between forty and fifty thousand pounds of steel a day. (Laughs) I know it's hard to believe—from four hundred pounds to three- and four-pound pieces. It's dying.

. . . It's hard to take pride in a bridge you're never gonna cross, in a door you're never gonna open. You're mass-producing things and you never see the end of it. (Muses) I worked for a trucker one time. At least I could see the truck depart loaded. In a steel mill, forget it. You don't see where nothing goes.

I got chewed out by my foreman once. He said, "Mike, you're a good worker but you have a bad attitude." My attitude is that I don't get excited about my job. I do my work but I don't say whoopee-doo. The day I get excited about my job is the day I go to a head shrinker. How are you gonna get excited about pullin' steel? How are you gonna get excited when you're tired and want to sit down?

It's not just the work. Somebody built the pyramids. Somebody's going to build something. Pyramids, Empire State Building—these things just don't happen. There's hard work behind it. I would like to see a building, say, the Empire State, I would like to see on one side of it a foot wide strip from top to bottom with the name of every bricklayer, the name of every electrician, and all the names. So when a guy walked by, he could take his son and say, "See, that's me over there on the forty-fifth floor, I put the steel beam in." Picasso can point to a painting. What can I point to? Everybody should have something to point to.

Heather Lamb, another Midwesterner, is employed in a newer, service-sector job. Her work as a long-distance telephone operator provides little more autonomy and personal satisfaction than Mike Lefevre finds in the steel mill.

It's a strange atmosphere. You're in a room about the size of a gymnasium, talking to people thousands of miles away. You come in contact with at least thirty-five an hour. You can't exchange any ideas with them. They don't know you, they never will. You feel like you might be missing people. You feel like they put a coin in the machine and they've got you. You're there to perform your service and go. You're kind of detached.

. . . A big thing is not to talk with a customer. If he's upset, you can't say more than, "I'm sorry you've been having trouble." If you get caught talking with a customer, that's one mark against you. You can't help but want to talk to them if they're in trouble or they're just feeling bad or something. For me it's a great temptation to say, "Gee, what's the matter?" You don't feel like you're really that much helping people.

. . . It's a hard feeling when everyone's in a hurry to talk to somebody else, but not to you. Sometimes you get a feeling of needing to talk to somebody. Somebody who wants to listen to you other than, "Why didn't you get me the right number?"

It's something to run into somebody who says, "It's a nice day out, operator. How's your day, busy?" You're so thankful for these people. You say, "Oh yes, it's been an awful day. Thank you for asking."

SOURCE: Terkel (1974).

## Labor Unions

As work has shifted from the primary to the secondary labor market, hard times have befallen **labor unions,** *organizations of workers that attempt to improve wages and working conditions through strategies including negotiations and strikes.* Membership in labor unions increased rapidly in the United States after 1935, rising to more than one-third of the non-farm labor force after World War II. In terms of absolute numbers, union membership peaked during the 1970s at almost 25 million.

Since then, the union rolls have steadily declined to about 16 percent of the non-farm labor force, or

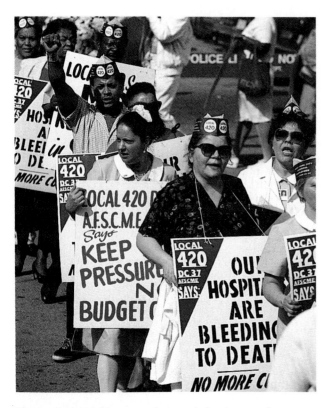

The postindustrial economy has eroded union membership in recent decades. As workers with lower-paying service jobs struggle to make ends meet, however, many are turning to unions in an effort to improve their situation. The American Federation of State, County, and Municipal Employees (AFSCME), a largely service-sector union, is now gaining strength.

about 20 million men and women. In global perspective, unions now claim a far lower portion of workers in the United States than in other industrial societies: more than 90 percent of workers in Denmark and Sweden belong to unions, for example, as do half in Great Britain, and about one third in Canada, Switzerland, and Japan.

Several factors have contributed to this decline. First, the highly unionized industrial sector of the U.S. economy has suffered greatly in recent decades, as already noted. Tens of thousands of unionized workers in steel, automobile, and other industries have lost their jobs. Much of this decline stems from the increasingly global economy; U.S. manufacturers are exporting jobs abroad in search of less expensive labor. At home, the management of many plants facing economic problems succeeded in forcing concessions from workers including,

in some cases, the dissolution of labor unions. Second, few of the new service jobs are unionized. Third, the political climate of the 1980s, under the Reagan and Bush administrations, was generally hostile to union interests (Goldfield, 1987).

Since 1990, the drop in union membership appears to have stabilized. Perhaps, as anxiety about job security rises, more workers are making union membership a higher priority (Marry, 1992).

## Professions

The *professions* constitute a privileged category of work in the postindustrial economy of the United States. Many kinds of work are commonly called professional: we speak of professional tennis players, professional exterminators, even professional con artists. Used this way, a professional pursues some activity for a living in contrast to the *amateur* (from Latin meaning "lover"), who acts simply out of love for the activity itself.

In its more traditional usage, a **profession** is *a prestigious, white-collar occupation that requires extensive formal education.* The term suggested that certain work involved a profession—or public declaration—of faith or willingness to abide by certain principles. Traditional professions include the ministry, medicine, law, and academia (W. Goode, 1960). Today, we recognize more occupations as professions, to the extent that they have the following four characteristics (Ritzer, 1972).

1. **Theoretical knowledge.** Mere jobs involve technical skills, but professionals claim a theoretical understanding of some field based on extensive schooling and regular interaction with peers. Anyone can master first-aid skills, for example, but physicians are set apart because of their theoretical understanding of human health and illness.

2. **Self-regulated training and practice.** While most workers are directly accountable to superiors and are subject to routine, on-the-job supervision, professionals are typically self-employed (Zald, 1971). Professionals participate in associations that set standards for performing or "practicing." Associations also expect their members to conform to a formal code of ethics.

3. **Authority over clients.** Many jobs—sales work, for example—require people to respond directly to the desires of customers. By contrast, professionals expect their "clients" to follow their direction

and advice. Professionals claim this authority based on possessing knowledge that "lay people" lack.

4. **Community orientation rather than self-interest.** The traditional "professing" of faith or obligation was a way for professionals to declare their intentions to serve the needs of clients or the broader community rather than their own self-interest. Most business executives readily admit to working in pursuit of personal financial gain, and this is one reason that engaging in commerce was not one of the traditional professions. Professionals such as priests or college professors, however, rarely admit to such motives. They prefer to think of their work as contributing to the well-being of others. Some professionals, including physicians, are even barred by professional codes from advertising. This aura of altruism also makes many professionals reluctant to discuss the fees that contribute to their high incomes.

Besides the traditional professions, a number of other occupations can be described as *new professions*. These occupations, which include architecture, social work, and accounting, share most of the characteristics just presented.

Many new service occupations in the postindustrial economy have also sought professional standing, a process known as *professionalization*. Members of an occupation often initiate a claim to professional standing by labeling their work in a new way. The new name suggests that they employ special, theoretical knowledge and has the added benefit of distancing them from their field's previously less distinguished reputation. Government bureaucrats, for example, become "public policy analysts," and dogcatchers are reborn as "animal control specialists." Interested parties may form a professional association that will formally attest to their specialized skills. This organization then begins to lobby for the legal right to license those who perform the work in question. It also develops a code of ethics, modeled on those of traditional professions, which emphasizes the occupation's contribution to the community. A professional association may also establish schools or other training facilities, and perhaps start a professional journal. All of this is done in an attempt to win public acceptance of the occupation's professional standing (Abbott, 1988).

Not every category of workers tries to claim full professional status. Some *paraprofessionals*, including paralegals and medical technicians, possess specialized skills but lack the extensive theoretical education required of professionals.

## Self-Employment

*Self-employment*—in effect, earning a living without working for a large organization—was once commonplace in the United States. Rural farms were owned and operated by families, and self-employed workers in the cities owned shops and other small businesses or sold their skills on the open market. C. Wright Mills (1951) estimated that in the early nineteenth century about 80 percent of the U.S. labor force was self-employed. With the onset of the Industrial Revolution, however, that picture changed dramatically. By 1870, the proportion of self-employed workers had plummeted to one-third, and by 1940, the share had dropped further to one-fifth.

There has been a slight *rise* in self-employment in recent years, suggesting that this is one dimension of the postindustrial economy (Steinmetz & Wright, 1989). In 1991, the government estimated that 8.2 percent of the labor force (10.1 percent of men and 6.0 percent of women) were self-employed. The one sector of the economy where self-employment is still pronounced is agriculture; there, about half of men and one-third of women are self-employed (Steinmetz & Wright, 1989; U.S. Department of Labor, 1992).

Professionals—especially lawyers and physicians—have always been well represented among the self-employed because their schooling and skills have high market value. But most self-employed workers in the United States are not professionals. They are small business owners, plumbers, carpenters, free-lance writers, editors, artists, and long-distance truck drivers. Overall, the self-employed are more likely to have blue-collar occupations than white-collar work.

Our society has always painted an appealing picture of working independently: no time clocks to punch, no rigid routines, and no one looking over your shoulder. For those excluded from organizations by prejudice or discrimination, self-employment has served as a strategy to increase economic opportunity (Evans, 1989). Further, self-employment holds the potential—although rarely realized—of earning a great deal of money. But for all its advantages, self-employment presents workers with special problems. Many are vulnerable to fluctuations in the economy: about one-third of small businesses fold in less than five years (Form, 1982). Another common problem is that the self-employed lack pension and health-care benefits generally provided to employees of large organizations.

## Unemployment

Work serves as a source not only of income but of personal satisfaction, social prestige, and individual identity. For this reason, unemployment causes both financial hardship and psychological stress (Riegle, 1982).

Some unemployment is found in every society. Few young people entering the labor force find a job immediately; some older workers temporarily leave the labor force while seeking a new job or because of a strike; others suffer from long-term illnesses; and still others who are illiterate or without skills cannot perform useful work. But unemployment is not just a personal problem; it is also a product of the economy itself. Capable and willing workers lose their jobs when economic recession occurs, if occupations become obsolete, or as factories close in the face of rising foreign competition. In recent decades, furthermore, the emerging postindustrial economy has shattered the job security of workers in many traditional blue-collar occupations (Kasarda, 1983).

In predominantly capitalist societies like the United States, the unemployment rate rarely dips below 5 percent of the labor force. Public officials generally view this level of unemployment as natural, and sometimes even describe it as "full employment." An "unemployment problem" is publicly acknowledged only when the unemployment rate exceeds 7 or 8 percent (Albrecht, 1983). In principle, predominantly socialist societies consider work to be each person's right and obligation, so the government may create jobs to keep the unemployment rate low. In practice, however, unemployment is just as great a problem in these societies.

In early 1992, 8.5 million people over the age of sixteen were unemployed—about 7.1 percent of the U.S. civilian labor force. In some regions of the country, including parts of West Virginia and New Mexico, unemployment may exceed twice the national rate. Unemployment declined through the 1980s from almost 10 percent at the beginning of the decade to about 5 percent in 1989, rising again with the recession of the early 1990s.

Unemployment is more common in the secondary than the primary labor market. Figure 19–3 shows the official unemployment rate for various segments of the U.S. population in 1991 (U.S. Department of Labor, 1992). Unemployment among African Americans stood more than twice as high (12.4 percent) as among whites (6.0 percent), due to the historical concentration of people of color in the secondary labor market (DiPrete, 1981). Younger people also confront high levels of unemployment, with jobless rates of 36.3 percent for black

During the Great Depression, a time of catastrophic unemployment in the United States, Isaac Soyer painted *Employment Agency*, a powerful statement of the personal collapse and private despair that can afflict men and women who are out of work.

*(Isaac Soyer,* Employment Agency. Collection of the Whitney Museum of American Art. Purchase 37.44. Photo by Geoffrey Clements, N.Y.)*

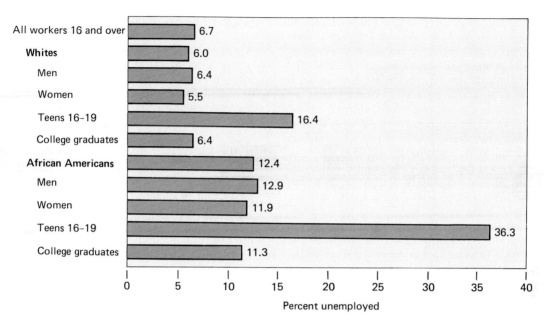

**Figure 19–3** Official U.S. Unemployment Rate among Various Categories of Adults, 1991
(*U.S. Department of Labor, 1992*)

teens and 16.4 percent for white teens. This racial pattern continues even among college graduates, who typically work in the primary labor market, with unemployment among African Americans topping 11.3 percent compared to 6.4 percent among whites.

In racial categories, men now have higher levels of unemployment than women. A decade ago, women contended with higher joblessness than men. The economic recession that has hit male-dominated blue-collar industrial jobs especially hard accounts for this change.

Official unemployment statistics, based on monthly national surveys, generally understate unemployment for two reasons. First, to be counted among the unemployed, a person must be actively seeking work. Especially during economic recessions, many people become discouraged after failing to find a job and stop looking. These "discouraged workers" are not counted among the unemployed. Second, many people unable to find jobs for which they are qualified take "lesser" employment: a former college professor, for example, may drive a taxi while seeking a new teaching position. Such people are included among the employed, although they might better be described as *underemployed*. Official statistics also may overlook the fact that some people who are out of work receive income from odd jobs or illegal activity. Overall, however, the actual level of un-

employment is probably several percentage points above the official figure.

## The Underground Economy

Unlike socialist economies that have traditionally condemned market forces, the capitalist U.S. economy embraces "free enterprise." Yet, even in the United States, economic transactions are subject to government regulations that require extensive records and regular reports. Any violation of these regulations places transactions within the **underground economy**, *economic activity involving income or the exchange of goods and services that is not reported to the government.*

On a small scale, evidence of the underground economy can be found everywhere: sales representatives from different companies swap customer samples on a weekly basis; teenagers baby-sit for parents in their neighborhoods; a family makes some extra money by holding a garage sale. All these things generate income that people are unlikely to report to the government. A larger segment of the underground economy consists of crime. Income from crimes such as illegal drug sales, prostitution, bribery, theft, illegal gambling, and loan-sharking almost always goes unreported.

But the single largest segment of the underground economy involves "honest" people who fail to accurately report their legally obtained income on income tax forms. Self-employed people like carpenters, physicians, and owners of small businesses may understate their incomes; waiters, waitresses, and other service workers may not report their full income from tips. Even relatively small omissions and misrepresentations on individual income tax returns add up to billions of dollars in the underground economy (Simon & Witte, 1982).

Exactly how large is the underground economy? Estimates suggest that perhaps 10 percent of economic activity in the United States goes unreported (Gutmann, cited in Simon & Witte, 1982). In 1992, the gross domestic product of the United States exceeded $5 trillion, so the underground economy may have amounted to $500 billion—more than the combined GDP of all the Scandinavian countries.

## Social Diversity in the Workplace

A revolution is now under way in the workplace. This has nothing to do with the change in the nature of jobs—from factory to service work—that we have already discussed; rather, this involves a fundamental shift in the composition of the U.S. labor force. In brief, this change is known as the *workplace diversity revolution*.

Traditionally, white men have formed the mainstay of the U.S. labor force. As explained in Chapter 12 ("Race and Ethnicity"), however, demographic shifts in the United States are sharply increasing our society's proportion of racial and ethnic minorities. During the 1980s, the increase in African Americans (13 percent) was twice as great as for whites (6 percent); the rise in the Hispanic population (above 50 percent), and in the numbers of Asian Americans (topping 100 percent), were greater still. These increases, taken together, point to a

## A DECADE OF CHANGE

# The Work Force of the Twenty-First Century

During the 1980s, the demographic profile of the United States changed significantly, with a marked rise in the share of the population represented by minorities. Looking ahead through the 1990s, we can expect continued transformation in the social composition of the population—and thus the labor force.

The figure shows that the number of white men in the U.S. labor force is projected to rise by a modest 8 percent during the 1990s. The rate of increase among African-American male workers will be far greater, at 24 percent. Among Hispanic men, the rise will be a whopping 50 percent. Among women, projected increases across the board are larger than for men, meaning that a greater share of workers in the United States will be women as we approach the new century. But, here again, the gains

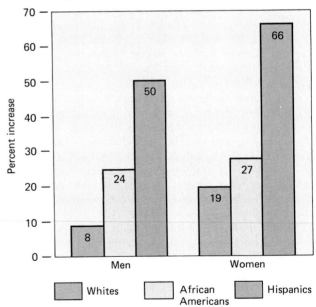

Projected Increase in the Numbers of People in the U.S. Labor Force, 1990–2000

*Hispanics can be of any race (U.S. Department of Labor)

"minority-majority" in the United States about halfway through the coming century. This change is already having profound consequences in businesses across the country. The box takes a closer look at how the increasing social diversity of our society is affecting the workplace in the 1990s.

## Technology and Work

The central feature of the emerging postindustrial economy is the computer and other new information technologies. Throughout history, technology has defined the kinds of skills that a society seeks and rewards; to some extent, then, technology also determines what kinds of *people* join in the productive system. The industrial era, with its emphasis on physically demanding factory work, was skewed toward men. The rise of information technol-

ogy has encouraged the entry of women into the labor force.

The computer-based Information Revolution is changing the conditions of work and the workplace. Shoshana Zuboff (1982) points to five ways in which computers have already altered the character of work. First, she suggests, *computers are deskilling labor.* Just as industrial machinery deskilled the master craftworker of an earlier era, so computers now threaten the skills of managers. Why? Simply because more and more business decisions are based on computer modeling, in which a machine signals a company to "buy" or "sell," or leads a passive manager to approve or reject a loan. Second, *work is becoming more abstract.* Industrial workers typically have a "hands-on" relationship with their product; postindustrial workers manipulate symbols in pursuit of some abstract business goal. Third, Zuboff explains, *computers limit workplace interaction.* The Information Revolution

---

among minorities will be greatest of all: a 19 percent rise among whites will be surpassed by a 27 percent jump among African Americans, and a 66 percent boost in Hispanics.

When you add up all these factors, non-Hispanic, white men—the traditional backbone of the U.S. labor force—will represent only 10 percent of growth in the labor force during the 1990s. By the end of the decade, they will amount to just 40 percent of all workers, and their numbers will continue to drop. This means that, in the twenty-first century, few businesses will be able to survive by relying solely on the efforts of white men. On the other side of the coin, companies that begin now to plan for growing social diversity in the labor force will have a competitive advantage.

Responding effectively to work-

place diversity means more than maintaining affirmative action programs, which are primarily aimed at recruiting. As important as fair hiring policies are, companies face a broader challenge—and a greater opportunity—that involves transforming the workplace environment to ensure the fullest use of all workers. Employees, after all, are any company's most important resource. There are several dimensions to the process of ensuring that this resource is used to advantage. First, companies must realize that the needs and concerns of women and people of color may not always be the same as those of white men. For example, the importance of child care will increase in the workplace during the next century; the ability to manage cultural diversity will also be vital. Second, businesses have to devise education programs and person-

nel policies that effectively defuse tensions that often accompany social differences. Rules to prevent all kinds of harassment related to gender and race will create an environment that allows the full efforts of all workers to come to the fore. Third, companies will have to reflect on current promotion practices. At present, according to a survey of Fortune 500 companies, only 2 percent of top executives are women, and just 1 percent are members of other minorities. Any informal "glass ceiling" that prevents advancement by skilled minorities clearly will have the effect of discouraging achievement in the competitive labor market of the 1990s and beyond. In effect, then, any such barriers deprive companies of their largest source of talent —women and other minorities.

SOURCES: Bureau of National Affairs (1990) and Crispell (1990).

often leads to social isolation as workers perform most of their work at computer terminals. Fourth, *computers demand new standards for productivity*. Because information can be processed so quickly, in other words, organizations must redefine their expectations for employees who utilize new technology. Fifth, *computers enhance the supervision and control of workers*. Using computers, supervisors can monitor worker output precisely and continuously. Workers now have to contend with ever-present management, which is far from typical in the industrial workplace.

Zuboff's broader point is that technology is not socially neutral; rather it shapes the way we work. Understandably, then, while workers may find some dimensions of the Information Revolution pleasing, they are likely to oppose others.

# Corporations

Corporations lie at the core of today's capitalist economies. A **corporation** is *an organization with a legal existence including rights and liabilities apart from those of its members*. An organization that is legally incorporated, in other words, becomes an entity unto itself able to enter into contracts and own property. Of roughly 20 million businesses in the United States, about 4 million (25 percent) are incorporated (*Statistics of Income Bulletin*, 1991).

The idea of legal incorporation arose about a century ago to provide two benefits to owners of large businesses. First, incorporation shields owners from the legal liabilities of their businesses. This legal strategy protects personal wealth from lawsuits arising from business debts or harm to consumers. Second, incorporation confers advantages under the tax laws of the United States that increase the profits of owners.

Chapter 9 ("Social Stratification") explains that most large corporations are owned by millions of stockholders (as well as by other corporations) rather than by single families. This dispersion of corporate ownership has to some extent spread wealth by making more people small-scale capitalists. Ralf Dahrendorf (1959) adds that the day-to-day operation of a corporation is the task of white-collar executives who are responsible to the stockholders. In practice, however, a great deal of corporate stock is owned by a small number of the corporation's top executives and directors. These major stockholders comprise a small economic elite, which owns and oper-

ates the richest and most powerful U.S. businesses. Thus the proliferation of corporations has not substantially changed how large businesses operate and it has only slightly affected the distribution of wealth in the United States (Useem, 1980).

## Economic Concentration

Profit-making corporations range in size from one-person businesses to veritable giants such as the major automobile manufacturers that employ hundreds of thousands of people in the United States and abroad. About half of U.S. corporations are small, with assets worth less than $100,000. The largest corporations, however, dominate our country's economy.

The first truly giant corporation was United States Steel, formed in 1901 from the merger of several steel companies. Leading this mega-corporation, industrialist J.P. Morgan controlled two-thirds of all steel production in the early decades of the twentieth century. Worth billions of dollars at that time, U.S. Steel's assets would have funded the operation of the federal government for almost two years (Baltzell, 1964; Fusfeld, 1982).

Throughout this century, the growth of corporations has resulted in an increasing concentration of national and international economic power. The productive assets of the 200 largest manufacturing corporations in 1950 were surpassed by those of the biggest one hundred companies in 1970 (Fusfeld, 1982). Of more than 4 million U.S. corporations in 1989, 347 had total assets exceeding $1 billion. Taken together, these economic giants owned 70 percent of all corporate assets and received 72 percent of all corporate profits (U.S. Bureau of the Census, 1991).

Table 19–4 shows the twenty largest corporations in the United States in 1990, ranked by sales. At the top of the list, General Motors had $125 billion in sales and $180 billion in total assets. GM's sales during that year are about as much as the combined tax revenue of half the states. GM also employed more people than did the governments of all the states on the West Coast, including Alaska and Hawaii. Such economic concentration suggests that a few giant corporations control many U.S. markets.

## Conglomerates and Corporate Linkages

Economic concentration has spawned **conglomerates,** *giant corporations composed of many smaller corporations*. Conglomerates, which begin as corporations, seek

**Table 19–4** THE TWENTY LARGEST INDUSTRIAL CORPORATIONS IN THE UNITED STATES, 1990 (RANKED BY SALES)

| Corporation | Product | Sales ($ billions) | Assets ($ billions) | Number of Employees |
|---|---|---|---|---|
| General Motors | Motor vehicles | 124.7 | 180.0 | 761,400 |
| Exxon | Oil refining | 105.5 | 87.7 | 104,000 |
| Ford Motor | Motor vehicles | 97.7 | 173.6 | 381,400 |
| International Business Machines (IBM) | Office equipment | 69.0 | 87.6 | 378,500 |
| General Electric | Electronics | 58.4 | 153.9 | 295,000 |
| Mobil | Oil refining | 57.8 | 41.7 | 67,600 |
| Sears, Roebuck | Retail stores | 56.0 | 96.3 | 480,000 |
| Philip Morris Co. | Tobacco products | 44.3 | 46.6 | 161,600 |
| Texaco | Oil refining | 40.9 | 26.0 | 38,100 |
| E.I. du Pont de Nemours | Chemicals | 39.7 | 38.1 | 144,900 |
| Chevron | Oil refining | 38.6 | 35.1 | 54,500 |
| Citicorp | Banks | 38.4 | 217.0 | 93,500 |
| American Telephone & Telegraph (AT&T) | Electronics | 37.3 | 43.8 | 278,600 |
| Wal-Mart Stores | Retail stores | 32.7 | 11.4 | 299,000 |
| K-mart | Retail stores | 32.3 | 13.9 | 369,000 |
| Chrysler | Motor vehicles | 30.6 | 46.4 | 109,900 |
| Amoco | Oil refining | 28.0 | 32.2 | 54,100 |
| Boeing | Aerospace | 27.6 | 14.6 | 161,700 |
| Procter & Gamble | Chemicals | 25.8 | 20.6 | 84,100 |
| American Express | Financial services | 24.3 | 137.7 | 107,200 |

SOURCE: "The Forbes 500 Annual Directory," *Forbes*, Vol. 147, no. 9 (April 29, 1991): Special issue.

greater profits by entering new markets. In the past, corporations grew as they spun off new companies; during the 1980s, "takeovers" of existing companies became more common. Forging a conglomerate is also a way to diversify a company, so that new products can provide a hedge against declining profits in the original market. Faced with declining sales of tobacco products, for example, R.J. Reynolds merged with Nabisco foods, forming a conglomerate called RJR-Nabisco. Another example is Coca-Cola. Although its original market is still growing, Coke now produces fruit drinks, coffee, bottled water, feature films, and television programs. Beatrice Foods is another corporate "umbrella" containing more than fifty smaller corporations that manufacture well-known products including Reddi-Whip, Wesson cooking oils, Peter Pan peanut butter, Hunt's foods, Tropicana fruit juices, La Choy foods, Orville Redenbacher popcorn, Max Factor cosmetics, Playtex clothing, and Samsonite luggage (Beatrice, 1985).

Besides conglomerates, corporations are also linked by extremely wealthy families who own their stock. For example, when Pittsburgh banking magnate Richard K. Mellon died in 1970, his family reportedly owned a controlling interest in six major corporations (Fusfeld, 1982). Today, linkage more often takes the form of corporations owning each other's stock. Because they are able to own property just as individuals do, corporations invest heavily in one another. Joint ventures, which promise to benefit all parties, frequently accompany stock linkages (Herman, 1981).

One more type of linkage among corporations is the **interlocking directorate**, *a social network of people who serve simultaneously on the boards of directors of many corporations.* These connections give corporations access to insider information that can be extremely valuable. When founded in 1901, for example, U.S. Steel was linked through its board to more than one hundred other corporations. Such economic inbreeding now violates antitrust laws that forbid direct linkages if the corporations compete with one another. Yet beneficial linkages persist among noncompeting corporations with common interests—for example, a corporation building tractors may share directors with one that manufactures tires. Indirect linkages also occur when, for example, a member of General Motors's board of directors and a member of Ford's board of directors both sit on the board of Exxon.

Research reveals that interlocking directorates remain an important trait of corporate life (Marlios, 1975; Herman, 1981; Scott & Griff, 1985). Beth Mintz and Michael Schwartz (1981) found General Motors to be linked through its board of directors to twenty-nine other major corporations. The members of these boards, in turn, serve as directors of almost 700 additional corporations. Indirect linkages among corporations, Mintz and Schwartz noted, commonly involve major banks and insurance companies, which seek to protect the financial well-being of U.S. corporations as a whole.

Finally, not all corporate linkages are formal. Gwen Moore (1979) has described how social networks (discussed in Chapter 7, "Groups and Organizations") informally link members of the corporate elite. In other words, corporate executives travel in many of the same social circles, allowing them to exchange valuable information. Michael Useem (1979) concludes that such networks enhance not only the economic clout of big businesses, they also expand the influence of corporate leaders in political, social, and charitable organizations.

Corporate linkages do not necessarily oppose the public interest, but they do concentrate power and they sometimes encourage illegal activity. Price-fixing, for example, is legal in much of the world (the Organization of Petroleum Exporting Countries—OPEC—meets regularly to try to set oil prices), but not in the United States. By their nature, however, linkages encourage price-fixing, especially when only several corporations control an entire market.

## Corporations and Competition

The capitalist economic model assumes businesses operate independently and competitively. In the United States, however, the entire economy is not competitive. On the contrary, the competitive sector includes mostly smaller businesses and self-employed people. Large corporations at the core of the American economy fall within the *noncompetitive sector*. Large corporations are not truly competitive, first, because of their extensive linkages. Second, many markets are dominated by a small number of corporations.

From a business point of view, a company would maximize profits by achieving a **monopoly**, *domination*

*of a market by a single producer*. With no competitors, a company can simply dictate prices. A century ago, the federal government saw the public danger in this and limited monopolies by law, beginning with the Sherman Anti-Trust Act of 1890.

Such legislation has eliminated total monopolies, but limited competition persists in the form of **oligopoly,** or *domination of a market by a few producers*. Oligopoly seems to be inherent in industrial-capitalism. Entering the automobile manufacturing market today, for example, would take a staggering investment of billions of dollars, and even then there is no certainty of competing effectively against existing automobile manufacturers that have merged to form ever-larger corporations. Certainly the successful entry of foreign-owned corporations into the U.S. automobile market shows that oligopolies can be challenged. But from the point of view of big business, competition means *risk*, and amounts to a threat to corporate profits.

Growing corporate power has implications for government. The capitalist model minimizes government intervention in the economy in favor of allowing market forces free reign. But corporate power is now so great— and competition among corporations so limited—that government regulation is often the only means to protect the public interest. Government oversight of at least much of the economy is now a fact of life in the United States. Yet, in the view of some critics, the government can hardly be called an adversary of large corporations. The government is, they point out, the single biggest customer of large corporations, and it frequently intervenes to support struggling corporations. More correctly, then, corporations and government typically work in concert to make the entire economy more stable and to make businesses more profitable (Madsen, 1980).

## Corporations and the Global Economy

Corporations have grown in size and power so fast that they will soon account for most of the world's economic activity. The largest corporations—centered in the United States, Japan, and Western Europe—have spilled across national borders and now view the entire world as one vast marketplace.

As discussed in Chapter 11 ("Global Inequality"), multinationals are large corporations that produce and market products in many different nations. Beatrice Foods, for example, operates factories in thirty countries and sells products in more than one hundred. General

The expansion of Western multinational corporations has altered patterns of consumption throughout the world, creating a homogeneous "corporate culture" that is—for better or worse—undermining countless traditional ways of life.

Motors, Ford, Exxon, and the other huge multinationals listed in Table 19–4 earn much—and in some cases most—of their profits outside the United States.

Corporations become multinational in pursuit of their primary goal: making money. About three-fourths of the world's people live in Third-World societies where most of the planet's resources are found. Worldwide operations, then, offer access to vast markets, cheap labor, and plentiful raw materials. Developing an international profile has the added bonuses of permitting corporations to lower their tax bills and to move money from country to country, profiting from fluctuating currency values.

The effects of capitalist expansion to the poor societies of the Third World are hotly debated, as Chapter 11 ("Global Inequality") explains in detail. On one side of the controversy, modernization theorists argue that multinationals are the key to world economic development (Rostow, 1978; Madsen, 1980; Berger, 1986). In the face of staggering problems of poverty and hunger, multinationals unleash the great productivity of the capitalist economic system. For instance, Exxon corporation alone outproduces almost any Third-World nation. During the 1980s, Exxon's annual sales averaged several times the combined gross national product of all seven Central American countries.

Corporate expansion, modernization theorists argue, provides poor societies with needed employment in the secondary (manufacturing) and tertiary (service) sectors. Multinationals also import capital to the Third World and introduce new technology—especially manufacturing techniques—that together accelerate economic growth. Multinationals thus offer countries in which they operate short-term advantages by paying wages and taxes, and stimulate long-term development by expanding the local economy with new products and services.

On the other side, dependency theorists claim that multinationals have intensified global inequality (Vaughan, 1978; Wallerstein, 1979; Delacroix & Ragin, 1981; Bergesen, 1983). Multinational investment, they argue, actually creates few jobs. Instead, tremendously powerful multinationals frequently inhibit the development of labor-intensive local industries, the real source of employment. Critics of multinationals also charge that they generally produce expensive consumer goods for export to rich societies, rather than generating food and other necessities needed by the local people.

Far from assisting in the economic development of Third-World societies, dependency theorists conclude, multinationals make poor societies poorer and increasingly reliant on rich societies of the capitalist First World.

From this perspective, the growth of multinational corporations amounts to little more than an extension of historical colonialism: a neocolonialism now concerned with profit rather than direct political control. As one defender of multinationals asserted, "We are not without cunning. We shall not make Britain's mistake. Too wise to govern the world, we shall simply own it" (cited in Vaughan, 1978:20).

## The Economy of the Twenty-first Century

In recent years the rate of economic change has accelerated, just as it did in 1890, as if to anticipate the arrival of a new century. The biggest changes have reverberated through socialist societies of Eastern Europe and the former Soviet Union. Socialism, which at its peak organized the productive lives of about one-fourth of humanity, seems to be in decline, although the People's Republic of China, Cuba, and other nations still hold steadfastly to government-based economies.

Capitalism, too, has seen marked changes and now operates with a significant degree of government regulation. The most significant change in the capitalist system is the emergence of global corporations. The global reach of today's giant businesses means that U.S. corporations have expanded into more parts of the world. On the other side of the coin, foreign-based corporations are increasing their investment in the United States.

Perhaps, as some analysts suggest, we are nearing the end of "the American century." A sign of impending change was the 1989 purchase of New York's Rockefeller Center—a prominent symbol of U.S. capitalism—by Japan's Mitsubishi corporation. Another turning point occurred in 1990, when for the first time, foreign corporations owned more of the United States than U.S. corporations owned abroad ("Buy America," 1989). Foreign investors now have title of half the commercial property in downtown Los Angeles, 40 percent in Houston, 35 percent in Minneapolis, and 25 percent in Manhattan (Selimuddin, 1989). Growing industrial production overseas, benefiting from new factories, a highly motivated workforce, and the latest technology, has also reduced our country's competitiveness in numerous areas. The

Our planet's resources support human life. But how those resources should be used, and who should control the economic destiny of our planet, remain controversial questions. One point of view is expressed by artist Ed McGowin in his painting *Grown Men Playing with the Planet Earth* (1991).

(Ed McGowin, Grown Men Playing with the Planet Earth. *1991. Oil/canvas/wood. 52" × 52". Collection of Dain Bosworth Incorporated; photo courtesy of Hokin Kaufman Gallery, Chicago.)*

world's largest steel corporations and automobile manufacturers are now Japanese, as is virtually the entire domestic market in home electronics.

What will be the long-term effects of all these changes? One conclusion seems clear: our economic future will depend less on the performance of individual *national* economies. Instead, the world's societies are becoming increasingly interconnected in a global economic system. The emergence of the postindustrial economy in the United States is certainly linked to increasing industrial production abroad, especially in Asia's Pacific Rim. Finally, the ever-pressing issue of global inequality looms large. Whether the world economy ultimately reduces or deepens the disparity between rich and poor societies will likely steer our planet toward peace or belligerence.

# Summary

1.  The economy is a major social institution by which goods and services are produced, distributed, and consumed.

2.  In technologically simple societies, economic activity is subsumed within the family. In agrarian societies, the economy becomes distinct from the family. Industrialization sparks significant economic expansion due to new sources of energy, factories, mass production, and specialization. In postindustrial economies, the majority of workers provide services rather than contributing to the manufacture of goods.

3.  The primary sector of the economy generates raw materials; the secondary sector manufactures various goods; the tertiary sector produces services. In preindustrial societies, the primary sector predominates; the secondary sector is of greatest importance in industrial societies; the tertiary sector prevails in postindustrial societies.

4.  The economies of today's industrial societies may be described in terms of two models. Capitalism is based on private ownership of productive property and the pursuit of personal profit in a competitive marketplace. Socialism is based on collective ownership of productive property and the pursuit of collective well-being through government control of the economy.

5.  Although the U.S. economy is predominantly capitalist, our government is widely involved in economic life. Government plays an even greater economic role in the democratic socialist societies of Western Europe. The former Soviet Union has slowly introduced some market elements into its historically centralized economy; many nations of Eastern Europe are making similar changes, with some limited success.

6.  Capitalism is highly productive, providing a high overall standard of living. Socialist economies are less productive but generate more economic equality.

7.  Agricultural work has declined in the United States during this century. The number of blue-collar jobs has also diminished; such work now involves only one-fourth of the labor force. Today, about two-thirds of American workers have white-collar service jobs.

8.  A profession is a special category of white-collar work based on theoretical knowledge, occupational autonomy, authority over clients, and an emphasis on community service.

9.  Work in the primary labor market provides far more rewards than work in the secondary labor market. Most new jobs are in the secondary labor market's service sector.

10. Today, 8 percent of U.S. workers are self-employed. Although many professionals fall into this category, most self-employed workers have blue-collar occupations.

11. Capitalist societies tend to maintain an unemployment rate of at least 5 percent. Socialist societies, too, struggle with high unemployment.

12. The underground economy represents about 10 percent of the economic activity in the United States, including most criminal business as well as legal income unreported on income tax forms.

13. Corporations form the core of the U.S. economy. The largest corporations, which are conglomerates, account for most corporate assets and profits.

14. The competitive sector of the U.S. economy encompasses smaller businesses. Large corporations dominate the noncompetitive sector.

15. Multinational corporations have grown in number and size during this century. The consequences for global economic development are a matter of continuing controversy.

# Key Concepts

**capitalism** an economic system in which productive resources are privately owned

**communism** a hypothetical economic and political system in which all members of society have economic and social equality

**conglomerates** giant corporations composed of many smaller corporations

**corporation** an organization with a legal existence including rights and liabilities apart from those of its members

**democratic socialism** an economic and political system that combines significant government intervention in the economy with free elections

**economy** the institutionalized system for production, distribution, and consumption of goods and services

**interlocking directorate** a social network of people who serve simultaneously on the boards of directors of many corporations

**labor unions** organizations of workers that attempt to improve wages and working conditions through various strategies, including negotiations and strikes

**monopoly** domination of a market by a single producer

**oligopoly** domination of a market by a few producers

**postindustrial economy** a productive system based on service work and high technology

**primary labor market** occupations that provide extensive benefits to workers

**primary sector** the part of the economy that generates raw materials directly from the natural environment

**profession** a prestigious, white-collar occupation that requires extensive formal education

**secondary labor market** jobs that provide minimal benefits to workers

**secondary sector** the part of the economy that transforms raw materials into manufactured goods

**socialism** an economic system in which productive resources are collectively owned

**tertiary sector** the part of the economy that generates services rather than goods

**underground economy** economic activity involving income or the exchange of goods and services that is not reported to the government

# Suggested Readings

One of sociology's best contemporary thinkers examines the social consequences of capitalism.

> Peter L. Berger. *The Capitalist Revolution: Fifty Propositions about Prosperity, Equality, and Liberty.* New York: Basic Books, 1986.

This textbook focuses on work in the United States, with an emphasis on patterns of conflict within the workplace.

> George Ritzer and David Walczak. *Working: Conflict and Change.* 4th ed. Englewood Cliffs, NJ: Prentice Hall, 1990.

The first of these books, a sociological classic, explores the emergence of a postindustrial society. The second, published a decade later, argues that manufacturing remains crucial to the U.S. economy and to our ability to develop high-wage service occupations.

> Daniel Bell. *The Coming of Post-Industrial Society: A Venture in Social Forecasting.* New York: Harper Colophon, 1976.

> Stephen S. Cohen and John Zysman. *Manufacturing Matters: The Myth of the Post-Industrial Economy.* New York: Basic Books, 1987.

In light of the economic struggles currently going on in Eastern Europe, this collection of essays, exploring this region's social and economic history, takes on new importance.

> Daniel Chirot, ed. *The Origins of Backwardness in Eastern Europe: Economics and Politics from the Middle Ages Until the Early Twentieth Century.* Berkeley: University of California Press, 1989.

This is among the first sociological accounts of the economic and political changes in Eastern Europe.

> William Echikson. *Lighting the Night: Revolution in Eastern Europe.* New York: Morrow, 1990.

Technology and corporate expansion have also worked to transform both the First and Second Worlds.

> Richard McKenzie and Dwight Lee. *Quicksilver Capital: How the Rapid Movement of Wealth Has Changed the World.* New York: The Free Press, 1991.

This study suggests that traditional notions about gender continue to shape the workplace today.

> Rita Mae Kelly. *The Gendered Economy: Work, Careers, and Success.* Newbury Park, CA: Sage, 1991.

These two books analyze the rise and decline of labor unions in the last half-century.

Daniel B. Cornfield. *Becoming a Mighty Voice: Conflict and Change in the United Furniture Workers of America.* New York: Russell Sage Foundation, 1989.

Michael Goldfield. *The Decline of Organized Labor in the United States.* Chicago: University of Chicago, 1987.

How have specific occupational groups—such as physicians and lawyers—historically claimed the right to control particular services as professional jurisdictions?

Andrew Abbott. *The System of Professions: An Essay on the Division of Expert Labor.* Chicago: University of Chicago Press, 1988.

This analysis highlights the economic reasons for tax evasion and other dimensions of the underground economy.

Frank A. Cowell. *Cheating the Government: The Economics of Evasion.* Cambridge, MA: The MIT Press, 1990.

Although farming has received growing attention in recent decades, the role of the 1 million American women in farming is rarely studied. This book describes farmwork, household work, and community life among farm women today.

Rachel Ann Rosenfeld. *Farm Women: Work, Farm, and Family in the United States.* Chapel Hill, NC: University of North Carolina Press, 1985.

This comparative study probes one important dimension of the economy—attitudes toward work.

Tomotsu Sengoku. *Willing Workers: The Work Ethics in Japan, England, and the United States.* Westport, CT: Quorum Books, 1985.

The first of these books provides an overview of the increasing social diversity of the workplace in the United States. The second highlights how people of color stand in the corporate economy.

Marilyn Loden and Judy B. Rosener. *Workforce America! Managing Employee Diversity as a Vital Resource.* Homewood, IL: Business One Irwin, 1991.

Floyd and Jacqueline Dickens. *The Black Manager: Making it in the Corporate World.* Rev. ed. New York: American Management Association, 1991.

# 20

# Health
# and Medicine

Melody Barrett, a nineteen-year-old sophomore at an exclusive private college in Minnesota, sits restlessly in the waiting room of the school medical clinic. She feels annoyed and fearful: her roommate has pressured her to see the doctor, and she is afraid her parents will be angry if they find out that she is ill. *There isn't anything wrong*, she keeps telling herself. Her parents, both lawyers, live forty miles away in Minneapolis. They expect Melody home for the weekend, but she is trying to think up an excuse for not going.

This young woman's problem is failing health due to starvation. Far from believing that she is starving, however, she thinks of herself as *fat*. She knows that she weighs only eighty-seven pounds, and she expects the doctor to warn her that she weighs far too little for a woman five feet, five inches tall. But for over three years Melody has been concerned—her roommate would say *obsessed*—with being thin.

Melody Barrett's problem, familiar to many college students, is *anorexia nervosa*,[1] a disorder characterized by what specialists term "severe caloric restriction," or intense, often compulsive dieting. Like many diseases, anorexia nervosa has social as well as biological sources:

90 to 95 percent of its victims are *females*, most of them *white* and from *affluent* families. Many women who contend with eating disorders are strongly pressured by their parents to be high achievers. Although Melody Barrett's case is unusually severe, research suggests that one-third to one-half of college-aged women actively try to lose weight, although most of them would not be considered overweight. About one in seven do so to the point that their behavior falls within the clinical description of an eating disorder (Levine, 1987; Robinson, 1987).

To better appreciate the social foundation of eating disorders for women, consider a comment once made by the Duchess of Windsor: "A woman," she observed, "cannot be too rich or too thin." Women fall victim to eating disorders because our culture places such importance on their physical appearance, with slenderness the ideal of femininity (Parrott, 1987). Some researchers suggest that this society socializes young women to believe that they are never "too thin to feel fat." Such an attitude pushes women toward a form of "mass starvation" that some critics claim "compares with foot-binding, lip-stretching, and other forms of woman mutilation" found in other cultures (Wooley, Wooley, & Dyrenforth, 1979; Levine, 1987).

Health is the concern of physicians and other medical professionals. Sociologists, too, study health because, as this chapter explains, social forces greatly shape the

---

[1] This profile of victims of anorexia nervosa is based on Levine, 1987. Another eating disorder, *bulimia*, involves binge eating coupled with induced vomiting to inhibit weight gain. The two diseases have similar victim profiles (cf. Striegel-Moore, Silberstein, & Rodin, 1986).

557

well-being of the U.S. population and people throughout the world.

# What Is Health?

Common sense suggests that health is simply the absence of disease. The World Health Organization, however, defines the ideal of **health** as *a state of complete physical, mental, and social well-being* (1946:3). This more sociological definition underscores the major theme of this chapter, that *health is as much a social as a biological issue.*

## Health and Society

The health of any population is shaped by important characteristics of the surrounding society as a whole.

1. *Health relates to a society's cultural patterns.* People evaluate health based on standards that vary from culture to culture. René Dubos (1980; orig. 1965) points out that early in this century, yaws, a contagious skin disease, was so common in tropical Africa that societies there considered it normal. There is some truth, then, in the observation that health is having the same diseases as one's neighbors (Quentin Crisp, cited in Kirk & Madsen, 1989).

   What the members of a society view as healthy is also closely linked to what they deem to be *morally* good; by the same token, they often define as illness what they judge to be ethically wrong. Because many people in the United States object to homosexuality on moral grounds, they sometimes call this sexual orientation "sick," although it is quite natural from a medical point of view. Many members of our society, especially men, view as normal and desirable a competitive, stressful way of life, even though stress is related to some two-thirds of physician visits. Stress also underlies heart disease, which is the leading cause of death in the United States (Wallis, 1983). Ideas about what constitutes good health, therefore, mesh into a type of social control that promotes conformity to cultural norms.

   Because they are embedded in culture, standards of health change over time. Early in this century, some prominent physicians condemned women who pursued a college education, warning that doing so placed an unhealthy strain on the female brain; others denounced people who masturbated as ruining their own health (Smith-Rosenberg & Rosenberg, 1984; Money, 1985). During the same era, few physicians recognized that the growing popularity of cigarette smoking posed a threat to health. Today, of course, we view each of these issues quite differently.

2. *Health relates to a society's technology and social resources.* The level of health people come to define as normal also depends on their society's technology. Looking back to a time when we had little control over the environment and living standards were low, people routinely contended with malnutrition, poor or nonexistent sanitation, all sorts of occupational hazards, and a host of infectious diseases. Only as industrialization raised the standard of living did conceptions of health correspondingly rise.

   In global perspective, contrasts of this kind persist today. What many people throughout the Third World learn to accept as the norm for health, most people in the United States would consider intolerable. In the most disadvantaged societies of the world, half the babies born each year die in infancy as a direct result of poverty (George, 1977; Harrison, 1984).

3. *Health relates to social inequality.* Every society on earth unequally distributes the resources that promote personal well-being. The physical, mental, and emotional health of wealthier women and men in the United States is far better than that of poor people, as we shall explain presently. This pattern starts at birth, with infant mortality highest among the poor; it persists through old age. Affluent people, on average, live years longer than poor people do.

## Historical Patterns of Health

Because health has an important social dimension, we find pronounced changes in human well-being over the long course of history. What we commonly think of as revolutionary events of the past—the development of agriculture, the Industrial Revolution, and the emergence of scientific medicine—have all had a major impact on patterns of health.

## Health in Preindustrial Societies

Members of the earliest hunting and gathering societies, described in Chapter 4 ("Society"), labored continually to secure an adequate supply of food. Simple technology greatly limited their ability to sustain a healthful environment. As Gerhard and Jean Lenski (1991) suggest, because each mother had to breast-feed an infant for a year or more, a food shortage or the birth of another child often meant abandoning at least one child. But children fortunate enough to survive infancy were still vulnerable to a host of injuries and illnesses. Nearly half the members of hunting and gathering societies died before age twenty, and few lived to see forty.

The agricultural revolution that marked the onset of "civilization" greatly expanded the supply of food and other resources. While this development enhanced the health of elites, peasants and slaves fared no better than before, typically living in crowded, unsanitary shelters. Facing a daily struggle with hunger, hard work, and frequently abusive treatment, this peasant majority suffered from widespread poor health.

Through much of history, the growth of cities threatened health even more. Concentrations of people living in conditions of little or no sanitation meant disease was ever-present and easily spread. In medieval Europe, for example, even rich urbanites lived amid human waste and other refuse, and the situation only became worse as the cities grew (Mumford, 1961). From time to time, the spread of infectious disease, including plague, wiped out a sizable portion of a city's population. A great plague struck London in 1665, for example, and killed thousands of people during the better part of a year. Reddish spots on the skin accompanied by sneezing marked the onset of the plague, and people could only fill their pockets with herbs and flowers hoping these would ward off the disease. So frightening was the experience of this plague centuries ago that it remains with us still in the form of an innocent children's rhyme (Gray 1970, cited in Spates & Macionis, 1987:57):

> *Ring-a-ring-a-roses,*
> *A pocket full of posies*
> *'Tishoo, 'tishoo,*
> *We all fall down.*

## Health in Industrial Societies

The Industrial Revolution in Europe and North America had a dramatic effect on health, but not immediately. At the outset, as factories in the mid-eighteenth century

Medieval medical practice was heavily influenced by astrology, so that physicians and lay people alike attributed disease to astral influence; this is the root of our word "influenza." In this woodcut by Swiss artist Jost Amman (1580), midwives attend a childbirth as astrologers cast a horoscope for the newborn.

drew millions of people from the countryside to the cities, health problems actually became worse. Even the few workers who were well paid lived in crowded, contaminated tenements, and rich and poor alike traversed city streets that were rife with crime. Factory smoke fouled the air, and the hazard this presented to people went unrecognized until well into the twentieth century. Factories were dangerous, and workplace accidents happened routinely. No laws protected the safety of early industrial workers and few employers thought these hired hands worthy of much concern.

During the nineteenth century, health in Western Europe and North America gradually began to improve. At first glance, this change may seem to be a result of medical advances, which occurred after mid-century, but the death rate in Western Europe and North America actually began to decline even before that (Illich, 1976; McKeown, 1979; Mahler, 1980). Industrialization itself—apart from any medical breakthroughs—brought improving health by slowly raising the standard of living, giving more people access to better nutrition and safer housing.

But scientific medicine did play a part in people's improving health, especially in cities plagued with infectious diseases. To illustrate, in 1854 John Snow examined residential patterns of cholera victims in London and traced the source of this disease to contaminated drinking water (Mechanic, 1978). Before long, scientists identified the cause of cholera as bacteria, and eventually they developed protective vaccines. Armed with this knowledge, early environmentalists also campaigned against the age-old practice of discharging raw sewage into rivers used for drinking water. By the early twentieth century, death rates from infectious diseases declined sharply.

Over the long term, industrialization has had a dramatic, beneficial effect on people's health. Leading killers in 1900 were influenza and pneumonia, which together accounted for one-fourth of all deaths. Today these diseases cause fewer than 3 percent of deaths in the United States. As Table 20–1 indicates, various infectious diseases including tuberculosis, stomach and intestinal disorders, diseases of early infancy, and diphtheria—all leading causes of death in 1900—no longer pose a major threat to health.

With infectious diseases now brought under control, chronic conditions like heart disease, cancer, and cerebrovascular diseases such as stroke eventually claim almost two-thirds of the population of the United States. Changing social patterns play a part here, too: the increasing use of work-saving devices reduce healthful exercise in the course of daily life, and people are smoking cigarettes, a practice rare a century ago. Also, our diet draws heavily on meat and eggs, providing 60 percent more cholesterol than the American Heart Association recommends. Consequently, we are now more likely to die from heart disease than are the Japanese, whose diet is based on fish (Wallis, 1984).

Because people today succumb from chronic conditions rather than acute infections, death is now associated with advancing age. A century ago, death commonly struck people of any age, reflected in a life expectancy of forty-eight years for men and fifty-one years for women in the United States. For people born in 1990, by contrast, government estimates place life expectancy at seventy-two years for men and seventy-nine years for women. In essence, we are now fortunate to live long enough to die from the chronic illnesses of old age, heart disease, cancer, and stroke.

**Table 20–1  THE CHANGING CAUSES OF DEATH IN THE UNITED STATES**

The Ten Leading Causes of Death in 1900
1. Influenza and pneumonia
2. Tuberculosis
3. Stomach and intestinal diseases
4. Heart disease
5. Cerebral hemorrhage
6. Kidney disease
7. Accidents
8. Cancer
9. Diseases of early infancy
10. Diphtheria

The Ten Leading Causes of Death in 1990
1. Heart disease
2. Cancer
3. Cerebrovascular diseases
4. Accidents
5. Lung disease (noncancerous)
6. Pneumonia and influenza
7. Diabetes
8. Suicide
9. Cirrhosis and related liver disease
10. Homicide

SOURCES: Information for 1900 is from William C. Cockerham, *Medical Sociology*, 2nd ed. (Englewood Cliffs, NJ: Prentice-Hall, 1986), p. 24; information for 1990 is from U.S. National Center for Health Statistics, *Monthly Vital Statistics Report*, Vol. 39, No. 11 (March 8, 1991): 14–15.

## Global Patterns of Health

In contrast to our remarkable progress in combating infectious disease, in the Third World striking poverty (see Chapter 11, "Global Inequality") makes health much worse than in industrial societies. People in poor countries expect to live roughly sixty years, ten years less than the First-World average (Mahler, 1980). In Africa, life expectancy is barely fifty, and in the poorest societies in the world, such as Cambodia and Ethiopia, the figure drops to forty.

According to the World Health Organization, one billion of the world's people—one in five—suffer from poor health due to poverty. Ill health stems directly from the cruel reality of malnutrition—not having enough to eat or consuming only one kind of food, as the box explains.

In impoverished countries, sanitary drinking water may be as scarce as the chance for a balanced diet.

# Poverty: The Leading Cause of Death in the Third World

Widespread famine in Africa during the 1980s brought home to people in the affluent United States the image of starving children. Some of the children portrayed by the mass media appeared bloated, while others seemed to have shriveled to little more than skin drawn tightly over bones. Both of these deadly conditions, Susan George explains, are direct consequences of poverty.

Children with bloated bodies are suffering from protein deficiency. In West Africa this condition is known as *kwashiorkor*, which means literally "one-two." The term derives from the mothers' common practice of abruptly weaning a first child upon the birth of a second. Deprived of mother's milk, an infant may receive virtually no protein. Children with shriveled bodies are being deprived of both protein and calories, the result of eating little food of any kind.

In either case, children usually do not die of starvation, strictly speaking. More precisely, their weakened condition makes them vulnerable to stomach ailments such as gastroenteritis or diseases like measles. The death rate from

measles is a thousand times greater in parts of Africa than in North America.

Depending on a single food also undermines nutrition, causing a deficiency of protein, vitamins, and minerals. Millions of people in the Third World suffer from goiter, a debilitating, diet-related disease of the thyroid gland. Pellagra, a disease common to people who consume only corn, is equally seri-

ous, frequently leading to insanity. Those who consume mostly processed rice are prone to beriberi.

A host of diseases virtually unknown to members of rich societies are a common experience of life—and death—in the Third World.

SOURCE: Based, in part, on George (1977).

Unsafe water is a major cause of the infectious diseases that imperil Third-World adults and children. The leading causes of death in the United States a century ago, including influenza, pneumonia, and tuberculosis, are still widespread killers in poor societies. Additionally, substandard sanitation promotes the growth of parasites such as hookworms, tapeworms, and roundworms, giving rise to additional illnesses (Harrison, 1984; Newman & Matzke, 1984).

To make matters worse, medical personnel are few and far between in the Third World. In some of the poorest societies—in central Africa, for example—many people never consult a physician. Global Map 20–1 on page 562 illustrates the state of medical care throughout the world.

Against this backdrop of overarching poverty and minimal medical care, it is no wonder that Third-World societies have high death rates at all stages of life, espe-

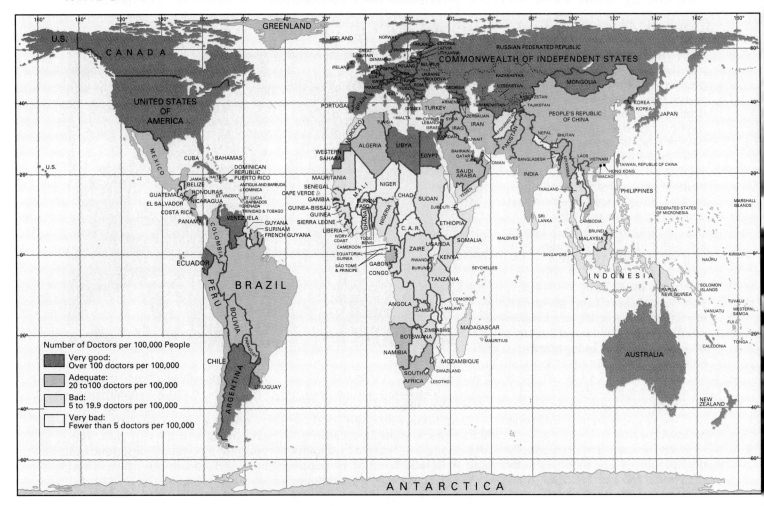

**Global Map 20–1** Medical Care in Global Perspective

Medical doctors, widely available to people in the First World, are perilously scarce in poor societies. While traditional forms of healing do improve health, antibiotics and vaccines—vital for controlling the infectious diseases that plague the Third World—are often in short supply. In poor societies, therefore, death rates are high, especially among infants.

cially in childhood. Paul Harrison (1984) estimates that 10 percent of Third-World children die in their first year of life; in the poorest societies, half the children never reach adulthood. Children of the Third World today, that is, die at the same rate as European children did in 1750 (George, 1977).

Improving Third-World health poses a monumental challenge. First, poverty and poor health form a vi-

cious circle: poverty (through malnutrition and inadequate medical care) breeds disease, which, in turn, limits people's ability to work to improve their economic situation (Harrison, 1984). As was explained in Chapter 11 ("Global Inequality"), the combined effects of simple technology in the Third World and concentrations of wealth in the First World make it unlikely that we will soon see a dramatic reduction in global poverty. The prognosis for improving the physical, mental, and social well-being of the world's poorest people, then, remains bleak.

One issue further complicates the problem of world health: as new medical technology brings infectious diseases under control, the populations of poor nations increase. But poor countries lack the resources to ensure the well-being of the populations they have now, so population growth only makes matters worse. Thus, reducing death rates through medical advances carries with it the moral obligation to help reduce birth rates as well.

# Health in the United States

In comparison with the Third World, the United States has very favorable patterns of health. To survey health in our society, we begin with an overview of how health is distributed throughout the population, and then move on to examine several contemporary issues that affect the health of everyone.

## Social Epidemiology: The Distribution of Health

**Social epidemiology** is *the study of how health and disease are distributed throughout a society's population.* Early social epidemiologists examined the origin and spread of epidemic diseases; John Snow's research on cholera, noted earlier, is but one example. Modern social epidemiologists try to link patterns of health to physical and social environments (Cockerham, 1986). For example, they might investigate rates of heart disease for people of various age categories, the two sexes, or according to class and race.

## Age and Sex

During this century, a rising standard of living and improved medical care in the United States have enhanced the health of people of almost every age. One exception is young adults, who suffer more accidental deaths than in the past, mostly due to automobile mishaps. Generally, however, members of our society are blessed with good health and substantial longevity: according to government projections, 74 percent of men and 85 percent of women born since 1980 will live to at least age sixty-five (U.S. Bureau of the Census, 1991).

As these numbers suggest, women have somewhat better health than men. Females have a biological advantage that renders them less likely than males to die before or immediately after birth. Then, as socialization takes over, males learn to be more aggressive and individualistic, resulting in higher rates of accidents, violence, and suicide. Our cultural definition of masculinity encourages males to be competitive at work, to repress their emotions, and to engage in hazardous behaviors like smoking and excessive drinking. While providing men with greater social and economic privileges, then, conventional gender distinctions also entail greater health risks.

## Social Class and Race

Social epidemiologists have established a strong link between health and social class from the beginning of life. Infant mortality—the death rate among newborns—is twice as high among the poor as it is for privileged people. While the richest children in our society have health that rivals that found anywhere in the world, our poorest children are as vulnerable as those in many Third-World countries, including Sudan and Lebanon.

Table 20–2 shows that a person's perception of health is strongly influenced by income. Almost 80 per-

**Table 20–2  ASSESSMENT OF PERSONAL HEALTH BY INCOME, 1990**

| Family Income | Excellent | Very Good | Good | Fair | Poor |
|---|---|---|---|---|---|
| $35,000 and over | 49.7% | 29.3% | 17.2% | 3.1% | 0.8% |
| $20,000–$34,999 | 39.2 | 30.5 | 22.3 | 6.2 | 1.8 |
| $10,000–$19,999 | 30.4 | 27.6 | 27.9 | 10.3 | 3.8 |
| Under $10,000 | 25.8 | 23.4 | 29.2 | 14.2 | 7.4 |

SOURCE:  U.S. National Center for Health Statistics, *Current Estimates from the National Health Interview Survey United States*, 1990, Series 10, No. 181 (Washington, DC: U.S. Government Printing Office, 1991), Table 70, p. 113.

cent of adults in families with incomes over $35,000 evaluate their health as excellent or very good, while less than half the people whose families earn less than $10,000 make this claim. Conversely, while only about 4 percent of high-income people describe their health as fair or poor, almost one-fourth of low-income people respond this way.

Bear in mind that the causal link here works both ways: just as income affects health, so does health affect income. People whose family income is under $10,000 miss some twenty-seven days of school or work each year due to illness, while members of families earning over $35,000 lose only ten days of productive activity for this reason (Adams & Benson, 1990; U.S. Department of Health and Human Services, 1991).

Chapter 12 ("Race and Ethnicity") stated that African Americans run triple the risk of poverty that whites do. The consequences of this disparity show up clearly in health statistics: African Americans are more likely to die in infancy and to suffer the effects of violence and illness as adults. Further, on average, life expectancy at birth for blacks is five years fewer than for whites, a disparity that increased during the 1980s. Table 20–3 shows the average life expectancy for U.S. children born in 1990. For whites, it exceeds seventy-six years; for African Americans, it is about seventy-one years. Sex is an even stronger predictor of health than race, since black females born in 1990 can expect to outlive males of any race. Table 20–3 also indicates that while 75 percent of white males born in 1990 will live to sixty-five, only about 63 percent of African-American males will. The comparable chances for women are about 86 percent for whites and 78 percent for blacks.

In the United States, as elsewhere in the world, poverty condemns people to crowded, unsanitary environments that breed infectious diseases. Although tuberculosis is no longer a widespread threat to health in the United States, the rate of TB is once again on the rise. Their higher risk of poverty makes African Americans four times as likely as whites to die from this disease. Poor people of all races also suffer from nutritional deficiencies. Twenty percent of our population—some 50 million people—try to get by with a substandard diet and minimal medical care. The results are predictable: while wealthy women and men typically die in old age of chronic illnesses such as heart disease and cancer, poor people generally die younger from infectious diseases that prey on the poor.

Poverty also breeds stress and violence. Frustration and despair have become more pronounced among our nation's urban underclass. The leading cause of death for African-American males aged fifteen to twenty-four—who are heavily represented among the urban poor—is *homicide*. In 1990 about 5,000 African Americans were killed by other African Americans—roughly the number of black soldiers killed in the entire Vietnam War. Drug use, especially the escalating use of crack cocaine, has sent the level of inner-city violence skyrocketing for people of all races.

But, in some respects, privilege also carries risks to health. In fact, when affluence results from stress-producing competition, or encourages a sedentary lifestyle and the consumption of rich food, the wealthy pay the price in terms of high death rates from heart disease (Fuchs, 1974; Wallis, 1984). Nevertheless, wealth also confers decided health advantages: a safer environment, living with less fear, and access to better medical care when illness strikes (Lin & Ensel, 1989). The facts are conclusive: affluent people live longer and suffer less from illness than do other members of our society. Here, again, we see how the distribution of health depends on how society operates.

## Environmental Pollution

In global perspective, the idea that human beings must live in harmony with the natural world has formed a central theme of many cultures, especially in Asia. Only recently, however, have we in the West come to embrace this position, and only after causing considerable damage to the environment.

By their very nature, industrial societies disrupt the ecological balance. Few members of our society can imagine living without automobiles and factories, but

**Table 20–3** LIFE EXPECTANCY FOR U.S. CHILDREN BORN IN 1990

|                   | Females | Males  | Both Sexes |
|-------------------|---------|--------|------------|
| Whites            | 79.6    | 72.7   | 76.2       |
|                   | (86%)   | (75%)  | (81%)      |
| African Americans | 75.0    | 67.7   | 71.4       |
|                   | (78%)   | (63%)  | (70%)      |
| All races         | 79.0    | 72.1   | 75.6       |
|                   | (73%)   | (85%)  | (79%)      |

Figures in parentheses indicate the chances of living to age 65.

SOURCE: U.S. Bureau of the Census, 1991.

they both pollute the air, producing a well-documented threat to health. In Los Angeles, where this problem is especially serious, officials warn that the air itself poses a health risk about half the days of the year. Thus modern technology, while raising our standard of living, has also introduced new health hazards.

Industrial wastes arouse public concern as well. For more than half a century, some industries across the country have been haphazardly disposing of poisonous chemicals. They have poured toxic substances into local sewage systems or discharged them directly into rivers and streams. Dumps that dot our national landscape now contain steel drums filled with dangerous chemicals that gradually leach into the soil and groundwater.

National attention was drawn to the issue of toxic wastes in 1980, when the residents of Love Canal, a neighborhood in Niagara Falls, New York, discovered deadly dioxin seeping into their homes and yards, which had been built on the site of an old petrochemical dump. In 1983 the entire population of Times Beach, Missouri, had to abandon their homes because oil contaminated with dioxin had been sprayed on the roads.

There are some 30,000 dump sites in the United States where hazardous waste poses a danger to water supplies. The Environmental Protection Agency has cited 1,200 of these that require urgent action, but only about twenty-seven were cleaned up substantially during the 1980s. Bureaucratic delays and budgetary constraints have slowed the cleanup; environmentalists also disagree on whether the hazards of air pollution and global warming are more serious than those of dump sites.

A final environmental issue that affects human health is nuclear power. In 1990, 111 nuclear reactors in the United States produced about 20 percent of the electricity consumed in this country (U.S. Department of Energy, 1991). An inexpensive source of energy, nuclear power also spares finite supplies of coal and oil. But nuclear power has the major drawback that a serious malfunction could release radiation—as deadly as fallout from an atomic bomb—into the atmosphere, threatening life for hundreds of miles. This danger is more than hypothetical: accidents at nuclear reactor plants have been reported since they first began operating in the early 1950s. Serious malfunctions occurred at reactors near Ottawa, Canada (1952), near Liverpool, England (1957), and at Three Mile Island near Harrisburg, Pennsylvania (1979). The most serious accident to date—a meltdown of the reactor core at the Chernobyl plant near Kiev in the former Soviet Union in 1986—spread radiation throughout much of the world. The immediate death toll was only thirty but, over the long term, casualties from radiation exposure will probably reach the thousands.

In addition to the danger of reactor accidents, nuclear power plants produce waste materials that remain highly radioactive for hundreds of thousands of years. Currently, we have no way to dispose of such wastes without risking future contamination of the environment.

## Cigarette Smoking

Many threats to health are matters of individual behavior, and cigarette smoking tops the list of preventable hazards. Cigarette smoking became common in the United States only about the time of World War I. Despite evidence of its dangers—especially rising rates of lung cancer a generation later—most people remained unaware of the harm posed by cigarettes and viewed smoking as socially acceptable and even fashionable. Now smoking is recognized as the leading preventable cause of illness and death among people in the United States, and this practice is coming to be defined as a mild social deviance.

Despite continued advertising by cigarette manufacturers (banned from television and radio in 1971), per capita consumption of cigarettes has fallen since 1963. Even so, in 1990, the United States produced more than 650 billion cigarettes. The popularity of smoking peaked in the mid-1950s at about 45 percent of adults; by 1970, some 37 percent of adults smoked cigarettes, and the proportion slid to 27 percent by 1990 (National Institute of Drug Abuse, 1991). More and more campuses across the country are responding to the health hazards of smoking tobacco by banning the practice in public buildings.

As most smokers realize, the nicotine in cigarette smoke is physically addictive. Thus people may become physically dependent on tobacco, as well as relying on the drug as a means of coping with stress. This psychological dependency explains why the divorced and separated are more likely to smoke, as are the unemployed and people in the military services. Blue-collar workers tend to smoke more than white-collar workers, and people with less schooling smoke more than their more educated counterparts. African Americans and whites are now about equally likely to smoke; a slightly smaller share of Hispanics smoke. In terms of sex, men of all races (30 percent) still smoke more than women (24 percent). But cigarettes—the only form of tobacco use to gain

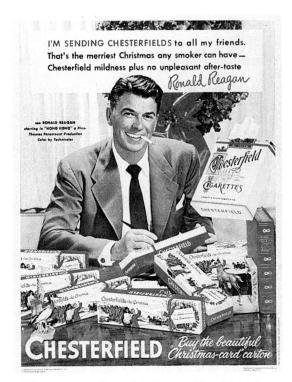

I'M SENDING CHESTERFIELDS to all my friends. That's the merriest Christmas any smoker can have— Chesterfield mildness plus no unpleasant after-taste

*Ronald Reagan*

see RONALD REAGAN starring in "HONG KONG" a Pine-Thomas Paramount Production Color by Technicolor

CHESTERFIELD

*Buy the beautiful Christmas-card carton*

Fifty years ago, film celebrities were hired by tobacco companies to help sell cigarettes, despite growing evidence of the harm caused by smoking.

popularity among women—have taken a growing toll on women's health. In 1987, lung cancer surpassed breast cancer as a cause of death among women in the United States.

During the 1930s, medical researchers noted a sharp rise in smoking-related diseases such as lung cancer. Studies showed that roughly twenty years of smoking was generally required for lung cancer to develop. But not until the 1960s did the government take the dangers of tobacco use seriously. The official turnaround was partly provoked by a rising incidence of lung cancer among women, who had begun smoking in large numbers during the 1940s. By the mid-1960s, government reports revealed a direct link between smoking cigarettes—as well as cigars and pipes—and heart disease; cancer of the mouth, throat, and lungs; and lung diseases such as bronchitis and emphysema. Some 430,000 men and women die prematurely each year as a result of cigarette smoking—about the same number of U.S. soldiers who died in all of World War II. About 115,000

of these deaths are due to lung cancer. Beyond raising their risk of fatal illnesses, smokers also experience more frequent minor illnesses such as flu, and pregnant women who smoke increase the likelihood of spontaneous abortion and prenatal death. Research indicates that even nonsmokers exposed to cigarette smoke have a higher risk of smoking-related diseases (Shephard, 1982).

Tobacco was a $25 billion industry in the United States in 1990. The tobacco industry still maintains that because the precise link between cigarettes and disease has not been specified, the health effects of smoking remain "an open question" (Rudolph, 1985). But the tobacco industry is not breathing as easily today as it once did. Laws mandating a smoke-free environment are rapidly proliferating. Furthermore, courts have increased the liability of cigarette manufacturers in lawsuits brought by victims of smoking-related illnesses, or their survivors.

One response of the tobacco industry has been to sell more of their products abroad—especially in the Third World—where regulation of tobacco sales and advertising is less strict, and antismoking sentiments have not dampened enthusiasm for tobacco products. In the United States, however, more and more smokers are giving up the habit, taking advantage of the fact that someone who has not smoked for ten years has about the same pattern of health as a lifelong nonsmoker.

## Sexually Transmitted Diseases

Sexual activity, while a source of individual pleasure and vital to the continuation of the species, can transmit a large number of illnesses. Commonly called *venereal diseases* (from Venus, the Roman goddess of love), sexually transmitted illnesses date back to humanity's beginnings; references to these maladies are even found in the Bible. The culture of the United States has traditionally viewed sex with ambivalence; while we celebrate it in advertising and throughout the mass media, we also tend to think of sex as sinful. Not surprisingly, then, some people regard venereal diseases not simply as illnesses, but as punishment for immorality.

In global perspective, sexually transmitted diseases (STDs) pose a very serious health problem; the World Health Organization estimates that 250 million new cases of STD are reported annually. This health problem is also great—and growing—in the United States. The incidence of STDs—there are fifty of them in all—soared during the "sexual revolution" of the 1960s. In essence, this revolution redefined sex as a natural and pleasant way to express affection that could be enjoyed whether or not people were married. Before this time, estimates held that two out of three men but only about one in ten women had premarital sexual intercourse; by 1990, the figures had risen to three out of four men and two out of three women.

In this climate of sexual permissiveness, sexually transmitted diseases became an exception to the general pattern by which infectious diseases have declined during this century. With the rise in STDs—and especially acquired immune deficiency syndrome (AIDS)—the second half of the 1980s witnessed a sexual counterrevolution that prompted individuals to reexamine their values and behavior (Kain, 1987; Kain & Hart, 1987). The following sections provide a brief overview of several common STDs.

### Gonorrhea and Syphilis

Gonorrhea and syphilis are very old diseases, each caused by a microscopic organism almost always transmitted by sexual contact. Untreated, gonorrhea can cause sterility; syphilis can damage major organs and result in blindness, mental disorders, and death. In the past, our society severely stigmatized victims of gonorrhea and syphilis, seeing these diseases as the "wages of sin" among social outcasts such as prostitutes.

Roughly 600,000 cases of gonorrhea and 40,000 cases of syphilis are reported each year, and the actual number may well be several times greater (Masters, Johnson, & Kolodny, 1988; Centers for Disease Control, 1992). Both diseases are more common among people of color than whites. Reporting suggests that almost 80 percent of infections involve African Americans, 15 percent affect whites, and 5 percent afflict Hispanics. African Americans also had the highest rate of syphilis, accounting for 76 percent of cases; whites and Hispanics each accounted for about 12 percent (Moran et al., 1989; Centers for Disease Control, 1991).

Most cases of gonorrhea and syphilis are easily cured with penicillin, an antibiotic drug developed in the 1940s. Although some strains of these diseases resist efforts at treatment, neither disease currently represents a serious health threat in the United States.

### Genital Herpes

Genital herpes received widespread public attention during the 1980s. An estimated 20 to 30 million adults in the United States (one in seven) are infected with the genital herpes virus. The infection rate among people of color, however, is estimated to be about twice as high (Moran et al., 1989).

Although far less serious than gonorrhea and syphilis, herpes is currently incurable. Patients may exhibit no symptoms or they may experience periodic, painful blisters on the genitals accompanied by fever and headache. Although it is not fatal to adults, women with active genital herpes can transmit the disease to a child during a vaginal delivery, and it can be deadly to a newborn. In such cases, therefore, women usually give birth by cesarean section.

### AIDS

The most serious of all sexually transmitted diseases is acquired immune deficiency syndrome, or AIDS. Although AIDS may have appeared as early as the 1960s, researchers identified it only in 1981. Although much has been learned since then, AIDS is incurable and fatal. About 45,000 new cases were reported in the United States during 1991, raising the total by early 1992 to

Experts—and the public—disagree as to the best strategy for combating the spread of HIV. Liberals support the distribution of condoms to young people because condom use significantly reduces the chances for sexual transmission of the virus. Conservatives object to this policy, claiming it encourages casual sex, which, for them, is the heart of the problem. From this point of view, rethinking the notion that young people should be sexually active is a better approach.

more than 205,000 individuals with AIDS, of which 135,000 have already died (Centers for Disease Control, 1992). AIDS is now the second leading killer of young men in the United States. The incidence of infection is rising fastest among women, especially those who are poor. AIDS has moved into the top five killers of young women nationwide, and is already the leading killer of young women of color in some urban areas.

AIDS is caused by a human immunodeficiency virus (HIV). This virus attacks white blood cells, the core of the immune system that the body mobilizes to fight infections. As these cells are destroyed, a person with AIDS becomes vulnerable to a wide range of infectious diseases that eventually bring on death. Technically, then, AIDS kills people indirectly by rendering them unable to fight off common infections.

Estimates place the number of people worldwide who are infected with HIV as high as 10 million, a figure that could increase three- or fourfold by the end of this decade. Global Map 20–2 shows that the African continent (more specifically, countries below the Sahara Desert) has the highest HIV infection rate and currently accounts for almost two-thirds of all cases worldwide. In the cities of central African nations such as Burundi, Rwanda, Uganda, and Kenya, roughly one-fifth of all young adults are infected with HIV (Tofani, 1991). North America represents about 10 percent of global HIV. In the United States, estimates placed the number of infected persons in 1992 at roughly 1 million.

People carrying HIV do not immediately contract AIDS, however. On the contrary, the majority of people with the virus show no symptoms whatever, and most are unaware of their own infection. Symptoms of AIDS usually do not appear for at least a year. Within about five years, some 25 percent of infected persons will develop AIDS; most infected people will eventually develop the disease. According to estimates, about 400,000 people in the United States will have the active disease by 1995. This means that the infection rate is continuing to rise, although at a slightly lower rate of increase. As the death toll mounts, AIDS has turned out to be nothing less than catastrophic—potentially the most serious epidemic of modern times.

Transmission of HIV almost always occurs through blood, semen, or breast milk. This means that AIDS is not spread through casual contact with an infected person; one cannot become infected by shaking hands or hugging an infected person. There is no recorded case of the virus being transmitted through coughing and sneezing, through the sharing of towels, dishes, or telephones, or through water in a bath, pool, or hot tub. The risk of transmitting AIDS through saliva (as in kissing) is extremely low. Oral and especially genital sex are dangerous, however, although the risk of transmitting the infection can be greatly reduced (but not eliminated) by use of latex condoms. In the age of AIDS, abstinence or an exclusive relationship with an uninfected person is the only sure way to avoid sexual transmission of AIDS. Self-interest demands that no one enter a sexual relationship lightly or casually.

While fear of AIDS is rampant, there are some grounds for comfort. In the United States, there is no danger of becoming infected by donating blood, and receiving a blood transfusion (in the past a source of infection) is now virtually safe. Infected women can pass HIV to their newborn children, although present evidence indicates that there is less than a 50 percent chance of this occurring. The bottom line is that AIDS is a deadly disease—but it is also hard to get.

These facts suggest that people can protect themselves by avoiding the behaviors that place them at high risk for becoming infected with HIV. The first is *anal sex*, which can cause rectal bleeding that allows easy transmission of HIV from one person to another. Anal sex is therefore extremely dangerous and, the greater the number of sexual partners, the greater the risk. Anal sex is commonly practiced by gay men, in some cases with multiple partners. This is the reason that homosexual and bisexual men comprise about 60 percent of those with AIDS. In response to the devastating effect of AIDS on gay communities across the United States, gays (as well as nongays) have shunned sexual promiscuity in recent years (McKusick et al., 1985).

*Sharing needles* used to inject drugs is the second most prevalent high-risk behavior. At present, intravenous drug users account for 25 percent of people with AIDS. Casual sex sometimes accompanies drug use; therefore, having sex with an intravenous drug user also constitutes a high-risk behavior. Because this kind of drug use is more common among poor people, AIDS is increasingly becoming a disease of the socially disadvantaged. Overall, 54 percent of AIDS patients are white, yet African Americans (12 percent of the population) account for 29 percent of people with AIDS, and half of all women with the disease. Hispanics (7 percent of all people in the United States) represent 17 percent of all AIDS cases and 20 percent of women with AIDS (Bowles & Robinson, 1989; Centers for Disease Control, 1992). The rise of AIDS among women of color stands out as a recent trend: this disease is now the leading

**Global Map 20–2** HIV Infection of Adults in Global Perspective

Infection of adults with HIV is not spread evenly around the world. Approximately two-thirds of all cases in the world are recorded in sub-Saharan Africa where, in many countries, HIV has become a runaway epidemic. Such a high infection rate reflects the prevalence of other venereal diseases and infrequent use of condoms, both of which enhance heterosexual transmission of HIV. Regions of the world with moderate rates of infection include South and Southeast Asia, which together account for 10 percent of global infections, and South and North America, which each represent another 10 percent of all cases of HIV. The incidence of infection is lower still in Europe. Least affected by HIV are the societies of North Africa and the Middle East and also the nations of Australia and New Zealand.

cause of death among young women in the New York metropolitan region. Among children, AIDS and minorities are even more closely linked: almost 80 percent of AIDS patients under thirteen are people of color (U.S. Department of Health and Human Services, 1989; Centers for Disease Control, 1992).

*Using any drug,* including alcohol, also increases the risk of being infected with HIV to the extent that it

Paul Marcus's sculpture *The Junkie* graphically depicts the loss of humanity that often accompanies serious drug abuse. The age of AIDS has added another deadly consequence of intravenous drug use: the transmission of HIV through the sharing of needles. Some cities now have programs providing clean needles to addicts despite opposition on the grounds that doing so encourages illegal drug use.

impairs judgment. In other words, even people who understand what places them at risk of infection may act less responsibly once they are under the influence of alcohol, marijuana, or some other drug.

In 1991, officials concluded, only 6 percent of people with AIDS in the United States were infected with HIV through heterosexual contact (although heterosexuals, infected in various ways, account for almost 30 percent of AIDS cases). The likelihood of a runaway "breakout" of AIDS into the heterosexual population now seems less likely than it did several years ago (Fumento, 1989). Heterosexual activity can and does trans-

mit AIDS, however, and the risk rises with the number of sexual partners a person has, especially if any partner falls into a high-risk category. Worldwide, heterosexual relations are the primary means of HIV transmission, accounting for two-thirds of all infections (Eckholm & Tierney, 1990).

In our country, the "third wave" of AIDS—after gay men and intravenous drug users—is now ravaging the urban poor. HIV is already getting out of control in cities such as Miami and New York, where the use of crack cocaine fuels casual sex and prostitution, which spread the deadly virus.

AIDS goes far beyond a medical problem and individual tragedies; it has also thrown our health-care system into financial crisis. The cost of treating a single person with AIDS already runs to hundreds of thousands of dollars and this figure may rise as new therapies are developed. In 1992, national expenditures for AIDS and HIV exceeded $4 billion, an already staggering total that will certainly increase throughout this decade. Added to the direct costs of treatment and research are tens of billions of dollars in lost earnings and productivity. Government health programs, private insurance, and personal savings will meet only a small fraction of this total. Taking all these factors into account, then, we see that AIDS represents both a medical and a social problem of monumental proportions.

The government responded slowly to the AIDS crisis, largely because gays and intravenous drug users are widely viewed as deviant. More recently, money allocated for AIDS research has increased rapidly, and progress is being made. For example, researchers have found that some drugs, such as AZT, suppress the symptoms of the disease but do not as yet lengthen the lives of people infected with HIV. Nevertheless, educational programs remain the most effective weapon against AIDS, since prevention is the only way to stop a disease that currently has no cure.

## Ethical Issues: Confronting Death

Health involves not only medical concerns but also ethical issues. For example, Chapter 14 ("Aging and the Elderly") explained that our society is now facing a dilemma as to whether we should continue to allocate more and more resources to provide medical care for elderly people at the expense of the growing needs of the young (Callahan, 1987). Other vexing ethical issues surround death. These questions arise mainly because technological changes now give human beings greater control over life itself.

**When is a person dead?** In defining death, common sense suggests that we reach this point when breathing ceases and the heart stops beating. But advancing medical technology has made this definition obsolete. Respiration can be sustained by machines, just as a heart that has stopped beating can be revived or even replaced. Furthermore, both breathing and heartbeat may continue in the absence of any brain activity.

Today, in short, experts confront the difficult question of specifying the line that separates life and death. Currently, medical and legal experts in the United States view death as an irreversible state involving no response to stimulation, no movement or breathing, no reflexes, and no indication of brain activity (Ladd, 1979; Wall, 1980).

**Do people have a right to die?** Today, medical personnel, family members, and patients themselves face the agonizing burden of deciding when a terminally ill person should die. In 1990, twenty-six-year-old Nancy Cruzan fell into an irreversible coma after an automobile accident. Physicians exhausted their efforts and solemnly assured Cruzan's parents that their daughter would never recover. Certain that their daughter would never wish to live in a permanent vegetative state, the Cruzans sought to let Nancy die, which required a legal decision in their favor. The couple took their case all the way to the U.S. Supreme Court.

In 1990, the court issued a judgment that established a patient's right to die. The justices declared that any person deemed competent could choose to refuse medical treatment or to decline nutrition. Because the Cruzans were able to present "clear and convincing evidence" that this would be their daughter's wish, the court endorsed removing the feeding tube that was keeping her alive. Nancy Cruzan died twelve days later (Mauro, 1990).

Ten thousand men and women in this country are in the same kind of permanent vegetative state as Nancy Cruzan (Howlett, 1990). Thousands more, faced with a terminal illness that may cause suffering, consider ending their own life. Thus courts and government commissions continue to wrestle with the ethical dilemma pitting *patients' rights* against the medical principle that we should provide all appropriate care to those in need.

A 1983 presidential commission developed some guidelines for helping patients and others confront death. First, the commission stated, the primary obligation of physicians and hospitals is to protect a patient's life. Doctors must explain every medical option available to a patient or, when a patient is incapacitated, to family members. When this is done, terminally ill patients have the right to refuse heroic treatment that may extend their lives but offer no hope of recovery. According to the commission, however, a family decision such as that faced by the Cruzans must be made in the interest of the patient—no one else.

Second, the commission suggested that physicians honor any patient's *living will*, a statement of a person's intention regarding heroic treatment in the event of catastrophic illness. Laws in most states support this principle. In the absence of a living will, or if the patient is a

The vexing problem of whether or when a society should allow suffering people to die is nowhere better illustrated than in the life of Dax Cowart. After being critically burned in a propane-gas explosion, Cowart begged for a gun to shoot himself, and protested every effort by medical specialists to save him. Now, almost twenty years later, Cowart has forged a life worth living—he graduated from law school and is married. But he still maintains that doctors should have complied with his wishes and let him die.

newborn child, physicians and hospitals must provide any treatment that may be reasonably expected to sustain life. Here again, however, a parent or other close family member, in consultation with physicians, may decide to refuse further medical intervention. According to the commission, all decision-makers should act in the interest of the patient, not themselves or other family members.

**What about mercy killing?** *Mercy killing* is the common term for **euthanasia**, *assisting in the death of a person suffering from an incurable disease.* Euthanasia (from the Greek, meaning "a good death") poses an ethical dilemma, since such an act is, on the one hand, an expression of kindness that, on the other hand, causes the death of another person.

Although legal support for a patient's right to die has increased in the United States, assisting in the death of another person is still quite controversial. In 1992, for example, Jack Kevorkian, a physician who helped two women end their lives with his "suicide machine," was arrested in Michigan and charged with murder. No one thinks that the women involved—who ended their lives rather than continuing to suffer from terminal illnesses—thought of Kevorkian as their murderer. But our society is uneasy about legally empowering physicians to actively end a life in response to a patient's request.

The debate breaks down roughly as follows. Those who view life—even with suffering—as preferable to death categorically reject euthanasia. People who recognize circumstances under which death is preferable to life support euthanasia, but they face the practical problem of determining just when a person's life is no longer worth living. Such a decision is always difficult, and family members confront this matter at a time already marked by stress and sorrow. People may express their love of a dying person in various ways, as these examples suggest. After requesting physicians to revive the heart of her dying father, one daughter recently said:

> "I'm glad they brought him back. He was old, but that doesn't mean he should stop living. He was still alive, and as long as he's alive, he should be saved."

Another daughter, however, insisted that physicians not prolong the life of her ninety-eight-year-old mother:

> "If my mother's heart stopped beating, I don't want them pounding on her chest and destroying her body any more than it was. For what? Revive her for another day or another two weeks?" (cited in Kleiman, 1985:11)

Adding to the burden of family members who must decide the fate of a dying patient is the ever-present concern with medical expenses. A single attempt to revive a patient whose heart has stopped may cost $1,500. Two weeks of heroic lifesaving efforts may result in tens of thousands of dollars in medical bills. Opponents of euthanasia fear that such costs cannot help but affect a family's decision regarding heroic treatment.

Ethical standards for dealing with dying patients are gradually emerging, a product of the interplay of physicians, lawyers, clergy, philosophers, patient rights groups, and others (Flynn, 1991). Such standards—and hospital bioethics committees to interpret them—are needed more than ever before, since about half of all deaths in the United States now occur while people are attached to life-prolonging equipment (Humphrey, 1991). Presently, wide support exists for the concept of *passive* euthanasia (or, in common language, "pulling the plug"), illustrated by the Cruzan case, in which heroic treatment is withheld. Support is weaker for *active* euthanasia, illustrated by the Kevorkian case, in which a family member or physician directly assists in ending a life.

## Medicine

**Medicine** is *an institutionalized system for combating disease and improving health.* Medicine forms a vital part of a broader concept of **health care,** which is *any activity intended to improve health.* Medicine has undergone many changes over the course of its long history.

Throughout most of human history, individuals and their families did what they could to enhance their own health. Medicine emerges as a multifaceted social institution when societies become more complex and their members assume various formal, specialized roles. Traditional preindustrial societies recognize medical specialists, who have knowledge of the healing properties of certain plants, and who often combine such skills with astute insights into the emotional and spiritual needs of the ill (Ayensu, 1981). Traditional healers—from acupuncturists to herbalists—are sometimes dismissed by the ethnocentric members of industrial societies as "witch doctors," but they do improve human health, and they continue to combat some of the world's greatest health problems.

As societies industrialize, a system of formal training and licensing empowers people to assist patients in improving their health. Although families still treat their own minor illnesses, they increasingly rely on a host of specialists—from anesthesiologists to x-ray technicians—to provide health care in offices and hospitals established for these purposes.

## The Rise of Scientific Medicine

Health care in the United States is now dominated by *scientific medicine*, which applies the logic of science to research and the treatment of illness. At our country's founding, various approaches to medicine distinguished herbalists, druggists, midwives, and even ministers. In the seventeenth century, about one in 600 adults engaged in some form of healing arts—about the same proportion as today—but there was little consensus about how this work should be done (Stevens, 1971). Even the medical elite of the time—men who had received formal medical training in Europe—still knew little by today's standards, and their skills were often surpassed by those of herbalists and midwives. Unsanitary instruments, lack of anesthesia, and a large measure of ignorance made surgery a terrible ordeal in which surgeons killed as many patients as they saved.

Gradually, however, specialists learned more about human anatomy, physiology, and biochemistry. Early in the nineteenth century, medical societies appeared across the United States as doctors established themselves as self-regulating professionals. Formal colleges of medicine, which numbered more than 400 by the end of the last century, offered training in the field. The increase in the number of medical schools paralleled the growth in the number of hospitals (Stevens, 1971). Medical societies required those who wished to practice or teach medical skills to obtain licenses, and these organizations enforced conformity to specific medical standards.

The standards that lay at the heart of this new profession were established largely through the efforts of the American Medical Association (AMA). The founding of the AMA itself in 1847 signified acceptance of the scientific model of medicine, and the organization widely publicized the medical successes of its members to further improve their own public image. Scientific researchers were touted for tracing the cause of life-threatening illnesses to bacteria and viruses, and also for developing vaccines to prevent disease.

Still, alternative approaches to health care, such as regulating nutrition, also had many defenders. The AMA responded boldly—some thought arrogantly—to

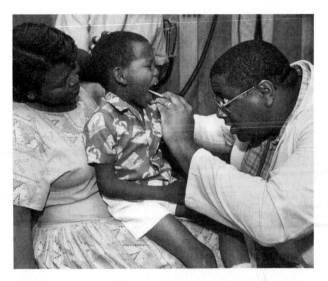

The rise of scientific medicine sparked stunning achievements in our ability to control disease. But it also effectively reduced the number of African Americans in the medical professions and opposed many kinds of healers who traditionally have served rural areas. Michael Cheers, MD has tried to turn the tide by transforming an abandoned restaurant into a medical clinic in Tchula, Mississippi. Cheers, who is also an ordained minister and jazz pianist, treats people who cannot afford to pay for care by accepting donations and by working overtime in hospital emergency rooms.

these challenges by asserting the superiority of its own approach. It won a victory in the early 1900s as state licensing boards agreed to certify only those physicians who had the skills and knowledge approved by the AMA (Starr, 1982). Once they had won control of the certification process, the AMA acted quickly to close down schools teaching other approaches. Before long, the practice of medicine was limited mainly to those with an M.D. degree. In the process, as the AMA intended, both the prestige and income of physicians rose dramatically. Men and women with M.D. degrees have become among the highest-paid workers in the United States with 1990 earnings, on average, of about $150,000.

Some practitioners of other approaches, such as osteopathic physicians, concluded that they had no choice but to fall in line and follow AMA standards. Thus osteopaths (with D.O. degrees), originally concerned with manipulating the skeleton and muscles, today treat illness in much the same way as medical doctors (with M.D. degrees). Other practitioners—such as chiropractors, herbal healers, and midwives—held to their traditional roles, but at a high cost: all have been relegated to fringe areas of the medical profession. With far less social prestige and income than physicians, such professionals now have a small, if devoted, following in the United States (Gordon, 1980).

The rise of scientific medicine, taught in expensive, urban medical schools, also changed the social profile of doctors. During the nineteenth century, many rural medical colleges trained people of modest financial means. But the AMA soon closed most of these schools, alleging that their standards were low and their facilities inadequate. Furthermore, the AMA denigrated the more traditional forms of health care in which women had long played a role. Some medical schools did train women and people of color but, with little public support or financial resources, few of these schools survived. The number of medical schools in the United States steadily dropped to a low of about seventy-seven in 1950, with the number of women and people of color in medicine following the same pattern (Starr, 1982; Huet-Cox, 1984). In 1992, 84 percent of physicians were men, while 97 percent of nurses were women.

In sum, as the AMA established physicians as scientific professionals, it simultaneously restricted the practice of medicine to a small, affluent elite—those admitted to expensive and often discriminatory medical schools. Medicine, in effect, became dominated by white men, most of them from urban, privileged families (Stevens, 1971; Starr, 1982). The result has been a shortage of physicians in rural areas as well as a lack of physicians drawn from the ranks of women and other minorities.

## Holistic Medicine

The achievements of the scientific medical model are impressive. Yet, especially in recent decades, this model has been tempered by the more traditional notion of **holistic medicine**, *an approach to health care that emphasizes prevention of illness and takes account of the whole person within a physical and social environment.*

A holistic approach is not necessarily in opposition to the model of scientific medicine. But advocates of holistic medicine point out that rigidly adhering to the scientific orientation focuses on diseases and injuries rather than on prevention of illness and overall well-being. Holistically oriented practitioners charge that at least some physicians have become preoccupied with drugs, surgery, artificial organs, and high technology; in the process, these healers have narrowed their focus,

concentrating on symptoms rather than people, and disease rather than health. Drugs and surgery can be vital forms of treatment, and holistic healers do not discount them. But they contend that these techniques should fit within a broader view of health that takes account of a person's entire life and environment. Thus holistic medicine reaches beyond medical doctors; in this view, a wide variety of other trained personnel—physical therapists, nutritionists, counselors, clergy, and even acupuncturists and teachers of meditation—can work with physicians as a team to improve the physical, mental, and social well-being of patients. In the holistic approach to health care, then, the following are major concerns (Gordon, 1980).

1. **Patients are people.** Holistic practitioners are concerned not only with symptoms, but with how each person's environment and lifestyle encourage or inhibit health. For example, the likelihood of illness increases under stress caused by the death of a family member, engaging in intense competition at work, or the daily burden of poverty (Duhl, 1980). This broad approach also leads holistic practitioners to expand the bounds of conventional medicine to actively combat environmental pollution and other dangers to public health.

2. **Responsibility, not dependency.** Holistic medicine tries to shift responsibility for health from physicians to people themselves. At the extreme, scientific medicine defines health as a complex issue only doctors can understand, thereby fostering dependency on the part of patients. While recognizing the need for experts, especially in a crisis, the holistic approach holds that professional healers should work to empower people by helping them to engage in health-promoting behavior (Ferguson, 1980). Holistic medicine favors an *active* approach to *health*, whereas scientific medicine more often takes a *reactive* approach to *disease*.

3. **Personal treatment environment.** Conventional medicine has shifted health care from the home to impersonal offices and hospitals, which are disease-centered rather than health-oriented, and which reinforce uninformed reliance on medical experts. While holistic medicine understands the need for hospitalization in cases of severe illness, it favors situating health care in personal, relaxed settings.

4. **Optimum health for all.** In principle, the holistic view extends health care beyond treating disease

to promoting the highest possible level of well-being for everyone. Even women and men who think they are "well" can work to realize "a state of extraordinary vigor, joy, and creativity" (Gordon, 1980:17).

On the broadest level, holistic medicine seeks to reestablish the personal social ties that commonly united healers and patients before the era of impersonal specialists. The AMA currently recognizes more than fifty specific areas of medical practice, and a growing proportion of M.D.s are entering these high-paying specialties rather than more holistic family practice. Thus, while technological advances surely improve medicine in some respects, they may actually diminish the profession in others.

## Medicine and Economics in Global Perspective

As medicine has come to rely on high technology, the costs of health care in industrial societies have skyrocketed. Various countries use different strategies to help people meet these expenses.

### Medicine in Socialist Societies

In societies with predominantly socialist economies, the government provides medical care directly to the people. It is an axiom of socialism that all citizens have the right to medical care on the same terms. To translate this ideal of equity into reality, people do not rely on their private financial resources to pay physicians and hospitals; rather, the government funnels public funds to pay medical costs. The state owns and operates medical facilities and pays salaries to practitioners, who are government employees.

***People's Republic of China.*** The People's Republic of China, a poor, agrarian society that is only beginning to industrialize, faces the daunting task of attending to the health of more than a billion people. Traditional healing arts, including acupuncture and the prescription of medicinal herbs, are still widely practiced in China. In addition, a holistic concern for the interplay of mind and body—a tradition whose roots extend back thousands of years—figures prominently in the Chinese approach to health care (Sidel & Sidel, 1982b; Kaptchuk, 1985).

As part of experimental market reforms, China introduced some private forms of medical care during the 1980s, but by the end of the decade the government had reestablished tight control over every area of life, including health care. Consequently, all medical facilities are now government operated. China's so-called barefoot doctors, roughly comparable to paramedics in the United States, have brought some modern methods of medical care to millions of peasants in remote rural villages. Glancing back at Global Map 20–1, we can see that medical care in China—measured in terms of the number of doctors—is adequate by world standards.

***The Commonwealth of Independent States.*** The former Soviet Union is in the process of sweeping transformation as its state-dominated economy moves toward a market system. In line with these momentous shifts, the scheme for providing medical care is also likely to change. Until 1992, at least, the government provided medical care funded from taxes (Fuchs, 1974; Knaus, 1981). As is the case in the People's Republic of China, people did not choose their own physician, but reported to a government health facility near their home.

Physicians in the former Soviet Union have had lower prestige and income than their counterparts in the United States. They have received about the same salary as skilled industrial workers, a reflection of socialist attempts at economic equality. During the recent market-

While providing basic care for the people, the medical system of the former Soviet Union has been highly impersonal and bureaucratic. In this Moscow hospital—one of the nation's best—a team of surgeons performs eye operations on eight patients in assembly-line fashion.

driven price increases, many physicians complained that their salaries had dropped in value to the point that they could scarcely afford to buy food. Worth noting, too, is that about 70 percent of Commonwealth physicians are women, compared with about 20 percent in the United States, and, as in the United States, occupations dominated by women offer fewer financial rewards.

Under the Soviet system, the number of physicians was high by world standards, and these women and men succeeded in meeting most of the basic needs of a large population. However, rigid bureaucracy resulted in highly standardized and impersonal medical care. As the nation adopts market reforms, uniformity will likely diminish and consumer choices will increase. But disparities in quality of care among various segments of the population may well intensify.

### Medicine in Capitalist Societies

Societies with predominantly capitalist economies limit government welfare programs, including health care. Citizens provide for themselves in accordance with their own resources and personal preferences. As Chapter 19 ("The Economy and Work") explains, capitalist societies have substantial economic inequality. Paying for good health is simply beyond the means of a significant part of the population. Therefore every capitalist society provides some government assistance. Most of these nations—with the noteworthy exception of the United States—offer a comprehensive health program to the entire population.

*Sweden.* In 1891 Sweden instituted a compulsory, comprehensive system of government medical care. Citizens of this Scandinavian country pay for this program with their taxes, which are among the highest in the world. Typically physicians receive salaries from the government rather than fees from patients, and most hospitals are government managed. Because this medical system resembles that of socialist societies, it is often described as **socialized medicine**, *a medical-care system in which most medical facilities are owned and operated by the government, and most physicians are salaried government employees.*

*Great Britain.* In 1948 Great Britain instituted socialized medicine as an outgrowth of a medical insurance program begun in 1911. However, the British did not do away with private care; instead, they devised a "dual system" of medical services. Thus all British citizens are entitled to medical care provided by the National Health Service, but those who can afford to may purchase more extensive—and expensive—care from doctors and hospitals that operate privately.

*Canada.* Canada offers yet another scheme to pay for medical care. The Canadian government pays doctors and hospitals—who operate privately—for the services they provide according to a schedule of fees set annually by the federal government and provincial governments in consultation with professional medical associations. Thus Canada has government-funded and -regulated medical care but, because practitioners operate privately, not true socialized medicine. Moreover, some physicians work entirely outside the government-funded system, charging whatever fees they wish (Grant, 1984; Vayda & Deber, 1984).

Canada's system has the advantage of providing care for everyone at a total cost that is one-third less than that needed to operate the (nonuniversal) medical system in the United States. At the same time, however, the Canadian system makes less use of state-of-the-art technology and responds more slowly to people's needs, often requiring those who need major surgery to wait months or even a year (Rosenthal, 1991).

*Japan.* Physicians in Japan operate privately, and a combination of private insurance and government programs pays medical costs. As Chapter 7 ("Groups and Organizations") notes, Japanese corporations take a wide-ranging interest in the welfare of their employees, and many provide medical care as an employee benefit. For those outside such privately funded programs, government medical insurance covers 70 percent of all costs, and the elderly receive free care (Vogel, 1979).

Despite differences among these programs, the medical-care systems of capitalist societies other than the United States have three major benefits in common. First, basic medical care is available to everyone regardless of income. Second, government programs protect citizens from the financial hardships of a catastrophic illness, which can overwhelm even the well-to-do. Third, a system of subsidized care encourages people to use medical facilities regularly not just to treat, but to prevent, illness.

## Medicine in the United States

The United States is unique among the industrialized societies of the world in having no government-sponsored medical program for every citizen. On average, European governments pay for about 75 percent of medical costs; by contrast, the U.S. government pays 40 percent (Lohr, 1988). The government does pay most medical expenses, but only for some categories of people. For the most part, then, medicine in the United States is a private, profit-making industry in which more money buys better care. Called a **direct-fee system**, ours is *a medical-care system in which patients pay directly for the services of physicians and hospitals.*

Affluent people in the United States can purchase top-flight medical care, yet the poor fare far worse than their counterparts in Europe. This translates into relatively high death rates among both infants and adults in the United States compared to many European countries (Fuchs, 1974; United Nations, 1991).

Why does the United States have no national health-care program? First, members of our society have historically favored limited government. When European societies were designing national medical-care plans a century ago, the U.S. government was playing only a small role in society. Second, despite the growth of government in the last fifty years, political support for a national medical program has not been strong, even among members of labor unions, who have concentrated instead on winning health-care benefits from employers. A third reason for the lack of a national health-care program has been the historical opposition of the AMA and the private insurance industry, both powerful special-interest groups (Starr, 1982).

Health insurance became a central issue in the 1992 presidential campaign. Both major political parties endorsed a greater government role in funding medical care, and the idea won new support from both the AMA and insurance companies. It appears that this country will soon join other industrial nations in guaranteeing at least some medical coverage for everyone.

But making care available to everyone is not the only issue. The cost of technologically sophisticated medicine is extremely high. As Figure 20–1 shows, expenditures for medical care increased almost forty-fold between 1950 and 1990, from just over $12 billion to more than $666 billion. In the United States, we spent about 5 percent of the gross national product on medical care in 1950; by 1990, such care was absorbing almost 12 percent of GNP. This amounted to $2,354 per person for 1991, higher than any other industrial society and double that spent by, for example, the Germans or the Japanese (Whitney, 1991). Without a program of socialized medicine or comprehensive federal health insurance, how do people pay for medical care?

**Figure 20–1**  The Rising Cost of Medical Care in the United States

*(U.S. Bureau of the Census, 1970; Health Insurance Association of America, 1991)*

***Private insurance programs.***  In 1990, 150 million people, or about 61 percent of the population, received some medical-care benefits from a family member's employer or labor union. Another 35 million (14 percent) purchased some private coverage on their own. Most large-scale private programs such as Blue Cross and Blue Shield pay most, but not all, medical costs. Overall, three-fourths of the U.S. population have some private medical insurance (Health Insurance Association of America, 1991; U.S. Bureau of the Census, 1991).

***Public insurance programs.***  In 1965 Congress enacted legislation creating Medicare and Medicaid. Medicare pays some of the medical expenses of men and women over sixty-five; in 1990 it covered almost 33 million women and men, or about 13 percent of the population.

During the same year, Medicaid, a medical insurance program for the poor, provided benefits to some 24 million people, or about 10 percent of the population. After World War II, the U.S. Veterans Administration granted veterans free medical care in government-operated hospitals; about 10 million people, or roughly 4 percent of the population, receive VA benefits. In all, close to 27 percent of the U.S. adult population now receives medical-care benefits from the government, but most of these people are also covered by private insurance programs.

***Health Maintenance Organizations.*** An increasing number of people in the United States belong to a **health maintenance organization** (HMO), *an organization that provides comprehensive medical care to subscribers for a fixed fee.* In 1990 there were 556 HMOs in the United States with over 33 million members, or almost 14 percent of the population. HMOs vary in their costs and benefits, and none provides full coverage. Since membership cost is fixed regardless of the services people use, these organizations have a financial interest in keeping their subscribers healthy, and therefore many have adopted a preventive approach to health (Ginsburg, 1983).

In all, 85 percent of the U.S. population rely on some medical insurance coverage, either private or public. Yet this coverage may fall short, first, because the health-insurance plans of some 50 million people pay only part of the costs of treating a major illness, threatening even middle-class people with financial ruin. Second, no program covers every medical need; even Medicare and Medicaid exclude many medical services, such as dental care (Eve, 1984). Third, and most serious, some 35 million men, women, and children in the United States (about 14 percent of the population) have no medical insurance at all. Another 30 million people lose their medical coverage temporarily each year due to layoffs, changing jobs, or for other reasons (Altman et al., 1989; *Sourcebook of Health Insurance Data*, 1989; Hilts, 1991).

Caught in a terrible bind, most of those with no insurance are poor or moderate-income people who simply cannot afford to become ill. Neither can these people afford to purchase the medical care they need to remain healthy. And, as is the case with poverty generally, children fall through the cracks in our system more than anyone else: about one in five children (one in four among African Americans and one in three among Hispanics) live in families with no health insurance of any kind.

# Theoretical Analysis of Health and Medicine

Each of the major theoretical paradigms in sociology provides a means of organizing and interpreting the facts and issues presented in this chapter.

## Structural-Functional Analysis

Structural-functional analysis rests on the image of society as a complex system that is stable and internally well-integrated. Talcott Parsons (1951) included the good health of its members as a societal imperative. From a social-systems point of view, Parsons viewed illness as dysfunctional, undermining individuals' ability to contribute to the operation of society.

Parsons also recognized that every society must have an established means for dealing with those who are ill. How this is done, of course, depends on a society's available technology and cultural system. Our society is among the most technologically complex in the world, and our medical care reflects this. Similarly, this nation's historical emphasis on private funding for medical care is consistent with our cultural value of individual self-reliance.

### The Sick Role

One of the most important ideas contributed by the structural-functional analysis of health is the **sick role**, *patterns of behavior defined as appropriate for people who are ill.* As developed by Parsons, the sick role has four characteristics.

1. *Illness provides exemption from routine responsibilities.* In everyday life, individuals perform their roles as students, parents, and employees. Serious illness, Parsons claims, relaxes or suspends normal social responsibilities. To prevent abuse of this license, people cannot simply declare themselves ill; they must enlist the support of others—especially a recognized medical expert—before assuming the sick role.

2. *A person's illness is not deliberate.* We assume that sick people are not responsible for their ailments; illness is something that has happened to them. Therefore, the failure of ill people to fulfill

routine responsibilities should carry no threat of punishment.

3. *A sick person must want to be well.* We also assume that the people who are ill want to be well. Thus people suspected of feigning illness to escape responsibility or to receive special attention have no legitimate claim to the sick role.

4. *An ailing person must seek competent help.* An additional obligation assumed by people who are ill is seeking competent assistance and cooperating with health-care practitioners. Anyone who fails to seek medical help or to follow doctor's orders gives up any claim on the sick role's exemption from routine responsibilities.

### The Physician's Role

Parsons perceived the sick person and the healer as functionally linked. He described the physician's role as providing medical care as needed by the patient. Just as a person in the sick role is expected to pursue health by seeking competent help, so the physician is expected to do whatever will cure illness. Sometimes doing so is impossible, but physician and patient initially work from the premise that the patient will recover.

Parsons claimed that the physician's role confers power over the patient. This hierarchy is rooted in the cultural norm that ailing individuals must cooperate with physicians, and it is strengthened by the physician's special knowledge. Physicians expect patients to comply with their requests and to supply personal information, even that shared with no one else. Parsons noted that the power of physicians also carries responsibility to use this information only for legitimate medical purposes.

The physician's role varies from society to society, and reflects a country's attitude toward hierarchy. In Japan, for example, strong tradition gives physicians considerable authority, so that they share less information with patients than their counterparts in the United States. The box on page 580 probes this cultural disparity.

*Critical evaluation.*   Parsons's functionalist analysis explains how notions about illness and strategies for providing medical care fit into broader patterns of social organization. The concept of the sick role, in other words, represents the accommodation of society to illness. Others have noted that the sick role also applies to some non-illness situations, such as pregnancy (Myers & Grasmick, 1989). One limitation of this concept is that it is

more easily applied to acute conditions (like the flu) than chronic disease (like heart disease), which may not be reversible. Moreover, affluent people have more opportunity to assume the sick role than poor people, who cannot afford not to work even when they are ill.

Critics charge that Parsons's view of the physician's role supports the idea that doctors—rather than people themselves—bear the primary responsibility for health. Treatment-oriented physicians respond to acute illness, of course, but a more prevention-oriented approach to health would cast physicians as equal partners along with patients in the pursuit of health.

## Symbolic-Interaction Analysis

Viewed according to the symbolic-interaction paradigm, society appears less as a grand system than a complex and changing reality. This means that health and medical care are human creations based on social definitions.

### The Social Construction of Illness

Any state of health or illness is a matter of socially constructed reality, as described in Chapter 6 ("Social Interaction in Everyday Life"). In a society where most people suffer from malnutrition, therefore, they may consider an underfed child to be quite normal. Similarly, for decades the members of our own society defined smoking cigarettes as a matter of personal taste, and today many people give little thought to the deleterious effects on health of a rich diet.

How we *respond* to serious illness is also based on social definitions which may or may not square with medical facts. For instance, people with AIDS contend with fear and sometimes outright bigotry that has no basis in medical fact.

Even the "expert opinions" of medical professionals are influenced by nonmedical factors. In one piece of research, David Mechanic (1978) noted that during periods when productivity lagged behind demand in the former Soviet Union, physicians were less likely to excuse workers from their jobs. Similarly, military doctors may define flu symptoms as illness during peacetime but overlook this evidence in desperate times of war. Closer to home, college students have been known to dismiss signs of illness on the eve of a vacation, yet dutifully march in to the infirmary before a difficult examination. In each case, people and medical experts do not simply assess health in some objective way; rather, they negotiate

# Breaking Bad News: Comparing Japanese and U.S. Physicians

Japanese emperor Hirohito died in 1988 without knowing why. The word leaked out to the public that the traditional Japanese ruler succumbed to intestinal cancer, but doctors never told him the bad news. This ignorance is far from uncommon: in Japan, physicians routinely conceal the fact of terminal illness from patients. A Japanese specialist in bioethics explains:

> In Japan, the art of medicine is regarded as an expression of loving kindness—part of the art of *Jin*, the fundamental teaching of Confucian ideas. There is the belief that giving the patient hope until the last minute will give him a fighting spirit.

Proceeding from this perspective, Japanese physicians take responsibility for every decision that affects a patient's well-being. Thus professional standards demand that they withhold information about the seriousness of an illness. The Japanese are not alone in this practice; physicians throughout the Third World follow the same precepts.

Physicians in the United States acted the same way three decades ago. In 1961, an article in the *Journal of the American Medical Association* reported that just one in eight U.S. physicians believed in discussing a terminal illness with a dying patient.

John Collier's painting *Sentence of Death* portrays perhaps the most difficult ordeal a physician can face: informing a patient of impending death. Until recently, U.S. physicians routinely withheld such a diagnosis in the belief that the patient was better off not knowing of a terminal condition. Although now this practice is far less common in the United States, it continues in Japan and in many other countries of the world.

What changed this practice? The *patient rights movement*, which has gathered the greatest support in the United States, has rewritten the rules for the physician-patient relationship. The public has steadily demanded—often with support from the courts—that physicians disclose to patients more and more medical information. Researchers have backed up this policy by demonstrating that such disclosure reduces patients' anxieties, strengthens their bond with physicians, and allows terminally ill people to better plan how to use whatever time is left.

European societies are following closely behind the United States in advancing patient rights. Japan, too, is starting to change its ways in this regard, as physicians and the public are considering people's right to be told the truth, even when the news is bad.

SOURCE: Based on Darnton & Hoshia (1989).

the definition of a situation based on a host of considerations.

How a medical situation is defined can also affect how somebody actually feels. Medical experts have long noted the existence of *psychosomatic* disorders (a fusion of Greek words for "mind" and "body"), in which a person's state of mind influences physical well-being (Hamrick, Anspaugh, & Ezell, 1986). Sociologist W. I. Thomas (1931) pointed out that as a situation is defined as real, it becomes real in its consequences.

### The Social Construction of Treatment

In Chapter 6 ("Social Interaction in Everyday Life"), we used the dramaturgical approach of Erving Goffman to explain how physicians craft their physical surroundings ("the office") and present themselves to others to foster specific impressions of competence and power.

Sociologist Joan Emerson (1970) further illustrates this process of reality construction by analyzing a situation familiar to women, a gynecological examination carried out by a male doctor. After observing seventy-five such examinations, she explains that this situation is especially precarious because it is vulnerable to misinterpretation. Why? Simply because the man's touching of a woman's genitals—conventionally viewed as a sexual act and possibly even an assault—must, in this case, be defined as impersonal and professional. To ensure that this reality dominates the setting, the medical staff carefully structures their personal performances to remove sexual connotations as completely as possible.

Emerson notes several ways in which the medical staff seeks to do this. The examination is restricted to a specific setting used for no other purpose—a room whose decor and equipment are decidedly medical in character. All personnel wear medical uniforms, never clothing that could be worn in other, nonmedical situations. The staff tries to make the patient feel that such examinations are simply routine although, from the patient's point of view, they may be quite unusual.

Furthermore, although rapport between physician and patient is important, this is established before the examination begins. Once under way, the male physician's performance is matter of fact, suggesting to the patient that inspecting the genitals is no different from surveying any other part of the body. A woman is usually present during the examination in the role of nurse. Not only does she assist the physician, but her presence dispels any impression that a man and woman are "alone in a room" (Emerson, 1970:81).

The need to manage situational definitions has long been overlooked by medical schools. This omission is unfortunate because, as Emerson's analysis shows, understanding how reality is socially constructed in the examination room is just as crucial as mastering the medical skills involved. Fortunately, medical professionals are gradually coming to recognize the importance of sociological insights. At the Southwestern Medical School in Dallas, Texas, for example, Professor David Hemsell urges all his medical students to gain a better understanding of this process from the patient's point of view by actually climbing onto an examination table and placing their feet in the metal stirrups with their legs apart. Hemsell claims, "The only way to understand women's feelings is to be there." He adds, "You can see the impact of being in that position hit them in the face like a two-by-four." Imagine the even greater impact on the men if they were required to do this without wearing their trousers.

***Critical evaluation.*** One strength of the symbolic-interaction paradigm lies in revealing the relative meaning of sickness and health. What is normal or deviant, healthful or harmful, depends on a host of factors, many of which are not, strictly speaking, medical. Another contribution lies in showing how all medical procedures involve a subtle interaction between patient and physician.

A problem with this approach is that it seems to deny that there are any objective standards of well-being. Certain physical conditions do indeed cause specific, negative changes in human capacities, however we define them. And people who lack sufficient nutrition and safe water, for example, suffer the ill effects of their unhealthy environment however they define their surroundings.

## Social-Conflict Analysis

Social-conflict analysis takes a different approach by linking health and medical care to social inequality. Sociologists using this paradigm have developed three major criticisms of capitalist societies with regard to health.

### Unequal Access to Medical Care

Personal health is the foundation of social life. Yet by defining medical care as a commodity for purchase, capitalist societies skew health in favor of the wealthy. As we have already noted, this problem is especially serious in the United States because our country stands out as having no comprehensive, national medical-care program. Critics of this situation—including some members of Congress—support the expansion of government-funded medical care to the entire population, so that everyone has access to high-quality medical care. Vested interests, especially the medical establishment, support doing so only if the emerging program remains predominantly private rather than government controlled.

### Medical Care and the Profit Motive

For others, however, even a program of socialized medicine would not go far enough. More radical critics claim that patterns of health in capitalist countries inevitably reflect the class system itself. Thus, they maintain, the strikingly unequal distribution of wealth in the United States makes equal medical care impossible, despite government efforts. Only a significant redistribution of economic resources would make medical care uniformly available (Bodenheimer, 1977; Navarro, 1977).

From this point of view, capitalist medical care amounts to another big business that provides a poor product. Physicians, hospitals, and producers of drugs and medical supplies comprise multibillion-dollar corporate conglomerates (Ehrenreich, 1978). The quest for ever-increasing profits, these critics suggest, encourages questionable medical practices, including performing unnecessary tests and surgery and an overreliance on drugs (Kaplan et al., 1985). For example, some 1 million men and women enter a hospital each year because of an adverse reaction to some medical drug (Illich, 1976). Then there are periodic scandals about unsafe medical products and procedures. For example, more than 2 million women in the United States had silicone breast implants under the assumption that the commonly used plastic packets of silicone were safe. Recently, however, it became clear that these implants—which have a tendency to rupture, causing significant harm—are not safe enough, a fact apparently known to Dow Corning, their major manufacturer, for decades.

Of the roughly 30 million surgical operations performed in the United States each year, three-fourths were "elective," meaning that they were intended to promote a patient's long-term health rather than being prompted by a medical emergency. Critics charge that the extent of such surgery reflects not just the medical needs of patients but the financial interests of surgeons and hospitals (Illich, 1976). Some suggest that at least 10 percent of elective surgery could safely be refused or deferred, saving patients more than $1 billion each year. More important, since about one in two hundred patients dies from elective surgery (because surgery itself is dangerous), 13,000 lives a year are needlessly lost (Sidel & Sidel, 1982a). Finally, critics point out, the United States has been all too tolerant of physicians having a direct financial interest in the tests and procedures they order for their patients (Pear & Eckholm, 1991). For some critics, this crystallizes the core problem with U.S. medicine: health care should be motivated by a concern for people, not profits.

### Medicine as Social Control

A final issue raised by social-conflict analysts is that medical care operates as a means of social control. Because we think of science as a path to objective truth, our scientifically based medical establishment has enjoyed broad support. But is scientific medicine as politically neutral as it claims to be?

For one thing, the medical establishment has long opposed government-operated health-care programs. Although medical officials decry such proposals as eroding quality care, critics charge that the real issue is the erosion of profits. Moreover, the medical establishment has a history of racial and sexual discrimination, invoking through the years "scientific" facts to protect the interests of the wealthy white men who dominate the medical profession (Leavitt, 1984). The box provides several illustrations of how the banner of science has been used to support sexism in the United States. Such practices subsided as more women and people of color joined the ranks of physicians, although critics contend that such biases—albeit more subtle—still pervade the U.S. medical establishment (Zola, 1978; Brown, 1979).

Even today critics view scientific medicine as a means of maintaining class inequality. A scientific approach to illness tends to focus on bacteria, viruses, and biological processes, while giving short shrift to social patterns that affect health such as wealth and poverty. From the scientific perspective, in other words, indigent people become ill because of poor sanitation and a diet lacking in vital nutrients, even though poverty may lie at the root of these ills. In this way, critics charge, scientific medicine effectively depoliticizes the issue of health in the United States by reducing social and political issues to simple biology.

*Critical evaluation.* Social-conflict analysis provides still another view of the relationships among health,

# Medicine and Victorian Women: Science or Sexism?

A century ago medical science reacted strongly to the changing roles of women. With men firmly in control, the medical establishment staunchly opposed greater sexual equality.

Medical opinion labeled conventional gender distinctions as both natural and inevitable. Beyond differences in size and strength, physicians pronounced men inherently rational while claiming that women are dominated by emotions and hypersensitive nervous systems. Thus women's highest calling was childbearing. Writing in 1890, one physician remarked that "the Almighty, in creating the female sex, had taken the uterus and built up a woman around it" (cited in Smith-Rosenberg & Rosenberg, 1984:13). In short, as far as women were concerned, medical opinion equated health with motherhood, arguing that childless women risked a life wreaked by physical and mental illness.

The Victorian medical establishment also obstructed women's demands for schooling. Physicians warned that too much thinking rendered a woman weak and sickly and decreased her capacity to bear healthy children. Confronting the notion of an educated woman in 1901, one gynecologist complacently predicted, "She may become highly cultured and accomplished and shine in society, but her future husband will discover too late that he has married a large outfit of headaches, backaches, and spine aches, instead of a woman fitted to take up the duties of life" (cited in Smith-Rosenberg & Rosenberg, 1984:16). Another member of the Harvard medical faculty warned that "If she puts as much force into her brain education as a boy, the brain or the special apparatus [the reproductive system] will suffer" (cited in Bollough & Voght, 1984:30).

Victorian physicians also drew on so-called scientific reasoning to oppose women's control over their sexuality. Women, they argued, had no interest in sexual activity beyond having children, and had neither the desire nor the ability to achieve orgasm. By contrast, if a man failed to reach sexual climax, he risked a dangerous buildup of nervous energy. Male orgasms, unimpeded by contraceptive devices such as condoms, were also said to enhance a woman's health by "bathing the female reproductive organs" (cited in Smith-Rosenberg & Rosenberg, 1984:19). Well into this century, in fact, the American Medical Association opposed contraception and abortion, citing allegedly medical grounds.

Some Victorians saw this pseudo-science for what it was. Martha Carey Thomas, president of Bryn Mawr College, won much support for her contention that men holding such ungenerous attitudes toward women were themselves "pathological, blinded by neurotic mists of sex, unable to see that women form one-half of the kindly race of normal, healthy human creatures in the world" (cited in Bollough & Voght, 1984:34).

medicine, and our society. There is little doubt that many people think of medicine in terms of artificial hearts, CAT scans, and other sophisticated technology while overlooking the fact that many people lack the most basic medical care.

One objection to the conflict approach is that it minimizes the advances in health in the United States wrought by scientific medicine. While there is plenty of room for improvement, the overall health of the U.S. population has become better in recent decades.

To sum up, sociology's three major theoretical paradigms convincingly argue that health and medicine are social issues. The famous French scientist Louis Pasteur (1822–1895) spent much of his life studying how bacteria cause disease. Before his death, the record indicates, he remarked that health depends much less on bacteria than on the social environment in which bacteria operate (Gordon, 1980:7). Explaining Pasteur's insight is sociology's essential contribution to understanding human health.

# Summary

1. Health is a social and biological issue and depends on the extent and distribution of a society's resources. Culture shapes definitions of health as well as patterns of health care.

2. Through most of human history, health has been poor by today's standards. Health improved dramatically in Western Europe and North America in the nineteenth century, first because industrialization raised living standards, and later as medical advances brought infectious diseases under control.

3. Infectious diseases were the major killers at the beginning of this century. Today most people in the United States die in old age of heart disease, cancer, or stroke.

4. Health in the Third World is generally poor, because of inadequate sanitation and malnutrition. Life expectancy is about twenty years less than in the United States; in the poorest nations, half the children do not survive to adulthood.

5. In the United States, three-fourths of children born today can expect to live to at least age sixty-five. Throughout the life course, women have relatively better health than men, and people of high social position enjoy better health than others.

6. Industrialization has raised our society's standard of living and thus improved health. However, environmental pollution, especially from industrial wastes, threatens the future health of our population.

7. Cigarette smoking increased during this century to become the greatest preventable cause of death in the United States. Now that the health hazards of smoking are known and social tolerance for tobacco use has declined, cigarette consumption has waned.

8. Sexually transmitted diseases are a health issue of growing concern. In the 1980s the spread of genital herpes transformed patterns of sexuality away from casual sex toward greater selectivity and commitment. The spread of AIDS, a fatal and incurable disease, has reinforced this shift.

9. Because of advancing medical technology, an increasing number of ethical issues surround death and the rights of the dying. Because of the capability to sustain life artificially, death now commonly results from a human decision.

10. Historically a family concern, health care is now the responsibility of trained specialists. The model of scientific medicine underlies the U.S. medical establishment.

11. The holistic approach to medicine balances science and technology with other procedures that promote health as well as treat disease. Highlighting the need for professional healers to gain personal knowledge of patients and their environment, holistic healers encourage people to assume greater responsibility for their own health.

12. Socialist societies define medical care as a right that governments offer equally to everyone. Capitalist societies view medical care as a commodity to be purchased, although most capitalist governments support medical care through socialized medicine or national health insurance.

13. The United States is the only industrialized society with no comprehensive medical-care program. In a direct-fee system like ours, most people have private health insurance, government-sponsored insurance, or membership in a health maintenance organization. One in five adults in the United States lacks any such coverage and thus cannot afford to pay for medical care.

14. Structural-functional analysis links health and medicine to other social structures. Central to structural-functional analysis is the concept of the sick role, in which illness allows release from routine social responsibilities as long as patients seek to regain their health.

15. The symbolic-interaction paradigm investigates how health and treatments for illness are largely matters of subjective perception and social definition.

16. Social-conflict analysis focuses on the unequal distribution of health and medical care. It criticizes U.S. medical care for overly relying on drugs and surgery and for overemphasizing the biological rather than the social causes of illness.

# Key Concepts

**direct-fee system** a medical-care system in which patients pay directly for the services of physicians and hospitals

**euthanasia** (mercy killing) assisting in the death of a person suffering from an incurable illness

**health** a state of complete physical, mental, and social well-being

**health care** any activity intended to improve health

**health maintenance organization (HMO)** an organization that provides comprehensive medical care to subscribers for a fixed fee

**holistic medicine** an approach to health care that emphasizes prevention of illness and takes account of the whole person within a physical and social environment

**medicine** an institutionalized system for combating disease and improving health

**sick role** patterns of behavior that are defined as appropriate for those who are ill

**social epidemiology** the study of how health and disease are distributed in a society's population

**socialized medicine** a health-care system in which most medical facilities are owned and operated by the government, and most physicians are salaried government employees

# Suggested Readings

This book probes many of the issues raised in this chapter.

> Peter E.S. Freund and Meredith B. McGuire. *Health, Illness, and the Social Body*. Englewood Cliffs, NJ: Prentice Hall, 1991.

Describing rituals of exorcism in Sri Lanka, the first of the following books explores forms of healing that defy understanding in Western terms. The second, a collection of essays, examines the wide variety of approaches to health care in African societies.

> Bruce Kapferer. A *Celebration of Demons*. New York: Berg, 1990.

> Brian M. de Toit and Ismail H. Abdalla, eds. *African Healing Strategies*. New York: Trado-Medic, 1985.

These books delve into the history of medicine from the perspective of gender conflict. The first reports on women's exclusion from the emerging medical establishment. The second explains how female midwives were gradually replaced by male obstetricians.

> Regina Markell Morantz-Sanchez. *Sympathy and Science: Women Physicians in American Medicine*. New York: Oxford University Press, 1985.

> Jane B. Donegan. *Women & Men Midwives: Medicine, Morality, and Misogyny in Early America*. Westport, CT: Greenwood Press, 1985.

Few issues reveal the interplay of medicine and ethics as clearly as abortion. This reference work provides a comprehensive overview of publications on all sides of this topic.

> Richard Fitzsimmons and Joan P. Diana. *Pro-Choice/Pro-Life: An Annotated, Selected Bibliography*. Westport, CT: Greenwood Press, 1991.

The effects of illness often ripple through an entire family, straining and distorting relationships. Alcoholism is a case in point.

> Ramona M. Asher. *Women With Alcoholic Husbands: Ambivalence and the Trap of Codependency*. Chapel Hill: University of North Carolina Press, 1992.

Here are four recent books concerned with the AIDS epidemic. The first highlights the social dimensions of this catastrophic disease; the second is of special concern to faculty and students; the third includes a dozen essays on how our society has responded to this crisis; and the fourth criticizes the medical establishment and the press for exaggerating the scope of the AIDS epidemic.

> Dorothy Nelkin, David P. Willis, and Scott V. Parris, eds. A *Disease of Society: Cultural and Institutional Responses to AIDS*. Cambridge, UK: Cambridge University Press, 1991.

> Jackie R. McClain and Tom E. Matteoli. *Confronting AIDS on the Campus and in the Classroom: A Guide for Higher Education*. Washington, DC: College and University Personnel Association, 1989.

> David E. Rogers and Eli Ginzberg, eds. *Public and Professional Attitudes Towards AIDS Patients: A National Dilemma*. Boulder, CO: Westview, 1989.

> Michael Fumento. *The Myth of Heterosexual AIDS*. New York: Basic Books, 1989.

# Population
# and
# Urbanization

In 1519 a band of Spanish conquistadors led by Hernando Cortés reached Tenochtitlán, the capital of the Aztec empire. What they saw stunned them—a lake-encircled city, teeming with over 300,000 people, more than the population of any European city at that time. Gazing down broad streets, exploring stone temples, and entering the magnificent royal palace filled with golden treasures, Cortés and his soldiers wondered if they were dreaming.

Cortés soon woke up and set his mind to looting the city. At first, he was unable to overcome the superior forces of the Aztecs and their leader Montezuma, but the determined leader spent two years raising a vast army and finally managed to destroy Tenochtitlán. In its place, Cortés constructed a new city in the European fashion—*Ciudad Imperial de México*—Mexico City.

Today Mexico City is once more fighting for its life. Its population has soared in recent decades and experts predict that, by the end of the 1990s, the city will be home to 30 million people—one hundred times the number that astonished Cortés. This huge population is grappling with a host of problems common to Third-World societies, including poverty, foreign debt, poor health, and a rapidly deteriorating environment.

Rising populations, vast urban sprawl, and desperate poverty—this combination burdens much of the world today. This chapter examines both population growth and urbanization—two powerful forces that have shaped and reshaped our planet for thousands of years.

Increasing population may turn out to be the most serious problem facing the world in the coming century; it is all but certain that this vital drama will be played out in cities of unprecedented size.

## Demography: The Study of Population

From the point at which the human species emerged some 200,000 years ago until recently, the population of the entire earth remained quite low at some 20 million —about the same number of people that live in southern California today. Life for our ancestors was anything but certain, as they were vulnerable to a wide range of diseases and frequent natural disasters. Across hundreds of centuries, however, our species has managed to flourish. Ironically, perhaps, global population is now so large (about 5.4 billion in 1992) and growing so rapidly (by almost 100 million each year) that the future of humanity is again uncertain.

The causes and consequences of this growth form the core of **demography,** *the study of human population.* Demography (from the Greek, meaning "description of people") is closely related to sociology, but focuses on the size, age, and sex composition of a population as

587

well as people's movements from one region to another. Although much demographic research is quantitative, demography is more than a numbers game. The discipline poses crucial questions about the effects of population growth and how it may be controlled.

Demographic analysis proceeds from several basic concepts.

## Fertility

Any study of human population must concern itself with how many people are born. **Fertility** is *the incidence of childbearing in a society's population.* Women are capable of childbearing from the onset of menstruation (typically in the early teens) to menopause (usually in the late forties). During this time, a woman could conceivably bear more than twenty children, but this *fecundity*, or potential childbearing, is sharply reduced by health, financial concerns, cultural norms, and personal choice.

Demographers often measure fertility using the **crude birth rate,** *the number of live births in a given year for every thousand people in a population.* A crude birth rate is calculated by dividing the number of live births in a given year by a society's total population, and multiplying the result by 1,000. In the United States in 1990 there were about 4.2 million live births in a population of 253 million (U.S. Bureau of the Census, 1991). According to this formula, then, there were 16.6 live births for every thousand people, or a crude birth rate of 16.6.

This birth rate is "crude" because it is based on the entire population, not just women and men in their childbearing years. For this reason, making comparisons using crude birth rates can be misleading because one society may have a higher proportion of women of childbearing age than another. A crude birth rate also tells us nothing about how birth rates differ among people of various races, ethnicities, and religions. But this measure does have the strength of being easy to calculate, and it is widely regarded as a good measure of a society's overall fertility. Table 21–1 shows that the crude birth rates of the United States and other industrial societies are low in world context.

## Mortality

Population size is also affected by **mortality,** *the incidence of death in a society's population.* Corresponding to the crude birth rate, demographers use a **crude death rate,**

**Table 21–1 FERTILITY AND MORTALITY RATES IN GLOBAL PERSPECTIVE, 1990**

| | Crude Birth Rate | Crude Death Rate | Infant Mortality Rate |
|---|---|---|---|
| **North America** | | | |
| United States | 17 | 9 | 10 |
| Canada | 14 | 7 | 7 |
| **Europe** | | | |
| Belgium | 12 | 11 | 6 |
| Commonwealth of Independent States | 18 | 10 | 24 |
| Denmark | 12 | 11 | 6 |
| France | 14 | 9 | 6 |
| Spain | 11 | 8 | 6 |
| United Kingdom | 14 | 11 | 7 |
| **Latin America** | | | |
| Chile | 21 | 6 | 18 |
| Cuba | 18 | 7 | 12 |
| Haiti | 45 | 16 | 107 |
| Mexico | 29 | 5 | 33 |
| Nicaragua | 39 | 8 | 65 |
| Puerto Rico | 19 | 8 | 17 |
| **Africa** | | | |
| Algeria | 37 | 9 | 87 |
| Cameroon | 42 | 15 | 120 |
| Egypt | 34 | 10 | 90 |
| Ethiopia | 45 | 15 | 116 |
| Nigeria | 46 | 17 | 119 |
| South Africa | 35 | 8 | 52 |
| **Asia** | | | |
| Afghanistan | 44 | 18 | 154 |
| Bangladesh | 42 | 14 | 136 |
| India | 30 | 11 | 89 |
| Israel | 22 | 7 | 9 |
| Japan | 11 | 7 | 5 |
| Vietnam | 30 | 8 | 50 |

SOURCE: U.S. Bureau of the Census, *Statistical Abstract of the United States 1991* (Washington, DC: U.S. Government Printing Office, 1991).

defined as *the number of deaths in a given year for every thousand people in a population.* The crude death rate is calculated as the number of deaths in a given year divided by the total population, and multiplied by 1,000. In 1990 there were 2.2 million deaths in the total U.S. population of 253 million, yielding a crude death rate of 8.7. As Table 21–1 shows, this rate is low by world standards.

A third widely used demographic measure is the **infant mortality rate,** *the number of deaths in the first* year of life for each thousand live births in a given year. This rate is derived from dividing the number of deaths of children under one year of age by the number of live births during the same year and multiplying the result by 1,000. In 1990 there were 42,600 infant deaths and about 4.1 million live births in the United States. Dividing the first number by the second and multiplying the result by 1,000 produces an infant mortality rate of 10.4.

Like other demographic variables, this rate conceals considerable variation among segments of the U.S. population. For example, infant mortality rates of poor people are twice those of well-to-do people, just as African Americans have an infant mortality rate of about 19, twice the rate for whites (Stockwell, Swanson, & Wicks, 1987; U.S. Bureau of the Census, 1991). But infant mortality offers a good general measure of overall quality of life. Table 21–1 shows that infant mortality in the United States, while low compared to poor countries, is somewhat higher than it is in Canada, Denmark, and other nations that make medical care more readily available to their people.

Societies with a low infant mortality rate have a high **life expectancy**, *how long a person, on the average, can expect to live.* Males born in 1990 can expect to live 72.1 years, while females can expect to live 79.0 years. Life expectancy in rich, First-World countries is about twenty years greater than it is in poor, Third-World societies.

## Migration

Population size also changes as people move from one place to another. Demographers define **migration** as *the movement of people into and out of a specified territory.* Migration is sometimes involuntary, as illustrated by the forcible transport of 10 million Africans to the Western Hemisphere as slaves (Sowell, 1981). Other migration is voluntary; in this case, people typically are motivated to move by complex "push-pull" factors. Dissatisfaction with life in a poor rural village may "push" people to begin the process of migration. A common "pull" factor is the attraction of a big city, where people assume opportunity is greater. As we shall explain later in this chapter, migration underlies much of rapid urban growth in the Third World. Migration can result from many factors, ranging from religious or political oppression (which brought millions of people to our shores in the past) to simply seeking a more agreeable climate (which is drawing millions of people to the so-called "sunbelt" today).

The movement of people into a territory—commonly termed *immigration*—is measured as an *in-migration rate* calculated as the number entering an area for every thousand people in the population. Movement out of a territory—or *emigration*—is measured as an *out-migration rate*, that is, the number leaving for every thousand people. Both types of migration usually occur simultaneously; demographers describe the net result of in-migration and out-migration as the *net-migration rate*.

African-American artist Jacob Lawrence completed a series of paintings that he titled *The Migration of the Negro* (1940–1941) to document a major population movement among people of color from the rural South to the urban centers of the Northeast and Midwest.

(Jacob Lawrence, The Migration of the Negro. Panel 1: During the World War There Was a Great Migration North by Southern Negroes. 1940–41. Tempera on masonite. 11½ × 17½". The Phillips Collection.)

## Population Growth

Fertility, mortality, and migration affect the size of a society's population. Demographers derive the *natural growth rate* of a population by subtracting the crude death rate from the crude birth rate. The natural growth rate of the American population in 1990 was 7.9 per thousand (the crude birth rate of 16.6 minus the crude death rate of 8.7), or 0.8 percent annually. During the 1990s, demographers predict, the growth rate of the U.S. population will remain low, but this is not the case for many regions of the world, as is shown in Global Map 21–1.

The global map shows that the population growth in the industrialized regions of the world is well below average. In Europe, the current rate of growth is just 0.2 percent, and it is falling rapidly in Japan and elsewhere in the First World. By contrast, annual growth rates equal or exceed the world average throughout the Third World—including Asia (currently about 1.7 percent) and Latin America (overall, about 1.8 percent). The greatest population surge is in Africa, where annual growth averages 3.1 percent. To understand the significance of these figures, consider that an annual growth of 2 percent (as in Latin America) doubles a population in thirty-five years, and a 3 percent growth rate (as in Africa) reduces the *doubling time* of a society's population to only twenty-four years. The rapid population growth of the poorest countries is deeply troubling because of their inability to support the populations they have now.

## Population Composition

Demographers also study the composition of a society's population at any point in time. One simple variable is the **sex ratio**, *the number of males for every hundred females in a given population.* In 1990 the sex ratio in the United States was 95.0, or 95.0 males for every 100 females. Sex ratios typically fall below 100 because, as was noted in Chapter 20 ("Health and Medicine"), women typically outlive men.

A more complex and subtle way to describe the composition of a population is the **age-sex pyramid**, *a graphic representation that divides a population into various categories based on age and sex.* Figure 21–1 presents the age-sex pyramid for the United States in 1990. The left side indicates the number of males of different ages, while the right side shows the corresponding number

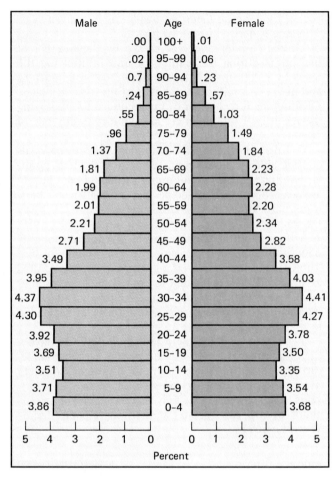

**Figure 21–1**   Age-Sex Population Pyramid for the United States, 1990

*(U.S. Bureau of the Census, 1991)*

of females. The rough pyramid shape results from higher mortality as people age. Also note that, after about age thirty, women increasingly outnumber men in the United States. The greater population share between the ages of twenty and forty-four represents the high birth rate from the mid-1940s to the late 1960s, commonly called the *baby boom.* The contraction just below age twenty shows that the baby boom was followed by a *baby bust*: a sharp decline in the birth rate. From a peak of 25.3 in 1957, the crude birth rate dropped to 15.3 in 1986 (and rose again to 16.6 by 1990).

The bulges and contractions in a society's age-sex

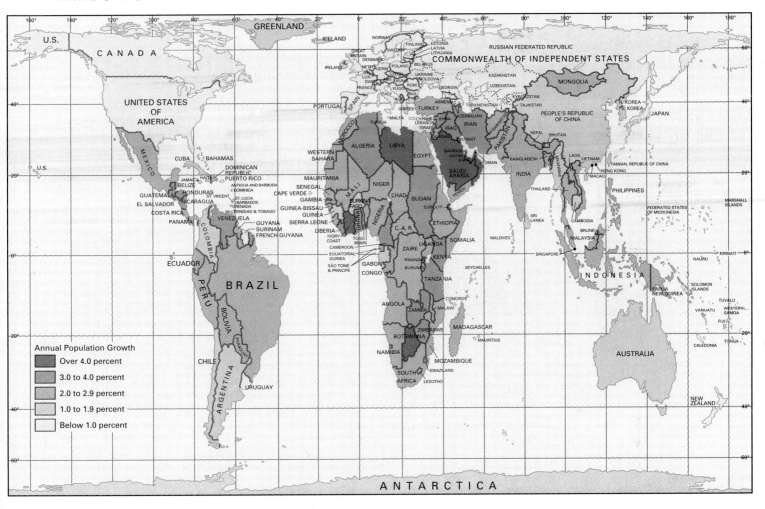

**Global Map 21–1**   Population Growth in Global Perspective
The richest societies of the world—including the United States, Canada, and the nations
of Europe—have growth rates below 1 percent. The nations of Latin America and Asia
typically have growth rates of about 2 percent, which double a population in thirty-five
years. The continent of Africa has an overall growth rate of 3.1 percent, which cuts the
doubling time to less than twenty-four years. In global perspective, we see that a society's
standard of living is closely related to its rate of population growth, meaning that population
is rising fastest in the world regions that can least afford to support more people.

pyramid provide important clues to its demographic history. Even more important, we can use these pyramids
to predict future population patterns. Figure 21–2 on
page 592 compares the age-sex pyramids of a rich country,

Switzerland, and a poor nation, Bangladesh. The relatively boxlike pyramid for Switzerland reveals a birth
rate that has long been very low, and which recently
has dropped even further. With fewer women entering

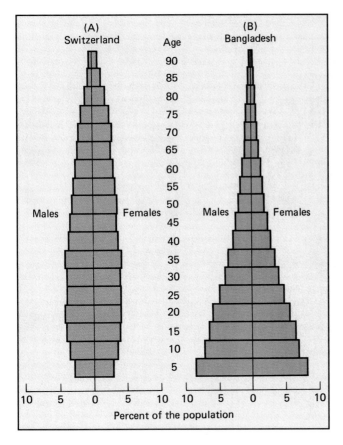

**Figure 21–2** The Demographic Composition of Switzerland and Bangladesh

*(Newman & Matzke, 1984)*

their childbearing years, population growth is likely to remain low. The Swiss pattern is more or less replicated by other industrial societies.

Bangladesh, a typical Third-World society, offers a dramatic contrast. The sharp point near the top of the pyramid is produced by high death rates after what we think of as middle age. The extremely wide base reveals the birth rate to be very high. Fertility is likely to rise even more, since the majority of females have yet to enter their childbearing years. Worldwide, the median age is only twenty-four—compared to thirty-three in the United States and thirty-five in Europe—making future population increases in poor countries all but inevitable. Unless effective birth control is available and utilized, exploding population will further strain limited social resources throughout the Third World.

# History and Theory of Population Growth

Through most of human history, people considered large families desirable since human labor was the key to productivity. Additionally, until the development of rubber condoms 150 years ago, birth control was uncertain at best. Paralleling high birth rates were high death rates—the result of the diseases for which there was no cure. Occurring together, high fertility and high mortality more or less canceled each other out, so population grew slowly. The world's population at the dawn of civilization in about 6000 B.C.E. (no more than 50 million) increased steadily if slowly across the millennia that followed, as is shown in Figure 21–3. When societies did manage population gains, they were often abruptly erased by periodic outbreaks of deadly plague, such as the Black Death, which swept across Western Europe in the mid-fourteenth century.

A demographic shift occurred about 1750 as the earth's population turned sharply upward, reaching 1 billion a century later. As explained presently, this increase was more the result of a drop in mortality than a jump in fertility. But the result was dramatic. Reaching a global population of 1 billion had taken forty thousand years to accomplish, but the 2 billion mark was attained in 1930—in just another eighty years. In other words, not only was population increasing, but the *rate* of growth was also rising quickly. A third billion was added by 1962—after just thirty-two years—and a fourth billion by 1974, a scant twelve years later. Although the rate of growth has recently stabilized, this pace continues,

**Figure 21–3** The Growth of World Population

Among the poorest countries on earth, Bangladesh is struggling to meet the needs of approximately 120 million people in a land area smaller than the state of Wisconsin. With a high birth rate, that nation's population problem is likely to become more serious in the future.

with our planet passing the 5 billion level in 1987. In no previous century did the world's population even double. In the twentieth century, however, it has increased *fourfold*.

Demographic projections are really informed guesswork. Currently, experts predict that world population will exceed 6 billion early in the coming century, and it probably will reach 8 billion by 2025. Little wonder, then, that global population has become a matter of urgent concern.

## Malthusian Theory

It was the sudden population growth some two centuries ago that sparked the development of demography as a discipline in the first place. One of the first efforts to explain population growth was made by Thomas Robert Malthus (1766–1834), an English clergyman and economist. His conclusion was as much a warning as an explanation, since he saw population growth driving the world toward social chaos.

Malthus (1926; orig. 1798) began by arguing that population growth was the simple result of the timeless passion between the sexes. As people reproduce, he con-

tinued, population should increase faster and faster according to what mathematicians call a geometric progression, as illustrated by the series of numbers 2, 4, 8, 16, 32, and so on. Malthus was left with the sobering realization that world population could soon soar out of control.

Malthus was confident that food production would also increase, but not as fast as people would multiply. Resources would expand only in arithmetic progression (as in the series 2, 3, 4, 5, 6, and so on) because, even with technological innovations in agriculture, farmland is limited. Malthus's analysis led to a startling vision of a future in which population would outstrip our planet's resources, leading ultimately to catastrophic starvation.

But what of efforts to limit population growth? Malthus imagined two possibilities. First were *positive checks* to growth, such as famine, disease, and war. Second were *preventive checks*, including artificial birth control, sexual abstinence, and delayed marriages. The clergyman's religious principles precluded birth control, and his common sense told him people would not abstain from sex or marry later, unless they were facing imminent famine. His forecast ended on a decidedly pessimistic note, earning him the title of the "dismal parson."

*Critical evaluation.* Fortunately, Malthus's predictions were flawed in several ways. First, by the middle of the nineteenth century, the birth rate in Europe began to drop—partly because children were becoming less of an economic asset, and partly because people did embrace artificial birth control. Second, Malthus underestimated human ingenuity: advances in irrigation, fertilizers, and pesticides greatly increased the output of farmers, and industrial technology resulted in unforeseen increases in the production of other goods.

But Malthus was also criticized, not for his answers, but for asking the wrong questions. Karl Marx denounced Malthus for ignoring the role of social inequality as a cause of abundance or a source of famine. According to Marx (1967; orig. 1867), Malthus seemed to think that human suffering was a "law of nature," rather than a result of human mischief in the form of the capitalist economy.

Still, we should not entirely dismiss Malthus's dire prediction. First, daunting problems of population growth and limited resources remain. As Malthus suggested, habitable land, clean water, and unpolluted air are certainly finite. Moreover, technology is no miracle solution to our problems. As technology has boosted economic productivity, it has also created new and threatening problems, such as environmental pollution, described in Chapter 20 ("Health and Medicine"). Similarly, medical advances have lowered the death rate but, in so doing, have increased world population.

Second, the press of population growth and the gnawing effects of hunger are less evident to North Americans than to people in the Third World. The United States, after all, is among the richest nations of the world. In the poorest societies of Africa, Asia, and Latin America, rapid population growth is approaching the catastrophe Malthus envisioned. The 3 percent growth rate currently found in much of Africa, for example, will double that region's population before the year 2020. And, throughout the Third World, almost one-fifth of the world's people are already in jeopardy due to poverty.

Third, although there is no doubt that short-run population growth has been far less than that feared by Malthus, in the long run, as Paul Ehrlich (1978) points out, *no rate of increase can be sustained indefinitely.* For this reason, the entire world has a direct interest in planning and programs that will control our planet's population.

## Demographic Transition Theory

Malthus's rather crude analysis of population growth has been superseded by **demographic transition theory,** *the thesis that population patterns are linked to a society's level of technological development.*

This relationship is evident by comparing the three stages of technological development shown in Figure 21–4. Stage 1—preindustrial agrarian societies—have high birth rates because adults value children as a source of labor and because effective birth control does not exist. Death rates, too, are high, since a low standard of living and primitive medical technology promote deadly infectious diseases. Overall, high mortality neutralizes high fertility, yielding slow population growth, a trend that lasted for thousands of years before the Industrial Revolution began in eighteenth-century Europe.

Stage 2—the onset of industrialization—brings a demographic transition as population surges upward. This increase results from expanding food supplies and more effective controls on disease so that, while birth rates remain high, death rates fall sharply. Malthus developed his ideas in this context, which explains his pessimism about the future. Most Third-World societies today are in this high-growth stage.

**Figure 21–4** Demographic Transition Theory

In Stage 3—a fully industrialized economy—the birth rate drops, curbing population growth once again. This happens, first, because sophisticated technology makes effective birth control widely available. People embrace this technology because a higher standard of living makes children expensive to raise, effectively transforming them from economic assets to liabilities. Having fewer children also permits women more time to work outside the home. As birth rates begin to fall into line with low death rates, fertility and mortality are balanced and once again population growth is slow.

Western industrial societies have been in this third stage for much of this century. Recall, for example, that annual growth rates for populations in Europe and North America are now below 1 percent. A few poor societies, such as the People's Republic of China, have managed to hold population growth at about 2 percent through sweeping government programs. But, without industrial development, most Third-World societies appear to be locked in a spiral of dangerously high population growth.

*Critical evaluation.* Demographic transition theory suggests that technology holds the key to population growth. Instead of the runaway population increase Malthus feared, in other words, this analysis foresees limited population growth and material plenty as a result of technological development.

Demographic transition theory dovetails with modernization theory, one approach to global development detailed in Chapter 11 ("Global Inequality"). Modernization theorists take the optimistic view that the Third World will solve its population problem as poor societies gradually adopt industrial technology and raise their living standards. But critics—notably those who endorse dependency theory—argue that current global economic arrangements will only ensure the continued poverty of Third-World societies. Unless there is a significant redistribution of global resources, they claim, our planet will become increasingly divided into industrialized "haves" enjoying low population growth and nonindustrialized "have-nots" struggling in vain to feed soaring populations.

## World Population Today

Drawing on demographic transition theory, we can briefly highlight important differences in the demographic standing of industrial and developing societies.

### Industrial Societies

Soon after the Industrial Revolution began, annual population growth in Western Europe and North America peaked at about 3 percent. Then, as industrialization proceeded, it declined, and since 1970, annual growth has remained below 1 percent in the United States. Well within Stage 3 of demographic transition theory, rich nations appear close to the population replacement level of 2.1 births per woman, a point termed **zero population growth,** *the level of reproduction that maintains population at a steady state.* Several European societies have already shown a decrease in population, prompting some analysts to suggest that postindustrial societies may experience a fourth demographic stage, as populations actually decline (van de Kaa, 1987). Because the U.S. population is still relatively young—with a median age of thirty-three in 1990—population growth is expected to continue for at least several decades. But the "graying of the United States," discussed in Chapter 14 ("Aging and the Elderly"), partly reflects the smaller proportion of children to older people as well as the trend of people living longer.

Factors pushing fertility downward include the higher costs of raising children, the increasing proportion of women in the labor force, and the growing number of people choosing to marry at a later age or to remain childless. During the last generation, contraceptive use has increased to about two-thirds of women in the childbearing years. Similarly, voluntary sterilization has increased dramatically and is now the most common form of birth control in the United States. Even Catholics, whose religious doctrine prohibits artificial birth control, no longer differ from other Americans in their contraceptive practices (Westoff & Jones, 1977; Moore & Pachon,

1985). Abortion has been legal since 1973, and each year women terminate some 1.4 million pregnancies in this fashion (Centers for Disease Control, 1991). Poor families are still somewhat larger than average and, as noted in Chapter 10 ("Social Class in the United States"), the largest category of the U.S. poor is children. Overall, however, population growth in the United States and other industrial societies does not present the pressing problem that it does in poor societies.

### Less-Developed Societies

Today only disappearing hunting and gathering societies (see Chapter 4, "Society") are still within demographic transition theory's Stage 1. These isolated societies, until recently untouched by industrial technology, have high birth and death rates and, consequently, low population growth. Most world societies—in Latin America, Africa, and Asia—have predominantly agrarian economies with limited industrialization, placing them in Stage 2. Advanced medical technology supplied to these areas by industrial societies has sharply reduced death rates, but

The birthrate in Europe has dropped so low that some analysts foresee an absolute decline in population in this world region. In France, the government has turned to advertising to encourage people to have children. The ad implies children are becoming so rare that this baby can remark: "It appears that I am a sociocultural phenomenon." At the bottom right is added, "France needs children."

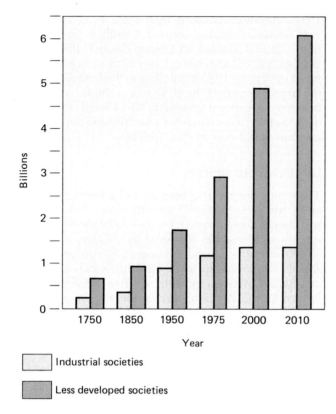

**Figure 21–5** Population Distribution, Industrial and Less-Developed Societies, 1750–2010

*(Piotrow, 1980; U.S. Bureau of the Census, 1991)*

birth rates remain high. Figure 21–5 shows the predictable result. These countries have experienced 80 percent of the world's population increase during this century, and they currently account for about two-thirds of the earth's people. Demographers predict that this percentage will increase to more than three-fourths when the global population exceeds 6 billion (U.S. Bureau of the Census, 1991).

Birth rates are high in the Third World today for the same reasons they were high everywhere for most of human history. In agrarian societies, children are vital economic assets, frequently working eight- or ten-hour days to contribute to their families' income. Parents also look to their offspring for economic support in old age. The economic value of children, coupled with high infant mortality, understandably encourages parents to have large families. Throughout the Third World, families average four or five children; in rural areas, the

number may reach six or even eight (The World Bank, 1991).

The social position of women also figures as a crucial factor in today's population picture. Agrarian societies are strongly patriarchal, defining women's primary responsibilities as bearing and raising children. In Latin America, a combination of economic need, traditional patriarchy, and Roman Catholic doctrine discourages many women from using birth control devices, with predictable demographic consequences. In much of Africa, many women in poor villages have never had the opportunity to use effective birth control (Salas, 1985). In some Asian countries, women have little access to effective contraception, although in others—notably India and China—governments have launched bold, even intrusive, programs to control fertility. The current situation in the People's Republic of China, the world's most populous society, is examined in the box.

There is a further connection between the social position of women and population growth. In short, if restricted to the traditional roles of child rearing and homemaking, women are likely to have many children. Similarly, men with economic and educational opportunities are more likely to define their masculinity in terms

Sex selection, the use of amniocentesis to determine the sex of a fetus leading to a decision to abort females, has become a popular practice in traditional, patriarchal societies of the world. This poster, by an organization in Bombay, India, reads "Once the woman becomes pregnant, after determination of the sex, everywhere there is murder of girls. Let's stop sex determination."

*(From "Sex Selection in India as a Bad Investment," an article by Les Levidow, in the premiere issue of* Science as Culture, *a quarterly published by Free Association Books in London. This poster was created by the Forum Against Sex Discrimination and Sex Pre-Selection Techniques in Bombay.)*

## Birth Control in China

P. R. China

Third-World governments have responded to rapid population growth with a variety of programs aimed at reducing fertility. The People's Republic of China has one-fifth of the world's people, with a population of 1.2 billion in 1990. Furthermore, more than half the Chinese people are under thirty, raising the specter of a baby boom without parallel in human history. As a result, since 1979, the Chinese government has pursued a tough policy limiting couples to a single child.

Local officials strongly encourage couples to delay childbirth and, once a child is born, to submit to sterilization or abort subsequent pregnancies. One-baby couples receive income bonuses, and single children are promised priority in school enrollment, health care, and, later, in employment and housing. In various ways, the government transmits a clear message: family planning is each couple's social responsibility. The results of this program have been significant, as the annual growth rate dropped from 2.0 percent in the 1960s to about 1.8 percent in the 1980s.

But like many government policies, this program spawned a number of unexpected problems. First, widespread sterilization during the early 1980s provoked international protest that China was forcing its people to undergo surgery. Second, the one-child policy has encouraged parents to abort female fetuses or even to kill female infants. Chinese cultural traditions confer on sons the duty of caring for elderly parents; daughters, by contrast, serve their husband's parents. Thus most Chinese couples shudder at the prospect of growing old without a son. A third problem is that privileges accorded to only children are now disproportionately enjoyed by sons, increasing sexual inequality in China.

By 1990, the government reacted to these strains with some leniency. Yet the price of unregulated growth appears higher: at the present rate of growth, the population will double by 2025, undermining the struggle of a vast society to raise its standard of living.

SOURCES: The World Bank (1984), Brophy (1989a, 1989b), and Tien (1989).

---

other than virility. Thus formal education and rewarding work hold the keys not only to a society's economic development, but to population control as well. Research suggests, to cite just two examples, that in Sudan (Africa) and Colombia (South America) women with seven years of schooling had half as many children as those with no schooling at all (Ross, 1985; Salas, 1985).

Efforts to control fertility have met with some success: in many Third-World countries, average family size fell by over 20 percent between 1975 and 1985 (Salas, 1985). This decline appears to be continuing, although perhaps at a slower rate. But the capacity to control population growth depends on reducing fertility sharply, since death rates are falling in most parts of the world.

In point of fact, population growth in the Third World is due *primarily* to declining death rates. After about 1920, when Europe and North America began to export advances in scientific medicine, nutrition, and sanitation to Third-World countries, mortality in these societies fell dramatically. Since that time, inoculations against infectious diseases and the use of antibiotics and insecticides have continued to curb death rates with stunning effectiveness. For example, in Sri Lanka, malaria caused half of all deaths in the mid-1930s; a decade later, the use of insecticide to kill malaria-carrying mosquitoes cut the death toll from this disease by 50 percent (Ehrlich, 1978). Although we hail such an achievement, over the long term this technological advance sent Sri Lanka's population soaring. Similarly, India's infant mortality rate fell from 130 in 1975 to 90 in 1990, but this decline helped boost that nation's population to more than 850 million.

In sum, although infant mortality and life expectancy in Third-World countries are still unfavorable when compared to richer nations, both have improved. More children throughout the world now survive to adulthood; however, they then proceed to have children of their own. This is why birth control programs are now vital in parts of the world where "death control" policies worked well several generations ago (Piotrow, 1980).

## The Importance of Demography

Demographic analysis sheds light on how and why the world is experiencing unprecedented population growth. Only through such study can humankind address this pressing problem.

But even if we grasp the causes and scope of the problem, controlling global population is a monumental task. As we have seen, the rate of population growth is currently greatest in the poorest societies of the world, those that lack the productive capacity to support their present populations, much less their future ones. Most of the privileged inhabitants of the First World are spared the trauma of poverty, and most of us recognize the consequences of adding almost 100 million people to our planet each year. Beyond the drain on food supplies, however, these millions need housing, education, and employment—all in tragically short supply. The well-being of the entire world may ultimately depend on resolving many of the economic and social problems of poor, overly populated countries and bridging the widening gulf between the "have" and "have-not" societies. Describing recent population growth as "a great wave," one official of the United States government concluded:

> I see the world population movement as the effort to construct a breakwater—a structure that will stop the wave and prevent it from engulfing and sweeping away centuries of human development and civilization. (cited in Gupte, 1984:323)

## Urbanization: The Growth of Cities

For most of human history, the small populations found around the world lived in nomadic groups, moving as they depleted vegetation or following migratory game. As civilization emerged in the Middle East some 8,000 years ago, widely scattered settlements were built for the first time, but these held only a small fraction of the earth's people. Today the largest single cities contain

as many people as the entire planet did then, and these cities will likely become even larger.

**Urbanization,** then, is *the concentration of humanity into cities.* Urbanization both redistributes population in a society, and it also transforms many patterns of social life. We will follow these changes in terms of three urban revolutions—the emergence of cities, the growth of industrial cities, and the explosive growth in Third-World cities—that are the focus of much of the rest of this chapter.

## The Evolution of Cities

In the long course of human history, cities are a recent development. After hundreds of thousands of years of evolutionary development, our ancestors grasped the idea of the city only about 10,000 years ago. Two factors set the stage for the *first urban revolution*: the emergence of permanent settlements.

One factor was the changing ecology: as glaciers began to melt at the end of the last ice age, people migrated toward warm regions with fertile soil. The second was changing technology: at about the same time, humans discovered how to raise animals and crops. Whereas hunting and gathering had required small bands of people to continually migrate, pastoralism and horticulture forced people to remain in one place and build permanent settlements (Lenski, Lenski, & Nolan, 1991). Domesticating animals and plants also generated a material surplus, which freed some people from the need to produce food in favor of activities like building shelters, making tools, weaving clothing, and leading religious rituals. In this context, the founding of cities stands as a truly revolutionary move; cities raised living standards significantly and enhanced productive specialization to a degree never seen before.

### The First Cities

Historians believe the first city was Jericho, a settlement to the north of the Dead Sea in disputed land currently occupied by Israel. About 8000 B.C.E., Jericho contained some 600 people (Kenyon, 1957; Hamblin, 1973; Spates & Macionis, 1987). By 4000 B.C.E., cities had become far more numerous, flourishing across the Fertile Crescent between the Tigris and Euphrates rivers in present-day Iraq and, soon afterward, along the Nile River in Egypt. Some settlements, with populations as high as 50,000, became centers of urban empires dominating

Early urban settlement in Latin America often took the form of ceremonial centers. Here is the massive Pyramid of the Sun at Teotihuacan, near Mexico City.

large regions. Priest-kings wielded absolute power over lesser nobility, administrators, artisans, soldiers, and farmers. Slaves, captured in frequent military campaigns, provided labor to build monumental structures like the pyramids of Egypt (Wenke, 1980; Stavrianos, 1983; Lenski, Lenski, & Nolan, 1991).

Cities originated independently in at least three other areas of the world. Several large, complex cities dotted the Indus River region of present-day Pakistan by about 2500 B.C.E. Scholars date Chinese cities from around 2000 B.C.E. In Central and South America, urban centers began somewhat later, about 1500 B.C.E. In North America, however, Native American societies rarely formed settlements; significant urbanization, therefore, did not begin until the arrival of European settlers in the sixteenth century (Lamberg-Karlovsky, 1973; Change, 1977; Coe & Diehl, 1980).

### Preindustrial Cities in Europe

Urbanization in Europe began about 1800 B.C.E. on the Mediterranean island of Crete. Spreading throughout Greece, the drive for urbanization gave rise to more than one hundred city-states, of which Athens is the most famous. During its Golden Age, lasting barely a century after 500 B.C.E., Athens exemplified the positive potential of urban life. The Athenians, numbering about 300,000 and living in an area of roughly one square mile, developed and advanced cultural elements still central to the Western way of life, including philosophy, the arts, the principles of democracy, and a mixture of physical and mental fitness symbolized by the Olympic games (Mumford, 1961; Carlton, 1977; Stavrianos, 1983). Yet for all its achievements, Athenian society depended on the labor of slaves, who made up nearly one-third of the population. And democratic principles notwithstanding, Athenian men denied the rights of citizenship to women and foreigners (Mumford, 1961; Gouldner, 1965).

As Greek civilization faded, the city of Rome grew to almost 1 million inhabitants and became the center of a vast empire. By the first century C.E., the militaristic Roman Empire encompassed much of northern Africa, Europe, and the Middle East. In the process, Rome widely diffused its language, arts, and technological innovations. After centuries of regional domination, the Roman Empire gradually fell into disarray by the fifth century C.E., a victim of its own gargantuan size, internal corruption, and militaristic appetite. In many respects, Athens and Rome were polar opposites, one moderate and learned, the other drawn to excess and militarism. Yet, between them, the Greeks and Romans founded cities all across Europe, including London, Paris, and Vienna.

The fall of the Roman Empire initiated an era of urban decline and stagnation that lasted some 600 years. Cities drew back within defensive walls, typically with no more than about 25,000 people. Competing warlords battled for territory, inhibiting trade and cultural exchange. About the eleventh century, the "dark ages" came to an end as a semblance of peace allowed economic activity to bring cities to life once again.

As trade increased, medieval cities slowly removed their walls, but they retained their narrow, winding, and usually filthy streets. As their economies expanded, London, Brussels, and Florence teemed with people from all walks of life: artisans, merchants, priests, peddlers, jugglers, nobles, and servants. Typically, different occupational groups such as bakers, keymakers, and carpenters lived in distinct sections or "quarters"; evidence of this practice remains today in the names of streets in many old cities. In the medieval cities of Europe, cathedrals towered above all other buildings, signifying the preeminence of Christianity.

By today's standards, medieval cities were surprisingly personal (Sjoberg, 1965). Family ties were strong, and the people inside each city "quarter" shared a trade and sometimes a religious and ethnic tradition. In some cases, this clustering was involuntary; religious and ethnic minorities were restricted by law to certain districts. For example, Jews were targets of extensive prejudice and discrimination in an era dominated by the Roman Catholic Church. Laws in Venice and later in most of Europe confined Jews to areas known as *ghettos*.

### Industrial-Capitalist Cities in Europe

Throughout the Middle Ages, commerce steadily increased, creating an affluent urban middle class or *bourgeoisie* (a French word meaning "of the town"). By the fifteenth century, the wealth-based power of the bourgeoisie rivaled the traditional dominance of the hereditary nobility. The expanding European colonization of much of the world further bolstered the might of the new trading class.

By about 1750 the trade-based economy of most cities was given an enormous boost as the Industrial Revolution got under way. In a short span of time, this tremendous economic expansion triggered a *second urban revolution* beginning in Europe and soon spreading to North America. Factories unleashed vast new productive power, drawing people to cities in unprecedented numbers. As Table 21–2 shows, during the nineteenth century the population of Paris soared from 500,000 to over 3 million, and London literally exploded from 800,000 to 6.5 million (A. Weber, 1963, orig. 1899; Chandler & Fox, 1974). Most of this increase was due to migration from rural areas by people seeking a better standard of living.

As industrialization proceeded, cities changed in more ways than just the size of their populations. Because business stood at its heart, the industrial-capitalist city evolved a typical urban form. The old, irregular alleys that marked the medieval city gave way to broad, straight streets that could accommodate the flow of ever-increasing commercial traffic, including motor vehicles. Steam and electric trolleys also criss-crossed the new cities, sometimes on the ground, sometimes above (the "elevated lines") and sometimes below (the "subways"). Cities also took on a patchwork character, as Lewis Mumford (1961) explains, because commercial interests dictated that land be divided into regular-sized lots that facilitated the real-estate industry. Finally, the cathedrals—icons of the medieval cities—were soon dwarfed by the epitome of industrial-capitalist living: the brightly lit, towering, and frantic central business district. In this center of the New City, corporate-owned skyscrapers proclaimed the power of the capitalist economy.

Industrialization also transformed urban social life.

**Table 21–2  POPULATION GROWTH IN SELECTED INDUSTRIAL CITIES OF EUROPE (IN THOUSANDS)**

| City | Year | | | |
|------|------|------|------|------|
| | 1700 | 1800 | 1900 | 1990* |
| Amsterdam | 172 | 201 | 510 | 725 |
| Berlin | 100 | 172 | 2,424 | 3,022 |
| Lisbon | 188 | 237 | 363 | 2,396 |
| London | 550 | 861 | 6,480 | 9,170 |
| Madrid | 110 | 169 | 539 | 4,451 |
| Paris | 530 | 547 | 3,330 | 8,709 |
| Rome | 149 | 153 | 487 | 3,021 |
| Vienna | 105 | 231 | 1,662 | 2,313 |

\* for urban area

SOURCE: Based on data from Tertius Chandler and Gerald Fox, *3000 Years of Urban History* (New York: Academic Press, 1974), pp. 17–19; and U.S. Bureau of the Census, *World Population Profile*, Washington, DC: U.S. Government Printing Office, 1991.

With increasing size and a focus on business rather than family ties, cities became impersonal; people could "walk lonely in the crowd." Crime rates rose. Inequality remained striking, with a handful of industrialists living in palatial splendor while most men, women, and children performed exhausting work in factories for bare subsistence.

Table 21–2 shows that European cities continued to grow into the twentieth century, although at a declining rate. As the frenetic pace of growth subsided, organized efforts by workers to improve their plight led to legal regulation of the workplace, better housing, and the right to vote. Early in this century, residents of virtually every city boasted of access to public services including water, sewerage, and electricity. While many city-dwellers, even today, remain in poverty, the city has partly fulfilled its historic promise—to provide a rising standard of living for most people.

## The Growth of U.S. Cities

Inhabiting this continent over tens of thousands of years, Native Americans were migratory people, establishing few permanent settlements. Cities first took root only after European colonization began. The Spanish made an initial settlement at St. Augustine, Florida, in 1565, and the English founded Jamestown, Virginia, in 1607.

New Amsterdam (later called New York) was established by the Dutch in 1624, and what began as a village soon overshadowed smaller settlements. In 1990, the United States contained 195 cities with a population of more than 100,000, and three-fourths of our people lived in cities that cover a scant one-sixth of the country's land area. This represents a remarkable transformation over the course of about 350 years; a brief overview of this process must begin in the colonial era.

## Colonial Settlement: 1624–1800

What we think of today as the metropolises of New York and Boston were, at their founding, tiny settlements in a vast wilderness. Dutch New Amsterdam at the tip of Manhattan Island (1624) and English Boston (1630) each resembled medieval towns of Europe, with narrow, winding streets that still delight pedestrians (and frustrate motorists) in lower Manhattan and downtown Boston. New Amsterdam was walled on its north side, the site of today's Wall Street. Boston, the largest colonial settlement, had a population of only 7,000 in 1700.

The rational and expansive culture of capitalism soon transformed these quiet villages into thriving towns with grid-like streets bustling with activity. Figure 21–6 contrasts the traditional shape of colonial New Amsterdam with the regular design of Philadelphia founded in 1680 after an additional half-century of economic development.

Even as the first settlements grew and the United States gained its independence from Great Britain, ours was still an overwhelmingly rural society. In 1790 the government's first census counted a national population of only 4 million, a scant 5 percent of whom lived in cities (see Table 21–3 on page 602). The vast majority of people lived on farms and in small villages scattered up and down the Eastern seaboard.

## Urban Expansion: 1800–1860

With the debut of the nineteenth century, towns began springing up from coast to coast, as transportation routes opened the American West. In 1818 the National Road (now Interstate-40) funneled migrants from Baltimore and the surrounding Middle-Atlantic region into the Ohio Valley. A decade later the Baltimore and Ohio Railroad transported even more people and products in less time. People pushed northward and westward from New York along the Erie Canal (1825) to the Great Lakes, sparking the development of cities along the way,

**Figure 21–6**   The Street Plans of Colonial New Amsterdam and Philadelphia
The plan of colonial New Amsterdam, shown at left, reflects the preindustrial urban pattern of walls enclosing a city of narrow, irregular streets. Colonial Philadelphia, founded fifty years later, reflects the industrial urban pattern of accessible cities containing wide, regularly spaced, parallel and perpendicular streets to facilitate economic activity.

**Table 21–3 THE URBAN POPULATION OF THE UNITED STATES, 1790–1990**

| Year | Population (millions) | Percent Urban |
|------|------|------|
| 1790 | 3.9 | 5.1 |
| 1800 | 5.3 | 6.1 |
| 1820 | 9.6 | 7.3 |
| 1840 | 17.1 | 10.5 |
| 1860 | 31.4 | 19.7 |
| 1880 | 50.2 | 28.1 |
| 1900 | 76.0 | 39.7 |
| 1920 | 105.7 | 51.3 |
| 1940 | 131.7 | 56.5 |
| 1960 | 179.3 | 69.9 |
| 1980 | 226.5 | 73.7 |
| 1990 | 253.0 | 75.2 |

SOURCE: U.S. Bureau of the Census.

including Albany, Syracuse, Buffalo, Cleveland, and Detroit. To understand the importance of water transportation during this period, just consider that virtually every one of the largest U.S. cities was founded on some sort of waterway.

By 1860 the proportion of city-dwellers in the United States had risen to one-third. To some, this increase constituted progress toward better living, but others mourned the gradual passing of traditional agrarian life.

It was at this point that rural-urban tensions grew especially pronounced, with adversaries trading negative stereotypes that pitted "ignorant country cousins" against "shady city slickers" (Callow, 1969).

Interestingly, the Industrial Revolution proceeded far more rapidly in the northern states than in the South, which experienced limited urbanization. By the time of the Civil War, New York City's population was ten times that of Charleston. Historians cite the tension between the industrial-urban North and the agrarian-rural South as one of the major causes of the Civil War (Schlesinger, 1969).

### The Metropolitan Era: 1860–1950

The Civil War gave an enormous boost to industrialization, as factories strained to produce the instruments of combat. But even after the guns fell silent, factories roared ahead, drawing millions of rural people to the cities in search of better jobs. To their numbers were added a huge wave of immigrants: tens of millions of men and women—most from Europe—were blending their various ways of life into the dynamic new urban mix. Table 21–4 shows the rapid growth of U.S. cities in the late nineteenth century.

As the Industrial Revolution reached its full stride, cities teemed with unprecedented numbers of people. In 1900 New York boasted 4 million residents, and Chicago—a city of scarcely 100,000 people in 1860—was

**Table 21–4 POPULATION GROWTH IN SELECTED U.S. CITIES, 1870–1990**

| City | Population (in thousands) | | | | | | |
|------|------|------|------|------|------|------|------|
| | 1870 | 1890 | 1910 | 1930 | 1950 | 1970 | 1990 |
| Baltimore | 267 | 434 | 558 | 805 | 950 | 905 | 736 |
| Boston | 251 | 448 | 671 | 781 | 801 | 641 | 574 |
| Chicago | 299 | 1,100 | 2,185 | 3,376 | 3,621 | 3,369 | 2,784 |
| Dallas | 7 | 38 | 92 | 260 | 434 | 844 | 1,007 |
| Detroit | 80 | 206 | 466 | 1,569 | 1,850 | 1,514 | 1,028 |
| Los Angeles | 6 | 50 | 319 | 1,238 | 1,970 | 2,812 | 3,485 |
| Milwaukee | 71 | 204 | 374 | 578 | 637 | 717 | 628 |
| New Orleans | 191 | 242 | 339 | 459 | 570 | 593 | 497 |
| New York* | 942 | 2,507 | 4,767 | 6,930 | 7,892 | 7,896 | 7,323 |
| Philadelphia | 674 | 1,047 | 1,549 | 1,951 | 2,072 | 1,949 | 1,586 |
| St. Louis | 311 | 452 | 687 | 822 | 857 | 622 | 397 |
| San Francisco | 149 | 299 | 417 | 634 | 775 | 716 | 724 |

* Population figures for New York in 1870 and 1890 reflect that city as presently constituted.

SOURCE: U.S. Bureau of the Census.

closing in on 2 million. This dizzying growth marked the coming of the **metropolis**, *a large city that socially and economically dominates the surrounding area*. Dozens of metropolises became the manufacturing, commercial, and residential centers of the United States.

As their populations grew, the physical shape of the metropolis continued to change as well. In 1850, few buildings could be found that exceeded three or four stories. By the 1880s, industrial technology was producing steel girders and mechanical elevators so that builders were raising structures ten stories above the ground. And this, of course, was only the beginning. By 1930, New York's Empire State Building was hailed as an urban wonder, a true "skyscraper" stretching 102 stories into the clouds. Then, too, railroads and highways enabled cities to expand outward so that, by the end of World War I, the United States reached a milestone as a majority of the population lived in cities. The rural-urban controversy that had simmered throughout the nineteenth century had ended: the United States had become, and would remain, an urban society.

### Urban Decentralization: 1950-Present

The industrial metropolis reached its peak about 1950. Since then, something of a turnaround has occurred as people have deserted the downtowns in a process known as *urban decentralization* (Edmonston & Guterbock, 1984). Another look at Table 21–4 shows that the largest central cities of the Northeast and Midwest stopped growing or actually lost population in the decades after 1950. For example, the 1990 census count found New York to have half a million fewer people than at mid-century.

But decentralization has not brought an end to urbanization. On the contrary, cities are once again evolving into a different form. Instead of densely populated central cities, our urban landscape now looks more and more like vast urban regions, a trend that is closely tied to the expansion of suburbs.

## Suburbs and Central Cities

Just as central cities flourished a century ago, we have recently witnessed the expansion of **suburbs**, *urban areas beyond the political boundaries of a city*. Suburbs began to grow rapidly late in the nineteenth century as railroad and trolley lines enabled people to live beyond the commotion of the city while still being able to commute to

work "downtown" (Warner, 1962). The first suburbanites were the well-to-do people imitating the pattern of the European nobility who alternated between their country estates and town houses (Baltzell, 1979). But the growth of suburbs was also fueled by racial and ethnic intolerance: rising immigration was adding to the social diversity of central cities, prompting many people to flee to homogeneous, high-prestige enclaves beyond the reach of the masses. In time, of course, less wealthy people also came to view a single-family house on its own piece of leafy suburban ground as part of the American Dream.

The economic boom of the late 1940s, coupled to the mobility provided by increasingly affordable automobiles, made this dream come true for more and more people. After World War II, men and women eagerly returned to family life, igniting the baby boom described earlier in this chapter. Since central cities offered little space for new housing construction, suburbs blossomed almost overnight. The government weighed in with economic assistance in the form of guaranteed bank loans, which further encouraged the purchase of suburban homes.

Some of the most successful postwar suburbs were designed for moderate-income people. Levittown, built on potato fields of New York's Long Island in the late 1940s, inaugurated a trend toward inexpensive suburban housing (Wattel, 1958). What some dismissed as prefabricated, cookie-cutter houses were nonetheless purchased by eager families just as fast as they were built. By 1970 more of the U.S. population lived in the suburbs than remained in central cities.

As population decentralized, businesses also began to migrate to the suburbs. Older people today can recall trips "downtown" to shop but, by 1970, the suburban mall had replaced "main street" as the center of retail trade (Rosenthal, 1974; Tobin, 1976; Geist, 1985). Manufacturing interests, too, began to eye the suburbs where there was relief from high taxes, soaring crime rates, and traffic congestion. The postwar interstate highway system with its beltways encircling central cities made the move to new industrial parks all but irresistible.

Decentralization was not good news for everyone, however. Rapid suburban growth soon threw older cities of the Northeast and Midwest into financial chaos. Population decline meant reduced tax revenues. Further, cities lost their more affluent residents to the suburbs and were left to provide expensive social programs for the poor who remained. The predictable result was inner-city decay after 1950 (Gluck & Meister, 1979; Sternlieb & Hughes, 1983). Some major cities, such as Cleveland

and New York, actually plummetted to the edge of financial bankruptcy. Especially to whites, deteriorating inner cities were places to leave, synonymous with low-quality housing, crime, drugs, unemployment, the poor, and minorities. This perception fed on itself, fueling wave after wave of "white flight" and urban decline. Suburbs may have their share of poor housing, congestion, and crime, but they still appeal to many people because they have remained largely white while the inner-city population contains a greater share of people of color (Clark, 1979; Logan & Schneider, 1984; Stahura, 1986; Galster, 1991).

The official response to the plight of the central cities was **urban renewal,** *government programs intended to revitalize cities.* Federal and local funds have paid for the rebuilding of many inner cities. Yet critics of urban renewal programs charge that they have benefitted business communities while doing little to meet the housing needs of low-income residents (Jacobs, 1961; Greer, 1965; Gans, 1982).

## Postindustrial Sunbelt Cities

Along with the new postindustrial economy (see Chapter 19, "The Economy and Work"), people are not only spilling beyond the boundaries of central cities, they are also migrating from the Snowbelt to the Sunbelt. The Snowbelt—the traditional industrial heartland of the United States—includes the Northeast and Midwest, and contained almost 60 percent of the population in 1940. By 1975, however, the Sunbelt—the South and the West—passed the Snowbelt in overall population; by 1990, the Sunbelt was home to 55.6 percent of the population.

This demographic shift is shown in Table 21–5, which compares the ten largest cities in the United States in 1950 and in 1990. In 1950, eight of the ten largest U.S. cities were industrial cities of the Snowbelt; in 1990, by contrast, six of the top ten were postindustrial cities of the Sunbelt. The box provides a snapshot of how our country's urban profile changed during the 1980s.

Why are Sunbelt cities faring so well? Unlike their counterparts in the Snowbelt, they are postindustrial cities that grew *after* urban decentralization began. Since suburbs take the form of a politically independent ring enclosing the Snowbelt cities, outward migration drew people out of central cities. Newer Sunbelt cities, by

**Table 21–5   THE TEN LARGEST CITIES IN THE UNITED STATES, 1950 AND 1990**

| 1950 | | |
|---|---|---|
| Rank | City | Population |
| 1 | New York | 7,892,000 |
| 2 | Chicago | 3,621,000 |
| 3 | Philadelphia | 2,072,000 |
| 4 | Los Angeles | 1,970,000 |
| 5 | Detroit | 1,850,000 |
| 6 | Baltimore | 950,000 |
| 7 | Cleveland | 915,000 |
| 8 | St. Louis | 857,000 |
| 9 | Boston | 801,000 |
| 10 | San Francisco | 775,000 |

| 1990 | | |
|---|---|---|
| Rank | City | Population |
| 1 | New York | 7,323,000 |
| 2 | Los Angeles | 3,485,000 |
| 3 | Chicago | 2,784,000 |
| 4 | Houston | 1,631,000 |
| 5 | Philadelphia | 1,586,000 |
| 6 | San Diego | 1,111,000 |
| 7 | Detroit | 1,028,000 |
| 8 | Dallas | 1,007,000 |
| 9 | Phoenix | 983,000 |
| 10 | San Antonio | 936,000 |

SOURCE:   U.S. Bureau of the Census.

contrast, are not locked in by suburbs, so these cities have simply expanded outward, gaining population in the process. Chicago, for example, covers 228 square miles, whereas Houston is now over 556. Through physical expansion, Sunbelt cities have retained population even as people move outward from the city's center, added new population as surrounding towns are enveloped, and enlarged their tax base to gain financial strength.

The great sprawl of the typical Sunbelt city does have drawbacks, however. Traveling across town is time-consuming, and automobile ownership is almost a necessity. Lacking a dense center, Sunbelt cities also generate far less of the excitement and intensity that draws people to New York or Chicago. Critics have long tagged Los Angeles, for example, as a vast cluster of suburbs in search of a center.

# The Burgeoning Sunbelt Cities

Just as the twentieth century opened with tremendous urban growth in the North and Midwest, the twenty-first century will almost surely begin with rapid urban growth in the South and West. The official count from the 1990 census indicates that, taken as a whole, Snowbelt cities suffered a moderate drop in population, while population is soaring in the Sunbelt.

The figure provides a comparison across the 1980s for a dozen large U.S. cities: the six more populous Snowbelt cities and the six largest in the Sunbelt. As the figure shows, two of the six most populous Snowbelt cities posted slight increases in population, while the remaining four recorded substantial declines. The population in each of these six cities has decreased substantially since 1950, the point at which Snowbelt cities reached their peak population.

The picture is very different if we turn to the cities of the Sunbelt, where population has been growing rapidly since mid-century. All six of the largest Sunbelt cities registered population gains during the 1980s—even Houston and Dallas, which were hard hit by the economic downturn. The population growth in the other four is dramatic—similar to the explosive increases found in the Snowbelt a century ago.

Which cities—regardless of

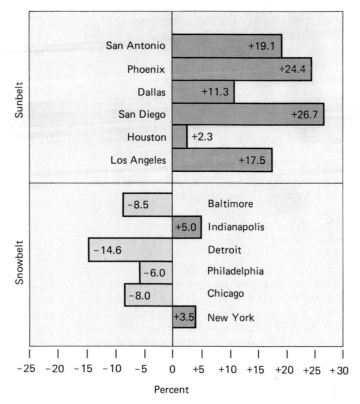

Percent Population Change, 1980–1990, for the Six Largest Snowbelt and Sunbelt Cities
SOURCE: U.S. Bureau of the Census.

population—grew fastest of all during the 1980s? Across the United States, Mesa, Arizona led the way with an 89 percent gain (to 288,000). Nine other cities had population increases of over 60 percent during the 1980s—every one in the Sunbelt.

## Megalopolis: Regional Cities

The decentralization of U.S. cities has produced large urban areas—regional cities—that contain numerous municipalities. In 1990 the Bureau of the Census (1991) recognized 284 heavily urbanized regions in the United States, which they call *metropolitan statistical areas* (MSAs). Each MSA contains at least one city with 50,000 or more people plus densely populated surrounding counties. Almost all of the fifty fastest-growing MSAs are located in the Sunbelt.

The biggest MSAs, containing more than 1 million people, are called *consolidated metropolitan statistical areas* (CMSAs). In 1990, there were twenty CMSAs. Heading the list was New York and adjacent urban areas in Long Island, western Connecticut, and northern New Jersey, with a total population of some 18 million. Next in size was the CMSA in Southern California that includes Los Angeles, Riverside, and Anaheim, with a population of almost 15 million (U.S. Bureau of the Census, 1991).

Some urban regions have grown so large that they have now collided with one another. For example, the CMSA centered around New York City is the centerpiece of a 400-mile long supercity extending from New England to Virginia. Witnessing such developments, French geographer Jean Gottmann (1961) first used the term **megalopolis** to designate *a vast urban region containing a number of cities and their surrounding suburbs*. A megalopolis is composed of hundreds of politically independent cities and suburbs; from an airplane at night, however, it looks like one continuous city. Other supercities of this kind are the eastern coast of Florida, much of Southern California, and an urban corridor extending from Cleveland to Chicago. Future urban regions will undoubtedly emerge, especially in the Sunbelt, where urban growth in the United States is currently the greatest.

# Understanding Cities: Theory and Method

Having sketched out the historical development of cities, we turn to various theoretical insights and research observations about city life. In short, what differences does urbanization bring to social life?

## European Theory: Urban Life Versus Rural Life

Various European sociologists were among the first to contrast urban and rural life. We will briefly introduce the contributions of two German sociologists, Ferdinand Toennies and Georg Simmel.

### Ferdinand Toennies: *Gemeinschaft* and *Gesellschaft*

In the late nineteenth century, when his society was awash in rapid change, the German sociologist Ferdinand Toennies (1855–1936) set out to chronicle the social traits emerging in the industrial metropolis (1963; orig. 1887). He contrasted rural and urban life using two concepts that have become an established part of sociology's terminology.

Toennies used the term **Gemeinschaft** (a German word roughly meaning "community") to refer to *a type of social organization in which people are bound closely together by kinship and tradition*. Rural villagers, Toennies explained, sustain enduring ties of kinship, neighborhood, and friendship. *Gemeinschaft*, then, describes any social setting in which people form what amounts to a single primary group. *Gemeinschaft* is essentially synonymous with Emile Durkheim's *mechanical solidarity*, discussed in Chapter 4 ("Society").

By and large, argued Toennies, *Gemeinschaft* is rarely found in the industrial city. On the contrary, urbanization enhances **Gesellschaft** (this German word roughly means "association"), which is *a type of social organization in which people typically have weak social ties and a great deal of self-interest*. As part of *Gesellschaft*, women and men are motivated by their own needs and desires rather than a desire to advance the well-being of everyone. City dwellers, Toennies suggested, have little sense of community and therefore look at others merely as the means of achieving their individual goals. *Gesellschaft* finds its parallel in Durkheim's concept of *organic solidarity*.

In short, then, to Toennies urbanization is the steady march from *Gemeinschaft* to *Gesellschaft*: the erosion of kinship and tightly integrated neighborhoods as society shifts to allow for greater cultural diversity, tolerance, and self-interest (cf. Wilson, 1991). Further, Toennies explained, *Gesellschaft* provides the social climate—the temporary and impersonal ties—characteristic of a society centered on economic pursuits. Thus Toennies took a basically negative view of modern, urban society—

Marc Chagall's painting *I and the Village* (1911) conveys the essential unity of rural life forged by tradition and common work on the land. By contrast, in his painting *The City* (1919), Ferdinand Léger communicates the disparate images and discontinuity of experience that are commonplace in urban areas. Taken together, these two paintings capture Toennies's distinction between *Gemeinschaft* and *Gesellschaft*.

(Marc Chagall, I and the Village. 1911. Oil on canvas. 63⅝ × 59⅝". Collection, The Museum of Modern Art, New York. Mrs. Simon Guggenheim Fund; Fernand Léger, The City. 1919. 91 × 117½. The Philadelphia Museum of Art [The A. E. Gallatin Collection.])

more so than Durkheim who, you will recall, saw in the urban world the benefits of expanding freedom and personal privacy.

### Georg Simmel: The Blasé Urbanite

We have already encountered the ideas of Georg Simmel in our discussion of how size affects the social dynamics of small groups (see Chapter 7, "Groups and Organizations"). Simmel also turned his characteristically micro-level focus to the question of how urban life shaped people's behavior and attitudes (1964; orig. 1905).

From the point of view of the individual, Simmel explained, the city is a crush of people, objects, and events. Understandably, he continued, the urbanite is easily overwhelmed with stimulation. Consequently, city people typically develop what Simmel termed a *blasé attitude*, as they learn to respond selectively to their surroundings. That is, they tune out much of what goes on around them in order to focus attention on what

seems to be important. City dwellers are not without sensitivity and compassion for others, although they sometimes may seem "cold and heartless." But urban detachment, as Simmel saw it, is better understood as a strategy for social survival by which people have to hold themselves aloof from much of their surroundings if they are to have the time and energy to engage those who really matter.

## U.S. Research: Observing the City

Sociologists in the United States soon joined their European colleagues in exploring the rapidly growing cities. The first major sociology program in the United States took root at the University of Chicago. In the late nineteenth century, Chicago was a major metropolis bursting with population and cultural diversity. Chicago's social life was the focus for generations of sociologists, and these researchers produced a rich understanding of many dimensions of urban life. Thus, while these early sociologists were inspired by the ideas of theorists like Toennies and Simmel, their unique contribution was in making the city a laboratory for actual research.

Perhaps the greatest urban sociologist of all was Robert Park, who for decades provided the leadership that established sociology as a respected academic discipline in the United States. Park is introduced in the box.

### Louis Wirth: Urbanism as a Way of Life

A second major figure in the Chicago School of urban sociology was Louis Wirth (1897–1952). Wirth's (1938) best-known contribution is a brief essay in which he systematically organized the ideas of Toennies, Simmel, Park, and others into a comprehensive theory of urban life.

Wirth began by identifying three factors that define urbanism: large population, dense settlement, and social diversity. These essential traits, he argued, make urban life impersonal, superficial, and transitory. Living among millions of others, urbanites have contact with many more people than rural residents do. Thus if city residents notice others at all, they know them in terms of *what they do*: as the school bus driver, the florist, or the clerk in the grocery store. Just as urban social relationships are highly specialized, Wirth continued, they are also an expression of self-interest. For example, shoppers see grocers as a source of food while grocers view shoppers as a source of income. These men and women may pleasantly exchange greetings, but they are both aware that friendship is not the reason for their interaction.

Limited interpersonal involvement, coupled with great social diversity, also make city dwellers more tolerant than rural villagers. Rural communities often jealously maintain their narrow traditions, but the heterogeneous population of a city rarely imposes a code of moral values on local residents (Wilson, 1985). Thus, concluded Wirth, cities operate like social "melting-pots."

Wirth's vision of the city belies a mixed view of urban living. While he acknowledged the freedom and privacy of urban living (echoing Durkheim and Park), he also saw in the anonymous rush of city life the loss of personal ties and the erosion of traditional morality (here, recalling Toennies). In sum, people find new excitement and opportunities in the city, but many important interpersonal connections are lost.

*Critical evaluation.* Both in Europe and the United States, early sociologists concentrated their research efforts on the city. After decades of additional research, however, we are in a better position to assess their conclusions.

Are cities distinctive? Yes, but probably not to the extent that some of the urban pioneers claimed. By and large, urban settings do have a weaker sense of community than do rural areas, but we can easily underestimate the strength of urban social ties just as we can exaggerate the social cohesion of rural life. While urbanites do treat most people impersonally, they also have a smaller number of close personal relationships. Further, the public anonymity of cities may mean that some people are lonely and aloof, but the majority remain well integrated with others and welcome the public privacy that cities afford (Keller, 1968; Cox, 1971; Macionis, 1978; Wellman, 1979; Lee et al., 1984). In addition, we need to remind ourselves that conflict has long characterized life in the countryside as well as the city.

On another level, we can now see that pioneering sociologists fell victim to another distortion: implying that urbanism neutralizes the effects of class, race, and ethnicity. Herbert Gans (1968) responded to Wirth's notion that urbanism is a single, general way of life by pointing out that there are many brands of urbanites: rich and poor, white and black, Anglo and Hispanic, women and men—all such categories are distinctive in the lives their members lead in cities. In fact, cities often intensify social differences. That is, we see the extent of social inequality and striking cultural diversity more clearly in cities—where categories of people have the greatest "critical mass"—than anywhere else (Spates & Macionis, 1987).

## Urban Ecology

Research into the social correlates of urbanism also extends to **urban ecology**, *the study of the link between the physical and social dimensions of cities.* Chapter 3 ("Culture") spotlighted cultural ecology, the investigation of how cultural patterns are related to the physical environment. Urban ecology is one application of this approach; it points up that cities are both physical and social realities and that these two facets of urbanism dovetail in many ways.

Consider, for example, why cities are located where they are. The first cities that accompanied the emergence of agriculture were established in fertile regions. Preindustrial societies concerned with defense built their cities on mountains or in other ways took advantage of the natural environment for self-protection. Athens is situ-

# Robert Ezra Park (1864–1944)

I suspect that I have actually covered more ground, tramping about in cities in different parts of the world, than any other living man. (1950:viii)

Robert Ezra Park was a man with a single consuming passion—the city. On the streets of the great cities of the world, he found the full range of human triumph and troubles. Through his thirty-year career at the University of Chicago, he led a group of dedicated sociologists in the direct, systematic observation of urban life.

Park acknowledged his debt to European sociologists such as Ferdinand Toennies and Georg Simmel (with whom Park studied in Germany). But Park created a new dimension in urban sociology by advocating the *direct observation* of the city rather than what he considered the armchair theorizing of the Europeans. At Park's urging, generations of sociologists at the University of Chicago rummaged through practically every corner of their city.

From this research, Park came to understand the city as a highly ordered mosaic of distinctive regions, including ethnic communities, vice areas, and industrial districts. These so-called "natural areas" all evolved in relation to one another over time. To Park, the city was a living social organism: truly the human kaleidoscope. This stunning variety of human experience, Park maintained, is the key to people's timeless attraction to cities:

The attraction of the metropolis is due in part to the fact that in the long run every individual finds somewhere among the varied manifestations of city life the sort of environment in which he expands and feels at ease; he finds, in short, the moral climate in which his particular nature obtains the stimulations that bring his innate dispositions to full and free expression. It is, I suspect, motives of this kind . . . which drove many, if not most, of the young men and young women from the security of their homes in the country into the big, booming confusion and excitement of city life. (1967:41; orig. 1925)

Park was well aware that many people saw the city as disorganized and even dangerous. Park recognized the element of truth in these concerns but, still, he found cities fascinating. So enamored was he that he devoted much of his life to exploring cities throughout the world. He firmly believed that urban places offered a better way of life—the promise of greater human freedom and opportunity—than could be found anywhere else.

SOURCES: Based on Park (1967; orig. 1925) and Park (1950).

---

ated on an outcropping of rock; Paris and Mexico City are centered on islands. After the Industrial Revolution, the unparalleled importance of economics situated cities near rivers and natural harbors that facilitated trade.

Urban ecologists also study the physical design of cities. They have developed several models explaining urban form.

***The concentric zone model.*** In 1925 Ernest W. Burgess, a student and colleague of Robert Park, visualized land use in Chicago and several other U.S. cities as a series of concentric zones rather like a bulls-eye. At the center of the city, Burgess observed, is a central business district, surrounded by a ring of factories. Beyond this commercial zone lie a succession of residential rings with housing that is more and more expensive the farther it stands from the noise and pollution of the city's center.

***The sector model.*** Investigating a greater number of cities, Homer Hoyt (1939) expanded the scope of Burgess's research. Hoyt concluded that distinctive districts often form wedge-shaped sectors. For example, a particularly fashionable area may be built along a finger of high ground. In San Francisco, wealthy residents of Nob Hill enjoy breathtaking views of the San Francisco

Bay. Similarly, industrial development in many cities extends outward along railroad lines or following the twists and turns of a river. In this way, Hoyt observed, specialized districts of a city grow in wedge-shaped sectors.

***The multiple-nuclei model.***   Chauncy Harris and Edward Ullman (1945) made an additional contribution to the urban ecology literature as they documented the onset of urban decentralization. As population spreads outward, they concluded, cities lose their single-center form in favor of a multiple-nuclei model, with many centers of business and manufacturing.

Looking closely at this process, Harris and Ullman identified two major reasons that specific endeavors spread out across a city. First, some activities may be antagonistic to others. Few people wish to live in the shadow of industrial areas, for example, and owners of fashionable retail shops want to distance themselves from pornography and vice areas such as Boston's Combat Zone. Thus the complexity and diversity of urban life yields a mosaic of distinctive districts. Second, economics also comes into play here. Industry usually prefers outlying industrial parks, where land is readily available and cheap, to the older, congested inner cities. People, too, are drawn to lower-cost land in the suburbs and, eventually, retail businesses follow them, giving rise to shopping malls miles from downtown. As a result, cities now have many distinctive centers of activity.

***Social area analysis.***   Social area analysis adds a new twist to urban ecology by investigating what people in specific neighborhoods have in common. Research in industrial cities in the United States and elsewhere has focused on three factors that explain a great deal about where people end up living: *family type*, reflecting marital status and family size; *social standing*, based on income and prestige; and *race and ethnicity* (Shevky & Bell, 1955; Johnston, 1976).

Researchers have concluded that families with children gravitate to areas offering large apartments or single-family homes and good schools. The rich generally seek high-prestige neighborhoods away from low-income people—sometimes in the suburbs, and often in exclusive central-city areas. People with a common cultural heritage tend to cluster together. The poor and some minorities, whose choices are limited, also live in distinct areas.

***An integrated analysis.***   Each of the models we have described provides a partial understanding of urban land use. Attempting to integrate them all, Brian Berry and Philip Rees (1969) argue that each factor plays a part

in shaping the city. In accordance with Burgess's theory, distinctive types of families disperse population in concentric zones, at least assuming there are no other influences. Families with few children tend toward the city's center, while those with more children live farther away. Differences of social standing generate the sector-shaped districts described by Hoyt; that is, the rich often occupy one "side of the tracks," while the poor inhabit the other. Racial and ethnic groups cluster together at various points throughout the city, in support of Harris and Ullman's multiple-nuclei model and the findings of social area analysis.

***Critical evaluation.***   After almost a century of research, urban ecologists have succeeded in linking the physical and social dimensions of urban life. But as ecologists themselves concede, their conclusions paint a very idealized picture of city life. Critics chime in that urban ecology errs by implying that cities take shape simply due to the choices people make; more accurately, from their point of view, urban development is guided by power elites rather than by "average" people (Molotch, 1976; Feagin, 1983). Another problem is that urban ecologists studied U.S. cities during a single historical period. What they have learned about industrializing cities has limited value for understanding preindustrial towns; similarly, even among industrial cities, socialist settlements are quite unlike their capitalist counterparts. Taken together, such concerns offer good reason to doubt that any single ecological model will account for the full range of urban diversity.

## Third-World Urbanization

Twice in human history the world has experienced a revolutionary expansion of cities. The first urban revolution began about 8000 B.C.E. when the first cities emerged, and this change spanned thousands of years as urban settlements sprang up on the various continents. The second urban revolution began about 1750 and lasted for two centuries as the Industrial Revolution sparked the rapid growth of cities in Europe and North America.

A third urban revolution was under way by 1950, but this time the change is not occurring in the industrial societies of the world where, as shown in Global Map 21–2, 75 percent of people already are city dwellers. Extraordinary urban growth is now taking place in the Third World, where, in 1950, only 25 percent of people

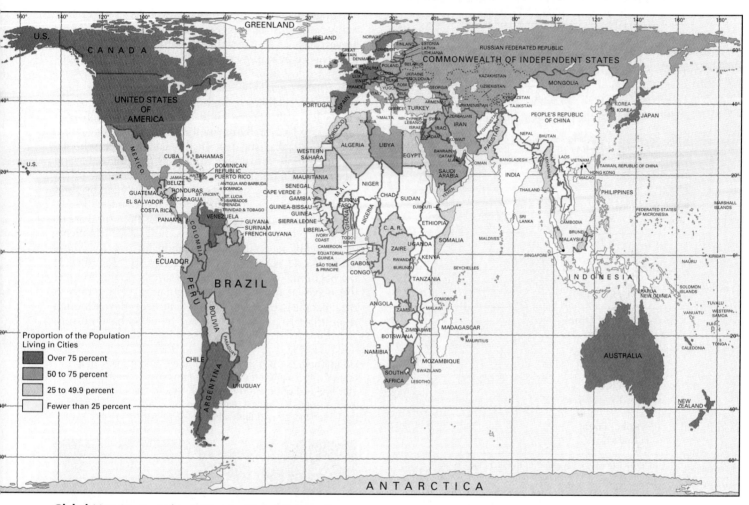

**Global Map 21–2**  Urbanization in Global Perspective

Urbanization is closely linked to economic development. Thus First-World nations—including the United States and Canada—have more than three-fourths of their populations in cities, while in the poorest countries of the Third World—found in Africa and Asia—fewer than one-fourth of the people live in urban centers. Urbanization is now extremely rapid in the Third World, however, with emerging "supercities" of unprecedented size.

lived in cities. Since then, about 40 percent of the Third-World population has clustered in cities; by 2000, half are expected to be urbanites. Put in other words, in 1950, only seven cities in the world had populations of over 5 million, and only two of these were in the Third World. By 1985, twenty-six cities had more than 5 million residents, and eighteen were in the Third World

(Fornos, 1986). By the end of this century, some Third-World cities will literally dwarf all but a few of the cities in industrialized societies.

Table 21–6 on page 612 looks a decade back and a decade ahead, comparing the size of the world's ten largest urban areas in 1980 and giving population estimates for 2000. In 1980, six of the top ten were in

Chapter 21  Population and Urbanization      611

**Table 21–6** THE WORLD'S TEN LARGEST URBAN AREAS, 1980 AND 2000

### 1980

| Urban Area | Population (in millions) |
|---|---|
| New York, U.S.A. | 16.5 |
| Tokyo–Yokohama, Japan | 14.4 |
| Mexico City, Mexico | 14.0 |
| Los Angeles–Long Beach, U.S.A. | 10.6 |
| Shanghai, China | 10.0 |
| Buenos Aires, Argentina | 9.7 |
| Paris, France | 8.5 |
| Moscow, U.S.S.R. | 8.0 |
| Beijing, China | 8.0 |
| Chicago, U.S.A. | 7.7 |

### 2000 (projected)

| Urban Area | Population (in millions) |
|---|---|
| Tokyo–Yokohama, Japan | 30.0 |
| Mexico City, Mexico | 27.9 |
| São Paulo, Brazil | 25.4 |
| Seoul, South Korea | 22.0 |
| Bombay, India | 15.4 |
| New York, U.S.A. | 14.7 |
| Osaka-Kobe-Kyoto, Japan | 14.3 |
| Tehran, Iran | 14.3 |
| Rio de Janeiro, Brazil | 14.2 |
| Calcutta, India | 14.1 |

SOURCES: United Nations and U.S. Bureau of the Census.

industrial societies, three of these in the United States. By the beginning of the next century, however, only four of the top ten will be situated in industrial nations: two in Japan, one in South Korea, and only one in the United States. Most will be in less economically developed societies of the Third World. These urban areas not only will be the world's largest, they will contain unprecedented populations. Relatively rich societies like Japan may have the resources to provide for urban settlements approaching 30 million people, but for poor societies, such as Mexico and Brazil, huge populations concentrated in limited areas will strain already overburdened services.

## Causes of Third-World Urban Growth

To understand the third urban revolution, recall that many nonindustrial societies are now entering the high-growth stage of demographic transition. Declining death rates caused by improved technology have fueled a population explosion in Latin America, Africa, and Asia. For urban areas, the rate of growth is *twice* as high because, in addition to high birth rates, millions of migrants leave the countryside each year in search of a better standard of living in the city. The urban areas offer more jobs, superior health care, better schools, and even basic conveniences such as running water and electricity. Political events have also intensified urban migration; in many societies, the seizure of land by elites has forced peasants to migrate to cities (London, 1987).

Cities do offer more opportunities than rural areas, but they provide no panacea for the massive problems generated by an escalating population and poverty. Many Third-World cities, such as Mexico City, described at the beginning of this chapter, are simply unable to meet the needs of much of their population. Thousands of rural people stream into Mexico City every day, although more than 10 percent of *current* residents have no run-

Hong Kong, the British colony on the Chinese mainland, is scarcely 400 square miles but contains some 6 million people. This yields a population density of 14,000 people per square mile, among the highest densities in the world. The comparable figure for the United States is 69.

ning water in their homes, 15 percent lack sewerage facilities, and half the trash and garbage produced each day cannot be processed. To make matters worse, exhaust from factories and cars chokes everyone, rich and poor alike (Friedrich, 1984). Like other major cities throughout Latin America, Africa, and Asia, Mexico City is surrounded by wretched shantytowns—settlements of makeshift homes built from discarded materials. As explained in Chapter 11 ("Global Inequality"), even city dumps are home to thousands of poor people, who pick through the waste hoping to find enough food and fuel to ensure their survival for another day.

### The Future of Third-World Cities

The problems now facing Third-World cities seem to defy solution, and the end of this remarkable urban growth is nowhere in sight. What hope is there of relieving the plight of people in these emerging megacities?

Earlier chapters have suggested two different answers to this question. One view, linked with modernization theory, holds that as the Third World undergoes industrialization (as Western Europe and North America did two centuries ago), greater productivity will push living standards upward and ease population growth. A second view, associated with dependency theory, dismisses such progress as illusory as long as Third-World societies remain economically dependent on rich societies.

Urbanist Jane Jacobs (1984), combining elements of each approach, asserts that expanding trade may solve some of these problems, but only if Third-World nations break trading ties with rich societies and build trading networks among themselves. Then their economies can move beyond providing only raw materials and inexpensive labor to wealthy corporate interests in rich societies.

Jacobs's argument, which embraces a middle ground, has drawn controversy from both camps. Analysts on the side of modernization theory warn that contact with rich societies is necessary for developing nations to obtain much-needed technology. Critics on the side of dependency theory assert that even breaking those ties would not resolve the growing crisis of Third-World cities: what is needed is a revolutionary redistribution of the wealth that is now controlled by a small segment of the population (Gilbert & Gugler, 1983). But almost everyone agrees on one important point: whatever the course of events, the drama of overpopulation in the Third World will be played out in the cities.

## The Historical Importance of Cities

Having finished our survey of urbanization, we end by stepping back and reflecting on the place of cities in the drama of human history. There can be no doubt that the city has figured strongly in our past. In fact the root of the word civilization is the Latin word civis—meaning a "city dweller." Like the ancient Romans, the early Greeks recognized this link; their word polis—meaning "city"—is the root of politics, which was the core of Greek life.

In global perspective, ours has been a nation ambivalent about urban life. As he assumed the presidency in 1800, Thomas Jefferson repudiated the city as a "pestilence to the morals, the health, and the liberties of man" (cited in Glaab, 1963:52). Almost a century later, on a visit to Chicago, English author and Nobel Prize winner Rudyard Kipling echoed those sentiments: "Having seen it, I urgently desire never to see it again. It is inhabited by savages" (cited in Rokove, 1975:22). Others have disagreed, of course, siding with the ancient Greeks, who viewed the city as the only place where humanity could expect to find the "good life."

Why do cities provoke such spirited and divergent reactions? The answer lies in their ability to encapsulate and intensify human culture. Cities have spawned some of the greatest human virtues (the cultural developments of classical Athens) as well generated some of the greatest human failings (the militarism and violence of classical Rome or Nazi Berlin). For over 350 years, the United States has undergone concerted urbanization as people have sought a better way of life, but ironically, many social problems—such as poverty, crime, racial tensions, and environmental pollution—are most pronounced in cities. In short, the city is an intricate weave of noble accomplishments and wretched shortcomings.

As we approach the twenty-first century, the greatest test of urban living will occur in societies of the Third World. Mexico City, São Paulo, and Bombay will contain almost unimaginable numbers of people. Throughout history, the city improved people's standard of living more than any other settlement pattern. The question facing humanity now is whether cities in poor societies will be able to meet the needs of vastly larger populations in the next century. The answer—which carries implications for international relations, global economic relations, and simple human justice—will affect all of us.

# Summary

1. Fertility and mortality, measured as crude birth rates and crude death rates, are major components of population growth. In global terms, fertility, mortality, and population growth in North America are relatively low.

2. Migration, another key demographic concept, has special importance to the historical growth of cities.

3. Age-sex pyramids allow demographers to describe the composition of a population and to project future population patterns.

4. Historically, world population grew slowly because high birth rates were largely offset by high death rates. In about 1750, however, a demographic transition began as world population rose sharply, mostly as a result of declining death rates.

5. Malthus claimed that population would grow faster than food supplies, eventually resulting in social calamity. Contradicting Malthus's ominous predictions, demographic transition theory holds that technological advance brings gradually declining birth rates. This leveling off has occurred in industrial societies, where population growth is now low. In the Third World, however, declining death rates coupled with continued high birth rates are swelling population to unprecedented levels.

6. Research has shown that lower birth rates and improved economic productivity in the Third World both result from bolstering the social position of women.

7. World population is expected to reach 8 billion by the year 2025. If this occurs, social problems related to poverty may overwhelm Third-World societies, where population growth is now greatest.

8. Closely related to population growth is urbanization. The first urban revolution began with the appearance of cities after 8000 B.C.E.; by the start of the common era, cities had emerged in every region of the world.

9. While members of nonurban societies must continually search for food, city dwellers engage in a wide range of productive specialization.

10. Preindustrial cities are characterized by small buildings and narrow, winding streets, personal social ties, and rigid patterns of social inequality.

11. A second urban revolution began about 1750 as the Industrial Revolution prompted rapid urban growth in Europe. The structure of cities changed, as planners created wide, regular streets, and social anonymity increased.

12. Urbanism came to North America with European settlers. A string of colonial towns dotting the Atlantic coastline gave way by 1850 to hundreds of new cities from coast to coast.

13. By 1920 a majority of the U.S. population lived in urban areas, and several metropolises encompassed millions of inhabitants.

14. Since 1950 U.S. cities have decentralized. The growth of the suburbs is one trait of the postindustrial city. Newer, rapidly growing Sunbelt cities are geographically larger than older, Snowbelt cities.

15. This decentralization has generated vast urban areas that the Census Bureau terms metropolitan statistical areas (MSAs), and even larger consolidated metropolitan statistical areas (CMSAs). As these urban areas expand, they may form a megalopolis—a vast urban sprawl.

16. Rapid urbanization in Europe during the nineteenth century led early sociologists to contrast rural and urban life. Ferdinand Toennies explained the process of urbanization in terms of the concepts of *Gemeinshaft* and *Gesellschaft*; Georg Simmel claimed that the overstimulation of city life produced a blasé attitude in urbanites.

17. At the University of Chicago, Robert Park hailed cities for permitting greater social freedom. Louis Wirth suggested that the size, density, and social heterogeneity of cities generated a way of life characterized by impersonality, self-interest, and tolerance of people's differences.

18. Urban ecology studies the interplay of the physical and social environment of the city. The concentric zone, sector, multiple-nuclei, and social area models each provide insights into urban land use.

19. A third urban revolution is now occurring in the Third World, where most of the world's largest urban areas will soon be found.

# Key Concepts

**age-sex pyramid** a graphic representation that divides a population into various categories based on age and sex

**crude birth rate** the number of live births in a given year for every thousand people in a population

**crude death rate** the number of deaths in a given year for every thousand people in a population

**demographic transition theory** the thesis that population patterns are linked to a society's level of technological development

**demography** the study of human population

**fertility** the incidence of childbearing in a society's population

*Gemeinschaft* a type of social organization in which people are bound closely together by kinship and tradition

*Gesellschaft* a type of social organization in which people have weak social ties and a great deal of self-interest

**infant mortality rate** the number of deaths in the first year of life for each thousand live births in a given year

**life expectancy** how long a person, on the average, can expect to live

**megalopolis** a vast urban region containing a number of cities and their surrounding suburbs

**metropolis** a large city that socially and economically dominates an urban area

**migration** the movement of people into and out of a specified territory

**mortality** the incidence of death in a society's population

**sex ratio** the number of males for every hundred females in a given population

**suburbs** urban areas beyond the political boundaries of a city

**urban ecology** the study of the link between the physical and social dimensions of cities

**urbanization** the concentration of humanity into cities

**urban renewal** government programs intended to revitalize cities

**zero population growth** the level of reproduction that maintains population at a steady state

# Suggested Readings

This text probes various demographic topics.

> John R. Weeks. *Population: An Introduction to Concepts and Issues*. 4th ed. Belmont, CA: Wadsworth, 1989.

This comparative analysis of twenty nations focuses on the availability of contraception and the effect of contraception policies on fertility.

> Elise F. Jones, Jacqueline Darroch Forrest, Stanley K. Henshaw, Jane Silverman, and Aida Torres. *Pregnancy, Contraception, and Family Planning in Industrialized Countries*. New Haven, CT: Yale, 1989.

These two books by noted population experts describe the current state of world population and offer straightforward suggestions about how to limit population growth.

> Rafael M. Salas. *Reflections on Population*. New York: Pergammon Press, 1984.

> Werner Fornos. *Gaining People, Losing Ground: A Blueprint for Stabilizing World Population*. Washington, DC: The Population Institute, 1986.

The first of these is a textbook that provides a historical and contemporary analysis of cities in North America and throughout the world. The second book profiles 300 cities in the United States including statistical data from the 1990 census.

> James L. Spates and John J. Macionis. *The Sociology of Cities*. 2nd ed. Belmont, CA: Wadsworth, 1987.

> Allan Carpenter. *Facts About the Cities*. Bronx, NY: H.W. Wilson, 1991.

This paperback examines the nature of community in today's world and considers how sociologists study community life.

> Larry Lyon. *The Community in Urban Society*. Chicago: Dorsey, 1987.

The central role of wealth and power in the growth and decline of U.S. cities is the focus of this paperback.

> Joe R. Feagin and Robert Parker. *Building American Cities: The Urban Real Estate Game*. 2nd ed. Englewood Cliffs, NJ: Prentice Hall, 1990.

# 22

# Collective Behavior and Social Movements

On February 1, 1990, four men walked into Woolworth's in Greensboro, North Carolina to share a meal. They sat down to what seemed to be an ordinary breakfast of eggs, grits, bacon, and coffee served by a smiling waitress. But the men were treated as celebrities and the event was news around the world.

Why? Thirty years earlier to the day, the same four—then college students—had seated themselves at the same lunch counter and requested a meal from the same waitress. She refused to serve them because, as African Americans, they were unwelcome in the segregated Greensboro Woolworth. The four young men sat there nervously, ignored by her but closely observed by a white police officer who periodically slapped his billy club into his bare hand. After an hour, the men got up and peacefully left. Their courageous action called attention to the racial exclusion then commonplace throughout the country, and helped ignite a major social movement for civil rights that sought to end such legal segregation.

People typically engage in organized and controversial action in order to transform the world in one way or another. A major focus of this chapter is **social movements,** *organized activity that encourages or discourages social change.* Social movements are perhaps the most important type of **collective behavior,** *activity involving a large number of people, often spontaneous, and typically in violation of established norms.* Other forms of collec-

tive behavior—each giving rise to controversy and some provoking change—are fashions and fads, riots, crowds, mass hysteria, and public opinion. This chapter surveys various topics that form the broad and internally diverse field of collective behavior. It then focuses on social movements, such as the women's movement in the United States and the democratic movements that recently swept through Eastern Europe and the former Soviet Union.

## Collective Behavior

Sociological inquiry into collective behavior in the United States dwindled about 1950, when sociologists shifted their focus to more established social patterns like the family and social stratification. Because collective behavior focused on actions generally deemed as unusual or deviant, many analysts apparently thought this area of inquiry to be less worthy. The numerous social movements that burst on the scene in the tumultuous 1960s, however, renewed sociological interest in various types of collective behavior (Weller & Quarantelli, 1973; G. Marx & Wood, 1975; Aguirre & Quarantelli, 1983; Turner & Killian, 1987; McAdam, McCarthy, & Zald, 1988).

617

## Studying Collective Behavior

Collective behavior presents sociologists with several significant challenges. First, the concept of collective behavior is *broad*, embracing a sometimes bewildering array of phenomena. It is far from obvious, for example, what traits fads, rumors, and mob behavior have in common. Furthermore, each of these activities has very different consequences for social change. Rumors may disrupt the life of a small town, clothing fads often challenge conventional standards of appearance, and mob behavior can result in loss of life and property as people confront authorities or one another.

A second difficulty is that collective behavior is *complex*. A rumor seems to come out of nowhere and circulates in countless different settings. For no apparent reason, one new form of dress "catches on" while another does not. Why would millions of people in Eastern Europe, after patiently enduring undemocratic rule for decades, suddenly and decisively sweep away their leaders?

Third, some collective behavior is *transitory*. Sociologists have extensively studied the family because it is an enduring element of social life. Fashions, rumors, and riots, by contrast, tend to arise and dissipate so quickly that they are difficult to track and study systematically.

Some researchers into collective behavior acknowledge these problems but add that they apply to most of the issues sociologists study. Benigno Aguirre and E. L. Quarantelli (1983) ask what social behavior is *not* complex and dynamic? Moreover, collective behavior is not always so elusive; no one is surprised by the crowds that form at sports events and musical festivals, and sociologists can study these gatherings firsthand or by examining videotapes or audio records. Researchers can even anticipate some natural disasters in order to study the human response they provoke. We know, for example, that forty to eighty major tornadoes occur in particular regions of the United States each year; therefore, sociologists can be prepared to initiate research on short notice (Miller, 1985). Researchers may also use historical documents to reconstruct details of an unanticipated natural disaster or riot.

But sociologists have not resolved all the problems inherent in this area of study. The most serious problem, Aguirre and Quarantelli maintain, is that theory still does not link all the diverse actions that fall under the term collective behavior. At present, here is how the situation stands. All collective behavior involves the action of a **collectivity**, by which sociologists mean *a large number of people whose minimal interaction occurs in*

Sociologists distinguish between a *group* and a *collectivity* on the basis of the extent of interaction, clarity of social boundaries, and character of norms. These people enjoying California's Huntington Beach are a loose collectivity rather than a well-defined group.

*the absence of well-defined and conventional norms.* Collectivities are of two kinds. *Localized collectivities* involve people in physical proximity to one another; this type is illustrated by crowds and riots. *Dispersed collectivities* comprise people who influence one another despite being spread over great distances; examples here include rumors, public opinion, and fashion (Turner & Killian, 1987).

Sociologists distinguish collectivities from social groups (see Chapter 7, "Groups and Organizations"), on the basis of three characteristics.

1. **Limited social interaction.** Group members interact directly and frequently. Interaction in localized collectivities such as mobs is limited and temporary. People participating in dispersed collectivities like a fad typically do not interact at all.

2. **Unclear social boundaries.** Limited interaction makes for weak social boundaries. Group members have a sense of common identity, which people engaged in collective behavior typically lack. Localized crowds may have a common object of attention (such as a despondent person on a ledge high above the street), but these people exhibit little sense of unity. Individuals involved in dispersed collectivi-

ties, such as "the public" that intends to vote for some political candidate, have even less of a sense of shared membership. The exception to this rule is a social movement that gives rise to well-defined factions; even here, however, it is often difficult to discern who falls within the ranks of, say, the pro-life or pro-choice movement.

3. **Weak and unconventional norms.** Conventional cultural norms usually regulate the behavior of group members. Some collectivities, such as people traveling on an airplane, operate according to social norms, but they usually amount to little more than respecting the privacy of the person sitting in the next seat. Other collectivities—such as emotional soccer fans who destroy property as they leave a stadium—rather spontaneously develop decidedly unconventional norms (Weller & Quarantelli, 1973; Turner & Killian, 1987).

## Crowds

An important concept in the study of collective behavior is the **crowd**, *a temporary gathering of people who share a common focus of attention and whose members influence one another.* Historian Peter Laslett (1984) points out that crowds are a modern development; in medieval Europe, 25,000 people assembled in one place only when major armies faced off on the field of combat. Crowds of this size routinely form in industrial societies; they are found at sporting events, rock concerts, and even the registration halls of large universities.

But all crowds are not alike. Herbert Blumer (1969) organized crowds into four types. A *casual crowd* is a loose collection of people who interact little, if at all. People who gather on the beach or collect at the scene of an automobile accident have only a passing awareness of one another. Few social patterns are typical of casual crowds beyond the momentary sharing of an interest.

A *conventional crowd* results from deliberate planning, as illustrated by a country auction, a college lecture, or a somber funeral. In each case, interaction typically conforms to norms deemed appropriate for the situation.

An *expressive crowd* forms around an event with emotional appeal, such as a religious revival, a wrestling match, or the New Year's Eve celebration in New York's Times Square. Excitement is the main reason people join expressive crowds in the first place, and this fact makes expressive crowds relatively spontaneous and exhilarating to those involved.

An *acting crowd* is a collectivity fueled by an intense, single-minded purpose, as in the case of people rushing the doors of a concert hall or fleeing from a building that is on fire. Acting crowds are ignited by emotions more powerful than those typical of expressive crowds, often reaching feverish intensity that sometimes erupts into mob violence.

Any gathering of people can change from one type of crowd to another. In 1985, for example, 60,000 fans assembled in a soccer stadium near Brussels, Belgium, to watch the European Cup Finals between Italy and Great Britain. Initially, they formed a conventional crowd. But by the time the game started, many of the British fans had become intoxicated and were taunting the Italians sitting in an adjacent part of the stands. At this point, an expressive crowd had formed. When the two sides began to throw bottles at each other, the scene exploded as the British surged like a human wave toward the Italians. An estimated 400 million television viewers watched in horror as this acting crowd became a rampaging mob trampling hundreds of helpless spectators. In minutes, thirty-eight people were dead and another 400 injured (Lacayo, 1985).

Deliberate action by a crowd is not the product simply of rising emotions. Participants in *protest crowds*—a fifth category that can be added to Blumer's list—engage in a variety of actions, including strikes, boycotts, sit-ins, and marches, that have political goals (McPhail & Wohlstein, 1983). For example, most campuses witness protest crowds who express views about a wide range of issues. These crowds vary in emotional intensity, ranging from conventional to acting crowds. Sometimes a protest gathering begins peacefully, but its members become aggressive when confronted with counter-demonstrators as illustrated by common clashes between pro-choice and pro-life activists.

## Mobs and Riots

As an acting crowd turns violent we may witness the birth of a **mob**, *a highly emotional crowd that pursues some violent or destructive goal.* Despite, or perhaps because of, their intense emotion, mobs tend to dissipate rather quickly. The duration of a mob incident also depends on whether its leadership tries to inflame or stabilize the crowd, and on the mob's precise objectives.

Lynching is the most notorious example of mob behavior in the United States. This term is derived from Charles Lynch, a Virginia colonist who sought to maintain law and order in his own way before formal courts

In this painting from his series *The Migration of the Negro* (1940–1941), African-American artist Jacob Lawrence captures the frenzy of a race riot. Many African-American men and women from the rural South were used as strike breakers by northern companies, a practice that provoked violent outbursts by angry white workers.

(Jacob Lawrence, The Migration of the Negro. #50. Tempera on gesso on composition board. 18 × 12". Collection, The Museum of Modern Art, New York. Gift of Mrs. David M. Levy.)

were established. The word soon became synonymous with terrorism and murder outside the legal system.

Lynching has always been colored by race. After the Civil War, as slaves gained political rights and economic opportunities, these free people of color threatened many whites who no longer had legally sanctioned superi-

ority. Especially in the South, whites' efforts to maintain their domination fueled lynch mobs as a highly effective form of social control. African Americans who questioned white superiority, or were even suspected of doing so, risked hanging or being burned alive at the hands of vengeful whites. Blacks and occasionally their white defenders became all-purpose scapegoats.

Lynch mobs—typically composed of low-status whites most threatened by the emancipation of slaves—reached a peak between 1880 and 1930. About 5,000 lynchings were recorded by police in that period; no doubt, many more occurred. Most of these crimes were committed in the Deep South, where an agrarian economy still depended on a cheap and docile labor force, but lynchings took place in virtually every state and victimized every minority. For example, on the western frontier, lynch mobs frequently targeted people of Mexican and Asian descent. In about 25 percent of the cases, whites lynched other whites. The lynching of women, however, was rare; only about a hundred such cases are known, almost all involving women of color (White, 1969, orig. 1929; Grant, 1975).

A violent crowd without any particular purpose is a **riot**, *a social eruption that is highly emotional, violent, and undirected.* Unlike the action of a mob, a riot usually has no clear goal. Long-standing anger generally fuels riots, which are sparked by some minor incident (Smelser, 1962). Rioters then indulge in seemingly random violence against property or persons. Whereas a mob action usually ends when a specific violent goal has been achieved (or decisively prevented), a riot tends to disperse only as participants run out of steam or community leaders or police gradually bring them under control.

Throughout our nation's history, riots have served as collective expressions of social injustice. Industrial workers, for example, have rioted to vent rage at their working conditions. In 1886 a bitter struggle by Chicago factory workers for an eight-hour workday led to the explosive Haymarket Riot, which left eleven dead and scores injured. Rioting born of anger and despair has also marked the history of this country's penal system. In addition, race riots have occurred with striking regularity. Early in this century, crowds of whites attacked African Americans in Chicago, Detroit, and other cities. In the 1960s, summers of violent riots rocked the minority ghettos of many cities as seemingly trivial events ignited violent anger at continuing prejudice and discrimination. In Los Angeles in 1992 an especially destructive riot was triggered by the acquittal of police officers involved in the beating of Rodney King. The turmoil left more than fifty dead, caused thousands of injuries, and millions of dollars' worth of property damage.

Riots are not always fired by hate. They can also stem from positive feelings, such as the high spirits characteristic of young people who flock to resort areas during spring break from college. In March of 1986, for example, the exuberance of vacationing students in Palm Springs, California, erupted into a riot leading to a hundred arrests after crowds of young men began throwing rocks and bottles at passing cars and stripping the clothing off terrified women (DeMott, 1986).

## Contagion Theory

What makes the behavior of crowds unconventional? Social scientists have developed several different explanations over the last century. One of the first, formulated by French sociologist Gustave Le Bon (1841–1931), is *contagion theory*. The essence of Le Bon's (1960; orig. 1895) argument is that crowds exert a hypnotic influence on their members. In the anonymity of a crowd, he claimed, people evade personal responsibility and surrender to a collective mind. As a crowd assumes a life of its own, individual members slip their social restraints and become irrational automatons driven by contagious emotion. As fear or hate resonates through the crowd, emotional intensity builds, hypnotizing individuals toward an unrestrained outburst. The predictable result, Le Bon concluded, is destructive violence.

*Critical evaluation.* Some of Le Bon's assertions—that crowds generate anonymity and sometimes emotion—are widely accepted as true. Yet, as Clark McPhail (1991) points out, Le Bon (and others who followed his lead) embraced the idea of "the maddening crowd" without systematic study. More recently, investigators who have completed empirical research have concluded that a crowd does not take on a life of its own, apart from the thoughts and intentions of members. For example, Norris Johnson (1987), investigating the 1979 tragedy at a Who concert in Cincinnati, where eleven people were crushed to death, discovered specific factors that contributed to the outbreak, including an inadequate number of entrance doors, an open-seating policy, and too little police supervision. Far from an episode of collective insanity, he concluded, that crowd was composed of many small groups of people valiantly trying to help each another.

## Convergence Theory

*Convergence theory* holds that motivations for collective action originate not in a crowd itself but rather in the setting where the action takes place. From this point of view, crowds form as like-minded individuals converge on the basis of a common attitude or interest. In 1985 a number of whites in southwest Philadelphia banded together to pressure an African-American couple to move from their neighborhood. Fearing violence, the couple fled; at this point, the crowd burned down the couple's home. In such instances, convergence theorists contend, the crowd itself did not generate violence; rather, racial hostility had been simmering for some time among many local people. This crowd, then, grew out of a convergence of people sharing an attachment to their traditionally white neighborhood, who opposed the presence of black residents, and who already had a propensity for violent action.

*Critical evaluation.* By linking crowds to broader social forces that operate in a particular setting, convergence theory places collective action in a clear context. From this perspective, crowd behavior is not irrational, as Le Bon maintained, but a result of individual decision making (Berk, 1974).

It is probably true, however, that people do some things in a crowd that they would not have the courage to do alone. In addition, crowds can intensify sentiments simply by creating a critical mass of like-minded people.

## Emergent-Norm Theory

Ralph Turner and Lewis Killian (1987) have developed an *emergent-norm theory* of crowd dynamics. While these researchers concede that crowds are not entirely predictable, they dismiss the notion that crowds are irrational, as Le Bon claimed. Similar interests may draw people together, but distinctive patterns of behavior emerge within the crowd itself.

Turner and Killian maintain that crowds begin as collectivities in which people have mixed interests and motives. Entering conventional or casual crowds, members understand what norms will guide their behavior. But the norms that steer less stable types of crowds—expressive, acting, and protest crowds—frequently surface only in particular settings. Usually leaders start the process of norm construction. For example, one member of the crowd at a rock concert holds up a lit cigarette

Whether a crowd of people intent on changing society is lionized for courage or condemned for disruptive behavior is a matter of political positions and value judgments. These Algerian marchers, who recently opposed Islamic fundamentalism as a threat to democracy, won their share of both praise and blame.

lighter to signal praise for the performers, and others follow suit; or a few people in an angry street crowd throw bricks through store windows, and a riot ensues.

In the infamous New Bedford, Massachusetts tavern rape in 1983, one man assaulted a twenty-one-year-old woman who had entered the bar to buy cigarettes, then he raped her on the floor. Five other men then joined in, repeatedly raping the woman for an hour and a half. Still others in the bar cheered the rapists; apparently as some people sized up the situation, they concluded that this brutal action was somehow acceptable, while the rest were too intimidated to voice opposition. In any case, no one in the bar responded in the conventional way by calling the police (*Time*, March 5, 1984).

*Critical evaluation.* Emergent-norm theory represents a symbolic-interaction approach to crowd dynamics. Turner and Killian maintain that crowd behavior is neither as irrational as contagion theory suggests, nor as purposeful as convergence theory implies. So while crowd behavior responds to participants' motives, it is guided by norms that emerge in a setting as the situation unfolds. This means that decision making plays a significant role in crowd behavior, even though it may not be evident to casual observers. For example, frightened people clogging the exits of a burning theater may appear to be victims of irrational panic but, from their point of view, fleeing a life-threatening situation is certainly a rational alternative to death (1972:10). Experience and common sense play a part in precisely how people respond to any such event, of course; leaders on the scene also have a hand in guiding crowd response.

Further, although people in a crowd may experience some pressure to conform, emergent-norm theory points out that not every participant embraces the emerging norms. Some assume leadership roles, others become lieutenants, rank-and-file followers, inactive bystanders, or opponents (Weller & Quarantelli, 1973; Zurcher & Snow, 1981).

## Crowds, Politics, and Social Change

In March 1770 a crowd of Boston citizens, angry at British domination, confronted an English soldier on the street. The soldier panicked and ran off to summon reinforcements. The ensuing clash, which came to be known as the Boston Massacre, left five Bostonians dead, and galvanized support for the colonies' independence. Three years later, another crowd of Bostonians gathered to angrily denounce British taxation policy. Soon afterward, some of their number dressed up as Native Americans and dumped tea from British commercial ships into Boston harbor, an event that history dubbed the Boston Tea Party (Kelley, 1982). The British and their colonial supporters deplored these examples of "mob action," but most colonists viewed the participants as patriots opposing injustice and paving the way for a new, democratic society.

Because crowds are linked to social change, they often provoke controversy. Defenders of the established social order have long feared and hated them. Gustave Le Bon's negative view of crowds as "only powerful for destruction" echoed the sentiments of members of the aristocracy (1960:18; orig. 1895). But collective action that privileged people condemn as destructive, the disadvantaged cheer as rightful protest against social wrongs.

But crowds do not share a single political cast: some call for change, some resist it. Throngs of Romans rallying to the Sermon on the Mount by Jesus of Nazareth, bands of traditional weavers destroying new industrial machinery that was making their skills obsolete, masses of marchers carrying banners and shouting slogans for or against abortion—these and countless other instances across the centuries show crowds to be an important means by which people challenge or support their society (Rudé, 1964; Canetti, 1978).

## Rumor and Gossip

Collective behavior is not limited to people in physical proximity. Sociologists use the term **mass behavior** to refer to *collective behavior among people dispersed over a wide geographical area.*

One example of mass behavior is **rumor,** *unsubstantiated information spread informally, often by word of mouth.* Rumors are a familiar part of social life. In the past, people spread rumors through face-to-face communication. Although this is still frequently the case, our modern technology—including telephones, computers, and especially the mass media—allows rumors to be transmitted more rapidly to a greater number of people.

Rumor has three essential characteristics.

1. *Rumor thrives in a climate of ambiguity.* Rumor grows when people lack definitive information about a topic they care about. For example, workers fearing a massive layoff may hear little from management, and may be suspicious of what they are told. Rumor, then, is an attempt to define reality in the absence of substantiated facts (Shibutani, 1966; Rosnow & Fine, 1976).

2. *Rumor is unstable.* As people spread a rumor, they alter its content so that, before long, many variations of truth emerge. People tend to change rumors by accentuating the parts that serve their interests. For example, workers play up the shortcomings of management as they transmit rumors; for their part, management tries to "spin" information in its own way.

3. *Rumor is difficult to stop.* The number of people aware of a rumor increases in geometric progression as one person spreads information to several others. Of course, some rumors dissipate with time but, in general, only clear, substantiated information that is widely dispersed will stop a rumor.

Rumor can trigger the formation of crowds or other collective behavior. For this reason, authorities often establish rumor-control hotlines in times of crisis as a form of information management and social control. Yet some rumors persist for years despite incontrovertible evidence to the contrary; the box on page 624 provides one notable example.

Closely related to rumor is **gossip,** *rumor about the personal affairs of others.* As Charles Horton Cooley (1962; orig. 1909) pointed out, while rumor involves issues or events of interest to a large segment of the public, gossip concerns a small circle of people who know a particular person. While rumors spread widely, then, gossip is typically localized.

Gossip can be an effective strategy for social control as its targets become aware that they are the subject of praise or scorn. People may also gossip about others to elevate their own standing as "insiders" in a social group. Those who gossip *too* often, however, may find themselves dismissed as disreputable. The need to control gossip suggests the power of this form of communication.

## Public Opinion

One form of highly dispersed collective behavior is *public opinion,* which was defined in Chapter 5 ("Socialization") as widespread attitudes toward controversial issues. Although we frequently speak about "the public" in singular terms, no single issue is of concern to everyone. More accurately, societies contain many publics. In industrial nations, publics wax and wane around issues such as water fluoridation, air pollution, handguns, foreign relations, child care, and thousands of other debates and activities. Although the members of a public may share an interest in a particular issue, typically they have a range of opinions about it. Public issues are thus important matters about which people disagree (Lang & Lang, 1961; Turner & Killian, 1987).

Because most individuals possess a wide range of interests and group affiliations, they belong simultaneously to many publics. Yet, on any given issue, 5 or 10 percent of people will offer no opinion on any public issue because of ignorance or apathy. As interest in an issue rises or falls, the public involved grows larger or smaller. For example, interest in the social position of women in the United States was strong during the decades of the women's suffrage movement but declined after women won the right to vote in 1920. Since the 1960s, a second wave of feminism has again created a public with strong opinions about a host of gender-related issues.

On any issue, not everyone's opinion carries the same clout. Some categories of people have more social influence than others because they are wealthier, more powerful, or better educated. As Chapter 18 ("Politics and Government") explained, many special-interest groups shape public policy in the United States even though they represent only a small fraction of the population. Physicians—just 2 percent of our people—have enormous influence on health-care policy because of

# The Rumored Death of Beatle Paul McCartney

The Beatles—John Lennon, Paul McCartney, George Harrison, and Ringo Starr—were probably the most celebrated rock band in the world during the 1960s. Their unprecedented fame, perhaps with a little help from the Beatles themselves, spawned a rumor that circulated over much of the world: the alleged death of Paul McCartney.

First heard in 1967, the rumor of McCartney's death spread rapidly. In 1969, the mass media were drawn in as a Detroit disk jockey announced several curious "facts":

1. At the end of the song "Strawberry Fields Forever" on the *Magical Mystery Tour* album, filtering out background noise allows the listener to hear a voice saying, "I buried Paul!"

2. A picture inside this album shows John, George, and Ringo wearing red carnations, while Paul is wearing a black flower.

3. The phrase "Number 9, Number 9, Number 9" from the song "Revolution No. 9" on the Beatles' *White Album*, when played backwards, seems to intone, "Turn me on, dead man!"

On the basis of these clues, millions of people began to in-

spect Beatle albums for other hints of McCartney's demise. And they found them:

4. The cover of the *Sergeant Pepper's Lonely Hearts Club Band* album (shown here) presents a grave with yellow flowers arranged in the shape of Paul's bass guitar.

5. On the inside of that album, McCartney wears an armpatch with the letters "OPD." Was the patch from some police department? Perhaps, but fans interpreted it to mean "Officially Pronounced Dead."

6. On the back cover of the same album, three Beatles are facing forward while McCartney has his back to the camera.

Soon after, a report in a University of Michigan newspaper

provided alleged details of McCartney's "death," including a photograph of a bloodied head said to be his. The Beatle, the story claimed, had been decapitated in an automobile crash early in November 1966 and sinister music company executives had secretly replaced Paul with a double.

Paul McCartney is, of course, very much alive and still jokes about the episode. Few doubt that the Beatles intentionally fabricated some of the clues to pique the interest of their fans. But the incident has a serious side, showing how quickly rumors may arise, and how they endure in a climate of distrust. During the late 1960s, many disaffected young people were quite ready to believe that the media and other powerful interests would conceal an event such as McCartney's death. Even when McCartney himself denied the rumor in a 1969 *Life* magazine interview, a distrustful youth subculture dismissed the story as unreliable. Thousands of readers also noticed that the back of the page containing McCartney's picture had an advertisement for an automobile: holding this page up to the light, the car lay across McCartney's chest and blocked his head!

SOURCE: Based on Rosnow & Fine (1976).

their specialized training and political organizing. In general, privileged people make use of their affluence, prestige, and social contacts to promote their opinions more effectively than others do. This helps to explain why the Equal Rights Amendment, calling for equality

under the law for women and men, has yet to be enacted into law despite support from about two-thirds of adults in the United States (N.O.R.C., 1991). What stopped the ERA, for better or worse, is that the vast majority of public officials in this country are men.

Political leaders, special-interest groups, and businesses all seek to influence public tastes and attitudes by using **propaganda,** *information presented with the intention of shaping public opinion.* Although the term has negative connotations, propaganda is not necessarily false. What determines whether or not we should view information as propaganda is the intention behind it. People generate propaganda to win over some audience to a particular viewpoint, not to encourage others to think carefully for themselves. Political speeches, commercial advertising, and even some college lectures disseminate propaganda with the goal of making people think or act in some specific way.

## Panic and Mass Hysteria

Panic and mass hysteria are closely related forms of collective behavior. A **panic** is *a form of localized collective behavior by which people react to a threat or other stimulus with emotional, irrational, and often self-destructive behavior.* The classic illustration of a panic is people responding to a fire in a crowded theater. As they flee in fear, they trample one another and block exits so that few actually escape. In other cases, the stimulus sparking a panic may be something desirable, like a sudden half-price sale in a popular discount store.

**Mass hysteria** is *a form of dispersed collective behavior by which people respond to a real or imagined event with irrational, frantic behavior.* Mass hysteria differs from a panic in that the people involved have little direct contact with one another. Mass hysteria is commonly a response to a perceived threat, although a positive event such as a film celebrity's appearance on campus might provoke such a reaction.

Whatever triggers the mass hysteria may or may not be real. The key is that a large number of people *think* it is and take it seriously. Parents' fears that their children may become infected with HIV from a schoolmate who has AIDS may stir as much hysteria in a community as the very real danger of an approaching hurricane. Moreover, actions of people in the grip of mass hysteria generally make the situation worse. At the extreme, mass hysteria leads to chaotic flight and crowds in panic. People who see others overcome by fear may become more afraid themselves, as hysteria feeds on itself.

On the night before Halloween in 1938, CBS radio broadcast a dramatization of H. G. Wells's novel *War of the Worlds* (Cantril, Gaudet, & Herzog, 1947; Koch, 1970). From a New York studio, a small group of actors began by presenting a program of "live dance music" heard by an estimated 10 million people across the United States. The program was suddenly interrupted by a "news report" of explosions on the surface of the planet Mars, and the subsequent crash landing of a mysterious cylinder near a farmhouse in New Jersey. The program then switched to an "on-the-scene reporter" who presented a chilling account of giant monsters equipped with death-ray weapons emerging from the spaceship. An "eminent astronomer," played by Orson Welles, somberly informed the audience that Martians had begun a full-scale invasion of Earth. At a time when most people relied on their radios for factual news and many were prepared to believe that intelligent life existed on Mars, this episode was chilling.

At the beginning, middle, and end of the program, an announcer identified the broadcast as a fictitious dramatization. Yet more than 1 million people apparently believed that the events were actually taking place as described. By the time the show was over, thousands were hysterical, gathering in the streets spreading news of the "invasion" while others flooded telephone switchboards with warnings to friends and relatives. Among those who jumped into their cars and fled were a college senior and his roommate.

> My roommate was crying and praying. He was even more excited than I was—or more noisy about it anyway; I guess I took it out in pushing the accelerator to the floor. . . . After it was all over, I started to think about that ride, I was more jittery than when it was happening. The speed was never under 70. I thought I was racing against time. . . . I didn't have any idea exactly what I was fleeing from, and that made me all the more afraid. (Cantril, Gaudet, & Herzog, 1947:52).

Mass hysteria, then, can build in a vicious cycle. The box on page 626 describes another classic example of mass hysteria in our nation's history, generated by totally fictitious accounts of witches in colonial Massachusetts.

## Fashions and Fads

Two additional types of collective behavior—fashions and fads—affect people dispersed over a large area. A **fashion** is *a social pattern favored for a time by a large number of people.* In contrast to more established norms, fashion is transitory, sometimes lasting only for months. Fashion characterizes the arts (including painting, music, drama, and literature), automobiles, language, architecture, and public opinion. The most widely recognized

## The Witches of Salem: Can Whole Towns Go Crazy?

The best-known example of mass hysteria in early U.S. history took place in 1692 in the village of Salem, Massachusetts, fifteen miles north of Boston. It is an example of mass hysteria that swept up an entire town, with deadly results.

The story began in the home of a local minister, Samuel Parris. He owned a slave woman named Tituba, who hailed from Barbados and was well-versed in the art of black magic. Tituba regularly enthralled a group of young girls by spinning tales that were undoubtedly beyond the bounds of conventional conversation in this devoutly pious Puritan community. Before long, two of the youngest girls began to display the most extraordinary behavior, writhing on the ground in apparent convulsions. Other young girls throughout the village soon mimicked this bizarre behavior, and horrified parents reached what seemed to be the only sensible conclusion: their children were bewitched.

The clergy stepped forward to demand that the girls identify those responsible for this "Satanic" outbreak. The girls pointed not only to Tituba but to two other older women. Brought to trial for witchcraft, Tituba provided an eerie and detailed account of beliefs about the "underworld" that she had learned in her youth, and

she hinted that many people in Salem were witches.

When the girls were pressed to identify other culprits, they spewed forth so many names that the jail soon overflowed with suspected sorceresses. As townspeople watched these events unfold, everyone became as terrified of being named a witch as they were of confronting one. Understandably, few were willing to defend any of the accused, lest they too be labeled as members of the evil coven. By the end of the summer of 1692, twenty people convicted of witchcraft had been put to death.

After reaching a fever pitch, the witchcraft hysteria began to subside. In the wake of the executions, some of Salem's citizens finally began to question the girls' accusations. No doubt, the young girls had been carried away by the immense power they were exercising over their patriarchal Puritan colony. They even accused strangers of sorcery. But as the accusations shifted from "outsiders" like Tituba to some of the founding fathers of the community, people with power began to fight back. It was then that, as quickly as they had invaded Salem, the "witches" departed.

SOURCE: Based on Erikson (1966).

examples of fashion are clothing and other aspects of personal appearance.

Lyn Lofland (1973) suggests that, in preindustrial societies, clothing and personal adornment reflect traditional *style* that changes little over the years. Categories of people—women and men, and members of various social classes and occupations—are easily recognized by distinctive clothes and characteristic hairstyles that visibly mark their social standing.

In industrial societies, however, style gives way

to fashion for two reasons. First, modern people are less tied to tradition and often eagerly embrace new ways of living. Second, the high social mobility of industrial societies heightens the significance of what people consume. German sociologist Georg Simmel (1971; orig. 1904) explained that people use fashion to craft their presentation of self, and seek approval and prestige as they do so. According to Simmel, affluent people are typically the trend setters, since they have the money to spend on luxuries that bespeak privilege. In the lasting phrase of U.S. sociologist Thorstein Veblen (1953; orig. 1899), fashion involves *conspicuous consumption*, meaning that people spend money simply to show off their wealth to one another.

Less affluent people understandably long to own the trappings of wealth, so they snap up less expensive copies of items that have become fashionable. In this way, a fashion moves downward in society. But as this happens the fashion eventually loses its prestige, with the wealthy moving on to something new. Fashions, in short, are born at the top of the social hierarchy— on the Fifth Avenues and Rodeo Drives of the rich— then they rise to mass popularity in bargain stores across the country, and soon are all but forgotten by everyone.

A curious reversal of this pattern sometimes occurs among more egalitarian-minded people. In this case, a fashion that originates among people of lower social position is mimicked by the rich who wish to identify with the masses. A classic example is the "upward mobility" of blue jeans, or dungarees (from a Hindi word for a coarse and inferior fabric). First worn by manual laborers, jeans gained popularity among the affluent, especially those who supported the struggles of the socially disadvantaged. Jeans became the uniform of political activists in the civil rights and antiwar movements in the 1960s and, gradually, of college students across the country. Author Tom Wolfe (1970) coined the phrase "radical chic" to satirize the desire of some rich people to look fashionably poor. By the 1980s, expensive designer jeans had become the rage among people of every political persuasion.

A **fad** is *an unconventional social pattern that people embrace briefly but enthusiastically*. Fads, sometimes called *crazes*, are commonplace in industrial societies and often define a decade. During the 1950s, two young entrepreneurs in California produced a brightly colored plastic version of a popular Australian toy, a three-foot-diameter hoop that one swung around the body by gyrating the hips. Dubbed the "hula hoop," this odd device soon swept the country as a national craze. Hula hoops disappeared almost as quickly as they emerged, but—

decades later—they have surfaced once again, this time in China. Streaking—running naked in public—had an even briefer moment in the sun, lasting a mere few months in early 1974. Their fleeting existence suggests that fads happen almost at random. But research reveals that the popularity of any fad depends on its acceptance by high-prestige people. In addition, as we see in the case of streaking, fads fade from the scene if subjected to official repression by police or other authority figures (Aguirre, Quarantelli, & Mendoza, 1988).

Fads and fashions share similar characteristics: both involve dispersed collectivities and last only a short time. But they also differ in several respects (Blumer, 1968; Turner & Killian, 1987). Fads are truly passing fancies— enthusiasms that capture the mass imagination but quickly burn out and disappear. Fashions, by contrast, reflect fundamental cultural values like individuality and sexual attractiveness and tend to evolve over time. In this way, a fashion but rarely a fad becomes incorporated into a society's culture. Streaking, for instance, came out of nowhere and soon vanished, while blue jeans originated in the rough mining camps of Gold Rush California a century ago and still influence clothing designs today. Such persistence explains the positive connotation of being called *fashionable* in contrast to the mildly insulting label *faddish*.

# Social Movements

Crowds, rumors, fashions, and the other forms of collective behavior we have examined usually have little enduring significance for society as a whole. Social movements, however, are deliberate and consequential forms of collective behavior.

As noted at the beginning of the chapter, a social movement involves organized activity that promotes or resists some dimension of change. Social movements stand apart from other types of collective behavior in three respects: they have a high degree of internal organization, they last longer, and their purpose is to reorganize or defend society in some respect.

Social movements are far more common today than in the past. Preindustrial societies are tightly integrated by tradition, making the emergence of social movements for change extremely rare. Industrial societies, however, foster diversity in the form of subcultures and countercultures so that social movements develop around a wide range of public issues. In recent decades, for example, homosexual men and women—supported by heterosexuals sympathetic to their political aims—have organized to win economic and legal parity with everyone else. The gay rights movement has already succeeded in securing legislation in several major cities forbidding various forms of discrimination based on sexual preference. Like any social movement that challenges conventional practices, this one has sparked a countermovement as traditionalists try to block greater social acceptance of homosexuality. In today's society, almost every significant public issue gives rise to both a social movement favoring change and an opposing countermovement (Lo, 1982).

## Types of Social Movements

Sociologists classify social movements in various ways (Aberle, 1966; Cameron, 1966; Blumer, 1969). One variable is *breadth*, since some movements target selected people while others try to change everyone. A second variable is *depth*, with some movements attempting to render only superficial changes in how we live, as others pursue radical transformation. Combining these variables, we can identify four types of social movements, shown in Figure 22–1.

*Alternative social movements* are the least threatening to the established social order, seeking limited change only in some segment of the population. Planned Parenthood, one example of an alternative social movement,

**Figure 22–1** Four Types of Social Movements
*(Aberle, 1966)*

|  | | BREADTH OF CHANGE | |
|---|---|---|---|
|  | | Specific individuals | Entire society |
| **DEPTH OF CHANGE** | Limited | 1 Alternative social movement | 3 Reformative social movement |
|  | Radical | 2 Redemptive social movement | 4 Revolutionary social movement |

encourages individuals of childbearing age to take the consequences of their sexual activity more seriously by practicing birth control.

*Redemptive social movements* also have a selective focus, but they attempt radical change in those they engage. Examples include fundamentalist Christian organizations that seek new members through conversion. The resulting transformation is sometimes so momentous that converts describe their experience as being "born again."

*Reformative social movements* seek only limited social change but encompass the entire society. The holistic health-care movement, described in Chapter 20 ("Health and Medicine"), is a reformative social movement that advocates revision of U.S. health-care practices. Reformative social movements generally work inside the existing political system. They can be progressive (promoting a new social pattern) or reactionary (countermovements trying to preserve the status quo or to return to past social patterns). In the ongoing debate about abortion in the United States, both the pro-life and pro-choice organizations are reformative social movements.

*Revolutionary social movements* have the most severe consequences of all. They seek basic transformation of a society. Sometimes pursuing specific goals, sometimes spinning utopian dreams, followers of these social movements reject existing social institutions as flawed while favoring some radically new alternatives. Until recently, most people in the United States linked revolutionary social movements to left-wing politics, but recent events in Eastern Europe and the Commonwealth of Independent States have shown that socialism, too, is subject to popular overthrow. Revolutionary social movements also emerge on the far right. In the United States, the John Birch Society and the political organization headed by Lyndon LaRouche each decry the erosion of our political system by socialism and seek to radically alter our social institutions in defense of individual freedoms (Broyles, 1978).

## Deprivation Theory

Because social movements are typically organized and enduring, sociologists find this form of collective behavior somewhat easier to explain than fleeting incidents of mob behavior or mass hysteria. One approach, *deprivation theory*, holds that social movements arise as a response to a perception of being deprived of what is deemed fair. People who think they lack sufficient income, satisfactory working conditions, important political rights, or basic social dignity may engage in organized collective behavior to bring about a more just state of affairs (Morrison, 1978; Rose, 1982).

The emancipation of Americans of African descent after the Civil War seemed to signal an end to white domination. However, the economic prosperity of many white farmers depended on low-cost black labor, so that many whites felt threatened by the apparent rise in the social position of African Americans. The whites' sense of loss was especially keen during economic downturns. As a result, various social movements emerged from the desire to keep African Americans "in their place" (Dollard et al., 1939). Some whites organized in support of segregationist Jim Crow laws, while others forged terrorist organizations like the Ku Klux Klan. The success of these movements enabled threatened whites to hold on to some relative advantages. For their part, African Americans had long experienced even greater deprivation, but they had relatively little opportunity to organize in the face of overwhelming white power. Not until well into this century did African Americans forge successful organizations seeking racial justice.

The deprivation approach is also evident in Karl Marx's prediction that industrial workers would organize in opposition to capitalism. Marx asserted that capitalism deprived workers by giving them low wages and little social power, thereby alienating them from their own creative potential. Labor unions and various political organizations of workers have arisen to redress grievances stemming from the deprivation experienced by working-class men and women.

As we noted in Chapter 7 ("Groups and Organizations"), deprivation is a relative concept (Stouffer et al., 1949; Merton, 1968). Regardless of their absolute amount of money and power, people tend to evaluate themselves in relation to some category of others or some standard of justice. **Relative deprivation**, then, is *a perceived disadvantage arising from some specific comparison.*

More than a century ago Alexis de Tocqueville (1955; orig. 1856) studied the social uprising that sparked the French Revolution. Why, he asked, did rebellion occur in progressive France rather than in more traditional Germany where, by any objective measure, peasants were worse off? Tocqueville's answer was that, as bad as their condition was, German peasants had known nothing but feudal servitude and thus had no basis for feeling deprived. French peasants, by contrast, had experienced various improvements in their lives, which whetted their appetite for even greater progress. Thus the French—not the Germans—felt a keen sense of relative

Under the domination of the Israeli government, Palestinians in the disputed territories claim that they have been reduced to second-class citizens. This keen sense of deprivation has led to years of protest, drawing both sides into violent conflict.

deprivation. In analyzing this apparent paradox, Tocqueville pinpointed one of the notable ironies of human history, that increasing prosperity, far from satisfying the population, is likely to promote a spirit of unrest (1955:175; orig. 1856).

Echoing Tocqueville's insight, James C. Davies (1962) suggests that as life gets better, people often take their rising fortunes for granted and come to expect even more. Relative deprivation can set in if the standard of living suddenly stops improving or, worse, begins to drop. As Figure 22–2 on page 630 illustrates, social movements aimed at changing society are most likely to arise when an extended period of improvement in the standard of living is followed by a shorter period of decline.

*Critical evaluation.* Deprivation theory reveals the limits of common sense as a predictor of discontent. People do not organize in opposition to their situation simply because they are suffering in an absolute sense; social movements aimed at change are propelled by a perception of relative deprivation. We can discern the broad appeal of this insight by noting that it is found in the work of thinkers as diverse as Marx and Tocqueville.

But since most people experience some sense of discontent all the time, we are left wondering why social movements emerge among certain categories of people and not others. A second problem is that deprivation theory has a tendency toward circular reasoning: deprivation is assumed to cause social movements, but the only evidence of deprivation is the social movement itself

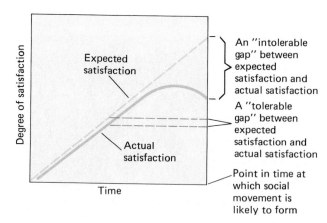

**Figure 22–2** Relative Deprivation and Social Movements
In this diagram, the solid line represents a rising standard of living over time. The dotted line represents the expected standard of living, which is typically somewhat higher. Davies describes the difference between the two as "a tolerable gap between what people want and what they get." If the standard of living suddenly drops in the midst of rising expectations, however, this gap grows to an intolerable level. At this point, social movements can be expected to form.

(Davies, 1962)

(Jenkins & Perrow, 1977). A third limitation of this approach is that it focuses more on the setting in which a social movement develops than on the movement itself (McAdam, McCarthy, & Zald, 1988). Fourth, some research suggests that relative deprivation turns out not to be a very good predictor of social movements (Muller, 1979).

## Mass-Society Theory

William Kornhauser's *mass-society theory* (1959) suggests that social movements attract socially isolated people who feel personally insignificant as part of the masses of large, complex societies. In this view, social movements are more *personal* than *political* in that they confer a sense of purpose and belonging on people otherwise adrift in society (Melucci, 1989). In this view, categories of people with weak social ties are most readily mobilized into a social movement. In societies characterized by strong social integration, on the other hand, social movements rarely come to the fore. Like Gustave Le Bon, whose ideas were explored earlier, Kornhauser offers a conservative and critical view of social movements. He regards activists as psychologically motivated individuals prone to deviance who join groups in which leaders can easily manipulate them and subvert democratic principles. Thus extremist social movements on both ends of the political spectrum typically gain their most ardent support from people who belong to few social groups.

*Critical evaluation.* The strength of Kornhauser's theory lies in its analysis of social movements in terms of both the people who join them and the characteristics of the larger society. One practical criticism is that, beginning with the contention that mass societies foster social movements, researchers run up against the problem of having no simple standard against which to measure the extent to which people form a "mass society." A more political criticism holds that placing the roots of social movements in human psychology tends to dismiss the importance of social justice. Put otherwise, this theory suggests that flawed people, rather than a flawed society, underlie the emergence of social movements.

Some research supports this approach; other evidence disputes its contentions. On the down side, a number of studies conclude that most people recruited by the Nazi movement in Germany were *not* socially isolated (Lipset, 1963; Oberschall, 1973). Similarly, urban rioters in the 1960s typically had strong ties to their communities (Sears & McConahay, 1973). Evidence also suggests that young people who join religious cults do not have particularly weak family ties (Wright & Piper, 1986). Finally, researchers who have examined the biographies of 1960s political activists find evidence of deep and abiding commitment to political goals rather than isolation from society or personal aberration (McAdam, 1988, 1989; Whalen & Flacks, 1989). On the up side, research by Frances Piven and Richard Cloward (1977) shows that a breakdown of routine social patterns seems to contribute to social movements among poor people. Also, in a study of the New Mexico State Penitentiary, Bert Useem (1985) found that suspending prison programs that promoted social ties among inmates led to an increase in chaotic and violent protest activity.

## Structural-Strain Theory

One of the most influential approaches to understanding social movements is *structural-strain theory*, developed by Neil Smelser (1962). This analysis identifies six factors that foster social movements. The more prevalent these conditions are, the greater the likelihood that a social movement will develop. Smelser's theory also offers clues as to what situations spark unorganized mobs or riots and which give rise to highly organized social movements. The pro-democracy movement that transformed Eastern Europe during the late 1980s illustrates Smelser's six factors.

1. **Structural conduciveness.** The roots of social movements lie in significant problems that beset a society. The generally low standard of living in Eastern Europe in recent decades, coupled with the lack of political participation by the majority of people, created widespread dissatisfaction.

2. **Structural strain.** Relative deprivation and other kinds of strain flow from the inability of a society to meet the expectations of its people. The pro-democracy movement in Eastern Europe gained strength because people there could readily see that their quality of life was far lower than that of their counterparts in Western Europe or than years of propaganda about prosperous socialism had led them to expect.

3. **Growth and spread of an explanation.** Any coherent social movement depends on a clear statement of a problem, its causes, and likely solutions. To the extent that these are well articulated, people are likely to express their dissatisfaction in an organized way. If not, frustration may eventually explode in the form of unorganized rioting. Intellectuals propounded the notion that the plight of Eastern Europe was caused by deep economic and political flaws; at the same time, movement leaders proposed strategies to increase democracy.

4. **Precipitating factors.** Discontent frequently festers for a long time, only to be transformed into collective action by a specific event. When Mikhail Gorbachev came to power in the Soviet Union in 1985 and implemented his program of *perestroika,* people in Eastern Europe seized a historic opportunity to reorganize their political and economic life, as Moscow relaxed its rigid control.

5. **Mobilization for action.** Widespread concern about a public issue sets the stage for collective action in the form of rallies, leafleting, building of alliances with sympathetic organizations, and similar activities. The initial success of the Solidarity movement in Poland—covertly aided by the Reagan Administration in the United States and the Vatican—mobilized people throughout Eastern Europe to press for change. The rate of change accelerated as reform movements gained strength:

progress that had taken a decade in Poland required only months in Hungary, and only weeks in other countries.

6. **Lack of social control.** The responses of established authorities, such as political officials, the police, and the military, largely determines the outcome of any social movement. Firm repression by the state can weaken or even destroy a social movement, as was seen by the crushing of pro-democracy forces in the People's Republic of China. By contrast, Gorbachev adopted a policy of nonintervention in Eastern Europe, which propelled the drive for change there. Ironically, the forces his program unleashed in these neighboring nations soon spread to the Soviet Union itself, ending the historic domination of the Communist Party and leading to a new political confederation in 1992. It also laid the groundwork for the three Baltic states—Estonia, Latvia, and Lithuania—to break away from the former Soviet Union and establish themselves as fully independent nations.

*Critical evaluation.* Smelser's approach recognizes the complexity of social movements and suggests how various factors encourage or inhibit their development. Structural-strain theory also explains how social problems may give rise to either organized social movements or more spontaneous mob action or rioting. It also is distinctly *social*, rather than psychological, in focus.

Yet Smelser's theory contains some of the same circularity of argument found in Kornhauser's analysis. Social movements are caused by strain, he maintains, but the only evidence of this underlying strain appears to be the emerging social movement itself. Finally, this theory overlooks several key factors, including the important role of resources such as the mass media or international alliances in the success or failure of a social movement (Oberschall, 1973; Jenkins & Perrow, 1977; McCarthy & Zald, 1977; Olzak & West, 1991).

## Resource-Mobilization Theory

*Resource-mobilization theory* adds an important dimension to our understanding of social movements. Drives for change are unlikely to succeed—or even get off the ground—without substantial resources, including money, human labor, office and communications facilities, contacts with the mass media, and a positive public image. In short, any social movement rises or falls on its ability to attract resources and mobilize people. The collapse of socialism in Eastern Europe was largely the work of dissatisfied people in those countries. But assistance from outside, in the form of fax machines, copiers, telecommunications equipment, money, and moral support, was critical in allowing first the Poles and then people in other countries to successfully oppose their leaders.

As this example demonstrates, outsiders are as important as insiders to the victory of a social movement, and outlanders typically play a crucial role in supplying resources (McCarthy & Zald, 1977; Killian, 1984; Baron, Mittman, & Newman, 1991; Burstein, 1991). Socially disadvantaged people, by definition, lack the money, contacts, leadership skills, and organizational know-how that a successful movement requires, and it is here that sympathetic outsiders fill the resource gap. In our own country, well-to-do whites, including college students, performed a vital service to the black civil rights movement in the 1960s, and affluent men as well as women have taken a leading role in the current women's movement. Even a small core of powerful resource people can sometimes be enough to link a fledgling social movement to a larger sympathetic audience and the practical resources it needs to get off the ground (Snow, Zurcher, & Ekland-Olson, 1980; Snow, Rochford, Jr., Worden, & Benford, 1986).

On the other side of the coin, a lack of resources frustrates efforts toward intentional change. The history of the AIDS epidemic offers a case in point. Initially, the government made a minimal response as the incidence of AIDS rose in the early 1980s. To a large extent, gay communities in cities like San Francisco and New York were left to shoulder the responsibility for treatment and educational programs on their own. Gradually, as the general public began to grasp the dimensions of the problem, state and local governments started to allocate more resources. Only after 1985 did escalating public concern prompt the federal government to provide significant funding to fight this disease. Galvanizing the public, members of the entertainment industry lent not only money and visibility but their prestige and credibility to the movement to combat this deadly disease. These extensive resources have transformed a fledgling social movement into a well-organized national and global coalition of political leaders, educators, and medical specialists.

*Critical evaluation.* The strength of resource-mobilization theory lies in its recognition that resources as well as discontent are necessary to the success of a social movement. This theory also emphasizes the interplay between social movements and other groups and organizations that are capable of providing or withholding valuable resources. Continuing research in this area suggests that a movement's position in the power structure also affects the strategies it can employ; violence, for example, is a resource that can be used by people initially seeking entry into a political system, but it can only be used defensively once an organization becomes established (Grant & Wallace, 1991).

Critics of this approach maintain that even relatively powerless segments of a population can promote successful social movements if they manage to organize effectively and have strongly committed members. Research by Aldon Morris (1981) shows that people of color drew largely on their own skills and resources to fuel the civil rights movement of the 1950s and 1960s. A second problem with this theory is that it overstates the extent to which powerful people are willing to challenge the status quo. Some powerful whites did provide valuable resources to the black civil rights movement but, generally speaking, white elites remained unsympathetic (McAdam, 1982, 1983).

Overall, the success or failure of a social movement turns on the outcome of a political struggle between challengers and supporters of intentional change. A strong and united establishment, perhaps aided by a countermovement, decreases the chances that any social movement will effect meaningful change. If, however, the established powers are divided, a movement's chances for success multiply.

## "New Social Movements" Theory

During the 1980s one more theoretical approach to social movements emerged in response to the changing character of these movements. What is now called *new social movements theory* investigates the distinctive features of recent social movements in mature industrial societies of North America and Western Europe (Melucci, 1980; McAdam, McCarthy, & Zald, 1988; Kriesi, 1989).

The most familiar contemporary social movements deal with global ecology, women's and gay rights, reducing the risks of war, and animal rights, among others. One distinctive feature of these movements is their national scope. As Chapter 18 ("Politics and Government") explained, the state has expanded to become the dominant center of power in all industrial societies, and government now sets countless policies that affect entire populations. Not surprisingly, then, social movements have also assumed national (and sometimes international) proportions. Second, while traditional social movements such as labor organizations are concerned primarily with economic issues, new social movements tend to focus on cultural change and enhancing the quality of our social and physical surroundings. The international ecology movement, for example, opposes practices that aggravate global warming and other environmental dangers. Third, whereas traditional social movements that strive for economic equality tend to elicit strong support from working-class people, the new social movements with their non-economic agendas usually draw disproportionate support from middle-class people.

***Critical evaluation.*** Because the "new social movements" theory is a recent development, sociologists are still assessing its utility. One clear strength of this analysis is its understanding of the vast power of the state to shape society, making government the target of large-scale social movements. This approach also spotlights the power of the mass media to unite people around the world in pursuit of political goals.

This approach garners criticism, however, for exaggerating the differences between "traditional" and "new" social movements. The women's movement, for example, focuses on many of the same issues—workplace conditions and pay—that have consumed the energies of labor organizations for decades.

Each of the five theories we have presented explains part of the complex process by which social movements arise. Table 22–1 summarizes the theories.

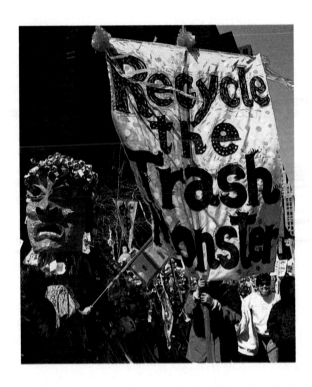

Environmentalists are a prominent example of what are called "new social movements." Such efforts for change typically involve people in many countries and are concerned with "quality of life" issues that participants believe are vital to the future of humanity. Here, throngs of people in New York participate in an Earth Day demonstration.

**Table 22–1  THEORIES OF SOCIAL MOVEMENTS: A SUMMARY**

| | |
|---|---|
| Deprivation Theory | People join as a result of experiencing relative deprivation. Social movement is a means of seeking change that brings participants greater benefits. Social movements are especially likely when rising expectations are frustrated. |
| Mass-Society Theory | People who lack established social ties are mobilized into social movements. Periods of social breakdown are likely to spawn social movements. Social movement is a means of gaining a sense of belonging and social participation. |
| Structural-Strain Theory | People join because of their shared concern about the inability of society to operate as they believe it should. The growth of a social movement reflects many factors, including a belief in its legitimacy and some precipitating event that provokes action. |
| Resource-Mobilization Theory | People may join for all of the reasons noted above and also because of social ties to existing members. The success or failure of a social movement depends largely on the resources available to it. Also important is the extent of opposition to its goals within the larger society. |
| "New Social Movement" Theory | People join motivated by a concern for "quality of life," not necessarily economic issues. Mobilization is national or international in scope. New social movements are a response to the expansion of the mass media, and also the power of the state in modern industrial societies to affect people's lives for good or ill. |

## Stages in Social Movements

Despite the many differences that set one social movement apart from others, all efforts at intentional change unfold in similar stages. Researchers have identified four phases in the life of the typical social movement (Blumer, 1969; Mauss, 1975; Tilly, 1978).

*Stage 1: Emergence.* Social movements are driven by the perception that all is not well. Some, such as the civil rights and women's movements, are born of widespread dissatisfaction. Others emerge only as a small vanguard group increases public awareness of some issue, as gay activists have done with respect to the threat posed by AIDS.

*Stage 2: Coalescence.* After emerging, a social movement must define itself clearly and develop a strategy for "going public." Leaders must determine policies, select tactics, build morale, and recruit new members. At this stage, the movement may engage in collective action like rallies or demonstrations to attract media attention in hopes of capturing the notice of the public. Additionally, the movement may form alliances with other organizations to gain necessary resources.

*Stage 3: Bureaucratization.* To become an established political force, a social movement must assume bureaucratic traits, as described in Chapter 7 ("Groups and Organizations"). As it becomes "routinized," a social movement depends less on the charisma and talents of a few leaders and relies more on a capable staff. Some social movements do not become established in this way, however. Many activist organizations on college campuses during the late 1960s were energized by a single charismatic leader and, consequently, did not endure for long. On the other hand, the well-established National Organization for Women (NOW), despite changing leadership, offers a steady voice on behalf of the women's movement.

At the same time, bureaucratization can sometimes hinder a social movement. Frances Piven and Richard Cloward (1977), reviewing social movements in U.S. history, noted that leaders sometimes become so engrossed in building an organization that they neglect the need to sustain sentiments of insurgency among their followers. In such cases, the radical edge of protest is lost.

*Stage 4: Decline.* Social movements are inherently dynamic, so a decline is not necessarily a demise (Wright, 1987). Eventually, however, most social movements lose their influence. Frederick Miller (1983) suggests four reasons why this may occur.

First, decline may simply signal success, as members see nothing more to accomplish. For example, the women's suffrage movement declined after it won for women in the United States the right to vote. Such clear-cut successes are rare, however, since few social movements have one specific goal. More commonly, gaining one victory adds impetus to new campaigns. Because issues related to gender extend far beyond voting, the women's movement has been reborn.

Second, a social movement may flag due to organizational factors, such as poor leadership, loss of interest among members, exhaustion of resources, repression by authorities, or excessive bureaucratization. Some people attracted by the dynamism of a new social movement lose interest when formal routines replace the excitement of early efforts at change. Fragmentation due to internal conflicts over goals and tactics is another common problem. Students for a Democratic Society (SDS), which developed out of the civil rights and antiwar movements of the 1960s, grew fragmented as some members decided to pursue more radical and often violent strategies to achieve their goals while others reverted to supporting traditional political parties as a way to press for change.

Third, a social movement may degenerate if the established power structure, through offers of money, prestige, and other rewards, succeeds in diverting leaders from their goals. "Selling out" is one facet of the iron law of oligarchy, noted in Chapter 7 ("Groups and Organizations"), by which organizational leaders may use their positions to enrich themselves. Jerry Rubin, a political activist of the late 1960s, parlayed his celebrity status as a rebel into a career in the New York financial world. But it actually works both ways: there are people who have left lucrative, high-prestige occupations to become activists too. Cat Stevens, a famous rock star of the 1970s, became a Muslim, changed his name to Yusuf Islam, and now promotes the spread of his religion.

Fourth and finally, the demise of a social movement may stem from repression. Those in power may crush a movement for social change by frightening away participants, discouraging new recruits, or even imprisoning leaders. The intensity of the state's reaction depends on how much of a threat the movement is deemed to be by officials with the power to crack down on it. The government of South Africa, for example, banned the African National Congress (ANC), a political organization seeking to overthrow the state-supported system of apartheid, so that even suspected members of the ANC

Although separated for centuries by social barriers, there is now hope that blacks and whites in South Africa will be able to forge a racially unified society. In a 1992 referendum, whites voiced their support for continued negotiations with the black majority towards a democratic government.

were subject to arrest. In 1990 the decades-old ban was lifted, with the release of ANC leader Nelson Mandela after twenty-seven years of imprisonment.

Beyond the reasons noted by Miller, a fifth cause of decline is that a social movement may "go mainstream." Some movements become an accepted part of the system—typically after realizing at least some of their goals—to the point that they no longer challenge the status quo. For example, the U.S. labor movement is now well established; its leaders control vast sums of money and, to some critics, at least, they now resemble the business tycoons they opposed in the past.

Figure 22–3 provides a graphic summary of the various stages of social movements.

## Social Movements and Social Change

Social movements exist to encourage—or to resist—social change. Whatever the intention, their success varies from case to case. Racial equality in the United States, still an unrealized goal, has certainly been advanced by the civil rights movement despite opposition from a handful of white supremacist countermovements like the Aryan Nation and the Ku Klux Klan.

Sometimes we overlook the success of past social movements and take for granted the changes that other people struggled so hard to win. Early labor movements in the United States, for example, battled for decades to end child labor in factories, to limit working hours, to make the workplace safer, and to establish what we now call the right to bargain collectively with employers. Legislation protecting the environment also grew out of successful social movements throughout this century. The women's movement in the United States has yet to attain full equality under the law for the sexes. But it has extended the legal rights and social opportunities of women to the extent that many young people are surprised to learn that—earlier in this century—women rarely worked for income and none were permitted to cast a vote.

This all leads to one overarching conclusion: we can draw a direct link between social movements and change. Social transformations such as the Industrial Revolution and the rise of capitalism sparked alliances among people intent on changing some dimension of their lives. By the same token, the efforts of workers, women, racial and ethnic minorities, and gay people have sent ripples of change throughout our society. Thus social change is both the cause and the consequence of social movements.

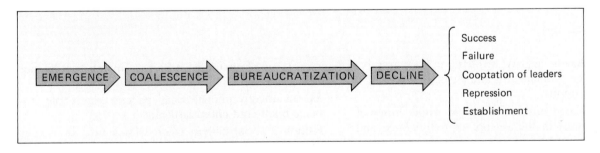

**Figure 22–3**   Stages in the Lives of Social Movements

# Summary

1. A collectivity differs from a social group in its limited social interaction, its vague social boundaries, and its weak and often unconventional norms.

2. Crowds, an important type of collective behavior, take various forms: casual crowds, conventional crowds, expressive crowds, acting crowds, and protest crowds.

3. Crowds that become emotionally intense and even violent spawn mobs and riots. Mobs pursue a specific goal; rioting is undirected destructiveness.

4. Contagion theory views crowds as anonymous, suggestible, and subject to escalating emotions. Convergence theory links crowd behavior to the traits of participants. Emergent-norm theory holds that crowds may develop their own behavioral norms.

5. Crowds have figured heavily in social change throughout history. Depending on political orientation, the observer perceives crowds as either detrimental or constructive.

6. Rumor, which thrives in a climate of ambiguity, is concerned with public issues; gossip, a closely related concept, deals with personal issues of local interest.

7. Public opinion consists of people's positions on issues of widespread importance. Such attitudes reflect people's social background. On any public issue a small proportion of the population claims to hold no opinion.

8. Mass hysteria is a type of collective behavior by which people anxiously respond to a significant event, real or imagined. In a spiral of panic, hysteria may lead to ineffective action, which provokes further frenzy.

9. In industrial societies, people employ fashion to gain social prestige. A fad, which is more unconventional than a fashion, is also of shorter duration but is embraced with greater enthusiasm.

10. A social movement entails deliberate activity intended to promote or discourage change. Social movements vary in the breadth and depth of their goals.

11. According to deprivation theory, social movements arise out of relative deprivation rather than anyone's absolute circumstances.

12. Mass-society theory suggests that people join social movements to gain a sense of belonging and social significance.

13. Structural-strain theory explains the development of social movements as a cumulative consequence of six factors. Well-formulated grievances and goals encourage the organization of social movements; undirected anger and frustration promote rioting.

14. Resource-mobilization theory ties the success or failure of a social movement to the availability of resources like money, human labor, and alliances with other organizations.

15. A typical social movement proceeds through specific stages. First, emergence occurs as leaders define a public issue requiring action; second, coalescence represents a movement's entry into public life; third, bureaucratization refers to a movement's increasingly formal organization, and fourth, a movement declines as a result of failure or, sometimes, success.

16. The accomplishment of social movements is evident in characteristics of society that people now take for granted. Just as movements produce change, so change itself sparks social movements.

# Key Concepts

**collective behavior** activity involving a large number of people, often spontaneous, and typically in violation of established norms

**collectivity** a large number of people whose minimal interaction occurs in the absence of well-defined and conventional norms

**crowd** a temporary gathering of people who share a common focus of attention and whose members influence one another

**fad** an unconventional social pattern that people embrace briefly but enthusiastically

**fashion** a social pattern favored for a time by a large number of people

**gossip** rumor about the personal affairs of others

**mass behavior** collective behavior among people dispersed over a wide geographical area

**mass hysteria** a form of dispersed collective behavior by which people respond to a real or imagined event with irrational, frantic behavior

**mob** a highly emotional crowd that pursues some violent or destructive goal

**panic** a form of localized collective behavior by which people react to a threat or other stimulus with emotional, irrational, and often self-destructive behavior

**propaganda** information presented with the intention of shaping public opinion

**relative deprivation** a perceived disadvantage arising from some specific comparison

**riot** a social eruption that is highly emotional, violent, and undirected

**rumor** unsubstantiated information spread informally, often by word of mouth

**social movement** organized activity that encourages or discourages social change

## Suggested Readings

These books probe in greater detail some topics covered in this chapter.

Ralph H. Turner and Lewis M. Killian. *Collective Behavior.* 3rd ed. Englewood Cliffs, NJ: Prentice Hall, 1987.

William Gamson. *The Strategy of Social Protest.* 2nd ed. Belmont, CA: Wadsworth, 1990.

Here is a historical account of how and why sociologists have understood (or, more accurately, misunderstood) crowd behavior.

Clark McPhail. *The Myth of the Maddening Crowd.* New York: Aldine De Gruyter, 1991.

This broad investigation of African-American politics in the United States contrasts various political movements that span fifty years.

Manning Marable. *Black American Politics: From the Washington Marches to Jesse Jackson.* London: Verso, 1985.

Chicano protest in the western United States, the focus of this book, is examined in terms of how some people express their suffering and why others may or may not respond.

John C. Hammerback, Richard J. Jensen, and José Angel Gutierrez. *A War of Words: Chicano Protest in the 1960s and 1970s.* Westport, CT: Greenwood Press, 1985.

This recent analysis further builds on the mass-society approach to social movements.

Alberto Melucci. *Nomads of the Present: Social Movements and Individual Needs in Contemporary America.* Philadelphia: Temple University Press, 1989.

This book analyzes three important social movements of a turbulent decade: the antiwar movement, the women's movement, and the civil rights movement.

Stewart Burns. *Social Movements of the 1960s: Searching for Democracy.* Boston: G.K. Hall/Twayne, 1990.

This valuable source of information on the peace movement in the United States traces its various expressions from the colonial period to the present.

Charles F. Howlett. *The American Peace Movement: References and Resources.* Boston: G.K. Hall, 1991.

The first of these books offers a historical overview of the gay and lesbian movements in the United States. The second concludes that when compared with the black civil rights movement, the gay movement has failed because of poor strategies.

Barry D. Adam. *The Rise of a Gay and Lesbian Movement.* Boston: Twayne, 1987.

Marshall Kirk and Hunter Madsen. *After the Ball.* Garden City, NY: Doubleday, 1989.

This account of one of the most stunning examples of collective behavior in recent years tries to explain the mass suicide of some 900 members of a sect called the People's Temple in Jonestown, Guyana.

John R. Hall. *Gone from the Promised Land: Jonestown in American Cultural History.* New Brunswick, NJ: Transaction, 1987.

Here is a personal account of a teenager's experiences during the Cultural Revolution in China from 1966 to 1969, which has been dubbed a mass movement out of control.

Gao Yuan. *Born Red: A Chronicle of the Cultural Revolution.* Stanford, CA: Stanford University Press, 1987.

These two books look at social movements in world perspective. The first explores how organizations of workers brought about change in Spain after the death of dictator Francisco Franco; the second highlights the tension between support for change and the status quo in poor societies of the Third World.

Robert M. Fishman. *Working-Class Organization and the Return to Democracy in Spain.* Ithaca, NY: Cornell University Press, 1990.

John Walton. *Reluctant Rebels: Comparative Studies of Revolution and Underdevelopment.* New York: Columbia University Press, 1984.

A noted global activist argues for a broad-based movement to renew our society's core cultural values.

Frances Moore Lappé. *Rediscovering America's Values.* New York: Ballantine Books, 1989.

# Social Change and Modernity

The firelight flickers in the gathering darkness. Chief Kanhonk sits, as he has done every evening for many years, ready to begin an evening of animated talk and storytelling.[1] These are the hours of every day when the Kaiapo, a small society of Brazil's Amazon region, celebrate their culture. As a traditional people with no written language, the Kaiapo elders rely on evenings before the fire to instruct their grandchildren in their people's history and way of life. In the past, evenings like this have been filled with tales of brave Kaiapo warriors fighting off Portuguese traders who came in pursuit of slaves and gold.

But as the minutes slip by, only a few older villagers assemble for the evening ritual. None of the children is to be found. "It is the Big Ghost," one old man grumbles, explaining the poor turnout. The "Big Ghost" has indeed descended upon them: its presence is evident in the soft glow spilling from windows of homes throughout the village. The Kaiapo children—and many adults as well—are watching television. The consequences of installing a satellite dish in the village three years ago have turned out to be greater than anyone imagined. In the end, what their enemies failed to do to the Kaiapo with guns they may do to themselves with prime-time

programming. Those around the fire sit in gloomy silence, knowing that their culture is once again under attack and may soon be gone (Simons, 1989).

The Kaiapo are distinctive members of the 230,000 native people who inhabit the country we call Brazil. They are easily identified by their striking body paint and ornate ceremonial dress. Recently, they have become rich as profits from gold mining and harvesting mahogany trees have flowed into the settlement. A favorite topic of conversation in the village is whether their new-found fortune is a blessing or a curse. To some, affluence means the opportunity to learn about the outside world through travel and television. Others, like Chief Kanhonk, express a different view. Sitting by the fire, he thinks aloud about how their wealth can help the Kaiapo to live better: "I have been saying that people must buy useful things like knives and fishing hooks. Television does not fill the stomach. It only shows our children and grandchildren white people's things." Bebtopup, the oldest priest, nods in agreement and adds, "The night is the time the old people teach the young people. Television has stolen the night" (Simons 1989:37).

The transformation of the Kaiapo raises profound questions about what causes social change; their current plight forces us to wonder whether change—even toward a higher material standard of living—is always for the better. Moreover, the drama of the Kaiapo is being played out around the globe as more and more traditional cul-

---

[1] This opening is a selective adaptation of the account provided by Simons (1989).

tures are drawn away from their past by a materialistic way of life modeled on the rich societies of the First World.

This chapter, then, examines social change as a process with both positive and negative consequences. Of particular interest to people in the United States is what sociologists call *modernity*, the product of social changes beginning with the Industrial Revolution. But we shall also consider how rich and powerful nations, like the United States, are involved in changes affecting the rest of the world.

## What Is Social Change?

Earlier chapters have examined human societies in terms of both stability and change. The relatively *static* social patterns include status and roles, social stratification, and the various social institutions. The *dynamic* forces that sometimes recast human consciousness, behavior, and needs include social conflict, innovations in technology, the development of formal organizations, the growth of cities, and social movements. It is factors of this kind that fuel **social change,** *the transformation of culture and social institutions over time.* The process of social change has four general characteristics.

1.  *Social change is universal although the rate of change varies.* "Nothing is constant except death and taxes," as the saying goes. However, social patterns related to death and dying have changed in recent centuries, as Chapter 5 ("Socialization") explained. Additionally, people today die at a much later age than in the past. And taxes, which emerged along with complex social organization, were unknown to most of our ancestors. In short, one would be hard pressed to identify anything that is not subject to the twists and turns of social change.

    Still, some societies change faster than others. Chapter 4 ("Society") explained that hunting and gathering societies were remarkably stable over thousands of years. As technology becomes more complex, a society's rate of social change increases (Lenski, Lenski, & Nolan, 1991), because technological advance multiplies the effect of discovery as any single invention is combined with cultural elements already in place.

    Moreover, even in a given society, some cul-

Increasing technological sophistication and the expansion of multinational corporations have made the world seem smaller, as products familiar to us are now eagerly consumed on the other side of the globe. Does this mean that thousands of historically distinctive ways of life will become a single global McCulture? What are the advantages and drawbacks of this expansion of First-World influence?

tural elements change more quickly than others. William Ogburn's (1964) theory of *cultural lag* recognizes that material culture—that is, things—usually changes faster than nonmaterial culture—ideas and attitudes (see Chapter 3, "Culture"). For example, medical devices that prolong the life of a seriously ill person have developed more rapidly than have ethical standards for deciding when and how to employ this technology.

2.  *Social change is sometimes intentional but often unplanned.* Industrial societies actively encourage many kinds of change. For example, scientists seek more efficient forms of energy, advertisers try to convince consumers that a new gadget is a "neces-

sity," and government officials seek ways to increase equality of opportunity among various categories of people. Yet even the experts rarely envision all the consequences of the changes they propose. Early automobile manufacturers understood that cars would allow people to travel in a single day distances that had required weeks or months a century before. But no one foresaw how profoundly the mobility provided by automobiles would affect families and reshape cities and suburbs, not to mention resulting in some 50,000 accidental deaths each year.

3. *Social change often generates controversy.* The historical record provides ample evidence that social change yields both good and bad consequences. Politically speaking, in other words, every social transformation wins support from some people and provokes opposition from others. Capitalists welcomed the Industrial Revolution because advancing technology increased productivity and profits. Many workers, however, fearing that machines would make their skills obsolete, strongly resisted "progress." Similarly, South African blacks have spoken almost with a single voice in support of the gradual weakening of apartheid. Although a majority of whites supported the 1992 referendum to end this system of racial separation, many harbor doubts about the long-term effects of this change. In the United States, changing patterns of social interaction between people of color and whites, between women and men, and between gays and heterosexuals give rise to tensions, misunderstandings, and an overall sense of unease.

4. *Social change has variable consequences.* Some social changes have only passing significance, whereas other transformations have far-reaching ramifications. At one extreme, fads, such as the "Teenage Mutant Ninja Turtles," arise and dissipate quickly. At the other, members of our society are still adjusting to powerful technological advances such as television half a century after its introduction. Today we can scarcely imagine how the computer-based Information Revolution will transform the entire world during the next century. Like the automobile and television, computers will have both positive and negative impacts, opening up new kinds of jobs while eliminating old ones, and facilitating the processing of information while compromising personal privacy.

# Causes of Social Change

Many factors underlie social change. Some change emerges within a particular society. But in a world linked by sophisticated communication and transportation technology, change in one place often prompts change elsewhere.

## Culture and Change

Culture is a dynamic system of symbols that continually gains new elements and loses others. Chapter 3 ("Culture") identified three important sources of cultural change. First, *invention* produces mechanical objects, ideas, and social patterns that reshape society to varying degrees. Rocket-propulsion research, beginning in the 1940s, has produced increasingly sophisticated vehicles for space flight. Today we take such technology for granted, and during the next century probably a significant number of people will travel in space.

A second process, *discovery*, occurs when people recognize existing elements of the world they hadn't noticed before or learn to see them in a new way. For example, medical advances offer a growing understanding of how the human body operates. Beyond the direct effects for human health, medical discoveries have also stretched life expectancy, setting in motion here what Chapter 14 ("Aging and the Elderly") calls the "graying of the United States."

Third, *diffusion* creates change as cultural elements spread from one society to another through trade, migration, and mass communication. Ralph Linton (1937) recognized that many familiar elements of our culture have come to us from other lands—for example, cloth (developed in Asia), clocks (invented in Europe), and coins (devised in Turkey). Generally, material things diffuse more readily than nonmaterial cultural traits. The Kaiapo, introduced at the beginning of this chapter, were quick to adopt television but have been reluctant to embrace the materialism and individualism that gradually seizes those who spend hours watching Western, commercial programming.

During its entire history, the United States has been transformed by cultural diffusion accompanying immigration. In recent decades, people from Latin America and Asia have been introducing new cultural patterns, clearly evident in the sights, smells, and sounds of cities across the country (Fallows, 1983; Muller & Espenshade, 1985). Conversely, the global power of the United States ensures that many elements of our culture—from the taste of hamburgers to the sounds of Harlem rap music to the skills of Harvard M.B.A.s—have diffused to other societies.

## Social Structure and Change

Tension and conflict within a society also produce social change. The link between social structure and social change stands at the core of Karl Marx's ideas (see especially Chapter 4, "Society," and Chapter 9, "Social Stratification"). Marx pointed to conflict between social classes as the engine of social change. In industrial-capitalist societies, he explained, the struggle between capitalists and workers drives society toward a system of socialist production. In the century since Marx's death, this model has proven simplistic; yet, he correctly foresaw that social conflict arising from inequality (involving race and gender as well as social class) would propel every society, including the United States, toward change. The last chapter ("Collective Behavior and Social Movements") described how movements supported by labor, people of color, women, and gay men and lesbians are continuing to reshape our society.

## Ideas and Change

Max Weber, too, contributed to our understanding of social change. While Weber acknowledged the importance of conflict based on material production, he traced the roots of social change to the world of ideas. He illustrated his argument by showing how people who display charisma (described in Chapters 17, "Religion," and 18, "Politics and Government") can convey a message that sometimes changes the world. Weber also spotlighted the importance of ideas by revealing how the world view of early Protestants drove them to embrace industrial capitalism (see Chapter 4, "Society"). Because industrial capitalism developed primarily in areas of Western Europe where the Protestant work ethic was strong, Weber (1958; orig. 1904–1905) concluded that the disciplined rationality of Calvinist Protestants was instrumental in this change.

Ideas also fuel social movements. Chapter 22 ("Collective Behavior and Social Movements") explained that a social movement may emerge from the decision to modify society in some manner (say, to clean up the environment) or from a sense that existing social arrangements must be reformed (Smelser, 1962). The international gay rights movement draws strength from the contention that homosexuals have been the targets of prejudice and discrimination, and that lesbians and gay men should enjoy rights equal to those of the heterosexual majority. The persisting opposition to the gay rights movement indicates the power of ideas—as ideology—to inhibit as well as to advance social change.

## The Natural Environment and Change

Because human societies interact with their natural environment, change in one tends to produce change in the other. Many Native American cultures viewed the natural world with reverence, living according to natural rhythms. European settlers who came to North America saw nature in a strikingly different way: as an adversary to be tamed and then molded to human purposes. Confronting a wilderness, these newcomers systematically cut down forests to provide space and materials for building, established towns, extended roads in every direction, and dammed rivers as sources of water and energy. Early in the seventeenth century, Manhattan Island was covered with woods and streams; today the center of New York City is twenty-two square miles of almost unbroken concrete and buildings that soar thousands of feet into the sky. Such construction reveals both our cultural determination to master the natural environment and the centrality of ideas like "growth" in our capitalist culture.

Despite its advantages, technological development increasingly threatens the natural environment. With our high standard of living, the people of the United States generate more than 300 billion pounds of refuse each year. Where is it to go? The operation of hundreds of millions of motor vehicles, tens of thousands of factories, and the routine use of dozens of household products all release hazardous chemicals into the air. Only in the last few decades have we begun to realize the potential hazardous effects of our way of life on our natural surroundings; devising workable solutions to this problem will surely require decades more.

Our way of life is also based on very high consumption of energy. As Global Map 23–1 shows, residents of rich countries, including the United States, are by far the highest energy users in the world, consuming one hundred times as much energy as people who live in the poorest societies of the Third World. Not only

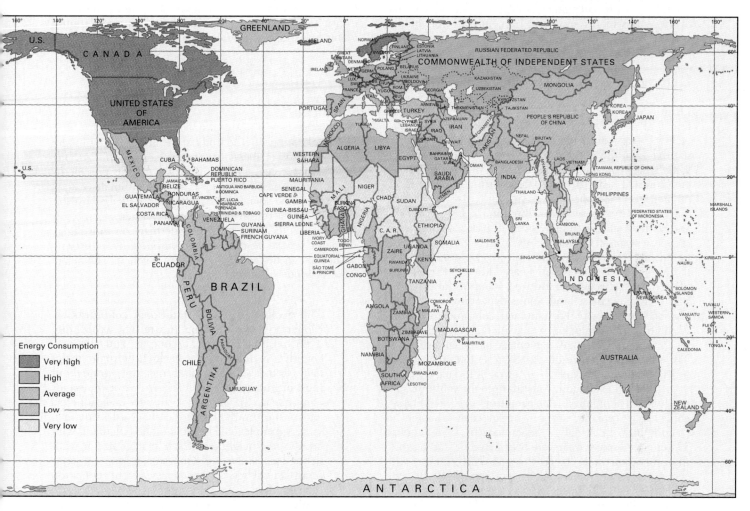

**Global Map 23–1** Energy Consumption in Global Perspective
The members of industrial societies consume far more energy than others on the planet.
The typical U.S. resident uses the same amount of energy in a year as one hundred people
in the Central African Republic. This means that the most economically productive societies
are also those that place the greatest burden on the natural environment.

does this pattern raise concerns about conservation of finite resources, it also highlights once again the material disparity that divides people of the world.

Just as people act on the natural environment, so does nature affect human societies, sometimes with devastating effect. Throughout history, entire civilizations have succumbed to natural disasters in the form of floods, volcanic eruptions, and earthquakes. A thriving civilization in ancient India was destroyed in about 1500 B.C.E. as the waters of the Indus River gradually rose. Four centuries later, devastating earthquakes ended an early civilization on the island of Crete (Hamblin, 1973; Stavri-

Chapter 23  Social Change and Modernity  643

anos, 1983). Today, life is still disrupted by such natural calamities. In recent years, earthquakes have killed tens of thousands in Armenia and Iran, just as droughts in central Africa have devastated the lives of millions.

## Demography and Change

Demographic factors (described in Chapter 21, "Population and Urbanization") also cause social change. Increasing population places escalating demands on the natural environment and shapes social relationships. In some small countries, notably the Netherlands and Japan, limited space already affects virtually every facet of life. For example, homes in Amsterdam are small and narrow in comparison to those in the United States, and staircases are extremely steep in order to make efficient use of space. In Tokyo, bus drivers routinely negotiate city streets that many American drivers would consider dangerously narrow for even a car. Although the United States and Canada have enjoyed a bounty of physical space, urbanization and industrialization have also changed our way of life and will continue to do so. About three-fourths of all North Americans live in cities, which cover only a small percentage of the land surface. The way of life that results barely resembles that found in the rural villages and small towns of the past.

Profound change also results from the shifting composition of a population. The people of the United States, collectively speaking, are growing older as Chapter 14 ("Aging and the Elderly") explained. In 1990, almost 13 percent of our people were over sixty-five, three times the proportion in 1900. By the year 2030, seniors will account for one in four U.S. residents (U.S. Bureau of the Census, 1991). Medical research and health-care services will increasingly focus on the elderly, and common stereotypes about old people will be challenged as more men and women enter this stage of life (Barberis, 1981). Life may change in countless additional ways as homes and household products are redesigned to meet the needs of older consumers.

Migration within and among societies is another demographic factor that often promotes dramatic social change. Between 1870 and 1930, tens of millions of foreign immigrants swelled the populations of industrial cities in the United States. Millions of rural Americans joined them. As a result, farm communities declined as metropolises expanded, and for the first time the United States became a predominantly urban society. In the process, cultural patterns from around the world diffused throughout the country. Similar changes are taking place today, as population shifts from Snowbelt to Sunbelt states, where they are being joined by immigrants from Latin America and Asia.

# Modernity

A central concept in the study of social change is **modernity,** *patterns of social life linked to industrialization.* In everyday usage, modernity refers to the present in relation to the past. Sociologists include within this catch-all concept the social patterns that arose along with the Industrial Revolution beginning in Western Europe in the mid-eighteenth century. **Modernization** thus designates *the process of social change initiated by industrialization.* Peter Berger (1977) notes four general characteristics of modernization.

1. **The decline of small, traditional communities.** Modernity involves "the progressive weakening, if not destruction, of the concrete and relatively cohesive communities in which human beings have found solidarity and meaning throughout most of history" (Berger, 1977:72). For thousands of years, in the camps of hunters and gatherers and in the rural villages of early North American settlers, people lived in small-scale settlements with family and neighbors. Each person had a well-defined place in a traditional world, based on sentiments and beliefs that were passed from generation to generation. Living in small primary groups certainly limited the range of personal experience, but it conferred a strong sense of identity, belonging, and purpose.

   Small, isolated communities still exist in the United States, of course, but they are now home to only a small percentage of people. Even for rural families, efficient communication and rapid transportation have changed the meaning of physical space so that no one is now isolated from events in the society as a whole and in the larger world. For everyone, too, the family no longer is the unrivaled center of everyday life. As Talcott Parsons (1966) noted, modern living is played out in distinct institutional settings including schools, workplaces, hospitals, prisons, and places of worship.

In response to the accelerated pace of change in the late nineteenth century, Paul Gauguin (1848–1903) left his native France for the South Seas where he was captivated by a simpler and seemingly timeless way of life. He romanticized this environment in his 1894 painting *Mahana no Atua (Day of the Gods)*.

*(Paul Gauguin, Day of the Gods [Mahana no Atua]. 1894. Oil on canvas. 68.3 × 91.5 cm. The Art Institute of Chicago, Helen Birch Bartlett Memorial Collection.)*

2. **The expansion of personal choice.** People in traditional, preindustrial societies view their lives as being shaped by forces beyond human control—gods, spirits, or simply fate. Jealously protecting their traditions, these societies grant members a narrow range of personal choices.

   As the power of tradition diminishes, a society's members come to see their lives as an unending series of options. Berger calls this process *individualization*. Many people in the United States, for instance, adopt one "lifestyle" or another, since a way of life that one person finds suitable may hold little appeal for another. Recognizing alternatives in everyday life, of course, parallels a willingness to embrace change. Modern people, then, readily imagine the world being different from what it is.

3. **Increasing diversity in beliefs.** In preindustrial societies, strong family ties and powerful religious beliefs enforce conformity, discouraging diversity and change. Modernization promotes a more rational, scientific world view, in which traditional beliefs lose their force and morality becomes a matter of individual attitude. The growth of cities, the expansion of impersonal, formal organizations, and the social mix of immigrants from around the world combine to foster a diversity of beliefs and behavior

as well as a tolerant openness to those who differ from ourselves.

   Chapter 17 ("Religion") spotlighted *secularization*, the historical decline in the importance of religion. The weakening of religious doctrine, and especially the separation of church and state, helps to expand the range of personal beliefs in modern societies. Of course, faced with such bewildering choices, many modern people look to religion for meaning and direction. This is why, as support for the more established churches has declined in the United States, fundamentalist religious activity has flourished (Stark & Bainbridge, 1981; Johnstone, 1983).

4. **Future orientation and growing awareness of time.** People in modern societies share a distinctive appreciation of time. First, we tend to think more about the future, while preindustrial people are past-oriented and guided by traditions. Modern people, moreover, look toward the future, typically imagining that life will be enhanced by inventions and discoveries. Second, modern societies organize daily routines according to precise units of time. With the introduction of clocks in the late Middle Ages, Europeans began to think in terms of hours and minutes. Why? Because of the growing importance of economic activity. Industrial technology

depends on the precise measurement of time; in addition, the Industrial Revolution prompted capitalists, preoccupied with profits, to proclaim, "Time is money!" Berger suggests that one shorthand way of gauging a society's degree of modernization is to note what proportion of people wear wristwatches.

According to Berger, then, modernization emancipates people from the tyranny of tradition, but leaves them without the comforting security of heritage and roots. No longer do people live in tightly knit communities where traditional religious beliefs provide each person with a strong sense of belonging but little individual freedom. Modern societies offer far more autonomy but less sense of purpose and fewer enduring social ties.

Finally, recall that modernization is one of the causes of sociology itself. As Chapter 1 ("The Sociological Perspective") explained, the discipline originated in the wake of the Industrial Revolution in Western Europe, at a time and place where social change was proceeding most intensely. Early European and U.S. sociologists attempted to describe and explain the rise of modern society and its consequences—both good and bad—for human beings.

## Ferdinand Toennies: The Loss of Community

The German sociologist Ferdinand Toennies, who is introduced in the box, produced a highly influential account of modernization, detailed in Chapter 21 ("Population and Urbanization"). Like Peter Berger, whose work he influenced, Toennies viewed modernization as the progressive loss of human community, or *Gemeinschaft*, which provided personal ties, a sense of group membership, and loyalty within small communities. The Industrial Revolution undermined this strong social fabric by introducing a businesslike emphasis on facts and efficiency. European and North American societies gradually became rootless and impersonal and people came

## PROFILE

# Ferdinand Toennies (1855–1936)

Can traditional human virtues such as selflessness and honor survive in the modern world? This question guided the work of Ferdinand Toennies, who, along with Max Weber and Georg Simmel, helped to establish sociology as an academic discipline in Germany.

Born to a wealthy family in the German countryside, Toennies received an extensive education. He also learned a great deal from observing the world about him—especially how the Industrial Revolution was transforming Germany and other European countries. Toennies's work reveals a deep concern with the common-sense notion of "progress"; he had serious qualms about whether "progress" was actually improving the quality of life in modern societies. His influential book *Gemeinschaft*

*and Gesellschaft* (1963; orig. 1887) is therefore both a chronicle of modernization and an indictment of an increasingly impersonal world.

Toennies's thesis is that traditional societies, built on kinship and neighborhood, nourish collective sentiments, morality, and honor. Modernization washes across traditional society like an acid, eroding human community and unleashing rampant individualism. Toennies stopped short of asserting that modern society was in a basic sense "worse" than societies of the past, and he made a point of praising the spread of rational, scientific thinking. Nevertheless, the growing individualism and selfishness of modern society troubled him considerably. Knowing that there could be no return to the past, he looked to the future, hoping that perhaps some new form of social organization would combine traditional collective responsibility and modern rationality.

SOURCE: Based on Cahnman & Heberle (1971).

George Tooker's painting *The Subway* depicts a common problem of modern life: weakening social ties and eroding traditions create a generic humanity in which everyone is alike yet each person is an anxious stranger in the midst of others.

to associate mostly on the basis of self-interest—a state Toennies called *Gesellschaft* (1963; orig. 1887).

Much of the United States early in this century approximated Toennies's concept of *Gemeinschaft*. Families that had lived in small villages and towns for many generations were tightly integrated into a hard-working, slow-moving way of life. This social world was circumscribed in space as well as in its way of life. Telephones (invented in 1876) were rare even after 1915, when the first coast-to-coast call made history. Living without television (introduced in 1939 and rare until the 1950s), families entertained themselves, often gathering with friends in the evening—much like Brazil's Kaiapo—to share stories, sorrows, or song. Without rapid transportation (although Henry Ford's assembly line began in 1908, cars became common only after World War II), many people thought of their own town as their entire world.

Inevitable tensions and conflicts—sometimes based on race, ethnicity, and religion—characterized small communities of the past. According to Toennies, however, the traditional ties of *Gemeinschaft* bound people of a community together, "essentially united in spite of all separating factors" (1963:65).

Modern societies are closer to Toennies's concept of *Gesellschaft*, in which people are "essentially separated in spite of uniting factors" (1963:65). In large cities, for example, most people live among strangers, and ig-

nore people they pass on the street. Trust is hard to come by in a mobile and anonymous society; in a recent survey, a majority of adults in the United States claimed that "you can't be too careful" in dealing with people (N.O.R.C., 1991:195). No wonder, as one news report indicated, 15 million men and women attend weekly support groups—also made up of strangers—in which they establish temporary emotional ties and find someone who is willing simply to *listen* (Leerhsen, 1990).

A major contributor to rootlessness in the United States is our high level of geographic mobility. Table 23–1 on page 648 shows that one in six households in the United States reported moving during the year because of a new job, divorce, or simply in search of something better.

Modern life is not completely devoid of *Gemeinschaft*. Even in a world of strangers, friendships are often strong and lasting. Traditions are especially pronounced in many ethnic neighborhoods where residents maintain their local community ties. But in cosmopolitan districts of large cities, an indifference to those outside of an immediate circle—the attitude that disturbed Toennies in the 1880s—continues to pose an ethical dilemma today, as the box on page 649 explains.

***Critical evaluation.*** Toennies's theory of *Gemeinschaft* and *Gesellschaft* is the most widely cited model for describing modernization. The theory's strength lies in its

**Table 23–1**  MOVING ON IN THE MODERN UNITED STATES

| | Residence in 1990 | | | | |
|---|---|---|---|---|---|
| Region | Same House as 1989 | Different House than in 1989 | Different House Same County | Different County Same State | Different State |
| Northeast | 87.4% | 11.9% | 7.6% | 2.4% | 2.0% |
| Midwest | 83.9 | 15.8 | 9.6 | 3.1 | 3.1 |
| South | 80.6 | 18.8 | 11.1 | 3.7 | 3.9 |
| West | 77.2 | 21.7 | 14.0 | 3.8 | 3.9 |
| Total U.S. | 82.1 | 17.3 | 10.6 | 3.3 | 3.3 |

SOURCE:  U.S. Census Bureau, *Geographical Mobility. March 1989 to March 1990* (Washington, DC: U.S. Government Printing Office, 1991), pp. 19–20.

synthesis of various dimensions of change—growing population, the rise of cities, greater impersonality. However, Toennies's approach falls short by failing to specify which factors are cause and which are effect. Critics have also asserted that Toennies favored—perhaps even romanticized—traditional societies.

## Emile Durkheim: The Division of Labor

The French sociologist Emile Durkheim, whose work is discussed in Chapter 4 ("Society"), shared Toennies's interest in the profound social changes wrought by the Industrial Revolution. For Durkheim, modernization is marked by the increasing *division of labor*, or specialized economic activity, that accompanies industrialization (1964b; orig. 1893). Whereas everyone in traditional societies performs similar daily activities, modern societies function by having people carry out highly distinctive roles.

Durkheim claimed that members of preindustrial societies are held together by *mechanical solidarity*—social bonds that result from shared moral sentiments and a sense that everyone is basically alike and belongs together. Mechanical solidarity depends on a minimal division of labor so that, guided by tradition, everyone's life is basically the same. Durkheim's mechanical solidarity mirrors Toennies's *Gemeinschaft*.

As the division of labor becomes more pronounced, a society develops *organic solidarity*—bonds of mutual dependency based on specialization. In simple terms, modern societies lose their bonds of likeness but, in the process, discover a new source of solidarity in their differences. Now specialized in their pursuits, people find that they are dependent on others to meet most of

their needs. Organic solidarity corresponds to Toennies's concept of *Gesellschaft*.

Despite obvious similarities, Durkheim and Toennies interpreted modernity somewhat differently. To Toennies, modern *Gesellschaft* lacks social solidarity—the inevitable result of the gradual change from "natural" and "organic" traditions of the rural past to the "artificial" and "mechanical" life of contemporary, industrial cities. Durkheim disagreed, maintaining that the modern city is no less natural than the village. He made this point by reversing Toennies's language: labeling modern society as "organic" and traditional societies as "mechanical" because they were so regimented. Thus Durkheim viewed modernization not so much as a loss of community as a *change* in the basis of community—from bonds of likeness (kinship and neighborhood) to economic interdependence (the division of labor). Durkheim's view of modernity is both more complex and more positive than that of Toennies.

*Critical evaluation.*  Durkheim's work stands alongside that of Toennies, which it closely resembles, as a highly influential analysis of modernity. Of the two, Durkheim is clearly the more optimistic; still, he feared that modern societies would become so internally diverse that they would collapse into *anomie*, a condition in which norms and values are so weak and inconsistent that society provides little moral guidance to individuals. As noted in Chapter 4 ("Society"), modern individuals prone to anomie will tend toward egocentrism, placing their own needs above those of others.

Evidence supports Durkheim's contention that anomie plagues modern societies. Suicide rates, which Durkheim considered a prime index of anomie, have risen during this century. Moreover, the vast majority of U.S. adults report that they see moral questions not in clear terms of right and wrong but as "shades of gray" (N.O.R.C., 1991:403).

On the other hand, shared norms and values are still strong enough to give most people a sense of meaning and purpose. Additionally, whatever the hazards of anomie and atomization, most people seem to value the privacy and personal autonomy that modern society affords.

## Max Weber: Rationalization

Max Weber held that ideas and beliefs stand out as causes of social change; his thesis is detailed in Chapter 4 ("Society"). For Weber, then, modernity amounts to the progressive replacement of a traditional world view by a rational way of thinking.

In preindustrial societies, tradition acts as a constant brake to change. To traditional people, "truth" is roughly synonymous with *what has always been* (1978:36; orig. 1921). In modern societies, however, people see truth as the product of deliberate calculation. Because they value efficiency more than reverence for the past, individuals embrace whatever new social patterns allow them to achieve their goals. A rational view of the world, then, leads people to seek out and assess various options according to their specific consequences rather than according to any absolute standard of rightness.

Echoing the claim of Toennies and Durkheim that industrialization weakens tradition, Weber declared that modern society had become "disenchanted." What were once unquestioned truths have become subject to matter-of-fact calculations in a more rational world. Embracing rational, scientific thought, in short, modern society turns away from the gods.

Weber's work thus explores various modern "types"—notably the capitalist, the scientist, and the

## CRITICAL THINKING

# Modern Society: What Do We Owe Others?

In today's society, how much should we bother with the lives of others? Few people would want to go back to the "tyranny of the tribe" by which people in traditional communities suspiciously monitor one another's every activity. But does the modern notion of "individual freedom" mean that we should be indifferent to everyone around us, including those in need?

Modern society poses a dilemma that we might describe as the principle of privacy versus the principle of human community. We don't expect others to interfere in our lives, yet we do expect others to display basic human concern for us. Trying to strike the right balance is no easy task.

Consider the 1964 murder of Kitty Genovese in New York City. On one level, the crime was all too common. Returning from work late at night, Genovese was stabbed to death in the parking lot near her apartment building. But investigators made a stunning discovery: the brutal attack had lasted more than thirty minutes and was observed by at least thirty-eight of her neighbors, not one of whom came to her assistance or even called the police. For months after the attack, people across the country debated the issue of just what people in a modern, industrial society owe one another.

For some, the murder of Kitty Genovese brings to mind the New Testament book of Luke (10:30–37), in which Jesus is asked "Who is my neighbor?" He responds with the tale of the Good Samaritan. The story begins with a man on the road to Jericho being robbed and left for dead; several travelers then passed by without offering him any help. Then a Samaritan stopped, attended to the man's wounds, took him to an inn, and then left money to pay for further care. The Samaritan made no effort to establish a personal relationship with the victim; he did not even try to learn his name. The victim, it seems, was just another stranger. But while the Samaritan behaved impersonally, he also acted compassionately, doing what was necessary for a fellow human being in need.

This ancient biblical parable offers an important lesson for today's world. We certainly do not want to become personally involved with everyone we meet. But we must never allow ourselves to become indifferent to the humanity of those around us.

bureaucrat—all of whom share the rational and detached world view he believed was coming to dominate human interaction.

*Critical evaluation.* Compared with Toennies, and especially Durkheim, Weber was a profound critic of modern society. He recognized that science could produce technological wonders, yet he worried that it was carrying us away from more basic questions about the meaning and purpose of human existence. Weber feared that rationalization, especially in bureaucracies, would erode the human spirit with endless rules and regulations.

Some critics of Weber maintained that the alienation he attributed to bureaucracy actually stems from social inequality. This contention leads us to the ideas of Karl Marx.

## Karl Marx: Capitalism

While other analysts of modernity examined shifting patterns of social order, Marx focused on social conflict. For Marx, modern society was synonymous with capitalism; in his view, the Industrial Revolution was primarily a *capitalist revolution.* As Chapter 4 ("Society") explained, Marx asserted that the bourgeoisie emerged in medieval Europe as a social class intent on wresting control of society from the feudal nobility. The bourgeoisie were finally successful when the Industrial Revolution placed a powerful new productive system under their control.

Marx agreed that modernity weakened small-scale communities (as described by Toennies), increased the division of labor (as noted by Durkheim), and fostered a rational world view (as asserted by Weber). But, he saw these factors simply as conditions necessary for capitalism to flourish. Capitalism draws people from farms and small towns into an ever-expanding market system centered in the cities; specialization underlies efficient factories; and rationality is exemplified by the capitalist's relentless quest for profits.

Earlier chapters painted Marx as a spirited critic of capitalist society, but his vision of modernity also contains significant optimism. Unlike Weber, who viewed modern society as an "iron cage" of bureaucracy, Marx believed that social conflict in capitalist social systems would produce revolutionary social change and, ultimately, lead to an egalitarian form of socialism. Such a society, he claimed, would allow the wonders of industrial technology to enrich the lives of the many rather than the few—and thereby rid the world of the prime

A sure sign of modernization is that people shun traditional activities such as farming in favor of specialized productive roles. Hoping to secure a day's work in Mexico City, these men offer their services as electricians, contractors, painters, and plumbers.

source of social conflict and dehumanization. While Marx's evaluation of modern capitalist society was highly negative, then, he envisioned a future with greater human freedom, blossoming human creativity, and a renewed sense of human community.

*Critical evaluation.* Marx's theory of modernization draws together many threads of change in a fabric dominated by capitalism. Yet Marx may have underestimated the significance of bureaucracy in shaping modern societies. The stifling effects of formal organization on humanity turned out to be as bad—or worse—in socialist societies, as their governmental apparatus expanded, than the dehumanizing impact of capitalism. The recent upheavals in Eastern Europe and the former Soviet Union reveal the depth of popular opposition to entrenched bureaucracies.

## Understanding Modernity: The Theory of Mass Society

The rise of modernity is a complex process involving many transformations, described in previous chapters and summarized in Table 23–2. How is one to make sense of so many changes going on all at once? One broad approach—drawing on the ideas of Toennies, Durkheim, and Weber—understands modernization as the formation of *mass societies* (Dahrendorf, 1959; Korn-

**Table 23–2**  TRADITIONAL AND MODERN SOCIETIES: DIMENSIONS OF DIFFERENCE

| | Characteristics of Traditional Societies | Characteristics of Modern Societies |
|---|---|---|
| | **Scale of Life** | |
| | Small scale; population typically small and widely dispersed in rural villages and small towns | Large scale; population typically large and concentrated in cities |
| | **Cultural Patterns** | |
| Values | Homogeneous; sacred character; few subcultures and countercultures | Heterogeneous; secular character; many subcultures and countercultures |
| Norms | High moral significance; little tolerance of diversity | Variable moral significance; high tolerance of diversity |
| Orientation | Present linked to past | Present linked to future |
| Technology | Preindustrial; human and animal energy | Industrial; advanced energy sources |
| | **Social Structure** | |
| Status and role | Few statuses, most ascribed; few specialized roles | Many statuses, some ascribed and some achieved; many specialized roles |
| Relationships | Typically primary; little anonymity and privacy | Typically secondary; considerable anonymity and privacy |
| Communication | Face-to-face | Face-to-face communication supplemented by mass media |
| Social control | Informal gossip | Formal police and legal system |
| Social stratification | Rigid patterns of social inequality; little mobility | Fluid patterns of social inequality; considerable mobility |
| Gender patterns | Pronounced patriarchy; women's lives centered on the home | Declining patriarchy; increasing number of women in the paid labor force |
| Family | Extended family as the primary means of socialization and economic production | Nuclear family retains some socialization function but is more a unit of consumption than of production |
| Religion | Religion guides world view; little religious pluralism | Religion weakens with the rise of science; extensive religious pluralism |
| Education | Formal schooling limited to elites | Basic schooling becomes universal, with growing proportion receiving advanced education |
| State | Small-scale government; little state intervention into society | Large-scale government; considerable state intervention into society |
| Economy | Based on agriculture; some manufacturing within the home; little white-collar work | Based on industrial mass production; factories become centers of production; increasing white-collar work |
| Health | High birth and death rates; brief life expectancy because of low standard of living and simple medical technology | Low birth and death rates; longer life expectancy because of higher standard of living and complex medical technology |
| | **Social Change** | |
| | Slow; change evident over many generations | Rapid; change evident within a single generation |

hauser, 1959; Nisbet, 1966, 1969; Baltzell, 1968; Stein, 1972; Berger, Berger, & Kellner, 1974).

Formally defined, a **mass society** is *a society in which industrialization proceeds and bureaucracy expands while traditional social ties grow weaker.* A mass society emerges with the erosion of traditional kinship and neighborhood. Socially atomized, the members of modern societies typically experience feelings of uncertainty and personal powerlessness.

Why? Because, first, the scale of modern life increases to the point that impersonality and cultural diversity overwhelm the individual and drain meaning from people's lives. Second, the government expands to the extent that it manages many aspects of daily life, taking over tasks that used to be carried out by strong families and cohesive neighborhoods (like social welfare programs for the indigent and care of the elderly). In place of kith and kin, in short, we now contend with the directives of strangers—often nameless officials in distant and unresponsive bureaucracies. We now take a closer look at each of these two arguments.

### Expanding Scale of Social Life

Mass-society theory argues, first, that the scale of modern life has increased exponentially. Before the Industrial Revolution, Europe and North America formed an intricate mosaic of countless rural villages and small towns. In these small communities, which inspired Toennies's concept of *Gemeinschaft,* people lived out their lives surrounded by kin and guided by a shared heritage. In these communities, gossip was an informal, yet highly effective, means of ensuring rigid conformity to community standards. Limited community size, social isolation, and a strong, traditional religion combined to generate cultural homogeneity—the mechanical solidarity described by Durkheim. For example, in England before 1690, law and local custom demanded that everyone regularly participate in the Christian ritual of Holy Communion (Laslett, 1984). Similarly, only Rhode Island among the New England colonies offered any support for the notion of religious dissent. Because social differences were repressed, subcultures and countercultures rarely flourished and the pace of social change was slow. Also, social position was more or less set at birth, with little social mobility.

A surge in population, the growth of cities, and the specialization of economic activity during the Industrial Revolution gradually changed all this. People came to be known by their function (for example, as the "doctor" or the "bank clerk") rather than by their kinship group or hometown. The majority of people regarded others simply as a mass of strangers. The face-to-face communication of the village was eventually replaced by the mass media—newspapers, radio, and television—that only furthered the process of social atomization. Large organizations steadily assumed more and more responsibility for daily needs that had once been fulfilled by family, friends, and neighbors; universal public education enlarged the scope of learning; police, lawyers, and courts supervised a formal criminal justice system. Even charity became the work of faceless bureaucrats working for the Red Cross and various public welfare agencies.

Geographical mobility, mass communications, and exposure to diverse ways of life undermined traditional values. Less certain about what was worth believing, people became more tolerant of social diversity, more and more trumpeting the merits of individual rights and freedom of choice. Subcultures and countercultures multiplied. Making categorical distinctions among people fell out of favor; to treat someone a particular way based on race, sex, or religion came to be defined as backwards and unjust. In the process, minorities who have long lived at the margins of society have gained greater power and broader participation. Yet, mass-society theorists fear, transforming people of various backgrounds into a generic mass may end up dehumanizing everyone.

### The Rise of the State

In the small-scale, preindustrial societies of Europe, government amounted to little more than a local noble, who had limited control over the population. A royal family formally reigned over an entire nation but, without efficient transportation or communication, the power of even absolute monarchs fell far short of that wielded by today's political leaders.

Technological innovation allowed government to expand, and the centralized state grew in size and importance. At the time the United States gained independence from Great Britain, the federal government was a tiny organization whose function was primarily national defense. Since then, government has entered more and more areas of social life—regulating wages and working conditions, establishing standards for products of all kinds, educating the population, and providing financial assistance to the ill and the unemployed. Taxes have correspondingly soared, so that today's average worker labors for four months a year merely to pay for various government services.

In a mass society, power resides in large bureaucracies, leaving people in local communities little control over their lives. For example, state officials mandate that local schools must have a standardized educational program, local products must be government-inspected and carry government-approved labels, and every citizen must maintain extensive records for purposes of taxation. While such regulations may protect people and enhance uniformity of treatment, they depersonalize human decision making and limit the autonomy of neighborhoods, families, and individuals.

*Critical evaluation.* The theory of mass society acknowledges that the transformation of small-scale societies has positive aspects, but tends to see in historical change the loss of an irreplaceable heritage. Modern societies increase individual rights, magnify tolerance for social differences, and raise standards of living. But they seem prone to what Max Weber feared most—excessive bureaucracy—as well as to Toennies's self-centeredness and to Emile Durkheim's anomie. Their size, complexity, and tolerance of diversity all but doom traditional values and family patterns, leaving individuals isolated, powerless, and materialistic. As was noted in Chapter 18 ("Politics and Government"), only about half of women and men eligible to vote do so. But should we be surprised that people in vast, impersonal societies tend to conclude that no one person can make a difference?

Critics of mass-society theory contend that it romanticizes the past. They remind us that many people in the small towns of America's past were actually quite eager to set out for a better life in the cities. And who would actually wish to give up the improved standard of living that industrial technology has made possible? Another limitation of the mass-society approach is that it offers little praise for deliberate efforts to lessen social inequality. Mass-society analysis, critics claim, attracts support from social and economic conservatives who defend conventional morality and capitalist values, while showing indifference to the historical plight of women and other minorities.

## Understanding Modernity: The Theory of Class Society

A second interpretation of modernity derives largely from the ideas of Karl Marx. From this point of view, modernity takes the form of a **class society**, *a capitalist society with pronounced social stratification.* According to this theory, the widespread feelings of powerlessness in modern society stem from pervasive social inequality. While this approach concurs that modern societies have grown to a mass scale, class-society theorists claim that the heart of modernization is an expanding capitalist economy. Inherent in capitalist societies are pronounced inequality and social conflict, even if the extent of inequality has diminished to some degree compared to what it was a century ago (Miliband, 1969; Habermas, 1970; Polenberg, 1980; Blumberg, 1981; Harrington, 1984).

### Capitalism

Class-society theory holds that the increasing scale of social life in modern times has resulted from the insatiable appetite of capitalism. Because a capitalist economy pursues ever-increasing profits, both production and consumption expand as long as there is money to be made. Marx considered the Industrial Revolution to be a significant stage in the enlarging capitalist economic system.

According to Marx, capitalism emphasizes "naked self-interest" and individual greed (1972:337; orig. 1848). This self-centeredness undermines the social ties that once cemented small-scale communities. Capitalism also fosters impersonality and anonymity by transforming people into commodities, both as a source of labor and a market for capitalist production. The net result is that capitalism reduces human beings to cogs in the machinery of material production.

Science, the key to greater productivity, also serves as a modern ideology to justify capitalism. In preindustrial Europe, the nobility defended their right to rule with traditional notions of moral obligation and responsibility. In modern societies, capitalists legitimize their way of life by encouraging people to view their own well-being as a *technical* puzzle to be solved by engineers and other experts rather than through the pursuit of social justice (Habermas, 1970). A capitalist culture, for example, encourages us to find the solution to illness in scientific medicine rather than in eliminating poverty, which for many people undermines health in the first place.

Businesses also raise the banner of scientific logic when they claim that efficiency is achieved only through continual growth. As Chapter 19 ("The Economy and Work") explained, capitalist corporations have reached enormous size and control almost unimaginable wealth. Nevertheless, to increase profits even more, they have gained "global reach" by becoming multinationals that operate throughout the world. From the class-society point of view, then, the expanding scale of life is not so much a function of "Gesellschaft" as it is the inevitable and destructive consequence of capitalism.

### The Persistence of Social Inequality

Modernity has gradually eroded some of the rigid categorical distinctions that divided preindustrial societies. Class-society theory maintains, however, that elites persist albeit in a different form: capitalist millionaires now occupy society's highest echelons rather than family-based nobility. In the United States, we may have no hereditary monarchy, but the richest 5 percent of the population nevertheless controls more than half of all property. As Paul Blumberg (1981) notes, despite a rising standard of living in the United States during this century, a small minority still enjoys great wealth while many people live in a state of desperate poverty.

What of the state, which mass-society theory suggests has an expanding role in combating social problems? Marx was skeptical that government could accomplish more than minor reforms. The capitalist state, he reasoned, could not bring about meaningful change because it was designed to protect the wealth and privileges of capitalists. Other class-society theorists add that, while it may be true that working people and minorities enjoy greater political rights and economic benefits today than in years past, these changes are the fruits of political struggle, not expressions of government benevolence. And, they continue, despite our pretensions of democracy, power still rests primarily in the hands of those with money. Throughout the 1980s conservative political leaders, in the name of economic growth and free-market efficiency, curtailed government funding for programs that benefited less privileged families (Harrington, 1984; Jacob, 1986).

*Critical evaluation.* Table 23–3 spells out key differences in the interpretations of modernity offered by class-society theory and mass-society theory. In place of mass-society theory's focus on the increasing scale of social life and the rise of large organizations, class-society theory stresses the expansion of capitalism and persistent social inequality. Class-society theory also dismisses Durkheim's argument that people in modern societies suffer from moral collapse and anomie. Instead, in this view, the malaise of modern life has as its roots alienation and powerlessness. Not surprisingly, then, the class-society interpretation of modernity enjoys widespread support among social and economic liberals and radicals who favor greater equality and extensive regulation of the capitalist marketplace.

**Table 23–3  TWO INTERPRETATIONS OF MODERNITY: A SUMMARY**

| | Key Process of Modernization | Key Effects of Modernization |
|---|---|---|
| Mass-society theory | Industrialization; growth of bureaucracy | Increasing scale of life; rise of the state and other formal organizations |
| Class-society theory | Rise of capitalism | Expansion of capitalist economy; persistence of social inequality |

One problem with class-society theory lies right at its core: most people in the United States do not want their society to be rigidly egalitarian; there is widespread support for unequal rewards, at least as far as they reflect differences in personal talents and efforts (N.O.R.C., 1991). Moreover, class-society theory ignores many ways in which modern societies have grown more egalitarian by lessening the significance of race, ethnicity, religion, and sex in daily interactions. Such categorical distinctions are still made, of course, but they are now widely defined as social problems. As Chapter 10 ("Social Class in the United States") explained, we have considerable social inequality in our society today, but the population of the United States has become much more equal since the onset of the Industrial Revolution.

Critics of the class-society approach also point out that this theory implies that a centralized economy would cure the ills of modern living. But few people would argue that socialism, at least in its various expressions around the world, has proved itself capable of generating a high standard of living. Furthermore, many social problems found in the United States—including unemployment, homelessness, industrial pollution, and unresponsive government—were commonplace in the formerly socialist nations of Eastern Europe and in the former Soviet Union.

## Modernity and the Individual

Both mass- and class-society theories focus on broad patterns of social change since the Industrial Revolution. Each "macro-level" approach also offers "micro-level" insights into how modernity shapes individual lives.

## Mass Society: Problems of Identity

Modernity liberated individuals from small, tightly knit communities of the past. In historical context, most people in today's modern societies possess unprecedented privacy and freedom to express their individuality. Mass-society theory suggests, however, that extensive social diversity, atomization, and rapid social change make it difficult for many people to establish any internally coherent identity at all (Wheelis, 1958; Riesman, 1970; Berger, Berger, & Kellner, 1974).

Chapter 5 ("Socialization") explained that people forge distinctive personalities based on their social experience. The small, homogeneous, and slowly changing societies of the past gave each member a firm foundation for building a meaningful personal identity. For example, the Amish communities that still flourish in the United States and Canada provide their members with strong historical and cultural roots. There, young men and women know the meaning of being Amish—that is, they understand how they should think and behave—and most learn to embrace this life as "natural" and right. Not everyone born into an Amish community can tolerate these demands for conformity, but most members establish a coherent and satisfying personal identity (Hostetler, 1980).

Mass societies, with their characteristic diversity and rapid change, provide only shifting sands on which to build a personal identity. Left to make their own life decisions, people confront a bewildering range of options. Autonomy has little value without standards for making choices; in a tolerant mass society, no one path seems more compelling than the next. Not surprisingly, many people shuttle from one identity to another, changing their lifestyle in search of an elusive "true self." They may join one or another social movement in search of purpose and belonging, and even experiment with various religions hoping to find a system of beliefs that "fits" them. This difficulty in developing an identity is not psychological, although it is often treated as an individual problem. Rather, many people grappling with modern life suffer from the widespread "relativism" of their society, unsure which way the moral compass points because they have lost the security and direction once made clear by tradition.

For David Riesman (1970; orig. 1950), modernization brings on changes in **social character**, that is, *personality patterns common to members of a society*. Preindustrial societies promote what Riesman terms **tradition-directedness**, *rigid personalities based on conformity to time-honored ways of living*. Members of traditional societies model their lives on what has gone before so that what is "good" is equivalent to "what has always been." Tradition-directedness, then, brings to the level of individual experience Toennies's *Gemeinschaft* and Durkheim's mechanical solidarity. Tradition-directed character makes people culturally conservative so that they think and act alike. Unlike the conformity found in modern societies, this uniformity is not an attempt to mimic one another. Instead, because everyone draws on the same cultural foundation, defined as the one proper way to live, homogeneity is the result. Amish women and men exemplify people with tradition-directed character; in the Amish culture, conformity ties everyone to ancestors and descendents in an unbroken chain of righteous living according to the historical demands of God (Hostetler, 1980).

A tradition-directed personality is likely to be defined as deviant by members of a diverse and rapidly changing society. Modern people, by and large, prize

Affluent people in the United States have such a wide range of choices about how to live that they often speak of their "lifestyles" as something they shape for themselves. For most of humanity, however, tradition and lack of opportunity generate a more fixed existence and a more well-defined personal identity.

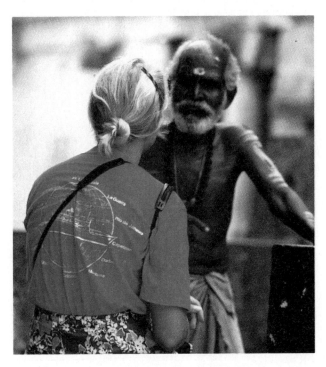

personal flexibility, the capacity to adapt, and sensitivity. Riesman calls this type of social character **other-directedness,** *highly variable personality patterns among people open to change and likely to imitate the behavior of others.* Because their socialization occurs within societies that are continuously in flux, other-directed people typically display greater superficiality, inconsistency, and change. They try on different roles and identities, sometimes like so many pieces of new clothing, and engage in various "performances" as they move from setting to setting (Goffman, 1959). In a traditional society, such "shiftiness" marks a person as untrustworthy, but in a modern society, the ability to fit in virtually anywhere is a valued personal trait (Wheelis, 1958).

In societies that value the up-to-date rather than the traditional, people look to members of their own generation as significant role models rather than looking up to their elders. Following the same reasoning, "peer pressure" can sometimes seem irresistible to people with no enduring standards to guide them. Our society urges individuals to be true to themselves. But when social surroundings change so rapidly, how can people determine to which self they should be true? This problem

Mass-society theory explains the collapse of the social fabric in U.S. cities as the result of rapid social change and the erosion of tradition. Class-society theory, by contrast, suggests that social inequality diminishes the likelihood of meaningful human community.

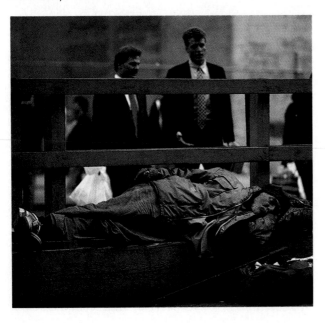

is at the root of the identity crisis so widespread in industrial societies today. "Who am I?" is a question that many of us struggle to answer. In sociological terms, this personal problem doesn't reflect a personal crisis but rather the inherent instability of modern mass society.

### Class Society: Problems of Powerlessness

Class-society theory paints a different picture of modernity's effects on individuals. This approach maintains that persistent social inequality undermines modern society's promise of individual freedom. For some, modernity delivers great privilege, but for others, modern life means coping every day with powerlessness. For people of color, the challenges of modern life are typically even greater. Similarly, women enjoy increasing participation in modern societies, but they continue to run up against traditional barriers of sexism. Elderly people as well encounter the impediment of ageism. In short, this approach rejects mass-society theory's claim that people suffer from too much freedom. Instead, class-society theory holds that a majority of people in the United States are still denied full participation in social life.

Class-society theorists hail the struggle to empower individuals, which has been gaining strength. For example, employees seek greater control of the workplace, consumers press for more say in the marketplace, and citizens try to make government more responsive to their needs (Toffler, 1981).

On a global scale, as Chapter 11 ("Global Inequality") explained, the expanding scope of world capitalism has placed more of the earth's population under the influence of multinational corporations. As a result, about two-thirds of the world's income is concentrated in the richest societies, which contain only about 15 percent of its people. Class-society theorists therefore ask: Is it any wonder that throughout the Third World people are also seeking greater power to shape their own lives?

Such problems led Herbert Marcuse (1964) to challenge Max Weber's contention that modern society is rational. Marcuse labels modern society irrational because it fails to meet the basic needs of so many people. While modern capitalist societies produce unparalleled wealth, poverty remains the daily plight of millions and, in global terms, billions of people. Moreover, Marcuse argues, technological advances rarely empower people; instead, technology tends to reduce their control over their own lives. High technology generally means that a corps of specialists—not the vast majority of people themselves—control events and dominate discussion, whether the issue is energy production for communities or health care for individuals. Specialists define ordinary people as ill-equipped for decision making, so that the public learns to defer to elites of one kind or another. And elites, from this point of view, have little concern for the common interest. Despite the popular view that technology *solves* the world's problems, Marcuse concludes, it may be more accurate to say it *causes* them. In sum, class-society theory asserts that people suffer because modern societies have concentrated both wealth and power in the hands of a privileged few.

## Modernity and Progress

In modern societies, most people expect—and applaud—social change. People link modernity to the idea of *progress* (from Latin, meaning "a moving forward"), a state of continual improvement. By contrast, we denigrate stability as a form of stagnation.

This chapter began by describing the Kaiapo of Brazil, for whom affluence has broadened opportunities but weakened traditional heritage. In examining the Kaiapo, we notice that social change is too complex to be simply equated with progress. More precisely, whether or not we see a given change as progress depends on our underlying values. A rising standard of living among the Kaiapo—or, historically, among people in the United States—has helped make lives longer and more comfortable. But affluence has also fueled materialism at the expense of spiritual life, creating ambivalence toward change in the minds of many people. In a recent survey, adults in the United States were divided on the idea of scientific change; aware of its benefits, many also think that science "makes our way of life change too fast" (N.O.R.C., 1991:388).

Many people also celebrate modern society's recognition of basic human rights. The assertion that people have rights simply by virtue of their humanity is a distinctly modern idea that can be found in the U.S. *Declaration of Independence* and the United Nations' *Declaration of Human Rights* (Berger, Berger, & Kellner, 1974). But, as Chapter 3 ("Culture") explained, we now have something of a "culture of rights" that often overlooks the duties and obligations we have to one another. The contrast between the modern idea of individual dignity and the traditional notion of personal duty and honor is highlighted in the box on page 658.

In principle, the idea that individuals should have considerable autonomy in shaping their own lives has wide support in the United States. Thus many people will applaud the demise of traditional conceptions of honor as progress. Yet, as people exercise their freedom of choice, they inevitably challenge social patterns cherished by those who maintain a more traditional lifestyle. For example, people may choose not to marry. Some may remain single, others may live with someone without marrying, have children outside of marriage, or form a partnership with a member of their own sex. To those who support individual choice, such changes symbolize progress; to those who value traditional family patterns, however, these developments signal societal decay (Wallis, 1985).

Even technological advance has controversial aspects. Rapid transportation and efficient communication have improved our lives in many respects. However, complex technology has also weakened traditional attachments to hometowns and even to family. Industrial technology has also unleashed an unprecedented threat to the natural environment and, in the form of nuclear weapons, imperiled the future of humanity. In short, then, social change gives rise to uncertainty, unforeseen complexity, and controversy, making sweeping assumptions about the modern world—whether ringing endorsements of "progress" or stinging indictments of unfamiliar new social forms—risky at best.

# Modernization in Global Perspective

Sometimes social change proceeds haphazardly, sometimes deliberately. Some change that is desperately needed has not occurred at all, as in much of the Third World, where almost 1 billion people struggle daily against life-threatening poverty.

Two competing views of the causes of global poverty were presented in Chapter 11 ("Global Inequality"). *Modernization theory* claims that in the past the entire world was poor and that technological change, especially the Industrial Revolution, has enhanced human productivity and raised living standards. From this point of view, the solution to global poverty lies in encouraging technological development in less developed regions.

For reasons suggested earlier, however, global modernization may be difficult. Recall that David Riesman portrayed preindustrial people as *tradition-directed*. By

# Traditional Honor and Modern Dignity

Honor occupies about the same place in contemporary usage as chastity. An individual asserting it hardly invites admiration, and one who claims to have lost it is an object of amusement rather than sympathy. (1974:83)

Honor is a human virtue that seems distinctly out of place in modern society. Honor means acting according to traditional cultural norms. Since traditional norms varied for different categories of humanity, honor also means behaving like the kind of person you are. Men and women gain honor by acting differently, for example. *He* is expected to act protectively toward *her*, while *she* is expected to be mindful of traditional norms including the need to defer graciously to *him*. Honor, in short, cannot be separated from strong morality and rigid social distinctions—between men and women, nobles and serfs, one's own family and outsiders. Through conformity, however, honor is available to people of every social station. During the Middle Ages, European no-

bles claimed honor when they performed their feudal obligations toward their social inferiors and displayed proper respect for their peers. Similarly, commoners acted honorably when they fulfilled their duties to their superiors and everyone else.

With modernization, cultural norms have become weaker and more variable, and categorical distinctions among people have been challenged by drives for social equality. Modern culture holds that all people should be treated as social equals. Therefore, although the concept of honor survives among some ethnic categories and traditional occupations, such as the military, it has less appeal to most members of modern societies.

Modernization enhances concern for people as *individuals*, which is expressed in the concept of *dignity*. Whereas various categories of people have distinctive codes of honor, dignity is a universal human trait, originating in the inherent value of everyone. We

recognize the dignity of others when we acknowledge our common humanity by overlooking social differences.

In the spirit of modern dignity, women may object to men treating them as women rather than as individuals. The male practices of holding open a door for a woman and paying for a shared meal may be honorable in the traditional sense, but are more likely to be viewed as affronts to the dignity of women by underscoring social differences based on sex.

As a result, the significance of honor is fading in modern societies. The cultural diversity and rapid social change sweeping across modern societies makes traditional scripts for living suspect, at best. In contrast to codes of honor that guided human interaction in the past, human beings now value individual self-worth and aspirations to self-determination. This forms the essence of dignity.

SOURCE: Based on Berger, Berger, and Kellner (1974).

---

embracing a way of life rooted in the past, they may resist change. According to modernization theory, the world's rich societies should deliberately intervene in poor societies to encourage productive innovation. First-World nations must export technology to the Third World, welcome students from abroad, and provide foreign aid to stimulate economic development.

The review of modernization theory in Chapter 11 suggests that the success of these policies has been limited. Even where the greatest efforts have been made, resistance to change has compromised the results. Traditional people such as Brazil's Kaiapo have gained wealth

by selling their resources on world markets, but only at the cost of being drawn into the "global village" where concern for money replaces traditional values. In some societies, notably some Islamic societies like Iran, rapid modernization has sparked a powerful backlash from segments seeking to restore traditional culture.

A daunting problem facing advocates of modernization theory, then, is that modernity may bring higher living standards but, in the process, sweep a society into a global mass culture of Western pop music, trendy clothes, and fast food. One Brazilian anthropologist expressed uncertainty about the future of the Kaiapo: "At least they quickly understood the consequences of watching television. . . . Now [they] can make a choice" (Simons, 1989:37).

But not everyone views modernization as a viable option. According to a second approach to global inequality, *dependency theory*, contemporary poor societies are at a distinct disadvantage even if they want to pursue modernization. From this point of view, the major barrier to economic development is not traditionalism but the global domination of rich, capitalist societies of the First World. Initially, as Chapter 11 explained, this system took the form of colonialism, whereby European societies seized control of much of Latin America, Africa, and Asia. Trading relationships soon enriched England, Spain, and other colonial powers, as their colonies, at the same time grew poorer. Almost all societies subjected to this form of domination are now politically independent, but colonial-style ties continue in the form of multinational corporations based in rich societies operating throughout the world.

In effect, dependency theory asserts, rich societies achieved their modernization at least partly at the expense of poor nations, which provided valuable resources and human labor. Even today, the Third World remains locked in a disadvantageous economic relationship with the First World, dependent on rich societies to buy their raw materials and in return provide them with whatever high-priced manufactured products they can afford. Continuing ties with rich societies appear likely to perpetuate current patterns of global inequality.

Dependency theory implies that social change occurs outside the control of individual societies. In this view, the fate and fortune of individual nations worldwide is tied to their position in the global economy. Thus, change to improve the plight of people in the Third World will require corresponding changes in First-World societies.

Whichever approach one finds more convincing, we can no longer isolate the study of the United States from the rest of the world. At the beginning of the twentieth century, a majority of people in even the richest societies lived in relatively small settlements with limited awareness of others. Now, at the threshold of the twenty-first century, people everywhere participate in a far larger human drama. The world seems smaller because the lives of all its people are increasingly linked. We now discuss the relationships among societies in the same way that people a century ago talked about the expanding ties among towns and cities. Surely one of the essential tasks of the twenty-first century will be managing global diversity as the people of the world find their lives linked in more and more ways.

The century now coming to an end has witnessed unparalleled human achievement. Yet solutions to many of the timeless problems of human existence—including finding meaning in life, eradicating poverty, and resolving internal conflicts—remain elusive. To this list of pressing matters, new concerns have been added, such as managing the global environment and maintaining world peace. One source of optimism as we approach the twenty-first century is that we look ahead with an unprecedented understanding of human society.

The future of our world lies not in isolation, by which societies jealously protect their culture, nor in confederation, by which everyone enthusiastically embraces a single way of life. The challenge of the next century will be *managing diversity*, a skill made more necessary as communications technology, economic expansion, and the need to confront global problems draw the disparate peoples of the world closer together. In the emerging conversation of nations, we should not assume that the richest and most powerful societies of the world should do all the talking. On the contrary, the keys to long-term peace and ecological survival may well lie in rediscovering the many human truths that form the common sense of our more traditional neighbors.

# Summary

1. Every society changes continuously, although with varying speed and consequences. Whether social change is intentional or unplanned, it is usually controversial.

2. Social change occurs in several ways, including the cultural processes of invention and discovery within a society, and cultural diffusion from one society to another. Another source of social change is found in social structure—tensions and conflicts within society itself. Patterns of culture and ways of thinking can either encourage or inhibit social change. Finally, the natural environment and population dynamics also influence the pace and direction of social change.

3. Modernity refers to the social consequences of industrialization. According to Peter Berger, the general characteristics of modernity are the weakening of small traditional communities, the expansion of personal choice, the increasing diversity in patterns of belief, and a keener awareness of time, especially the future.

4. Ferdinand Toennies described modernization as the transition from *Gemeinschaft* to *Gesellschaft*. This process signifies the progressive loss of community amid growing individualism.

5. Emile Durkheim linked modernization to an expanding division of labor. Mechanical solidarity, based on common activities and shared beliefs, gradually gives way to organic solidarity, in which specialization makes people interdependent.

6. Max Weber described the rise of modernity as the replacement of traditional patterns of thought by rationality. He feared that rational organization would dehumanize modern society.

7. According to Karl Marx, modernity amounts to the triumph of capitalism over feudalism. Viewing capitalist societies as fraught with social conflict, he anticipated revolutionary change leading to a more egalitarian socialist society.

8. In the view of mass-society theorists, modernity increases the scale of life and transfers to government and other formal organizations the responsibility for many tasks previously performed informally by the family and neighbors. Mass-society theory holds that cultural diversity and rapid social change lead individuals in modern societies to develop variable personal identities and to have difficulty finding certainty and meaning in their lives.

9. Class-society theory holds that capitalism underlies Western modernization. According to this approach, widespread powerlessness in modern societies stems from capitalism's propensity to concentrate wealth and power in the hands of a few.

10. People in the United States commonly associate modernity with social progress. This simplistic view overlooks the often deleterious effects of social change. Social change is an exceedingly complex process; from any point of view, the consequences of modernity can be perceived as good and bad.

11. In a global context, modernization theory advocates intentional intervention to stimulate the development of poor societies. Advocates of this approach argue that global poverty primarily stems from traditionalism.

12. Dependency theory argues that a society's potential for development depends on its position in the world economic system. Poor, Third-World societies are unlikely to duplicate the path to modernization of rich, First-World societies because they have become dependent on these rich societies.

# Key Concepts

**class society** a capitalist society with pronounced social stratification

**mass society** a society in which industrialization proceeds and bureaucracy expands while traditional social ties grow weaker

**modernity** patterns of social life linked to industrialization

**modernization** the process of social change initiated by industrialization

**other-directedness** highly variable personality patterns among people open to change and likely to imitate the behavior of others

**social change** the transformation of culture and social institutions over time

**social character** personality patterns common to members of a society

**tradition-directedness** rigid personalities based on conformity to time-honored ways of living

# Suggested Readings

This paperback text surveys social change in a world perspective.
> Daniel Chirot. *Social Change in the Modern Era.* New York: Harcourt Brace Jovanovich, 1986.

Many people in the United States think of growth as inherently good. The notion of growth is hardly simple, however, as this book explains.
> Henry Teune. *Growth.* Newbury Park, CA: Sage, 1988.

This paperback traces Western societies from the ancient empires that marked the onset of civilization to the end of the Middle Ages just before the Industrial Revolution.
> Constance Brittain Bouchard. *Antiquity and the Middle Ages: Life and Society in the West.* New York: Harcourt Brace Jovanovich, 1988.

The following highly readable books are filled with fascinating insights about the modern world.
> Peter Berger, Brigitte Berger, and Hansfried Kellner. *The Homeless Mind: Modernization and Consciousness.* New York: Vintage Books, 1974.

> Peter L. Berger. *Facing Up to Modernity: Excursions in Society, Politics, and Religion.* New York: Basic Books, 1977.

Here we grasp the implications of modernity through detailed comparisons with preindustrial England.
> Peter Laslett. *The World We Have Lost: England Before the Industrial Age.* 3rd ed. New York: Charles Scribner's Sons, 1984.

Many of the consequences of major events in history are unpredictable. This book examines changes in U.S. society—attitudes toward sex, gender, and homosexuality—that were part of the legacy of World War II.
> John Costello. *Virtue Under Fire: How World War II Changed Our Social and Sexual Attitudes.* Boston: Little, Brown, 1986.

This book takes a popular-culture approach to social change in the United States, exploring the transformations in roadside architecture during the twentieth century.
> Chester H. Liebs. *Main Street to Miracle Mile: American Roadside Architecture.* Boston: New York Graphic Society/ Little, Brown, 1985.

These two books—the first a collection of articles by many well-known thinkers—delve into the implications of technological changes during this century and suggest likely future developments.
> Albert H. Teich, ed. *Technology and the Future.* 5th ed. New York: St. Martin's Press, 1990.

> O. B. Hardison, Jr. *Disappearing Through the Skylight: Culture and Technology in the Twentieth Century.* New York: Viking, 1989.

This book examines social change in traditional societies with a focus on music: how Western music is influencing traditional musical patterns in a number of countries.
> Bruno Nettl. *The Western Impact on World Music: Change, Adaptation, and Survival.* New York: Schirmer Books, 1985.

This analysis of the U.S. economy and workforce offers projections about change over the 1990s.
> William B. Johnston and Arnold E. Packer. *Workforce 2000: Work and Workers for the Twenty-First Century.* Indianapolis: Hudson Institute, 1987.

Probing economic development and the changes that accompany it, this analysis contrasts rural and urban development as well as its different consequences for men and women.
> Tony Barnett. *Social and Economic Development: An Introduction.* New York: Guilford Press, 1989.

A well-known social critic explores the state of politics, religion, and progress in today's world in this wide-ranging discussion.
> Christopher Lasch. *The True and Only Heaven: Progress and Its Critics.* New York: W. W. Norton, 1991.

This critical analysis of the 1980s stresses the need for grassroots activism to reshape the world of the next century.
> David C. Korten. *Getting to the 21st Century: Voluntary Action and the Global Agenda.* West Hartford, CT: Kumarian Press, 1990.

This collection of essays offers crucial insights into how change in the United States affects transformations in other societies of the world.
> Mike Featherstone, ed. *Global Culture: Globalization, Nationalism, and Modernity.* Newbury Park, CA: Sage, 1990.

# Glossary

**absolute poverty** a deprivation of resources that is life threatening

**achieved status** a social position that is assumed voluntarily and that reflects a significant measure of personal ability and effort

**activity theory** an analysis of aging linking personal satisfaction in old age to a high level of activity

**Afrocentrism** highlighting the viewpoint of people of African descent

**ageism** prejudice and discrimination against the elderly

**age-sex pyramid** a graphic representation that divides a population into various categories based on age and sex

**age stratification** the unequal distribution of wealth, power, and privileges among people of different ages

**agriculture** the technology of large-scale farming using plows powered by animals or advanced energy

**alienation** the experience of separation resulting from powerlessness

**animism** the belief that natural objects are conscious forms of life that can affect humanity

**anomie** Durkheim's designation of a condition in which society provides individuals with little moral guidance

**anticipatory socialization** the process of social learning directed toward gaining a desired position

**arms race** a mutually reinforcing escalation of military might

**ascribed status** a social position that is received at birth or involuntarily assumed later in the life course

**assimilation** the process by which minorities gradually adopt patterns of the dominant culture

**authoritarianism** any political system that denies popular participation in government

**authority** power that people perceive as legitimate rather than coercive

**bilateral descent** a system tracing kinship through both females and males

**blue-collar occupations** work involving mostly manual labor

**bureaucracy** an organizational model rationally designed to perform complex tasks efficiently

**bureaucratic inertia** the tendency of bureaucratic organizations to persist over time

**bureaucratic ritualism** a preoccupation with organizational rules and regulations as ends in themselves rather than as the means to organizational goals

**capitalism** an economic system in which productive resources are privately owned

**capitalists** people who own factories and other productive enterprises

**caste system** a system of social stratification based on ascription

**cause and effect** a relationship between two variables in which change in one (the independent variable) causes change in another (the dependent variable)

**charisma** in religious terms, evidence of God's favor in the behavior of an individual

**charismatic authority** power legitimized through extraordinary personal abilities that inspire devotion and obedience

**church** a type of religious organization that readily seeks accommodation with the larger society

**civil religion** a quasi-religious loyalty binding individuals in a basically secular society

**class conflict** Marx's term for the struggle between social classes over the distribution of wealth and power in society

**class consciousness** Marx's term for workers' recognition of their unity as a social class in opposition to capitalists and to capitalism itself

**class society** a capitalist society with pronounced social stratification

**class system** a system of social stratification based on individual achievement

**cohabitation** the sharing of a household by an unmarried couple

**cohort** a category of people with a common characteristic, usually their age

**collective behavior** activity involving a large number of people, often spontaneous, and typically in violation of established norms

**collectivity** a large number of people whose minimal interaction occurs in the absence of well-defined and conventional norms

**colonialism** the process by which some nations enrich themselves through political and economic control of other countries

**communism** a hypothetical economic and political system in which all members of society have economic and social equality

**concept** a mental construct that represents some part of the world, inevitably in a somewhat simplified form

**concrete operational stage** Piaget's term for the level of human development at which people first use logic to understand their surroundings

**conglomerates** giant corporations composed of many smaller ones.

**control** the ability to neutralize the effect of one variable in order to assess the relationships among other variables

**conversion** a personal transformation resulting from adopting new religious beliefs

**corporation** an organization with a legal existence including rights and liabilities apart from those of its members

**correlation** a relationship between two (or more) variables

**counterculture** social patterns that strongly oppose popular culture

**credentialism** the requirement that a person hold an advanced degree as a condition of employment

**crime** the violation of norms formally enacted into criminal law

**crimes against property** (property crimes) crimes that involve theft of property belonging to others

**crimes against the person** (violent crimes) crimes against people that involve violence or the threat of violence

**criminal justice system** a formal system that responds to alleged violations of the law using police, courts, and punishment

**criminal recidivism** subsequent offenses by people previously convicted of crimes

**crowd** a temporary gathering of people who share a common focus of attention and whose members influence one another

**crude birth rate** the number of live births in a given year for every thousand people in a population

**crude death rate** the number of deaths in a given year for every thousand people in a population

**cult** a religious organization with roots outside the dominant religious traditions of a society

**cultural ecology** a theoretical paradigm that explores the relationship of human culture and the physical environment

**cultural integration** the close relationship among various parts of a cultural system

**cultural lag** disruption in a cultural system resulting from the unequal rates at which different cultural elements change

**cultural relativism** the practice of judging a culture by its own standards

**cultural transmission** the process by which one generation passes culture to the next

**cultural universals** traits found in every culture

**culture** the beliefs, values, behavior, and material objects shared by a particular people

**culture shock** personal disorientation that accompanies exposure to an unfamiliar way of life

**deductive logical thought** reasoning that transforms general ideas into specific hypotheses suitable for scientific testing

**democracy** a type of political system in which power is exercised by the people as a whole

**democratic socialism** an economic and political system that combines significant government intervention in the economy with free elections

**demographic transition theory** the thesis that population patterns are linked to a society's level of technological development

**demography** the study of human population

**denomination** a church, not linked to the state, in a society that recognizes religious pluralism

**dependency theory** a model of economic and social development that explains global inequality in terms of the historical exploitation of poor societies by rich ones

**dependent variable** a variable that is changed by another (independent) variable

**descent** the system by which members of a society trace kinship over generations

**deterrence** the attempt to discourage criminality through punishment

**deviance** the recognized violation of cultural norms

**direct-fee system** a medical-care system in which patients pay directly for the services of physicians and hospitals

**discrimination** treating various categories of people unequally

**disengagement theory** an analysis of aging linking disengagement by elderly people from positions of social responsibility to the orderly operation of society

**division of labor** specialized economic activity

**dramaturgical analysis** the investigation of social interaction in terms of theatrical performance

**dyad** a social group with two members

**ecclesia** a church that is formally allied with the state

**economy** the institutionalized system for production, distribution, and consumption of goods and services

**education** the various ways in which knowledge—including factual information and occupational skills as well as cultural norms and values—is transmitted to members of a society

**ego** Freud's designation of a person's conscious attempt to balance innate pleasure-seeking drives with the demands of society

**empirical evidence** information we are able to verify with our senses

**endogamy** marriage between people of the same social group or category

**ethnicity** a shared cultural heritage

**ethnocentrism** the practice of judging another culture by the standards of one's own culture

**ethnomethodology** the study of the everyday, common-sense understandings that people have of the world

**Eurocentrism** the dominance of European (esp. English) culture

**euthanasia** (mercy killing) assisting in the death of a person suffering from an incurable illness

**exogamy** marriage between people of different social groups or categories

**experiment** a research method for investigating cause and effect under highly controlled conditions

**expressive leadership** group leadership that emphasizes collective well-being

**extended family** (consanguine family) a social unit including parents, children, and other kin

**fad** an unconventional social pattern that people embrace briefly but enthusiastically

**faith** belief anchored in conviction rather than scientific evidence

**false consciousness** Marx's description of any belief suggesting that the shortcomings of individuals, rather than society, are responsible for widespread social problems

**family** a relatively permanent social group of two or more people, who are related by blood, marriage, or adoption and who usually live together

**family of orientation** the family into which a person is born and receives early socialization

**family of procreation** a family in which people have or adopt children of their own

**family violence** emotional, physical, or sexual abuse of one family member by another

**fashion** a social pattern favored for a time by a large number of people

**female infanticide** the practice of aborting female fetuses and neglecting, or even actively killing, infant girls by parents who would prefer to raise boys

**feminism** the advocacy of social equality for the sexes, in opposition to patriarchy and sexism

**feminization of poverty** a trend by which women represent an increasing proportion of the poor

**fertility** the incidence of childbearing in a society's population

**First World** industrial societies that have predominantly capitalist economies

**folkways** norms that have little moral significance

**formal operational stage** Piaget's term for the level of human development at which people use highly abstract thought and are able to imagine alternatives to reality

**formal organization** a large secondary group that is formally organized to facilitate achieving its goals efficiently

**functional illiteracy** the lack of basic reading and writing skills needed for everyday life

**Gemeinschaft** a type of social organization in which people are bound closely together by kinship and tradition

**gender** society's division of humanity, based on sex, into two distinctive categories

**gender identity** traits that females and males, guided by their culture, incorporate into their personalities

**gender roles** (sex roles) attitudes and activities that a culture links to each sex

**gender stratification** a society's unequal distribution of wealth, power, and privilege between the two sexes

**generalized other** George Herbert Mead's term for widespread cultural norms and values we use as a reference in evaluating ourselves

**genocide** the systematic annihilation of one category of people by another

**gerontocracy** a form of social organization in which the elderly have the most wealth, power, and privileges

**gerontology** the study of aging and the elderly

*Gesellschaft* a type of social organization in which people have weak social ties and a great deal of self-interest

**gossip** rumor about the personal affairs of others

**government** formal organizations that direct the political life of a society

**"groupthink"** a limited understanding of some issue due to group conformity

**Hawthorne effect** a change in a subject's behavior caused by the awareness of being studied

**health** a state of complete physical, mental, and social well-being

**health care** any activity intended to improve health

**health maintenance organization** (HMO) an organization that provides comprehensive medical care to subscribers for a fixed fee

**hermaphrodite** a human being with some combination of female and male internal and external genitalia

**hidden curriculum** ideas and behavior that support the status quo, taught in subtle ways to students

**holistic medicine** an approach to health care that emphasizes prevention of illness and takes account of the whole person within a physical and social environment

**homogamy** marriage between people who are socially alike

**horticulture** technology based on using hand tools to cultivate plants

**humanizing bureaucracy** fostering an organizational environment that develops human resources

**hunting and gathering** simple technology to hunt animals and gather vegetation

**hypothesis** an unverified statement of a relationship between variables

**id** Freud's designation of the human being's basic drives

**ideal culture** social patterns consistent with cultural values and norms

**ideal type** an abstract statement of the essential characteristics of any social phenomenon

**ideology** cultural beliefs that reflect and support the interests of certain categories of people

**incest taboo** a cultural norm forbidding sexual relations or marriage between certain kin

**income** occupational wages or salaries and earnings from investments

**independent variable** a variable that causes change in another (dependent) variable

**inductive logical thought** reasoning that builds specific observations into general theory

**industrialism** technology that powers sophisticated machinery with advanced fuels

**infant mortality rate** the number of deaths in the first year of life for each thousand live births in a given year

**ingroup** a social group commanding a member's esteem and loyalty

**institutional discrimination** discrimination that is a normative and routine part of the economy, the educational system, or some other social institution

**instrumental leadership** group leadership that emphasizes the completion of tasks

**intergenerational social mobility** upward or downward social mobility of children in relation to their parents

**interlocking directorate** a social network of people who serve simultaneously on the boards of directors of many corporations

**interview** a series of questions administered personally by a researcher to respondents

**intragenerational social mobility** a change in social position occurring during a person's lifetime

**juvenile delinquency** the violation of legal standards by the young

**kinship** social ties based on blood, marriage, or adoption

**labeling theory** the assertion that deviance and conformity result from the response of others

**labor unions** organizations of workers that attempt to improve wages and working conditions through various strategies, including negotiations and strikes

**language** a system of symbols that allows members of a society to communicate with one another

**latent functions** the unrecognized and unintended consequences of any social pattern

**liberation theology** a fusion of Christian principles with political activism, often Marxist in character

**life expectancy** how long a person, on average, can expect to live

**looking-glass self** Cooley's assertion that the self is based on how others respond to us

**macro-level orientation** a focus on broad social structures that characterize society as a system

**magnet schools** schools that attract students through special facilities and programs promoting educational excellence

**mainstreaming** the integration of students with disabilities into the educational program as a whole

**mandatory education laws** legal requirements that children receive a minimum of formal education

**manifest functions** the recognized and intended consequences of any social pattern

**marriage** a socially approved relationship, involving economic cooperation and allowing sexual activity and childbearing, that is expected to be relatively enduring

**mass behavior** collective behavior among people dispersed over a wide geographical area

**mass hysteria** a form of dispersed collective behavior by which people respond to a real or imagined event with irrational, frantic behavior

**mass media** impersonal communications directed toward a vast audience

**mass society** a society in which industrialization proceeds and bureaucracy expands while traditional social ties grow weaker

**master status** a status that has exceptional importance for social identity, often shaping a person's entire life

**material culture** tangible elements of culture such as clothing and cities

**matriarchy** a form of social organization in which females dominate males

**matrilineal descent** a system tracing kinship through females

**matrilocality** a residential pattern in which a married couple lives with or near the wife's family

**mean** the arithmetic average of a series of numbers

**measurement** the process of determining the value of a variable in a specific case

**mechanical solidarity** Durkheim's term for social bonds, common to preindustrial societies, based on shared moral sentiments

**median** the value that occurs midway in a series of numbers arranged in order of magnitude or, simply, the middle case

**medicalization of deviance** the transformation of moral and legal issues into medical matters

**medicine** an institutionalized system for combating disease and improving health

**megalopolis** a vast urban region containing a number of cities and their surrounding suburbs

**meritocracy** a system of social stratification based on personal merit

**metropolis** a large city that socially and economically dominates an urban area

**micro-level orientation** a focus on situational patterns of social interaction

**migration** the movement of people into and out of a specific territory

**military-industrial complex** the close association between the federal government and defense industries

**minority** a category of people, distinguished by physical or cultural traits, who are socially disadvantaged

**miscegenation** the biological process of interbreeding among racial categories

**mob** a highly emotional crowd that pursues some violent or destructive goal

**mode** the value that occurs most often in a series of numbers

**modernity** patterns of social life linked to industrialization

**modernization** the process of social change begun by industrialization

**modernization theory** a model of economic and social development that explains global inequality in terms of differing levels of technological development among world societies

**monarchy** a type of political system in which power is passed from generation to generation in a single family

**monogamy** a form of marriage that joins one female and one male

**monopoly** domination of a market by a single producer

**monotheism** belief in a single divine power

**mores** norms that have great moral significance

**mortality** the incidence of death in a society's population

**multiculturalism** an educational program seeking to recognize the past and present cultural diversity of American society and to promote the equality of cultural traditions

**multinational corporation** a large corporation that operates in many different countries

**neocolonialism** a new form of international, economic exploitation that involves not direct political control but the operation of multinational corporations

**neolocality** a residential pattern in which a married couple lives apart from the parents of both spouses

**network** a web of social ties that links people who may have little common identity and interaction

**nonmaterial culture** intangible elements of culture such as values and norms

**nonverbal communication** communication using body movements, gestures, and facial expressions rather than speech

**norms** rules and expectations by which a society guides the behavior of its members

**nuclear family** (conjugal family) a social unit composed of one or, more commonly, two parents and children

**nuclear proliferation** the acquisition of nuclear-weapons technology by more and more societies

**objectivity** the state of personal neutrality in conducting research

**oligarchy** the rule of the many by the few

**oligopoly** domination of a market by a few producers

**operationalizing a variable** specifying exactly what is to be measured in assigning a value to a variable

**organic solidarity** Durkheim's designation of social bonds, common to industrial societies, based on specialization

**organizational environment** a range of factors outside an organization that affect its operation

**other-directedness** highly variable personality patterns among people open to change and likely to imitate the behavior of others

**outgroup** a social group toward which one feels competition or opposition

**overeducation** a situation in which workers have more formal education than the performance of their occupations requires

**panic** a form of localized collective behavior by which people react to a threat or other stimulus with emotional, irrational, and often self-destructive behavior

**participant observation** a method in which researchers systematically observe people while joining in their routine activities

**pastoralism** technology that supports the domestication of animals

**patriarchy** a form of social organization in which males dominate females

**patrilineal descent** a system tracing kinship through males

**patrilocality** a residential pattern in which a married couple lives with or near the husband's family

**peace** the absence of war

**peer group** people who interact regularly, usually with common interests, social position, and age

**personality** a person's fairly consistent pattern of thinking, feeling, and acting

**personal space** the surrounding area over which a person makes some claim to privacy

**plea bargaining** a legal negotiation in which the prosecution reduces a defendant's charge in exchange for a guilty plea

**pluralism** a state in which racial and ethnic minorities are distinct but have social parity

**pluralist model** an analysis of politics in which power is dispersed among many competing interest groups

**political action committee** (PAC) an organization formed by a special-interest group, independent of political parties, to pursue specific aims by raising and spending money

**political parties** organizations operating within the political system that seek control of government

**political revolution** the overthrow of one political system in order to establish another

**political state** a formal government claiming the legitimate use of coercion to support its rule

**politics** the institutionalized system by which a society distributes power and makes decisions

**polyandry** a form of marriage that joins one female with more than one male

**polygamy** a form of marriage that unites three or more people

**polygyny** a form of marriage that joins one male with more than one female

**polytheism** belief in many gods

**population** the people who are the focus of research

**positivism** a means to understand the world based on science

**postindustrial economy** a productive system based on service work and high technology

**power** the ability to achieve desired ends despite possible resistance from others

**power-elite model** an analysis of politics holding that power is concentrated among the rich

**prejudice** a rigid and irrational generalization about a category of people

**preoperational stage** Piaget's term for the level of human development in which the individual first uses language and other symbols

**presentation of self** the ways in which individuals, in various settings, try to create specific impressions in the minds of others

**primary group** a small social group in which relationships are both personal and enduring

**primary labor market** occupations that provide extensive benefits to workers

**primary sector** the part of the economy that generates raw materials directly from the natural environment

**primary sex characteristics** the genitals, used to reproduce the human species

**profane** that which is defined as an ordinary element of everyday life

**profession** a prestigious white-collar occupation that requires extensive formal education

**proletariat** people who provide labor necessary for the operation of factories and other productive enterprises

**propaganda** information presented with the intention of shaping public opinion

**public opinion** the attitudes of people throughout a society about one or more controversial issues

**qualitative research** inquiry based on subjective impressions

**quantitative research** inquiry based on the analysis of numerical data

**questionnaire** a series of questions presented to subjects

**race** a category composed of men and women who share biologically transmitted traits deemed socially significant

**racism** the belief that one racial category is innately superior or inferior to another

**rationality** deliberate, matter-of-fact calculation of the most efficient means to accomplish any particular goal

**rationalization of society** Weber's characterization of the historical change from tradition to rationality as the dominant mode of thought

**rational-legal authority** (bureaucratic authority) power legitimized by legally enacted rules and regulations

**real culture** actual social patterns that typically only approximate cultural values and norms

**reference group** a social group that serves as a point of reference for people making evaluations or decisions

**rehabilitation** reforming the offender to preclude subsequent offenses

**relative deprivation** a perceived disadvantage arising from some specific comparison

**relative poverty** the deprivation of some people in relation to those who have more

**reliability** the quality of consistent measurement

**religion** a system of beliefs and practices based on recognizing the sacred

**religiosity** the importance of religion in a person's life

**religious fundamentalism** a conservative religious doctrine that opposes intellectualism and worldly accommodation in favor of restoring a traditional otherworldly focus

**replication** repetition of research by others in order to assess its accuracy

**research method** a strategy for systematically conducting research

**resocialization** deliberate control of an environment intended to radically alter an inmate's personality

**retribution** an act of moral vengeance by which a society subjects an offender to suffering comparable to that caused by the offense

**retrospective labeling** the interpretation of someone's past consistent with present deviance

**riot** a social eruption that is highly emotional, violent, and undirected

**ritual** formal, ceremonial behavior

**role** patterns of expected behavior attached to a particular status

**role conflict** incompatibility among the roles corresponding to two or more different statuses

**role set** a number of roles attached to a single status

**role strain** incompatibility among roles corresponding to a single status

**routinization of charisma** the transformation of charismatic authority into some combination of traditional and bureaucratic authority

**rumor** unsubstantiated information spread informally, often by word of mouth

**sacred** that which is defined as extraordinary, inspiring a sense of awe, reverence, and even fear

**sample** a part of a population selected to represent the whole

**Sapir-Whorf hypothesis** the assertion that people perceive the world only in terms of the symbols provided by their language

**scapegoat** a person (or category of people), typically with little power, who is unfairly blamed for the troubles of others

**schooling** formal instruction under the direction of specially trained teachers

**science** a logical system that bases knowledge on direct, systematic observation

**secondary analysis** a research method in which a researcher utilizes data collected by others

**secondary group** a large and impersonal social group based on some special interest or activity

**secondary labor market** jobs that provide minimal benefits to workers

**secondary sector** the part of the economy that transforms raw materials into manufactured goods

**secondary sex characteristics** physical traits, other than the genitals, that distinguish physiologically mature females and males

**Second World** industrial societies that are currently transforming their socialist economies

**sect** a type of religious organization that resists accommodation with the larger society

**secularization** a historical trend away from the supernatural and the sacred

**segregation** the physical and social separation of categories of people

**self** George Herbert Mead's term for a dimension of personality encompassing an individual's self-conception

**sensorimotor stage** Piaget's term for the level of human development in which people experience the world only through sensory contact

**sex** the division of humanity into biological categories of female and male

**sexism** the belief that one sex is innately superior to the other

**sex ratio** the number of males for every hundred females in a given population

**sexual harassment** comments, gestures, or physical contact of a sexual nature that is deliberate, repeated, and unwelcome

**sexual orientation** the manner in which people experience sexual arousal and achieve sexual pleasure

**sick role** patterns of behavior appropriate for those who are ill

**social change** the transformation of culture and social institutions over time

**social character** personality patterns common to members of a society

**social conflict** struggle between segments of society over valued resources

**social-conflict paradigm** a framework for building theory based on the assumption that society is a complex system characterized by inequality and conflict that generate social change

**social construction of reality** the process by which individuals creatively shape reality through social interaction

**social control** the process by which members of a society encourage conformity to cultural norms

**social dysfunction** the undesirable consequence of any social pattern for the operation of society

**social epidemiology** the study of how health and disease are distributed in a society's population

**social fact** Durkheim's term for any social pattern that people confront as an objective reality beyond themselves

**social function** the consequence of any social pattern for the operation of society

**social group** two or more people who identify with one another and have a distinctive pattern of interaction

**social institution** a major sphere of social life organized to meet a basic human need

**social interaction** the process by which people act and react in relation to others

**socialism** an economic system in which productive resources are collectively owned

**socialization** lifelong social experience by which individuals develop human potential and learn patterns of their culture

**socialized medicine** a health-care system in which most medical facilities are owned and operated by the government, and most physicians are salaried government employees

**social marginality** the state of being excluded from social activity as an "outsider"

**social mobility** changes in people's positions in a system of social stratification

**social movement** organized activity that encourages or discourages social change

**social protection** rendering an offender incapable of further offenses either temporarily during a period of incarceration or permanently by execution

**social stratification** a system by which society ranks categories of people in a hierarchy

**social structure** a relatively stable pattern of social behavior

**society** people who interact in a limited territory and share a culture

**sociobiology** a theoretical paradigm that studies ways in which biological forces affect human culture

**sociocultural evolution** the Lenskis' term for the process of social change that results from gaining new cultural information, particularly technology

**socioeconomic status** a composite social ranking based on various dimensions of social inequality

**sociology** the scientific study of human society

**special-interest group** a political alliance of people who share an interest in some economic or social issue

**spurious correlation** an apparent, although false, relationship between two (or more) variables caused by some other variable

**state terrorism** the use of violence, generally without support of law, against individuals or groups by a government or its agents

**status** a recognized social position that an individual occupies

**status consistency** consistent standing across various dimensions of social inequality

**status set** all the statuses a person holds at a given time

**stereotype** a set of prejudices concerning some category of people

**stigma** a powerfully negative social label that radically changes a person's self-concept and social identity

**structural-functional paradigm** a framework for building theory based on the assumption that society is a complex system whose parts work together to promote stability

**structural social mobility** a shift in the social position of large numbers of people due more to changes in society than to individual efforts

**subculture** cultural patterns that distinguish some segment of a society's population

**suburbs** urban areas beyond the political boundaries of a city

**superego** Freud's designation of the presence of culture within the individual in the form of internalized values and norms

**survey** a research method in which subjects respond to a series of questions in a questionnaire or interview

**symbol** anything that carries a particular meaning recognized by members of a culture

**symbolic-interaction paradigm** a theoretical framework based on the assumption that society is continuously recreated as human beings construct reality through interaction

**technology** the application of cultural knowledge to the task of living in a physical environment

**terrorism** violence or the threat of violence employed by an individual or group as a political strategy

**tertiary sector** the part of the economy that generates services rather than goods

**theoretical paradigm** a set of fundamental assumptions that guides thinking and research

**theory** the process of linking facts together to explain something

**Third World** primarily agrarian societies, in which most people are poor

**Thomas theorem** the assertion that situations that are defined as real are real in their consequences

**total institution** a setting in which people are isolated from the rest of society and manipulated by an administrative staff

**totalitarianism** a political system that denies popular participation in government and extensively regulates people's lives

**totem** an object in the natural world imbued with sacred qualities

**tracking** categorically assigning students to different types of educational programs

**tradition** sentiments and beliefs passed from generation to generation

**traditional authority** power that is legitimized through respect for long-established cultural patterns

**tradition-directedness** rigid personalities based on conformity to time-honored ways of living

**transsexuals** people who feel they are one sex though biologically they are the other

**triad** a social group with three members

**underground economy** economic activity involving income or the exchange of goods and services that is not reported to the government

**urban ecology** the study of the link between the physical and social dimensions of cities

**urbanization** the concentration of humanity into cities

**urban renewal** government programs intended to revitalize cities

**validity** the quality of measuring precisely what one intends to measure

**values** culturally defined standards of desirability, goodness, and beauty that serve as broad guidelines for social life

**variable** a concept whose value changes from case to case

**victimless crimes** violations of law in which there are no readily apparent victims

**war** armed conflict among the people of various societies, directed by their governments

**wealth** the total amount of money and valuable goods that any person or family controls

**white-collar crime** crimes committed by people of high social position in the course of their occupations

**white-collar occupations** higher-prestige work involving mostly mental activity

**zero population growth** the level of reproduction that maintains population at a steady state

# References

ABBOTT, ANDREW. *The System of Professions: An Essay on the Division of Expert Labor.* Chicago: University of Chicago Press, 1988.

ABERLE, DAVID F. *The Peyote Religion Among the Navaho.* Chicago: Aldine, 1966.

ABZUG, ROBERT H. *Inside the Vicious Heart: Americans and the Liberation of Nazi Concentration Camps.* New York: Oxford University Press, 1985.

ADAMS, P. F., and V. BENSON. "Current Estimates from the National Health Interview Survey, 1989." U.S. National Center for Health Statistics. *Vital Health Statistics,* Vol. 10, No. 176. Washington, DC: U.S. Government Printing Office, 1990.

ADORNO, T. W., ET AL. *The Authoritarian Personality.* New York: Harper and Brothers, 1950.

AGUIRRE, B. E., E. L. QUARANTELLI, and JORGE L. MENDOZA. "The Collective Behavior of Fads: Characteristics, Effects, and Career of Streaking." *American Sociological Review.* Vol. 53, No. 4 (August 1988):569–84.

AGUIRRE, BENIGNO E., and E. L. QUARANTELLI. "Methodological, Ideological, and Conceptual-Theoretical Criticisms of Collective Behavior: A Critical Evaluation and Implications for Future Study." *Sociological Focus.* Vol. 16, No. 3 (August 1983):195–216.

AKERS, RONALD L., MARVIN D. KROHN, LONN LANZA-KADUCE, and MARCIA RADOSEVICH. "Social Learning and Deviant Behavior." *American Sociological Review.* Vol. 44, No. 4 (August 1979):636–55.

ALAM, SULTANA. "Women and Poverty in Bangladesh." *Women's Studies International Forum.* Vol. 8, No. 4 (1985):361–71.

ALBA, RICHARD D. *Italian Americans: Into the Twilight of Ethnicity.* Englewood Cliffs, NJ: Prentice Hall, 1985.

ALBON, JOAN. "Retention of Cultural Values and Differential Urban Adaptation: Samoans and American Indians in a West Coast City." *Social Forces.* Vol. 49, No. 3 (March 1971):385–93.

ALBRECHT, WILLIAM P., JR. *Economics.* 3rd ed. Englewood Cliffs, NJ: Prentice-Hall, 1983.

ALLAN, EMILIE ANDERSEN, and DARRELL J. STEFFENSMEIER. "Youth, Underemployment, and Property Crime: Differential Effects of Job Availability and Job Quality on Juvenile and Young Adult Arrest Rates." *American Sociological Review.* Vol. 54, No. 1 (February 1989):107–23.

ALLEN, MICHAEL PATRICK, and PHILIP BROYLES. "Campaign Finance Reforms and the Presidential Campaign Contributions of Wealthy Capitalist Families." *Social Science Quarterly.* Vol. 72, No. 4 (December 1991):738–50.

ALLSOP, KENNETH. *The Bootleggers.* London: Hutchinson and Company, 1961.

ALTMAN, DREW, ET AL. "Health Care for the Homeless." *Society.* Vol. 26, No. 4 (May/June 1989):4–5.

AMERICAN COUNCIL ON EDUCATION. "Senior Women Administrators in Higher Education: A Decade of Change, 1975–1983." Washington, DC: 1984.

AMERICAN COUNCIL ON EDUCATION, as reported in "Number of Black Students Still Falling, Study Finds." *The Chronicle of Higher Education.* Vol. XXXIV, No. 11 (November 11, 1987):2.

AMERICAN SOCIOLOGICAL ASSOCIATION. "Code of Ethics." Washington, DC: 1984.

ANDERSON, DANIEL R., and ELIZABETH PUGZLES LORCH. "Look at Television: Action or Reaction?" In Jennings Bryant and Daniel R. Anderson, eds., *Children's Understanding of Television: Research on Attention and Comprehension.* New York: Academic Press, 1983:1–33.

ANDO, FAITH H. "Women in Business." In Sara E. Rix, ed., *The American Woman: A Status Report 1990–91.* New York: W.W. Norton, 1990:222–30.

ANG, IEN. *Watching Dallas: Soap Opera and the Melodramatic Imagination.* London: Methuen, 1985.

ANGELO, BONNIE. "The Pain of Being Black" (an interview with Toni Morrison). *Time.* Vol. 133, No. 21 (May 22, 1989):120–22.

———. "Assigning the Blame for a Young Man's Suicide." *Time.* Vol. 138, No. 2 (November 18, 1991):12–14.

ARCHER, DANE, and ROSEMARY GARTNER. *Violence and Crime in Cross-National Perspective.* New Haven: Yale University Press, 1987.

ARENDT, HANNAH. *The Origins of Totalitarianism.* Cleveland, OH: Meridian Books, 1958.

———. *Between Past and Future: Six Exercises in Political Thought.* Cleveland, OH: Meridian Books, 1963.

ARIÈS, PHILIPPE. *Centuries of Childhood: A Social History of Family Life.* New York: Vintage Books, 1965.

———. *Western Attitudes Toward Death: From the Middle Ages to the Present.* Baltimore, MD: The Johns Hopkins University Press, 1974.

ARJOMAND, SAID AMIR. *The Turban for the Crown: The Islamic Revolution in Iran.* New York: Oxford University Press, 1988.

ASANTE, MOLEFI KETE. *The Afrocentric Idea.* Philadelphia: Temple University Press, 1987.

———. *Afrocentricity.* Trenton, NJ: Africa World Press, 1988.

ASCH, SOLOMON. *Social Psychology.* Englewood Cliffs, NJ: Prentice Hall, 1952.

ASTONE, NAN MARIE, and SARA S. McLANAHAN. "Family Structure, Parental Practices and High School Completion." *American Sociological Review.* Vol. 56, No. 3 (June 1991):309–20.

ATCHLEY, ROBERT C. "Retirement as a Social Institution." *Annual Review of Sociology.* Vol. 8. Palo Alto, CA: Annual Reviews, Inc., 1982:263–87.

———. *Aging: Continuity and Change.* Belmont, CA: Wadsworth, 1983; 2nd ed., 1987.

AVIS, GEORGE. "Access to Higher Education in the Soviet Union." In J. J. Tomiak, ed., *Soviet Education in the 1980s.* London: Croom Helm, 1983:199–239.

AYENSU, EDWARD S. "A Worldwide Role for the Healing Powers of Plants." *Smithsonian.* Vol. 12, No. 8 (November 1981):87–97.

BABBIE, EARL. *The Practice of Social Research.* 6th ed. Belmont, CA: Wadsworth, 1992.

BACHRACH, PETER, and MORTON S. BARATZ. *Power and Poverty.* New York: Oxford University Press, 1970.

BAHL, VINAY. "Caste and Class in India." Paper presented to the Southern Sociological Society, Atlanta, April, 1991.

BAILEY, WILLIAM C. "Murder, Capital Punishment, and Television: Execution Publicity and Homicide Rates." *American Sociological Review.* Vol. 55, No. 5 (October 1990):628–33.

BAILEY, WILLIAM C., and RUTH D. PETERSON. "Murder and Capital Punishment: A Monthly Time-Series Analysis of Execution Publicity." *American Sociological Review.* Vol. 54, No. 5 (October 1989):722–43.

BAINBRIDGE, WILLIAM SIMS, and DANIEL H. JACKSON. "The Rise and Decline of Transcendental Meditation." In Bryan Wilson, ed., *The Social Impact of New Religious Movements.* New York: The Rose of Sharon Press, 1981:135–58.

BAKER, MARY ANNE, CATHERINE WHITE BERHEIDE, FAY ROSS GRECKEL, LINDA

Carstarphen Gugin, Marcia J. Lipetz, and Marcia Texler Segal. *Women Today: A Multidisciplinary Approach to Women's Studies*. Monterey, CA: Brooks/Cole, 1980.

Bales, Robert F. "The Equilibrium Problem in Small Groups." In Talcott Parsons et al., eds., *Working Papers in the Theory of Action*. New York: Free Press, 1953:111–15.

Bales, Robert F., and Philip E. Slater. "Role Differentiation in Small Decision-Making Groups." In Talcott Parsons and Robert F. Bales, eds., *Family, Socialization and Interaction Process*. New York: Free Press, 1955:259–306.

Ballantine, Jeanne. *The Sociology of Education*. 2nd ed. Englewood Cliffs, NJ: Prentice Hall, 1989.

Baltes, Paul B., and K. Warner Schaie. "The Myth of the Twilight Years." *Psychology Today*. Vol. 7, No. 10 (March 1974):35–39.

Baltzell, E. Digby. *The Protestant Establishment: Aristocracy and Caste in America*. New York: Vintage, 1964.

———. "Introduction to the 1967 Edition." In W. E. B. DuBois, *The Philadelphia Negro: A Social Study*. New York: Schocken, 1967; orig. 1899.

———, ed. *The Search for Community in Modern America*. New York: Harper & Row, 1968.

———. "The Protestant Establishment Revisited." *The American Scholar*. Vol. 45, No. 4 (Autumn 1976):499–518.

———. *Philadelphia Gentlemen: The Making of A National Upper Class*. Philadelphia, PA: University of Pennsylvania Press, 1979; orig. 1958.

———. *Puritan Boston and Quaker Philadelphia*. New York: Free Press, 1979.

———. "The WASP's Last Gasp." *Philadelphia Magazine*. Vol. 79 (September 1988):104–7, 184, 186, 188.

Banfield, Edward C. *The Unheavenly City Revisited*. Boston, MA: Little, Brown, 1974.

Barash, David. *The Whispering Within*. New York: Penguin Books, 1981.

Barberis, Mary. "America's Elderly: Policy Implications." *Population Bulletin*. Vol. 35, No. 4 (January 1981). Population Reference Bureau.

Barker, Eileen. "Who'd Be a Moonie? A Comparative Study of Those Who Join the Unification Church in Britain." In Bryan Wilson, ed., *The Social Impact of New Religious Movements*. New York: The Rose of Sharon Press, 1981:59–96.

Baron, James N., Brian S. Mittman, and Andrew E. Newman. "Targets of Opportunity: Organizational and Environmental Determinants of Gender Integration within the California Civil Service, 1979–1985." *American Journal of Sociology*. Vol. 96, No. 6 (May 1991):1362–1401.

Barone, Michael, and Grant Ujifusa. *The Almanac of American Politics*. Washington, DC: Barone and Co., 1981.

Barrow, George M., and Patricia A. Smith. *Aging, the Individual, and Society*. 2nd ed. St. Paul, MN: West, 1983.

Barry, Kathleen. "Feminist Theory: The Meaning of Women's Liberation." In Barbara Haber, ed., *The Women's Annual 1982–1983*. Boston: G. K. Hall, 1983:35–78.

Bassuk, Ellen J. "The Homelessness Problem." *Scientific American*. Vol. 251, No. 1 (July 1984):40–45.

Bateson, C. Daniel, and W. Larry Ventis. *The Religious Experience: A Social-Psychological Perspective*. New York: Oxford, 1982.

Bauer, P. T. *Equality, the Third World, and Economic Delusion*. Cambridge, MA: Harvard University Press, 1981.

Beatrice Company, Inc. *Annual Report 1985*. Chicago: Beatrice, 1985.

Becker, Howard S. *Outside: Studies in the Sociology of Deviance*. New York: Free Press, 1966.

Bedell, George C., Leo Sandon, Jr., and Charles T. Wellborn. *Religion in America*. New York: Macmillan, 1975.

Beeghley, Leonard. *The Structure of Social Stratification in the United States*. Needham Heights, MA: Allyn & Bacon, 1989.

Beigel, Hugo G. "Romantic Love." *American Sociological Review*. Vol. 16, No. 3 (June 1951):326–34.

Bell, Alan P., Martin S. Weinberg, and Sue Kiefer-Hammersmith. *Sexual Preference: Its Development in Men and Women*. Bloomington, IN: Indiana University Press, 1981.

Bellah, Robert N. *The Broken Covenant*. New York: Seabury, 1975.

Bellah, Robert N., Richard Madsen, William M. Sullivan, Ann Swidler, and Steven M. Tipton. *Habits of the Heart: Individualism and Commitment in American Life*. New York: Harper & Row, 1985.

Belsky, Jay, Richard M. Lerner, and Graham B. Spanier. *The Child in the Family*. Reading, MA: Addison-Wesley, 1984.

Bem, Sandra Lipsitz. "Gender Schema Theory: A Cognitive Account of Sex-Typing." *Psychological Review*. Vol. 88, No. 4 (July 1981):354–64.

Benedict, Ruth. "Continuities and Discontinuities in Cultural Conditioning." *Psychiatry*. Vol. 1 (May 1938):161–67.

———. *The Chrysanthemum and the Sword: Patterns of Japanese Culture*. New York: New American Library, 1974; orig. 1946.

Benet, Sula. "Why They Live to Be 100, or Even Older, in Abkhasia." *The New York Times Magazine* (December 26, 1971):3, 28–29, 31–34.

Benjamin, Bernard, and Chris Wallis. "The Mortality of Widowers." *The Lancet*. Vol. 2 (August 1963):454–56.

Bennett, Neil G., David E. Bloom, and Patricia H. Craig. "The Divergence of Black and White Marriage Patterns." *American Journal of Sociology*. Vol. 95, No. 3 (November 1989):692–722.

Bennett, Stephen Earl. "Left Behind: Exploring Declining Turnout among Noncollege Young Whites, 1964–1988." *Social Science Quarterly*. Vol. 72, No. 2 (June 1991):314–33.

Benokraitis, Nijole, and Joe Feagin. *Modern Sexism: Blatant, Subtle, and Overt Discrimination*. Englewood Cliffs, NJ: Prentice Hall, 1986.

Berardo, F. M. "Survivorship and Social Isolation: The Case of the Aged Widower." *The Family Coordinator*. Vol. 19 (January 1970):11–25.

Berg, Ivar. *Education and Jobs: The Great Training Robbery*. New York: Praeger, 1970.

Berger, Brigitte, and Peter L. Berger. *The War Over the Family: Capturing the Middle Ground*. Garden City, NY: Anchor/Doubleday, 1983.

Berger, Peter L. *Invitation to Sociology*. New York: Anchor Books, 1963.

———. *The Sacred Canopy: Elements of a Sociological Theory of Religion*. Garden City, NY: Doubleday & Company, Inc., 1967.

———. *Facing Up to Modernity: Excursions in Society, Politics, and Religion*. New York: Basic Books, 1977.

———. *The Capitalist Revolution: Fifty Propositions About Prosperity, Equality, and Liberty*. New York: Basic Books, 1986.

Berger, Peter, Brigitte Berger, and Hansfried Kellner. *The Homeless Mind: Modernization and Consciousness*. New York: Vintage Books, 1974.

Berger, Peter L., and Hansfried Kellner. *Sociology Reinterpreted: An Essay on Method and Vocation*. Garden City, NY: Anchor Books, 1981.

Berger, Peter L., and Thomas Luckmann. *The Social Construction of Reality: A Treatise in the Sociology of Knowledge*. Garden City, NY: Anchor, 1967.

Bergesen, Albert, ed. *Crises in the World-System*. Beverly Hills, CA: Sage Publications, 1983.

Berk, Richard A. *Collective Behavior*. Dubuque, IA: Wm. C. Brown, 1974.

Bernard, Jessie. *The Female World*. New York: Free Press, 1981.

———. *The Future of Marriage*. New Haven, CT: Yale University Press, 1982; orig. 1973.

Bernard, Larry Craig. "Multivariate Analysis of New Sex Role Formulations and Personality." *Journal of Personality and Social Psychology*. Vol. 38, No. 2 (February 1980):323–36.

Berry, Brian L., and Philip H. Rees. "The Factorial Ecology of Calcutta." *American Journal of Sociology*. Vol. 74, No. 5 (March 1969):445–91.

Berscheid, Ellen, and Elaine Hatfield. *Interpersonal Attraction*. 2nd ed. Reading, MA: Addison-Wesley, 1983.

Berube, Allan. *Coming Out Under Fire: The History of Gay Men and Women in World War Two*. New York: The Free Press, 1990.

Best, Raphaela. *We've All Got Scars: What Boys and Girls Learn in Elementary School*. Bloomington, IN: Indiana University Press, 1983.

Bingham, Amy. "Division I Dilemma: Making the Classroom a Priority for Athletes." *The Kenyon Journal*. Vol. II, No. 3 (November 1987):2.

*Black Issues in Higher Education*. "Black Graduate Students Decline." Vol. 4, No. 8 (July 1, 1987):1–2.

Blau, Judith R., and Peter M. Blau. "The Cost of Inequality: Metropolitan Structure and Violent Crime." *American Sociological Review*. Vol. 47, No. 1 (February 1982):114–29.

Blau, Peter M. *Exchange and Power in Social Life*. New York: Wiley, 1964.

———. *Inequality and Heterogeneity: A Primitive Theory of Social Structure*. New York: The Free Press, 1977.

BLAU, PETER M., TERRY C. BLUM, and JOSEPH E. SCHWARTZ. "Heterogeneity and Intermarriage." *American Sociological Review*. Vol. 47, No. 1 (February 1982):45–62.

BLAU, PETER M., and OTIS DUDLEY DUNCAN. *The American Occupational Structure*. New York: John Wiley, 1967.

BLAUSTEIN, ALBERT P., and ROBERT L. ZANGRANDO. *Civil Rights and the Black American*. New York: Washington Square Press, 1968.

BLOOM, LEONARD. "Familial Adjustments of Japanese-Americans to Relocation: First Phase." In Thomas F. Pettigrew, ed., *The Sociology of Race Relations*. New York: Free Press, 1980:163–67.

BLUM, ALAN, and GARY FISHER. "Women Who Kill." In Delos H. Kelly, ed., *Criminal Behavior: Readings in Criminology*. New York: St. Martin's Press, 1980:291–301.

BLUMBERG, ABRAHAM S. *Criminal Justice*. Chicago: Quadrangle Books, 1970.

BLUMBERG, PAUL. *Inequality in an Age of Decline*. New York: Oxford University Press, 1981.

BLUMER, HERBERT G. "Fashion." In David L. Sills, ed., *International Encyclopedia of the Social Sciences*. Vol. 5. New York: Macmillan and Free Press, 1968:341–45.

———. "Collective Behavior." In Alfred McClung Lee, ed., *Principles of Sociology*. 3rd ed. New York: Barnes & Noble Books, 1969:65–121.

BLUMSTEIN, PHILIP, and PEPPER SCHWARTZ. *American Couples*. New York: William Morrow, 1983.

BNA COMMUNICATIONS INC. "The Challenge of Diversity: Equal Employment and Managing Difference in the 1990s." Summary report. Washington, DC: The Bureau of National Affairs, 1990.

BODENHEIMER, THOMAS S. "Health Care in the United States: Who Pays?" In Vicente Navarro, ed., *Health and Medical Care in the U.S.: A Critical Analysis*. Farmingdale, NY: Baywood Publishing Co., 1977:61–68.

BOFF, LEONARD and CLODOVIS. *Salvation and Liberation: In Search of a Balance Between Faith and Politics*. Maryknoll, NY: Orbis Books, 1984.

BOGARDUS, EMORY S. "Comparing Racial Distance in Ethiopia, South Africa, and the United States." *Sociology and Social Research*. Vol. 52, No. 2 (January 1968):149–56.

BOHANNAN, PAUL. *Divorce and After*. Garden City, NY: Doubleday & Company, 1970.

BOHLEN, CELESTINE. "Where the Fires of Hatred are Easily Stoked." *The New York Times* (August 4, 1991):E3.

BOHM, ROBERT M. "American Death Penalty Opinion, 1936–1986: A Critical Examination of the Gallup Polls." In Bohm, Robert M., ed., *The Death Penalty in America: Current Research*. Cincinnati: Anderson Publishing Co., 1991:113–45.

BOLLOUGH, VERN, and MARTHA VOGHT. "Women, Menstruation, and Nineteenth-Century Medicine." In Judith Walzer Leavitt, ed., *Women and Health in America*. Madison, WI: The University of Wisconsin Press, 1984:28–37.

BONILLA-SANTIAGO, GLORIA. "A Portrait of Hispanic Women in the United States." In Sara E. Rix, ed., *The American Woman 1990–91: A Status Report*. New York: W.W. Norton, 1990:249–57.

BONNER, JANE. Research presented in "The Two Brains." Public Broadcasting System telecast, 1984.

BOOTH, ALAN, and LYNN WHITE. "Thinking About Divorce." *Journal of Marriage and the Family*. Vol. 42, No. 3 (August 1980):605–16.

BOSWELL, TERRY E. "A Split Labor Market Analysis of Discrimination Against Chinese Immigrants, 1850–1882." *American Sociological Review*. Vol. 51, No. 3 (June 1986):352–71.

BOTT, ELIZABETH. *Family and Social Network*. New York: Free Press, 1971; orig. 1957.

BOTWINICK, JACK. "Intellectual Abilities." In James E. Birren and K. Warner Schaie, eds., *Handbook of the Psychology of Aging*. New York: Van Nostrand Reinhold, 1977:580–605.

BOULDING, ELISE. *The Underside of History*. Boulder, CO: Westview Press, 1976.

BOWLES, JACQUELINE, and WILLIAM A. ROBINSON. "PHS Grants for Minority Group HIV Infection Education and Prevention Efforts." *Public Health Reports*. Vol. 104, No. 6 (November-December 1989):552–59.

BOWLES, SAMUEL, and HERBERT GINTIS. *Schooling in Capitalist America: Educational Reform and the Contradictions of Economic Life*. New York: Basic Books, 1976.

BOYER, ERNEST L. *College: The Undergraduate Experience in America*. Prepared by The Carnegie Foundation for the Advancement of Teaching. New York: Harper & Row, 1987.

BRAITHWAITE, JOHN. "The Myth of Social Class and Criminality Reconsidered." *American Sociological Review*. Vol. 46, No. 1 (February 1981):36–57.

BRAND, DAVID. "The New Whiz Kids." *Time*. Vol. 130, No. 9 (August 31, 1987):42–46, 49, 51.

BREEN, LEONARD Z. "The Aging Individual." In Clark Tibbitts, ed., *Handbook of Social Gerontology*. Chicago: University of Chicago Press, 1960:145–62.

BRENNER, HARVEY. *Estimating the Social Costs of National Economic Policy: Implications for Mental and Physical Health and Criminal Aggression*. Joint Economic Committee, 94th Congress, October 26, 1976.

BRINTON, CRANE. *The Anatomy of Revolution*. New York: Vintage Books, 1965.

BRINTON, MARY C. "The Social-Institutional Bases of Gender Stratification: Japan as an Illustrative Case." *American Journal of Sociology*. Vol. 94, No. 2 (September 1988):300–34.

BROMLEY, DAVID G., and ANSON D. SHUPE, JR. *New Christian Politics*. Macon, GA: Mercer University Press, 1984.

BROPHY, GWENDA. "China, Part I." *Population Today*. Vol. 17, No. 3 (March 1989a):12.

———. "China: Part II." *Population Today*. Vol. 17. No. 4 (April 1989b):12.

BROWN, E. RICHARD. *Rockefeller Medicine Men: Medicine and Capitalism in America*. Berkeley, CA: University of California Press, 1979.

BROWNMILLER, SUSAN. *Femininity*. New York: Linden Press, Simon and Schuster, 1984.

BROWNSTEIN, RONALD, and NINA EASTON. *Reagan's Ruling Class: Portraits of the President's Top One Hundred Officials*. New York: Pantheon, 1983.

BROYLES, J. ALLEN. "The John Birch Society: A Movement of Social Protest of the Radical Right." In Louis E. Genevie, ed., *Collective Behavior and Social Movements*. Itasca, IL: F. E. Peacock, 1978:338–45.

BRUNO, MARY. "Abusing the Elderly." *Newsweek* (September 23, 1985):75–76.

BUCHHOLZ, MICHAEL, and JACK E. BYNUM. "Newspaper Presentation of America's Ages: A Content Analysis of Image and Role." *The Gerontologist*. Vol. 22, No. 1 (February 1982):83–88.

BUMPASS, L. "Children and Marital Disruption: A Replication and Update." *Demography*. Vol. 21, No. 1 (February 1984):71–82.

BURCH, ROBERT. Testimony to House of Representatives Hearing in "Review: The World Hunger Problem." October 25, 1983, Serial 98-38.

BURNHAM, WALTER DEAN. *Democracy in the Making: American Government and Politics*. Englewood Cliffs, NJ: Prentice Hall, 1983.

BURNS, JAMES A. "Discipline: Why Does It Continue To Be a Problem? Solution Is in Changing School Culture." *National Association of Secondary School Principals Bulletin*. Vol. 69, No. 479 (March 1985):1–47.

BURRIS, VAL. "The Social and Political Consequences of Overeducation." *American Sociological Review*. Vol. 48, No. 4 (August 1983):454–67.

BURSTEIN, PAUL. "Legal Mobilization as a Social Movement Tactic: The Struggle for Equal Employment Opportunity." *American Journal of Sociology*. Vol. 96, No. 5 (March 1991):1201–25.

BUSBY, LINDA J. "Sex Role Research on the Mass Media." *Journal of Communications*. Vol. 25 (Autumn 1975):107–13.

BUTLER, ROBERT N. *Why Survive? Being Old in America*. New York: Harper & Row, 1975.

BUTTERWORTH, DOUGLAS, and JOHN K. CHANCE. *Latin American Urbanization*. Cambridge, UK: Cambridge University Press, 1981.

"Buy America while Stocks Last." *The Economist*. Vol. 313, No. 7633 (December 16, 1989):63–66.

CAHNMAN, WERNER J., and RUDOLF HEBERLE. "Introduction." In *Ferdinand Toennies on Sociology: Pure, Applied, and Empirical*. Chicago: University of Chicago Press, 1971:vii–xxii.

CALLAHAN, DANIEL. *Setting Limits: Medical Goals in an Aging Society*. New York: Simon & Schuster, 1987.

CALLOW, A. B., JR., ed. *American Urban History*. New York: Oxford University Press, 1969.

CALMORE, JOHN O. "National Housing Policies and Black America: Trends, Issues, and Implications." In *The State of Black America 1986*. New York: National Urban League, 1986:115–49.

CAMERON, WILLIAM BRUCE. *Modern Social Movements: A Sociological Outline.* New York: Random House, 1966.

CAMPBELL, ANNE. *The Girls in the Gang.* 2nd ed. Cambridge, MA: Basil Blackwell, 1991.

CANETTI, ELIAS. *Crowds and Power.* New York: The Seabury Press, 1978.

CANTOR, MURIAL G., and SUZANNE PINGREE. *The Soap Opera.* Beverly Hills, CA: Sage Publications, 1983.

CANTRIL, HADLEY, HAZEL GAUDET, and HERTA HERZOG. *Invasion from Mars: A Study in the Psychology of Panic.* Princeton, NJ: Princeton University Press, 1947.

CAPLOW, THEODORE, ET AL. *Middletown Families.* Minneapolis, MN: University of Minnesota Press, 1982.

CARLEY, KATHLEEN. "A Theory of Group Stability." *American Sociological Review.* Vol. 56, No. 3 (June 1991):331–54.

CARLSON, NORMAN A. "Corrections in the United States Today: A Balance Has Been Struck." *The American Criminal Law Review.* Vol. 13, No. 4 (Spring 1976):615–47.

CARLTON, ERIC. *Ideology and Social Order.* London: Routledge & Kegan Paul, 1977.

CARMICHAEL, STOKELY, and CHARLES V. HAMILTON. *Black Power: The Politics of Liberation in America.* New York: Vintage, 1967.

CARROLL, GINNY. "Who Foots the Bill?" *Newsweek.* Special Issue (Fall/Winter, 1990):81–85.

CARTER, STEPHEN L. *Reflections of an Affirmative-Action Baby.* New York: Basic Books, 1991.

CENTER FOR THE STUDY OF SPORT IN SOCIETY. *1991 Racial Report Card: A Study in the NBA, NFL, and Major League Baseball.* Boston: Northeastern University, 1991.

CENTERS FOR DISEASE CONTROL. Report included in "Blacks' Syphilis Rate Up Sharply." *The New York Times* (May 17, 1991):A19.

———. *HIV/AIDS Surveillance.* Vol. 40, Nos. 51 & 52 (January 3, 1992). Atlanta: The Centers, 1992.

CHAGNON, NAPOLEON A. *Yąnomamö.* 3rd ed. New York: Holt, Rinehart and Winston, 1983.

———. "Life Histories, Blood Revenge, and Warfare in a Tribal Population." *Science.* Vol. 239, No. 4843 (February 26, 1988):985–92.

CHANDLER, TERTIUS, and GERALD FOX. *3000 Years of Urban History.* New York: Academic Press, 1974.

CHANGE, KWANG-CHIH. *The Archaeology of Ancient China.* New Haven, CT: Yale University Press, 1977.

CHAPPELL, NEENA L., and BETTY HAVENS. "Old and Female: Testing the Double Jeopardy Hypothesis." *The Sociological Quarterly.* Vol. 21, No. 2 (Spring 1980):157–71.

CHAPPLE, STEVE, and REEBEE GAROFALO. *Rock 'n' Roll Is Here to Pay: The History and Politics of the Music Industry.* Chicago: Nelson-Hall, 1977.

CHERLIN, ANDREW. *Marriage, Divorce, Remarriage.* Cambridge, MA: Harvard University Press, 1981.

CHERLIN, ANDREW, and FRANK F. FURSTENBERG, JR. "The American Family in the Year 2000." *The Futurist.* Vol. 17, No. 3 (June 1983):7–14.

CHILDREN'S DEFENSE FUND. *Child Poverty in America.* Washington, DC, 1991.

CHIP1 *Social Survey Software.* Datasets by J. Bruner and J. J. Macionis. Hanover, NH: Zeta Data/Englewood Cliffs. NJ: Prentice Hall, 1991.

CHOWN, SHEILA M. "Morale, Careers and Personal Potentials." In James E. Birren and K. Warner Schaie, eds., *Handbook of the Psychology of Aging.* New York: Van Nostrand Reinhold, 1977:672–91.

CLANCY, PAUL, and GAIL OBERST. "First Comes Love, Then Comes Live-In." *USA Today* (March 28, 1985):1A, 2A.

CLARK, CURTIS B. "Geriatric Abuse: Out of the Closet." In *The Tragedy of Elder Abuse: The Problem and the Response.* Hearings before the Select Committee on Aging, House of Representatives, July 1, 1986:49–50.

CLARK, JUAN M., JOSE I. LASAGA, and ROSE S. REGUE. *The 1980 Mariel Exodus: An Assessment and Prospect: Special Report.* Washington, DC: Council for Inter-American Security, 1981.

CLARK, MARGARET S., ED. *Prosocial Behavior.* Newbury Park, CA: Sage, 1991.

CLARK, THOMAS A. *Blacks in Suburbs.* New Brunswick, NJ: Rutgers University Center for Urban Policy Research, 1979.

CLINARD, MARSHALL B. *Cities with Little Crime: The Case of Switzerland.* Cambridge, UK: Cambridge University Press, 1978.

CLINARD, MARSHALL, and DANIEL ABBOTT. *Crime in Developing Countries.* New York: Wiley, 1973.

CLOWARD, RICHARD A., and LLOYD E. OHLIN. *Delinquency and Opportunity: A Theory of Delinquent Gangs.* New York: Free Press, 1966.

COAKLEY, JAY J. *Sport in Society: Issues and Controversies.* 3rd ed. St. Louis, MO: C. V. Mosby, 1986; 4th ed., 1990.

COCKERHAM, WILLIAM C. *Medical Sociology.* 2nd ed. Englewood Cliffs, NJ: Prentice Hall, 1982; 3rd ed., 1986.

COE, MICHAEL D., and RICHARD A. DIEHL. *In the Land of the Olmec.* Austin, TX: University of Texas Press, 1980.

COHEN, ALBERT K. *Delinquent Boys: The Culture of the Gang.* New York: Free Press, 1971; orig. 1955.

COHEN, LLOYD R. "Sexual Harassment and the Law." *Society.* Vol. 28, No. 4 (May-June, 1991):8–13.

COHEN, MICHAEL. "Restructuring the System." *Transaction.* Vol. 26, No. 4 (May/June 1989):40–48.

COHN, BOB. "The Lawsuit Cha-Cha." *Newsweek* (August 26, 1991):58–59.

COHN, RICHARD M. "Economic Development and Status Change of the Aged." *American Journal of Sociology.* Vol. 87, No. 2 (March 1982):1150–61.

COLEMAN, JAMES S., and THOMAS HOFFER. *Public and Private High Schools: The Impact of Communities.* New York: Basic Books, 1987.

COLEMAN, JAMES, THOMAS HOFFER, and SALLY KILGORE. *Public and Private Schools: An Analysis of Public Schools and Beyond.* Washington, DC: National Center for Education Statistics, 1981.

COLEMAN, JOHN R. "Homeless on the Streets of New York." In John J. Macionis and Nijole V. Benokraitis, eds., *Seeing Ourselves: Classic, Contemporary, and Cross-Cultural Readings in Sociology.* 2nd ed. Englewood Cliffs, NJ: Prentice Hall, 1992.

COLEMAN, RICHARD P., and BERNICE L. NEUGARTEN. *Social Status in the City.* San Francisco, CA: Jossey-Bass, 1971.

COLEMAN, RICHARD P., and LEE RAINWATER. *Social Standing in America.* New York: Basic Books, 1978.

COLLINS, RANDALL. "A Conflict Theory of Sexual Stratification." *Social Problems.* Vol. 19, No. 1 (Summer 1971):3–21.

———. *The Credential Society: An Historical Sociology of Education and Stratification.* New York: Academic Press, 1979.

———. *Sociological Insight: An Introduction to Nonobvious Sociology.* New York: Oxford University Press, 1982.

———. *Weberian Sociological Theory.* Cambridge, UK: Cambridge University Press, 1986.

COLLOWAY, N. O., and PAULA L. DOLLEVOET. "Selected Tabular Material on Aging." In Caleb Finch and Leonard Hayflick, eds., *Handbook of the Biology of Aging.* New York: Van Nostrand Reinhold, 1977:666–708.

COMTE, AUGUSTE. *Auguste Comte and Positivism: The Essential Writings.* Gertrud Lenzer, ed. New York: Harper Torchbooks, 1975.

CONGREGATION FOR THE DOCTRINE OF THE FAITH. *Instruction on Respect for Human Life in Its Origin and on the Dignity of Procreation: Replies to Certain Questions of the Day.* Vatican City, 1987.

CONRAD, PETER, and JOSEPH W. SCHNEIDER. *Deviance and Medicalization: From Badness to Sickness.* Columbus, OH: Merrill, 1980.

CONTRERAS, JOSEPH. "A New Day Dawns." *Newsweek* (March 30, 1992):40–41.

COOLEY, CHARLES HORTON. *Social Organization.* New York: Schocken Books, 1962; orig. 1909.

———. *Human Nature and the Social Order.* New York: Schocken Books, 1964; orig. 1902.

COPPOCK, MARJORIE L. "Women's Leadership Involvement in Community Volunteer Organizations." Paper presented to Southwestern Sociological Association, Dallas, Texas, 1987.

CORSARO, WILLIAM A., and THOMAS A. RIZZO. "*Discussione* and Friendship: Socialization Processes in the Peer Culture of Italian Nursery School Children." *American Sociological Review.* Vol. 53, No. 6 (December 1988):879–94.

COSER, LEWIS A. *Masters of Sociological Thought: Ideas in Historical and Social Context,* 2nd ed. New York: Harcourt Brace Jovanovich, 1977.

COTTLE, THOMAS J. "What Tracking Did to Ollie Taylor." *Social Policy.* Vol. 5, No. 2 (July-August 1974):22–24.

COTTRELL, JOHN, and THE EDITORS OF TIME-LIFE. *The Great Cities: Mexico City.* Amsterdam: 1979.

COUNCIL ON INTERNATIONAL EDUCATIONAL EXCHANGE. *Educating for Global Competence: The Report of the Advisory Committee for International Educational Exchange.* New York: The Council, 1988.

COUNTS, G. S. "The Social Status of Occupations: A Problem in Vocational Guidance." *School Review.* Vol. 33 (January 1925):16–27.

COURTNEY, ALICE E., and THOMAS W. WHIPPLE. *Sex Stereotyping in Advertising.* Lexington, MA: D.C. Heath, 1983.

COWGILL, DONALD, and LOWELL HOLMES. *Aging and Modernization.* New York: Appleton-Century-Crofts, 1972.

COX, HAROLD. *Later Life: The Realities of Aging.* Englewood Cliffs, NJ: Prentice-Hall, 1984.

COX, HARVEY. *The Secular City.* Rev. ed. New York: Macmillan, 1971; orig. 1965.

———. *Turning East: The Promise and Peril of the New Orientalism.* New York: Simon and Schuster, 1977.

———. "Church and Believers: Always Strangers?" In Robbins, Thomas, and Dick Anthony. *In Gods We Trust: New Patterns of Religious Pluralism in America.* 2nd ed. New Brunswick, NJ: Transaction, 1990:449–62.

CRISPELL, DIANE. "Working in 2000." *American Demographics.* Vol. 12, No. 3 (March 1990):36–40.

CROUSE, JAMES, and DALE TRUSHEIM. *The Case Against the SAT.* Chicago: University of Chicago Press, 1988.

CRYSTAL, GRAEF S. "How Much CEOs Really Make." *Fortune* (June 17, 1991):72–80.

CUFF, E. C., and G. C. F. PAYNE, EDS. *Perspectives in Sociology.* London: Allen and Unwin, 1979.

CUMMING, ELAINE, and WILLIAM E. HENRY. *Growing Old: The Process of Disengagement.* New York: Basic Books, 1961.

CURRIE, ELLIOTT. *Confronting Crime: An American Challenge.* New York: Pantheon, 1985.

CURTISS, SUSAN. *Genie: A Psycholinguistic Study of a Modern-Day "Wild Child."* New York: Academic Press, 1977.

CUTRIGHT, PHILLIP. "Occupational Inheritance: A Cross-National Analysis." *American Journal of Sociology.* Vol. 73, No. 4 (January 1968):400–16.

DAHL, ROBERT A. *Who Governs?* New Haven, CT: Yale University Press, 1961.

———. *Dilemmas of Pluralist Democracy: Autonomy vs. Control.* New Haven, CT: Yale University Press, 1982.

DAHLIN, MICHAEL. "Perspectives on Family Life of the Elderly in 1900." *The Gerontologist.* Vol. 20, No. 1 (February 1980):99–107.

DAHRENDORF, RALF. *Class and Class Conflict in Industrial Society.* Stanford, CA: Stanford University Press, 1959.

DALY, MARTIN, and MARGO WILSON. *Homicide.* New York: Aldine De Gruyter, 1988.

DAMON, WILLIAM. *Social and Personality Development.* New York: W. W. Norton, 1983.

DANIELS, ROGER. "The Issei Generation." In Amy Tachiki et al., eds., *Roots: An Asian American Reader.* Los Angeles: UCLA Asian American Studies Center, 1971:138–49.

DANNEFER, DALE. "Adult Development and Social Theory: A Reappraisal." *American Sociological Review.* Vol. 49, No. 1 (February 1984):100–116.

DARNTON, NINA, and YURIKO HOSHIA. "Whose Life Is It, Anyway?" *Newsweek.* Vol. 113, No. 4 (January 13, 1989):61.

DAVIES, CHRISTIE. *Ethnic Humor Around the World: A Comparative Analysis.* Bloomington: Indiana University Press, 1990.

DAVIES, JAMES C. "Toward a Theory of Revolution." *American Sociological Review.* Vol. 27, No. 1 (February 1962):5–19.

DAVIES, MARK, and DENISE B. KANDEL. "Parental and Peer Influences on Adolescents' Educational Plans: Some Further Evidence." *American Journal of Sociology.* Vol. 87, No. 2 (September 1981):363–87.

DAVIS, JAMES A. *Social Differences in Contemporary America.* New York: Harcourt Brace Jovanovich, 1987.

DAVIS, KINGSLEY. "Extreme Social Isolation of a Child." *American Journal of Sociology.* Vol. 45, No. 4 (January 1940):554–65.

———. "Final Note on a Case of Extreme Isolation." *American Journal of Sociology.* Vol. 52, No. 5 (March 1947):432–37.

DAVIS, KINGSLEY, and WILBERT MOORE. "Some Principles of Stratification." *American Sociological Review.* Vol. 10, No. 2 (April 1945):242–49.

DAVIS, SHARON A., and EMIL J. HALLER. "Tracking, Ability, and SES: Further Evidence on the 'Revisionist-Meritocratic Debate.'" *American Journal of Education.* Vol. 89 (May 1981):283–304.

DECKARD, BARBARA SINCLAIR. *The Women's Movement: Political, Socioeconomic, and Psychological Issues.* 2nd ed. New York: Harper & Row, 1979.

DEDRICK, DENNIS K. Personal communication, 1990.

DEDRICK, DENNIS K., and RICHARD E. YINGER. "MAD, SDI, and the Nuclear Arms Race." Manuscript in development. Georgetown, KY: Georgetown College, 1990.

DEGLER, CARL. *At Odds: Women and the Family in America From the Revolution to the Present.* New York: Oxford University Press, 1980.

DELACROIX, JACQUES, and CHARLES C. RAGIN. "Structural Blockage: A Crossnational Study of Economic Dependency, State Efficacy, and Underdevelopment." *American Journal of Sociology.* Vol. 86, No. 6 (May 1981):1311–47.

DEMOTT, JOHN S. "Wreaking Havoc on Spring Break." *Time.* Vol. 127, No. 14 (April 7, 1986):29.

DEPARLE, JASON. "Painted by Numbers, 1980s are Rosy to G.O.P., While Democrats See Red." *The New York Times* (September 26, 1991a):B10.

———. "Poverty Rate Rose Sharply Last Year as Incomes Slipped." *The New York Times* (September 27, 1991b):A1, A11.

*Der Spiegel.* "Third World Metropolises Are Becoming Monsters; Rural Poverty Drives Millions to the Slums." In *World Press Review* (October 1989).

DEVINE, JOEL A. "State and State Expenditure: Determinants of Social Investment and Social Consumption Spending in the Postwar United States." *American Sociological Review.* Vol. 50, No. 2 (April 1985):150–65.

DEWEY, JOHN. *Experience and Education.* New York: Collier Books, 1968; orig. 1938.

DIAMOND, MILTON. "Sexual Identity, Monozygotic Twins Reared in Discordant Sex Roles and a BBC Follow-Up." *Archives of Sexual Behavior.* Vol. 11, No. 2 (April 1982):181–86.

DICKENS, CHARLES. *The Adventures of Oliver Twist.* Boston: Estes and Lauriat, 1886; orig. 1837–1839.

DIPRETE, THOMAS A. "Unemployment over the Life Cycle: Racial Differences and the Effect of Changing Economic Conditions." *American Journal of Sociology.* Vol. 87, No. 2 (September 1981):286–307.

DIZARD, JAN E., and HOWARD GADLIN. *The Minimal Family.* Amherst: The University of Massachusetts Press, 1990.

DOBSON, RICHARD B. "Mobility and Stratification in the Soviet Union." *Annual Review of Sociology.* Vol. 3. Palo Alto, CA: Annual Reviews, Inc., 1977:297–329.

DOBYNS, HENRY F. "An Appraisal of Techniques with a New Hemispheric Estimate." *Current Anthropology.* Vol. 7, No. 4 (October 1966):395–446.

DOLLARD, JOHN, ET AL. *Frustration and Aggression.* New Haven, CT: Yale University Press, 1939.

DOMHOFF, G. WILLIAM. *Who Rules America?* Englewood Cliffs, NJ: Prentice-Hall, 1967.

———. *The Higher Circles: The Governing Class in America.* New York: Vintage, 1971.

———. *The Powers That Be: Processes of Ruling Class Domination in America.* New York: Vintage, 1979.

———. *Who Rules America Now? A View of the '80s.* Englewood Cliffs, NJ: Prentice Hall, 1983.

———. "The Growth Machine and the Power Elite: A Theoretical Challenge to Pluralists and Marxists Alike." Paper presented to the American Political Science Association. Washington, DC: 1984.

DONOVAN, VIRGINIA K., and RONNIE LITTENBERG. "Psychology of Women: Feminist Therapy." In Barbara Haber, ed., *The Women's Annual 1981: The Year in Review.* Boston: G. K. Hall, 1982:211–35.

DOUGLASS, RICHARD L. "Domestic Neglect and Abuse of the Elderly: Implications for Research and Service." *Family Relations.* Vol. 32 (July 1983):395–402.

DOW, UNITY. Personal communication, 1990.

DOYAL, LESLEY, with IMOGEN PENNELL. *The Political Economy of Health.* London: Pluto Press, 1981.

DOYLE, JAMES A. *The Male Experience.* Dubuque, IA: Wm. C. Brown, 1983.

DUBOIS, W. E. B. *The Philadelphia Negro: A Social Study.* New York: Schocken, 1967; orig. 1899.

———. "The Social Effects of Emancipation (1913)." In John J. Macionis and Nijole V. Benokraitis, eds. *Seeing Ourselves: Classic, Contemporary,* and Cross-Cultural Readings in Sociology. 2nd ed. Englewood Cliffs, NJ: Prentice Hall, 1992.

DUBOS, RENÉ. Man Adapting. New Haven, CT: Yale University Press, 1980; orig. 1965.

DUHL, LEONARD J. "The Social Context of Health." In Arthur C. Hastings et al., EDS., Health for the Whole Person: The Complete Guide to Holistic Medicine. Boulder, CO: Westview Press, 1980:39–48.

DURDEN, GAREY C., JASON F. SHOGREN, and JONATHAN I. SILBERMAN. "The Effects of Interest Group Pressure on Coal-Strip Mining Legislation." Social Science Quarterly. Vol. 72, No. 2 (June 1991):239–50.

DURKHEIM, EMILE. The Division of Labor in Society. New York: Free Press, 1964a; orig. 1895.

———.The Rules of Sociological Method. New York: Free Press, 1964b; orig. 1893.

———. The Elementary Forms of Religious Life. New York: Free Press, 1965; orig. 1915.

———. Suicide. New York: Free Press, 1966; orig. 1897.

———. Selected Writings. Anthony Giddens, ed. Cambridge, UK: Cambridge University Press, 1972.

———. Sociology and Philosophy. New York: Free Press, 1974; orig. 1924.

DWORKIN, ANDREA. Intercourse. New York: Free Press, 1987.

DZIECH, BILLIE WRIGHT, and LINDA WEINER. The Lecherous Professor: Sexual Harassment on Campus. Boston, MA: Beacon Press, 1984.

EBAUGH, HELEN ROSE FUCHS. Becoming an EX: The Process of Role Exit. Chicago: University of Chicago Press, 1988.

ECKHOLM, ERIK. "Malnutrition in Elderly: Widespread Health Threat." The New York Times (August 13, 1985):19–20.

ECKHOLM, ERIK, and JOHN TIERNEY. "AIDS in Africa: A Killer Rages On." The New York Times (September 16, 1990):A1, 14.

EDMONSTON, BARRY, and THOMAS M. GUTERBOCK. "Is Suburbanization Slowing Down? Recent Trends in Population Deconcentration in U.S. Metropolitan Areas." Social Forces. Vol. 62, No. 4 (June 1984):905–25.

EDWARDS, DAVID V. The American Political Experience. 3rd ed. Englewood Cliffs, NJ: Prentice Hall, 1985.

EDWARDS, RICHARD. Contested Terrain: The Transformation of the Workplace in the Twentieth Century. New York: Basic Books, 1979.

EHRENREICH, BARBARA. The Hearts of Men: American Dreams and the Flight from Commitment. Garden City, NY: Anchor, 1983.

EHRENREICH, JOHN. "Introduction." In John Ehrenreich, ed., The Cultural Crisis of Modern Medicine. New York: Monthly Review Press, 1978:1–35.

EHRLICH, PAUL R. The Population Bomb. New York: Ballantine Books, 1978.

EISEN, ARNOLD M. The Chosen People in America: A Study of Jewish Religious Ideology. Bloomington, IN: Indiana University Press, 1983.

EISENSTEIN, ZILLAH R., ED. Capitalist Patriarchy and the Case for Socialist Feminism. New York: Monthly Review Press, 1979.

EISLER, BENITA. The Lowell Offering: Writings by New England Mill Women 1840–1845. Philadelphia and New York: J. B. Lippincott Company, 1977.

EITZEN, D. STANELY. Social Problems. Boston: Allyn and Bacon, 1980.

EKMAN, PAUL. "Biological and Cultural Contributions to Body and Facial Movements in the Expression of Emotions." In A. Rorty, ed., Explaining Emotions. Berkeley: University of California Press, 1980a:73–101.

———. Face of Man: Universal Expression in a New Guinea Village. New York: Garland Press, 1980b.

———. Telling Lies: Clues to Deceit in the Marketplace, Politics, and Marriage. New York: W.W. Norton, 1985.

EKMAN, PAUL, WALLACE V. FRIESEN, and JOHN BEAR. "The International Language of Gestures." Psychology Today (May 1984):64–69.

ELAM, STANLEY M., LOWELL C. ROSE, and ALEC M. GALLUP. "The 23rd Annual Gallup Poll of the Public's Attitudes Toward Public Schools." Phi Delta Kappan, Vol. 73 (September 1991):41–56.

EL-ATTAR, MOHAMED. Personal communication, 1991.

ELIAS, ROBERT. The Politics of Victimization: Victims, Victimology and Human Rights. New York: Oxford University Press, 1986.

ELKIN, FREDERICK, and GERALD HANDEL. The Child and Society: The Process of Socialization. 4th ed. New York: Random House, 1984.

ELKIND, DAVID. The Hurried Child: Growing Up Too Fast Too Soon. Reading, MA: Addison-Wesley, 1981.

ELLIOT, DELBERT S., and SUZANNE S. AGETON. "Reconciling Race and Class Differences in Self-Reported and Official Estimates of Delinquency." American Sociological Review. Vol. 45, No. 1 (February 1980):95–110.

ELMER-DEWITT, PHILIP. "The Revolution that Fizzled." Time. Vol. 137, No. 20 (May 20, 1991):48–49.

EMBER, MELVIN, and CAROL R. EMBER. "The Conditions Favoring Matrilocal versus Patrilocal Residence." American Anthropologist. Vol. 73, No. 3 (June 1971):571–94.

EMBER, MELVIN M., and CAROL R. EMBER. Anthropology. 6th ed. Englewood Cliffs, NJ: Prentice Hall, 1991.

EMBREE, AINSLIE T. The Hindu Tradition. New York: Vintage Books, 1972.

EMERSON, JOAN P. "Behavior in Private Places: Sustaining Definitions of Reality in Gynecological Examinations." In H. P. Dreitzel, ed., Recent Sociology. Vol. 2. New York: Collier, 1970:74–97.

ENGELS, FRIEDRICH. The Origin of the Family. Chicago: Charles H. Kerr and Company, 1902; orig. 1884.

ERIKSON, ERIK H. Childhood and Society. New York: W. W. Norton, 1963; orig. 1950.

———. Identity and the Life Cycle. New York: W. W. Norton, 1980.

ERIKSON, KAI T. Wayward Puritans: A Study in the Sociology of Deviance. New York: John Wiley, 1966.

———. Everything in Its Path: Destruction of Community in the Buffalo Creek Flood. New York: Simon and Schuster, 1976.

ERIKSON, ROBERT S., NORMAN R. LUTTBEG, and KENT L. TEDIN. American Public Opinion: Its Origins, Content, and Impact. 2nd ed. New York: Wiley, 1988.

ETZIONI, AMITAI. A Comparative Analysis of Complex Organization: On Power, Involvement, and Their Correlates. Revised and enlarged ed. New York: Free Press, 1975.

———. "Too Many Rights, Too Few Responsibilities." Society. Vol. 28, No. 2 (January/February 1991):41–48.

ETZIONI-HALEVY, EVA. Bureaucracy and Democracy: A Political Dilemma. Rev. ed. Boston: Routledge & Kegan Paul, 1985.

EVANGELAUF, JEAN. "Student Financial Aid Reaches $20.5 Billion, but Fails to Keep Pace with Rising College Costs, Study Finds." The Chronicle of Higher Education. Vol. XXXIV, No. 14 (December 2, 1987):A33, A36.

EVANS, M. D. R. "Immigrant Entrepreneurship: Effects of Ethnic Market Size and Isolated Labor Pool." American Sociological Review. Vol. 54, No. 6 (December 1989):950–62.

EVE, SUSAN BROWN. "Age Strata Differences in Utilization of Health Care Services among Adults in the United States." Sociological Focus. Vol. 17, No. 2 (April 1984):105–20.

FALK, GERHARD. Personal communication, 1987.

FALLOWS, JAMES. "Immigration: How It's Affecting Us." The Atlantic Monthly. Vol. 252 (November 1983):45–52, 55–62, 66–68, 85–90, 94, 96, 99–106.

FALUDI, SUSAN. Backlash: The Undeclared War Against American Women. New York: Crown, 1991.

Family Economics Review. "Updated Estimates of the Cost of Raising a Child." Vol. 2, No. 4 (1989):30–31.

FANTINI, MARIO D. Regaining Excellence in Education. Columbus, OH: Merrill, 1986.

FARRELL, MICHAEL P., and STANLEY D. ROSENBERG. Men at Midlife. Boston, MA: Auburn House, 1981.

FEAGIN, JOE. The Urban Real Estate Game. Englewood Cliffs, NJ: Prentice Hall, 1983.

FEAGIN, JOE R. "The Continuing Significance of Race: Antiblack Discrimination in Public Places." American Sociological Review. Vol. 56, No. 1 (February 1991):101–16.

FEATHERMAN, DAVID L., and ROBERT M. HAUSER. Opportunity and Change. New York: Academic Press, 1978.

FENNELL, MARY C. "The Effects of Environmental Characteristics on the Structure of Hospital Clusters." Administrative Science Quarterly. Vol. 29, No. 3 (September 1980):489–510.

FERGUSON, TOM. "Medical Self-Care: Self Responsibility for Health." In Arthur C. Hastings et al., eds., Health for the Whole Person: The Complete Guide to Holistic Medicine. Boulder, CO: Westview Press, 1980:87–109.

FERGUSSON, D. M., L. J. HORWOOD, and F. T. SHANNON. "A Proportional

Hazards Model of Family Breakdown." *Journal of Marriage and the Family*. Vol. 46, No. 3 (August 1984): 539–49.

FINKELHOR, DAVID. *Child Sexual Abuse: New Theory and Research*. New York: The Free Press, 1984.

FINKELSTEIN, NEAL W., and RON HASKINS. "Kindergarten Children Prefer Same-Color Peers." *Child Development*. Vol. 54, No. 2 (April 1983):502–8.

FIORENTINE, ROBERT. "Men, Women, and the Premed Persistence Gap: A Normative Alternatives Approach." *American Journal of Sociology*. Vol. 92, No. 5 (March 1987):1118–39.

FIREBAUGH, GLENN, and KENNETH E. DAVIS. "Trends in Antiblack Prejudice, 1972–1984: Region and Cohort Effects." *American Journal of Sociology*. Vol. 94, No. 2 (September 1988):251–72.

FISCHER, CLAUDE S., ET AL. *Networks and Places: Social Relations in the Urban Setting*. New York: Free Press, 1977.

FISCHER, CLAUDE W. *The Urban Experience*. 2nd ed. New York: Harcourt Brace Jovanovich, 1984.

FISHER, ELIZABETH. *Woman's Creation: Sexual Evolution and the Shaping of Society*. Garden City, NY: Anchor/Doubleday, 1979.

FISHER, ROGER, and WILLIAM URY. "Getting to YES." In William M. Evan and Stephen Hilgartner, eds., *The Arms Race and Nuclear War*. Englewood Cliffs, NJ: Prentice Hall, 1988:261–68.

FISHMAN, PAMELA M. "Interactional Shitwork." *Heresies: A Feminist Publication on Art and Politics*. Vol. 2 (May 1977):99–101.

——. "The Work Women Do." *Social Problems*. Vol. 25, No. 4 (April 1978):397–406.

FISKE, ALAN PAIGE. "The Cultural Relativity of Selfish Individualism: Anthropological Evidence that Humans Are Inherently Sociable." In Margaret S. Clark, ed., *Prosocial Behavior*. Newbury Park, CA: Sage, 1991:176–214.

FITZPATRICK, JOSEPH P. *Puerto Rican Americans: The Meaning of Migration to the Mainland*. Englewood Cliffs, NJ: Prentice Hall, 1971.

——. "Puerto Ricans." In *Harvard Encyclopedia of American Ethnic Groups*. Cambridge, MA: Harvard University Press, 1980:858–67.

FITZPATRICK, MARY ANNE. *Between Husbands and Wives: Communication in Marriage*. Newbury Park, CA: Sage, 1988.

FLAHERTY, MICHAEL G. "A Formal Approach to the Study of Amusement in Social Interaction." *Studies in Symbolic Interaction*. Vol. 5. New York: JAI Press, 1984:71–82.

——. "Two Conceptions of the Social Situation: Some Implications of Humor." *The Sociological Quarterly*. Vol. 31, No. 1 (Spring 1990).

FLORIDA, RICHARD, and MARTIN KENNEY. "Transplanted Organizations: The Transfer of Japanese Industrial Organization to the U.S." *American Sociological Review*. Vol. 56, No. 3 (June 1991):381–98.

FLYNN, PATRICIA. "The Disciplinary Emergence of Bioethics and Bioethics Committees: Moral Ordering and its Legitimation." *Sociological Focus*. Vol. 24, No. 2 (May 1991):145–56.

*Forbes*. Special Issue. "The Forbes 500 Annual Directory." Vol. 147, No. 9 (April 29, 1991).

FORD, CLELLAN S., and FRANK A. BEACH. *Patterns of Sexual Behavior*. New York: Harper & Row, 1951.

FORM, WILLIAM. "Self-Employed Manual Workers: Petty Bourgeois or Working Class?" *Social Forces*. Vol. 60, No. 4 (June 1982):1050–69.

FORNOS, WERNER. "Growth of Cities Is Major Crisis." *Popline*. Vol. 8, No 3 (March 1986):4.

FORREST, HUGH. "They Are Completely Inactive . . ." *The Gambier Journal*. Vol. 3, No. 4 (February 1984):10–11.

FOWLER, FLOYD J., JR., and THOMAS W. MANGIONE. *Standardized Survey Interviewing: Minimizing Interviewer-Related Error*. Newbury Park, CA: Sage, 1989.

FRANK, ANDRÉ GUNDER. *On Capitalist Underdevelopment*. Bombay: Oxford University Press, 1975.

——. *Crisis: In the World Economy*. New York: Holmes & Meier, 1980.

——. *Reflections on the World Economic Crisis*. New York: Monthly Review Press, 1981.

FRANKLIN, JOHN HOPE. *From Slavery to Freedom: A History of Negro Americans*. 3rd ed. New York: Vintage Books, 1967.

FRAZIER, E. FRANKLIN. *Black Bourgeoisie: The Rise of a New Middle Class*. New York: Free Press, 1965.

FREDRICKSON, GEORGE M. *White Supremacy: A Comparative Study in American and South African History*. New York: Oxford University Press, 1981.

FREEMAN, DEREK. *Margaret Mead and Samoa: The Making and Unmaking of an Anthropological Myth*. Cambridge, MA: Harvard University Press, 1983.

FRENCH, MARILYN. *Beyond Power: On Women, Men, and Morals*. New York: Summit Books, 1985.

FRIEDMAN, EUGENE A., and ROBERT J. HAVIGHURST. *The Meaning of Work and Retirement*. Chicago: University of Chicago Press, 1954.

FRIEDRICH, CARL J., and ZBIGNIEW BRZEZINSKI. *Totalitarian Dictatorship and Autocracy*. 2nd ed. Cambridge, MA: Harvard University Press, 1965.

FRIEDRICH, OTTO. "A Proud Capital's Distress." *Time*. Vol. 124, No. 6 (August 6, 1984):26–30, 33–35.

——. "United No More." *Time*. Vol. 129, No. 18 (May 4, 1987):28–37.

FUCHS, VICTOR R. *Who Shall Live*. New York: Basic Books, 1974.

——. "Sex Differences in Economic Well-Being." *Science*. Vol. 232 (April 25, 1986):459–64.

FUGITA, STEPHEN S., and DAVID J. O'BRIEN. "Structural Assimilation, Ethnic Group Membership, and Political Participation among Japanese Americans: A Research Note." *Social Forces*. Vol. 63, No. 4 (June 1985):986–95.

FUJIMOTO, ISAO. "The Failure of Democracy in a Time of Crisis." In Amy Tachiki et al., eds., *Roots: An Asian American Reader*. Los Angeles: UCLA Asian American Studies Center, 1971:207–14.

FUMENTO, MICHAEL. *The Myth of Heterosexual AIDS*. New York: Basic Books, 1989.

FURSTENBERG, FRANK F., JR. "The New Extended Family: The Experience of Parents and Children after Remarriage." Paper presented to the Changing Family Conference XIII: The Blended Family. University of Iowa, 1984.

FURSTENBERG, FRANK F., JR., J. BROOKS-GUNN, and S. PHILIP MORGAN. *Adolescent Mothers in Later Life*. New York: Cambridge University Press, 1987.

FUSFELD, DANIEL R. *Economics: Principles of Political Economy*. Glenview, IL: Scott, Foresman, 1982.

GAGLIANI, GIORGIO. "How Many Working Classes?" *American Journal of Sociology*. Vol. 87, No. 2 (September 1981):259–85.

GALLUP, GEORGE, JR. *Religion in America*. Princeton, NJ: Princeton Religion Research Center, 1982.

GALSTER, GEORGE. "Black Suburbanization: Has It Changed the Relative Location of Races?" *Urban Affairs Quarterly*. Vol. 26, No. 4 (June 1991):621–28.

GANS, HERBERT J. *People and Plans: Essays on Urban Problems and Solutions*. New York: Basic Books, 1968.

——. *Deciding What's News: A Study of CBS Evening News, NBC Nightly News, Newsweek and Time*. New York: Vintage, 1980.

——. *The Urban Villagers: Group and Class in the Life of Italian-Americans*. New York: Free Press, 1982; orig. 1962.

GARDNER, R. ALLEN, and BEATRICE T. GARDNER. "Teaching Sign Language to a Chimpanzee." *Science*. Vol. 165 (1969):664–72.

GARFINKEL, HAROLD. "Conditions of Successful Degradation Ceremonies." *American Journal of Sociology*. Vol. 61, No. 2 (March 1956):420–24.

——. *Studies in Ethnomethodology*. Cambridge, UK: Polity Press, 1967.

GEERTZ, CLIFFORD. "Common Sense as a Cultural System." *The Antioch Review*. Vol. 33, No. 1 (Spring 1975):5–26.

GEIST, WILLIAM. *Toward a Safe and Sane Halloween and Other Tales of Suburbia*. New York: Times Books, 1985.

GELLES, RICHARD J., and CLAIRE PEDRICK CORNELL. *Intimate Violence in Families*. 2nd ed. Newbury Park, CA: Sage, 1990.

GELMAN, DAVID. "Who's Taking Care of Our Parents?" *Newsweek* (May 6, 1985):61–64, 67–68.

GEORGE, SUSAN. *How the Other Half Dies: The Real Reasons for World Hunger*. Totowa, NJ: Rowman & Allanheld, 1977.

GERSTEL, NAOMI. "Divorce and Stigma." *Social Problems*. Vol. 43, No. 2 (April 1987):172–86.

GERTH, H. H., and C. WRIGHT MILLS, EDS. *From Max Weber: Essays in Sociology*. New York: Oxford University Press, 1946.

GESCHWENDER, JAMES A. *Racial Stratification in America*. Dubuque, IA: Wm. C. Brown, 1978.

GIBBONS, DON C. *Delinquent Behavior*. 3rd ed. Englewood Cliffs, NJ: Prentice Hall, 1981.

GIBBONS, DON C., and MARVIN D. KROHN. *Delinquent Behavior*. 4th ed. Englewood Cliffs, NJ: Prentice Hall, 1986.

674    References

GIBBS, NANCY. "When Is It Rape?" *Time*. Vol. 137, No. 22 (June 3, 1991a):48–54.

———. "The Clamor on Campus." *Time*. Vol. 137, No. 22 (June 3, 1991b):54–55.

GIDDENS, ANTHONY. *Sociology: A Brief but Critical Introduction*. New York: Harcourt Brace Jovanovich, 1982.

GIELE, JANET ZOLLINGER. "Women's Work and Family Roles." In Janet Zollinger Giele, ed., *Women in the Middle Years: Current Knowledge and Directions for Research and Policy*. New York: John Wiley and Sons, 1982:115–50.

GILBERT, ALAN, and JOSEF GUGLER. *Cities, Poverty, and Development*. New York: Oxford University Press, 1983.

GILBERT, DENNIS, and JOSEPH A. KAHL. *The American Class Structure: A New Synthesis*. 3rd ed. Homewood, IL: The Dorsey Press, 1987.

GILLETT, CHARLIE. *The Sound of the City: The Rise of Rock and Roll*. New York: Pantheon, 1983.

GILLIGAN, CAROL. *In a Different Voice: Psychological Theory and Women's Development*. Cambridge, MA: Harvard University Press, 1982.

GIMENEZ, MARTHA E. "Silence in the Classroom: Some Thoughts about Teaching in the 1980s." *Teaching Sociology*. Vol. 17, No. 2 (April 1989):184–91.

GINSBURG, PAUL B. "Market-Oriented Options in Medicare and Medicaid." In Jack B. Meyer, ed., *Market Reforms in Health Care: Current Issues, New Directions, Strategic Decisions*. Washington, DC: American Enterprise Institute for Public Policy Research, 1983:103–18.

GIOVANNINI, MAUREEN. "Female Anthropologist and Male Informant: Gender Conflict in a Sicilian Town." In John J. Macionis and Nijole V. Benokraitis, eds., *Seeing Ourselves: Classic, Contemporary, and Cross-Cultural Readings in Sociology*. 2nd ed. Englewood Cliffs, NJ: Prentice Hall, 1992:27–32.

GLAAB, CHARLES N. *The American City: A Documentary History*. Homewood, IL: Dorsey Press, 1963.

GLADUE, BRIAN A., RICHARD GREEN, and RONALD E. HELLMAN. "Neuroendocrine Response to Estrogen and Sexual Orientation." *Science*. Vol. 225, No. 4669 (September 28, 1984):1496–99.

GLASS, DAVID V., ED. *Social Mobility in Britain*. London: Routledge & Kegan Paul, 1954.

GLAZER, NATHAN, and DANIEL P. MOYNIHAN. *Beyond the Melting Pot*. 2nd ed. Cambridge, MA: M.I.T. Press, 1970.

GLENN, CHARLES L., and FRANMARIE KENNEDY-KEEL. "Commentary." *Education Week*. Vol. V, No. 21 (February 5, 1986):21.

GLENN, NORVAL D., and BETH ANN SHELTON. "Regional Differences in Divorce in the United States." *Journal of Marriage and the Family*. Vol. 47, No. 3 (August 1985):641–52.

GLOCK, CHARLES Y. "The Religious Revival in America." In Jane Zahn, ed., *Religion and the Face of America*. Berkeley, CA: University of California Press, 1959:25–42.

———. "On the Study of Religous Commitment." *Religious Education*. Vol. 62, No. 4 (1962):98–110.

GLUCK, PETER R., and RICHARD J. MEISTER. *Cities in Transition*. New York: New Viewpoints, 1979.

GLUECK, SHELDON, and ELEANOR GLUECK. *Unraveling Juvenile Delinquency*. New York: Commonwealth Fund, 1950.

GOETTING, ANN. "Divorce Outcome Research." *Journal of Family Issues*. Vol. 2, No. 3 (September 1981):350–78.

———. "The Six Stations of Remarriage: Developmental Tasks of Remarriage after Divorce." *Family Relations*. Vol. 31, No. 2 (April 1982):213–22.

———. Personal communication, 1989.

GOFFMAN, ERVING. *The Presentation of Self in Everyday Life*. Garden City, NY: Anchor, 1959.

———. *Asylums: Essays on the Social Situation of Mental Patients and Other Inmates*. Garden City, NY: Anchor, 1961.

———. *Stigma: Notes on the Management of Spoiled Identity*. Englewood Cliffs, NJ: Prentice Hall, 1963.

———. *Interactional Ritual: Essays on Face to Face Behavior*. Garden City, NY: Anchor, 1967.

———. *Gender Advertisements*. New York: Harper Colophon, 1979.

GOLD, ALLAN R. "Increasingly, Prison Term is the Price for Polluters." *The New York Times* (February 15, 1991):B6.

GOLDBERG, STEVEN. *The Inevitability of Patriarchy*. New York: William Morrow and Co., 1974.

———. Personal communication, 1987.

GOLDEN, FREDERIC. "Here Come the Microkids." *Time*. Vol. 119, No. 18 (May 3, 1982):50–56.

GOLDFARB, JEFFREY C. *Beyond Glasnost: The Post-Totalitarian Mind*. Chicago: University of Chicago Press, 1989.

GOLDFIELD, MICHAEL. *The Decline of Organized Labor in the United States*. Chicago and London: University of Chicago Press, 1987.

GOLDSBY, RICHARD A. *Race and Races*. 2nd ed. New York: Macmillan, 1977.

GOLDSMITH, H. H. "Genetic Influences on Personality from Infancy." *Child Development*. Vol. 54, No. 2 (April 1983):331–35.

GOODE, WILLIAM J. "The Theoretical Importance of Love." *American Sociological Review*. Vol. 24, No. 1 (February 1959):38–47.

———. "Encroachment, Charlatanism, and the Emerging Profession: Psychology, Sociology and Medicine." *American Sociological Review*. Vol. 25, No. 6 (December 1960):902–14.

GORDON, JAMES S. "The Paradigm of Holistic Medicine." In Arthur C. Hastings et al., eds., *Health for the Whole Person: The Complete Guide to Holistic Medicine*. Boulder, CO: Westview Press, 1980:3–27.

GORDON, MILTON M. *Assimilation in American Life*. New York: Oxford University Press, 1964.

GORING, CHARLES BUCKMAN. *The English Convict: A Statistical Study*. Montclair, NJ: Patterson Smith, 1972; orig. 1913.

GORTMAKER, STEVEN L. "Poverty and Infant Mortality in the United States." *American Journal of Sociology*. Vol. 44, No. 2 (April 1979):280–97.

GOTTMANN, JEAN. *Megalopolis*. New York: Twentieth Century Fund, 1961.

GOUGH, KATHLEEN. "The Origin of the Family." *Journal of Marriage and the Family*. Vol. 33, No. 4 (November 1971):760–71.

GOULD, STEPHEN J. "Evolution as Fact and Theory." *Discover* (May 1981):35–37.

GOULDNER, ALVIN. *Enter Plato*. New York: Free Press, 1965.

———. "The Sociologist as Partisan: Sociology and the Welfare State." In Larry T. Reynolds and Janice M. Reynolds, eds., *The Sociology of Sociology*. New York: McKay, 1970a:218–55.

———. *The Coming Crisis of Western Sociology*. New York: Avon Books, 1970b.

GOVE, WALTER R. "The Relationship Between Sex Roles, Marital Status, and Mental Illness." *Social Forces*, Vol. 51, No. 3 (September 1972):34–44.

———. "Sex, Marital Status, and Psychiatric Treatment." *Social Forces*, Vol. 58, No. 3 (September 1979):89–94.

GRANOVETTER, MARK. "The Strength of Weak Ties." *American Journal of Sociology*. Vol. 78, No. 6 (May 1973):1360–80.

GRANT, DON SHERMAN II, and MICHAEL WALLACE. "Why Do Strikes Turn Violent?" *American Journal of Sociology*. Vol. 96, No. 5 (March 1991):1117–50.

GRANT, DONALD L. *The Anti-Lynching Movement*. San Francisco, CA: R and E Research Associates, 1975.

GRANT, KAREN R. "The Inverse Care Law in the Context of Universal Free Health Insurance in Canada: Toward Meeting Health Needs Through Public Policy." *Sociological Focus*. Vol. 17, No. 2 (April 1984):137–55.

GRAY, PAUL. "Whose America?" *Time*. Vol. 137, No. 27 (July 8, 1991):12–17.

GREELEY, ANDREW M. *Why Can't They Be Like Us? America's White Ethnic Groups*. New York: E.P. Dutton, 1971.

———. *Ethnicity in the United States: A Preliminary Reconnaissance*. New York: John Wiley, 1974.

———. *Religious Change in America*. Cambridge: Harvard University Press, 1989.

GREENBERG, DAVID F. *The Construction of Homosexuality*. Chicago: University of Chicago Press, 1988.

GREER, SCOTT. *Urban Renewal and American Cities*. Indianapolis: Bobbs-Merrill, 1965.

GREGORY, PAUL R., and ROBERT C. STUART. *Comparative Economic Systems*. 2nd ed. Boston, MA: Houghton Mifflin, 1985.

GRIFFIN, RICHARD WAYNE, and SANDRA KERANEN GRIFFIN. "Theoretical Aspects of Insurgency Among the Powerless." Paper presented to the Southwestern Sociological Association, Little Rock, Arkansas, 1989.

GRISWOLD, WENDY. "The Fabrication of Meaning: Literary Interpretation in the United States, Great Britain, and the West Indies." *American Journal of Sociology*. Vol. 92, No. 5 (March 1987):1077–1117.

GROSS, JANE. "New Challenge of Youth: Growing Up in a Gay Home." *The New York Times* (February 11, 1991):A1, B7.

GRUENBERG, BARRY. "The Happy Worker: An Analysis of Educational and Occupational Differences in Determinants of Job Satisfaction." *American Journal of Sociology*. Vol. 86, No. 2 (September 1980):247–71.

GUPTE, PRANAY. *The Crowded Earth: People and the Politics of Population*. New York: W.W. Norton, 1984.

GURAK, DOUGLAS T., and JOSEPH P. FITZPATRICK. "Intermarriage among Hispanic Ethnic Groups in New York City." *American Journal of Sociology*. Vol. 87, No. 4 (January 1982):921–34.

GUTMAN, HERBERT G. *The Black Family in Slavery and Freedom, 1750–1925*. New York: Pantheon Books, 1976.

GWARTNEY-GIBBS, PATRICIA A. "The Institutionalization of Premarital Cohabitation: Estimates from Marriage License Applications, 1970 and 1980." *Journal of Marriage and the Family*. Vol. 48, No. 2 (May 1986):423–34.

GWARTNEY-GIBBS, PATRICIA A., JEAN STOCKARD, and SUSANNE BOHMER. "Learning Courtship Aggression: The Influence of Parents, Peers, and Personal Experiences." *Family Relations*. Vol. 36, No. 3 (July 1987):276–82.

HAAS, LINDA. "Domestic Role Sharing in Sweden." *Journal of Marriage and the Family*. Vol. 43, No. 4 (November 1981):957–67.

HABERMAS, JÜRGEN. *Toward a Rational Society: Student Protest, Science, and Politics*. Jeremy J. Shapiro, trans. Boston, MA: Beacon Press, 1970.

HACKER, HELEN MAYER. "Women as a Minority Group." *Social Forces*. Vol. 30 (October 1951):60–69.

———. "Women as a Minority Group: 20 Years Later." In Florence Denmark, ed., *Who Discriminates Against Women*. Beverly Hills, CA: Sage, 1974:124–34.

HADDEN, JEFFREY K., and CHARLES E. SWAIN. *Prime Time Preachers: The Rising Power of Televangelism*. Reading, MA: Addison-Wesley, 1981.

HAGAN, JOHN, A. R. GILLIS, and JOHN SIMPSON. "The Class Structure of Gender and Delinquency: Toward a Power-control Theory of Common Delinquent Behavior." *American Journal of Sociology*. Vol. 90, No. 6 (May 1985):1151–78.

HAGAN, JOHN, and PATRICIA PARKER. "White-Collar Crime and Punishment: The Class Structure and Legal Sanctioning of Securities Violations." *American Sociological Review*. Vol. 50, No. 3 (June 1985):302–16.

HAGAN, JOHN, JOHN SIMPSON, and A. R. GILLIS. "Class in the Household: A Power-Control Theory of Gender and Delinquency." *American Journal of Sociology*. Vol. 92, No. 4 (January 1987):788–816.

HAIG, ROBIN ANDREW. *The Anatomy of Humor: Biopsychosocial and Therapeutic Perspectives*. Springfield, IL: Charles C. Thomas, 1988.

HALBERSTAM, DAVID. *The Reckoning*. New York: Avon, 1986.

HALLINAN, MAUREEN T., and RICHARD A. WILLIAMS. "Interracial Friendship Choices in Secondary Schools." *American Sociological Review*. Vol. 54, No. 1 (February 1989):67–78.

HAMBLIN, DORA JANE. *The First Cities*. New York: Time-Life, 1973.

HAMEL, RUTH. "Raging Against Aging." *American Demographics*. Vol. 12, No. 3 (March 1990):42–45.

HAMMOND, PHILIP E. "Introduction." In Philip E. Hammond, ed., *The Sacred in a Secular Age: Toward Revision in the Scientific Study of Religion*. Berkeley, CA: University of California Press, 1985:1–6.

HAMRICK, MICHAEL H., DAVID J. ANSPAUGH, and GENE EZELL. *Health*. Columbus OH: Merrill, 1986.

HANDLER, JOEL F., and YEHESKEL HASENFELD. *The Moral Construction of Poverty: Welfare Reform in America*. Newbury Park, CA: Sage, 1991.

HANDLIN, OSCAR. *Boston's Immigrants 1790–1865: A Study in Acculturation*. Cambridge, MA: Harvard University Press, 1941.

HANEY, CRAIG, CURTIS BANKS, and PHILIP ZIMBARDO. "Interpersonal Dynamics in a Simulated Prison." *International Journal of Criminology and Penology*. Vol. 1 (1973):69–97.

HANNAN, MICHAEL T., and GLENN R. CARROLL. "Dynamics of Formal Political Structure: An Event-History Analysis." *American Sociological Review*. Vol. 46, No. 1 (February 1981):19–35.

HANSEN, KAREN V., and ILENE J. PHILIPSON, EDS. *Women, Class, and the Feminist Imagination: A Socialist-Feminist Reader*. Philadelphia: Temple University Press, 1990.

HARBERT, ANITA S., and LEON H. GINSBERG. *Human Servies for Older Adults*. Columbia, SC: University of South Carolina Press, 1991.

HARDEN, MIKE. "Rest Assured that Eventually You'll Get Your Money's Worth." *The Columbus Dispatch* (November 19, 1989):C1.

HARDOY, JORGE E. "Two Thousand Years of Latin American Urbanization." In Jorge E. Hardoy, ed., *Urbanization in Latin America: Approaches and Issues*. Garden City, NY: Anchor Books, 1975.

HAREVEN, TAMARA K. "The Life Course and Aging in Historical Perspective." In Tamara K. Hareven and Kathleen J. Adams, eds., *Aging and Life Course Transitions: An Interdisciplinary Perspective*. New York: Guilford Press, 1982:1–26.

HARLAN, WILLIAM H. "Social Status of the Aged in Three Indian Villages." In Bernice L. Neugarten, ed., *Middle Age and Aging: A Reader in Social Psychology*. Chicago: University of Chicago Press, 1968:469–75.

HARLOW, CAROLINE WOLF. *Female Victims of Violent Crime*. Bureau of Justice Statistics report. Washington, DC: U.S. Government Printing Office, 1991.

HARLOW, HARRY F., and MARGARET KUENNE HARLOW. "Social Deprivation in Monkeys." *Scientific American*. Vol. 207 (November 1962):137–46.

HARRIES, KEITH D. *Serious Violence: Patterns of Homicide and Assault in America*. Springfield, IL: Charles C Thomas, 1990.

HARRINGTON, MICHAEL. *The New American Poverty*. New York: Penguin Books, 1984.

HARRIS, CHAUNCEY D., and EDWARD L. ULLMAN. "The Nature of Cities." *The Annals*. Vol. 242 (November 1945):7–17.

HARRIS, LOUIS, AND ASSOCIATES. *The Myth and Reality of Aging in America*. Washington, DC: National Council on Aging, 1976.

HARRIS, MARVIN. *Cows, Pigs, Wars and Witches: The Riddles of Culture*. New York: Vintage Books, 1975.

———. "Why Men Dominate Women." *New York Times Magazine* (November 13, 1977):46, 115–23.

———. *Good to Eat: Riddle of Food and Culture*. New York: Simon and Schuster, 1985.

———. *Cultural Anthropology*. 2nd ed. New York: Harper & Row, 1987.

HARRISON, PAUL. *Inside the Third World: The Anatomy of Poverty*. 2nd ed. New York: Penguin Books, 1984.

HARTMANN, BETSY, and JAMES BOYCE. *Needless Hunger: Voices from a Bangladesh Village*. San Francisco: Institute for Food and Development Policy, 1982.

HAVIGHURST, ROBERT J., BERNICE L. NEUGARTEN, and SHELDON S. TOBIN. "Disengagement and Patterns of Aging." In Bernice L. Neugarten, ed., *Middle Age and Aging: A Reader in Social Psychology*. Chicago: University of Chicago Press, 1968:161–72.

HAVILAND, WILLIAM A. *Anthropology*. 4th ed. New York: Holt, Rinehart and Winston, 1985.

HAYNEMAN, STEPHEN P., and WILLIAM A. LOXLEY. "The Effect of Primary-School Quality on Academic Achievement Across Twenty-nine High- and Low-Income Countries." *American Journal of Sociology*. Vol. 88, No. 6 (May 1983):1162–94.

HEALTH INSURANCE ASSOCIATION OF AMERICA. *Source Book of Health Insurance Data*. Washington, DC: The Association, 1991.

HEILBRONER, ROBERT L. *The Making of Economic Society*. 7th ed. Englewood Cliffs, NJ: Prentice-Hall, 1985.

HELGESEN, SALLY. *The Female Advantage: Women's Ways of Leadership*. New York: Doubleday, 1990.

HELMUTH, JOHN W. "World Hunger Amidst Plenty." *USA Today*. Vol. 117, No. 2526 (March 1989):48–50.

HENLEY, NANCY, MYKOL HAMILTON, and BARRIE THORNE. "Womanspeak and Manspeak: Sex Differences in Communication, Verbal and Nonverbal." In John J. Macionis and Nijole V. Benokraitis, eds., *Seeing Ourselves: Classic, Contemporary, and Cross-Cultural Readings in Sociology*, 2nd ed. Englewood Cliffs, NJ: Prentice Hall, 1992:10–15.

HERITAGE, JOHN. *Garfinkel and Ethnomethodology*. Cambridge, UK: Polity Press, 1984.

HERMAN, DIANNE F. "The Rape Culture." In John J. Macionis and Nijole V. Benokraitis, eds., *Seeing Ourselves: Classic, Contemporary, and Cross-Cultural Readings in Sociology*. 2nd ed. Englewood Cliffs, NJ: Prentice Hall, 1992.

HERMAN, EDWARD S. *Corporate Control, Corporate Power: A Twentieth Century Fund Study*. New York: Cambridge University Press, 1981.

HERRNSTEIN, RICHARD J. *IQ and the Meritocracy*. Boston: Little, Brown, 1973.

HERRSTROM, STAFFAN. "Sweden: Pro-Choice on Child Care." *New Perspectives Quarterly*. Vol. 7, No. 1 (Winter 1990): 27–28.

HERTY, ROBERT. "The Collective Representation of Death." In *Death and the Right Hand*. Aberdeen: Cohen and West, 1960:84–86.

HESS, STEPHEN. "Reporters Who Cover Congress." *Society*. Vol. 28, No. 2 (January-February 1991):60–65.

HEWLETT, SYLVIA ANN. *A Lesser Life: The Myth of Women's Liberation in America*. New York: William Morrow, 1986.

———. "The Feminization of the Work Force." *New Perspectives Quarterly*. Vol. 7, No. 1 (Winter 1990):13–15.

HILSMAN, ROGER. *The Politics of Governing America*. Englewood Cliffs, NJ: Prentice-Hall, 1985.

HILTS, PHILIP J. "Demands to Fix U.S. Health Care Reach a Crescendo." *The New York Times* (June 9, 1991):1, 5.

HIROSHI, MANNARI. *The Japanese Business Leaders*. Tokyo: University of Tokyo Press, 1974.

HIRSCHI, TRAVIS. *Causes of Delinquency*. Berkeley, CA: University of California Press, 1969.

HIRSCHI, TRAVIS, and MICHAEL GOTTFREDSON. "Age and the Explanation of Crime." *American Journal of Sociology*. Vol. 89, No. 3 (November 1983):552–84.

HIRSCHMAN, CHARLES, and MORRISON G. WONG. "Socioeconomic Gains of Asian Americans, Blacks, and Hispanics: 1960–1976." *American Journal of Sociology*. Vol. 90, No. 3 (November 1984):584–607.

HOCHSCHILD, ARLIE, WITH ANNE MACHUNG. *The Second Shift: Working Parents and the Revolution at Home*. New York: Viking, 1989.

HODGE, ROBERT W., DONALD J. TREIMAN, and PETER H. ROSSI. "A Comparative Study of Occupational Prestige." In Reinhard Bendix and Seymour Martin Lipset, eds., *Class, Status, and Power: Social Stratification in Comparative Perspective*. 2nd ed. New York: Free Press, 1966:309–21.

HOERR, JOHN. "The Payoff from Teamwork." In *Business Week*, No. 3114 (July 10, 1989):56–62.

HOGAN, DENNIS P., and EVELYN M. KITAGAWA. "The Impact of Social Status and Neighborhood on the Fertility of Black Adolescents." *American Journal of Sociology*. Vol. 90, No. 4 (January 1985):825–55.

HOLLAND, DOROTHY C., and MARGARET A. EISENHART. *Educated in Romance: Women, Achievement, and College Culture*. Chicago: The University of Chicago Press, 1990.

HOLM, JEAN. *The Study of Religions*. New York: Seabury Press, 1977.

HOLMES, LOWELL. "A Tale of Two Studies." *American Anthropologist*. Vol. 85, No. 4 (December 1983):929–35.

HOLT, THOMAS C. "Afro-Americans." In *Harvard Encyclopedia of American Ethnic Groups*. Cambridge, MA: Harvard University Press, 1980:5–23.

HONEYWELL, ROY J. *The Educational Work of Thomas Jefferson*. Cambridge, MA: Harvard University Press, 1931.

HOOK, ERNEST B. "Behavioral Implications of the XYY Genotype." *Science*. Vol. 179 (January 12, 1973):139–50.

HOSTETLER, JOHN A. *Amish Society*. 3rd ed. Baltimore: Johns Hopkins University Press, 1980.

HOUSE OF REPRESENTATIVES. *A.I.D. and Third World Women, the Unmet Potential*. Hearing held May 11, 1988. Washington, DC: U.S. Government Printing Office, 1988.

HOUT, MICHAEL, and ANDREW M. GREELEY. "The Center Doesn't Hold: Church Attendance in the United States, 1940–1984." *American Sociological Review*. Vol. 52, No. 3 (June 1987):325–45.

HOWE, NEIL, and WILLIAM STRAUSS. "America's 13th Generation." *The New York Times* (April 16, 1991).

HOWLETT, DEBBIE. "Cruzan's Struggle Left Imprint: 10,000 Others in Similar State." *USA Today* (December 27, 1990):3A.

HOYT, HOMER. *The Structure and Growth of Residential Neighborhoods in American Cities*. Washington, DC: Federal Housing Administration, 1939.

HOYT, MARY FINCH. "The New Prime Time." *USA Weekend* (December 13–15, 1985):4.

HRUSCHKA, PETER D. Personal communication, 1990.

HSU, FRANCIS L. K. *The Challenge of the American Dream: The Chinese in the United States*. Belmont, CA: Wadsworth, 1971.

HUBER, JOAN, and GLENNA SPITZE. "Considering Divorce: An Expansion of Becker's Theory of Marital Instability." *American Journal of Sociology*. Vol. 86, No. 1 (July 1980):75–89.

HUET-COX, ROCIO. "Medical Education: New Wine in Old Wine Skins." In Victor W. Sidel and Ruth Sidel, eds., *Reforming Medicine: Lessons of the Last Quarter Century*. New York: Pantheon Books, 1984:129–49.

HULS, GLENNA. Personal communication, 1987.

HUMPHREY, DEREK. *Final Exit: The Practicalities of Self-Deliverance and Assisted Suicide for the Dying*. Eugene, OR: The Hemlock Society, 1991.

HUMPHRIES, HARRY LEROY. *The Structure and Politics of Intermediary Class Positions: An Empirical Examination of Recent Theories of Class*. Unpublished Ph.D. dissertation. Eugene, OR: University of Oregon, 1984.

HUNNICUT, BENJAMIN K. *Work Without End*. Philadelphia: Temple University Press, 1988.

———. "Are We All Working Too Hard? No Time for God or Family." *The Wall Street Journal* (January 4, 1990).

HUNT, MORTON. *Sexual Behavior in the 1970s*. Chicago: Playboy Press, 1974.

HUNTER, FLOYD. *Community Power Structure*. Garden City, NY: Doubleday, 1963; orig. 1953.

HUNTER, JAMES DAVISON. *American Evangelicalism: Conservative Religion and the Quandary of Modernity*. New Brunswick, NJ: Rutgers University Press, 1983.

———. "Conservative Protestantism." In Philip E. Hammond, ed., *The Sacred in a Secular Age*. Berkeley, CA: University of California Press, 1985:50–66.

———. *Evangelicalism: The Coming Generation*. Chicago: The University of Chicago Press, 1987.

HURN, CHRISTOPHER. *The Limits and Possibilities of Schooling*. Boston: Allyn and Bacon, 1978.

HWANG, SEAN-SHONG, STEVEN H. MURDOCK, BANOO PARPIA, and RITA R. HAMM. "The Effects of Race and Socioeconomic Status on Residential Segregation in Texas, 1970–1980." *Social Forces*. Vol. 63, No. 3 (March 1985):732–47.

HYMAN, HERBERT H., and CHARLES R. WRIGHT. "Trends in Voluntary Association Memberships of American Adults: Replication Based on Secondary Analysis of National Sample Survey." *American Sociological Review*. Vol. 36, No. 2 (April 1971):191–206.

ILLICH, IVAN. *Medical Nemesis: The Expropriation of Health*. New York: Pantheon Books, 1976.

INSTITUTE FOR PHILOSOPHY AND PUBLIC POLICY. "The Graying of America." Vol. 8, No. 2 (Spring 1988):1–5.

IRISH, MARIAN D., JAMES W. PROTHRO, and RICHARD J. RICHARDSON. *The Politics of American Democracy*. 7th ed. Englewood Cliffs, NJ: Prentice-Hall, 1981.

IRWIN, JOHN. *Prison in Turmoil*. Boston, MA: Little, Brown, 1980.

ISAY, RICHARD A. *Being Homosexual: Gay Men and Their Development*. New York: Farrar, Straus, Giroux, 1989.

JACOB, JOHN E. "An Overview of Black America in 1985." In James D. Williams, ed., *The State of Black America 1986*. New York: National Urban League, 1986:i-xi.

JACOBS, DAVID. "Inequality and Police Strength." *American Sociological Review*. Vol. 44, No. 6 (December 1979):913–25.

JACOBS, JANE. *The Death and Life of Great American Cities*. New York: Random House, 1961.

———. *The Economy of Cities*. New York: Vintage, 1970.

———. *Cities and the Wealth of Nations*. New York: Random House, 1984.

JACQUET, CONSTANT H., and ALICE M. JONES. *Yearbook of American and Canadian Churches 1991*. Nashville, TN: Abingdon Press, 1991.

JAEGER, ART, and ROBERT GREENSTEIN. "Poverty Rate and Household Income Stagnate as Rich-Poor Gap Hits Post-War High." Washington, DC: Center on Budget and Policy Priorities, 1989.

JAGAROWSKY, PAUL A., and MARY JO BANE. *Neighborhood Poverty: Basic Questions*. Discussion paper series H–90–3. John F. Kennedy School of Government. Cambridge: Harvard University, 1990.

JAGGER, ALISON. "Political Philosophies of Women's Liberation." In Laurel Richardson and Verta Taylor, eds., *Feminist Frontiers: Rethinking Sex, Gender, and Society*. Reading, MA: Addison-Wesley, 1983.

JAMES, DAVID R. "City Limits on Racial Equality: The Effects of City-Suburb

Boundaries on Public-School Desegregation, 1968–1976." *American Sociological Review*. Vol. 54, No. 6 (December 1989):963–85.

JANIS, IRVING. *Victims of Groupthink*. Boston, MA: Houghton Mifflin, 1972.
———. *Crucial Decisions: Leadership in Policymaking and Crisis Management*. New York: Free Press, 1989.

JAYNES, GERALD DAVID, and ROBIN M. WILLIAMS, eds. *A Common Destiny: Blacks and American Society*. Washington, DC: National Academy Press, 1989.

JEFFERSON, THOMAS. Letter to James Madison, October 28, 1785. In Julian P. Boyd, ed., *The Papers of Thomas Jefferson*. Princeton: Princeton University Press, 1953:681–83.

JENCKS, CHRISTOPHER. "Genes and Crime." *The New York Review* (February 12, 1987):33–41.

JENCKS, CHRISTOPHER, ET AL. *Inequality: A Reassessment of the Effect of Family and Schooling in America*. New York: Basic Books, 1972.

JENKINS, BRIAN M. "Statements About Terrorism." In *International Terrorism, The Annals of the American Academy of Political and Social Science*. Vol. 463 (September 1982). Beverly Hills, CA: Sage Publications:11–23.
———. "Terrorism Remains a Threat." Syndicated column, *The Columbus Dispatch* (January 14, 1990):D-1.

JENKINS, J. CRAIG, and CHARLES PERROW. "Insurgency of the Powerless: Farm Worker Movements (1946–1972)." *American Sociological Review*. Vol. 42, No. 2 (April 1977): 249–68.

JOHNSON, DIRK. "Census Finds Many Claiming New Identity: Indian." *The New York Times* (March 5, 1991):A1, A116.

JOHNSON, JULIE. "Do We Have Too Many Lawyers?" *Time*. Vol. 138, No. 8 (August 26, 1991):54–55.

JOHNSON, NORRIS R. "Panic at 'The Who Concert Stampede': An Empirical Assessment." *Social Problems*. Vol. 34, No. 4 (October 1987):362–73.

JOHNSON, PAUL. "The Seven Deadly Sins of Terrorism." In Benjamin Netanyahu, ed., *International Terrorism*. New Brunswick, NJ: Transaction Books, 1981:12–22.

JOHNSTON, R. J. "Residential Area Characteristics." In D. T. Herbert and R. J. Johnston, eds., *Social Areas in Cities. Vol. 1: Spatial Processes and Form*. New York: Wiley, 1976:193–235.

JOHNSTONE, RONALD L. *Religion in Society: A Sociology of Religion*. 2nd ed. Englewood Cliffs, NJ: Prentice Hall, 1983.

JOINT ECONOMIC COMMITTEE. *The Concentration of Wealth in the United States: Trends in the Distribution of Wealth Among American Families*. Washington, DC: United States Congress, 1986.

JONES, DAVID A. *History of Criminology: A Philosophical Perspective*. Westport, CT: Greenwood Press, 1986.

JONES, RUTH, and WARREN E. MILLER. "Financing Campaigns: Macro Level Innovation and Micro Level Response." *The Western Political Quarterly*. Vol. 38, No. 2 (June 1985):187–210.

JONES, TERRY. "Foul Ball in the Front Office: Racial Practices in Baseball Management." *The Black Scholar*. Vol. 18, No. 3 (May/June 1987):16–24.

JOSEPHY, ALVIN M., JR. *Now That the Buffalo's Gone: A Study of Today's American Indians*. New York: Alfred A. Knopf, 1982.

KAELBLE, HARTMUT. *Social Mobility in the 19th and 20th Centuries: Europe and America in Comparative Perspective*. New York: St. Martin's Press, 1986.

KAIN, EDWARD L. "A Note on the Integration of AIDS Into the Sociology of Human Sexuality." *Teaching Sociology*. Vol. 15, No. 4 (July 1987):320–23.
———. *The Myth of Family Decline: Understanding Families in a World of Rapid Social Change*. Lexington, MA: Lexington Books, 1990.

KAIN, EDWARD L., and SHANNON HART. "AIDS and the Family: A Content Analysis of Media Coverage." Presented to National Council on Family Relations, Atlanta, 1987.

KALISH, CAROL B. "International Crime Rates." Bureau of Justice Statistics *Special Report*, May 1988. Washington, DC: U.S. Government Printing Office, 1988.

KALISH, RICHARD A. "The New Ageism and the Failure Models: A Polemic." *The Gerontologist*. Vol. 19, No. 4 (August 1979):398–402.
———. *Late Adulthood: Perspectives on Human Development*. 2nd ed. Monterey, CA: Brooks/Cole, 1982.

KALMUSS, DEBRA, and JUDITH A. SELTZER. "Continuity of Marital Behavior in Remarriage: The Case of Spouse Abuse." Unpublished paper. November 1984.

KAMINER, WENDY. "Volunteers: Who Knows What's in It for Them." *Ms.* (December 1984):93–94, 96, 126–28.

KANTER, ROSABETH MOSS. *Men and Women of the Corporation*. New York: Basic Books, 1977.
———. *The Change Masters: Innovation and Entrepreneurship in the American Corporation*. New York: Simon and Schuster, 1983.
———. "All That Is Entrepreneurial Is Not Gold." *The Wall Street Journal* (July 22, 1985):18.
———. *When Giants Learn to Dance: Mastering the Challenges of Strategy, Management, and Careers in the 1990s*. New York: Simon and Schuster, 1989.

KANTER, ROSABETH MOSS, and BARRY A. STEIN. "The Gender Pioneers: Women in an Industrial Sales Force." In R. M. Kanter and B. A. Stein, eds., *Life in Organizations*. New York: Basic Books, 1979:134–60.

KANTER, ROSABETH MOSS, and BARRY STEIN. *A Tale of "O": On Being Different in an Organization*. New York: Harper & Row; 1980.

KANTROWITZ, BARBARA. "Mothers on Their Own." *Newsweek* (December 23, 1985):66–67.

KAPLAN, ERIC B., ET AL. "The Usefulness of Preoperative Laboratory Screening." *Journal of the American Medical Association*. Vol. 253, No. 24 (June 28, 1985):3576–81.

KAPTCHUK, TED. "The Holistic Logic of Chinese Medicine." In Shepard Bliss et al., eds., *The New Holistic Health Handbook*. Lexington, MA: The Steven Greene Press/Penguin Books, 1985:41.

KARP, DAVID A., and WILLIAM C. YOELS. "The College Classroom: Some Observations on the Meaning of Student Participation." *Sociology and Social Research*. Vol. 60, No. 4 (July 1976):421–39.

KASARDA, JOHN D. "Entry-Level Jobs, Mobility and Urban Minority Employment." *Urban Affairs Quarterly*. Vol. 19, No. 1 (September 1983):21–40.

KAUFMAN, MARC. "Becoming 'Old Old'." *The Philadelphia Inquirer* (October 28, 1990):1-A, 10-A.

KAUFMAN, POLLY WELTS. "Women and Education." In Barbara Haber, ed., *The Women's Annual, 1981: The Year in Review*. Boston, MA: G. K. Hall and Company, 1982:24–55.

KAUFMAN, ROBERT L., and SEYMOUR SPILERMAN. "The Age Structures of Occupations and Jobs." *American Journal of Sociology*. Vol. 87, No. 4 (January 1982): 827–51.

KAUFMAN, WALTER. *Religions in Four Dimensions: Existential, Aesthetic, Historical and Comparative*. New York: Reader's Digest Press, 1976.

KEATING, NORAH C., and PRISCILLA COLE. "What Do I Do with Him 24 Hours a Day? Changes in the Housewife Role After Retirement." *The Gerontologist*. Vol. 20, No. 1 (February 1980):84–89.

KELLER, HELEN. *The Story of My Life*. New York: Doubleday, Page and Company, 1903.

KELLER, SUZANNE. *The Urban Neighborhood*. New York: Random House, 1968.

KELLEY, JACK. "Births Out of Wedlock Opposed." *USA Today* (August 16, 1985):6A.

KELLEY, ROBERT. *The Shaping of the American Past. Vol. 2: 1865 to the Present*. 3rd ed. Englewood Cliffs, NJ: Prentice-Hall, 1982.

KEMP, ALICE ABEL, and SHELLEY COVERMAN. "Marginal Jobs or Marginal Workers: Identifying Sex Differences in Low-Skill Occupations." *Sociological Focus*. Vol. 22, No. 1 (February 1989):19–37.

KENISTON, KENNETH. "Working Mothers." In James M. Henslin, ed., *Marriage and Family in a Changing Society*. 2nd ed. New York: Free Press, 1985:319–21.

KENNICKELL, ARTHUR, and JANICE SHACK-MARQUEZ. "Changes in Family Finances from 1983 to 1989: Evidence from the Survey of Consumer Finances." *Federal Reserve Bulletin* (January 1992):1–18.

KENYON, KATHLEEN. *Digging Up Jericho*. London: Ernest Benn, 1957.

KERCKHOFF, ALAN C., RICHARD T. CAMPBELL, and IDEE WINFIELD-LAIRD. "Social Mobility in Great Britain and the United States." *American Journal of Sociology*. Vol. 91, No. 2 (September 1985):281–308.

KESSLER, RONALD D., and PAUL D. CLEARY. "Social Class and Psychological Distress." *American Sociological Review*. Vol. 45, No 3 (June 1980):463–78.

KII, TOSHI. "Recent Extension of Retirement Age in Japan." *The Gerontologist*. Vol. 19, No. 5 (October 1979):481–86.

KILBOURNE, BROCK K. "The Conway and Siegelman Claims Against Religious

Cults: An Assessment of Their Data." *Journal for the Scientific Study of Religion.* Vol. 22, No. 4 (December 1983):380–85.

KILGORE, SALLY B. "The Organizational Context of Tracking in Schools." *American Sociological Review.* Vol. 56, No. 2 (April 1991):189–203.

KILLIAN, LEWIS M. "Organization, Rationality and Spontaneity in the Civil Rights Movement." *American Sociological Review.* Vol. 49, No. 6 (December 1984):770–83.

KING, KATHLEEN PIKER, and DENNIS E. CLAYSON. "The Differential Perceptions of Male and Female Deviants." *Sociological Focus.* Vol. 21, No. 2 (April 1988):153–64.

KING, MARTIN LUTHER, JR. "The Montgomery Bus Boycott." In Walt Anderson, ed., *The Age of Protest.* Pacific Palisades, CA: Goodyear, 1969:81–91.

KING, PATRICIA. "When Desegregation Backfires." *Newsweek.* Vol. 144, No. 5 (July 31, 1989):56.

KINSEY, ALFRED, ET AL. *Sexual Behavior in the Human Male.* Philadelphia: W. B. Saunders, 1948.

———. *Sexual Behavior in the Human Female.* Philadelphia: W.B. Saunders, 1953.

KIPP, RITA SMITH. "Have Women Always Been Unequal?" In Beth Reed, ed., *Towards a Feminist Transformation of the Academy: Proceedings of the Fifth Annual Women's Studies Conference.* Ann Arbor, MI: Great Lakes Colleges Association, 1980:12–18.

KIRK, MARSHALL, and PETER MADSEN. *After the Ball: How America Will Conquer its Fear and Hatred of Gays in the '90s.* New York: Doubleday, 1989.

KITANO, HARRY H. L. "Japanese." In *Harvard Encyclopedia of American Ethnic Groups.* Cambridge, MA: Harvard University Press, 1980:561–71.

———. *Race Relations.* 3rd ed. Englewood Cliffs, NJ: Prentice Hall, 1985.

KITSON, GAY C., and HELEN J. RASCHKE. "Divorce Research: What We Know, What We Need to Know." *Journal of Divorce.* Vol. 4, No. 3 (Spring 1981):1–37.

KITTRIE, NICHOLAS N. *The Right To Be Different: Deviance and Enforced Therapy.* Baltimore, MD: The Johns Hopkins University Press, 1971.

KLEIMAN, DENA. "Changing Way of Death: Some Agonizing Choices." *The New York Times* (January 14, 1985):1, 11.

KLEIN, SUSAN SHURBERG. "Education." In Sarah M. Pritchard, ed., *The Women's Annual, Number 4, 1983–1984.* Boston, MA: G.K. Hall and Company, 1984:9–30.

KLEUGEL, JAMES R., and ELIOT R. SMITH. *Beliefs About Inequality: Americans' Views of What Is and What Ought to Be.* New York: Aldine de Gruyter, 1986.

KLUCKHOHN, CLYDE. "As An Anthropologist Views It." In Albert Deuth, ed., *Sex Habits of American Men.* New York: Prentice Hall, 1948.

KNAUS, WILLIAM A. *Inside Russian Medicine: An American Doctor's First-Hand Report.* New York: Everest House, 1981.

KNOKE, DAVID, and RICHARD B. FELSON. "Ethnic Stratification and Political Cleavage in the United States, 1952–1968." *American Journal of Sociology.* Vol. 80, No. 3 (November 1974):630–42.

KOCH, HOWARD. *The Panic Broadcast: Portrait of an Event.* Boston: Little, Brown, 1970.

KOHLBERG, LAWRENCE, and CAROL GILLIGAN. "The Adolescent as Philosopher: The Discovery of Self in a Postconventional World." *Daedalus.* Vol. 100 (Fall 1971):1051–86.

KOHN, MELVIN L. *Class and Conformity: A Study in Values.* 2nd ed. Homewood, IL: The Dorsey Press, 1977.

KOHN, MELVIN L., and CARMI SCHOOLER. "Job Conditions and Personality: A Longitudinal Assessment of Their Reciprocal Effects." *American Journal of Sociology.* Vol. 87, No. 6 (May 1982):1257–83.

KOLATA, GINA. "When Grandmother Is the Mother, Until Birth." *The New York Times* (August 5, 1991):1, 11.

KOMAROVSKY, MIRRA. *Blue Collar Marriage.* New York: Vintage Books, 1967.

———. "Cultural Contradictions and Sex Roles: The Masculine Case." *American Journal of Sociology.* Vol. 78, No. 4 (January 1973):873–84.

———. *Dilemmas of Masculinity: A Study of College Youth.* New York: W.W. Norton, 1976.

KORNHAUSER, WILLIAM. *The Politics of Mass Society.* New York: Free Press, 1959.

KOZOL, JONATHAN. *Prisoners of Silence: Breaking the Bonds of Adult Illiteracy in the United States.* New York: Continuum, 1980.

———. "A Nation's Wealth." *Publisher's Weekly* (May 24, 1985):28–30.

———. *Illiterate America.* Garden City, NY: Doubleday, 1985.

———. *Rachel and Her Children: Homeless Families in America.* New York: Crown Publishers, 1988.

KRAMARAE, CHERIS. *Women and Men Speaking.* Rowley, MA: Newbury House, 1981.

KRAMARAE, CHERIS, BARRIE THORNE, and NANCY HENLEY. "Sex Similarities and Differences in Language, Speech, and Nonverbal Communication: An Annotated Bibliography." In Barrie Thorne, Cheris Kramarae, and Nancy Henley, eds., *Language, Gender and Society.* Cambridge: Newbury House, 1983:150–331.

KRIESI, HANSPETER. "New Social Movements and the New Class in the Netherlands." *American Journal of Sociology.* Vol. 94, No. 5 (March 1989):1078–16.

KRISBERG, BARRY, and IRA SCHWARTZ. "Rethinking Juvenile Justice." *Crime and Delinquency.* Vol. 29, No. 3 (July 1983):333–64.

KUBEY, ROBERT W. "Television and Aging: Past, Present, and Future." *The Gerontologist.* Vol. 20, No. 1 (February 1980):16–35.

KÜBLER-ROSS, ELISABETH. *On Death and Dying.* New York: Macmillan, 1969.

KUHN, THOMAS. *The Structure of Scientific Revolutions.* 2nd ed. Chicago: University of Chicago Press, 1970.

KURTZ, LESTER R. *The Nuclear Cage: A Sociology of the Arms Race.* Englewood Cliffs, NJ: Prentice Hall, 1988.

KUZNETS, SIMON. "Economic Growth and Income Inequality." *The American Economic Review.* Vol. XLV, No. 1 (March 1955):1–28.

———. *Modern Economic Growth: Rate, Structure, and Spread.* New Haven, CT: Yale University Press, 1966.

LACAYO, RICHARD. "Blood in the Stands." *Time.* Vol. 125, No. 23 (June 10, 1985):38–39, 41.

LACAYO, RICHARD. "Law and Disorder." *Time.* Vol. 137, No. 13 (April 1, 1991):18–21.

LADD, JOHN. "The Definition of Death and the Right to Die." In John Ladd, ed., *Ethical Issues Relating to Life and Death.* New York: Oxford University Press, 1979:118–45.

LADNER, JOYCE A. "Teenage Pregnancy: The Implications for Black Americans." In James D. Williams, ed., *The State of Black America 1986.* New York: National Urban League, 1986:65–84.

LAI, H. M. "Chinese." In *Harvard Encyclopedia of American Ethnic Groups.* Cambridge MA: Harvard University Press, 1980:217–33.

LAMAR, JACOB V., JR. "Redefining the American Dilemma." *Time.* Vol. 126, No. 19 (November 11, 1985):33, 36.

LAMBERG-KARLOVSKY, C. C., and MARTHA LAMBERG-KARLOVSKY. "An Early City in Iran." In *Cities: Their Origin, Growth, and Human Impact.* San Francisco: Freeman, 1973:28–37.

LANDALE, NANCY S., and STEWART E. TOLNAY. "Group Differences in Economic Opportunity and the Timing of Marriage: Blacks and Whites in the Rural South, 1910." *American Sociological Review.* Vol. 56, No. 1 (February 1991):33–45.

LANDERS, ANN. Syndicated column: *The Dallas Morning News* (July 8, 1984):4F.

LANDERS, RENÉ M. "Gender, Race, and the State Courts." *The Radcliffe Quarterly.* Vol. 76, No. 4 (December 1990):6–9.

LANE, CHARLES. "Defying the Stereotypes." *Newsweek* (July 15, 1991):18–19.

LANE, DAVID. "Social Stratification and Class." In Erik P. Hoffman and Robbin F. Laird, eds., *The Soviet Polity in the Modern Era.* New York: Aldine, 1984:563–605.

LANG, KURT, and GLADYS ENGEL LANG. *Collective Dynamics.* New York: Thomas Y. Crowell, 1961.

LAPPÉ, FRANCES MOORE, and JOSEPH COLLINS. *World Hunger: Twelve Myths.* New York: Grove Press/Food First Books, 1986.

LAPPÉ, FRANCES MOORE, JOSEPH COLLINS, and DAVID KINLEY. *Aid as Obstacle: Twenty Questions about Our Foreign Policy and the Hungry.* San Francisco: Institute for Food and Development Policy, 1981.

LASLETT, BARBARA. "Family Membership, Past and Present." *Social Problems.* Vol. 25, No. 5 (June 1978):476–90.

LASLETT, PETER. *The World We Have Lost: England Before the Industrial Age.* 3rd ed. New York: Charles Scribner's Sons, 1984.

LEACOCK, ELEANOR. "Women's Status in Egalitarian Societies: Implications for Social Evolution." *Current Anthropology.* Vol. 19, No. 2 (June 1978):247–75.

LEAVITT, JUDITH WALZER. "Women and Health in America: An Overview."

In Judith Walzer Leavitt, ed., *Women and Health in America*. Madison, WI: University of Wisconsin Press, 1984:3–7.

LE BON, GUSTAVE. *The Crowd: A Study of the Popular Mind*. New York: The Viking Press, 1960; orig. 1895.

LEE, BARRETT A., R. S. OROPESA, BARBARA J. METCH, and AVERY M. GUEST. "Testing the Decline of Community Thesis: Neighborhood Organization in Seattle, 1929 and 1979." *American Journal of Sociology*. Vol. 89, No. 5 (March 1984):1161–88.

LEERHSEN, CHARLES. "Unite and Conquer." *Newsweek* (February 5, 1990):50–55.

LEIFER, ERIC M. "Inequality Among Equals: Embedding Market and Authority in League Sports." *American Journal of Sociology*. Vol. 96, No. 3 (November 1990):655–83.

LEMERT, EDWIN M. *Social Pathology*. New York: McGraw-Hill, 1951.

———. *Human Deviance, Social Problems, and Social Control*. 2nd ed. Englewood Cliffs, NJ: Prentice Hall, 1972.

LENGERMANN, PATRICIA MADOO, and RUTH A. WALLACE. *Gender in America: Social Control and Social Change*. Englewood Cliffs, NJ: Prentice Hall, 1985.

LENSKI, GERHARD. *Power and Privilege: A Theory of Social Stratification*. New York: McGraw-Hill, 1966.

LENSKI, GERHARD, and JEAN LENSKI. *Human Societies: An Introduction to Macrosociology*. 3rd ed. New York: McGraw-Hill, 1978; 4th ed., 1982; 5th ed., 1987.

LENSKI, GERHARD, JEAN LENSKI, and PATRICK NOLAN. *Human Societies: An Introduction to Macrosociology*. 6th ed. New York: McGraw-Hill, 1991.

LEONARD, EILEEN B. *Women, Crime, and Society: A Critique of Theoretical Criminology*. New York: Longman, 1982.

LESLIE, GERALD R., and SHEILA K. KORMAN. *The Family in Social Context*. 7th ed. New York: Oxford University Press, 1989.

LESTER, DAVID. *The Death Penalty: Issues and Answers*. Springfield, IL: Charles C. Thomas, 1987.

LEVER, JANET. "Sex Differences in the Complexity of Children's Play and Games." *American Sociological Review*. Vol. 43, No. 4 (August 1978):471–83.

LEVIN, JACK, and WILLIAM C. LEVIN. *Ageism: Prejudice and Discrimination Against the Elderly*. Belmont, CA: Wadsworth, 1980.

LEVINE, MICHAEL P. *Student Eating Disorders: Anorexia Nervosa and Bulimia*. Washington, DC: National Educational Association, 1987.

LEVINSON, DANIEL J., with CHARLOTTE N. DARROW, EDWARD B. KLEIN, MARIA H. LEVINSON, and BRAXTON MCKEE. *The Seasons of a Man's Life*. New York: Alfred A. Knopf, 1978.

LEVITAN, SAR A., and ISAAC SHAPIRO. *Working but Poor: America's Contradiction*. Baltimore, MD: Johns Hopkins University Press, 1987.

LEVY, FRANK. *Dollars and Dreams: The Changing American Income Distribution*. New York: Russell Sage Foundation, 1987.

LEWIS, FLORA. "The Roots of Revolution." *The New York Times Magazine* (November 11, 1984):70–71, 74, 77–78, 82, 84, 86.

LEWIS, OSCAR. *The Children of Sanchez*. New York: Random House, 1961.

LEWONTIN, R. C., STEVEN ROSE, and LEON J. KAMIN. *Not In Our Genes: Biology, Ideology, and Human Nature*. New York: Pantheon, 1984.

LIAZOS, ALEXANDER. "The Poverty of the Sociology of Deviance: Nuts, Sluts and Preverts." *Social Problems*. Vol. 20, No. 1 (Summer 1972):103–20.

LICHTER, DANIEL R. "Race, Employment Hardship, and Inequality in the American Nonmetropolitan South." *American Sociological Review*. Vol. 54, No. 3 (June 1989):436–46.

LIEBERSON, STANLEY. *A Piece of the Pie: Black and White Immigrants Since 1880*. Berkeley, CA: University of California Press, 1980.

LIEBOW, ELLIOT. *Tally's Corner*. Boston, MA: Little, Brown, 1967.

LIN, NAN, and WALTER M. ENSEL. "Life Stress and Health: Stressors and Resources." *American Sociological Review*. Vol. 54, No. 3 (June 1989):382–99.

LIN, NAN, WALTER M. ENSEL, and JOHN C. VAUGHN. "Social Resources and Strength of Ties: Structural Factors in Occupational Status Attainment." *American Sociological Review*. Vol. 46, No. 4 (August 1981):393–405.

LINCOLN, JAMES R., and ARNE L. KALLEBERG. "Work Organization and Workforce Commitment: A Study of Plants and Employees in the U.S. and Japan." *American Sociological Review*. Vol. 50, No. 6 (December 1985):738–60.

LING, PYAU. "Causes of Chinese Emigration." In Amy Tachiki et al., eds.,

*Roots: An Asian American Reader*. Los Angeles, CA: UCLA Asian American Studies Center, 1971:134–38.

LINK, BRUCE G., FRANCIS T. CULLIN, JAMES FRANK, and JOHN F. WOZNIAK. "The Social Rejection of Former Mental Patients: Understanding Why Labels Matter." *American Journal of Sociology*. Vol. 92, No. 6 (May 1987):1461–1500.

LINK, BRUCE G., BRUCE P. DOHRENWEND, and ANDREW E. SKODOL. "Socio-Economic Status and Schizophrenia: Noisome Occupational Characteristics As a Risk Factor." *American Sociological Review*. Vol. 51, No. 2 (April 1986):242–58.

LINTON, RALPH. "One Hundred Percent American." *The American Mercury*. Vol. 40, No. 160 (April 1937):427–29.

———. *The Study of Man*. New York: D. Appleton-Century, 1937.

LIPSET, SEYMOUR MARTIN. *Political Man: The Social Bases of Politics*. Garden City, NY: Doubleday Anchor Books, 1963.

LIPSET, SEYMOUR MARTIN, and REINHARD BENDIX. *Social Mobility in Industrial Society*. Berkeley, CA: University of California Press, 1967.

LISKA, ALLEN E. *Perspectives on Deviance*. 3rd ed. Englewood Cliffs, NJ: Prentice Hall, 1991.

LISKA, ALLEN E., and MARK TAUSIG. "Theoretical Interpretations of Social Class and Racial Differentials in Legal Decision Making for Juveniles." *Sociological Quarterly*. Vol. 20, No. 2 (Spring 1979):197–207.

LISKA, ALLEN E., and BARBARA D. WARNER. "Functions of Crime: A Paradoxical Process." *American Journal of Sociology*. Vol. 96, No. 6 (May 1991):1441–63.

LITTMAN, MARK S. "Poverty in the 1980s: Are the Poor Getting Poorer?" *Monthly Labor Review*. Vol. 112, No. 6 (June 1989):13–18.

LO, CLARENCE Y. H. "Countermovements and Conservative Movements in the Contemporary U.S." *Annual Review of Sociology*. Vol. 8. Palo Alto, CA: Annual Reviews, Inc., 1982:107–34.

LOFLAND, LYN. *A World of Strangers*. New York: Basic Books, 1973.

LOGAN, JOHN R., and MARK SCHNEIDER. "Racial Segregation and Racial Change in American Suburbs, 1970–1980." *American Journal of Sociology*. Vol. 89, No. 4 (January 1984):874–88.

LOHR, STEVE. "British Health Service Faces A Crisis in Funds and Delays." *The New York Times* (August 7, 1988):1, 12.

LONDON, BRUCE. "Structural Determinants of Third World Urban Change: An Ecological and Political Economic Analysis." *American Sociological Review*. Vol. 52, No. 1 (February 1987):28–43.

LONG, EDWARD V. *The Intruders: The Invasion of Privacy by Government and Industry*. New York: Frederick A. Praeger, 1967.

LORD, WALTER. *A Night to Remember*. Rev. ed. New York: Holt, Rinehart and Winston, 1976.

LORENZ, KONRAD. *On Aggression*. New York: Harcourt, Brace and World, 1966.

LOY, PAMELA HEWITT, and LEA P. STEWART. "The Extent and Effects of Sexual Harassment of Working Women." *Sociological Focus*. Vol. 17, No. 1 (January 1984):31–43.

LUBENOW, GERALD C. "A Troubling Family Affair." *Newsweek* (May 14, 1984):34.

LUKAS, J. ANTHONY. "Wilding—As American as Tom Sawyer." *The New York Times* (May 28, 1989):sec. 4, p. 15.

LUND, DALE A. "Conclusions about Bereavement in Later Life and Implications for Interventions and Future Research." In Dale A. Lund, ed., *Older Bereaved Spouses: Research With Practical Applications*. Taylor-Francis-Hemisphere, 1989:217–31.

LUND, DALE A., MARGARET F. DIMOND, MICHAEL S. CASERTA, ROBERT J. JOHNSON, JAMES L. POULTON, and J. RICHARD CONNELLY. "Identifying Elderly With Coping Difficulties After Two Years of Bereavement." *Omega*. Vol. 16, No. 3 (1985):213–24.

LUTZ, CATHERINE A. *Unnatural Emotions: Everyday Sentiments on a Micronesia Atoll and Their Challenge to Western Theory*. Chicago: University of Chicago Press, 1988.

LUTZ, CATHERINE, and GEOFFREY M. WHITE. "The Anthropology of Emotions." In Bernard J. Siegel, Alan R. Beals, and Stephen A. Tyler, eds., *Annual Review of Anthropology*. Palo Alto, CA: Annual Reviews, Inc. Vol. 15 (1986):405–36.

LYND, ROBERT S. *Knowledge For What? The Place of Social Science in American Culture*. Princeton, NJ: Princeton University Press, 1967.

LYND, ROBERT S., and HELEN MERRELL LYND. *Middletown in Transition.* New York: Harcourt, Brace & World, 1937.

MA, LI-CHEN. Personal communication, 1987.

MACCOBY, ELEANOR EMMONS, and CAROL NAGY JACKLIN. *The Psychology of Sex Differences.* Palo Alto, CA: Stanford University Press, 1974.

MACE, DAVID, and VERA MACE. *Marriage East and West.* Garden City, NY: Doubleday (Dolphin), 1960.

MACIONIS, JOHN J. "Intimacy: Structure and Process in Interpersonal Relationships." *Alternative Lifestyles.* Vol. 1, No. 1 (February 1978):113–30.

———. "The Search for Community in Modern Society: An Interpretation." *Qualitative Sociology.* Vol. 1, No. 2 (September 1978):130–43.

———. "A Sociological Analysis of Humor." Presentation to the Texas Junior College Teachers Association, Houston, 1987.

———. "Sociology in the 1990s: Reaching for the World." *VUES: Newsletter of the Section on Undergraduate Education* (Summer 1991):4. Washington, DC: American Sociological Association.

MACKAY, DONALD G. "Prescriptive Grammar and the Pronoun Problem." In Barrie Thorne, Cheris Kramarae, and Nancy Henley, eds., *Language, Gender and Society.* Cambridge: Newbury House, 1983:38–53.

MACKLIN, ELEANOR D. "Nonmarital Heterosexual Cohabitation: An Overview." In Eleanor D. Macklin and Roger H. Rubin, eds., *Contemporary Families and Alternative Lifestyles: Handbook on Research and Theory.* Beverly Hills, CA: Sage, 1983:49–74.

MADSEN, AXEL. *Private Power: Multinational Corporations for the Survival of Our Planet.* New York: William Morrow, 1980.

MAHLER, HALFDAN. "People." *Scientific American.* Vol. 243, No. 3 (September 1980): 67–77.

MAJKA, LINDA C. "Sexual Harassment in the Church." *Society.* Vol. 28. No. 4 (May-June, 1991):14–21.

MAJOR, BRENDA. "Gender Patterns in Touching Behavior." In Clara Mayo and Nancy M. Henley, eds., *Gender and Nonverbal Behavior.* New York: Springer Verlag, 1981:15–37.

MALTHUS, THOMAS ROBERT. *First Essay on Population 1798.* London: Macmillan, 1926; orig. 1798.

MANGAN, J. A., and ROBERTA J. PARK. *From Fair Sex to Feminism: Sport and the Socialization of Women.* London: Frank Cass, 1987.

MARCUSE, HERBERT. *One-Dimensional Man.* Boston, MA: Beacon Press, 1964.

MARE, ROBERT D. "Change and Stability in Educational Stratification." *American Sociological Review.* Vol. 46, No. 1 (February 1981):72–87.

———. "Five Decades of Educational Assortative Mating." *American Sociological Review.* Vol. 56, No. 1 (February 1991):15–32.

MARGOLICK, DAVID. "Rape in Marriage Is No Longer Within the Law." *The New York Times* (December 13, 1984):6E.

MARKOFF, JOHN. "Remember Big Brother? Now He's a Company Man." *The New York Times* (March 31, 1991):7.

MARLIOS, PETER. "Interlocking Directorates and the Control of Corporations: The Theory of Bank Control." *Social Science Quarterly.* Vol. 56, No. 3 (December 1975):425–39.

MARRY, MARCUS. "New Hope for Old Unions?" *Newsweek* (February 24, 1992):39.

MARSDEN, PETER. "Core Discussion Networks of Americans." *American Sociological Review.* Vol. 52, No. 1 (February 1987):122–31.

MARSHALL, SUSAN E. "Ladies Against Women: Mobilization Dilemmas of Anti-Feminist Movements." *Social Problems.* Vol. 32, No. 4 (April 1985):348–62.

MARTIN, RICHARD C. *Islam: A Cultural Perspective.* Englewood Cliffs, NJ: Prentice-Hall, 1982.

MARTIN, WILLIAM. "The Birth of a Media Myth." *The Atlantic.* Vol. 247, No. 6 (June 1981):7, 10, 11, 16.

MARULLO, SAM. "The Functions and Dysfunctions of Preparations for Fighting Nuclear War." *Sociological Focus.* Vol. 20, No. 2 (April 1987):135–53.

MARX, GARY T., and JAMES L. WOOD. "Strands of Theory and Research in Collective Behavior." In Alex Inkeles et al., eds., *Annual Review of Sociology.* Vol. 1. Palo Alto, CA: Annual Reviews, Inc., 1975:363–428.

MARX, KARL. Excerpt from "A Contribution to the Critique of Political Economy." In Karl Marx and Friedrich Engels, *Marx and Engels: Basic Writings on Politics and Philosophy.* Lewis S. Feurer, ed. Garden City, NY: Anchor Books, 1959:42–46.

———. *Karl Marx: Early Writings.* T. B. Bottomore, ed. New York: McGraw-Hill, 1964a.

———. *Karl Marx: Selected Writings in Sociology and Social Philosophy.* T. B. Bottomore, trans. New York: McGraw-Hill, 1964.

———. *Capital.* Friedrich Engels, ed. New York: International Publishers, 1967; orig. 1867.

———. "Theses on Feuer." In Robert C. Tucker, ed., *The Marx-Engels Reader.* New York: W. W. Norton, 1972:107–9; orig. 1845.

MARX, KARL, and FRIEDRICH ENGELS. "Manifesto of the Communist Party." In Robert C. Tucker, ed., *The Marx-Engels Reader.* New York: W. W. Norton, 1972:331–62; orig. 1848.

———. *The Marx-Engels Reader.* Robert C. Tucker, ed. New York: W. W. Norton, 1977.

MASHEK, JOHN W., and PATRICIA AVERY. "Women Politicians Take Off the White Gloves." *U.S. News and World Report* (August 15, 1983):41–42.

MASSERMAN, JULES H., and VICTOR M. URIBE. *Adolescent Sexuality.* New York: Charles C. Thomas, 1990.

MASSEY, DOUGLAS S., and NANCY A. DENTON. "Hypersegregation in U.S. Metropolitan Areas: Black and Hispanic Segregation Along Five Dimensions." *Demography.* Vol. 26, No. 3 (August 1989):373–91.

MASTERS, WILLIAM H., VIRGINIA E. JOHNSON, and ROBERT C. KOLODNY. *Human Sexuality.* 3rd ed. Glenview, IL: Scott, Foresman/Little, Brown 1988.

MATTHEWS, MERVYN. "Long Term Trends in Soviet Education." In J. J. Tomiak, ed., *Soviet Education in the 1980s.* London: Croom Helm, 1983:1–23.

MATTHIESSEN, PETER. *In the Spirit of Crazy Horse.* New York: Viking Press, 1983.

———. *Indian Country.* New York: Viking Press, 1984.

MATZA, DAVID. *Delinquency and Drift.* New York: John Wiley, 1964.

MAURO, TONY. "Cruzan's Struggle Left Imprint: Private Case Triggered Public Debate." *USA Today* (December 27, 1990):3A.

MAUSS, ARMAND L. *Social Problems of Social Movements.* Philadelphia, PA: Lippincott, 1975.

MAY, ELAINE TYLER. "Women in the Wild Blue Yonder." *The New York Times* (August 7, 1991):21.

MAYO, KATHERINE. *Mother India.* New York: Harcourt, Brace and Co., 1927.

McADAM, DOUG. *Political Process and the Development of Black Insurgency, 1930–1970.* Chicago: University of Chicago Press, 1982.

———. "Tactical Innovation and the Pace of Insurgency." *American Sociological Review.* Vol. 48, No. 6 (December 1983):735–54.

———. *Freedom Summer.* New York: Oxford University Press, 1988.

———. "The Biographical Consequences of Activism." *American Sociological Review.* Vol. 54, No. 5 (October 1989):744–60.

McADAM, DOUG, JOHN D. McCARTHY, and MAYER N. ZALD. "Social Movements." In Neil J. Smelser, ed., *Handbook of Sociology.* Newbury Park, CA: Sage, 1988:695–737.

McBROOM, WILLIAM H., and FRED W. REED. "Recent Trends in Conservatism: Evidence of Non-Unitary Patterns." *Sociological Focus.* Vol. 23, No. 4 (October 1990):355–65.

McCARTHY, JOHN D., and MAYER N. ZALD. "Resource Mobilization and Social Movements: A Partial Theory." *American Journal of Sociology.* Vol. 82, No. 6 (May 1977):1212–41.

McGRATH, ELLIE. "Preparing to Wield the Rod." *Time.* Vol. 121, No. 4 (January 23, 1984):57.

McGUIRE, MEREDITH B. *Religion: The Social Context.* 2nd ed. Belmont, CA: Wadsworth, 1987.

McHENRY, SUSAN. "Rosabeth Moss Kanter." In *Ms.* Vol. 13 (January 1985):62–63, 107–8.

McKEOWN, THOMAS. *The Role of Medicine: Dream, Mirage, or Nemesis?* Princeton, NJ: Princeton University Press, 1979.

McKUSICK, LEON, ET AL. "Reported Changes in the Sexual Behavior of Men at Risk for AIDS, San Francisco, 1982–84—The AIDS Behavioral Research Project." *Public Health Reports.* Vol. 100, No. 6 (November-December 1985):622–29.

McLANAHAN, SARA. "Family Structure and the Reproduction of Poverty." *American Journal of Sociology.* Vol. 90, No. 4 (January 1985):873–901.

McNEIL, DONALD G., JR. "Should Women Be Sent Into Combat?" *The New York Times* (July 21, 1991):E3.

McPHAIL, CLARK. *The Myth of the Maddening Crowd.* New York: Aldine De Gruyter, 1991.

McPHAIL, CLARK, and RONALD T. WOHLSTEIN. "Individual and Collective Behaviors Within Gatherings, Demonstrations, and Riots." *Annual Review of Sociology.* Vol. 9. Palo Alto, CA: Annual Reviews, Inc., 1983:579–600.

McRae, Susan. *Cross-Class Families: A Study of Wives' Occupational Superiority.* New York: Oxford University Press, 1986.

McRoberts, Hugh A., and Kevin Selbee. "Trends in Occupational Mobility in Canada and the United States: A Comparison." *American Sociological Review.* Vol. 46, No. 4 (August 1981):406–21.

Mead, George Herbert. "Teaching of Science in College." *Science.* Vol. 24 (1906):390–97.

———. *Mind, Self, and Society.* Charles W. Morris, ed. Chicago: University of Chicago Press, 1962; orig. 1934.

Mead, Margaret. *Coming of Age in Samoa.* New York: Dell, 1961; orig. 1928.

———. *Sex and Temperament in Three Primitive Societies.* New York: William Morrow, 1963; orig. 1935.

Mechanic, David. *Medical Sociology.* 2nd ed. New York: Free Press, 1978.

Meltzer, Bernard N. "Mead's Social Psychology." In Jerome G. Manis and Bernard N. Meltzer, eds., *Symbolic Interaction: A Reader in Social Psychology.* 2nd ed. Boston, MA: Allyn & Bacon, 1977:15–27; 3rd ed., 1978.

Melucci, Alberto. "The New Social Movements: A Theoretical Approach." *Social Science Information.* Vol. 19, No. 2 (May 1980):199–226.

———. *Nomads of the Present: Social Movements and Individual Needs in Contemporary Society.* Philadelphia: Temple University Press, 1989.

Melville, Keith. *Marriage and Family Today.* 3rd ed. New York: Random House, 1983.

Merton, Robert K. "Social Structure and Anomie." *American Sociological Review.* Vol. 3, No. 6 (October 1938):672–82.

———. *Social Theory and Social Structure.* New York: Free Press, 1968.

———. "Discrimination and the American Creed." In *Sociological Ambivalence and Other Essays.* New York: The Free Press, 1976:189–216.

Messner, Steven R. "Economic Discrimination and Societal Homicide Rates: Further Evidence of the Cost of Inequality." *American Sociological Review.* Vol. 54, No. 4 (August 1989):597–611.

Michels, Robert. *Political Parties.* Glencoe, IL: Free Press, 1949; orig. 1911.

Milgram, Stanley. "Behavioral Study of Obedience." *Journal of Abnormal and Social Psychology.* Vol. 67, No. 4 (1963):371–78.

———. "Group Pressure and Action Against a Person." *Journal of Abnormal and Social Psychology.* Vol. 69, No. 2 (August 1964):137–43.

———. "Some Conditions of Obedience and Disobedience to Authority." *Human Relations.* Vol. 18 (February 1965):57–76.

Miliband, Ralph. *The State in Capitalist Society.* London: Weidenfeld and Nicolson, 1969.

Miller, Arthur G. *The Obedience Experiments: A Case of Controversy in Social Science.* New York: Praeger, 1986.

Miller, David L. *Introduction to Collective Behavior.* Belmont, CA: Wadsworth, 1985.

Miller, Frederick D. "The End of SDS and the Emergence of Weatherman: Demise Through Success." In Jo Freeman, ed., *Social Movements of the Sixties and Seventies.* New York: Longman, 1983:279–97.

Miller, Mark. "Under Cover, In the Closet." *Newsweek* (January 14, 1991):25.

Miller, Michael. "Lawmakers Begin to Heed Calls to Protect Privacy." *The Wall Street Journal* (April 11, 1991):A16.

Miller, Walter B. "Lower Class Culture as a Generating Milieu of Gang Delinquency." In Marvin E. Wolfgang, Leonard Savitz, and Norman Johnston, eds., *The Sociology of Crime and Delinquency.* 2nd ed. New York: John Wiley, 1970:351–63; orig. 1958.

Millet, Kate. *Sexual Politics.* Garden City, NY: Doubleday, 1970.

Mills, C. Wright. *White Collar: The American Middle Classes.* New York: Oxford University Press, 1951.

———. *The Power Elite.* New York: Oxford University Press, 1956.

———. *The Social Causes of World War Three.* New York: Simon and Schuster, 1958.

———. *The Sociological Imagination.* New York: Oxford University Press, 1959.

Mink, Barbara. "How Modernization Affects Women." *Cornell Alumni News.* Vol. III, No. 3 (April 1989):10–11.

Mintz, Beth, and Michael Schwartz. "Interlocking Directorates and Interest Group Formation." *American Sociological Review.* Vol. 46, No. 6 (December 1981):851–69.

Mirowsky, John. "The Psycho-Economics of Feeling Underpaid: Distributive Justice and the Earnings of Husbands and Wives." *American Journal of Sociology.* Vol. 92, No. 6 (May 1987):1404–34.

Mirowsky, John, and Catherine Ross. "Working Wives and Mental Health." Presentation to the American Association for the Advancement of Science. New York, 1984.

———. *The Social Causes of Psychological Distress.* Hawthorne, NY: Aldine de Gruyter, 1989.

Mitchell, William L. "Lay Observations on Retirement." In Frances M. Carp, ed., *Retirement.* New York: Behavioral Publications, 1972:199–217.

Molnar, Stephen. *Human Variation: Races, Types, and Ethnic Groups.* 2nd ed. Englewood Cliffs, NJ: Prentice Hall, 1983.

Molotch, Harvey. "The City as a Growth Machine." *American Journal of Sociology.* Vol. 82, No. 2 (September 1976):309–33.

Molotch, Harvey L., and Deirdre Boden. "Talking Social Structure: Discourse, Domination, and the Watergate Hearings." *American Sociological Review.* Vol. 50, No. 3 (June 1985):273–88.

Money, John. *The Destroying Angel: Sex, Fitness & Food in the Legacy of Degeneracy Theory, Graham Crackers, Kellogg's Corn Flakes & American Health History.* Buffalo, NY: Prometheus Books, 1985.

Money, John, and Anke A. Ehrhardt. *Man and Woman, Boy and Girl.* New York: New American Library, 1972.

Monk-Turner, Elizabeth. "Sex, Educational Differentiation, and Occupational Status: Analyzing Occupational Differences for Community and Four-Year Entrants." *The Sociological Quarterly.* Vol. 24, No. 3 (July 1983):393–404.

———. "The Occupational Achievement of Community and Four-Year College Graduates." *American Sociological Review.* Vol. 55, No. 5 (October 1990):719–25.

Montague, Ashley. *The Nature of Human Aggression.* New York: Oxford University Press, 1976.

Moore, Gwen. "The Structure of a National Elite Network." *American Sociological Review.* Vol. 44, No. 5 (October 1979):673–92.

———. "Structural Determinants of Men's and Women's Personal Networks." *American Sociological Review.* Vol. 55, No. 5 (October 1991):726–35.

Moore, Joan, and Harry Pachon. *Hispanics in the United States.* Englewood Cliffs, NJ: Prentice Hall, 1985.

Moore, Wilbert E. "Modernization as Rationalization: Processes and Restraints." In Manning Nash, ed., *Essays on Economic Development and Cultural Change in Honor of Bert F. Hoselitz.* Chicago: University of Chicago Press, 1977:29–42.

———. *World Modernization: The Limits of Convergence.* New York: Elsevier, 1979.

Moran, John S., S. O. Aral, W. C. Jenkins, T. A. Peterman, and E. R. Alexander. "The Impact of Sexually Transmitted Diseases on Minority Populations." *Public Health Reports.* Vol. 104, No. 6 (November-December 1989):560–65.

Morris, Aldon. "Black Southern Sit-in Movement: An Analysis of Internal Organization." *American Sociological Review.* Vol. 46, No. 6 (December 1981):744–67.

Morrison, Denton E. "Some Notes Toward Theory on Relative Deprivation, Social Movements, and Social Change." In Louis E. Genevie, ed., *Collective Behavior and Social Movements.* Itasca, IL: F. E. Peacock, 1978:202–9.

Morrow, Lance. "Rough Justice." *Time.* Vol. 137, No. 13 (April 1, 1991):16–17.

Moskos, Charles C. "Female GIs in the Field." *Society.* Vol. 22, No. 6 (September/October 1985):28–33.

Mottaz, Clifford J. "Some Determinants of Work Alienation." *The Sociological Quarterly.* Vol. 22, No. 4 (Autumn 1981):515–29.

Mueller, Daniel P., and Philip W. Cooper. "Children of Single Parent Families: How Do They Fare as Young Adults?" Presentation to the American Sociological Association, San Antonio, Texas, 1984.

Muller, Edward N. *Aggressive Political Participation.* Princeton, NJ: Princeton University Press, 1979.

Muller, Thomas, and Thomas J. Espenshade. *The Fourth Wave: California's Newest Immigrants.* Washington, DC: The Urban Institute Press, 1985.

Mumford, Lewis. *The City in History: Its Origins, Its Transformations, and Its Prospects.* New York: Harcourt, Brace & World, 1961.

MURDOCK, GEORGE P. "Comparative Data on the Division of Labor by Sex." *Social Forces.* Vol. 15, No. 4 (May 1937):551–53.

———. "The Common Denominator of Cultures." In Ralph Linton, ed., *The Science of Man in World Crisis.* New York: Columbia University Press, 1945:123–42.

MURDOCK, GEORGE PETER. *Social Structure.* New York: Free Press, 1965; orig. 1949.

MURPHY, ROBERT F. *An Overture to Social Anthropology.* Englewood Cliffs, NJ: Prentice Hall, 1979.

MURRAY, MEGAN BALDRIDGE. "Innovation Without Geniuses." In *Yale Alumni Magazine and Journal.* Vol. XLVII, No. 6 (April 1984):40–43.

MURRAY, PAULI. *Proud Shoes: The History of an American Family.* New York: Harper & Row, 1978.

MYDANS, SETH. "Study of Indians' Remains: Science or Sacrilege?" *The New York Times* (October 19, 1990).

MYERS, DAVID G. *Psychology.* New York: Worth, 1986.

MYERS, SHEILA, and HAROLD G. GRASMICK. "The Social Rights and Responsibilities of Pregnant Women: An Application of Parsons' Sick Role Model." Paper presented to Southwestern Sociological Association, Little Rock, Arkansas, March 1989.

NATIONAL CENTER FOR EDUCATION STATISTICS. *Digest of Education Statistics 1983–84.* Washington, DC: U.S. Government Printing Office, 1983.

NATIONAL CENTER FOR EDUCATION STATISTICS. *Digest of Education Statistics: 1990.* Washington, DC: U.S. Government Printing Office, 1990:244.

NATIONAL COMMISSION ON EXCELLENCE IN EDUCATION. *A Nation at Risk.* Washington, DC: U.S. Government Printing Office, 1983.

NATIONAL INSTITUTE OF DRUG ABUSE. U.S. Department of Health and Human Services. *National Household Survey on Drug Abuse: Main Findings 1990.* Rockville, MD: U.S. Government Printing Office, 1991.

NAVARRO, VICENTE. "The Industrialization of Fetishism or the Fetishism of Industrialization: A Critique of Ivan Illich." In Vicente Navarro, ed., *Health and Medical Care in the U.S.: A Critical Analysis.* Farmingdale, NY: Baywood Publishing Co., 1977:38–58.

NEIDERT, LISA J., and REYNOLDS FARLEY. "Assimilation in the United States: An Analysis of Ethnic and Generation Differences in Status and Achievement." *American Sociological Review.* Vol. 50, No. 6 (December 1985):840–50.

NELSON, HARRY, and ROBERT JERMAIN. *Introduction to Physical Anthropology.* 3rd ed. St. Paul, MN: West, 1985:22–24.

NEUGARTEN, BERNICE L. "Grow Old with Me. The Best Is Yet to Be." *Psychology Today.* Vol. 5 (December 1971):45–48, 79, 81.

———. "Personality and the Aging Process." *The Gerontologist.* Vol. 12, No. 1 (Spring 1972):9–15.

———. "Personality and Aging." In James E. Birren and K. Warner Schaie, eds., *Handbook of the Psychology of Aging.* New York: Van Nostrand Reinhold, 1977:626–49.

NEUHOUSER, KEVIN. "The Radicalization of the Brazilian Catholic Church in Comparative Perspective." *American Sociological Review.* Vol. 54, No. 2 (April 1989):233–44.

NEW HAVEN JOURNAL COURIER. "English Social Structure Changing." November 27, 1986.

NEWMAN, JAMES L., and GORDON E. MATZKE. *Population: Patterns, Dynamics, and Prospects.* Englewood Cliffs, NJ: Prentice Hall, 1984.

NEWMAN, WILLIAM M. *American Pluralism: A Study of Minority Groups and Social Theory.* New York: Harper & Row, 1973.

*1991 Green Book.* U.S. House of Representatives. Washington, DC: U.S. Government Printing Office, 1991.

NISBET, ROBERT. "Sociology as an Art Form." In *Tradition and Revolt: Historical and Sociological Essays.* New York: Vintage Books, 1970.

NISBET, ROBERT A. *The Sociological Tradition.* New York: Basic Books, 1966.

NORBECK, EDWARD. "Class Structure." In *Kodansha Encyclopedia of Japan.* Tokyo: Kodansha, 1983:322–25.

N. O. R. C. *General Social Surveys, 1972–1991: Cumulative Codebook.* Chicago: National Opinion Research Center, 1991.

NUMBERS, RONALD L. "Creationism in 20th-Century America." *Science.* Vol. 218, No. 5 (November 1982):538–44.

NUNN, CLYDE Z., HARRY J. CROCKETT, JR., and J. ALLEN WILLIAMS, JR. *Tolerance for Nonconformity.* San Francisco, CA: Jossey-Bass Publishers, 1978.

OAKES, JEANNIE. "Classroom Social Relationships: Exploring the Bowles and Gintis Hypothesis." *Sociology of Education.* Vol. 55, No. 4 (October 1982):197–212.

———. *Keeping Track: How High Schools Structure Inequality.* New Haven, CT: Yale University Press, 1985.

OBERSCHALL, ANTHONY. *Social Conflict and Social Movements.* Englewood Cliffs, NJ: Prentice-Hall, 1973.

O'DEA, THOMAS F., and JANET O'DEA AVIAD. *The Sociology of Religion.* 2nd ed. Englewood Cliffs, NJ: Prentice Hall, 1983.

OFFIR, CAROLE WADE. *Human Sexuality.* New York: Harcourt Brace Jovanovich, 1982.

OGBURN, WILLIAM F. *On Culture and Social Change.* Chicago: University of Chicago Press, 1964.

O'HARE, WILLIAM. "In the Black." *American Demographics.* Vol. 11, No. 11 (November 1989):25–29.

———. "The Rise of Hispanic Affluence." *American Demographics.* Vol. 12, No. 8 (August 1990):40–43.

O'HARE, WILLIAM, and JAN LARSON. "Women in Business: Where, What, and Why." *American Demographics.* Vol. 13, No. 7 (July 1991):34–38.

OKIMOTO, DANIEL. "The Intolerance of Success." In Amy Tachiki et al., eds., *Roots: Asian American Reader.* Los Angeles, CA: UCLA Asian American Studies Center, 1971:14–19.

OLZAK, SUSAN. "Labor Unrest, Immigration, and Ethnic Conflict in Urban America, 1880–1914." *American Journal of Sociology.* Vol. 94, No. 6 (May 1989):1303–33.

OLZAK, SUSAN, and ELIZABETH WEST. "Ethnic Conflict and the Rise and Fall of Ethnic Newspapers." *American Sociological Review.* Vol. 56, No. 4 (August 1991):458–74.

O'REILLY, JANE. "Wife Beating: The Silent Crime." *Time.* Vol. 122, No. 10 (September 5, 1983):23–24, 26.

ORLANSKY, MICHAEL D., and WILLIAM L. HEWARD. *Voices: Interviews with Handicapped People.* Columbus, OH: Charles E. Merrill, 1981:85, 92, 133–34, 172. Copyright 1981. Reprinted by permission of the publisher.

ORSHANSKY, MOLLIE. "How Poverty is Measured." *Monthly Labor Review.* Vol. 92, No. 2 (February 1969):37–41.

OSTLING, RICHARD N. "Jerry Falwell's Crusade." *Time.* Vol. 126, No. 9 (September 2, 1985):48–52, 55, 57.

———. "Technology and the Womb." *Time.* Vol. 129, No. 12 (March 23, 1987):58–59.

OSTRANDER, SUSAN A. "Upper Class Women: The Feminine Side of Privilege." *Qualitative Sociology.* Vol. 3, No. 1 (Spring 1980):23–44.

———. *Women of the Upper Class.* Philadelphia, PA: Temple University Press, 1984.

OUCHI, WILLIAM. *Theory Z: How American Business Can Meet the Japanese Challenge.* Reading, MA: Addison-Wesley, 1981.

OWEN, DAVID. *None of the Above: Behind the Myth of Scholastic Aptitude.* Boston, MA: Houghton Mifflin, 1985.

PALMORE, ERDMAN. "Predictors of Successful Aging." *The Gerontologist.* Vol. 19, No. 5 (October 1979a):427–31.

———. "Advantages of Aging." *The Gerontologist.* Vol. 19, No 2 (April 1979b):220–23.

———. "What Can the USA Learn from Japan About Aging?" In Steven H. Zarit, ed., *Readings in Aging and Death: Contemporary Perspectives.* New York: Harper & Row, 1982:166–69.

PAMPEL, FRED C., KENNETH C. LAND, and MARCUS FELSON. "A Social Indicator Model of Changes in the Occupational Structure of the United States: 1947–1974." *American Sociological Review.* Vol. 42, No. 6 (December 1977):951–64.

PARCEL, TOBY L., CHARLES W. MUELLER, and STEVEN CUVELIER. "Comparable Worth and Occupational Labor Market: Explanations of Occupational Earnings Differentials." Paper presented to the American Sociological Association, New York, 1986.

PARENTI, MICHAEL. *Inventing Reality: The Politics of the Mass Media.* New York: St. Martin's Press, 1986.

PARK, ROBERT E. *Race and Culture.* Glencoe, IL: The Free Press, 1950.

———. "The City: Suggestions for the Investigation of Human Behavior in the Human Environment." In Robert E. Park and Ernest W. Burgess, *The City.* Chicago: University of Chicago Press, 1967; orig. 1925:1–46.

PARKINSON, C. NORTHCOTE. *Parkinson's Law and Other Studies in Administration.* New York: Ballantine Books, 1957.

PARROTT, JULIE. "The Effects of Culture on Eating Disorders." Paper presented to Southwestern Social Science Association, Dallas, Texas, March 1987.

PARSONS, TALCOTT. "Age and Sex in the Social Structure of the United States." *American Sociological Review*. Vol. 7, No. 4 (August, 1942):604–16.

————. *Essays in Sociological Theory*. New York: Free Press, 1954.

————. *The Social System*. New York: Free Press, 1964; orig. 1951.

————. *Societies: Evolutionary and Comparative Perspectives*. Englewood Cliffs, NJ: Prentice Hall, 1966.

PARSONS, TALCOTT, and ROBERT F. BALES, EDS. *Family, Socialization and Interaction Process*. New York: Free Press, 1955.

PATCHEN, MARTIN. "The Escalation of Inter-Nation Conflicts." *Sociological Focus*. Vol. 20, No. 2 (April 1987):95–110.

PATTERSON, GREGORY A. "Black Middle Class Debates Merits of Cities and Suburbs." *The Wall Street Journal* (August 6, 1991):B1.

PAUL, ELLEN FRANKEL. "Bared Buttocks and Federal Cases." *Society*. Vol. 28. No. 4 (May-June, 1991):4–7.

PEAR, ROBERT. "Women Reduce Lag in Earnings, But Disparities With Men Remain." *The New York Times* (September 4, 1987):1, 7.

PEAR, ROBERT, with ERIK ECKHOLM. "When Healers are Entrepreneurs: A Debate Over Costs and Ethics." *The New York Times* (June 2, 1991):1, 17.

PEDERSEN, DANIEL. "The Swedish Model: Lessons for the Left." *Newsweek* (March 5, 1990):30–31.

PENNINGS, JOHANNES M. "Organizational Birth Frequencies: An Empirical Investigation." *Administrative Science Quarterly*. Vol. 27, No. 1 (March 1982):120–44.

PEREZ, LISANDRO. "Cubans." In *Harvard Encyclopedia of American Ethnic Groups*. Cambridge, MA: Harvard University Press, 1980: 256–60.

PERSELL, CAROLINE HODGES. *Education and Inequality: A Theoretical and Empirical Synthesis*. New York: Free Press, 1977.

PESCOSOLIDO, BERNICE A., and SHARON GEORGIANNA. "Durkheim, Suicide, and Religion: Toward a Network Theory of Suicide." *American Sociological Review*. Vol. 54, No. 1 (February 1989):33–48.

PESSEN, EDWARD. *Riches, Class, and Power: America Before the Civil War*. New Brunswick, NJ: Transaction, 1990.

PETER, LAURENCE J., and RAYMOND HULL. *The Peter Principle: Why Things Always Go Wrong*. New York: William Morrow, 1969.

PETERS, THOMAS J., and ROBERT H. WATERMAN, JR. *In Search of Excellence: Lessons From America's Best-Run Companies*. New York: Warner Books, 1982.

PHILLIPSON, CHRIS. *Capitalism and the Construction of Old Age*. London: The Macmillan Press, 1982.

PHYSICIANS' TASK FORCE ON HUNGER IN AMERICA. "Hunger Reaches Blue-Collar America." Report issues 1987.

PILLEMER, KARL. "Maltreatment of the Elderly at Home and in Institutions: Extent, Risk Factors, and Policy Recommendations." In U.S. Congress. House, Select Committee on Aging and Senate, Special Committee on Aging. *Legislative Agenda for an Aging Society: 1988 and Beyond*. Washington, DC: U.S. Government Printing Office, 1988.

PINDERHUGHES, DIANNE M. "Political Choices: A Realignment in Partisanship Among Black Voters?" In James D. Williams, ed., *The State of Black America 1986*. New York: National Urban League, 1986:85–113.

PINES, MAYA. "The Civilization of Genie." *Psychology Today*. Vol. 15 (September 1981):28–34.

PIOTROW, PHYLLIS T. *World Population: The Present and Future Crisis*. Headline Series 251 (October 1980). New York: Foreign Policy Association.

PIRANDELLO, LUIGI. "The Pleasure of Honesty." In *To Clothe the Naked and Two Other Plays*. New York: Dutton, 1962:143–98.

PITT, MALCOLM. *Introducing Hinduism*. New York: Friendship Press, 1955.

PIVEN, FRANCES FOX, and RICHARD A. CLOWARD. *Poor People's Movements: Why They Succeed, How They Fail*. New York: Pantheon, 1977.

————. *Why Americans Don't Vote*. New York: Pantheon, 1988.

PLOMIN, ROBERT, and TERRYL T. FOCH. "A Twin Study of Objectively Assessed Personality in Childhood." *Journal of Personality and Sociology Psychology*. Vol. 39, No. 4 (October 1980):680–88.

POLENBERG, RICHARD. *One Nation Divisible: Class, Race, and Ethnicity in the United States Since 1938*. New York: Pelican Books, 1980.

POLLACK, OTTO, and ELLEN S. WISE. *Invitation to a Dialogue: Union and Separation in Family Life*. New York: SP Medical and Scientific Books, 1979.

POLSBY, NELSON W. "Three Problems in the Analysis of Community Power." *American Sociological Review*. Vol. 24, No. 6 (December 1959):796–803.

POMER, MARSHALL I. "Labor Market Structure, Intragenerational Mobility, and Discrimination: Black Male Advancement Out of Low-Paying Occupations, 1962–1973." *American Sociological Review*. Vol. 51, No. 5 (October 1986):650–59.

POPENOE, DAVID. "Family Decline in the Swedish Welfare State." *The Public Interest*. No. 102 (Winter 1991):65–77.

POPKIN, SUSAN J. "Welfare: Views from the Bottom." *Social Problems*. Vol. 17, No. 1 (February 1990):64–79.

PORTES, ALEJANDRO. "The Rise of Ethnicity: Determinants of Ethnic Perceptions Among Cuban Exiles in Miami." *American Sociological Review*. Vol. 49, No. 3 (June 1984):383–97.

PORTES, ALEJANDRO, and LEIF JENSEN. "The Enclave and the Entrants: Patterns of Ethnic Enterprise in Miami Before and After Mariel." *American Sociological Review*. Vol. 54, No. 6 (December 1989):929–49.

POWELL, CHRIS, and GEORGE E. C. PATON, EDS. *Humour in Society: Resistance and Control*. New York: St. Martin's Press, 1988.

PREMACK, DAVID. *Intelligence in Ape and Man*. Hillsdale, NJ: Lawrence Erlbaum Associates, 1976.

PURCELL, PIPER, and LARA STEWART. "Dick and Jane in 1989." *Sex Roles*. Vol. 22, Nos. 3–4 (1990):177–85.

PUTKA, GARY. "SAT To Become A Better Gauge." *The Wall Street Journal* (November 1, 1990):B1.

————. "Whittle Develops Plan to Operate Schools for Profit." *The Wall Street Journal* (May 15, 1991):B1.

QUEENAN, JOE. "The Many Paths to Riches." *Forbes*. Vol. 144, No. 9 (October 23, 1989):149.

QUINNEY, RICHARD. *Class, State and Crime: On the Theory and Practice of Criminal Justice*. New York: David McKay, 1977.

RADIN, NORMA. "Primary Caregiving and Role-Sharing Fathers." In Michael E. Lamb, ed., *Nontraditional Families: Parenting and Child Development*. Hillsdale, NJ: Lawrence Erlbaum Aassociates, 1982:173–204.

RANDALL, VICKI. *Women and Politics*. London: Macmillan Press, 1982.

RAPHAEL, RAY. *The Men from the Boys: Rites of Passage in Male America*. Lincoln and London: University of Nebraska Press, 1988.

RECKLESS, WALTER C. "Containment Theory." In Marvin E. Wolfgang, Leonard Savitz, and Norman Johnstone, eds., *The Sociology of Crime and Delinquency*. 2nd ed. New York: John Wiley, 1970:401–5.

RECKLESS, WALTER C., and SIMON DINITZ. "Pioneering with Self-Concept as a Vulnerability Factor in Delinquency." *Journal of Criminal Law, Criminology, and Police Science*. Vol. 58, No. 4 (December 1967):515–23.

REED, RODNEY J. "Administrator's Advice: Causes and Remedies of School Conflict and Violence." *National Association of Secondary School Principals Bulletin*. Vol. 67, No. 462 (April 1983):75–79.

REICH, ROBERT B. "As the World Turns." *The New Republic* (May 1, 1989):23, 26–28.

————. *The Work of Nations: Preparing Ourselves for 21st-Century Capitalism*. New York: Alfred A. Knopf, 1991.

REID, SUE TITUS. *Crime and Criminology*. 3rd ed. New York: Holt, Rinehart and Winston, 1982; 6th ed. Fort Worth, TX: Holt, 1991.

REIMAN, JEFFREY H. *The Rich Get Richer and the Poor Get Prison: Ideology, Class, and Criminal Justice*. 2nd ed. New York: John Wiley & Sons, 1984; 3rd ed., 1990.

REIMERS, CORDELIA W. "Sources of the Family Income Differentials Among Hispanics, Blacks, and White Non-Hispanics." *American Journal of Sociology*. Vol. 89, No. 4 (January 1984):889–903.

REMOFF, HEATHER TREXLER. *Sexual Choice: A Woman's Decision*. New York: Dutton/Lewis, 1984.

RENICK, TIMOTHY M. "From Apartheid to Liberation: Calvinism and the Shaping of Ethical Belief in South Africa." *Sociological Focus*. Vol. 24, No. 2 (May 1991):129–43.

RICHARDSON, JAMES T. "Definitions of Cult: From Sociological-Technical to Popular Negative." Paper presented to the American Psychological Association, Boston, August, 1990.

RIDGEWAY, CECILIA, and DAVID DIEKEMA. "Dominance and Collective Hierarchy Formation in Male and Female Task Groups." *American Sociological Review*. Vol. 54, No. 1 (February 1989):79–93.

RIDGEWAY, CECILIA L. *The Dynamics of Small Groups.* New York: St. Martin's Press, 1983.

RIEFF, PHILIP. "Introduction." In Charles Horton Cooley, *Social Organization.* New York: Schocken Books, 1962.

RIEGEL, KLAUS F. "History of Psychological Gerontology." In James E. Birren and K. Warner Schaie, eds., *Handbook of the Psychology of Aging.* New York: Van Nostrand Reinhold, 1977:70–102.

RIEGLE, DONALD W., JR. "The Psychological and Social Effects of Unemployment." *American Psychologist.* Vol. 37, No. 10 (October 1982):1113–15.

RIESMAN, DAVID. *The Lonely Crowd: A Study of the Changing American Character.* New Haven, CT: Yale University Press, 1970; orig. 1950.

RILEY, MATILDA WHITE, ANNE FONER, and JOAN WARING. "Sociology of Age." In Neil J. Smelser, ed., *Handbook of Sociology.* Newbury Park, CA: Sage Publications, 1988:243–90.

RITZER, GEORGE. *Man and His Work: Conflict and Change.* New York: Appleton-Century-Crofts, 1972.

———. *Sociological Theory.* New York: Alfred A. Knopf, 1983:63–66.

ROBERTS, J. DEOTIS. *Roots of a Black Future: Family and Church.* Philadelphia, PA: The Westminster Press, 1980.

ROBINSON, DAWN. "Toward a Synthesis of Sociological and Psychological Theories of Eating Disorders." Paper presented to Southwestern Social Science Association, Dallas, Texas, March 1987.

ROBINSON, VERA M. "Humor and Health." In Paul E. McGhee and Jeffrey H. Goldstein, eds., *Handbook of Humor Research, Vol II, Applied Studies.* New York: Springer-Verlag, 1983:109–28.

ROESCH, ROBERTA. "Violent Families." *Parents.* Vol. 59, No. 9 (September 1984):74–76, 150–52.

ROETHLISBERGER, F. J., and WILLIAM J. DICKSON. *Management and the Worker.* Cambridge, MA: Harvard University Press, 1939.

ROHLEN, THOMAS P. *Japan's High Schools.* Berkeley, CA: University of California Press, 1983.

ROKOVE, MILTON L. *Don't Make No Waves, Don't Back No Losers.* Bloomington, IN: Indiana University Press, 1975.

ROMAN, MEL, and WILLIAM HADDAD. *The Disposable Parent: The Case for Joint Custody.* New York: Holt, Rinehart and Winston, 1978.

ROOF, WADE CLARK. "Socioeconomic Differentials Among White Socioreligious Groups in the United States." *Social Forces.* Vol. 58, No. 1 (September 1979):280–89.

———. "Unresolved Issues in the Study of Religion and the National Elite: Response to Greeley." *Social Forces.* Vol. 59, No. 3 (March 1981):831–36.

ROOF, WADE CLARK, and WILLIAM McKINNEY. *American Mainline Religion: Its Changing Shape and Future.* New Brunswick, NJ: Rutgers University Press, 1987.

ROOS, PATRICIA. "Marriage and Women's Occupational Attainment in Cross-Cultural Perspective." *American Sociological Review.* Vol. 48, No. 6 (December 1983):852–64.

ROSE, ARNOLD M. "The Subculture of the Aging: A Topic for Sociological Research." In Bernice L. Neugarten, ed., *Middle Age and Aging: A Reader in Social Psychology.* Chicago: University of Chicago Press, 1968:29–34.

ROSE, JERRY D. *Outbreaks.* New York: Free Press, 1982.

ROSEN, ELLEN ISRAEL. *Bitter Choices: Blue-Collar Women in and out of Work.* Chicago: University of Chicago Press, 1987.

ROSENBAUM, RON. "A Tangled Web for the Supreme Court." *The New York Times Magazine* (March 12, 1989):60.

ROSENFELD, RACHEL A., and ARNE L. KALLEBERG. "A Cross-National Comparison of the Gender Gap in Income." *American Journal of Sociology.* Vol. 96, No. 1 (July 1990):69–106.

ROSENTHAL, ELISABETH. "Canada's National Health Plan Gives Care to All, With Limits." *The New York Times* (April 30, 1991):A1, A16.

ROSENTHAL, JACK. "The Rapid Growth of Suburban Employment." In Lois H. Masotti and Jeffrey K. Hadden, eds., *Suburbia in Transition.* New York: New York Times Books, 1974:95–100.

ROSKIN, MICHAEL G. *Countries and Concepts: An Introduction to Comparative Politics.* Englewood Cliffs, NJ: Prentice Hall, 1982.

ROSNOW, RALPH L., and GARY ALAN FINE. *Rumor and Gossip: The Social Psychology of Hearsay.* New York: Elsevier, 1976.

ROSS, CATHERINE E., JOHN MIROWSKY, and JOAN HUBER. "Dividing Work, Sharing Work, and In-Between: Marriage Patterns and Depression." *American Sociological Review.* Vol. 48, No. 6 (December 1983):809–23.

ROSS, SUSAN. "Education: A Step Ladder to Mobility." *Popline.* Vol. 7, No. 7 (July 1985):1–2.

ROSSI, ALICE S. "Gender and Parenthood." In Alice S. Rossi, ed., *Gender and the Life Course.* New York: Aldine, 1985:161–91.

ROSSIDES, DANIEL W. *Social Stratification: The American Class System in Comparative Perspective.* Englewood Cliffs, NJ: Prentice Hall, 1990.

ROSTOW, W. W. *The Stages of Economic Growth: A Non-Communist Manifesto.* Cambridge, UK: Cambridge University Press, 1960.

ROSTOW, WALT W. *The World Economy: History and Prospect.* Austin, TX: University of Texas Press, 1978.

ROUDI, NAZY. "The Demography of Islam." *Population Today.* Vol. 16, No. 3 (March 1988):6–9.

ROWE, DAVID C. "Biometrical Genetic Models of Self-Reported Delinquent Behavior: A Twin Study." *Behavior Genetics.* Vol 13, No. 5 (1983):473–89.

ROWE, DAVID C., and D. WAYNE OSGOOD. "Heredity and Sociological Theories of Delinquency: A Reconsideration." *American Sociological Review.* Vol. 49, No. 4 (August 1984):526–40.

RUBENSTEIN, ELI A. "The Not So Golden Years." *Newsweek* (October 7, 1991):13.

RUBIN, BETH A. "Class Struggle American Style: Unions, Strikes and Wages." *American Sociological Review.* Vol. 51, No. 5 (October 1986):618–31.

RUBIN, LILLIAN B. *Intimate Strangers: Men and Women Together.* New York: Harper & Row, 1983.

RUBIN, LILLIAN BRESLOW. *Worlds of Pain: Life in the Working-Class Family.* New York: Basic Books, 1976.

RUBINSON, RICHARD. "Class Formation, Politics, and Institutions: Schooling in the United States." *American Journal of Sociology.* Vol. 92, No. 3 (November 1986):519–48.

RUDÉ, GEORGE. *The Crowd in History: A Study of Popular Disturbances in France and England, 1730–1848.* New York: John Wiley & Sons, 1964.

RUDOLPH, BARBARA. "Tobacco Takes a New Road." *Time.* Vol. 126, No. 20 (November 18, 1985):70–71.

RUMBERGER, RUSSELL. *Overeducation in the U.S. Labor Market.* New York: Praeger, 1981.

RUSSELL, DIANA E. H. *Rape in Marriage.* New York: Macmillan, 1982.

RYAN, WILLIAM. *Blaming the Victim.* Rev. ed. New York: Vintage, 1976.

RYTINA, JOAN HUBER, WILLIAM H. FORM, and JOHN PEASE. "Income and Stratification Ideology: Beliefs About the American Opportunity Structure." *American Journal of Sociology.* Vol. 75, No. 4 (January 1970):703–16.

SABATO, LARRY J. *PAC Power: Inside the World of Political Action Committees.* New York: Norton, 1984.

SACKS, HOWARD L. Letter to the author, 1986.

SAGAN, CARL. *The Dragons of Eden.* New York: Ballantine, 1977.

SALAS, RAFAEL M. "The State of World Population 1985: Population and Women." *Popline.* Vol. 7, No. 7 (July 1985):4–5.

SALE, KIRKPATRICK. *The Conquest of Paradise: Christopher Columbus and the Columbian Legacy.* New York: Knopf, 1990.

SALHOLZ, ELOISE. "The Future of Gay America." *Newsweek* (March 12, 1990):20–25.

SALINE, CAROL. "Bleeding in the Suburbs." *Philadelphia.* Vol. 75, No. 3 (March 1984):81–85, 144–51.

SALTMAN, JULIET. "Maintaining Racially Diverse Neighborhoods." *Urban Affairs Quarterly.* Vol. 26, No. 3 (March 1991):416–41.

SAMPSON, ANTHONY. *The Changing Anatomy of Britain.* New York: Random House, 1982.

SAMPSON, ROBERT J. "Urban Black Violence: The Effects of Male Joblessness and Family Disruption." *American Journal of Sociology.* Vol. 93, No. 2 (September 1987):348–82.

SAMPSON, ROBERT J., and JOHN H. LAUB. "Crime and Deviance Over the Life Course: The Salience of Adult Social Bonds." *American Sociological Review.* Vol. 55, No. 5 (October 1990):609–27.

SAPIR, EDWARD. "The Status of Linguistics as a Science." *Language.* Vol. 5 (1929):207–14.

———. *Selected Writings of Edward Sapir in Language, Culture, and Personality.* David G. Mandelbaum, ed. Berkeley, CA: University of California Press, 1949.

SAUNDERS, JANICE MILLER, and JOHN N. EDWARDS. "Extramarital Sexuality: A Predictive Model of Permissive Attitudes." *Journal of Marriage and the Family.* Vol. 46, No. 4 (November 1984):825–35.

SCAFF, LAWRENCE A. "Max Weber and Robert Michels." *American Journal of Sociology*. Vol. 86, No. 6 (May 1981):1269–86.

SCHAEFER, RICHARD T. *Racial and Ethnic Groups*. Boston: Little, Brown, 1979.

SCHAIE, K. WARNER. "Intelligence and Problem Solving." In James E. Birren and R. Bruce Sloane, eds., *Handbook of Mental Health and Aging*. Englewood Cliffs, NJ: Prentice-Hall, 1980:262–84.

SCHEFF, THOMAS J. *Being Mentally Ill: A Sociological Theory*. 2nd ed. New York: Aldine, 1984.

SCHELLENBERG, JAMES A. *Masters of Social Psychology*. New York: Oxford University Press, 1978:38–62.

SCHLAFLY, PHYLLIS. "Mothers, Stay Home; Your Kids Need You." *USA Today* (May 30, 1984):10A.

SCHLESINGER, ARTHUR. "The City in American Civilization." In A.B. Callow, Jr., ed., *American Urban History*. New York: Oxford University Press, 1969:25–41.

SCHLESINGER, ARTHUR, JR. "The Cult of Ethnicity: Good and Bad." *Time*. Vol. 137, No. 27 (July 8, 1991):21.

SCHMIDT, ROGER. *Exploring Religion*. Belmont, CA: Wadsworth, 1980.

SCHOOLER, CARMI, JOANNE MILLER, KAREN A. MILLER, and CAROL N. RICHTAND. "Work for the Household: Its Nature and Consequences for Husbands and Wives." *American Journal of Sociology*. Vol. 90, No. 1 (July 1984):97–124.

SCHREINER, TIM. "Your Cost to Bring Up Baby: $142,700." *USA Today* (October 19, 1984):1D.

SCHUMANN, HANS WOLFGANG. *Buddhism: An Outline of Its Teachings and Schools*. Wheaton, IL: The Theosophical Publishing House, Quest Books, 1974.

SCHUR, EDWIN M. *Labeling Women Deviant: Gender, Stigma, and Social Control*. New York: Random House, 1984.

SCHUTT, RUSSELL K. "Objectivity versus Outrage." *Society*. Vol. 26, No. 4 (May/June 1989):14–16.

SCHWARTZ, FELICE N. "Management, Women, and the New Facts of Life." *Harvard Business Review*. Vol. 89, No. 1 (January-February 1989):65–76.

SCHWARTZ, JOE. "Rising Status." *American Demographics*. Vol. 11, No. 1 (January 1989):10.

SCHWARTZ, MARTIN D. "Gender and Injury in Spousal Assault." *Sociological Focus*. Vol. 20, No. 1 (January 1987):61–75.

SCHWARTZ-NOBEL, LORETTA. *Starving in the Shadow of Plenty*. New York: McGraw-Hill, 1981.

SCOTT, JOHN, and CATHERINE GRIFF. *Directors of Industry: The British Corporate Network, 1904–1976*. New York: Blackwell, 1985.

SCOTT, W. RICHARD. *Organizations: Rational, Natural, and Open Systems*. Englewood Cliffs, NJ: Prentice Hall, 1981.

SEARS, DAVID O., and JOHN B. McCONAHAY. *The Politics of Violence: The New Urban Blacks and the Watts Riot*. Boston: Houghton Mifflin, 1973.

SELIMUDDIN, ABU K. "The Selling of America." *USA Today*. Vol. 117, No. 2525 (March 1989):12–14.

SELLIN, THORSTEN. *The Penalty of Death*. Beverly Hills, CA: Sage Publications, 1980.

SELTZER, ROBERT M. *Jewish People, Jewish Thought: The Jewish Experience in History*. New York: Macmillan, 1980.

SEN, K. M. *Hinduism*. Baltimore, MD: Penguin, 1961.

SENGOKU, TAMOTSU. *Willing Workers: The Work Ethics in Japan, England, and the United States*. Westport, CT: Quorum Books, 1985.

SENNETT, RICHARD, and JONATHAN COBB. *The Hidden Injuries of Class*. New York: Vintage, 1973.

SEWELL, WILLIAM H., ARCHIBALD O. HALLER, and GEORGE W. OHLENDORF. "The Educational and Early Occupational Status Attainment Process: Replication and Revision." *American Sociological Review*. Vol. 35, No. 6 (December 1970):1014–27.

SHANAS, ETHEL. "Social Myth as Hypothesis: The Case of the Family Relations of Old People." *The Gerontologist*. Vol. 19, No. 1 (February 1979):3–9.

SHAPIRO, NINA. "Botswana Test Case." *Chicago Tribune* (September 15, 1991):1.

SHAW, CLIFFORD R., and HENRY D. McKAY. *Juvenile Delinquency in Urban Areas*. Chicago: University of Chicago Press, 1972; orig. 1942.

SHAWCROSS, WILLIAM. *Sideshow: Kissinger, Nixon and the Destruction of Cambodia*. New York: Pocket Books, 1979.

SHEEHAN, TOM. "Senior Esteem as a Factor in Socioeconomic Complexity." *The Gerontologist*. Vol. 16, No. 5 (October 1976):433–40.

SHEEHY, GAIL. *Passages: Predictable Crises of Adult Life*. New York: E. P. Dutton, 1976.

SHELDON, WILLILAM H., EMIL M. HARTL, and EUGENE McDERMOTT. *Varieties of Delinquent Youth*. New York: Harper, 1949.

SHELER, JEFFERY L. "Lobbyists Go for It." *U.S. News & World Report*. Vol. 98, No. 23 (June 17, 1985):30–34.

SHEPHARD, ROY J. *The Risks of Passive Smoking*. London: Croom Helm, 1982.

SHERRID, PAMELA. "Hot Times in the City of London." *U.S. News & World Report* (October 27, 1986):45–46.

SHEVKY, ESHREF, and WENDELL BELL. *Social Area Analysis*. Stanford, CA: Stanford University Press, 1955.

SHIBUTANI, TAMOTSU. *Improvised News: A Sociological Study of Rumor*. Indianapolis, IN: Bobbs-Merrill, 1966.

SHIPLER, DAVID K. *Russia: Broken Idols, Solemn Dreams*. New York: Penguin Books, 1984.

SHIPLEY, JOSEPH T. *Dictionary of Word Origins*. Totowa, NJ: Roman & Allanheld, 1985.

SHOCKEY, JAMES W. "Overeducation and Earnings: A Structural Approach to Differential Attainment in the U.S. Labor Force (1970–1982)." *American Sociological Review*. Vol. 54, No. 5 (October 1989):856–64.

SIDEL, RUTH, and VICTOR W. SIDEL. *The Health Care of China*. Boston, MA: Beacon Press, 1982b.

———. *A Healthy State: An International Perspective on the Crisis in United States Medical Care*. Rev. ed. New York: Pantheon, 1982a.

SILLS, DAVID L. "The Succession of Goals." In Amitai Etzioni, ed., *A Sociological Reader on Complex Organizations*. 2nd ed. New York: Holt, Rinehart and Winston, 1969:175–87.

SILVERSTEIN, MICHAEL. In Jon Snodgrass, ed., *A Book of Readings for Men Against Sexism*. Albion, CA: Times Change Press, 1977:178–79.

SIMMEL, GEORG. *The Sociology of Georg Simmel*. Kurt Wolff, ed. New York: Free Press, 1950:118–69.

———. "The Mental Life of the Metropolis." In Kurt Wolff, ed., *The Sociology of Georg Simmel*. New York: Free Press, 1964:409–24; orig. 1905.

———. "Fashion." In Donald N. Levine, ed., *Georg Simmel: On Individuality and Social Forms*. Chicago: University of Chicago Press, 1971; orig. 1904.

SIMON, CARL P., and ANN D. WITTE. *Beating the System: The Underground Economy*. Boston: Auburn House, 1982.

SIMON, DAVID R., and D. STANLEY EITZEN. *Elite Deviance*. 3rd ed. Boston: Allyn & Bacon, 1990.

SIMONS, CAROL. "Japan's *Kyoiku* Mamas." In John J. Macionis and Nijole V. Benokraitis, eds., *Seeing Ourselves: Classic, Contemporary, and Cross-Cultural Readings in Sociology*. Englewood Cliffs, NJ: Prentice Hall, 1989:281–86.

SIMONS, MARLISE. "The Amazon's Savvy Indians." *The New York Times Magazine* (February 26, 1990):36–37, 48–52. Copyright © 1989 by the New York Times Company.

SIMPSON, GEORGE EATON, and J. MILTON YINGER. *Racial and Cultural Minorities: An Analysis of Prejudice and Discrimination*. 4th ed. New York: Harper & Row, 1972.

SINGER, DOROTHY. "A Time to Reexamine the Role of Television in Our Lives." *American Psychologist*. Vol. 38, No. 7 (July 1983):815–16.

SINGER, JEROME L., and DOROTHY G. SINGER. "Psychologists Look at Television: Cognitive, Developmental, Personality, and Social Policy Implications." *American Psychologist*. Vol. 38, No. 7 (July 1983):826–34.

SIVARD, RUTH LEGER. *World Military and Social Expenditures, 1987–88*. 12th ed. Washington, DC: World Priorities, 1988.

SIZER, THEODORE R. *Horace's Compromise: The Dilemma of the American High School*. Boston, MA: Houghton Mifflin, 1984.

SJOBERG, GIDEON. *The Preindustrial City*. New York: Free Press, 1965.

SKOCPOL, THEDA. *States and Social Revolutions: A Comparative Analysis of France, Russia, and China*. Cambridge, UK: Cambridge University Press, 1979.

SKOLNICK, ARLENE. *The Psychology of Human Development*. New York: Harcourt Brace Jovanovich, 1986.

SKOLNICK, ARLENE S. *The Intimate Environment: Exploring Marriage and the Family*. 5th ed. New York: HarperCollins, 1992.

SLATER, PHILIP. *The Pursuit of Loneliness*. Boston, MA: Beacon Press, 1976.

SLATER, PHILIP E. "Contrasting Correlates of Group Size." *Sociometry*. Vol. 21, No. 2 (June 1958):129–39.

SMART, NINIAN. *The Religious Experience of Mankind*. New York: Charles Scribner's Sons, 1969.

SMELSER, NEIL J. *Theory of Collective Behavior*. New York: Free Press, 1962.

SMILGAS, MARTHA. "The Big Chill: Fear of AIDS." *Time*. Vol. 129, No. 7 (February 16, 1987):50–53.

SMITH, ADAM. *An Inquiry into the Nature and Causes of the Wealth of Nations*. New York: The Modern Library, 1937; orig. 1776.

SMITH, DOUGLAS A. "Police Response to Interpersonal Violence: Defining the Parameters of Legal Control." *Social Forces*. Vol. 65, No. 3 (March 1987):767–82.

SMITH, DOUGLAS A., and PATRICK R. GARTIN. "Specifying Specific Deterrence: The Influence of Arrest on Future Criminal Activity." *American Sociological Review*. Vol. 54, No. 1 (February 1989):94–105.

SMITH, DOUGLAS A., and CHRISTY A. VISHER. "Street-Level Justice: Situational Determinants of Police Arrest Decisions." *Social Problems*. Vol. 29, No. 2 (December 1981):167–77.

SMITH, ROBERT ELLIS. *Privacy: How to Protect What's Left of It*. Garden City, NY: Anchor Press/Doubleday, 1979.

SMITH-LOVIN, LYNN, and CHARLES BRODY. "Interruptions in Group Discussions: The Effects of Gender and Group Composition." *American Journal of Sociology*. Vol. 54, No. 3 (June 1989):424–35.

SMITH-ROSENBERG, CAROL, and CHARLES ROSENBERG. "The Female Animal: Medical and Biological Views of Woman and Her Role in Nineteenth Century America." In Judith Walzer Leavitt, ed., *Women and Health in America*. Madison, WI: University of Wisconsin Press, 1984:12–27.

SNELL, MARILYN BERLIN. "The Purge of Nurture." *New Perspectives Quarterly*. Vol. 7, No. 1 (Winter 1990):1–2.

SNOW, DAVID A., E. BURKE ROCHFORD, JR., STEVEN K. WORDEN, and ROBERT D. BENFORD. "Frame Alignment Processes, Micromobilization, and Movement Participation." *American Sociological Review*. Vol. 51, No. 4 (August 1986):464–81.

SNOW, DAVID A., LOUIS A. ZURCHER, JR., and SHELDON EKLAND-OLSON. "Social Networks and Social Movements: A Macrostructural Approach to Differential Recruitment." *American Sociological Review*. Vol. 45, No. 5 (October 1980):787–801.

SNOWMAN, DANIEL. *Britain and America: An Interpretation of Their Culture 1945–1975*. New York: Harper Torchbooks, 1977.

SOUTH, SCOTT J., and STEVEN F. MESSNER. "Structural Determinants of Intergroup Association: Interracial Marriage and Crime." *American Journal of Sociology*. Vol. 91, No. 6 (May 1986):1409–30.

SOWELL, THOMAS. *Ethnic America*. New York: Basic Books, 1981.

SOYINKA, WOLE. "Africa's Culture Producers." *Society*. Vol. 28, No. 2 (January/February 1991):32–40.

SPATES, JAMES L. "Sociological Overview." In Alan Milberg, ed., *Street Games*. New York: McGraw-Hill, 1976a:286–90.

———. "Counterculture and Dominant Culture Values: A Cross-National Analysis of the Underground Press and Dominant Culture Magazines." *American Sociological Review*. Vol. 41, No. 5 (October 1976b):868–83.

———. "The Sociology of Values." In Ralph Turner, ed., *Annual Review of Sociology*. Vol. 9. Palo Alto, CA: Annual Reviews, 1983:27–49.

SPATES, JAMES L., and JOHN J. MACIONIS. *The Sociology of Cities*. 2nd ed. Belmont, CA: Wadsworth, 1987.

SPATES, JAMES L., and H. WESLEY PERKINS. "American and English Student Values." *Comparative Social Research*. Vol. 5. Greenwich, CT: Jai Press, 1982:245–68.

SPECTOR, LEONARD S. "Nuclear Proliferation Today." In William M. Evan and Stephen Hilgartner, eds., *The Arms Race and Nuclear War*. Englewood Cliffs, NJ: Prentice Hall, 1988:25–29.

SPEER, JAMES A. "The New Christian Right and Its Parent Company: A Study in Political Contrasts." In David G. Bromley and Anson Shupe, eds., *New Christian Politics*. Macon, GA: Mercer University Press, 1984:19–40.

SPEIZER, JEANNE J. "Education." In Barbara Haber, ed., *The Women's Annual 1982–1983*. Boston: G.K. Hall, 1983:29–54.

SPENCER, GARY. *Projections of the Population of the United States, by Age, Sex, and Race: 1988 to 2080*. Washington, DC: U.S. Government Printing Office, 1989.

SPENDER, DALE. *Man Made Language*. London: Routledge & Kegan Paul, 1980.

SPITZER, STEVEN. "Toward a Marxian Theory of Deviance." In Delos H. Kelly, ed., *Criminal Behavior: Readings in Criminology*. New York: St. Martin's Press, 1980:175–91.

SRINIVAS, M. N. *Social Change in Modern India*. Berkeley, CA: University of California Press, 1971.

STACEY, JUDITH. *Patriarchy and Socialist Revolution in China*. Berkeley: University of California Press, 1983.

STACK, CAROL B. *All Our Kin: Strategies for Survival in a Black Community*. New York: Harper & Row, 1975.

STAHURA, JOHN M. "Suburban Development, Black Suburbanization and the Black Civil Rights Movement Since World War II." *American Sociological Review*. Vol. 51, No. 1 (February 1986):131–44.

STAPLES, BRENT. "Where Are the Black Fans?" *New York Times Magazine* (May 17, 1987):26–34, 36.

STAPLES, ROBERT, and ALFREDO MIRANDE. "Racial and Cultural Variations Among American Families: A Decennial Review of the Literature on Minority Families." *Journal of Marriage and the Family*. Vol. 42, No. 4 (August 1980):157–72.

STARK, EVAN, and ANN FLITCRAFT. "Domestic Violence and Female Suicide Attempts." Presentation to American Public Health Association, New York, 1979.

STARK, RODNEY. "The Rise of a New World Faith." *Review of Religious Research*. Vol. 26, No. 1 (September 1984):18–27.

———. *Sociology*. Belmont, CA: Wadsworth, 1985.

STARK, RODNEY, and WILLIAM SIMS BAINBRIDGE. "Of Churches, Sects, and Cults: Preliminary Concepts for a Theory of Religious Movements." *Journal for the Scientific Study of Religion*. Vol. 18, No. 2 (June 1979):117–31.

———. "Secularization and Cult Formation in the Jazz Age." *Journal for the Scientific Study of Religion*. Vol. 20, No. 4 (December 1981):360–73.

STARK, RODNEY, and CHARLES Y. GLOCK. *American Piety: The Nature of Religious Commitment*. Berkeley, CA: University of California Press, 1968.

STARR, PAUL. *The Social Transformation of American Medicine*. New York: Basic Books, 1982.

*Statistics of Income Bulletin*. Vol. 11, No. 3 (Winter 1991–92).

STAVRIANOS, L. S. *A Global History: The Human Heritage*. 3rd ed. Englewood Cliffs, NJ: Prentice Hall, 1983.

STEELE, SHELBY. *The Content of Our Character: A New Vision of Race in America*. New York: St. Martin's Press, 1990.

STEIN, MAURICE R. *The Eclipse of Community: An Interpretation of American Studies*. Princeton, NJ: Princeton University Press, 1972.

STEINMETZ, GEORGE, and ERIK OLIN WRIGHT. "The Fall and Rise of the Petty Bourgeoisie: Changing Patterns of Self-Employment in the Postwar United States." *American Journal of Sociology*. Vol. 94, No. 5 (March 1989):973–1018.

STEPHENS, JOHN D. *The Transition from Capitalism to Socialism*. Urbana, IL: University of Illinois Press, 1986.

STERNLIEB, GEORGE, and JAMES W. HUGHES. "The Uncertain Future of the Central City." *Urban Affairs Quarterly*. Vol. 18, No. 4 (June 1983):455–72.

STEVENS, GILLIAN, and GRAY SWICEGOOD. "The Linguistic Context of Ethnic Endogamy." *American Sociological Review*. Vol. 52, No. 1 (February 1987):73–82.

STEVENS, ROSEMARY. *American Medicine and the Public Interest*. New Haven, CT: Yale University Press, 1971.

STIEHM, JUDITH HICKS. *Arms and the Enlisted Woman*. Philadelphia: Temple University Press, 1989.

STOCKWELL, EDWARD G., DAVID A. SWANSON, and JERRY W. WICKS. "Trends in the Relationship Between Infant Mortality and Socioeconomic Status." *Sociological Focus*. Vol. 20, No. 4 (October 1987):319–27.

STODDARD, SANDOL. *The Hospice Movement: A Better Way to Care for the Dying*. Briarcliff Manor, NY: Stein and Day, 1978.

STONE, LAWRENCE. *The Family, Sex and Marriage in England 1500–1800*. New York: Harper & Row, 1977.

STONE, ROBYN. *The Feminization of Poverty and Older Women*. Washington, DC: U.S. Department of Health and Human Services, 1986.

STONE, ROBYN, GAIL LEE CAFFERATA, and JUDITH SANGL. *Caregivers of the Frail Elderly: A National Profile*. Washington, DC: U.S. Department of Health and Human Services, 1987.

STOUFFER, SAMUEL A., ET AL. *The American Soldier: Adjustment During Army Life*. Princeton, NJ: Princeton University Press, 1949.

STRANG, DAVID. "From Dependency to Sovereignty: An Event History Analysis of Decolonization 1870–1987." *American Sociological Review*. Vol. 55, No. 6 (December 1990):846–60.

STRAUS, MURRAY A., and RICHARD J. GELLES. "Societal Change and Change in Family Violence from 1975 to 1985 as Revealed by Two National Surveys." *Journal of Marriage and the Family*. Vol. 48, No. 4 (August 1986):465–79.

STREIB, GORDON F. "Are the Aged a Minority Group?" In Bernice L. Neugarten, ed., *Middle Age and Aging: A Reader in Social Psychology*. Chicago: University of Chicago Press, 1968:35–46.

STRIEGEL-MOORE, RUTH, LISA R. SILBERSTEIN, and JUDITH RODIN. "Toward an Understanding of Risk Factors for Bulimia." *American Psychologist*. Vol. 41, No. 3 (March 1986):246–63.

SUDNOW, DAVID N. *Passing On: The Social Organization of Dying*. Englewood Cliffs, NJ: Prentice Hall, 1967.

SUMNER, WILLIAM GRAHAM. *Folkways*. New York: Dover, 1959; orig. 1906.

SUNG, BETTY LEE. *Mountains of Gold: The Story of the Chinese in America*. New York: Macmillan, 1967.

SURO, ROBERTO. "Hispanics in Despair." *The New York Times: Education Life* (November 4, 1990):section 4a, page 25.

SUTHERLAND, EDWIN H. "White Collar Criminality." *American Sociological Review*. Vol. 5, No. 1 (February 1940):1–12.

SUTHERLAND, EDWIN H., and DONALD R. CRESSEY. *Criminology*. 3rd ed. Philadelphia: J.B. Lippincott, 1930; 8th ed., 1970; 10th ed., 1978.

SUZUKI, DAVID, and PETER KNUDTSON. *Genethics: The Clash Between the New Genetics and Human Values*. Cambridge, MA: Harvard University Press, 1989.

SWARTZ, STEVE. "Why Michael Milken Stands to Qualify for Guinness Book." *The Wall Street Journal*. Vol. LXX, No. 117 (March 31, 1989):1, 4.

SZYMANSKI, ALBERT. *Class Structure: A Critical Perspective*. New York: Praeger, 1983.

SZASZ, THOMAS S. *The Manufacturer of Madness: A Comparative Study of the Inquisition and the Mental Health Movement*. New York: Dell, 1961.

———. *The Myth of Mental Illness: Foundations of a Theory of Personal Conduct*. New York: Harper & Row, 1970; orig. 1961.

TAEUBER, KARL, and ALMA TAEUBER. *Negroes in Cities*. Chicago: Aldine, 1965.

TAJFEL, HENRI. "Social Psychology of Intergroup Relations." *Annual Review of Psychology*. Palo Alto, CA: Annual Reviews, 1982:1–39.

TANNEN, DEBORAH. *You Just Don't Understand Me: Women and Men in Conversation*. New York: William Morrow, 1990.

TANNENBAUM, FRANK. *Slave and Citizen: The Negro in the Americas*. New York: Vintage Books, 1946.

TAVRIS, CAROL, and SUSAN SADD. *The Redbook Report on Female Sexuality*. New York: Delacorte Press, 1977.

TAVRIS, CAROL, and CAROLE WADE. *The Longest War: Sex Differences in Perspective*. 2nd ed. New York: Harcourt Brace Jovanovich, 1984.

TAYLOR, JOHN. "Don't Blame Me: The New Culture of Victimization." *New York Magazine* (June 3, 1991):26–34.

TERKEL, STUDS. *Working*. New York: Pantheon Books, 1974:1–2, 57–59, 65, 66, 69, 221–22. Copyright © 1974 by Pantheon Books, a Division of Random House, Inc.

THEEN, ROLF H. W. "Party and Bureaucracy." In Erik P. Hoffmann and Robbin F. Laird, eds., *The Soviet Polity in the Modern Era*. New York: Aldine, 1984:131–65.

THEODORSON, GEORGE A., and ACHILLES G. THEODORSON. *A Modern Dictionary of Sociology*. New York: Barnes and Noble Books, 1969.

THOITS, PEGGY A. "Self-labeling Processes in Mental Illness: The Role of Emotional Deviance." *American Journal of Sociology*. Vol. 91, No. 2 (September 1985):221–49.

THOMAS, EDWARD J. *The Life of Buddha as Legend and History*. London: Routledge & Kegan Paul, 1975.

THOMAS, PIRI. *Down These Mean Streets*. New York: Signet, 1967.

THOMAS, W. I. "The Relation of Research to the Social Process." In Morris Janowitz, ed., *W. I. Thomas on Social Organization and Social Personality*. Chicago: University of Chicago Press, 1966:289–305; orig. 1931.

THOMPSON, ANTHONY PETER. "Emotional and Sexual Components of Extramarital Relations." *Journal of Marriage and the Family*. Vol. 46, No. 1 (February 1984):35–42.

THORNBERRY, TERRANCE, and MARGARET FARNSWORTH. "Social Correlates of Criminal Involvement: Further Evidence on the Relationship Between Social Status and Criminal Behavior." *American Sociological Review*. Vol 47, No. 4 (August 1982):505–18.

THORNE, BARRIE, CHERIS KRAMARAE, and NANCY HENLEY, EDS. *Language, Gender and Society*. Cambridge: Newbury House, 1983.

THORNTON, ARLAND. "Changing Attitudes Toward Separation and Divorce: Causes and Consequences." *American Journal of Sociology*. Vol. 90, No. 4 (January 1985):856–72.

THUROW, LESTER C. "A Surge in Inequality." *Scientific American*. Vol. 256, No. 5 (May 1987):30–37.

TIBBITTS, CLARK. "Can We Invalidate Negative Stereotypes of Aging?" *The Gerontologist*. Vol. 19, No. 1 (February 1979):10–20.

TIEN, H. YUAN. "Second Thoughts on the Second Child." *Population Today*. Vol. 17, No. 4 (April 1989):6–9.

TIENDA, MARTA, and DING-TZANN LII. "Minority Concentration and Earnings Inequality: Blacks, Hispanics, and Asians Compared." *American Journal of Sociology*. Vol. 93, No. 1 (July 1987):141–65.

TIGER, LIONEL, and JOSEPH SHEPHER. *Women in the Kibbutz*. New York: Harcourt Brace Jovanovich, 1975.

TILLY, CHARLES. *From Mobilization to Revolution*. Reading, MA: Addison-Wesley, 1978.

———. "Does Modernization Breed Revolution?" In Jack A. Goldstone, ed., *Revolutions: Theoretical, Comparative, and Historical Studies*. New York: Harcourt Brace Jovanovich, 1986:47–57.

*Time*. "The Crime That Tarnished a Town." Vol. 123, No. 10 (March 5, 1984):19.

TITTLE, CHARLES R., and WAYNE J. VILLEMEZ. "Social Class and Criminality." *Social Forces*. Vol. 56, No. 22 (December 1977):474–502.

TITTLE, CHARLES R., WAYNE J. VILLEMEZ, and DOUGLAS A. SMITH. "The Myth of Social Class and Criminality: An Empirical Assessment of the Empirical Evidence." *American Sociological Review*. Vol. 43, No. 5 (October 1978):643–56.

TOBIN, GARY. "Suburbanization and the Development of Motor Transportation: Transportation Technology and the Suburbanization Process." In Barry Schwartz, ed., *The Changing Face of the Suburbs*. Chicago: University of Chicago Press, 1976.

TOCH, THOMAS. "The Exodus." *U.S. News and World Report*. Vol. 111, No. 24 (December 9, 1991):68–77.

TOCQUEVILLE, ALEXIS DE. *The Old Regime and the French Revolution*. Stuart Gilbert, trans. Garden City, NY: Doubleday Anchor Books, 1955; orig. 1856.

———. *Democracy in America*. Garden City, NY: Doubleday Anchor Books, 1969; orig. 1834–1840.

TOENNIES, FERDINAND. *Community and Society (Gemeinschaft und Gesellschaft)*. New York: Harper & Row, 1963; orig. 1887.

TOFANI, LORETTA. "AIDS Ravages a Continent, and Sweeps a Family." *The Philadelphia Inquirer* (March 24, 1991):1, 15–A.

TOFFLER, ALVIN. *The Third Wave*. New York: Bantam Books, 1981.

TOMIAK, JANUSZ. "Introduction." In J. J. Tomiak, ed., *Soviet Education in the 1980s*. London: Croom Helm, 1983:vii–x.

TOOMEY, BEVERLY, RICHARD FIRST, and JOHN RIFE. Research described in "Number of Rural Homeless Greater than Expected." Ohio State *Quest* (Autumn 1990):2.

TREAS, JUDITH. "Socialist Organization and Economic Development in China: Latent Consequences for the Aged." *The Gerontologist*. Vol. 19, No. 1 (February 1979):34–43.

TREIMAN, DONALD J. "Industrialization and Social Stratification." In Edward O. Laumann, ed., *Social Stratification: Research and Theory for the 1970s*. Indianapolis, IN: Bobbs-Merrill, 1970.

TROELTSCH, ERNST. *The Social Teaching of the Christian Churches*. New York: Macmillan, 1931.

TROIDEN, RICHARD R. *Gay and Lesbian Identity: A Sociological Analysis*. Dix Hills, NY: General Hall, 1988.

TUMIN, MELVIN M. "Some Principles of Stratification: A Critical Analysis." *American Sociological Review*. Vol. 18, No. 4 (August 1953):387–94.

———. *Social Stratification: The Forms and Functions of Inequality*. 2nd ed. Englewood Cliffs, NJ: Prentice Hall, 1985.

TURNER, RALPH H., and LEWIS M. KILLIAN. *Collective Behavior*. 2nd ed. Englewood Cliffs, NJ: Prentice-Hall, 1972; 3rd ed., 1987.

Tygiel, Jules. *Baseball's Great Experiment: Jackie Robinson and His Legacy.* New York: Oxford University Press, 1983.

Tyler, S. Lyman. *A History of Indian Policy.* Washington, DC: United States Department of the Interior, Bureau of Indian Affairs, 1973.

Tyree, Andrea, Moshe Semyonov, and Robert W. Hodge. "Gaps and Glissandos: Inequality, Economic Development, and Social Mobility in 24 Countries." *American Sociological Review.* Vol. 44, No. 3 (June 1979):410–24.

Uchitelle, Louis. "But Just Who is That Fairy Godmother?" *The New York Times* (September 29, 1991):section 4, page 1.

United Nations. *World Economic Survey 1988: Current Trends and Policies in the World Economy.* New York: United Nations Publications, 1988.

United Nations Development Programme. *Human Development Report 1991.* New York: Oxford University Press, 1991.

U.S. Bureau of the Census. *Household and Family Characteristics: March 1990 and 1989.* Current Population Reports, Series P-20, No. 447. Washington, DC: U.S. Government Printing Office, 1990.

U.S. Bureau of the Census. *Fertility of American Women: June 1990.* Current Population Reports, Series P–20, No. 454. Washington, DC: U.S. Government Printing Office, 1991.

U.S. Bureau of the Census. "Get the Scoop on 1990 Metro Area Population." *Census and You.* Vol. 29, No. 9 (September 1991). Washington, DC: U.S. Government Printing Office, 1991.

U.S. Bureau of the Census. *Marital Status and Living Arrangements: March 1990.* Current Population Reports, Series P-20, No. 450. Washington, DC: U.S. Government Printing Office, 1991.

U.S. Bureau of the Census. *Money Income of Households, Families, and Persons in the United States: 1990.* Current Population Reports, Series P-60, No. 174. Washington, DC: U.S. Government Printing Office, 1991.

U.S. Bureau of the Census. Press release on homeless count (CB91-117). Washington, DC: U.S. Government Printing Office, 1991.

U.S. Bureau of the Census. "Where Does Your City Rank?" *Census and You.* Vol. 26, No. 7 (July 1991). Washington, DC: U.S. Government Printing Office, 1991.

U.S. Bureau of the Census. Current Population Survey. Unpublished data for March 1991. Supplied by the bureau, 1992.

U.S. Bureau of Justice Statistics. *Recidivism of Prisoners Released in 1983.* Washington, DC: U.S. Government Printing Office, 1989.

U.S. Congress. House. Select Subcommittee On Children, Youth, And Families. *U.S. Children and Their Families: Current Conditions and Recent Trends, 1989.* Washington, DC: U.S. Government Printing Office, 1989.

U.S. Department of Commerce. *United States Department of Commerce News.* CB91-221. Washington, DC: U.S. Government Printing Office, 1991.

U.S. Department of Education. National Center for Education Statistics. *The Condition of Education, 1991, Vol. 2, Postsecondary Education.* Washington, DC: U.S. Government Printing Office, 1991.

U.S. Department of Energy. *Annual Energy Review 1990.* Washington, DC: U.S. Government Printing Office, 1991.

U.S. Department of Health and Human Services. *Alcohol, Drug Abuse, and Mental Health News.* Vol. 15, No. 8 (October 1989).

U.S. Department of Health and Human Services. *Vital and Health Statistics: Current Estimates from the National Health Interview Survey, 1990.* Series 10, No. 181. Hyattsville, MD: U.S. Government Printing Office, 1991.

U.S. Department of Justice. *Criminal Victimization in the United States, 1987.* Washington, DC: U.S. Government Printing Office, 1987.

U.S. Department of Labor. Bureau of Labor Statistics. *Employment and Earnings.* Vol. 38, No. 9 (September). Washington, DC: U.S. Government Printing Office, 1991.

U.S. Department of Labor. Bureau of Labor Statistics. *Employment and Earnings.* Vol. 39, No. 1 (January). Washington, DC: U.S. Government Printing Office, 1992.

Useem, Bert. "Disorganization and the New Mexico Prison Riot of 1980." *American Sociological Review.* Vol. 50, No. 5 (October 1985):677–88.

Useem, Michael. "The Social Organization of the Corporate Business Elite and Participation of Corporate Directors in the Governance of American Institutions." *American Sociological Review.* Vol. 44, No. 4 (August 1979):553–72.

———. "Corporations and the Corporate Elite." In Alex Inkeles et al., eds., *Annual Review of Sociology.* Vol. 6. Palo Alto, CA: Annual Reviews, 1980:41–77.

Useem, Michael, and Jermoe Karabel. "Pathways to Corporate Management." *American Sociological Review.* Vol. 51, No. 2 (April 1986):184–200.

U.S. Federal Bureau of Investigation. *Crime in the United States 1990.* Washington, DC: U.S. Government Printing Office, 1991.

U.S. Federal Election Commission. *FEC Final Report on 1988 Congressional Campaigns Shows $459 Million Spent.* Washington, DC: The Commission, 1989a.

U.S. Federal Election Commission. *Federal Election Commission Record.* Vol. 15, No. 8 (August 1989b).

U.S. House of Representatives, Select Committee on Children, Youth, and Families. *Abused Children in America: Victims of Neglect.* Washington, DC: U.S. Government Printing Office, 1987.

U.S. National Center for Health Statistics. *Current Estimates from the National Health Survey, 1989.* Washintgon, DC: U.S. Government Printing Office, 1990.

U.S. National Center for Health Statistics. *Vital Statistics of the United States, 1988, Vol. 1, Natality.* Washington DC: U.S. Government Printing Office, 1990.

U.S. Women's Bureau. *Employers and Child Care: Benefiting Work and Family.* Washington, DC: U.S. Government Printing Office, 1989.

Unruh, John D., Jr. *The Plains Across.* Urbana: University of Illinois Press, 1979.

Van De Kaa, Dirk J. "Europe's Second Demographic Transition." *Population Bulletin.* Vol. 42, No. 1 (March 1987). Washington, DC: Population Reference Bureau.

Van Den Haag, Ernest, and John P. Conrad. *The Death Penalty: A Debate.* New York: Plenum Press, 1983.

Van Valey, T. L., W. C. Roof, and J. E. Wilcox. "Trends in Residential Segregation." *American Journal of Sociology.* Vol. 82, No. 4 (January 1977):826–44.

Vatz, Richard E., and Lee S. Weinberg. *Thomas Szasz: Primary Values and Major Contentions.* Buffalo, NY: Prometheus Books, 1983.

Vaughan, Mary Kay. "Multinational Corporations: The World as a Company Town." In Ahamed Idris-Soven et al., eds., *The World as a Company Town: Multinational Corporations and Social Change.* The Hague: Mouton Publishers, 1978:15–35.

Vayda, Eugene, and Raisa B. Deber. "The Canadian Health Care System: An Overview." *Social Science and Medicine.* Vol. 18, No. 3 (1984):191–97.

Veblen, Thorstein. *The Theory of the Leisure Class.* New York: The New American Library, 1953; orig. 1899.

Viguerie, Richard A. *The New Right: We're Ready to Lead.* Falls Church, VA: The Viguerie Company, 1981.

Vines, Gail. "Whose Baby Is It Anyway?" *New Scientist.* No. 1515 (July 3, 1986):26–27.

Vinovskis, Maris A. "Have Social Historians Lost the Civil War? Some Preliminary Demographic Speculations." *Journal of American History.* Vol. 76, No. 1 (June 1989):34–58.

Vogel, Ezra F. *Japan as Number One: Lessons for America.* Cambridge, MA: Harvard University Press, 1979.

Vogel, Lise. *Marxism and the Oppression of Women: Toward a Unitary Theory.* New Brunswick, NJ: Rutgers University Press, 1983.

Vold, George B., and Thomas J. Bernard. *Theoretical Criminology.* 3rd ed. New York: Oxford University Press, 1986.

Von Hirsh, Andrew. *Past or Future Crimes: Deservedness and Dangerousness in the Sentencing of Criminals.* New Brunswick, NJ: Rutgers University Press, 1986.

Vonnegut, Kurt, Jr. "Harrison Bergeron." In *Welcome to the Monkey House.* New York: Delacorte Press/Seymour Lawrence, 1968:7–13; orig. 1961.

Waite, Linda J., Gus W. Haggstrom, and David E. Kanouse. "The Consequences of Parenthood for the Marital Stability of Young Adults." *American Sociological Review.* Vol. 50, No. 6 (December 1985):850–57.

Walker, Jack L. "The Origins and Maintenance of Interest Groups in America." *The American Political Science Review.* Vol. 77, No. 2 (June 1983):390–406.

Wall, Thomas F. *Medical Ethics: Basic Moral Issues.* Washington, DC: University Press of America, 1980.

WALLERSTEIN, IMMANUEL. *The Modern World-System: Capitalist Agriculture and the Origins of the European World-Economy in the Sixteenth Century.* New York: Academic Press, 1974.

———. *The Capitalist World-Economy.* New York: Cambridge University Press, 1979.

———. "Crises: The World Economy, the Movements, and the Ideologies." In Albert Bergesen, ed., *Crises in the World-System.* Beverly Hills, CA: Sage Publications, 1983:21–36.

———. *The Politics of the World Economy: The States, the Movements, and the Civilizations.* Cambridge (UK): Cambridge University Press, 1984.

WALLERSTEIN, JUDITH S., and SANDRA BLAKESLEE. *Second Chances: Men, Women, and Children a Decade after Divorce.* New York: Ticknor & Fields.

WALLIS, CLAUDIA. "Stress: Can We Cope?" *Time.* Vol. 121, No. 23 (June 6, 1983):48–54.

———. "Hold the Eggs and Butter." *Time.* Vol. 123, No. 13 (March 26, 1984):56–63.

———. "Children Having Children." *Time.* Vol. 126, No. 23 (December 9, 1985):78–82, 84, 87, 89–90.

WALTON, JOHN, and CHARLES RAGIN. "Global and National Sources of Political Protest: Third World Responses to the Debt Crisis." *American Sociological Review.* Vol. 55, No. 6 (December 1990):876–90.

WARNER, SAM BASS, JR. *Streetcar Suburbs.* Cambridge, MA: Harvard University and M:I.T. Presses, 1962.

WARNER, W. LLOYD, and J. O. LOW. *The Social System of the Modern Factory.* Yankee City Series, Vol. 4. New Haven, CT: Yale University Press, 1947.

WARNER, W. LLOYD, and PAUL S. LUNT. *The Social Life of a Modern Community.* New Haven, CT: Yale University Press, 1941.

WATSON, JOHN B. *Behaviorism.* Rev. ed. New York: W. W. Norton, 1930.

WATSON, RUSSELL. "A Hidden Epidemic." *Newsweek* (May 14, 1984):30–36.

WATTEL, H. "Levittown: A Suburban Community." In William Dobriner, ed., *The Suburban Community.* New York: G. P. Putnam's Sons, 1958:287–313.

WAXMAN, CHAIM I. *The Stigma of Poverty: A Critique of Poverty Theories and Policies.* 2nd ed. New York: Pergamon Press, 1983.

WEBER, ADNA FERRIN. *The Growth of Cities.* New York: Columbia University Press, 1963; orig. 1899.

WEBER, MAX. *The Protestant Ethic and the Spirit of Capitalism.* New York: Charles Scribner's Sons, 1958; orig. 1904–1905.

———. *General Economic History.* Frank H. Knight, trans. New York: Collier Books, 1961; orig. 1919–1920.

———. *Economy and Society.* G. Roth and C. Wittich, eds. Berkeley, CA: University of California Press, 1978.

WECHSLER, D. *The Measurement and Appraisal of Adult Intelligence.* 5th ed. Baltimore, MD: Williams and Wilkins, 1972.

WEEKS, JOHN R. "The Demography of Islamic Nations." *Population Bulletin.* Vol. 43, No. 4 (December 1988).

WEINBERG, GEORGE. *Society and the Healthy Homosexual.* Garden City, NY: Anchor Books, 1973.

WEINER, ANNETTE B. "Ethnographic Determinism: Samoa and the Margaret Mead Controversy." *American Anthropologist.* Vol. 85, No. 4 (December 1983):909–19.

WEINRICH, JAMES D. *Sexual Landscapes: Why We Are What We Are, Why We Love Whom We Love.* New York: Charles Scribner's Sons, 1987.

WEISNER, THOMAS S., and BERNICE T. EIDUSON. "The Children of the 60s as Parents." *Psychology Today* (January 1986):60–66.

WEITZMAN, LENORE J. *The Divorce Revolution: The Unexpected Social and Economic Consequences for Women and Children in America.* New York: Free Press, 1985.

WEITZMAN, LENORE J., DEBORAH EIFLER, ELIZABETH HODAKA, and CATHERINE ROSS. "Sex-Role Socialization in Picture Books for Preschool Children." *American Journal of Sociology.* Vol. 77, No. 6 (May 1972):1125–50.

WELLER, JACK M., and E. L. QUARANTELLI. "Neglected Characteristics of Collective Behavior." *American Journal of Sociology.* Vol. 79, No. 3 (November 1973):665–85.

WELLFORD, CHARLES. "Labeling Theory and Criminology: An Assessment." In Delos H. Kelly, ed., *Criminal Behavior: Readings in Criminology.* New York: St. Martin's Press, 1980:234–47.

WELLMAN, BARRY. "The Community Question: Intimate Networks of East Yorkers." *American Journal of Sociology.* Vol. 84, No. 5 (March 1979):1201–31.

WENKE, ROBERT J. *Patterns of Prehistory.* New York: Oxford University Press, 1980.

WERMAN, JILL. "Who Makes What?" *Working Woman* (January 1989):72–76, 80.

WESOLOWSKI, WLODZIMIERZ. "Transition from Authoritarianism to Democracy." *Social Research.* Vol. 57, No. 2 (Summer 1990):435–61.

WESTERMAN, MARTY. "Death of the Frito Bandito." *American Demographics.* Vol. 11, No. 3 (March 1989):28–32.

WESTOFF, CHARLES F., and ELISE F. JONES. "The Secularization of U.S. Catholic Birth Control Practices." *Family Planning Perspective.* Vol. X, No. 5 (September/October 1977):203–7.

WHALEN, JACK, and RICHARD FLACKS. *Beyond the Barricades: The Sixties Generation Grows Up.* Philadelphia, PA: Temple University Press, 1989.

WHEELIS, ALLEN. *The Quest for Identity.* New York: W. W. Norton, 1958.

WHITAKER, MARK. "Ten Ways to Fight Terrorism." *Newsweek* (July 1, 1985):26–29.

WHITE, RALPH, and RONALD LIPPITT. "Leader Behavior and Member Reaction in Three 'Social Climates.'" In Dorwin Cartwright and Alvin Zander, eds., *Group Dynamics.* Evanston, IL: Row, Peterson, 1953:586–611.

WHITE, WALTER. *Rope and Faggot.* New York: Arno Press and The New York Times, 1969; orig. 1929.

WHITMAN, DAVID. "Shattering Myths about the Homeless." *U.S. News & World Report* (March 20, 1989):26, 28.

WHITNEY, CRAIG R. "British Health Service, Much Beloved but Inadequate, is Facing Changes." *The New York Times* (June 9, 1991):11.

WHORF, BENJAMIN LEE. "The Relation of Habitual Thought and Behavior to Language." In *Language, Thought, and Reality.* Cambridge, MA: The Technology Press of M.I.T./New York: Wiley, 1956:134–59; orig. 1941.

WHYTE, WILLIAM FOOTE. *Street Corner Society.* 3rd ed. Chicago: University of Chicago Press, 1981; orig. 1943.

WHYTE, WILLIAM H., JR. *The Organization Man.* Garden City, NY: Anchor, 1957.

WIARDA, HOWARD J. "Ethnocentrism and Third World Development." *Society.* Vol. 24, No. 6 (September–October 1987):55–64.

WIATROWSKI, MICHAEL A., DAVID B. GRISWOLD, and MARY K. ROBERTS. "Social Control Theory and Delinquency." *American Sociological Review.* Vol. 46, No. 5 (October 1981):525–41.

WILCOX, CLYDE. "Support for the Christian Right Old and New: A Comparison of Supporters of the Anti-Communism Crusade and the Moral Majority." *Sociological Focus.* Vol. 22, No. 2 (May 1989):87–97.

WILKERSON, ISABEL. "Interracial Marriage Rises, Acceptance Lags." *The New York Times* (December 2, 1991):1, 10.

WILL, GEORGE F. "No Psycho-Socio Babble Lessens the Fact That Evil Was the Crux of Central Park Rape." *The Philadelphia Inquirer* (May 1, 1989).

WILLIAMS, RHYS H., and N. J. DEMERATH III. "Religion and Political Process in an American City." *American Sociological Review.* Vol. 56, No. 4 (August 1991):417–31.

WILLIAMS, ROBIN M., JR. *American Society: A Sociological Interpretation.* 3rd ed. New York: Alfred A. Knopf, 1970.

WILLIAMSON, JEFFREY G., and PETER H. LINDERT. *American Inequality: A Macroeconomic History.* New York: Academic Press, 1980.

WILSON, ALAN B. "Residential Segregation of Social Classes and Aspirations of High School Boys." *American Sociological Review.* Vol. 24, No. 6 (December 1959):836–45.

WILSON, BRYAN. *Religion in Sociological Perspective.* New York: Oxford University Press, 1982.

WILSON, CLINTY C., II, and FÉLIX GUTIÉRREZ. *Minorities and Media: Diversity and the End of Mass Communication.* Beverly Hills, CA: Sage Publications, 1985.

WILSON, EDWARD O. *Sociobiology: The New Synthesis.* Cambridge, MA: Belknap Press of the Harvard University Press, 1975.

———. *On Human Nature.* New York: Bantam Books, 1978.

WILSON, JAMES Q. *Bureaucracy: What Government Agencies Do and Why They Do It.* New York: Basic Books, 1991.

WILSON, JAMES Q., and RICHARD J. HERRNSTEIN. *Crime and Human Nature.* New York: Simon and Schuster, 1985.

WILSON, JOHN. *Religion in American Society: The Effective Presence.* Englewood Cliffs, NJ: Prentice-Hall, 1978.

WILSON, LOGAN. *American Academics Then and Now.* New York: Oxford University Press, 1979.

WILSON, THOMAS C. "Urbanism and Tolerance: A Test of Some Hypotheses Drawn from Wirth and Stouffer." *American Sociological Review.* Vol. 50, No. 1 (February 1985):117–23.

———. "Urbanism, Migration, and Tolerance: A Reassessment." *American Sociological Review.* Vol. 56, No. 1 (February 1991):117–23.

WILSON, WILLIAM JULIUS. "The Black Underclass." *The Wilson Quarterly.* Vol. 8 (Spring 1984):88–99.

———. "Studying Inner-City Social Dislocations: The Challenge of Public Agenda Research." *American Sociological Review.* Vol. 56, No. 1 (February 1991):1–14.

WINN, MARIE. *Children Without Childhood.* New York: Pantheon Books, 1983.

WINNICK, LOUIS. "America's 'Model Minority'." *Commentary.* Vol. 90, No. 2 (August 1990):22–29.

WIRTH, LOUIS. "Urbanism As a Way of Life." *American Journal of Sociology.* Vol. 44, No. 1 (July 1938):1–24.

WITKIN-LANOIL, GEORGIA. *The Female Stress Syndrome: How to Recognize and Live with It.* New York: Newmarket Press, 1984.

WOLF, NAOMI. *The Beauty Myth: How Images of Beauty Are Used Against Women.* New York: William Morrow, 1990.

WOLFE, DAVID B. "Killing the Messenger." *American Demographics.* Vol. 13, No. 7 (July 1991):40–43.

WOLFE, TOM. *Radical Chic.* New York: Bantam, 1970.

WOLFGANG, MARVIN E., ROBERT M. FIGLIO, and THORSTEN SELLIN. *Delinquency in a Birth Cohort.* Chicago: University of Chicago Press, 1972.

WOLFGANG, MARVIN E., TERRENCE P. THORNBERRY, and ROBERT M. FIGLIO. *From Boy to Man, From Delinquency to Crime.* Chicago: University of Chicago Press, 1987.

WOLFINGER, RAYMOND E., and STEVEN J. ROSENSTONE. *Who Votes?* New Haven, CT: Yale University Press, 1980.

WOLFINGER, RAYMOND E., MARTIN SHAPIRO, and FRED J. GREENSTEIN. *Dynamics of American Politics.* 2nd ed. Englewood Cliffs, NJ: Prentice Hall, 1980.

WONG, BUCK. "Need for Awareness: An Essay on Chinatown, San Francisco." In Amy Tachiki et al., eds., *Roots: An Asian American Reader.* Los Angeles, CA: UCLA Asian American Studies Center, 1971:265–73.

WOODWARD, C. VANN. *The Strange Career of Jim Crow.* 3rd rev. ed. New York: Oxford University Press, 1974.

WOODWARD, KENNETH L. "Rules for Making Love and Babies." *Newsweek.* Vol. 109, No. 12 (March 23, 1987):42–43.

———. "Feminism and the Churches." *Newsweek.* Vol. 13, No. 7 (February 13, 1989):58–61.

———. "Talking to God." *Newsweek.* Vol. 119, No. 1 (January 6, 1992):38–44.

WOOLEY, ORLAND W., SUSAN C. WOOLEY, and SUE R. DYRENFORTH. "Obesity and Women—II: A Neglected Feminist Topic." *Women's Studies International Quarterly.* Vol. 2 (1979):81–92.

THE WORLD BANK. *World Development Report 1984.* New York: Oxford University Press, 1984.

———. *World Development Report 1991: The Challenge of Development.* New York: Oxord University Press, 1991.

WORLD HEALTH ORGANIZATION. *Constitution of the World Health Organization.* New York: World Health Organization Interim Commission, 1946.

WREN, CHRISTOPHER S. "In Soweto-by-the-Sea, Misery Lives On as Apartheid Fades." *The New York Times* (June 9, 1991):1, 7.

WRIGHT, ERIK OLIN, and BILL MARTIN. "The Transformation of the American Class Structure, 1960–1980." *American Journal of Sociology.* Vol. 93, No. 1 (July 1987):1–29.

WRIGHT, JAMES D. "Address Unknown: Homelessness in Contemporary America." *Society.* Vol. 26, No. 6 (September/October 1989):45–53.

WRIGHT, QUINCY. "Causes of War in the Atomic Age." In William M. Evan and Steven Hilgartner, eds., *The Arms Race and Nuclear War.* Englewood Cliffs, NJ: Prentice Hall, 1987:7–10.

WRIGHT, STUART A. "Social Movement Decline and Transformation: Cults in the 1980s." Paper presented to the Southwestern Social Science Association, Dallas, Texas, March 1987.

WRIGHT, STUART A., and WILLIAM V. D'ANTONIO. "The Substructure of Religion: A Further Study." *Journal for the Scientific Study of Religion.* Vol. 19, No. 3 (September 1980):292–98.

WRIGHT, STUART A., and ELIZABETH S. PIPER. "Families and Cults: Familial Factors Related to Youth Leaving or Remaining in Deviant Religious Groups." *Journal of Marriage and the Family.* Vol. 48, No. 1 (February 1986):15–25.

WRONG, DENNIS H. "The Oversocialized Conception of Man in Modern Sociology." *American Sociological Review.* Vol. 26, No. 2 (April 1961):183–93.

YATES, RONALD E. "Growing Old in Japan; They Ask Gods for a Way Out." *Philadelphia Inquirer* (August 14, 1986):3A.

YBARRA, LEA. *Conjugal Role Relationships in the Chicano Family.* Unpublished doctoral dissertation, University of California, 1977 (cited in Nielsen, 1990).

YODER, EDWIN M., JR. "Offering Sociology as Theology." *The Philadelphia Inquirer* (May 5, 1990).

YODER, JAN D., and ROBERT C. NICHOLS. "A Life Perspective: Comparison of Married and Divorced Persons." *Journal of Marriage and the Family.* Vol. 42, No. 2 (May 1980):413–19.

ZALD, MAYER N. *Occupations and Organizations in American Society.* Chicago: Markham, 1971.

ZANGWILL, ISRAEL. *The Melting Pot.* Macmillan, 1921; orig. 1909.

ZASLAVSKY, VICTOR. *The Neo-Stalinist State: Class, Ethnicity, and Consensus in Soviet Society.* Armonk, NY: M. E. Sharpe, 1982.

ZEITLIN, IRVING M. *The Social Condition of Humanity.* New York: Oxford University Press, 1981.

ZHOU, MIN, and JOHN R. LOGAN. "Returns of Human Capital in Ethnic Enclaves: New York City's Chinatown." *American Sociological Review.* Vol. 54, No. 5 (October 1989):809–20.

ZILL, NICHOLAS. National Survey conducted by Child Trends, Inc., Washington, DC, 1984. Reported by Marilyn Adams. "Kids Aren't Broken by the Breakup." *USA Today* (December 20, 1984):5D.

ZIMBARDO, PHILIP G. "Pathology of Imprisonment." *Society.* Vol. 9 (April 1972):4–8.

ZIPP, JOHN F. "Perceived Representativeness and Voting: An Assessment of the Impact of 'Choices' vs. 'Echoes.'" *The American Political Science Review.* Vol. 79, No. 1 (March 1985):50–61.

ZIPP, JOHN F., and JOEL SMITH. "A Structural Analysis of Class Voting." *Social Forces.* Vol. 60, No. 3 (March 1982):738–59.

ZOLA, IRVING KENNETH. "Medicine as an Institution of Social Control." In John Ehrenreich, ed., *The Cultural Crisis of Modern Medicine.* New York: Monthly Review Press, 1978:80–100.

ZUBOFF, SHOSHANA. "New Worlds of Computer-Mediated Work." *Harvard Business Review.* Vol. 60, No. 5 (September-October 1982):142–52.

ZURCHER, LOUIS A., and DAVID A. SNOW. "Collective Behavior and Social Movements." In Morris Rosenberg and Ralph Turner, eds., *Social Psychology: Sociological Perspectives.* New York: Basic Books, 1981:447–82.

# Photo Credits

**CHAPTER 1** Patrick Rouillard/The Image Bank, xxvi; Jacques Chenet/Woodfin Camp & Associates, 1; Paul Liebhardt, 2; Sepp Seitz/ Woodfin Camp & Associates, 4; Dan Ford Connolly/Picture Group, 10; Brown Brothers, 11; New York Public Library, 12; The Bettmann Archive, 13; © The Pierpont Morgan Library, 15 (l.); Archive Photos, 15 (r.); New York Public Library Picture Collection, 18; Brown Brothers, 20; The Bettmann Archive, 21 (t.); Brown Brothers, 21 (b.); Private Collection. Courtesy of Pucker Safrai Gallery, Boston. Photograph by David N. Israel, 24.

**CHAPTER 2** Steve Elmore/The Stock Market, 30; Bob Daemmrich/ The Image Works, 31; Heard Museum, Phoenix, Arizona, 33; Tony Stone Worldwide, 36; Paul Liebhardt, 40; H. E. Edgerton, 41; Reuters/ Bettmann, 44; Mike Greenlar/The Image Works, 45; Paul Liebhardt, 49; Luis Villota/The Stock Market, 51; John Giordano/SABA, 53; The Museum of Modern Art, New York. Gift of Mr. and Mrs. Robert C. Scull, 56.

**CHAPTER 3** Daniel Laine/Actuel, 60; Napoleon A. Chagnon, 61; Paul Liebhardt, 63 (top r., l., & m., m.l., m.r., b.l.); David Austen/ Stock, Boston, 63 (m.m.); Jack Fields/Photo Researchers, 63 (b.r.); Gerhard Hinterleitner/Gamma Liaison, 64; Paul Liebhardt, 68; Sally Swain, from *Great Housewives of Art*. Copyright © 1988, 1989 by Sally Swain. Used by permission of Viking Penguin, a division of Penguin Books U.S.A., Inc. 70; Dennis Stock/Magnum Photos, 73 (l.); Catherine Ursillo/Photo Researchers, 73 (r.); M. Courtney-Clarke, 74; The Bettmann Archive, 77 (l.); The Granger Collection, 77 (r.); Catherine Smith/Impact Visuals, 78; Paul Liebhardt, 82; Gerd Ludwig, 84; Paul Liebhardt, 85; Peter Menzel, 87; Tom Leas, U.S. Department of Defense, Still Media Records Center, 89.

**CHAPTER 4** Terra Museum of American Art, Chicago, 92; Frank Whitney/The Image Bank, 93; Courtesy of the Lenskis. Photo by Will Owens, 95; Four By Five, Inc., 96 (l.); Anthro-Photo, 96 (r.); James R. Holland/Stock, Boston, 97; Robert Frerck/Woodfin Camp & Associates, 98; Culver Pictures, Inc., 101; Brown Brothers, 104; Scala/Art Resource, 105; Bridgeman Art Library/Art Resource, 107; Alfred/SIPA, 109; New York Public Library Picture Collection, 111; Private Collection, 114; Roger Ressmeyer/Starlight, 115; The Bettmann Archive, 116; Paul Liebhardt, 118.

**CHAPTER 5** Hampton University Museum, 122; John McDonough/ *Sports Illustrated*, 123; Suzanne Szasz/Photo Researchers, 125 (l.); Mimi Forsyth/Monkmeyer Press, 125 (m.); Tom Pollack/Monkmeyer Press, 125 (r.); First appeared in the June 1990 *Atlantic Monthly* in an article entitled "Growing Up Scared" by Karl Zinmeister, 126; Mary Evans/Sigmund Freud Copyrights, courtesy of W. E. Freud, 128; Elizabeth Crews, 130; Courtesy of the University of Chicago Archives, 131; Yale University Art Gallery. Bequest of Edith M. K. Wetmore, 132; Nancy Seissel/New York Times Pictures, 136; Audrey Gottlieb/Monkmeyer Press, 137; Brown Brothers, 139; Paul Liebhardt, 144.

**CHAPTER 6** Michael Ging/The Arizona Republic, 150; Trevor Wood/Stockphotos/The Image Bank, 151; Paul Liebhardt, 153; John Focht, 156; Smithsonian Institution. Gift of William T. Evans, 157; Paul Liebhardt, 158; Kit King/Gamma Liaison, 161 (u.l.); Alan Weiner/ Gamma Liaison, 161 (u.m.); Ellis Herwig/The Picture Cube, 161 (u.r.); Lynn McLaren/The Picture Cube, 161 (l.l.); Richard Pan/Stockphotos/The Image Bank, 161 (l.m.); Paul Steel/The Stock Market, 161 (l.r.); David Johnson, *Time* Magazine, April 22, 1985, p. 59; Bob Daemmrich/The Image Works, 165; Paul Liebhardt, 166; Courtesy Knave Productions, Inc., 169; "Trading Places" copyright © 1983 by Paramount Pictures, 171.

**CHAPTER 7** John Eastcott/Yva Momatiuk/Woodfin Camp & Associates, 174; Copyright 20th Century Fox Film Corporation/NBC, 175; Homer Sykes/Impact Photos, London, 176; Frederic Stevens/SIPA, 180; The Picture Cube, 181; Private Collection, 182; Harriet Gans/ The Image Works, 184; Ann States/SABA, 185; Biblioteque Nationale, 187; Paul Liebhardt, 191; Bill Varie/The Image Bank, 192; The Metropolitan Museum of Art, George A. Hearn Fund, 193; George Merillon/ Gamma Liaison, 194; Julie Houck, 195; Ethan Hoffman/Picture Project, 197; Karen Kasmauski/Woodfin Camp & Associates, 198.

**CHAPTER 8** Michael Going/The Image Bank, 204; Andrew Lichtenstein/Impact Visuals, 205; Alon Reininger/Woodfin Camp & Associates, 206; John Paul Filo, 207; Jacques Chenet/Woodfin Camp & Associates, 209; Archive Photos, 211 (l.); Capital Features/The Image Works, 211 (r.); Stephen Shames/Matrix from the book *Outside the Dream*, Aperture/Children's Defense Fund, 212; UPI/Bettmann Newsphotos, 213; Martin Rogers/Stock, Boston, 217; Will & Deni McIntyre/Photo Researchers, 218; Collection of Peter Schindler, 220; Damion Clayton, 221; SIPA Pool, 224; David Austen/Woodfin Camp & Associates, 228 (l.); Bob Daemmrich/Stock, Boston, 228 (r.); Natsuko Utsumi/Gamma Liaison, 231; Pushkin State Museum, Moscow, 233.

**CHAPTER 9** Lisl Dennis/The Image Bank, 238; Ken Marshall; Collection of Joseph M. Ryan, 239; Sebastiao Salgado/Magnum Photos, 240; Frederic Reglain/Gamma Liaison, 243; Reuters/Bettmann, 244; Sygma, 246; Giraudon/Art Resource, 249; Art Resource, 252 (l.); The Jacob A. Riis Collection. Museum of the City of New York, 252 (r.); The Granger Collection, 255.

**CHAPTER 10** William Strode/Woodfin Camp & Associates, 262; Paul Liebhardt, 263; Michael Grecco/Stock, Boston, 269; Abbas/Magnum, 271 (l.); Burt Glinn/Magnum, 271 (r.); Roger Prigent/Sygma, 273; Stephen Shames/Matrix from the book *Outside the Dream*, Aperture/Children's Defense Fund, 275; Ralf-Finn Hestoft/SABA, 277; FPG International, 283; Philadelphia Museum of Art. William H. and Camille O. Cosby Collection, 285; John Chiasson/Gamma Liaison, 287.

**CHAPTER 11** Collection, The Museum of Modern Art, New York. Gift of M. M. Warburg, 290; Gerard Rancinan/Sygma, 291; G. V. Faint/The Image Bank, 293 (t.l.); Peter Turnley/Black Star, 293 (t.r.); Pablo Bartholomew/Gamma Liaison, 293 (b.r.); Pablo Bartholomew/Gamma Liaison, 295; Paul Liebhardt, 296; Bonnie Freer/Rapho/Photo Researchers, 299 (l.); Viviane Moss/The Stock Market, 299 (r.); Paul Liebhardt, 301; Paul Liebhardt, 302; ARCHIV/Photo Researchers, 304; Paul Liebhardt, 306; The Granger Collection, 309; Reuters/Bettman, 311; Paul Liebhardt, 313.

**CHAPTER 12** Norman Prince, San Francisco, CA. Mural by Ruby Newman & Selma Brown, 318; Haviv/SABA, 319; Paul Liebhardt, 320 (u.l., u.m., l.l., l.m.); Robert Caputo/Stock, Boston, 320 (u.r.); Lisl Dennis/The Image Bank, 320 (l.r.); Raveendran/Agence France Press, 326; The Bettmann Archive, 327 (t.); Culver Pictures, Inc., 327 (l.l.); Schomburg Center/New York Public Library, 327 (l.m.); UPI/Bettmann, 327 (l.r.); Chester Higgins Jr./Photo Researchers, 330; The Bettmann Archive, 332; Eric Haase/Contact/Woodfin Camp & Associates, 333; UPI/Bettmann, 336; Terrence McCarthy/*The New York Times*, 340; National Archives Photo. Courtesy of the National Japanese American Historical Society, 342.

**CHAPTER 13** Larry Fried/The Image Bank, 348; Jacky Gucia/The Image Bank, 349; Michel Tcherevkoff/The Image Bank, 350; Co Rentmeester/The Image Bank, 353; Courtesy of Pennsylvania State University, 358; Courtesy of Revlon, 360; Private Collection, 364; Charles Gupton/Stock, Boston, 366; Rob Crandall/Picture Group, 370; Courtesy of the National Organization of Women, 373; Robert Fox/Impact Visuals, 375; Ken Sax/Shooting Star, 377.

**CHAPTER 14** Paul Liebhardt, 380; Rob Crandall/Picture Group, 381; Daemmrich/The Image Works, 383; Sharon Farmer, from "Songs of My People." © New African Visions, Inc., 386; Eve Arnold/Magnum Photos, 390; The Museum of Modern Art, New York. Gift of Lincoln Kirstein. Photograph © 1992, 392; Scala/Art Resource, 399; Stanley B. Burns, M.D./The Burns Archives, 400.

**CHAPTER 15** Collection of Marilyn Lanfear, Texas. Photo courtesy Bernice Steinbaum Gallery, New York City, 404; Michael O'Neill, 405; Farrell Grehan/Photo Researchers, 407; Steve Sands/Outline Press, 412; The National Gallery, London, 416; Laguna Art Museum, Austin, TX, 421; David Schreiber/The Torrance (CA) Daily Breeze, 426; James Skovmand, The San Diego Union-Tribune, 429; Stu Rossner/Stock, Boston, 433.

**CHAPTER 16** Robert Caputo, 438; Richard Kalvar/Magnum Photos, 439; Hans Neleman/The Image Bank, 443; Paul Liebhardt, 446; The Bettmann Archive, 448; Chester Higgins from "Songs of My People." © New African Visions, Inc., 451; AP/Wide World Photos, 456; Courtesy Literacy Volunteers of America, Inc., 460.

**CHAPTER 17** Raghu Rai/Magnum Photos, 466; Eric Haase/CONTACT/Woodfin Camp & Associates, 467; Hans Hoefer/Woodfin Camp & Associates, 468; Ira Wyman/Sygma, 471; Gilles Peress/Magnum Photos, 475; British Library, London. Bridgeman/Art Resource, 481; Paul Liebhardt, 483; Jan Lukas/Photo Researchers, 484; The Metropolitan Museum of Art, New York. Fletcher Fund, 487; New Britain Museum of American Art, Connecticut. Harriet Russell Stanley Fund, 489.

**CHAPTER 18** Andy Hernandez/SIPA, 496; Eve Arnold/Magnum Photos, 497; JB Pictures, 498; The Metropolitan Museum of Art, New York. Wolfe Fund, 500; The Prado, Madrid. Giraudon/Art Resource, 506; T. W. Wood Art Gallery, 514; Reuters/Bettmann, 519.

**CHAPTER 19** Louis Psihoyos/Matrix, 528; Vince Dewitt/Impact Visuals, 529; Museum of Textile History, 531; Harald Sund/The Image Bank, 536 (l.); Sygma, 536 (r.); Savino/The Image Works, 542; Collection of Whitney Museum of American Art. Photo by Geoffrey Clements, N.Y., 544; Mayer/Gamma Liaison, 551; Collection of Dain Bosworth Incorporated. Photo courtesy of Hokin Kaufman Gallery, Chicago, 552.

**CHAPTER 20** Frank Fournier/Contact/Woodfin Camp & Associates, 556; Susan Rosenberg/Photo Researchers, 557; The Granger Collection, 559; W. Campbell/Sygma, 561 (l.); Peter Magubane/Black Star, 561 (r.); Cecil Fox/Science Source/Photo Researchers, 566; Marty Katz, 567; P.P.O.W. Gallery, New York, 570; Ruven Afanadore, 571; D. Michael Cheers from "Songs of My People." © New African Visions, Inc., 573; Sam Garcia, 575; The Mansell Collection Limited, 580.

**CHAPTER 21** Hunter Museum of Art, Chattanooga, Tennessee. Gift of the Benwood Foundation, 586; Stephanie Maze/Woodfin Camp & Associates, 587; The Phillips Collection, 589; Terry Madison/The Image Bank, 593; N. Maceschal/The Image Bank, 595; Erich Hartmann/Magnum Photos, 599; Collection, The Museum of Modern Art, New York. Mrs. Simon Guggenheim Fund, 607 (l.); The Philadelphia Museum of Art. The A. E. Gallatin Collection, 607 (r.); The University of Chicago Library, 609; Fred Mayer/Magnum Photos, 612.

**CHAPTER 22** Ron Haviv/SABA, 616; AP/Wide World Photos, 617; Stephen Wilkes/The Image Bank, 618; Collection, The Museum of Modern Art, New York. Gift of Mrs. David M. Levy, 620; Jalil Bonhar/Wide World Photos, 622; Chris Pullo, 624; The Granger Collection, 626; Shlomo Arad/JB Pictures, 629; Donna Binder/Impact Visuals, 633; Jon Jones/Sygma, 635.

**CHAPTER 23** James Willis/Tony Stone Worldwide, 638; Mauri Rautkari/WWF Photolibrary, 639; G. V. Faint/The Image Bank, 640; The Art Institute of Chicago. Helen Birch Bartlett Memorial Collection, 645; Bildarchiv Preussischer Kulturbesitz, 646; Whitney Museum of American Art, New York, 647; Stephanie Maze/Woodfin Camp & Associates, 650; Paul Liebhardt, 655; Andrew Holbrooke/Black Star, 656; Kevin Bubriski/The Film Study Center, Harvard University, 659.

# Index

## Name Index

**700** Index

# Subject Index

# About the Author

John J. Macionis (pronounced ma-SHOW-nis) was born and raised in Philadelphia, Pennsylvania. He received his bachelor's degree from Cornell University and his doctorate in sociology from the University of Pennsylvania. His publications are wide-ranging, focusing on community life in the United States, interpersonal intimacy in families, effective teaching, the importance of global analysis to sociology, and the anatomy of humor. He is coauthor of the popular urban text *The Sociology of Cities*, and he has coedited the companion volume to this text, *Seeing Ourselves: Classic, Contemporary, and Cross-Cultural Readings in Sociology*. He has also written a brief version of this book, *Society: The Basics*.

John Macionis is currently professor of sociology at Kenyon College in Gambier, Ohio. He has served as chair of the Anthropology-Sociology Department, director of Kenyon's multidisciplinary program in humane studies, and chair of the college's faculty.

Professor Macionis teaches a wide range of upper-level courses, but his favorite course is Introduction to Sociology, which he teaches every semester. He enjoys extensive contact with students, making an occasional appearance on campus with his guitar and inviting each of his students to enjoy a home-cooked meal. He also is a frequent visitor to other campuses and enjoys participating in teaching programs abroad. Much of his time is spent raising son McLean, about whom he remarks, "It's amazing that an infant who knows so little can teach you so much!"

The author welcomes comments and suggestions about this book. Write to Kenyon College, Gambier, Ohio 43022. His internet address is MACIONIS@KENYON.EDU

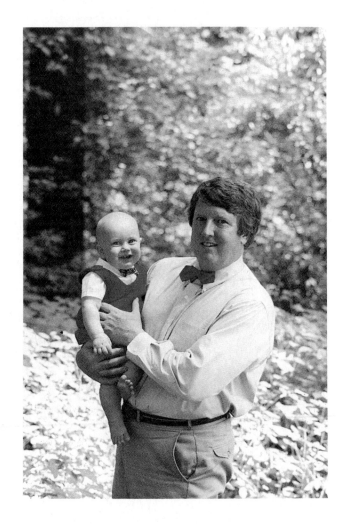